FRANCE

B. Kaufmann/MICHELIN

Executive Editorial Director David Brabis

Chief Editor Cynthia Clayton Ochterbeck

THE GREEN GUIDE FRANCE

Editor Gwen Cannon

Principal Writer Jason T. Strand

Production Coordinator Allison Michelle Simpson

Cartography Alain Baldet, Michèle Cana, Peter Wrenn

Photo Editor Brigitta L. House

Proofreader Gaven R. Watkins

Layout Allison Michelle Simpson, Nicole D. Jordan

Cover Design Laurent Muller

Interior Design Agence Rampazzo

Production Pierre Ballochard, Renaud Leblanc

Contact Us : The Green Guide
Michelin Travel Publications
One Parkway South
Greenville, SC 29615
USA
☎ 1-800-423-0485
www.michelintravel.com
michelin.guides@us.michelin.com
or
Hannay House, 39 Clarendon Road
Watford, Herts WD17 1JA, UK
☎ 1-1923-205-240 - Fax 01923-205-241
www.ViaMichelin.com
TheGreenGuide-uk@us.michelin.com

Special Sales : For information regarding bulk sales, customized editions
and premium sales, please contact our Customer
Service Departments:
USA   1-800-423-0485
UK   (01923) 205 240
Canada   1-800-361-8236

Note to the reader

One Team...
A Commitment to Quality

There's just one reason our team is dedicated to producing quality travel publications—you, our reader. We want you to get the maximum benefit from your trip—and from your money. In today's multiple-choice world of travel, the options are many, perhaps overwhelming.

In our guidebooks, we try to minimize the guesswork involved with travel. We scout out the attractions, prioritize them with star ratings, and describe what you'll discover when you visit them.

To help you orient yourself, we provide colorful and detailed, but easy-to-follow maps. Floor plans of some of the major museums help you plan your tour.

Throughout the guides, we offer practical information, touring tips and suggestions for finding the best views, good places for a break and interesting shops.

Lodging and dining are always a big part of travel, so we compile a selection of hotels and restaurants that we think convey the feel of the destination, and organize them by geographic area and price. We also highlight shopping, recreational and entertainment venues, especially the popular spots.

If you're short on time, driving tours are included so you can hit the highlights and quickly absorb the best of the destination.

For those who love to experience a place on foot, we add walking tours, often with a map. And we list other companies who offer boat, bus or guided walking tours of the area, some with culinary, historical or other themes.

In short, we test and retest, check and recheck to make sure that our guidebooks are truly just that: a personalized guide to help you make the most of your visit. After all, we want you to enjoy traveling as much as we do.

The Michelin Green Guide Team
michelin.guides@us.michelin.com

PLANNING YOUR TRIP

INTRODUCTION TO FRANCE

SYMBOLS

🖐	**Tips to help improve your experience**
👍	**Details to consider**
💰	**Entry fees**
🚶	**Walking tours**
🔑	**Closed to the public**
🕐	**Hours of operation**
🕓	**Periods of closure**
▷▷	**See also, time permitting**

TABLE OF CONTENTS

DISCOVERING FRANCE

Principal Sights

TOULOUSE ★★★ Highly recommended

Autun ★★ Recommended

Giverny ★ Interesting

Montélimar Other sight described
in this guide.

Seaside resorts ⌂, spas ♯ and winter resorts ❄ are classified
according to the quality and range of facilities offered.

Shown on this map are the towns and sights in the alphabetical section of the guide, with the
additional sites attached to them, as well as principal resorts.

A number of other places, monuments, historical events and natural sites appear in this guide
and may be found in the index.

0   100 km

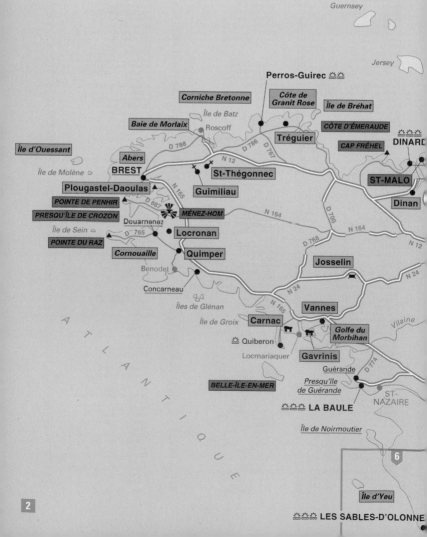

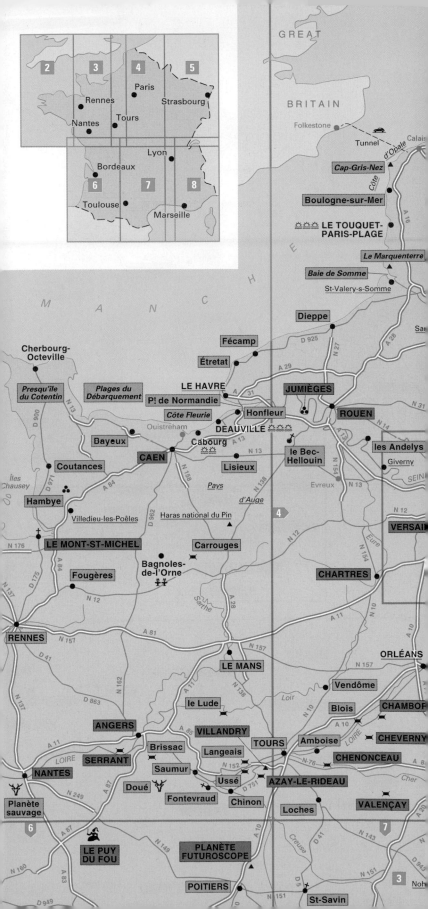

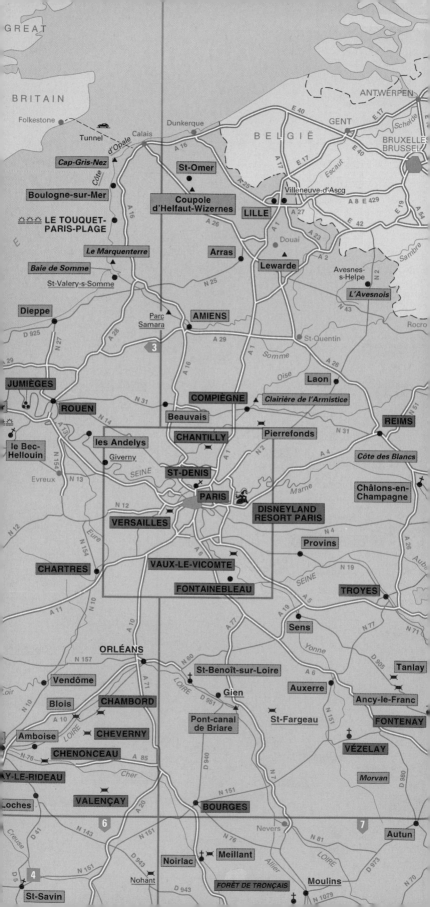

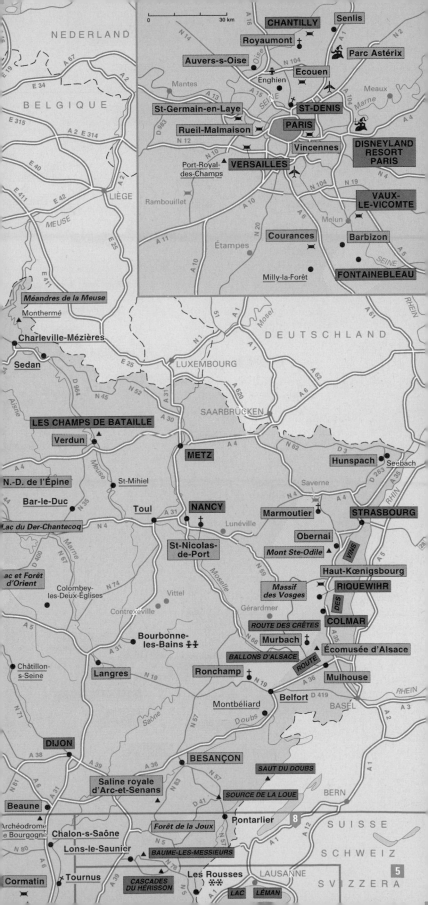

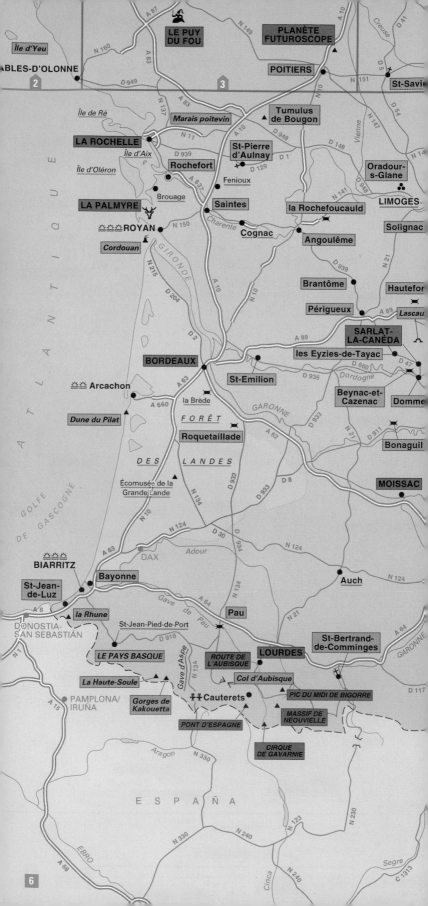

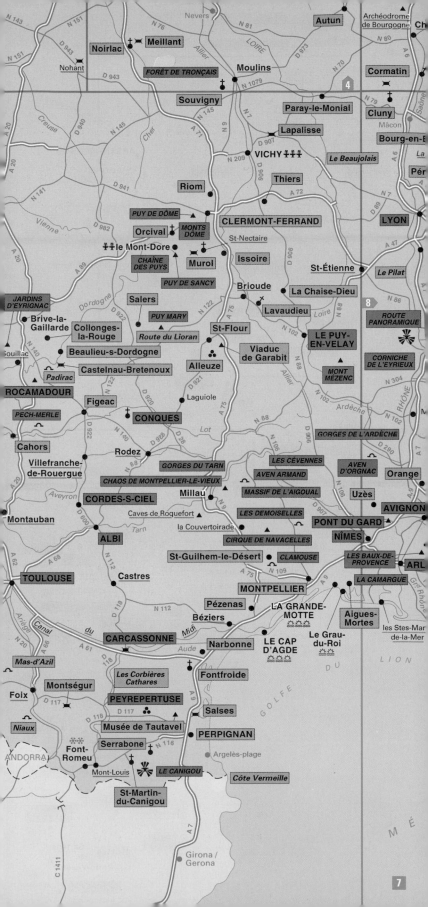

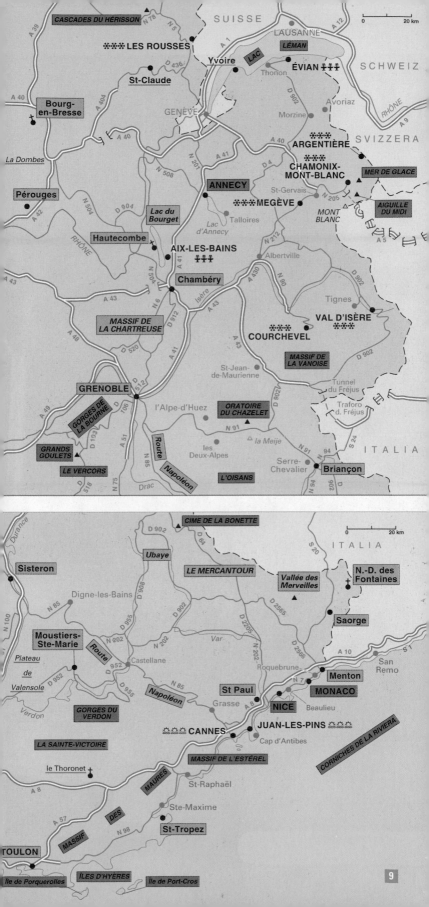

CASCADES DU HÉRISSON

SUISSE

LAUSANNE

LAC LÉMAN

***LES ROUSSES

Yvoire

ÉVIAN ♱♱♱

SCHWEIZ

St-Claude

Thonon

GENÈVE

Avoriaz

SVIZZERA

Bourg-en-Bresse

Morzine

RHÔNE

La Dombes

***ARGENTIÈRE

CHAMONIX-MONT-BLANC

MER DE GLACE

Pérouges

ANNECY

St-Gervais

AIGUILLE DU MIDI

Lac du Bourget

***MEGÈVE

Talloires

MONT BLANC

Lac d'Annecy

Hautecombe

AIX-LES-BAINS ♱♱♱

Albertville

Chambéry

Tignes

VAL D'ISÈRE ***

MASSIF DE LA CHARTREUSE

***COURCHEVEL

MASSIF DE LA VANOISE

St-Jean-de-Maurienne

GRENOBLE

Tunnel du Fréjus

Traforo d. Fréjus

l'Alpe-d'Huez

ORATOIRE DU CHAZELET

ITALIA

GORGES DE LA BOURNE

Route Napoléon

les Deux-Alpes

△ la Meije

GRANDS GOULETS

Serre-Chevalier

Briançon

LE VERCORS

Drac

L'OISANS

CIME DE LA BONETTE

ITALIA

Ubaye

Durance

Sisteron

LE MERCANTOUR

Vallée des Merveilles

N.-D. des Fontaines

Digne-les-Bains

Saorge

Moustiers-Ste-Marie

Route Napoléon

Castellane

Var

San Remo

Plateau de Valensole

Roquebrune

Menton

St Paul

MONACO

Verdon

GORGES DU VERDON

Grasse

NICE

Beaulieu

LA SAINTE-VICTOIRE

⌂⌂⌂ CANNES

JUAN-LES-PINS ⌂⌂⌂

CORNICHES DE LA RIVIERA

le Thoronet

MASSIF DE L'ESTÉREL

Cap d'Antibes

MAURES

St-Raphaël

DES

Ste-Maxime

St-Tropez

MASSIF

TOULON

île de Porquerolles

ÎLES D'HYÈRES

île de Port-Cros

9

Krug champagne cellar

IDEAS FOR YOUR VISIT

Main Tourist Resorts

Most of the resort areas listed below have a wide range of accommodation and leisure facilities and are therefore characterised only in terms of their setting or other special features.

★★Aix-en-Provence – 🕭 *See Index* – Spa – Casino – 18C spa complex built next to site of Roman baths.

★★Aix-les-Bains – Spa – Palais de Savoie Casino and Nouveau Casino – prestigious "Season" – Parks – Lakeside esplanade★ – Dr Faure Museum★.

★★Ajaccio – 🕭 *See Index* – Sandy beach – Casino – Place Maréchal-Foch – other beaches around Ajaccio Bay.

★L'Alpe-d'Huez – Mountain resort (1 860-3 350m/6 100-10 990ft) with winter sports– Lac Blanc Summit★★★ (*by cableway and cable-car*): view of Écrins Massif and Mont Blanc – Lake Besson★ (6.5km – 4mi).

★Amélie-les-Bains – Spa – Casino – Restored Roman baths – Montdony Gorges.

★★★Annecy – 🕭 *See Index* – Swimming in lake – Lakeside★★★ – Riverside walk.

★★Arcachon – 🕭 *See Index* – Sandy beach – Casino – Seafront with views over Arcachon Bay.

Argelès-Gazost – Spa – Panorama of the Pyrenees.

Argelès-Plage – Casino – Sandy beach at northern end of Côte Vermeille★★.

★★Avoriaz – Mountain resort (winter sports).

★Ax-les-Thermes – Spa – Mountain resort with winter sports (1 400-2 400m/4 590-7 870ft) – Ladres Valley – Bonascre Plateau★ (View★★ of Ariège heights and Andorra mountains).

★★Bagnères-de-Bigorre – Spa – Casino – Salut spa complex and park★.

★★Bagnoles-de-l'Orne – Spa – Casino – Lake★ – Park★ – Roc-au-Chien Walk★ (in Tessé-la-Madeleine).

★Bandol – Sandy beach – Casino – Jean-Moulin avenue★.

Barèges – Spa – Mountain resort with winter sports (1 250-2 350m/4 100-7 710ft) – Lienz Plateau – Font d'Ayré funicular.

★★★La Baule – 🕭 *See Index* – Sandy beach – Thalassotherapy centre – Casino – Seafront★★ – Dryades Park★ – La-Baule-les-Pins★★.

★★Beaulieu-sur-Mer – Sandy beach – Casino – Villa Kerylosa (setting★) – Fourmis Bay★.

★★Belle-Ile – 🕭 *See Index* – Thalassotherapy centre.

★Bénodet – Sandy beach – Casino – Pyramide lighthouse (panorama★ over Cornouaille coast and Glénan islands).

★★★Biarritz – 🕭 *See Index* – Sandy beach with rocks – Thalassotherapy centre – Casino – La Perspective viewpoint★★ – St-Martin Point (view★) – Vierge Rock★ – Museum of the Sea★.

Le Boulou – Spa – Casino – Setting at foot of Albères Mountains.

★★La Bourboule – Spa – Fenestre Park★ – Charlannes Plateau.

★★Cabourg – Sandy beach – Casino – Marcel-Proust Promenade.

Canet-Plage – Sandy beach – Casino – Active sports centre.

★★★Cannes – 🕭 *See Index* – Sandy beach – Fleurs Casino, Palm Beach Casino, Casino Municipal) – Boulevard de la Croisette★★ – La Croisette Point★ – Super-Cannes Observatory (panorama★★★) – La Castre Museum★.

★★Cap-d'Antibes – Sandy beach with rocks – Round tour★★ – La Garoupe Plateau (panorama★★) – Thuret Gardens★.

★Capvern-les-Bains – Spa – View of Pyrenees.

Carnac – Thalassotherapy centre.

★Cauterets – Spa – Mountain resort with winter sports (930-2 340m/3 050-7 680ft) – Casino Esplanade – Espagne Bridge★★ – Lutour Valley★ and Falls★★; Jeret Valley★★.

★★★Chamonix – 🕭 *See Index* – Mountain resort with winter sports (1 035-3 842m/3 400-12 604ft) – Setting at foot of Aiguille du Midi with view of Mont-Blanc.

★★**Châtelguyon** – Spa – Casino – Prades Valley★ – Enval Gorge★.

Chaudes-Aigues – Spa – Source of the River Par – Neighbourhood saints in niches.

★**Combloux** – Mountain resort with winter sports (1 000-1 853m/3 280-6 080ft) – View★ of Mont-Blanc.

★**Contrexéville** – Spa – Casino – La Folie Lake.

★★**Courchevel** – Mountain resort with winter sports (1 300-2 700m/4 260-8 860ft) – Panorama★ – La Saulire *(cableway and cable-car)*: panorama★★.

★**Dax** – Spa – Casino – Warm springs – *9km – 6mi northeast:* Buglose (birthplace of St Vincent de Paul).

★★★**Deauville** – 🕭 *See Index* – Sandy beach – Summer and Winter Casinos – Boardwalk★ (Promenade des Planches).

★**Les Deux-Alpes** – Twin mountain resorts (L'Alpe-du-Mont-de-Lans and L'Alpe-de-Venosc) with winter sports (1 650-3 560m/5 410-11 680ft) – From L'Alpe-de-Venosc: La Croix viewpoint★ and Cimes viewpoint★ *(by cableway).*

★★**Dieppe** – 🕭 *See Index* – Pebble beach – Casino – Boulevard de la Mer (view★) – Boulevard du Maréchal-Foch.

★★★**Dinard** – 🕭 *See Index* – Sandy beach with rocks – Thalassotherapy centre – Casino – Moulinet Point (view★★) – Grande Plage beach★ – Clair de Lune Promenade★.

★**Divonne** – 🕭 *See Index* – Spa – Casino – Park.

★**Douarnenez** – Thalassotherapy centre.

★**Enghien** – Spa – Casino – Lake★.

★★★**Évian** – 🕭 *See Index* – Spa – Casino – English Garden.

★★**Font-Romeu** – Mountain resort with winter sports (1 850-2 204m/6 070-7 230ft) – Casino – Hermitage★ (Camaril★★) – Calvary (panorama★★ over the Cerdagne).

★★**Gérardmer** – 🕭 *See Index* – Spa – Mountain/forest setting – Winter sports (870-1 130m/2 850-3 710ft) – Lake★.

★★★**La Grande-Motte** – 🕭 *See Index* – Sandy beach – Casino – Modern resort architecture.

★**Hossegor** – Sandy beach – Casino – Lakeside Promenade★.

★★**Juan-les-Pins** – 🕭 *See Index* – Sandy beach – Casino: Eden Beach – Fine coastal setting.

★★**Luchon** – Spa – Mountain setting with winter sports at Super-Bagnères (1 420-2 260m/4 660-7 420ft) – d'Étigny avenues.

★★★**Megève** – 🕭 *See Index* – Alpine setting with winter sports (1 067-2 350/3 510-7 710ft) – Casino – Mont d'Arbois *(by cable-car)*: panorama★★★ over Aravis mountains and Mont-Blanc.

★★**Menton** – 🕭 *See Index* – Pebble beach – Casino du Soleil – Promenade du Soleil★★ – Carnolès Palace Museum★.

★★**Les Menuires** – Mountain resort with winter sports (1 067-2 350m/3 500-7 710ft) – Mont de la Chambre★★

★★**Le Mont-Dore** – Spa – Mountain resort with winter sports (1 350-1 850m/4 430-6 070ft) – Casino – Promenade des Artistes★ – Salon du Capucin (funicular).

★★★**Monte-Carlo** – 🕭 *See Index* – Sandy beach with rocks – Grand Casino, Casino du Sporting Club, Casino Loews – Museum of Dolls and Automata★.

★★**Morzine** – 🕭 *See Index* – Mountain setting with winter sports (1 000-2 460m/3 280-8 070ft) – Meeting point of six valleys – Le Pléney *(cable-car)*: panorama.

★★★**Nice** – 🕭 *See Index* – Pebble beach – Casino-club.

★**Perros-Guirec** – Sandy beach – Thalassotherapy centre – Casino – Le Château Point (view★) – Viewing table (view★) – Douaniers Path★★.

★**Plombières** – Spa – Casino – Park designed by Haussmann.

★**Pornichet** – 🕭 *See Index* – Sandy beach – Casino – Boulevard des Océanides.

★**Propriano** – Sandy beach – Valinco Bay★.

Quiberon – 🕭 *See Index* – Sandy beach with rocks – Thalassotherapy centre – Casino – Côte Sauvage★★.

★★★**La Rochelle** – 🕭 *See Index* – Sandy beach – Casino.

★**Roscoff** – 🕭 *See Index* – Thalassotherapy centre – Sandy beaches with some pebbles – Aquarium★ – Notre-Dame-de-Kroaz-Betz Church★ (Belfry★, alabaster statues★).

★★**Royan** – Sandy beach – Casino (at Pontaillac) – Seafront★ – Notre-Dame Church★.

★★**Royat** – Spa – Casino – Set among foothills of Monts Dômes – Spa Park and Bargoin Park

★★**Les Sables-d'Olonne** – Sandy beach – Casino de la Plage – Casino des Sports – Remblai promenade★ – Fishermen's quarter.

★★**St-Cast-le-Guildo** – Sandy beach – St-Cast Point (view★★) – La Garde Point (view★★).

★★**St-Gervais** – Spa – Mountain resort with winter sports (850-2 350m/2 790-7 710ft) – Bettex scenic route★★★ – Eagle's Nest and Bionassay glacier★★ (Mont-Blanc mountain railway).

★★**St-Jean-de-Luz** – 🔥 See Index – Sandy beach – Casino.

★★★**St-Malo** – 🔥 See Index – Sandy beach – Thalassotherapy centre – Casino.

★★**St-Nectaire** – 🔥 See Index – Spa.

★**St-Raphaël** – Sandy beach – Casino – Sheltered setting at foot of Esterel Massif – Seafront.

St-Trojan – Sandy beach – Pinetum.

★★**St-Tropez** – 🔥 See Index – Sandy beach – Harboura and quaysides – L'Annonciade Museum★★ – View★ from harbour wall – View★ from citadel.

★**Ste-Maxime** – Sandy beach – Casino – Panorama★ from semaphore.

★**Serre-Chevalier** – Winter sports.

★**Super-Lioran** – Mountain resort with winter sports (1 160-1 830m/3 810-6 000ft) – Plomb du Cantal★ (cable-car): panorama★★.

★★**Talloires** – Bathing in the lake – Lakeside setting★★★ (Petit Lac d'Annecy).

★★**Thonon** – Spa.

★★★**Le Touquet-Paris-Plage** – 🔥 See Index – Sandy beach – La Forêt and Quatre Saisons Casinos – Seafront promenade – Woodland – Lighthouse (view★★).

★★**Trégastel** – Sandy beach – Rocky coastline of the Breton Corniche★ – White Shore (La Grève blanche) footpath★.

★★**Trouville** – Sandy beach – Casino – Corniche road★ – Boardwalk (Promenade des Planches).

★★**Le Val-André** – Sandy beach – Casino – Pléneuf Pointa (View★★) – Promenade de la Guette★.

★★★**Val-d'Isère** – Mountain resort with winter sports (1 850-3 450m/6 070-11 320ft) – Rocher de Bellevarde (cable-car): panorama★★★ – Tête du Solaise (cable-car): panorama★★.

★★**Val-Thorens** – Mountain resort with winter sports (1 067-3 200m/7 546-10 499ft) – Cime de Carona★ (by cable-car).

★★★**Vichy** – 🔥 See Index – Spa – Élysée Palace Casino, Grand Casino – Sources Park★ – Allier Park★.

★**Villard-de-Lans** – Mountain resort with winter sports (1 050-2 170m/3 450-7 120ft) – Vercors Regional Park setting – Bourne Gorge★★★.

★★★**Vittel** – Spa – Casino – Landscape park★.

The Islands of France

🔥 See also **Michelin Green Guides** to: *Normandy, Brittany, Atlantic Coast, Provence, French Riviera, and Corse (in French)*.

France has an extensive coastline (2 700km - 1 678mi) along which are dotted idyllic islands, some as small as a field and others very large – Corsica is three times the size of a small country such as the Grand Duchy of Luxembourg. The islands are perfect destinations for a change of scenery and pace; their isolation as well as an air of mystery and charm add to the fascination of a way of life shaped by the sea.

The list below includes the principal islands ranging from north to south and west to east.

ÎLES DU PONANT

(English Channel-Atlantic Ocean)

Îles Chausey★: *65ha - 0.25sq mi* at high tide attached to **Granville**.

Île de Bréhat★: *318ha - 1.2sq mi; 10min* crossing from **Arcouest** near **Paimpol**.

Île de Batz: *357ha - 1.4sq mi; 15min* crossing from **Roscoff.**

Île d'Ouessant★★: the westernmost island off the Atlantic coast. *1 558ha - 6sq mi, highest point 60m - 197ft; 2hr 30min* crossing from **Brest** or *1hr 30min* from **Conquet**.

Île de Molène: *100ha - 0.38sq mi; 30min* crossing from **Pointe St-Matthieu.**

UNESCO World Heritage List

In 1972, the United Nations Educational, Scientific and Cultural Organization (UNESCO) adopted a Convention for the preservation of cultural and natural sites. To date, more than 150 States Parties have signed this international agreement,
which has listed over 500 sites "of outstanding universal value" on the World Heritage List. Each year, a committee of representatives from 21 countries, assisted by technical organisations (ICOMOS – International Council on Monuments and Sites; IUCN – International Union for Conservation of Nature and Natural Resources; ICCROM – International Centre for the Study of the Preservation and Restoration of Cultural Property, the Rome Centre), evaluates the proposals for new sites to be included on the list, which grows longer as new nominations are accepted and more countries sign the Convention. To be considered, a site must be nominated by the country in which it is located.

The protected cultural heritage may be monuments (buildings, sculptures, archaeological structures etc) with unique historical, artistic or scientific features; groups of buildings (such as religious communities, ancient cities); or sites (human settlements, examples of exceptional landscapes, cultural landscapes) which are the combined works of man and nature of exceptional beauty. Natural sites may be a testimony to the stages of the earth's geological history or to the development of human cultures and creative genius or represent significant ongoing ecological processes, contain superlative natural phenomena or provide a habitat for threatened species.

Signatories of the Convention pledge to co-operate to preserve and protect these sites around the world as a common heritage to be shared by all humanity.

Some of the most well-known places which the World Heritage Committee has inscribed include: Australia's Great Barrier Reef (1981), the Canadian Rocky Mountain Parks (1984), The Great Wall of China (1987), the Statue of Liberty (1984), the Kremlin (1990), Mont-Saint-Michel and its Bay (France, 1979), Durham Castle and Cathedral (1986).

UNESCO World Heritage Sites included in this guide are:

1 – Mont-St-Michel and its bay. Green Guide Normandy.
2 – Chartres Cathedral. Green Guide Northern France.
3 – Versailles: Château and Gardens. Green Guide Northern France.
4 – Vézelay: Basilica and Hill. Green Guide Burgundy-Jura.
5 – Caves with prehistoric art in the Vallée de la Vézère. Green Guide Dordogne-Berry-Limousin.
6 – Fontainebleau: Palace and Gardens. Green Guide Northern France.
7 – Amiens Cathedral. Green Guide Northern France.
8 – Orange: Roman theatre and surrounding area, Triumphal Arch. Green Guide Provence.
9 – Arles: Roman and Romanesque monuments. Green Guide Provence.
10 – Fontenay Abbey. Green Guide Burgundy-Jura.
11 – Arc-et-Senans: Saline royale. Green Guide Burgundy-Jura.
12 – Nancy: Place Stanislas, Place de la Carrière, Place d'Alliance. Green Guide Alsace-Lorraine-Champagne.
13 – Saint-Savin-sur-Gartempe: Abbey church. Green Guide Atlantic Coast.
14 – Gulfs of Girolata and Porto, Scandola Nature Reserve, bays (calanches) in Piana, Corsica. Green Guide Corse (in French).
15 – Pont du Gard. Green Guide Provence.
16 – Strasbourg: Cathedral, Grande Île. Green Guide Alsace-Lorraine-Champagne.
17 – Reims: Cathedral, Palais du Tau, Basilique St-Rémi.Green Guide Alsace-Lorraine-Champagne.
18 – Paris: banks of the Seine from L'Arsenal to Pont d'Iéna (Île de la Cité, Île St-Louis), vistas and monuments (Place de la Concorde, Église de la Madeleine, Chambre des Députés, Pont Alexandre-III, Grand Palais, Petit Palais, Les Invalides, École Militaire, Champ-de-Mars, Palais de Chaillot). Green Guide Paris.
19 – Chambord: Château and Park. Green Guide Châteaux of the Loire.
20 – Bourges: Cathédrale St-Étienne. Green Guide Dordogne-Berry-Limousin.
21 – Avignon: Centre historique. Green Guide Provence.
22 – Canal du Midi. Green Guide Pyrénées-Languedoc-Roussillon.

Île de Sein: *50ha - 0.19sq mi, highest point 6m - 20ft; 1hr* crossing from **Audierne.**

Îles de Glénan: a group of 10 islets, mostly uninhabited, attached to **Fouesnant.**

Île de Groix★: *1 770ha - 7sq mi, highest point 49m - 160ft; 45min* crossing from **Lorient.**

Îles du Golfe de Morbihan★★: Among the string of islets in the bay, the most noteworthy are **Île-aux-Moines**★, *310ha - 1.2sq mi,* and **Île d'Arz**, *324ha - 1.25sq mi.*

Belle-Île-en-Mer★★: *8 400ha - 48sq mi; 1hr* crossing from **Quiberon.**

Île d'Houat: *288ha - 1sq mi; 1hr* crossing from **Quiberon**.

Île d'Hoedic: *209ha - 0.8sq mi; 1hr 30min* crossing from **Quiberon** via **Houat.**

Île d'Yeu★★: *2 300ha - 9sq mi;* this island is the farthest from the mainland; *1hr 15min* crossing from **Fromentine.**

Île d'Aix★: *129ha - 0.5sq mi; 20min* crossing from **Fouras.**

Île de Noirmoutier, Île de Ré★ and **Île d'Oléron**★: These are linked to the mainland by a road bridge.

ÎLES DU LEVANT

(Mediterranean Sea)

Archipel du Frioul: Île de Pomègues and **Île Ratonneau** linked by Frioul harbour, **Îlot d'If**★★: *1hr 30min* excursion from **Marseille.**

Îles des Calanques: Maire, Jarre, Calseraigne, Riou are great spots for underwater fishing.

Île de Bendor★: *7min* from **Bandol.**

Îles d'Hyères★★★: **Porquerolles**★★★, *1 254ha - 5sq mi, 20min crossing from Giens; Port-Cros*★★, *640ha - 2.5sq mi, 45min* crossing from **Port-de-Miramar**; **Île du Levant**, *996ha - 3.8sq mi, 35min* crossing from **Le Lavandou.**

Îles de Lérins★★: **St-Honorat**★★, *60ha - 0.2sq mi;* **Ste-Marguerite**★★, *210ha - 0.8sq mi, 30min* crossing from **Cannes** or **Juan-les-Pins.**

Îles Sanguinaires★★: *60min* crossing from **Ajaccio.**

Îles Lavezzia: *30min* crossing from **Bonifacio.**

Leisure Activities

Information and brochures for sporting and outdoor facilities available may be obtained from the French Government Tourist Office or from the local tourist information centres shown within the *Discovering France* section of this guide.

WINE TOURS

In the various regions, wine tours which take in the main wine-producing areas and cellars are signposted. For information apply to the Tourist Information Centre. Buying your own wine directly from the grower can be an adventurous and satisfying holiday occupation. Signs announce farm-gate sales (*vins-vente directe*) or wine tasting and sales (*dégustation vente*).

CRAFTS

Many arts-and-crafts studios (weaving, wrought iron, pottery) on the coast and inland are open to visitors in summer. For courses apply to the Tourist Information Centre.

CYCLING HOLIDAYS

The Fédération Française de Cyclotourisme: 8 rue Jean-Marie-Jégo, 75013 Paris, ☎ (01) 45 80 30 21 supplies itineraries covering most of France, mentioning mileage, difficult routes and sights to visit.
You can also contact the Fédération Française de Cyclisme, 5 rue de Rome, 93561 Rosny-sous-Bois Cedex ☎ (01) 49 35 69 00.
Lists of cycle hire businesses are available from the Tourist Information Centres. The main railway stations also hire out cycles which can be returned at a different station.

HIKING

Short-, medium- and long-distance footpath Topo-Guides are published by the Fédération Française de la Randonnée Pédestre – Comité National des Sentiers de Grande Randonnée. These give detailed maps of the paths and offer valuable information to the hiker, and are on sale at the Information Centre: 64 rue de Gergovie, 75014 Paris. ☎ (01) 45 45 31 02; or by mail order from McCarta, 15 Highbury Place, London N5 1QP, ☎ (0171) 354 1616.

Arral/IMAGES TOULOUSE

Canoeing

FISHING

Current brochures: folding map *Fishing in France* (*Pêche en France*) published and distributed by the Conseil Supérieur de la Pêche, 134 avenue de Malakoff, 75016 Paris, ☎ (01) 45 02 20 20; also available from the departmental fishing organisations. For information about regulations contact the Tourist Information Centres or the offices of the Water and Forest Authority (Eaux et Forêts).

CRUISING

The extensive network of canals and rivers of France can be explored at leisure (maximum speed 6km/h). For information on boat hire, apply to the Syndicat national des loueurs de bateaux de plaisance, port de Javel Haut, 75015 Paris, ☎ (01) 44 37 04 00. Charges usually include boat hire, insurance, technical assistance. Some charter companies offer bicycles which enable visitors to go shopping and for rides or excursions along the towpath or to neighbouring villages. Visitors usually operate the locks on small canals by themselves; otherwise, it is customary to give a hand to the lock-keeper.

Two publishers produce collections of guides to cruising on French canals. Both series include numerous maps and useful information and are provided with English translations. The publishers are: Grafocarte, 125 rue J.-J. Rousseau, 92130 Issy-les-Moulineaux, ☎ (01) 41 09 19 00;
Guides Vagnon, Les Éditions du Plaisancier, 100 avenue du Général-Leclerc, 69641 Caluire Cedex, ☎ (04) 78 23 31 14.

SAILING

Many resorts have sailing clubs offering courses. In season it is possible to hire boats with or without crew; apply to the Fédération Française de Voile: 55 avenue Kléber, 75784 Paris. ☎ (01) 44 05 81 00.

CANOEING

Apply to Fédération Française de Canoe-Kayak, 87 quai de la Marne, 94340 Joinville-le-Pont, ☎ (01) 45 11 08 50. A guide is published annually indicating schools and places where canoeing may be practised.

MOTOR BOATING AND WATER-SKIING

Enquire at the local Tourist Information Centre or at the resort. Anyone who intends to drive a powered boat (6hp – 50hp) within five nautical miles of a French harbour must qualify for a sea certificate (*carte mer*). Beyond the 5-mile limit an additional sea permit (*permis mer*) is required. Yachts and boats with engines of less than 6hp are exempt.

SCUBA-DIVING

Apply to the Fédération Française d'Études et de Sports Sous-Marins, 24 quai de Rive Neuve, 13007 Marseille, ☎ (04) 91 33 99 31. The federation publishes *Subaqua*, a bimestrial journal on diving in France.

WIND SURFING

The sport, which is subject to certain regulations, is permitted on lakes and in sports and leisure centres. Apply to sailing clubs. Boards may be hired on all major beaches.

RIDING AND PONY TREKKING

Apply to the Délégation Nationale au Tourisme Équestre (DNTE), Parc de l'Île Saint-Germain, 170 quai Stalingrad, 92130 Issy-les-Moulineaux, ☎ (01) 46 48 83 93, which publishes an annual handbook covering the whole of France.

HUNTING

For all enquiries apply to **Saint-Hubert Club de France**, 10 rue de Lisbonne, 75008 Paris, ☎ (01) 45 22 38 90.

GOLF

For location, addresses and telephone numbers of golf courses in France, consult the map *Golfs, les Parcours français,* published by Edition Plein Sud based on **Michelin maps.** You can also contact the Fédération Française de Golf, 69 avenue Victor-Hugo, 75016 Paris, ☎ (01) 44 17 63 00.

SKIING

For all enquiries contact the Club Alpin Français, 24 avenue de Laumière, 75019 Paris, ☎ (01) 53 72 88 00.

CLIMBING

Excursions with qualified instructors are organised by sections of the Club Alpin Français (apply to the above address for information on regional sections) or by local guides. For information apply to the Tourist Information Centres or to the Fédération Française de la Montagne et de l'Escalade, 8 quai de la Marne, 75019 Paris, ☎ (01) 40 18 75 50.

SPELEOLOGY

Apply to the Speleology sections of the Club Alpin Français (see under Skiing and Mountaineering).

GLIDING

Apply to the Fédération Française de Vol à voile, 29 rue de Sèvres, 75006 Paris, ☎ (01) 45 44 04 78.

Shopping

OPENING HOURS

Department stores are open Monday to Saturday, 9am to 6.30pm-7.30pm. Smaller, more specialised shops may close during the lunch hour. Food stores (grocers, wine merchants and bakeries) are open from 7am to 6.30pm-7.30pm; some open on Sunday mornings. Many food stores close between noon and 2pm and on Mondays. Hypermarkets are usually open until 9pm-10pm.

WHAT YOU CAN TAKE HOME

Travellers to America cannot bring back food and plant products, especially cheeses and fruit. Americans are allowed to take home, tax-free, up to US$400 worth of goods, Canadians up to CND$300, British up to £ 136, Australians up to AUS$400 and New Zealanders up to NZ$700.

MARKETS

When travelling around France make sure you have a look around the different local markets – an important domestic institution – or the various agricultural fairs which are held regularly throughout the year.

VALUE-ADDED TAX

In France a sales tax (*TVA* or VAT) is added to purchases. For non-Europeans, this tax can be refunded as long as you have bought more than 175€ worth of goods at the same time and in the same shop. This fixed amount may vary, so it is advisable to check with the VAT-refund counter (*service de détaxe*). Collect the appropriate forms at the time of purchase and present to Customs officials on leaving France for processing. Customs Information Centre: ☎ 08 25 30 82 63 *(0.15€/min)* or www.douane.gouv.fr.

Books

Copies of titles mentioned below may be obtained through public libraries.

France Today by J Ardagh (*Penguin 1990*)

The French by T Zeldin (*Collins Harvill 1988*)

The Identity of France 1. History and Environment by F Braudel (*Fontana 1989*)

A Traveller's History of France by R Cole *(Windrush 1988)*

French and English by R Faber *(Faber 1975)*

Britain and France: Ten Centuries by D Johnson F Bedarida and F. Crouzet *(Dawson 1980)*

The Lives of the Kings and Queens of France by the Duc de Castries *(Weidenfeld 1979)*

Searching for the New France by J Hollifield and G Ross *(Routledge)*

The Lost World of the Impressionists by A Bellony-Rewald *(Galley 1976)*

French Architecture by P Lavedan *(Penguin 1956)*

The Wine Lover's Guide to France by M Busselle *(Pavilion, Michael Joseph 1986)*

The Food Lover's Guide to France by P Wells *(Eyre and Spottiswoode)*

The Wines and Winelands of France – Geological Journeys by L Pomerol *(Edition du BRGM)*

The Wine Regions of France by Michelin *(2005)*

1000 Charming Hotels and Guesthouses by Michelin *(2005)*

Films

Alps: La Route Napoléon *(1953)* by J Delannoy (villages in the Alpes-de-Haute-Provence).

Alsace-Lorraine: La Grande Illusion *(1937)* by Jean Renoir *(Colmar and around Neuf-Brisach).*

Atlantic Coast: Moderato Cantabile *(1960)* by P Brook *(Blaye, Gironde);* **Les Demoiselles de Rochefort** *(1966)* by J Demy.

Berry: Tous les Matins du Monde *(1992)* by A Corneau *(Château de Bodeau near Rougnat).*

Brittany: Les Vacances de Monsieur Hulot – *Monsieur Hulot's Holidays (1951)* by J Tati.

Burgundy-Jura: Mayerling *(1968)* by T Young *(Pontarlier).*

Champagne: Camille Claudel *(1988)* by B Nuytten; **Au Revoir les Enfants** *(1988)* by L Malle.

Châteaux of the Loire: La Règle du Jeu *(1939)* by C Renoir *(Château de la Ferté-St-Aubin).*

Corsica: Napoléon *(1927)* by A Gance *(Ajaccio, Grotte de Casone, Pointe des Sanguinaires).*

Dordogne-Berry-Limousin: Les Misérables *(1935)* by R Boleshawski *(Sarlat, Montpazier).*

Flanders: Germinal *(1993)* by C Berri *(Oignies, Astres).*

French Riviera: To Catch a Thief *(1956)* by A Hitchcock *(Monaco);* **Pierrot le Fou** *(1965)* by J.-L. Godard.

Ile-de-France: La Belle et la Bête *(1945)* by Jean Cocteau; **La Guerre des Boutons** *(1961)* by Y Robert *(Rambouillet);* **La Haine** *(1995)* by M Kassovitz *(Paris Suburbs).*

Normandy: Les Parapluies de Cherbourg *(1963)* by J Demy *(Cherbourg).*

Provence: Marius *(1931)* by Pagnol *(Marseille);* **Crin Blanc** *(1953)* by A Lamorisse *(Camargue);* **Jean de Florette** and **Manon des Sources** *(1986)* by C Berri; **La Gloire de mon Père** and **Le Château de ma Mère** *(1990)* by Y Robert *(Marseille, Allauch, Grambois).*

Pyrenees-Languedoc-Tarn Gorges: 37°2 le Matin – *Betty Blue (1986)* by J J Beineix *(Gruissan, Marvejols);* **Le Retour de Martin Guerre** *(1982)* by D Vigne.

Rhône Valley: L'Horloger de Saint-Paul *(1973)* by B Tavernier *(Lyon).*

When to Go

SEASONS

To give the visitor a general idea of the weather in France, below is a temperature chart which covers the entire country. **Spring**, **summer** and **autumn** are the best seasons to visit France but there is a region for every season. The summer period can be beautiful but crowds are much larger, so it would be wiser to travel either in June or September when French children are still at school.

CLIMATE

For an overview of a specific region of the country, see the **Michelin Green Guide** series, which cover 24 regions of France (13 of the guides are in English), such as Normandy, Brittany, the French Riviera, Provence, etc. In general the French climate is a moderate one; extremes of either heat or cold are rare for the most part, so that outdoor activity of some kind is almost always possible. Inland the winters are chilly and darkness comes early, especially in the northern latitudes. As spring turns to summer, the days become long and warm and by June the sun lingers well into the evening. Spring and autumn provide opportunities to explore the outdoors and enjoy the lovely countryside and coastal areas of France. In winter, snowfall throughout much of the interior of the country, as well as in the mountainous regions near Italy, permits a wide array of winter sports, such as downhill skiing and snowboarding. However, gray skies in this period are not unusual for much of the country, especially in Paris.

WEATHER FORECAST

National forecast: ☏ 32 50. Information a bout the weather is also available online at www.meteofrance.com.

WHAT TO PACK

Year-round, it is advisable to have a raincoat or hooded coat, and umbrella. Warmer wear, including a hat, neck scarf and gloves, is necessary in early spring, late autumn and winter. In summer it can be cool in the evening in some parts of the country, so taking some warmer clothing is recommended. Comfortable footwear is essential for sightseeing.

Temperature chart throughout France												
	Jan	Feb	Mar	Apr	May	Jun	Jul	Aug	Sep	Oct	Nov	Dec
	9	10	15	17	20	23	25	25	23	18	12	8
Bordeaux	1	2	4	9	12	13	13	13	12	8	4	2
	8	9	11	13	15	18	19	20	18	15	11	9
Brest	4	3	4	7	8	11	12	13	11	8	6	4
	7	8	13	16	19	23	25	25	22	16	11	7
Clermont	-1	-1	2	5	7	11	13	12	10	6	3	0
	5	8	13	16	20	23	26	26	23	16	10	6
Grenoble	-3	-2	2	5	8	12	14	13	11	6	3	-1
	5	6	10	13	17	20	22	22	19	14	9	6
Lille	0	0	2	4	7	10	12	12	10	7	3	1
	12	13	14	17	20	23	26	26	24	20	16	13
Nice	4	4	5	9	12	16	18	16	12	8	5	
	7	7	12	15	19	22	24	24	21	15	10	6
Paris	1	1	3	6	9	12	14	14	11	8	4	2
	12	13	16	18	21	25	28	28	25	20	15	12
Perpignan	3	4	7	9	12	16	19	18	16	12	8	5
	3	5	11	15	19	23	24	25	20	14	8	4
Strasbourg	-2	-1	1	4	6	11	13	13	10	5	2	-1
Maximum temperatures in red; minimum temperatures in black.												

Calendar of Events

This list includes a selection of festivals and events likely to be of interest to the visitor, further details of which can be obtained from the telephone numbers shown after the name of the town.

Religious and Civic Festivals

LATE FEBRUARY

Nice
☏ 04 93 87 16 28
Carnival
Chalon-sur-Saône
☏ 03 85 48 39 79
Carnival, Winter Fur and Pelt Fair
Le Touquet
☏ 02 21 99 05 43
Motorbike Race along the beach

MAUNDY THURSDAY

Le Puy-en-Velay
☏ 04 71 09 38 41
White Penitents Procession
Saugues
☏ 04 71 77 84 46
White Penitents Procession
(at nightfall)

GOOD FRIDAY

Arles-sur-Tech
☏ 04 68 39 11 99
Black Penitents Procession
Burzet
☏ 04 75 94 41 03
The Passion re-enacted
Collioure
☏ 04 68 82 15 47
Penitents Procession
Perpignan
☏ 04 68 66 30 30
Black Penitents Procession
Roquebrune-Cap-Martin
☏ 04 93 35 62 87
Procession of the
Entombment of Christ
Sartène
☏ 04 95 77 05 11
U Catenacciu Procession

EASTER SUNDAY

St-Benoit-sur-Loire
☏ 02 38 35 72 43
Easter Service

EASTER MONDAY

Cassel
☏ 03 28 42 40 13
Carnival of the Giants Reuze-Papa and
Reuze-Maman

APRIL

Chartres
☏ 02 37 21 54 03
Students' Pilgrimage

MID-APRIL

Gérardmer
☏ 03 29 63 00 80
Flower Festival

EARLY MAY

Orléans
☏ 02 38 79 23 86
Joan of Arc Festival

MID MAY

St-Tropez
☏ 04 94 97 45 21
Procession in honour
of St-Tropez (Bravade)
Tréguier
☏ 02 96 92 30 19
Pardon of St-Ives
Mont-St-Michel
☏ 02 33 60 14 30
Feast of St Michael in Spring

LATE MAY

Rouen
☏ 02 35 74 41 77
Joan of Arc Festival
Pomarez
☏ 05 58 89 33 32
Les Stes-Maries-de-la-Mer
☏ 04 90 47 82 55
Gypsy Pilgrimage

WHIT

Honfleur
☏ 02 31 89 23 30
Seamen's Festival

EARLY JUNE

La Rochelle
☎ 05 46 44 62 44
International Regatta

Utah Beach-Omaha Beach
☎ 02 33 41 31 18
Commemoration of the D-Day
Landings (American sector)

Gold-Juno-Sword
☎ 02 31 86 53 30
Commemoration of the D-Day
Landings (Anglo-Canadian sector).
*The two events are combined every
five years.*

MID-JUNE

Chambord
☎ 02 47 55 09 16
Game Fair

Le Mans
☎ 03 43 40 24 24
24-hour car race

EARLY JULY

Douai
☎ 03 27 88 26 76
Carnival of the Giant Gayant
and his family

MID-JULY

Carcassonne
☎ 04 68 25 07 04
Illumination of the City

LATE JULY

Ste-Anne-d'Auray
☎ 02 97 57 68 80
Great Pardon of Ste-Anne

EARLY AUGUST

Bayonne
☎ 05 59 59 31 31
Corrida and Street Festival

Colmar
☎ 03 89 20 25 50
Alsatian Wine Festival

MID-AUGUST

Béziers
☎ 04 67 36 73 73
Feria

Carcassonne
☎ 04 68 25 07 04
Medieval Festival

Chamonix
☎ 04 50 53 00 88
Mountain Guides Festival

Pomarez
☎ 05 58 89 33 32
Running of the Cows

St-Palais
☎ 05 59 65 95 77
Basque Festival

LATE AUGUST

Boulogne-sur-Mer
☎ 03 21 31 68 38
Pilgrimage to Notre-Dame-de-
    Boulogne

Concarneau
☎ 02 98 97 01 44
Festival of the Blue Nets

Monteux
☎ 04 90 66 33 96
Fireworks Festival

EARLY SEPTEMBER

Dinan
☎ 02 96 39 22 43
Ramparts Festival
(every two years)

Lille
☎ 03 20 30 81 00
Grand jumble sale

Le Mas Soubeyran
☎ 04 66 85 02 72
National Protestant Assembly

LATE SEPTEMBER

Mont-St-Michel
☎ 02 33 60 14 30
Feast of the Archangel St Michael

MID-NOVEMBER

Beaune
☎ 03 80 22 24 51
Auction sale of the wines of the
Hospices de Beaune

EARLY DECEMBER

Marseille
☎ 04 91 54 91 11
Santons Fair

Mont-Ste-Odile
☎ 03 88 95 80 53
Pilgrimage
(the most important in Alsace)
Strasbourg
☎ 03 88 52 28 28
Christmas Market

DECEMBER 25

Les-Baux-de-Provence
☎ 04 90 97 34 39
Shepherds' Midnight Mass

Son et Lumière in the Loire Valley
The theme of the shows may change periodically. The list below is only a selection.
Amboise
☎ 02 47 57 14 47
"At The Court of King François"
Azay-le-Rideau
☎ 02 47 45 42 04
"The Imaginary World of the Château d'Azay-le-Rideau"
Blois
☎ 02 54 78 72 76
"The Story of Blois"
Chenonceau
☎ 02 47 23 90 07
"The Ladies of Chenonceau"
Cheverny
☎ 02 54 42 69 03
"The River Loire down the ages"
Loches
☎ 02 47 59 07 98
"The Strange Story of Bélisane"
Le Lude
☎ 02 43 94 60 09
"Spectacular Historical Events"
Valençay
☎ 02 54 00 04 42
"Esclarmonde"
You are advised to book accommodation well in advance at festival times, even out of season.

Cultural Festivals
The following list includes some of the more important annual festivals:

Aix-en-Provence
☎ 04 42 17 34 00
July
International music Festival

ALBI
☎ 05 63 54 22 30
June
Theatre
July
Music

ARLES
☎ 04 90 96 76 06
2nd week July
International Photo Festival

AVIGNON
☎ 04 90 82 67 08
2nd fortnight July
Dramatic art

BELFORT
☎ 03 84 54 24 24
late November
Cinema

BELLAC
☎ 05 55 68 10 44
late June/early July
Drama, music

BESANÇON
☎ 03 81 80 73 26
September
Classical music-Young Conductors Competition

BÉZIERS
☎ 04 67 36 73 73
1st fortnight in July
Classical music

BOURGES
☎ 02 48 70 61 11
late April/early May
Music Festival

CANNES
☎ 04 42 66 92 20
May
International Film Festival

CARCASSONNE
☎ 04 68 25 33 13
July
Theatre, music and dance

CARPENTRAS
☎ 04 90 63 46 35
2nd fortnight in July
Music and dance

LA CHAISE-DIEU
☎ 04 71 00 01 16
late August/early September
French religious music

CHARTRES
☎ 02 37 21 54 03
July and August
Religious music

CHAUMONT-SUR-LOIRE
☎ 02 54 20 99 22
mid-June/mid-October
International Garden Festival

DEAUVILLE
1st fortnight in September
American film Festival

DIVONNE
☎ 04 50 40 34 16
2nd fortnight in June
Chamber music

ENTRECASTEAUX
☎ 04 94 04 42 86
2nd fortnight in August
Chamber music

ÉVIAN
☎ 04 50 75 04 26
mid-May
Music

GANNAT
☎ 04 70 90 12 67
2nd fortnight in July
International folk music

JUAN-LES-PINS
☎ 04 93 33 95 64
2nd fortnight in July
World Jazz Festival

LANNION
☎ 02 96 37 07 35
mid-July/late August
Organ and choral music

LILLE
☎ 03 20 52 74 23
October-November
Music, dance and theatre

LORIENT
☎ 02 97 21 24 29
early August
Celtic festival

LYON
☎ 04 72 40 26 26
2nd fortnight in September
even years: dance; odd years: music and contemporary art

MONTAUBAN
☎ 05 63 63 60 60
early August
Choreography

NANTES
☎ 02 40 47 04 51
early July
Folkways

ORANGE
☎ 04 90 34 24 24
2nd fortnight in July
Music and opera

PAU
☎ 05 59 27 85 80
mid-June/mid-July
Theatre, music and dance

PRADES
☎ 04 68 96 33 07
late July/mid-August
Chamber music (Festival Pablo Casals)

LE PUY-EN-VELAY
☎ 04 71 09 38 41
mid-September
Renaissance Festival

QUIMPER
☎ 02 98 55 53 53
4th Sunday in July
Cornouaille Festival

RENNES
☎ 02 99 30 38 01
early July
Theatre, music, dance and poetry

ST-CÉRÉ
☎ 05 65 38 29 08
mid-July/late August
Music

ST-DONAT-SUR-L'HERBASSE
☎ 04 75 45 10 29
late July/early August
Bach Festival

ST-GUILHEM-LE-DÉSERT
☎ 04 67 63 14 99
July/August
Baroque Music

ST-MALO
☎ 02 99 40 42 50
late October
Comics Festival

ST-RÉMY-DE-PROVENCE
☎ 04 90 92 16 31
mid-July/mid-September
Organ music

SALON-DE-PROVENCE
☎ 04 90 42 12 12
July
Jazz/Rock

SARLAT
☎ 05 53 31 10 83
late July/early August
Theatre

SCEAUX
☎ 01 46 60 07 79
mid-July/late September
Classical and chamber music

TOULOUSE
☎ 05 61 11 02 22
late June/late August
Classical, Jazz and Folk Music

VAISON-LA-ROMAINE
☎ 04 90 36 12 92
July and August
Theatre and dance-Folklore

VANNES
☎ 02 97 47 24 34
15 August
Arvor Festival (folk music)

VERSAILLES
☎ 01 39 50 36 22
May to October every Sunday
Fountain display with music
☎ 01 39 50 36 22
2 weekends July 2
weekends
Illuminations of the Neptune Basin, fireworks display and fountain display with music

Useful Words and Phrases

SIGHTS

abbaye . . . . .abbey
beffroi . . . . .belfry
chapelle . . . . chapel
château. . . . . .castle
cimetière . . . . cemetery
cloître . . . . .cloisters
cour . . . . courtyard
couvent. . . . . .convent
écluse . . . . .lock (canal)
église. . . . . church
fontaine . . . . fountain
halle. . . . . covered market
jardin . . . . .garden
mairie . . . . .town hall
maison . . . . .house
marché . . . . .market
monastère . . . . monastery
moulin. . . . . windmill
musée . . . . museum
parc . . . . park
place . . . . square
pont. . . . . bridge
port . . . . .port/harbour
porte . . . . gateway
quai . . . . .quay
remparts. . . . . .ramparts
rue . . . . .street
statue . . . . statue
tour . . . . .tower

NATURAL SITES

abîme . . . . chasm
aven . . . . .swallow-hole
barrage. . . . . dam
belvédère. . . . . .viewpoint
cascade. . . . . waterfall
col. . . . . pass
corniche . . . . ledge
côte . . . . .coast, hillside
forêt. . . . . .forest
grotte . . . . cave
lac. . . . . .lake
plage . . . . .beach
rivière . . . . river
ruisseau. . . . . .stream
signal. . . . . beacon
source . . . . spring
vallée. . . . . valley

ON THE ROAD

car park. . . . . parking
driving licence . .permis de conduire
east. . . . . .Est
garage (for repairs) . . . . .garage
left . . . . gauche
motorway/highway . . . . . .autoroute
north . . . . .Nord
parking meter. . . . . .horodateur
petrol/gas. . . . . essence
petrol/gas station . . .station essence
right. . . . . .droite
south . . . . .Sud
toll . . . . péage
traffic lights . . . . .feu tricolore
tyre. . . . . .pneu
west . . . . .Ouest
wheel clamp . . . . sabot
zebra crossing. . . . . . . passage clouté

TIME

today . . . . aujourd'hui
tomorrow. . . . . demain
yesterday .hier
winter . . . . .hiver
spring . . . . .printemps
summer. été
autumn/fall . . . . .automne
week . . . . semaine
Monday. .lundi
Tuesday. .mardi
Wednesday . . . . .mercredi
Thursday. . . . . .jeudi
Friday. . . . . .vendredi
Saturday . . . . samedi
Sunday . . . . dimanche

NUMBERS

0 . . . . zéro
1 . . . . un
2 . . . . .deux
3 . . . . trois
4 . . . . quatre
5 . . . . cinq
6 . . . . six
7 . . . . sept
8 . . . . .huit
9 . . . . neuf
10 . . . . .dix
11 . . . . .onze
12 . . . . .douze
13 . . . . treize
14 . . . . .quatorze

15	quinze
16	seize
17	dix-sept
18	dix-huit
19	dix-neuf
20	vingt
30	trente
40	quarante
50	cinquante
60	soixante
70	soixante-dix
80	quatre-vingt
90	quatre-vingt-dix
100	cent
1000	mille

SHOPPING

bank	banque
baker's	boulangerie
big	grand
butcher's	boucherie
chemist's	pharmacie
closed	fermé
cough mixture	sirop pour la toux
cough sweets	cachets pour la gorge
entrance	entrée
exit	sortie
fishmonger's	poissonnerie
grocer's	épicerie
newsagent, bookshop	librairie
open	ouvert
post office	poste
push	pousser
pull	tirer
shop	magasin
small	petit
stamps	timbres

FOOD AND DRINK

beef	bœuf
beer	bière
butter	beurre
bread	pain
breakfast	petit-déjeuner
cheese	fromage
dessert	dessert
dinner	dîner
fish	poisson
fork	fourchette
fruit	fruits
glass	verre
chicken	poulet
ice cream	glace
ice cubes	glaçons
ham	jambon
knife	couteau
lamb	agneau
lunch	déjeuner
lettuce salad	salade
meat	viande
mineral water	eau minérale
mixed salad	salade composée
orange juice	jus d'orange
plate	assiette
pork	porc
restaurant	restaurant
red wine	vin rouge
salt	sel
spoon	cuillère
sugar	sucre
vegetables	légumes
water	de l'eau
white wine	vin blanc
yoghurt	yaourt

TRAVEL

airport	aéroport
credit card	carte de crédit
customs	douane
passport	passeport
platform	voie
railway station	gare
shuttle	navette
suitcase	valise
train ticket	billet de train
plane ticket	billet d'avion
wallet	portefeuille

CLOTHING

coat	manteau
jumper	pull
raincoat	imperméable
shirt	chemise
shoes	chaussures
socks	chaussettes
stockings	bas
suit	costume
tights	collants
trousers	pantalon

COMMON WORDS

goodbye	au revoir
hello/good morning	bonjour
how	comment
excuse me	excusez-moi
thank you	merci
yes/no	oui/non
I am sorry	pardon

why . . . . .pourquoi
when . . . . quand
please . . . . s'il vous plaît

USEFUL PHRASE

Do you speak English? . . . .
   Parlez-vous anglais?
I don't understand. . . . .
   Je ne comprends pas
Talk slowly . . . .
   Parlez lentement
Where's...? . . . .
   Où est...?
When does the ... leave? . . . .
   A quelle heure part...?
When does the ... arrive? . . . .
   A quelle heure arrive...?
When does the museum open?. . . . . .
   A quelle heure ouvre le musée?
When is the show?. . . . .
   . . . . .A quelle heure est la
   représentation?

When is breakfast served? . . . .
   . . . . .A quelle heure sert-on le
   petit-déjeuner?
What does it cost? . . . .
   Combien cela coûte?
Where can I buy a newspaper in
   English? . . . .Où puis-je acheter un
   journal en anglais?
Where is the nearest petrol/gas
   station? . . .Où se trouve la station
   essence la plus proche?
Where can I change traveller's
   cheques? Où puis-je échanger des
   traveller's cheques?
Where are the toilets? . . . .
   Où sont les toilettes?
Do you accept credit cards? . . . .
   . . . . . .Acceptez-vous les cartes de
   crédit?

GASTRONOMIC TERMS

*See Gastronomy of France in the
Introduction.*

KNOW BEFORE YOU GO

Useful Web Sites

www.ambafrance-us.org, www.ambafrance-uk.org

The French Embassy has a web site in the US and UK providing basic information (geography, demographics, history), a news digest and business-related information. It offers special pages for children, pages devoted to culture, language study and travel, and links to other selected French sites (regions, cities, ministries).

www.franceguide.com

The French Government Tourist Office/ Maison de la France site is packed with practical information and tips for those travelling to France.

www.FranceKeys.com

This site has plenty of practical information for visiting France. It covers all the regions, with links to tourist offices and related sites. Very useful for planning the details of your tour in France!

www.franceway.com

This is an online magazine which focuses on culture and heritage. For each region, there are also suggestions for activities and practical information on where to stay and how to get there.

ViaMichelin.com

This site has maps, tourist information, suggestions on hotels and restaurants, and a route planner for numerous locations in Europe. In addition, you can look up weather forecasts, traffic reports and service station location, particularly useful if you will be driving in France.

French Tourist Offices

For information, brochures, maps and assistance in planning a trip to France, travellers should contact the official tourist office in their own country:

Australia-New Zealand

BNP Building, 12 Castlereagh Street, Sydney, New South Wales 2000.
☏ (2) 9231 5244
Fax (2) 9231 8682

Canada

1981 Av McGill College, Suite 490, Montreal, QUE H3A 2W9.
☏ (514) 288 4264
Fax (514) 845-4868/(416) 767 6755

Republic of Ireland

35 Lower Abbey St, Dublin
☏ (1) 703 4046
Fax (1) 874 7324

United Kingdom

178 Piccadilly, London W1V 0AL.
☏ (0891) 244 123 (France Information Line, £0.50/min)
Fax (0171) 493 6594
email piccadilly@mdlf.demon.co.uk

United States

France On Call Hotline: 900-990-0040 (US$0.50/min)
for information on hotels, restaurants and transportation.

East Coast: 444 Madison Avenue, 16th floor, New York, NY 10022.
☏ (212) 838 7800, Fax (212) 838 7855

West Coast: 9454 Wilshire Bld, Suite 715, Beverly Hills, CA 90212-2967.
☏ (310) 271 2693, Fax (310) 276 2835

NATIONAL TOURIST OFFICES

France has a national network of regional tourist offices that will provide you with brochures and other information useful in planning your trip and answering your questions.

Fédération nationale des comités régionaux de tourisme
17 av.de l'Opéra, 75001 Paris, ☏ 01 47 03 03 10.
www.fncrt.com

Fédération nationale des comités départementaux de tourisme
280 boulevard St-Germain, 75007 Paris. ☏ (01) 44 11 10 20.

Fédération nationale des offices de tourisme et syndicats d'initiative
280 boulevard St-Germain, 75007 Paris. ☏ (01) 44 11 10 30.

REGIONAL TOURIST OFFICES

Alsace Lorraine Champagne
Alsace
39 av. des Champs-Élysées, 75008 Paris, ☏ 01 53 83 10 10.

20a r. Berthe-Molly, BP 247, 68005 Colmar Cedex, ☏ 03 88 25 01 66.
www.tourisme-alsace.com

Lorraine

2 r. de l'Échelle, 75001 Paris, ☎ 01 40 07 04 67.

Abbaye des Prémontrés, BP 97, 54700 Pont-à-Mousson, ☎ 03 83 80 01 80. www.crt-lorraine.fr

Champagne-Ardenne

15 av. Mar.-Leclerc, BP 319, 51013 Châlons-en-Champagne Cedex, ☎ 03 26 21 85 80. www.tourisme-champagne-ardenne.com

Atlantic Coast

Aquitaine

Cité Mondiale, 23 parvis des Chartrons, 33074 Bordeaux Cedex, ☎ 05 56 01 70 00. www.crt.cr-aquitaine.fr

Poitou-Charentes

68 r. du Cherche-Midi, 75006 Paris, ☎ 01 42 22 83 74.

62 r. Jean-Jaurès, 86002 Poitiers Cedex, ☎ 05 49 50 10 50. www.poitou-charentes-vacances.com

Auvergne The Rhone Valley

Auvergne

194 bis r. de Rivoli, 75001 Paris, ☎ 01 44 55 33 33. www.maisondelauvergne.com

44 av. des États-Unis, 63057 Clermont-Ferrand Cedex 1, ☎ 04 73 29 49 49. www.crt-auvergne.fr

Rhône-Alpes

104 rte de Paris, 69260 Charbonnières-les-Bains, ☎ 04 72 59 21 59. www.rhonealpes-tourisme.com

Brittany

Bretagne

203 bd St-Germain, 75007 Paris, ☎ 01 53 63 11 50.

1 r. Raoul-Ponchon, 35069 Rennes Cedex, ☎ 02 99 28 44 30. Info ☎ 02 99 36 15 15. www.touismebretagne.com

Burgundy Jura

Bourgogne

BP1602, 21035 Dijon Cedex, ☎ 03 80 28 02 80. www.bourgogne-tourisme.com

Franche-Comté

2 bd de la Madeleine, 75009 Paris, ☎ 01 42 66 26 28.

La City, 4 r. Gabriel-Plançon, 25044 Besançon Cedex, ☎ 03 81 25 08 08. www.franche-comte.org

Chateaux of the Loire

Centre-Val de Loire

6 r. Cassette, 75006 Paris, ☎ 01 53 63 02 50.

37 av. de Paris, 45000 Orléans, ☎ 02 38 79 95 00. www.loirevalleytourism.com

Pays de la Loire

6 r. Cassette, 75006 Paris, ☎ 01 53 63 02 50. 2 r. de la Loire, BP 20411, 44204 Nantes Cedex 2, ☎ 02 40 48 24 20. www.loirevalleytourism.com

Corsica

Corse

ATC, 17 bd Roi-Jérôme, BP 19, 20181 Ajaccio, ☎ 04 95 51 00 00. www.visit-corsica.com

Dordogne Berry Limousin

Limousin

30 r. Caumartin, 75009 Paris, ☎ 01 40 07 04 67.

27 bd de la Corderie, 87031 Limoges Cedx, ☎ 05 55 45 18 80. www.tourismelimousin.com

French Alps

Alpes-Dauphiné-Isère

2 pl. André-Malraux, 75001 Paris, ☎ 01 42 96 08 43/56. www.isere-tourisme.com

Hautes-Alpes

4 av. de l'Opéra, 75001 Paris, ☎ 01 42 96 05 08.

Savoie

31 av. de l'Opéra, 75001 Paris, ☎ 01 42 61 74 73. www.maisondesavoie.com

French Riviera

Riviera-Côte d'Azur

55 prom. des Anglais, BP 1602, 06011 Nice Cedex 1, ☎ 04 93 37 78 78. www.guideriviera.com

Languedoc Roussillon Tarn Gorges

Aveyron

46 r. Berger, 75001 Paris, ☎ 01 42 36 84 63. www.maison-aveyron.com

Languedoc-Roussillon

20 r. de la République, 34000 Montpellier, ☎ 04 67 22 81 00. www.cr-languedocroussillon.fr/tourisme

Lozère

4 r. Hautefeuille, 75006 Paris, ☎ 01 43 54 26 64. www.lozere-tourisme.com

Midi-Pyrénées

15 r. St-Augustin, 75002 Paris, ☎ 01 42 86 51 86.

54 bd de l'Embouchure, BP 2166, 31022 Toulouse Cedex 2, ☎ 05 61 13 55 55. www.tourisme.midi-pyrenees.com

Normandy

Normandie

Le Doyenné, 14 r. Charles-Corbeau, 27000 Évreux, ☎ 02 32 33 79 00. www.normandy-tourism.org

Northern France & Paris Region

Île-de-France

91 av. des Champs-Élysées, 75008 Paris, ☎ 01 56 89 38 00. www.paris-ile-de-france.com

Nord-Pas-de-Calais

6 pl. Mendès-France, 59028 Lille Cedex, ☎ 03 20 14 57 57. www. crt-nordpasdecalais.fr

Paris

127 av. des Champs-Élysées, 75008 Paris, ☎ 08 92 68 31 12. www.paris-touristoffice.com

Picardie

3 r. Vincent-Auriol, 80011 Amiens Cedex 1, ☎ 03 22 22 33 63

Provence

Provence-Alpes-Côte d'Azur

Les Docks, Atrium 10.5, 10 pl. de la Joliette, BP 46214, 13567 Marseille Cedex 02, ☎ 04 91 56 47 00.

International Visitors

EMBASSIES AND CONSULATES

Australia: Embassy, 4 rue Jean-Rey, 75015 Paris, ☎ (01) 40 59 33 00, Fax (01) 40 59 33 10

Canada: Embassy, 35 avenue Montaigne, 75008 Paris, ☎ (01) 44 43 29 00, Fax (01) 44 43 29 99

Republic of Ireland: Embassy, 4 rue Rude, 75016 Paris, ☎ (01) 44 17 67 00, Fax (01) 45 00 84 17

New Zealand: Embassy, 7 ter rue Léonard-de-Vinci, 75016 Paris, ☎ (01) 45 00 24 11, Fax (01) 45 01 26 39

UK: Embassy, 35 rue du Faubourg St-Honoré, 75008 Paris, ☎ (01) 42 66 91 42, Fax (01) 42 66 95 90

Consulate, 16 rue d'Anjou, 75008 Paris, ☎ (01) 42 66 06 68 (visas)

Consulate, 9 avenue Hoche, 75008 Paris, ☎ 01 42 66 38 10

Consulate, 24 avenue Prado, 13006 Marseille, ☎ (04) 91 15 72 10, Fax (04) 91 37 47 06

Consulate, Victoria Center, 20 chemin Laporte, 31300 Toulouse, ☎ (05) 61 15 02 02

USA: Embassy, 2 avenue Gabriel, 75008 Paris, ☎ (01) 43 12 22 22, Fax (01) 42 66 97 83

Consulate, 2 rue St-Florentin, 75001 Paris, ☎ (01) 44 29 40 00

Consulate, 12 boulevard Paul-Peytral, 13006 Marseille, ☎ (04) 91 54 92 00

DOCUMENTS

Passport – Visitors entering France must be in possession of a valid national passport. Citizens of one of the European Union countries need only a national identity card. In case of loss or theft, report to the embassy or consulate and the local police. A leaflet entitled *Get It Right Before You Go*, on the dos and don'ts of staying in France, is available from the French Government Tourist Office.

Visa – No **entry visa** is required for European Union, US, Canadian and New Zealand citizens as long as their stay in France does not exceed three months. Australians require a visa and should apply for one at the nearest French consulate. Citizens of other countries should check with a French consulate or travel agent.

US citizens should read the **Consular Information Sheets** (and Public Announcements or Travel Warnings, If applicable) provided by the Department of State which describe entry requirements, currency regulations, unusual health conditions, security information and special information about driving and road conditions. They also provide addresses and emergency telephone numbers for US embassies and consulates. Contact any of the regional passport agencies or US embassies and consulates abroad, or the Office of American Citizens Services, Bureau of Consular Affairs, U.S. Dept. of State, Washington, DC 20520. This info can also be found at travel.state.gov, or by calling the **Overseas Citizens Services** (☎ 1-888-407-4747 or 1-202-501-4444) if you are already abroad.

CUSTOMS REGULATIONS

Apply to the **Customs Office** (*UK*) for a leaflet entitled *A Guide for Travellers* on customs regulations and the full range of duty-free allowances. **The US Customs Service**, PO Box 7407, Washington, DC 20044, ☎ 202-927-5580, offers a free publication *Know Before You Go* for US citizens. There are no customs formalities for holidaymakers bringing caravans into France for a stay of less than six months. No customs document is necessary for pleasure-boats and outboard motors for a stay of less than six months, but the registration certificate should be kept on board.

Accessibility

The sights described in this guide which are easily accessible to people of reduced mobility are indicated in the *Admission times and charges* by the symbol ♿.

On TGV and Corail trains, operated by the national railway (SNCF), there are special wheelchair slots in 1st class carriages available to holders of 2nd-class tickets. On Eurostar and Thalys special rates are available for accompanying adults. All airports are equipped to receive physically disabled passengers.

Web-surfers can find information for slow walkers, mature travellers and others with special needs at www. access-able.com. For information on museum access for the disabled contact La Direction, Les Musées de France, Service Accueil des Publics Spécifiques, 6 rue des Pyramides, 75041 Paris Cedex 1, ☎ 01 40 15 35 88. The **Michelin Guide France** and the **Michelin Camping Caravaning France** indicate hotels and camp sites with facilities suitable for physically handicapped people.

Information is also available from the **Comité National Français de Liaison pour la Réadaptation des Handicapés**, 236 bis rue de Tolbiac, 75013 Paris, ☎ (05) 53 80 66 66, and the **Association France Handicaps**, 9 rue Luce-de-Lancival, 77340 Pontault-Combault, ☎ (01) 60 28 50 12.

GETTING TO FRANCE

By Air

The various national and other independent airlines operate services to **Paris** (Roissy-Charles de Gaulle and Orly airports), **Bordeaux, Lyon, Mulhouse, Toulouse, Marseille, Nice, Montpellier, Perpignan.** North American airlines usually operate flights to Paris. Regional airports are widely connected to both Parisian airports. There are also package-tour flights with a rail or coach link-up, as well as Fly-Drive schemes. Information, brochures and timetables are available from the airlines or travel agents.

By Rail

British Rail and **French Railways (SNCF)** operate a daily service via the Channel Tunnel on Eurostar in 3 hours between **London** (Waterloo International Station, ☏ 03 45 88 18 81) and **Paris** (Gare du Nord) – bookings and information: ☏ 09 90 33 00 03. Fast inter-city services from Paris to most towns throughout France run several times a day. For further information, contact the SNCF or your travel agent. There are rail passes offering unlimited travel, and group-travel tickets offering services for parties. **Eurodomino Rover** tickets for unlimited rail travel over 3, 5 or 10 days are available in the UK, along with other kinds of tickets. Information and bookings from **Rail Europe Travel Centre**, 178 Piccadilly, London W1V 0BA, ☏ (08708) 371 371, or **British Rail International**, PO Box 303, Victoria Station, London SW1V 1JY, ☏ (0990) 848 848, Fax (0171) 839 3341, or from travel agencies. **Eurailpass, Flexipass** and **Saver Pass** are options available in the US for travel in Europe and must be purchased in the US from Rail Europe Inc., ☏ 1-800-438-7245 or 1-800-4-EURAIL.
Tickets bought in France must be validated (*composter*) by using the orange automatic date-stamping machines at the platform entrance (failure to do so may result in a fine). A worthwhile investment is the Thomas Cook European Rail timetable which gives train schedules throughout France (and Europe) as well as useful information on rail travel.
The French railway company SNCF operates a telephone information, reservation and prepayment service in English from 7am to 10pm (French time). In France call ☏ 08 36 35 35 39 (when calling from outside France, leave out the initial 0) or visit www.sncf.com.

By Coach/Bus

Eurolines operate regular coach services between London and many towns throughout the country:
London: 52 Grosvenor Gardens, Victoria, London, SW1 0AU.
☏ (01582) 404 511 (information)
☏ (0990) 143 219 (ticket sales)
Paris: 28 avenue du Général de Gaulle, 93541 Bagnolet.
☏ (01) 49 72 51 51

By Car

Drivers from the British Isles can easily travel to France. Numerous **cross-Channel services** (passenger and car-ferries, hovercraft, SeaCat and via the Channel Tunnel operate accross the English Channel and St George's Channel). For details contact travel agencies or:

Brittany Ferries, The Brittany Centre, Wharf Road, Portsmouth, Hants PO2 8RU. ☏ (0990) 360 360, Fax (01705) 873 237.

Hoverspeed, Western Docks, Dover, Kent CT17 9TG. ☏ (01304) 240 241, Fax (01304) 240 088.

Irish Ferries, 50 West Norland Street, Dublin 2. ☏ (1) 6 610 511.

P&O European Ferries, Channel House, Channel View Road, Dover, Kent CT17 9TJ. ☏ (0990) 980 980, Fax (01304) 223 464.

Sally Line, Argyle Centre, York Street, Ramsgate, Kent CT11 9DS. ☏ 0990 595 522.

Sea France Ltd, Eastern Dock, Dover, Kent CT16 1JA. ☏ (01304) 212 696, Fax (01304) 240 033.

Le Shuttle, Customer Services Centre, PO Box 300, Folkestone, Kent CT19 4QW. ☏ (0990) 353 535.

Stena Line, Charter House, Park Street, Ashford, Kent TN24 8EX. ☏ (0990) 707 070, Fax (01233) 202 361.

To choose the most suitable route between one of the ports along the north coast of France and your destination, use the **Michelin France Tourist and Motoring Atlas**, **Michelin map 726** (which gives travel times and mileages) or **Michelin Local Maps** (with yellow covers).

DRIVING IN FRANCE

DOCUMENTS

Nationals of the EU member countries require a valid **national driving licence**. Nationals of non-EU countries should obtain an **international driving licence** (obtainable in the US from the American Automobile Association and the America Touring Alliance, cost for members: US$10, for non-members under US$20). Drivers must carry with them the vehicle's registration papers (log-book) and a current insurance certificate. A nationality plate of the approved size should be displayed near the registration plate on the back of the vehicle.

INSURANCE

Insurance cover is compulsory and although an international insurance certificate (green card) is no longer a legal requirement in France for vehicles registered in Great Britain, it is the most effective proof of insurance cover and is internationally recognised by the police and other authorities. Most British insurance policies give the minimum third-party cover required in France (check with your insurance company) – but be warned that this amounts to less than it would in the UK. Certain UK motoring organisations (AA, RAC) offer special accident insurance and breakdown service programmes for members (the AA also has a programmes for non-members), and motorists should check available programmes with their own insurance company.

Members of the **American Automobile Association** should obtain the free brochure *Offices To Serve You Abroad*. The affiliated organisation for France is the **Automobile Club National**, 5 rue Auber, 75009 Paris, ☎ (01) 44 51 53 99.

HIGHWAY CODE

The minimum age to drive in France is 18 years old. Traffic drives on the right. It is compulsory for the front-seat and back-seat passengers to wear **seat belts** where they are fitted. Children under the age of 10 should not travel in the front of the car.

Full or dipped headlights must be switched on in poor visibility and at night; use sidelights only when the vehicle is stationary. Headlight beams should be adjusted for driving on the right. It is illegal to drive with faulty lights in France, so it is advisable to take a spare set of bulbs with you.

In the case of a **breakdown**, a red warning triangle or hazard warning lights are obligatory. Drivers should watch out for unfamiliar road signs and take great care on the road. In built-up areas **priority** must be given to vehicles coming **from the right.** However, traffic on main roads outside built-up areas (indicated by a yellow

SPEED LIMITS

Although liable to modification these are as follows:

– toll motorways *(péage)* 130kph/80mph (110kph/68mph when raining);

– dual carriage roads and motorways without tolls 110kph/68mph (100kph/62mph when raining);

– other roads 90kph/56mph (80kph/50mph when raining) and in towns 50kph/31mph;

– outside lane on motorways during daylight, on level ground and with good visibility – minimum speed limit of 80kph/50mph.

diamond sign) and on roundabouts has priority. Vehicles must stop when the lights turn red at road junctions (where they may filter to the right only where indicated by a flashing amber arrow).

The regulations on **drinking and driving** (maximum-permissible blood alcohol content: 0.50g/litre) and **speeding** are strictly enforced – usually by an on-the-spot fine and/or confiscation of the vehicle.

PARKING REGULATIONS

In town there are zones where parking is either restricted or subject to a fee; tickets should be obtained from the ticket machines (*horodateurs* – small change necessary) and displayed inside the windscreen on the driver's side; failure to display may result in a heavy fine (and, in extreme cases, removal of the offending vehicle!). In some towns there are "blue" parking zones (*zone bleue*), marked by a blue line on the pavement or a blue signpost with a P and a small square underneath. In this particular case motorists should display a cardboard "parking disc" which can be adjusted to display their time of arrival and which allows a stay of up to 1hr 30min (2hr 30min over lunchtime) free. These discs are on sale in supermarkets or petrol stations (ask for a *disque de stationnement*).

Petrol

In France 4 different types of petrol (US: gas) are available:
sans plomb 95 – unleaded 95 octane
super – super leaded
sans plomb 98 – unleaded 98 octane
diesel/gazole – diesel
Petrol is more expensive in France compared to the USA and the UK. The French Tourist Office issues a map showing the location of cheaper petrol stations within a mile or so of motorway exits, usually in a hypermarket complex

---

ROUTE PLANNING

For 24-hour motorway information dial (01) 47 05 90 01.
The road network is excellent and includes many motorways. The roads are very busy during the holiday period (particularly weekends in July and August), and to avoid traffic congestion it is advisable to follow the recommended secondary routes (signposted *Bison Futé* or *itinéraires bis*: ☎ (01) 48 94 33 33 – national centre). The motorway network includes rest areas *(aires)* every 10-15km/5-10mi and petrol stations, usually with restaurant and shopping complexes, about every 40km/25mi, so that long-distance drivers have no excuse not to stop for a rest now and then.

TOLLS

In France, most motorway sections are subject to a toll (*péage*). This can be expensive especially if you take the motorway all the way south. Tolls can be paid in cash or with a credit card (Visa, Mastercard).

CAR RENTAL

There are car rental agencies at airports, railway stations and in all large towns throughout France. European cars usually have manual transmission. Those wishing to rent a car with automatic transmission must book it in advance and should bear in mind that cars of this type are available only in large towns and cities. The minimum age for car rental is 21 years, although in some cases motorists under 23 years of age will be able to rent a car only through a travel agent. It is relatively expensive to rent a car in France; Americans in particular will notice the difference and should consider booking a car from home before leaving, or taking advantage of Fly-Drive schemes. Drivers between 21 and 25 years old may find that they have to pay an additional fee. Those who rent a car before leaving home should make sure that they inform the car rental company that they intend to take the car to France, so that their rental contract includes insurance for the car while on French soil.

Reservation Numbers in France:
(charge per min applies for certain numbers beginning 08)
Avis: ☎ (08) 20 05 05 05
   www.avis.fr
Europcar: ☎ (08) 25 35 83 58
   www.europcar.fr
Budget: ☎ (08) 25 00 35 64
   www.budget.fr
Hertz: ☎ (01) 41 91 95 25
   www.hertz.fr

WHERE TO STAY AND EAT

Address Books

Hotel and restaurant listings fall within the *Discovering France* section of the guide.; they can be found in green boxes titled Address Books. To enhance your stay, hotel selections have been chosen for their location, comfort, value for the money, and in many cases, their charm. French cuisine is as varied as it is delicious. We have highlighted an array of eateries primarily for their atmosphere, location and regional delicacies. The Legend at the back of the guide explains the symbols and abbreviations used in the Address Books. For an even greater selection, use the **Michelin Guide France**, with its famously reliable star-rating system and hundreds of establishments throughout France.

Where to Stay

FINDING A HOTEL

The **Address Books** (see above) in this guide describe a number of lodgings arranged by price category. They appear in the many of the cities and towns described in the guide. For an even greater selection, use the **Michelin Guide France**, with its famously reliable star-rating system and hundreds of establishments throughout France. The **Michelin Charming Places to Stay** guide contains a selection of 1 000 hotels and guest houses at reasonable prices.

Be sure to book ahead to ensure that you get the accommodation you want, not only in the tourist season but year round, as many towns fill up during trade fairs, arts festivals etc. Some places require an advance deposit or a reconfirmation. Reconfirming is especially important if you plan to arrive after 6pm.
For further assistance, **Loisirs Accueil** is a booking service that has offices in some French départements. Contact information: *280 boul St-Germain - 75007 Paris* ☎ *01 44 11 10 44 - www.resinfrance.com or www. loisirsaccueilfrance.com*. A guide good-value, family-run hotels, *Logis et Auberges de France*, is available from the French Tourist Office, as are lists of other kinds of accommodation such as

hotel-châteaux, bed-and-breakfasts etc. Another resource, which publishes a catalog for each French *département*, for vacation villas, apartments or chalets is the **Fédération nationale Clévacances France** *(54 bd de l'Embouchure - BP 52166 - 31022 Toulouse Cedex -* ☎ *05 61 13 55 66 - www.clevacances.com)*.
Relais et Châteaux provides information on booking in luxury hotels with character: 15 rue Galvani, 75017 Paris, ☎ 01 45 72 90 00.

ECONOMY CHAIN HOTELS

If you need a place to stop en route, these lodgings can be useful, as they are inexpensive (30-45€ for a double room) and generally located near the main road. While breakfast is available, there may not be a restaurant; rooms are small, with a television and bathroom. Central reservation numbers:

– Akena ☎ 01 69 84 85 17

– B&B ☎ 0 803 00 29 29 (inside France); 33-2 98 33 75 00 (from outside France)

– Mister Bed ☎ 01 46 14 38 00

– Villages Hôtel ☎ 03 80 60 92 70

The hotels listed below are slightly more expensive (from 45€), and offer a few more amenities and services. Central reservation number:

– Campanile, Climat de France, Kyriad ☎ 01 64 62 46 46

Many chains have on-line reservations: www.etaphotel.com; www.ibishotel. com.

RENTING A COTTAGE, BED AND BREAKFAST

The **Maison des Gîtes de France** is an information service on self-catering accommodation in France. Gîtes usually take the form of a cottage or apartment decorated in the local style where visitors can make themselves at home, or bed and breakfast accommodation (chambres d'hôtes) which consists of a room and breakfast at a reasonable price. Contact the Gîtes de France office in Paris: 59 rue St-Lazare, 75439 Paris Cedex 09, ☎ 01 49 70 75 75, or their representative in the UK, Brittany Ferries (address above). The Internet site, www.gites-de-france. fr, has a good English version. From the site, you can order catalogues for different regions illustrated with photographs of the properties, as well as specialised catalogues (bed and breakfasts, farm stays etc). You can also surf on www.loire-valley-holidays.com to view and book cottages in Touraine and contact the local tourist offices which may have lists of available properties and local bed and breakfast establishments.

The Web site www.enpaysdelaloire.com comprises thousands of short descriptive texts on accommodation etc. The site is already active in French.

HOSTELS, CAMPING

To obtain an International Youth Hostel Federation card (there is no age requirement, and there is a senior card available too) you should contact the IYHF in your own country for information and membership applications (US ☎ 202 783 6161; UK ☎ 1727 855215). There is a booking service on the internet (iyhf.org), which you may use to reserve rooms as far as six months in advance.

There are two main youth hostel associations (auberges de jeunesse) in France, the **Ligue Française pour les Auberges de la Jeunesse** (67 rue Vergniaud, 75013 Paris, ☎ 01 44 16 78 78; www.auberges-de-jeunesse.com) and the **Fédération Unie des Auberges de Jeunesse** (4 boulevard Jules-Ferry, 75011 Paris, ☎ 01 43 57 02 60, Fax 01 43 57 53 90).There are numerous officially graded camp sites with varying standards of facilities throughout the country. The **Michelin Camping Caravaning France** guide lists a selection of camp sites. The area is very popular with campers in the summer months, so it is wise to reserve in advance.

Where to Eat

FINDING A RESTAURANT

Turn to the green-coloured Address Books within the *Discovering France* section for descriptions and prices of selected places to eat in the different locations covered in this guide. The Legend at the back of the guide explains the symbols and abbreviations used in these Address Books. Use the **Michelin Guide France**, with its famously reliable star-rating system and hundreds of establishments all over France, for an even greater choice.

If you would like to experience a meal in a highly rated restaurant from the Michelin Guide, be sure to book ahead. In the countryside, restaurants usually serve lunch between noon and 2pm and dinner between 7.30-10pm. It is not always easy to find something in-between those two meal times, as the non-stop restaurant is still a rarity in the provinces. However, a hungry traveller can usually get a sandwich in a café, and ordinary hot dishes may be available in a brasserie.

Another guide series to help you with your culinary quest is Michelin's **Les Guides Gourmands** for the individual regions such as Provence, Normandy, Northern France, French Riviera, etc. In French restaurants and cafés, a service charge is included. Tipping is not necessary, but French people often leave the small change from their bill on their table, or about 5% for the waiter in a nice restaurant.

For a glossary of gastronomic terms and for information on local specialities, ☙ *see the section titled Gastronomy in France in the Introduction.*

BASIC INFORMATION

Electricity

The electric current is 220 volts. Circular two-pin plugs are the rule. An electrical adaptor may be necessary (these are on sale at most airports).

Telephones

Most public phones in France use prepaid phone cards (*télécartes*). Some telephone booths accept credit cards (Visa, Mastercard/Eurocard). *Télécartes* (50 or 120 units) can be bought in post offices, branches of France Télécom, cafés that sell cigarettes *(tabac)* and newsagents, and can be used to make calls in France and abroad. Calls can be received at phone boxes where the blue bell sign is shown. Depending on the length of your visit and on how often you plan on using the phone, you may want to consider buying a cell phone with a coverage plan that fits your needs. There are a variety of options you can choose from making it less expensive than you might imagine. The mobile phone companies **Orange** (www.orange.com) and **Bouygues** (www.bouyguestelecom.fr) are good places to look. You can also consider renting a cell phone (✆ *See Cell Phones*).

Emergency numbers:

Police: 17
Fire *(Pompiers):* 18
Ambulance *(SAMU):* 15

NATIONAL CALLS

French telephone numbers have 10 digits. Numbers begin with 01 in Paris and the Paris region; 02 in northwest France; 03 in northeast France; 04 in southeast France and Corsica; 05 in southwest France. The French ringing tone is a series of long tones and the engaged (busy) tone is a series of short beeps.

International information, UK
✆ 00 33 12 44
International information, USA/Canada
✆ 00 33 12 11
International operator
✆ 00 33 12 + country code
Local directory assistance
✆ 12

INTERNATIONAL CALLS

To call France from abroad, dial the country code (33) + 9-digit number (omit the initial 0). When calling abroad from France dial 00, followed by the country code, followed by the area code and number of your correspondent.

International dialling codes:
Australia: 61
Eire: 353
United Kingdom: 44
Canada: 1
New Zealand: 64
United States: 1
To use your personal calling card dial:
AT&T ✆ 0 800 99-0011
BT ✆ 0 800 99-0044
MCI ✆ 0 800 99-0019
Mercury ✆ 0 800 99-00 944
Sprint ✆ 0 800 99-0087
Canada Direct ✆ 0 800 99-0016

Cheap rates with 50% extra time are available from private telephones to the UK on weekdays between 9.30pm and 8am, from 2pm on Saturdays and all day on Sundays and holidays. Cheap rates to the USA and Canada are from 2am to noon all week, and to Australia between 9.30pm and 8am Monday to Saturday and all day Sunday.

Toll-free numbers in France begin with 0 800.

MINITEL

France Télécom operates a system offering directory enquiries, travel and entertainment reservations, and other services (cost varies between 0.02€-1.41€/min). These small computer-like terminals can be found in some post offices, hotels and France Télécom agencies and in many French homes. **3614 PAGES E** is the code for directory assistance in English (turn on the unit, dial 3614, hit the "connexion" button when you get the tone, type in "PAGES E", and follow the instructions on the screen). For route planning, use Michelin services **3615 MICHELIN** and **3617 MICHELIN** (information sent by fax). www.minitel.fr.

CELL PHONES

In France these have numbers which begin with 06. Two-watt (lighter, shorter reach) and eight-watt models are on the market, using the Itinéris (France Télécom) or SFR network. Cell phone rentals (delivery or airport pickup provided):
Ellinas Phone Rental ☎ (01) 47 20 70 00
Euro Exaphone ☎ (01) 44 09 77 78
Rent a cell Express ☎ (01) 53 93 78 00

Emergencies

First aid, medical advice and chemists' night-service rotas are available from chemists/drugstores (*pharmacie* identified by a green cross sign). It is advisable to take out comprehensive insurance cover, as tourists undergoing medical treatment in French hospitals or clinics have to pay for it themselves. Nationals of non-EU countries should check with their insurance companies about policy limitations. Reimbursement can then be negotiated with the insurance company according to the policy held. All prescription drugs should be clearly labelled; it is recommended to carry a copy of prescriptions. American Express offers only to its cardholders a service, "Global Assist", for any medical, legal or personal emergency: ☎ (01) 47 16 25 29.
British and Irish citizens should apply to their local post office for **Form E111** (application form included in the brochure *Health Advice for Travellers* available from the post office). Form E111 entitles the holder to urgent treatment for accident or unexpected illness in EU countries. A refund of part of the costs of treatment can be obtained on application in person (recommended) or by post to the local French Social Security offices (*Caisse Primaire d'Assurance Maladie).*

Money

TIPPING

Since a service charge is automatically included in the price of meals and accommodation in France, any additional tipping is up to the visitor, generally small change, and generally not more than 5%. Taxi drivers and hairdressers are usually tipped 10-15%.

CURRENCY

There are no restrictions on the amount of currency visitors can take into France. Visitors wishing to export currency in foreign banknotes in excess of the given allocation from France should complete a currency declaration form on arrival.

Coins and notes – ♿ *See illustration at the end of this chapter.* The unit of currency in France is the **euro** (€). One euro is divided into 100 cents or *centimes d'euro.* Old franc notes can still be exchanged by the Banque de France until early 2012.

BANKS AND CURRENCY EXCHANGE

Banks are generally open from 9am to 4.30pm (smaller branches may close for lunch) and are closed on Monday or Saturday (except if market day). Some branches are open for limited transactions on Saturday. Banks close early on the day before a bank holiday. A passport is necessary as identification when cashing cheques (travellers' or ordinary) in banks. Commission charges vary and hotels usually charge more than banks for cashing cheques for non-residents. By far the most convenient way of obtaining French currency is the **24-hr cash dispenser** or ATM (*distributeur automatique de billets* in French), found outside many banks and post offices and easily recognisable by the CB (Carte Bleue) logo. Most accept international credit cards (don't forget your PIN) and some even give instructions in English. Note that American Express cards can be used only in dispensers operated by the Crédit Lyonnais bank or by American

Express. Foreign currency can also be exchanged in major banks, post offices, hotels or private exchange offices found in main cities and near popular tourist attractions.

CREDIT CARDS

American Express, Visa, Mastercard/Eurocard and Diners Club are widely accepted in shops, hotels, restaurants and petrol stations. If your card is lost or stolen call the appropriate 24-hour hotlines:
American Express ☎ (01) 47 77 72 00
Visa ☎ (01) 42 77 11 90
Mastercard/Eurocard ☎ (01) 45 67 84 84
Diners Club ☎ (01) 47 62 75 50
You should also report any loss or theft to the local police who will issue you with a certificate (useful proof to show the credit card company).

Post/Mail

Look for the bright yellow *La Poste* signs. Main post offices open Monday to Friday from 8am to 7pm, Saturday from 8am to noon. Smaller branch post offices generally close at lunchtime between noon and 2pm and finish for the day at 4pm. There are often automatic tellers *(guichets automatiques)* inside which allow you to weigh packages and buy postage and avoid a line. You may also find that you can use a Minitel, change money, make copies, send faxes and make phone calls in a post office. To mail a letter from the street look for the bright yellow post boxes. Stamps are also sold in newsagents and cafés that sell cigarettes *(tabac)*. Stamp collectors should ask for *timbres de collection* in any post office (there is often a *philatélie* counter). France uses a five-digit postal code that precedes the name of the city or town on the last line of the address. The first two digits indicate the *département* and the last three digits identify the *commune* or local neighborhood. www.laposte.fr.

Postage via airmail to:
  UK: letter (20g) 0.50€;
  North America: letter (20g) or postcard 0.90€;
  Australia and New Zealand: letter (20g) or postcard 0.90€.

Public Holidays

The following are days when museums and other monuments may be closed or may vary their hours of admission:

1 January	New Year's Day *(Jour de l'An)*
Mar-Apr	Easter Sunday and Monday *(Pâques)*
1 May	May Day
8 May	V E Day
	Ascension Day *(Ascension)*
	Whit Sunday and Monday *(Pentecôte)*
14 July	France's National Day (Bastille Day)
15 August	Assumption *(Assomption)*
1 November	All Saints' Day*(Toussaint)*
11 November	Armistice
25 December	Christmas Day *(Noël)*

Local Radio

These usually give frequent updates on traffic, local demonstrations, etc as well as information on local cultural events. To find the local stations, ask at the Tourist Office or in the local newspapers.

Time Difference

France is one hour ahead of Greenwich Mean Time (GMT).
When it is **noon in France,** it is:
  11am in London
  7pm in Perth
  11am in Dublin
  9pm in Sydney
  6am in New York
  11pm in Aucklan
  3am in Los Angeles

In France "am" and "pm" are not used but the 24-hour clock is widely applied.

Conversion Tables

Weights and measures

		🇬🇧
1 kilogram (kg)	2.2 pounds (lb)	2.2 pounds
1 metric ton (tn)	1.1 tons	1.1 tons

to convert kilograms to pounds, multiply by 2.2

1 litre (l)	2.1 pints (pt)	1.8 pints
1 litre	0.3 gallon (gal)	0.2 gallon

to convert litres to gallons, multiply by 0.26 (US) or 0.22 (UK)

1 hectare (ha)	2.5 acres	2.5 acres
1 square kilometre (km²)	0.4 square miles (sq mi)	0.4 square miles

to convert hectares to acres, multiply by 2.4

1 centimetre (cm)	0.4 inches (in)	0.4 inches
1 metre (m)	3.3 feet (ft) - 39.4 inches - 1.1 yards (yd)	
1 kilometre (km)	0.6 miles (mi)	0.6 miles

to convert metres to feet, multiply by 3.28 . kilometres to miles, multiply by 0.6

Clothing

Women	🇪🇺	🇺🇸	🇬🇧		🇪🇺	🇺🇸	🇬🇧	Men
	35	4	2½		40	7½	7	
	36	5	3½		41	8½	8	
	37	6	4½		42	9½	9	
Shoes	38	7	5½		43	10½	10	Shoes
	39	8	6½		44	11½	11	
	40	9	7½		45	12½	12	
	41	10	8½		46	13½	13	
	36	4	8		46	36	36	
	38	6	10		48	38	38	
Dresses &	40	8	12		50	40	40	Suits
Suits	42	12	14		52	42	42	
	44	14	16		54	44	44	
	46	16	18		56	46	48	
	36	08	30		37	14½	14,5	
	38	10	32		38	15	15	
Blouses &	40	12	14		39	15½	15½	Shirts
sweaters	42	14	36		40	15¾	15¾	
	44	16	38		41	16	16	
	46	18	40		42	16½	16½	

Sizes often vary depending on the designer. These equivalents are given for guidance only.

Speed

kph	10	30	50	70	80	90	100	110	120	130
mph	6	19	31	43	50	56	62	68	75	81

Temperature

Celsius (°C)	0°	5°	10°	15°	20°	25°	30°	40°	60°	80°	100°
Fahrenheit (°F)	32°	41°	50°	59°	68°	77°	86°	104°	140°	176°	212°

To convert Celsius into Fahrenheit, multiply °C by 9, divide by 5, and add 32.
To convert Fahrenheit into Celsius, subtract 32 from °F, multiply by 5, and divide by 9.

Notes and Coins

The euro banknotes were designed by Robert Kalinan, an Austrian artist. His designs were inspired by the theme "Ages and styles of European Architecture." Windows and gateways feature on the front of the banknotes, bridges feature on the reverse, symbolising the European spirit of openness and co-operation. The images are stylised representations of architecture typical of each period, rather than specific structures.

Classical

Baroque and Rococo

Romanesque

19C Iron and glass

Gothic

Renaissance

20C Modern

Euro coins have one face common to all 12 countries in the European single currency area or "Eurozone" (currently Austria, Belgium, Finland, France, Germany, Greece, Ireland, Italy, Luxembourg, The Netherlands, Portugal and Spain) and a reverse side specific to each country, created by their own national artists.

Euro banknotes look the same throughout the Eurozone. All Euro banknotes and coins can be used anywhere in this area.

A.Leprince / Michelin

a. 🏰 *Luxury hotel ?*

b. 🧑 *"Bib Hotel": accommodation at moderate prices ?*

c. 🐴 *Very quiet hotel ?*

Can't decide ?

Find out more with the Michelin Guide Collection!

- A collection of 13 titles
- 30 000 hotels around Europe
- 1 600 town plans
- The best addresses in every price category

Discover the pleasure of travel with the Michelin Guides

Le Trayas — Pointe de Mambois

G. Gauthier/PIX

THE LANDSCAPE

Topography

France has a happy location in the European continent – not detached from it like the British Isles, nor projecting far to the west like Iberia, nor set deep in its interior like the countries of Central Europe, yet in touch with the resources and the life of the whole of Western Europe and the seas around it, Atlantic, Channel, Mediterranean and North Sea. These seas together with the other natural frontiers, the Alps and Pyrenees and the River Rhine, define the compact shape of the "hexagon". Within this unified and robust framework there flourishes a geographical identity which is unmistakably French yet of an unrivalled local richness and variety. Less a paradox than a wonderful synthesis, this coexistence of unity and diversity is the work of both Nature and Man.

> "La France est diversité"
> (France is diversity)
> Fernand Braudel

GEOLOGICAL HISTORY

It has been said that the whole of Earth's history – the building of the planet – can be traced within the confines of France. The country's complex geological history starts in the Primary era (600 million years ago), when the Hercynian folding was responsible for the raising up of the great mountain ranges which were the ancestors of today's Massif Central, Armorican Peninsula, Vosges and Ardennes.

In Secondary times (beginning 200 million years ago), the Paris region, Aquitaine, the Rhône and Loire valleys and the southern part of the Massif Central all lay under the sea which gradually filled them with sedimentary deposits.

New mountain ranges reared up in the Tertiary era (beginning 60 million years ago): the Alps, Pyrenees, the Jura and Corsica. The shock-waves of this violent mountain-building were felt far afield, particularly in the Massif Central where great volcanoes erupted.

The Quaternary age (2 million years ago) saw an alternation of warm and cold periods; glaciers advanced and retreated and rivers swelled and shrank, sculpting much of the land surface into its present forms.

CLIMATE AND RELIEF

In climatic terms too, France gathers into herself the patterns of the continent as a whole; Atlantic, Continental and Mediterranean influences are all present, contributing decisively to the formation of soils and their mantle of vegetation as well as to the processes which have shaped the geological foundation into the patterns of today's relief.

The north of the country is largely composed of great sedimentary basins, scarp (côtes) and vale country, drained by slow-flowing rivers like the Seine and the Loire. At the extremities of these lowlands are rugged areas formed of Primary rocks, the much-eroded granites of Brittany and the gneisses and schists of the Ardennes, and the higher massifs of the Vosges and the centre. Beyond lie the fertile plains of Aquitaine and Languedoc while the corridor carved by the Rhône and Saône links the north and south of the country. Finally come the "young" mountains of the Jura, Alps and Pyrenees; their high peaks and ranges, while forming fine natural frontiers, are by no means impermeable to political, commercial and cultural currents.

Regions of France

Few parts of the country are unfavourable to human settlement; France is still a largely rural country, with a relatively even spread of population. Great cities and conurbations exist, but beyond them spreads a spacious countryside, uncrowded but rarely deserted, created over the centuries by the efforts of its inhabitants, whose collective understanding of the places where they live is expressed in every detail of the local landscape. The layout of fields, the pattern of crops and woodlands, the grouping of the population in hamlets, villages and towns, the materials and styles of building, all combine to proclaim the individuality of the innumerable localities or *pays* which themselves contribute to the identity of the larger regions listed below and which form the subject of the 24 Michelin regional guides (13 in English).

PARIS

The presence of a number of islands in the Seine made a convenient crossing

The Pyramid at the Louvre, Paris

point here for the prehistoric North-South trade route. Under the Gauls, urban development was confined to the Île de la Cité, though Roman Lutetia spread southwards over today's Latin Quarter. It was the Capetian kings who made Paris their capital, thereby giving it the dominant role in the country's political and cultural life which it has exercised ever since.

Until modern times, Paris tended to be tightly circumscribed by successive rings of fortifications (the wall of Philippe Auguste in the 13C, the wall of Charles V in the 14C, and the wall of the Farmers-General in the late 18C), giving the city a much more densely built-up character than, say, London. Within these boundaries, a succession of bold building and planning projects, spread over the centuries, has helped give the city its distinct identity.

Renaissance urbanism was responsible for the layout of the Marais district, centred on the Place des Vosges, where the French town mansion, the *hôtel*, took on its definitive form, while the Baroque sense of drama and movement in the townscape is seen in the grand perspectives opened up on the Invalides, Champ-de-Mars and above all the Champs-Élysées.

Neo-Classical monumentality was favoured by Napoleon I in his attempt to make Paris a fittingly Imperial capital, but the greatest planned transformation of all was undertaken in the 19C by Napoleon III and his Prefect, Baron Haussmann, who drove great axial boulevards through the dense web of ancient streets and laid out splendid

green spaces like the Bois de Boulogne and the Parc Monceau. In the late 19C and early 20C it was the new institution of the international exhibition which gave the *"Ville Lumière"* some of its most characteristic monuments, the Eiffel Tower, the Grand Palais and Petit Palais, and the Palais de Chaillot.

Under the influence of Le Corbusier and many others, the aesthetics of Parisian architecture have been radically revamped since 1945: UNESCO (1957), the Palais de la Défense (CNIT, 1958), the Maison de la Radio et de la Télévision (1963), the Montparnasse Tower (1973), the Palais des Congrès (1974). This trend was to be confirmed in subsequent years with the building in central Paris of several major landmarks, designed by prominent contemporary architects: the Palais Omnisports de Paris-Bercy (1984), the City of Science and Industry and the Géode Cinema at La Villette (1986), the Opera-Bastille (1989), La Grande Arche at La Défense (1989), the Louvre Pyramid (1989), the Ministry of Finance building at Bercy (1990), the Richelieu Wing (1994), an important stage of the "Grand Louvre" project (1981-98), the City of Music at La Villette (1995) and the Bibliothèque de France (1996).

ILE-DE-FRANCE

This historic region, the kernel from which the French state has grown, is called Île-de-France (literally: Island of France) because of its location marked by the rivers Seine, Aisne, Oise and Marne. Where its limestone plateaux have been cut into by the rivers, lush valleys have been formed, contrasting with the vast arable tracts of the Beauce, Vexin and Brie. A girdle of greenery surrounds the capital; there are great forests like those of Fontainebleau, Halatte, Chantilly, Ermenonville and Rambouillet, into which merge the landscapes of leisure and pleasure with which the mighty surrounded their châteaux, the parks and gardens of Versailles, Chantilly, Vaux-le-Vicomte and others. The region's privileged position has left it an exceptional legacy of fine building, ranging from innumerable parish churches to the great monuments of the Gothic dawn, such as St-Denis, and Chartres.

From Corot's time, the landscapes of the Île-de-France have moved artists to render their subtleties in paint, the Seine valley above all becoming the great axis of Impressionist activity.

The capital has long burst its bounds to invigorate its region with urban activity of all kinds; its established towns have expanded rapidly to accommodate new populations, aided by new foundations, planned towns like St-Quentin-en-Yvelines, Marne-la-Vallée and Cergy-Pontoise. One indication of the importance of the region in the country's economic life; covering only 2% of the area of France, it now employs 22% of the economically active population.

THE LOIRE VALLEY

This "garden of France" with its abundant horticultural crops, its flowers and its vineyards, has also been called "a home spun cloak with golden fringes", are ference to the contrast between the fertile valleys of the Loire and its tributaries and the low, somewhat bleak plateaux that separate them.

Rising far to the southeast in the Massif Central, France's longest (some 1 000km – 620 miles) river was once a busy waterway, connected to the Seine basin by the Briare Canal. Many of the towns along its banks bear traces of this former activity, from Gien, rebuilt after its bombing in the Second World War, to Orléans, once the Loire's foremost port, Blois, Tours, Langeais, Saumur... But, as on the Rhône, navigation was never easy, and once the railways came, the Loire was left to its caprices.

Below Gien, the valley opens out and the river describes a great bend partly enclosing the immense heathy tract of the Sologne, rich in game. But it is from Orléans onward that the Loire exercised, and continues to exercise, its greatest

attraction; its gentle landscapes and soft light encouraged the kings, courtiers and magnates to build the Renaissance châteaux for which the region is famous, Blois, Chambord, Azay and others, their elegance and architectural exuberance contrasting with the sterner fortresses of an earlier age like the great castle at Angers. Other building has a distinctive character too, often with white walls of tufa and roofs of slate, while there are trogloditic dwellings, notably around Amboise and Tours.

BRITTANY

Populated by Celtic settlers who arrived here from Cornwall in the 5C, Brittany retains many affinities with the other Celtic lands fringing the Atlantic. Its identity, quite distinct from that of the rest of France, is expressed in language (Breton, akin to Welsh) and traditions as well as in its landscape.

The province turns its face towards the sea. Its extraordinarily indented coastline, 1 200km – 750 miles long, was given its name **Armor** ("country near the sea") by the Gauls. Its cliffs, reefs, rocky headlands and offshore islands are battered by Atlantic breakers, while its narrow drowned valleys (abers) and sandy bays are washed by tides of exceptional range (up to 15m – 49ft).

Much of France's fishing fleet operates from Brittany and there are naval bases, shipyards and commercial harbours too. All around the coast are resorts, some smart (Dinard), some simple.

Inland is the **Argoat** ("country of the wood"), once thickly afforested, now a mixture of bocage countryside and wilder landscapes of heath and moor rising to wind-blown granite heights (like **Trévezel Rock** 384m – 1 229ft and **Ménez Hom** 330m – 1 083ft) commanding vast prospects. The Monts d'Arrée and Montagnes Noires mark the natural boundaries of the Lake Guerlédan region and the Châteaulin basin.

From the Loire estuary to the Aulne valley, the **Atlantic coast** with its picturesque harbours, resorts, villages and distinctive geographical features (Gulf of Morbihan, Guérande and Crozon Peninsulas) is backed by a varied landscape: the Lanvaux moorlands, the Grande Brière, the Guérande salt flats and the Nantes region. The **Channel coast** from Fougères and the Rennes basin to the large harbour at Brest and the Ile d'Ouessant is punctuated by historic towns (Guingamp, Morlaix, Tréguier), elegant resorts and dramatic corniches and headlands (Cap Fréhel, Pointe St-Mathieu).

The province's long and mysterious past makes itself felt in the abundance of prehistoric remains, menhirs, dolmens, and the great lines of megaliths around Carnac. Granite, outcropping nearly everywhere, distinguishes Breton building, whether in church or chapel, castle or château, harbour wall or humble house, and is used to great effect in the robust and expressive forms of churchyard calvaries.

NORMANDY

Taking its name from the Norsemen or Normans, this old dukedom extends from the western edge of the Paris Basin towards the Breton peninsula. To many it is reminiscent of southern England, not only in its shared heritage of glorious Norman architecture, but also in the lush, pastoral countryside of the *bocage,* with its small hedged fields, abundant trees and woodlands, apple orchards, sunken lanes and scattered hamlets.

Lower Normandy (Basse-Normandie), like Brittany, is built of old rocks, the sandstones, granites and schists of the Primary era. The Cotentin peninsula projects into the English Channel dividing the Bay of the Seine from the Gulf of St-Malo with its dramatic tides washing Mont St-Michel and the rocky Channel Islands (Anglo-Norman Islands in French). To the southeast lies the *bocage* – its hedgebanks offered excellent cover to the German defence in 1944.

On either side of the Seine Valley extends **Upper Normandy** (Haute-Normandie) centred on the historic city of Rouen. To the south is the Pays d'**Auge**, quintessential *bocage* country, famous for its ciders, cheeses and Calvados. To the north stretches the vast chalk plain of the Pays de **Caux**, good arable land, bordered by the Channel coast with its white cliffs and hanging valleys.

A diversity of resources has given rise to an exceptional variety in the materials and styles of building; Norman masons fashioned the fine Caen limestone into great ecclesiastical edifices on both sides of the Channel, while humbler structures were built from cob, chalk, pebbles in mortar, brick, timber, shingles and thatch.

Normandy's coast is the nearest to Paris, and while much has changed since Marcel Proust watched Albertine playing at diabolo, its cliffs and beaches continue to attract visitors and holiday-makers.

FLANDERS, ARTOIS, PICARDY

Before the rising sea cut its way through the Straits of Dover at the end of the last Ice Age, the chalklands of southern England and the North of France were one; even today the broad fields of the old provinces of **Artois** (capital Arras) and **Picardy** (capital Amiens) recall the English downland, while a gap of only some 30km – 19 miles separates Cap Gris-Nez from the South Foreland and Shakespeare Cliff.

In the claylands of the Pays de Bray, the Vimeux and the Bas Boulonnais is *bocage* countryside, but most of the North's landscapes are open, with few field boundaries to check the view. This high-yielding arable land is broken by a number of valleys like that of the Somme making its way slowly to the sea, its alluvial soils intensively exploited by market gardeners whose tiny plots of land are linked by narrow canals. Many of the towns are sited by these sluggish streams, like Amiens, its superb cathedral a reminder that the region, together with the Île-de-France, was the cradle of Gothic architecture. With few dramatic hills, man-made verticals take on more importance, not only cathedral spires and church towers, but also the bright white concrete watertowers, the volcanic cones of pit-heaps or lines of electricity pylons marching majestically to the horizon. Much of the North is built of brick, from singlestoreyed roadside cabin to tall town house, though grander buildings may merit stone.

In close succession along the coast are the ports of Boulogne, Calais and Dunkirk, making this one of France's most important outlets to the sea. As well as chalk and limestone cliffs, there are extensive areas of land reclaimed from the sea, impressive dune systems and fine sandy beaches overlooked by resorts like Le Touquet.

The edges of the chalk country are marked by other, very different landscapes. Northeast is French **Flanders**, consisting largely of polderlands having much in common, including language, with the adjoining Low Countries. Inland is France's "Black country", the *pays noir* of the great coalfield stretching from Béthune to Valenciennes and running into the vast conurbation of a million people formed by Lille-Tourcoing-Roubaix. Further eastward, the green pastures of the more hilly Thiearache and Avenois country anticipate the landscapes of the nearby Ardennes. As the Île-de-France is approached, extended wooded tracts appear, like the forest of Compiègne, impressive relics of the Gaulish forest which once extended from the Paris basin to the eastern frontier.

The North is indeed a frontier land, open to the Northern European Plain, an invasion route for successive waves of would-be conquerors, its countryside today studded with the memorials to the victims of two world wars, its place-names redolent of bloody struggles, defeats and victories.

CHAMPAGNE, ARDENNES

The eastern rim of the Paris Basin is formed by an outward-facing series of limestone escarpments pierced by rivers flowing northwest such as the Marne, Aube and Seine. Alluvial deposits carried by the watercourses have created the soft contours of the landscape.

Around Reims, the steep, sometimes cliff-like slopes of the Côte de l'Île-de-France carry the vineyards which since the days of Dom Pérignon have produced the world's most prestigious sparkling wine. Beyond stretch the sweeping Champagne chalklands, once notorious for their meagre soils, but now, with the use of artificial fertilisers, one of France's most productive agricultural regions. To the east are the Champagne claylands, an area of mostly mixed farming and woodlands, where great artificial lakes, designed to regulate the flow of Seine and Marne, have become important recreational areas.

Further eastward still is the Barrois plateau and the escarpment of the Côte des Bars, a favoured site for towns like Bar-le-Duc, Bar-sur-Aube and Bar-sur-Seine, while to the north, forming a buffer between Champagne and Lorraine, is the vast Argonne forest.

The upper valleys of both Marne and Seine lead to an extensive and well-wooded limestone upland, the Plateau de Langres, named after the old fortified town sited on one of its spurs.

The French **Ardennes** form a small part of an ancient massif stretching away into southeastern Belgium and merging with the uplands of the German Eifel. This is one of Europe's most extensive areas of forest, with fine stands of oak and beech as well as conifers, all sheltering abundant game. Sometimes described as "impenetrable", the Ardennes have rarely proved a reliable barrier to the passage of armies, least of all in the spring of 1940. Below Charleville-Mézières the meandering Meuse cuts into the plateau, accompanied by a string of industrial towns.

ALSACE, LORRAINE, VOSGES

Alsace forms France's window onto Central Europe. Its capital, Strasbourg, was a free city, part of the Holy Roman Empire, until the days of Louis XIV; together with the other towns and villages along this left bank of the Rhine it has a picturesqueness of decidedly Germanic character. The Rhine itself is both a frontier and, with the Alsace Canal, a great international waterway, flowing through the broad rift valley defined by the Black Forest to the east, the Vosges uplands to the west.

The towns avoid the river and its once-unpredictable moods; its course leads it through a mysterious and little-frequented landscape of reed swamps, stagnant backwaters and old cut-offs. On the infertile sands and gravels brought down from the Alps grow forests like that of Haguenau, almost 140km2 – 54sq miles, 2/3 of which consists of Scots pine and the rest of hornbeam, beech and oak. But most of the Alsace countryside wears a cheerful air, particularly when the orchards are in blossom or when the grape-harvest is being collected in the famous vineyards of the foothills, where each eminence seems crowned by some ruined stronghold.

Above these lower slopes rise the **Vosges** themselves, their rounded granite summits in the south (the Ballons) contrasting with the more rugged forms of the red sandstone outcropping in the north. The latter is both attractive and easily worked, furnishing building material for many a castle, church or cathedral. In the valleys of these uplands, whose breadth rather than height once hindered communication, are glacial lakes, while the slopes are clad with splendid forests giving way near the summits to rich pastures, the Hautes Chaumes. Laid out for strategic puposes in the First World War, the high-level Route des Crêtes now forms a fine north-south tourist route.

Lorraine owes its name to ancient Lotharingia, central of the three kingdoms into which Charlemagne's inheritance was divided. To the west, the landscape is one of alternating outcrops of limestone and clay, the former giving rise to the escarpments of the Côte de Moselle and Côte de Meuse overlooking these northward-flowing rivers. Eastward to the foot of the Vosges extends the Lorraine plateau, a mixed-farming area of monotonous appearance.

The presence of coal, iron-ore and salt led to the development of heavy industry in adjoining Luxembourg and

Saarland as well as in Lorraine (Longwy, Thionville) itself. Fortress towns stud this much-contested province: Bitche, Metz, Verdun.

THE JURA

These limestone uplands, part of them in Switzerland, run in a great arc for some 240km – 150 miles from Rhine to Rhône, corresponding roughly to the old province known as the Franche-Comté. The limestones from which they were formed were folded along a northeast-southwest axis into long parallel ridges and valleys by the pressure exerted on them in the Alpine-building period; the exceptionally massive development of the limestone beds (they reach a maximum thickness of some 1 300m – 4 300ft) has led to the term "Jurassic" passing into geological usage for rocks of this age and type (cf the oolitic limestone of the English Cotswolds). Many characteristic features of limestone country occur, like great natural amphitheatres or *cirques* (Cirque de Baume), gorges, caves and chasms, while the regular pattern of valleys and ridges stepping down westwards can be easily appreciated from a number of high viewpoints like the Grand Colombier (1,571m – 5,151ft).

Owing to the high rainfall, extensive forests of beech and oak, firs and spruce (covering 40% of the land surface), and vast upland pastures, this is a verdant landscape. Water is everywhere present, rising from springs and resurgences to feed rushing torrents, spill over spectacular falls (like the Cascades du Hérisson) and fill some 70 lakes. Winters are harsh here, sometimes burying the sturdily-built isolated farmhouses to the eaves of their spreading roofs, and encouraging the development of woodcarving skills during the long months of enforced indoor activity. Woodmanship and forestry have long been supplemented by upland farming (the Jura is famous for its Comté and other cheeses) and at times by other occupations of an industrial character, salt production at Salins and Lons-le-Saunier, clock- and watchmaking at Besançon, and metal-working, now mostly gone.

The margins of the upland have their own interest; where the westernmost and lowest ridge drops to the Bresse plain is the *Bon Pays*, an attractively variegated countryside including many vineyards, while at the foot of the great cliff falling away from the highest, easternmost ridge towards Geneva and its lake is the Pays de Gex, very much part of the hinterland of the great Swiss city.

BURGUNDY

Burgundy's unity is based more on history than on geography. Fortunately located on the great trade route linking northern Europe to the Mediterranean, the territory was consolidated in the 15C by the diplomatic skills of its great Dukes; it consists of a number of *pays* of varying character, though its heartland lies in the limestone plateaux stretching eastward from the Auxerre area to the country around the ducal capital, Dijon.

The old dukedom's heritage of Romanesque architecture is outstanding, but the village scene is characteristic too, the colours of the countryside repeated in the warm red roofs and mellow limestone walls of the houses clustered around a modest church made of the same materials.

Towards the east, the elevated land terminates in escarpments dropping down to the wide valley of the Saône. Of these, La Côte is the most renowned, its slopes producing some of the world's finest wines, its centuries of prosperity made manifest in the large and comfortable houses of the wine-growers. To the south lies the Mâconnais where the

Burgundy landscape

steep faces of the escarpment are turned towards the interior. This is a region of vine-covered hillsides and pastureland.

Standing apart from the province, and long isolated from the wider world through poor communications, is the **Morvan**, a granite massif of poor soils cut by a network of rivers, lonely farmsteads and scattered hamlets and extensive forests, its highest point being Haut-Folin (901m – 2 956ft). The lower slopes have been turned into pastureland. The region's unspoilt natural landscapes are a great attraction.

To the west and north of the Morvan are other pays, the plateaux and hills of the Nivernais stretching away to the Loire, the moorlands and pastures of the Gâtinais and Puisaye, while to the south the lower reaches of the Saône are bordered by the broad Bresse plain, famous for its beef, pork and delicately-fleshed poultry.

BERRY, LIMOUSIN

Little touched by industrialisation or mass tourism, these two regions seem to represent the quintessence of rural France.

Berry centres on Bourges, which with its great cathedral was once the seat of the French court. The vast limestone plateau which forms the area's heartland was settled as long ago as Neolithic times and is now devoted to large-scale arable farming. In contrast are the intimate *bocage* landscapes of the valleys of the Boischaut, the vines and orchards of the Sancerrois and the Brenne marshlands, a nature reserve of the first importance with innumerable ponds and little sandstone knolls covered in pine and broom.

Limousin is the name of the old province around Limoges forming the northwestern extremity of the Massif Central. Much of it is a quiet countryside of hedgerows, ponds and shady meadows, drained by rivers flowing westwards towards Saintonge and the Dordogne. In contrast is the Montagne, its name derived more from the rigour of its climate than from altitude since

nowhere does it rise above 1,000m – about 3,300ft; the Plateau des Millevaches is a thinly-peopled upland, grazed by sheep and cattle, blasted by wind and rain and with a high snowfall. The province's urban pattern is one of old market towns with solid, granite-walled and slate-roofed houses.

MANCHE

Cherbourg-Octeville

Cotentin

Caen

NOR

St-Malo

Bocage normand

Brest

M^{ts} d'Arrée 384

MASSIF

BRETAGNE

M^{gnes} Noires

Rennes

Maine

Lorient

ARMORICAIN

Angers

VA

LOIRE

Nantes

VENDÉE

POITOU

la Rochelle

CHARENTE

ATLANTIQUE

Angoulême

GIRONDE

Bordeaux

GU

BAS

LANDES

AQ

GAS

Biarritz

Pays Basque

Pau

Béarn

P Y R

Somport 1632

3298

Vignemale

0   100 km

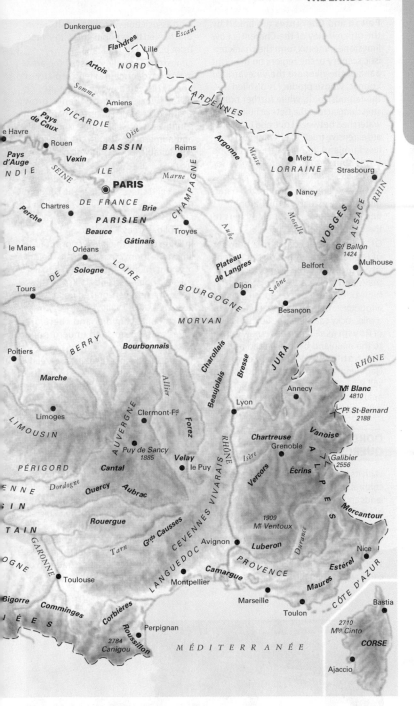

POITOU, VENDÉE, CHARENTES

Between the estuaries of the Loire and the Gironde, France faces the breezes and breakers of the Atlantic with a generally flat but otherwise fascinatingly varied coastline. There are great marshy tracts like the Marais Breton and above all the Marais Poitevin, low cliffs, vast mud-flats shimmering at low tide and dune systems bordering splendid sandy beaches. Landscapes inland are equally varied. Like Brittany, the **Vendée** has a granite foundation; its *bocage* countryside is one of deep lanes and scattered farmsteads, while its heaths and moors rise to 295m – 968ft at Puy Crapaud.

Poitou and **Charentes** are linked by the green valley of the Charente. Low limestone plateaux form the characteristic scenery of the region; on the right bank of the river are the vineyards of Cognac, whose product is distilled into the famous spirit, while further north, stretching across the Gate of Poitou, the watershed between Loire and Charente, are extensive tracts of open, almost treeless farmland. In places the limestone forms spurs, good defensive sites for towns like Angoulême.

To the south is the Gironde, the name given to the estuary of the Garonne; its fine beaches extend from Meschers to the Coubre headland.

Off this western coast are a number of islands, each with a distinct identity. **Noirmoutier** is connected to the mainland by a causeway covered at high tide. **Yeu**, further south, has an altogether more Breton character, with a wild, rocky coastline. The holiday island of **Ré** with its salt marshes is now linked to the mainland by a new road bridge. **Aix**, fortified by Vauban, was where Napoleon spent his last days on French soil, while **Oléron**, France's largest island apart from Corsica, enjoys a remarkably mild climate.

DORDOGNE: PÉRIGORD, QUERCY

With its hills, its mature and varied agricultural landscapes, its deciduous woodlands and its mellow stone buildings, this is a welcoming region, not unlike parts of southern England, albeit with a more genial climate and a general atmosphere of good living. Perhaps it is this pleasing synthesis of the familiar and the mildly exotic, more than the traces of the area's long association with the English Crown, that has led to its popularity with visitors from beyond the Channel.

Limestone underlies most of the area, in **Périgord** forming extensive plateaux deeply dissected by the Dordogne and other rivers; along the banks grow southern crops like maize, tobacco and sunflowers, as well as grass and cereals and numerous walnut trees. The soil is also suitable for the cultivation of strawberries.

On the higher land there are woodlands of oak and chestnut, and in the Périgord Noir, evergreen oaks too. The region is famous for the truffles which grow at the foot of oak trees.

In **Quercy** the thick layers of Jurassic limestone form *causses,* lying at a height of about 300m – 1 000ft, with a sparse cover of juniper, scrubby oaks and carob trees. These sheep-grazed uplands are dissected by dry valleys and spectacular canyons and there are caves and chasms and underground watercourses.

The area has been settled since very early times. Evidence of its attractiveness to prehistoric people extends beyond tools and implements to wall paintings and engravings, low reliefs and decorated bone, ivory and stone. As well as stunning examples of medieval settlement seeming to have grown organically from its site (Rocamadour, St-Cirq-Lapopie), there are numerous reminders of the Anglo-French struggle, from the geometrically planned towns *(bastides)* laid out by both parties to help consolidate their hold on the territory (Monpazier), to rugged strongholds like Beynac and Bonaguil. The medieval and later importance of the towns is expressed in a fine tradition of building in limestone (Sarlat).

Château de Belcastel and the river Dordogne

AUVERGNE

The Auvergne forms the core of the **Massif Central**. It is a volcanic landscape, unique in France – its forms range from the classic cones of the Monts Dômes to the rugged shapes of the much-eroded Monts Dore and the great Cantal volcano, and to the lava flows which seem to have only just cooled into immobility. In the Cézallier area, the streams of lava have piled up on one another to surround the flattened dome of the Signal du Luguet; at La Cheire d'Aydat, the molten torrent has taken on a crystalline pattern, while around St-Flour it has formed the great stretches of upland known locally as *planèzes*. Elsewhere, the lava has filled valley floors, protecting them from the erosion wearing away the hills around and giving rise to the phenomenon of relief inversion (Polignac, Carlat, Gergovie). At Bort-les-Orgues and Le Puy there are curious crystalline formations resembling organ-pipes.

The volcanic activity has created an array of lakes and other water-bodies; at Aydat and Guéry a lava flow has blocked a valley, trapping its waters, while the same effect has been produced at Chambon and Montcineyre by a volcano erupting in the valley itself. Elsewhere, as at Chauvet, the hollows produced by a series of volcanic exposions have filled with water. Lakes have also formed inside a crater (Bouchet, Servière) or within the steep walls of an explosion crater (Gour de Tazenat, Pavin).

This great variety of relief makes for fine upland walking country, while the towns and villages of sombre granite have their own allure, heightened by the presence of some of France's finest Romanesque churches. The Auvergne is a mainly agricultural region, the grazing grounds of the higher land complemented by the rich alluvial soils of the series of basins through which the Allier flows northward towards the **Bourbonnais** with its *bocage* countryside of rich pasturelands. Industry is present too, notably at Clermont-Ferrand (Michelin), the provincial capital overlooked from a height of 1 465m – 4 806ft by the old volcano of the Puy de Dôme.

The area is famous for its springs, the spas which have grown up around them (Vichy) and for the bottling and marketing of mineral water.

THE RHÔNE VALLEY

Together with its tributary, the Saône, which joins it at Lyon, this great river has long served as a communications corridor of the first importance, linking northwestern Europe to the Mediterranean. Though its valley seems to divide the ancient uplands to the west from the younger, folded rocks of the Alps to the east, its geological structure is of some complexity; at Vienne and St-Vallier the river carves its way through some of the outermost granitic bastions of the Massif Central, while at Valence it flows between one of the last terraces of the Dauphiné and the limestone ridge of Crussol backing onto the granite mass of the Vivarais.

The area around the great city of Lyon itself is marked by centuries of industrial activity. Downstream, the river's course takes it through a succession of narrow gorges and broad basins, where châteaux perched on spurs alternate with an attractive pattern of red-roofed villages set among vineyards (some of them first planted in pre-Roman times) and orchards, though industry is present too. The southern character of the landscape becomes ever more pronounced, olives and evergreen oaks appearing just below Montélimar.

Fed by Alpine thaws, the Rhône's currents could be dangerously swift, its level unpredictable, its bed mobile. Until the incorporation of the Dauphiné, Dromme and the Papal lands around Avignon into the French kingdom, it was a frontier too, a further obstacle to easy commerce. Towns tended to develop in pairs, one on the east "foreign" bank, one on the west "French" bank, like Vienne/Ste-Colombe, Valence/St-Péray, Avignon/Villeneuve-lès-Avignon... The very diverse character of the river's banks and the frequency with which it is joined by wide tributaries made it difficult to form a satisfactorily continuous towpath, and later to engineer railway lines. But the Rhône has been tamed; decades of construction (18 dams, 13 power stations and locks) now allow 2 000-tonne barges to reach Lyon. Nevertheless, the improved waterway carries only a fraction of the total traffic using its corridor; it is supplemented by the A6 motorway, two national highways, a main-line railway on each bank (one carrying TGV traffic), a gas pipeline, and an oil pipeline.

To the west of the river runs an escarpment marking the edge of the Massif Central. Close to the old industrial area centred on St-Étienne is Mont Pilat (1 432m – 4,698ft) offering a number of splendid viewpoints over the Rhône valley (Crêt du l'Oeillon). Southward lie the basalt plateaux of the Velay and the lava flows and limestone country of the Vivarais, cut by the spectacular Ardèche gorges.

PROVENCE AND THE RHÔNE DELTA

The Rhône flows into the sea in the centre of France's Mediterranean coastline, the Midi (South). Here, "the climate has imposed a unifying stamp reflected in both the landscape and the way of life" (J Sion) and Mediterranean influences are supreme, from the extensive remains of the six centuries of Roman occupation to the traditional triumvirate of wheat, vine and olive alternating with the remnants of the natural forest (evergreen oaks, pines) and the infertile but wonderfully aromatic *garrigues* (arid scrubland).

Among the fertile Provençal plains stand the *mas,* shallow-roofed pantiled farmsteads protected from the fierce sun by stone walls with few window openings. Crops and buildings are shielded from the violence of the master-wind from the north, the *mistral,* by serried ranks of cypresses. The plains are flanked by ranges of limestone hills running east-west, including the picturesque Alpilles, the rugged Luberon range and the Vaucluse plateau with its chasms, gorges and great resurgent spring at Fontaine-de-Vaucluse.

The Provençal landscape and the intensity of the light have played a key role in the evolution of modern painting; Mt Ste-Victoire never ceased to fascinate Paul Cézanne, while Arles and the countryside around was made to reflect the tormented spirit of Vincent van Gogh.

The 20 million cubic metres of sand, gravel and silt brought down annually by the Rhône has created the vast deltaic plain of the **Camargue**, a lonely place of salt marshes and lagoons, populated by herdsmen and wildfowl. Before it changed its course to join the Rhône, the Durance too flowed directly into the sea through the Lamanon Gap, depositing vast quantities of boulders and pebbles to form the Grande Crau, a stony wasteland scorched by summer sun and blasted by the *mistral* in winter and increasingly invaded by the industries spawned by Marseille, France's great Mediterranean port and second city.

TARN GORGES: CÉVENNES, LOWER LANGUEDOC

Along the southern edge of the Massif Central stretch the **Grands Causses**, vast limestone tablelands of striking severity.

They are laced with corniche roads offering unforgettable views over the deep canyons and gorges hollowed out by the Tarn and its tributaries. Below the surface is a "speleologist's paradise" of caves and chasms, and the endlessly weird forms produced by dissolution and deposition. Where dolomite occurs, weathering has resulted in the fantastic pinnacles and castellations of the rocky chaos known as Montpellier-le-Vieux.

The *causses* are bounded by landscapes of surprising diversity. The lava flows of the Aubrac area have given rise to a countryside of immensely broad horizons, one of France's least-populated areas. The **Cévennes**, mostly designated a National Park, consist of lowering granite summits overlooking deep and narrow valleys separated by crests *(serres)*, a secret and long-impenetrable area which merges southward with the Mediterranean vegetation of the *garrigues*.

Cirque de Gavarnie

J. Joffre/ IMAGES TOULOUSE

The central plain of **Lower Languedoc** (capital: Montpellier) with its vast and highly productive vineyards, is bordered by a chain of brackish lakes, separated from the sea by sandy bars. Old towns like Sète (created in the 17C by Louis XIV) are complemented by planned modern resorts such as La Grande Motte with its modern apartment buildings in ziggurat form.

Far to the southwest, the ancient rocks of the Montagne Noire form the last outpost of the Massif Central. Behind it stretches the varied countryside of the Segalas and the great granite block of the Sidobre.

THE PYRENEES

Dividing France from Spain, these mountains, the "most satisfactory of France's frontiers", run some 400km – 250 miles from Atlantic to Mediterranean.

In the west is the **Basque country**, topographically and linguistically distinct, though many of the valleys descending northwards at right angles to the main crestline form *pays* (**Béarn, Bigorre**) with their own character and traditions. Here is spectacular mountain scenery: jagged ridges, great natural amphitheatres streaked with waterfalls, high-altitude lakes and rushing torrents, all in contrast to the well-cultivated valley bottoms with their scattering of white houses.

The centre of the range is formed by the splendid Maladetta Massif rising high above the **Comminges** country and the most venerable of the Pyrenees' many spas, Luchon. Northwards, a vast fan-shaped area of ridges and valleys has been formed from glacial debris brought down from the mountains and by subsequent river action. Prolonged westwards by the valleys of the turbulent Adour and its tributaries, this landscape gives way to varied cropland along the course of **Aquitaine's** principal river, the Garonne. Here, the kindly climate and rich alluvial soils have allowed each town to develop its own specialised product, like the plums of Agen, which, dried, become delicious prunes. The ancient English province of **Guyenne** grew up around the confluence of Garonne and Dordogne, an area devoted then as now to the production of the world's most coveted wines. Beyond the provincial capital of Bordeaux, the Garonne widens out into the broad estuary of the Gironde.

The Atlantic coast (Côte d'Argent) south of Grave Point at the mouth of the estuary runs in a straight line almost to the Spanish border, interrupted only by the great Bay of Arcachon. Behind the vast sandy beaches rise the highest sand dunes in Europe, while inland are the **Landes**, once an immense, ill-drained waste, now successfully planted with profitable pinewoods.

Among the former statelets of the Pyrenees like the Pays de Foix, Andorra alone preserves its independence. The watershed between Atlantic and Mediterranean is crossed by the Canal du Midi, built as early as 1680 to link sea to ocean. The former capital of Languedoc, Toulouse, is France's sixth largest city, an important industrial centre. All around and northward in the **Albigeois** too,

lies rich farming country, the granary of Southern France.

At the Mediterranean extremity of the Pyrenees lies **Roussillon**, France's Catalan province, the often snow-covered peak of Canigou (2 784m – 9 134ft) a symbol to Catalans on both sides of the border. At a lower level lie the upland basins of the Cerdagne and the Capcir, then come the forests and pastures of the Vallespir (Tech valley), the rugged Aspres hills, and finally the plain of Roussillon itself, a great market-garden with its vines and abundant fruit and vegetable crops. The province is bounded to the south by the rocky Côte Vermeille, where the Albères mountains descend to the sea through the Banyuls vineyards and scattered cork oaks clinging to the steep slopes. Few contrasts could be greater than the one between this charmingly irregular coastline with its ancient port-resort of Collioure and the sweeping beaches to the north, backed by the planned modern tourist developments of Languedoc-Roussillon.

THE FRENCH ALPS

Stretching 370km – 230 miles from the Mediterranean to Lake Geneva, the French Alps display all the varieties of mountain scenery, from the sublimity of bare rock and eternal snow to the animation of densely-settled valleys. Nowhere more than among these incomparable mountains does human habitat show such close adaptation to natural conditions. Centuries of endurance and ingenuity have overcome formidable obstacles and brought all possible resources into play, not only settling valley floors, but pushing grazing and cultivation to its highest limits and developing widely-varied local traditions of living and building. Whether grouped sociably in village or hamlet or standing proudly in isolation, the traditional farmhouse combines under a single roof, with a minimum of openings, virtually all the functions of the farm (residence, barn, storage, drying). Building form, orientation and choice of materials (stone, slate, timber, shingles) all reflect the resources of the locality, reinforcing a sense of place which is already strong in these valley *pays*.

In modern times the Alps have become a vast playground, welcoming visitors at all seasons to sophisticated resort and remote cabin alike. The mountains have never discouraged communication, rather channelling it through valleys linked by pass routes where necessary. The grandiose works of the railway engineers have been followed by steady improvement of the road network, opening up to the touring motorist such spectacular itineraries as the Route des Grandes Alpes.

The northern boundary of the French Alps and part of the country's frontier with Switzerland is marked by the great sweep of **Lake Geneva**. To the south of the superb lake rise the Alps of Savoy, first the Chablais and Faucigny country, then the famous peaks and glaciers around the great white mountain, Mont-Blanc. Westward lie other graceful stretches of water, Lake Annecy, Le Bourget Lake, still in a mountain setting, but bordered by flower-bedecked resorts and villages and a countryside of human scale, patterned by woodlands, fruit and nut trees, crops and pasture, a landscape in cheerful contrast to the sometimes severe countenance of the higher land.

An important southwest-northeast communication route is formed by the Sub-Alpine Furrow, a broad and prosperous valley in which Grenoble, the metropolis of the Alps, sits at the confluence of Isère and Drac. The latter river and its tributaries rise among the crystalline rocks of the **Écrins** mountains, while the headwaters of the Isère flow through the **Vanoise** massif, with its deep valleys and vast pastures the site of France's first National Park.

The western rampart of the Alps is formed by a succession of massifs, **Bauges, Chartreuse, Vercors** the latter an extraordinary natural fortress of giddy limestone cliffs.

Beyond Briançon, hard up against the Italian border, the mountains are lit by the strong light of the Mediterranean. Here, among splendid forests of larch and high grazing grounds, settlement reaches its maximum altitude in Europe in villages like St-Véran (2 040m – 6 693ft); the houses exhibit extreme adaptation to rigours of site and climate.

Further south still, the scene is often one of striking severity, bare rock rising from vegetation of increasingly Mediterranean character, the olive tree making its appearance in the middle reaches of the Durance, the main watercourse of the Southern Alps.

The stark summit of Mount Ventoux overlooks the Comtat plain, while eastwards lie the most desolate tracts of the whole Alpine region, the Pre-Alps and high plateaux of Provence; here torrential streams have scored deep gorges like that of the Grand Canyon of the Verdon.

In **Upper Provence** (Haute-Provence), and particularly in the Maritime Alps which form the backdrop to the French Riviera, the proximity of the Mediterranean world makes itself felt again in the numerous fortified hill-top villages, with their houses of stone, pantiled roofs and fountains splashing in shady squares.

The richness of the natural heritage of the French Alps is reflected in the number of National (Mercantour, Écrins as well as Vanoise) and Regional (Vercors, Queyras) Parks set up to protect these incomparable landscapes and enhance the visitors' experience of them.

THE FRENCH RIVIERA

The Riviera's brilliant light, abundant sunshine, exotic vegetation and dramatic combination of sea and mountains have made it a fashionable place of pleasure since its "discovery" in the 19C; it is the archetypal holiday coast against which all others must be measured.

Between Nice and Menton, the Pre-Alps plunge almost sheer into the sea. The coast is densely built up, the resorts linked by triple corniche roads. Further north are the Maritime Alps, dissected by the upper valleys of the Var, Tinée, Vésubie and Roya, and, on the Italian border, the great crystalline massif of the **Mercantour** (Cime du Gélas 3 143m – 10 312ft). To the west of Nice the coast flattens out, forming wide bays with fine beaches.

The bustle of the coast is in contrast to the quieter charm of the interior, with its valleys carpeted in olive groves, its spectacular gorges, and its many hill-villages built to protect the population from the perils which proximity to the coast might bring. The limestone plateaux of the Provence tableland are separated from the sea by two massifs, Esterel and Maures. The jagged rocks of brightly-coloured porphyry making up the **Esterel massif** are best appreciated from the coast road leading from St-Raphaël to Cannes. The Estérel has been largely denuded of its former forest, but to the west, the **Maures massif** retains much of its fine cover of pine, cork oak and chestnut. Its coastline has great promontories and narrow tongues of land extending into the sea, defining wide bays like that of the Gulf of St-Tropez. Offshore are the densely-vegetated Hyères Islands, detached from the mainland in geologically recent times.

The Toulon coast, with its outstanding roadstead, is characterised by vertical cliffs interrupted by a number of attrac-

Villefranche-sur-Mer

tive beaches. To the north rise the rugged limestone heights of the Provençal Ranges; Mount Faron overlooks the great French naval port from an elevation of 584m – 1 916ft.

CORSICA

The mountainous "Island of Beauty", the name given to Corsica by the ancient Greeks, lies some 170km – just over 100 miles off the coast of mainland France. With its intense light, its superbly varied and dramatic coast and its wild and rugged interior, it is a place of utterly distinct natural identity, enhanced by the succession of peoples who have been attracted here to settle or to rule; these have included megalith builders and mysterious Torreans, Greeks and Romans, Pisans and Genoese, French and British, though the somewhat absurd interlude of the Anglo-Corsican Viceroyalty of 1794-96 seems to have left little trace.

The gulfs of Corsica's west coast are of extraordinary beauty, the jagged headlands and precipitous porphyry cliffs rising from the Golfe de Porto being especially memorable. The Cap Corse promontory prolongs the island's backbone of schistic rocks 40km – 25 miles northwards into the sea. The coastal plains of Bastia and Aléria to the east constitute the only substantial areas of flat land; their agricultural prosperity has revived in recent years, largely through the enterprise of resettled *pieds-noirs* from Algeria.

The interior is penetrated by a skeletal network of narrow and winding roads as well as by a remarkable one metregauge railway. Here are villages of tall granite houses overlooking deep gorges, as well as superb forests of oak, Corsican pine and sweet chestnut, *garrigue* and *maquis* vegetation. Above the tree line rise the high bare summits, all the more imposing because of their proximity to the sea. Much of inland Corsica is now protected as a Regional Nature Park, through which GR 20, one of Europe's finest long-distance footpaths, threads its way.

HISTORY

The great sweep of prehistory has left abundant traces in France, and it is to Frenchmen that much of our knowledge of prehistoric times is due. 🕭 *See Les EYZIES-DE-TAYAC: Prehistory.*

Ancient times

BC 5000 Megalithic culture flourishes in Brittany (Carnac), then in Corsica, lasting for over 2 500 years.

8C Celtic tribes from central Europe arrive in Gaul where they build the fortified settlements known as oppidums.

600 Greek traders found a number of cities, including Marseille, Glanum (🕭 *see ST-RÉMY-DE-PROVENCE*) and Aléria in Corsica.

2C Celtic culture, which had spread as far as Brittany, gives way to both Germanic and Roman influences. The port of Fréjus, on the Mediterranean coast, is founded in 154 by the Romans as a link on the sea-route to their possessions in Spain. By the year 122 they have established themselves at Aix, and four years later at Narbonne.

58-52 Julius Caesar's Gallic Wars. He defeats the Veneti in 56 BC (🕭 *see VANVES*), then himself suffers defeat at the hands of Vercingetorix (🕭 *see CLERMONT-FERRAND*) in 52 BC, though the latter's surrender comes only a few months later.

AD 1C During the reign of Augustus Roman rule in Gaul is consolidated and expanded (🕭 *see NÎMES*). Fréjus is converted into a naval base and fortified.

5C The monasteries set up by St Martin at Ligugé and by St Honorat at Lérins reinforce Christian beliefs and mark the beginning of a wave of such foundations (by St Victor at Marseille, by St Loup at Troyes, by St Maxime at Riez).

The Merovingians (418-751)

451 Merovius, king of the Salian Franks (from the Tournai area in present-day Belgium), defeats Attila the Hun (🕭 *see CHÂLONS-EN-CHAMPAGNE*). It is to him that the dynasty owes its name.

476 Fall of the Roman Empire in the West; Gaul occupied by barbarian tribes.

496 Clovis, grandson of Merovius and King of the Franks, is baptised in Reims.

507 Defeat of the Visigoths under Alaric II at Vouillé (🕭 *see POITIERS*) by Clovis.

6C Accompanied by Christian missionaries, settlers from Britain arrive in the Breton peninsulas, displacing the original Celtic inhabitants. But they too are overcome, first by the Franks (in the 9C), then by the Angevins (11C).

732 The Arab armies invading France are defeated at Moussais-la-Bataille (🕭 *see POITIERS*) by Charles Martel.

THE CAROLINGIANS (751-986)

751 Pepin the Short has himself elected king by an assembly of magnates and bishops at Soissons, sending the powerless Childeric, last of the Merovingians, to a monastery.

800 Charlemagne is crowned Emperor of the West in Rome.

842 The Strasbourg Oaths.

843 By the Treaty of Verdun, the Carolingian Empire is divided between

St-Martin cutting his cloak

the sons of Louis I, Charles the Bald receiving the territories to the west, roughly corresponding to modern France.

850 Nominoé (🕮 *see VANNES*) wrests eastern Brittany and the Rais country south of the Loire from its Frankish rulers.

910 Foundation of the great abbey at Cluny.

911 By the Treaty of St-Clair-sur-Epte, Charles the Simple and the Viking chief Rollo create the Duchy of Normandy.

The Capetians (987-1789)

THE DIRECT CAPETIANS (987-1328)

987 A descendant of Robert the Strong, Hugh Capet, Duke of "France", ousts Charles of Lorraine and has himself elected. By having his son crowned during his own lifetime, he consolidated his family's rule, which nevertheless does not become truly hereditary until the accession of Philippe Auguste in 1180.

1066 **William Duke of Normandy** (🕮 *see BAYEUX and CAEN*) sets out for the English coast from Dives. His victory over Harold at the Battle of Hastings leads to his coronation as King of England, though technically speaking he is still a vassal of the French king.

1095 The First Crusade is preached at Clermont-Ferrand.

1137 Louis VII weds Eleanor of Aquitaine (🕮 *see BORDEAUX)*; the annulment of their marriage 15 years later is a disaster for the dynasty.

Foundation of the School of Medicine at Montpellier.

1204 Gaillard Castle falls to Philippe Auguste, who goes on to conquer Normandy, Maine, Touraine and Anjou.

1209 Start of the Albigensian Crusade.

1214 Victory at the Battle of Bouvines (🕮 *see LILLE)*; for the first time, a genuinely French patriotism appears.

1244 Cathars burnt at the funeral pyre at Montségur.

1270 St Louis (Louis IX) dies aboard ship off Tunis on his way to the Eighth Crusade.

The House of Valois (1328-1589)

THE HUNDRED YEARS WAR – 1337-1475

Extending over six reigns, the war was both a political and dynastic struggle between Plantagenets and Capetians over who should rule in France. Accompanied by plague (including the Black Death of 1348) and religious confusion, it was a time of tribulation for the people of France, harassed as they were by bands of outlaws as well as by the English soldiery.

In 1337, Philippe VI of Valois resisted the claims to his throne made by Edward III of England (the grandson on his mother's side of Philippe le Bel (the Fair). This marked the beginning of the war. Three years after the French defeat at Crécy, Philippe VI purchased the Dauphiné (up to then a territory of the Empire) from its ruler, Humbert II, thereby extending French rule far to the east of the Rhône.

In 1356 King John the Good was defeated by the Black Prince at the Battle of Poitiers (🕮 *see POITIERS)*.

Under Charles V, Du Guesclin succeeded in restoring internal order. But at this point in their conflict, both adversaries were beset by problems of their own, caused in England by the minority of Richard II. In France, Charles VI too was under age, then affected by madness. The War between Armagnacs and Burgundians began and the Church was torn by the Great Schism (🕮 *see AVIGNON)*. Following the English victory at Agincourt (🕮 *see ST-OMER)* and the assassination of John the Fearless of Burgundy at Montereau (🕮 *see DIJON)*, the Treaty of Troyes, promising the French crown to the English king, seemed to extinguish any hope of the future Charles VII succeeding.

In 1429, however, after having picked out the king from among the courtiers assembled at Chinon, Joan of Arc recaptured Orléans, thereby preventing Salisbury's army from crossing the Loire and meeting up with the English troops who had been stationed in central and southwestern France following the Treaty of Brétigny in 1360. On 17 July, Charles VII was crowned in Reims cathedral; in 1436 Paris was freed, followed by Normandy and Guyenne. In 1453, the French victory at Castillon-la-Bataille was the last important clash of arms in the war, which was formally brought to an end by the Treaty of Picquigny.

1515 Accession of François I; Battle of Marignano and the signing of peace in perpetuity with Switzerland.

1520 Meeting of François I and Henry VIII of England at the Field of the Cloth of Gold at Guînes.

1539 The Ordinance of **Villers-Cotterêts**, one of the bases of French law, is promulgated by François I. Among its 192 articles are ones decreeing the keeping of parish registers of births and deaths, as well as law reform outlawing the founding of guilds and instituting secret criminal investigation and the compulsory use of French instead of Latin in legal matters. By this time, provincialism was on the way out, supplanted by a truly national consciousness, the outcome of three centuries of shared ordeals and triumphs.

1541 Calvin's "Institutes of the Christian Religion" is published. In it, this native Frenchman (born at Noyon) attempts to stem the fissiparous tendencies of the Reformation and to proclaim its universality. Style, structure and significance combine in this work to make it the first great classic of French literature.

1559 Treaty of Le Cateau-Cambrésis (👉 *see ST-QUENTIN*).

1560 The Amboise Conspiracy, harbinger of the looming political and religious crisis.

François I in 1525 by Jean Clouet (Musée du Louvre, Paris)

EXPLORER

THE WARS OF RELIGION – 1562-1598

This is the name given to the 36-year-long crisis marked by complex political as well as religious conflict. During the latter half of the 16C, the French monarchy was in poor shape to withstand the looming hegemony of Spain, with political life in chaos and debt reaching incredible dimensions. The firm stand taken on religion by Spain and Italy on the one hand and by the Protestant countries on the other was missing in the France of Catherine de' Medici's regency, where both parties jostled for favour and a policy of appeasement applied.

The nobility took advantage of the situation, seeking to bolster their power base in the provinces and, under cover of religion, to grasp the reins of government. The Catholic League was formed by the Guise and Montmorency families, supported by Spain and opposed by the Bourbon, Condé and Coligny factions, Huguenots all, with English backing.

Though historians distinguish eight wars separated by periods of peace or relative tranquillity, the troubles were continuous:

in the country, endless assassinations, persecutions and general lawlessness; at court, intrigues, volte-faces and pursuit of particular interests. Actual warfare, threatened ever since the Amboise Conspiracy, began at Wassy in 1562, following a massacre of Protestants. The names of Dreux, Nîmes, Chartres, Longjumeau, Jarnac, Montcontour, St-Lô, Valognes, Coutras, Arques, Ivry follow in bloody succession.

The Peace of St-Germain in 1570 showed a general desire for reconciliation, but only two years later came the St Bartholomew's Day Massacre in which some 20 000 Huguenots died.

The States General were convened at Blois at the request of the supporters of the League who were opposed to the centralisation of power into royal hands. Fearful of the power enjoyed by Duke Henri of Guise, head of the Catholic League and the kingdom's best military commander, King Henri III had him assassinated in the château at Blois one cold morning in December 1588, only to be cut down himself by a fanatical monk the following year.

This left the succession open for the Huguenot Henry of Navarre, the future Henri IV. By formally adopting the Catholic faith in 1593 and by promulgating the Edict of Nantes in 1598, this able ruler succeeded in rallying all loyal Frenchmen to his standard, putting at least a temporary end to the long-drawn-out crisis.

The Bourbons (1589-1789)

HENRI IV – 1589-1610

Though his political manœuvrings and his personal conduct did not endear him to everybody, Henri IV put France's affairs

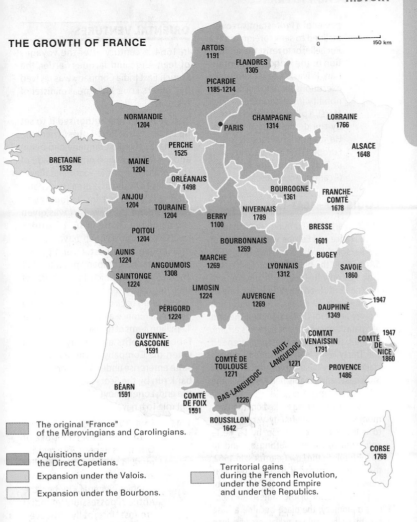

THE GROWTH OF FRANCE

0   150 km

ARTOIS
1191

FLANDRES
1305

PICARDIE
1185-1214

NORMANDIE
1204

CHAMPAGNE
1314

LORRAINE
1766

● PARIS

PERCHE
1525

ALSACE
1648

BRETAGNE
1532

MAINE
1204

ORLÉANAIS
1498

ANJOU
1204

TOURAINE
1204

BOURGOGNE
1361

FRANCHE-
COMTÉ
1678

POITOU
1204

BERRY
1100

NIVERNAIS
1789

BRESSE
1601

AUNIS
1224

BOURBONNAIS
1269

MARCHE
1269

BUGEY

ANGOUMOIS
1308

LYONNAIS
1312

SAVOIE
1860

SAINTONGE
1224

LIMOSIN
1224

AUVERGNE
1269

1947

PÉRIGORD
1224

DAUPHINÉ
1349

GUYENNE-
GASCOGNE
1591

COMTAT
VENAISSIN
1791

1947

COMTÉ
DE
NICE
1860

COMTÉ DE
TOULOUSE
1271

HAUT-
LANGUEDOC
1271

PROVENCE
1486

BÉARN
1591

COMTÉ
DE FOIX
1591

BAS-LANGUEDOC
1226

ROUSSILLON
1642

CORSE
1769

The original "France"
of the Merovingians and Carolingians.

Aquisitions under
the Direct Capetians.

Expansion under the Valois.

Expansion under the Bourbons.

Territorial gains
during the French Revolution,
under the Second Empire
and under the Republics.

on a firm footing once more, attaching the provinces of Bresse and Bugey to the kingdom and setting great architects like Du Cerceau and Métezeau to work on projects in Paris such as the Place des Vosges and the Louvre Gallery, and La Rochelle and Charleville in the provinces. Important economic reforms were undertaken, and the king's old Huguenot friend, Maximilien de Béthune, Duke of Sully, set the nation's finances in order, dug canals and laid out new roads and port facilities.

In 1600, the landowner Olivier de Serres published his great work on progressive farming technique "The Theatre of Agriculture and Field Husbandry", supporting Sully in his contention that "tilling and stockkeeping are the two breasts from which France feeds". The king's concern with his people's well-being found expression too in his famous statement "a chicken in the pot every Sunday".

1610 Louis XIII becomes King. The country's trade flourishes with the development of inland ports and there are fine planned expansions to a number of towns (Orléans, La Rochelle, Montargis, Langres). The reign is marked by an aristocratic rebellion, as well as by the pioneering work of St Vincent de Paul in social welfare (hospitals, Sisters of Mercy). In the field of ideas, Descartes publishes his "Discourse on Method" (1637), with its reasoning based on systematic questioning ("Cogito, ergo sum"), a starting point for the intellectual revolution which, among other achievements, led to the invention of analytical geometry.

1624 The King's First Minister, Richelieu (1585-1642), is successful in his attempts to reduce the power of a Protestantism over-inclined to seek foreign aid (La Rochelle) or to resist the unification of the kingdom (Montauban, Privas). A few exemplary executions serve to humble the nobility (Montmorency, Cinq-Mars), a process carried further by the demolition of castles. He strengthens France's role in Europe (Thirty Years War) and, in 1635, founds the Academy (Académie française).

LOUIS XIV – 1643-1715

The 72 years of the Sun King's reign marked both France and Europe with the force of his personality (👉 see PARIS and VERSAILLES). At the time of his accession, the king was only five years old and Anne of Austria confirmed Mazarin in his role as first minister. Five days later, the French victory at Rocroi (1643) signalled the end of Spanish dominance of Europe's affairs. In 1648, the Peace of Westphalia ended the Thirty Years War, confirmed France's claim to Alsace (apart from Strasbourg and Mulhouse) and established French as the language of diplomacy.

In 1657, while the king looked on, the two-month siege of Montmédy was brought to a triumphant conclusion by La Ferté and Vauban, thereby putting an end to Spanish rule in the Low Countries. In 1662, the king's first year of personal rule was crowned by the purchase of the port of Dunkirk, a result of the statesman Lionne's diplomacy; the place became a base for smugglers and for privateers like Jean Bart operating in the service of the king. Anglo-French rivalry for control of the seas (👉 see BELLE-ILE) now became the main theme of international politics. In 1678, the Treaty of Nijmegen marked the end of the war with Holland, the giving-up of the Franche-Comté and of 12 strongholds in Flanders by Spain, and the reconquest of Alsace. This was a high point in Louis' reign and in French expansion, insured by Vauban's work in fortifying the country's new frontiers. The politics of religion were not always straightforward; for 20 years, the king was in conflict with the Pope in what was known as the Affair of the Régale; in 1685 came the Revocation of the Edict of Nantes with all its dire consequences, and in 1702, the suppression of the camisard revolt (👉 see ANDUZE). The monarch's later years were clouded by the country's economic exhaustion, though the Battle of Denain in 1712 saved France from invasion by the Austro-Dutch armies and led to the end of the War of the Spanish Succession.

ORIENTAL VENTURES

In 1664, a century after the voyages of Jean Ango and Jacques Cartier, the French East India Company was revived by Colbert, Louis XIV's great minister of finance.

Two years later he authorised it to set up bases both at **Port-Louis** (where the original East India Company had been) and on waste ground on the far side of the confluence of the Scorff and Blavet rivers. In 1671 the first great merchantman was fitted out for its journey to the East, and the new port was given the name of L'Orient in 1671 (**Lorient** in 1830). Anglo-French naval rivalry now began in earnest. Over a period of 47 years the Company put a total of 76 ships into use, which, in the course of their long and often dangerous voyages, would bring back cargoes of spices and porcelain (France alone importing over 12 million items of the latter). The initially fabulous profits eventually declined when the Company became a kind of state enterprise under the control of the bank run by the Scots financier Law. In the end, Lorient moved from a commercial role to a naval one.

1715   Louis XV succeeds to the crown at the age of five; the Duke of Orleans is Regent. The reign is marked by indecision, frivolity and corruption; many of France's colonies (Senegal, Québec, the Antilles, possessions in India) are lost. Internally, however, the country prospers, benefiting from a wise economic policy; the standard of living improves and a long period of stability favours agricultural development (introduction of the potato, artificial extension of grazing lands). Lorraine is absorbed into France in 1766, and Corsica in 1769.

1774   Louis XVI becomes King. Lafayette takes part in the American War of Independence, brought to an end by the Treaty of Versailles in 1783.

The spirit of scientific enquiry leads to rapid technological progress, the growth of industry (textiles, porcelain, steam power) and to endeavours such as Lalande's astronomical experiments and the Montgolfier brothers' balloon flights at Annonay in 1783.

The French Revolution (1789-1799)

The Revolution, opening up the continent of Europe to democracy, was the outcome of the long crisis affecting the Ancien Régime.

Hastened along by the teachings of the thinkers of the Enlightenment as much as by the inability of a still essentially feudal system to adapt itself to new social realities, the Revolution broke out following disastrous financial mismanagement and the emptying of the coffers of the state. The main events unfolded in Paris but their repercussions were felt in the provincial cities (Lyon, Nantes...) as well as in the countryside.

The year 1789 heralded a number of major historical events for France. The Estates General were renamed the National Assembly, the Bastille was stormed, privileges were abolished (night of 4 July) and the Rights of Man were proclaimed. Two years later, in 1791, the king, fleeing with his family, was arrested in Varennes (22 June) and brought back to Paris, where he was suspended from office on 30 September. The following year the Convention (1792-95) was signed, while in Valmy (20 September) Kellermann and Dumouriez saved France from invasion by forcing the Prussians to retreat; on 22 September France is proclaimed a one and indivisible Republic. The major landmarks of 1793 were the execution of Louis XVI (21 January), the Vendée revolt, the crushing of the Lyon uprising and the siege of Toulon (July-December). In 1795 France adopted the metric system. In 1799 Napoleon overthrew the **Directory** (*9 November*) and declared himself First Consul of the Republic. Finally, in 1801, the Code Napoléon was promulgated throughout the country.

THE VENDÉE

This is the name given to the Royalist-led but popular uprising in western France in 1793 in reaction to the excesses of the Convention. The bocage countryside of much of the area favoured the guerrilla warfare waged by the "Whites" (Catholic royalists) against "Blues" (Republicans), who brought in the Alsatian general Kléber. In the winter of 1794 thousands of Whites were executed at Nantes, Angers, Fontenay... while the countryside was ravaged by mobile columns of vengeful soldiery (known as the infernal columns of General Turreau). Still resistance continued, until finally put to an end by the more conciliatory policies of Hoche.

La Marseillaise by Rude – Arc de Triomphe

A. Eli/MICHELIN

The Empire (1804-1815)

1804 On 2 December, Napoleon is crowned Emperor of the French in Notre-Dame by Pope Pius VII. The territorial acquisitions made in the course of the French Revolution now have to be defended against a whole series of coalitions formed by the country's numerous enemies.

1805 Napoleon gives up his planned invasion of England, abandoning the great camp set up at Boulogne for that purpose. The Royal Navy's victory at Trafalgar gives Britain control of the seas, but France's

1806 armies win the Battles of Ulm and Austerlitz (Slavkov).

1806 Intended to bring about England's economic ruin, the Continental Blockade pushes France into further territorial acquisitions.

1808 Some of the best French forces bogged down in the Peninsular War.

1812 Napoleon invades Russia. The Retreat from Moscow.

1813 The Battle of Leipzig. The whole of Europe lines up against France. Not even Napoleon's military genius can prevent the fall of Paris and the Emperor's farewell at Fontainebleau (20 April 1814).

The Restoration (1815-1830)

1814 Louis XVIII returns from exile in England.

1815 The Hundred Days (20 March-22 June); the attempt to re-establish the Empire ended by the victory of the Allies at Waterloo. Louis XVIII once more on the throne. France returns to the frontiers of 1792. Talleyrand's efforts at the Congress of Vienna help bring France back into the community of European nations. Execution of Marshal Ney.

The July Monarchy (1830-1848)

1830 Charles X's "Four Ordinances of St-Cloud" violate the Constitution and lead to the outbreak of revolution. There follow the "Three Glorious Days" (27, 28 and 29 July) and the flight of the Bourbons. Louis-Philippe becomes King.

1837 France's first passenger-carrying railway is opened between Paris and St-Germain-en-Laye.

Second Republic and Second Empire (1848-1870)

1848 On 10 December, Louis Napoléon is elected President of the Republic by universal suffrage.

1851 On 2 December, Louis Napoléon dissolves the Legislative Assembly and declares himself President for a 10-year term.

1852 A plebiscite leads to the proclamation of the Second Empire (Napoleon III).

1855 The World Fair is held in Paris.

1860 Savoy and the county of Nice elect to become part of France.

1869 Freedom of the Press is guaranteed.

1870 War declared on Prussia on 19 July. On 2 September, defeat at Sedan spells the end of the Second Empire. Two days later Paris rises and the Republic is proclaimed. But the way to the capital lies open, and soon Paris is under siege.

The Republic (1870-the present day)

1870 Following the disaster at Sedan, the Third Republic is proclaimed on 4 September.

1871 The Paris Commune (21-28 May). By the Treaty of Frankfurt France gives up all of Alsace (with the exception of Belfort) and part of Lorraine.

1881 Jules Ferry secularises primary education, making it free and, later, compulsory.

1884 Trade unions gain formal recognition.

1885 Vaccination in the treatment of rabies (Pasteur).

Inauguration of the Eiffel Tower (World Fair).

1894 The Dreyfus Affair divides the country. Forged evidence results in this Jewish General Staff captain being unfairly imprisoned for spying.

1897 Clément Ader's heavier-than-air machine takes to the air at Toulouse.

1904 Entente Cordiale.

1905 Separation of Church and State.

1914 Outbreak of the First World War. On 3 August the German armies attack through neutral Belgium but are thrown back in the Battle of the Marne. Four years of trench warfare follow, a bloody climax being reached in

1916-17 around the fortress city of Verdun, where the German offensive is held, at immense cost in lives on both sides.

In 1919 the signing of the Treaty of Versailles brings the First World War to an end.

1934 France is deeply divided; on 6 February, the National Assembly is attacked by right-wing demonstrators. Two years later, Léon Blum forms his Popular Front government.

1939 Outbreak of the Second World War. In June 1940 France is overrun by the German army and Marshal Pétain's government requests an armistice. Much of the country is occupied (the north and the whole of the Atlantic seaboard), but the "French State" with its slogan of "Work, Family, Fatherland" is established at Vichy and collaborates closely with the Germans. France's honour is saved by General de Gaulle's Free French forces, active in many theatres of the war, and by the courage of the men and women of the Resistance.

In 1942, the whole country is occupied, and the French fleet scuttles itself at Toulon. In June 1944 the Allies land in Normandy, and in the South of France in August. Paris is liberated and the German surrender signed at Reims on 7 May 1945.

This major conflict, which inflamed all continents, is detailed in this guide under the places which it affected most in France.

1947 The Fourth Republic established. Its governments last an average of six months.

1954 Dien Bien Phu falls to the Vietminh. France abandons Indo-China and grants Morocco and Tunisia their independence (1956).

1958 The Algerian crisis leads to the downfall of the Fourth and the establishment of the Fifth Republic under De Gaulle. Civil war is narrowly averted. Nearly all its French population leaves Algeria, which becomes independent in 1962.

Charles de Gaulle

PIX, Paris

1958 The Fifth Republic established. The European Economic Community (EEC) comes into effect.

The new constitution inspired by General de Gaulle is voted by referendum.

1962 Referendum establishing that the future President of the Republic be elected by universal suffrage.

1967 Franco-British agreement to manufacture Airbus.

1968 The "events of May"; workers join students in mass protests, roughly put down by riot police. The Gaullists triumph in national elections, but it is a hollow victory and De Gaulle, defeated in the referendum of April 1969, retires to continue writing his memoirs.

1969 Georges Pompidou is elected President (16 June).

1974 Valéry Giscard d'Estaing is elected President (19 May).

1981 François Mitterrand is elected President (10 May).

Inauguration of the TGV line between Paris and Lyon (2h 40min); Paris-Marseille (1981); and Paris-Bordeaux (1990).

1994 Inauguration of the Channel Tunnel (6 May).

1995 Jacques Chirac is elected President (7 May).

2002 1 Jan, dubbed "€ Day," marks the beginning of circulation for Euro notes and coins.

2005 Prince Rainier III of Monaco dies (6 Apr). His son Prince Albert takes power.

Contemporary France

Although France is ranked among the five leading countries in the world in terms of international trade, it remains a nation with a strong **rural tradition,** even if the number of people employed in farming is on the decline. The French have stayed close to their native land, either by acquiring a cottage in the country or by inheriting a family estate.

For most French people, the qualities associated with this ancestral land are encapsulated in the traditional **village** – the village where one was born, where one has chosen to live or where one spends one's holidays. Leaving aside the differences attributed to climatic conditions and building materials, all villages feature common characteristics: the **main street** (Grand'rue) lined with small shops, the **marketplace,** where local cattle fairs used to be held, and of course, the **church**, whose chimes continue to herald the fortunes and misfortunes of the community. Although they see a surge of activity during municipal and trade fairs, French villages lead quiet, peaceful lives most of the year. Only the traditional **café** and the **boules playing ground** echo the conversations of the locals idly debating on the meaning of life.

Although a series of decentralisation reforms was implemented in 1982, Paris and her eleven million inhabitants remain the administrative core of the country, ruling supreme over the provinces.

The seat of political power and an important centre for world trade, "the city of lights" is also a privileged stopover for tourists, on account of its wealth of architectural marvels, its museums and its high cultural standards.

Over the past decades, a number of **regional capitals** have been created, striking a balance between the capital and small country villages. These new urban zones are resolutely turned towards the future and illustrate the thriving activity of the French regions.

This brief description would not be complete without mentioning the **French.** Frequently misunderstood by foreign visitors, believed to be grumpy, unhelpful and unresponsive to outside influences, they are nonetheless always ready to defend their traditions and support a just cause. To those who make the effort of going towards them, the French will always extend a warm, genuine welcome.

Art in France

ABC OF ARCHITECTURE

Ecclesiastical architecture

CLERMONT FERRAND (Puy-de-Dôme) – Ground plan of Basilique Notre-Dame-du-Port (11C-12C)

Latin-cross plan, the transverse aisle forming the **transept**

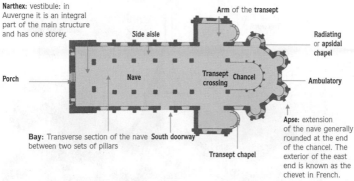

Narthex: vestibule: in Auvergne it is an integral part of the main structure and has one storey.

Arm of the **transept**

Side aisle

Radiating or apsidal chapel

Porch

Nave

Transept crossing

Chancel

Ambulatory

Apse: extension of the nave generally rounded at the end of the chancel. The exterior of the east end is known as the chevet in French.

Bay: Transverse section of the nave between two sets of pillars

South doorway

Transept chapel

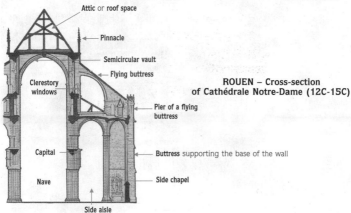

Attic or roof space

Pinnacle

Semicircular vault

Flying buttress

Clerestory windows

Pier of a flying buttress

ROUEN – Cross-section of Cathédrale Notre-Dame (12C-15C)

Capital

Buttress supporting the base of the wall

Nave

Side chapel

Side aisle

MOISSAC – South doorway of the 12C abbey church

Torus: a large convex moulding separating the covings

Historiated tympanum (decorated with narrative scenes and figures, here Christ in Majesty)

Coving: concave moulding

Archivolt: series of mouldings curving round an arch

Lintel

Medallion

Embrasure: arch shafts, splaying sometimes adorned with statues or columns

Pier adorned with interlaced lions

Engaged piers supporting the arched mouldings

Scallop motif

R. Corbel/MICHELIN

73

ORCIVAL – Notre-Dame Basilica (12C)

Most of the Romanesque churches of the Auvergne belong to a school which developed in the 11C 12C and is considered one of the most unusual in the history of art in the western world

Relieving arch: releves the weight of the wail above an opening.

Two storeyed **octagonal bell-tower:** its thrusts are but tressed by the chevet, nave and the arms of the transept.

Twin windows

Transept

Semicircular window

Gable-wall

Window

Modillions: scroll shaped projecting mouldings supporting the cornice.

String-course with billet moulding: ornamental frieze consisting of bands of raised short cylindrical or square blocks placed at regular intervals.

Radiating or **apsidal** chapel

Buttress: external support for a wall, built against it.

Cornice adorned with chequered motif

Chevet: the east end is the most beautiful and most characteristic of the Auvergne churches owing to the original layout of the various levels.

R. Corbel/MICHELIN

CHARTRES – West front of Cathédrale Notre-Dame (12C-13C)

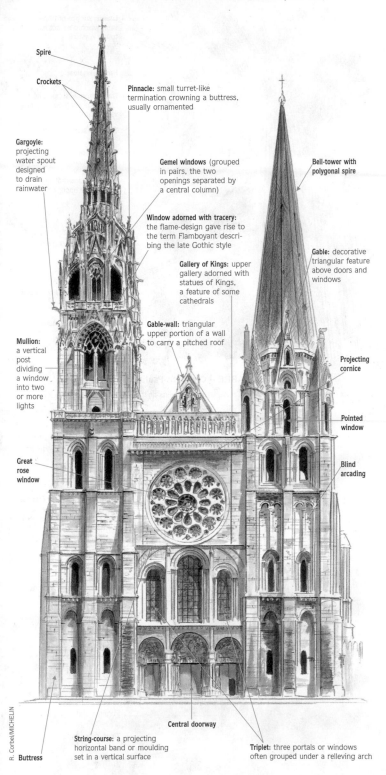

Spire

Crockets

Pinnacle: small turret-like termination crowning a buttress, usually ornamented

Gargoyle: projecting water spout designed to drain rainwater

Gemel windows (grouped in pairs, the two openings separated by a central column)

Bell-tower with polygonal spire

Window adorned with tracery: the flame-design gave rise to the term Flamboyant describing the late Gothic style

Gable: decorative triangular feature above doors and windows

Gallery of Kings: upper gallery adorned with statues of Kings, a feature of some cathedrals

Gable-wall: triangular upper portion of a wall to carry a pitched roof

Mullion: a vertical post dividing a window into two or more lights

Projecting cornice

Pointed window

Great rose window

Blind arcading

Central doorway

String-course: a projecting horizontal band or moulding set in a vertical surface

Triplet: three portals or windows often grouped under a relieving arch

R. Corbel/MICHELIN

Buttress

SENLIS – Cathédrale Notre-Dame (12C-13C)

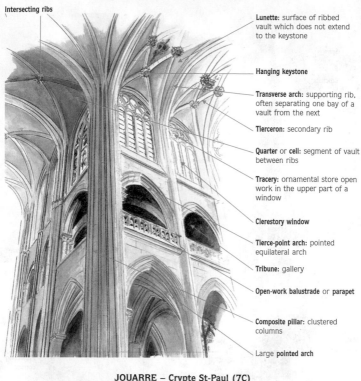

Intersecting ribs

Lunette: surface of ribbed vault which does not extend to the keystone

Hanging keystone

Transverse arch: supporting rib, often separating one bay of a vault from the next

Tierceron: secondary rib

Quarter or **cell:** segment of vault between ribs

Tracery: ornamental store open work in the upper part of a window

Clerestory window

Tierce-point arch: pointed equilateral arch

Tribune: gallery

Open-work balustrade or **parapet**

Composite pillar: clustered columns

Large **pointed arch**

JOUARRE – Crypte St-Paul (7C)

The crypts of Jouarre Abbey built in the CarolIgian period are among the earliest examples of funerary religious architecture popular in the Middle Ages.

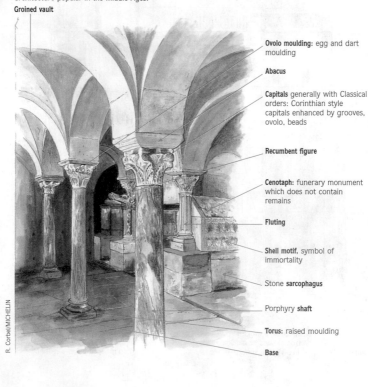

Groined vault

Ovolo moulding: egg and dart moulding

Abacus

Capitals generally with Classical orders: Corinthian style capitals enhanced by grooves, ovolo, beads

Recumbent figure

Cenotaph: funerary monument which does not contain remains

Fluting

Shell motif, symbol of immortality

Stone **sarcophagus**

Porphyry **shaft**

Torus: raised moulding

Base

R. Corbel/MICHELIN

THANN – Choir stalls in Collégiale St-Thiébaut (14C-early 16C)

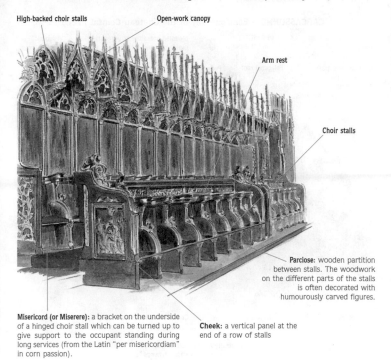

High-backed choir stalls

Open-work canopy

Arm rest

Choir stalls

Parciose: wooden partition between stalls. The woodwork on the different parts of the stalls is often decorated with humourously carved figures.

Misericord (or Miserere): a bracket on the underside of a hinged choir stall which can be turned up to give support to the occupant standing during long services (from the Latin "per misericordiam" in corn passion).

Cheek: a vertical panel at the end of a row of stalls

ALBI – Rood screen in Cathédrale Ste-Cécile (16C)

The **rood screen** was designed to separate the chancel (reserved for the clergy) from the nave (where the congregation gathered) and carry the Crucifix (rood). This example in Albi is typical of the Flamboyant Gothic style.

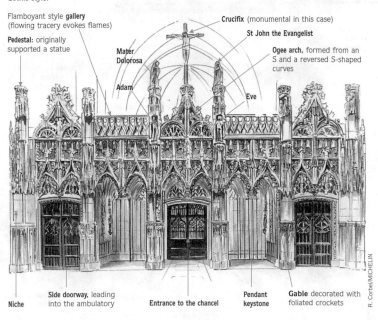

Flamboyant style **gallery** (flowing tracery evokes flames)

Pedestal: originally supported a statue

Mater Dolorosa

Adam

Crucifix (monumental in this case)

St John the Evangelist

Ogee arch, formed from an S and a reversed S-shaped curves

Eve

Niche

Side doorway, leading into the ambulatory

Entrance to the chancel

Pendant keystone

Gable decorated with foliated crockets

R. Corbel/MICHELIN

Military architecture

CARCASSONNE – East gateway of the Château Comtal (12C)

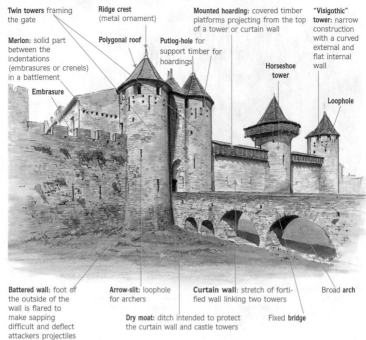

Twin towers framing the gate

Merlon: solid part between the indentations (embrasures or crenels) in a battlement

Embrasure

Ridge crest (metal ornament)

Polygonal roof

Putlog-hole for support timber for hoardings

Mounted hoarding: covered timber platforms projecting from the top of a tower or curtain wall

"Visigothic" tower: narrow construction with a curved external and flat internal wall

Horseshoe tower

Loophole

Battered wall: foot of the outside of the wall is flared to make sapping difficult and deflect attackers projectiles

Arrow-slit: loophole for archers

Dry moat: ditch intended to protect the curtain wall and castle towers

Curtain wall: stretch of fortified wall linking two towers

Fixed bridge

Broad **arch**

Château de BONAGUIL (13C – early 16C)

Bonaguil Castle, rebuilt from 1483 to 1510 by Béranger de Roquefeuil, is a good example of the improvements made to a defensive stronghold to take account of the development of firearms.

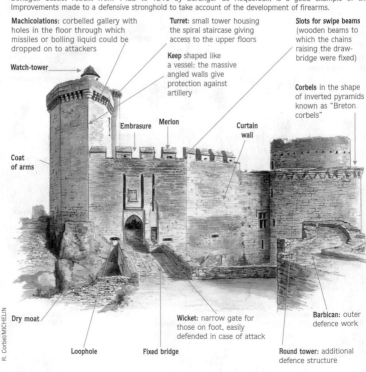

Machicolations: corbelled gallery with holes in the floor through which missiles or boiling liquid could be dropped on to attackers

Watch-tower

Coat of arms

Turret: small tower housing the spiral staircase giving access to the upper floors

Keep shaped like a vessel: the massive angled walls give protection against artillery

Embrasure   **Merlon**

Curtain wall

Slots for swipe beams (wooden beams to which the chains raising the draw-bridge were fixed)

Corbels in the shape of inverted pyramids known as "Breton corbels"

Dry moat

Loophole

Wicket: narrow gate for those on foot, easily defended in case of attack

Fixed bridge

Barbican: outer defence work

Round tower: additional defence structure

R. Corbel/MICHELIN

NEUF-BRISACH (1698-1703)

The polygonal stronghold was developed in the early 16C as firearms became more common in warfare: the cannon mounted on one structure covered the "blind spot" of the neighbouring position. This stronghold was built by Vauban, opposite the formidable Breisach, handed back to the Hapsburgs under the Treaty of Ryswick (1697).

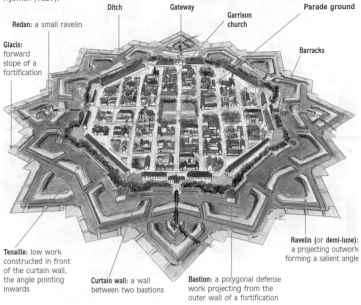

Ditch **Gateway** **Garrison church** **Parade ground**

Redan: a small ravelin

Glacis: forward slope of a fortification

Barracks

Tenaille: low work constructed in front of the curtain wall, the angle pointing inwards

Curtain wall: a wall between two bastions

Bastion: a polygonal defense work projecting from the outer wall of a fortification

Ravelin (or demi-lune): a projecting outwork forming a salient angle

Civil architecture

BLOIS – Château, François-1er staircase (16C)

The spiral stairway is built inside an octagonal staircase half set into the façade. It opens onto the main courtyard in a series of balconies which form loggias. The king and his court would view all sorts of entertainment from here: the arrival of dignitaries, jousting, hunting or military displays.

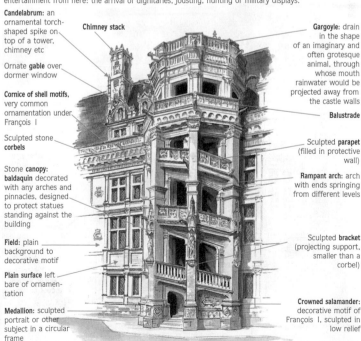

Candelabrum: an ornamental torch-shaped spike on top of a tower, chimney etc

Chimney stack

Ornate **gable** over dormer window

Cornice of shell motifs, very common ornamentation under François I

Sculpted stone **corbels**

Stone **canopy: baldaquin** decorated with any arches and pinnacles, designed to protect statues standing against the building

Field: plain background to decorative motif

Plain surface left bare of ornamentation

Medallion: sculpted portrait or other subject in a circular frame

Gargoyle: drain in the shape of an imaginary and often grotesque animal, through whose mouth rainwater would be projected away from the castle walls

Balustrade

Sculpted **parapet** (filled in protective wall)

Rampant arch: arch with ends springing from different levels

Sculpted **bracket** (projecting support, smaller than a corbel)

Crowned salamander: decorative motif of François I, sculpted in low relief

R. Corbel/MICHELIN

SERRANT – Château (16C-17C)

Imperial dome (pointed dome, vertical section of which is an ogee)

Balustrade: low protective wall composed of balusters

Corner tower

Dormer window surmounted by a broken pediment

Œil-de-bœuf window: small and circular ("bull's eye")

Triangular pediment

Main building, or *corps-de-logis*

Attic: small extra upper storey

Lantern

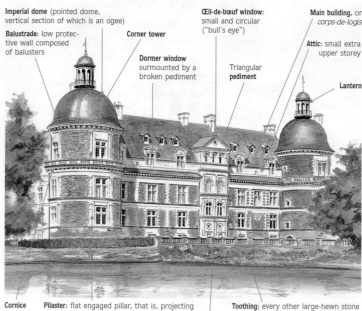

Cornice

Pilaster: flat engaged pillar, that is, projecting only slightly from the wall behind it

Avant-corps: part of a building projecting from the rest of the façade for the entire height of the building, roof included

Toothing: every other large-hewn stone is left projecting from the stone-work framing the windows for a more solid and more decorative bond with the adjoining schist walls

BORDEAUX – Palais de la Bourse (18C)

Flaming urn: a characteristic feature in Classical architecture

Triangular pediment with allegorical carving

Œil-de-bœuf: a small, circular window ("bull's-eye")

Trophy: decorative carving of arms grouped around a breast plate or helmet

Dentils: a frieze of small, rectangular blocks

Architrave: the lowest part of the entablature resting directly upon the columns

Ionic capital: capital with a spiral volute

Mullioned window

Cartouche: a panel ornately framed and usually bearing an inscription

Column offset from the wall

Fanlight: upper section of a door or window

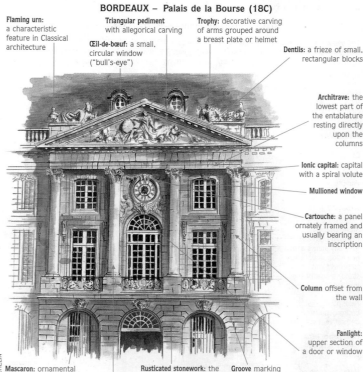

R. Corbel/MICHELIN

Mascaron: ornamental sculpture on keystone or voussoir

Colossal order spanning several storeys

Rusticated stonework: the massive blocks are dressed to a flat surface with chamfered edges

Groove marking the join between dressed stone blocks

A SURVEY OF FRENCH ART

From Prehistory to the Gallo-Roman Era

PREHISTORY

While stone and bone tools appeared in the Lower Paleolithic period, prehistoric art did not make its entrance until the Upper Paleolithic (350 to 100 centuries BC), and reached its peak in the Magdalenian Period (*see Les EYZIES-DE-TAYAC for the chronology of prehistoric eras)*. The art of engraved wood and ivory objects together with votive statuettes developed alongside the art of wall decoration, as is well illustrated in France by caves in the Dordogne, the Pyrenees, the Ardèche and the Gard. Early artists used pigments with a mineral base for their cave paintings and sometimes took advantage of the natural shape of the rock itself to execute their work in low relief.

The Neolithic revolution (6500 BC), during which populations began to settle, brought with it the advent of pottery as well as a different use of land and a change in burial practices – some megaliths (dolmens and covered passageways) are ancient burial chambers. Menhirs, a type of megalith found in great numbers in Brittany (Carnac and Locmariaquer), are as yet of unknown origin.

The discovery of metal brought prehistoric civilisation into the Bronze Age (2300-1800 BC) and then into the Iron Age (750-450 BC). Celtic art showed perfect mastery of metalwork as in the tombs of Gorge-Meillet, Mailly-le-Camp, Bibracte and Vix in which the treasures consist of gold torques (necklaces) and other items of jewellery, various coins and bronzeware.

THE GALLO-ROMAN ERA AND THE EARLY MIDDLE AGES

When the Romans conquered Gaul (2C-1C BC), they introduced the technique of building with stone. In cities, the Empire's administrative centres, the centralised power of Rome favoured a style of architecture that reflected its strength and prestige and imposed its culture. Theatres (Orange and Vienne), temples (the Square House or Maison Carrée in Nîmes), baths, basilicas and triumphal arches were constructed, while the local aristocracy took to building Roman villas with frescoes and mosaics (Vaison-la-Romaine and Grand). The presence of the Romans has had a lasting effect on the shape of France in terms of town-planning, roads, bridges and aqueducts (Pont du Gard). Towards the end of the late Empire, official recognition of the Christian church in the year 380 prompted the first examples of Christian architecture, among them the baptisteries of Fréjus, Riez, and Poitiers.

During the great barbarian invasions of the 5C, figurative art, unknown to Germanic peoples, gave place to abstract (intertwining, circular shapes) and animal motifs. The technique of *cloisonné* gold and silverware (Childeric's treasure) became widespread.

Merovingian art (6C-8C), a synthesis of styles, included elements of antique, barbarian and Christian art (the Dunes hypogeum near Poitiers and the crypt in Jouarre) out of which evolved medieval art.

The **Carolingian Renaissance** (9C) was marked by a great flowering of illuminated manuscripts and ivory-carving (the Dagulf psalter in the Louvre) and by a deliberate return to imperial, antique art forms (Aix-la-Chapelle and the oratory of Germigny-des-Prés).

The altar in churches of the period is sometimes raised above a vaulted area of the chancel known as the crypt which was originally on the same level as the nave (St-Germain of Auxerre and St-Philibert-de-Grand-Lieu.

Lady of Brassempouy, St-Germain-en-Laye

Romanesque Period (11C–12C)

In the early 11C, after the disturbances of the year 1000 (decadence of the Carolingian dynasty and struggles between great feudal barons), the spiritual influence and power of the Church gave rise to the birth of Romanesque architecture.

ROMANESQUE ARCHITECTURE

Early Romanesque edifices were characterised by the widespread use of stone vaulting which replaced timber roofs, the use of buttresses and a return to architectural decoration (as in the churches of St-Martin-du-Canigou, and St-Bénigne in Dijon). The darkness of the nave was explained by the fact that for structural reasons wide openings could not be cut into the walls supporting the vaulting. The basilica plan with nave and side aisles, sometimes preceded by a porch, predominated in France although some churches were built to a central plan (the church of Neuvy-St-Sépulcre). Depending on the church, the east end might have been flat or have had apsidal chapels; it was often semicircular with axial chapels (as in the church of Anzy-le-Duc) or may have featured radiating chapels. More complex designs combined an ambulatory with radiating chapels (the churches of Conques and Cluny).

The first attempts at embellishment led to a revival of sculptural decoration of which the lintel of St-Genis-les-Fontaines Church is one of the earliest examples. Tympana, archivolts, arch shafts and piers were covered with carvings of a religious or profane nature (as in the illustration of the *Romance of Renart* in the church of St-Ursin in Bourges). Interior decoration consisted mainly of frescoes (the churches of St-Savin-sur-Gartempe and Berzé-la-Ville) and carved capitals with the occasional complex theme (as in the chancel capitals in Cluny).

The Romanesque decorative style drew largely upon three main models, the Oriental (griffins and imaginary animals) which was spread by the Crusades, the Byzantine (illustrations of Christ in Majesty and a particular style for folds) and the Islamic (stylised foliage and pseudo-Kufic script).

REGIONAL CHARACTERISTICS

The Romanesque style spread throughout France affecting some areas earlier than others and developing special stylistic features according to the region. It first appeared in the south and in Burgundy, reaching the east of France at a much later date.

Romanesque architecture in the **Languedoc** owes much to Toulouse's St-Sernin Basilica, whose tall lantern tower pierced by ornamental arcading served as a model for many local bell-towers. The sculptures on the Miégeville doorway, completed in 1118, have a distinctive style, with highly expressive folds and a lengthening of the figures which is repeated in Moissac and, to a lesser extent, in St-Gilles-du-Gard.

In **Saintonge-Poitou**, the originality of the edifices derives from the great height of the aisles which serve to reinforce the walls of the nave and thus lend balance to the barrel vaulting. The gabled façades, flanked by lantern towers, are covered in ornamental arcading with statue niches and low relief (as in the church of Notre-Dame-la-Grande in Poitiers).

In **Auvergne**, the transept crossing is often covered by a dome, buttressed by high, quadripartite vaulting and supported on diaphragm arches. This constitutes an oblong mass which juts out above the roof beneath the bell-tower. The use of lava, a particularly difficult stone to carve, explains the limited sculptural decoration (as in the churches of St-Nectaire, Notre-Dame-du-Port in Clermont-Ferrand and that of Orcival). The tympana lintels are gable-shaped.

The development of the Romanesque in **Burgundy** was strongly influenced by the Abbey of Cluny (now destroyed) with its great chancel with radiating chapels, a double transept and the hint of direct lighting in the nave through slender openings at the base of the barrel vaulting. The churches of Paray-le-Monial and Notre-Dame in La Charité-sur-Loire were built on the Cluniac model.

The basilica of Sainte-Madeleine in Vézelay in the north of the Morvan, with its harmonious, simplified church body and its covering of groined vaults, was also to influence churches in the region.

In the **Rhine** and **Meuse** regions, architectural characteristics from the Carolingian era, with an Ottonian influence, tend to prevail. This is borne out by double chancels and transepts (as in Verdun) and a central plan and interior elevation like that of the Palatine Chapel in Aachen (as in Ottmarsheim).

Lastly, until a relatively late date the churches in **Normandy** faithfully retained the custom of a timber roof (as in Jumièges and Bayeux). As stone

D. Goudouneix/ EXPLORER

St-Nectaire

vaulting was introduced decorative ribs gradually came into use (as in St-Étienne in Caen). The monumental size of the edifices and their harmoniously proportioned façades with two towers, are also typical of the Anglo-Norman Romanesque style.

Apart from these regional features some buildings owe their individuality to their function. The **pilgrimage churches**, for instance, had an ambulatory around the chancel, transept aisles and two aisles on either side of the nave to give pilgrims easy access to the relics they wished to venerate. The main churches of this kind on the way to Santiago de Compostela were St Faith in Conques, St-Sernin in Toulouse, St-Martial in Limoges and St-Martin in Tours (the two latter have since been destroyed).

ROMANESQUE RELIGIOUS ART

Liturgical items at the time consisted of church plate, manuscripts, precious fabrics and reliquaries. Church treasure would often include a Virgin in Majesty made of polychrome wood or embossed metal decorated with precious stones. The blossoming of **Limousin enamelware** marked a great milestone in the history of the decorative arts during the Romanesque period when it

was exported throughout Europe. The *champlevé* method consisted of pouring the enamel into a grooved metal surface of gilded copper. Enamel was used in a number of ways to decorate items ranging from small objects such as crosses, ciboria and reliquaries to monumental works like altars (high altar of **Grandmont** abbey church and items in the Cluny Museum, Paris).

Gothic Period (12C–15C)

ARCHITECTURE

Transitional Gothic – In about 1140, important architectural innovations in St-Denis Cathedral, such as intersecting ribbed vaulting and pointed arches in the narthex and chancel, heralded the dawn of the Gothic style.

In the late 12C, there were further innovations common to a group of buildings in Ile-de-France and in the north of France. They included ogives and mouldings which extended down from the vaulting into bundles of engaged slender columns around the pillars of great arches. Capitals were simplified, became smaller with time and gradually diminished in importance. New concepts

83

of sculptural decorating, including the appearance of statue-columns, affected building façades. In Sens Cathedral, the rectangular layout of the bays called for sexpartite vaulting with alternating major and minor pillars to support large arches. The major pillars supported three ribs while the minor ones supported a single intermediary rib. Apart from sexpartite vaulting with alternating supports, this early Gothic architecture typical of Sens, Noyon and Laon was also characterised by a four-storeyed elevation, great arches, tribunes, a triforium and tall bays.

In the years 1180-1200, in Notre-Dame Cathedral in Paris, raised vaults were reinforced by the addition of flying buttresses on the outside of the edifice while inside, alternating supports disappeared. These new measures gave rise to the emergence of a transitional style which led to Lanceolate Gothic.

Lanceolate Gothic – The Gothic style was at its peak during the reigns of Philippe Auguste (1180-1223) and St Louis (1226-70). The rebuilding of Chartres Cathedral (1210-30) gave rise to a model for what is known as the Chartres family of cathedrals (Reims, Amiens and Beauvais) which included oblong plan vaulting, a three-storeyed elevation (without tribunes) and flying buttresses. The chancel with its double ambulatory and the transept arms with side aisles made for a grandiose interior. The upper windows in the nave were divided into two lancets surmounted by a round opening.

The façades were subdivided into three horizontal registers, as in the cathedrals of Laon and Amiens. The doorways were set in deep porches with gables while above them was an openwork rose window with stained glass. A gallery of arches ran beneath the bell-towers.

There are a number of variations of Lanceolate Gothic in France. An example is Notre-Dame Church in Dijon where the ancient section of the sexpartite vaulting has been preserved.

Development of the Gothic style to the 15C – The improvement in vaulting from a technical point of view, in particular the use of relieving arches, meant that the supporting function of walls was reduced and more space could be given over to windows and stone tracery as in St-Urbain's Basilica in Troyes and the Sainte-Chapelle in Paris (1248). This gave rise to the **High Gothic** style in the north of France from the end of the 13C to the late 14C. (Examples include the chancel in Beauvais Cathedral, Évreux

Cathedral and the north transept of Rouen Cathedral.)

Gothic architecture in the centre and southwest of France developed along unusual lines in the late 13C. Jean Deschamps, master mason of Narbonne Cathedral, designed a massively proportioned building in which the vertical upsweep of the lines was interrupted by wide galleries above the aisles. St Cecilia's Cathedral in Albi diverged completely from Gothic models in the north of France through the use of brick and a buttress system inherited from the Romanesque period. Throughout the 14C, church interiors were filled with sculptural decoration in the form of rood screens, choir screens, monumental altarpieces and devotional statues.

From the late 14C, development of the main principles of Gothic architecture came to a halt but decorative devices grew apace giving rise to the elaborate **Flamboyant Gothic** style with its gables, lancet arches, pinnacles and exuberant foliage. This ornamentation, occasionally referred to as Baroque Gothic, also played a part in civil architecture. An example is the Great Hall in the Law Courts at Poitiers, carved by Guy de Dammartin in the last 10 years of the 14C. Riom's Sainte-Chapelle, built for the Duke Jean de Berry, is another early example. Flamboyant Gothic in France left its mark on a good number of public and religious edifices (Palais Jacques Cœur in Bourges and the façade of St-Maclou Church in Rouen) as well as on liturgical furnishings (the choir screen and rood screen in Ste-Cécile's Cathedral in Albi).

Amiens Cathedral

S. Chirol

Throughout the Gothic period castle architecture remained faithful to feudal models (Angers Castle, the walled city of Cordes and the mountain fortress of Merle Towers) and did not develop further until the beginning of the Renaissance.

SCULPTURE, DECORATIVE ARTS AND PAINTING

Gothic sculpture – Progress towards naturalism and realism, the humanism of the Gothic style, can be seen in the statuary and sculptural decoration of the time. Statue-columns of doorways in the 12C tended still to be rigidly hieratic but in the 13C took on greater freedom of expression as may be seen in Amiens and Reims (the Smiling Angel). New themes emerged including the Coronation of the Virgin which first appeared in Senlis in 1191 and thereafter became a popular subject.

Stained glass – The four main areas producing stained glass in France in the 12C were St-Denis, Champagne, the west (Le Mans, Vendôme and Poitiers) and a group of workshops in the Rhine area in eastern France. Master glassworkers developed an intense blue-coloured glass known as Chartres blue which was to become famous. The invention of silver yellow in 1300-10 led to a more translucent enamelled glass with a subtler range of colour.

The combination of stained glass and Gothic architecture gave rise to larger bays – formerly opaque wall space could be opened up and filled with glass, thanks to new support systems. The fragility of stained glass explains the fact that there are very few original medieval windows intact today; many have been replaced by copies or later works. The windows of Chartres, Évreux and the Sainte-Chapelle are precious testimonies to the art.

Illumination and painting – The art of illumination reached its peak in the 14C when artists freed from University supervision produced sumptuous manuscripts, including Books of Hours, for private use. Among them were Jean Pucelle (*Les Heures de Jeanne d'Évreux*) and the Limbourg brothers (*Les Très Riches Heures du Duc de Berry,* dating from the early 15C).

Easel painting first made its appearance in France in 1350 (the portrait of John the Good, now in the Louvre, is an example). Italian and more particularly

St Michael (detail from the Polyptych of The Last Judgement), Beaune

H. Champolliou/OUEST-FRANCE

Flemish influences, evident as much in depiction of landscape as in attention to detail, may be seen in works by great 15C artists like **Jean Fouquet, Enguerrand Quarton** and the **Master of Moulins**.

The Renaissance

Gothic art persisted in many parts of France until the middle of the 16C. In the Loire region, however, there were signs of a break with medieval traditions as early as the beginning of the century.

ITALIAN STYLE AND EARLY RENAISSANCE

Renaissance aesthetics in Lombardy, familiar in France since the military campaigns of Charles VIII and Louis XII at the end of the 15C, at first affected only architectural decoration, through the introduction of motifs from Antiquity such as pilasters, foliage and scallops (as in the tomb of Solesmes, Château de Gaillon). Little by little, however, feudal, military and defensive architecture gave way to a more comfortable style of seigniorial residence. The Château de Chenonceau (begun before 1515) and that of Azay-le-Rideau (1518-27) are examples of this development, particularly in their regular layout, the symmetry of the façades and the beginnings of a new type of architectural decoration. However, it was the great royal undertakings of the time that brought about the blossoming of the Renaissance style in France.

ARCHITECTURE UNDER FRANÇOIS I (1515-1547)

The Façade des Loges (1520-24) in the Château de Blois (begun in 1515) is a free replica of the Vatican loggia in Rome. While the castle's irregular fenestration recalls the old medieval style, its great novelty is the preoccupation with Italianate ornamentation. During the reign of François I, the Château de Chambord (1519-47) which combines French architectural traditions (corner towers, irregular roofs and dormer windows) with innovative elements (symmetrical façades, refined decoration and a monumental internal staircase) served as a model for a good many of the Loire castles including Chaumont, Le Lude and Ussé.

After his defeat at the Battle of Pavia in 1525, François I left his residences in the Loire valley to turn his attention to those in Ile-de-France. In 1527 building began on the Château de Fontainebleau under the supervision of Gilles Le Breton. The interior decoration by artists from the **First School of Fontainebleau** was to have a profound influence on the development of French art.

The Italian artist **Rosso** (1494-1540) introduced a new system of decoration to France that combined stuccowork, wood panelling and allegorical frescoes which drew upon humanistic, philosophical and literary references and were painted in acid colours. The Mannerist style, characterised by the influence of antique statuary, a lengthening of lines and overabundant ornamentation, became more pronounced after **Primaticcio** (1504-70) arrived at the court in 1532.

The influence of this art could be felt until the end of the century in works by sculptors such as **Pierre Bontemps, Jean Goujon** (reliefs on the Fountain of the Innocents in Paris) and **Germain Pilon** (monument for the heart of Henri II in the Louvre) and painters like Jean Cousin the Elder. Court portraitists, on the other hand (**Jean** and **François Clouet** and **Corneille de Lyon**), were more influenced by Flemish traditions.

HENRI IV AND PRE-CLASSICISM

After the Wars of Religion (1560-98) new artistic trends revived the arts and heralded the dawn of Classicism. Royal interest in town-planning gave rise to the regular, symmetrical layout of squares (Place des Vosges and Place Dauphine in Paris) and to the harmonisation of the buildings that surrounded them (ground-level arcades and brick and stone façades). These were copied in the provinces (Charleville and Montauban) foreshadowing the royal squares of the 17C, France's *Grand Siècle*.

The Fontainebleau style of adornment continued to develop under the auspices of the **Second School of Fontainebleau**. This was made up of all the court painters working during the reign of Henri IV and the regency of Marie de' Medici. The style was further shaped by decoration in other royal palaces including the Tuileries, the Louvre and Château-Neuf in St-Germain-en-Laye. **Toussaint Dubreuil** (1561-1602), **Ambroise Dubois** (1542-1614) and **Martin Fréminet** (1567-1619) continued the Mannerism of Fontainebleau (light effects, half-length figures and a lengthening of perspectives) in their works and at the same time sought greater classicism as well as a revival of themes from contemporary literature (*La Franciade* by Ronsard).

In the late 16C, castle architecture took on a new form with a single main building centred around a projecting section flanked by corner pavilions (Rosny-sur-Seine, and the Château de Gros-Bois). Right-angled wings were done away with and façades were given a brick facing with stone courses.

During the regency period, the architect Salomon de Brosse (Palais de Justice in Rennes, Palais du Luxembourg in Paris) designed sober, impressive monuments with a clarity of form which contained some of the characteristics of Classical architecture.

16C DECORATIVE ARTS

The 16C was a productive period for jewellery-making, in particular for small brooches fastened in the hair or hat and pendants which were used as articles of dress or simply as collectors' items. **Étienne Delaune** (1518-83) was one of the great goldsmiths of the time.

There was rich regional variety in ceramics. Beauvaisis produced famous blue-tinged stoneware. Following the example of Italy, Lyon and Nevers manufactured majolica (glazed and historiated earthenware). The decorative arts in Saintonge were dominated by **Bernard Palissy** (c 1510-c 1590) who, apart from making a great many plates covered in reptiles, fish and seaweed, all modelled from nature, also decorated the grotto at the Château d'Écouen and that of the Tuileries. Some of his ceramics (nymphs in a country setting) were influenced by engravings from the Fontainebleau School.

The technique for painted enamel on copper with permanent colours was developed in Limoges in the 15C during the reign of Louis XI. J C Pénicaud and especially **Léonard Limosin** (1501-75) excelled in the technique, which was favoured in portrait painting by the French court.

French Classicism in the Early 17th Century

ARCHITECTURE

Three famous architects, **Jacques Lemercier** (c 1585-1654), **François Mansart** (1598-1666) and **Louis le Vau** (1612-70), played an essential part in drawing up the standards for the French Classical architectural style.

J Lemercier, who built the Château de Rueil, the town of Richelieu and the Église de la Sorbonne in Paris, supported the Italian style which was particularly evident in religious architecture: two-storeyed façades and projecting central sections with columns and triangular pediments. F Mansart was even more inventive (**Château de Balleroy, Château de Maisons-Laffitte** and the Gaston of Orléans Wing in the Château de Blois). From his time on, castle plans with a central pavilion and projecting section, architectural decoration that accentuated horizontal and vertical lines, and the use of orders (Doric, Ionic and Corinthian), remained constant features of Classical architecture. Le Vau, who began his career before the reign of Louis XIV by designing town houses (Hôtel Lambert in Paris) for the nobility and the upper middle classes, favoured

a grandiose style of architecture characteristic of Louis XIV Classicism (Château de Vaux-le-Vicomte).

PAINTING

The French school of painting blossomed as a result of Simon Vouet's (1590-1649) return to France in 1627 after a long stay in Rome and the foundation of the Royal Academy of Painting and Sculpture in 1648. References to Italian painting, in particular Venetian (richness of colour) and Roman (dynamism of composition), albeit tempered by a concern for order and clarity, are evident in the work of Vouet and that of his pupil **Eustache le Sueur** (1616-55). Painters such as **Poussin** (1595-1665) and **Philippe de Champaigne** (1602-74) produced highly intellectual works that drew upon philosophical, historical and theological themes – all emblematic of French Classicism.

Other trends in French painting flourished in the first half of the century. The realism of the Italian painter Caravaggio influenced the Toulouse school of which the major artist was **Nicolas Tournier** (1590-post 1660). In Lorraine, **Georges de la Tour** (1593-1652) was deeply affected by Caravaggio's style, notably in the use of light and shade and the portrayal of people from humble backgrounds. The **Le Nain** brothers, Antoine (c 1588-1648), Louis (c 1593-1648) and Mathieu (c 1607-77), who painted first in Laon and then in Paris, belonged to a trend known as "painters of reality" that favoured genre scenes, drawing more upon the world of the landed upper-middle classes than that of peasant farmers. Their work bore the stamp of Flemish craftsmanship.

SCULPTURE

Sculpture in the early 17C was influenced by contemporary Italian models. **Jacques Sarrazin** (1588-1660), who studied in Rome, worked in a moderate, Classic mode that derived from Antiquity and also drew upon paintings by Poussin (decoration in the Château de Maisons-Laffitte and the tomb of Henri of Bourbon in the Château de Chantilly). François Anguier (Montmorency Mausoleum in the Lycée chapel in Moulins) and his brother Michel (sculptural decoration on the St-Denis gateway in Paris) showed a more Baroque tendency in their treatment of dynamism and the dramatic stances of their sculptures.

Musée du Louvre/ RMN

Wealth by Vouet

Versailles Classicism

During the reign of Louis XIV (1643-1715) the centralisation of authority and the all-powerful Royal Academy gave rise to an official art that reflected the taste and wishes of the sovereign. The Louis XIV style evolved in Versailles and spread throughout France where it was imitated to a lesser degree by the aristocracy in the late 17C.

The style was characterised by references to Antiquity and a concern for order and grandeur, whether in architecture, painting or sculpture. French resistance to Baroque, which had but a superficial effect on French architecture, was symbolised by the rejection of Bernini's projects for the Louvre. One of the rare examples of the style is Le Vau's College of Four Nations (today's Institute of France) which consists of a former chapel with a cupola and semi-circular flanking buildings.

In Versailles **Louis le Vau** and later **Jules Hardouin-Mansart** (1646-1708) favoured a majestic type of architecture: rectangular buildings set off by projecting central sections with twin pillars, flat roofs and sculptural decoration inspired by Antiquity.

Charles le Brun (1619-90), the leading King's Painter, supervised all the interior decoration (paintings, tapestries, furniture and *objets d'art*), giving the palace remarkable homogeneity. There were dark fabrics and panelling, gilded stuccowork, painted coffered ceilings, and copies of Greco-Roman statues. The decoration became less abundant towards the end of the century.

In 1662, the founding of the **Gobelins**, the "Royal Manufactory for Crown Furniture", stimulated the decorative arts. A team of painters, sculptors, warp-weavers, marble-cutters, goldsmiths and cabinet-makers worked under Charles le Brun, achieving a high degree of technical perfection. Carpets were made at the Savonnerie factory in Chaillot. The massive furniture of the period was often carved and sometimes gilded. Boulle marquetry, a combination of brass, tortoiseshell and gilded bronze, was one of the most sumptuous of the decorative arts produced at the time.

Versailles park, laid out by **Le Nôtre** (1613-1700), fulfilled all the requirements of French landscape gardening with its emphasis on rigour and clarity. Its geometrically tailored greenery, long axial perspectives, fountains, carefully designed spinneys and allegorical sculptures reflect the ideal of perfect order and control over nature.

Sculptures were placed throughout the gardens. Many of the works were by the two major sculptors of the time, **François Girardon** (1628-1715) and **Antoine Coysevox** (1640-1720) who drew upon mythology from Antiquity. The work of **Pierre Puget** (1620-94), another important sculptor, was far more tortured and Baroque – an unusual style for the late 17C.

French Rocaille (1715-1750)

The 18C style in France grew from a reaction against the austerity and grandeur of the Louis XIV style, which was considered ill-adapted to the luxurious life and pleasures of the aristocracy and the upper-middle classes during the regency of Philippe of Orléans (1715-23) and the reign of Louis XV (1723-74). Rocaille was an 18C Rococo style or ornamentation based on rock and shell motifs.

ARCHITECTURE

Rocaille architecture, at least on the outside, remained faithful to some of the principles of Classical composition – plain buildings with symmetrical façades and projecting central sections crowned by a triangular pediment – but the use of Classical orders became less rigid and systematic. The most representative examples of this new type of architecture were town houses such as the Hôtel de Soubise by **Delamair** and Hôtel Matignon by **Courtonne**, both in Paris.

The majestic formal apartments of the previous century gave way to smaller, more intimate rooms such as boudoirs and studies.

Inside, woodwork, often white and gold, covered the walls from top to bottom (Hôtel de Lassay in Paris and the Clock Room or Cabinet de la Pendule in Versailles). The repertoire of ornamentation included intertwining plant motifs, curved lines, shells and other natural objects. Paintings of landscapes and country scenes were inserted in the woodwork above doors or in the corners of ceilings. **Verberckt**, who worked in Versailles for Louis XV, was an exceptionally skilled interior decorator.

PAINTING

The generation of painters working at the turn of the century was influenced by Flemish art. Artists such as **Desportes**

The Oval Salon in the Hôtel de Soubise

(1661-1743), **Largillière** (1656-1746) and **Rigaud** (1659-1743) painted sumptuously decorative still-lifes and formal portraits. Secular themes including scenes of gallantry *(fêtes galantes)*, and fashionable society life became popular. **Watteau** (1684-1721), **Boucher** (1703-70), **Natoire** (1700-77) and **Fragonard** (1732-1806) reflected the taste of the day in their elegant genre scenes, some with mythological overtones, of pastoral life and the game of love.

Religious painting was not neglected in spite of these trends. Charles de la Fosse (1636-1716), one of Le Brun's pupils, Antoine Coypel (1661-1722) and especially **Restout** (1692-1768) adapted it to the less stoical ideals of the 18C by stripping it of too strong a dogmatism. There was a revival in portraiture during the 18C. **Nattier** (1685-1766), official painter of Louis XV's daughters, produced likenesses in mythological guise or half-length portraits which were far less pompous than the usual court picture. The pastellist **Quentin de la Tour** (1704-88) excelled in portraying his subjects' individual temperament and psychology rather than their social rank by concentrating more on faces than dress and accessories.

The lesser genres (still-lifes and landscapes), scorned by the Academy but favoured by the middle classes for the decoration of their homes, blossomed considerably at the time. **Chardin** (1699-1779) painted simple still-lifes in muted tones and Flemish-inspired scenes of everyday life, giving them a realistic, picturesque quality.

SCULPTURE

Baroque influence swept through sculpture in the first half of the century. The **Adam** brothers (Neptune Basin at Versailles), **Coustou** (1677-1746) (Horses of Marly), and **Slodtz** (1705-64) introduced the style's expressiveness into their work to lend movement and feeling. The main characteristics of Baroque art were flowing garments, attention to detail and figures shown in action.

In contrast, the contemporary work of **Bouchardon** (1698-1762) who trained in Rome and was therefore influenced by Antique sculpture, tended to be more Classical (Fountain in the Rue de Grenelle in Paris).

DECORATIVE ARTS

The rise of fashionable society brought with it a great need for luxury furniture that matched the style of woodwork inside elegant homes. New types of furniture were created: after commodes (chests of drawers) came writing-desks – upright or inclined, escritoires, chiffoniers and countless small tables. For the comforts of conversation there were wing-chairs and deep easy chairs. There were also *voyeuses* or conversation chairs (special seats in gaming houses placed behind players to allow spectators to watch) and all manner of sofas and seats on which to recline (couches, lounging-chairs, divans and settees). Curved lines were favoured, as were rare and precious materials like exotic woods and lacquered panelling often set off by floral marquetry and finely

"Bachelier" vase, 18C, Sèvres

chased gilded bronze. Among the great rocaille cabinet-makers were Cressent, Joubert and Migeon, while the principal seat carpenters of the time were Foliot, Sené and Cresson.

The **Vincennes Porcelain Factory** moved to **Sèvres** in 1756 and produced luxury items of which some were decorated in deep blue known as Sèvres blue. Gilt ornamentation was theoretically used only for royal services. Rocaille gold and silver plate was adorned with reed motifs, crested waves, scroll-work and shells often arranged in asymmetrical patterns. **Thomas Germain** (1673-1748), one of the most prestigious names in the trade, supplied the princely tables of the time.

Neo-Classical Reaction

The middle of the century brought a reaction against rocaille on moral and aesthetic grounds. The style was considered to be too florid and frivolous, the result of decadence in both morals and the arts. Classical models from Antiquity and the 17C were then deemed the only recourse to revive proper artistic creation.

ARCHITECTURE

The new style of architecture that emerged was more austere and tended towards the monumental. Sculptural decoration on façades grew more restrained and the Doric order became widespread (Église St-Philippe-du-Roule

by J F Chardin in Paris). Some buildings, like the Église Ste-Geneviève (the present-day Panthéon) in Paris by **G Soufflo**t (1713-80), were direct copies of Antique models. Louis XVI commissioned men like **Victor Louis** (1731-1802) who designed the Bordeaux theatre, **A T Brongniart** (1739-1813) and **J F Bélanger** (1744-1818) for most of the great architectural undertakings of the time. The philosophical influence of the Enlightenment led to a keen interest in the architecture of functional, public buildings such as the Royal Salt-works in Arc-et-Senans by **Claude-Nicolas Ledoux** (1736-1806).

SCULPTURE

Sculptors distanced themselves from rocaille extravagance by striving towards a natural portrayal of anatomy. E M Falconet (1716-91), P Julien (1731-1804) and G C Allegrain (1710-95) drew upon Greco-Roman models for their greatly admired sculptures of female bathers. **J A Houdon** (1741-1828), one of the greatest sculptors of the late 18C, made busts of his French and foreign contemporaries (Voltaire, Buffon and Madame Adélaïde for the first, and Benjamin Franklin and George Washington for the second) which constituted a veritable portrait gallery. The busts, executed in an extremely realistic manner, many without wigs or articles of dress to detract from the faces, were the culmination of modelled portraiture in France. Houdon also sculpted tombs and mythological statues. **J B Pigalle** (1714-85) maintained the style of sculpture predominant at the beginning of the century that the neo-Classical reaction had not managed to stifle entirely (mausoleum of the Marshal de Saxe in the Église St-Thomas in Strasbourg).

PAINTING

In the 1760s, attempts by the Royal Academy to restore a style of painting known as the grand manner encouraged the emergence of new themes such as antique history, civic heroism and 17C tragedies. These were adopted by painters like **J L David** (1748-1825), **J B M Pierre** (1714-89) and **J F P Peyron** (1744-1814). The style drew upon low-reliefs and statuary from Antiquity and followed the principles of composition used by painters like Poussin and other 17C masters.

Works by **J M Vien** (1716-1809) and **J B Greuze** (1725-1805) showed a less austere approach to painting, with more room for sensibility and emotion, that heralded the romanticism that was to blossom after the Revolution.

DECORATIVE ARTS

Louis XVI furniture kept some of the characteristics inherited from the beginning of the century such as the use of precious materials and chased gilt bronze ornamentation, but curves and sinuous shapes gave way to straight lines. As far as decoration was concerned, while the floral motifs and ribbons of the past were maintained, ovoli friezes, Greek fretwork and fasces were willingly introduced. **René Dubois** (1738-99) and **Louis Delanois** (1731-92) initiated the Greek style derived from Antique furniture seen in friezes at Herculaneum and Pompeii. Prestigious artists of the genre included Oeben and Riesener while Carlin followed by Beneman and Levasseur specialised in furniture adorned with plaques of painted porcelain.

At the end of the century new decorative motifs including lyres, ears of corn, wickerwork baskets and hot-air balloons were imported from England.

The technique of hard-paste porcelain that was introduced into France at the beginning of the 1770s took the lead over soft-paste porcelain in the factory at Sèvres. Figurines of **biscuit** porcelain (white, fired, unglazed pottery) shaped on models by Fragonard, Boucher and other artists, became very popular.

The iconoclasm that prevailed during the **Revolution** marked a break in the history of French art although the neo-Classical movement continued into the early 19C. The Louvre opened in 1793 paving the way for many more museums in France.

19th Century

ART DURING THE FIRST EMPIRE

After his investiture in 1804, Napoleon favoured the emergence of an official style of art by commissioning palace decoration (Tuileries, destroyed in 1870, and Fontainebleau) and paintings that related the great events of the Empire. The artists to benefit from the Emperor's patronage were men like J L David and his pupils **A J Gros** (1771-1835) and **A L Girodet-Trioson** (1767-1824).

Paintings of the time took on new themes derived from the romanticism in contemporary literature, orientalism and an interest in the medieval. National historic anecdotes were painted by artists who, like the troubadours, praised heroic deeds and fine sentiment.

Artistic development in the realm of architecture was less innovative. Napoleon commissioned large edifices commemorating the glory of the *Grande Armée* including the Carrousel Arch, the column in Place Vendôme and the Temple de la Madeleine (now a church). The official architects **Percier** (1764-1838) and **Fontaine** (1762-1853) were responsible for the overall supervision of the undertakings, setting models not only for buildings but also for decoration at official ceremonies and guidelines for the decorative arts.

Ambitious town-planning projects like the reconstruction of Lyon were also completed under the Empire.

Former royal palaces were refurnished. The style of First Empire furniture derived from the neo-Classical with massive, quadrangular, commodes and jewel-cases made of mahogany with gilt bronze plating and Antique decorative motifs. **Desmalter** (1770-1841) was the main cabinet-maker of the imperial court. The sculptors **Chaudet** (1763-1810) and **Cartellier** (1757-1831) supplied models for furniture ornamentation in the neo-Classical style which also inspired their statues. After the Egyptian Campaign motifs like sphinxes and lotuses began to appear in the decorative arts.

RESTORATION AND THE JULY MONARCHY

Two major trends affected French art between 1815 and 1848. The first was the gradual disappearance of the neo-Classical style which, however, still influenced church building (Notre-Dame-de-Lorette and St-Vincent-de-Paul in Paris); and the second was the birth of historicism, a style that fostered regard for the architecture of the past, particularly of the medieval period (Église Notre-Dame in Boulogne-sur-Mer and Marseille Cathedral by Léon Vaudoyer). The trend was furthered by the founding of the *Monuments Historiques* (a body set up for the classification and preservation of the national heritage) in 1830 and the enthusiasm of **Viollet-le-Duc (1814-79)**.

THE SECOND EMPIRE

On the accession of Napoleon III the arts in general were affected by a spirit of **eclecticism**. The Louvre, completed by Percier's disciple Visconti (1791-1853) and **H Lefuel** (1810-80), and the Paris Opera by **Garnier** (1825-98) were among the greatest undertakings of the century. References to architectural styles of the past (16C, 17C and 18C) were present everywhere. Nevertheless, the introduction of new materials like glass and cast iron (the Gare du Nord by Hittorff and the Église St-Augustin by V Baltard) showed the influence of technological progress and a new rational approach to building.

Baron Haussmann (1809-91), Prefect of the *département* of the Seine, laid down the principles for a public works programme that was to modernise the capital. Prefect C M Vaïsse carried out a similar plan in Lyon.

Academicism reigned over the **painting** of the time. **Cabanel** (1823-83), **Bouguereau** (1825-1905) and the portraitist **Winterhalter** (1805-73) drew their inspiration just as easily from Antique statuary as from works by 16C Venetian masters or Rococo ornamentation. However, **Courbet** (1819-77), **Daumier** (1808-79) and **Millet** (1814-75) formed an avant-garde group that fostered realism in painting with subjects from town and country life.

Ingres (1780-1867) who represented the Classical trend, and **Delacroix** (1798-1863), the great romantic painter of the century, were both at the height of their powers.

Great architectural projects stimulated the production of **sculpture. Carpeaux** (1827-75), responsible for the high-relief of Dance on the façade of the Paris Opera, transcended the eclecticism of his time by developing a very personal style that was reminiscent of, and not simply a copy of, Flemish, Renaissance and 18C art. Dubois (1829-1905), Frémiet (1824-1910) and Guillaume (1822-1905) were more academic in their approach.

A taste for pastiche prevailed in the decorative arts. The shapes and ornamental motifs of the Renaissance, the 16C and 18C were reproduced on furniture and *objets d'art*. The advent of **industrialisation** affected certain fields. The goldsmith Christofle (1805-63) and the bronze-founder Barbedienne (1810-92) made luxury items for the imperial court as well as mass-produced articles for new clients among the rich upper-middle classes.

LATE 19C ARTISTIC TRENDS

Architecture during the Third Republic was mainly marked by edifices built for Universal Exhibitions held in Paris (the former Palais du Trocadéro, the Eiffel Tower, the Grand-Palais and the Pont Alexandre-III). The pompous style of the buildings with their exotic ornamentation derived from the trend for eclecticism.

In the 1890s **Art Nouveau** architects, influenced by trends in England and Belgium, distanced themselves from the official style of the day. They harmonised decoration on façades with that inside their buildings and designed their creations as a whole – stained glass, tiles, furniture and wall-paper. Decoration included plant motifs, stylised flowers, Japanese influences and asymmetrical patterns. **Guimard** (1867-1942) was the main proponent of the style in France (Castel Béranger in Paris and entrances to the capital's metro stations).

The decorative arts followed the Art Nouveau movement with works by the cabinet-maker **Majorelle** (1859-1929) and the glass and ceramics artist **Gallé** (1846-1904) in Nancy.

In the field of painting, the **Impressionists** began exhibiting their work outside official salons in 1874. **Monet** (1840-1926), **Renoir** (1841-1919) and **Pissarro** (1830-1903) breathed new life into the technique and themes of landscape painting by working out of doors, studying the play of light in nature and introducing new subjects drawn from contemporary life. **Manet** (1832-83) and **Degas** (1834-1917) joined the group temporarily.

Between 1885 and 1890, Neo-Impressionists like **G Seurat** (1859-91) and **Signac** (1863-1935) brought the Pointillist (painting with small dots) technique known as divisionism to a climax. The Dutch painter **Van Gogh** (1853-90) settled in France in 1886. His technique of using pure and expressionist colours with broad swirling brushstrokes cou-

The Garden by Claude Monet

National Gallery Washington D.C. A-Hinous/EDIMEDIA Paris.

pled with his belief that expression of emotional experience should override impressions of the external world were to have a great influence on early-20C painters. **Cézanne** (1839-1906) and **Gauguin** (1848-1903), who were influenced by primitive and Japanese art, partly dispensed with Impressionism to give more importance to volume. In 1886, seeking new inspiration, Gauguin moved to Pont-Aven, a small town east of Concarneau in Brittany that had often been visited by the painter Corot in the 1860s. Fellow artists **Émile Bernard** and **Paul Sérusier** formed the Pont-Aven School that favoured synthesist theories and symbolic subjects which paved the way for the **Nabis**.

Among the Nabis were artists like **Denis** (1870-1943), **Bonnard** (1867-1947) and **Vuillard** (1868-1940) who advocated the importance of colour over shape and meaning.

Sculpture at the end of the century was dominated by the genius of **Rodin** (1840-1917). His expressionistic, tormented, symbolic work stood free from formal academic conventions and was not always understood in his time.

20th Century

AVANT-GARDE MOVEMENTS

At the beginning of the 20C, proponents of the avant-garde reacted against the many trends of the 19C including the restrictions laid down by official art, academicism in painting and Art Nouveau in architecture.

The **Stijl** movement was characterised in architecture by simple, geometric buildings adorned with sober low-reliefs. One of its most magnificent examples was the Théâtre des Champs-Élysées by the Perret brothers with sculptural decoration by **Bourdelle** (1861-1929). In the field of sculpture, the artists **Maillol** (1861-1944), **Bartholomé** (1848-1928) and **J Bernard** (1866-1931) opposed Rodin's aesthetic concepts and produced a very different type of art by simplifying their figures, in some cases to the point of schematic representation.

Fauvism was the great novelty at the Autumn Salon of **painting** in 1905. A Derain (1880-1964), A Marquet (1875-1947) and M de Vlaminck (1876-1958) broke up their subject-matter through the vivid and arbitrary use of colour, a technique which was to pave the way for non-figurative painting. After an early period with the fauvist movement, **Matisse** (1869-1904) went his own way developing a personal style based on the exploration of colour.

A further major avant-garde movement in painting followed on from **Cézanne's** (1839-1906) structural analysis in which he broke up his subject matter into specific shapes. The trend was taken up by artists like **Braque** (1882-1963) and **Picasso** (1881-1973) whose exploration led to **Cubism**, a new perception of reality based not on what the eye saw but on an analytical approach to objects, depicting them as a series of planes, usually in a restricted colour range. The style dominated their work from 1907 to 1914.

Members of the *Section d'Or* (golden section) Cubist group like A Gleizes, J Metzinger and F Léger (his early works) were less revolutionary and more figurative. The main contribution to French cubism in the field of sculpture came from Henri Laurens who was influenced by Braque.

Surrealism breathed new life into the art world in the 1920s and 1930s. It was a subversive art form that created an irrational, dreamlike, fantasy universe. For the first time chance and promptings from the subconscious were integrated into the creative process. Duchamp (1887-1968), **Masson** (b 1896), **Picabia** (1879-1953) and **Magritte** (1898-1967) all formed part of the movement.

ARTISTIC CREATION SINCE 1945

Abstract art began to affect the field of painting after the Second World War. **Herbin** defined it as the triumph of mind over matter. In 1949 he published *Non-figurative, Non-objective Art (L'Art non figuratif non objectif)* and greatly influenced young artists of the

La joie de vivre or Antipolis (1946) by Picasso (detail)

Musée Picasso, Antibes

geometric abstract art movement. All his works from the 1950s onwards have been one-dimensional patterns of letters and simple geometric shapes painted in pure colours.

The **lyrical abstract** artists focused on the study of colour and texture. **Riopelle** applied his paint with a knife while **Mathieu** applied it directly from the tube. **Soulages**, who was influenced by art from the Far East, produced meditative, expressive work in shades of black.

Nicolas de Stael's art constituted a link between abstract and figurative in that his abstract compositions were the result of observations of real objects which could sometimes be distinguished in the final work.

Some artists like **Fautrier** worked with very thick paint to which they added other materials including sand.

There was an important revival in architecture with **Le Corbusier** (1897-1965) whose buildings fulfilled functional requirements with great clarity of form (Cité Radieuse in Marseille and Ronchamp Chapel).

In the 1960s, **New Realism** *(Nouveau Réalisme)*, a form of pop art, with **Pierre Restany** as its leading theoretician, attempted to express the reality of daily life in modern consumer society. Industrial items, the symbols of this society, came under critical scrutiny – they were accumulated, broken up (by the artist **Arman**), compressed and assembled (by **César**) or trapped in glass.

Yves Klein (1928-62) took his adherence to New Realism a step further in his *Monochromes* by trying to capture and express space, energy and the universal essence of objects. He worked in pure colours and created I B K, or International Klein Blue. He rejected formal and traditional values as did **Dubuffet** (1901-85) who, in 1968, wrote a pamphlet entitled *Asphyxiating Culture (Asphyxiante culture)* which made a stand for permanent revolution, derision and the unexpected. Dubuffet's later paintings and sculptures consisted of puzzles of coloured or black and white units.

Since the 1960s, the problems posed by town-planning have led to a re-evaluation of the relationship between architecture and sculpture and an attempt to reconcile the two arts. Architects and sculptors often work together as in the case of the project by Ricardo Bofill and D Karavan in Cergy-Pontoise northwest of Paris, and artists are increasingly being asked to modify townscapes (Buren's columns in the Palais-Royal in Paris).

The **Support-Surface** movement (**Claude Viallet, Pagès** and **Daniel Dezeuze**) of the 1970s reduced painting to its pure material state by focusing on the support itself or the way the paint was applied. Paintings were removed from their stretchers and cut up, suspended and folded.

The 1980s saw the return of **Figuration** in manifold ways. References to tradition are evident in the work of artists like **Gérard Garouste** and **Jean-Charles Blais**.

The great vitality of contemporary art can be seen in the extremely wide variety of styles and trends favoured by artists today.

Évry Cathedral

J-L. Bohin/ EXPLORER

FURNITURE FROM BASSE-NORMANDIE

Box bed (Pays d'Auge – 18C)

Longcase clock (St-Lô – 19C)

Marriage wardrobe (Bayeux – 18C)

Dairy cupboard (Avranchin – 18C)

Kitchen dresser (Cotentin – 19C)

Sideboard (Vire – 19C)

Collection Musée du Meuble Normand, Villedieu-les-Poêles

GASTRONOMY OF FRANCE

An Introduction

France is the land of good food and good living and it has a host of regional specialities. In addition to the **Michelin Guide France,** which describes hundreds of hotels and restaurants throughout the country, here are examples of traditional fare.

SOUPS AND CONSOMMÉS

The best-known are cream of asparagus (*velouté d'asperges*), leek and potato (*soupe de poireaux-pommes de terre*), onion (*soupe à l'oignon or gratinée*), lobster (*bisque de homard*), *garbure* (a thick soup with cabbage popular in south-western France), and *cotriade* (Breton fish soup), all of which are served at the start of a meal.

HORS D'ŒUVRES

There are countless ways to begin a meal and French chefs have boundless imagination in this respect. The following, though, deserve a special mention: *salade niçoise* (tomatoes, anchovies, onions, olives), *salade lyonnaise* (using various meats with seasoning and a dressing of oil, vinegar and shallots), and *salade cauchoise* (celery, potatoes and ham). Another good start to a meal is a

flamiche (a leek quiche that is a speciality of Picardy), or a *ficelle* (a ham pancake with a mushroom sauce). *Tapenade* is one of the traditional dishes of Provence (black olive purée into which are blended capers, anchovies and tuna fish). Or you may prefer *quiche lorraine* (made with ham or bacon and cream) or *pissaladière* (provençal quiche with onions, tomatoes and anchovies). No mention of starters would be complete without seafood and shellfish, such as oysters from Belon, Cancale or Marennes, shrimps, prawns and clams.

MAIN COURSES

There are two main "families" of main course – fish or meat accompanied by all sorts of vegetables depending on the season, or served with a *gratin dauphinois* (potatoes, eggs and milk), not to be confused with *gratin savoyard* (potatoes, eggs and stock). *Bouillabaisse* is the famous stew from Marseille made with three types of fish (scorpion fish, red gurnard and conger eel), seasoned with saffron, thyme, garlic, bay, sage and fennel. *Brandade* is a creamy blend of mashed cod with olive oil, milk and a few cloves of garlic; it is a speciality of Nîmes. In Brittany, what better than lobster *à l'armoricaine*, mussels in cream

Bouillabaisse

S. Sauvignier/MICHELIN

(*moules à la crème*), shad or pike with Nantes-style "white butter sauce" (*brochet au beurre blanc*), worthy rivals of Dieppe-style sole (*sole dieppoise*) or the shrimps (*crevettes*) and cockles (*coques*) of Honfleur in Normandy, and of the bass grilled with fennel (*loup grillé au fenouil*) or baked over a fire of vine shoots (*au sarment de vigne*), a dish that is popular in Provence and on the Riviera.

Kougelhopf

There are so many regional dishes that we can do no more than provide a glimpse of the delights in store.

The best-known meat dishes include Strasbourg sauerkraut (*choucroute* - cabbage, potatoes, pork, sausages and ham), Toulouse or Castelnaudary *cassoulet* (bean stew with pieces of goose or duck and pork-meat products), Caen-style tripe (*tripes à la mode de Caen*), Rouen pressed duck (*canard au sang*), Burgundy *meurette* (wine sauce) that is as good an accompaniment for poached eggs as for brains or beef – cooked Burgundy-style, of course! Also well worth a mention are Auvergne *potée* (cabbage, piece of pork, bacon and turnips) or its cousin from Franche-Comté (cabbage, Morteau or Montbéliard sausage), *aligot* (a creamy blend of fresh tomme cheese and mashed potato seasoned with garlic) from Chaudes-Aigues, *tripoux* from Aurillac, Basque-style chicken (*poulet basquaise* with tomatoes and pimentoes), rabbit (*lapin*) *chasseur* and rabbit *forestier* (with mushrooms and diced bacon).

CHEESE

There is such a wide range of cheeses in France that it is difficult to know them all, so it is worth defining the main "families":

I – Soft cheeses

a) Cheese with surface mould (Brie de Meaux, Camembert, Chaource, etc)
b) Cheese with washed rind (Livarot, Reblochon, Munster, Vacherin, etc)
c) Cheese with natural rind (Tomme de Romans, Cendres de Bourgogne, Brie de Melun, etc)

II – Hard pressed non-boiled cheeses

(Cantal, Fourme de Laguiole, Gapron d'Auvergne, etc)

III – Hard pressed boiled cheeses

(Emmental de Savoie, Comté de Franche-Comté, Beaufort de Savoie, and Beaufort de Dauphiné, etc)

IV – Blue cheeses

a) Blue cheeses with natural crust (Bleu de Bresse, Bleu de Corse, Fourme de Montbrison, etc)

b) Scraped blue cheeses (Roquefort, Bleu d'Auvergne, Bleu des Causses, etc).

V – Processed Cheeses

Such as Crème de Gruyère, spreads with walnuts or grapes, and a whole range of cheese spreads.

FRUIT AND DESSERTS

There are innumerable **desserts** to round off a meal. Apart from the baskets of fruit, strawberries and cream or strawberries in red wine, fruit salads and macedoines using all the orchard fruits, there are apple, pear, and peach compotes, and all sorts of cakes, such as *tarte Tatin* (a caramelised tart cooked with the filling underneath), Grenoble walnut cake (*gâteau aux noix*), Breton *far* (a baked custard dessert), gingerbread (*pain d'épices*) in the Gâtinais region, *clafoutis* (a blend of milk and eggs mixed with fruit and baked in the oven), and *kougelhopf* from Alsace baked in the form of a ring and served as a dessert or as an afternoon snack. Not to mention all the crème caramels, baked cream desserts, and soft meringues with custard sauce (*île flottante*) that are found in nearly every region of France.

THE WINES OF FRANCE

For wine lovers, the Michelin guide **The Wine Regions of France** offers a comprehensive introduction to French winemaking and features driving itineraries for 14 main wine regions of the country: Alsace, Beaujolais, Le Bordelais (Bordeaux wines), Burgundy, Champagne, Cognac, Corse (Corsican wines) Jura, Languedoc-Roussillon, Loire Valley, Provence, Rhone Valley, Savoie-Bugey and the Southwest. Descriptions of over 500 restaurants, hotels and guest houses are included in this guide to enhance your journey through these regions.

See also the **Michelin Green Guide** for the specific region in which you are interested, for example the *Green Guide Provence* describes Provençal wines.

The official French wine Web site, www. wines-france.com, features information about grapes, wine labels, France's wine regions and more.

Food Glossary

Aïoli . . . . Garlic mayonnaise

Andouille . . . . Large chitterling sausage

Andouillettes . . . . Chitterling sausages

Angélique . . . . Angelica

Anis . . . . Aniseed confectionery

Asperges . . . . Asparagus

Bergamotes . . . . . Orange-flavoured sweets

Berlingots . . . . Humbugs

Bêtises . . . . Hard mints

Beurre blanc . . . White butter sauce

Bouillabaisse . . . . Seafood stew

Bourride . . . . Fish soup

Brandade . . . . Creamed salt-cod

Cagouilles . . . . Snails

Calissons . . . . Almond and crystal-lised fruitsweetmeats

Canard au sang . . . . . . Pressed duck

Cassoulet . . . . Stew with haricot beans and pork rinds

Cedrats confits . . . Crystallised citrus fruit

Cèpes . . . . Cèpe mushrooms

Charcuterie . . . . . . Smoked, cured or dried meats

Chipirones . . . . Small cuttlefish, often stuffed

Choucroute . . . . Sauerkraut

Confiseries . . . . Confectionery

Confits . . . . . . Goose preserved in fat

Crêpes dentelles . . . . Thin pancakes

Dragées . . . . Sugared almonds

Escargots . . . . Snails

Esturgeons . . . . Sturgeon

Far . . . . Flan with prunes

Ficelles picardes . . . Ham pancakes with mushroom sauce

Foie gras . . . . Goose liver

Fouace . . . . Dough cakes

Fraises . . . . Strawberries

Fruits confits . . . . . . Crystallised fruit

Galettes . . Thick pancakes or waffles

Gâteau d'amandes . . . Almond cake

Garbure . . Meat and vegetable stew

Gratins . . . . Dishes with a crusty topping

Jambon . . . . Ham

Jambon cru des Ardennes . . . . Ardennes cured ham

Kouign-Amam . . . . Cake

Kougelhopf . . . . Plain yeast cake

Lamproies . . . . Lampreys

Macarons . . . . Macaroons
Madeleines . . . . Small sponge cakes
Magrets . . . . Breast of duck
Marrons glacés . . . . Crystallised chestnuts
Massepains . . . . Marzipan cakes
Matelote . . . . Eel stew
Meurette . . . . Wine sauce
Mouclade . . . . Mussel stew
Moutarde . . . . Mustard
Mouton de pré-salé . . Salt-pasture . . . . lamb
Noix . . . . Nuts
Nougat . . . . Sugar, honey and nut . . . . sweetmeat
Nougatine . . . . . Caramel syrup and . . . . almond sweetmeat
Ortolans . . . . Buntings
Oursins . . . . Sea urchins
Pain d'épice . . . . . Spiced honey cake
Pâté d'alouette . . . . Lark paté
Pâté de merle . . . . Blackbird paté
Pauchouse . . . . . Fish stew with wine
Pieds de cochon . . . . . . Pigs' trotters
Piperade Sweet pepper and tomato omelette

Poulardes . . . . Chickens
Pralines . . . . Caramelised almond confectionery
Pruneaux . . . . Prunes
Quenelles . . . . Poached meat or fish dumplings
Quenelles de brochet . . . . Poached Pike dumplings
Quiche (Lorraine) . . Egg, cream and bacon flan
Rillettes . . . . Potted pork
Rillons . . . . Potted chopped pork
Saupiquet . . . . Spiced wine sauce
Saucisse de Morteau . . . . . Morteau sausage
Saucisson . . . . Dried sausage
Soupe au pistou . . . Vegetable soup with basil
Touron . . Soft almond confectionery
Tourteau fromager . Goats' cheese gateau
Tripes . . . . Tripe
Tripoux . . . . Stuffed tripe
Truffes . . . . Truffles
Volailles . . . . Poultry

Château de Chaumont

Massif de l'AIGOUAL★★★

MICHELIN MAP 339 G 4

GREEN GUIDE LANGUEDOC ROUSSILLON TARN GORGES

The immense forces involved in the formation of the Alps in the Tertiary era acted on the ancient granitic foundation of this landscape, uplifting it to form a massif which reaches its highest point at **Mont Aigoual**★★★ (1 567m – 5 141ft). Subsequent erosion, all the more vigorous because of high precipitation and the low elevation of the surrounding country, has created a landscape of long straight ridges cut by deep ravines. These well-watered highlands make a striking contrast to the arid landscapes of the neighbouring *causses* where any rainfall is immediately absorbed by the porous limestone.

A Bit of History

From 1875 onwards a massive programme of reafforestation was undertaken by the state; the forest today covers some 14 000ha – 50 square miles. Tree growth is particularly vigorous on the more exposed western slopes. In the last 20 years conifers have been added to the beeches planted in the 19C, and there are sweet chestnuts too, the traditional tree of the Cévennes, growing at altitudes of 600-900m (2 000-3 000ft).

Visit

Panorama★★★

From the viewing table at the top of the meteorological station the view extends over the Causses and the Cévennes. In winter it is sometimes possible to see both Mont-Blanc and the Maladeta Massif in the Pyrenees, though at other times haze or fog may reduce the extent of the view.

AIGUES-MORTES★★

POPULATION 4,999

MICHELIN MAP 339 K 7

GREEN GUIDE PROVENCE

Few places evoke the spirit of the Middle Ages as vividly as Aigues-Mortes sheltering behind its ramparts in a landscape of marshland, lakes and salt-pans. 🖪 *Pl. St-Louis, 30220 Aigues-Mortes,* ☎ *04 66 53 73 00. www.ot-aiguesmortes.fr.*

▸ **Orient Yourself:** Take the tourist train around Aigues-Mortes for an overview of what there is to see and do. Shops, restaurants and hotels lie within the city walls. A traditional market can be found on Ave. Frederic-Mistral.

🙂 **Don't Miss:** Climb to the top of the Tour de Constance (53 steps) for an impressive panorama over the town.

🕓 **Organizing Your Time:** See the fortifications first, allowing at least 45min for your visit. Then visit the town site before taking the Excursions.

🅿 **Parking:** Parking is available at the lot at the foot of the ramparts.

A Bit of History

In 1240, Louis IX (St Louis), then 26 years old, was perturbed by the lack of French involvement in the kind of commerce undertaken by the merchant fleets of Pisa and Genoa. He was also very much taken by the idea of a Crusade, but he lacked a Mediterranean port and a French king could not countenance sailing from a foreign harbour (at this time Provence was part of the Holy Roman Empire, Sète did not exist, and Narbonne was silting up). Louis' solution was to buy a site from a priory and grant a charter to the township which began to develop on what up to then had been virtually an island. The new settlement was laid out more or less on the geometrical lines of a bastide and was linked to the sea via an artificial channel.

Aigues-Mortes Ramparts

D. Pazery/MICHELIN

Visit

Tour de Constance★★

Access by place Anatole-France. 🚇 🕐 *May-Aug: daily 10am-7pm; Sep-Apr: daily 10am-5.30pm. Last admission 1hr before closing.* 🕐 *Closed 1 Jan, 1 May, 1 and 11 Nov, and 25 Dec.* ⌦ *6.10€ (under 18 years: no charge).* ☎ *04 66 53 61 55. www.monum.fr.*

The tower (1241-49) rests on wooden piles and was intended to be a symbol of royal power as much as a purely military installation. The layout of its elaborate internal defences (staircases, winding passageways, portcullises) is typical of the Capetian dynasty, and its fine walls of Beaucaire limestone stand out boldly against the surrounding sandy landscape. Its turret originally served as a lighthouse, the sea being only 3km – 2 miles away at the time. On 28 August 1248 the king embarked for the Sixth Crusade aboard a fleet of 38 Genoese vessels drawn up in the Grau Louis channel. Twenty-two years later, on 1 July 1270, he set out from here once more, on the Crusade (the Eighth) which, for him, was to prove fatal. St Louis succumbed as the fleet lay off Tunis.

Remparts★★

🕐 *Same hours as Tour de Constance.*

The ramparts were never seen by St Louis. They were begun in 1272 on the orders of Philippe le Hardi (the Bold) and their completion led to Aigues-Mortes becoming the Capetian kingdom's principal Mediterranean harbour.

At the end of the 13C Philippe le Bel (the Fair) improved the port and completed the defences, adding 20 massive towers to protect the gateways and provide enfilading fire along the walls themselves.

In the 14C Aigues-Mortes' population totalled 15 000, but its waterways began to silt up and the sea to retreat; the Constance Tower (Tour de Constance) lost its military significance altogether and became a prison, housing Knights Templar and rebel barons; for more than a century after the revocation of the Edict of Nantes in 1665 Huguenots were incarcerated here too.

The silting up of the port and the incorporation of Marseilles into the French kingdom in 1481 helped push Aigues-Mortes into decline and the coup-de-grâce was the founding (17C) and subsequent development of Sète.

AIX-EN-PROVENCE★★

POPULATION 123 842

MICHELIN MAP 340 H-I 4

GREEN GUIDE PROVENCE

The old capital of Provence has kept much of its 17C and 18C character: the elegance of its mansions, the charm of its squares, the majesty of its avenues and the loveliness of its fountains. It is also a lively city whose large student population is much in evidence on the busy café terraces. The new part of town is rapidly expanding and attracting more and more residents; it has established itself as a city of the arts, a thermal spa and an important centre for industry and the tourist trade. *2 pl. du Gén.-de-Gaulle, 13100 Aix-en-Provence, ☎ 04 42 16 11 61. www.aixenprovencetourism.com.*

▶ **Orient Yourself:** For an overview of the city, take a 2hr tour of Aix; for details, contact the tourist office (*2 pl. du Gén.-de-Gaulle - 13100 - ☎ 04 42 16 11 61; www.vpah.culture.fr*).

Don't Miss: Vieil Aix, the charming old town of Aix.

Organizing Your Time: Even if you take the guided tour, it's worth a walk down the Cours Mirabeau to see the aristocratic 17C buildings and to visit the many shops and cafés lining the street. Then head north through Vieil Aix to the Hôtel Boyer d'Eguilles to see the Muséum d'histoire naturelle, before continuing north to the Cathédrale St-Sauveur. Allow at least four hours.

Also See: Thermes Sextius, Aix's thermal spa *(day tickets available, 55 Cours Sextius ☎ 0 800 639 699, toll-free within France; www.thermes-sextius.com; Mon-Fri 8.30am-7.30pm, Sat 8.30am-1.30pm and 2.30pm-6.30pm).*

A Bit of History

Twenty years later the sway of Rome was threatened by the fierce Cimbrians, a Germanic people capable of chasing the legions from the field of battle. At the same time the Teutons, another Germanic group, were on the move southward, but their attempt to make their way into Italy via the Maritime Alps was frustrated by the Roman general Marius who crushed them in a great battle near the foot of Mount Ste-Victoire to the east of Aix.

Aquae Sextiae was subsequently destroyed by the Lombards (AD 574) and by Saracens; its deserted buildings served as a quarry for building materials for a good six centuries. In the 12C its fortunes were restored by the Counts of Provence who made it their place of residence. The last and most illustrious of the line was King **René** (1409-80), Duke of Anjou, Lorraine and Bar, King of Naples, and the ally of Charles VII of France against the English and Burgundians. The enlightened monarch supported literature and the arts and completed Aix' cathedral. Though a benevolent ruler, he was also a strict administrator. Towards the end of his life he made Charles of Maine his heir; Charles however was to die without issue, enabling Louis XI to incorporate Provence into France (1486).

Harsh times intervened; invasion by Imperial troops, feuding, and religious conflict. While the Aix Parliament was putting up a strong resistance to Richelieu's centralising policies, an administrative caste grew and prospered and the peaceful period ushered in by Cardinal Mazarin saw the extension and rebuilding of the city on Classical lines; judges, lawyers and rural notables built themselves the sober but distinguished urban residences that contribute so much to the charm of the Old Town (Vieil Aix) today (rusticated doorways, mask and scroll decoration, stucco-work and ornate staircases).

The intellectual life fostered by King René continued to flourish and the roll-call of great men who were born or who lived in Aix is a long one. It includes the 17C astronomer Fabri de Peiresc who in 1636 drew the first map of the moon. In the 18C there was the elegant portrait-painter Jean-Baptiste van Loo, Vauvenargues, that most optimistic of moralists, and **Count Mirabeau**, the great orator; the latter, meeting only contempt and rejection from his peers, gained election to the Estates-General in 1789 as a representative, not of the nobility, but of the Third Estate. Finally there is Paul Cézanne (1839-1906), one of the founders of modern painting; his many studies of Mount Ste-Victoire are justly renowned. The room devoted to him in Aix's museum, the Musée Granet, houses among other paintings his Still Life with Sugar-bowl, Nude at the Mirror and the monumental Bathers.

Aix-en-Provence - Address Book

Église St-Jean-de-Malte – *rue Cardinale* Open daily, 10am-noon and 3-7pm. Possibility of guided tours in Jul and Aug. ☎ 04 42 38 25 70.

Cézanne Tour – Mid-Mar to mid-Oct, Thur, 10am; ask at the tourist office - ☎ 04 42 16 11 61 - www.aixenprovencetourism.com.

For coin ranges, see the Legend at the back of the guide.

EATING OUT

⌣ **Chez Charlotte** – *32 r. des Bernardines* ☎ *04 42 26 77 56 -* ◷ *Open for lunch and dinner.* ◷ *Closed Aug, Sun, and Mon.* Upon entering you are greeted with a nostalgic atmosphere. The main eating area's decor is dedicated to the cinema. Offering traditional and seasonal cuisine, the owner gives special attention to every dish.

⌣ **Le Basilic Gourmand** – *6 r. du Griffon (a small street NE of townhall from rue Paul-Bert) -* ☎ *04 42 96 08 58 -* ◷ *Open for lunch and dinner, except Sun and Mon, open all evenings Jul - Aug. Terrace.* Light Mediterranean cuisine in a space with antique decor and warm, saffron-tones.

⌣⌣ **Chez Antoine "Côté Cour"** – *19 cours Mirabeau -* ☎ *04 42 93 12 51 -* ◷ *Closed Mon lunch and Sun.* This is a retreat with a luminous, verdant patio-veranda. All the flavours of Provence and Italy are at your fingertips. Try *aux aubergines à la parmesane* and *aux calamars farcis.* This is a place to be sure to visit.

⌣⌣⌣ **La Vieille Auberge** – *63 rue Espariat -* ☎ *04 42 27 17 41 -* ◷ *closed 5-19 Jan and Mon lunchtime.* Set in a small square, which is lively in the evenings, this restaurant offers a rustic setting with exposed beams and columns and a huge fireplace in Rognes stone. Original cooking, with a good choice of dishes, and a seductive choice of regional wines.

WHERE TO STAY

⌣⌣ **La Manoir** – *8 rue d'Entrecasteaux -* ☎ *04 42 26 27 20 – msg@hotelmanoir.com –* ◷ *closed 7-30 Jan –* P *– 40 rooms –* ⌷ *11€.* A lovely old building, formerly a hat factory. Part of an adjoining 14C cloister has been converted into a summer terrace, creating a unique atmosphere.

⌣⌣ **Prieuré** – *3km/1.9mi N of Aix-en-Provence, on the Sisteron road –* ☎ *04 42 21 05 23 – 22 rooms –* ⌷ *6.50€.* A former 17C priory which benefits from a peaceful setting. The romantically decorated bedrooms overlook an elegant park designed by Lenôtre.

⌣⌣ **Hôtel St-Christophe** – *2 avenue Victor-Hugo –* ☎ *04 42 26 01 24 – saintchristophe@francemarket.com –* P *– 51 rooms –* ⌷ *8.50€.* This hotel is right in the centre of the city, near cours Mirabeau, and rooms are decorated in either a 1930s or Provençal style. The lively Brasserie Léopold is decorated in the Art Deco style and offers regional cuisine and typical brasserie dishes. Pavement terrace in fine weather.

⌣⌣ **Hôtel des Augustins** – *3 rue Masse –* ☎ *04 42 27 28 59 – hotel.augustins@wanadoo.fr –29 rooms –* ⌷ *10€.* Stone vaulting and stained glass are reminders of the origins of this hotel, a stone's throw from cours Mirabeau, which was originally a 15C convent. The rooms, of which two have terraces with rooftop views, are decorated in a modern style.

ON THE TOWN

Café des Deux Garçons – *53 cours Mirabeau –* ☎ *04 42 26 00 51 – www.les2garcons.com –* ◷ *daily 7am-2am.* Bordered by plane trees, cours Mirabeau is mainly frequented by Aix's bourgeoisie in search of a little fresh air on the terraces of one of its 13 cafés. The Deux Garçons café, more familiarly known as "le 2 G", is the oldest and most famous of these cafés and dates from 1792. Cézanne and Zola used to meet here every afternoon.

Château de la Pioline – *260 r. Guillaume-du Vair, Les Milles –* ☎ *04 42 52 27 27 – www.chateaudelapioline.fr –* ◷ *daily 24hr.* The bar of this hotel-restaurant (which dates from the 16C) is adorned with highly prestigious furnishings, such as those from the Medici hall (to commemorate the illustrious Catherine de' Medici) and the Louis XVI hall. Don't miss the large terrace overlooking the 4ha/10 acre French garden.

SHOPPING

Markets – Traditional market every morning in place Richelme and every Tuesday, Thursday, and Saturday in place des Prêcheurs and place de la Madeleine. Flower market every Tuesday, Thursday and Saturday in place de l'Hôtel de Ville, and in place des Prêcheurs on other days.

Antiques – Antique market every Tuesday, Thursday and Saturday in place Verdun. Antiques fairs take place in the center of town, throughout the year. Check with the tourist office. Village des **Antiquaires du Quartier de Lignane**, *RN 7, Lignane, 13540 Puyricard.* The place to hunt for antiques.

Crafts – Makers of vases, ceramics, fabrics, baskets and jewellery display their wares on cours Mirabeau at the end of Mar, in mid-May, mid-Jun, mid-October, and mid-Nov.

Calissons – The legend has it that these treats were invented to sweeten up Jeanne for her marriage to King René. It seems she felt much happier about her fate after savouring a *calisson* made of equal parts of almonds, sugar and candied melon. **Calissons du Roy René**, *10 rue Clemenceau – ☎ 04 42 26 67 86 – www.calisson.com;* **Maison L. Béchard**, *12 cours Mirabeau –☎ 04 42 26 06 78 – bechard-aix@wanadoo.fr* (for *calissons* and biscuits, this is an Aix institution, having celebrated its 100th anniversary in 2001).

Aperitifs – The definitive shop for Provençal liquors and aperitifs is **Liquoisterie de Provence**, *36 av. de la Grand-Béude, 13770 Venelles – ☎ 04 42 54 94 65 – www.versinthe.net.* Free tour and tasting.

Santons Fouque – *65 cours Gambetta,* ☎ *04 42 26 33 38 – www.santonsfouque.fr.* Visit the atelier where these figurines are made.

Books – Cité du Livre, *8-10 rue des Allumettes* bookstore is a haven for book lovers - ☎ *04 42 91 98 88.*

EVENTS

International Opera and Music Festival
Founded in 1948 by Gabriel Dussurget, this prestigious festival takes place every summer in the courtyard of the archiepiscopal palace which is converted into a theatre for the event. Concerts and recitals are held in the cathedral, the cloisters of St-Saveur and the Hôtel Maynier d'Oppède. The festival focuses on important operas (in particular those by Mozart) as well as Baroque opera and contemporary music. Among the many illustrious artists who have contributed to the high standards of the festival are conductors Hans Rosbaud and Carlo Maria Giulini and the acclaimed singer Teresa Berganza. Working alongside the musicians, world-famous directors (Jorge Lavelli, Pier Luigi Pozzi) and set designers (Balthus, Derain, Masson) have also contributed to the creation of some unforgettable performances.

Santon Fair – These figurines can be purchased from the end of November until the end of December along cours Mirabeau.

Wine Festival – Festivals des vins et Coteaux d'Aix – *cour Mirabeau – last Sunday in July.*

Dance Festival – *end of July - August.* ☎ *04 42 96 05 01 – www.danse-a-aix.com.*

Sights

Vieux Aix★★

Elegant 17C-19C mansions with corner statues, pleasant squares and charming fountains combine to give the old town its distinctive character.

Cours Mirabeau★★

Fountains splash under the canopy of fine plane trees shading this most pleasant of boulevards from the fierce Provençal sun. It was laid out on the line of the 15C ramparts by Mazarin's brother who was also responsible for the construction of the district immediately to the south. This was planned in a systematic way to give the mansions a formal façade to the north and a sunny garden to the south. Aristocratic residences line the south side of the Cours Mirabeau, distinguished by the warm patina of their Rognes stone, their sculptured doorways and their balconies of wrought iron held up by caryatids and atlantes of the school of Pierre Puget.

Hôtel Boyer d'Eguilles

It houses a natural history museum, the **Muséum d'histoire naturelle (**🕐 *Open daily 10 am-noon, 1-5pm;* 🕐 *closed 1 Jan, 1 May, 25 Dec.* ⊕ *2.50€.* ☎ *04 42 27 91 27).* Attributed to Puget, it marks the transition from Baroque to Rococo and has a beautiful ironwork staircase of 1678.

Place d'Albertas★

A fine mansion of 1724 and fountain of 1745 are complemented by other 18C buildings with soaring first-floor pilasters and graceful balconies contrasting with the more robust appearance of the ground floor which has semicircular arches and rusticated stonework.

Hôtel de ville

The city's traditional centre of administration and justice. The building, designed by Pierre Pavillon, has a façade much divided up by pilasters and entablatures but relieved by an elegant ironwork balcony. The treatment of the courtyard (**cour★** intérieure – 1671) is on strictly Classical lines.

The square was laid out in the 18C. The nearby 16C Clock Tower (Tour de l'Horloge) has a bell hung high in a wrought-iron cage.

Cathédrale St-Sauveur

Cathédrale St-Sauveur★

The interesting baptistery (**baptistère** ★) is of Merovingian date (4C); eight ancient columns, probably from a Roman basilica nearby, have been used to hold up the 18C octagonal cupola crowning the Gallo-Roman structure. In the nave is the **Triptych of the Burning Bush** ★★, painted around 1475 by Nicolas Froment; it is one of the masterpieces of the Second School of Avignon, integrating a religious subject, a landscape derived from Italian Quattrocento models, and Flemish decorative elements (precious stones, mirrors, folds of clothing).

The doorway panels (**vantaux** ★) of 1500-08 *(masked by false doors)* represent Prophets and Sibyls, and the roof of the delightful Romanesque cloisters (**cloître** ★) (*Guided tours Apr-Nov: daily except during services 9am-noon and 2pm-6pm; Dec-Mar: daily except during services 10am-noon and 2.30pm-5.30pm; 04 42 23 98 90)* rests on delicate columns. In the time of the Emperor Augustus this was the site of the Forum of Aquae Sextiae.

Every year, in July and August, the **International Festival of Music and Lyrical Art**, one of the most prestigious events of its kind in Europe, turns the old city of Aix into the capital of music. Since 1948, stunning performances of Mozart's operas have revealed not only new "voices" (Teresa Stich-Randall, Teresa Berganza, Régine Crespin, Luigi Alva) but also budding directors of great talent. The splendid sets are often designed and executed by famous painters of the calibre of G Whakevitch, Cassandre and Balthus.

Musée des Tapisseries – 17C-18C tapestries *Wed-Mon 10am-5pm. Closed Tue, 1 Jan, 1 May and 25 Dec. 2€. 04 42 21 05 78.* Église St-Jean-de-Malte – **Nave** ★. **Musée Granet** ★ – fine arts and archeology *Wed-Mon 10am-noon, 2-6pm. Closed Tue and public holidays. No charge. 04 42 38 14 70.* Église Ste-Marie-Madeleine – **statue of Our Lady** ★, **triptych** ★ *Weekdays 9am-noon, 3-6pm. Closed Jul and Aug.* **Fondation Vasarely** ★ *Mon-Fri 10am-1pm, 2-6pm, Sat-Sun 10am-7pm (Nov-Mar: 6pm). Last admission 1hr before closing. Closed 1 Jan, 1 May, 25 Dec. 7€. 04 42 20 01 09. www.fondationvasarely.com.* Fontaine des Quatre Dauphins ★.

AJACCIO★★

POPULATION 52,315

MICHELIN MAP 345 A-B 7-8

GREEN GUIDE CORSE (IN FRENCH)

Ajaccio occupies a natural amphitheatre looking out over its splendid bay. The town was founded in 1492 by the Office of St George which governed Corsica on behalf of the Republic of Genoa. Native Corsicans were forbidden residence there until 1553, when, in the course of the first French intervention in the island, it was taken by the legendary military adventurer Sampierro Corso (1498-1567), born in the village of Bastelica 25km – 15 miles to the northeast. *3 bd du Roi-Jérôme, 20181 Ajaccio (Aiacciu), ☎ 04 95 51 53 03. www.tourisme.fr/ajaccio.*

A Bit of History

It was here, at 1am on 13 September 1943, that the first Free French forces to land on the territory of France itself were disembarked from the submarine *Casabianca*, under Commander L'Herminier.

Ajaccio's historic importance is due above all to its being the birthplace of **Napoleon Bonaparte**; his extraordinary career not only arose out of the political realities of his time but also changed them decisively. The town continues to revere the memory of its "glorious child prodigy". Born on 15 August 1769, the son of Charles-Marie Bonaparte and Letizia Romolino, he was admitted to the military school at Brienne (*Aube*) at the age of 10. At 27 he married Josephine Tascher de la Pagerie, the widow of General Beauharnais, before directing the Italian campaign (Battle of Arcole) and, two years later, the expedition to Egypt. In 1804, taking the title of Napoleon I, he crowned himself Emperor of the French. On 26 August the following year he launched the Grand Army (*Grande Armée*) against Austria from the encampment at Boulogne whence he had threatened England with invasion. By 1807, at the age of 38, he dominated Europe.

It was then, however, that the various coalitions originally formed to resist the French Revolution were turned against the Empire. England was deeply involved in them all, in the colonies and on the high seas as well as in Europe. Though bloated and prematurely aged, Napoleon rose to the challenge, never more formidable than from 1809 on, the years of struggle against the Fifth and Sixth Coalitions. But France and her Emperor were now out of touch with a changed Europe; the ideology of the Revolution, disseminated by France's territorial conquests, had awakened a strong desire for national independence among the peoples of Europe and ranged them against her. The Napoleonic Age was brought to a close on 18 June 1815 by the Battle of Waterloo; the last farewells at Malmaison on 29 June were followed by embarkation aboard the *Bellerophon* at Aix Island on 15 July and by exile on St Helena, where "General Bonaparte" died on 5 May 1821.

Sights

Musée Fesch★★

♿ ⏱ *Apr-Jun and Sep: 9.15am-12.15pm, 2.15-5.15pm, Mon 1-5.15pm; Jul and Aug: Tue-Fri 9am-6.30pm (Fri evening 9pm-midnight), Mon 1.30-6pm, Sat-Sun and public holidays 10.30am-6pm; Oct-Mar: daily except Sun and Mon 9.15am-12.15pm,2.15-5.15pm. ⊚ 5.35€. ☎ 04 95 21 48 17 . www.musee-fesch.com.*

This has France's most important collection of **Italian paintings**★★ outside the Louvre, together with a number of French and Spanish works. Entry to the museum is on the second level, via the main courtyard. Temporary exhibits are housed here, while on the level above can be seen 15C paintings by Jacopo Sellajo, Lorenzo di Credi, **Bellini** (*Mary with the Infant Jesus)*

Bonaparte by David

Musée du Louvre/GIRAUDON

and **Botticelli** (*Virgin with Garland*). There are two outstanding works from the 16C: Veronese's **Leda** and the second **Man with Glove** by Titian.

Maison Bonaparte

Apr-Sep: Tue-Sun 9am-noon, 2-6pm, Mon 2-6pm; Oct-Mar: Tue-Sun 10am-noon, 2-5pm, Mon 2-5pm. Last admission 15min before closing. 4€, no charge 1st Sunday in the month. 04 95 21 43 89.

The Genoese-style house came into the Bonaparte family's possession in 1743; Napoleon is supposed to have been born on a couch in the antechamber on the first floor. His father's modest earnings and the income from landholdings at Mielli, Egitto, Salines and Sposata did not suffice for a life of luxury. It was Letizia, "a most remarkable woman", who directed the household and who brought up her children with a wise mixture of discipline and tenderness. In May 1793, Bonaparte, loyal to Republican ideas, was forced by the followers of Pascal Paoli to abandon the house; the building was sacked and the adjoining family properties laid waste.

On her return to Ajaccio in 1798, Letizia put the house back in order with the help of her half-brother, Abbot Fesch (a future cardinal). The work was financed in part by a grant from the Directory, in part by sums sent to his brother Joseph by Napoleon (now in Egypt), enabling him to acquire the upper storeys and the adjoining house. On his return from Egypt on 29 September 1799, Bonaparte stopped off at Ajaccio to see the family home. He is supposed to have slept in the alcove on the second floor. After six days he slipped away via a trap-door, never to see his birthplace again.

Place Letizia

Napoleon was anxious to have an appropriate setting for the house where he was born. The square was laid out on the site of a number of demolished buildings. There is a bust of the Emperor's son, the "Aiglon" (Eaglet).

Place Maréchal-Foch

This fine square, the focus of Ajaccio's outdoor social life, is shaded by palm trees; its upper part is dominated by a marble statue by Laboureur of Napoleon as First Consul.

Musée Napoléonien

First floor of the Town Hall. Daily except Sat-Sun 9am-11.45am, 2-5.45pm (mid-Sep to mid-Jun: 4.45pm). 2.30€ (under 15 years: no charge). 04 95 51 52 53.

In the museum, Napoleon's baptism certificate (21 July 1771) in Genoese dialect, family pictures, portraits and statues, make a moving display which draws serious historians as well as faithful admirers. Also shown is a bronze cast of a death mask made on St Helena.

ALBI★★★

POPULATION 46,579

MICHELIN MAP 338 D 6, E 7

GREEN GUIDE LANGUEDOC ROUSSILLON TARN GORGES

The whole of Albi, from the bridges spanning the Tarn to the extraordinary cathedral, is made of brick which owes its rosy hue to the clays dug from the river's bed.

▶ **Orient Yourself:** To get a better idea of the massive proportions of the cathedral, take a look at it from a distance, preferably the bridge across the Tarn (the Pont du 22-Août), or from one of the streets of Old Albi, which opens onto the cathedral square.

Don't Miss: A boat trip on the Tarn (**Berges du Tarn** *Jun-Sep: Sun, Tue and Thu 11.25am-noon, 2-6pm; Fri and Sat 10.45am-noon, 2-6.30pm; Mon and Wed 10.45am-noon, 2-5.15pm; 5€ for 30min, children under 12 years: 3€; 15€ for 2hr, children under 12 years: 10€; closed Oct-Jun).*

Organizing Your Time: Start the day at "la Berbie" on Place Ste-Cécile, opposite the cathedral. Drop in to sample some local specialities at "Pâtisserie Galy" on rue Saunal. Plan a boat trip on the Tarn, and end the day at one of the pubs this student town has to offer: "Connemara", "Estabar" or "Shamrock".

Albi - Address Book

VISIT

Guided Tour of the Old Town *(1hr) –* organised by the Tourist Office, mid-Jul-late Aug: Mon-Sat except public holidays at 12.15pm. Book at the Tourist Office. 4€ (under 14s: no charge).

Walks – Three walks allow the visitor to discover Albi : the circuit Pourpre goes through the heart of old Albi and takes in the main historic sites, characters and monuments; the circuit Or focuses on the growth of Albi over two thousand years; the circuit Azur leads along the banks of the Tarn, taking in the Pont Vieux and the Pont Neuf, and provides some fine views of the town (routes marked by explanatory signposts in three languages). Depart from the Tourist Office.

For coin ranges, see the Legend at the back of the guide.

EATING OUT

Le Poisson d'Avril – *17 r. d'Engueysse -* ☎ *05 63 38 30 13 -* closed *Mon noon and Sun Oct-Apr.* This restaurant in a typical old Albi house 200m/220yd from the cathedral has an unusual interior decor designed like the inside of a barrel, with wooden beams. Prices are moderate and food is not heavy.

Le Table du Sommelier – *20 r. Porta -* ☎ *05 63 46 20 10 -* closed *Sun and Mon.* The proprietor sets the scene here perfectly, with cases of wine piled high in the entrance and rustic dining room with mezzanine floor. Beyond appearances, this wine-focused bistro serves refined cuisine using the freshest ingredients.

Le Robinson – *142 r. Édouard-Branly -* ☎ *05 63 46 15 69 - robinsonalbi@yahoo. com –* closed *Nov-Feb, Tue noon and Mon.* This isle of green on the banks of the Tarn is acceible from the pont Neuf. Dating from the 1920's, the old-fashioned dance hall has an exuberant charm. The food is simple and the welcome warm. Dream away the evening!

Jardin des Quatre Saisons - *19 bd de Strasbourg -* ☎ *05 63 60 77 76 -* closed *Sun evening and Mon.* A friendly welcome from the owners awaits, along with a good selection of wines and traditional cuisine. A little away from the centre, this remains a reliable favourite.

Le Moulin de La Mothe – *R. de Lamothe -* ☎ *05 63 60 38 15 - restaurant_ moulin_delamothe@wanadoo.fr -* closed *school holidays in Feb and Oct/ Nov, Tues evening from 15 Sep-30 Apr, Sun evening and Wed.* In fine weather, this restaurant on the banks of the Tarn attracts a crowd. It has a terrace overlooking the park and the river. In cooler weather, the light and airy dining room offers the same view.

WHERE TO STAY

George V - *29 av. du Mar.-Joffre -* ☎*05 63 54 24 16 – info@hotelgeorgev.com – 9 rms.* It is worth searching out this cosy establishment with its typical local style in the station district. Rooms are a generous size and some have a fireplace. At the first sign of fine weather, make the best of the pleasant shade of the little courtyard.

Chambre d'hôte Le Moulin d'Ambrozy – *81120 Lombers - 14km/9mi south of Albi on the N112 and then the D71 -* ☎*05 63 79 17 12 –* – *3 rms.* This authentic 17C mill in open countryside is experiencing a new lease of life, its attractive rooms with many personal touches including fine furniture such as a four poster bed, plus pleasant gardens and swimming pool. Dinner draws inspiration from seasonal specialities.

Cantepau – *9 r.Cantepau -* ☎*05 63 60 75 80 -* closed *25 Dec-11 Jan -* - *33 rms.* Wicker furniture, subdued hues and fans give this hotel a colonial feel following its recent revamp.Friendly welcome.

Hôtel Mercure – *41 bis r. Porta -* ☎*05 63 47 66 66 – h1211-gm@accor-hotels. com -* - *56 rms.* This modern hotel has an original setting, in an old 18C red-brick mill on the banks of the Tarn. The functional rooms offer a view of the river and cathedral. Guests can enjoy the same view from the dining room.

SIT BACK AND RELAX

La Berbie – *17 pl. Ste-Cécile -* ☎ *05 63 54 13 86 -* Jul-Aug: daily 9.30am-11pm; Sep-Jun: Wed-Mon 9.30am-8pm. This attractive tea room on Place Ste-Cécile, opposite the cathedral, serves a wide range of tea, coffee, home-baked pastries, ice-cream sundaes and pancakes. Luncheon menu.

ON THE TOWN

Albi "the red", named after its red-brick façades, is a beautiful city. Visitors might like to start their day at "la Berbie" on Place Ste-Cécile, opposite the imposing cathedral. Then we recommend dropping in to sample some local specialities at "Pâtisserie Galy". During the day, a boat trip on the Tarn is a must, in order to appreciate the beauty of the city at its best. At the end of the day, this student town offers plenty of pleasant places to spend the evening, such as the "Connemara", "Estabar" or "Shamrock".

SHOPPING

In the streets of the Old Town (especially rues Mariès, Ste-Cécile et Verdrusse) are a variety of antique shops and boutiques. Also, visitors cannot miss the many shops selling local food and drink.

L'Artisan Pastellier – *5 r. Puech-Bérenguier -* ☎ *05 63 38 59 18 - artisan.pastellier@*

wanadoo.fr – ⏰Tue-Sat 10am-noon, 2-7pm, Mon mid-Jun to mid-Sep and Sun in Aug 3-6.30pm - ⏰closed 20 Jan-10 Feb, 14 Jul, 15 Aug, Sun and Mon out of season. Near the Maison du vieil Alby, this shop is a poem in blue. Made from pastel leaves, this irresitable colour is used to shade local crafts and fabrics. Claire and her husband prepare artists' materials of quality including inks for caligraphy. The owners know everthing there is to know about pastel and are happy to answer questions.

Marché biologique – Pl. F.-Pelloutier – ⏰Tue 5-7pm. In addition to organic produce, local craftwarer and books are also on sale here.

Markets– Pl. Ste-Cécile. A big market is held on Saturday on place Ste-Cécile: fruit, vegetables, foie gras (in season), mushrooms, garlic from Lautrec, charcuterie from Lacaune et Gaillac wines.

Patisserie J.P. Galy – 7 r. Saunal – ☎ 05 63 54 13 37 - Tues -Sat 9.45am-7pm - ⏰closed 1 week in Feb and 4 weeks Sep-early Oct and holidays. For 14 years, Galy pastrycooks have been supplying local people and visitors with fine pastries, many of which are local specialities (try out the following: navettes, gimblettes, croquants aux amandes, jeannots à l'anis, croissants aux pignons). These delicacies sell like cakes and it is worth paying a visit earl, the day to avoid disappointment.

RECREATION

Boat Trip on the Tarn – Berges du Tarn - ☎ 05 63 43 59 63 - www.mairie-albi.fr - ⏰Jun- Sep: Sun, Tue and Thu 11.25am-noon, 2pm-6.30pm Fri and Sat 10.45am-noon, 2pm-6.30pm, Mon and Wed 10.45am-noon, 2pm-5.15pm - 5€ (for 30min, children under 12: 3€); 15€ (for 2hr, children under 12: 10€). The boat in question is in fact a flat-bottomed barge, a gabarre, used for transporting goods until the 19C and now used for pleasure trips. Leaving the old harbour at the foot of the ramparts of the Palais de la Berbie, the barge travels along the Tarn past the old Albi mills, and the locks at the Moulin de Gardès and Moulin de la Mothe.

CALENDAR OF EVENTS

Free Organ Concerts in the Cathedral - Wed and Sun afternoons in Jul and Aug.

Le festival de théâtre - early Jul, ☎ 05 63 49 48 80.

Carnaval - Feb.

Le Grand Prix automobile d'Albi - Sep.

A Bit of History

At the beginning of the 13C the city was one of the centres of the dualist Cathar doctrine, dubbed the "Albigensian heresy" by a fearful Church. The subsequent "Albigensian Crusade" was directed on the spiritual side by St Dominic; on the ground, armies moved in from north and east to commit the terrible atrocities of Béziers, Carcassonne, Minerve and Lavaur. The Capetian kings took advantage of the troubles, which lasted from 1208 to 1229, to gain a foothold in Languedoc, but the Albigensian heresy itself was finally stamped out only by the Inquisition and the ghastly funeral pyre at Montségur (👆 see Château de MONTSÉGUR).

Sights

Cathédrale Ste-Cécile★★★

Construction of the cathedral, extending over two centuries, began in 1282 at a time when work on the neighbouring Berbie Palace, the bishops' residence, and on that of the Dominicans at Toulouse, was already well advanced. For the bishops, the status of the church was inextricably linked to its temporal power and they therefore gave their cathedral the appearance of a fortress. In the 19C the formidable edifice acquired the three upper storeys of its keep-like bell-tower, its machicolations and its inspection gallery.

Inside, the perfect simplicity of the single broad nave with its Southern French Gothic side chapels passes almost unnoticed, such is the exuberance of the Flamboyant decorative scheme. The rood screen (**jubé**★★★), one of the few to have survived, is also one of the most sumptuous. In the 15C and 16C all the greater churches possessed such a screen; it separated the clergy, in the choir, from the lay worshippers in the nave; during services readings would be given from its gallery. This example dates from 1485, as does the screen closing off the choir (**chœur**)(👆 ⏰ Daily 9am-noon, 6.30pm; Jun-Sep: 9am-6.30pm; call in advance for guided tour, 1hr30min; 1€; 05 63 43 23 43); its arches and gables, columns and arcading all show the extraordinary skill and attention to detail of the craftsmen who worked the white limestone. The naturalistic poses and facial expressions typical of Gothic art are here brought to life. Old Testament figures are on the outside, those from the New Testament inside of the choir, where there are two rows of 66 stalls. The vaults were painted to 1512 by Bolognese artists; they repay study with binoculars.

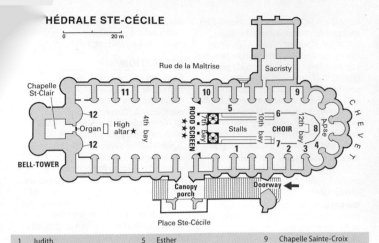

HÉDRALE STE-CÉCILE

1	Judith	5	Esther	9	Chapelle Sainte-Croix
2	Prophet Zephaniah	6	Charlemagne	10	Painting of the Holy Family
3	Prophet Isaish	7	Constantine	11	Chapelle du Rosaire
4	Prophet Jeremiah	8	Statue of Virgin and child	12	Last Judgement

The hallucinatory **Last Judgement** is a masterpiece of late-15C mural painting; it was unfortunately disfigured by the installation in the 17C of the great organ. But it is nevertheless possible to admire the upper part depicting the Heavenly Kingdom: on the left the Apostles, haloed in gold, and the saints as well as the elect bearing the book of their life held open; on the right the damned, punished by their sin itself.

Palais de la Berbie★

🕐 Jun–Sep: daily 9am–noon, 2–6pm; Jul and Aug: daily 9am–6pm; Apr and May: daily 10am–noon, 2–6pm; Oct–Mar: daily except Tue 10am–noon, 2–5pm (Mar and Oct: 5.30pm). 🕐 Closed 1 Jan, 1 May, 1 Nov, 25 Dec. 💶 4.50€ (under 14 years: no charge). ☎ 05 63 49 48 70.

The former Bishops' Palace houses a museum, the **Musée Toulouse-Lautrec**★★. Henri de Toulouse-Lautrec (1864-1901) was born in Albi at the Hôtel du Bosc and was crippled in early life by two accidents. He is revealed here as one of the great painters of everyday life; his vision of the depravity and decadence of late-19C Paris is communicated with restraint and compassion (*Jane Avril, Mademoiselle Lucie Bellanger, Au bal de l'Élysée-Montmartre*).

◖◗ **Vieil Albi**★★ (Old Town).

Ecomusée d'**ALSACE**★★

ALSACE ECOMUSEUM

MICHELIN MAP 315 H 9

GREEN GUIDE ALSACE LORRAINE CHAMPAGNE

An open-air museum founded in 1984 as part of a plan to save the local heritage comprises some 60 old buildings dotted over an area of 15 hectares – 37 acres. The old buildings dating from the 15C to 19C, which were saved from demolition and carefully dismantled and re-erected to create a village setting, are fine examples of rural habitat from the various regions of Alsace. The museum which is constantly evolving also includes industrial structures; next door to the museum are the restored buildings of a potassium mine which was worked from 1911 to 1930.

Visit

🕐 Mar–Sep: daily 10am–6pm; Jul and Aug: daily 9.30am–7pm; Jan–Feb and Oct to n daily 10am–5pm; mid-Nov to mid-Dec: Sundays only. 💶 14.50€ (children: 9€ under 4 years: no charge). ☎ 03 89 74 44 74. www.ecomusee-alsace.com.

ALSATIAN DWELLINGS

Potter's house in Outre-Forêt

Fisherman's house in the Reid

Farmstead in Kochersberg

House in the vineyards of Alsace

Farmhouse in the Sundgau

Walk around the half-timbered buildings grouped by region (Sundgau, Reid, Kochersberg, Bas-Rhin) and complete with courtyards and gardens, to appreciate the development of building techniques and the varied architecture of farm buildings according to the regions and periods.

Specific buildings such as a fortified structure, a chapel, a school and a wash-house evoke community life in a traditional Alsatian village. Old plant varieties are grown in a typical field which also serves for farming demonstrations.

An area devoted to fun-fairs includes a rare merry-go-round (1909). Visitors will also discover the age-old crafts of carpenters and masons, as well as the evolution of living conditions, from the reconstructed interiors complete with kitchens, alcoves and "stube", the living area with its terracotta stove.

AMBOISE★★

POPULATION 10,982

MICHELIN MAP 317-O 4

GREEN GUIDE CHÂTEAUX OF THE LOIRE

Amboise is a bridge-town, built at the foot of an escarpment already fortified in Gallo-Roman times, on which stand the proud remains of its great château. ⏸ *Quai du Gén.-de-Gaulle, 37400 Amboise, ☎ 02 47 57 09 28. www.amboise-valdeloire.com.*

Visit

Château★★

🕐 *Mid to end Mar, Sep and Oct: daily 9am-6pm; Jul and Aug: daily 9am-7pm; Apr-Jun: daily 9am-6.30pm; early to mid-Nov: daily 9am-5.30pm; mid-Nov to end Jan: daily 9am-noon, 2-4.45pm; early Feb to mid-Mar: daily 9am-noon, 1.30-5.30pm.* 🕐 *Closed 1 Jan and 23 Dec.* ⏲ *7.50€ (7-14 years: 4.20€). ☎ 02 47 57 00 98.*

The 15C saw the Golden Age of Amboise. Charles VIII was born here in 1470; from his 22nd year onwards he carried on the work begun by his father, Louis XI. By the time he left on his Italian campaign, work was well in hand on a number of projects: the round towers, the great Gothic roof of the wing overlooking the Loire, and the Flamboyant St-Hubert Chapel, which served as an oratory for Anne of Brittany and has particularly fine Flemish door panels. In 1496 Charles returned from Italy, dazzled by what he had seen, and bringing with him not only works of art but a whole retinue of artists, architects (Fra Giocondo and Il Boccadoro), sculptors, cabinet-makers and gardeners.

With these Italians came a taste for Antiquity and a decorative sense unknown at the time in France (doorways resembling triumphal arches, inlaid ceilings, superimposed arches, etc). Charles' liking for luxury enhanced the prestige of the monarchy; his promotion of the artistic ideas of the Renaissance was continued by Louis XII and even more by François I, under whom château life became a whirl of princely gaiety with festivals, entertainments, hunting parties. However, this first French château of the Renaissance was destined to disappear; partly demolished by the troops of Louis XIII, it was further dismantled on the orders of Napoleon's Senate. Now it is known only from an engraving by Du Cerceau.

Less than a year after the Treaty of Le Cateau-Cambrésis came the **Amboise Conspiracy**, a bloody precursor of events to follow. Led by La Renaudie, 1 500 Huguenots marched on Blois where, on 15 March 1560, they demanded guarantees of freedom of worship from the young François II. They were in fact planning to seize the King and force him to denounce the Guises, their bitter enemies. But forewarned, the Court fled to Amboise which was easier to defend. As the conspirators began to arrive at the château they were arrested. Savage punishment was meted out; it is even thought that Catherine de' Medici, François II and his young wife Mary Stuart enjoyed the last gasps and grimaces of the condemned swinging from balcony and battlement as an after-dinner entertainment.

Clos-Lucé★

🕐 *Jul and Aug: daily 9am-8pm; Apr-Jun and Sep-Oct: daily 10am-7pm; Feb-Mar and Nov-Dec: daily 10am-6pm; Jan: daily 10am-5pm.* 🕐 *Closed 1 Jan, 25 Dec.* ⏲ *11€ (children: 6.50€) ☎ 02 47 57 00 73.*

It was to this manor house of red brick with stone dressings that François I invited **Leonardo da Vinci** in 1516.

The great Florentine was then 64. At Amboise he neither painted nor taught, devoting himself instead to organising royal festivities, designing a château at Romorantin for Louise of Savoy, François' mother, planning the drainage of the Sologne and amusing himself with mechanical inventions which lack of motive power kept on the drawing-board.

AMIENS

POPULATION 156 120

MICHELIN MAP 301 G 8

GREEN GUIDE NORTHERN FRANCE AND THE PARIS REGION

It was in the middle years of the 4C on a high road near Amiens that a young Roman officer took pity on a beggar freezing in the icy wind. Slicing his cloak in two with his sword, he shared it with the poor wretch. Later ordained, then Bishop of Tours, the former soldier was eventually canonised as St Martin, patron saint of France.

▶ **Orient Yourself:** Amiens, which is listed as a "Town of Art and HIstory," offers discovery tours *(2hr)* Sat at 2.30pm *(daily except Sun from mid-Jun to mid-Sep)*. 5.50€. Information at the tourist office or on www.amiens.com/tourisme. Shopping enthusiasts will particularly enjoy rue du Hocquet and place du Don. Walk across the River Somme to explore the narrow streets of Quartier St-Leu, which contain craft and antique shops, cafés and restaurants.

Especially for Kids: Within the Hortillonnages, the Île aux Fagots has an aquarium and insectarium that invites children to discover ecology and its problems (picnic areas). **Théâtre des Marionnettes-Chés Cabotans d'Amiens** *(31 r. Édouard-David 80000 Amiens;* ⏱ *shows mid-Jul to mid-Aug, Mon-Fri 6pm;* ⏱ *closed from Sep to mid-Oct and from 24 Dec-early Jan;* ⏺ *5-10€;* ☎ *03 22 22 30 90)* – Amiens is famous for its puppets. See a show or just examine the fine detail and craftsmanship of the displayed "cabotans."

P **Parking:** Parking is available in the place St. Michel, next to the cathedral.

A Bit of History

Amiens gained its charter in 1117, and in 1477, on the death of Charles le Téméraire (the Bold) this ancient capital of Picardy became subject to the French Crown. In the 17C its textile industry prospered (Amiens velvet), largely thanks to Colbert's economic policies. The city suffered in both World Wars, in 1918 during the Ludendorff Offensive, in 1940 during the Battle of France.

The famous names associated with the city include: **Pierre Choderlos de Laclos** (1741-1803), military engineer and author of *Les Liaisons Dangereuses (Dangerous Liaisons)*, Charles Tellier (1828-1913), inventor of refrigeration (1872), **Jules Verne**

Puppets

Amiens is famous for its string puppets dating back to about 1785. Known in the Picardy dialect as a **cabotan**, the puppet is about 50cm – 19in in height. It is carved out of wood and operated from above. The character **Lafleur** is the king of St-Leu (a district which existed in medieval times) and the leader of the *cabotans*; he is undoubtedly the most expressive embodiment of the spirit and character of the Picardy people.

Since the 19C, but arguably from an earlier date, this mythical, truculent, bold, irreverent and brave character with a fiery temper has expressed plain common sense and described the pride and nobility of the province in the language of his ancestors. Even from a distance, he is recognisable by his impressive stature, by his characteristic gait, and most of all by his 18C valet's livery of fine red Amiens velvet. He is often accompanied by his wife Sandrine and his best friend Tchot Blaise. His motto is "Drink, walk and do nothing".

In the 19C each of the 20 quarters in the city had its own puppet theatre. With the arrival of the cinema and sporting events at the turn of the century, however, the theatres gradually closed down.

Amiens - Address Book

🗐 *6 bis r. Dusevel, 80000 Amiens,* ☎ *03 22 71 60 50. www.amiens.com/tourisme.*

TOURS

🚶 Guided tours *(90min-2hr)* highlighting the art and history of Amiens offered mid-Jun to mid-Sep.daily except Sun at 2.30pm; rest of the year Sat. at 2.30pm. 5.50€. Contact the Tourism Office *(above).*

For coin ranges, see the Legend at the back of this guide.

EATING OUT

🍽🍽 **Le Bouchon** – *10, rue Alexandre Fatton* – ☎ *03 22 92 14 32* – 🕐 *closed Sun evening, Sep to Jun.* A Parisian-style bistro near the railway station specialising in typically Lyonnais dishes and traditional cuisine of the region; a relaxed, "no fuss" atmosphere.

🍽 **Le Vivier** – *593, route de Rouen* – ☎ *03 22 89 12 21* – 🕐 *closed 3-18 Aug, Christmas to New Year, Sun evenings and Mon.* Specialising in seafood dishes.

🍽 **Ale factory (Les Artisans Brasseurs)** *18 port d'Amont, quartier St Leu* – ☎ *03 22 72 69 85* – 🕐 *closed mid-Jul to mid-Aug, Sat lunch and Sun.* A brick building set on the banks of the Somme. Alsatian specialities *(flammeküches* and sauerkrauts) are served, in addition to more traditional dishes, all to be washed down with one of the beers brewed on the site. The décor is a blend of wood and metal.

🍽 **Le T'chiot Zinc** – *18 rue de Noyon* – ☎ *03 22 91 43 79* – 🕐 *closed Mon lunch and Sun.* Housed in a former bakery built in 1643, this highly charming eatery has a typical bistro decor with alcoves and photos of Old Amiens. The menu proposes solid, traditional cuisine, featuring suckling pig and the mouth-watering caqhuse: pork cooked with onions, white wine and *crème fraîche.*

🍽🍽 **Les Marissons** – *Pont de la Dodane* – ☎ *03 22 92 96 66* – *les-marissons@les-marissons.fr* – 🕐 *closed 31 Dec to 4 Jan, Sat lunch, Sun and Wed lunch.* Search no further! The place to be in the Saint-Leu quarter is right here, in this old maritime workshop transformed into a restaurant. The flowery mini-garden becomes a terrace in summer, while in winter diners sit under the sloping wooden frame in a pleasant decor of handsome beams and round tables.

🍽 **L'Os à Mœlle** – *12 r. Flatters* – ☎ *03 22 92 75 46* – 🕐 *closed 2 to 21 jan, Sun evening, Mon and Tue.* In this small restaurant in the centre of the village, be prepared to sample bone marrow! Behind its modest façade and with a décor in the style of a bistrot *spécialités du terroir* are served.

WHERE TO STAY

🛏 **Hôtel Alsace-Lorraine** – *18 rue de la Morlière* – ☎ *03 22 91 35 71* – *www.alsace-lorraine.fr.st –13 rms:* 🍽 *6.50€.* You won't regret having chosen this comfortable little hotel hidden behind an imposing carriage entrance just a five-minute walk from the train station. The rooms, brightened with colourful fabrics, give onto the charming inner courtyard, guaranteeing a good night's sleep.

🛏🛏 **Hôtel Carlton** – *42 rue de Noyon* – ☎ *03 22 97 72 22* – *www.lecarlton.fr* – *24 rms:* 🍽 *10€.* Go beyond the 19C facade of this attractive building and discover the modern, agreeably plush interior. Every room features waxed furniture and murals. Their restaurant, Le Bistrot, is more simply decorated; grilled meat is the mainstay here.

🛏🛏 **Mme Lemaitre (Bed and Breakfast)** – *26 r. Principale, 80480 Creuse – 14km/8.5mi SW of Amiens* – ☎ *03 22 38 91 50 – closed winter* – 🍽 *6 rms.* A gorgeous late-18C residence nestled in a spacious garden featuring ancient trees. White walls and furniture with a regional slant characterize the comfortable bedrooms. Downstairs, there's a snug sitting room warmed by a handsome period fireplace.

🛏🛏 **Le Petit Chateau (Bed and Breakfast)** – *2 rue Grimaux, 80480 Dury - 6km/3.6mi S of Amiens via N 1 dir. Beauvais* – ☎ *03 22 95 29 52* – *alainsaguez@ libertysurf.fr* – 🍽 *4 rms.* Offering all the advantages of the countryside, yet only 10 minutes from downtown Amiens, a massive 19C residence whose comfortable guest rooms (all non-smoking) are housed in an outbuilding. Collecting old automobiles is the owner's hobby, and he will be delighted to show you his treasures.

ON THE TOWN

Texas Café – *13 rue des Francs-Mûriers, Quartier Saint-Leu* – ☎ *03 22 72 19 79* – 🕐 *Tue-Sat 10pm-5am;* 🕐 *closed Sun-Mon.* This enormous 'saloon' of brick and wood hosts various theme evenings that are always very animated. Come have a drink (beer and cocktails), dance, flaunt your lovely voice (karaoke), or play billiards or darts.

Vents et Marées – *48 r. du Don* – ☎ *03 22 92 37 78.* 🕐 *Mon-Sat 5pm-3am.* Walk down an iron staircase to enter this café designed as a barge docked upon the water. With its singular ambience, particularly hospitable welcome and permanent exhibition of comic strip pages, the place has a soul of its own.

SHOWTIME AND ART

"Amiens, the cathedral in living colour" – The artist Skertzò uses light effects to highlight the polychromatic entranceways of the Amiens cathedral's western facade. The presentation, based on scientific data, is truly mesmerizing! It is held from mid-June to September at dusk, and from mid-December to early January at 8pm. Commentary in French and then English.

Comédie de Picardie – *62 rue des Jacobins* – ☎ *03 22 22 20 20* – *www.comdepic.com* – ⏱ *Mon-Fri 1pm-7pm, Sat 1pm-6pm.* ⏱ *Closed Aug, public holidays, Sun except performance days. 11 to 46€.* This venerable old manor, entirely restored, houses a very pretty 400-seat theatre. The region's creative and dramatic hub, it produces 15 different shows for a total of 250 performances per season.

La Lune des Pirates – *17 quai Bélu* – ☎ *03 22 97 88 01* – *www.lalune.net.* ⏱ *Closed mid-Jul to end Aug (tickets at Fnac).* Formerly a very popular café, the Pirates' Moon has become a showcase for contemporary music. It also holds exhibitions and cultural happenings.

Maison de la Culture d'Amiens – *Pl. Léon-Gontier* – ☎ *03 22 97 79 77* – *www.maisondelaculture-amiens.com.* ⏱ *Tue-Fri noon-7pm, Sat-Sun 2pm-7pm* – ⏱ *closed public holidays and Mon.* Two halls (1070 and 300 seats), a movie theatre devoted to art and experimental films and two exhibition rooms. Embracing all cultures, this complex offers an unusually interesting and eclectic selection of events from year to year. Programmes at the reception.

Théâtre de Marionnettes – *Chés Cabotans d'Amiens* – 🧒 *31 rue Édouard-David, quartier St-Leu* – ☎ *03 22 22 30 90* – *www.ches-cabotans-damiens.com.* ⏱ *Exhibitions: Apr-Aug from Tue to Sun 10am-noon, 2pm-6pm except Sun morning; mid-Oct to Mar from Tue to Sun 2pm-6pm. Performances: mid-Jul-mid-Aug from Tue to Sun: 6pm; 15 Oct to end Mar: Sun (except public holidays and Christmas week) 3pm; additional shows during school holiday weekdays at 2.30pm – 10 € (children: 5 €).* An actor performs, a marionette becomes alive. The puppets all have their own history and language (French or Picard) plus remarkably expressive faces that can be admired in the ground-floor exhibition. This fascinating show for all audiences takes place in a veritable miniature theatre with a beautifully designed set.

Laurent-Devime – *80260 St-Gratien* – ☎ *03 22 40 16 71.* This storyteller offers entertainment in a variety of forms: Picard evenings, storytelling walks in the country or city, marionettes and shows inspired by *kamishibaï*, Japanese image-based theatre. Traditional Picardy games workshop.

SHOPPING

Atelier de Jean-Pierre Facquier – *67 rue du Don* – ☎ *03 22 92 49 52 or 03 22 39 21 74* – ⏱ *Tue-Fri 2pm-6.30pm, Sat 10am-noon, 2pm-6pm* – ⏱ *closed 1 week in summer.* Transforming them into traditional and invented wooden figurines, Monsieur Facquier carves life into pieces of wood before your eyes. Madame Facquier sews their clothes using fabric chosen with care. Each unique character is a genuine work of art.

Caveau St-Loupien - La Galerie Gourmande – *19 rue de la République-Galerie des Jacobins* - ☎ *03 22 72 40 40* - *www.caveau-saint-loupien.com* - ⏱ *Mon 2.30pm-7.30pm, Tue-Sat 10.30am-7.30pm, public holidays (mornings).* A specialist in regional gastronomy: here you will find a vast selection of local mustards, wine jellies, red fruit preserves, terrines and regional dishes in addition to just about every sort of beer and ale brewed in Picardy, locally produced lemonades and syrups (rose, violet, lavender and others), Picard aperitifs and, naturally, genuine Amiens macaroons.

Jean Trogneux – ☎ *03 22 71 17 17.* The city's speciality since the 16C, the Amiens macaroon, with its blend of almonds and honey, is ever popular. The Trogneux family, confectioners and chocolatiers for five generations, sell more than two million of them every year! The shop also carries a nice selection of local products.

Marché sur l'eau – The local market gardeners, who grow their produce in canal-bordered, floating wetlands (*hortillonnages*), come to market Saturday mornings, Place Parmentier. Once a year, on 3rd Sunday in June, market is held as in years gone by. The gardeners, wearing traditional attire, come via flat-bottomed boats and unload their produce onto the docks.

Le Petit Poucet – *52 rue des Trois-Cailloux* – ☎ *03 22 91 42 32.* This attractive pink-faced establishment is very popular with the people of Amiens who come here for a slice of quiche, a ficelle picarde (baked crepes, stuffed and rolled), or a mixed salad for lunch, a delectable chocolate for tea, or a box of divine pastries to enjoy at home.

(1828-1905), born in Nantes, author of *20 000 Leagues under the Sea* and *Around the World in Eighty Days*, **Édouard Branly** (1844-1940), whose radioconductors made wireless telegraphy possible, and Roland Dorgelès (1885-1973), author of *Croix de bois (Cross of Wood)*, a realistic account of trench warfare.

Traditionally, Amiens has always been an important crossroads and a major centre for the arts and the economy. In 1964 it became the seat of a university.

Sights

Cathédrale Notre-Dame★★★

🕐 *Apr- Sep: daily 8.30am-6.30pm; Oct-Mar: daily 8.30am-5.30pm.* 🕐 *Closed 1 Jan.*
☎ *03 22 80 03 41.*

The harmonious building was begun in 1220 and completed 68 years later, an achievement made possible by its architect, Robert de Luzarches, who had all the stonework cut to its finished dimensions before it left the quarry, then simply assembled on site.

The cathedral is in Gothic Lanceolate style, with three-storey elevations including a blind triforium in nave and transept. The wonderfully elegant nave is the highest in France (42.5m – 140ft).

At an early date problems arose through water from the Somme penetrating the foundations; movement occurred along the length of the building, evidence of which can be seen in cracks in the nave near the transept. The weight of the vaults aggravated the effect; to remedy it, in the 16C a brace of Toledo steel was inserted into the triforium, heated red-hot, and allowed to cool. For four centuries it has served its purpose admirably. The building was further strengthened by increasing the number of buttresses at the east end and by adding side chapels in the form of double aisles to the nave in order to spread the downward forces as widely as possible.

The famous slender steeple rising above the crossing was built by the master carpenter Cardon in two years (1528-29).

Much of the cathedral's decoration is of very high quality indeed: the sculpture of the west front (including the noble figure of Christ known as the "Beau Dieu"), and the rose windows of the main façade, including the 16C Sea Window (rose de la Mer), of the north transept – the 14C Window of the Winds (rose des Vents), and of the south transept – the 15C Window of Heaven (rose du Ciel). Inside, the wrought-iron choir screen dates from the 18C and the oak choir stalls from the beginning of the 16C. The third chapel of the north aisle houses a remarkable Romanesque Crucifixion probably influenced by oriental art. Christ's feet are nailed to the Cross separately; clad in a long robe, He wears His royal crown in glory. The figure was carved before the arrival in Paris of the relics of the Passion (including the Crown of Thorns) purchased by St Louis; it thus pre-dates Western awareness of the medical realities of Christ's agony.

Hortillonnages★

🕐 *Guided tours* 🚣 *(50min) Apr to end Oct: by boat, 2pm onwards. Maison des hortillonnages, 54, bd Beauvillé.* ☞ *5€ (children 2.50€).* ☎*03 22 92 12 18.*

The small allotments known as **aires** which stretch over an area of 300ha – 749 acres amid a network of canals or **rieux** fed by the many arms of the Somme, have been worked since the Middle Ages by market gardeners or *hortillons*. They supplied the local population with fruit and vegetables. At present, fruit trees and flowers are tending to replace vegetables and the gardeners' sheds are becoming weekend holiday homes.

Central doorway, Cathedral Notre-Dame

S. Sauvignier/ MICHELIN

▶▶ **Musée de Picardie**★★ – archeology, painting ♿ ⏰ *Tue-Sun 10am-12.30pm, 2-6pm.* ⏰ *Closed Mon,1 Jan, 1 and 8 May, 14 Jul, 11 Nov, 25 Dec.* ⊶ *4€, no charge 1st Sunday in the month.* ☏*03 22 97 14 00.* **Hôtel de Berny**★.

Château d'**ANCY-LE-FRANC**★★

MICHELIN MAP 319

GREEN GUIDE BURGUNDY JURA

Designed by Sebastian Serlio, one of the Italian architects attracted to the French court in 1541 by François I, this **château** was begun in 1546 and completed 50 years later for Antoine III of Clermont-Tonnerre. It marks the end of the early, Italian-influenced French Renaissance in all its brilliance.

Visit

⏰ *Guided tours* ➶ *(1hr) Apr to mid-Nov: daily except Mon 10.30am, 11.30am, 2pm, 3pm and 4pm (Apr-Sep: a tour at 5pm also).* ⏰ *Closed Nov to Easter.* ⊶ *7€ (children under 11 years: 4€).* ☏ *03 86 75 14 63. www.chateau-ancy.com.*

The exterior gives an impression of great order and dignity, combining a symmetry worthy of Bramante with a masterly handling of spaces and surfaces according to the rules of the Golden Section. The treatment of the courtyard is particularly subtle, with its deeply-sunken twin pilasters topped by Corinthian capitals and separating scalloped niches.

The interior is equally fine. The Judith Room has a coffered ceiling painted by a pupil of Primaticcio, Cornelius van Haarlem. There are ancient bindings in the library, secret cabinets from Italy, and a monochrome study of musculature in dell'Abbate's *Battle of Pharsalus* and, in the Salon des Arts, oval medallions by Primaticcio representing the Liberal Arts.

Les **ANDELYS**★★

POPULATION 8 455

MICHELIN MAP 304

GREEN GUIDE NORMANDY

The site of Les Andelys commands the Seine valley and the old highway linking Paris and Rouen. Its exceptional strategic value was appreciated by Richard the Lionheart, son of Henry II Plantagenet and Eleanor of Aquitaine, Duke of Normandy as well as King of England. In 1196 he decided to break the agreement concluded at Louviers with the king of France, and construct the mightiest fortress of the age to protect his possessions from French ambition. Within the year, so legend has it, the great work was complete, and Richard was able to cry aloud "See my fine yearling!"

Visit

Château Gaillard★★

⏰ *Mid-Mar to mid-Nov: Wed-Mon 10am-1pm, 2-6pm. Last admission 1hr before closing.* ⏰ *Closed Tue, 1 May.* ⊶ *3€.* ☏ *02 32 54 04 16.*

The stronghold must certainly have been an impressive sight; with its 17 towers, eight-foot-thick walls, its cliff-top site and with three successive rings of defences and moats protecting its keep, it was virtually impregnable. Impregnable that is, save by means of a ruse, and it was in this way that King Philippe Auguste succeeded in taking it in 1274 after a siege of eight months. This victory enabled him to incorporate Normandy, Maine, Anjou and Touraine into the French kingdom. In 1419, four years after Agincourt, Henry V of England took it back. La Hire, companion to Joan of Arc, won it again for France 10 years later, only to lose it to Henry once more. It finally passed into French possession under Charles VII in 1449.

Principat d'**ANDORRA**★★

Principality of ANDORRA

POPULATION 62 400

MICHELIN MAP 343 G-H-I 9-10

GREEN GUIDE LANGUEDOC ROUSSILLON TARN GORGES

Andorra, which has a total area of 464km2/179sq mi (about one and a third times the area of the Isle of Wight), lies at the heart of the Pyrenees; the high plateaux and tributary valleys are served by narrow mountain tracks. It is divided into seven "parishes" or administrative units. ▯ *R. Dr-Vilanova, Andorra La Vella, ☎ 82 02 14. Office du tourisme de la principauté d'Andorre, av. de l'Opéra, 75001 Paris, ☎ 01 42 61 50 55. 3615 Andorra. www.tourisme-andorre.net.*

A Bit of History

Until 1993, Andorra was a co-principality under a regime of dual allegiance, a legacy from the medieval feudal system. Under such a contract, two neighbouring lords (until 1993 the Bishop of Urgell and the President of the French Republic) would define the limits of their respective rights and authority over a territory that they held in common fief. Andorra is now a member of the UN.

The development of hydro-electric power and tourism, with the construction of special holiday villages ("urbanitzacio") and the influx of foreign visitors, is having a profound impact on the Andorran economy and its traditional way of life, although tobacco remains the main crop in the valley of Sant Juliá de Lòria and the Catalan *aplech* (pilgrimage) is a popular event.

Sights

Andorra la Vella

The capital of the Andorran valleys, huddled on a terrace above the Gran Valira valley, is a bustling commercial town. Once away from the busy main axis, however, the heart of Andorra la Vella has kept its peaceful old streets and the **Casa de la Vall** (⊙ *Jun-Oct: Sat-Thu 9.15am-1pm, 3pm-7pm; Fri and public holidays 10am-2pm; rest of the year: daily except Sun and public holidays 9.15am-1pm, 3pm-5pm; ⏴ call in advance for guided tour, 30min; ⊙ closed 1 and 6 Jan, 14 Mar, 1 May, 24 Jun, 8 Sep, 21, 25 and 26 Dec; no charge*) which is both Andorra's Parliament building and its Law Courts. The General Council holds session here.

To the east Andorra-la-Vella merges with the lively town of Escales above which rises **Caldea**, a large water-sports complex famous for its futuristic architecture (Turkish baths, bubble beds, hot marble, etc).

Estany d'Engolasters (Lake Engolasters)

On the Engolasters plateau, where there are pastures as well as sports grounds used by the residents of Andorra la Vella, the outstanding landmark is the lovely Romanesque bell-tower of **San Miguel.**

At the end of the road, cross the crest under the pine trees and walk downhill to the dam, which has raised the level of the lake (alt 1 616m – 5 272ft) by 10m – 33ft. The waters of the lake reflect the dark forest which lines its shores.

Santuari de Meritxell (Meritxell Sanctuary)

Beyond Encamp, the road negotiates a defile before reaching the hamlet of **Les Bons**, which occupies a spectacular sitea perched on a rocky spur beneath the ruins of a defensive castle and the chapel of Sant Roma. Nearby stands the chapel of **Notre-Dame-de-Meritxell**, rebuilt in 1976, which is the national shrine.

Canillo

The church built right against the rock has the tallest bell-tower in Andorra (27m – 88ft). Nearby is a white charnel-house; such buildings are a common sight in countries of Iberian culture.

Sant Joan de Caselles

⊙ *Guided tours ⏴ Jul-Aug: 10am-1pm, 4pm-7pm; rest of the year: by appointment, AINA ☎ (00-376) 85 14 34.*

This church, with its three-storeyed bell-tower, is a particularly fine example of Romanesque Andorran architecture. The altarpiece (1525) behind the attractive wrought-iron parclose screen is the work of the Master of Canillo and depicts the Life of St John and his apocalyptic visions. During the last restoration (in 1963) a Romanesque **Crucifixion**★ was found; the stucco fragments of the Christ figure were fixed back onto the wall in its original setting.

Port d'Envalira★★

The road may be closed owing to heavy snowfall but is usually reopened within 24 hours. Alt 2 407m – 7 823ft. A good road runs through this pass which is the highest in the Pyrenees and marks the watershed between the Mediterranean (Valira) and the Atlantic (Ariège). There is a **panorama** taking in the Andorra mountains.

Pas de la Casa

Alt 2 091m – 6 861ft. This frontier village, the highest in Andorra, has become a major ski resort.

Ordino

Leave the car in the upper village in the square near the church. Downhill from the church this village has a network of picturesque streets well worth exploring. The church has attractive wrought-iron gates; these are a common feature in churches near the old Catalan forges. Near the church is another example of this craft, in the erstwhile residence of a blacksmith, "Don Guillem's" house, which boasts a splendid wrought-iron balcony (18m – 59ft long).

ANGERS★★★

POPULATION 206 276

MICHELIN MAPS 317 E-F-G 4

GREEN GUIDE CHÂTEAUX OF THE LOIRE

The Rivers Loir, Sarthe, Mayenne and Oudon flow through a tranquil bocage landscape before joining together to form the Maine just above Angers, itself only 8km – 5 miles upstream from the Loire. Two geological systems meet here; the sedimentary rocks of the Paris basin to the east and the schists of the Armorican Massif to the west, the latter quarried since the 12C at nearby Trélazé.

▸ **Orient Yourself**: Angers, which is listed as a "Town of Art and HIstory," offers discovery tours (2hr). Information at the tourist office or on www.vpah.culture.fr. ▯ *7 pl. du Président-Kennedy, 49051 Angers,* ☎ *02 41 23 50 00. www.angers-tourisme.com.* Find a variety of shops and cafés in the Place du Ralliement and along the Rue d'Alsace and the Rue St. Julien. Angers also has many public parks and gardens: Jardin des Plantes, Jardin du Mail (bandstand), Jardin Médiéval (at the foot of the castle), French-style gardens in the moat and Parcs de l'étang St-Nicolas on the outskirts of town *(usually open from 8am to 8pm in summer and from 8am to 5pm in winter).*

⊚ **Don't Miss**: Tenture de l'Apocalypse, a 14C tapestry depicting the Apocalypse of St. John.

⊙ **Organizing Your Time:** After visiting the Château (2hr) allow at least half a day to walk through the steets of the Old Town.

▣ **Parking**: Parking and tourist information available on the southeast side of the château (Esplanade du Port-Ligny).

A Bit of History

On 9 June 1129, Geoffrey Plantagenet, stepson of Fulk Nerra, married William the Conqueror's granddaughter, the proud Mathilda, whose inheritance of both Normandy and England made her the most desirable of brides. Twenty-three years later an equally significant marriage took place, that of Henry II, Geoffrey's son, to Eleanor of Aquitaine, the divorced wife of Louis VII. Two months later Henry became King of England, thereby extending the frontiers of the Angevin state to Scotland in the north and the Basque country in the south. By contrast, the Capetian kingdom to the east cut a sorry figure, its capital, Paris, seeming little more than an overgrown village in comparison with Angers.

Angers Address Book

PRACTICAL INFORMATION

TOURISM OFFICE

7 Pl. du Président Kennedy, 49100 ANGERS, ☎ 02 41 23 50 10. www.angers-tourisme.com.

TOURS

Discovery tours of Angers, emphasizing art and history (2hr). For information and reservations, contact the tourist office *(above)*.

For coin ranges, see the Legend at the back of the guide

EATING OUT

◉◉ **La Ferme** – *2 pl. Freppel* – ☎ *02 41 87 09 90* – 🕓 *closed 20 Jul-12 Aug, Sun evening and Wed – reservations required.* A well-known restaurant near the cathedral, where you can enjoy traditional local cooking in a simple setting. The terrace is one of the nicest in town.

◉◉ **Provence Caffé** – *9 pl. du Ralliement* – ☎ *02 41 87 44 15* – 🕓 *closed 3 Jan, 1 Aug-24 Aug, 19 Dec, Sun and Mon – reservations required.* This popular restaurant next to the Hôtel St-Julien is often full both at lunchtime and in the evenings. The patron is from the south of France and the menu reflects this, with its Mediterranean flavours. The dining room has a Provençal atmosphere too. Carefully prepared cuisine at moderate prices.

◉◉ **Le Relais** – *9 r. de la Gare* – ☎ *02 41 88 42 51* – *le.relais@libertysurf.fr* – 🕓 *closed 22 Aug-13 Sep, 24 Dec-4 Jan, Sun and Mon.* The woodwork and the murals in this charming tavern recall the vineyard and the harvest. The traditional cooking is satisfying and simple, at affordable prices.

WHERE TO STAY

◉ **Hôtel Mail** – *8 r. des Ursules* – ☎ *02 41 25 05 25* – *hoteldumailangers@yahoo.fr* - 🅿 – *26 rooms* – 🖙 *7€.* The thick walls of this former Ursuline convent in a peaceful street prevent the noise from the nearby town centre from penetrating. The fairly spacious rooms have a personal touch and are under the sloping roof on the top floor.

◉ **Chambre d'hôte Le Grand Talon** – *3 rte des Chapelles* – *49800 Andard* – *11km/6.8mi E of Angers on N 147 (towards Saumur) then D 113* – ☎ *02 41 80 42 85* – 🖙 *3 rooms.* This elegant 18C house just outside Angers, decked out with leafy vines of Virginia creeper, is a haven of peace. You can picnic in the park, or relax in the lovely square courtyard. The rooms are pretty and the owners extend a very warm welcome.

◉◉ **Le Progrès** – *26 r. Denis-Papin* – ☎ *02 41 88 10 14* – 🕓 *closed 7-15 Aug, 24 Dec-1 Jan. 41 rooms* – 🖙 *6.10€.* Conveniently located near the train station, this is a friendly place with modern, well-lit and practical rooms. Before setting out to tour the château, enjoy your coffee in the breakfast room, with its decor inspired by the bright colours of Provence.

◉ **Hôtel Cavier** – *La Croix-Cadeau* – *49240 Avrillé* – *8km/5mi NW of Angers on N 162* – ☎ *02 41 42 30 45* – *lecavier@lacroixcadeau.fr* - 🅿 – *43 rooms* – 🖙 *7.50€.* The sails of this 18C windmill still turn! Inside its old stone walls is the dining room, near the original machinery. Modern bedrooms in a recent wing. Terrace next to the outdoor pool.

ON THE TOWN

L'Écubier – *20 r. Château-Gontier* – ☎ *02 41 88 15 26* – 🕓 *Mon-Sat 6pm-2am.* In this small wine bar, the wood panelling is reminiscent of a ship's hold, the atmosphere is friendly and the conversation absorbing. Those who enjoy Loire wines can come and sample Muscadet, red Anjou, St-Nicolas-de-Bourgueil, or a glass of mead. Theatre and gallery (painting and sculpture).

Pub Saint-Aubin – *71 r. St-Aubin* – ☎ *02 41 87 42 30* – 🕓 *daily 9am-1am* - 🕓 *closed 1 Jan and 25 Dec.* This brasserie seems to be transforming itself into a high-class restaurant. Anjou wines hold pride of place, for the owner is the son of a wine-grower. The pub is popular with local business people.

SHOWTIME

Nouveau Théâtre d'Angers – *12 pl. Imbach* – ☎ *02 41 88 99 22* – *www.nta-angers.fr* – 🕓 *box office Mon-Sat 11am-7pm.* This national drama centre manages several venues for the performing arts: the Beaurepaire Theatre (theatre, music and dance) and the Atelier Jean Dasté (theatre).

SIT BACK AND RELAX

Les Délices de la Tour – *Chocolats Benoît* – *1 r. des Lices* – ☎ *02 41 88 94 52* – *benoit-chocolats@worldonline.fr* – 🕓 *Mon-Sat 9.15am-12.30pm, 2-7.30pm.* Since 1975, this shop has been a haven for those who love fine chocolate. Anne-Françoise Benoît, an extraordinary chocophile, has created a bright and fragrant environment for selling more than 70 flavours of chocolate, sweet and bitter, classic and inventive. Her concoctions include some surprising ingredients such as fennel, tea and ginger.

Maison du vin de l'Anjou – *5 bis pl. Kennedy* – ☎ *02 41 88 81 13* - *www. interloire.com* – 🕓 *May-Sept: Tue-Sun*

9am-1pm, 3-6.30pm; Oct-Apr Dec: Tue-Sat. 9am-1pm, 3-6.30pm - ○ closed Jan-Feb and public holidays. In the centre of town, near the château, this wine shop offers a good selection of Anjou and Saumur wines, which you can taste.

OUTDOOR LEISURE ACTIVITIES

Parc de loisirs du Lac de Maine – This 200ha/494-acre park offers various facilities such as swimming, tennis, windsurfing, canoeing, kite-flying etc.

Maison de la Nature et de l'Environnement – This nature information centre organises various activities including environment-awareness courses.

Public Gardens and Parks – They are usually open from 8am to 8pm in summer and from 8am to 5.30pm in winter: Jardin des Plantes, Jardin du Mail (bandstand), Jardin Médiéval (at the foot of the castle), French-style gardens in the moat and Parcs de l'étang St-Nicolas on the outskirts of town. ☎ 02 41 22 53 26.

Boat Trips – Various possibilities including a combined tourist-train ride and mini boat trip on the River Maine and a dinner/cruise by candlelight. *Batellerie promenade l'Union, cale de la Savatte, 49100 Angers,* ☎ *02 41 42 12 12.*

Golf Club d'Angers – *Moulin de Pistrait - 49320 St-Jean-des-Mauverts* ☎ *02 41 91 96 56 - golf.angers@infonie.fr -* ○ *daily 9am-7pm.* 18 holes, par 70.

In 1203, with the 81-year-old Eleanor living in retirement at Fontevraud, King Philippe Auguste succeeded in incorporating Anjou into the French kingdom, together with Normandy, Maine, Touraine and Poitou, all territories of John Lackland (the Plantagenets, contrary to feudal law, had effectively allowed these lands to become English possessions). In 1471, King **René** let Anjou pass into the hands of Louis XI.

Angevin (or Plantagenet) Vaulting – This type of vault marks the transition from Romanesque to Gothic in a particularly elegant way. Curved vaults (with the central keystone some 3m – 10ft higher than that of the supporting arches) probably originated in the late-11C domes of Eleanor of Aquitaine's homeland, with their quadripartite arches and slender ribs. The characteristic Angevin vault is identifiable by the middle of the 12C, notably in the vaulting of the nave of the cathedral, **Cathédrale St-Maurice★★**, with its transverse arches with double roll mouldings by Normand le Doué. By the end of the century the vaulting has become lighter; the number of ribs increases, springing from slender columns, as in the choir and transepts of St Maurice. At the beginning of the 13C it reaches its peak of development: lateral support is dispensed with; the structure dissolves into a graceful web of liernes, as in the hospital ward of the former St John's Hospital, resting on a small number of slim columns, as in the early-13C ceiling of the choir (**chœur★★**) of the church, **Église St-Serge★** (○ *Daily except certain Sun afternoons;* ☎ *02 41 43 66 76).*

Sights

Château★★★

○ *Guided tours* ⬥ *(1hr) May to early Sep: daily 9.30am-6.30pm; early Sep to end Apr: daily 10am-5.30pm. Last admission 45min before closing.* ○ *Closed 1 Jan, 1 May, 1 and 11 Nov, 25 Dec.* ⬥ *5.50€ (under 17 years: no charge), no charge 1st Sunday in the month from Oct to Mar.* ☎ *02 41 87 43 47. www.monum.fr.*

It was rebuilt by Louis IX from 1228 to 1238 on the surviving Roman foundations; this splendid example of medieval military architecture was intended to counter any threat arising from the territorial ambitions of the Dukes of Brittany. The site's natural potential for defence is particularly evident where the substantial walls overlook the river; with their 17 towers in alternating courses of dark schist and white freestone they must indeed have constituted a formidable deterrent. The moats were dug in 1485 by Louis XI.

In the reign of Henri III during the Wars of Religion, the towers were reduced in height by Philibert Delorme (1562), the former Abbot of St-Serge, who also formed terraces to give the defenders a clear field of fire.

Tenture de l'Apocalypse★★★

375-80. This wonderful tapestry, originally 168m – 550ft long and 5m – 16ft high, the oldest and most important to have been preserved. According to Jean Lurçat 92-1966) who discovered it in 1938 and whose artistic career was inspired by it, it ne of the greatest works of Western art". The 76 extant scenes are closely based e Apocalypse of St John, and are impressive in their masterly scale, composition sign. Commissioned by the Duke of Anjou Louis I, this superb tapestry was

Château d'Angers

executed by the master weaver **Nicolas Bataille,** most likely in Robert Poinçon's Parisian workshop after cartoons by Hennequin of Bruges; it draws its inspiration from the illuminations of a manuscript belonging to King Charles V.

Tenture de la Passion et Tapisseries mille-fleurs★★

Located in the Governor's Lodging, the fine collection of Flemish tapestries includes the 16C *Lady at the Organ* and *Penthesilea* and above all the three-part *Passion* of the late 15C with its rich colours and graceful angels carrying the instruments of the Passion.

Hôpital St-Jean★

Founded in 1174 and in use for 680 years, the former hospital now houses the **Musée Jean-Lurçat** (&. ◔ *Jun-Sep: daily 10am-7pm ; Oct-Jun: daily except Mon 10am-noon, 2-6pm;* ◔ *closed 1 Jan, 1 May, 14 Jul, 1 and 11 Nov, 25 Dec;* ◉ *4€;* ☎ *02 41 05 38 37 or 02 41 05 38 38; www.angers.fr)* In the hospital ward with its Angevin vaulting is Lurçat's series of tapestries known as **Le Chant du Monde**★★ (The Song of the World), 10 huge compositions symbolising the contradictions of the modern world. Lurçat's achievement marked the revival of the art of tapestry.

◔◔ **Maison d'Adam**★; **Galerie David d'Angers**★ – sculpture ◔ *Jun-Sep: daily 10am-7pm (Fri 9pm); Oct-May: daily except Mon 10am-noon, 2-6pm.* ◔ *Closed 1 Jan, 1 May, 14 Jul, 1 and 11 Nov, 25 Dec.* ◉ *4€.* ☎ *02 41 87 21 03.* **Romanesque arcade**★★ (in the Prefecture) – **Hôtel Pincé**★ – Musée Turpin de Crissé: archeology, Oriental art ◔ *as for the Galerie David-d'Angers.* ◉ *2 €.* ☎ *02 41 18 24 40.* **La Doutre district**★ – Château Pignerolles musée européen de la Communication★.

Excursions

Château de Serrant

◔ *Guided tours* 👁 *(1hr) Jul-Aug: daily 10am-5.15pm; Apr-Jun and Sep to mid-Nov: daily except Mon and Tue 10am-noon, 2-5.15pm.* ◉ *9€.* ☎ *02 41 39 13 01.*
👁 *See illustration in Introduction: Art – Architecture – 18km – 11mi southwest of Angers.*
Although built over a period of three centuries (16C to 18C), this elegant moa mansion has great unity of style. Its massive round towers and the contrast betw the dark schist and the white tufa give it considerable character.

Apartments

The furnishings are splendid. Sumptuous Flemish tapestries hang in the dining room. Of particular note are the great Renaissance staircase, the coffered ceilings on the first floor, the library with its 10 000 volumes and the state rooms where both Louis XIV and Napoleon Bonaparte were received. There are many works of art: Flemish and Brussels tapestries, a very fine Italian cabinet, and a bust of Empress Marie-Louise by Canova.

ANGOULÊME★★

POPULATION 42 876

MICHELIN MAP 324 K-L-M 5-6

GREEN GUIDE ATLANTIC COAST

From its lofty promontory Angoulême's stately upper town (**ville haute**★★) overlooks the Anguienne and Charente 70m – 230ft below. The character of the lower town is quite different, busy with paper-making and engineering.

▸ **Orient Yourself:** Angoulême, which is listed as a "Town of Art and HIstory," offers discovery tours. Information available from the Heritage Dept. ☎ 05 45 38 70 79 or www.vpah.culture.fr.

A Bit of History

The vain and darkly witty Guez de Balzac (1597-1654), though famous as one of the original members of the Académie française and as a champion of literary French, eventually buried himself away in his native town. Another Balzac, Honoré (1799-1850), added to the city's literary renown when he became a citizen by adoption.

Charles Augustin de Coulomb, born here in 1736, owes his reputation to his having perfected the torsion balance and to his "Law" of 1785 confirming Newton's law of gravitation.

In 1806 a daring exploit was carried out on the city's northern ramparts (**remparts**); the 77-year-old General Resnier launched himself into the void in a flying-machine of his own invention. The general suffered a broken leg, and a plan for the invasion of England by this method was shelved.

Visit

Cathédrale St-Pierre★

Extensively destroyed by the Calvinists, the cathedral was restored in 1634 and again from 1866 onwards by Abadie.

The early-12C statuary of the west front (**façade**★★) is, happily, mostly intact; more elaborate than the other façades typical of the region around Angoulême, its themes include the Ascension (treated as at Cahors) and the Last Judgement.

Particularly noteworthy among the 70 statues and low-reliefs are the superb Christ in Majesty surrounded by the Evangelists, the medallions of saints and a battle scene inspired by the *Song of Roland* (lintel of the first doorway to the right).

◖◗ Centre National de la Bande Dessinée et de l'Image – strip-cartoon centre ♿ ◷ *Jul-Aug: Mon-Fri 10am-7pm, Sat-Sun 2-7pm; rest of the year: daily except Mon 10am-6pm, Sat-Sun 2-6pm.* ◷ *Closed 1 Jan, 1 May, 25 Dec.* ◈ *5€ (children 7-18 years: 2.50€).* ☎ *05 45 38 65 65.*

ANNECY★★★

POPULATION 49 644

MAP P 9 – MICHELIN MAP 328 J-K 5

GREEN GUIDE FRENCH ALPS

Annecy's setting is a perfect composition of lakes and mountains, the meeting point of the Bauges massif to the south and the gentler hilly country stretching northwards towards Geneva. Originally a settlement of lake-dwellers, then a Gallo-Roman township, the city shifted its site in the Middle Ages from Annecy-le-Vieux to the lower slopes of the Semnoz, finally settling under the walls of its castle by the Thiou, whose rapid waters once supplied the motive power for its many mills.

🖫 *Centre Bonlieu, 1 r. J.-Jaurès, 74000 Annecy,* ☏ *04 50 45 00 33. www.lac-annecy.com.*

▶ **Orient Yourself:** Annecy, a "Town of Art and HIstory," offers discovery tours (2hr). 5.30€. Information at the tourist office or on www.vpah.culture.fr.

A Bit of History

In the 16C Annecy became the regional capital, displacing Geneva, abandoned by its overlords who had tired of the incessant squabbling between Calvinist burghers and diehard Catholics. In the 17C it was the home of **St Francis of Sales**, provost of the cathedral and bitter opponent of Calvinism which had spread throughout the Chablais area. In 1604 he met St Jeanne de Chantal, widow of Rabutin Chantal, grandmother of Mme de Sévigné, and founder of the Order of the Visitation at Annecy. In what is now the St Francis of Sales Library (Bibliothèque Salésienne) he wrote his *Introduction to a Devout Life*. In 1608, together with Antoine Favre, he founded the *Académie florimontaine*, 30 years before the *Académie française*.

Sights

Le vieil Annecy★★

The picturesque old town lies on the banks of the Thiou as it runs out from the lake; from its bridges can be seen the highly-folded skyline of Mont Veyrier as well as the **Palais de l'Isle**★ (a former prison which nowadays houses the **musée de l'histoire d'Annecy**– 🕓 *as for the château-museum–*👌 *see below;* 👓 *3.20€, children under 12 years: no charge; no charge 1st Sun in the month.* ☏ *04 50 33 87 30*– presenting the town's history) rising out of the bed of the stream like the prow of a ship. **Rue Ste-Claire**★ with its arcades and gabled houses has kept its 17C appearance.

It was in the courtyard of the Bishops' Palace on a spring morning in 1728 that a meeting took place between Jean-Jacques Rousseau and Mme de Warens.

Overlooking the old town, the **château**★ (🕓 *Jun-Sep: daily 10.30am-6pm; Oct-May: daily except Tue 10am-noon, 2-5pm; last admission 45min before closing;* 🕓 *closed 1 Jan, Easter Sun and Mon, 1 May, 1 and 11 Nov, 25 Dec;* 👓 *4.70€, children under 12 years: no charge; no charge 1st Sun in the month from Oct-May;* ☏ *04 50 33 87 30*), the former residence of the lords of Geneva, retains its defensive character. It houses a museum and an observatory.

Le lac★★★

🕓 *Apr to end Oct: several types of boat trips with commentaries (1hr).* 👓 *9.80€. May to mid-Sep: boats stopping at various places (2hr).* 👓 *12.10€. Lunch trip and dinner-dance on board the MS Libellule. Times and reservations: Compagnie des Bateaux du lac d'Annecy,* ☏ *04 50 51 08 40. www.annecy-croisieres.com.*

Fine vista from the **Avenue d'Albigny**. Overlooked by the Semnoz, this lovely lake in its glaciated valley site is know as the "Pearl of the Alps".

◐◐**Jardins de l'Europe**★ – arboretum; **Musée de la Cloche**★ – 14C to 19C bells – at Sevrier *5km – 3mi south.*

Excursions

Talloires★★

This little resort has a most charming **setting**★★★ overlooking the narrows dividing the Grand Lac to the north from the Petit Lac to the south. From the lakeside there are fine views of the Entrevernes Mountain and, nearer at hand, the wooded promontory of the Château de Duingt.

Palais de l'Isle

ARCACHON★★

POPULATION 11 770

MICHELIN MAP 335 D 6-7

GREEN GUIDE ATLANTIC COAST

The site of Arcachon was no more than a pinewood when, in 1852, the Pereire brothers, who had just bought up the loss-making railway line from Bordeaux to La Teste, had the inspired idea of extending it further seawards. This gave the green light to a building boom and Arcachon was born. It became popular as a winter resort as well as a place for summer holidays.

A Bit of History

The town comprises four distinct quarters: a winter resort (**ville d'hiver**★), with villas in varied architectural styles sheltering among the pines; a summer resort (**ville d'été**), boasting a fine seafront and the attractive **Boulevard de la Mer**★; and the fashionable autumn and spring districts (**ville d'automne et ville de printemps**) with opulent houses situated near Pereire park.

Sights

Bassin★ (Bay)

Boat trip in a pinasse-Thiers landing stage. ⏱ All year round: from Arcachon to Cap Ferret. 🚢 9.50€; round trip around the Île aux Oiseaux 13€. High season: 🚢 guided tour of the oyster beds 10.50€, visit to the Banc d'Arguin reserve 15€, tour around the coast 13.50€. Departure from: Thiers and Eyrac landing stages (Arcachon), Bélisaire landing stage (to Cap-Ferret), Moulleau landing stage, Andernos landing stage. The boatmen are professional seafarers working as fishermen and oyster farmers. Their boats are available to take you for a trip round the Île aux Oiseaux, to take you line or game fishing, to take you for a trip round the oyster beds or to Cap-Ferret or Andernos, as you wish. Pinasses for hire (boats used traditionally by the oyster farmers). ☎ 05 57 72 28 28.

Bordered by the resorts of Arcachon, Andernos and the wooded dunes of the Cap Ferret peninsula, this vast bay, with Bird Island (Île aux Oiseaux) at its centre, extends over an area of 25 000ha – nearly 100sq miles, four-fifths of which is exposed at low tide. With its great stretches of oyster beds totalling 1 800ha – 4 500 acres in all, Arcachon is one of the main oyster-farming areas.

Dune du Pilat★★ *7.5km – 4.5mi south.*

This dune, the highest (114m – 374ft) and longest (2 800m – over 3 000yds) in Europe, is still in the process of formation. On its landward side it drops almost sheer to the pine woodland.

The top of the dune offers the best of all views over the Silver Coast **(Côte d'Argent)**. This long, straight shore with its magnificent sandy beaches and splendid Atlantic rollers stretches 230km – 140 miles from the mouth of the Gironde to the Nivelle. Apart from the harbours at Arcachon and Capbreton, it affords little hospitality to sailors. Every year some 15 cubic metres of sand per linear metre of coastline are deposited by the ocean, building up dunes which in places rival the cliffs of Normandy in height and which, in 1774, swallowed up the church at Soulac. The problem they present was tackled by Bremontier (1738-1809), a Bordeaux engineer, who succeeded in checking the invading dunes on a front of 5km – 3 miles. Their advance was finally stopped during the period of the Restoration (1815-48). The dunes have been responsible for the formation of lakes some distance from the coast but linked to it by channels (courants). The **panorama**★★ of the ocean and the local pine forest reveals the romantic aspect of the region, especially at dusk.

ARC-ET-SENANS★★

POPULATION 1 277

MICHELIN MAP 321 E 4

GREEN GUIDE BURGUNDY JURA

Erected 1775-80, the Classical buildings of the former royal salt-works are an extraordinary essay in utopian town planning of the early Industrial Age.

Visit

Saline Royale★★

Only the cross-axis and half the first ring of buildings envisaged by the architect **Claude-Nicolas Ledoux** (1736-1806) were actually completed; what we see today is however enough to evoke the idea of an ideal 18C city. His plan was ambitious; a whole town laid out in concentric circles with the Director's Residence at the centre, flanked by storehouses (Bâtiments des sels), offices and workshops, and extending out to include a church, a market, public baths and recreational facilities. Ledoux's vision makes him one of the forerunners of modern architecture and urban design. The quality of the architecture is striking; highly original but dignified, it has a pervasive symbolism; not only is there the use of the Director's Residence as a focal point, but decorative elements too are exploited, like rock formations or the petrified overflow from great urns representing the salt-works' basic resource. Unity of style, use of materials, the arrangement of columns and pediments, all reveal the influence of the 16C Italian architect **Palladio**.

Gorges de l'ARDÈCHE★★★

ARDÈCHE GORGES

MICHELIN MAP 331 I-J 7-8

GREEN GUIDE PROVENCE

The Ardèche rises 1 467m – 4 813ft up in the Mazan Massif to the north of the Col de la Chavade and flows 119km – 67 miles before joining the Rhône. The river is notorious for its spring floods and sudden spates which are capable of increasing its flow by a factor of 3 000 (the spate of 22 September 1890 brought down 28 bridges).

A Bit of History

Ardèche plateau – Consisting of the Gras uplands to the north and the Orgnac uplands to the south, the Ardèche plateau contrasts strongly with the high valley and orchard country between Pont-de-Labeaume and Vallon. Its thick beds of much-fissured grey limestone were built up from the sediments deposited in the seas of the Secondary Era. Its surface was exposed and uplifted during the formation of the Alps in Tertiary times and is faulted in places. The vegetation cover consists of scrubby evergreen oaks, box and juniper, and there are jackdaws, shrikes and various birds of prey.

The proximity of the great migration route formed by the Rhône valley meant that prehistoric people came here very early indeed; it may well have been here that the invention of the bow took place, together with the domestication of the dog, the beginnings of agriculture and the making of pottery. The galleries at Orgnac III sheltered auroch-hunters who were probably the contemporaries of Tautavel Man (⌾ *see Les EYZIES-DE-TAYAC)*; at St-Marcel-d'Ardèche there is evidence of the presence of agriculturalists in the warmer times which followed the last Ice Age some 10 000 years ago, and of pastoralists at Vallon-Pont-d'Arc in the Neolithic era. The dolmens and cave-dwellings near St-Remèze date from the Bronze Age.

Visit

Aven d'Orgnac★★★
South bank. ⌾ *See Aven d'ORGNAC.*

Aven de Marzal★
North bank. At the bottom of this deep swallowhole, 130m – 426ft from the surface, the Gallery of Diamonds is made up of glittering crystals of calcite.

Vallon-Pont d'Arc

A museum, **Musée du Monde souterrain**, presents a display of equipment used by the great explorers of these subterranean realms. Nearby, another museum, the **Zoo préhistorique**, featuring reproductions of prehistoric animals, attracts many visitors.

Gorges: From Vallon-Pont-d'Arc to Pont-St-Esprit

47km – 29mi. The meanders of the river mark the course it originally followed on the ancient surface of the plateau before cutting down through the rocks as they were uplifted during the Alpine-building Tertiary period. Great sweeps of vertical cliffs, dramatic meanders cut deep into the limestone, and rapids alternating with calm stretches of water combine to form a splendid object-lesson in the geography of river formation.

Pont-d'Arc★★

Spanning the full width of the river, the arch of this gigantic natural bridge is 34m – 112ft high and 59m – 194ft wide. In geological terms it is a recent phenomenon, caused by the action of the river, which, helped by the presence of fissures and cavities in the limestone, has succeeded in eroding away the base of a meander.

Haute Corniche (Scenic route)★★★

The road links a number of splendid viewpoints. From the Serre de Tourre can be seen the Pas du Mousse meander, where the river has still to cut through the wooded isthmus; the view from the Morsanne Needles (Aiguilles de Morsanne) gives a good idea of the structure of the plateau as it dips down to the south.

Limestone ridges can be viewed from Gournier, while the rock spires of the Cathedral Rock (Rocher de la Cathédrale) lend this natural monument the appearance of a ruined cathedral.

The Templars' Belvedere (Balcon des Templiers) commands a fine prospect of the Templars' Wall (Mur des Templiers), whose high cliffs (220m – 720ft) dominate the spectacular meander far below. On a rocky spur in the valley stand the ruins of a leper hospital built by the Templars.

ARLES★★★

POPULATION 54 309

MICHELIN MAP 340 C 3

GREEN GUIDE PROVENCE

Arles is an important centre of Provençal life, proud of its traditions and famed for both its Roman and its early-medieval heritage. Far from being stuck in the past, Arles is a lively town that ably integrates its traditions with a sense of modernity. It is also France's largest commune covering 77 000ha – 30sq miles.

▶ **Orienting Yourself:** Arles, which is listed as a "Town of Art and HIstory," offers discovery tours (1hr30min). 4€. Information at the tourist office. ☎ 04 90 18 41 20. www.tourisme.ville-arles.fr. As soon as you exit the highway into Arles (coming from Nîmes, Avignon or Aix-en-Provence) you will find yourself on boulevard des Lices, the busy town center which runs along the remains of the ancient ramparts.

 **Don't Miss:** Van Gogh spent a productive period of his career in Arles. Replications of his paintings are displayed throughout the town, outside the various cafes and monuments he depicted.

🕐 **Organizing Your Time:** There are visitor passes available (12€) at the tourist office or any of the monuments and museums (except Museon Arlaten). This may be worth buying if you plan to visit the many historic public buildings, the museums and the Église St-Trophime. Expect to spend a full day if you want to see everything, but don't neglect the many shops and cafés along boulevard des Lices and boulevard Clemenceau.

🅿 **Parking:** Park under the plane trees of boulevard Georges-Clemenceau. It is a mistake to venture into Old Arles' maze of alley-ways by car!

A Bit of History

The Rome of the Gauls – The ancient Celtic-Ligurian town was colonised by the Greeks of Marseille as early as the 6C BC, and went on to play an important role in Roman rule in southern France. Following his victory over the Teutons, Marius used his prisoners to dig a canal linking Arles with the sea (much nearer at the time), thus enabling the city to be supplied readily from Rome. Later, at the end of the Gallic Wars, Caesar established a veterans' colony; the fleet he used to defeat Marseille (49 BC) was also built here. Subsequently Arles became an important sea and river

Arles - Address Book

TOURS AND DISCOUNTS

Tours of the Town – 🔍 Guided tours (1hr30min) 4€. Contact the tourist office for information and hours (🏠 ☎ *04 90 18 41 20. www.tourisme.ville-arles.fr).*

Monuments and Museums – At the tourist office, you can buy a single pass (🎟13.50€) for all sights and museums, except the Museon Arlaten.

Les Alpilles Train – 🖑 *see Les ALPILLES.*

ENTERTAINMENT

The newspaper Le César, available free of charge for tourists at the Tourist Office and other cultural spots, gives listings of shows in the city.

Le Méjan – *Pl. Nina-Berberova -* ☎ *04 90 49 56 78.* Evening and afternoon musicals, jazz concerts, lectures, conferences, and exhibitions in the chapel Saint-Martin-du-Méjan.

SHOPPING

Markets – **Traditional** market every Wed in boulevard Émile-Combes and every Sat in boulevard des Lices and boulevard Clemenceau. **Antique** market first Wed of the month in boulevard des Lices. **Christmas** market the end of November.

Provençal Fabrics – *Les Étoffes de Romane (maison Carcassonne), 10 boulevard des Lices -* ☎ *04 90 93 53 70.*

Patisserie – **De Moro,** *24 rue du Prés.-Wilson (near the Espace Van Gogh) –* 🕐 *closed Sun and public holidays.* ☎ *04 90 93 14 43.* Specializes in delicious almond biscuits.

Provençal Furniture – **Melani Fréderic**, *route d'Eyguères, Pont-de-Crau, 13200 Arles,* ☎ *04 90 49 72 83.* The workshops can be visited in small groups by appointment only.

Fashion and Jewelry – **Christian Lacroix**, *rue de la République* – ☎ *04 90 96 11 16.*

Books – **Librarie Actes Sud** – *Pl. Nina-Berberova, Le Mejan –* ☎ *04 90 49 56 77.* Find the latest publications of this local publishing house. **La Boutique des Passionnés** – *14 r. Réattu (town center, walknig pedestrian zone) -* ☎ *04 90 96 59 93 - www.passion.toros.com -* 🕐 *Mon, 2-7pm, Tues-Sat 9am-7pm, Sun in Dec.* 🕐 *Closed public hoildays.* At once a book and music shop, this is a gold mine for *tauromachie*

and for music from the south.

Crafts – Maison Chave – *14 rd-pt des Arènes –* ☎ *04 90 96 15 22 –* 🕐 *May-Sept: Tue-Sat 9am-7pm; low season 9am-12.30pm, 2-7pm –* 🕐 *Closed Jan.* In this workshop, four craftsmen model and decorate santons, and a wide choice of figures is on sale. Exclusive hand-made santons, using two or three different types of clay, made here for three generations.

Olive Oil – Huiles Jamard – *46 rue des Arènes –* ☎ *04 90 49 70 73 – pjamard@aol.com –* 🕐 *Tue-Sat 11am-12.30pm, 4-6pm –* 🕐 *closed 25 Dec to 2 Jan – prices for bottles of oil range from 6.10€ to 18.29€, according to the variety.* Provençal olive oil, but also varieties from Spain, Greece and Italy, each with its particular flavour. Pierre, the master oil producer and former engineer will allow you to taste the different types of oil, accompanied by anecdotes about the secrets of their manufacture.

EVENTS

Rencontres Internationales de la Photographie – Throughout this international photography festival (*from July to mid-Sept*) there are evenings at the Roman theatre, exhibitions, courses, talks, and activities in the field of photography in various locations throughout the town. *For more information: 10 rond-point des Arènes,* ☎ *04 90 96 76 06 – www.rencontres-arles.com.*

Fête des Gardians – *1 May.* A mass in the Provençal dialect is held in Collégiale Notre-Dame-de-la-Major. This includes the blessing of horses, typical Camargue games, dancing to the sounds of pipes and drums as well as beautiful girls competing for the title of "Queen" of Arles.

Tauromachia – The architectural beauty of the amphitheatre acquires even greater appeal when **bullfights** and Camargue races take place and one can almost breathe a sense of antiquity. As well as shows organized on specific occasions, bullfights also take place during the ferias at Easter (*Easter weekend*), and during the Rice Festival (*second weekend in Sept*) which sees the participation of tauromachy's most illustrious figures. With the arrival of spring come the **Camargue races**, although the most important of these races take place during the **fêtes d'Arles** with **Cocarde d'Or** (*early*

July) and in the finals of the **Trophée des As**, which takes place every two years in October, alternating with Nîmes.

Booking: **Bureau des Arènes** *(to the right of the main entrance),* ☎ 04 90 96 03 70, *www.label-camargue.com).*

Festival Les Suds – *second half of July. www.suds-arles.com.* World music festival. *For coin ranges, see Legend at the back of the guide.*

WHERE TO EAT

🍴**La Charcuterie** – *51 rue des Arènes –* ☎ 04 90 96 56 96 – *restaurant.la-charcuterie@wanadoo.fr –* ⏰ *Closed 1-15 Aug, 23 Dec-6 Jan, Sun and Mon except Jul and weekends in May.* A real reveller from Lyons, the jovial proprietor couldn't have chosen a better spot for this old charcuterie with its marble counters. Pork lovers can treat themselves to a range of carefully chosen products, from Arles sausages to pig's trotters from Lyons.

🍴**Le Criquet** – *21 R. Porte-de-Laure –* ☎ 04 90 96 80 51 – ⏰ *Closed end of Dec to end of Feb and Wed.* Go for the charming dining room with its beams and exposed stonework rather than the terrace in this little restaurant near the amphitheatre. Once you're comfortably seated, savour the young chef's *bourride* (a kind of fish soup) and other specialities.

🍴🍴**Jardin de Manon** – *14 avenue des Alyscamps –* ☎ 04 90 93 38 68 – ⏰ *Closed 4-24 Feb, 21 Oct-10 Nov.* This restaurant, situated just outside the city centre, is aptly named. Its interior courtyard terrace, full of trees and flowers, will appeal to lovers of alfresco dining. There are two dining rooms with wood panelling and the local cooking, which uses seasonal market produce, offers good value for money.

🍴🍴**Lou Calèu** – *27 r. Porte-de-Laure - montée Vauban -* ☎ 04 90 49 71 77 - *contact@lou-caleu.com -* ⏰ *Closed 5 Jan-15 Feb .* A real classic: fresh salads, *taureau* stew, lamb with rosemary. All Arle's delights are at your fingertips. An excellent wine list. The place for the ultimate gourmet.

WHERE TO STAY

🛏 **Le Relais de Poste** – *2 r. Molière -* ☎ 04 90 52 05 76 - *le.relais.de.poste@ wanadoo.fr -* ⏰ *Closed Jan - 15 rooms: -* 🛏 6€. A couple steps from the boulevard des Lices and the espace Van-Gogh, this centrally-based hotel was once the 18C postal relay. The restaurant evokes its era, with beams and frescos. The rooms are simple and warmly decorated with Provençal textiles.

🛏🛏 **Hôtel du Musée** – *11 r. du Grand-Prieuré -* ☎ 04 90 93 88 88 - *contact@ hoteldumusee.com.fr -* ⏰ *Closed Jan - 28 rooms -* 🛏 7€. Facing the Musée Réattu, this is hotel was built in the 17C : a labyrinth of green pathways through intimate courtyards, the rooms are tranquile and warm. An absolutely charming place!

🛏🛏 **Muette** – *15 r. des Suisses -* ☎ 04 90 96 15 39 - ⏰ *Closed for Feb vacation - 18 rooms -* 🛏 6€. A beautiful building (originally from the 15C and 17C) at home in the heart of historic Arles. Visible stone in veritable Provençal rooms guarantee that the walls are soundproof.

🛏🛏🛏 **Hôtel Calendal** – *5 rue Porte-de-Laure -* ☎ 04 90 96 11 89 – *contact@ lecalendal.com – 38 rooms -* 🛏 7€. This hotel has all the stylishness of Provençal interiors with its colourful façade, pretty inner shaded garden and cosy sitting room. Blue and yellow make up the colour scheme of furniture, fabrics and ceramics. Small tearoom.

🛏🛏🛏 **Mireille** – *2 place St-Pierre, Trinquetaille –* ☎ 04 90 93 70 74 – *contact@ hotel-mireille.com –* ⏰ *Closed 4 Nov-14 Mar –* 🅿 *– 34 rooms –* 🛏11€. Dive into the swimming pool in total peace in this hotel situated outside the city centre. Good size rooms with vibrant colours and Provençal furniture. Airy dining room with red and yellow fabrics.

🛏🛏🛏🛏 **Hôtel D'Arlatan** – *26 rue Sauvage, near place du Forum –* ☎ 04 90 93 56 66 – *hotel-arlatan@wanadoo.fr –* ⏰ *closed 5 Jan to 8 Feb –* 🅿 *– 41 rooms* 🛏 *10.50€.* Fall under the spell of this old mansion dating from the 15C, a stone's throw from place du Forum. Admire the underground Roman fragments through the glass floor of the bar and the drawing room. Rooms furnished with antiques and pretty fabrics. Small courtyard planted with trees where breakfast is served in the summer.

ON THE TOWN

Far from being stuck in the past, Arles is a lively town that integrates its traditions with a sense of modernity. Between a bullfight and the International Photography Festival, the craft market and the music programme, set aside a few moments to sit at the sidewalk cafes that Van Gogh so skilfully depicted.

Bar de l'Hôtel Nord Pinus – *place du Forum –* ☎ 04 90 93 44 44 – *www.nord-pinus.com –* ⏰ *daily 10am-1am.* An essential stopping place in Arles, the small bar of the Hotel Nord Pinuas, dating from the 17C has indiscriminately entertained artists, writers, film stars, and bullfighters: Picasso, Jean Cocteau, Yves Montand, Nimeno 2, Ruiz Miguel, Jean Giono. The charm of this place is made of small details such as its boat-shaped lamps, the bullfighting bar, squat armchairs and, in the background, refined flamenco music.

Café Van Gogh – *11 place du Forum –* ☎ 04 90 96 44 56 – ⏰ *low season: daily 9am-midnight; July-Aug 9am-2am.* This café, with its large terrace in place du Forum owes its fame to Vincent Van Gogh who made it the subject of one of his paintings in 1888: "This is a nocturnal painting with no blackness, nothing but beautiful blue and violet and green and, in this setting, the lit square takes on the hue of sulphur yellow and lime. It amuses me enormously to paint in this square at night" (extract from a letter from Van Gogh to his sister Wilhelmina, dated September 1888).

L'Entrevue – 23 Quai Marx-Dormoy – ☎ 04 90 93 37 28 – ⏲ Oct-May: 8.30am-midnight; June-Sept: 8.30-2am. It is a well known fact that Arles is the birthplace of the flourishing Actes Sud publishing house: the publishers of Paul Auster and Nina Berberova are also responsible for the creation of this café-restaurant that is the cultural hub of the ancient Roman capital. On the other side of the square there is a space for concerts, readings, plays, and photography exhibitions.

port. Under Augustus the city prospered, exploiting its pivotal position in the Roman highway system. Later still it became the administrative and political capital of both parts of Gaul, celebrating its status with many fine buildings.

Sights

Théâtre antique★★

⏲ May-Sep: daily 9am-6.30pm; Mar-Apr and Oct: daily 9am-noon, 2-6pm; Nov-Feb: daily 10am-noon, 2-6pm. Last admission 30min before closing. ⏲ Closed 1 jan, 1 May, 1 Nov and 25 Dec. ⚏ 3€. ☎ 04 90 49 36 74.

It is one of the most important Roman theatres, and it dates from the end of the 1C BC. Two fine columns in African breccia and Italian marble still stand elegantly among the ruins. The theatre was quarried for its stone as early as the 5C; in the 9C it was made into a redoubt, subsequently disappearing completely under houses and gardens. It was excavated in the 19C.

Arènes★★

⏲ Jun-Sep: daily 9am-6.30pm (Wed 2pm); May: daily 9am-6.30pm; Mar-Apr and Oct: daily 9am-6pm; Nov-Feb: daily 10am-5pm. Last admission 30min before closing. ⏲ Closed from All Saint's Day (1 Nov) to Easter Mon, second weekend in Sep, 1 Jan, 1 May, 1 Nov, and 25 Dec. ⚏ 5.50€. ☎ 04 90 49 35 97. ▯ Information on guided tours from the tourist office.

With a capacity of 20 000 spectators, this amphitheatre dates from the reign of Vespasian (c AD 75). Its good state of preservation is due to the role it played as a fortress in the 5C and 6C at a time when the Empire was crumbling in the face of the barbarian assault. It was then that its topmost gallery disappeared, if indeed it was ever built. The amphitheatre is of later construction and even larger than its counterpart at Nîmes and illustrates clearly the power of the architecture of Antiquity. Hellenistic influence is apparent in the horizontal entablature of the cornices and in the flat slabs which cover the galleries in place of the usual Roman vaults.

G. Magnin/MICHELIN

Roman Amphitheatre

Cryptoportiques★ (Cryptoporticus)

⊶ *Closed for security reasons.* ☎ *04 90 49 36 74.*

In the basement of a museum, the **Musée d'art chrétien.** These impressive 1C store-rooms enabled the forum above to be built on the level in spite of the sloping site. The sarcophagi in the museum show scenes testifying to the spread of Christianity in the Rhône valley as early as the reign of Constantine (about 350). Those of Imago and of the Hunt are particularly interesting.

Église St-Trophime★

🕐 *As for the Arènes.* 🕐 *Closed 1 Jan, 1 May, 1 Nov and 25 Dec.* ⊸ *3.50€*

The church was rebuilt from 1080 onwards. Its porch **(portail★★)** is one of the master-pieces of late-12C Provençal Romanesque architecture. The arrangement of columns and design of the frieze hark back to Roman work like the municipal arch at Glanum (🜄 *see ST-RÉMY-DE-PROVENCE)* and the 4C sarcophagi at nearby Alyscamps and Trinquetaille. The fact that the stone from which the church is built was taken from the Roman Theatre further strengthens a sense of continuity with the Classical past. The cloisters **(cloître★★)** were built after 1150 and are renowned for their sculpture. Particularly fine are the corner pillars of the north gallery and the capitals, foliated or decorated with Biblical scenes.

Hôtel de Ville

The Classical façade of the Town Hall exemplifies the second phase of the Louis XIV style in architecture. The vestibule on the ground floor has a fine flat vault (**voûte**★ – 1684) supported by 20 columns along the walls. It is the work of Hardouin-Mansart and the details of its construction used to be an object-lesson to journeymen on their way around France. Note particularly the groins, some curved, some out of true, and also the perfect stonework of the arches.

◗◗ **Musée d'Art païen★** – ancient art. **Musée d'Art chrétien★★** – Museon Arlaten – Provençal culture and traditions 🕐 *Jun-Aug: Tue-Sun 9.30am-1pm and 2-6.30pm; Apr-May and Sep: Tue-Sun 9.30am-12.30pm and 2-6pm; Oct-Mar: Tue-Sun 9.30am-12.30pm and 2-5pm. Last admission 1hr before closing.* 🕐 *Closed Mon, Oct-Jun, 1 Jan, 1 May, 1 Nov, 25 Dec.* ⊸ *4€, no charge first Sun and last Wed in the month.* ☎ *04 90 93 58 11.* **Musée Réattu★** – paintings, **Picasso Bequest★** 🕐 *May-Sep: daily 10am-12.30pm and 2-7pm; Mar-Apr and Oct: daily 10am-12.30pm and 2-5.30pm; Nov-Feb: daily 1-5.30pm. Last admission 30min before closing.* 🕐 *Closed 1 Jan, 1 May, 1 Nov, 25 Dec.* ⊸ *4€.* ☎ *04 90 49 38 34.* **Palais Constantin★** – largest baths in Provence 🕐 *Same hours as for the Théâtre antique.* **Alyscamps★** – necropolis, *Allow half a day.* 🕐 *Same hours as the Théâtre antique.* ⊸ *3.50€.* ☎ *04 90 49 35 67.*

ARRAS★★

POPULATION 79 607

MICHELIN MAP 301 J 5-6

GREEN GUIDE NORTHERN FRANCE AND THE PARIS REGION

The Abbey of St-Vaast formed the nucleus around which the capital of Artois grew in the Middle Ages. Between the 12C and the 14C it gained various municipal privileges from the Counts of Artois encouraging an economy based on corn, cloth and money-changing. The city prospered; poetic and literary societies thrived in which Arras' notables could enjoy hearing themselves lampooned by minstrels and entertainers. In the 15C, Artois passed into the hands of the Dukes of Burgundy, ensuring steady orders until c 1460 for its tapestry industry whose products treated profane subjects with a high degree of realism. 🄸 *Hôtel de ville, pl. des Héros, 62000 Arras,* ☎ *03 21 51 26 95. www.ot-arras.fr.*

▶ **Orient Yourself:** Arras, which is listed as a "Town of Art and History," offers discovery tours Jul-Aug. Information at the tourist office or www.vpah.culture.fr.

A Bit of History

Maximilian Robespierre was born in Arras in 1758 to a well-to-do legal family. He too was called to the Bar before becoming a Deputy in 1789, a Republican in 1792, and a prominent member of the Committee of Public Safety in 1793. Frank, determined, indifferent to favours, "Robespierre the Incorruptible" embodied the spirit of the Revolution. Backed by Saint-Just and Couthon, he harried plotters and crushed deviationists, going so far as to take part in the condemnation of his allies, the Girondins. Discredited in the end by the consequences of his extremist ideology, he fell victim to the guillotine on 27 July 1794.

Sights

Les Places★★ (Main Squares)

Dating from the 11C, the **Grand'Place, Place des Héros** and the **Rue de la Taillerie** linking them celebrate the city's status as an important regional market centre. Their present splendidly harmonious appearance is the fruit of the city fathers' purposeful civic design initiatives in the 17C and 18C. The existing Spanish Plateresque buildings of the 16C and 17C (Arras was effectively under Spanish rule from 1492 to 1640) were given Flemish Baroque façades from 1635 onward. The 155 brick and stone houses rest on 345 columns: their arcading sheltered traders and clients alike. With few projections, their regularly-proportioned façades give an impression of great unity, relieved by a rich variety of detail. This includes curvilinear gables, arcades with pilasters or corbelling, decorative tie-bars, and a number of sculpted merchants' signs (a whale, a harp and a bell, among others). To the north of the Grand'Place a brick building with a stone-built ground floor is topped by a stepped gable, the only one of its kind.Arras' civic pride was symbolised by the construction of its Town Hall, **Hôtel de Ville**★(Jul and Aug: Wed and Sun 3pm; 2€; 03 21 51 26 95; www. ot-arras.fr) in 1572; its bell-tower **(beffroi)** (May-Sep: Tue- Sat 9am-6.30pm, Sun 10am-1pm, 2.30-6.30pm, Mon 9am-noon, 2-6pm; Oct-Apr: Tue-Sat 9am-noon, 2-6pm, Sun 10am-12.30pm, 2.30-6.30pm, Mon 10am-noon, 2-6pm; 2.30€. 03 21 51 26 95) blends Flemish Gothic with Henri II-style ornamentation. It was destroyed in the First World War but rebuilt in 1919.

Ancienne abbaye St-Vaast★★ Apr-Sep: daily 10am-noon, 2-6pm; Oct-Mar: Mon-Fri 10am-noon,2pm-5pm, Sat-Sun 10am-noon, 2pm-6pm. 3.05€, no charge 1st Sun and 1st Wed in the month. 03 21 71 26 43. **Musée des Beaux-Arts**★ Daily 9.30am-noon, 2-5.30pm, Thu 9.30am-5.30pm. Closed Tue, 1 Jan, 1 and 8 May, 14 Jul, 1 and 11 Nov, 25 Dec. 4€, no charge 1st Wed and 1st Sun in the month. 03 21 71 26 43.

R. Decottignies/DIAPHOR

Grand 'Place

Excursions

Vimy

10 km – 6mi north. The summit of this chalky ridge was taken by the Canadian Expeditionary Force, part of the British Third Army, in April 1917. It is crowned by the Canadian Memorial (**mémorial canadien de Vimy ★**). There are extensive views over a farmed landscape dotted with the conical tips of coal mines. To the west are the cemetery and basilica of Notre-Dame-de-Lorette, and nearby, in the scrubby woodland, can be found some of the entrenchments and pitted landforms left by trench warfare.

Parc ASTÉRIX★★

ASTERIX PARK

MICHELIN MAP 305 G 6

GREEN GUIDE NORTHERN FRANCE AND THE PARIS REGION

Asterix the Gaul, hero of the famous cartoon strip by Goscinny and Uderzo, provides the theme for this fun park (50ha – 123 acres). It is a fantasy world for all ages which offers a journey into the past: carefully reconstructed 'historical' sections, various attractions and shows, as well as audio-visual displays add to the fun.

Visit

🚸 ⏱ *Apr-Aug: daily except certain Mondays and Fridays (May and Jun: call for opening days and times). Sep to mid-Oct: Wed and Sat-Sun. Times vary according to the time of year: 10am-6pm or 9.30am-7pm (summer period). Opening days and times liable to modification.* ⏱ *Closed from mid-Oct to end Mar.* 🎫 *31€ (children: 23€, children under 3 years: no charge).* ☎ *08 92 68 30 10 or 03 44 62 34 34. www.parcasterix.fr.*

To explore this enchanting world, start at the Via Antiqua lined with stalls symbolising Asterix's journeys across Europe. Six areas illustrate various themes: the **Village Astérix** is a veritable Gallic village with its huts; the **Menhir Express ★** is the highlight of a Stone Age village built on piles (**Domaine Lacustre**); 10 centuries of history are illustrated in the **Rue de Paris**; a lake, **Grand Lac**, is a popular spot with thrilling attractions (**Goudurix ★, Tonnerre de Zeus**); Icarus's flight (Vol d'Icare) and performing dolphins in an auditorium, **Théâtre de Poséidon,** are the main interests of the section on Ancient Greece (**Grèce Antique**); in the Roman city (**Cité Romaine**) contests between gladiators are held in the arena and there is an exciting descent into Hell (**Descente du Styx ★**).

Col d'AUBISQUE★★

AUBISQUE PASS

MICHELIN MAP 342 J-K 5

GREEN GUIDE ATLANTIC COAST

The main east-west axis of the Pyrenees is interrupted by a series of long narrow valleys running roughly north-south. Each of these valleys forms a distinct unit, with a characteristic landscape and way of life which often have more in common with the lowlands to the north or even with Spain than with the valleys on either side. A number of high passes permit east-west communication; the Tourmalet Pass at 2 114m – 6 936ft is the highest, but the Aubisque Pass (Col d'Aubisque – 1 709m – 5 608ft) separating the Béarn from the Bigorre country is the most spectacular.

Visit

From the southern summit of the pass *(TV relay station – 30min return on foot)* the immense **panorama ★★★** extends over rocky slopes to the gentler, man-made landscape of the valleys far below, as well as taking in the magnificent rock formations of the Cirque de Gourette, marked from left to right by the Grand Gabizos, Pène Blanque and the Pic de Ger.

AUCH★

POPULATION 23 136

MICHELIN MAP 336 E 6-7, C-D-E-F 8

GREEN GUIDE LANGUEDOC ROUSSILLON TARN GORGES

The origins of Auch go back to a fortified settlement of the Basques situated on the left bank of the Gers. For 2 000 years the city served as a staging-post on the old Toulouse-Bordeaux highway; its alignment avoided the treacherously-shifting course of the middle Garonne to the north.

A Bit of History

The real d'Artagnan, Charles de Batz, was from this district. Another citizen remembered with pride is d'Etigny, who, as the city's Intendant, was responsible for its revival in the 18C. He was the first of a series of able administrators to reside in the former Bishops' Palace; its façade is distinguished by a rhythmic sequence of fluted pilasters.

Sights

Cathédrale Ste-Marie★★

🕐*Closed at lunchtime (except mid-Jul to end Sep). Pre-recorded commentaries on the building available at the entrance. Audio tour of the gallery and windows available ⊶ 2€, identity document retained as guarantee.*

The cathedral's ambulatory contains a masterly series of Renaissance stained-glass windows **(vitraux★★)**, completed in 1517 by the Gascon Arnaud de Moles. They are remarkable for their composition, their sophisticated use of colour (subtle nuances and gradations and half-tones, all in strong contrast to the pure colours, rigidly separated, of the Gothic), and for the way in which the central figure of each window is surrounded by vignettes elucidating its symbolism and prefiguration (a characteristic humanist device of the time). Adam and Eve, Jonah, and the Nativity are exceptionally fine.

The choir stalls **(stalles★★★ -** 🕐 *Apr to mid-Jul: daily 8.30am-noon, 2-6pm; mid-Jul to end Sep: daily 8.30am-6pm; Oct-Mar: daily 9.30am-noon, 2-5pm;* ⊶ *1.50€)*, an inspired work completed in 1554, are peopled by 1 500 different figures in an extraordinary wealth of detail. The backs are carved with representations of biblical and other personages; the faces crowding the dividers, elbow-rests, the panels and niches of the backs and the misericords provide an interest and stimulation which are inexhaustible. The opulence characteristic of the Flamboyant style survives in this work of the Renaissance.

AULNAY★★

POPULATION 1 462

MICHELIN MAP 322 G 3

GREEN GUIDE ATLANTIC COAST

Originally in the province of Poitiers, Aulnay was apportioned to Saintonge by virtue of the division of France into *départements* by the Constituent Assembly on 22 December 1789.

Visit

Église St-Pierre★★

This fine Romanesque church stands among the cypresses of its ancient burial ground with its Gothic Hosanna Cross. It was built between 1140 and 1170 at a time when Eleanor of Aquitaine ruled southwestern France as queen first to Louis VII, then to Henry II of England. Its structure, notably its tribune-less triple nave, is essentially in the Romanesque style typical of the Poitou area, while its sculpture is characteristic of Saintonge.

Although somewhat marred by massive 15C buttresses, the west front is remarkable for its sumptuously decorated arches and its large-scale figure sculptures. In the left portal is a poignant representation of St Peter hanging upside-down on his cross. Considering himself unworthy of the same treatment as his Master, he demanded this even crueller form of crucifixion for himself. This method of execution was not uncommon, even before the days of Nero; by lowering its centre of gravity, the cross could be made smaller, and thus less costly.

The doorway of the south transept has lofty corner columns and a great relieving arch; the second arch, supported by sitting atlantes and showing the Prophets and Apostles, is an achievement of the 13C Saintonge school of sculpture.

Within, the central window of the apse is famous for its unusually rich carving, characteristic of the level which decorative art had reached in the High Middle Ages. The capitals of the columns in the nave are also worthy of attention, as is the bell-tower with its 18C slate-clad spire; its lower levels are particularly attractive in spite of the insensitive addition of extra height in the 15C.

AUTUN★★

POPULATION 17 906

MICHELIN MAP 320 F 8

GREEN GUIDE BURGUNDY JURA

Autun was founded by the Emperor Augustus, half a century after Caesar's conquest of Gaul. The hilly site bestrode the Roman road linking Lyon with Sens and overlooked the wide Vale of Arroux. Rome was taken as the model for the new town; its walls (6km – 4mi in length) soon sheltered fine civic buildings (a theatre, an amphitheatre) and a thriving commercial life. From their stronghold at Bibracte on **Mont Beuvray** 29km – 18mi away to the west, the Gallic Aedui tribe watched the city's growth with fascination and ended up moving there themselves. In the Middle Ages the city consolidated itself on the upper part of its site.  *2 av. Charles-de-Gaulle, 71400 Autun, ☎ 03 85 86 80 38. www.autun.com.*

▶ **Orient Yourself:** Autun, which is listed as a "Town of Art and History," offers discovery tours (2hr). Information at the tourist office or on www.vpah.culture.fr.

Visit

Cathédrale St-Lazare★★

The great sandstone edifice was built from 1120 to 1146 and named after the friend of Christ whom He raised from the dead and whose relics had been brought here from Marseille shortly before. Though its external appearance was altered by the addition of a tower and steeple in the 15C, it remains essentially a building of the Burgundian Romanesque style; its barrel-vaulted nave has slightly pointed arches (an early example) and a blind triforium designed to enliven an otherwise bare wall. With a gallery identical to that of the city's Roman Arroux Gate (Porte d'Arroux), this triforium is striking evidence of the continuing influence of Antiquity well into the 12C.

The glory of the cathedral is its 12C Burgundian sculpture, most of it the achievement of Master Gislebertus, who came from Vézelay in 1125 and worked here for 20 years. The tympanum **(tympan★★★)** over the central doorway dates from about 1135 and has the Last Judgement as its subject. Less mystical in feeling than its equivalent at Moissac which pre-dates it by some 30 years, it exhibits supreme mastery of technique and in the boldness of its design outshines all other contemporary work. What might pass for naïve or grotesque elsewhere here becomes a powerful means for expressing a hierarchy of spiritual values. Look carefully for example at the joy of the saved, the agony of the damned and the use of scale in the treatment of the figure of Christ, the Apostles and other figures. The same mastery is evident in the capitals **(chapiteaux★★)** in the nave (lighting) and in the chapter-house, where more capitals (originally in the choir) are displayed at eye-level.

▶▶ **Musée Rolin★** – ⏰ *Apr-Sep: Wed-Mon 9.30am-noon, 1.30-6pm; Oct-Mar: Mon, Wed-Sat,10am-noon, 2-5pm, Sun 10am-noon, 2.30-5pm.* ⏰ *Closed Tue, 1 Jan, 1 May, 14 Jul, 1 and 11 Nov, 25 Dec.* ∞ *3.20€.* ☎ *03 85 52 09 76*– Gallo-Roman collections, paintings, sculpture. **Porte St-André★** – Gallo-Roman gate.

AUXERRE★★

POPULATION 38 819

MICHELIN MAP 319 E-F-G 5

GREEN GUIDE BURGUNDY JURA

Capital of Lower Burgundy, Auxerre is a port on the navigable River Yonne. The countryside around consists of arable plateaux with much woodland, cut by valleys with slopes planted with vineyards and orchards. The city is sited on the west bank of the river and served as an important staging-post on the great Roman highway which led from Lyon to Boulogne via Autun and Lutetia (Paris). 🔲 *1 quai de la République, 89000 Auxerre,* ☎ *03 86 52 06 19. www.ot-auxerre.fr.*

Visit

Abbaye St-Germain★

🔍 *Self-guided tour of the museum, guided tour of the crypt (45min) Wed-Mon 10am-6.30pm (Oct-May: Wed-Mon 10am-noon, 2-6pm).* ⏰ *Closed Tue, 1 Jan, 1 and 8 May, 1 and 11 Nov, 25 Dec.* ∞ *4.20€ (under 16: no charge) (combined ticket including entrance to the musée Leblanc-Duvernoy), no charge 1st Sun in the month.* ☎ *03 86 18 05 50.*

The city's most venerable building, a focus of interest for historian and archeologist. It is named after St Germanus (378-448), born in Auxerre and its first bishop, the successor to St Martin in the great work of converting Gaul to Christianity. A small basilica was probably erected over the saint's tomb early in the 6C by Clothilde, the wife of King Clovis. This building was extended in 841 to include an outer nave to the west and a crypt to the east; the relics were moved here on completion of the work 18 years later.

The abbey crypt **(crypte★)** therefore houses a raised cavity which was hollowed out in the 9C to hide the tomb from raiding Norsemen. In addition there is a false tomb designed to lead them astray, plus various other works carried out subsequently. In that part of the crypt dating from Merovingian times (6C) where the oratory was originally located, there are two oak beams carried on Gallo-Roman columns and also a 5C monogram of Christ. From the Carolingian period (8C-10C) there is a fresco showing the bishops of Auxerre, floor-tiling, and most moving of all, a capital based crudely on the Ionian Order, proof of the aesthetic poverty of the time.

The mid-12C bell-tower, a remarkable Romanesque structure, was isolated from the rest of the building by the destruction of several bays in the 19C. The eight sides of its squat spire have an almost imperceptible bulge.

⊙⊙ **Cathédrale St-Étienne**★★ – ⏰ *7.30am-6pm; Tour of the treasury and crypt from Easter to All Saint's Day (1 Nov) 9am-6pm, Fri 2-6pm; the rest of the year daily except Sun 10am-5pm.* ☎ *03 86 52 23 29* – crypt, **treasury**★, **stained glass**★.

AVEN ARMAND★★★

MICHELIN MAP 338 M 5

GREEN GUIDE LANGUEDOC ROUSSILLON TARN GORGES

To the west of the Cévennes extends one of France's most remote landscapes, the Causses, arid limestone tablelands cut deeply by canyons. The monotonous tracts of the Causse Méjean leave a desolate impression; occasional groupings of drystone houses, patches of oats in the grudgingly fertile depressions known as sotchs, attempts at reafforestation with black pines on the slopes.

Visit

⏰ *Guided tours* 〰 *(1hr) mid-May to mid-Sep: daily 9.30am-6.15pm; end-Mar to mid-May and mid-Sep to early Nov: daily 9.30am-noon, 1.30-5pm.* ⊛ *8€ (children: 5.50€).* ☎ *04 66 45 61 31. www.aven-armand.com.*

Deep within the limestone of the Causse Méjean the subterranean waters have created one of the wonders of the natural world, the **Aven Armand**, a great chasm discovered in 1897 by Louis Armand, one of the collaborators of the pioneer speleologist Edouard-André Martel. Here the limestone has been eroded and dissolved to form a vast cavern, its floor littered with rock fallen from its roof. Four hundred stalagmites, the "Virgin Forest", make an extraordinary spectacle.

Aven Armand

AVIGNON★★★

POPULATION 181 136

MICHELIN MAP 332 B-C 10

GREEN GUIDE PROVENCE

Protected by its ramparts, the historic core of Avignon is a lively centre of art and culture. For 68 years it was the residence first of seven French Popes, then of three others once Pope Gregory XI had returned to Rome in 1377, then of the Papal Legates who remained here until the city was reunited with France in 1791.

▶ **Orient Yourself:** Avignon, which is listed as a "Town of Art and History", offers discovery tours (2hr) for 7€ and 10€. Apr-Oct: Tue, Thu and Sat at 10am; Nov-Mar: Sat at 10am. Information at the tourist office or on www.vpah.culture.fr. Get a great view of Avignon's skyline from across the Rhône, especially if you are approaching the city in the evening. In addition to the guided tours mentioned above, there is a sightseeing train *(45min)* that runs most of the year (🕐 *mid-Mar to mid-Oct: daily 10am-8pm; mid-Sep to mid-Oct: daily 10am-7pm;* ⊛ *7€, 4€ children;* ☎ *04 05 60 05 55; www.petittrainavignon.fr).*

🐾 **Don't Miss:** A great view of the city from the **Terrasse des Grands Dignitaires** in the Palais des Papes.

🕐 **Organizing Your Time:** With so much to do in Avignon, allow yourself at least 2 hours to visit the Palais des Papes and the Pont St-Bénézet before exploring the rest of the city. Many sights can be visited at a reduced rate by obtaining a "carte-pass" at specific sights or the Avignon tourist information centre (🛈 *41 cours Jean-Jaurès, 84000 AVIGNON,* ☎*04 32 74 32 74, www. avignon-tourisme.com).*

🅿 **Parking :** Parking is available in the underground car park (fee) at the Palais des Papes.

A Bit of History

At the beginning of the 14C the Popes had begun to feel the need to escape from the pressures of the turbulent political life of Rome. Avignon formed part of the Papal territories, albeit attached to Provence and under the protection of the Holy Roman Empire. In addition it occupied a central position in the Europe of the time. The case for moving there was made with some force by Philippe le Bel (the Fair), conceivably not without the ulterior motive of involving the Papacy in his own political manœuvrings. In 1309 Pope Clement V took the plunge, and Avignon thus became the capital of Christianity. The following year the Pope had to accept the dissolution of the Order of the Templars.

Palais des Papes

S. Sauvignier/MICHELIN

Avignon - Address Book

TOURISM

📍 *41 cours Jean-Jaurès, 84000 Avignon,* ☎ *04 32 74 32 74. www.ot-avignon.fr.*

TOURS AND DISCOUNTS

Pass – The city offers a tourist pass, valid for two weeks and offering significant price reductions for visitors to Avignon and Villeneuve-les-Avignon (museums and monuments, guided tours of the town, boat and tourist train trips, coach excursions). To obtain it, simply pay full price at one of the sites mentioned on the pass. Therafter, you will qualify for Pass reductions. Show it each time you purchase a a ticket. Ask about the Pass at the tourist office.

Avignon by Boat – *(45mn) audioguide tour, from pont Saint-Bénezet and along the Rhône.* ◷ *July-Aug: 1-6pm (each hour); May-June, and Sept: 1pm, 2pm, 3pm, 3.30pm, and 4.45pm.* 🎟 *8€.* ☎ *04 32 74 32 74 (tourist office).*

Sightseeing Train –*Guided visit through Avignon (45mn).* ◷ *Mid-Mar to mid-Sept: 10am-8pm; mid-Sept to mid-Oct: 10am-7pm - 7 € (under 9 years, 4€). Departs from the place du palais des Papes.* ☎ *04 50 60 05 55 - www.petittrainavignon.fr.*

Trips on the Rhône – ♿ "Grands Bateaux de Provence,"organizes several full day roundtrip boat outings from Avignon along the Rhône, to such destinations as Arles, Châteauneuf-du-Pape, the Camargue, etc. ☎ *04 90 85 62 25 - www. avignon-et-provence.com/mireio .*

Coach Excursion – Provence Vision (Cars Lieutaud) – *36, bd Saint-Roch (near the central train station),* ☎ *04 90 86 36 75, contact@cars-lieutaud.fr, or, inquire and make reservations at the tourist office –* Offers half and full-day excursions from Avignon to the Camrague, Pont du Gard, Fontaine de Vaucluse, the Alpilles, a Lavender tour (Coustellet, Gordes, Abbaye de Sénanque), a wine tour (Orange and Châteauneuf du Pape). A tour of Avignon proper is also offered.

SHOPPING

Markets – **Les Halles Centrales,** *Place Pie, traditional covered market,* ◷ *open daily except Mon, 6am-1.30pm.* **Flower market** every Saturday in *place des Carmes.* **Fair** Sat and Sun, *rempart St-Michel.* **Flea market** every Sunday in *place des Carmes.*

Honey – **Miellerie des Butineuses**, *189 rue de la Source, 84450 St-Saturnin-lès-Avignon,* ☎ *04 90 22 47 52 – www.miellerie. fr.* Honey, pollen, and royal jelly, as well as honey-based products.

Chocolate – **Puyricard**, *33 rue Joseph-Vernet,* ☎ *04 90 85 96 33.* ◷ *Open Mon, 2-7pm; Tues-Sat, 9am-12pm and 4-7pm. Closed Mon and July-Aug.* Chocolate lovers go no further: herein find some 92 varieties of chocolate in all its possible forms.

Pastries and Confections – Nicole Poutet – *15 rue des Trois-Faucons -* ☎ *04 90 82 08 31 –* ◷ *Mon-Sat, 7.30am-8pm; Sun, 7.30am-6pm.* ◷ *Closed 15-28 Feb and 15-31 Aug.* Are you familiar with *papalines?* This speciality of Avignon was created in 1960 by the current owner's father: pink delicacies filled with an exquisite liqueur made from oregano, a plant of the Comtat Venaissin.

Home decor – Terre è Provence – *26 r. de la République -* ☎ *04 90 85 56 45 - terre-provence@waandoo.fr -* ◷ *Mon-Sat, 10am-1.30pm, 2-7pm (June-Aug: 10am-7pm).* In the same family for several generations, this shop is dedicated to all that is Provence : table settings, textiles with Provençal prints, pottery, and porcelain and many lovely ideas for your home.

EVENTS

The Festival : Mainstream and Fringe Events – Theatre, dance, lectures, exhibitions, meetings, and concerts given in the main courtyard of the Palais des Papes, in the municipal theatre, in the many cloisters and churches of the town, as well as at Villeneuve-lès-Avignon and other outlying areas, such as the Boulbon quarry (Carrière de Boulbon), Montfavet or Châteaublanc. Fringe events are dotted around the town.

Booking – Programmes and tickets are available at the Bureau du Festival d'Avignon, Cloître Saint-Louis - *20 r. du Portail-Boquier - 84000 Avignon,* ☎ *04 90 27 66 50 - réservations* ☎ *04 90 14 14 14.* From the first two weeks of June onwards it is also possible to make reservations by internet (*www.festival-avignon.com*), by minitel 3615 FNAC, at FNAC booking counters, and at the main office located at St-Louis d'Avignon (20 *rue Portail-Bocquier).* Festival programmes are available by mail: send a check for 5€ to: *Avignon Public Off, BP 5, 75521 Paris Cedex 11* (☎ *01 48 05 01 19, contact@avignon-off. org, www.avignon-off.org).*

Hivernales d'Avignon – This choreography festival takes place in February but it never attains the atmosphere of the summer festival as the shows (luckily) take place indoors. ☎ *04 90 82 33 12. www.hivernales-avignon.com.*

Horse Festival – In January this event includes dressage, show jumping, competitions, and shows at the sports stadium. ☎ *04 90 84 02 04. www.cheval-passion.com.*

For coin ranges, see Legend at the back of the guide.

EATING OUT

🍽 **Le Mesclun - Le Petit Bistrot de Brunel** – *46 r. de la Balance -* ☎ *04 90 86 14 60 -* ◷ *closed evenings Sun, and Mon.* There's no better place for lunch, be it on the shaded terrace or inside. The daily dishes and menu mingle market freshness, Provence, and gastronomy with the zest of good cheer. The choice spot to take a pause between excursions.

⊜⊜ **Le Grand Café** – *cours Maria-Casares, La Manutention* – ☎ *04 90 86 86 77* – 🕐 *closed Jan, Sun and Mon except July-Aug – booking recommended.* Backing onto the buttresses of the Palais des Papes, these old barracks have become an essential part of local life. Locals and tourists all flock here to savour inventive cooking with Provençal accents. Pleasant décor that combines the styles of a Parisian bistro and a Viennese café. There is also an attractive terrace.

⊜⊜ **Au Coin des Halles** – *4 r. Grivolas -* ☎ *04 90 82 93 49* – 🕐 *closed Sun and public holidays.* Enjoy this central spot among the Avignonnais, with its reading space and two little dining areas, all infused with jazzy music. And check out the menu: simple dishes, like a delicious *reblochon* cheese tart, a *salade landaise*, a winter squash soup.

⊜⊜ **Entrée des Artistes** – *1 place des Carmes* – ☎ *04 90 82 46 90* – 🕐 *closed 23 Dec-3 Jan, 17 Aug-8 Sept, Sat and Sun.* The dining room of this restaurant is decorated in the style of a Parisian bistro, with its old posters and movie memorabilia. Tables are placed close together and the cooking is traditional. Service is friendly and there is a real scent of the Mediterranean in the air.

⊜⊜ **Le Moutardier** – *15 place du Palais-des-Papes* – ☎ *04 90 85 34 76* – *moutardier@wanadoo.fr* – 🕐 *closed 6-25 Jan, 24 Nov-19 Dec, and Wed from Oct-Mar.* This 18C building, listed in France's National Heritage, makes an exceptional setting for a simple, fresh meal. There is a pleasant atmosphere, both in the bistro room, where frescoes depict the story of "The Pope's mustard maker," and on the terrace facing the Palais des Papes.

⊜⊜⊜ **Compagnie des Comptoirs** – *83 r. Joseph-Vernet, Le Cloître des Arts -* ☎ *04 90 85 99 04 - jc.toussaint@ lacompagniedescomptoirs.com -* 🕐 *closed Sun and Mon.* Inspired by the colonial trading posts of the French East Indies Company, this restaurant, situated in the 14C cloisters, is the "in" place to eat. The bar decor is glass and bamboo, there are colonial etchings in the dining rooms, and the terrace is decked out with a palm tree and straw huts. The menu combines the flavours of East Asia with those of southern France.

WHERE TO STAY

⊝ **Hôtel Le Provençal** – *13 r. Joseph-Vernet* – ☎ *04 90 85 25 24 - hotel. leprovencal@wanadoo.fr - 11 rooms –* 🛏 *5€.* Le Provençal offers the advantage of being in the very heart of Avignon without being too pricey, a rare mix for this town. Moreover, the rooms are comfortable and decent.

⊝⊜ **Hôtel Médiéval** – *15 rue de la Petite-Saunerie* – ☎ *04 90 86 11 06 – hotel. medieval@wanadoo.fr –* 🕐 *closed 3 Jan-7 Feb – 34 rooms -* 🛏 *7€.* A simple hotel in the city centre, the Médiéval also offers special reduced rates for stays of a week or longer. Some rooms (studios) have kitchenettes. A stone's throw from the Palais des Papes, this is a wonderful base for exploring the heart of Avignon (and for picking up market delights at Les Halles!). The owner and staff are very welcoming and helpful.

⊝⊜ **Chambre d'hôte La Prévôté** – *354 chemin d'Exploitation – 84210 Althen-les-Paluds – 17km/10.5mi northeast of Avignon towards Carpentras* – ☎ *04 90 62 17 06 – prevote@aol.com –* 🕐 *closed Nov-1 Mar –* 🛏 *– 5 rooms –* 🛏 *5€.* After a peaceful night spent in one of the spacious, colourful rooms of this *mas*, you will certainly enjoy breakfast, which is served in the shade of the vine arbour or under the chestnut tree. Let your gaze roam over the apple trees or have a dip in the swimming pool.

⊝⊜⊜ **Hôtel Garlande** – *20 rue Galante* – ☎ *04 90 80 08 85 – hotel-de-garlande@ wanadoo.fr –* 🕐 *closed Jan – 11 rooms -* 🛏 *6.10€.* Situated in two renovated old houses in a peaceful street, this small, family-run hotel is close to the church of St Didier. Colourful rooms with Provençal floral fabrics.

⊝⊜⊜ **Hôtel Cloître St-Louis** – *20 rue Portail Boquier* – ☎ *04 90 27 55 55 – hotel@ cloitre-saint-louis.com –* 🅿 *– 77 rooms -* 🛏 *16€ - restaurant 38/55€.* Situated in 16C cloisters, part of this hotel was designed by the architect Jean Nouvel. The building uses a variety of materials including glass, steel, and stone. Rooms are stylishly minimalist. Pool and solarium on the roof. Sunday mass in the chapel at the heart of the hotel.

ON THE TOWN

La Cave Breysse – *41 r. des Teinturiers -* ☎ *04 90 86 00 44 -* 🕐 *Open 6-10.30pm.* A very popular wine bar, this is a nice place to enjoy a well-priced glass of wine or an aperitif, and to take in the night, the ambiance, and the festivities.

Café In&Off – *place du Palais-des-Papes –* ☎ *04 90 85 48 95 – www.cafeinoff.com –* 🕐 *Summer: daily 7.30am-10pm and until 3am during the festival; rest of year: 7.30am-8pm –* 🕐 *closed from mid-Nov to the end of Feb.* Don't miss the only café that enjoys unbeatable views of the Palais des Papes. The interior is not lacking in appeal but the terrace is definitely the highpoint of this café.

Cloître des Arts – *83 rue Joseph-Vernet -* ☎ *0490861232 - www.avignon-et-provence.com/gambrinus. -* 🕐 *Daily 7am-1.30pm except Sun. During the festival 7am-3am.* 🕐 *Closed the first fortnight of Jan.* Sixty varieties of beers from all over the world and a relaxed atmosphere attract beer enthusiasts of all ages, whether among friends or with the family.

Woolloomooloo – *16 bis rue des Teinturiers -* ☎ *04 90 85 28 44 - www.wooll. com -* 🕐 *Daily noon-1am.* Bearing a long, wild cry for a name, this bar-restaurant nevertheless occupies the very civilised site of a former printing works inthe oldest street of the city. The myriad objects brought back by the owner from his worldwide travels adorn this place Everything from musical evenings in the bar to exotic dishes (always using fresh produce from the market) evokes travel.

SHOWTIME

Le Rouge Gorge – *10 bis rue Peyrolerie -* ☎ *04 90 14 02 54 - www.le.rougegorge.fr -* 🕐 *Tues-Sun 8.30pm-3am.* 🕐 *Closed July-Aug.* The only cabret in Avignon, the Rouge-Gorge, modestly sheltered by thePalais des Papes, unveils the sensual charms of its show every Friday and Saturday from 8.30pm, while two Sundays a month there is an operetta lunch. During the week the atmosphere remains lively with numerous themed evenings (Corsican, Latino, Oriental).

Between them, the Papal court and the administration of the Church built with enthusiasm, transforming the appearance of the city.

An influential centre for art and culture, Avignon owes much to Jean Vilar, who founded the Drama Festival **(Festival d'art dramatique)** in 1947. This prestigious annual event led to a blossoming of the arts which has served as a model to many other towns in Provence. As well as stage productions, Avignon hosts a variety of different cultural events: films, exhibitions, poetry readings, concerts, mime performances, ballets, etc. It is also keen on fostering international co-operation.

Sights

Palais des Papes★★★

🕐 *Mid-Mar to Jun and Oct: daily 9am-7pm; Nov to mid-Mar: daily 9.30am-5.45pm. Last admission 1hr before closing.* 👛 *9.50€ (7.50€ early Nov to mid-Mar); 9.50€, 11.50€ combined ticket with pont St-Bénézet.* ☎ *04 90 27 50 83. www.palais-des-papes.com.*
The Old Palace (Palais Vieux) lies to the north, the New Palace (Palais Nouveau) to the south. The huge feudal structure, fortress as well as palace, conveys an overwhelming impression of defensive strength with its high, bare walls, its massive corbelled crenellations and stalwart buttresses.

The Popes at Avignon

The building of the Old Palace to accommodate the Church's archives and treasures was begun in 1334 by Benedict XII, a former Cistercian of austere ways. The Consistory (Consistoire), St John's Chapel (Chapelle St-Jean), Banqueting Hall (Grand Tinel), St Martial's Chapel (Chapelle St-Martial) and three state rooms all date from this period.

Clement VI followed him in 1342. A great patron of the arts, desirous of increasing the wealth and influence of the Church, he was responsible for the New Palace (Great Audience Chamber – Grande Audience, Small Audience Chamber – Petite Audience, and Clementine Chapel – Chapelle Clémentine) and succeeded in buying Avignon from Jeanne of Provence.

At the time France could stand comparison with Italy in architecture and sculpture, but not in painting. Clement called in Italian artists **(First School of Avignon);** Simone Martini painted the fresco in the Consistory, Matteo Giovanetti decorated the Wardrobe Room (Chambre de la Garde-robe) using the foliage motifs popular at the time. The latter's mastery is evident too in his treatment of perspective in St Martial's Chapel and in his courtly Prophets in the Great Audience Chamber.

In response to the fears awakened by the Battle of Poitiers and the troubles of the Hundred Years War, Innocent VI rebuilt the city's ramparts, using techniques of military engineering already obsolete (fewer machicolations, towers exposed on the side facing the town).

Sadly, little is left to remind us of the princely life of the Papal court; all the furniture has gone, as has most of the decoration.

Second School of Avignon

Dissatisfied with the accession of Gregory XI, the cardinals at Rome elected another Pope in 1378, Clement VII, who returned to Avignon. A confusing period lasting 37 years followed in which two, sometimes three Popes (at Pisa as well as at Rome and Avignon) vied with and excommunicated each other. The Great Schism divided the West, threw Christianity into disarray, troubled men's minds and extinguished all artistic activity at the Papal court. This started up again at Avignon in 1418 with the establishment of the rule of the Papal Legates, who created an island of calm in the midst of general European anarchy.

The Second School of Avignon (1440-1500) is marked by a compromise between the stylisation and the light effects of the Italians (15C works in the Museum of the Petit Palais) and the mystical realism of the Flemish masters. A "French" type of painting emerged, its main protagonist Enguerrand Quarton (his *Pietà* from Villeneuve-lès-Avignon is in the Louvre) together with Josse Lieferinxe and Nicolas Froment (whose triptych of *The Burning Bush* is in the cathedral at Aix-en-Provence).

Pont St-Bénézet★★

♿ 🕐 *Jul: daily 9am-9pm; Aug-Sep: daily 9am-8pm; mid-Mar-Jun and Oct: daily 9am-7pm; Nov to mid-Mar: daily 9.30am-5.45pm. Last admission 1hr before closing.* ⛶ *4€; 11.50€ combined ticket with Palais des Papes.* ☎ *04 90 85 60 16.*

Begun in 1177, according to legend, by the shepherd-boy Bénézet himself, founder of the Bridge Brotherhood (Frères Pontifes). Until the Brotherhood built the Pont-St-Esprit more than a century later it was the only stone bridge over the Rhône. It helped the economic development of Avignon long before becoming a useful link with Villeneuve when the Cardinals built their villas there. Eighteen of its arches were carried away by the floodwaters of the river in the 17C.

▶▶ **Petit Palais★★** – 🕐 *Oct to end May: Wed-Mon 9.30-1pm, 2-5.30pm; Jun to end Sep: Wed-Mon 10am-1pm, 2-6pm.* 🕐 *Closed Tue, 1 Jan, 1 May, 14 Jul, 1 Nov, 25 Dec.* ⛶ *6€.* ☎ *04 90 86 44 58.* Local and Italian paintings. **Rocher des Doms★★ – views★★.** Cathédrale – **cupola★. Ramparts★. Musée Calvet★** 🕐 *Wed-Mon 10am-1pm, 2-6pm.* 🕐 *Closed Tue, 1 Jan, 1 May, 25 Dec.* ⛶ *6€.* ☎ *04 90 86 33 84* - prehistory, metalwork, fine arts. Musée Louis-Vouland 🕐 *May-Oct: Tue-Sat 10am-noon, 2-6pm, Sun and public holidays 2-6pm; Nov-Apr: Tue-Sun 2-6pm.* 🕐 *Closed Mon, 1 Jan, 1 May, 25 Dec.* ⛶ *4€.* ☎ *04 90 86 03 79.–* **faience★.** Hôtel des Monnaies – **façade★. Musée lapidaire★** ♿ 🕐 *Wed-Mon 10am-1pm, 2-6pm.* 🕐 *Closed Tue, 1 Jan, 1 May, 25 Dec.* ⛶ *2€ (children under 12years: no charge).* ☎ *04 90 86 33 84 or 04 90 85 75 38.* Église St-Didier – **frescoes★.**

Excursions

Villeneuve-lès-Avignon★

2km/1mi west, on the west bank of the river. At the point where St Bénézet's bridge touched French territory Philippe le Bel built a small fort (only a tower remains). Half a century later, feeling hemmed in at Avignon, the Cardinals crossed the river and built themselves 15 fine houses (*livrées*) here.

At the same time, Jean le Bon (John the Good) erected the St-André fortress on the hill which was already crowned by an abbey. Protected by its walls and with a splendid twin-towered gatehouse, this vast building complex offers (from its Romanesque Chapel of Notre-Dame de Belvézet) one of the finest views over the Rhône valley. In the foreground is the gateway, Porte St-André, and beyond, on the far bank, the Palace of the Popes.

Chartreuse du Val de Bénédiction★

In 1352 the General of the Carthusian Order had been elected Pope but humbly refused the throne. Pope Innocent VI, elected in his stead, founded this charterhouse to commemorate the gesture. It soon became the greatest in France. It has a monumental 17C gateway, small cloisters and graveyard cloisters, the latter fringed by the cells of the Fathers. The church contains the founder's tomb.

Strictly speaking, it was not St Bruno who founded the Order of Carthusians. But, by living the life of a hermit in the wild setting of the Chartreuse Massif (1084-90), it was he who was responsible for establishing the rigorous asceticism incorporated in the Order's constitution of 50 years later.

Château d'AZAY-LE-RIDEAU★★★

MICHELIN MAP 31 L 5

GREEN GUIDE CHÂTEAUX OF THE LOIRE

In a verdant setting where the waters of the Indre act as reflecting pools, the **château d'Azay-le-Rideau** was built for the financier Gilles Berthelot from 1518 to 1529.

Visit

🕐 ╾╼ *Guided tours Apr-Sep: daily 9.30am-6pm (Jul and Aug: 7pm); Oct-Mar: daily 10am-12.30pm, 2-5.30pm. Last admission 45min before closing.* 🕐 *Closed 1 Jan, 1 May, 25 Dec.* 🞉 *6.10€ (under 18 years: no charge), no charge 1st Sun in the month (Nov-Mar).* ☎ *02 47 45 42 04. www.monum.fr.*

In architectural terms it is French Gothic work of the 15C, with a corbelled sentry-walk, steep-pitched roof, great stumps of chimneys, mullioned windows and a heavily-ribbed door. But its defences (machicolated cornice, pepperpot towers and turrets) are purely decorative, the owner's status symbols.

By contrast, the decoration shows the influence of the Italianate style used in the François I wing at Blois: Florentine shells in the gable of the great dormer window, pilasters, moulded entablatures and above all the grand staircase with straight flights (at Blois it is still in the form of a spiral) and rectangular landings (still curved at Chenonceau). The interior is particularly notable for the French-style ceiling in the dining room and the chimneypiece in the François I Room.

Excursions

Marnay

6 km – 3.5mi west of Azay-le-Rideau via D57 then into D20. The **Musée Maurice-Dufresne★** *(♿ 🕐 May-Sep: daily 9.15am-6.45pm; Feb-Apr and Oct-Nov: daily 9.15am-5.45pm;* 🕐 *Closed Dec-Jan;* 🞉 *10€, children: 5€;* ☎ *02 47 45 36 18)* houses several machines linked to the history of locomotion.

BAR-LE-DUC★

POPULATION 17 545

MICHELIN MAP 307 B 6, E 5

GREEN GUIDE ALSACE LORRAINE CHAMPAGNE

This old capital of the Duchy of Bar is sited on the limestone plateau just back from the Côte des Bars, the escarpment marked by ancient strongholds like Bar-sur-Seine and Bar-sur-Aube. In appearance it suggests the proximity of Lorraine. The lower town laid out along the Ornain and the Rhine-Marne canal is industrial in character. The city became a possession of the Capetian kings in 1301 when Philippe le Bel (the Fair) persuaded the Count of Bar to accept him as sovereign. In 1484, it was absorbed by the Duchy of Lorraine and incorporated into France at the same time as that province, in 1766.

Visit

Ville haute★ (Upper Town)

Here, in the Place St-Pierre, are a number of houses dating from the 15C, 16C and 17C. The castle (now a museum) already dominated its surroundings in the 6C; its window-mouldings and carved imposts are characteristic of the Rhenish Renaissance. St Stephen's Church (Église St-Étienne) has a curious late-18C belfry-cum-porch in the medieval style; within are two works by the 16C master Ligier Richier, a relatively conventional figure of *Christ (behind the altar)*, and a striking **Skeleton★★** which owes much to advances in dissection technique and is far removed from the serene recumbent figures of the Middle Ages.

Excursions

La "Voie Sacrée" (Sacred Route)

During the Battle of Verdun there were only two routes for supplies, reinforcements and removal of the wounded not to be cut by enemy gunfire. Both linked Verdun with Bar-le-Duc; one was a narrow-gauge railway with a capacity of up to 2 000 tons a day, the other a winding secondary road (today's N35), 56km – 35mi long, and barely 6m – 20ft wide. It was this vital artery which became the *"Voie Sacrée"* of France's hard-pressed soldiers, the *poilus*. Its surface was quickly wrecked by the solid tyres of the 8 500 lorries—Berliets especially, but also Renaults and Peugeots—which used it every day, transporting 90 000 tons of material per week, but it was kept open by 10 000 Territorials constantly shovelling roadstone from quarries dug in the fields alongside.

St-Mihiel★

33km – 20mi northeast. Like many of the other towns along the Meuse, St-Mihiel's importance is due to its role as a river crossing in this zone where Gallic and Germanic claims to sovereignty have so often clashed.

As early as September 1914, the invading German army established the St-Mihiel salient, thus cutting the direct valley route to Verdun and making the beleaguered city's reinforcement entirely dependent on the state of the Voie Sacrée.

St-Mihiel's ancient abbey was founded in the 8C and rebuilt in the 17C, but the town is best known for its elegant hall-church dedicated to St Stephen which houses the celebrated **Sepulchre★★** by Ligier Richier, a native of the town. More theatrical in its effect than its equivalent at Chaumont, it was started in 1554 and never completed, because Richier, attracted by the ideas of the Reformation, left for Geneva in 1565. Nevertheless, the work reveals a strong sense of design and a dramatic intensity characteristic of the richness of provincial sculpture in Renaissance France.

La BAULE

POPULATION 14 688

MICHELIN MAP 316 B 4

GREEN GUIDE BRITTANY

Perhaps the ultimate in modern seafront development in northwestern France, the resort of La Baule is an attraction on a European scale. Such has not always been the case. It was only in 1879 that construction of the town began, after 400ha – 1000 acres of maritime pines had been planted to halt the steady encroachment of the sand dunes. The older houses retain much of their original charm and stand mostly hidden behind the more recent constructions, along the various shaded and well laid-out avenues.

Visit

Miles of beautiful and well-frequented sandy beaches protected by the headlands, Pointes de **Penchâteau** and **Chémoulin** to the northwest and southeast respectively, numerous hotels and apartment complexes, some comfortable, others luxurious, the proximity of delightful resorts such as **Le Croisica, Le Pouliguen★** and **Pornichet★**, with their pleasure-boat harbours, make La Baule, together with its neighbour **La Baule-les-Pins★★**, the ideal spot for discovering the splendour of the **"Côte d'Amour"** and the **Guérande Peninsula.**

Les **BAUX-DE-PROVENCE**★★★

POPULATION 437

MICHELIN MAP 340 D 3

GREEN GUIDE PROVENCE

With its ruined castle and deserted houses capping an arid rocky spur plunging abruptly to steep ravines on either side, the old village of Baux has the most spectacular of **sites**★★★. Baux has given its name to bauxite, a mineral first discovered here in 1822 and which gave rise to the aluminium industry.

🕐 **Organizing Your Time:** A walk through the streets of Les Baux is a magical experience, as long as they are not too crowded or full of souvenir sellers (unavoidable in the summer months). Give yourself an hour to take in the village and at least 45 minutes for the chateau.

🅿 **Parking:** The D78 approaches from Fontvielle and the first few houses of the old village clinging to the hillsides come into view suddenly in a bend. Park the car in one of the car parks *(unlimited parking: 4€, parking meter: 3€)*, however in high season it will probably be necessary to park by the side of the road some way down from the village and climb the rest of the hill on foot.

Sights

Town

The 17C former Town Hall (Hôtel de ville) has rooms with ribbed vaulting. The original entrance into the town is guarded by a gate (Porte Eyguières). The **Place St-Vincent**★, pleasantly shaded by elms and lotus-trees, has a terrace giving views of the small Fontaine Valley and Val d'Enfer. The church (Église St-Vincent) dates from the 12C; dressed in their long capes, the shepherds from the Alpilles hills come here for their **Christmas festival**★★, celebrated at Midnight Mass. The **Rue du Trencat**★ was carved into the living rock which has subsequently been pitted and eroded by wind and rain.

Château

🕐 *Jun-Aug: daily 9am-7.30pm; Mar-May and Sep-Nov: daily 9am-6.30pm; Dec-Feb: daily 9am-5pm.* ✆ *7.30€ (7-17 years: 3.50€).* ☎ *04 90 54 55 56. www.chateau-baux-provence.com.*
By the 11C the lords of Baux, "that race of eagles," were among the most powerful rulers in the south of France. Their turbulent ways, together with their support for the Reformation, were a great irritant to Louis XIII who in 1632 ordered the castle and ramparts to be dismantled; this was the town's death-blow.

Château and Chapelle Ste-Blaise

S. Sauvignier/MICHELIN

From the remains of the 13C keep a fine **panorama**★★ unfolds over the Alpilles with the windmills of Fontvieille to the west. One of them is Daudet's Mill (Moulin de Daudet). It was here that **Alphonse Daudet**, the Nîmes-born author, is supposed to have written his delightful *Letters from My Mill*, creating the characters of the Woman of Arles *(L'Arlésienne)*, Monsieur Seguin's goat, the Pope's grumpy mule and Dom Balaguère the gourmand.

◖◗ **Cathédrale d'images★** – ○ *Apr-Sep: daily 10am-7pm; Oct-Dec: daily 10am-6pm.* ○ *Closed 8 Jan to mid-Feb.* ⊙ *7.30€ (children: 3.50€).* ☎ *04 90 54 38 65. www. cathedrale-images.com* – audio-visual show. **Musée Yves Brayer★** ○ *Apr-Sep: daily 10am-12.30pm, 2-6.30pm; Oct-Dec and mid-Feb to end Mar: daily except Tue. 10am-12.30pm, 2-5.30pm.* ⊙ *4€.* ☎ *04 90 54 36 99. www.yvesbrayer.com.* – retrospective collection of the local artist.

Aiguilles de **BAVELLA**★★★

MICHELIN MAP 345 E 9

GREEN GUIDE CORSE (IN FRENCH)

From the Bavella Pass, Col de Bavella, there is a splendid view of the jagged Bavella or Asinao Peaks in a spectacular stark setting; the changing light plays on the sheer rock walls rising above the pine trees at the base.

Visit

Forêt de Bavella★★

The dense forest growing at an altitude of 500m to 1 300m (1 640ft – 4 265ft) has been repeatedly damaged by fire and has been extensively replanted with maritime and laricio pines, cedars and fir trees. A hunting preserve shelters herds of wild sheep which can be glimpsed perched high up on the sheer rocks. Just before the pass are low buildings formerly used as sheep-pens, and an inn, **Auberge du Col**, which is the starting-point for hikes around the pass to the Trou de la Bombe and La Pianona.

Col de Bavella

The mountain ridge crowning the island is indented by the Bavella Pass (alt 1 218m – 3 996ft) marked by a cross and the statue of **Notre-Dame-des Neiges.** The setting and the panorama over the summits are spectacular. To the west the Bavella Peaks rise above the forest of twisted pine trees while to the east the rock wall of Calanca Murata and the jagged ridge of red rock of Punta Tafonata di Paliri stand out against the backdrop of the Tyrrhenian Sea.

BAYEUX★★

POPULATION 14 704

MICHELIN MAP 303 H 4

GREEN GUIDE NORMANDY

The old capital of the lush pasturelands of the Bessin district, happily unscathed, was the first French town to be liberated, on D-Day + 1, 7 June 1944. Bayeux was the home town of Alain Chartier (1385-1433), the chronicler who spared no effort in rousing all manner of Frenchmen to save their country in the Hundred Years War. Five centuries later, on D-Day + 7, General de Gaulle "on foot, going from street to street, visibly moved" made his first speech on French soil. Later, on 16 June, he was to set out his principles for the establishment of a new constitution.  *Pont St-Jean, BP 343, 14400 Bayeux,* ☎ *02 31 51 28 28. www.bayeux-tourism.com.*

Bayeux - Address Book

For coin ranges see Legend at the back of the guide.

EATING OUT

La Cassonade – *35 r. du Bienvenu -* ☎ *02 31 92 47 32 -* 🕐 *Closed end of Dec.* Located in the heart of old Bayeux, this place is a must. Crepes and buckwheat *galettes*, salads and omelettes will satisfy the hungry and not-so hungry. Colourful dining room and reasonable prices.

Le Pommier – *40 r. des Cuisiniers -* ☎ *02 31 21 52 10 -* 🕐 *Open Tue evening and Wed, except during July-Aug -* 🕐 *Closed 7 - 28 Feb, 21 Nov - 2Dec.* No place could be more centrally located, near the Cathedral, its inviting apple-green façade announcing its rich Norman cuisine: smoked ham, *tripes à la mode de Caen*, cream sauces and of course apples. There are also vegetarian dishes. The vaulted dining-room with stone walls adds charming authenticity.

Hostellerie St-Martin – *14480 Creully -* ☎ *02 31 80 10 11 hostellerie. stmartin@ wanadoo.fr.* Today it's a restaurant, but in olden times the large vaulted rooms dating from the 16C housed the village market. Exposed stone, a fireplace, sculptures and a view of the wine cellar make up the curious decor. Classic cuisine. A few bedrooms.

Le Petit Bistrot – *2 r. du Bienvenu -* ☎ *02 31 51 85 40 -* 🕐 *Closed Jan, Sun and Mon - reserv. advisable .* An inventive cuisine prepared by a keen chef is the main attraction of this small establishment facing the cathedral. Original dishes inspired by Mediterranean cuisine are served in a Provençal-style decor with an ochre colour scheme, water colours and drawings.

WHERE TO STAY

La Ferme des Châtaigniers Bed and Breakfast – *14400 Vienne-en-Bessin - 7.5km/4.6mi E of Bayeux via D 126 -* ☎ *02 31 92 54 70 - 3 rooms.* Set apart from the farmhouse, this converted farm building contains simple yet pleasant, comfortable rooms. Guests have the use of a fitted kitchen. Peace and quiet is guaranteed in this house set in the fields.

Le Grand Fumichon Bed and Breakfast – *14400 Vaux-sur-Aure - 3km/1.9mi N of Bayeux via D 104 -* ☎ *02 31 21 78 51 - duyckja@wanadoo.fr - 4 rooms.* Once part of Longues-sur-Mer Abbey, this fortified 17C farm, with its square courtyard and characteristic porch, is today a dairy and cider-making farm. The attic rooms are plain but pleasant.

Hôtel Reine Mathilde – *23 r. Larcher -* ☎ *02 31 92 08 13 hotel-reinemathilde@ wanadoo.fr , www.hotel-reinemathilde. com -* 🕐 *Closed 15 Nov to 15 Feb - 16 rooms:* . If you wish to stay in the old town, this small family hotel is conveniently situated a stone's throw from the cathedral and the famous tapestry. Exposed beams and light-wood furniture. Plain rooms, some of them with sloping ceilings.

Le Manoir de Crépon Bed and Breakfast – *14480 Crépon -* ☎ *02 31 22 21 manoirdecrepon@wanadoo.fr -* 🕐 *Closed 10 Jan to 10 Feb - 5 rooms.* This 17C and 18C house is typical of the area, with its oxblood-coloured roughcast. You will like the stone floors and fireplaces, the vast, tastefully furnished bedrooms and the authentic atmosphere of the former kitchen converted into a breakfast room.

SHOPPING

Naphtaline – *16 parvis de la Cathédrale -* ☎ *02 31 21 50 03 -* 🕐 *Open Apr-3 Oct: 10am-7pm; Nov: 2-6.60pm; Mar and Dec: 11am-12.30pm, 2-6.30pm,* 🕐 *Closed Jan and Feb, Sundays and holidays off-season.* Two boutiques housed in a fine 18C building offer antique and modern lace, Bayeux porcelain and reproductions of traditional tapestries woven on Jaquard looms.

ON THE TOWN

Café Inn – *67 r. St-Martin -* ☎ *02 31 21 11 37-* 🕐 *Open daily 9am-7pm,* 🕐 *Closed Sundays and holidays.* Coffee beans are roasted on the spot and 75 sorts of tea are served in a bustling ambiance. Light meals of salades, omelettes and quiches are offered as prelude to the delicious *Tarte Tatin*, an upside-down apple pie.

Duke William knights Harold. They set out together for Bayeux (detail of the Bayeux Tapestry).

Courtesy Ville de Bayeux

The Norman Conquest

Edward the Confessor died without issue. His favourite, Harold, had sworn on sacred relics at Bayeux to honour the claim to the English throne of William the Bastard, Duke of Normandy (Edward's cousin). Whether through weakness or because of ambition, he reneged on his pledge. Secure in the support of the Pope and the neutrality of the King of France, encouraged by his barons and with the resources of the rich cities of Caen and Rouen at his disposal, William organised a punitive expedition in the space of seven months.

The main part of the Norman fleet was assembled at Dives *(48km – 30mi east);* its 3 000 ships carried 50 000 soldiers and cavalry who were landed on the coast of Sussex on 28 September 1066. Within a few days, battle had been joined just inland from Hastings and the Saxon army routed. Duke William had become the Conqueror. Shortly after his great victory, at a coronation ceremony in Westminster Abbey on 25 December, he accepted the crown of England.

Though in accordance with feudal law, the situation was an ambiguous one: William was both King of England and Duke of Normandy; the latter title made him a vassal of the King of France. Difficulties soon arose, becoming even more serious in 1152 as a result of the divorce of Louis VII and Eleanor of Aquitaine, and were to be resolved only at the end of the Hundred Years War.

Sights

Tapisserie de la Reine Mathilde★★★

♿ ⏱ *Mid-Mar to early Nov: daily 9am-6.30pm; May-Aug: daily 9am-7pm; early Nov to mid-Mar: daily 9.30am-12.30pm, 2-6pm.* ⏱ *Closed 1 Jan, 2 Jan (morning), 24 (afternoon), 25, 26 Dec (morning) and 31 Dec (afternoon).* 🎫 *7.50€ (ticket combined with the Baron-Gérard Museum and the Museum of Religious Art).* ☎ *02 31 51 25 50.*

This extraordinary masterpiece of embroidery was probably made in England soon after the Conquest. It tells of the consequences of Harold's failure to keep the oath he swore at Bayeux recognising William's right to succeed Edward the Confessor.

Its 58 episodes with headings recount the epic of the Norman invasion with striking truthfulness; in addition it is an irreplaceable source of information on the ships, weapons, clothes and way of life of the middle of the 11C.

Cathédrale Notre-Dame★★

Bayeux' much-venerated "mother-church" bears the marks of the many changes it has undergone over the centuries.

Of the Romanesque church (1049-97) there survive above all the groin-vaulted crypt and the lower part of the nave, with its walls and cornerstones profusely decorated in the 12C with interlacing, knotwork and low-relief sculpture. In the second half of the 12C the nave pillars were encased in slim columns, its arches doubled and the aisles given rib vaults.

In the 13C, the high watermark of the Gothic, the Romanesque galleries were replaced and the new work supported by twin-spanned flying buttresses. Of the same period is the superb chancel with its radiating chapels, elegant triforium, Norman gallery and the four fluted pillars at its semicircular eastern end. The 13C also saw the covering-up of the Romanesque façade by new doorways and a gable, together with the construction of the transepts with their three-pointed arches and gallery with a fretwork design.

Later additions included the building of side chapels along the aisles (14C), frescoes in the springs of the nave and, in a niche in the crypt, an octagonal storey over the crossing (15C), and the embellishment of the cathedral with furnishings and works of art (16C, 17C and 18C). In the 19C the tower was in danger of collapsing; its foundations were rebuilt and the external lantern added.

▶▶ **Musée mémorial de la Bataille de Normandie★** – ♿ ⏱ *May to mid-Sep: daily 9.30am-6.30pm; mid-Sep to end Apr: daily 10am-12.30pm, 2-6pm.* ⏱ *Closed mid to end Jan, 1 Jan, 25 Dec.* 🎫 *5.50 € (children: 2.50€)* ☎ *02 31 51 46 90–* Musée Baron Gérard (♿ temporarily in the Hôtel du Doyen) ⏱ *Jul-Aug: daily 10am-12.30pm and 2-7pm; Sep-Jun: daily 10am-12.30pm and 2-6pm.* ⏱ *Closed 1 Jan and 25 Dec.* 🎫 *2.60€ (ticket combined with the Bayeux Tapestry Museum and the Museum of Religious Art).* ☎ *02 31 92 14 21.*

BEAULIEU-SUR-DORDOGNE★★

POPULATION 1 265

MICHELIN MAP 329 M-6

GREEN GUIDE DORDOGNE BERRY LIMOUSIN

Beaulieu's Benedictine abbey, which had fallen on difficult times, placed itself under the authority of Cluny in 1076. Its restoration began 25 years later.

Sights

Église St-Pierre★★

🕐 *Daily 8am-7pm (summer: 7am-8pm).* 🏃‍♂️ *Guided tours available Jul-Aug: 10am-noon, 2.30-6pm (Casa Association; ☎ 01 46 51 39 30; www.guidecasa.com). ☎ 05 55 91 18 78.*

This is the former abbey church. Situated on the borders of the Auvergne, Limousin and Quercy, it recalls Conques (tribunes and ambulatory), le Dorat and Solignac (Limoges-style arching, restrained decoration), and Cahors (treatment of the chancel).

Its fine doorway **(portail★★)**, dating from 1125, is the work of artists from Toulouse. It still has the stylisation of the Romanesque (highly compartmentalised composition, jambs and piers like those at Moissac, treatment of the folds of clothes as at Souillac and Cahors), but it also anticipates the more subtle presentation of personality characteristic of the Gothic (the expressive features of the Apostles). The theme is the opening stages of the Last Judgement, with the dead being summoned from their graves. The ecstasy of the Apostles, the magnificence of the Cross and of the instruments of the Passion, the display of Christ's wounds and the subjugation of Evil represented by monsters, all proclaim the imminence of judgement.

◐◑ **Vierge romane★** (Romanesque figure of Our Lady – in the Treasury).

BEAUNE★★

POPULATION 21 289

MICHELIN MAP 320 I-J 6-7

GREEN GUIDE BURGUNDY JURA

The epicentre of one of the world's great wine regions, Beaune is also renowned for its artistic heritage. Fortified in 1368, it was the residence of the Dukes of Burgundy before they moved to Dijon. 🛈 *1 r. de l'Hôtel-Dieu, 21200 Beaune, ☎ 03 80 26 21 30. www.ot-beaune.fr.*

▶ **Orient Yourself:** Beaune, which is listed as a "Town of Art and History", offers discovery tours (1hr30min) from early Jul to mid-Sep at 3pm. Information at the tourist office or on www.vpah.culture.fr.

A Bit of History

La Côte – The vineyards stretch north and south from Beaune, as fine as they are prestigious. The vine was first planted here in Gallo-Roman times; the area devoted to it increased in the Middle Ages thanks to the clearing of waste and woodland by the monastic foundations. The reputation of the wines of Burgundy grew in the 15C along with the rise of its Ducal court. In the following century the great vineyards came into their own, as the monks mortgaged their lands and control passed into the hands of financial interests from the towns, eager to maximise returns from all their landholdings.

The "Côte" is formed by a long, straight escarpment rising above the alluvial plain of the Saône, fissured in places by deep combes. At its foot, depending on detailed conditions of soil, drainage, exposure and microclimate, grow the great vines, the most precious enclosed by walls. To the north is the **Côte de Nuits**, celebrated for its noble red wines made from the choice Pinot Noir grape (Nuits, Vosne, Vougeot, Chambolle, Morey, Gevrey). To the south is the **Côte de Beaune** where the same grape makes other great red wines (Beaune, Pommard, Volnay, Chassagne-Montrachet, Santenay,

Beaune - Address Book

For coin ranges, see the Legend at the back of the guide.

EATING OUT

🍽 **Le Bouchon** – *Pl. de l'Hôtel-de-Ville - 21900 Meursault - 8km/5mi SW of Beaune by N 74 - ☎ 03 80 21 29 56 - ⏱ closed 20 Nov-28 Dec Sun evenings and Mon.* Le Bouchon is a small, popular restaurant in the town centre with a thriving local clientele. Regional dishes are served in a simply decorated dining room with small but pretty square tables.

🍽 **Le Bénaton** – *25 R. du Fg-Bretonnière - ☎ 03 80 22 00 26 - lebenaton@club-internet.fr - ⏱ closed 30 Nov to 8 Dec, Wed and Thu except in high season.* Small restaurant far from the madding crowd with a pretty covered terrace for the summer days. Pleasant dining room with stone walls and bright decorative hues. Attractive quality/price ratio for light yet delicious meals made with fresh seasonal produce.

🍽 **Le P'tit Paradis** – *25 R. Paradis - ☎ 03 80 24 91 00 - ⏱ closed 8-16 Mar, 9-17 Aug, 21 Nov to-14 Dec, Mon and Tue.* The pretty dining room and terrace border a flowering garden. Contemporary cuisine incorporates regional flourishes, and wines are selected from boutique producers.

🍽 **Ma cuisine** – *Passage Ste-Hélène - ☎ 03 80 22 30 22 - cave-sainte-helene@ wanadoo.fr - ⏱ closed August, Christmas holidays, Wed, Sat and Sun.* Located along a tiny street, this small dining room sports the colours of Provence. Regional wines on the wine list.

🍽 **Le Caveau des Arches** – *10 Bd Perpreuil - ☎ 03 80 22 10 37 - restaurant. caveau.des.arches@wanadoo.fr - ⏱ closed 24 Jul to 25 Aug, 23 Dec-17 Jan Sun and Mon.* In summer remember to bring a cardigan with you as the vaulted dining rooms of this restaurant set up on the ramparts can be somewhat chilly. Admire the ruins of an old bridge which once gave access to the city. Traditional Burgundy cooking.

WHERE TO STAY

🛏 **Chambre d'Hôte Le Meix des Hospices** – *R. Basse (near the church) - 71150 Demigny - 10km/6.2mi S of Beaune by D 18 - ☎ 03 85 49 98 49 - ⏱ closed 1st wk of Jul and last wk of Aug. - 🚫 - 3 rooms.* This former hospice annexe consists of several outbuildings arranged around a square courtyard. The quiet, simple rooms, one of which is set up beneath the eaves, are sparsely appointed with modern furniture. The dining room features exposed beams, stone flooring and a fireplace.

🛏 **Hôtel du Parc** – *21200 Levernois - 5km/3.1mi SW of Beaune by rte de Verdun-sur-le-Doubs, D 970 then D 111L - ☎ 03 80 24 63 00 - hotel.le.parc@wanadoo.fr - ⏱ closed 28 Nov-27 Jan - 🅿 - 25 rooms - 🍴 6€.* Covered with Virginia creeper and bursting with flowers in summertime, this hotel is quite simply charming. The two buildings are separated by a small patio. Bright, sober accommodation. The park at the back looks out over peaceful meadows.

🛏 **Hôtel Le Cep** – *27 R. Maufoux - ☎ 03 80 22 35 48 - resa@hotel-cep-beaune. com - 🅿 - 61 rooms - 🍴 15€.* Ravishing 16C house in the old quarter. The bedrooms, decorated in old-fashioned style, carry the names of famous vintages from the Côte-d'Or. Breakfast is served in the vaulted cellar or, weather permitting, in the courtyard with its pretty Renaissance arcades and medallions.

🛏 **Hostellerie du Château de Bellecroix** – *Rte de Chalon - 71150 Chagny - 18km/11.2mi SW of Beaune by N 74 then N 6 - ☎ 03 85 87 13 86 - chateau.de. bellecroix@wanadoo.fr - ⏱ closed 19 Dec-13 Feb and Wed out of season - 🅿 - 20 rooms - 🍴 13€.* The two towers of this 18C château stand amid wooded parkland. Nearby lie the turrets of a former 12C Knights Templar commandery belonging to the Order of Malta. The bedrooms are appointed with antique furniture. There are some fine replicas of medieval wainscoting in the dining hall.

SIT BACK AND RELAX

Bouché – *1 pl. Monge - ☎ 03 80 22 10 35 - Tue-Sun 8am-8pm, Sun 8am-1pm and 3-8pm.* Step inside this pretty tearoom and you'll find lovely gift boxes ready to fill with tantalizing house specialties, among them chocolate "snails", candied chestnuts and candied fruits. At table, you'll have to chose between *tarte vigneronne*, *millefeuille*, or any of the 20 or so specially created sweets.

Palais des gourmets – *14 Pl. Carnot - ☎ 03 80 22 13 39 - May-Sep daily 7am-7.30pm ; Oct-Apr Tue-Sun 7am-7pm - ⏱ closed. Tue Oct-Apr.* This delightful *patisserie*-tea room serves many a local delicacy, including *cassissines* (blackcurrant fruit jelly flavoured with blackcurrant liqueur), *roulés au cointreau* (pancakes with a Cointreau filling) and chocolate medallions depicting the Hôtel-Dieu.

ON THE TOWN

Le Bistrot Bourguignon – *8 R. Monge - ☎ 03 80 22 23 24 - le.bistrot.bourguignon@ wanadoo.fr - ⏱ open Tue-Sat 11am-3pm, 6-11pm - ⏱ closed mid-Feb to mid-Mar.* Relax on the charming terrace or sink into one of the comfortable armchairs inside this old house, sipping a glass of excellent wine to the strains of a few popular songs.

Place Carnot – This large, recently restored square has many outdoor cafés where you can sit in the sun all day. The perfect place to have breakfast, lunch or dinner!

WINELOVERS' PARADISE

L'Athenaeum de la Vigne et du Vin – *5 r. de l'Hôtel-Dieu - ☏ 03 80 25 08 30 - althenaeum@wanadoo.fr - ⏰ open daily 10am-7pm - ⏰ closed 25 Dec and 1 Jan.* This bookshop has earned quite a reputation as the ultimate authority on the art of oenology, Burgundy and fine gastronomy. It also presents a collection of miscellaneous items related to wine: corkscrews, glasses and cellarman's knives.

Cave Patriarche Père & Fils – *5-7 R. du Collège - ☏ 03 80 24 53 78 - www.patriarche.com - ⏰ open Oct-Mar: daily 10-11.30am, 2-5.30pm (Sa-Su 5pm); Apr-Sep: daily 9.30-11.30am, 2-5.30pm - ⏰ closed 25 Dec and 1 Jan.* Burgundy's largest cellars (15 000m2/18 000sq yd) are housed in a former convent dating from the 14C and 16C. Guided tours and tasting sessions of 13 different wines.

Caves de La Reine Pédauque – *Porte St-Nicolas - ☏ 03 80 22 23 11 - www.reine-pedauque.com - ⏰ open end of Nov to Mar: daily 10am-noon, 2-5pm; Apr-Nov: daily 9.30am-12.30pm, 2-7pm - ⏰ closed Christmas and Jan.* After exploring the 18C vaulted cellars, visitors may take part in a wine tasting session around an imposing round marble table! An opportunity not to be missed!

La Cave des Cordeliers – *6 R. de l'Hôtel-Dieu - ☏ 03 80 25 o8 85 - ⏰ open Oct-Apr: daily 10.30-11.30am, 2-5.30pm; May-Sep: daily 9.30am-noon, 2-6pm - ⏰ closed 25 Dec and 1Jan.* The Couvent des Cordeliers, built in 1242, provides a splendid backdrop to these wine cellars, which you can visit before tasting six fine Burgundy wines. In the courtyard, note the 1580 low relief depicting the Adoration of the Magi.

Le Comptoir Viticole – *1 R. Samuel-Legay - ☏ 03 80 22 15 73 - 222.comptoir-viticole. com - ⏰ open Mon 9am-noon, 2-7pm; Tue-Sat8am-noon, 2-7pm - ⏰ closed Sun and public holidays.* Wine buffs and amateur vignerons will adore this shop, which sells all manner of devices related to winemaking: bottling machines, corkscrews, bottle racks, jeroboams, balthasars.

Marché aux Vins – *2 R. Nicolas-Rolin - ☏ 03 80 25 08 20 - www.marcheauxvins. com - ⏰ open mid-Jun to late Aug: daily 9.30am-7pm; Sep to mid-Jun: 9.30am-noon, 2-6.30pm - ⏰ closed 25-26 Dec and 1-2 Jan.* Housed in Beaune's oldest church (13C and 14C) opposite the famous hospice, this wine market offers 18 wines of between 3 and 15 years of age, to be sipped and relished slowly. If requested, a cellar containing some extremely rare vintages, which have been maturing since 1911, can also be opened to visitors.

Vins de Bourgogne Denis-Perret – *40 R. Carnot - ☏ 03 80 22 35 47 - contact@denisperret.fr - ⏰ open May-Oct: Mon-Sat 9am-7pm, Sun 9am-noon; the rest of the year Mon-Sat 9am-noon, 2-7pm, ⏰ closed public holiday afternoons and Sun out of season.* Five wine-growers and a group of landowners have teamed up to offer you some of the most prestigious names from the Burgundy region— Romanée-Conti, Clos-Vougeot, Montrachet, Chambertin. Such a rich selection could easily leave you speechless but, not to worry, several young oenologists are there to help you make your choice and to suggest the best dishes to go with each wine.

Mercurey), and where the Chardonnay makes the finest of white wines (Meursault, Puligny-Montrachet). On the third Sunday in November the auction takes place in Beaune of the wines of the Hospices.

The Hospices: a Charitable Foundation of the 15C – In 1443, **Nicolas Rolin** (1377-1461), Chancellor to Philippe le Bon (the Good), founded the Hôtel-Dieu hospital in Beaune. Few rises have been as meteoric as his. Born of a modest Autun family, he became a lawyer, then a counsellor to John the Fearless. In 1422 he was promoted to the high rank of Chancellor by Philip the Good. While expertly promoting the prestige and interests of his master, he also acquired favour, fortune and power for himself to an unprecedented degree. It was he who succeeded in detaching Burgundy from its alliance with England and reconciling her with France by the Treaty of Arras in 1435.

Whether out of remorse for scruples forgotten while furthering his ambition, concern of a man aged 66 for his soul, or genuine interest in the welfare of the needy, he founded a free hospital and guaranteed a perpetual income for it from a 1 300ha – 3 200-acre estate of woodland, arable land and vines between Aloxe-Corton and Meursault; today, the income from 58ha – 143 acres of great vines suffices for the maintenance and restoration of this venerable institution.

In 1457 Rolin fell into disgrace; he died at Autun four years later.

Hôtel-Dieu

Sights

Hôtel-Dieu★★

♿ ⏰ *End Mar to mid-Nov: daily 9am-6.30pm; mid-Nov to end Mar: daily 9-11.30am, 2-5.30pm.* ⊚ *5.40€.* ☎ *03 80 24 45 00. www.hospices-de-beaune-tm.fr.*

For 520 years, Rolin's foundation cared for the sick, from 1451 to 1971. It has come down to us intact. With its fine architecture, its elegant decoration (ironwork, gabled dormers, weathervanes), its multi-coloured glazed tiles and its old well, it seems more a palace of luxury than a place for the poor. Although the internal courtyard in Flemish-Burgundian style, the pharmacy, the nuns' quarters, the kitchens are fascinating, it is the Great Hall (Grand'Salle) which most completely evokes the spiritual dimension of the hospitals of yesteryear. It remained in service up to 1959.

Polyptych of the Last Judgement★★★

Rolin himself commissioned this work from Rogier van der Weyden to go over the altar of the Great Hall. The master, with the help of assistants, completed it between 1443 and 1451. In its expression of emotion at this crucial moment and in its perfection of detail (which can be inspected with the aid of a giant magnifying-glass), it is one of the greatest of Gothic paintings. At the time, its masterly evocation of the outcome to be expected from the living of a blameless life must have been reassuring too.

▶▶ **Musée du vin de Bourgogne★** – ⏰ *Wed-Mon 9.30am-6pm (Dec-Mar: 5pm). Last admission 30min before closing.* ⏰ *Closed Tue, 1 Jan and 25 Dec.* ⊚ *5.40€.* ☎ *03 80 22 08 19* – relates the history of Burgundian vineyards. **Collégiale Notre-Dame★** – tapestries★★. **Hôtel de la Rochepot★**.

Excursions

Châteauneuf★

37km – 23 miles northwest. The old fortified market town in its picturesque **setting★** is famous for its castle which commanded the road from Dijon to Autun. The charming narrow streets are lined with old houses. The southern approach provides the best view immediately after crossing the Canal de Bourgogne.

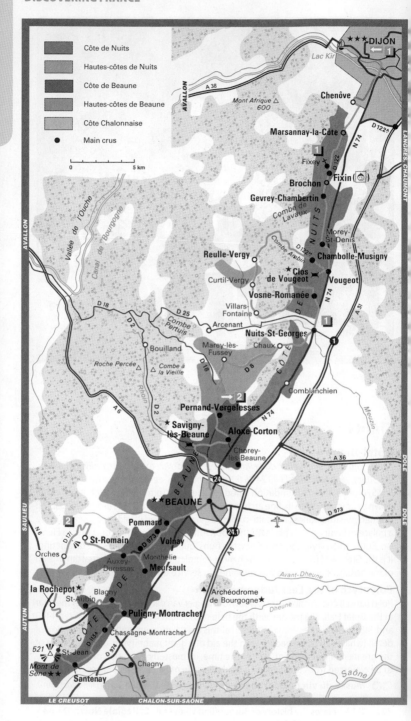

Château★

The imposing fortress girt by thick walls flanked by massive towers was built in the 12C and remodelled in the 15C. A drawbridge framed by huge round towers gives access to the courtyard.

BEAUVAIS★★

POPULATION 57 704

MICHELIN MAP 305 D 4

GREEN GUIDE NORTHERN FRANCE AND THE PARIS REGION

A fortified city rising from the surrounding marshlands, Beauvais became a town in its own right as early as 1099. It was here in 1357 that the peasants' revolt known as the Jacquerie had its beginnings. The physicist Gilles Personne de Roberval was born here in 1602; in 1647, he proved the existence of atmospheric pressure (measured the following year by Pascal at the foot and summit of the Puy de Dôme), and in 1670 achieved fame through his invention of beam scales; he was also known as an opponent of Descartes' philosophy. *1 r. Beauregard, 60000 Beauvais, ☎ 03 44 15 30 30.*

▶ **Orient Yourself:** Beauvais, which is listed as a "Town of Art and History", offers discovery tours (2hr) from Apr-Sep on Sun at 3pm. 4€. Information at the tourist office or on www.vpah.culture.fr.

Sights

Cathédrale St-Pierre★★★

🕒 *Son et lumière display (30min) at 10.40am, 11.40am, 2.40pm, 3.40pm 4.40pm (Jul and Aug: additional show at 12.40pm and 5.40pm; winter: at 11.40am, 2.40pm, 3.40pm).* 🕒 *Closed 1 Jan.* 🎫 *4€ (children: 1€).* ☎ *03 44 48 11 60.*

Only three western bays remain of the Carolingian cathedral. In 1225 the decision was taken by the Bishop of Beauvais to build the biggest and highest cathedral of the age in honour of St Peter. Its vaults were to top 48 metres – 157ft. Construction of the choir began in 1238 and by 1263 was completed. In 1272 the vault collapsed; it was rebuilt but fell again in 1284. Work had to start immediately on strengthening the abutments, building new buttresses, increasing the number of flying buttresses at the east end and using them like external struts at the very base of the roof, 40m – 131ft above ground, concealing the sheer daring of the original enterprise.

The interior was treated similarly. In the southern bays, additional pillars underpinned the structure above. The windows were given more lancets to subdivide and strengthen them, glazing was added to the elevation, lightening it considerably.

After the Hundred Years War, Martin Chambiges began the construction of the transepts and crossing. He designed the great gable and rose window of the south transept, then, instead of starting on the nave, he built the crossing tower. It was completed in 1539, a century later, but 11m – 36ft higher, than the tower of Strasbourg Cathedral. With no nave to buttress it, however, the great structure collapsed in 1573.

There is much decorative work to admire, from the Renaissance doors of the south portal, to the stained-glass windows (**vitraux**★★) created by the Beauvais workshops founded by Ingrand Leprince. The south transept has beautiful hues of green in the triforium and a rose window by Nicolas Leprince, and the figures of the Sibyls in the north transept. Tapestries are exhibited regularly; their fame is linked to the work of Jean-Baptiste Oudry who was in charge of the Beauvais manufactory from 1734 to 1753. The astronomical clock (**horloge astronomique**★) is of interest.

Église St-Étienne★

The aisles of the Romanesque nave have one of the earliest of ribbed vaults; the transverse arches have a slight horse-shoe shape and the ribbing is archaic in form. On the north side of the choir is a Jesse Window (**vitrail de l'Arbre de Jessé**★★★). Jesse's descendants are depicted against a luminous blue background; the design of the window, its colours and transparency make it a rare masterpiece.

▶▷ **Musée Départemental de l'Oise**★ – 🕒 *Jul to Sep: Wed-Mon 10am-6pm; Sep to end Jun: Wed-Mon 10am-noon, 2-6pm.* 🕒 *Closed Tue, 1 Jan, Easter, Whitsun, 1 May, 1 Nov, 25 Dec.* 🎫 *2€, no charge Wed.* ☎ *03 44 11 43 83* – paintings, sculpture and tapestries.

Abbaye du **BEC-HELLOUIN**★★

MICHELIN MAP 304 E 6

GREEN GUIDE NORMANDY

The prestigious abbey rivalled that of Jumièges, its influence in matters of doctrine and oratory being without parallel.

A Bit of History

In the year 1042, **Lanfranc** (1005-89) appeared before the abbey gates. This great yet humble man, a fine teacher and master of jurisprudence, was in flight from the success his teaching had brought him at Avranches. Three years later, a sense of duty led him to start teaching again, making Le Bec one of the great intellectual centres of the West. After the Conquest, Lanfranc, who had become Duke William's Counsellor, was made Archbishop of Canterbury and Primate of all England. He took his church vigorously in hand, staffing its higher ranks with clerics from Le Bec.

His successor at Le Bec was St Anselm (1033-1109), his former pupil, a philosopher and distinguished theologian whose thinking was of an almost experimental rigour in its drive for truth. His *Proslogion*, written here in 1078, is held to be one of the great sources of Western thought. In 1093 he too became Archbishop of Canterbury.

In England Le Bec owned great estates which were lost at the Dissolution following Henry VIII's break with Rome (1534). But the Abbey's spiritual prestige remained intact, with both English Churches – Anglican and Roman Catholic – claiming St Anselm's succession and maintaining links with Le Bec which were broken only when the monks were expelled in 1792. They returned in 1948.

Destruction, Desecration, Restoration – The monks remaining at Le Bec were driven out at the time of the French Revolution. The Abbey's copper and lead, and the bronze from its bells were melted down, and its tapestries, archives, books and furniture dispersed. In 1809, following a decree which authorised the demolition of churches where there were two or more to a parish, the 13C abbey church and its chapter-house were used as quarries.

From 1802 for nearly a century the abbey served as a remount depot and stud. In 1901 it was put in the charge of the Ministry of War.

Visit

🕐 *Guided tours*  *(45min) Jun-Sep: daily except Tue at 10.30am, 3pm, 4pm, 5pm, Sat at 10.30am, 3pm, 4pm, Sun and public holidays at noon, 3pm, 4pm; Oct-May: daily except Tue at 10.30am, 3pm, 4pm, Sun and public holidays at noon, 3pm, 4pm, by appointment; Jan: self-guided visits on Tue.* ⊗ *4.60€.* ☎ *02 32 43 72 60.*

Since 1948 considerable reconstruction has taken place, particularly of the St-Nicolas Tower of 1467 and the Abbot's Lodging of 1735. But the great Abbey Church, whose 42m – 140ft choir was one of the wonders of the Christian world, has gone, though its spiritual power is undiminished.

BELFORT★

POPULATION 75 509

MICHELIN MAP 321 K 1, 314 J 7

GREEN GUIDE BURGUNDY JURA

Belfort is divided by the Savoureuse into two distinct parts. On the river's west bank are extensive industrial and commercial areas and housing estates; on the east bank, at the foot of the rock on which the castle is sited, is the "impregnable" citadel built by Vauban. This 17C fortified town is the great military engineer's masterpiece. In the 19C, as pressure built up on the town to expand, its ramparts were demolished.

A Bit of History

An Invasion Route – Lying between the Jura to the south and the Vosges to the north, the route through the Belfort Gap (Trouée de Belfort) or Burgundian Gate (Porte de Bourgogne) has drawn successive waves of invaders, Celts, Germanic tribes, soldiers of the Holy Roman Empire. Belfort's history is a battered one.

In the course of the Franco-Prussian War of 1870, 40 000 German troops were held up for a month before Belfort by the Mobile Guards commanded by Colonel Denfert-Rochereau. Retiring in good order into the citadel, he and his men withstood a 103-day siege, consenting to march out (with full battle honours) only on the direct orders of the French government, 21 days after the armistice signed at Versailles. In the struggle between President Thiers and Bismarck, the German Chancellor, over the cession of French territory, this exemplary resistance made it possible for Belfort to escape the fate of Alsace and Lorraine; it became instead the centre of its own tiny territory.

In November 1944 the advance of the First French Army through the Belfort Gap towards the Rhine was held up by the retreating Wehrmacht. The night attack of 19 November on the Salbert Fort (northwest of the town) by Commandos of the Army of Africa led to Belfort's liberation on 22 November; the thrust in the direction of Mulhouse could now continue.

Visit

Le Lion★★

🕐 *Apr-Sep: Wed-Mon 10am-noon, 2-6pm; Oct-Mar: Wed-Mon 10am-noon, 2-5pm.* 🕐 *Closed Tue, 1 Jan, 25 Dec.* ⊚ *3.90€ (under 18 years: no charge), no charge second Sun in the month.* ☎ *03 84 54 25 51.*

The great beast (22m – 72ft long and 11m – 36ft high) carved from red Vosges sandstone just below the castle symbolises the spirit and strength of Belfort's defenders in 1870, and marks the response of the French people to their heroism. It is the work of **Frédéric Bartholdi** (1834-1904) of Colmar, who here gave free rein to his patriotic fervour and ardent creativity. It was he who sculpted the *Trois Sièges (Three Seats)* monument in the town's Place de la République as well as *Liberty Lighting the World* at the entrance to New York harbour.

◑◑ **Le Camp retranché**★★(the Citadel) – 🕐 *Guided tours* 🔊 *(1hr) Jul-Sep: daily 10am-noon, 2-6pm.* ☎ *03 84 54 25 51.*

Excursions

Pays de Montbéliard

19km – 12mi south. The principality of Montbéliard was converted early to Lutheranism, a result of its having been attached to the Duchy of Württemberg in 1397. Its annexation by France dates from 1793. Powerful families lived here, like the Moussons, the Montfaucons and the Châlons, whose name is recalled by Montbéliard's round-towered château. The great biologist **Jean Cuvier** was born here.

The industrial progress which marked the reign of Louis XVI produced interesting developments in the area. In 1773, **Georges-Frédéric Japy**, a farrier and grandson of a locksmith, started a clock-making works, which spawned other factories around Paris and in the North of France producing metalwork, electrical goods, typewriters and mechanical dolls.

Jean-Pierre Peugeot was descended from a long line of mill-owners (corn, dyes, tanning). In 1811, at his Sous-Cratet mill near Herimoncourt, he started working in metal, not without some set-backs. His sons, Armand and Eugène, went on to found an important industrial group, beginning with their bicycle factory in 1886 and the manufacture of a number of steam tricycles in 1889. At Sochaux is the **Musée Peugeot**★ which tells the story of this famous name. There are coffee-mills, bicycles, tools, and a vis-à-vis of 1892; among the other vehicles note especially a Double Phaeton of 1906, a Bébé Torpedo of 1913, a two-door Eclipse of 1936 and a 404 Diesel Records coupé of 1965.

BELLE-ÎLE★★★

POPULATION 4 489

MICHELIN MAP 308 L-M 10-11

GREEN GUIDE BRITTANY

Belle-Île's interest lies as much in its history as in its wonderful coastline. In the Middle Ages the island belonged to the Counts of Cornouaille and was often raided by pirates (French as well as Dutch and English) because of its wealth in grain.

Sights

Le Palais

This is the island's capital, its natural harbour dominated by the citadel and the fortifications protecting the town. In 1548 an English attack had been repulsed, but the incident made Henri II aware of England's continuing interest in Aquitaine and France's Atlantic coast generally. His response was to build a fort along more solid lines than the previous monastic château.

In 1572, during the Wars of Religion, Albert de Gondi was charged with the defence of the island; he was responsible for constructing the dungeons of the Le Palais gateway. The following year the island was taken by Gabriel de Lorgues. It was this gentleman, also known as Montgomery, who had fatally wounded Henri II at a joust in Paris, then, turned Huguenot, and fearful of Catherine de' Medici's revenge, had escaped from the St Barthomew's massacre (1572) to England. His sacking of the island came in between two inconclusive battles off La Rochelle, all serving to justify in retrospect the King's policy at the Treaty of Le Cateau-Cambrésis.

Citadelle Vauban★

🕒 Apr-Oct: daily 9.30am-6pm; Jul and Aug: daily 9am-7pm; Nov-Mar: daily 9.30am-noon, 2-5pm. ⚬ 6.10€ (children: 3.05€) no charge 3rd Sat-Sun in Sep. ☎ 02 97 31 84 17.

The proximity of Belle-Île to the ports of the south coast of Brittany (e.g. Lorient) and the mouth of the Loire (Nantes) gave it great importance in the fight for the control of the high seas conducted by England and France, an aspect of that rivalry between them which was the dominating factor in international politics from the reign of Louis XIV to the fall of Napoleon. In the search for outlets for her growing manufactures, England came frequently into conflict with France, herself in pursuit of new overseas territories but with the additional burden of defending long land frontiers.

In 1658, the island came into the hands of Chancellor **Fouquet**. He consolidated the defences and installed 200 new batteries to defend against attack from the sea.

In 1674, at the time of the Dutch Wars, 70 ships of the United Provinces' fleet dropped anchor off Grands Sables beach. At this point Vauban was working at St Malo, Rochefort, Blaye and St-Martin-de-Ré, but from 1682, the great military engineer adapted the citadel to the needs arising from improvements in the technology of war, convert-

Aiguilles de Port-Coton

G. Targat/MICHELIN

ing an old chapel (Henri II Tower) into a powder-magazine with a projecting roof to fend off broadsides, rebuilding the old arsenal as well as laying out an officers' walk (Promenade des Officiers) with a gallery giving fine sea views.

In 1696, during the War of the League of Augsburg *(1)* the English succeeded in taking the nearby islands of Houat and Hoëdic, and at one point landed on Belle-Île itself. From 1710 to 1713, during the War of the Spanish Succession, they based themselves at Grands Sables. This was the time at which Acadia and Newfoundland were taken from France. In 1723, the old Louis XIII bastion was altered and became the Sea Bastion (Bastion de la Mer). In 1746, during the War of the Austrian Succession, the English fleet sank the royal ship *L'Ardent* between Le Palais and Quiberon. In 1761, during the Seven Years War, in which France lost Guadeloupe and Martinique in the Antilles as well as Pondicherry, Belle-Île's citadel fell after 38 days of siege. For two years, under the guns of a fleet of 130 vessels, the island became a virtual colony, governed by General Hodgson. By the Treaty of Paris, signed 10 February 1763, France recovered the Antilles but lost Canada; England gave back Belle-Île but made herself a Mediterranean base on Ibiza, convenient for her designs on Corsica.

In 1775 the Louis XVI Arsenal was the final major project carried out in the citadel. Three years later, the American War of Independence made it more necessary than ever to assert French sea power along the Breton coast and protect free access to its ports.

Anglo-French rivalry continued during both Revolution and Empire. In 1793 the Convention had to come to terms with the loss of Pondicherry, confront an Anglo-Spanish fleet off Toulon, in 1794 accept the loss of the Antilles and squash the Anglo-Corsican Kingdom, and in 1795 defeat the emigré forces at Quiberon. In 1802, while still First Consul, Napoleon had Le Palais fortified; later, as Emperor, he had to face the loss of the Antilles again while dealing with the successive coalitions ranged against him.

Côte Sauvage★★★

Belle-Île is a remnant of the ancient coastline of Brittany which once ran from the Penmarch peninsula to the Île d'Yeu. The rise in sea-level following the retreat of the glaciers at the end of the last Ice Age some 8 000 years ago led to its separation from the mainland.

The Côte Sauvage, literally "wild coast", runs from the Pointe des Poulains to the Pointe de Talud. Battered by the Atlantic waves, the schists of which the island's plateau is composed have been formed into spectacular coastal scenes.

Port-Donnant★★ has a splendid sandy beach between high cliffs but is known for its great rollers and perilous currents.

The **Aiguilles de Port-Coton**★★ are pyramids hollowed out into caverns and grottoes. The different colours of the rock have been exposed by the action of the sea.

 **Sauzon**★; **Pointe des Poulains**★★; **Port-Goulphar**★.

BESANÇON★★

POPULATION 122 623

MICHELIN MAP 321 G 3

GREEN GUIDE BURGUNDY JURA

Besançon is the capital of the Franche-Comté. The **site**★★★ of the historic core of the city is unusual, framed as it is by a series of hills and enclosed by a meander of the Doubs emerging from the Lomont Mountains by way of the Rivotte Valley.

The strategic value of the site, already remarked on by Caesar, gave rise to a Gallo-Roman settlement; the Black Gate (Porte Noire), a 2C triumphal arch, survives. The axis formed by the Roman highway has become the modern Grande-Rue in the heart of old Besançon (**Vieille ville**★). Already in Roman times, Besançon was an important stopping point on the commercial route to the Rhine, the Alps and Italy. *2 pl. de la 1ʳᵉ-Armée-Française, 25000 Besançon, ☎ 03 81 80 92 00. www. besancon.tourisme.com.*

Every year, in early September, the city stages a music festival, the **Festival International de Musique de Besançon et de Franche-Comté**, during which a prize is awarded to the best young conductor.

▶ **Orient Yourself:** Besançon, which is listed as a "Town of Art and History," offers various discovery tours. Information at the tourist office or on www.vpah.culture.fr.

A Bit of History

A city under Spanish rule, then French – In 1493, Emperor Maximilian of Austria granted the Franche-Comté to his son Philip the Fair who married Joan the Mad, heiress of Spain. Their son Charles V thus inherited Spain from his mother and Habsburg lands, among them Flanders and the Franche-Comté, from his father. Having been Imperial, then Burgundian territory, the Franche-Comté, in the 16C, became Spanish.

The era marked a high point in the province's commercial life, illustrated by the rise of the Granvelle family. Starting from a humble peasant background in the Loue Valley, Perrenot, one of their number, became Chancellor to Charles V and built himself the **Palais Granvelle**★. This fine example of civil architecture of the 16C has a three-storey façade, divided by five horizontal bands of decoration, and a high mansard roof with crowstep gables. Its proportions and decorative details are those of the Early Renaissance (basket-handle arches, mouldings) while other features are quite new (Tuscan columns, and the superposition of Ionic and composite orders).

In 1674 Louis XIV conquered the Franche-Comté. He made Besançon, rather than Dole, the capital of the new French province, and, fully aware of the vulnerability of the new frontier, ordered Vauban to make the city impregnable. In carrying out his task the great engineer razed part of the Spanish fortifications of 1668 and from 1675 to 1711 constructed the citadel (**citadelle**★★); its great strength is best appreciated from the sentry-walk along the encircling ramparts. One prominent look-out is named for the King, another for the Queen (Guérites du Roi, de la Reine).

Besançon Address Book

For coin ranges, see the Legend at the back of the guide.

EATING OUT

🖾 **Au Petit Polonais** – *81 R. Granges - ☎ 03 81 81 23 67 - jean-michel.viennot@wanadoo.fr -* 🕐 *closed 14 Jul-15 Aug, Sat evenings and Sun.* In 1870 this restaurant was founded by a Pole, whose story is recounted on the menu. Simple, unpretentious setting. Traditional and regional cuisine. Warm, congenial atmosphere.

🖾 **Le Cavalier Rouge** – *3 R. Mégevand - ☎ 03 81 83 41 02 - fermé dim. et lun. soir.* A trendy urban atmosphere welcomes groups of regulars, who talk shop over specialties of the day. Quick service.

🖾 **Le Chaland** – *Prom. Micaud, near Pont Brégille - ☎ 03 81 80 61 61 - chaland@chaland.com -* 🕐 *closed Sat lunchtime.* Settle into the restaurant on this charming old barge moored along the Doubs, offering views of the old town and the Promenade Micaud. In fair weather, meals are served on the upper deck, from where you can see the cormorants circling above the water.

🖾🖾 **Barthod** – *22 R. Bersot - ☎ 03 81 82 27 14 -* 🕐 *closed Sun and Mon.* Sit down on the charming terrace bursting with bushes and potted plants and admire the view of the nearby waterfall. The owner is a wine buff who proposes lovingly prepared menus (prices include wine) washed down by an interesting selection

of vintages. Don't forget to drop by the shop on your way out.

WHERE TO STAY

🖾 **Hôtel du Nord** – *8 R. Moncey - ☎ 03 81 81 34 56 - hoteldunord3@wanadoo.fr -* 🅿 - 🖾 *5.40€.* Situated in the historic quarter, this hotel is a perfect base for venturing out into the old town. The spacious, traditional rooms are equipped with all modern conveniences.

🖾🖾 **Relais des Vallières** – *3 R. P.-Rubens – 4km/2.5mi from Besançon by Bd. de l'O – ☎ 03 81 52 02 02 - relaisvallieres@wanadoo.fr -* 🅿 *– 49 rooms -* 🖾 *6€.* Near the Micropolis expo park, this hotel offers clean, comfortable rooms (those at the rear are quieter); a few boast balconies. Buffet-style meals in the bistrot-style restaurant.

🖾🖾 **Hôtel Citotel Granvelle** – *13 R. du Gén.-Lecourbe - ☎ 03 81 81 33 92 -* 🅿 - *28 rooms -* 🖾 *6,50€.* This stone building boasts an ideal location just steps from the historic town centre. Comfortable rooms giving onto a paved interior courtyard. Buffet breakfast.

SIT BACK AND RELAX

Brasserie 1802 – *Pl. Granvelle - ☎ 03 81 82 21 97 -* 🕐 *closed 1 Jan and 25 Dec.* Since it's named for the year Victor Hugo was born, you'd think this brasserie would carry the weight of history but no, it's as hip as they come. The menu features local products transformed into contemporary cuisines. Wide, shady terrace.

Brasserie du Commerce – *31 R des Granges -* ☎ *03 81 81 33 11 -* 🕐 *open daily 8am-1am -* 🕐 *closed 24, 25 Dec-1, 2 Jan.* This brasserie founded back in 1873 has retained its original decor and has become something of an institution. Its old-fashioned atmosphere is indeed charming but its popularity is such that, on some evenings, it is almost impossible to find a table, or a seat!

Le Vin et l'Assiette – *97 R. Battant -* ☎ *03 81 81 48 18 - le.vin@wanadoo.fr -* 🕐 *Tue-Sat 9am-9.30pm -* 🕐 *closed 1 Jan, 1 May, Ascension, 2 weeks in Aug, 1 Nov, 25 Dec, Sun and Mon.* This former wine-grower's cellar in the old quarter is housed in a 14C building which is an officially listed site. Wine buffs will be able to taste wine by the glass, accompanied by a plate of *rosette* (dry pork sausage) or Comté cheese.

Baud – *4 Grande-Rue -* ☎ *03 81 81 20 12 - ste-baud@baud-traiteur.fr -* 🕐 *Tue 2-7pm, Wed-Sat 7.30am-noon and 2-6:30pm.* This family business has literally become an institution in Besançon on account of the delicious food it provides: cakes and pastries, ice cream, take-away dishes. If the terrace is crowded, just grin and bear it: it's definitely worth the wait.

SHOPPING

Courbet – *71 R. de Dole -* ☎ *03 81 52 02 16 -* 🕐 *open Tue-Sat 6.30am-12.30pm and .30-7.15pm.* 🕐 *closed public and Feb holidays and late Jul-mid-Aug.* You've everything to gain by stepping inside this fine gourmet shop. There's an astounding variety of fine prepared dishes including meat specialties, salads, savoury tarts and cheeses.

La Ferme Comtoise – *12 R. Battant -* ☎ *03 81 81 38 78 - thierry.lfc@wanadoo.fr -* 🕐 *Tue-Sat 9am-12.30pm and 3-7.30pm, Sun 9am-12.30pm; Jun-Sept 9am-12.30pm and 4-7.30pm.* 🕐 *closed 1 week in Sept.* Entering this tempting shop, with its old-fashioned utensils and tools, is like stepping inside a cheese museum. *Bleu de Gex, mamirolle, comté, morbier;* the treasured cheeses of the region are all represented, along with yogurts, jams, sausages and a selection of Jura wines.

Besançon's defences were later completed by the forts of Chaudanne, Beauregard and Brégille, as its military role superseded its commercial one.

Most of the great **clock-making firms** are represented at Besançon. Some of the most important advances in the art have been made here or in the Jura.

1660: **Mayet** created the first centre of clock-making in the province at Morbier.

1766: **Antide Janvier,** born at St-Claude, succeeded in making a planetarium. He subsequently manufactured astronomical clocks and opened a school of clock-making in Paris.

1771: **Georges-Frédéric Japy** (🕐 *see BELFORT*) set up the first workshop to produce watch-makers' callipers. In 1777 he founded a factory for machine engraving.

1790: **Laurent Mégévand** opened a clock manufactory.

1798: **Louis Perron** invented the double-pin escapement (a century later this invention was exploited in America when mass-production of alarm-clocks started); between 1817 and 1827 he made clocks and watches of highly original design.

1889: **Frederic L'Epée** exhibited musical boxes and manufactured escapement bearings.

1897: **Leroy** started to make the most complicated watch in the world, completed only in 1904 *(in the museum).*

1920: **Maurice Favre-Bulle** produced the first electric clock.

1952: **CETEHOR** launched a clock powered by daylight. In the same year Lip made Europe's first electric watch.

1958: More innovations from **Lip**, first an electric wrist-watch, then in 1967, a quartz micro-oscillator for watches and, in 1971, the first French quartz wrist-watches.

A room on the first floor of the **Musée des Beaux-Arts** provides plenty of evidence of the long tradition of clock-and watch-making in the Franche-Comté.

Hour-glasses, the earliest way of measuring the passage of time, a multiple-faced sundial anticipating the table-clocks of the 16C, alarm-watches and fob-watches of the 17C and 18C, hanging wall-clocks of the early Rococo style (c 1710-30) and fine products of the 19C, the movements of striking clocks, bracket clocks, grandfather clocks, all proclaim the skill that has long gone into the making of timepieces and elevated the design of their cases into works of art.

🔵🔵 **Cathédrale St-Jean** – 🕐 *Daily except Tue 9am-6pm–* **Painting of the Virgin with Saints**★, **St-Jean Rose Window**★ (Rose de St-Jean). **Astronomical Clock**★ (Horloge astronomique) – 🔲 🕐 *Guided tours* 〰️ *(30min) Apr-Sep: Wed-Mon 9.50am,*

10.50am, 11.50am, 2.50pm, 3.50pm, 4.50pm, and 5.50pm; Oct-Mar: Wed-Mon 9.50am, 10.50am, 11.50am, 2.50pm, 3.50pm, 4.50pm and 5.50pm. 🕐 Closed Tue, Jan, 1 May, 1 and 11 Nov, 25 Dec. 🎟 2.50€ (under 18 years: no charge). ☎ 03 81 81 12 76. **Musées de la Citadelle**★ – Natural History Museum, Zoo, aquarium, insectarium, 🕐 end Mar-Jun and early Sep-Oct: daily 9am-6pm; Jul and Aug: daily 9am-7pm; Nov-Mar: daily except Tue 10am-5pm. 🕐 Closed 1 Jan and 25 Dec. **Folk Museum (Musée comtois) and Resistance and Deportation Museum,** 🕐 same hours as Natural History Museum, except 🕐 closed Tue Nov-Mar. 🎟 7€, ticket valid for all citadel museums (children: 4€). ☎ 03 81 87 83 33. www.citadelle.com. **Musée des Beaux-Arts et d'Archéologie**★★ – ♿ 🕐 Wed-Mon 9.30am-noon, 2-6pm. 🕐 Closed Tue, 1 Jan, 1 May, 1 Nov, 25 Dec. 🎟 3€ (under 18 years: no charge), no charge Sun and certain holidays. ☎ 03 81 87 80 49. **Préfecture**★. **Bibliothèque municipale**★ –Temporary exhibits. ☎ 03 81 83 26 63– manuscripts, incunabula, drawings, etc.

BEYNAC-ET-CAZENAC★★

MICHELIN MAP 329 H 6

GREEN GUIDE DORDOGNE BERRY LIMOUSIN

One of the great castles of Périgord, **Château de Beynac**★★ is famous for its history, its architecture and for its setting (**panorama**★★ from the nearby Calvary).

Visit

🕐 Mar-Sep: daily 10am-6pm; Jun-Sep: daily 10am-6.30pm; Oct-Feb: daily 10am to dusk, Dec-Feb: daily noon-dusk. Call for admission price information. ☎ 05 53 29 50 40.
Defended on the north side by double walls, it looms over the river from a precipitous height of 150m – 500ft. Crouching beneath its cliff is a tiny village, once the home of the poet Paul Eluard as well as of the creator of Bibendum, O'Galop. A square keep existed here as early as 1115; it was strengthened at the time of the great rivalry between the Capetians and Plantagenets. During the Hundred Years War, the Dordogne frequently marked the border between French and English territory; stirring times for Beynac, face to face with its rival Castelnaud on the cliffs opposite. Once the English had finally departed, Périgord was organised into four baronies: Beynac, Biron, Bourdeilles, and Mareuil. The castle still has its great Hall of State.

BIARRITZ★★★

POPULATION 28 742

MICHELIN MAP 324 C-D 2

GREEN GUIDE ATLANTIC COAST

With its splendid beaches of fine sand and modern facilities of all kinds (including its own airport, five golf courses and a conference centre), this Basque Coast resort enjoys an international reputation.

A Bit of History

Over a century ago, Biarritz was a place of no particular distinction, its beaches attracting people from nearby Bayonne. Fame came suddenly, with the visits of Empress Eugénie and Napoleon III, followed by many of the illustrious names of the period. Queen Victoria was here in 1889, and after 1906 Biarritz became one of the favourite resorts of Edward VII.
Now enhanced by modernisation, Biarritz continues to offer pleasures which never pall, its beaches, promenades and gardens to either side of the rocky promontory of the Plateau de l'Atalaye remaining as attractive as ever.
The shape of the seabed in this part of the Bay of Biscay and the orientation of the beaches produce fine Atlantic rollers, the delight of surf-riders.

Biarritz - Address Book

For coin ranges, see the Legend at the back of the guide.

EATING OUT

La Goélette – *4 r. du Port-Vieux -* ☎ *05 59 24 84 65 -* ⏰ *closed 1 Dec-11 Jan.* Take a break from shopping and treat yourself to a meal in this pleasant restaurant surrounded by boutiques. The decor is inspired by the nearby sea – blue and white tones, fishing nets, and other nautical objects. Cuisine with an accent on fish and salads.

Tikia – *1 pl. Ste-Eugénie -* ☎ *05 59 24 46 09 .* Tikia means 'small' in Basque. It's true that there's not much space in this little restaurant, but its attractive ambience makes it a pleasant place to linger. The decor has a cabin-type feel, with varnished wood panelling on the walls, porthole-shaped mirrors and other marine knick-knacks. Giant kebabs on the menu.

La Pizzeria des Arceaux – *20-24 av. Édouard-VII -* ☎ *05 59 24 11 47 -* ⏰ *closed 6-26 May, 14 Nov-6 Dec, Sun eve and Mon.* This lively pizzeria just a stone's throw from the city hall is particularly popular with a young, trendy crowd. Attractive decor with tile frescos and mirrors and an excellent choice of desserts.

Le Clos Basque – *12 rue Louis-Barthou -* ☎ *05 59 24 24 96 -* ⏰ *closed 16 Feb-5 Mar, 23 Jun-3 Jul, 19 Oct-6 Nov, Sun eve and Mon except in Jul-Aug.* Excellent local cuisine and a warm, friendly atmosphere mean that there's rarely a spare table in this popular restaurant. Exposed beams and *azulejos* tiles add an Iberian flavour to the decor.

Plaisir des Mets – *5 rue du Centre -* ☎ *05 59 24 34 66 -* ⏰ *closed 15-30 Jun, 15-30 Nov, Mon noon and Tue noon in Jul and Aug, Tue eve and Wed from Sep-Jun.* This attractive small restaurant is situated near the market hall, just a few hundred yards from the sea. The contemporary cuisine served here highlights seasonal, regional produce. Light, modern decor in restful shades of white and blue.

WHERE TO STAY

Hôtel Gardenia – *19 av. Carnot -* ☎ *05 59 24 10 46 - www.hotel-gardenia.com -* ⏰ *closed Dec-Feb. - 19 rooms.* This central hotel with a pink facade has all the charm of a private home. Its quiet, attractive rooms are regularly re-decorated and its reception and salon have just been refurbished. Reasonable prices considering the location.

Hôtel Atalaye – *6 r. des Goëlands, Plateau de l'Atalaye -* ☎ *05 59 24 06 76 - contact@hotelatalaye.com –* ⏰ *closed 14 Nov-15 Dec - 24 rooms.* This imposing turn-of-the century villa owes its name to the superb Atalaye plateau overlooking the Atlantic ocean. The rooms here are gradually being refurbished – those with a sea view are the most attractive. Free parking nearby.

Chambre d'hôte Maison Berreterrenea – *Quartier Arrauntz - 64480 Ustaritz - 11km/6.6mi SE of Biarritz. Take the D 932, Arrauntz exit -* ☎ *05 59 93 05 13 -* ✉ *- 4 room.* Facing a cider apple orchard, this 17C Basque house dominates the Valley of the Nive. Now a bed and breakfast, the house has been sympathetically renovated in traditional style, with whitewashed stone walls. Simply furnished rooms adorned with beams and old beams.

Hôtel Maïtagaria – *34 av. Carnot -* ☎ *05 59 24 26 65 –* ⏰ *closed 1-15 Dec - 17 rooms.* A warm, friendly reception in this little hotel near the garden, just 500m/550yd from the beach. The rooms, of varying sizes, are bright and functional and were recently renovated. Small flower-filled garden in the back.

Le Petit Hôtel – *11 r. Gardères -* ☎ *05 59 24 87 00 - www.petithotel-biarritz.com - 12 rooms.* This appealing hotel is ideally located for exploring the town or spending time on the beach. Its soundproofed rooms have been renovated in tones of blue or yellow; all have Internet access. The hotel has a seminar room above its restaurant, just 100m/110yd from the hotel.

BARS AND CAFES

L'Impérial (Hôtel du Palais) – *1 av. de l'Impératrice -* ☎ *05 59 41 64 00 - www. hotel-du-palais.com.* ⏰ *daily 9am-midnight -* ⏰ *closed Feb.* "La Villa Eugénie", the scene of Napoleon III's love affair with the Empress Eugénie, became the majestic Hôtel du Palais in 1893. Enjoy a glass of champagne and savour the atmosphere in the hotel's elegant bar, the Impérial, where a pianist makes the ambience complete from 8 to 11 every evening.

Le Caveau – *4 r. Gambetta -* ☎ *05 59 24 16 17 -* ⏰ *daily 10.30pm-5am.* One of the trendiest bar-discotheques in the region, Le Caveau is popular with locals and visitors, as well as the inevitable stars on holiday. *The* place to be seen in Biarritz.

La Santa Maria – *Espl. du Port-Vieux -* ☎ *05 59 24 92 25 -* ⏰ *Apr-Jun, Oct daily 10am-2am; Jul-Sep daily 9am-3am.* The splendid view of the Rocher de la Vierge and the Port Vieux beach is one of the attractions of this little bar perched on a rock. A terrace, a few stools and a bar counter in a cave make this a pleasant, unpretentious spot where you can sample tapas while listening to the little orchestra.

ENTERTAINMENT

Gare du Midi – 21 bis av. du Mar.-Foch - ☎ 05 59 22 37 10 - www.biarritz.tm.fr - tickets available from the tourist office: ⏰ daily 10am-6pm. The city's main theatre, with a seating capacity of 1 400, puts on a range of plays, music concerts and ballets. It is also the home of the Biarritz ballet company.

Casino de Biarritz – 1 av. Édouard-VII - ☎ 05 59 22 77 77 - www.lucienbarriere.com - ⏰ Sun-Thu 10am-3am, Fri-Sat until 4am. Located on the Grande Plage, this enormous casino has a table games room (roulette, Black Jack) and 180 slot machines as well as Le Café de la Plage brasserie, Le Baccara restaurant, Le Flamingo discotheque, a show room (theatre, dance) and a ballroom.

SHOPPING

Cazaux et fils – 10 r. Broquedis - ☎ 05 59 22 36 03 – ⏰ Mon-Sat 10am-12.30pm and 3pm-7pm, public hols by appointment. The Cazaux family has been involved in making ceramic pottery since the 18C. Jean-Marie Cazaux is happy to talk about his profession, describing it as 'austere and solitary'. The boutique also offers personalised creations - every step can be undertaken according to the customer's wishes, from extracting the clay to hand-painting the finishing touches.

Fabrique de chistéras Gonzalez – 6 allée des Liserons - 64600 Anglet - ☎ 05 59 03 85 04 – ⏰ Mon-Fri 9am-noon and 2-7pm; tours 5pm Mon, Wed and Fri – ⏰ closed Sat afternoon, Sun and public hols. Founded in 1887, the Gonzalez company produces hand-made *cestas* (wicker scoops that prolong the protective *pelota* glove). In one hour, you'll learn everything there is to know about the history and manufacture of *pelotas* and *cestas*.

Chocolats Henriet – Pl. Clemenceau - ☎ 05 59 24 24 15 – chocolat.henriet@wanadoo.fr - ⏰ daily 9am-7pm. Established after WWII, Henriet is the local guiding light in chocolates and confectionery, featuring *calichous* (Échiré butter and fresh cream caramels), and *rochers de Biarritz* (bitter chocolate, orange rinds, almonds). Serge

Couzigou, maître chocolatier responsible for the creation of the Musée du Chocolat (located 4 Ave. de la Marne), has been running the shop for the past twenty years.

Maison Arostéguy – 5 av. Victor-Hugo - ☎ 05 59 24 00 52 - www.maison-arosteguy.com - ⏰ Mon-Sat 9.30am-1pm and 3-7.30pm - ⏰ closed 25 Dec. Founded in 1875, this famous Biarritz grocery store (formerly the 'Epicerie du Progrès') has kept its original walls, shelves and facade. The shop specialises in regional fare and also stocks many products difficult to find elsewhere: rare bottles of Bordeaux, prestigious Armagnacs, Basque products, flavoured teas and spices.

SPORT AND LEISURE

Euskal-Jaï Fernand Pujol – R. Cino-del-duca - ☎ 05 59 23 91 09 – ⏰ open match days. This pelota Basque school organizes cesta punta competitions nearly every Wednesday and Saturday from June to September.

Hippodrome des Fleurs – Av. du Lac Marion - ☎ 05 59 43 91 56 – ⏰ open racing days. Horse races have been held here on July and August evenings for over fifty years. This trotters' hippodrome has an 800m cindered track with sharp bends.

Piscine municipale – Bd du Gén.-de-Gaulle - ☎ 05 59 22 52 52 – www.biarritz.fr - ⏰ schedule varies depending on the school calendar. Located on the shore, this municipal complex features heated seawater pools as well as a jacuzzi, a hammam and a sauna.

Thermes Marins – 80 r. de Madrid - ☎ 05 59 23 01 22 - www.thermesmarins-biarritz.com - ⏰ Apr-Oct, Mon-Fri 8.30am-12.30pm and 2.30pm-6.30pm, Sat 8.30am-12.30pm, Sun 10am-noon and 4-7pm; Nov-Mar Mon-Fri 9am-noon and 2.30-6.30pm, Sat 8.30am-12.30pm, Sun 10am-noon and 4-7pm – ⏰ closed one week in Jan. This spa featuring a leisure pool and jacuzzi proposes various treatments, such as affusion or underwater showers, seaweed treatment booths, massages, sea-air bath booths.

Visit

Promenades

Pleasantly shaded and landscaped streets lead from the main beach (Grande Plage) to the Virgin's Rock (**Rocher de la Vierge** ★). To the south is the viewpoint (Perspective de la Côte des Basques) offering an uninterrupted **view** ★★ towards the mountain peaks of the Basque Country.

▶▶ **Musée Bonnat** ★★– ⏰ Jul-Aug: daily 10am-6.30pm (Wed: 9.30pm); May-Jun and Sep-Oct: daily except Tue 10am-6.30pm; Nov-Apr: daily except Tue 10am-12.30, 2-6pm. ⏰ Closed public holidays (except Jul-Aug). ☞ 5.50€, no charge 1st Sun in the month. ☎ 05 59 59 08 52. **Musée Basque** ★★ – ⏰ Daily except Mon 10am-12.30pm, 2-6pm (May-Oct: daily 10am-6.30pm). ⏰ Closed public holidays. ☞ 5.50€, no charge 1st Sun in the month. ☎ 05 59 46 61 90. www.musee-basque.com – one of the finest regional ethnographic museums in France. **Cathédrale Ste-Marie** ★ (**Cloisters** ★).

Excursions

Bayonne★★

Biarritz, Anglet and Bayonne merge with one another to form a single urban area (conurbation 169 378) of which Bayonne, with its busy quaysides and old streets, is the commercial centre. Its harbour on the estuary of the Adour handles maize, sulphur and chemical products.

The town gave its name to the bayonet which was invented by Basque armourers and was first used in 1703 by the French infantry.

The picturesque Rue du Pont-Neuf is flanked by arcades and tall houses. The delicious smells wafting from the pastry-shops and confectioners emphasise the importance of the chocolate-making industry which began here in the 17C.

Route Impériale des cimes★

Bayonne to Hasparren 25km – 16mi. This section of Napoleon I's scenic highway was part of an overall project to link Bayonne with St-Jean-Pied-de-Port for strategic reasons. It follows a highly sinuous alignment and affords fine **views**★ of the Basque coast and countryside.

BITCHE

POPULATION 5 517

MICHELIN MAP 307 P 4

GREEN GUIDE ALSACE LORRAINE CHAMPAGNE

Among the forests of the "Little Vosges" between Alsace and Lorraine, the fortress-town of Bitche stands guard over the frontier.

Visit

Citadelle★

🕐 *Mid-Mar to mid-Nov: tour (with infrared listening device, 2hr) 10am-5pm (6 pm Jul and Aug).* ⌨ *7€/6€, according to the season, (children: 5€/4€).* ☎ *03 87 96 18 82 or* ☎ *03 87 06 16 16.*

...castle stood here as early as the 12C. In 1683, on the orders of Louis XIV, Vauban ...w up plans for a citadel. Fifteen years later, when the terms of the Treaty of Ryswick ...ed France to abandon Lorraine, his work was razed to the ground. The citadel ...built by Louis XV in 1741.

...ciate the formidable strength of the place (its massive red sandstone founda- ...complexity of its defensive system of moats, bastions, glacis) it is necessary ...nd *(30min,* ▶ *take the path before the second gateway).*

The Maginot Line

the interval between the two World Wars, France decided to build a line of forti-
cation in case of another conflict with Germany. The lessons of the Great War and
the atrocities caused by gas, tanks and planes forced military authorities to rethink
the defensive system of open trenches and isolated fortresses. The Maginot Line
with its strongly fortified sectors, behind continuous fronts from 20 to 60 km (13 to
38 miles) long, and permanent underground fortifications, was better adapted to
modern warfare.

By the end of the 1930s, the Maginot Line – named after the War Minister André
Maginot – was completed along the Franco-German border, stretching from Switzerland to the vicinity of the Belgian frontier near Montmédy. The north section was
never completed owing to financial and political problems. In 1940 the German army
invaded France via Belgium.

The Line was composed of huge fortresses with smaller defence posts or simple
blockhouses. They were not all linked together but each fort was connected to its
ammunition depot by long underground tracks, using small electric trains. The entire
line formed a secret city where soldiers could live in a "peaceful" world surrounded
by cooks, surgeons, hairdressers and other guilds.

After the war, the line was part of the NATO defence organisation, but in 1965 France
ceased to maintain the line in working order and eventually sold the different subs-
tructures to towns, associations and even individuals. Several fortresses have now
been restored and can be visited, taking the tourist back to the atmosphere of the
pre-war years.

The citadel lost its strategic value at the beginning of the 20C.

Fort de Simserhof★

4km – just over 2mi west. This fort, one of the most important structures on the Maginot
Line, was completed in 1935. It could house a combined arms garrison of 1 200 men
(infantry, artillery, engineers) with three months' autonomy (food, gasoline, ammunition). From the outside, only the east-facing entrance block can be seen with its
seven-tonne reinforced door, its side slit, its shooting and observation post.

BLOIS★★

POPULATION 65 132

MICHELIN MAP 318 C-D-E-F 5-6-7

GREEN GUIDE CHÂTEAUX OF THE LOIRE

**Blois looks northwards to the Beauce and south to the Sologne, and is situated
at that point on the Loire at which the limestone landscapes around Orléans
give way almost imperceptibly to the chalk country of Touraine downstream.
Originally defended by a medieval castle, the town was transformed from 1503
onwards when the kings moved there from Amboise, bringing in their train all
the trades devoted to satisfying the royal taste for luxury.**

▶ **Orient Yourself:** Blois, which is listed as a "Town of Art and History," offers 2hr
discovery tours. Information at the tourist office or on www.vpah.culture.fr.

Visit

Chateau★★★

🕐 *Apr-Sep: daily 9am-6pm; Sep-Mar: daily 9am-12.30pm, 2-5.30pm. Last admission
30min before closing.* 🕐 *Closed 1 Jan and 25 Dec.*  *6.50€ (children: 2€), no charge
1st Sun in the month (Nov-Mar).* ☎ *02 54 90 33 32 www.ville-blois.fr – for Illustration
see Introduction: Art – Architecture.*

The whole development of secular French architecture from feudalism to the
sicism of Louis XIII's reign can be traced at Blois.

The medieval remains include the round towers, spiral stairways and steep-
roofs of the Foix Tower and the Chamber of the States-General of 1205; with
elled ceiling, this is where the States-General held its Assemblies in 1576

Blois Address Book

PRACTICAL INFORMATION

TOURISM OFFICE

▤ 3 av. J.-Laigret, 41000 Blois, ☎ 02 54 90 41 41.

TOURS

⚓ Discovery tours *(2hr)*. Information at the tourist office or on www.vpah.culture.fr.

For coin ranges, see the Legend at the back of the guide.

EATING OUT

⊖⊖▤ **Le Bistrot du Cuisinier** – *20 quai Villebois-Mareuil* – ☎ 02 54 78 06 70 – bistrot.du.cuisinier@wanadoo.fr – ◷ *closed 24 Sep-4 Oct and 21 Dec-4 Jan.* You'll find a real bistro atmosphere here. The decor is simple, and from the front dining room there is a splendid view of Blois and the Loire. The cordial and inventive owner has established monthly themes for his culinary creations, and encourages you to try different wines by the glass. The children's menu will tempt the fussiest eaters to try something new and special.

⊖▤ **Au Bouchon Lyonnais** – *25 r. des Violettes* – ☎ 02 54 74 12 87 – ◷ *closed Jan, Sun and Mon except public holidays* – *reservation recommended.* Located just at the bottom of the hill crowned by the château, this restaurant is a favourite with residents of Blois, who enjoy the rustic decor with exposed beams and stone walls. The menu features regional fare.

⊖▤ **Au Rendez-vous des Pêcheurs** – *27 r. Foix* – ☎ 02 54 74 67 48 – ◷ *closed 2-14 Jan, 29 Jul-20 Aug, Mon lunchtime and Sun* – *reservation recommended.* A provincial-style bistro in the old part of Blois. Stained-glass windows filter the light in the quiet dining room. Fish features prominently among the fresh market produce on the menu.

WHERE TO STAY

⊖▤ **Hôtel Anne de Bretagne** – *31 av. J.-Laigret* – ☎ 02 54 78 05 38 – ◷ *closed 9 Jan-6 Feb – 28 rooms* – ⊿ 6€. This small family hotel is near the castle and the terraced Jardin du Roi. The rooms are decorated in attractive colours and well soundproofed; those on the third floor are under the sloping roof.

⊖⊖▤ **Chambre d'hôte La Villa Médicis** – *1 r. St-Denis, Macé – 41000 St-Denis-sur-Loire – 4km/2.5mi NE of Blois on N 152 towards Orléans* – ☎ 02 54 74 46 38 – *reservation required in winter – 6 rooms.* Marie de Medici came to take the waters at the springs in the park in which this 19C villa was built, as a hotel for spa patrons at the time. Enjoy a peaceful stay in one of the rooms or the suite. Breakfast is served in the park in summer.

⊖⊖▤ **Chambre d'hôte Domaine des Bidaudières** – *R. du Peu-Morier – 37210*

Vouvray – 3km/1.8mi W of Vouvray towards Château-Renault – ☎ 02 47 52 66 85 – www.bandb-loire-valley.com – ⌷ – *6 rooms.* The rooms in this 18C castle have plenty of character, with four-poster beds, carefully chosen fabrics, and views of the park, lake or vineyards surrounding the property. The breakfast nook is carved into the cliff side, or you may choose to sit under the veranda.

⊖⊖▤ **Chambre d'hôte Château de Nazelles** – *16 r. Tue-la-Soif (behind the post office) – 37530 Nazelles-Négron – 3km/1.8mi N of Négron on D 5* – ☎ 02 47 30 53 79 – *3 rooms.* It would be hard to remain indifferent to the charms of this 16C property, built on a hillside and designed by Thomas Boyer, architect of the Château de Chenonceau. The rooms display a successful mix of ancient and modern styles. There is a swimming pool hewn out of natural rock and a terraced garden.

⊖⊖▤ **Chambre d'hôte Château de Montgouverne** – *37210 Rochecorbon* – ☎ 02 47 52 84 59 – *6 rooms.* Set among the vineyards of Vouvray, this 18C castle with its pretty pepper-pot towers is an incentive to prolong your stay. Each room and suite has its own individual style. French-style garden for pleasant strolls.

ON THE TOWN

⊖ **Le Boulot** – *9 r. Henri-Drussy* – ☎ 02 54 74 20 20 – ◷ *Mon-Sat noon-2pm and from 6pm.* The moustachioed owner opened his first pizzeria in the small town of Blois over 20 years ago. He is eager to share his knowledge about wine, and offers a different choice of wines by the glass every week, to be enjoyed with the dish of the day or a snack.

Rond-point de la Résistance – There are three cafés near this roundabout by the river. It is more pleasant to go late in the evening, to avoid the car exhaust fumes: L'Époque, Le Maryland and Le Colonial Café. Nearby are tobacconists and newsagents which stay open late.

Rue Foulerie – In this narrow street on the edge of the old part of town you will find a disco, a piano bar and a couple of pubs.

SHOPPING

Rue du Commerce – Rue du Commerce and the adjacent streets in this pleasant pedestrian-only district (rue du Rebrousse-Pénil, rue St-Martin) offer all kinds of shopping opportunities.

SIT BACK AND RELAX

La Salsa – *4 ruelle Ronceraie* – ☎ 02 54 78 28 67 – sekou-kassogué@wanadoo.fr – ◷ *Tue-Sun 8pm-2am.* A cross between an old-fashioned youth club and Savoyard chalet-restaurant in appearance, this bar is rather out of the ordinary, perhaps because it started out as a cooperative and the present owner, who took over when the co-op failed, still has a certain contempt for commerce. The atmosphere is very easy-going, to the beat of salsa and African music.

Le Bistrot – *12 r. Henry-Drussy –* ☏ *02 54 78 47 74 –* ⏰ *daily 8am-2pm except Sun noon-2am.* The attractive, slightly old-fashioned decor of this bistro provides a contrast to the crowd of smart young regulars, who are quite happy to listen to accordion music or the Sex Pistols, as the mood strikes. "Everyone knows each other, but I don't know everyone" admits the owner, whose long terrace set among the acacias in place Ave-Maria is much in demand on fine days.

SON ET LUMIÈRE

Alain Decaux of the Académie Française wrote the texts that retrace the history of Blois – "a thousand years' history spanning 10 centuries of splendour" – and they are read by famous French actors including Michael Lonsdale, Fabrice Luchini, Robert Hossein, Pierre Arditi and Henri Virlojeux. Enormous projectors, combining photographs with special lighting effects, and the very latest in sound transmission systems make for a lively, entertaining and visually stimulating show, despite there being no live actors participating in the show.

Performances (45min) every evening between 9.30pm and 10.30pm (sunset) from late April to mid-September; Ascension-Whitsun: weekend only. 9.50€ (children: 4.50€). ☏ *02 54 78 72 76.*

The transition from the Gothic to the Renaissance is evident in the Charles of Orléans Gallery and particularly in the Louis XII Wing of 1498-1501. Louis had been born at Blois in 1462 and, together with Anne of Brittany, carried out a number of improvements including the construction of a new wing. This was right up to date with its triumphal arch doorways, Italianate arabesque decoration applied to the three Gothic pillars on the courtyard side, and the use of galleries to link rooms rather than having them run directly into one another.

Built only 15 years later, possibly by Claude de France, the François I wing exemplifies the preoccupation with ornamentation that swept in with the first phase of the French Renaissance. The work remained incomplete but the new taste for sumptuous decoration is very apparent, not only in the Façade des Loges (built 7m – 23ft in front of the old rampart) with its still-irregular fenestration, but also in Pierre Trinquart's François I staircase; though somewhat over-restored in the view of some archeologists, this is a richly decorated masterpiece with openings between its buttresses forming a series of balconies. The much-modified interior includes, on the first floor, Catherine de' Medici's study with its secret cupboards, and on the second floor, Henri III's apartments, scene of the murder of Henri de Guise.

The style of Louis XIII appears in the Gaston of Orléans Wing (1632-37). The King's brother employed François Mansart, who, however, failed to deploy the full range of his talents, his work here being stiff rather than dignified. Building stopped when the birth of Louis XIV put paid to his uncle's hopes of succeeding to the throne.

▶▶ **Église St-Nicolas★**. Hôtel d'Alluye (**galleries★**) ⏰ *Mon-Fri 10am-noon, 2-4pm by appointment 4 days in advance, contact Mrs Terré, 8, r. St-Honoré, 41000 Blois.* ⏰ *Closed Sat-Sun and public holidays. No charge.* ☏ *02 54 56 38 00.*

Château de BONAGUIL★★

MICHELIN MAP 336 I 2

GREEN GUIDE DORDOGNE BERRY LIMOUSIN

This majestic fortress on the border of Périgord Noir (Black Périgord, so-called because of its extensive woods) and Quercy, makes a stunning sight. It exemplifies the state of military architecture of the late 15C and of the 16C.

Visit

⏰ *Jun-Aug: daily 10am-6pm; Apr-May: daily 10.30am-1pm, 2.30pm-5.30pm; Sep: daily 10.30am-1pm, 2.30pm-5pm; Feb-Mar: daily 11am-1pm, 2.30pm-5.30pm; Oct: daily 11am-1pm, 2.30-5pm; Nov: Sun, school and public holidays 11am-1pm, 2.30-5pm; Dec: school holidays 2.30-5pm.* ⏰ *Closed Jan, 25 Dec.* ⊜ *4.50€ (7-16 years: 3€).* ☏ *05 53 71 90 33.*

The castle *(illustration – 👌 see Introduction: Art – Architecture)* was enla
around the existing 13C keep, and further extended between 1482 an
unusual in that underneath its old-fashioned appearance of a traditional stro
is actually remarkably well adapted to the new firearms then coming into use, a
has loopholes for both cannon and muskets. Furthermore, it was conceived no
offensive establishment to hold down territory or to threaten a rival, but as a plac
refuge, able to withstand any attack, with its firearms used in a purely defensive ro
In 1480-1520 this was something new, and anticipated the idea of the fort.
At a time when the châteaux along the Loire were being turned from castles into
country houses, Bonaguil was, however, something of an anachronism.

BONIFACIO★★★

POPULATION 2 683

MICHELIN MAP 345 D-E 11

GREEN GUIDE CORSE (IN FRENCH)

Greek and Roman remains have been found at Bonifacio and there is evidence
that the site was occupied in prehistoric times, but the town's history really begins when Bonifacio, Marquis of Tuscany, gave it his name. The place's strategic
value in terms of control of the Western Mediterranean was appreciated by the
Genoese, who succeeded in taking it by trickery in 1187, and set up a colony here
eight years later.

Most of the rulers of Europe cast an envious eye on Bonifacio at one time or another; the town was besieged many times, most notably in 1420 by King Alfonso
V of Aragon. Legend has it that his soldiers cut the famous stairway of 187 steps
into the cliff-face in the course of a single night.

Visit

Site★★★
Bonifacio is magnificently sited on a long, narrow promontory protecting its "fjord"
in the far south of Corsica and it is reached from the rest of the island across a vast,
arid plain. The town is divided in two, the **"Marine"**★, the port quarter offering a

J.L. Gallo/MICHELIN

ge for warships, fishing boats and pleasure craft, and the Upper Town
~e★★) overlooking the sea from 60m – 200ft-high cliffs. Its old houses,
~em with four or five storeys, are joined together by what appear to be flying
~es but are in fact rainwater channels feeding the town's cisterns.

~eat loggia of the Church of Ste-Marie-Majeure is built over a cistern with a
~city of 650m3 – about 140 000 gallons; under Genoese rule this is where the
~airs of the town were deliberated upon by four elders, who were elected for three
~onths at a time. Twice a week the *podesta*, the mayor, who lived opposite, would
mete out justice from here.

◖◖ **Église St-Dominique★★** – ◷ *Daily 9am-8pm, possibility of a guided visit.* ⬿
2€. ⓘ *Information available at the tourist office.* ☎ *04 95 73 11 88.*

Excursions

Grotte du Sdragonato★

45min by boat. The dragon's cave is dimly lit by a shaft in the shape of Corsica in reverse.
12km – 7 miles away across the sometimes choppy waters of the Bonifacio Straits
(Bouches de Bonifacio) is Sardinia. The trip gives good views of the high limestone
cliffs of the promontory and of the King of Aragon's steps.

BORDEAUX★★★

POPULATION 696 367

MICHELIN MAP 335 H 5

GREEN GUIDE ATLANTIC COAST

**"Take Versailles, add Antwerp, and you have Bordeaux", was how the city was
defined by Victor Hugo impressed by its 18C grandeur and its splendid tidal river.
Bordeaux had, however, played an important role in the affairs of France long
before Versailles had been thought of.**

▸ **Orient Yourself:** Find the Galerie des Grands-Hommes, which is a nice central
location for discovering Bordeaux. Appealing boutiques and confectioneries are
plentiful here and along the cours George Clemenceau to the east. Head south to
see the newly restored 18C buildings of Vieux Bordeaux, the charming old town.
For a more extensive introduction to Bordeaux, consider one of the guided tours
offered by the tourist office.

◉ **Don't Miss:** The extensive collection of paintings in the Musée des Beaux-Arts.

Kids **Especially For Kids:** Croiseur
Colbert– Take a tour of this anti-
aircraft warship which was first
launched in 1959 and has been
birthed in Port de la Lune since
1993.

◔ **Also See:** Of course, there are
Bordeaux's world-famous wines.
Take an excursion to the Bordeaux
Vineyards, you won't regret it.

A Bit of History

Eleanor's Dowry – In 1137, Bordeaux'
St Andrew's Cathedral was the setting
for the wedding of the king's son (the
future Louis VII) to Eleanor (◔ *see
ANGERS*), the only daughter of Duke
William of Aquitaine. The bride's dowry
consisted of practically the whole of
southwestern France. But, after 15
years of marital discord, the mismatch
of a marriage broke up when the great

Fontaine des Girondins

Bordeaux - Address Book

For coin ranges, see the Legend at the back of the guide.

EATING OUT

A QUICK BITE

La Table du Pain – *6 pl. du Parlement - ☎ 05 56 81 01 00 – ⏱ closed 1 Jan and 25 Dec.* This very successful restaurant genre originated in Belgium. The dining room – blond stone walls, old shelves and waxed pine furnishings – is quite inviting. The menu proposes a wide selection of sandwiches, toasts and salads.

A LEISURELY MEAL

Lou Magret – *62 r. St-Rémi - ☎ 05 56 44 77 94 - ⏱ closed 7-21 Jul, Sun and public holidays.* If overwhelmed by the choice of restaurants in this street, try this pleasant establishment whose speciality is canard de Chalosse, duck served grilled or with a delicious sauce. No-frills decor and outdoor terrace.

Bar Cave de la Monnaie – *34 r. Porte-la-Monnaie - ☎ 05 56 31 12 33 – latupinalatupina.com - ⏱ closed Sun.* This very young wine bar decorated with photos of old Bordeaux bistros has an original flair. Customers choose their dishes first (omelettes or salads), then they draw their glass of Bordeaux from one of four taps in the wall. Affordable prices.

Chez Mémère – *11 r. de la Devise - ☎ 05 56 81 88 20.* Under the vaulted ceiling of this 16C workshop, discover the flavour and ambience of a fine meal chez mémère (at granny's): garbure landaise (soup), agneau de Pauillac, encornets frais aux piments d'Espelette... and, at the end of the week, la sanguette, a sort of black pudding made of poultry blood.

Le Bistro du Musée – *37 pl. Pey-Berland - ☎ 05 56 52 99 69 - ⏱ closed 2 weeks Christmas, 3 weeks in Aug and Sun.* This bistro with a pretty green wood entrance makes a promising impression from the start. Thoughtful decor with exposed stone walls, oak parquet, moleskin seats and wine paraphernalia. Southwest cuisine and a fine Bordeaux wine menu.

Hôtel des 4 Sœurs – *6 bis cours du 30-Juillet - ☎ 05 56 81 19 20 – 4sœursmailcity.com – 34 rooms – ▭ 8€.* Close by the Grand Théâtre, this café founded in 1841 is charming indeed with its stucco, mirrors, mosaic and red velvet wall seats. Choose an *omelette aux cêpes*, *a jambon piperade*, a *morue basquaise* or some *chipirons frais à l'encre* with a glass of wine.

Café Louis – *2 pl. de la Comédie - ☎ 05 56 44 07 00.* Intelligent renovations have given new life to this ex-brasserie of the Grand Théâtre de Bordeaux, built in the 18C. The interior design - gilded pilasters, high ceiling with frescos and crystal chandeliers - is based on glory past. Pleasant terrace under the arcades. Traditional menu.

WHERE TO STAY

Hôtel Clemenceau – *4 cours Georges-Clemenceau - ☎ 05 56 52 98 98 - clemenceauhotel-bordeaux.com - ⏱ closed 15 days late Dec - 45 rooms- ▭ 4.50€.* Those who enjoy discovering the city by foot will appreciate this hotel established in an 18C building. Simple, air-conditioned rooms. Nice view of the roofs of Bordeaux from the breakfast room.

Hôtel Acanthe – *12 r. St-Rémi - ☎ 05 56 81 66 58 - info@canthe-hotel-bordeaux.com - ⏱ closed 23-30 Dec - reserv. required - 20 rooms- ▭ 5.50€.* A central location and very reasonable prices are the strong points of this recently renovated hotel. The bright rooms are big enough and well sound-proofed, and the reception is agreeable.

Hôtel Opéra – *35 r. de l'Esprit-des-Lois - ☎ 05 56 81 41 27 - hotel.opera@wanadoo.fr - ⏱ closed 24 Dec to 2 Jan - 27 rooms - 6€.* Near the Grand Théâtre et the Allées de Tourny, here's a modest little family hotel. The reception is courteous and the rooms are functional. Those on the street are well sound-proofed. Good value for the euro.

Hôtel Notre-Dame – *36 r. Notre-Dame - ☎ 05 56 52 88 24 - hotelnotredamefree.fr - 21 rooms - ▭ 5.90€.* An unpretentious little family hotel in an 18C house just behind the Quai des Chatrons. Rooms small but well-kept; reasonable prices.

Hôtel Presse – *6 r. de la Porte-Dijeaux - ☎ 05 56 48 53 88 - infohoteldelapresse.com - ⏱ closed 25 Dec to 2 Jan - 27 rooms - ▭ 8€.* In the pedestrian shopping quarter of the old city, this is a nice little hotel despite the rather difficult access by automobile. Superb stairway with crimson carpets. Modern, functional, yet cosy rooms.

Hôtel Continental – *10 r. Montesquieu - ☎ 05 56 52 66 00 – continentalhotel-le-ontinental.com – ⏱ closed 24 Dec to 3 Jan - 50 rooms - ▭ 7€.* In the old city, here's a venerable 18C mansion with a fine staircase in the hall. Breakfast room under a glass roof. Modern rooms with waxed wood furnishings.

ON THE TOWN

Bodega Bodega – *4 r. des Piliers-de-Tutelle. - ☎ 05 56 01 24 24 – Mon-Sat noon-2:30pm, 7pm-2am, Sun 7pm-2am.* The exuberance of the Spanish music and the range of flavours as you savour a variety of tapas will transport you to Castille, at least for the evening.

Chez Brunet – *9 r. de Condé - ☎ 05 56 51 35 50 – Tue-Sat 10am-2pm, 5pm-10pm –*

🕐 *closed 1st week of Jan and and 3 wks in Aug*. A charming woman runs this little restaurant where you can discover one of the region's specialities – oysters with grilled sausages.

SHOWTIME

L'Onyx – *11 r. Fernand-Philippart – Quartier St-Pierre* ☎ *05 56 44 26 12 – www.theatreonyx.net - office:* 🕐 *6pm-8pm performance evenings; Oct-May: Wed:1-6pm, Thu-Fri:9.30-12pm, 1-6pm –* 🕐 *closed Jul-Sep – 12.5€*. The oldest café-theatre of the city, L'Onyx is a requisite stop for discovering local culture.

La Boîte à Jouer – *50 r. Lombard -* ☎ *05 56 50 37 37 (reserv.) –* 🕐 *ticket office: Wed-Sat 8pm; performances 8:30pm –* 🕐 *closed Jul-Sep*. This theatre has two small rooms (60 and 45 seats) where lesser regional, national or international troupes specialized in contemporary or musical theatre perform.

Opéra de Bordeaux-Grand théâtre – *Pl. de la Comédie- BP 95 -* ☎ *05 56 00 85 95 - www.opera-bordeaux.com -* 🕐 *ticket office: Tue-Sat 11am-6pm;* 🕐 *closed public holidays*. The Grand Théâtre de Bordeaux is one of the most handsome of France - its architectural assets are a showpiece for its impressive cultural wealth. Henri Tomasi's *Sampiero Corso* (1956), Jean-Michel Damase's *Colombe* (1961) and the French adaptation of Benjamin Britten's *Gloriana* (1967) are among the significant performances that were first staged here. Symphonies, operas and ballets are performed here under excellent acoustic conditions.

Théâtre Fémina – *20 r. de Grassi -* ☎ *05 56 79 06 69 – depending on shows*. With 1 100 seats, this handsome edifice sets the stage for plays, comedies, operettas, dance and concerts.

Théâtre du Port-de-la-Lune – *Sq. Jean-Vauthier - BP7 Quartier Ste-Croix* ☎ *05 56 91 98 00 –* 🕐 *ticket office:Tue-Sat 1pm-7pm –* 🕐 *closed 25 July to 25 August, Sun, Mon and public holidays*. This theatre's repertoire includes classic and contemporary drama staged by the Centre Dramatique National Bordeaux Aquitaine.

SHOPPING

Librairie Mollat – *15 r. Vital-Carles -* ☎ *05 56 56 40 40 - www.mollat.com -* 🕐 *Mon-Sat 9:30am-7pm –* 🕐 *closed Sun except 2 Sun. before Christmas and public holidays*. France's first independent bookstore is still a veritable regional institution.

Baillardran Canelés – *Galerie des Grands-Hommes -* ☎ *05 56 79 05 89 –* 🕐 *Mon-Sat 8:30am-7:30pm*. Located in the Grands-Hommes market, this boutique makes delicious *canelés*, the small brown Bordelais cakes, irresistibly delicate and caramelised, that take on the shape of the ribbed (canelé) cake tins they're baked in. Crisp outside, they're soft and spongy inside.

Cadio-Badie – *26 allées de Tourny -* ☎ *05 56 44 24 22 – cadiotbadie.com -* 🕐 *Mon 9am-noon, 2pm-7pm, Tue-Sat 9am-7pm –* 🕐 *closed 2 weeks in Aug, Sun and, public holidays except Christmas and Easter*. You can't help but be charmed by the old-fashioned style of this appealing boutique founded in 1826. Their truffes and Armagnac-flavoured *bouchons bordelais* are worth a special trip.

Chocolaterie Saunion – *56 cours Georges-Clemenceau -* ☎ *05 56 48 05 75 –* 🕐 *Mon 2pm-7:15pm, Tue-Sat 9:30am-12:30pm, 1:30pm-7:15pm –* 🕐 *closed 15-22 Aug, Sun and Mon morning, public holidays except Christmas, New Year and Easter*. One of the most illustrious chocolate confectioners of Bordeaux – a must.

Conseil Interprofessionnel des Vins de Bordeaux – *1 cours du XXX Juillet -* ☎ *05 56 00 22 66 - www.vins-bordeaux.fr - Mon-Fri 9am-5pm –* 🕐 *closed Sat-Sun and public holidays*. This is where you'll find ample information about Bordeaux wines and vineyards – workshops, tastings. Several different wine cellars are to be found around this centre, including La Vinothèque Bordeaux (8 cours du XXX Juillet), L'intendant (2 allées de Tourny) and Bordeaux Magnum (3 rue Gobineau).

Darricau – *7 pl. Gambetta -* ☎ *05 56 44 21 49 - www.darricau.com -* 🕐 *Mon-Fri 10am-7pm, Sat 11am-7pm –* 🕐 *closed 1 to 15 Aug and public holidays*. Since the turn of the century, this chocolatier pampers the city with the irresistible *pavé Gambetta* (praline with raisins soaked in wine), Bordeaux bottle-shaped chocolates (*confits de sauterne* or *de médoc*), la *cadichonne* (crunchy vanilla) and *niniches* (soft caramel with dark chocolate).

SPORTS

Centre de Voile de Bordeaux-Lac – *Bd du Parc des Expositions - 33520 Bruges -* ☎ *05 57 10 60 35 – voile-bordeaux-lacwanadoo.fr -* 🕐 *Mon-Fri 9am-noon, 2pm-6:30pm –* 🕐 *closed 12 Apr,1, 8, 20, 31 May, 14 Jul and Sun*. This sailing centre organizes boat and wind-surfing courses for young and old alike.

statesman, Abbot Suger of St-Denis, was no longer there to pacify the quarrelsome couple in the interests of his policy of expanding the kingdom. In 1152 the Council of Beaugency annulled the marriage. Eleanor had won back her freedom and her dowry. Two months later she married Henry Plantagenet, Duke of Normandy, Count of Anjou, ruler of Touraine and Maine.

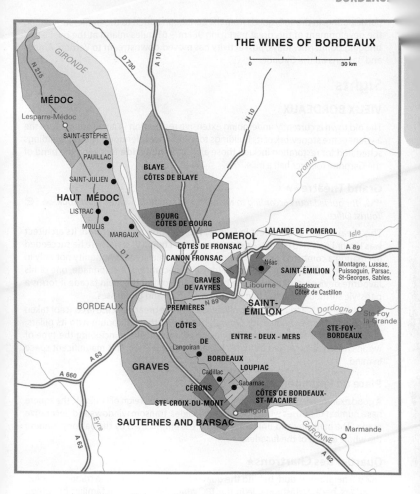

THE WINES OF BORDEAUX

0   30 km

MÉDOC

Lesparre-Médoc

SAINT-ESTÈPHE

PAUILLAC

SAINT-JULIEN

HAUT MÉDOC

LISTRAC

MOULIS

MARGAUX

BLAYE
CÔTES DE BLAYE

BOURG
CÔTES DE BOURG

POMEROL

LALANDE DE POMEROL

CÔTES DE FRONSAC

CANON FRONSAC

Néac

SAINT-ÉMILION

Montagne, Lussac,
Puisseguin, Parsac,
St-Georges, Sables.

GRAVES
DE VAYRES

Libourne

Bordeaux
Côtes de Castillon

BORDEAUX

PREMIÈRES

SAINT-
ÉMILION

Ste-Foy
la-Grande

CÔTES

DE

ENTRE - DEUX - MERS

STE-FOY-
BORDEAUX

Langoiran

BORDEAUX

GRAVES

Cadillac

LOUPIAC

CÉRONS

Gabarnac

CÔTES DE BORDEAUX-
ST-MACAIRE

STE-CROIX-DU-MONT

Langon

SAUTERNES AND BARSAC

Marmande

Another two months and her new husband inherited the English crown, becoming Henry II of England. It was a disaster for the House of Capet; the conflict it heralded between England and France would last three centuries.

From 1360, Bordeaux served as a base for the Black Prince in the expeditions against the French-held possessions in the southwest. Finally, in 1453, at Castillon-la-Bataille, Bordeaux and Guyenne (Old English for Aquitaine) were won back for France in the final battle of the Hundred Years War.

The Intendants – These high-ranking representatives of the French Crown in the provinces, first appointed by Richelieu, were made an effective instrument of government by Colbert. Their broad vision of a well-planned city to replace the tangle of medieval streets brought them into conflict with the local population, but in the course of the 18C they succeeded in transforming Bordeaux, giving it the Classical face it wears today. The work of Claude Boucher, Tourny, Dupré and St-Maur can be seen in the grandiose set-pieces of urban design: the quaysides, the Place de la Bourse, the great avenues, the Town Hall (Hôtel de Ville), and the Grand Théâtre.

The Girondins – In the course of the French Revolution the Bordeaux *députés*, including Condorcet and Vergniaud, formed the grouping known as the Girondins. Essentially bourgeois in attitude, they enjoyed a majority in the Legislative Assembly and during the first few months of the Convention. But because of their federalist tendencies they were held responsible for the state of the country by the Montagnard faction, who accused them of conspiring against the Revolution. Twenty-two of them were tried in May 1793, condemned to death and executed.

...ort – It was the English demand for wine under English rule that introduced Bordeaux ...seafaring, and promoted the expansion of the area under vines. Even during the ...ndred Years War claret continued to flow north to England, and right up to the ...the trade took the form of an annual event, with Dutch as well as English ships participating. In the 18C, goods from the Caribbean added to the traffic, stimulating the development of this great port lying 98km – 61 miles inland at the river's first bridging point. Nowadays, port activity has moved downstream to Verdon, Ambès and Bassens on the Gironde.

Sights

VIEUX BORDEAUX

The old town is currently undergoing extensive restoration in an effort to return the ancient ochre stonework of its buildings to its original splendour. The 18C buildings scheduled for restoration include those along the **quayside** following the bend of the Garonne for over half a mile.

Grand Théâtre★★

🚶 *1hr guided tours according to the rehearsal schedule, visitors must book.* ⊜ *5€. Tourist Office.*

This theatre, one of the finest in France, has recently been restored. Its architect was Victor Louis (1731-1802), a proponent of the Louis XVI style; here he succeeded in creating a combined theatre and concert hall which recalls Antiquity not only in its sheer scale but also in its restrained use of decoration. A colonnade, one of his favourite devices, runs around the building; in front of the main façade it forms a peristyle surmounted by 12 huge statues of muses and goddesses.

The interior too is a triumph, not only because of the great staircase (a concept taken up again by Garnier in his Paris Opera), but also in the auditorium with its pillars, ramps and cantilevered boxes. The design of the balconies, including the type of wood chosen, was carried out with the acoustic quality of this magnificent space in mind.

Place du Parlement★

A good example of the urban planning carried out in the reign of Louis XV, the square has a number of houses with groundfloor arcades, transom windows and decorative masks. The harmony and unity of the square is emphasised by the balcony running the whole length of the façades.

Quartier des Chartrons★

This old neighbourhood, behind the quayside devoted to the wine trade and ships' chandlers, became fashionable in the 18C when the city's great families built their town houses here. Some of the streets (Rue Notre-Dame, Cours de la Martinique, Cours Xavier Arnozan) have many fine dwellings with classical façades, attics, wrought-iron balconies (balconsa) and transom windows with entablatures.

Esplanade des Quinconces

The sheer size (about 126 000m² – 150 700sq yds) of this esplanade is impressive. It was laid out on the site of the old Château de la Trompette during the Restoration (early 19C).

Monument aux Girondins

It consists of a column (50m – 164ft high) topped by Liberty casting off her chains and two bronze fountains (fontainesa) symbolising the Triumph of the Republic (facing the Grand Théâtre) and the Triumph of Concord.

◗◗ **Musée des Beaux-Arts★★** – ♿ ◷ *Wed-Mon 11am-6pm.* ◷ *Closed Tue and public holidays.* ⊜ *4€ (temporary exhibit: 5.50€), no charge 1st Sunday in the month.* ☎ *05 56 10 25 25.* **Cathédrale St-André★**. **Basilique St-Michel★** ◷ 🚶 *Daily guided tours 1st and 2nd Sun in the month 3-5pm.* ☎ *05 56 94 30 50.* **Place de la Bourse★★**. Église Ste-Croix – **façade★**. **Musée d'Aquitaine★★** – ♿ ◷ *Tue-Sun 11am-6pm.* ◷ *Closed Mon and public holidays.* ⊜ *6€, no charge 1st Sunday in the month.* ☎ *05 56 01 51 00. www.mairie-bordeaux.fr.* **Musée d'Art Contemporain★** – ♿ ◷ *Tue, Thu-Sun 11am-6pm, Wed 11am-8pm.* ◷ *Closed Mon and public holidays.* ⊜ *5.50 €, no charge 1st Sunday in the month.* ☎ *05 56 00 81 50* – **Entrepôt Lainé★★**. **Croiseur Colbert★** – a post-WWII cruiser. 🧒 ◷ *Jul-Aug: daily 10am-8pm; Jun: daily 10am-7pm; Apr-May an Sep: Mon-Fri 10am-6pm, Sat-Sun, public and school holidays 10am 7pm; Oct-Mar a zone C school holidays: Wed, Sat-Sun and school holidays: 10am-6pm. Last admiss 1hr before closing.* ◷ *Closed 1 Jan, 25 Dec.* ⊜ *7.50€.* ☎ *05 56 44 96 11.*

Excursions

The Bordeaux Vineyards★

The Bordeaux wine region which extends over approximately 135 000 hectares – 333 585 acres in the Gironde *département* is the largest vineyard producing quality wines in the world.

The areas to the north produce red wines: Médoc on the west bank of the Gironde with Bourg on the east bank, and St-Émilion and Pomerol north of the Dordogne. The remaining area is devoted to white wines: Entre-Deux-Mers between the Dordogne and the Garonne, and Graves and Sauternes to the south.

Haut Médoc

It boasts the most prestigious "châteaux" which uphold a wine-making tradition dating back to the reign of Louis XIV. Some of the châteaux and the famous cellars are open to visitors, in particular Château Margaux, **Château Mouton-Rothschild**★ and Château Lafite.

St-Émilion★★

The region is famous for its full-bodied and fragrant red wines produced under the strict control of the Jurade, a guild founded in the Middle Ages which was reconvened in 1948. ⓒ *See ST-ÉMILION.*

Sauternes

The vineyards on the slopes of the lower valley of the Ciron produce renowned white wines, in particular Château Yquem. The grapes are picked by hand at the "noble rot" stage when the flavour is highly concentrated.

Musée des Tumulus de **BOUGON**★★

MICHELIN MAP 322 F 6

GREEN GUIDE ATLANTIC COAST

This important Megalithic site lies hidden in a wood near Bougon, a village known today for its goat's cheese. There is also a museum of modern design.

Visit

&. Kids ◷ *Jul and Sep: Thu-Tue 10am-6.30pm, Wed 1-6.30pm; Oct-Dec: Mon-Tue, Thu-Fri 10am-5.30pm, Wed, Sat and Sun: 1-5.30pm; Feb-Jun: Mon-Tue, Thu-Fri 10am-6pm, Wed, Sat, and Sun: 2-6pm. Jan: Sun 1-5.30pm.* ◷ *Closed 1 Jan and 25 Dec.* ⌧ *3.90€ (6-18 years: 1.50€), no charge 1st Sat in the month (Oct-Jun).* ☎ *05 49 05 12 13. www. deux-sevres.com/musee-bougon.*

A Megalithic Necropolis – The complex comprises five *tumuli* or barrows (ancient burial mounds), either circular or rectangular in shape, which were built by Neolithic tribes living in the neighbourhood; of the tribes' dwellings, however, little or no trace remains. The funerary monuments are among the oldest in the world; some structures date back to c 4700 BC (2 000 years earlier than the Pyramids of Egypt).

An elegant modern peristyle built of metal and glass on the original limestone foundation surrounds a ruined Cistercian priory. It is the startingpoint of a discovery tour ranging from prehistory to the building of the necropolis.

The outer faces of the barrows are constructed of concentric, drystone walls. Inside, beneath the earth roofs, are **passage graves.** The 300 or so skeletons found in the chambers were grouped together, confirming that the barrows were designed as collective burial places, though reserved for important members of the tribe. They were probably also places of worship.The site was abandoned c 2000 BC.

BOULOGNE-SUR-MER★★

POPULATION 95 930

MICHELIN MAP 301 C 3

GREEN GUIDE NORTHERN FRANCE AND THE PARIS REGION

Boulogne's location along the chalk cliffs facing the English coast made it a cross-Channel port at an early date. It was from here that Emperor Claudius set sail to conquer Britain; he established regular boat services to Dover and built an enormous 12-storey landmark tower 200 Roman feet high which stood until the 16C.

Fishing has long been the town's mainstay, the activities of the ship-owners' guild being regulated as early as 1203. Today's fishing fleet ties up alongside the Quai Gambetta, its catch of fresh fish the largest in continental Europe. Boulogne's other deep-water docks and basins make it France's second passenger port and tenth largest commercial port.

▶ **Orient Yourself:** Boulogne-sur-Mer, which is listed as a "Town of Art and History," offers thematic tours every day in Jul and Aug at 3pm except Tue. Check the tourist office or on www.vpah.culture.fr for information.

Sights

Ville haute★★

The upper town, Boulogne's historic core built on the site of the Roman fortress, is still surrounded by its 13C ramparts.

Colonne de la Grande Armée★★

◷ *Mid-Jun to end Sep: daily except Mon and Tue: 10am-12.30pm, 2.30-6.30pm; Oct 7 Nov and Christmas vacation to mid-Jun: Fri and Sat 10am-noon, 2-4pm.* ◷ *Closed rest of the year.* ⌧ *2.50€.* ☎ *03 21 80 43 69–3km – 2mi north.*

This monument commemorates the army assembled here by Napoleon in 1¢ for the invasion of England. The project was abandoned when the entry of Russ and Austria into the war in August 1805 forced him to strike camp and redeploy h₁ forces. A little to the west is the scene of the second great ceremony at which the award of the Légion d'Honneur was made (16 August 1804). A marker shows where the Emperor's throne was set up.

◐◐ Basilique Notre-Dame – **dome**★, **crypt**★ (🕐 *Tue-Sun 2-5pm;* 🕐 *closed Mon, 1 Jan, 25 Dec;* 🎫 *2€;* ☎ *03 21 99 75 98) and* **treasury**. **Château-Musée**★ 🕐 *Daily 10am-noon, 2-5pm (Sun and public holidays 5.30pm). Call for prices.* ☎ *03 21 10 02 20.* **Nausicaa**★★★ ♿ 🄺🄸🄳🄳 🕐 *Sep-Jun: daily 9.30am-6.30pm (Jul and Aug: 8pm). Last admission 1hr before closing.* 🕐 *Closed first 3 weeks in Jan, 25 Dec (morning).* 🎫 *15.50€ (children: 14€).* ☎ *03 21 30 99 99. www.nausicaa.fr – national sea centre.*

Excursion

Côte d'Opale★ – ♿ *See CALAIS: Excursions.*

BOURG-EN-BRESSE★★

POPULATION 40 972

MICHELIN MAP 328 C-D-E 3-4

GREEN GUIDE BURGUNDY JURA

Bourg is the capital of the Bresse area, a fertile plain much liable to flooding and fa-mous for its delicately-fleshed poultry. To the south extend the Dombes; its many irregularly-shaped meres mark the furthest extent of the Alpine glaciers.

A Bit of History

"Fortune infortune fort une" – The sadly appropriate motto of **Margaret of Austria** (1480-1530) can be translated as "Fate was very hard on one woman." As a child of two, Margaret lost her mother, Mary of Burgundy. At three, she was chosen by Louis XI as the wife of the Dauphin Charles VIII because of her Burgundian inheritance; a form of wedding took place at Amboise. Then, at the age of 11, she was repudiated by the Crown in favour of Anne of Brittany and the marriage annulled. At the age of 21 she married John of Castile who left her a widow after less than a year. At 24

she re-married, this time to Philibert le Beau (the Fair). He too was soon dead, of a cold caught while out hunting. For Margaret this was enough; from then on her life was devoted to prayer and to looking after the lands she had inherited.

Adversity had strengthened her character; her rule over Burgundy, the Franche-Comté and Artois was marked by skilled diplomacy, financial rigour and great political wisdom. As a result, her father, the Emperor Maximilian, made her Regent of the Low Countries on the death of her brother Philippe 'e Beau (the Fair) in 1506. Margaret, ⌐ow 26 years old, moved to Brussels d decided to transform the humble ⌐y of Brou into a monastery, partly ⌐ilment of a vow made 24 years ⌐ by her mother-in-law, Margaret ⌐on, partly to assert her own ⌐us and achievement and to ⌐ her love for her husband.

Ph. Gajic/MICHELIN

Margaret of Austria, stained glass window in Brou church

sit

glis de Brou★★

🕐 *Apr-Sep: daily 9am-12.30pm, 2-6pm; mid-Jun to mid-Sep: daily 9am-6pm; Oct-Mar: daily 9am-noon, 2-5pm.* 🕐 *Closed 1 Jan, 1 May, 1 and 11 Nov, 25 Dec.* 🔗 *6.10€ (combined ticket includes a visit to the museum and the cloister)* 🔗 *Guided tours available.* ☎ *04 74 22 83 83.*

The church (1513-32) is in late-Gothic style, harmonious but perhaps over-exuberant. The work was undertaken by a Flemish master builder and a team of artists and craftsmen, mostly from Flanders. Their decoration of the church is already much influenced by the Renaissance.

In the elegant nave built of pale stone from the Jura, a finely sculptured balustrade was substituted for the more usual triforium. The stone rood screen (**jubé★★**) has three basket-handle arches and is profusely decorated with leaves, cable-moulding and scrolls.

The 74 choir stalls (**stalles★★**) were built in the space of two years by local carpenters. An array of statuettes represents figures from the Old Testament (on the right) and from the New Testament (on the left). In the Margaret of Austria chapel (**Oratoire★★★**) is an altarpiece representing the Seven Joys of the Virgin, a masterwork of amazing craftsmanship. There are also superb stained-glass windows (**vitraux★★**) inspired by works by Dürer and Titian.

The three tombs (**tombeaux★★★**) give the church its truly regal character. On the right is that of Margaret of Bourbon. To conform to the taste of her time, it was housed in a Gothic niche with Flamboyant decoration. Philibert the Fair's tomb, in the middle, is completely Renaissance in character; up above, the prince, clad in decorative armour, lies recumbent, watched over by cherubs, while below his cadaver is guarded by delightful little statues representing his virtues. Margaret of Austria's tomb, on the left, forms part of the parclose screen; she is first shown lying in state on a black marble slab, then, underneath, in her shroud. Its richly carved canopy incorporates her motto.

▷▷ **Musée★** (in the monastery) – 🕐 *Apr-Sep: daily 9am-12.30pm, 2-6pm; Jun to mid-Sep: daily 9am-6pm; Oct-Mar: daily 9am-noon, 2-5pm.* 🕐 *Closed 1 Jan, 1 May, 1 and 11 Nov, 25 Dec.* 🔗 *6.10€.* ☎ *04 74 22 83 83.*– painting, sculpture, decorative arts.

BOURGES★★★

POPULATION 94 731

MICHELIN MAP 323 K 4-6

GREEN GUIDE DORDOGNE BERRY LIMOUSIN

Bourges was already a place of some importance at the time of the conquest of Gaul; in 52 BC it was sacked by Julius Caesar, who is supposed to have massacred 40 000 of its inhabitants. In the 4C the city became the capital of the Roman province of Avaricum, part of Aquitaine. Its significance increased over the years, but it was only at the end of the 14C that it took on a national role, when **Jean de Berry**, the dynamic son of John the Good, made his capital. A great patron, he made Bourges a centre of the arts to rival Dijon (Court of the Dukes of Burgundy) and Avignon (the Papal court), commissioning works like the Très Riches Heures from the Limbourg brothers, perhaps the most exquisite miniatures ever painted.

▶ **Orient Yourself:** A 45min ride on the tourist train gives you a nice look at Bourge history and architecture. (🕐 *Apr to mid-Nov: daily, train leaves every 15min in fr of the Tourist Office; contact M. Sary for more info;* ☎ *06 08 60 54 56).* There are 2hr guided tours offered by the tourist office for 5.50€.

Shopping: The main shopping area is in the pedestrian centre of town wh can take a pleasant stroll along rue Coursarlor and rue Mirabeau (near t' Jacque-Cœur), or rue Bourbonnoux and rue Moyenne (near the cathe

Bourges - Address Book

TOURIST INFORMATION

Guided tours – Bourges, which has been officially designated as a "Town of Art and History", offers guided tours (1hr 30min/2hr) with qualified local guides. *For information, contact the tourist office (☎ 02 48 23 02 60) or log on to www.bourges-tourisme.com.*

P'tit train touristique – The city's tourist train provides a 45min overview of the city's history and architecture. Operates daily, Apr to early-Nov (departures every 15min from the tourist office). *For information, call ☎ 06 08 60 54 56.*

For coin ranges, see the Legend at the back of the guide.

EATING OUT

⊜ **Le Bourbonnoux** – *44 r. Bourbonnoux* - ☎ 02 48 24 14 76 - *restaurant. bourbonnoux@wanadoo.fr -* 🕐 *closed 11-21 Feb, 16-26 Apr, 16 Aug-3 Sep, Sun eve Nov-Jun, Sat lunchtime and Fri.* The restaurant is in a street lined with craft shops, just a few steps away from St-Étienne Cathedral. The welcome is warm and the dining room is pleasantly decorated with bright colours and exposed beams. Popular with locals.

⊜⊜ **Le Bistro Gourmand** – *5 pl. de la Barre -* ☎ 02 48 70 63 37 - *reserv. recommended.* A delightful bistro specialising in regional and Lyonnais cuisine. The sober decor here is enhanced by gentle candlelight. The terrace looks onto the Église Notre-Dame.

⊜⊜ **La Table Savoyarde** – *14 r. Florentin-Labbé -* ☎ 02 48 24 57 94 - 🕐 *closed the first 3 weeks in Aug, Sun lunchtime and Mon.* As the name suggests, the focus here is on the cuisine of Savoy, with a menu that includes cheese fondues, *raclettes*, *tartiflettes* etc. Wooden skis, clogs, cow bells and other typically Savoyard objects adorn the cool stone vaults of this former coal cellar.

⊜⊜ **La Courcillière** – *R. de Babylone -* ☎ 02 48 24 41 91 - 🕐 *closed Wed, Sun eve and Tue eve.* Located in the Les Marais district just a stone's throw from the city centre, this pleasant, rustic restaurant has a terrace by the water facing the gardens. Down-to-earth and reasonably priced cuisine.

⊜⊜ **D'Antan Sancerrois** – *50 r. Bourbonnoux -* ☎ 02 48 65 96 26 - 🕐 *closed 1 Jan, 1-20 Aug, 25 Dec, Sun and Mon.* This pretty bistro used to be home to a 15C alderman who kept company with the Duchesse de Berry. The handsome rustic decor features an amusing collection of porcelain tureen lids. Traditional fare and good service.

WHERE TO STAY

⊜⊜ **Chambre d'hôte Château de Bel** – *Lieu-dit le Grand-Chemin - 18340*

Arcay - 16km/10mi S of Bourges on the D 73 - ☎ 02 48 25 36 72 - 🕐 *open all year -* 🛏 - *6 rooms.* Surrounded by spacious grounds, this 19C château is both calm and comfortable. The vast entrance hall leads to the dining room with its massive fireplace. Large rooms on the upper floor. Mountain bikes available for rent.

⊜⊜ **Hôtel Christina** – *5 r. Halle -* ☎ 02 48 70 56 50 - *info@le-christina.com - 71 rooms.* This hotel is the perfect base for discovering the city centre. Two categories of well-maintained bedrooms are available: cosy and chic, or smaller and functional.

⊜⊜ **Hôtel Les Tilleuls** – *7 pl. Pyrotechnie -* ☎ 02 48 20 49 04 - *lestilleuls.bourges@ wanadoo.fr -* 🅿 - *39 rooms.* Situated in a quiet part of town, this hotel offers guests accommodation in the main building and an annex, where the rooms are less spacious, more basic, but with the benefit of air-conditioning. Children's play area in the garden. Solarium.

⊜⊜⊜ **Best Western Hôtel d'Angleterre** – *1 pl. des Quatre-Piliers -* ☎ 02 48 24 68 51 - 🕐 *closed 24 Dec-1 Jan -* 🅿 - *30 rooms.* The city's former court of justice is located close to the Palais Jacques-Cœur. All necessary creature comforts in the bedrooms (most with air-conditioning), where the decor is sober yet modern. Buffet breakfast. Friendly staff.

BARS AND CAFÉS

Pub des Jacobins – *Enclos des Jacobins -* ☎ 02 48 24 61 78 - 🕐 *open Mon-Sat, 4pm-3am -* 🕐 *closed Sun.* This piano-bar is whole-heartedly devoted to jazz, as demonstrated by the photos of musicians covering the walls. Top-quality concerts are held here once a month. The pub specialises in cocktails.

Pub Jacques Cœur – *1 r. d'Auron -* ☎ 02 48 70 72 88 - 🕐 *open Mon-Sat, 10am-2am -* 🕐 *closed Sun.* This 16C half-timbered residence, now a pub, was built on the site where Jacques Cœur, a wealthy and influential 15C merchant and councillor to King Charles VII, was born. Sloping and lopsided, this antique building is the most photographed of Bourges. Concerts are frequently held here.

ENTERTAINMENT

Maison de la Culture de Bourges – *Pl. André-Malraux -* ☎ 02 48 67 74 70 - *www. mcbourges.com -* 🕐 *ticket office open Tue-Sat, 2-7pm -* 🕐 *closed 13 Jul-20 Aug and 1 May.* Opened by André Malraux, then Minister of Culture, this was the first Maison de la Culture in France. This lively and popular venue hosts plays, dance performances and classical music and jazz concerts. Cinema and café.

Les Nuits Lumières de Bourges – ☎ 02 48 23 02 60 - ⏱ Every evening in Jul-Aug and during the Printemps de Bourges festival; May-Jun and Sep: Thu-Sat. No charge. A walk through the historic city centre at night to view illuminated buildings (2hr 30min). Blue lanterns mark the way.

LEISURE ACTIVITIES

Base de Voile du Val-d'Auron – 23 chemin Grand Mazières - ☎ 02 48 20 07 65. ⏱ Open 9am-noon and 2-6pm. ⏱ Closed Oct-Apr and Mon. This watersports centre at the Val d'Auron Lake covering 85 ha/210 acres offers a range of activities, including swimming, canoeing, fishing and rowing.

SHOPPING

The main shopping area is in the pedestrianised area that includes rue Coursarlor and rue Mirebeau (near the palais Jacques-Cœur), and rue Bourbonnoux and rue Moyenne (near the cathedral).

Markets – Every Saturday morning, the listed Halle au Blé comes to life with 200 stallholders selling all types of food. A permanent daily market is also held at the Halle St-Bonnet (⏱ open 7.30am-1pm and 3-7.30pm), selling fresh seasonal produce, local cheeses and other regional specialities. On Sunday mornings, stalls

selling bric-a-brac, inexpensive clothes etc add to the charm of this popular market.

La Maison des Forestines – 3 pl. Cujas - ☎ 02 48 24 00 24 - mdforestines@wanadoo.fr - ⏱ open Mon, 3-7pm; Tue-Sat 9.30am-12.15pm and 2-7.15pm. This chocolate/confectionery business founded in 1825 occupies an attractive Haussmann-style building. The shop, with its coffered ceiling and superb Gien china, produces irresistible house specialities such as the Forestine, a chocolate praline with a satiny sugar coating created in 1879, the Amandine and Noisette (created in 1885) and the Richelieu, a nougatine filled with an almond and pistachio creme, created in 1890.

Domaine de Coquin – ☎ 02 48 64 84 51 - ⏱ open Mon-Fri, 8am-7pm, Sun and public hols, 9am-noon. Francis Audiot is a wine-producer whose family has been producing excellent white wines for the past 150 years.

Épicerie du Berry – 41 r. Moyenne (îlot Victor-Hugo) - ☎ 02 48 70 02 38. This small boutique at the foot of the cathedral only sells regional products such as sablés de Nançais (a type of shortcake biscuit), pasta from La Chapelle de St-Ursin, tortillons (goat's cheese pastries) and Monin syrups.

Visit

Cathédrale St-Étienne★★★

⏱ Guided tours 🕿 (45min) Jul-Aug: 9.45am, 11am, 12.15pm, 2.15pm, 3.15pm, 3.45pm, 4.15pm, 5pm and 5.45pm; May-Jun: 10am, 11.15am, 2.30pm, 3.45pm, 5pm; Apr-Sep: 10.15, 11.15pm, 2.30pm, 3.45pm, 5pm; Oct-Mar: 10am, 11.15pm, 2.30pm, 3.30pm, 4.30pm. ⏱ Closed 1 Jan, 1 May, 1 and 11 Nov, 25 Dec. 🎫 6.10€ (under 18 years: no charge), crypt and North tower. 8.50€ combined ticket with Palais Jacques-Cœur. ☎ 02 48 65 49 44.

In the 12C, Bourges was the seat of an archbishopric linked by tradition to the royal territories to the north, whereas the regions to the southwest came under the sphere of influence of the Angevin kingdom. The great new cathedrals of the Ile-de-France were taking shape, and the Archbishop, Henri de Sully, Primate of Aquitaine, dreamed of a similar great edifice for his city.

In drawing up his plans, the anonymous architect exploited all the new techniques of the Gothic in order to control and direct the thrusts exerted by and on his great structure. Other innovations of his included leaving out the transepts, retaining six sexpartite bays and incorporating the Romanesque portals of the old cathedral into the north and south doorways of the new building.

By 1200 the crypt was completed, by 1215, the choir. In 1220 the great nave with its splendid row of two-tiered flying buttresses was ready. Over-enthusiastic restoration at the start of the 19C included the remodelling of the external gables and the unfortunate addition of round windows, balustrades and pinnacles.

The huge west front **(façade ouest)** has five doorways, anticipating the nave and four aisles adorned with the radiating motifs of the High Gothic (mid 13C-14C) style; they were begun in 1230. Ten years later the two right-hand portals were in place. By 1250, the central portal (Last Judgement) had been finished. But 60 years later, subsidence made it necessary to prop up the South Tower by means of a massive pillar-buttress and to strengthen the west front. This was to no avail; on 31 December 1506, the north tower fell in ruins. Guillaume Pellevoysin, the new architect, worked for 30 years on its replacement and on the construction of the two left-hand portals; he included many architectural and decorative features of the Early Renaissance.

The east end **(chevet)** has the Gothic windows of the lower church inserted between the base of the chapels and the buttresses. Three-sided chapels radiate out from the outer ambulatory, while the inner ambulatory is spanned by the first tier of the double flying buttresses; the upper spans pierce the structure to hold the vault of the choir in place. The Lanceolate Gothic style here reaches a high point in its development. Inside, the nave and four aisles **(nefs)**, completed in 1270, make a striking impression by virtue of their great height and the light filtering through the stained glass. The outer aisles, lined by chapels, are already 9m – 30ft from floor to vault, the inner aisles, with a blind triforium, reach 21m – 70ft, while the nave rises to a full 37.15m – 122ft. With no gallery, and limited by the great size of its arches it is covered by a sexpartite vault; the alternating sequence of major and minor piers is cunningly disguised by the shafts wrapped around the columns. This rare arrangement was to be repeated soon afterwards in the choir at Le Mans. Beneath the choir a crypte **(crypte★★)** of the same layout takes up a 6m – 20ft change in level of the ground. A fine example of a 13C crypt, it has an outer ambulatory with triangular vaulting and arcades mounted on twisted diagonal arches to allow the keystones to be set properly.

The stained glass **(vitraux★★★)** – some of the finest in the whole of France – demonstrates the whole evolution of the art of glass-making between the 12C and 17C. The 13C windows in the choir recall the techniques of the master glass-makers of Chartres. The great nave is illuminated by light streaming in through all its windows, from the lowest (in the side chapels), from the double windows in the inner aisles, and from the highest, which reach almost to the vaults of the central nave itself.

Palais Jacques Cœur★★

⏱ *Guided tours* ⚓ *(1hr) Jul and Aug: 9.30am-7pm; May-Jun: 9.30am-12.15pm, 2-6.15pm; Sep-Apr: 10am -12.15pm, 2-5.15pm.* ⏱ *Closed 1 Jan, 1 May, 1 and 11 Nov, 25 Dec.* ✆ *6.10€ (under 17 years: no charge)* ☎ *02 48 24 79 41.*

The son of a Bourges fur-trader, Jacques Cœur (1395-1456) started out as a goldsmith, first at the court of Jean de Berry, then with Charles VII. He soon became aware of the economic recovery just beginning and of the opportunities opening up in the Mediterranean. Before long he had many commercial interests and he supplied the royal court with luxury goods and became the king's Minister of Finance. At the peak of his career at the age of 50 he decided to build himself a worthy residence.

His palace, begun in 1445, was completed in the short space of 10 years. It shows how the will to build had revived after the stagnation due to war and also demonstrates the success of the Flamboyant Gothic style. It is a sumptuous building, incorporating certain pioneering comforts like a bath-house and an arcaded courtyard. Other innovations it contributed to the evolution of late-medieval domestic architecture included the provision of a large number of rooms with independent access, sculptures indicating the purpose of the rooms served by the various staircases, and, in the chapel, two oratories reserved for the proprietor and his wife.

▶▶ **Hôtel Cujas★** (Berry Provincial Museum) ⏱ *Jan-Mar: Mon, Wed-Sat 10am-noon, 2-5pm, Sun. 2-5pm; Apr-Jun and Sep-Dec: Mon, Wed-Sat 10-noon, 2-6pm, Sun 2-6pm; Jul and Aug: Mon, Wed-Sat 10am-12.30pm, 1.30-6pm, Sun 1.30-6.30pm.* ⏱ *Closed Tue, 1 Jan, 1 May, 1 and 11 Nov, 25 Dec. No charge.* ☎ *02 48 57 81 15.* **Hôtel Lallemant★** ⏱ *Jan-Mar: Tue-Sat 10am-noon, 2-5pm, Sun 2-5pm; Apr-Jun and Sep-Dec: Tue-Sat 10-noon, 2-6pm, Sun 2-6pm; Jul and Aug: Tue-Sat 10am-12.30pm, 1.30-6pm, Sun 1.30-6.30pm.* ⏱ *Closed Mon, 1 Jan, 1 May, 1 and 11 Nov, 25 Dec. No charge.* ☎ *02 48 57 81 17* – decorative arts. Hotel des Échevins (Musée Maurice-Estève★). Jardin des Prés-Fichaux★.

Lac du **BOURGET**★★

MICHELIN MAP 333 H-I 3-4

GREEN GUIDE FRENCH ALPS

his is France's largest (4 500ha – 11 000 acres) and most celebrated lake. It lies in laciated valley between the southern end of the Jura and the foothills of the ; its waters were once fed directly by the Rhône and stretched right to the of the Grand Colombier. Today it is linked to the river by the Savières Canal cross the marshy Chantagne valley. Its steep western shore is dominated peaks of the Dent du Chat and the Mont de la Charvaz.

ne lake and its banks form a rich and unusual habitat for wildlife. In its waters
ive pollans, migratory members of the salmon family, together with crayfish,
originally imported a century ago from New England. Its varied birdlife includes
300 cormorants which winter on the west bank at La grande Cale.

A Bit of History

It was on the shores of the lake that **Alphonse de Lamartine** (1790-1867) found his
Muse. A young, distinguished consumptive, idling his time away between Burgundy,
Italy and Paris, he met Mme Charles, Julie, here in October 1816. Though she was to
die only 14 months later, it was through her that Lamartine achieved his maturity as
a poet, while she, in turn, was immortalised as Elvire. In March 1820 his *Méditations
poétiques* were published, a distillation of tender memories expressed in "a harmonious and half-blurred language which seems to flow below the level of consciousness"
(Geoffrey Brereton). They brought him instant literary fame. In 1830 he turned to
politics, establishing himself as an idealistic orator of considerable power. Though in
opposition from 1833, his popularity was immense. In February 1848 it was he who
proclaimed the Provisional Government and succeeded in saving the tricolour. But
after Napoleon III's coup d'état of 2 December he was obliged to retire to his country
estate. Plagued by debts, he sold his property and published many volumes on political history, and a potted *Course in Literature*. The last months of his life were eased by
the proceeds of a national collection, patronised by Napoleon III.

Visit

Abbaye royale de Hautecombe★★

Restored in the 19C in a somewhat emphatic style, the church houses the tombs
of 42 princely members of the House of Savoy. Over the centuries these rulers had
looked westwards from their capital at Turin at the irritating chain of the Alps which
split their domain in two. In 1857, in a determined effort to overcome this obstacle,
Victor-Emmanuel II had a railway tunnel 13.7km – 8.5 miles long bored between
Bardonecchia and Modane. This was the first tunnel to pierce the Alpine barrier;
ironically, by the time of its completion in 1872, it lay entirely in French territory, since
Savoy had opted for France in the plebiscite of 1860.

The abbey's little lakeside harbour has an unusual 12C building **(grange batelière)**
with covered moorings, allowing goods to be unloaded and stored under the same
roof.

◗◗ **Tour du lac**★★ (Lakeside road).

BRANTÔME★★

POPULATION 2 080

MICHELIN MAP 329 E 3

GREEN GUIDE DORDOGNE BERRY LIMOUSIN

Few landscapes are as generously endowed as the smiling countryside of Perigord with its gently-sloping fields, walnut trees, solid stone farmhouses and meandering rivers hemmed in by limestone cliffs.

At its heart lies Brantôme, its **setting**★★ by the banks of the Dronne making it the most delightful of riverside villages. It has old dwellings with slate roofs built like little manor houses, a crooked bridge seen across the tranquil surface of the water, great trees growing on the lawns of its lovely gardens. The 18C abbey has a fine west front and a Romanesque bell-tower (**clocher**★★) (& ☉ *Guided tours* ◠◟ *(1hr15min) mid-Jun to end Jun and early Sep to mid-Sep : daily except Tue 10.30am-noon, 2-6pm, Sun 2-6pm; Jul and mid-Aug: daily 10am-7pm, Sun 2.30-6pm; ◠ 6€. ☏ 05 53 05 80 63).*

A Bit of History

Pierre de Bourdeilles (1540-1614) was commendatory abbot here. In 1589 he retired to the abbey after a fall from a horse, having also fallen from favour at court as the Bourbons replaced the Valois. Under the nom-de-plume of Brantôme, this former courtier and soldier of fortune amused himself with his memoirs, published posthumously as the *Lives (les Vies) of Illustrious Ladies, Illustrious Men, Great Leaders, and of Gallant Ladies*. These lively tales of licentious exploits have many piquant portraits penned by a chronicler whose own days of merry-making were sadly over.

East bank of the River Dronne

J.-P. Clapham/MICHELIN

Château de la **BRÈDE**★

MICHELIN MAP 335 H 6

GREEN GUIDE ATLANTIC COAST

In the peaceful countryside of the Graves area the **Château de la Brède**, protected by its moat, still keeps its aristocratic 15C appearance. It was the birthplace of **Charles Montesquieu** (1689-1755), Baron de la Brède, a magistrate of Bordeaux, who took pleasure in the life of a country gentleman, devoting much time to the management of his vines, but also wrote extensively (*Persian Letters* – 1724) and travelled widely, notably to England, where he spent two decisive years (1729-31), returning with that somewhat idealised notion of English constitutionalism prevalent among French political thinkers of the 18C. Twenty years of philosophical reflection and hard writing led to the publication in 1748 of his L'Esprit des lois (The Nature of Laws), in which he expanded the theory of the separation of legislative, executive and judicial powers, sole guarantee of the citizen's liberty. Its 31 volumes are hardly read today but went through 22 editions in 18 months at the time. With them, political writings enter the mainstream of French literary history.

Visit

  Guided tours (30min) *Jul-Sep: daily except Tue 2-6.30pm; Easter to end Jun: Sat-Sun and public holidays 2-6pm; Oct to mid-Nov: Sat-Sun and public holidays 2-5.30pm.* 6€.

In the château, the bedroom **(chambre)** with its original furnishings and library **(bibliothèque)** comprising some 7 000 volumes help to evoke the life and work of this sympathetic figure.

BREST★

POPULATION 201 480

MICHELIN MAP 308 A 4, E 4-5

GREEN GUIDE BRITTANY

Although used as a port by Gauls and Romans, Brest really became important only in the 13C. The town had to be completely rebuilt after the Second World War in which it suffered four years of air attack and a 43-day siege.

The Rue de Siam runs in a straight line between the arsenal and Place de la Liberté; it formed the main axis of the ancient town and its fame was spread world-wide by the sailors who frequented it.

A Bit of History

In 1341, at the start of his struggle with Jeanne de Penthièvre for the Breton succession, Jean de Montfort allowed his ally, Edward III of England, to occupy Brest. Digging themselves well in, the English refused to budge, even when peace came and the Treaty of Guérande had been signed, three sieges notwithstanding. They were persuaded to relinquish their prey only in 1397, under the terms of the marriage contract between the new ruler of England, Richard II, and Isabella, the daughter of Charles VI. A French garrison moved in and has been there ever since. At the beginning of the 17C, Richelieu's wish was to have French naval forces which could be permanently ready for action. Aware of the potential of Brest (as of Toulon), he founded the naval dockyard on the banks of the Penfeld river; its first warship was launched as early as 1634. His work was continued by Colbert, who created a college of marine guards as well as schools of gunnery, hydrography and naval architecture. The yard was further improved by Duquesne who also built the ramparts that Vauban improved in his turn in 1683. A number of sculptors were employed in the port, among them Coysevox who worked on figureheads and the decoration of poops. Breton sculpture of the late 17C was much influenced by the work of these naval craftsmen-artists.

In the 18C, the fortifications at **Le Quélern** out on the channel (le Goulet) linking the Brest roadstead to the sea are evidence of the need to safeguard French naval power at the time of the American War of Independence.

Christ washing the disciples' feet, the Calvary, Plougastel-Daoulas

MICHELIN

Visit

Cours Dajot★

This fine promenade was laid out in 1769 on the old ramparts. It gives splendid **views**★★ of the activity of the port and of the great roadstead of 150km² – 58sq mi fed by the estuaries of the Elorn, Daoulas, Faou and Aulne and almost closed off by the Roscanvel Peninsula. On the right the Brest Channel (Goulet de Brest) opens out; this channel (55m – 180ft deep, 2km – 1.25mi wide and 5km – 3mi long) is a spectacular example of a coastline drowned by the rise in sea-level which accompanied the final melting of the glaciers. The same phenomenon produced the abers, the drowned valleys of Lower Brittany (aber Wrac'h, aber Benoît, aber Ildut), the rivers of the south coast of Brittany (Auray, Pont-Aven, Etel, as well as the *rias* of Galicia and their counterparts in Devon, Cornwall and South Wales and the coves *(calanques)* in the Provençal mountain range (Cassis).

Musée des Beaux Arts★

◷ *Mon, Wed-Sat 10-noon, 2-6pm, Sun. 2-6pm.* ◷ *Closed Tue and public holidays (except 14 Jul and 15 Aug.* ◷ *4€ (under 18 years: no charge), no charge 1st Sun in the month .* ☎ *02 98 00 87 96.*

The collections illustrate the advances made by the painters of the Pont-Aven School, for example *Yellow Sea (Mer jaune)* by Lacombe, as well as a curious study of the town of Ys (✆ *see QUIMPER*), Manet's *Parrots*, and *Bouquet of Roses* by Suzanne Valadon.

Pont de Recouvrance

This is Europe's biggest lifting bridge, with an 87m – 285ft span. The *aber* of the Penfeld winds upstream between steep banks past the naval dockyard and base founded in the 17C.

Château – Together with the tower (Tour Tanguy) on the opposite bank of the Penfeld, this is a reminder of Brest's historic fortifications.

Oceanopolis★★

Kids ♿ ◷ *Apr-Aug: daily 9am-6pm; Sep -Mar: daily except Mon 10am-5pm, Sun, public holidays, and school holidays (all zones) 10am-6pm.* ◷ *Closed 1 Jan, 2 weeks in Jan (call for more info) and 25 Dec.* ◷ *15€ (children 4-17 years: 10.50€).* ☎ *02 98 34 40 40. www. oceanopolis.com– Moulin Blanc Marina.*

In this ultra-modern building, shaped like a giant crab, discover the marine life of Brittany's coastal waters in the saltwater aquariums (downstairs), and the many sea birds of the coast in their nesting places on the cliff face (entrance level).

Excursions

Calvaire de Plougastel-Daoulas★★

11km – 7 mi east, south of the church. The calvary was built from 1602 to 1604 by the Priget brothers to mark an outbreak of plague four years earlier. Its 180 figures are sculpted in the round; a certain stiffness of posture is set off by the size of the heads and the vigorous expressions. The 28 scenes illustrate the life of Christ (the Nativity, the Washing of Feet) and above all the Passion (Arrest and Scourging) and the Resurrection.

The monument itself is built from ochre Logonna sandstone in nice contrast to the episodes shown in **kersanton**, a dark igneous coarse-textured rock of the diorite family containing much black mica. This used to be extracted at water-level from an inlet off the Brest roadstead; it is easy to work and hardens with exposure. It was this stone which helped establish the reputation of the sculpture made at Le Folgoët and for many years was the material used in Finistère for gravestones.

The Abers★

The term *aber* is of Celtic origin and is found in Scottish and Welsh place names such as Aberdeen, Aberdour, Aberystwyth, Abersoch. In Brittany *abers* are picturesque, fairly shallow estuaries on the low, rocky northwest coast of Finistère. Harbours are suitable only for yachts and other sailing craft.

The entrance to the **aber Wrac'h** is guarded by the small seaside resort of the same name near which there are fine views of the lighthouse on Vierge Island, the tallest in France (82.5m – 270ft). A **scenic road**★ runs along the rugged coastline through a number of charming resorts.

BRIANÇON★★

POPULATION 11 041

MICHELIN MAP 334 H 3

GREEN GUIDE FRENCH ALPS

Briançon is best viewed from the terraces of the fortress (**citadelle**) where stands the 9m – 30ft-high statue of **France**★ sculpted by **Antoine Bourdelle**. This is the highest town in Europe (1 321m – 4 334ft), sited at the meeting-point of the valleys forming the upper part of the Durance basin. Since ancient times, two great routes into Italy have met here, one coming from the Romanche valley via the Col de Lautaret, the other following the Durance up from Embrun.

A Bit of History

The strategic value of the site was appreciated by the Gauls. It seems likely that the survivors of the Germanic tribes routed by the Roman general Marius outside Aix-en-Provence found their way here, and Briançon may have provided a refuge too for some of the persecuted members of the Vaudois, a pre-Protestant sect in the 15C. The town played an important commercial and military role, the latter enhanced by the presence of great rock bars lending themselves naturally to fortification. The forts (Dauphin, Sallettes, les Trois-Têtes, Anjou, Randouillet) built by Vauban in the 17C proved their effectiveness in the year of Waterloo, when General Eberlé's triumphant resistance here held off the invading Austro-Sardinians for three months.

▶ **Orient Yourself:** Briançon, which is listed as a "Town of Art and History," offers 2hr discovery tours daily in Jul and Aug at 10am and 3pm; in Sep on Wed, Fri and Sat at 3pm; and Oct-May on Fri and Sat at 2.30pm. They cost 4.80€ and more information is available from the Heritage Dept. and on www.vpah.culture.com.

Visit

Ville haute ★★(Upper Town)

In January 1692, the War of the League of Augsburg had been raging for six years; mercenaries in the pay of Vittorio-Amadeo II, Duke of Savoy, invaded the Dauphiné and put Briançon to the torch – only two houses out of 258 escaped the conflagration. Vauban was working in Burgundy, but was immediately dispatched by Louis XIV to Briançon (which he knew already) with a brief to rebuild the town and make it impregnable. A week sufficed for the great engineer to draw up his plans, but age and ill health made it impossible for him to supervise their execution, and he was to deplore a number of modifications and compromises made to his project.

With its gate (Porte Pignerol) and its fortified church, Briançon-Vauban, in contrast to the lower town Briançon-Ste-Catherine, still has the look of a frontier town of Louis XIV's reign, while its narrow, steeply-sloping streets, especially the **Grande Gargouille**★ (also known as the Grande Rue), express the drama of its precipitous site.

◖◗ **Pont d'Asfeld**★. **Fort des Salettes**★. **Prorel**★★ Jul-Aug: (25min, continuous) 9.45am-5.30pm. 9€ round trip (pedestrian). ☎ 04 92 25 55 00.

BRIARE

POPULATION 6 070

MICHELIN MAP 318 N 6

GREEN GUIDE BURGUNDY JURA

Briare is a busy town on the banks of the Loire, known for its ceramic floor mosaics and its stoneware.

Visit

Pont-Canal★

The Loire was used by river traffic from the 14C to the 19C, but the navigation companies found it difficult to cope with the river's irregular flow on the one hand, and shallowness on the other. To rectify this, and as part of his policy of economic unification, Henri IV began building the Briare Canal in 1604; completed in 1642, it linked the basins of the Loire and the Seine via its junction with the River Loing at Montargis. It was the first connecting canal in Europe.

The Loire Lateral Canal (1822-38) extends it south to Digoin. It crosses the Loire at Briare on an aqueduct built 1890-94 (58 years after those at Le Guétin and Digoin). The channel is the longest in the world (662.68m – 2 174ft 2in). It rests on 15 granite piers designed by G Eiffel; their loading is constant, irrespective of the presence of barges or the weight of their cargo, a nice illustration of Archimedes' principle.

B. Henry/CEDRI

Pont-Canal

BRIOUDE★

POPULATION 7 295

MICHELIN MAP 331 C 2

GREEN GUIDE AUVERGNE RHÔNE VALLEY

Brioude is the market centre of the southern Limagne, an ancient lake-bed, now a fertile plain which contrasts with the ruggedness of the surrounding mountains.

Visit

Basilique St-Julien★★

This was built at the spot where, according to tradition, Julian, a centurion of a Roman legion based at Vienne, was martyred in 304. For many years it attracted throngs of pilgrims on the road which, beyond Le Puy, passed through Langogne and Villefort, at the time the only route between the Auvergne and Languedoc. Work on the present building began with the narthex in 1060, and was completed in 1180 with the construction of the choir and east end. The nave was raised in height and given a ribvault in 1259.

The east end (**chevet**★★) is one of the final examples of Romanesque architecture in the Auvergne. Its five slate-roofed radiating chapels have richly-decorated cornices and capitals, above which runs a band of mosaic masonry. The south porch (**porche**★) has kept its typical Auvergne five-sided lintel, its wrought-iron strap-hinges and two fine bronze knockers. The warm colouring of the interior is due to the combination of sandstones and basalts of red, pink and brown hue. The nave is paved with cobblestones laid in the 16C and only recently exposed again.

The presence locally of both sandstones and marble was a distinct advantage to the four, possibly even six, masons' workshops responsible for the decoration of the church during the 12C and 13C. The capitals (**chapiteaux**★★) are exceptional; note particularly (in the south aisle near the entrance) an armed knight, perhaps a participant involved in the First Crusade (which had been preached at Clermont-Ferrand), together with a usurer (the sculptor's social comment on this curse of the Middle Ages). Further up the south aisle are two 14C works, the Virgin Birth and Our Lord as a Leper. There are murals too, not, unfortunately, very well preserved, but covering an area of 140m – about 1 300sq ft. There are two outstanding subjects, the figure of St Michael in the first bay of the nave, and the composition in the gallery of the narthex (south room): Christ in Glory, the Chosen and the Damned, the Virtues and the Vices and 100 angels, and, on the timber wall, a stunning 13C Fall of Satan.

Excursion

Lavaudieu★
10km – 6mi southeast. The 11C Benedictine priory, attached to the great abbey at La Chaise-Dieu, has charming cloisters (**cloître**★) with timber-built galleries and 14C **frescoes**★ in the chapel and refectory.

Château de **BRISSAC**★★

MICHELIN MAP 317 G 4

GREEN GUIDE CHÂTEAUX OF THE LOIRE

The château, set in a fine park shaded by magnificent cedar trees★, is unusual both for its height and for the juxtaposition of two buildings; they were not meant to stand side by side but the latter building was supposed to replace the earlier. As the original building had been damaged during the Wars of Religion, Duke Charles de Cossé commissioned a new residence designed by Jacques Corbineau, the architect responsible for the citadel at Port-Louis in Lorient. Work ceased at the latter's death in 1621 and the château was left as we see it today.

Visit

🕐 *Guided tours* ⌁ *(45min) Apr-Jun and mid-Sep to end Oct: daily except Tue 10am-noon, 2.15-5.15pm; Jul to mid-Sep: daily 10am-5.45pm.* ⌑ *8€ (children: 6€).* ☎ *02 41 91 22 21. www.brissac.net.*

The château has an unfinished main façade flanked by medieval towers. The central pavilion and the left wing are abundantly ornamented with rusticated pilasters and statues in niches. The right wing, which would have replaced the Gothic tower, was never built.

The 17C French painted **ceilings** are often embellished with sculptures; the walls are hung with superb **tapestries**. The Louis XIII staircase leads to the imposing guard room (Salle des Gardes), to the bedchamber where Louis XIII and his mother, Marie de' Medici, had a short-lived reconciliation after the Battle of Ponts-de Cé (1620), and to the Hunt Room (Chambre des Chasses) hung with magnificent 16C Flemish tapestries.

North of Brissac, on the road to Angers, stands a fine windmill with a chamber hollowed out at ground level.

BROUAGE ★

POPULATION 498

MICHELIN MAP 324 D 4

GREEN GUIDE ATLANTIC COAST

A victim of the retreating coastline, the ancient port of Brouage – its ships once sailed to the Baltic – now lies among extensive grazing lands, which themselves were once washed by the sea. The great explorer of Canada and founder of Quebec City, Samuel Champlain, was born here in 1570. During the Wars of Religion the men of La Rochelle isolated Brouage by scuttling a number of ships weighed down with rocks in the channel linking it to the sea.

In the early 17C the English had attacked this coastline frequently, besieging the Ile de Ré and actively supporting the Protestant rebels of La Rochelle. Richelieu decided to make Brouage "the arsenal of the Atlantic," and built a new town protected by ramparts. But in spite of Vauban's efforts, the port and channel silted up and the marshes became disease-ridden; Brouage, once the rival of La Rochelle, was abandoned in favour of the new port of Rochefort.

Visit

Remparts★★
Built from 1630 to 1640, these ramparts are a fine example of defences of the pre-Vauban era, with gun-slits, fortified gateways and elegant corbelled turrets. Louis XIV came here after his wedding to Maria-Theresa at St-Jean-de-Luz, less to inspect the fortifications than to dream about his lost love, Marie Mancini, who had fled here in sorrow six months previously after her uncle, Cardinal Mazarin, had frowned on their passion.

Excursion

Zoo de la Palmyre★★
32km – 20mi south. The zoo in its undulating setting shaded by maritime pines and oak trees, extends over an area of 14ha – 34 acres in La Palmyre Forest. Pink flamingoes perch by a waterfall tumbling down the rock face. Panels *(in French)* along a pleasant trail (about 4km – 2.5mi) explain the character and way of life of over 1 500 animals from the five continents. It is fascinating to observe the many types of small monkeys with piercing eyes and the antics of imposing gorillas, as well as the giant bats living in a cave with a star-studded vault, and lion cubs in the nursery.

CAEN ★★★

POPULATION 189 000

MICHELIN MAP 303 E-J 3-4

GREEN GUIDE NORMANDY

Capital of Lower Normandy, Caen is an important river port, thanks to the canal linking it to the Orne. Its proximity to France's second-largest iron-ore deposits has led to the development of works producing more than 1 million tons of steel a year. The city was the birthplace of **François Malherbe** (1556), the poet and grammarian hailed by the eminent writer, Boileau, as a purifier of the French language.

> **Orient Yourself:** The pedestrian precinct, between place St-Pierre and place de la République and bounded by rue St-Pierre and boulevard du Maréchal-Leclerc, is ively both day and night. North of here, near the château, in the small Vangueux strict, several pubs and restaurants have opened in fine houses spared by the Caen, which is listed as a "Town of Art and History," offers discovery tours ucted by guide-lecturers approved by the Ministry of Culture and Com- ation. Information at the tourist office or on www.vpah.culture.fr

Caen - Address Book

For coin ranges, see the Legend at the back of the guide.

EATING OUT

Alcide – *1 pl. Courtonne -* ☎ *02 31 44 18 06 -* ⏰ *Closed 20-31 Dec, Fri evening off-season and Sat.* This restaurant by the canal offers good fare at moderate prices. You can choose between the bar and the dining room with its bistro-style furniture. Bright ambience thanks to the light-reflecting mirrors.

Maître Corbeau – *8 r. Buquet -* ☎ *02 31 93 93 00 -* ⏰ *Closed first 3 weeks of Aug, Christmas school holidays and 1 Jan.* This place is entirely dedicated to cheese: boxes, advertisements, implements etc. Of course, in this original setting, your task will be to choose between this cheese and that cheese, hot cheese, cold cheese and warm cheese! The establishment's generous helpings draw local connoisseurs.

P'tit B – *15 r. Vaugueux -* ☎ *02 31 93 50 76 -1eptitb@wanadoo.fr .* Charming 17C house with a rustic interior artfully modernized, including a superb fireplace. Relaxed atmosphere, a view of the kitchen and seasonal dishes.

Le Bouchon du Vaugueux – *12 r. Graindorge -* ☎ *02 31 44 26 26 -* ⏰ *Closed 3 weeks in Aug, Sun-Mon - reserv. required.* This tavern (*bouchon*) is situated near the château and old Caen. Crowded tables add to the friendly ambience. Two fixed-price menus to be discovered on the slate menu du jour.

L'Insolite – *16 r. du Vaugueux at the foot of the château -* ☎ *02 31 43 83 87 -* ⏰ *Closed Sun-Mon except Jul-Aug - reserv. advisable.* Take the time to discover this half-timbered 16C house with its unexpected, novel decor, a successful blend of rustic and old-fashioned styles featuring frescoes, mirrors and dried flowers. Fish and seafood dishes on the menu. Well-stocked cigar humidor.

Pub William's – *Pl Courtonne 13 r. des Prairies-St-Gilles -* ☎ *02 31 93 45 52 -* ⏰ *Closed 1 week in Feb, 3 weeks in Aug, Sun and public holidays.* The business people of Caen frequent this British-style "pub", with its warm atmosphere, elegant bar and attractive wood furniture. In the winter, a fireplace adds to the comfort. Traditional cuisine with fresh market produce.

Auberge de l'Île Enchantée – *On the banks of the River Orne - 14123 Fleury-sur-Orne - 4km/2.5mi S of Caen via D 562 -* ☎ *02 31 52 15 52 -* ⏰ *Closed 24 Feb to 8 Mar, 13-28 Jul, Sun evening, Wed evening and Mon.* You too will be enchanted with this riverside inn. The view from the panoramic dining room overlooking the River Orne is lovely, the atmosphere is warm and the owners' menus are in line with current tastes.

WHERE TO STAY

Hôtel St-Étienne – *2 r. de l'Académie -* ☎ *02 31 86 35 82 - 11 rooms* ⌷ . This house, going back to the 1789 Revolution, is located in a quiet district close to the Abbaye-aux-Hommes. Note the fine wooden staircase with its beautiful patined woodwork and the smart bedrooms, some of them with fireplaces. Breakfast served in the dining room.

Hôtel Central – *23 pl. J.-Letellier -* ☎ *02 31 86 18 52 - accueil@centralhotel-caen.com - 25 rooms* ⌷ As its name suggests, this hotel is located in the town centre, which makes it convenient for visiting the castle or browsing round this busy shopping area. Basic comfort at very reasonable prices.

Hôtel du Havre – *11 r. du Havre -* ☎ *02 31 86 19 80 - hotelduhavreaol@aol.com - 19 rooms* ⌷ . Located near La Prairie and its racecourse, this post-war hotel offers modern, colourful and well-soundproofed rooms at very attractive prices.

Hôtel Bernières – *50 r. de Bernières -* ☎ *02 31 86 01 26 - hotelbernieres@wanadoo.fr - 17 rooms* ⌷ . Don't walk right by the discreet entrance of this hotel, for you would regret its convivial welcome, the charming breakfast room and drawing room and the delightful bedrooms. The owner's dried-flower bouquets add a personal touch to the pleasant surroundings.

Le Bristol – *31 r. du 11-Novembre -* ☎ *02 31 84 59 76 - hotelbristol@wanadoo.fr - 24 rooms* ⌷ . Those who would rather distance themselves from the bustle of the centre city will appreciate this hotel just a minute from the Orne and the racetrack. The bedrooms, recently updated, are all identical: yellow tones, modern furnishings, sound beds and efficient double-glazed windows.

Quatrans – *17 r. Gemare -* ☎ *02 31 86 25 57 - hotel-des-quatrans@wanadoo.fr - 32 rooms* ⌷ . A few steps from the city centre, this family establishment offers practical rooms enlivened with brighly coloured fabrics; the rooms in the back are quieter.

A PLEASANT INTERLUDE

Stiffler – *72 r. St-Jean -* ☎ *02 31 86 08 94 - www.stifflertraiteur.com -* ⏰ *Open Tue-Sat 9am-1pm, 2.30-7.30pm, Sun 8am-noon.* This magnificent pastry shop offers specialties such as the celebrated *charlotte aux fruits de saison,* the *bavaroise au chocolat,* or the *méringue aux amandes* Sit down for a few minutes to enjoy the bounty. At the delicatessen counter, th are delicious prepared dishes and sala for a quick lunch as well.

ON THE TOWN

Caen is a highly convivial and lively town. Don't hesitate to take a stroll in the pedestrian district; you will be pleasantly greeted by all the shopkeepers. In the evening a tour of the small Vaugueux district is recommended: several pubs and restaurants have opened in fine houses spared by the war. If all this does not make you want to become a regular visitor, it must be because you're settling in Caen for good!

Centre dramatique national de Normandie (Comédie de Caen) – *32 r. des Cordes -* ☎ *02 31 46 27 29 - www.cdn-normandie.com -* ◷ *Opening times follow the calendar of performances: Mon-Sat -* ◷ *Closed July-Aug.* The programming explores all the possibilities of the theatre. Classical plays alternate with contemporary ones in an attempt to show the public how drama is continually evolving. Two halls, one of 300 seats and one of 700 seats.

Théâtre de Caen – *135 blvd du Mar.-Leclerc -* ☎ *02 31 30 48 00 - www.theatre. caen.fr - following the calendar of performances -* ◷ *Ticket office Open Tues-Sat: 12.30-6.30pm.* ◷ *Closed Jun-Sep – 6 to 50€ depending on programme.* Inaugurated in 1963, this vast theatre with over 1 000 seats was entirely renovated in 1991. Operas, ballets and performances of contemporary dance alternate with theatre, classical concerts, jazz sessions and traditional music programmes. Concerts are free on Saturday at 5pm from October to May.

SHOPPING

Librairie Guillaume – *98 r. St-Pierre -* ☎ *02 31 85 43 13 - librairie.gen.calv. guillaume@wanadoo.fr -* ◷ *Mon: 2-7.30pm, Tue-Sat: 9am-1pm, 2.30-7pm.* ◷ *Closed Sun.* The carved-wood façade of this splendid bookshop dates from 1902. There is a choice of books about the region and, on the upper floor, a first-rate selection of antique books.

Poupinet – *8 r. St-Jean -* ☎ *02 31 86 07 25-* ◷ *Tue-Thu: 8am-1pm, 3-8pm, Fri,Sat: 8am-8pm, Sun 8am-1pm,* ◷ *Closed July.* To taste authentic *tripes à la mode de Caen,* you must visit Poupinet, where you can buy this specialty put up in jars. You can also find an enormous range of regional specialties including pâtés, terrines, country-style blood puddings, pork ears in jelly, and prepared dishes of highest quality.

MARKETS

Marché St-Pierre (Sun), rue de Bayeux (Tue), boulevard Leroy (Wed and Sat), boulevard de la Guérinière (Thu), Marché St-Sauveur (Fri), Christmas Market (Dec).

LEISURE

Hippodrome de Caen – *La Prairie -* ☎ *02 31 85 42 61 -* ◷ *Open Mar-Jun, Sep-Nov -* ◷ *Closed Jul-Aug.* This racecourse, nearly 2km/1.2mi long, in located in the heart of Caen. On the second floor, the panoramic restaurant offers a lovely view of the city. Visits are organised on mornings when races are held (30 times a year). Absolutely worth a visit.

Festyland – 🔲 *- Boulevard Péripherique 50 N, exit for Carpiquet, 14650 Carpiquet -* ☎ *02 31 75 04 04 - www.festyland.com -* ◷ *Open off-season: Wed: 1.30-6.30pm, Sat-Sun and public holidays 11am-6.30pm; school holidays 10.30am-7pm. June: Mon, Tues, Thu 10am-6pm. Wed. Sat-Sun 11am-6.30. July-Aug: daily 11am-6pm.* ◷ *Closed late Sept to end Mar. 10€ (children under 12: 9€).* This leisure park offers some 30 attractions, including: giant loop the loop, bumper boats, nautical trail, old bangers, babyland, clockwork horses, 1900-style merry-go-round, water toboggans. Three daily shows (including a circus show) for young children. Food service available in the park.

PARKS AND GARDENS

Caen is a "green city" with hundreds of acres of parks and gardens, open every morning at 8am during the week and 10am on weekends; closing times vary with the season. Tours are available and there are exhibits throughout the summer months.

The **Prairie**, a 90hectare/36 acre green space in the centre of the city, dates from the middle ages. The small lake is frequented by acquatic birds.

Parc floral de la Colline-aux-oiseaux, *av. Amiral-Montbatten, 14000 Caen.*

Jardin Botanique – ◷ *Open daily from 2-5pm.* This 300-year-old garden is the oldest in Caen and contains remarkable greenhouses with exotic plants.

Le parc Michel-d'Ornano, part of the Abbaye-aux-Dames, is a superb garden "à la française."

◷ **Organizing Your Time:** Allow yourself 1hr30min for the Château and the nearby museums (Musée des Beaux-Arts, Musée de Normandie, and Musée de la Poste et des Techniques de Communication). You will need about 2hr for the Abbeys.

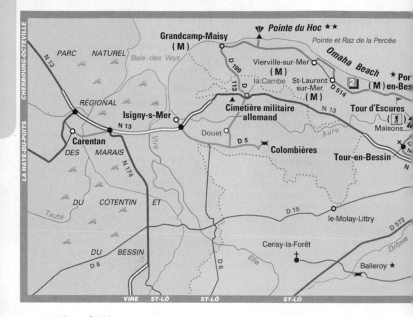

A Bit of History

Caen Stone

The Jurassic limestone quarried locally, often a light creamy colour, was used not only here but also in some of the great buildings undertaken by the Normans in England (Canterbury Cathedral, the White Tower at the Tower of London and Westminster Abbey).

"Caen the Crucible"

Chester Wilmot's pithy epithet (from The Struggle for Europe) evokes the sufferings undergone by the city during the summer of 1944 as well as the strategic role it played in the Battle of Normandy.

The first shells fell on Caen on D-Day itself; the city burned for 11 days. Liberated by the Canadians on 9 July, it was then continuously bombarded for another month by the Germans. The inhabitants huddled in the abbey (Abbaye aux Hommes), the hospital (Hospice du Bon Sauveur) and the quarries at Fleury; the final shell fell on 20 August. In the meantime a bitter battle was waged over the crossing of the Odon, an operation which cost the British more casualties than the crossing of the Rhine. But Montgomery's hammer-blows in the Caen sector helped lead to the break-out by the American armies further west, the pincer movement which crushed the Wehrmacht at Falaise Gap, and the subsequent liberation of most of France.

The City of the Normans

Caen's architectural heritage is essentially the creation of the Norman school of the Romanesque and reveals the affection felt by William, Duke of Normandy, and his wife Mathilda for the city.

After the invasions of the Norsemen in the 9C and 10C, and the establishment of the Dukedom of Normandy, the Benedictines set to work under the enthusiastic patronage of the Dukes. Their abbey churches were the first major religious buildings in Normandy. Externally, they are distinguished by the robust towers framing their west fronts, and by high lanterns over the crossing; internally by their generous dimensions and well-lit structure, and by the deliberate adoption of a timber roof rather than a stone barrel vault. Another Norman speciality is the inspection passage running just below the level of the upper windows.

Proud Mathilda

Caen's importance grew in the 11C when it was chosen as their place of residence by William and his young bride Mathilda of Flanders. The Duke's wooing of his distant cousin had originally met with a rebuff, proud Mathilda having no time for the illegitimate offspring of Duke Robert the First's liaison with "La Belle Arlette" of Falaise. But, mad with love and anger, William returned to Lille and chastised his intended wife. Mathilda was won over, and accepted his proposal. They were married in about 1050, in the face of Papal opposition which arose because of their kinship. This led to

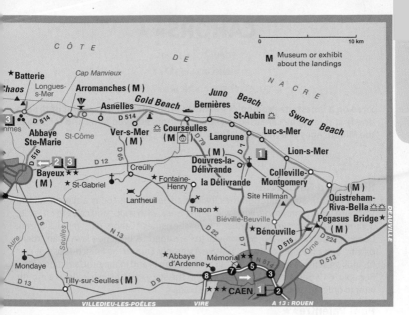

their excommunication and the placing of Normandy under an interdict. In 1059 the great Bishop Lanfranc succeeded in having these sanctions lifted and the couple made amends, William by founding the Abbey for Men (Abbaye aux Hommes), Mathilda by founding the Abbey for Women (Abbaye aux Dames).

When William left to conquer England, faithful Mathilda became Regent and ruled the Duchy with a firm hand.

Sights

Église St-Étienne★★

The church of the **Abbey for Men** was founded by the Conqueror; it was begun in 1066 and took 12 years to build. The west front with its soaring towers (the octagonal spires were added in the 13C) dates from this time.The nave is vast; it is a fine example of Romanesque construction with great square bays divided in two by minor piers and with high galleries over the aisles. The clerestory was altered in the 12C when the timber roof was replaced by sexpartite vaulting.

The great lantern-tower over the crossing is probably the work of Lanfranc and William themselves; in its simple perfection it is a masterpiece of Romanesque art.

The choir which was extended and altered in the 13C is a very early specimen of Norman Gothic which was to set the standard for buildings all over the province.

Château★

This great fortress perched on a bluff overlooking the city was built by William in 1060, and subsequently strengthened and extended. From its ramparts there are extensive views over Caen.

Église de la Trinité★★

The Norman building with its nave of nine bays, round-headed arches, and blind arcades in the triforium was founded by Mathilda in 1062 as the church of the **Abbey for Women**. As at St Stephen's, the upper storey was altered when the timber roof was replaced by sexpartite vaulting.

The choir with its spacious 11C groined vaults has Mathilda's tomb at its centre. The crypt is well preserved.

▶▶ **Musée des Beaux-Arts**★★ &. ⏱ *Wed-Mon 9.30am-6pm.* ⏱ *Closed Tue,1 Jan, Easter, 1 May, Ascension, 1 Nov, 25 Dec.* ⊗ *4€ (during temporary exhibits), call for prices during other periods, no charge Wed (under 18: no charge).* ☎ *02 31 30 47 70.* **Musée de Normandie**★★ ⏱ *Wed-Mon 9.30am-6pm.* ⏱ *Closed Tue, 1 Jan, Easter, 1 May, Ascension, 1 Nov, 25 Dec.* ⊗ *1.60€, no charge Sun.* ☎ *02 31 30 47 60. www.ville-caen.fr/mdn* archeology and ethnography. **Église St-Pierre**★ ⏱ *Daily 8.30am-noon, 2-6pm, Sun 2.30-6pm.* – **east end**★★. **Hotel d'Escoville**★. **Église St-Nicolas**★ *(cemetery)* ⏱ *Mar-Oct: daily 8am-6pm; Nov-Feb: daily 8am-5pm. No charge.*

CAHORS★★

POPULATION 19 735

MICHELIN MAP 337 E 5

GREEN GUIDE DORDOGNE BERRY LIMOUSIN

Sited on a limestone promontory almost surrounded by a meander of the Lot (the first river to be canalised in France), Cahors enjoyed fame and fortune in the Middle Ages as a commercial and university city.

Visit

Boulevard Gambetta

Running north-south through the city, this ancient axis is today a typically lively southern town promenade, lined with plane trees, with shops and cafés to one side, administrative buildings to the other. It bears the name of Cahors' most famous citizen, **Léon Gambetta** (1838-82), who moved to Paris aged 18, became a lawyer, an ardent patriot, and a member of the Legislative Assembly. During the Franco-Prussian War he took an active part in the downfall of Napoleon III and in the proclamation of the Republic on 4 September 1870; he escaped the siege of Paris in a balloon a month later in order to organise the Army of the Loire.

Pont Valentré★★

The city's merchants were responsible for building this superb six-arched stone bridge; its construction lasted from 1308 to 1378. Its fortifications are a reminder of the importance attached to the defence of Cahors by Philippe le Bel (the Fair), whose relationship with the city was based on an act of pariage (equality between a feudal lord and a town).

Cathédrale St-Étienne★

In these much-troubled lands it was wise to fortify a place of worship as was done here. The cathedral is one of the first of the domed churches of Aquitaine; its twin domes (18m – 59ft in diameter, 32m – 105ft in height) are early examples of the systematic use of broken arches (lateral and transversal arches). They also have empirically designed pendentives, somewhat flattened and certainly far from the perfectly curved design.

Pont Valentré

Cahors - Address Book

For coin ranges, see the Legend at the back of the guide.

EATING OUT

Le Dousil – *124 r. Nationale -* ☎ *05 65 53 19 67 -* ⊙ *closed 10 days in Feb, 10 days in Oct, Sun and Mon.* This wine bar near the town's covered market offers an extensive list of over 100 vintages. The decor includes a traditional zinc counter and stone walls. The menu includes a choice of sandwiches, *charcuterie* and daily specials.

Le Rendez-Vous – *49 r. Clément-Marot -* ☎ *05 65 22 65 10 -* ⊙ *closed 29 Apr-14 May, 28 Oct-12 Nov, Sun and Mon - reserv. recommended.* Located close to the cathedral, Le Rendez-Vous has developed a reputation for its modern cuisine. The mix of colourful contemporary decor and old stonework combine well in the dining room and mezzanine extension. Attractive à la carte and fixed menu options.

La Garenne – *In Saint-Henri, 7km/4.5mi N towards Brive -* ☎ *05 65 35 40 67 -* ⊙ *closed Feb, 1-15 Mar, Mon eve and Tue eve (except Jul-Aug) and Wed.* This typically Quercy-style building once served as a stable. Cosy interior decor featuring exposed beams, stone walls, attractive, locally made furniture and typical country objects. The main attraction here is the delicious regional cuisine.

Auberge du Vieux Douelle – *46140 Douelle - 8km/5mi W of Cahors on the D 8 -* ☎ *05 65 20 02 03 - aubergededouelle@aol.com -* ⊙ *closed over Christmas week.* The dining room in the vaulted cellar of this popular inn, known locally as "Chez Malique", is decked out with bright red tablecloths. Meats are grilled over a wood fire; salads and a buffet are also available. Terrace and pool in the summer. A few rooms available.

WHERE TO STAY

Hôtel Les Chalets – *46090 Vers - 14km/8.7mi E of Cahors on the D 653 -* ☎ *05 65 31 40 83 - les.chalets.vers@wanadoo.fr -* ⊙ *closed Jan Sun evenings and Mon Oct-Apr - 23 rooms.* This small modern hotel situated in an attractive leafy setting is particularly welcoming. The bedrooms, with balconies or small gardens, overlook the river. A quiet and peaceful retreat, with gentle background noise courtesy of a waterfall. Swimming pool in summer.

Chambre d'hôte Le Clos des Dryades – *46090 Vers - 19km/11.4mi NE of Cahors on the D 653, towards St-Cirq-Lapopie and the D 49 road to Cours -* ☎ *05 65 31 44 50 -* ⊙ *closed 15 Nov-15 Feb -* 🍴 *- 5 rooms.* Nestled deep in the woods, this house with its tiled roof is the perfect place to get away from it all. The rooms are comfortable and the large swimming pool is a great place to cool off on a hot summer's day. Two self-catering cottages are also available.

Chambre d'hôte Les Poujades – *Flaynac - 46090 Pradines - 5km/3⁄.1mi N of Cahors on the D 8 -* ☎ *05 65 35 33 36 -* 🍴 *- 2 rooms.* A flower garden and shady trees surround this typical Quercy house, from where you can enjoy a wonderful view of the Château de Mercuès, the Cahors vineyards and the outskirts of the town. The decor is a little on the sombre side, but is compensated by the warm welcome. One holiday cottage available.

Hôtel A l'Escargot – *5 bd Gambetta -* ☎ *05 65 35 07 66 -* ⊙ *closed Feb school hols, Dec and Sun out of season - 9 rooms.* Near the Tour Jean-XXI, this hotel occupies the old palace built by the pontiff's family. Functional bedrooms with colourful furnishings, plus a renovated breakfast room.

Chambre d'hôte Domaine de Labarthe – *46090 Espère - 8km/5mi NW of Cahors on the D 911 -* ☎ *05 65 30 92 34 -* 🍴 *- reserv. required - 3 rooms.* Guests at this manor house, complete with dovecote, are assured the warmest of welcomes. The rooms are pretty, and fresh flowers and biscuits await you on arrival. All the rooms open onto the garden and pool.

SHOPPING

Market – *Pl. de la Halle.* A traditional market is held on Wednesday and Saturday mornings, with numerous stalls run by farmers selling a range of local produce.

Les Délices du Valentré – *21 bd Léon-Gambetta -* ☎ *05 65 35 09 86 -* ⊙ *open Tue-Sun.* This pastry chef makes *Coque de Cahors*, a *brioche* with candied citron and flavoured with orange water, and *Cabecou*, a chocolate sweet.

Château de Haute-Serre – *Georges Vigouroux - 8km/5mi S of Cahors on the D 6 towards Lalbenque - 46230 Cieurac -* ☎ *05 65 20 80 20 - g-vigouroux.fr -* ⊙ *open 10am-noon and 2-6pm -* ⊙ *closed holidays from 1 Nov to the day before Easter.* This estate, in a wonderful location on a hill with views of vineyards and the Causses du Lot, is one of Cahors' best-known wineries. Guided tours of the cellars and vineyards.

LEISURE ACTIVITIES

L'Archipel – *Quai Ludo-Rollès. Water sports and leisure centre -* ☎ *05 65 35 05 86 / 31 38 -* ⊙ *closed mid-Sep to mid-Jun.* This summer pool offers lots of fun activities for kids, including slides, hydro-massage, bubble baths, fountains and a games area.

Stade Nautique de Regourd – *Base Nautique de Regourd -* ☎ *05 65 30 08 02 or 05 65 22 15 23 - fabian.gouthier@free.fr -* ⊙ *open Oct-May, Sat, Sun and public hols, 3-6pm; Jun and Sep, Wed, Sat and Sun,*

2-7pm; Jul-Aug, Mon-Fri, 3-7pm, Sat-Sun, 2-8pm - ☾ closed Nov-May. Water-skiing, wakeboarding and kneeboarding.
Alliance Nautique Cahors – Port Bullier - ☎ 06 80 14 96 77 - ☾ open Easter-15 Sep - 30min: 18€; 1hr: 28€; 1hr 30min: 38€. Hire a small, quiet and easy-to-handle electrically powered boat to explore the

River Lot from a different perspective. No permit required.

EVENTS

Festival de Blues - mid-Jul. ☎ 05 65 35 99 99.

Festival du Quercy Blanc - late-Jul to mid-Aug. ☎ 05 65 31 83 12.

The north door **(portail nord★★)** depicts the Ascension. It was built in the 13C and shows the moment at which Christ is beginning to rise and the angels are stilling the fears of the disciples. The sculptors who created it had learned their skills at Moissac, and the compartmentalisation of the different scenes recalls the Languedoc School.

◗◖ **Barbacane et Tour St-Jean★**.

CALAIS

POPULATION 101 768

MICHELIN MAP 301 E 2

GREEN GUIDE NORTHERN FRANCE AND THE PARIS REGION

The proximity of the English coast a mere 38km – 24 miles away has determined the destiny of Calais, looking out over the straits to which, in French at least, it has given its name (Pas de Calais = Straits of Dover in English). The port handles more passengers than any other in France, being both the railhead for England and the point of departure for the great cities of the Continent.

In May 1347, eight months after his victory at Crécy over Philippe VI which marked the beginning of the Hundred Years War, Edward III succeeded in starving Calais into submission. The town was to remain English for more than two centuries until the Duke of Guise seized it in January 1558, just over a year before the Treaty of Le Cateau-Cambrésis. The loss of England's last possession in France provoked Mary Tudor's bitter comment "When I am dead and opened, you shall find 'Calais' lying in my heart."

A Bit of History

In 1520 the famous meeting beween Henry VIII and François I took place at the Field of the Cloth of Gold, between Guînes and Ardres to the southwest of Calais. The proposed alliance in opposition to Charles V was not however concluded, no doubt in some measure owing to the ostentatious display indulged in by both sovereigns.

Visit

Monument des Bourgeois de Calais★★

In front of the Town Hall (Hôtel de ville). Rodin's group of bronze figures (1895) commemorates the self-sacrificing action of Eustache de Saint-Pierre and his five fellowcitizens; emaciated by the eight long months of siege, barefoot and clad in long robes, they came before Edward III offering themselves for execution provided the king spared their fellow-citizens. Edward accepted their plea and spared them too, doubtless with an eye to the governability of his new conquest. Rodin's huge talent comes over triumphantly in these vibrant figures, haughty in their humiliation.
Other examples of this sculpture may be seen in London (near the Houses of Parliament), in Los Angeles (at the Norton Simon Inc. Museum of Art) and in Washington (at the Hirshhorn Museum and Sculpture Garden).

◗◖ **Views★★** from the lighthouse (*Phare*). **Musée des Beaux Arts et de** **Dentelle★** ⟨ ☾ Mon, Wed-Fri 10am-noon, 2-5.30pm, Sat 10am-noon, 2-6.30pm, 2-6.30pm. ☾ Closed Tue and public holidays. ⟨ 5€ during the summer exhibit, 3€ rest of year, no charge Wed. ☎ 03 21 46 48 40.– history and artistic development of the tow

Excursion

CÔTE D'OPALE★

The road linking Calais and Boulogne takes the visitor along the most spectacular part of this coastline with its high chalk cliffs, heathlands and vast sandy beaches backed by grassy dunes.

Blériot-Plage

The little resort has a fine beach stretching as far as Cap Blanc-Nez. On a cliff-top knoll is the obelisk commemorating the **Dover Patrol**, mounted continuously between 1914 and 1918 to protect the vital supply routes across the English Channel. At Les Baraques just to the west of the resort is a monument marking **Edouard Blériot's** flight across the Channel in 1909.

The Channel Tunnel

Between **Blériot-Plage** and **Sangatte** can be seen the French terminal for the Channel Tunnel *(at Coquelles 3km – 1.9mi from the coast)*. Today the tunnel connecting Britain to the road and rail networks of continental Europe is a reality. The inauguration of the triple tunnel system in 1994 was the realisation of a series of dreams and schemes – many far-fetched. The passenger vehicle and freight shuttles (Le Shuttle) and the high-speed trains (Eurostar) make the crossing in about 35 minutes from Chariton Terminal near Folkestone to the French terminal near the village of Coquelles. Trains run round the clock with two to four departures per hour during the day and one an hour at night. The tunnel system consists of two single track rail tunnels and one service tunnel for safety and ventilation. The tunnels are 50.5 km – 31 miles long and run for most of the way 40m – 131ft under the seabed.

Cap Blanc-Nez★★

From the top of the white cliffs the **view**★ extends from Calais to Cap Gris-Nez and right across the Channel to the English coast.

Wissant

With its superb beach of fine hard sand, one of France's main centres for land yachting, Wissant enjoys its privileged position in the middle of the National Conservation Area which includes both Cap Gris-Nez and Cap Blanc-Nez.

Cap Gris-Nez★★

This splendid limestone headland marks the point where the English Channel joins the North Sea.

Ever since the end of the last Ice Age when the rise in sea-level cut the land bridge which once linked Britain and France, Cape "Grey-nose" has protected the Flanders coastline to the north and influenced the way in which it has evolved. The chalk cliffs to the south have been eroded over the centuries to form promontories divided by deep combes, while to the north, longshore drift is continually adding to the sands of Wissant Bay. In fine weather, the cape affords a **view**★ of the white cliffs of the English coast.

Ambleteuse

This picturesque village lies at the mouth of the River Slack, at the half-way point between Boulogne and Cap Gris-Nez. The approach to the beach is commanded by **Fort Mahon**, a 17C structure built by Vauban to protect Ambleteuse in its days as a base for the French Navy. Part of the fleet assembled by Napoleon to invade England (see BOULOGNE-SUR-MER) was stationed here.

Wimereux

This sizeable family resort is pleasantly situated between Cap d'Alprech to the south and the cliffs running up to Cap Gris-Nez in the north.

From the raised seafront promenade there are fine views over the Channel and along the coast from the monument (**Colonne de la Grande Armée**) to the port of Boulogne.

Beyond the promenade, a footpath leads towards the headland (**Pointe aux Oies**) where the future Napoleon III landed in the course of his abortive attempt to raise the population of Boulogne against Louis-Philippe.

Boulogne-sur-Mer★ – See BOULOGNE-SUR-MER.

La **CAMARGUE**★★

MICHELIN MAP 340 A-E 4-5 AND 339 J-M 7-8

GREEN GUIDE PROVENCE

The immense alluvial plain of 95 000ha – 367sq miles is the product of the interaction of the Rhône and Mediterranean and the winds. This most original area is divided into three distinct regions: a cultivated region north of the delta, salt-marshes near Salin-de-Giraud and to the west of the Petit Rhône, and the nature reserve to the south.

Visit

Parc Naturel Régional de Camargue

The nature park covers an area of 85 000ha – 328sq miles in the Rhône delta, including the communes of Arles and Stes-Maries-de-la-Mer. Together with the nature reserve, **Réserve Nationale de Camargue,** it aims to protect the fragile ecological system of the region with its exceptional variety of flora and fauna – there are some 400 bird species. The traditional image of the Camargue is associated with the herds **(manades)** and the horsemen **(gardians)**. Many horse owners hire out their mounts for organised rides among the animals.

The *manade* designates livestock and all that relates to the upkeep of the herd: herdsmen, pastureland, horses, etc. The *gardian*, an experienced rider, is the symbol of the *manade* with his large felt hat and long three-pronged stick; he watches over the herd, cares for the sick animals and selects the bulls for the bullfights.

Les-Stes-Maries-de-la-Mer

At the heart of the Camargue is situated Les-Stes-Maries-de-la-Mer marked by a fortified church. The town, which is now at some distance from the coastline of medieval times, is protected by dikes to counter the encroachment of the sea.

Nineteen centuries of pilgrimage – According to Provençal legend, c AD 40 a boat carrying Mary, the mother of James, Mary Salome, the mother of James Major and John, Mary Magdalene, Martha and her brother Lazarus, was cast at sea. Under divine protection it came to rest on the shore where Stes-Maries now stands. The two Marys and their black servant Sarah remained in Camargue; their burial place became a shrine. A Gypsy Celebration (**Pèlerinage des Gitans**★★, 24-25 May), a lively and colourful event, draws gypsies from all over the world.

▶▶ **Musée camarguais at Pont de Rousty** ⬢ ⏱ *Jul and Aug: daily 10am-6pm; Apr-Jun and Sep: daily 9am-6pm; Oct-Mar: daily except Tue 10am-5pm. Last admission 1hr before closing.* ⏱ *Closed 1 Jan, 1 May, 25 Dec.* ⬢ *5€.* ☎ *04 90 97 10 82. www.parc-camargue.fr.* **Centre d'information de la Camargue:** ⬚ *information centre at* **Ginès**. ⏱ *Apr-Sep: daily 9am-6pm; Oct-Mar: daily except Fri 9.30am-5pm.* ⏱ *Closed 1 Jan, 1 May, 25 Dec.*

Camargue horses

CANAL DU MIDI

MICHELIN MAP 343 H-I 4, J-K 5 AND 339 A-K 1-3, A-F 9

GREEN GUIDE LANGUEDOC ROUSSILLON TARN GORGES

The pass (Seuil de Naurouze, alt 194m – 636ft) forms the watershed between Atlantic and Mediterranean; the notion of a canal enabling shipping to avoid the long route via Gibraltar had preoccupied not only the Romans but also François I, Henri IV and Richelieu. The natural obstacles, however, seemed insurmountable.

In 1662, **Pierre-Paul Riquet** (1604-80) succeeded in interesting Colbert in his project; with the latter's support he gained the necessary authorisations four years later. But the canal was to prove his ruin; all the work had to be carried out at his own expense and he died six months before the opening. In 1825 Riquet's successors, finally freed of the burden of debt, built an obelisk here to commemorate the great man and his work. The canal passed into state ownership in 1897.

A Bit of History

The canal, which became obsolete in the 19C as modernisation did not keep up with technical progress, provides a perfect illustration of pre-industrial techniques. The completed Canal du Midi is 240km – 149 miles long and has 103 locks; it is used mainly by boats hired out to tourists. In 1996 it was nominated as a World Heritage site by UNESCO.

CANNES★★★

POPULATION 68 676

MICHELIN MAP 341 B-D 5 AND P-Q 5

GREEN GUIDE FRENCH RIVIERA

Spread out between the Suquet Heights and La Croisette Point on the shore of La Napoule Bay, Cannes owes its popularity to the beauty of its **setting**★★, its mild climate and its magnificent festivals. In 1834, the former Lord Chancellor of Britain, Lord Brougham, was on his way to Italy when he was prevented from entering what was then Sardinian territory because of a cholera epidemic in Provence. Forced to retrace his steps, he made an overnight stop at Cannes, at the time no more than a fishing village. Enchanted by the place, he returned to it every winter, establishing a trend among the English aristocracy and stimulating Cannes' first period of growth.

▶ **Orient Yourself:** Locals and visitors congregate along the elegant **Boulevard de la Croisette**★★ with its succession of delightful gardens. To one side extends the resort's splendid sandy beach, while the landward side of the boulevard is lined with the dignified and impeccably maintained façades of luxury hotels and exclusive boutiques.

At the eastern end of La Croisette is a marina, busy with yachts and pleasure craft, and at its western end another, overlooked by the Festival and Conference Centre (Palais des Festivals et des Congrès). It is here that the Cannes Film Festival is held every May, the town's most spectacular and prestigious event.

Don't Miss: Le Suquet , the old town of Cannes. From the Mount Chevalier Tower (Tour du Mont Chevalier) there is a fine **view**★ over beach and bay, the Lérins Islands and the Esterel Heights.

Organizing Your Time: Allow yourself at least 2hr to visit Le Suquet and the marina.

Excursion

Massif de L'Esterel★★★

40km – 24mi west by N98. The massif's jagged relief of volcanic rock (red porphyry) worn by erosion dips vertically into the deep blue sea between La Napoule and St-Raphael. The rugged coastline is fringed with rocks, islets and reefs. From its highest peak, **Mont Vinaigre**★★★ (alt 618m – 2 027ft), a vast panorama unfolds over the surrounding area. The pine and cork-oak forests clothing the wild and lonely massif have been ravaged by fire in recent years.

Cannes - Address Book

PRACTICAL INFORMATION

TOURISM OFFICES

Cannes – *Palais des Festivals, 1, La Croisette – 06400 –* ☎ *04 93 39 24 53* (**Train Station Branch** – *Aile Est of the Gare SNCF –* ☎ *04 93 99 19 77). www.cannes.fr.*

Le Cannet – *Avenue du Campon – Le Cannet –* ☎ *04 93 45 34 27. www.lecannet.com.*
For coin ranges, see the Legend at the back of the guide.

EATING OUT

☞ **Côte d'Azur** – *3 Rue Jean-Daumos –* ☎ *04 93 38 60 02 –* ⏱ *Closed evenings and Sun.* Modest restaurant with a friendly ambience and cosy setting with period furnishings. The traditional cooking attracts a great many locals. Low prices guaranteed.

☞ **Aux Bons Enfants** – *80 Rue Meynadier* – ⏱ *Closed Aug, 24 Dec-2 Jan, Sat evening Oct to Apr, and Sun –* ✄ *– reservations highly recommended.* Simplicity, generosity and congeniality are the hallmarks of this informal establishment where there's no telephone and customers are required to pay in cash. A true locals' hangout since 1935, with tasty Mediterranean dishes.

☞☞ **Le Comptoir des Vins** – *13 Boulevard de la République –* ☎ *04 93 68 13 26 – www.comptoirdesvins.com –* ⏱ *Closed Feb, evenings Mon-Wed, Sun and public holidays.* This handsomely stocked wine boutque leads to a colorful dining area where light snacks can be served, washed down with a glass of wine.

☞☞ **Le Caveau 30** – *45 Rue F.-Faure –* ☎ *04 93 39 06 33.* Large restaurant comprising two dining rooms done up in the style of a 1930 brasserie. The terrace overlooks a shaded square popular among boules players. Fish and seafood are the specialities of the house.

☞☞ **Au Poisson Grillé** – *8 Quai St-Pierre – Vieux Port –* ☎ *04 93 39 44 68.* Appropriately located in the old port, this fish restaurant was opened back in 1949. It serves grilled fish alongside many other Mediterranean dishes, in a warm setting of varnished wood evoking the interior of a luxury cabin. Attentive service at affordable prices.

☞☞☞ **Fred L'Écailler** – *7 Place de l'Étang –* ☎ *04 93 43 15 85 – http://fredlecailler. com.* A large neon sign marks the entrance to this rustic-style restaurant whose walls are draped with fishing nets. The tiny square affords a glimpse of village life with its bustling activity and daily games of pétanque. Fine selection of freshly caught fish and seafood.

☞☞☞ **Côté Jardin** – *12 Avenue St-Louis –* ☎ *04 93 38 60 28 –* ⏱ *Closed 1-11 Jan and Sun –* ▦. Just off the Boulevard Carnot, this Provençal-style restaurant attracts the locals with its covered terrace and courtyard seating.

WHERE TO STAY

☞ **Le Chanteclair** – *12 Rue Forville –* ☎ *04 93 39 68 88 –* ⏱ *Closed 15 Oct-3 Jan –* ✄ *– 15 rooms –* ▭. After walking through a building, you will discover this friendly hotel laid out on several floors, offering a selection of variously priced rooms depending on the level of comfort. Pleasant inner courtyard where breakfast is served in summer.

☞ **Hôtel National** – *9 Rue du Maréchal-Joffre –* ☎ *04 93 39 91 92 – hotel nationalcannes@wanadoo.fr – 17 rooms –* ▤▭. The main advantage of this hotel is its location near the Palais des Festivals and the sea. The bedrooms designed in white and grey with tiled bathrooms are on the small side but they are clean and carefully maintained.

☞☞ **Hôtel Albert 1** – *68 Avenue de Grasse –* ☎ *04 93 39 24 04 –* ⏱ *Closed 1-15 Dec –* 🅿 *– 11 rooms –* ▭. In a quiet, residential area tucked away from the town center, this villa houses a small, family-run business that will give you a warm welcome. Have breakfast on the shaded terrace enhanced by the intoxicating aroma of pink oleander.

☞☞ **Hôtel Appia** – *6 Rue Marceau –* ☎ *04 93 06 59 59 – www.appia-hotel.com –* ⏱ *Closed 21 Nov-27 Dec – 31 rooms –* ▤▭. Practicality takes precedence over comfort in this downtown hotel where t' well-kept, smallish rooms are both air-conditioned and soundproofed. Pristi bathrooms.

○◎🛏 **Villa L'Églantier** – *14 Rue Campestra* – ☎ *04 93 68 22 43* – � – *4 rooms*. Impressive white villa dating from 1920, surrounded by palm trees and other exotic species, dominating the city of Cannes. The large, peaceful rooms are all extended by a terrace or a balcony.

○◎🛏 **Le Cavendish** – *11 Boulevard Carnot* – ☎ *04 97 06 26 00* – *www. cavendish-cannes.com* – *34 rooms* – 🍽 🅿 🖥. A beautiful Belle Epoch era building with a 1920s elevator and a stylish, contemporary decor, this family-run hotel is a comforting retreat in the center of Cannes. Breakfast includes homemade jams and cakes, and every evening is a free open bar Happy Hour in the lounge.

○◎🛏 **Le 3.14 Hôtel** – *5 Rue François Einesy* – ☎ *04 92 99 72 00* – *www.3-14hotel. com* – 🍽 🅿 🖥 – *80 rooms*. As one of the only design boutique hotels in Cannes, this exotic and trendy establishment around the corner from the Carlton is a breath of fresh air. In the lobby live love birds and a Murano glass fountain welcome you, while each of the five floors is decorated according to a different continent theme: America, Europe, Africa, Asia and Oceania. The rooftop spa, swimming pool and jacuzzi, private beach, and a stunning Mahatma bar and restaurant make it hard to leave this pampering cocoon of a hotel.

ON THE TOWN

The best way to get to know this glamorous city is to frequent its luxury hotel bars: order a cocktail on the terrace of the Ritz-Carlton hotel, on the beach of the Majestic or in the piano-bar of the Martinez.

L'Amiral – *73 Boulevard de la Croisette* – ☎ *04 92 98 73 00* – *www.hotel.martinez. com* – 🕓 *Daily 10am-2am*. Attached to the Martinez Hotel, this bar is by far the most popular meeting place along the coast. It owes its reputation to the head barman and to Jimmy, the American piano player. Live music every evening from 8pm.

Le Bâoli – *Port Pierre Canto, Boulevard de la Croisette* – ☎ *04 93 43 03 43* – 🕓 *Wed-Sat from 8pm (off-season Fri-Sat from 8pm)*. The hottest night spot in Cannes with beachfront views over the bay, this luxurious bar-restaurant-nightclub with the exotic decor can host up to 1500 partygoers in high season. Popular with the international jet-set crowd and beautiful locals.

SHOPPING

Market – *Marché de Forville:* 🕓 *daily 7am-1pm except Mondays in low season;* fine stalls displaying fresh regional produce.

Allées de la Liberté – Flower market every morning. Popular flea market on Saturdays.

Shopping streets – Rue Meynadier: tempting window displays of food and craftwork in a lively pedestrian area. Rue d'Antibes: luxury clothes and luggage.

Cannolive – *16 Rue Vénizelos* – ☎ *04 93 39 08 19* – 🕓 *Open 8am-noon, 2.15-7pm.* – 🕓 *Closed Sun, Mon morning, and two weeks in Dec.* This shop boasts an incredible choice of Provençal products to take back home: household linen, *tapenades,* crockery, *santons,* soap, and even Lérina liqueur from the nearby islands for those who get seasick!

Vilfeu Père et Fils – *19 Rue des Etats-Unis* – ☎ *04 93 39 26 87* – 🕓 *Open Thurs-Mon 11am-7pm (Jul-Aug daily 10am-midnight).* – 🕓 *Closed 15 Oct-Apr.* For 30 years this family has perfected their home-made ice cream with the freshest ingredients. Some of the startling flavors include saffron, thyme, rosemary and olive oil.

La Ferme Savoyarde – *22 Rue Meynadier* – ☎ *04 93 39 63 68* – 🕓 *Open Tue-Sat 7am-12.30pm, 4-7.30pm (open Sun morning Jul-Aug).* Not only is this the preferred cheese boutique of the local Cannois, but they also ship their Chèvre de Provence, Camembert de Calvados and Brie with Truffles to four-star hotels around the world. Ask for your cheeses "sous-vide" if you plan on traveling with them.

LEISURE ACTIVITIES

For sailing, deep-sea diving or water-skiing, contact the Tourism Office or visit www. france-nautisme.com.

Beaches – Not all the beaches on La Croisette charge a fee (details of prices are listed at the top of the steps), or belong to a hotel (located opposite). There are also three free beaches, one of which is located behind the Palais du Festival. The other public beaches lie west of the old port, on Boulevard Jean-Hibert and Boulevard du Midi, at Port Canto and on Boulevard Gazagnaire beyond La Pointe.

Ponton Majestic Ski Nautique – *Boulevard de la Croisette* – ☎ *04 92 98 77 47/ 06 11 50 77 53* – 🕓 *Apr-Oct daily 8am until dusk.* If you want to get away from the bustling crowds, why not try your hand at water-skiing or parasailing?

TOURS AND TRANSPORTATION

TAM – *Gare routière, Place de l'Hôtel-de-Ville* – ☎ *04 93 39 11 39* – *www.rca.tm.fr.* These buses operate between Cannes and Nice, including direct service to the airport.

Train Station – *SNCF Gare de Cannes* – ☎ *0 892 35 35 35* – *www.ter-sncf.com/paca.* This train station is served by SNCF trains, the TGV, and the local TER trains (service between Mandelieu-La-Napoule and Vintimille).

Les Trains Touristiques – *Cannois de Loisirs, La Croisette* – ☎ *06 14 09 49 39* – 🕓 *10am-11pm (in summer; until dusk off-season).* – 🕓 *Closed Nov* – ◎ *8€ (child* under 10 years, 5€). This tiny train does tours of La Croisette and Le Suquet with commentary in English. Departs from in front of Majestic Plage.

Trans Côte d'Azur – *3 Quai des Îles* – ☎ *04 92 98 71 30* – ⏰ *Feb-Oct daily 8.30am-noon, 1.30-6pm (Jul-Aug 8am-7pm).* ⛴ *10€ (child 5€). www.trans-cote-azur.com.* Regular service to the Île Ste-Marguerite (15 minutes), plus seasonal tours to l'Île de Porquerolles, Monaco, Saint-Tropez, San Remo, la Corniche d'Or, etc.

Planaria– *Quai des Îles* – ☎ *04 92 98 71 38* – ⏰ *May-Sep hourly 8am-12.30pm, 2-6pm*

(Oct-Apr until 5pm, fewer departures). ⛴ *10€ (child 5€). www.abbayedelerins.com.* Regular service to Île St-Honorat *(15 min).*

CALENDAR OF EVENTS

International Film Festival – 10 days in May; free open-air cinema retrospectives on the beach (official screenings open to accredited professionals only). *www. festival-cannes.org.*

Nuits Misicales du Suquet – End of July; classical concerts on the esplanade in front of the Église du Suquet. ☎ *04 92 99 33 83.*

CAP CORSE★★★

MICHELIN MAP 345 F 1-2

GREEN GUIDE CORSE (IN FRENCH)

The Cap Corse promontory is the mountain range which prolongs the island's ridge of schistous rock 40km – 25 miles into the sea.

A Bit of History

A Seafaring People – In contrast to the rest of the Corsican population, local inhabitants responded to the call of the sea and took up trade and travel to distant lands. In the 19C they set up the first trading-posts in North Africa. A large number emigrated to South America; many became prosperous and built great houses in colonial or Renaissance style in their native village. These styles have influenced the architecture of the region.

▸ **Orient Yourself:** The west and east sides of Cap Corse are in sharp contrast. The indented west coast is dominated by a high ridge with sheer cliffs plunging into the sea. The east coast which has a softer elevation and runs in a fairly straight line boasts fine beaches and valleys suitable for cultivation or grassland.

🕐 **Organizing Your Time:** Take a picturesque corniche road to discover villages clinging to defensive sites, tiny sandy beaches, and marinas nestling in an inlet.

CARCASSONNE★★★

POPULATION 43 470

MICHELIN MAP 344 E-F 3

GREEN GUIDE LANGUEDOC ROUSSILLON TARN GORGES

The centre of the wine-producing Aude department, Carcassonne is also a fortified town which by some wave of a magic wand seems to have been preserved untouched since the end of the Middle Ages.

🕐 **Organizing Your Time:** Take at least 2hr to visit the fortified town. Remember that the Château Comtal can only be visited as part of a guided tour.

🅿 **Parking:** When you visit the fortified town, leave the car in one of the car parks outside the walls in front of the gateway to the east, Porte Narbonnaise.

A Bit of History

This extraordinary vision of medieval military architecture crowns an escarpment commanding the great communication route which links Toulouse with the Mediterranean. The site was first fortified by the Gauls; their entrenched camp served Roman, Visigoth and Frank in turn. In the 9C, Carcassonne became the capital of a county, then of a viscounty subject to Toulouse. In common with the rest of the South of Franc it enjoyed a long period of prosperity which was brought to an end by the Crusade mounted to put down the Albigensian Heresy.

On 1 August 1209 the army of crusaders under the orders of Simon de Montfort arrived beneath the walls of Carcassonne and put the city to siege. Within a fortnight it was all over, the defenders broken by lack of water and the seizure of their chief negotiator Raymond-Roger Trencavel. In 1240 his son tried to recapture his inheritance with the aid of the townspeople, but the attempt failed; Louis IX razed the fortifications and sentenced the inhabitants to seven years of exile for their treachery. After serving their term they were allowed to settle here again, but only on the far bank of the River Aude, today's Lower Town (Ville basse). This was laid out in typical *bastide* fashion and the line of its ramparts is now marked by the ring of boulevards.

Visit

LA CITÉ (THE FORTIFIED TOWN)★★★

Louis IX restored and reinforced the Cité both to hold down France's new territorial acquisitions and to defend the kingdom against Spain. His son Philippe le Hardi (the Bold) strengthened the defences still further, making Carcassonne, "the Virgin of Languedoc," virtually impregnable. During the Hundred Years War the Black Prince, unwilling to risk a frontal assault, contented himself with burning the Lower Town to the ground.

In 1659 Roussillon was incorporated into France, pushing the vulnerable frontier zone southward. This, together with the invention of modern artillery, meant that Carcassonne's strategic significance was now nil; abandonment and decay followed. Then, in the 19C, Romanticism brought the Middle Ages back into fashion; the writer **Prosper Mérimée,** with his taste for ruins, was made Government Inspector of Ancient Monuments; the architect **Viollet-le-Duc** surveyed the remains, wrote an enthusiastic report and in 1844 was put in charge of reconstructing the city. The restoration process lasted until 1910.

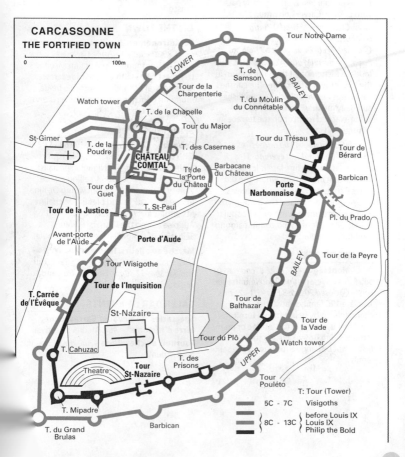

Carcassone - Address Book

For coin ranges, see the Legend at the back of the guide.

EATING OUT

A QUICK BITE

Le Bar à Vins – 6 r. du Plo – ☎ 04 68 47 38 38 - mhrc@wanadoo.fr – ⏰ daily 9am-2am – ⏰ closed Nov-Feb. Situated at the heart of the medieval Cité, this wine bar boasts a charming shady garden offering a view of the St-Nazaire basilica. Tapas and fast food.

A LEISURELY MEAL

La Tête de l'Art – 37 bis r. Trivalle - ☎ 04 68 47 36 36 - tilcke@tele2.fr – ⏰ closed Sun in winter - 🍴 - reservation recommended on weekends. Food and art go hand in hand in this restaurant specializing in pork dishes, which are served in rooms displaying works of modern painting and sculpture, in between figurines of the mascot itself.

Auberge de Dame Carcas – 3 pl. du Château - ☎ 04 68 71 23 23 - ⏰ closed Jan, noon and Wed. A friendly establishment in the medieval Cité. The good-natured atmosphere and generous menu no doubt contribute to its success – the dining rooms on four levels are regularly packed with people. Carvery on ground floor.

Chez Fred – 31 bd O.-Sarraut - ☎ 04 68 72 02 23 - contact@chez-fred.fr – ⏰ closed 9 Feb-2Mar, 20 Oct-3 Nov, Sat noon, Tue evening and Wed in winter. This modern bistro not far from the station in the lower town is full of life. The cuisine vascillates between Andalousian dishes and daily menus. Food is served in a white-washed room or on the terrace in summer.

L'Écurie – 43 bd Barbès - ☎ 04 68 72 04 04 - ⏰ closed Sun evening. This restaurant serving fine fare is located in magnificent old stables, where the old horses' stalls now separate the guests. This original setting and the garden-court which is pleasant in summer are popular with local residents, who count it among their favourite places to go.

WHERE TO STAY

Montségur – 27 allée d'Iéna - ☎ 04 68 25 31 41 – reservation@hotelmontsegur. com – ⏰ closed 20 Dec-3 Feb - 🅿 - 21 rms. This late 19C family mansion is characterized by beautiful old furniture. Breakfast is served in the lounge or on the terrace. 150m/160yd away is the restaurant Le Languedoc, run by the same family.

Chambre d'hôte La Maison sur la Colline – Lieu-dit Ste-Croix - 1km/0.6mi S of la Cité on rte de Ste-Croix - ☎ 04 68 47 57 94 - ⏰ closed 1 Dec – 15 Feb - 🍴 - reservation recommended in season - 5 rms. Perched on top of a hill, this restored old farm offers a spectacular view of the Cité from its garden. Rooms are spacious and furnished with old dyed objects, in a different colour for each room: blue, yellow, beige, white.. Breakfast is served by the pool in summer.

Hôtel Espace Cité – 132 r. Trivalle - ☎ 04 68 25 24 24 - infos@hotelespacecite. com - 48 rms. Modern hotel with attractive façade at the foot of the citadel. It offers a "budget accommodation" formula. Rooms are functional and clean, without grand luxury but with plenty of light. Warm welcome. Breakfast buffet.

Hôtel Le Donjon and les Remparts – 2 r. du Comte-Roger - ☎ 04 68 11 23 00 - info@bestwestern-donjon.com - 🅿 - 62 rms. Partly occupying a 15C orphanage at the heart of the Cité, this hotel combining old stonework and renovated decor offers three kinds of room to choose from: with white or rustic furniture in the main building, and modern style in the "Remparts" annex. Brasserie.

ON THE TOWN

Le Métronome – 3 av. du Mar.-Foch - ☎ 04 68 71 30 30 - daily 10-2am - ⏰ closed 1 week Jan. Le Métronome is one of Carcassonne's trendiest spots with its canalside terrace, large central bar and comfortable beige moleskin benches. Frequent concerts and a long list of tapas.

SHOPPING

Cabanel – 72 allée d'Iéna - ☎ 04 68 25 02 58 - cabanel@wanadoo.fr – ⏰ Mon-Sat 8am-noon, 2-7pm. This liqueur specialist has been here since 1868, selling a wide variety of unusual brews including Or-Kina (made from spices and plants), Micheline (its origins lost in medieval times), and Audoise (called the Cathars' liqueur). Selection of regional wines also available.

Marché aux fleurs. légumes and fruits – Pl. Carnot - ☎ 04 68 10 24 30 - ⏰ Tues, Thu and Sat 8am-12.30pm. Flowers, fruit and vegetables.

CALENDAR OF EVENTS

Spectacles médiévaux "Carcassonne, terre d'histoire" – Aug. Medieval festival.

Tournois de chevalerie – Aug. Jousting tournament.

Fortifications

See Introduction: Art – Architecture. Carcassonne's defences enable us to imagi~
what medieval siege warfare was like; they are a veritable catalogue of the architectura~
ingenuity that went into resisting an attack. There are drawbridges and fixed bridges
with portcullises, towers with projecting "beaks" or open on the inside, protected at
the top by hoardings and at the base by flared footings, curtain walls with a sentry-
walk behind the crenellations, watch-turrets, arrow-slits, machicolations... Even if the
attackers succeeded in breaking in, they could be pinned down by covering fire.

Château Comtal

Guided tours (30min) Apr-Sep: daily 9.30am-6pm; Oct-Mar: daily 9.30am-5pm.
*Closed 1 Jan, 1 May, 1 and 11 Nov, 25 Dec. Call for admission prices. No charge 1st Sun
in the month.* ☎ *04 68 11 70 70. www.monum.fr.*
Butting onto the Gallo-Roman ramparts, this was built in the 12C by the Viscounts,
the Trencavels. A deep ditch and a barbican separate it from the interior.

Enceinte intérieure

The inner ramparts were first built in the 6C by the Visigoths, though altered and
given extra height in the 13C. The original towers can be identified easily; they are
slender, rounded on the outside and flat on the inside. The 13C additions include the
remarkable "beaked" towers.

Enceinte extérieure

The outer ramparts were begun by Louis IX and completed by Philippe le Hardi (the
Bold). Most of the towers are open on the inside; if taken by the attackers they would
be difficult to defend against a counter-attack from within.
There are also completely enclosed towers acting as redoubts from which the defence
could harass any attackers who had succeeded in gaining entry to the inner ward.
It is possible to date the fortifications by the way in which materials are used. The
Gallo-Roman foundations are made up of large blocks fitted together without the
use of mortar. The work of the Visigoths is characterised by the use of cube-shaped
stones alternating with brick courses often laid in herring-bone fashion.
The Viscounts' buildings are constructed from yellowish sandstone laid rather crudely.
The walls built by the kings of France are made up of rectangular stones laid in a
regular fashion, smooth-faced under Louis IX, rusticated at the time of Philip the
Bold in order to withstand impacts more easily. The curtain-walls and towers of the
outer ramparts are unusual in that Roman or Visigothic work is visible at a higher
level than the 13C walling. This is because additional work had to be carried out on
the foundations when the ground level was lowered to form the outer ward.

▶▶ **Basilique St-Nazaire★ – stained glass★★, statues★★.**

CARNAC★

POPULATION 4 243

MICHELIN MAP 308 M 9

GREEN GUIDE BRITTANY

In the bleak Breton countryside just north of the little town of Carnac are some
of the world's most remarkable megalithic remains.

Visit

Megaliths★★

The area containing the megaliths is somewhat divided up by roads and a number
~f stones have been lost, but altogether it comprises 2 792 menhirs, arranged in
~ or 11 lines – *alignements* – including the **alignements du Ménec★★** with
~9 menhirs, the alignements de **Kermario★** with 1 029 and the alignements de
~scan★ with 594. As well as the lines there are also dolmens (burial places),
~chs (semicircles) and tumuli.
~hic culture flourished during the Neolithic period, from about 4670 to 2000
~s the creation of a settled population growing crops and with domestic
~n contrast to the hunter-gatherers of Paleolithic times), who produced

ned objects, pottery and basket-work and who traded in flints. The inhabitants
.arnac had commercial relations with people from Belgium and from Grand-Pres-
gny in the north of Poitou.

he markings on the megaliths represent an art of abstraction in contrast to the
figurative cave-art of the Upper Paleolithic, and the orientation of the lines in a
west-north-east direction adds to their enigmatic character. Various theories have
been advanced about their likely religious or astronomical significance.

The tumuli and dolmens which appeared 40 centuries before the birth of Christ are
collective burial-places, and the mounds covering them, a thousand years older than
the pyramids, may be "Mankind's most ancient built monuments."

Four thousand centuries previously, the Carnac area was inhabited by prehistoric
people, and, during the Lower Paleolithic, by nomads, contemporaries of the nomads
of Tautavel, Terra Amata and the Ardèche Valley.

In the 5C BC, the Celts moved here. In Gallo-Roman times there was the great villa
of the Bosseno. Later, the area was repopulated by immigrants from Britain and by
monks from Ireland.

Église St-Cornély★

In the centre of the old village of Carnac stands the church, one of the finest examples
of Renaissance monuments to be found in the Morbihan; it was built in 1639 and
dedicated to St Cornély, the patron saint of horned beasts; he is shown here on the
west front standing between two oxen.

The church's decoration dates from the 17C, 18C and 19C. The porch on the north
side is surmounted by a Baroque canopy in the form of a crown. Inside, the panelled
vaulting has 17C paintings showing scenes from the life of Christ, of John the Baptist
and of St Cornély himself. The 18C chancel grille and pulpit are of wrought iron.

◐◑ **Musée de Préhistoire J.-Miln-Z.-Le-Rouzic**★★ ᗷ ◷ *Jun-Sep: daily 10am-
12.30pm, 1.30-7pm; Oct-May: daily 10am-12.30pm, 1.30-6pm.* ◷ *Closed Wed morning,
Jan, 1 May, 25 Dec.* ᗌ *5€ (children: 2.50€).* ☎ *02 97 52 22 04. www.museedecarnac.
com.* **Tumulus St-Michel**★ ◷ *Daily 9am-7pm. No charge.*

CASSIS★

POPULATION 7 967

MICHELIN MAP 340 I 6

GREEN GUIDE PROVENCE

The little port of Cassis has a most attractive **setting**★ in a bay formed where the Provençal limestone ridges come down to the sea; to the east is **Cap Canaille**★★★, at 362m – 1 188ft the highest sea-cliff in France. At the beginning of the 20C, artists like Derain, Vlaminck, Matisse and Dufy were attracted here by the quality of the light.

Calanque d'En-Vau

Excursion

Les Calanques★★.

1hr by boat. To the west of Cassis the Puget Massif is cut into by inlets known as *calanques;* they occupy steep-sided valleys which were invaded by the sea when its level rose because of the melting of the glaciers at the end of the Ice Age. Sheltered by cliffs with a sparse cover of maritime pines, they make pleasant bathing-places. **En-Vau, Port-Pin** and **Port-Miou** are perhaps the most attractive.

The Cosquer Cave

The submarine cave situated near the tip of the headland at Cap Morgiou was discovered in 1985 by Henri Cosquer, a local diver. The sensational news of its painted decoration and engravings dating from the Paleolithic Age broke on 3 September 1991 and it was acclaimed as one of the high spots for rock art. Carbon dating techniques date the **hand prints** to c 27 000 BC and the animal drawings to c 17 000 BC, making them 1 000 to 2 000 years earlier than those at Lascaux, which are similar in style and technique. The marine fauna (seals, penguins, fish) is a rare feature which adds to the interest of this decorated cave, the oldest of this type in the world.

The cave was submerged as the level of the sea rose and its treasures were preserved. It will not be open to view owing to its inaccessibility. However, an exhibition on the site is presented at La Joliette docks in Marseille.

CASTRES★

POPULATION 44 812

MICHELIN MAP 338 E-F 9-10

GREEN GUIDE LANGUEDOC ROUSSILLON TARN GORGES

Built on the banks of the **Agout** river, Castres is an ideal starting-point for trips to the Sidobre, the heights of **Monts de Lacaune** and **Montagne Noire**. Castres is a thriving city with modern industries such as chemistry, pharmacology and robotics.

Visit

Musée Goya★

🕐 *Jul and Aug: daily 9am-6pm; Apr-Jun, Sep: daily except Mon 9am-noon, 2-6pm, Sun and public holidays 10am-noon, 2-6pm; Oct-Mar: daily except Mon 9am-noon, 2-5pm, Sun 10-noon, 2-5pm.* 🕐 *Closed 1 Jan, 1 May, 1 Nov, 25 Dec. 3€ summer, 2.30€ winter, no charge 1st Sun in the month (Oct-May). ☎ 05 63 71 59 30.*
Set up on the second floor of the former episcopal palace (presently the Town Hall), this museum specialises in Spanish painting and boasts an outstanding **collection**★★ of works by Goya, namely *Self-Portrait, The Disasters of War, Francisco del Mazo and The Junta of the Philippines led by Ferdinand VII.*

CAUDEBEC-EN-CAUX★

POPULATION 2 265

MICHELIN MAP 304 E 4

GREEN GUIDE NORMANDY

A market town since 1390 (market-day Saturday) on the north bank of the Seine, Caudebec possesses in **Église Notre-Dame**★ "the finest chapel in the kingdom" according to Henri IV; the monarch was struck by the harmonious relationship between this masterpiece of Flamboyant Gothic architecture and the sculpture which adorns it.

Visit

Among the architectural features note particularly the exquisitely carved spire, the parapet, the west front, and, within, the great nave and the pierced triforium which shows how the chalk of the region lent itself to being carved into intricate patterns.

The wealth of sculpture includes, on the west front, a number of small figures with intriguing poses and expressions on the jambs as well as the canopies. Inside, the Chapel of the Holy Sepulchre (Chapelle du Sépulcre) has statues from Jumièges Abbey while the keystone (clef de voûtea) of the Lady Chapel (Chapelle axiale) is an extraordinary seven-ton monolith with a 4.3m – 13ft pendentive. The font has panels with biblical scenes; each of the lower panels shows a scene from the New Testament while above it is the corresponding prophetic episode from the Old Testament.

Corniche des CÉVENNES★

MICHELIN MAP 339 G 4

GREEN GUIDE LANGUEDOC ROUSSILLON TARN GORGES

This highway was constructed at the beginning of the 18C in order to facilitate the movement of Louis XIV's troops engaged in putting down the Camisard rebellion.

Driving Tour

From Florac to Anduze

67km – 42mi. The scenic road follows a high ridge separating two rivers and leads past a number of splendid viewpoints, offering stunning panoramas over the characteristic landscape of the Cévennes with its long straight ridges, deep valleys and limestone plateaux known as *causses*.

- The eastern escarpment of the Causse Méjean stands out as the road rises towards St-Laurent-de-Trèves;
- Dinosaur remains 190 million years old were discovered at St-Laurent; from here, there are fine **views**★ extending over the causses and as far as Mont Aigoual and Mont Lozère;
- Le Can de l'Hospitalet was one of the meeting-places of the Camisards;
- At the Col des Faïsses there is a fine general view over the Cévennes;
- At Le Pompidou, the limestone gives way to schists, and chestnut trees begin to make their appearance. Further on is a network of long, narrow ridges.

La **CHAISE-DIEU**★★

POPULATION 778

MICHELIN MAP 331 E 2

GREEN GUIDE AUVERGNE THE RHÔNE VALLEY

Over 1 000m – 3 300ft up on the high granite plateau of Livradois, La Chaise-Dieu Abbey was already famous in the 11C. In the 12C its importance was second only to that of Cluny and by the 13C its influence extended to Bordeaux, Spain, Sicily and Switzerland, with altogether 300 dependent congregations. Its finest hour came with the election at Avignon in 1342 of Pope Clement VI; as Pierre Roger, he had once been a novice and monk here before becoming prelate at Rouen, Bishop of Arras and Archbishop of Sens. The abbey's decline set in after 1518, when commendam was instituted; abbots were henceforth appointed by the king, with fiscal, rather than religious, considerations taking first place. La Chaise-Dieu's commendatory abbots included Henri d'Angoulême, illegitimate son of Henri II, one of the assassins of the Huguenot leader Coligny; this pious churchman lost his life in a duel. Richelieu's reforms in the 17C failed to stop the slide into decadence which was brought to an end only by the abbey's dissolution at the time of the French Revolution.

Chaise-Dieu Music Festival

J.-L. Beltram

Visit

Église abbatiale de St-Robert★★

The granite west front with its twin towers (the spires have disappeared) speaks strongly of the abbey's former grandeur and austerity. The impression of rigour is somewhat relieved by the arching of the doorway, albeit mutilated by the Huguenots, which is approached via a monumental stairway.

Within, the structure is of a noble simplicity, a single-storeyed elevation, aisles almost equal to the nave in height, the arches reaching up to the flattened vaults. The sobriety of the granite is offset by the soaring eight-sided chamfered piers.

Chœur des Moines★★ - The Monks' chancel was built from 1344 to 1352 by Clement VI, who was also responsible for the New Palace at Avignon. A great patron of the arts, he had acquired a taste for the Gothic style of Northern France, and appointed the architect Hugues Morel to give his old monastery its abbey church. The result sets monastic values and the care of the needy above the ostentation prevailing at the Papal court, sacred geometry and its symbolism above decorative virtuosity. In 1348, Clement announced that he would be buried here.

The 14 Flemish **tapestries**★★★ (1500-18) of wool, linen and silk, came from Arras and Brussels. They illustrate scenes from the Life of Christ related to the corresponding prophetic episode of the Old Testament; the Temptation of Jesus, the Last Supper, and the empty Tomb are particularly fine. The tapestries are hung over the 15C stalls (**stalles★★**), 144 in number, fashioned from Limousin oak into floral or figurative patterns; those reserved for the Abbot and Dean, below the screen at the entrance to the choir, are decorated with more elaborate carvings.

Clement's tomb was much restored after its mutilation by the Huguenots who seized the abbey in 1572. It still lacks its mourning figures, but the effigy of this French Pope lies on his tomb in serene state.

Dance macabre (Dance of Death)★ - 1470. An obsessive preoccupation with death and decay appeared towards the end of the 15C during the last convulsions of the Hundred Years War. Sermons spoke of the horrors of death, tombstones portrayed decomposing bodies (rather than the calm of final repose), artists painted Christ's wounds (rather than Last Judgements), and the Dance of Death became a favourite decorative subject (even forming the subject of a painting at the court of Dijon). At La Chaise-Dieu, figures of the mighty, of great ladies, or of clergymen are shown next to their likeness in death. The work provided Honegger with the inspiration for his 1938 composition entitled the Dance of Death.

Travées de l'Ouest - Like the cloisters and Clement's Tower (Tour Clémentine), the west bays were built by Gregory IX, the nephew of Clement VI, in order to provide for the increasing number of pilgrims. In the 16C they were closed off by the construction of the screen and its balcony which extends into one bay of the nave.

A great organ was installed at the west end in 1683 and enlarged in 1726; the organ-case (**buffet★**) is elaborately sculpted and contrasts with the spirit prevailing in the architecture of the choir.

◖◗ **Cloître★**.

CHÂLONS-EN-CHAMPAGNE★★

POPULATION 62 452

MICHELIN MAP 306 I 9

GREEN GUIDE ALSACE LORRAINE CHAMPAGNE

Châlons originated on an island site in the Marne. It lies at the centre of the chalk-lands of Champagne, an extensive plateau once notorious for its poverty, but now one of France's most prosperous agricultural regions, thanks to the artificial fertilisers which enable rich crops of cereals and sugar-beet to be grown.

▶ **Orient Yourself:** Châlons-en-Champagne, which is listed as a "Town of Art and History," offers 2hr discovery tours Mon-Sat in Jul and Aug at 2.30pm, and only on Sat per month in low season. They cost 4.50€, and you can find more information at the tourist office or on www.vpah.culture.fr.

A Bit of History

The valley of the Aube to the southwest of the town was the setting in 451 for the series of battles known as the Catalaunian Fields (**Champs catalauniques**). Having given up his intention of sacking Paris, then known as Lutetia, because of the intervention of St Genevieve, Attila the Hun was engaged here by the Roman army under Aetius; after fierce fighting, he quit the battlefield and fled eastwards.

Châlons was the birthplace in 1749 of Nicolas Appert, a pioneer of the food industry and the inventor of a system of preserving food by sterilisation.

Visit

Cathédrale St-Étienne★★

The present building was begun around 1235 in the Lanceolate Gothic style invented 40 years previously at Chartres, though there is little evidence of stylistic development having taken place.

The cathedral is famous for its stained glass (**vitraux**), Renaissance as well as medieval. The 13C glass includes the tall windows in the choir, the north transept (with the wonderful hues of green characteristic of the region), and the first bay on the north side (the Tanners' window – note the hanging skins). The finest windows however are those of Renaissance date, in the side chapels of the south aisle, showing scenes from the Creation, the earthly Paradise, the Passion, the Life of Christ and the Lives of the Saints.

Église Notre-Dame-en-Vaux★

🕐 *Jun to mid-Sep: daily 10-noon, 2-6pm, Sun 2.30-6pm; mid-Sep to Jun: daily except Sun 10am-noon, 2-6pm.* ☏ *03 26 65 63 17.*

A typical early-Gothic church with a characteristic four-tier elevation. Particularly noteworthy is the ambulatory, inspired by the one at St-Rémi in Reims, together with the stained glass in the windows of the north aisle, again showing superb skill in the use of green.

To the left of the church, the **Musée du Cloître de Notre-Dame-en-Vaux★★** (🕐 *Apr-Sep: Wed-Mon 10am-noon, 2-6pm; Oct-Mar: Mon, Wed-Fri 10-noon, 2-5pm, Sat-Sun 10am-noon, 2-6pm;* 🕐 *closed Tue, 1 Jan, 1 May, 1 and 11 Nov, 25 Dec;* ⊜ *4.60€, no charge 1st Sun in the month Oct-May, call to verify;* ☏ *03 26 64 03 87*) houses **sculptures★★** from the old Romanesque cloisters.

CHALON-SUR-SAÔNE ★

POPULATION 62 452

MICHELIN MAP 320 J 9

GREEN GUIDE BURGUNDY JURA

Chalon is the urban centre for the fertile lowlands bordering the Saône as it makes its way between the Jura and the Massif Central.

▶ **Orient Yourself:** Chalon-sur-Saône, which is listed as a "Town of Art and History," offers discovery tours conducted by guide-lecturers approved by the Ministry of Culture and Communication. Information at the tourist office or on www.vpah. culture.fr.

A Bit of History

The river is fed by a number of canals; at Corre it is joined by the Eastern Canal (Canal de l'Est – completed 1882), at Pontailler by the canal from the Marne (1907), at St-Jean-de-Losne by both the Rhine-Rhône Canal (1833) and the Burgundy Canal (1832). But it is only at Chalon, where it is joined by the Central Canal (completed 1790), that it becomes one of Europe's great commercial waterways, flowing south to join the Rhône at Lyon. Long before the present age, however, the Saône had been an important commercial route; a large number of amphora bases were found at Chalon, proof that wine was imported here from Naples before the introduction of the vine to Burgundy by the Romans.

Since the 18C the banks of the river have been a favoured site for industry, which includes the heavy engineering firm Schneider du Creusot as well as electrical works and nuclear power plants.

The Origins of Photography – Joseph Nicéphore Niepce (1765-1833) was a native of Chalon. His restlessly inventive disposition had already led him to design an internal combustion engine in 1807. He lacked talent as a draughtsman, but was fascinated by lithography. At the age of 48 he set himself the task of recording images through the spontaneous action of light. He was already familiar with the optics of the camera obscura which had been studied by the Arab physicist El Hazen (11C), by Leonardo da Vinci and by various 18C men of science, among them Jacques Charles, the husband of Lamartine's Elvire.

After three years' work he succeeded in making and fixing a positive image, and on 28 May 1816 he sent his brother a print made at his home in St-Loup-de-Varennes (7km – 4mi south); this was the very first photograph. **Daguerre** popularised Niepce's discovery and others developed it (e.g. Fox Talbot and Bayard).

Progressive refinement and invention have led from Niepce's simple apparatus to photography as an art form, to the Hasselblad used in lunar exploration and to the snapshots in the family album.

Visit

Musée Nicéphore Niépce ★★

🔲 🕒 *Jul and Aug: daily 10-12.30pm,1.30-6pm; Sep-Jun: daily 9.30-11.45am, 2-5.45pm.* 🕒 *Closed public holidays.* 🔎 *3.10€, no charge Wed and 1st Sun in the month.* ☎ *03 85 48 41 98. ww.museeniepce.com.*

The museum is housed in the 18C Hôtel des Messageries on the banks of the Saône. The rich collection comprises photographs and early photographic equipment, including the earliest cameras ever made which were used by Joseph Nicéphore Niepce, as well as his first heliographs. There are also works by well-known contemporaries of Niepce in the world of photography.

◑◑ **Musée Denon** ★ 🕒 *Wed-Mon 9.30am-noon, 2-5.30pm.* 🕒 *Closed Tue, 1 Jan, Easter Mon, 1 and 8 May, Ascension Day, Pentecost Mon, 14 Jul, 15 Aug, 1 and 11 Nov, 25 Dec.* 🔎 *3.10€, no charge Wed and 1st Sun in the month.* ☎ *03 85 94 74 41.* – painting and archeological collections.

CHAMBÉRY★★

MICHELIN MAP 333 I 3-4

GREEN GUIDE FRENCH ALPS

Chambéry lies in a valley dividing the Chartreuse and Bauges massifs. It was chosen as their capital by the Counts of Savoy in 1232; they made good use of its strategic position astride the ancient lines of communication with Italy and kept their liking for the place even after their seat was shifted to Turin.

▶ **Orient Yourself:** Chambéry, which is listed as a "Town of Art and History," offers discovery tours conducted by guide-lecturers approved by the Ministry of Culture and Communication. Information at the tourist office or on www.vpah.culture.fr.

Visit

The famous **Fontaine des Éléphants** is sited in the Rue de Boigne; its arcades make an urban composition reminiscent of the town planning of Northern Italy.

The **Sainte-Chapelle**★, part of the **château**★(◷ *Guided tours* ✆ *(1hr) Jul and Aug: daily 10.30am, 2.30pm, 3.30pm, 4.30pm, Sun 2.30pm, 3.30pm, 4.30pm; May-Jun, Sep and shorter school holidays: daily 2.30pm; Oct-Apr: Sat-Sun and public holidays 2.30pm; ☞ 4€ ☎ 04 79 70 15 94)*, was built by Amadeus VIII to house the Holy Shroud, though this was removed to Turin when Savoy became part of France in 1860 (and is now known as the Turin Shroud). Its charm lies in its Flamboyant architecture, Renaissance stained glass and trompe-l'œil painted vaults.

The country house known as **Les Charmettes** (◷ *Apr-Sep: Wed-Mon 10am-noon, 2-6pm; Oct-Mar: Wed-Mon 10am-noon, 2-4.30pm; ◷ closed Tue and public holidays; ☞ 3.10€, no charge 1st Sun in the month. ☎ 04 79 33 39 44)* was where Mme de Warens and the writer Jean-Jacques Rousseau lived from 1736 to 1742.

◖◗ **Vieille ville**★. **Château**★. **Musée Savoisien**★ ◷ *Wed-Mon 10am-noon, 2-6pm.* ◷ *Closed Tue and public holidays.* ☞ *3.10€, no charge 1st Sun in the month.* ☎ *04 79 33 44 48*– prehistory, religious art, regional ethnography. Église St-Pierre de Lémenc – crypt.

Château de **CHAMBORD**★★★

MICHELIN MAP 318 G 6

GREEN GUIDE CHÂTEAUX OF THE LOIRE

The first of France's great Classical palaces, Chambord stands in a vast park enclosed by a 32km – 20 mile wall. Beyond stretches the forest of Sologne, teeming with the game which the rulers of France have long loved to hunt.

A Bit of History

At the age of 21, François I had just returned in triumph from his victory over the Swiss at Marignano which had given him possession of the Duchy of Milan. Dissatisfied with the old royal residence at Blois in spite of the improvements he had made, he had a vision of a dream castle to be built four leagues away on the forest edge. Leonardo da Vinci may have helped with the plans for this fabulous edifice; its feudal keep and corner towers belied its purpose as a palace of pleasure and status symbol for a Renaissance prince. The château was begun in 1519; later Philibert Delorme, Jean Bullant and the great Mansart all worked on it.

Hardly had Chambord started to rise from its foundations when the king suffered defeat and captivity at Pavia in 1525. On his return to France he judged it more suitable for a monarch to live close to his capital, at either Fontainebleau or St-Germain-en-Laye.

Visit

◷ *Apr-Sep: daily 9am-6.15pm; Oct-Mar: daily 9am-5.45pm. Last admission 30min before closing.* ◷ *Closed 1 Jan, 1 May, 25 Dec.* ☞ *7€ (under 18 years: no charge), no charge 1st Sun in the month (Oct-Mar).* ☎ *08 25 82 60 88. www.chambord.org.*

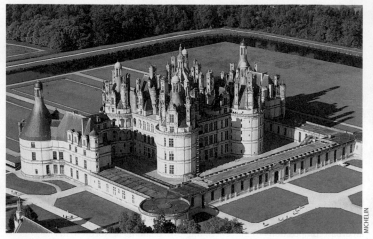

Château de Chambord

The château's double staircase is justly famous for its interlocking spirals opening onto internal loggias and for its vaults adorned with salamanders, François' crest.

The extraordinary roof terrace was where the king and his entourage spent much of their time watching tournaments and festivals or the start and return of the hunt; its nooks and crannies lent themselves to the confidences, intrigues and assignations of courtly life, played out against this fantastic background of pepperpot turrets, chimney stacks, dormers peeping from the roofs, false windows embellished with shells, all decorated with inset slatework and dominated by the splendid lantern.

The state rooms contain rich furnishings: wood panelling, tapestries, furniture, portraits, hunting collections.

CHAMONIX-MONT-BLANC★★★

POPULATION 9 700

MICHELIN MAP 328 M-O 5

GREEN GUIDE FRENCH ALPS

Chamonix is France's mountaineering capital. It lies at the foot of the famous 3 000m – 10 000ft Chamonix Needles (Aiguilles de Chamonix) at a point where the glacial valley of the Arve widens out. All around are the high mountains of the Mont Blanc Massif; this is the most renowned of the massifs of the French Alps, because of its dramatic relief, crystalline rocks and glacial morphology. The dome of the great White Mountain is visible from the town.

Site

The tongue of the 7km – 4 mile-long Glacier des Bossons hangs 500m – 1 650ft above the valley on the approach to Chamonix.

The Geneva naturalist **Horace Benedict de Saussure** based himself here in the course of his scientific studies in Savoy. In 1760, he offered a reward for the first ascent of Mont-Blanc. On 8 August 1786 Dr Michel Paccard and Jacques Balmat reached the summit, thereby inaugurating the age of mountaineering, as well as the development of the town as an Alpine resort.

Excursions

By cable-car or rack railway

Aiguille du Midi ★★★
Jul-Aug: daily 7.10am-5pm; May-Jun and Sep-Oct: daily 8.10am-4pm; Nov-Apr: daily 8.10am-3.30pm. Trip in two stages: Chamonix-Plan de l'Aiguille and Plan de l'Aiguille-

Aiguille du Midi. (departures every 30min). ☜ *35€ round trip.* ☏ *04 50 53 22 75, reservation possible in summer, call* ☏ *08 36 68 00 67. Allow at least 2hr round trip on the cable-car.*

The **panorama**★★★, especially from the central peak (3 842m – 12 605ft), is staggering, taking in the snowy splendours of the high mountains, Mont-Blanc, Mont-Maudit, the Grandes Jorasses, and the dome of the Goûter whose buttresses are buried in 30m – 100ft of ice. The domes and other rounded summits are of granite (Mont Blanc, Peuterey, Goûter), while the jagged shapes of the needles and spikes and the sharp ridges separating the snow-filled gullies are of schistous rocks (Drus, Grandes Jorasses).

The **Vallée Blanche**, also known as the Giant's Glacier (Glacier du Géant), can be reached by taking the cable-car (*teleferique*) to Pointe Helbronner. From here can be seen the glacial cirques with their flanks worn down by the incessant attacks of the ice. The snow builds up in the cirques, hardens to form névé (a granular substance, half-snow, half-ice), then becomes a slowly-moving crystalline mass of ice, fissuring into crevasses, dividing into ice pinnacles (séracs) and scooping out the valley as it descends. It is in this way that the glaciers of the Géant and Mont-Blanc-de-Tacul form the upper part of the Mer de Glace.

Mer de Glace★★★

2hr30min by rack railway and teleferique.

The view from the upper station of the railway built in 1908 takes in the whole of this world-famous "sea of ice". The glacier is 14km – 9 miles long, in places 400m – 1 300ft thick, and moves 90m – 300ft a year. The rocky material it carries with it scores and scratches the mountain walls on either side as well as giving the glacier its characteristic rather grimy appearance (as the ice evaporates grit is left on the surface). At the foot of the glacier this material is deposited, forming a terminal moraine.

Beyond, the eye is led from one soaring peak to another; this **panorama**★★★ is one of the most beautiful in the region; the Grand-Charmoz, the Grépon, Blaitière, the Tacul, Pointe Helbronner, Dent du Géant, Grandes Jorasses, the Drus, the Aiguille Verte du Montenvers.

◖◗ **Summit of the Brévent**★★★ ⓒ *Jun and Sep: daily 9am-4pm; Jul-Aug: daily 8am-5pm; Oct-May: daily 8.45am-5pm. Chamonix-Planpraz by rack railway (10min), Planpraz-Brévent by teleferique (10min).* ⓒ *Closed May and Oct to mid-Dec.* ☜ *18€ round trip* ☏ *04 50 53 22 75.* **La Flégère viewpoint**★★ *By teleferique* ⓒ *Jul and Aug: daily 7.40am-5.30pm; Jun and Sep: daily 8.40am-4.30pm; mid-Dec to mid-Apr: daily 8.45am-5pm.* ⓒ *Closed end Apr-May.* ☜ *16€ round trip.* ☏ *04 50 53 22 75.* Summit of the **Aiguille des Grands-Montets**★★★; **Bellevue**★★ (Les Houches) and the **Nid d'Aigle**★★ (glacier de Bionnassay – leave from St-Gervais-les-Bains).

Aiguille du Midi

J.C. Ligeon/FOC

Château de CHANTILLY★★★

MICHELIN MAP 305 F-G 6

GREEN GUIDE NORTHERN FRANCE AND THE PARIS REGION

A synonym for elegance, Chantilly evokes wonderful art collections, a great park and forest, and the cult of the horse as well as the château itself.

Visit

Château

Anne de Montmorency, the great Constable of France who served six monarchs (from Louis XII to Charles IX), had a Renaissance castle built here in 1528. The foundations of an earlier building (1386) were re-used by Pierre Chambiges. The finished building filled Charles V with admiration.

In 1560 the architect Jean Bullant designed a charming little château (Petit Château) to the south of the main building.

The Great Condé and his descendants later made the state rooms of the Petit Château into their living quarters; today, there is much to delight the eye, including Rococo woodwork, manuscripts, incunabula, silver caskets, icons, and, in the bedroom of Monsieur le Prince (the title given to the reigning prince of Condé), a chest of drawers by Riesener. The greatest treasure is in the Library (Cabinet des Livres); this is the **Limbourg** brothers' sumptuously illuminated *Book of Hours for the Duke of Berry (Les Très Riches Heures du Duc de Berry)* of about 1415, completed 60 years later by Jean Colombe (on display in reproduction).

Henri II of Bourbon-Condé acquired Chantilly through his marriage to Charlotte de Montmorency. Their son Louis II of Bourbon, known as the Great Condé, employed the men of talent of the time: Le Nôtre, who laid out the park and gardens (where the ornamental canals and their fountains so impressed Louis XIV that he determined to reproduce them on an even grander scale at Versailles); François Mansart, who redesigned the principal façade (thereby wiping out Chambiges' work) and the layout of the rooms; and Vatel, his major domo, who killed himself at a banquet, supposedly because the fish course had not been on time.

At the time of the French Revolution, the château was dismantled to first-floor level, the Petit Château was ruined and the park laid waste.

On his return from exile Louis-Joseph de Condé set about putting his house and grounds back into order. On his death, the estate passed into the hands of the Duke of Aumale (Henri of Orléans, the fifth son of Louis-Philippe), who rebuilt the great edifice (1875-83) in a neo-Renaissance style, bequeathing to the Institut de France what was now a palace, mausoleum and museum.

The château houses a museum (**musée★★**) (🕐 *Mar-Oct: daily 10am-6pm; Nov-Feb: daily 10.30am-12.45pm, 2-5pm, Sat-Sun and public holidays 10.30am-5pm;* ⊛ *7€, museum and park;* ☎ *03 44 62 62 62)* – manuscripts, furniture, paintings, sculpture – whose wealth would prove difficult to rival today.

Grandes Écuries★★

These were built in 1721 by Jean Aubert for Louis-Henri of Bourbon, the Great Condé's great-grandson. Much admired in its time, it is the finest example of 18C building at Chantilly to have come down to us. The stables house the **Musée vivant du Cheval et du Poney★** (🕐 *Apr-Oct: daily 10.30am-6.30pm, Sat-Sun and public holidays 10.30am-7pm; Nov-Mar: daily except Tue 2-6pm, Sat-Sun and public holidays 10.30am-6.30pm; last admission 1hr before closing;* ⊛ *8€, children 4-12 years: 5.50€;* ☎ *03 44 57 40 40, www. musee-vivant-du-cheval.fr)*, which has stalls from the time of the Duke of Aumale, historic harnessing, costumes, and all kinds of objects associated with equitation. Riding displays take place in the central rotunda.

More than 3 000 horses are stabled and trained in and around Chantilly; race-meetings and hunts both perpetuate the tradition begun on 15 May 1834 when France's first great official race-meeting was held, and maintain Chantilly's reputation as the country's thoroughbred capital.

▶▶ **Parc★★** ♿ 🕐 *Mar-Oct: Wed-Mon 10am-6pm; Nov-Feb: Mon, Wed-Fri 10.30am-12.45pm, 2-5pm, Sat-Sun and public holidays 10.30am-5pm.* 🕐 *Closed Tue.* ⊛ *3.50€.* ☎ *03 44 62 62 62. www.chateaudechantilly.com.* **Appartements des Princes★**. English gardens: 🕐 *Same hours as the park.*

CHAOURCE★

POPULATION 1 031

MICHELIN MAP 313 E 5

GREEN GUIDE ALSACE LORRAINE CHAMPAGNE

Chaource lies at the centre of that part of the old province of Champagne known as "Champagne humide" (Champagne wetlands), to distinguish it from the drought-ridden chalklands of "Champagne crayeuse" to the west.

Visit

The village has a particularly interesting Gothic church (**église**★) with a 12C chancel and a nave of the 15C and 16C. Restored after war damage, the church is a veritable museum of regional sculpture, some of which has come here from churches no longer in use. Much of the work has a touching simplicity and truthfulness. Some of it is exceptional, like the 15C *Man of Sorrows*, the 16C (but still Gothic in feeling) St Martha (in the Lady Chapel – Chapelle de la Vierge), the **Entombment**★★, the *Crib* and the *Pietà* in the Paradise Chapel to the north (Chapelle du Paradis).

CHARLEVILLE-MÉZIÈRES★

POPULATION 67 213

MICHELIN MAP 306 K 3-4

GREEN GUIDE ALSACE LORRAINE CHAMPAGNE

Here are two towns in one. Mézières is the administrative and military town, evolving from the 10C onward at the foot of the château guarding the isthmus formed by the triple meander of the Meuse to the south; Charleville is the commercial centre, built in the 17C within the broader central meander.

A Dramatic Figure – Arthur Rimbaud was born here in 1854; in his revolt against society, this great symbolist poet penetrated the realm of the subconscious (*Bateau ivre – The Drunken Boat*), anticipating the surrealists' attempts at spontaneous writing. He then gave up writing and embarked on a life of travel to the East. He died at the age of 37 in Marseille.

Visit

Place Ducale★★

Like the rest of the town, this square was built in 16 years from 1612. Its designer was Clément Métezeau, the younger brother of Louis Métezeau who completed the Place des Vosges in Paris in the same year. There is a strong similarity of style between these two important examples of Renaissance town planning: careful geometry of the elevations, use of brick with stone dressings, unity achieved by the regular design of the arcades. Louis XIII pediments and bull's-eye windows have been reinstated in some of the buildings.

On the west side of the square, the Law Courts (Palais de Justice) and the Town Hall (Hôtel de ville) are of later date and much less interesting in spite of their pilasters and projecting balconies.

In the centre of the square is the statue of Charles of Gonzaga who managed to get exemption from the salt tax for the town he had just founded and which bears his name.

CHARTRES★★★

POPULATION 39 595

MICHELIN MAP 311 E 5

GREEN GUIDE NORTHERN FRANCE AND THE PARIS REGION

Chartres' magnificent cathedral, the "Acropolis of France" (Rodin), still beckons to the pilgrim far off across the endless cornfields of the Beauce.

The area was occupied by the Carnutes, and Druids once worshipped here; there is also evidence of the pagan cult of a holy spring, and possibly also of a mother-goddess, whom the first missionaries may have christianised as a forerunner of the Virgin Mary.

A Bit of History

The old town (le Vieux Chartres★) lies at the point where the Eure cuts into the plain of the Beauce; its picturesque streets evoke the bustling activity of a medieval city of merchants and craftsmen. The banks of the Eure were once alive with the manifold trades of the riverside, millers, tanners, curriers, cobblers, fullers. Today, the old mill-races and laundry-houses have been restored, and a number of 17C houses have kept their embossed doorways topped by a bull's-eye. The most attractive townscape is to be found in the St-André quarter, by the riverbanks, and in Rue des Écuyers and Rue du Cygne. Loëns Granary (Grenier de Loëns) is a fine 12C building which once housed the tithes of grain and wine.

Chartres attracted pilgrims at an early date, first of all to Our Lady of the Underground Chapel (Notre-Dame-de-Sous-Terre), then to the cathedral which Bishop Fulbert built in the 11C but which was burnt down in 1194.

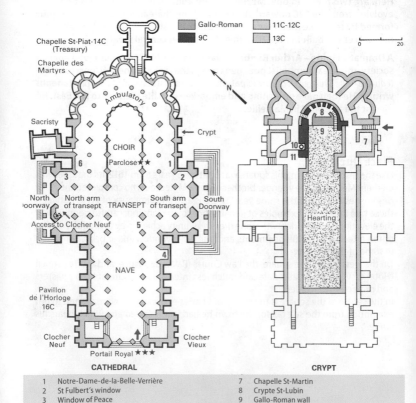

1	Notre-Dame-de-la-Belle-Verrière	7	Chapelle St-Martin
2	St Fulbert's window	8	Crypte St-Lubin
3	Window of Peace	9	Gallo-Roman wall
4	Chapelle Vendôme	10	Puits des Saints-Forts
5	Organ	11	Chapelle Notre-Dame-de-Sous-Terre
6	Vierge du Pilier		

Chartres - Address Book

TOURISM INFORMATION

Pl. de la Cathédrale, 28000 Chartres, ☎ *02 37 18 26 26. www.chartres-tourisme.com. For coin ranges, see the Legend at the back of the guide.*

EATING OUT

⊖ **Le Pichet** – *19 r. du Cheval-Blanc.* ☎ *02 37 21 08 35 – restaurant.pichet@voila.fr.* ◐ *Closed Tue evening and Wed.* Just down the street from the cathedral, a very friendly little bistro that suits our tastes. Inside, there is a pleasant jumble of bric-a-brac: wooden chairs, a collection of coffeepots, pitchers, old street signs and other good stuff. The food is traditional French cuisine.

⊖⊖ **Le Café Serpente** – *2 r. du Cloître Notre-Dame.* ☎ *02 37 21 68 81.* ◐ *Closed evenings of 24 and 31 Dec - reserv. requested in winter.* A bicycle on the ceiling, posters on the walls and enamelled plaques in the stairwell comprise the decor of this thoroughly genial old café opposite the cathedral. On your plates: appetizing salads, brasserie fare and authentic cuisine at all hours.

⊖⊖⊖ **Le Tripot** – *11 pl. Jean-Moulin.* ☎ *02 37 36 60 11.* ◐ *Closed last 2 weeks of Aug, Sun-Mon.* This house built in 1553 used to accommodate a *jeu de paume* (real tennis court) called 'Le Tripot' whose Latin motto meaning 'Belligerents: stay away' may still be seen above the front door. A timeless ultimatum! Well-preserved rustic interior and contemporary cuisine.

WHERE TO STAY

⊖ **La Ferme du Château (Bed and Breakfast)** – *in Levesville, 28300 Bailleau-l'Évêque – 8km/5mi NW of Chartres via N 154 and D 134.* ☎ *02 37 22 97 02. 3 rms* ⬚ *meals* ⊖⊖*.* This elegant Beauce farm offers pretty, comfortable rooms that have been decorated with a light hand. Neighbouring a small château, the farm is very quiet and its kind, hospitable owners are very discreet.

⊖⊖⊖ **Le Grand Monarque** – *22 pl. des Épars.* ☎ *02 37 18 15 15, info@bw-grand-monarque.com – 50 rms* ⬚ *12€ –restaurant* ⊖⊖⊖⊖*.* A 16C coaching inn at the heart of the city. The comfortable rooms have a personal touch; some are embellished with cheerfully flowered patterns and canopies while others are more sober. Snug dining room with ornamental wood carvings and works of art.

SHOPPING

Galerie de Chartres – *7 r. Collin-d'Harleville.* ☎ *02 37 88 28 28, www.interencheres.com –* ◐ *showings: Mon and Fri, 9am-noon, 2-6pm.* This establishment organises auctions for an international clientele every weekend in the 16C Eglise Sainte-Foy (ceramics, weapons, stamps, silverware, cameras, radios, etc.). It is one of the rare galleries to specialise in the sale of collectable dolls and toys.

Marché aux légumes et volailles – *Pl. Billard.* Each Saturday morning, the covered Vegetable and Poultry Market displays colourful stands featuring authentic Beauce produce. This carrousel of sights, tastes and fragrances is one of the most popular markets in the area.

Atelier Loire – *16 r. d'Ouarville, 28300 Léves – Just north of Chartres on the way to Dreux, 2km/1.2mi from the cathedral –* ☎ *02 37 21 20 71 – www.galerie-du-vitrail. com –* 🚶 *guided tours,* ◐ *Fri 2:30pm;* ◐ *closed Aug and public holidays.* A century-old, stately residence set amidst a park and adorned with stained-glass creations is the home of this atelier founded in 1946 by Gabriel Loire, and continued today by his grandchildren. The art and technique of making stained glass are carefully explained, beginning with artists' models (as designed by Adami, Miro or Fernand Léger, for example) and ending with the finished product created by master glass crafters. The visit, with its thousand hues and shades, is simply magical.

La Galerie du Vitrail – *17 Cloître Notre-Dame.* ☎ *02 37 36 10 03 – www.galerie-du-vitrail.com –* ◐ *mid-Apr to end Oct: Tue-Sat 9:45am-7pm, Sun and public holidays 10:30am-7pm; Nov to mid-Apr: Tue-Sat 10:30am-1pm, 2-7pm.* Come here to acquire first-class knowledge of stained-glass, from the show rooms featuring antique and contemporary works, to the boutique where stained glass mirrors, lamps and mobiles are presented. Madame Loire, who presides over La Galerie, is the only antique dealer in France specialised in this art form. Bookshop.

ON THE TOWN

Brûlerie les Rois Mages – *6 r. des Changes.* ☎ *02 37 36 30 52 –* ◐ *Tue-Sat 9:15am-12:15pm, 1:30-7:15pm.* Enter this "retro" coffee-roasting shop and choose among the wide variety of coffees roasted on site and the dozens of teas to enjoy in the brûlerie or take home.

La Chocolaterie – *14 pl. Marceau.* ☎ *02 37 21 86 92 –* ◐ *Tue-Sat, 8am-7:30pm; Sun-Mon 10am-7:30pm.* A highly useful address for stocking up on gourmet treats to take home as souvenirs, such as macaroons or Mentchikoffs, a local chocolate speciality. The very cosy tearoom offers sofas and a fireplace; there's a pleasant terrace in summer.

Visit

Cathédrale Notre-Dame★★★

& See *Introduction: Art – Architecture*. Reconstruction began immediately and was completed in the short space of 25 years. The north and south porches were added only 20 years later and the building consequently has a unity of style possessed by few other Gothic churches. Pilgrims have now been coming here for almost eight centuries to fill the vast transept and the great chancel with its double ambulatory, and to admire the 175 representations of the Virgin Mary which adorn the cathedral. The most celebrated pilgrim was probably the writer Charles Péguy, who came here in the years before the First World War. Chartres inspired this socialist and unorthodox Catholic with an essentially medieval vision of a renewed France, whose lasting force is seen in the young peoples' pilgrimages which his writings initiated and which still take place today.

The new cathedral raised the Transitional Gothic style to new levels of achievement. The bays of the nave, previously square in plan, are now oblong and have sexpartite vaults; the arches of arcades and windows are more pointed; a round opening is inserted in the space above the highest windows; the structural functions of galleries are taken over by flying buttresses, and a narrow triforium (still windowless) forms an inspection gallery. All this signifies the emergence of the Lanceolate style.

Gothic verticality reigns outside too, but the architect wisely kept two Romanesque masterworks, the Old Bell Tower (Clocher vieux) of 1145, a marvel of audacity and lightness, and the Royal Doorway, **Portail Royal**★★★, of the west front, with its long-bodied but intensely expressive sculpted figures.

The cathedral's interior is subtly lit by its superb stained glass (**vitraux**★★★) which covers a total area of 2 700m2 – 25 000sq ft and depicts 5 000 figures. Forty-five of the windows were donated by the city's guilds. Most of them date from the 12C and 13C and are the greatest achievement of this art form. "Chartres blue" is famous for its clarity and depth; its full range can best be seen in the wonderful Blue Madonna (Notre-Dame-de-la-Belle-Verrière) Window *(first window on the south side of the ambulatory)*. In 1964, the American Society of Architects gave a window (in the south transept) and in 1971 the German Friends of the Cathedral did likewise *(north transept)*.

◗◗ Musée des Beaux-Arts – **enamels**★ 🕐 *May-Oct: Mon, Wed-Sat 10am-noon, 2-6pm, Sun 2-6pm; Nov-Apr: Mon, Wed-Sat 10am-noon, 2-5pm, Sun 2-5pm.* 🕐 *Closed Tue, 1 Jan, 1 and 8 May, 1 and 11 Nov, 25 Dec.* ⊚ 2.45€. ☎ 02 37 36 41 39. **Église St-Pierre**★ – **stained glass**★.

Massif de La **CHARTREUSE**★★

MICHELIN MAP 333 H 5

GREEN GUIDE FRENCH ALPS

The relatively low, fir-clad Chartreuse upland is bounded by the narrow transverse valleys in which Grenoble and Chambéry are sited and by the Graisivaudan lowland. In appearance it is not unlike the subalpine country to the north, with its rugged summits and deep valleys formed from much folded and faulted beds of Jurassic limestone. It was in this isolated spot *(désert)* that St Bruno founded his monastery in 1084; it became the mother church of the celebrated Carthusian Order.

Sites

Charmant-Som★★★

🚶 *1hr30min round trip on foot*. Panorama taking in the Chamechaude peak, the Guiers-Mort valley and the site of the monastery in its deep valley.

Pas du Frou ★★

A deep ravine hollowed out by the Guiers-Vif.

Col du Granier ★★

This great rock-wall has been formed by erosion at the base of a syncline.

Bec du Margain★★

The summit of the Bec rises 820m – 2 700ft above the Graisivaudan, the best-known section of the Subalpine Trench which runs between the Central Alps and the Pre-Alps. First formed in ancient seas, then remodelled by the action of the glaciers and filled with the material brought down by the Isère, this busy valley is an important communication route. Its northwest flanks next to the Chartreuse are given over to farmland and vineyards, while the far side, under the shadow of the Belledonne, has a harsher, industrial character, with paper, chemical and engineering works and power stations. It was here, at Lancey, in 1891, that Aristide Berges converted the hydraulic installations of a paper-mill to the production of "white coal" – hydro-electric power. The **view** from here includes, from right to left, the Vercors, the Grandes Rousses, the Belledonne uplands, Mont-Blanc and the Bauges.

CHÂTILLON-SUR-SEINE★

POPULATION 6 862

MICHELIN MAP 320 H 2

GREEN GUIDE BURGUNDY JURA

Close to the Celtic oppidum on Mount Lassois near Vix (7km – 4.5mi north), Châtil-lon occupied a strategic location on the ancient north-south trade route. It was here that the Seine ceased to be navigable; as a result, the place developed all the facilities that transhipment needed, and grew prosperous on the merchandise being exchanged between Cornwall and Etruria – amber, tin, coral, ceramics.

Visit

Trésor de Vix★★

The first floor of the museum houses the treasure of Vix, grave goods found in the tomb of a 30-year-old queen who was buried at the very beginning of the 5C BC. They give some idea of the quality of material life of the élite of the time, who surrounded themselves with fine objects imported from Greece and Italy; the exhibits include a huge bronze vase, a masterpiece of Greek metalwork, Etruscan vases, gold jewellery (a diadem), and Gallic ironwork.

◖◗ **Source of the Douix★**.

Château de **CHENONCEAU**★★★

MICHELIN MAP 317 P 5

GREEN GUIDE CHÂTEAUX OF THE LOIRE

Chenonceau is a jewel of Renaissance architecture built 1513-21 on the site of a fortified mill on the River Cher by Thomas Bohier, François I's treasurer. It is a rectangular building with corner-towers; it stands on two piers of the former mill resting on the bed of the Cher. The library and the chapel are projecting structures to the left. Catherine de' Medici's two-storeyed gallery is built on the bridge spanning the river. This structure by Philibert Delorme has a Classical simplicity contrasting with the charming, ornate appearance of the older structure with its sculptures on the balustrades, roof and dormer windows.

A Bit of History

Over the years the place has been in the charge of six women, of whom three marked it strongly with their personality.

Catherine Briçonnet was the wife of Thomas Bohier. In his absence she supervised much of the building work. It is to her that we owe the central hall giving onto all the other rooms; its axial vault, broken by keystones, is a masterpiece. Another innova-tion is the introduction into the Loire Valley of an Italian staircase, that is, one that substitutes ramps for Gothic spirals, and is consequently much better adapted for receptions. However, here the returns are still curved and provided with steps.

In 1556 **Diane de Poitiers** commissioned Philibert Delorme, who had previously worked for her at Anet, to design the flower garden (*to the east*) as well as the bridge across the Cher.

Three years later, on the death of Henri II, **Catherine de' Medici** humiliated the former favourite by forcing her to exchange Chenonceau for Chaumont. Later, she added the two extra storeys to the bridge, laid out the gardens to the west and gave the windows their elaborate pediments.

Visit

🕐 *Mid-Mar to mid-Sep: daily 9am-7pm; mid to end Sep: daily 9am-6.30pm; early to mid-Mar and early to mid-Oct: daily 9am-6pm; mid to end Oct and mid to end Feb: daily 9am-5.30pm; early to mid-Feb and early to mid-Nov: daily 9am-5pm; mid-Nov to end Jan: daily 9am-4.30pm.* ∞ *9.50€ (children 7-18 years: 8€).* ☎ *08 20 20 90 90. www.chenonceau.com.*

There is much to see within the château; a fine fireplace by **Jean Goujon** (in the Salle Diane de Poitiers), the Library of 1521, the ceiling of the Green Cabinet (Cabinet Vert), the portrait of Diane by Primaticcio, the tapestries and mantelpiece of the Salon Louis XIV, a fine Renaissance creation with its wealth of scrolls, baskets of fruit, cornucopias and fantastic beasts.

Château de **CHEVERNY**★★★

MICHELIN MAP 318 F 7

GREEN GUIDE CHÂTEAUX OF THE LOIRE

Cheverny was built between 1604 and 1634 with that simplicity and distinction characteristic of the Classical architecture of the reigns of Henri IV and Louis XIII.

Visit

🕐 *Allow 45min. Jul-Aug: daily 9.15am-6.45pm; Apr-Jun and Sep: daily 9.15am-6.15pm; Oct and Mar: daily 9.15am-5pm; Nov-Feb: daily 9.45am-5pm; "feeding the dogs" early Apr to mid-Sep: daily 5pm; mid-Sep to end Mar: daily except Tue, Sat-Sun and public holidays 3pm.* ∞ *6.10€ (château and park), 10.50€ (château and permanent exhibit), 10.80€ (château and discovery of unusual sights in the park and canal).* ☎ *02 54 79 96 29. www.chateau-cheverny.com.*

Main façade, Château de Cheverny

Studio 3Bis/MICHELIN

The main façade is built in stone from **Bourré** *(28km – 17mi southwest)* which whitens and hardens with age. The elevation is strictly symmetrical, extending to either side of the well containing the staircase, and terminated by massive corner pavilions with square domes. The prominent slate roofs are in Louis XIII style, pierced with mansards and bull's-eye windows. The first-floor windows are crowned with scrolls; between them are medallions of Roman emperors (Julius Caesar in the central pediment). The elegant doorway is adorned with two concentric collars: outside, that of the Order of the Holy Ghost; inside, that of the Order of St Michael. The state rooms, served by a majestic Louis XIII ramped staircase with massive balustrades and rich sculptural decoration, contain a fine collection of furniture from the 17C to the 19C.

CHINON★★

POPULATION 8 627

MICHELIN MAP 317 J 5

GREEN GUIDE CHÂTEAUX OF THE LOIRE

Chinon occupies a sunny site on the Vienne surrounded by the fertile Veron countryside, and known for the mildness of its climate.

In 1494, **François Rabelais**, son of a Chinon lawyer, was born at La Devinière 8km – 5mi to the southwest. He studied medicine at Montpellier and then practised at Lyons. Under the guise of ribaldry, he imparted to the awakening middle classes a healthy contempt for pedantry and false culture, and a respect for a social morality founded on the rectitude of free and upright men.

Visit

Le Vieux Chinon★★

The old town, Joan of Arc's Ville-Fort (fortified town) has kept its medieval and Renaissance appearance. The old gabled houses with corner turrets and the 16C and 17C mansions, most of them in white tufa, make up a most evocative townscape.

The main axis is formed by the Rue Voltaire, formerly Haute-St-Maurice. Along it are ranged: the Gothic dwelling where Richard the Lionheart is supposed to have died in 1199 and where the States-General assembled in 1421 (now the museum); the Hôtel du Gouvernement with 17C arcades in its courtyard; the Palais du Bailliage; and the 16C Hôtel Poirier de Beauvais.

At the crossroads **(Grand Carroi★★)** the oldest houses of all press closely together. On her arrival from Vaucouleurs on Sunday 6 March 1429, **Joan of Arc** is thought to have used the coping of the well-head here to dismount from her horse. The following day she picked out the Dauphin hiding among his courtiers, and declared, "You are the heir of France and true son of the king, Lieutenant of the King of Heaven who is King of France", a touching scene calculated to still the Dauphin's worries about his legitimacy. From here, Joan was sent to Poitiers. Back in Chinon again, she was equipped and given a troop of soldiers and sallied forth to meet her extraordinary and tragic destiny.

Château★★

🕑 *Apr-Sep: daily 9am-7pm; Oct-Mar: daily 9.30am-5pm.* 🕑 *Closed 1 Jan and 25 Dec.* 💷 *6€ (12-18 years: 4.50€).* ☎ *02 47 93 13 45.*

The spur overlooking the town was the site of a Gallic oppidum, then of a fortress, long before Henry II of England (born at Le Mans in 1133) built the present castle to protect Anjou from Capetian designs. The castle was taken by Philippe Auguste in 1205 from John Lackland; it subsequently became a royal residence, was strengthened by Charles VII, but then abandoned by the court at the end of the 15C and gradually dismantled.

It was in the castle that the first meeting took place between Charles VII and Joan of Arc, here too that Agnes Sorel stayed, and here that the leading Templars were imprisoned in 1308. On 10 December 1498 the Papal legate Ludovico Borgia came to the castle to hand Louis XII the Bull annulling his marriage to Joan of France, thereby allowing him to marry Anne of Brittany.

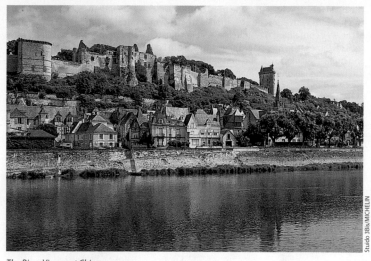

The River Vienne at Chinon

The remains of the castle include, to the east, St George's Fort (Fort St-Georges), watching over the most vulnerable approach, the Middle Castle (Château du Milieu), which has a 14C clock tower, the royal apartments and gardens giving a fine view over the old town, and finally the Coudray Fort (Fort de Coudray) at the far end of the spur.

Excursions

Champigny-sur-Veude★

15km – 9mi south. Erected in the first half of the 16C by Louis of Bourbon and his son, the château of Champigny was demolished in 1635 on the orders of Richelieu, who felt that it might outshine his own pile, then a-building not far away. It was used by him as a source of materials, and today only some outbuildings and the chapel remain.

Sainte-Chapelle★

With its two side galleries the St Louis Chapel is a jewel of Renaissance architecture. Toussaint Chesneau's splendid porch of 1570 has antique scrolls, strapwork and pilasters, as well as a terrace, the whole treated in a manner which anticipates Classicism.

The chapel is lit by splendid Renaissance stained glass (**vitraux★★**) of 1538-61, attributed to the brothers Pinaigrier, master craftsmen of Tours, trained in the school of Jean Fouquet and Bourdichon. Some of the glass may be from a Bourbonnais workshop. The subjects represented include 34 portraits of the Bourbon-Montpensier family, episodes from the life of Louis IX, and scenes of the Passion. The lustre of the glass, above all of the Prussian blues with a hint of reddish-browns, has no equal.

Richelieu★

25km – 15.5mi south. The town built for Cardinal Richelieu by Lemercier (1631-42) is a rare example of Classical town planning. Little remains of Richelieu's great château planned as the centrepiece of the vast park.

Musée de l'hôtel de ville. *Jul and Aug: guided tours (30 min) 10am-noon, 2-6pm; Jan-Jun and Sep-Dec: daily except Tue, Sat-Sun and public holidays 10am-noon, 2-6pm. 2€ museum and park. 03 47 58 10 13.* Steam railway (between Chinon and Richelieu). *Jul and Aug: Sat-Sun. Ask for information on departure times. 9.15€ return (from Richelieu to Ligré-Rivière). 02 47 58 12 97.*

CLERMONT-FERRAND★★

POPULATION 254 416

MICHELIN MAP 326 E-G 7-10

GREEN GUIDE AUVERGNE THE RHÔNE VALLEY

The site★★ of Clermont is unique; the old town, including the cathedral, is built on and from a volcano, whose black lava makes for an unusual townscape. To the north are the plateaux of Chanturgue and Les Côtes, once the site of a Gallic oppidum, and an example of the phenomenon known as relief inversion which has protected them from erosion and left them standing out from the surrounding country. To the west are the summits of the Puys, the mountain range which gives Clermont its incomparable setting, perhaps best viewed from the Place de la Poterne with its pretty fountain (**Fontaine d'Amboise**★) of 1515.

▶ **Orient Yourself:** Clermont-Ferrand, which is listed as a "Town of Art and History," offers 2hr discovery tours of Clermont from early Jul to mid-Sep on Mon, Wed, and Fri at 3pm, and on Tue and Thur at 8.30pm. Tours of Montferrand are on Tue, Thurs and Sat at 3pm. There are also theme tours, possibilities for a Sun visit to a museum or special temporary exhibits, and excursions. The cost is 5.70€. Check the tourist office or on www.clermont-fd.com for more information.

A Bit of History

Vercingétorix – By 58 BC, the security of the Roman Empire was no longer adequately secured simply by the possession of Gallia Narbonensis (corresponding roughly to modern Provence); all Gaul, with its agricultural produce and its trade routes for tin and amber, was to be the prize. Julius Caesar grasped at it, eager for glory, and, in the March of 52 BC marched his legions up to the gates of the great oppidum of the Arverni (the Celts who gave their name to the Auvergne). But within the space of a few days he met with a surprising defeat, which forced him to retreat through Berry, Burgundy and the Jura towards Italy. The victor of this encounter was the Gallic chieftain Vercingétorix (72-46 BC), whose spirited equestrian statue by Bartholdi stands at one end of Clermont's Place de Jaude. Before the summer was over, however, Caesar returned, this time winning a decisive battle, the site of which is still not certain. Vercingétorix had to wait six years in the Mamertine prison in Rome for execution of the sentence of death by strangulation meted out to him by Caesar.

D. Goudouneix/Explorer

Notre-Dame Cathedral in the old town centre

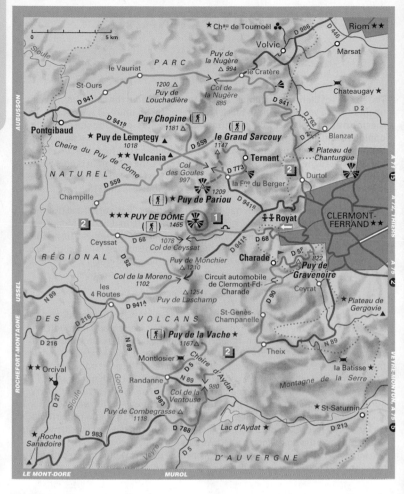

The First Crusade – On 28 November 1095 Pope Urban II, a former Clunaic monk, closed the Synod which had been held here at Clermont because of the stable conditions prevailing in the province. In the presence of a great crowd of archbishops, bishops, abbots, barons, knights and common people, he called for the reconquest of the Holy Land. Over the century following the Frankish, Norman and Danish invasions, the population of the Auvergne had grown to such an extent that the province could afford to see so many ardent crusaders depart with the ringing cry "It is God's will!" (*Dieu le veut!*); countless of them were to perish before Godfrey of Bouillon succeeded in taking Jerusalem three years later.

Blaise Pascal – To the southwest of the cathedral a slab marks the birthplace of this writer and thinker of genius, a man whose temperament made him quite unable to accept received ideas.

Though he was in poor health, his acute intelligence and interest in science showed itself at an early age; at 11 he was studying the laws of acoustics; at 12 he rediscovered, on his own, Euclid's 32nd proposition; at 16 he wrote his essay on conics which astounded Fermat and Descartes among others, and at 19 he invented an adding machine (*on display in Musée du Ranquet*). Subsequently he developed the idea of a hydraulic press, formulated the principle of hydrostatics and anticipated the probability theory.

At 33, after a mystical experience two years previously, he put his literary talents to work in the service of Jansenism. At 34, he wrote his Thoughts (*Pensées*) which has been called the greatest literary work in French of the 17C.

"The heart has its reasons that reason knows not" Blaise Pascal 1623-62.

28 September 1665 – 30 January 1666 (Les Grands Jours d'Auvergne) – Far removed from the seat of government, the feudal lords of the Auvergne had become

The Capital of the Motor Tyre

Two men, Aristide Barbier and Édouard Daubrée came together around 1830 to make agricultural machinery as well as gunshot, and rubber belts and tubes. In 1889, their factory was taken over by the brothers **André** and **Édouard Michelin**, the grandsons of Barbier. Building on their tradition of applying scientific method to the work of industry, the company has subsequently flourished through study of the client's real needs, scrupulous observation of reality and the consolidation of previous experience. This process has led via the detachable bicycle tyre of 1891, the car tyre of 1895, the low

pressure "Confort" tyre of 1923, the "Metalic" of 1937 (its steel-reinforced casing helped heavy road transport come of age), the radial tyre of 1946 (given the designation "X" in 1949), to today's achievements, with the introduction in the early 1990's of the new Michelin Energy tyre. This new "green" tyre technology – based on reduced rolling resistance – will enable the driver to make considerable savings on fuel.

PARIS-BORDEAUX 1895 · Ire VOITURE sur PNEUS MICHELIN · MICHELIN

petty tyrants, putting down the periodic peasant revolts with great ferocity. To overcome this lack of discipline, the king's commissioners arrived in Clermont on 28 September 1665 with full powers to deal with the situation and assert royal authority. 1 360 files were opened, but since the local nobility had fled to a man as soon as the first execution had taken place, most sentences were carried out in absentia, and effigies hanged in batches of 30. There was much rejoicing, restitution of confiscated property, and razing of castles which had escaped Richelieu's attention 40 years earlier. The power of the state and the force of the king's laws now prevailed throughout the land.

Sights

Basilique Notre-Dame du Port★★

See Introduction: Art – Architecture. This is the finest of the larger Romanesque churches of the Lower Auvergne, unforgettable in its beautiful simplicity. It was built around 1150 over a crypt of the 11C. Its south doorway differs from those of Quercy and Burgundy in the clear differentiation of its subjects, in spite of their having suffered damage. To the left of the door stands the figure of Isaiah, to the right that of John the Baptist. In the typically Auvergnat five-sided lintel is a highly-controlled, hierarchical composition, and above that, in the tympanum, a *Christ in Majesty* flanked by Seraphim. The south side of the building is also characteristic of the Romanesque style of the Auvergne, with its great buttressing arches, the three-bayed blind arcading and the polychrome stonework adorning the transept. The east end was much restored in the 19C.

Inside, both the structure itself and the materials from which it is built confirm the impression of robustness. The great arches at the crossing, though descended from the masterworks of Carolingian times, surpass them greatly in scale. Relieved by short arcades and patterned stonework, the high cross-walls support the splendid dome on pendentives, best seen from the steps up to the ambulatory.

The small, raised chancel (**chœur★★★**), admirably proportioned, is divided from the ambulatory by eight slender columns; their capitals (**chapiteaux★★**), together with those of the wall of the ambulatory, are among the finest in Auvergne because of their good state of preservation, their fascinating subjects, and their expressiveness.

In the crypt is an ancient, possibly Celto-Gallic well, together with a Black Virgin, a copy of a Byzantine icon, which has been worshipped here since the 13C.

Rue Pascal

Lined with lava-built residences of somewhat severe aspect, this is one of the typical streets of the old town (**Vieux Clermont★★**). No 22 has a façade in rusticated stone and a wrought-iron balcony, and a lava-patterned rose on the floor of the hall. No 4 (Hôtel de Chazerat) has an oval courtyard with Ionic pilasters. In the Place du Terrail is a pretty 17C fountain.

Cathédrale Notre-Dame-de-l'Assomption★★

The visitor coming here from Notre-Dame-du-Port is immediately struck by the revolutionary changes in architectural style which had occurred in the relatively short period of 100 years which separates the two buildings. The cathedral was begun in 1248 by Jean Deschamps, something along the lines of the new cathedrals of the north of France and recalling the High Gothic style. It symbolises the extension of Capetian power into the Auvergne. It has unusual terraces which hide the ambulatory and is built in sombre Volvic lava – its strength allowed the pillars to be more slender than usual. The west front, spires and first two bays of the nave are the work of **Viollet-le-Duc** in 1865.

The stained-glass medallions (**vitraux**★★) of the 12C-15C are copies of those in the Sainte-Chapelle in Paris. The warm tones of red and violet in the rose windows of the transepts are particularly striking. The **Treasury**★ (◷ *early Jul to mid-Sep: Mon-Sat 2.30-5pm;* ◷ *closed Sun, Mon, 14 Jul and 15 Aug;* ☎ *04 73 92 46 61)* displays 12C-19C collections of gold, silver and enamel ware.

A chapel (Chapelle St-Georges – *first chapel left in the ambulatory*) has a wall-painting showing a frieze of animals and the martyrdom of this patron saint of crusaders. In the axial chapel is a Romanesque Madonna, contemporary with those of Marsat and Orcival, and probably the descendant of the 10C Golden Madonna of Stephen II which was destroyed at the time of the French Revolution.

◖◗ **Vieux Montferrand**★★ (old town). **Musée d'Art Roger-Quilliot**★★ ◷ *Tue-Sun 10am-6pm.* ◷ *Closed Mon, 1 Jan, 1 May, 1 Nov, 25 Dec.* ⬯ *4€, no charge 1st Sun in the month.* ☎ *04 73 16 11 30.* **Église St-Léger**★ (fortified church at Royat).

CLUNY★★

POPULATION 4 430

MICHELIN MAP 320 H 11

GREEN GUIDE BURGUNDY JURA

The conditions for the future renown and prosperity of the great **Abbaye de Cluny**★★ existed at the very moment of its foundation.

A Bit of History

The abbey, founded in 910, lay deep in the forests of this frontier zone, far removed from the centres of power in either France or Germany; to the west the Carolingian king of France, Charles III, was absorbed by problems with Norse invaders; to the east, Ludwig IV was still an inexperienced adolescent, much weakened by rivalries between his barons and by troublesome Hungarians and Norsemen. The abbey's independence was absolute; it was subject to no authority other than that of the Pope himself; at the time when the great feudal estates were being broken up and seigneurial rights were crumbling, it answered – like its daughter houses and other dependencies – to no one but its elected abbot. In an unstable and entirely unscrupulous world, it represented in exemplary fashion the ascetic ideals of St Benedict. It thus became a powerful instrument for the Papacy in its own domains, in the struggle to maintain its authority in the face of the barons of Latium and in its ambitions for the reform of the Church.

Cluny's development was rapid, its prestige immense, and its influence pre-eminent at the very moment when Western culture was taking shape. In under a century, the abbey had amassed considerable political power as well as much property; already there were 1 184 daughter and dependent houses grouped in "provinces", but organised in a strictly hierarchical fashion. One hundred and fifty years later their numbers had risen to 3 000, scattered all over Europe. For two and a half centuries this capital of monasticism found leaders of exceptional calibre (St Mayeul, St Hugh, Peter the Venerable), some of whom ruled for a fruitful term of up to 60 years.

The government of such an empire was not of course without problems of conformity to its Rule and to its ideal of poverty. The fight against temptation required qualities of intellect and will compared with which the struggle against external threats was but a minor affair. The decline of the order began in the 13C, but its prosperity lasted until the 18C.

Sights

ÉGLISE ABBATIALE

The abbey church, started by St Hugh in 1088, was completed in 1130 under Peter the Venerable. Its destruction was begun in 1798 and continued until 1823. All that remains of the narthex are the lower parts of two towers; of the nave and its aisles, nothing at all; of the five bell-towers, the one known as "the Holy Water" (**Eau bénite★★**), a superb octagon, and another known as the Clock Tower (Tour de l'Horloge); of the great transept, the south arm with its two chapels and an octagonal vault (32m – 105ft high); of the minor transept, the chapel (Chapelle de Bourbon) with sculpted heads of the Prophets.

Bâtiments abbatiaux

The abbey buildings were rebuilt in the 18C.

Farinier

Reduced in height in the 18C. The flour store has a fine timber roof (13C) built like the hull of a boat, and eight capitals from the abbey.

 **Musée Ochier★** – sculpture.

Excursion

Château de Cormatin★★

13km – 8mi north. ⏱ 🚶 *Guided tours (45min) early Apr to end May: 10am-noon, 2-5.30pm (Jun-Sep: 6.30pm), mid-Jul to mid-Aug: 10am-6.30pm). The park is open to the public even when the château is closed.* 🎫 *6.50€.* ☏ *03 85 50 16 55. The château (4km – 2.5mi north of Taizé), probably built by Jacques II Androuet du Cerceau, is a good example of the Henri IV style (late 16C-early 17C): the monumental gates framed by antique orders, the basement built of stone and the windows decorated with mouldings. The mannerist style which evolved in the literary salons under Louis XIII (1610-43) reached its peak with the gilding and the lapis-lazuli decoration of the St Cecilia Room* (**Cabinet Ste-Cécile★★★**).

COGNAC★

POPULATION 19 528

MICHELIN MAP 324 I 5

GREEN GUIDE ATLANTIC COAST

For many years Cognac was a river port on the calm waters of the Charente, exporting salt – the best in the world, so said the Scandinavians – and, from the 11C, wine. In 1570, it was one of the four strongholds conceded to the Protestants under the Treaty of St-Germain.

A Bit of History

Cognac

The Ancients were fully aware of the properties of alcohol. It was studied in 1250 by Arnaud de Villeneuve who attributed quasi-miraculous powers to it. Of all the different kinds of spirit, it is cognac which has acquired a universal reputation. It was early in the 17C that the local vintners started to distil those of their wines that travelled badly, in order to help turnover, reduce excise dues and facilitate storage. The taste for the product spread first to Holland, Scandinavia and of course the British Isles, whose long association with brandy is reflected in some of the great names of Cognac, Hine, Martell, Hennessy.

A century later the accumulated stock became the subject of speculation. In addition, it was realised that ageing improved the quality of the spirit.

Cognac was first divided into regions in 1887; today they comprise Grande Champagne, Petite Champagne, Borderies, Fins Bois, Bons Bois and Bois Ordinaires, reflecting, in that order, a decreasing proportion of chalk in the soil, an increasing earthiness of the – *goût de terroir* – and ability to mature rapidly.

The production of cognac is the result of a two-stage distillation process, using the special still of the region. The 90 000ha – 220 000 acres of vineyards yield a white wine which is light, flowery and quite acid; it takes nine litres of it to make one of brandy. It is then kept in barrels made of porous oak from the Limoges district for at least two and a half years, during which time the brandy absorbs tannin and resins from the wood, and oxygen from the atmosphere, to which it loses 2 1/2% of its volume per annum – the "angels' portion", equivalent to 2 million bottles a year!

The making of cognac has given rise to a very distinct way of life. People here have a fine sense of irony and a love of independence which has expressed itself in revolts against salt-tax, in peasant rebellions at the time of Louis XIV and in the disturbances of the Wars of Religion; the chais where the cognac is stored, is the repository of the greater part of a family's savings.

Sights

Quartier Ancien
In the streets of the old part of the town on the west bank are a number of fascinating buildings. The Grande-Rue has a fine half-timbered example dating from the 15C, the Rue Saulnier a number of 16C houses with rusticated stonework and elaborate doorways and windows, while in the Rue de l'Île d'Or is the Hôtel de l'Échevinage (House of the Magistrates), distinguished by its corner niches.

The château was rebuilt by John the Good in 1450; its riverside façade has an austere air, enlivened somewhat by the King's Balcony of 1515, a grand loggia resting on a bracket carved in the shape of a salamander, the emblem of François I who was born here in 1494.

Les chais
All tours are guided (45min-1hr30min).
The cellars and storerooms (chais) spread out along the riverside quays, near the port and in the suburbs, house the casks in which the slow alchemy between spirit and oak occurs, bestowing its distinctive subtlety to the brandy of Cognac.

Hennessy
Guided tours (1hr15min) Jun-Sep: daily 10am-6pm; Mar-May and Oct-Dec: daily 10am-5pm; Closed 1 May. 6€ (under 16 years: no charge). ☎ 05 45 35 72 68. www.hennessy.com.
The business was founded in 1765 by a captain of Irish origin serving in Louis XV's Irish Brigade. His descendants still head the company today. A Cooperage Museum (Musée de la Tonnellerie) is devoted to the manufacture of brandy casks by craftsmen.

Rémy Martin
Guided tours by train (1hr30min) Jul-Aug: daily 10am-5.30pm; Apr-Jun and Sep-Oct: daily 10-11am, 1.30-4.30pm. Closed 1 May. Reservations recommended. 5€. ☎ 05 45 35 76 66. www.remy.com.
The distillery, founded in 1724, creates its cognac exclusively from the prestigious Grande Champagne and Petite Champagne vintages. A little train takes visitors on a tour of the plant.

Martell
Guided tours (1hr) Apr-Oct: 9.30am-5pm, Sat-Sun and public holidays 11am-5pm. 4€. ☎ 05 45 36 34 98. www.visitez-martell.com.
Founded in 1715 it is the oldest of the famous cognac distilleries. Three rooms of the founder's residence have been restored and convey the working environment of an entrepreneur in the early 18C.
Other cognac houses open their cellars to visitors: Camus, Otard, Prince Hubert de Polignac.

Musée du Cognac. – *Jun-Sep: daily except Tue 10am-noon, 2-6pm; Oct-May: daily except Tue 2-5.30pm. Closed 1 Jan, 1 and 8 May, Ascension, 14 Jul, 15 Aug, 1 and 11 Nov, 25 Dec. 2.20€. ☎ 05 45 32 07 25.*

COLLONGES-LA-ROUGE★★

POPULATION 379

MICHELIN MAP 329 K 5

GREEN GUIDE DORDOGNE BERRY LIMOUSIN

Collonges-la-Rouge boasts mansions, old houses and a Romanesque church built of red sandstone; rabbits thrive in the surrounding countryside dotted with nut orchards and vineyards. In the 13C the original simple village was granted franchises and other privileges by the county of Turenne. Later in the 16C it became a holiday centre favoured by the county dignitaries who built charming mansions and residences flanked by towers and turrets which give Collonges its special character.

Visit

The exclusive use of the traditional building stone and the balanced proportions of the various structures give a harmonious character to the town.

Some are of special interest: the **Maison de la Sirène** (🕐 *Easter to All Saints: 10am-noon, 3-6pm; ✆ 2€; contact Mme Foucher ☎ 05 55 84 08 03*) with an elegant carved porch; the imposing mansion **Hôtel des Ramades de Friac;** the **Château de Benge;** and the elegant **Castel de Vassinhac★** bristling with massive towers and pepperpot turrets.

Église

The church dates back to the 11C and 12C; it was fortified in the 16C during the Wars of Religion. The tympanum **(tympan★)** carved from the local white limestone is an unusual feature of this structure built of red sandstone. The bell-tower **(clocher★)** is a fine example of the Limousin Romanesque style.

COLMAR★★★

POPULATION 83 816

MICHELIN MAP 315 I 8

GREEN GUIDE ALSACE LORRAINE CHAMPAGNE

The capital of Upper Alsace is situated at the point where the Munster valley widens out into the broad plain of the Rhine. Since the 13C the town has prospered on the proceeds of the wine trade and boasts fine monuments. More recently, industries have spread along the Logelbach Canal.

▶ **Orient Yourself:** Locate the center of the Old Town at the Place de l'Ancienne Douane. The museum lies to your north, while south along the rue des Tanneurs you'll find picturesque flower-decked houses lining the canal of "Little Venice."

🅰 **Don't Miss:** The **Retable d'Issenheim**, the 16C masterpiece of **Matthias Grünewald** on display at the Musée Unterlinden.

Ⓚⓘⓓⓢ **Especially For Kids: Musée animé du Jouet et des Petits Trains** is housed in a former cinema, and its collections include numerous railway engines, trains, and dolls in many different materials (♿ 🕐 *Jul-Sep: daily 9am-6pm; Oct-Jun: daily except Tue 10am-noon, 2-6pm; last admission 30min before closing; 🕐 closed 10 days in Jan, 1 Jan, 1 May, 1 Nov and 25 Dec; 4€; ☎ 03 89 41 93 10*).

A Bit of History

In 1834 **Frédéric Bartholdi** was born here, the patriotic sculptor responsible not only for such striking achievements as the Lion of Belfort or the figure of General ▪pp here in Colmar, but also for the Statue of Liberty.

▪ween 1871-1918, when Alsace and Lorraine formed part of the German Reich, ▪town distinguished itself by its obstinate Frenchness. A particular irritant to ▪rity was the Colmar writer and caricaturist Jean-Jacques Waltz (1872-1951), ▪ as "Hansi", who was imprisoned at the outbreak of war in 1914, but escaped ▪ in the French army.

Colmar - Address Book

PRACTICAL INFORMATION

Tourist office – *4 r. des Hunterlinden,* ☏ *03 89 20 68 92, www.ot-colmar.fr*

Guided Tours – 🚶 Tours of the old town are organised from Jul-Sep. €4. Enquire at the tourist office.

Colmar by Night – The town's most beautiful buildings are lit up at night. *May-Sep, Sat evenings.* Christmas show: *late Nov-late Dec, Tue, Thu, Fri and Sat. Departures from tourist office, 7pm (1hr 15min).* €4.

Tourist Train – *Easter-Nov 1: commentary, departures every 30min Quai de la Sinn (opposite Unterlinden Museum), 9am-noon and 1.30-6pm,* €5.50 (2-12 year olds: €3). ☏ *03 89 24 19 82.*

Boat Trips – 🚤 *See Little Venice.*

For coin ranges, see the Legend at the back of the guide.

WHERE TO EAT

🍽 **Winstub La Krutenau** – *1 r. de la Poissonnerie –* ☏ *03 89 41 18 80 –* 🕐 *closed Christmas to end Jan, Sun and Mon out of season .* At this winstub beside the River Lauch you can go boating in Little Venice and eat a *flammekueche* on the flower-decked terrace beside the canal in summer. A fun way, with no obligations, to learn about this lovely part of Colmar – recommended.

🍽 **Le Caveau St-Pierre** – *24 r. de la Herse (Little Venice) –* ☏ *03 89 41 99 33 – michel. francois@caveaustpierre.com –* 🕐 *closed in Jan – booking advisable.* A pretty wooden footbridge across the Lauch leads to this 17C house, which offers a little slice of paradise with its rustic, local-style decor and a terrace stretching out over the water. Local cuisine.

🍽 **Schwendi Bier-U-Wistub** – *23-25 Grand'Rue –* ☏ *03 89 23 66 26 –* 🕐 *closed evenings on Christmas and New Year's Day.* You will instantly warm to this charming winstub with its ideal location in the heart of old Colmar. The principally wooden decor and the cooking, which is good quality and served in generous portions, are a tribute to Alsace. Huge terrace to be enjoyed in summer.

🍽 **La Maison Rouge** – *9 rue des Écoles –* ☏ *03 89 23 53 22 –* 🕐 *closed Sun.* The somewhat ordinary façade hides a delightful rustic interior. Regional and home-made cooking take pride of place.

🍽🍽 **Chez Bacchus** – *2 Grand'Rue – 68230 Katzenthal – 5km/3mi NW of Colmar, Kaysersberg direction, then D 10 –* ☏ *03 89 27 32 25 –* 🕐 *closed 7-31 Jan, 1 week in Jul and in Nov, open Thu-Sat evening from 1 Oct-14 Jul, Sun and 15 Jul-30 Sep every evening except Tue – booking advisable at weekends.* There's a lovely friendly atmosphere in this wine bar dating from 1789 in a winemaking village. Massive

exposed beams and helpings of Alsatian cuisine to match – guaranteed to satisfy the healthiest of appetites. Automated puppets will entertain the children with a lively show.

🍽🍽 **Winstub Brenner** – *1 r. de Turenne –* ☏ *03 89 41 42 33 –* 🕐 *closed 17 Feb-3 Mar, 23 Jun-3 Jul, 17-26 No, 24 Dec- 2 Jan, Tue and Wed.* The terrace by the Lauch in Little Venice is very popular on fine days. Not surprising, as the setting is ideal and the food, though simple, is served in generous portions. The whole of Colmar meets here with obvious enjoyment.

WHERE TO STAY

🏨 **Colbert** – *2 r. des Trois-Épis –* ☏ *03 89 31 05 - 50 rooms -* 🍴 €6. This functional hotel near the station provides a comfortable place to stay for those travelling by train. The rooms are well equipped with new bedding, effective soundproofing and air conditioning, and some have a balcony. Bar and disco for those in search of nightlife.

🏨 **Chambre d'hôte Les Framboises** – *128 r. des Trois-Épis – 68230 Katzenthal – 5km/3mi NW of Colmar, Kaysersberg direction then D 10 –* ☏ *03 89 27 48 85 – sarl.amrein@wanadoo.fr – 4 rooms.* Leave Colmar behind and head for the open countryside and this village among the vines. The proprietor distils his own *marc* (grape brandy) from Gewürztraminer and provides accommodation in wood-panelled attic rooms. Don't miss the puppet show in the mornings!

🏨🏨 **Hôtel Au Moulin** – *Rte d'Herrlisheim – 68127 Ste-Croix-en-Plaine – 10km/6.2mi S of Colmar on A 35 and D 1 –* ☏ *03 89 49 31 20 –* 🕐 *closed 5 Nov-31 Mar –* 🅿 *– 17 rooms -* 🍴 €8. This old mill deep in the country is perfect for those seeking peace and quiet. Its spacious rooms are all the same but nicely arranged. A small museum of old local objects has been created in a neighbouring building.

🏨🏨 **Hôtel Turenne** – *10 rte de Bâle –* ☏ *03 89 41 12 26 – helmlinger@turenne. com – 82 rooms -* 🍴 €7.50. On the edge of the old town, this hotel occupies a large, pleasing building with a pink and yellow façade. Its rooms have been nicely renovated and are well soundproofed. A few small but neat and reasonably priced single rooms are available.

🏨🏨🏨 **Hôtel Le Colombier** – *7 r. de Turenne –* ☏ *03 89 23 96 00 – info@hotel-le-colombier.com –* 🕐 *closed Christmas holidays – 24 rooms -* 🍴 €10. This lovely 15C house in old Colmar combines old stone and contemporary decor by retaining elements from its past, such as the superb Renaissance staircase. Contemporary furniture, modern paintings and carefully arranged room

ON THE TOWN

La Manufacture – *6 rte d'Ingersheim* - ☎ *03 89 24 31 78*. Programme of contemporary theatre, as well as music and dance.

Folk nights – *Pl. de l'Ancienne Douane* – 🕑 *May-Sep: Tue at 8.30pm*.

Théâtre municipal – *Pl. du 18-Novembre* - ☎ *03 89 20 29 01. culture@ville-colmar.com*. Classic plays, comedy and opera.

SHOPPING

Domaine viticole de la Ville de Colmar – *2 r. Stauffen* – ☎ *03 89 79 11 87* – *www.domaineviticolecolmar.com* – 🕑 *Mon-Fri 9.30am-12.30pm, 2-6pm, Sat 9am-noon*. Founded in 1895, this estate grows seven *cépages* and boasts a host of *grands crus* in addition to sparkling wines.

Caveau Robert-Karcher – *11 r. de l'Ours* – ☎ *03 89 41 14 42* – *www.vins-karcher.com* – 🕑 *daily 8am-noon, 1.30-7pm* – 🕑 *closed Sun afternoon, Good Friday, Easter, Christmas Day and Boxing Day*. The vineyards of this family business are north-west of Colmar, but the cellar, dating from 1602, is in a pedestrian street in the town centre. You can taste the whole range of Alsace wines and be shown around the cellar.

Fortwenger – *32 r. des Marchands* – ☎ *03 89 41 06 93* – *www.fortwenger.fr* – 🕑 *Mon-Fri 9.30am-12.30pm, 1.30-7pm, Sat 9.30am-12.30pm, 1.30-6.30pm, Sun 10am-12.30pm, 1.30-6pm*. It was in Gertwiller in 1768 that Charles Fortwenger founded his gingerbread factory, but this Colmar shop sells a wide range of delicious products, made with chocolate, honey, icing sugar, aniseed and cinnamon.

Maison des Vins d'Alsace – *Civa – 12 av. de la Foire-aux-Vins – BP1217* – ☎ *03 89 20 16 20* – *www.vinsalsace.com* – 🕑 *Mon-Fri 9am-noon, 2-5pm* – 🕑 *closed from Christmas to New Year's Day*. Five important local organisations concerned with Alsace wines are based in this centre. The visitor can study a map six metres (nearly 20 feet) long, showing all the winemaking villages and grands crus, as well as learn about the process of winemaking from hands-on models and a film.

The Colmar Pocket – In early February 1945 the French army under General de Lattre de Tassigny launched a pincer attack on Colmar to eliminate pockets of German resistance. On 1 February the German lines north of Colmar were overrun by American infantry troops; the following day the latter gave precedence to the French 5th armoured division of General Schlesser to enter Colmar.

Visit

Musée Unterlinden★★★

🕑 *May-Oct: daily 9am-6pm; Nov-Apr: daily except Tue 9-noon, 2-5pm*. 🕑 *Closed 1 Jan, 1 May, 1 Nov, 25 Dec*. ∞ *7€ (ages 12-17: 5€)*. ☎ *03 89 20 15 50. www.musee-unterlinden. com*

It is housed in a former 13C monastery. The ground floor is devoted to religious art and presents rich collections of paintings and sculpture dating from the late Middle Ages and the Renaissance.

GIRAUDON

Issenheim Altarpiece (central section)

Retable d'Issenheim★★★

In the chapel. In 1512 **Matthias Grünewald** was called to Issenheim 22km – 14mi south of Colmar to paint the **Issenheim altarpiece** for the chapel of the Antonite convent. This extraordinary work should be seen, not as a collection of separate masterpieces, but as an integrated whole, conceived and executed as a programme whose logic, while still puzzling to the specialist of today, probably lies in the convent superior's particular vision of the meaning of suffering. Everything contributes to the overall effect, not only the choice of themes and their relationship to one another, but also the pose and expression of the figures, the symbolic meaning of the various themes, animals and monsters, and even the use of colour. Note for example the figure of Mary Magdalene at the foot of the cross; her pose conveys both the attraction exercised over her by the figure of Christ as well as the revulsion she feels in the face of His agony. Note too the way contrast is handled, with the generally gloomy tone of the paintings shot through with flashes of light.

Grünewald's stature as one of the truly great masters of Western religious painting is fully revealed in the central panel of the altarpiece, the harrowing Crucifixion.

Ville Ancienne★★

The heart of the old town comprises the Place de l'Ancienne Douane, Rue des Marchands and Rue Mercière (Haberdasher Street). There are many picturesque old houses, with corner turrets, oriel windows and half-timbering, and balconies gay with flowers. Particularly striking are the **Maison Pfister★★**, with frescoes and medallions and a pyramidal roof, and the Old Customs House, **Ancienne Douane★** of 1480 with a timber gallery and canted staircase tower.

◐◐ **Église des Dominicains** ◔ *Apr-Dec: 10am-1pm, 3-6pm.* ⊜ *1.30€ (children 0.50€)* – **stained glass★** and **Virgin in the Rose Bower★★**. **Ancien Corps de Garde★** (Old Guard House). **"Little Venice"★**. **Maison des Têtes★**. Église St-Matthieu *Call in advance for guided tour.* ☎ *03 89 41 44 96* – **Crucifixion window★**.

COLOMBEY-LES-DEUX-ÉGLISES

POPULATION 660

MICHELIN MAP 313 J 4-5

GREEN GUIDE ALSACE LORRAINE CHAMPAGNE

Situated in the far south of Champagne on the borders of Burgundy and Lorraine, Colombey owes its fame to **General de Gaulle**. This great Frenchman was born in Lille in 1890; in 1933 he bought the country house here known as La Boisserie (now a museum – *musée*). Having withdrawn from affairs of state in 1969, he died here on 9 November 1970.

Visit

♿ ◔ *Mid-Apr to mid-Oct: daily 10am-12.30pm, 2-6.15pm, Sun 10am-6.15pm. Mid-Oct to Mid-Apr: 10am-12.30pm, 2-4.45pm. Possibilty of a guided tour (1hr).* ◔ *Closed Jan and Dec.* ⊜ *4€ (children under 12 years: no charge)* ☎ *03 25 01 52 52.*
Both the Memorial, a great cross of Lorraine dominating the village, and the general's tomb have become places of pilgrimage.

COMPIÈGNE★★★

POPULATION 57 057

MICHELIN MAP 305 H 4

GREEN GUIDE NORTHERN FRANCE AND THE PARIS REGION

The site of Compiègne had been appreciated by the Merovingians, long before Charles the Bald built a château here in the 9C. A fortified town grew up around this nucleus. In 1429, Philippe le Bon (the Good), Duke of Burgundy, had designs on

Château de Pierrefonds

Picardy, which he hoped to incorporate into his realm by means of a joint operation with the English. The French line of defence along the Oise was reinforced on the orders of Joan of Arc; disgusted with the inertia prevailing at Sully-sur-Loire where the French Court had established itself, she had come to Compiègne on her own initiative. But on the evening of 23 May 1430, she was seized by the Burgundians. Wary of possible consequences, Philip the Good sold her on to the English; one year later she was burnt at the stake in Rouen.

▸ **Orient Yourself:** Compiègne, which is listed as a "Town of Art and History," offers discovery tours from mid-May to mid-Jul and mid-Aug to mid-Oct on Sat-Sun and public holidays. Departure from the tourist office at 3.30pm. 5€. ☎ 03 44 40 01 00. Information at the tourist office or on www.vpah.culture.fr.

🕐 **Organizing Your Time:** The Palace will take you about 2hr to visit. The excursions will send you through the forested area surrounding Compiègne, one of the most beautiful of its type in France.

Sights

Le Palais★★★

Compiègne had been a royal residence since the time of the later Capetians, but Louis XV was dissatisfied with the ill-assorted and crumbling buildings inherited from his great-grandfather, and in 1738 he gave orders for the château to be reconstructed. The architect was **Ange-Jacques Gabriel,** who succeeded in building one of the great monuments of the Louis XV style. Begun in 1751, the great edifice made use of the foundations of the previous structure, partly for reasons of economy, partly because the site was pitted with old quarries. Gabriel chose to emphasise the horizontality of his buildings, stretching them out and providing them with flattened roofs with balustrades, themes he took up again in the Place de la Concorde and École Militaire in Paris. The palace was 40 years a-building; after Gabriel's retirement the work was carried on by his draughtsman, and a general movement in the direction of greater simplicity is very evident, with features like entablatures, ornamental window-brackets and attic floors tending to disappear. This evolution can be traced in the left wing of the main courtyard (1755), the principal façade facing the park, which was designed in 1775 and completed 10 years later (Napoleon's staircase of 1801 spoils the effect wished for by Gabriel), and the peristyle of 1783.

While the place was still a building site, it formed the background to the first meeting (1770) between Louis XVI and Marie-Antoinette; then in 1810, it was where Napoleon met Marie-Louise, the latter's great-niece.

Compiegne - Address Book

TOURISM INFORMATION

▯ Pl. de l'Hôtel-de-Ville, 60200 Compiègne, ☎ 03 44 40 01 00. www.mairie.compiegne. fr.
For coin ranges, see the Legend at the back of the guide.

EATING OUT

⊖ **Le Bistrot des Arts** – *35 cours Guynemer.* ☎ *03 44 20 10 10.* 🕐 *Closed Sat lunch and Sun.* Located on the ground floor of the Hôtel des Beaux-Arts, an appealing, authentic bistro decorated with various objects and etchings. In the kitchen, the chef concocts appetizing dishes using market-fresh produce.

⊖⊖ **Auberge du Buissonnet** – *825 r. Vineux, 60750 Choisy-au-Bac – 5km/3mi NE of Compiègne via N 31 and D 66.* ☎ *03 44 40 17 41.* 🕐 *Closed Sun evening, Tue evening and Mon.* Ask for a table near the bay windows of the dining room or on the terrace, weather permitting, and watch ducks and swans glide peacefully over the pond, then shake themselves off and waddle proudly toward the garden.

⊖⊖ **Le Palais Gourmand** – *8 r. Dahomey* – ☎ *03 44 40 13 13.* 🕐 *Closed 1 to 7 Mar, 2-23 Aug, 24-28 Dec, Sun evening and Mon .* This spruce timbered house (1890) has a string of rooms and an attractive verandah where heaters, Moorish pictures and mosaics create an agreeable atmosphere. Traditional cuisine.

⊖⊖ **Le Nord** – *Pl de la Gare.* ☎ *03 44 83 22 30.* 🕐 *Closed 25 Jul - 17 Aug, Sat lunch and Sun evening.* This has become quite an institution locally for its seafood dishes. The dining room is modern and bright.

WHERE TO STAY

⊖ **Auberge de la Vieille Ferme** – *60880 Meux.* ☎ *03 44 41 58 54 – auberge.vieille. ferme@wanadoo.fr.* 🕐 *Closed 28 Jul to 19 Aug, 22 Dec to 7 Jan and Sun evening –* ▯ *14 rms –* ▭ *9€ – restaurant* ⊖⊖. This old farmhouse built of Oise Valley brick offers rooms that are simple but well-kept and practical. The restaurant sports exposed beams, rustic furniture, a tile floor and gleaming copperware. The menu offers traditional and regional cuisine.

⊖⊖ **Hôtel Les Beaux Arts** – *33 cours Guynemer.* ☎ *03 44 92 26 26 – hotel@bw-lesbeauxarts.com – 35 rms –* ▭ *10€.* Located along the Oise waterfront, here's a contemporary hotel whose modern, well-soundproofed rooms have been furnished in teak or laminated wood. Some are larger and have a kitchenette.

SHOPPING

Les Halles du Grenier à Sel – *place du Change.* ☎ *03 44 23 19 55.* 🕐 *Tue-Sat, 8am-12.30pm, 3-7pm.* What better way to get close to the French way of doing things than to wander around a provincial market. This mini-market is at the centre of town, close to the beautiful church of St-Jacques *(open Sat 8am-7pm).*

ON THE TOWN

Sweet Home Pub – *49 r. St-Corneille.* ☎ *03 44 86 51 00 –* 🕐 *Mon 6pm-1am, Tue-Sat 11.30am-1am.* This is, without a doubt, the most enjoyable pub in town. Beyond the handsome wood facade, the owners hold highly entertaining evenings that feature folk and rock concerts, theatre, or literary readings.

During the Second Empire, Napoleon III made Compiègne his favourite residence, where he took much pleasure in the house-parties to which like-minded celebrities would be invited, some 80 at a time.
Inside, the palace is decorated and furnished in 18C and Empire style (chests of drawers, applied ornament, wall-cupboards, tapestries).

Musée de la Voiture et du Tourisme★★

🕐 *Guided tours* ☎ *(1hr) Wed-Sun 10am-6pm.* 🕐 *Closed Tue, 1 Jan, 1 May, 1 Nov, 25 Dec. Last admission 45 min before closing.* ☞ *4€ (under 18 years: no charge), no charge 1st Sun in the month.* ☎ *03 44 38 47 02. www.musee-chateau-compiegne.fr.*
In addition to 18C and 19C coaches, the vehicles exhibited include:the **Mancelle** of 1898, a steam mail-coach designed by Amédée Bollée;a No 2 **Panhard**;a Type **A Renault** of 1899 with direct drive;the **Jamais Contente** ("Never Satisfied") of 1899, an electric car with tyres by Michelin, the first to reach 100km/h-62.1mph;a Type C **Renault** of 1900, one of the first cars to have enclosed bodywork (by Labourdette);a **Citroën** half-track of 1924.

▶▶ **Hôtel de ville★. Musée de la Figurine historique★** ⚿ 🕐 *Mar-Oct: Tue-Sat 9am-noon, 2-6pm, Sun and public holidays 2-6pm; Nov-Feb: Tue-Sat 9am-noon, 2-5pm, Sun and public holidays 2-5pm.* 🕐 *Closed Mon, 1 Jan, 1 May, 14 Jul, 1 Nov, 25 Dec.* ☞ *2€ (under 18 years: no charge), no charge 1st Sun in the month.* ☎ *03 44 40 72 55. Musée Vivenel –* **Greek vases★★** *Mar-Oct:* 🕐 *Tue-Sat 9am-noon, 2-6pm, Sun 2-6pm; Nov-Feb: Tue-Sat 9am-noon, 2-5pm, Sun 2-5pm.* 🕐 *Closed Mon, 1 Jan, 1 May, 14 Jul, 1 Nov, 25 Dec.* ☞ *2€ (under 18 years: no charge), no charge 1st Sun in the month.* ☎ *03 44 20 26 04 –* archeology, fine arts.

Excursions

Clairière de l'Armistice★★

8km – 5mi east. This is the place where, at 5.15am on 11 November 1918, the armistice was signed which put an end to the First World War at 11am on the same day. At the time the site was sheltered by forest trees. A restaurant-car identical to the carriage **(wagon-bureau)** (⏱ *Apr to mid-Oct: Wed-Mon 9am-12.30pm, 2-6pm; mid-Oct to end Mar: Wed-Mon 10am-noon, 2-5pm;* ☎ *call in advance for guided tour;* ⏱ *closed Tue, 1 Jan, 25 Dec.* ⊙ *3€;* ☎ *03 44 85 14 18*) used by Marshal Foch displays the original objects handled by the delegates in 1918. **Ferdinand Foch** (1851-1929) is generally held to have been the architect of Allied victory in the Great War of 1914-18. He was born in Tarbes in the Pyrénées in an 18C middle-class home (now a museum). He taught strategy at the Military Academy (École de Guerre), then became its commandant. In 1914 he distinguished himself both in the Battle of the Frontiers in Lorraine and in the "Miracle of the Marne". After the German breakthrough in the Ludendorff offensive of early 1918, Foch was appointed supreme commander of the French and British armies. Promoted to marshal, it was he who launched the final Allied offensive on 8 August.

After the Battle of France in 1940, it was the turn of a French delegation to present itself here to the dignitaries of the Nazi regime in order to hear the victors' terms for an armistice. It was signed on the evening of 22 June. The clearing and its historic monuments were then ransacked by the occupation forces; only the statue of Marshal Foch was spared.

Château de Pierrefonds★★

14km – 9mi southeast. The stronghold seems to embody everything that a medieval castle should be as it looms over the village crouching at its feet. For the most part, however, it is a creation of the 19C.

Pierrefonds was part of the Duchy of Valois, and its castle, whose origins go back as far as Carolingian times, was rebuilt in the middle of the Hundred Years War by Louis d'Orléans, the brother of Charles VI, as part of a chain of defences between the rivers Oise and Ourcq. It was dismantled during the reign of Louis XIII. The castle ruins were bought by Napoleon I. In 1857 Louis Napoleon inspired by romantic ideals commissioned **Viollet-le-Duc** (1814-79) to restore the keep; four years later he was entrusted with a complete rebuilding of the castle for use as an Imperial residence and a picturesque place for receptions given to entertain the Emperor's guests at Compiègne. From the ramparts the view extends over the Vallée de Pierrefonds.

Little of Louis d'Orléans' building is left save the base of the walls and the towers visible from the track leading to the castle. Viollet-le-Duc's contributions, in the neo-Gothic style, are not without merit, but are notable more for originality than for strict historical accuracy, in terms of both architecture and decoration (arcading and gallery of the main façade in the courtyard, tribune in the chapel, roof of the Salle des Preuses). Nevertheless, it gives an excellent idea of a castle's defensive system prior to the age of cannon (north rampart walk).

Château de Blérancourt

31km – 19mi northeast. In the First World War, the château was taken over by Ann Morgan, who set up a temporary hospital here. Blérancourt subsequently became the headquarters for the organisation of relief for the civilian population.

When the war was over, Miss Morgan's efforts were directed towards the establishment of a museum of Franco-American history. In 1929, she presented the place to the French state, whereupon its name was changed to the **Musée National de la Coopération Franco-Américaine**. About a dozen rooms in the left wing (at present closed for reconstruction) are devoted to the American War of Independence.

The exhibits on show in the right wing (Pavillon Florence Gould) illustrate aspects of the long and close relationship between the two countries; there are displays on the 1801 Treaty of Friendship, the Louisiana Purchase, emigration to the United States, the Gold Rush, etc. Other rooms evoke the two World Wars, notably by means of relics of the **La Fayette** Squadron and of the American Field Service.

CONCARNEAU★

POPULATION 18 630

MICHELIN MAP 308 H 7

GREEN GUIDE BRITTANY

The growth of Concarneau is based on its importance as a fishing port. Trawlers and cargo-boats moor in the inner harbour up the estuary of the Moros, while the outer harbour is lively with pleasure craft. There are many vegetable and fish canneries and plenty of bustle as the catch is sold in the early morning at the "criée" (fish auction market).

Visit

Ville close (Walled Town)★★

On its islet in the bay, this was one of the strongholds of the ancient county of Cornouaille; as at Dinan and Guérande, its walls proclaim the determination of the citizens to maintain their independence, particularly in times of trouble (as during the War of the Breton Succession in 1341).

The English nevertheless seized the place in 1342, and were thrown out only by Du Guesclin in 1373.

The granite ramparts (**remparts**) (🕐 *mid-Jun to mid-Sep: daily 10am-9.30pm; Apr to mid-Jun and mid-Sep to mid-Nov: daily 10am-6pm; access to the ramparts is prohibited if weather conditions are not favourable and during the Filets bleus festival; 0.80€ high season, no charge low season; ☎ 02 98 97 01 44*) with their typically Breton corbelled machicolations, were started at the beginning of the 14C and completed at the end of the 15C. They were improved by Vauban at the end of the 17C at a time when England once more posed a threat to these coasts; he lowered the height of the towers and built gun emplacements into them.

The interior of the town gate is of the same period. It has impressive crenellations, regular stonework and gables. A Fishing Museum, **Musée de la Pêche**★ (🕐 *Jul-Aug: daily 9.30am-8pm; rest of the year: daily 10am-noon, 2-6pm; 🕐 closed last 3 weeks of Jan 6€, children 4€; ☎ 02 98 97 10 20*), is nearby.

At the heart of the walled town, Rue Vauban and Rue St-Guénolé are a demonstration of how medieval marketplaces arose more or less spontaneously through a simple widening of the street.

CONQUES★★★

POPULATION 362

MICHELIN MAP 338 G 3

GREEN GUIDE LANGUEDOC ROUSSILLON TARN GORGES

This tiny medieval town has a splendid hillside site★★ best seen from the rock, Rocher du Bancarel (*3km – 2mi south*).

Visit

Église St-Foy★★

Completely rebuilt between 1045 and 1060, this is one of the oldest Romanesque pilgrimage churches on the route to Santiago de Compostela. Its abbey had a chapel and hospice at Roncesvalles to serve the pilgrims as they made their way across the Pyrenees. Within, the spacious nave is flooded with light from the south tribune windows. The dimensions of the transept are exceptional and the ambulatory with its annular barrel vault is also remarkable.

The tympanum (**tympan**★★★) above the west door with its wealth of sculpture forms a striking contrast to the overall plainness of the west front. Traces of the original colouring can still be made out. It shows how sculpture had evolved away from the static solemnity characteristic of Burgundy and Languedoc, towards the greater freshness and spontaneity evident in the capitals of the churches of the Auvergne.

It may be that the weighing of souls taking place below the figure of Christ is an expression of the idea – entirely new at the beginning of the 12C – of the personal nature of the Last Judgement.

It seems likely that the tympanum was moved forward by the length of a bay and integrated with the west front in the 15C in order to extend the nave; this move would have led to the displacement of the statues in the north transept.

Trésor★★★

🕐 Apr-Sep: 9.30am-12.30pm, 2-6.30pm; rest of the year: 10-noon, 2-6pm. 🕐 Closed 1 Jan, 25 Dec. ✆ 5.50€. ☎ 08 20 82 08 03.

The treasury is among the most important in Europe. Its most precious object is the reliquary statue of St Faith (Ste-Foy).The saint's relics had been brought to Conques at the end of the 9C, when they were venerated by prisoners and by the blind. The statue was put together and added to over a long period; some of its features probably go back as far as the last years of the Roman Empire and consist of reused elements of Roman date (face-mask, intaglio work in precious stones, jewels); the gold and engraved crystal are of the Merovingian and Carolingian periods (7C-9C). At the close of the 10C the revered statue was renovated here at Conques and adorned with enamels, cabochons and other precious stones.

Four more of the treasures are of exceptional significance: the initial "A" given to the abbey, it is said, by Charlemagne (a fragment of the Holy Cross decorated in the 11C with intaglio work and with chased and gilded silver); two portable altars, one, St Faith's, in alabaster and chased silver, the other, Abbot Begon's, from the beginning of the 12C, in porphyry and silver inlaid with niello; and the reliquary of Pope Pascal with filigree work and diadems, also from the early 12C.

CORDES-SUR-CIEL★★★

POPULATION 932

MICHELIN MAP 338 D 6

GREEN GUIDE LANGUEDOC ROUSSILLON TARN GORGES

Nestling at the top of the peak, Puech de Mordagne, Cordes occupies a most attractive site★★ overlooking the Cérou valley.

Visit

The superb row of **Gothic houses (maisons gothiques★★)** dating from the 13C and 14C testify to the wealthy past of this quaint little town. Notice the **Maison du Grand Fauconnier★** and the **Maison du Grand Veneur★**. For more than 50 years, artists and craftsmen have contributed to preserving and restoring local tradition.

CORTE★

POPULATION 5 693

MICHELIN MAP 345 D 6

GREEN GUIDE CORSE (IN FRENCH)

Corte owes its fame to its site★ among gorges and ravines, as well as to two great men, Gaffori and Paoli, who were instrumental in making it one of the strongholds of Corsican patriotism.

A Bit of History

Jean-Pierre Gaffori (1704-53) was born here. He was a member of the Triumvirate ▪lected as "Protectors of the Nation", who took up arms against Genoa. In 1746, sup-◦rted by his indomitable wife Faustine, he succeeded in wresting the town from ◦e Genoese. Four years later the latter returned, taking the citadel but failing to ◦rcome the resolute defence of the old town; Gaffori's house still bears the marks ◦le by the Genoese guns.

In June 1751, Gaffori was made "General of the Nation" and granted executive power. But two years later he was killed in an ambush, betrayed by his brother.

After this assassination, an appeal was made for **Pascal Paoli** (1725-1807), then in exile in Italy, to return to his native land. He was proclaimed "General of the Nation" in his turn. By 1764, the island was united under his leadership, with only the Genoese coastal forts still able to hold out against him. For 14 years, watched closely by the European Powers, he made Corte his capital, drew up a constitution, founded a university, minted money, reformed the system of justice, encouraged industry and stimulated agricultural production.

Having failed to put down the Corsicans' long struggle for independence (1729-69) the Republic of Genoa requested the intervention of France. A mission of conciliation arrived, headed by the future French Governor, Marbeuf. Paoli, lacking somewhat in the skills of statesmanship, unwisely prevaricated, and was bypassed by events; on 15 May 1768, by the Treaty of Versailles, Genoa provisionally gave up its rights over the island to France. Paoli proclaimed a mass uprising, but was defeated at **Ponte Nuovo** on 8 May 1769.

Paoli went into exile, spent mostly in England, where he was lionised by the court of George III and was a friend of James Boswell. Amnestied at the outbreak of the French Revolution, he met with a triumphal reception in Paris before returning to Corsica. Later, after his denunciation as a counter-revolutionary, he sought aid from the English. Nelson's victories over the French at St-Florent, Bastia and Calvi did not however fulfil Paoli's hopes of independence under the English crown, but led to an Anglo-Corsican kingdom of limited duration (two years) and renewed exile in London for Paoli himself. He died there in 1807.

Visit

Ville haute★

Dominated by the citadel **(citadelle★)** perched high up on its rock, old Corte, with its cobbled and stepped streets and tall houses, still has the air of the island's capital it once was.

In the Place Paoli stands the statue of the great man, in bronze. Further up is the Place Gaffori, where, behind the monument to the General of the Nation, is his house, pitted with bullet holes from the siege of 1750. In the Rue de l'Ancien Collège is the old dwelling where Joseph Bonaparte was born. It was also the birthplace of Jean Thomas Arrighi de Casanova, one of the Empire's most brilliant generals.

A ramp opposite the National Palace (Palais National) leads to a viewpoint **(belvedère★)** on a peak standing out from the main promontory on which the citadel is built. It offers a fine view of the town in its setting bordered by the river valley, Gorges du Tavignano.

 **Chapelle Ste-Croix★. Musée de la Corse★★. Gorges de la Restonic★★.**

COUTANCES★★

POPULATION 9 715

MICHELIN MAP 303 D5

GREEN GUIDE NORMANDY

On its hilltop overlooking the woodlands and pastures (*bocage*) of the Cotentin peninsula, Coutances is famous as a cattle-breeding centre for Normandy dairy cows. The town is dominated by its cathedral, a wonderful synthesis of the local architectural traditions of Normandy and the Gothic style at the peak of its development.

Visit

Cathédrale★★★

The present building (1220-75) made use of some of the remains of Geoffroy de Montbray's Norman cathedral, as well as drawing on the experience gained in the recently-completed abbey at Fécamp.

The west front is framed by two towers, whose soaring lines (a regional characteristi... are further emphasised by the tall and narrow corner turrets. The great octago... lantern rises imposingly over the crossing; it too is flanked by turrets, and has st...

ingly delicate ribbing and slender openings. At the east end, the flying buttresses arch daringly over the double ambulatory to the point from which the ribs rise to support the choir vault. Within, the Lanceolate phase of the Gothic is evident in the features of the nave, which has clustered piers and highly moulded arches, a triforium with double openings and tall windows behind the typically Norman balustraded inspection gallery.

The transept is in a more advanced style. Here, great piers reinforced by splendidly soaring shafts carry the pendentives on which the elegant octagon of the lantern rests. Built in 1274, it is a masterpiece of ingenious construction. The lower level of the drum is formed by a balustrade and twin arches; above it, the columns of a second gallery support the ribs of the 16-part vault, while light floods in through 16 windows. The keystone is 40.85m – 134ft 4ins above the floor of the crossing.

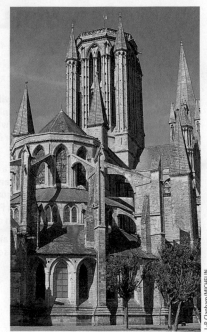

Lantern-tower of Coutances Cathedral

J.-P. Clapham/MICHELIN

The elevation of the choir and the inner ambulatory and the six coupled columns of the apse show the High Gothic style in all its perfection. Given the unusual height of the main arches, the search for an architecturally satisfying solution led to a lengthening of the clerestory windows and the omission of the triforium above the blind arcading (though the inspection gallery is retained), and justified the design of elaborate vaulting covering both the outer ambulatory and the radiating chapels.

◗◗ **Jardin des Plantes**★.

La **COUVERTOIRADE**★

POPULATION 148

MICHELIN MAP 338 L 7

GREEN GUIDE LANGUEDOC ROUSSILLON TARN GORGES

High up on the lonely Larzac limestone plateau (*causse*), La Couvertoirade is an old fortified settlement which once belonged to the Knights Templar. It has many robustly-built houses, typical of the region, with cisterns, outside stairways leading to the main floor, and a vaulted sheep-pen at ground level. Most date from the 17C.

The ramparts were erected around 1450, some 140 years after the Templars' Order had been disbanded, by the Knights of St John of Jerusalem; insecurity continued to prevail here in Upper Languedoc, even while the Hundred Years War was coming to an end in Guyenne.

Visit

Remparts: ⏱ *May-Aug: daily 10am-7pm; Mar-Jun and Sep-Nov: daily 10am-noon, ?-5pm.* ◉ *3€. Call in advance for guided tour (Jul-Aug),* ◉ *3€, 5€.* ☎ *05 65 58 55 59. www. lacouvertoirade.com.*

...lise forteresse: ⏱ *Jul-Aug: 10am-7pm; Apr-Jun: 10am-noon, 2-6pm; Mar and Sep to ...-Nov: 10am-noon, 2-5pm.* ☎ *05 65 58 55 59.*

...owers and the sentry-walk of the ramparts **(remparts)** are particularly interesting, ...he visitor should also see the fortified church **(église forteresse)** – disc-shaped ...t the entrance to the chancel, the dismantled 12C-13C castle, the old houses in ...pite, and the mansions, Hôtel de la Scipione and Hôtel de Grailhe.

DEAUVILLE★★★

POPULATION 4 261

MICHELIN MAP 303 M 3

GREEN GUIDE NORMANDY

While the neighbouring little town of Trouville began to attract visitors as early as the 1830s, Deauville, on the opposite bank of the River Touques, was created virtually out of nothing from the 1860s onward by the efforts of one man, a Dr Oliffe, physician to the British Ambassador in Paris as well as to the renowned French financier Donon.

Deauville owes its world-wide reputation as a luxury resort to the sumptuousness of its facilities and the elegance of its social and sporting calendar which extends over the whole year but reaches a peak in summer; there are regattas, golf and tennis championships, galas, the American Film Festival, international yearling horse sales and horse racing culminating in the Deauville Grand Prix.

Life in Deauville centres on the one hand around the Place de Morny and the yachting harbour, on the other around the seafront with its famous boardwalk, its casino and Port Deauville.

Excursions

Corniche Normande★★
From Deauville-Trouville to Honfleur via the D513 – *21km – 13mi*. This scenic route leads through typical Normandy countryside and affords fine views over the Seine Estuary.

Honfleur★★ – ⓒ *See HONFLEUR.*

Côte Fleurie★★
From Deauville-Trouville to Cabourg via the D513. – *19km – 12mi*. The road passes through a number of attractive small resorts with excellent recreational facilities, among them **Villers-sur-Mer★★, Houlgate★★** and **Cabourg★★.**

Les Plages du DÉBARQUEMENT★★

D-DAY LANDING BEACHES

MICHELIN MAP 303 F-K 3-4 , LOCAL MAP PP194-195

GREEN GUIDE NORMANDY

A Bit of History

Dawn of D-Day – A formidable armada, which consisted of 4 266 barges and landing craft together with hundreds of warships and naval escorts, sailed from the south coast of England on the night of 5 June 1944. As the crossing proceeded, airborne landings took place at **Pegasus Bridge** (near Caen) and Ste-Mère-Église which were intended to neutralise the enemy on either flank of the attack.

The Allied Landings – **Sword Beach** (Colleville-Montgomery, Lion-sur-Mer, St-Aubin), where British and Free French troops landed, marks the easternmost point of the invasion perimeter; to the west came the Canadians at **Juno Beach** (Bernières and Courseulles), the British again at **Gold Beach** (Ver-sur-Mer and Asnelles), then the Americans at **Omaha Beach** and **Utah Beach** (la Madeleine and the Varrevil" dunes at the base of the Cotentin peninsula).

The **Pointe du Hoc★★**, between Omaha and Utah Beaches, offered the enemy co mand of the entire invasion front, and was stormed by the Second Rangers Batta early on D-Day. The first Mulberry (artificial harbour) was in place at **Arromar** by the end of D-Day.

The Normandy invasion, and its significance in European and world history, is marked all along this coastline and its hinterland by military cemeteries, monuments, viewing points, museums and some features of the Atlantic Wall (Mur de l'Atlantique) – German battery **(batterie allemande)** at Longues-sur-Mer, bunker **(Grand Bunker** – ○ *Feb to mid-Nov: 10am-6pm (Apr-Sep: 9am-7pm),* ⌕ *6.10€.* ☎ *02 31 97 28 69.***)** at Ouistreham, etc.

Visit

Principal Military Cemeteries

Banneville-Sannerville (British)	Michelin map 54 fold 16
Bayeux (British)	Michelin map 54 fold 15
La Cambe (British)	Michelin map 54 fold 14
Cinetheaux (Canadian)	Michelin map 54 fold 16
Colleville-St-Laurent (American)	Michelin map 54 fold 14
Marigny (German)	Michelin map 54 fold 13
Huisnes-sur-Mer (German)	Michelin map 59 fold 7
Ranville (British)	Michelin map 54 fold 16
Reviers (Canadian)	Michelin map 59 fold 15
St-James (American)	Michelin map 54 fold 8
St-Manvieu-Norrey (British)	Michelin map 54 fold 15

Omaha Beach

Until 6 June 1944 this name existed only as an Allied code word designating one of the sections of Normandy coastline to be assaulted in the early hours of that fateful day. Including the beaches of St-Laurent, Colleville-sur-Mer and Vierville-sur-Mer, it was here that the US First Division made its first contact with French soil and it was here that the bloodiest engagement of D-Day was fought. The film *The Longest Day* directed by D Zanuck gives a realistic account of these dramatic events.

The St-Laurent military cemetery stands as a moving testimony to the thousands of young men who came from far shores to liberate an oppressed continent, and who were cut down here and on the other invasion beaches by a tenacious defence.

Utah Beach

This beach to the northeast of Carentan entered history together with Omaha Beach and the beaches along the Normandy coast following the landing of American forces on 6 June 1944. Despite murderous fire from the German coastal batteries, the troops of the American 4th Division managed only on 12 June to link up with the forces who had landed at Omaha Beach.

La Madeleine

There is a milestone – Borne 00, the first on the Road to Liberty – the route taken by the American forces from Normandy to the Ardennes (the first symbolic milestone – Borne 0 – stands in front of the town hall of Ste-Mère-Église). On an area of dunes which is now American territory rises a huge stele erected in 1984 on the 40th anniversary of D-Day to commemorate those who died in the bloody operations at Utah Beach.

▶▶ **Utah Beach: Musée du débarquement.** – ○ *Jun-Sep: 9.30am-7pm; Oct to mid-Nov and Apr: 10am-12.30pm, 2-6pm; Feb and Mar: 10am-12.30pm, 2-5.30pm.* ○ *Closed in Jan, 24 and 15 Dec.* ⌕ *4.50€.* ☎ *02 33 71 53 35.*

Grotte des DEMOISELLES★★★

MICHELIN MAP 339 H 5

GREEN GUIDE LANGUEDOC ROUSSILLON TARN GORGES

...ave was first discovered in 1770. Before the massive upheavals of the Alpine- ...ng period which raised the whole of the Massif Central far above its previous ...was probably a sea-cave. Its roof fell in, enlarging it still further, as well as ...up an aven – a deep narrow trench – on the Thaurac plateau above.

Visit

🕐 Guided tours 🏃‍♂️ (1hr) Apr-Jun and Sep: daily 9.45am-noon, 1.30-5.30pm; Jul and Aug: daily 9.45am-7pm; Oct-Mar: daily 9.45am-noon, 1.30-5.30pm. Last departure 30min before closing time. 🕐 Closed 1 Jan and 25 Dec. ✆ 7.90€, children 4.50€. ☎ 04 67 73 70 02; www.demoiselles.com.

Subsequent processes of evaporation and deposition of calcium carbonate within the cave (**grotte**) have produced a scale and diversity of forms which are quite extraordinary, from stalactites and stalagmites and translucent draperies, to the great columns and huge organ-case of this underground cathedral.

DIEPPE★★

POPULATION 35 894

MICHELIN MAP 304 G 2

GREEN GUIDE NORMANDY

As well as being the nearest seaside resort to Paris, Dieppe is also the most venerable; its famous sea-front lawns were laid out in 1863 by Empress Eugénie and Napoleon III. The first docks were built in 1839 and today it is one of the main cross-Channel ports, with regular car-ferry services to Newhaven. Its history as a port, however, goes back much further, to the days of the herring fisheries (beginning in the 11C), the English wool trade, and the import of spices from the Orient in Italian ships.

▶ **Orient Yourself:** Dieppe, which is listed as a "Town of Art and History", offers 2hr discovery tours for 5€ conducted by guide-lecturers approved by the Ministry of Culture and Communication.

A Bit of History

Dieppe Mariners – As early as the 14C, sailors from Dieppe were landing on the coast of the Gulf of Guinea and Jean Cousin was exploring the South Atlantic. In 1402 Jean de Bethencourt founded the first European colony on the Canary Islands. Jean Ango (1480-1541), whose privateers once captured a fleet of 300 Portuguese vessels, was responsible for equipping many a voyage of discovery to remote shores. The Parmentier brothers made their way as far as Sumatra as well as drawing up charts of the globe.

It was from Dieppe too that the Florentine Giovanni da Verrazano, in the service of France, set out on the journey that eventually took him through the Narrows named after him at the entrance to New York harbour (1524). In the 16C the great explorer **Samuel de Champlain**, a Dieppe ship-owner, sailed out from Honfleur to found the French colony of Quebec. Later the port traded in sugar from the Antilles and ivory from Guinea.

The Canadian Raid – On 19 August 1942, Dieppe was the main target of Operation Jubilee, the first sortie on French soil after June 1940 by Allied troops under the command of Admiral Mountbatten. Seven thousand men, mostly Canadians, landed at dawn at eight different places on the coast. The tank crews gave their lives to protect the retreat under heavy artillery fire and with heavy losses including 3 500 Canadian soldiers.

Visit

Dieppe ivories★

Dieppe ships had loaded elephant tusks from the West African coast ever since they had begun calling there on the return journey from Brazil in the early years of the 16C. The fragile ivory was filed and polished with great skill by artists encouraged to settle Dieppe by Jean Ango. Whalebone and the teeth of sperm whales were worked as w Production was interrupted when many of the craftsmen quit France after the revoca of the Edict of Nantes, but it started up again at the time of the rebuilding of the in the 18C. It was then that Jean Mauger and Michel Mollart, and later Pierre (1807-72) fashioned ravishing little objects very much in the spirit of the Rocc

Dieppe - Address Book

For coin ranges, see the Legend at the back of the guide.

EATING OUT

�e�e **Le New Haven** – *53 quai Henri IV -* ☎ *02 35 84 89 72 restaurant -newhaven@ wanadoo.fr -* ◷ *closed 1 week in Oct, 2 weeks in Jan, Tue and Wed except in July-Aug.* The young couple at the helm have opted to concentrate on the generous local specialties, made with care and the best ingredients. The specialties, such as liver of lotte on toast, are all from the sea, of remarkable freshness. The interior is nautical in theme, and the view on the marina is charming.

�e�e **L'Auberge d'Archelles** – *76880 Arques-la-Bataille -* ☎ *02 35 83 40 51 -* ◷ *closed 2 last weeks of Feb, 25 Aug - 6 Sept, Fri evening, Sat lunch and Sun evening off-season.* Located in a 16C stable, this inn and its terrace on the water are totally charming. Attractive interior where red brick rules. As for meals, your vegetables come directly from the kitchen garden just outside, and your meat is grilled in the fireplace in winter.

�e�e **Le Bistrot du Pollet** – *23 r. de Tête-de-Bœuf -* ☎ *02 35 84 68 57 -* ◷ *closed 10-24 Mar, Aug, Sun-Mon - reserv. essential.* This small bistro comes highly recommended with a pretty façade of marine tiles, yellow walls hung with old posters, tables close to each other encouraging conviviality, and flavoursome cuisine blending the best of surf and turf. No wonder the place is often packed!

�e�e�e **La Marmite Dieppoise** – *8 r. St-Jean -* ☎ *02 35 84 24 26 -* ◷ *closed Nov-Mar, 23, Sun evening, Thu evening and Mon.* The yellow-brick façade in the centre of town conceals a small restaurant with a faithful following. Cuisine with a spotlight on seafood; try the house speciality, the delectable *marmite dieppoise.*

WHERE TO STAY

◒◒ **Hôtel de la Plage** – *20 bd de Verdun -* ☎ *02 35 84 18 28 - 40 rooms -* ▭. This hotel, facing the beach and close to the town centre, offers a family atmosphere. Every room is functional, but you may prefer one overlooking the beach; the others are quieter.

◒◒ **La Villa Florida Bed and Breakfast** – *24 chemin du Golf -* ☎ *02 35 84 40 37 -* ⊟ - *3 rooms.* A surprising, modern house built from slate: bathed in light, the interior has been superbly designed. Each room, elegant and sober, has its own little terrace. The pretty garden gives onto the Dieppe golf course. Peace and quiet guaranteed; very warm welcome.

ON THE TOWN

Le Rade – *12 r. de la Rade -* ☎ *02 35 82 34 15 -* ◷ *Tue-Sun 5pm-2am, weekend until 4am; early Jan to Feb school holidays: Sat-Sun 5pm-2am -* ◷ *closed Mon and 1 week in Jan.* In French, *rade* evokes pubs typical of the old harbours where fishermen come to have a pint while smoking a warm pipe and discussing the day's catch. This *rade,* convivial and authentic, is a fine example of the genre.

LEISURE

⚓ **Armement Legros** – *Jean-Ango Marina, next to the tourist office -* ☎ *02 35 84 82 85 - daily from 2pm -* ◷ *closed Sep-Jun except public holidays.* Monsieur Legros proposes fishing trips and 40min sea cruises. Equipment may be rented. Invigorating and fun.

🚲 **Loca-cycles** – *17 r. d'Issoire -* ☎ *02 35 06 07 40 -* ◷ *Apr-Sep - 9.50€ half day, 14€ day, 24.50€ weekend.* Home delivery available.

In the castle is the **Museum**★ where many of these meticulously-crafted masterpieces are displayed; they include ship-models, busts, medallions, snuff-boxes, as well as objects of religious or mythological significance.

◑◑ **Cité de la Mer**★. **Église St Jacques**★. Notre-Dame de Bon Secours Chapel – **view**★.

Excursions

Côte D'Albâtre (Alabaster Coast)★
From Dieppe to Etretat

104km – 65mi. With its beaches and sheer white cliffs cut into by dry valleys *(valleuses)*, this is a landscape reminiscent of the coastline of much of southern England. The chalk continues inland to form the Caux region, a vast plateau whose farmsteads shelter from the winds behind massive tree-topped hedgebanks.

▸ *Leave Dieppe by the D75 in the direction of Pourville.*

A number of little resorts – **Pourville-sur-Mer, Ste-Marguerite-sur-Mer** and **Veu-les-les-Roses** – are sited at the seaward end of a succession of lush valleys, their half-timbered houses hidden among the hedgerows.

In **Varangeville-sur-Mer**, the graveyard of the 11-15C church which overlooks the sea and shelters the tomb of the Cubist painter, **Georges Braque**, and the stained glass of Chapelle St-Dominique (on the outskirts) by the artist are of interest.
Further along the way, the Gorge du Petit-Ailly and Vastérival are two typical dry valleys (valleuses). From the lighthouse, **Phare d'Ailly**★, the view extends for miles along the coast.

St-Valéry-en-Caux

In a gap in the cliffs halfway between Dieppe and Fécamp, St-Valéry (twin town, Inverness) is a fishing port as well as a popular resort. High up on a cliff (Falaise d'Amont) are two monuments, one commemorating the last stand of the 51st Highland Division in June 1940, the other to the airmen Coste and Bellemont who completed the first east-west crossing of the Atlantic from Paris to New York in 1930.

▶ Continue to **Fécamp**★★ (see FÉCAMP), Yport with its slate roofs, and **Étretat**★★ (see ÉTRETAT).

DIJON★★★

POPULATION 226 025

MICHELIN MAP 320 K 5-6

GREEN GUIDE BURGUNDY JURA

Close to some of the world's finest vineyards, Dijon, former capital city of the Dukes of Burgundy, straddles important north-south and east-west communication routes and has a remarkable artistic heritage.

▶ **Orient Yourself:** Dijon, which is listed as a "Town of Art and History," offers guided tours which serve as an excellent introduction to Dijon. Check the tourist office or on www.vpah.culture.fr for more information.

A Bit of History

The Great Dukes of Burgundy – Dijon had been the capital of Burgundy ever since the rule of Robert the Pious at the beginning of the 11C. In 1361 Philippe de Rouvres died without an heir, leaving the duchy without a ruler. In 1363, the French King Jean II le Bon (the Good) handed the duchy to his son Philippe, the first of an illustrious line of Valois Dukes who made the Burgundian court at Dijon one of the most brilliant of Europe.

Philippe became Duke in 1364, at the same time as his brother Charles V le Sage (the Wise) was acceding to the throne of France. Philippe stood out as the most able of four royal brothers; cool, analytical on the one hand, well-named "le Hardi" (the Bold) on the other. His marriage in 1369 to Margaret of Flanders made him the most powerful prince of Christian Europe. Anxious to provide a worthy burial place for himself and his successors, he founded the Champmol Charterhouse in Dijon in 1383, and set out to attract to the city the best sculptors, painters, goldsmiths and illuminators from his possessions in Flanders. They included Jean de Marville (who designed his tomb), Jean de Beaumetz from Artois (who worked for five years on the altar of the Charterhouse), Claus Sluter and Melchior Broederlam (who succeeded Marville as Court painter), and Malouel from Gelderland who gave Burgundian-Flemish style its distinct identity (his great circular *Pietà* can be seen in the Louvre).
In an attempt to redress the cultural balance in France's favour, Jean de Berry, virtual ruler of the kingdom as a consequence of Charles VI's growing madness, encouraged other artists to settle and work in Bourges, Poitiers and Riom.

Jean sans Peur (John the Fearless), Charles VI's cousin, became Duke in 1404 at the age of 33. While continuing to employ the artists chosen by his father, John nourished political ambitions, spurred on by the insanity of the king and the Dauphin's unease about his legitimacy. But John's attempt to make himself master of France came to an end in 1419, when he was assassinated on the bridge at Montereau on his way to negotiate with the Dauphin.
The odious crime of Montereau led to **Philippe le Bon** (the Good) inheriting the title at the age of 23. Burgundy's alliance with England helped Henry V acquire the Crown of France by the Treaty of Troyes in 1420. From this time on, Burgundy slowly

Dijon - Address Book

For coin ranges, see the Legend at the back of the guide.

EATING OUT

Café du Vieux Marché – *2 R. Claude-Ramey* - ☎ *03 80 30 73 61* - ⏱ *closed Sun.* This café located opposite the covered market is fronted by a pretty white and blue terrace. Simplicity and authenticity guaranteed. Light meals and snacks are available.

La Mère Folle – *102 R. Berbisey* - ☎ *03 80 50 19 76* - ⏱ *closed Tue.* This small restaurant in the town centre offers regional specialties on its menu such as *escargots, œufs en meurette,* and *sandre au Chablis.* Convivial atmosphere, good service and 1930s-style décor.

Les Deux Fontaines – *16 Pl. de la République* - ☎ *03 80 60 86 45* - ⏱ *closed 1 Jan, 10-25 August, 25 Dec, Sun and Mon.* Whitwashed walls, old banquettes, wood tables plastered with advertisements of yesteryear: it all makes for a nostalgic trip to bistrots past. Nostalgia reigns over the menu as well.

Le Bistrot des Halles – *10 R. Bannelier* - ☎ *03 80 49 94 15* - ⏱ *closed Sun and Mon.* A typical bistrot a stone's throw from the covered market. Choose one of the dishes chalked up on a slate and enjoy the warm and friendly ambience.

L'Auberge de la Charme – *21121 Prenois - 13km/8.1mi NW of Dijon by N 71 then D 104 heading towards the Circuit Automobile* - ☎ *03 80 35 32 84 - davidlacharme@aol.com* - ⏱ *closed Feb school holidays, 1-14 Aug, Sun evenings, Tue lunchtime and Mon – reservations required.* Bellows and other old-fashioned tools from the smithy adorn this flower-filled country inn. You will succumb to the rustic charm of the place and will be won over by its hearty and delicious meals.

La Dame d'Aquitaine – *23 Pl. Bossuet* - ☎ *03 80 30 45 65 - dame. aquitaine@wanadoo.fr* - ⏱ *closed 1-6 Jan, Mon lunchtime and Sun.* In the town centre, a porch, a paved courtyard and a long flight of steps will take you down to a superb vaulted dining hall dating back to the 13C. The decor is typically medieval, complete with tapestries, stained glass, sculpted columns and imposing chandeliers. Regional cuisine.

WHERE TO STAY

Jacquemart – *32 R. Verrerie* - ☎ *03 80 60 09 60 - hotel@hotel-lejacquemart.fr - 31 rooms* - ⏱ *6€.* The people of Dijon do love their Jacquemarts at Notre Dame. Simple, family-style rooms in a 17C building.

Hôtel Victor Hugo – *23 R. des Fleurs* - *03 80 43 63 45 -23 rooms* - ⏱ *5€.* You appreciate the thoughtful service at this traditional hotel. The rooms with their white roughcast walls are simple and quiet, despite their location near the town centre.

Hôtel Wilson – *Pl. Wilson* - ☎ *03 80 66 82 50 - hotelwilson@wanadoo.fr - 27 rooms* - ⏱ *10€.* This former post house has retained its traditional charm and charisma. The rooms are prettily decorated with light wood furniture. The exposed beams and luminosity make for a cosy atmosphere where one immediately feels at home.

ON THE TOWN

Theatres and Opera – Comedians and actors regularly ply the stages of the Théâtre du Sablier *(R. Berbisey)*, the Théâtre du Parvis-St-Jean *(Pl. Bossuet)*, the Bistrot de la Scène *(R. D'Auxonne).* In May the city hosts the Rencontres Internationales du Théâtre. The Théâtre National Dijon-Bourgogne is directed by Robert Cantarella. Classical music, opera and dance productions are held at the Auditorium and at the Opéra de Dijon *(Pl. du Théâtre).*

L'Agora Café – *10 Pl. de la Libération* - ☎ *03 80 30 99 42* - *Tue-Sat 11:30am-2am.* A piano-bar located in a former 16C convent chapel. Wide selection of whiskies, beers and cocktails in a quiet, convivial atmosphere. Piano performances on Sat. evenings. Patio open in summer.

Le Caveau de la Porte Guillaume – *Pl. Darcy - downtown* - ☎ *03 80 50 80 50 - www.bourgogne.net/hnord - daily 7am-2am.* ⏱ *closed 20 Dec-5 Jan.* Bordering the Hotel du Nord, this wine bar is an ideal spot for discussing (and sampling) the delights of the region, by the glass or by the bottle.

SIT BACK AND RELAX

Comptoir des Colonies – *12 Pl. François-Rude* - ☎ *03 80 30 28 22* - ⏱ *open Mon-Sat 8am-7.30pm* ⏱ *closed Sun.* Teas, coffees roasted in-house and hot chocolate await you in this colonial-style tea shop, which also has a leather and mahogany salon and a large sunny terrace.

Maison Millière – *10 R. de la Chouette* - ☎ *03 80 30 99 99 - www.maison-milliere.fr* - *Tue-Sun 10am-7pm.* This pleasant tearoom occupies a 15C structure that began as a fabric shop behind the Église Notre-Dame.

La Causerie des Mondes – *16 R. Vauban* - ☎ *03 80 49 96 59 - la.causerie.des.mondes@ wanadoo.fr* - ⏱ *open daily 11am-7pm, Sundays Oct-Mar 3-7pm.* - ⏱ *closed Mon.* Jute-covered walls, and Asiatic-themed decor, with a backdrop of mood music makes for an exotic atmosphere in this pleasant tearoom. More than 70 imported teas, 20 house-roasted coffees, chocolates and cakes to tempt you.

Mulot et Petitjean – *13 Pl. Bossuet -* ☎ *03 80 30 07 10 - mulot.petitjean@wanadoo.fr -* 🕐 *open Mon 2-7pm, Tue-Sat 9am-noon, 2-7pm.* This long-standing establishment, which originated in 1796, specialises in all forms of gingerbread: round biscuits filled with jam, crunchy *gimblettes* with almonds, and sweetmeats shaped as snails, fish, hens, eggs or clogs. The half-timbered house contains a sumptuous decor with marble and wood furniture dating from 1901.

SHOPPING

Marché des Halles – *Center of town - Tue, Thu and Fri mornings, and Sat.*

Nicot Yves – *48 R. Jean-Jacques-Rousseau -* ☎ *03 80 73 29 88 - nicotvins@infonie.fr -* 🕐 *Mon-Fri 8am-12.30pm, 3-8pm, Sat 8am-8pm, Sun 8am-12.30pm.* The proprietor, M Nicot, nurtures a veritable passion for wines in this shop. He also runs a school offering courses in wine tasting and oenology. Good selection of Burgundies.

Auger – *16 and 61 R. de la Liberté -* ☎ *03 80 30 26 28 -* 🕐 *Sun-Tue 10am-noon, 2-pm, Wed-Sat 9am-7pm.* One of the last producers of traditional gingerbread in Dijon (documents indicate the beginnings of gingerbread baking here as early as the 14C). You'll also find a good selection of regional products for sale.

Boutique Amora-Maille – *32 R. de la Liberté -* ☎ *03 80 30 41 02 -* 🕐 *Mon-Sat 9am-7pm -* 🕐 *closed public holidays.* Founded in 1777, this shop specialises in mustards and vinegars of Dijon. Take a look at the sign over the entrance.

L'Escargotière de Marsannay-le-Bois – *Rte d'Épagny - 21380 Marsannay-le-Bois -* ☎ *03 80 35 76 15 - sylvainmansuy@ wanadoo.fr -* 🕐 *10am-8pm.* In addition to sampling and purchasing snails, scallops and other fine prepared dishes, you can learn about how culinary snails are raised, harvested and transformed for consumption.

saw its cultural importance waning in favour of the Netherlands and Flanders, where Renaissance ideas were blossoming. Nevertheless, artistic production continued throughout his long reign of 48 years. Among the talents working at Dijon were Claus de Werve, Henri Bellechose from Brabant (whose St Denis altarpiece is in the Louvre), Rogier van der Weyden, and, it seems probable, Robert Campin, the likely **Master of Flémalle**. Working at Bruges in the service of the Duke was Van Eyck, the founder of the Flemish School, who was responsible for perfecting the techniques of painting in oils. At the same time, Nicolas Rolin, the Duke's Chancellor, was establishing the Hôtel-Dieu at Beaune.

The boundaries of the Burgundian state had never been more extensive nor the life of its court more exuberant; on his wedding-day in 1429, Philip founded the Order of the Golden Fleece; never had the French king and his court, lurking in relative obscurity at Bourges, been more pitiful.

But the alliance with England had now become embarrassing, even unpopular; it was beginning to threaten the dominance of Burgundy at the very moment when Joan of Arc was awakening national sentiment. Subtle policies were required; the Duke found it convenient to allow Charles VII to cross Burgundian territory in order to have himself crowned at Reims. Then, aged 33, Philip, who hitherto had always conducted himself like any other non-French monarch, submitted himself to the feudal authority of the French king, thus marking the beginning of the end of the interminable Hundred Years War.

Charles le Téméraire (the Bold) succeeded in 1467; he was the last and perhaps the most renowned of all the Valois Dukes of Burgundy. Consumed by ambition, he squandered his resources in the search for glory. But now, after a century, the balance of power had been reversed; the Duke found himself faced with the wily Louis XI, devoting himself stubbornly and with great effect to the interests of the French kingdom. Charles' death at the siege of Nancy in 1477 marked the end of the great days of the Burgundian dynasty, but not the end of the problems besetting the French throne. It was in the same year that Mary of Burgundy, Charles' daughter, married the Habsburg Maximilian, Holy Roman Emperor, in spite of her godfather Louis XI's fierce opposition. She was to be the mother of Philippe le Beau (the Fair), who in turn fathered the future Emperor Charles V. The recovery of Burgundy and the other land making up her dowry cost France more than two and a half centuries of struggle

Painting and Sculpture at the Time of the Dukes – As a great European centr artistic activity, Dijon tended towards a certain ostentation. But though the w of some of its artists may have been lacking in refinement, they more than ma for it by their sumptuousness, vigour and power.

Dijon

Sights

LA VILLE DUCALE (THE DUCAL CITY)

Palais des ducs et des États de Bourgogne★★

The ducal palace had been neglected since the death of Charles the Bold. In the 17C, it was restored and adapted and given a setting of dignified Classical buildings. At the time the city was concerned to emphasise its parliamentary role and needed a suitable building in which the States-General of Burgundy could meet in session. Plans were drawn up by Mansart. The exterior of the Great Hall of the States-General (Salle des États) recalls the Marble Court (Cour de Marbre) at Versailles. By contrast, the east wing with its peristyle anticipates the architectural style of the 18C.

Mansart was also responsible for the semicircular Place de la Libération (formerly Place Royale). With its arcades crowned by an elegant stone balustrade, it is designed to show off the main courtyard of the palace.

Musée des Beaux-Arts ★★

  May-Oct: Wed-Mon 9.30am-6pm; Nov-Apr: Wed-Mon 10am-5pm. Closed Tue, 1 Jan, 1 May, 25 Dec. 3.40€, no charge Sun. 03 80 74 52 09 .
The Fine Arts Museum is housed in the former ducal palace and in the east wing of the palace of the States-General.

Salle des Gardes★★★

On the first floor, in the former Banqueting Hall. This is the ducal palace's most important interior. Its centrepiece is formed by two tombs which before the French Revolution were in the chapel of the Champmol Charterhouse. The tomb of Philip the Bold was designed by Jean de Marville; its decoration was in the hands of Claus Sluter followed by his nephew Claus de Werve who succeeded in softening somewhat the severity of Marville's conception. Flamboyant Gothic inventiveness and exuberance are expressed in the procession of hooded mourners making its way around the cloisters formed by the four sides of the monument. Nearby, the tomb (**tombeau**★★★) of John the Fearless and Margaret of Bavaria is similar in style.

There are also two altarpieces dazzling in the richness of their decoration: one, sculpted by Jacques de Baerze and painted and gilded by Broederlam, shows **Saints and Martyrs**★★★; the other, depicting the Crucifixion, has famous paintings by Broederlam on the reverse side of its panels. A portrait of Philip the Good by Rogier van der Weyden (born in Tournai, a pupil of Van Eyck and perhaps of Campin too, then teacher to Memling) is remarkable for its psychological insight. In an adjoining room is a fine Nativity of 1425 by the Master of Flémalle.

Ancienne Chartreuse de Champmol★

Enter at 1 Boulevard Chanoine-Kir. Follow the signs reading "Puits de Moïse." Daily 10am-6pm. 03 80 42 48 01.
Entrance No 1 Boulevard Chanoine-Kir (now a hospital). All that is left of the Charterhouse is Moses' Well (**Puits de Moise**★★) and the chapel doorway (**portail de la chapelle**★), both the work of Claus Sluter, the foremost among the sculptors of the Dijon School. Born in Holland, he learnt his skills in Brabant and worked in Dijon from 1385 to 1404.

Moses' Well was originally the pedestal of a Calvary. The head of the figure of Christ is now in the Archeological Museum. Six great statues of Moses and the Prophets face outwards from the hexagonal base; their treatment shows a striking realism and sense of movement, notably in the folds of the clothing. The statues of Philip the Bold and Margaret of Flanders in the chapel doorway are thought to be actual portraits.

▶▶ **Rue des Forges**★. **Église Notre-Dame**★. Cathédrale St-Bénigne – **crypte**★ 🕐 *9am-6pm. Call in advance for guided tour information.* 🎟 *1€ offering.* ☎ *03 80 30 14 90.* **Musée Archéologique**★ 🕐 *Wed-Mon 9am-6pm.* 🕐 *Closed Tue, 1 Jan, 1 and 8 May, 14 Jul, 1 and 11 Nov, 25 Dec.* 🎟 *2.20€, no charge Sun.* ☎ *03 80 30 88 54.* **Église St-Michel**★.

DINAN★★

POPULATION 11 591

MICHELIN MAP 309 J 4

GREEN GUIDE BRITTANY

Dinan is situated at the head of the Rance estuary on which its little port is built, but the wall-girt town itself rises from the plateau 30m – 100ft above the river.

▶ **Orient Yourself:** Dinan, which is listed as a "Town of Art and History," offers various discovery tours. Information at the tourist office or on www.vpah.culture.fr.

A Bit of History

Bertrand du Guesclin (c 1315-80) – In the town is a statue of this redoubtable warrior. Jean le Bon (John the Good) had been taken prisoner by the English at the Battle of Poitiers in 1356. During the four years of captivity he spent in England he became aware of the extent to which feudal rights imposed limitations on royal power, and conceived the idea of a body of knights attached to the monarch. In pursuit of this aim, he took Du Guesclin into his service shortly after his release and return to France. This middle-aged knight had until then experienced little but rebuffs and difficulties due to his modest ancestry, lack of means and exceptionally ugly appearance. John's successor, Charles V, kept him on, doubtless in view of his great popularity and reckless bravery and his implacable hatred of the English (which at one point in his youth had led him to support Charles of Blois). In 1366, after ridding France of the "Free Companies" (marauding bands of mercenaries), he was made High Constable of France. He freed Périgord from English rule in 1370 and Normandy in 1378. In 1379 he handed his sword to the king rather than use it against his rebellious Breton compatriots. In 1380 he died beneath the walls of Châteauneuf-de-Randon in the south.

Sights

La Vieille Ville

The houses of the old town cluster together behind the 2.5km – 1 1/2 mile long circuit of walls, built by the Dukes of Brittany in the 14C in order to protect the place's commercial activity and to defend their domain against the Normans, the English, and, after the accession of Louis XI, the French.

Château★

🕐 *Jun-Sep daily 10am-6.30pm; Oct-May: daily 1.30-5.30pm.* 🕐 *Closed Jan.* 🎟 *4€.* ☎ *02 96 87 58 72.*

Begun by Duke John IV about the middle of the 14C. Its 15C towers project outwards in order to facilitate enfilading fire. The exceptionally fine machicolations of Duchess Anne's Keep (Donjon de la Duchesse Anne) are of interest.

Basilique St-Sauveur

The west front is much influenced by the Poitiers version of the Romanesque. In the north aisle is the Evangelists' Window, a fine example of late-15C Breton glass, famous for its yellows. In the north transept is the cenotaph containing the heart of Du Guesclin.

Vieilles maisons

Duke John was happy to let Dinan run its own affairs, and the town's consequent prosperity is reflected in the rebuilding of many old timber houses in stone. A most picturesque townscape results from the many buildings with overhanging upper storeys, angle-posts, halftimbering on stone footings, arcades carried on timber beams, and granite side-walls.

The most interesting houses are on Rue de l'Apport (the 15C Mère Pourcel House), **Place des Merciers**★ (triangular gables and porches), **Rue du Jerzual**★ which links the main part of the town with the port (15C and 16C shops where craftsmen have worked for six centuries) and on Place Du Guesclin (17C and 18C town houses).

DINARD★★★

POPULATION 9 918

MICHELIN MAP 309 J 3

GREEN GUIDE BRITTANY

On the magnificent estuary of the River Rance, Dinard is an elegant resort with sheltered sandy beaches and luxuriant Mediterranean vegetation flourishing in the mild climate.

A Bit of History

It was little more than a small fishing harbour, an offshoot of nearby St-Enogat, when in 1850 a rich American by the name of Coppinger decided to build himself a château here. He was followed two years later by a British family, who in turn attracted many of their fellow-countrymen; Dinard's period of fame had begun. Its success as a resort owed much to the fashion for sea-bathing which developed at the time of Napoleon III. It was formally inaugurated by Empress Eugénie in 1868, and by the end of the 19C its reputation rivalled that of Brighton; sumptuous villas and luxurious hotels abounded, frequented by an international smart set, their evenings spent in sophisticated revelry. Nowadays many of Dinard's grand hotels are no more than a memory, but plenty of well-tended villas remain to tell of past glories.

Visit

Le bord de mer (Beaches and Coastline)

Seaside promenades lead from the **Plage de l'Écluse**★ (or **Grande Plage**) to the Plage du Prieuré, giving fine views over the coast and the Rance estuary. From the **Pointe du Moulinet**★★, the view extends as far as Cap Fréhel to the west and to the ramparts of St-Malo to the east. In summer, the **Promenade du Clair de Lune**★ with its pretty parterres and Mediterranean plants forms an attractive setting for evening concerts.

◖◗ Aquarium et Musée de la Mer.

DISNEYLAND PARIS★★★

MICHELIN MAP 312 F 2

GREEN GUIDE NORTHERN FRANCE AND THE PARIS REGION

Nestling in the Brie Plain, 20 miles away from Paris, a leisure centre unique in Europe has been set up at Marne-la-Vallée. This huge complex, scheduled to expand until the year 2017, already includes a Disneyland Paris theme park, as well as numerous recreational activities and facilities for accommodation. These consist of six hotels, each focusing on one particular region in the United States, a camping and caravanning site, **Davy Crockett Ranch**, a 27-hole golf course (Golf Disneyland Paris), and an entertainment centre (**Disney Village**) portraying the American way of life. The resort also features restaurants, shops, a discotheque and a mounted show (**Buffalo Bill's Wild West Show**★★) reproducing the adventurous lifestyle of the Far West.

▶ **Orient Yourself:** Find the information desk in City Hall (Disneyland Park) where a program of the attractions is provided.

🕐 **Organizing Your Time:** To avoid long lines at popular attractions, it is recommended to visit them during the parade, at the end of the day or better still to get a **Fast Pass** issued by distributors outside the most popular attractions in both parks; this ticket bears a time slot of one hour during which time you may have access to the attraction within a few minutes.

Kids Especially for Kids: As you know, there is something here for children of all ages.

P **Parking:** There is parking available in the northeast portion of the park, but with both train and bus terminals, Disneyland Paris is easily accessible from Paris.

Visit

Parc Disneyland Paris★★★

🕐 *Jul-Aug: daily 9am-11pm (9pm for Walt Disney Studios); Sep to mid-Jan: Mon-Fri 10am-8pm, Sat-Sun and public holidays 9am-8pm; low season: Sun-Fri10am-8pm, Sat 9am-8pm.* ☎ *01 60 30 60 30.* ⬦ *For guided tours, contact the City Hall on Town Square in Main Street, USA: 7.62€ (children: 4.57€).* P *Parking: Cars 6.86€, motorcycles 3.81€.* ⬦ *Disneyland Passport in high season: 1 day: 40€ (children 3-11 years: 30€); 3 days: 109€ (children: 84€). 3-day passports allows entrance to both theme parks and can be used non-consecutively. Passes valid for 3 years. Readmission: to leave the park temporarily, visitors must have their hand stamped; visitors must keep passports and parking tickets.*

Like its counterparts in the United States and Japan, this resort is the perfect illustration of Walt Disney's dream: "a small, magic garden where both children and grown-ups could have fun together."

Disneyland Paris occupies a total area of 55 hectares – 135 acres and includes five lands devoted to a particular theme **(Main Street USA, Frontierland, Adventureland, Fantasyland and Discoveryland)**. Each land stages spectacular shows featuring amazing automata that move in sumptuous, elaborate settings. It also has its own boutiques and restaurants (table-service and self-service).

DOMME★★

POPULATION 1 030

MICHELIN MAP 329 I 7

GREEN GUIDE DORDOGNE BERRY LIMOUSIN

One of the many medieval fortified towns *(bastides)* founded in southwest France by both French and English, Domme was laid out by Philippe le Hardi (the Bold) in 1281. The normal rectangular plan of such settlements was here distorted in order to fit it to the rocky crag overlooking the Dordogne 145m – 475ft below.

Visit

Panorama★★★

There are splendid views over the alluvial valley of the Dordogne from the Barre belvedere or, better still, from the cliff-top walk (Promenade des Falaises – *no parapet*) just below the public gardens.

Although the river meanders here are not so well-formed as those upstream at Trémolat nor as perfect as the one at Luzech on the Lot, their sinuous pattern is enhanced in a most satisfactory way by the curving cliffs, lines of poplars and the layout of field boundaries and the crops growing within them.

The regularity of the river channel, the equilibrium reached between the forces of erosion and deposition, and the present stable state of the meanders mean that the Dordogne here is a regulated river. All around is the opulent landscape so characteristic of Périgord: castles perched on the heights, well-wooded slopes dotted with stone-built villages, and the rich alluvial lands with their lush meadows, walnut trees and crops of tobacco and corn.

Of all the creative artists who have come here seeking inspiration, the writer Henry Miller was perhaps the most affected; he described the area as perhaps the nearest thing to Paradise on earth.

DOMRÉMY-LA-PUCELLE★

POPULATION 182

MICHELIN MAP 307 E 8

GREEN GUIDE ALSACE LORRAINE CHAMPAGNE

Joan of Arc was born in this modest village in the Meuse valley on 6 January 1412. It was at Bois-Chenu 1.5km – 1 mile south that she heard the voices of St Catherine, St Margaret and St Michael calling upon her to deliver France from the misery inflicted on her by the English and their Burgundian allies. Having with some difficulty convinced the local lord, Robert de Baudricourt, of the divine nature of her mission, she left Vaucouleurs on 23 February 1429 at the age of 17. In the next 15 months there followed the journey to Chinon, the testing time at Poitiers, the relief of Orléans, the coronation at Reims, the campaigns of Paris, the Loire and the Oise; and finally the funeral pyre at Rouen, during the course of which there emerged for the first time the stirring of a truly French national feeling in opposition to the horrors of the Hundred Years War, the sufferings of the occupied territories and the insubordination of the Burgundians.

Visit

Maison natale de Jeanne d'Arc★

♿ ⏰ *Apr-Sep: daily 9am-noon, 1.30-6.30pm; Oct-Mar: daily except Tue 10am-noon, 2-5pm.* ⏰ *Closed 1 Jan, first 3 weeks of Jan, 25 Dec.* ✆ *3€ (children 6-12: 1.50€)* ☎ *03 29 06 95 86.*
Joan was born into a family of prosperous peasants. The modest home with its stout walls is moving in its simplicity (small museum).

Église

The church built in the early 15C contains a 12C font which witnessed Joan's christening ceremony.

◖◗ Basilique du Bois Chenu.

Le DORAT★★

POPULATION 2 203

MICHELIN MAP 325 D3

GREEN GUIDE DORDOGNE BERRY LIMOUSIN

Le Dorat lies in the gently rolling countryside of the old province of Marche, whose patchwork of pastureland feeds the yellowish-fawn Limousin cattle bought and sold in the great market at **St-Yrieix-la-Perche** 41km – 25 miles south of Limoges. The little town has a collegiate church of impressive size and harmonious proportions.

Visit

Collégiale St-Pierre★★

⏰ *Daily year-round.*  *Guided tours: daily except Sun and public holidays 10am-noon, 2.30-6pm. Call in advance. No charge.*
The great edifice was rebuilt in Romanesque style over a period of 50 years beginning 1112. It is firmly rooted in its region by virtue of its siting, the coarse granite from which it is built, and by a number of characteristic Limousin features. These include massive square west tower flanked by bell-turrets, the portal with its scalloped

archivolts, the openwork lantern (inspired by the one built 50 years earlier at St-Junien 45km – 28 miles south but vastly more original), and the mouldings used in the arches and arcades throughout the building.

The late-11C crypt **(crypte)** dedicated to St Anne has crudely hewn columns and simple capitals, only one of which is sculpted, openwork barrel vaulting in granite in the ambulatory and groined vaults in the chapels. Compared with the crypt in the church at Uzerche it shows the architectural progress achieved within a period of 50 years.

DOUAI

POPULATION 42 175

MICHELIN MAP 302 G 5

GREEN GUIDE NORTHERN FRANCE AND THE PARIS REGION

In the 11C and 12C, like Valenciennes, Douai provided winter quarters for merchants and merchandise using the great trading routes of Northern Europe. The town was laid out on both sides of the River Scarpe: on the west bank, the depots and workshops and a charterhouse (now a museum) on what was then an isolated site; on the east bank, the town centre, with its burghers' houses and monuments such as the bell-tower, town hall, Notre-Dame church and latterly some fine 18C residences. Douai was a free town from the late 12C, and from 1713-89 was the seat of the Parliament of Flanders, whose successor is the present Court of Appeal.

▸ **Orient Yourself:** Douai, which is listed as a "Town of Art and History," offers 2hr discovery tours May-Oct on Sun at 3.30pm. 4.50€. Information at the tourist office or on www.vpah.culture.fr.

A Bit of History

The painter **Jean Bellegambe** (1470-1534) was born here. He probably learnt his skills in Marmion's studio in Valenciennes before returning to work in his native town and its surroundings. His paintings, mostly of religious subjects, are medieval still in their treatment of familiar details, Renaissance in their decoration (colonnades, shells) and specifically Flemish in their realism. His Polyptych of the Trinity **(polyptyque d'Anchin★** – in the former Anchin charterhouse) is justly famous.

Around 1605, a number of Benedictine monks from England and Wales came to Douai and established the monastery of St Gregory the Great. It was here that the "Douai Bible", an English version of the Old Testament, was published in 1609. The monastery buildings were destroyed at the time of the French Revolution, and the community recrossed the Channel, eventually settling at Stratton-on-the-Fosse in Somerset, where they founded **Downside Abbey.**

Sights

Cortège des Gayants (Parade)

On the Sunday after 5 July, five giant figures of the Gayant family, dressed in medieval costume, are paraded though the town accompanied by folk groups: Gayant, the father (7.50m – 25ft tall, weighing 370kg – 816lbs), his wife Marie Cagenon (6.50m – 21ft tall) and their children Jacquot, Fillion and Binbin. The giants appear in town on the next two days. Gayant , the oldest giant in northern France (1530), is also the most popular. The inhabitants of Douai refer to themselves in jest as "Gayant's children".

Beffroi★

🕐 *Guided tours* 🐟 *(1hr) Jul and Aug: Mon-Sat 10am, 11am, 2pm, 3pm, 4pm and 5pm; Sep-Jun: Mon-Sat 11am, 3pm, 4pm and 5pm.* 🕐 *Closed Sun, 1 Jan and 25 Dec.* 🎫 *3.50€* ☎ *03 27 88 26 79. www.ville-douai.fr.*

The is one of the best belfries of its kind in the North of France. Both Victor Hugo and Corot were much taken by the Gothic tower of 1390 with its elaborate crown. The Flemish Renaissance courtyard front was rebuilt in 1860.

Les houillères (Northern Coalfield)

The Louis XV Aoust building (Hôtel d'Aoust) with its Rococo doorway and allegorical sculptures was the management headquarters for what used to be an important mining district. Douai lies on the edge of the great coalfield which extends from the Ruhr through southern Belgium into France. Between the Belgian border and Artois it runs for some 120km – 75mi; the six pits used to supply coking plants and power stations.

Coal was mined here from the 18C to 1990. The history of the area has been marked by such tragedies as the disaster at Courrières in 1906 when 1 200 miners lost their lives in a fire-damp explosion.

▷▷ **Musée de la Chartreuse**★ ◷ *Wed-Mon 10am-noon, 2-6pm.* ◷ *Closed Tue, 1 Jan, 1 May, Ascension Day, 14 Jul, 15 Aug, 1 and 11 Nov, 25 Dec.* ☞*Call in advance for guided tour.* ☜ *3€, no charge 1st Sunday in the month.* ☎ *03 27 71 38 80–* paintings, archeology, natural history.

Saut du **DOUBS**★★★

MICHELIN MAP 321 K 4

GREEN GUIDE BURGUNDY JURA

The gorges of the River Doubs downstream from Villers-le-Lac mark the frontier between France and Switzerland. The river has cut down deeply into the highly folded Jurassic limestone, but here its course has been blocked by eroded mate-rial to form Lake Chaillexon (Lac de Chaillexon). Its waters escape from the lake over the 28m – 92ft high Doubs Falls (Saut de Doubs).

◷ **Organizing Your Time:** Follow a footpath through the woods to reach the main viewpoint (*45min return*); beyond, a very steep path descends to the lake itself, from where there is another most impressive view of the falls crashing down into the narrow defile.

Saut du Doubs

DUNKERQUE

DUNKIRK

POPULATION 70 331

MICHELIN MAP 302 C 1

GREEN GUIDE NORTHERN FRANCE AND THE PARIS REGION

Dunkirk (Church of the Dunes in Flemish) was originally a fishing village, whose transformation into the principal port of Flanders began as early as the 14C. Handling timber from Scandinavia, wool from England and wine from Bordeaux, by the 17C it had become a pawn in the political manœuvres of the European powers. It was taken by Turenne after his victory in the Battle of the Dunes in 1658, but was given to England immediately afterwards in recognition of her help in the struggle against Spain. The town was repurchased by France in 1662, the crowning achievement of the shrewd diplomatic campaign waged on Louis XIV's behalf by the diplomat Lionne.

A Bit of History

It was now that Dunkirk became the abode of smugglers and of pirates pressed into the service of the king. In the course of Louis XIV's wars, a total of 3 000 foreign ships were captured or destroyed and the trade of the Netherlands completely wrecked. The most intrepid of these privateers was **Jean Bart** (1651-1702); his statue of 1848 by David d'Angers stands in the square named after him.

Demolition of the fortifications in 1713 (one of the conditions of the Treaty of Utrecht) brought about a decline in Dunkirk's fortunes, notwithstanding the efforts made by the Intendant Calonne in the mid-18C to improve the port facilities. Later, in Napoleon's scheme of things, Dunkirk played second fiddle to Antwerp.

The German breakthrough at Sedan in mid-May 1940 and subsequent dash to the coast near Abbeville had led to the Allied forces in the north being trapped with their backs to the sea.

Defeat was turned into partial victory by the "Miracle of Dunkirk", the name given to the successful evacuation between 27 May and 2 June of more than a third of a million troops from the beaches of Dunkirk itself and its outlying resorts of Malo, Zuydcoote and Bray-Dunes, an operation carried out in the face of intense bombardment on land and from the air.

Visit

Le port★★

Dunkirk is the third largest port in France with a total of over 37 million tonnes of traffic in 1994. A vast industrial zone has emerged, based on shipbuilding, steelworks, refineries and petrochemicals.

Jean Bart, "the king's official privateer"

During the wars fought by Louis XIV, the privateers of Dunkirk destroyed and captured 3 000 ships, took 30 000 prisoners and wiped out Dutch trade. The most intrepid of all the privateers was Jean Bart (1651-1702).

He was as famous as the privateers from St-Malo, Duguay-Trouin and Surcouf, and was a past master at raiding on the North Sea trade routes. Unlike pirates, who were outlaws attacking any and every passing ship, privateers were granted "letters patent" by the sovereign entitling them to attack warships or merchant vessels. In 1694 Jean Bart saved the kingdom from famine by capturing 130 ships loaded with wheat. His success owed much to the existence of an ultra-modern arsenal and the constant presence of a royal fleet. He was a simple, plain-spoken man but his exploits were many and varied. As a result, he was raised to the nobility in 1694, then three years later given the rank of Commodore. The following year he avoided a combat with nine large ships while taking the Prince de Conti to Poland. Once the threat was past, the prince commented that had they been attacked they would have been captured. Jean Bart replied that there had been no such danger as his son was in the munitions hold and the latter had orders to set light to a powder keg as soon as he gave the command.

◖◗ **Musée d'Art Contemporain**★ – ◷ *Daily except Tue 10am-12.15pm, 1.45-6pm.* ◷ *Closed 1 Jan, carnival Sunday, 1 May, 1 Nov, 25 Dec. 3.05€,* ◚ *no charge 1st Sunday in the month.* ☎ *03 28 59 21 65.* **Musée des Beaux-Arts**★ – ◷ *Daily except Tue 10am-12.15pm, 1.45-6pm.* ◷ *Closed 1 Jan, Sunday of the Dunkirk carnival, 1 May, 1 Nov, 25 Dec. 3.05€,* ◚ *no charge 1st Sunday in the month.* ☎ *03 28 59 21 65.* **Musée Portuaire**★ – ◷ *10am-12.45pm, 1.30-6pm (Jul and Aug: 10am-6pm).* ◷ *Closed 1 Jan, eve of Shrove Tuesday, 1 May, 25 Dec.* ◚ *3.81€.* ☎ *03 28 63 33 39.*

Basilique Notre-Dame de L'ÉPINE★★

MICHELIN MAP 306 I 9

GREEN GUIDE ALSACE LORRAINE CHAMPAGNE

The village nestles at the foot of its great pilgrimage church. Its houses, with a courtyard separating them from the road, eschew the crumbling local chalk in favour of half-timbering as their preferred building material.

Visit

The basilica (Basilique Notre-Dame) was started in 1410, beginning with the crossing and the lower walls of the nave, continuing with the west front in about 1450 and finishing with the east end in 1510. Its fine Flamboyant Gothic features include the slender gable over the main portal, the delicate openwork structure of the south spire (the north spire was rebuilt in the 19C), and the grotesque gargoyles **(gargouilles**★**)** which took the fancy of both the writers Huysmans and Victor Hugo.

Within, the round piers with their engaged columns are a throw-back to the Lanceolate Gothic style, while the false triforium seems to have been inspired by the one in Reims cathedral which is over 200 years older. The elegant rood screen and its monumental rood-beam are 15C work. The south side of the choir screen is Gothic; the north, Renaissance in date. The splendid Jesse Window *(in the easternmost bay of the south aisle)* is a masterpiece of local work in Renaissance style, carefully composed, with finely-modelled faces and an impressive range of green hues.

ÉTRETAT★★

POPULATION 1 565

MICHELIN MAP 304 B 3

GREEN GUIDE NORMANDY

Sited where a dry valley in the chalk country of the Caux region meets the sea, Étretat was a humble fishing village well into the 19C. It was then favoured by writers such as Maupassant and painters like Courbet and Eugène Isabey.

Two excursions on foot allow the visitor to appreciate the distinctive character of the "Alabaster Coast" (Côte d'Albâtre) with its chalk cliffs seamed by bands of dark flints and yellowish marls.

Visit

Falaise d'Aval★★★

⚐ *1hr round trip on foot from the end of the promenade.*

▶ *Take the steps and then the path to the clifftop known as Porte d'Aval.*

There are fine views of the magnificent Manneport Arch, the solitary 70m – 200ft Needle (Aiguille), the long shingle beach and the Amont Cliff on the far side of the bay. The play of colours changes constantly with the time of day and conditions of sky and sea.

Falaise d'Amont★★

1hr round trip on foot from the end of the promenade.

Cliffs at Étretat

Situated at the end of the promenade, the memorial was put up to mark the spot from which two aviators, Nungesser and Coli, were last glimpsed as they set out in their "White Bird" (*Oiseau Blanc*) on their attempt to make a non-stop westward crossing of the Atlantic (8 May 1927). It is not known whether these brave men perished under the ocean's waves or in the forests of New England.

A footpath with steps cut into the cliff leads to the sea.

ÉVREUX★★

POPULATION 57 968

MICHELIN MAP 304 G 7

GREEN GUIDE NORMANDY

The history of Évreux could read like a series of unmitigated disasters, from the burnings and sackings perpetrated by Vandals, Vikings and Plantagenets, to the more recent devastation wreaked from the air by Luftwaffe (in 1940) and Allied air forces (in 1944). But after each disaster the townspeople have recreated prosperity from ruin. Evidence of this spirit can be seen in the promenade laid out on the old Roman rampart on the banks of the River Iton, and in the treatment of the Clock Tower (Tour de l'Horloge) which was built by Henry V in 1417, two years after his victory over the French at Agincourt.

Sights

Cathédrale Notre-Dame★

The cathedral, begun in the 12C under Henry II of England and continued under the Norman and Plantagenet dynasties (the choir was completed in about 1260), is essentially a harmonious Gothic building of the 13C.

It did not escape the troubles which beset the town, much restoration having to take place for example after John the Good's siege in 1356 and during the reign of Louis XI (1461-83). In the 16C the aisles of the nave were rebuilt in Flamboyant style, and after the Second World War much of the upper part of the cathedral was replaced.

Vitraux★

See illustration Introduction: Art – Architecture.

The stained-glass windows give an excellent insight into the evolution of this art form.

Late 13C: the windows of the south aisle have a wonderful intensity of colour.

14C: in the fourth chapel on the right of the ambulatory it is noticeable how the glass has acquired a greater degree of elegance. The windows of the choir were installed in about 1330. Their clarity, the delicacy of their golden tones and the transparency of their colours are admirable, and illustrate the gradual change from translucent decoration to elaborate scenes which occurred from 1330 to the end of the century.

15C: the second window in the clerestory on the north side of the nave has very subtle grisaille effects which include a pearly white. The windows of the axial chapel are a fascinating source of information on the reign of Louis XI.

16C: there is a fine Last Judgement in the rose window of the north transept.

17C: glass in the third chapel of the north part of the ambulatory.

◖◗ Ancien évêché – **Musée**★★ ◷ Tue-Sun 10am-noon, 2-6pm. ◷ Closed Mon,1 Jan, 1 May, 1 and 11 Nov, 25 Dec. ⊛ 4€, no charge first Sun in th month. ☎ 02 32 31 81 90 – archeology, medieval religious art. Église St Taurin – **Châsse de St Taurin**★★ (reliquary).

Les **EYZIES-DE-TAYAC**★★

POPULATION 853

MICHELIN MAP 329 H 6

GREEN GUIDE DORDOGNE BERRY LIMOUSIN

The discovery here of cave-paintings and of shelters cut into the base of the cliffs contributed to the beginnings more than a century ago of the scientific investigation of prehistory.

Largely French in their origins, prehistoric studies got under way early in the 19C, following the work carried out by Boucher de Perthes in the Somme region, at Acheul and Abbeville. He was succeeded by other investigators, who concentrated their attention on the wealth of evidence here in the Vézère valley; among the eminent pioneers who laid the foundations on which modern archeology is based – Lartet, Mortillet, the abbots A and J Bouyssonie and Lemozi, Dr Capitan, D Peyrony, Rivière, Cartailhac, Lantier and Abbot Breuil – was an English banker, Henry Christy.

Prehistory

The Quaternary Age, the most recent and shortest of the periods into which geological history is divided, began some 2 000 millennia ago. During this time the great glaciers spread outwards from the high mountains, a result of the general cooling of the global atmosphere, but the period is marked above all by the movement into Asia and Europe of early people who had first made their appearance in Africa 1 000 millennia previously.

Grotto de Lascaux

J. Vertut

Towards the end of Tertiary times, about 3 000 000 years ago (1), it seems that the first glimmerings of reflective – not simply instinctive – thought occurred in the minds of the pre-hominids, thus distinguishing mankind's oldest ancestors from other species. For most purposes, the Quaternary Age as defined by geologists corresponds to "prehistoric times" as defined by anthropologists, and the Paleolithic, marked by the manufacture and use of knapped-flint tools, takes up most of the period.

Lower Paleolithic – 2 000 000 to 150 000 years BC. The first tools are made and various human species succeed one another, evolving all the time; Australopithecus from southern Africa, Pithecanthropus from Java, Sinanthropus from northern China, Atlanthropus from North Africa. Traces have been found of the encampments made by auroch hunters as they pursued their quarry across the steppes, notably in the Pyrenees (the skull found at the Caune d'Arago cavern near Tautavel, the jaw at Montmaurin). At Nice, studies have been made of the print made by a human foot and also of the Terra Amata site used by hunters in the Paillon and Var valleys, a beach now some 26m – 85ft above the present level of the Mediterranean.

To the same period belong the deposits found in the Lower Ardèche and around Carnac, as well as the bifaces and other flint tools discovered at Gouzeaucourt *(17km – 11mi south of Cambrai)*.

The fragments of skull belonging to Fontechevade Man *(southeast of La Rochefoucauld)* have been linked to the Tayacian culture marking the transition from the Lower to the Middle Paleolithic.

Middle Paleolithic – 150 000 to 35 000 years BC. A human skeleton of the Neanderthal type was found at Chapelle-aux-Saints near Brive-la-Gaillarde in 1908; Neanderthal Man first appeared about 150 000 years ago, possibly as a descendant of Atlanthropus, but died out some 35 000 years ago. The first tombs date from this period.

Upper Paleolithic – 35 000 to 10 000 years BC. Skeletons dating from the early part of this period were found at Cro-Magnon in the Dordogne in 1868. Cro-Magnon people were tall, with nimble hands and possessed of great inventiveness, the first examples of modern man, Homo sapiens. Another branch of the same species, characterised likewise by large brains, sophisticated language and self-awareness, is formed by the people known as the Chancelade race, remains of whom were discovered at Chancelade near Périgueux in 1888.

The Aurignacian and **Perigordian** cultures – the latter is marked by long migration periods – though contemporary, do not seem to have been in contact with each other and differ in a number of respects, although both are characterised by a continuous improvement in tool-making and the development of hunting techniques which allowed time to be set aside for the creation of works of art (line-drawings and paintings). Aurignacian industry (🌐 *see* **Aurignac**, *Green Guide Atlantic Coast*) brought forth very finely knapped flints, gravers and scrapers and perforated batons made from reindeer horn. The culture reached its peak about 25 000 years ago; its achievements can be seen in the famous drawings in the Pair-non-Pair caves at **Marcamps** (🌐 *see Green Guide Atlantic Coast)*, in the cave at La Grèze and in the shelter **(Abri du Poisson)**, all of which mark the beginnings of human activity in the lower Vézère valley.

Solutrean culture, named after the rock near Mâcon (Roche de **Solutré**★★, 🌐 *see Green Guide Burgundy Jura)* at the foot of which important discoveries were made, is well represented in the Dordogne. It is characterised by the manufacture of fine flint blades and weapons with serrated points and by the appearance of needles with eyes.

The warming-up of the climate at the end of the Magdalenian period encouraged people to live more in the open as at Pincevent and Étiolles in the Île-de-France. Later, in the Azilian period (named after the Mas d'Azil cave – in the Pyrenean foothills), people once again lived in caves, both in the Pyrenees and in the Dordogne. The Paleolithic was followed by the Mesolithic (10 000 to 7 500 years ago) which was marked by a decline in artistic output, although increasingly sophisticated implements were made like the miniaturised tools and new types of harpoon found at Mas d'Azil (🌐 *see Grotte du MAS D'AZIL)*. There followed the Neolithic, the period in which the first settled agricultural societies appear and which leads us out of prehistoric times into the era of writing and recorded history.

The slow pace of human progress stuns the imagination; it took people about 30 000 centuries to learn to polish stone; in contrast, the 50 centuries which followed saw the rise of the brilliant civilisations of the Near East and Egypt, and the discovery and use of metal (bronze).

Capital of Prehistory

There are almost 200 prehistoric sites in the Dordogne, more than half of them in the vicinity of Les Eyzies. The area has easily-accessible natural **caves** and shelters as well as rock projections forming a natural habitat. Prehistoric people have left many traces of their activities. Two hundred centuries before civilisations arose along the Tigris and the Nile, the valley of the Vézère was inhabited by accomplished artists who carved in ivory and reindeer horn and painted on the walls of caves.

Les Eyzies was one of humanity's capitals long before Nineveh; the deposits at **Laugerie-Haute** (& Apr-Sep: ✺ *Guided tours by appointment (45min, last admission 1hr before closing time)* ⊙ *9am-noon, 2-6pm; Mar and Oct: daily except Tue 9.30am-noon, 2-5.30pm; Nov-Feb: daily except Wed 10am-noon, 2-5pm.* ⊙ *Closed 1 Jan, 1 May, 1 and 11 Nov, 25 Dec.* ✆ *2.44€. As for information at the grotte de Font-de-Gaume.* ☎ *05 53 06 86 00.)* are all of six metres – 20ft thick; they reveal to us 7 000 years of civilisation (Solutrean and Magdalenian cultures).

▷▷ **Grotte du Grand-Roc**★★ ⊙ *Guided tours ✺ (30min) Apr-Oct: daily 10am-6pm; Jul and Aug: daily 9.30am-7pm; Nov-Mar: daily 10am-5pm.* ⊙ *Closed Jan and 25 Dec.* ✆ *6.50€ (children: 3.50€).* ☎ *05 53 06 92 70.*

Musée National de la Préhistoire★ ⊙ *Jul and Aug: daily 9.30am-6.30pm; Jun and Sep: daily except Tue 9.30am-6pm; Oct-May: daily except Tue 9.30am-12.30pm, 2-5.30pm. ✺ Call in advance for guided tour.* ⊙ *Closed 1 Jan and 25 Dec.* ✆ *4.50€ Mon-Sat, 3€ Sun (under 18 years: no charge), no charge 1st Sun in the month.* ☎ *05 53 06 45 45.*

Grotte de Font-de-Gaume★ ⊙ *Guided tours ✺ (45min) mid-May to mid-Sep: Sun-Fri 9.30am-5.30pm; mid-Sep to mid-May: Sun-Fri 9.30am-12.30pm, 2-5.30pm. Last departure 1hr30min before closing. Call in advance.* ⊙ *Closed Sat, 1 Jan, 1 May, 1 and 11 Nov, 25 Dec.* ✆ *6.10€.* ☎ *05 53 06 86 00.*

Le **FAOUËT**

POPULATION 2 869

MICHELIN MAP 308 J 6

GREEN GUIDE BRITTANY

Pleasantly sited in well-wooded countryside, this large village attests to the period of great prosperity which followed the troubled times brought about by the War of the Breton Succession. In the 15C, nine fairs a year were held here, leading to the construction of the great market hall.

Visit

Halle
Built at the beginning of the 16C, it is divided into three naves, each of 15 bays; its massive timber roof is covered with slates and supported on granite columns.

Excursion

Chapelle St-Fiacre★
2.5km – 1.5mi south. – The Breton countryside is dotted with many such isolated rural chapels. The Bouteville family were anxious to emulate their rivals, the great de Rohans, who were building the church and hospital at Kernascleden; begun in 1450, the chapel here took 30 years to complete and was probably endowed with a hospice for pilgrims and the sick.

Flanked by two bell-turrets, the west front is dominated by a central belfry with a tall spire and projecting balcony like that of the Kreisker Chapel ( *see ST-POL-DE-LÉON).* The Flamboyant rood screen **(jubé★★)** of 1480 is a superb example of Breton painted wood sculpture.

The 16C windows, divided horizontally, mark that moment in the art of stained glass when it evolves from a series of medallions to a planned composition. Particularly fine are the scenes of the Passion in the main window of the chancel, the Life of John the Baptist in the south transept, and a Jesse Tree and the Life of St Fiacre in the north transept.

FÉCAMP★★

POPULATION 20 808

MICHELIN MAP 304 C 3

GREEN GUIDE NORMANDY

Fécamp's main activity is still its port, a long-standing "capital" for cod fishing in French Newfoundland; today it caters for both industry (timber, bulk goods) and fishing (herring and mackerel). Several smoking and deep-freezing factories have been set up nearby.

As early as the 11C Fécamp had seen considerable monastic activity as a result of the efforts of Guglielmo da Volpiano. This energetic cleric had been Abbot of St-Bénigne at Dijon, where he had implemented the important reform which had originated from Cluny and which involved the worship of the Precious Blood and of the Holy Trinity. That master of the short story, **Guy de Maupassant** (1850-93), lived in the town and used it as the setting for much of his literary output.

▶ **Orient Yourself:** Fécamp, which is listed as a "Town of Art and History," offers discovery tours conducted by guide-lecturers approved by the Ministry of Culture and Communication. 5€. Information available at the Service Animation du Patrimoine (Heritage Dept.). ☎ 02 35 28 84 39. www.vpah.culture.fr.

Visit

Abbatiale de la Trinité★★
As big as any cathedral, the ancient abbey church marks an important stage in the evolution of Gothic architecture in Normandy. Built for the most part between 1168

Dormition of the Virgin

and 1219, it was much influenced by the developments taking place in the Île de France (use of tribunes as in the churches derived from St-Denis outside Paris, the combination of flying buttresses and triforium pioneered at Chartres, which made the tribunes redundant and which here is seen in the south wall of the chancel).

Norman regionalism reasserts itself however in a number of ways: in the slender lantern-tower high above the crossing, and in the inspection gallery at the base of the triforium windows.

In the south transept chapel is a beautiful **Dormition of the Virgin**★.

 **Palais Bénédictine**★★ ◷ *Mid-Jul to end Aug: 10am-7pm; end Mar to mid-Jul and Sep: 10am-1pm, 2-6.30pm; Feb-Mar and Oct-Dec: 10.30am-12.45pm, 2-6pm. Last admission 1hr before closing.* ◷ *Closed Jan and 25 Dec.* ⊛ *5.60€ (children under 12 years: no charge).* ☎ *02 35 10 26 10. www.benedictine.fr* – objets d'art, history and production of Benedictine. **Musée des Terres-Neuvas et de la Pêche**★ ♿ ◷ *Sep-Jun: daily except Tue 10am-noon, 2-5.30pm Jul-Aug: daily 10am-7pm.* ◷ *Closed 1 Jan, 1 May, 25 Dec.* ⊛ *3€ (under 18 years: no charge), ticket combined with the Musée des Arts et de l'Enfance.* ☎ *02 35 28 31 99.* **Musée Centre des Arts et de l'Enfance**★ ◷ *Sep-Jun: daily except Tue 10am-noon, 2-5.30pm; Jul-Aug: daily 10am-7pm.* ◷ *Closed 1 Jan, 1 May, 25 Dec.* ⊛ *3€ (under 18 years: no charge), ticket combined with the Musée des Terre-Neuvas et de la pêche.* ☎ *02 35 28 31 99* – ceramics, ivory, archeology, regional furniture.

FENIOUX★

POPULATION 133

MICHELIN MAP 324 G 4

GREEN GUIDE ATLANTIC COAST

The small village of Fenioux boasts an 11C country church, a fine example of Romanesque architecture, which is pleasing in its simplicity.

Visit

Église

On the south side of the building are the ruined cloisters of an earlier Carolingian edifice retained by the architects who reconstructed the rest of the church between 1000 and 1050.

The west front has perhaps the finest example of the didactic sculpture of the Saintonge School; the signs of the Zodiac emphasise the passage of time, the cycle of the months, the Wise and Foolish Virgins, and the Vices and Virtues (the triumph of Good over Evil). The little north doorway is charmingly decorated with leaves and with the flowers of the clematis which adorns so many houses in the Saintonge area. The belfry is a masterpiece of delicate construction in spite of a certain stiffness resulting from its restoration by followers of Viollet-le-Duc in the 19C.

Lanterne des Morts★

These unusual constructions were common in the region in the 11C and 12C. They consist of a sepulchre, steps leading up to an altar, a hollow column, the top of which housed an eternal flame, the whole surmounted by a little roof and a splendid cross. This is a particularly fine example with a hollow base framed by 14 columns, a moulded entablature, a lantern surrounded by smaller columns, and a pyramid-shaped roof of overlapping tiles surmounted by a cross.

FIGEAC★★

POPULATION 9 549

MICHELIN MAP 337 I 4

GREEN GUIDE DORDOGNE BERRY LIMOUSIN

Sprawled along the north bank of the Célé, Figeac's development began at the point where the Auvergne meets Upper Quercy. A commercial town, it had a prestigious past as is shown in the architecture of its tall sandstone town houses.

The small city's main industrial concern is Ratier, a company which specialises in aeronautical construction.

▸ **Orient Yourself:** Figeac, which is listed as a "Town of Art and history," offers 2hr discovery tours from Apr-Sep. 5€. Information at the tourist office or on www.vpah.culture.com.

A Bit of History

Jean-François Champollion – Champollion, the outstanding Orientalist, whose brilliance enabled Egyptology to make such great strides, was born at Figeac in December 1790. At the beginning of the 19C, Ancient Egyptian civilisation was still a mystery, since the meaning of hieroglyphics (the word means "sacred carving") had not yet been deciphered.

By the time Champollion was 14, he had a command of Greek, Latin, Hebrew, Arabic, Chaldean and Syrian. After his studies in Paris, he lectured in history, at the youthful age of 19, at Grenoble University.

He set himself the task of deciphering a polished basalt tablet, showing three different inscriptions (Egyptian hieroglyphics, demotic – simplified Egyptian script which appeared around 650 BC – and Greek), which had been discovered in 1799 by members of Napoleon's expedition to Egypt near Rosetta in the northwest Nile delta, from which it derives its name – the Rosetta Stone.

In 1826, he founded the Egyptology Museum at the Louvre Palace, Paris, and became its first curator. In 1831, he was appointed Professor of Archeology at the Collège de France; however, he gave only three lecture courses before dying a year later, worn out by all his hard work.

A. Kumrdjian, La Brède

Place des Écritures

Figeac - Address Book

For coin ranges, see the Legend at the back of the guide.

EATING OUT

À l'Escargot – *2 bis av. Jean-Jaurès -* ☎ *05 65 34 23 84 -* 🕐 *closed 21 Dec-10 Mar and Thu - reserv. recommended.* The regular clientele of this unassuming restaurant flock here for the simple, family-style fare and friendly ambience. Three generations of women have run the kitchen here.

La Dînée du Viguier – *R. Boutaric -* ☎ *05 65 50 08 08 -* 🕐 *closed 23 Jan-15 Feb, 15-22 Nov, Sun eve out of season, Sat lunchtime and Mon.* The restaurant in the Château Viguier du Roy combines medieval decor (high ceilings, painted beams and stone fireplace) with contemporary cuisine.

Ferme-Auberge Domaine des Villedieu – *46100 Boussac - 8km/5mi SW of Figeac on the D 13 and then the D 41 -* ☎ *05 65 40 06 63 - reserv. required .* An enchanting 18C farmhouse deep in the country. In keeping with their farming background, the owners serve their own produce in the wood-floored dining room and on the outdoor terrace. The restored farm buildings have been converted into a number of attractive guestrooms.

WHERE TO STAY

Champollion – *3 pl. Champollion -* ☎ *05 65 34 04 37 - 10 rooms.* The memory of the famous Egyptologist is everywhere in the centre of town, including this hotel, the town's medieval meat market. Although on the small side, the bedrooms are modern and well-maintained.

Le Pont d'Or – *2, av Jean-Jaurès -* ☎ *05 65 50 95 00 - www.hotelpontdor.com - 10 rooms.* A welcoming stone house on the banks of the Célé, with some rooms offering balconies overlooking the river. A yellow and orange colour scheme, contemporary furniture and immaculate bathrooms. Fitness room and rooftop swimming pool. In summer, breakfast is served on the riverside terrace.

LEISURE ACTIVITIES

Domaine de Loisirs du Surgié – *Chemin Moulin Surgie -* ☎ *05 65 34 59 00 - www. domainedesurgie.com -* 🕐 *open May-Sep, 11am-8pm.* This large (14ha/34.5-acre) outdoor watersports and leisure area is on the banks of the River Célé to the northeast of Figeac.

SHOPPING

Market – The town's weekly market is held on Saturdays (the largest one is the last Saturday of the month). Evening markets are held on Thursdays in July and August.

Visit

Le Vieux Figeac★

The old quarter, surrounded by boulevards which trace the line of the former moats, has kept its medieval town plan with its narrow and tortuous alleys.

The buildings, of elegant beige sandstone, exemplify the architecture of the 13C, 14C and 15C. Generally the ground floor was opened by large pointed arches and the first floor had a gallery of arcaded bays. Underneath the flat tiled roof was the soleilho, an open attic, which was used to dry laundry, store wood, grow plants, etc. Its openings were separated by columns or pillars in wood or stone, sometimes even brick, which held up the roof. Other noticeable period architectural features to be discovered during your tour of the old quarter are: corbelled towers, doorways, spiral staircases and some of the top storeys, which are half-timbered and of brick.

▷▷ **Hôtel de la Monnaie★** 🕐 *Jul-Aug: daily 10am-7.30pm; May-Jun and Sep: Mon-Sat 10am-noon, 2.30-6.30pm, Sun 10am-1pm; Oct-Apr: daily except Sun and public holidays 10am-noon, 2.30-6pm.* 🐽 *2€.* ☎ *05 65 34 06 25.* **Musée Champollion★** 🕐 *Mar-Jun: daily except Mon (excluding public holidays) 10am-noon, 2.30-6.30pm, Jul and Aug: daily 10am-noon, 2.30-6.30pm; Nov-Feb: daily except Mon 2-6pm.* 🕐 *Closed 1 Jan, 1 May, 25 Dec.* 🐽 *3.09€ (children: 1.86€).* ☎ *05 65 50 31 08.*

The Rosetta Stone

During the reigns of the first Ptolemaic kings (332-80 BC), Egyptian priests recorded the decrees issued at the end of their synods on basalt tablets which were then displayed in the main temples. The Rosetta Stone is one of these tablets, carved in 196 BC. By this time, the members of the clergy were the only people to be taught hieroglyphics, hence the need for a translation into three languages so that the decrees would be understood also by those people who used demotic script in Memphis and Greek in Alexandria. The content of the decrees was both political and economic, defining the respective powers of the clergy and the monarch, the extent of fiscal privileges and the nature of laws and taxes among other things. This is illustrated by the following extracts from the Rosetta Stone:

"whereas king PTOLEMY..., the son of King Ptolemy and Queen Arsinoe, the Gods Philopatores, has been a benefactor both to the temples and to those who dwell in them, ... he has dedicated to the temples revenues in money and corn and has undertaken much outlay to bring Egypt into prosperity, and to establish the temples, and has been generous with all his own means; and of the revenues and taxes levied in Egypt some he has wholly remitted and others has lightened, in order that the people and the others might be in prosperity during his reign; ...he has directed that the gods shall continue to enjoy the revenues of the temples and the yearly allowances given to them, both of corn and money, likewise also the revenues assigned to the gods from vine land and from gardens and other properties which belonged to the gods in his father's time."

Translation courtesy of the British Museum, London.

FILITOSA★★

MICHELIN MAP 345 C 9

GREEN GUIDE CORSE (IN FRENCH)

This fascinating site was discovered in 1946; the beginnings of Corsican history are all visible here, from the Neolithic (6000-2000 BC), to the Megalithic (3000-1000 BC) and the Torreen (1500-800 BC), and finally to the Roman.

A Bit of History

The **Megalithic people** interred their dead in caves or beneath dolmens. Peaceful in their ways, they made granite sculptures using tools fashioned from imported obsidian.

About 1800 BC they raised menhirs to their chiefs, prototypical statues in which the head is already distinct from the body. Around 1500 BC, the representation of anatomy becomes more precise, with the spine and shoulder-blades shown. Finally, in the hope of acquiring their powers, they depicted their enemies as armed men killed in combat; these are the Torreens.

The **Torreens** were a sea-faring, warlike people, technically advanced, with clothes made of leather, breastplates and weapons of bronze and iron. They had already harassed the empires around the edge of the Mediterranean and caused concern to the Egypt of Rameses III. But they were essentially a race of builders, and in time began to lead a more settled existence, involving trading and other links with the peoples of Italy and Sardinia. Over a period of some 500 years they gradually pushed the Megalithic people into the northern part of Corsica before they themselves abandoned the island around 800 BC, probably making for Sardinia.

Visit

Station préhistorique★★ *1hr*

🕐 *Apr to mid-Oct: 8am to dusk. Preferably in the middle of the day: good light to study the sculptures and engravings. Sound recordings in 4 languages.* 🎧 *5€.* ☎ *04 95 74 00 91.*
By the path leading to the prehistoric site stands the superb menhir known as Filitosa V bearing, in front, a long sword and an oblique dagger, and behind, anatomical or clothing details.

A stone wall built by the Megalithic people encloses the site. Within it, four striking groups of monuments testify to the domination exercised by the Torreens: the East Monument **(Monument Est)** which they filled in; the remains of huts **(cabanes)** which they re-used, the circular Central Monument **(Monument central)**, and the fragments of menhir-statues. The latter had been made by the Megalithic people; the Torreens cut them up and re-used them, face downwards, in the construction of the Central Monument, doubtless to signal their supremacy. Some of them, however, have been stood upright again, and Filitosa IX and XIII frame the way into the Central Monument. The West Monument **(Monument Ouest)** is Torreen, and is built on Megalithic foundations.

The five menhir-statues near an age-old olive-tree on the far slope of the valley mark the end of the Megalithic period in this area.

FOIX

POPULATION 9 660

MICHELIN MAP 343 H 7

GREEN GUIDE LANGUEDOC ROUSSILLON TARN GORGES

Foix is the name both of a region – pays de Foix – and of its capital on the Ariège between the high hills of the Plantaurel and the Pyrenees proper. In the Middle Ages the town enjoyed some importance as the capital of the colourful Counts of Foix.

A Bit of History

At the conclusion of the Albigensian Crusade, the Counts, who had favoured the heresy, were obliged to submit to the King of France. At the end of the 13C they inherited that other Pyrenean statelet, the Béarn, which still enjoyed its independence, and decided to reside there. Their fondness for Foix, their ancestral home, was undimmed, although they failed to maintain it properly, and in the end had to dismantle much of its massive fortifications. But the three great towers remained intact, symbols of their pride, property and power.

The greatest of the Counts was Gaston Febus (1331-91), a brilliant figure whose wide culture did not however stop him killing both his brother and his only son. Henri IV was a member of the family; his accession to the French throne in 1589 meant the formal union of the Pays de Foix with France.

Site

Panorama★

From the **Château** (🕐 Apr-Mai: 10.30am-noon, 2-5.30pm; Jun and Sep: 9.45am-noon, 2-6pm; Jul-Aug: 9.45am-6.30pm; Oct-Mar: daily except Mon and Tue, apart from school holidays, 10.30am-noon, 2-5.30pm; 🕐 closed Jan, 1st Mon in Sep, and 25 Dec; ⊚ 4€ , ages 6-18 2€; ☎ 05 34 09 83 83) rock high above the river there are extensive views over the surrounding region. To the southwest are the green Plantaurel hills, characterised by their remarkably regular relief. To the south are the Pyrenees themselves; among the many summits can be picked out the Trois Seigneurs (2 199m – 7 215ft) and St-Barthélemy (2 368m – 7 769ft). Eastward lies the high and windy Sault plateau from which rise a number of pointed peaks resembling the one on which the Cathar fortress of Montségur is built.

Excursions

Grotte de Niaux★★

Michelin map 343 H 8. Located in the Vicdessos valley, this cave is famed for its remarkably well-preserved prehistoric wall drawings, in particular those depicting animals in the "Black Hall" (Salon noir); the pure, sober lines and high craftsmanship mark the summit of Magdalenian art.

Parc pyrénéen de l'art préhistorique (Tarascon-sur-Ariège) ★★

At Lacombe, on the road to Banat. The park, devoted to cave paintings – there are some 12 decorated caves in the Ariège area – comprises a distinctive modern building housing a display area, the Grand Atelier, and an open space with exhibits featuring water and rock. An audio-tour of the Grand Atelier bringing into play the latest technological advances gives a comprehensive account of the discoveries of cave paintings.

FONTAINEBLEAU★★★

POPULATION 15 714

MICHELIN MAP 312 F 5

GREEN GUIDE NORTHERN FRANCE AND THE PARIS REGION

As early as the 12C, the Capetian kings had built a hunting lodge here, drawn by the abundant game which thrived in the vast forest.

🕐 **Organizing Your Time:** The exterior of the Palace will take you about an hour to move around, so you may want to tour this first before spending the majority of your time within the countless rooms of the palace.

A Bit of History

The woodland covers 25 000ha – 62 000 acres, much of it high forest of sessile oaks, Norway pines and beeches. It grows on the low east-west sandstone ridges, among the crags and boulders of stony wastelands, and in the sandy depressions between the ridges. The Forest is traversed by a network of well-signposted footpaths. Since the days of Colbert's Forestry Ordinance of 1669, "a masterpiece of forestry administration" (J L Reed), it has been carefully managed to ensure its long-term survival.

In spite of the forest's fame and popularity, it is the palace begun by François I which has made the reputation of Fontainebleau.

A taste for natural surroundings together with its role as a military base (notably for cavalry) led to the growth of the town of Fontainebleau in the 19C. Between 1947 and 1967 it was home to the headquarters of NATO.

Visit

Palais★★★

From the days of the Capetian kings to the time of Napoleon III, the Palace of Fontainebleau has been lived in, added to and altered by the sovereigns of France. Napoleon Bonaparte liked it; here, in contrast to Versailles, he was free of the overwhelming presence of Louis XIV, a formidable predecessor in the quest for glory. He called Fontainebleau "the house of Eternity", furnished it in Empire style and set about altering it for himself, for Josephine, and for Pope Pius VII.

In 1528, François I commissioned Gilles Le Breton to replace the existing medieval buildings with two structures linked by a gallery. Like his predecessor Charles VIII, while campaigning in Italy, François had acquired a taste for agreeable surroundings adorned with works of art. He brought in gifted and prolific artists who are known as the **First School of Fontainebleau**. They included Rosso (of Florence), Primaticcio (from Perugia), Niccolo dell'Abbate (from Parma), as well as architects, thinkers,

Cour du Cheval-Blanc or des Adieux

M. Beaugeois/PIX

Fontainebleau - Address Book

For coin ranges, see the Legend at the back of the guide.

EATING OUT

🍽️ **Croquembouche** – *43 r. de France –* ☎ *01 64 22 01 57.* 🕐 *Closed Aug, Christmas school holidays, Sun evening, Thu lunch and Wed.* A plain and simple restaurant in centre city frequented by regular patrons who appreciate the warm reception, the inviting dining room decorated in soothing colours, and the traditional food prepared from fresh produce.

🍽️ **L'Île aux Truites** – *6 chemin de la Basse-Varenne, 77870 Vulaines-sur-Seine - 7km/4.2mi E of Fontainebleau dir. Samoreau.* ☎ *01 64 23 71 87.* 🕐 *Closed 20 Dec to 25 Jan, Thu lunch and Wed – reserv. required.* A pretty thatched-roof country house well-situated on the banks of the Seine. Diners can savour trout and salmon culled from the restaurant's fish tank while enjoying an incomparable view of the river and forest. Summertime, meals are served outdoors.

WHERE TO STAY

🛏️ **Hôtel Victoria** – *112 r. de France.* ☎ *01 60 74 90 00 – resa@hotelvictoria.com –* 🅿️ *– 20 rms: –* 🍴 *7€.* This 19C building is a pleasant, relaxing place to stay. Most of the rooms on its three floors have been redone in shades of yellow and blue; five of them have a marble fireplace. Breakfast is served on the veranda or the terrace looking toward the garden.

🛏️ **Hôtel de la Chancellerie** – *1 r. de la Chancellerie.* ☎ *01 64 22 21 70 – hotel. chancellerie@gofornet.com – 25 rms –* 🍴

5.50€. This small hotel in the heart of the city is located in the former buildings of the chancellery. The small rooms are bright and practical and the reception is amiable. An appealing address for those on a budget.

ON THE TOWN

Le Franklin-Roosevelt – *20 r. Grande.* ☎ *01 64 22 28 73 –* 🕐 *Mon-Sat 10am-1am.* This wine bar aims to please. Note the inviting decor featuring mahogany furniture and red leatherette wall seats, the library dedicated to the period between 1890 and 1920, the intimate ambience with jazz in the background and some fine vintages on the wine menu. Heated terrace.

SHOPPING

La Ferme des Sablons – *19 r. des Sablons.* ☎ *01 64 22 67 25 –* 🕐 *Tue-Fri 8am-1pm, 3:30pm-7:30pm; Sat 8am-7:30pm; Sun 8am-1pm.* 🕐 *Closed Aug.* A third of the 130 varieties of cheese sold by this cheese shop are matured on site, including the house speciality, le Fontainebleau, a soft white cheese with cream. There is also a selection of local products. A pleasant, pastoral setting.

SPORT

Jeu de Paume de Fontainebleau – *Château de Fontainebleau.* ☎ *01 64 22 47 67 –* ♿ *-fontainebleau@wanadoo.fr –* 🕐 *daily 11am-7pm.* The jeu de paume, a sport whose descendants include tennis and squash, has been played since 1601 in this indoor court of the Château de Fontainebleau. Visitors can watch a match or try a game themselves.

cabinet-makers, goldsmiths, decorators… He also acquired works of art including Leonardo's Mona Lisa and paintings by Raphael. France was thus permeated by Renaissance taste, by Renaissance mathematics and by an appreciation of the rules of proportion derived from the architecture of Greece and Rome. The pleasures of life were savoured anew, and painters and sculptors abandoned religious subjects in favour of older divinities.

This era endowed the palace with many of its most splendid features: on the outside, the left wing and façade of the Court of the White Horse or Farewell Court (**Cour du Cheval-Blanc ou des Adieux**★★), the concave section of the Oval Court (**Cour Ovale**★), the Golden Gate (**Porte dorée**★) with its loggia painted by Primaticcio; and on the inside, the François I Gallery (**Galerie François I**★★★) by Rosso, the first important French interior to mix frescoes and stucco work, and the Ballroom (**Salle de bal**★★★) painted by Primaticcio and dell'Abbate and completed by Philibert Delorme in the reign of Henri II.

Henri II, Catherine de' Medici and Charles IX carried on the work initiated during this most creative and productive period.

Henri IV enlarged the palace further by building the real tennis court (Jeu de Paume), and the Diana Gallery (Galerie de Diane). He also completed the enclosure of the Oval Court. There was a change of style; the Second School of Fontainebleau looked to Flanders for its inspiration and found its artists in the Ile de France; oil was now the preferred medium for painting.

Louis XIII completed the Farewell Court. It was here, from the famous horse-shoe staircase built by Du Cerceau, that Napoleon bade his men farewell on 20 April 1814 following his abdication.

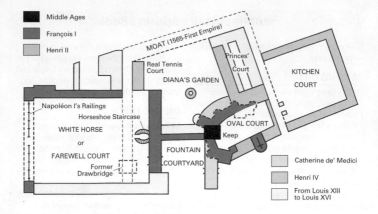

Ensemble des Grands Appartements★★★ *(First-floor State Rooms)* 🚻 🕐
*Jun-Sep: Wed-Mon 9.30am-6pm; Oct-May: Wed-Mon 9.30am-5pm. Last admission
45min before closing.* 🕐 *Closed Tue, 1 Jan, 1 May, 25 Dec.* ⊚ *5.50€ (under 18 years:
no charge), no charge 1st Sun in the month.* ☎ *01 60 71 50 60. www.musee-chateau-
fontainebleau.fr.* **Petits Appartements**★ *(Ground-floor State Rooms)* 🔍 *Guided
tours (1hr) daily. Call in advance the morning of your visit.* 🕐 *Jun-Sep: Wed-Mon
9.30am-6pm. Oct-May: Wed-Mon 9.30am-5pm.* 🕐 *Closed Tue, 1 Jan, 1 May, 25 Dec.*
⊚ *3€. (under 18 years: no charge).* ☎ *01 60 71 50 60.* **Musée Napoléon**★ 🚻 🕐
Guided tours 🔍 *(1hr) daily. Call in advance the morning of your visit. Jun-Sep:
9.30am-6pm; Oct-May: 9.30am-5pm.* 🕐 *Closed 1 Jan, 1 May, 25 Dec.* ⊚ *3€ (under
18 years: no charge).* ☎ *01 60 71 50 60.* **Gardens**★ *(Jardins).*

Châteaux in the Ile-de-France

Owing to its proximity to the seat of royal power and its immense prestige, the Ile-
de-France was for many centuries a choice setting for architectural and artistic innovations. The quest for glory and love of art have inspired sovereigns and courtiers to
build original and splendid mansions. Most of these are still extant and are a proud
testimony to their past glory.

Worth a Journey★★★
Palais de Versailles
Châteaux de Chantilly, Fontainebleau, Vaux-le-Vicomte

Worth a Detour★★
Châteaux de Breteuil, Champs, Courances, Dampierre, Écouen, Malmaison, St-Germain-en-Laye, Sceaux, Thoiry

Interesting★
Châteaux de Ferrières, Fleury-en-Bière, Grosbois, Guermantes, Maintenon, Maisons-
Laffitte, Marais, Rambouillet, La Roche-Guyon, Saussay

Also of Interest
Châteaux de Bourron, Blandy-les-Tours, Chevreuse, Courson, Malesherbes, St-Jean-
de-Beauregard

La **FONTAINE DE VAUCLUSE**

MICHELIN MAP 332 D 10

GREEN GUIDE PROVENCE

An excursion *(1hr round trip on foot)* from the village of the same name takes in
this resurgent spring which was famous enough to figure in Strabo's Geography
more than 2 000 years ago; the word Vauclusian is used world-wide to define
springs of this type.

Visit

Gushing forth at the foot of one of the cliffs marking the limits of the Vaucluse upland,
it is one of the most spectacular phenomena of its kind in the world.

It is fed by rain falling high up on the Vaucluse, the Ventoux Massif and Mount Lure; water penetrates these highly fissured limestone uplands with their 400-plus chasms (avens) and collects in a vast, still-unexplored cavern, from which it is forced out under pressure to the surface by way of a faultline.

For more than a century attempts have been made to explore the depths. In 1983 Hasenmayer went down 200m – 656ft below the surface; a remote-controlled video-equipped device reached a depth of 315m – 1 033ft in 1985 without however touching bottom.

Towards the end of the winter, the flow from the underground source can amount to 100 cubic meters– 3 631 cubic feet per second. At such times the waters of the River Sorgue foam and spray against the rocks, a magnificent natural spectacle. In the dry season screens of trees mark out the strata of the plateau which is pitted with pot-holes.

Abbaye de FONTENAY★★★

MICHELIN MAP 320 G 4

GREEN GUIDE BURGUNDY-JURA

Tucked away in its lonely valley near the River Brenne, Fontenay is very evocative of the self-sufficient life of a Cistercian abbey of the 12C.

A Bit of History

St Bernard (1091-1153) – By the end of the 11C there had arisen a longing for a greater degree of asceticism, spirituality and a renunciation of self in religious life, which could not be satisfied by the wealth and power represented by Cluny. One response was the founding of the Cistercian Order in 1198 by Robert, Abbot of Molesme, at **Cîteaux,** 23km – 14 miles south of Dijon. Bernard, a young nobleman born at the Château of Fontaine near Dijon, came to Cîteaux in 1112 and before long had restored the fortunes of the abbey, which had fallen on hard times. He was made responsible for establishing the abbey at **Clairvaux** on the River Aube; then, in 1118, at the age of 27, he founded Fontenay, his "second daughter."

St Bernard was one of the great spiritual leaders of the Middle Ages, a writer, preacher, theologian, philosopher and statesman. Though diminished physically by fasting and self-mortification, he was quite tireless. He could be gentle and humble, but above all possessed an extraordinary will which he put entirely to the service of the Church. By the time of his death, at Clairvaux, he had witnessed the founding of 167 Cistercian monasteries. At the end of the 13C their number had risen to 700 and the Order enriched by donations was no longer in a position to admonish Cluny.

Visit

Ancienne abbaye – ♿ ◷ 10am-noon, 2-5pm (Apr to mid-Nov 5.30pm). ⊜ 7.50€ (children: 3.75€). ☎ 03 80 92 15 00. Fontenay is the architectural expression of the ideas of St Bernard; its buildings form the perfect setting for monastic life led according to the Rule of St Benedict. The harmonious apportionment of time between prayer, work (manual as well as intellectual, unlike Cluny) and sleep found its physical equivalent in the functional arrangement of external and internal spaces: church, cloisters, chapter-house, scriptorium (where manuscripts were copied), dormitory and forge.

The ravages of time have left the abbey in a sad state. It was sacked by the English and plundered by marauding bands of mercenaries in the Hundred Years War; it suffered during the Wars of Religion and under the regime of commendam (when abbots were nominated by royal favour and were interested only in the revenues). It was sold during the French Revolution and became a paper mill. Since 1906 its owners have been endeavouring to restore it to its original condition.

The abbey church (**église abbatiale**) was built between 1139 and 1147. It is the first example of the "monastic simplicity" characteristic of the architecture promoted by St Bernard, and is laid out in the most straightforward way, with a square chancel and chapels of square plan. The nave has a broken barrel vault, solidly supported by cross-vaulted aisles. The lesson of Cluny, whose ambitious vault had collapsed in 1125, had clearly been learnt.

FONTEVRAUD L'ABBAYE★★

MICHELIN MAP 317 J 5

GREEN GUIDE CHÂTEAUX OF THE LOIRE

A Bit of History

The Order of Fontevraud was founded in 1099 as a result of the failure in France of Pope Gregory's reform which had been designed to enhance both the competence and the respectability of the clergy.

In many ways the Plantagenets considered themselves to be more Angevin than English, and chose the abbey as their last resting place. When Eleanor of Aquitaine died at Fontevraud in 1204, her husband Henry II and her son Richard the Lionheart were already buried here.

The Order was aristocratic in nature and accommodated both sexes. It was presided over by an abbess (this at a time when the cult of the Virgin Mary was growing and influencing the status of womanhood). The abbey formed the largest monastic grouping in France and comprised five distinct elements: St Mary (nuns), St-Jean-de-l'Habit (monks), St Benedict (hospice), St Lazarus (lepers) and St Mary Magdalene (fallen women).

Having suffered in their time from the assaults of Huguenots and Revolutionaries and from use as a penitentiary, the abbey buildings are now the subject of thoroughgoing restoration.

Visit

Église abbatiale★★

Built between 1104 and 1150, this abbey church is closer in style to the architecture of southwestern France than to that of the Île-de-France, with which Anjou had no political ties at the time.

Characteristically southwestern is the sequence of four domes forming the roof of the nave, while the delicately carved capitals with their foliated scrolls and palm leaves recall the workmanship of the Saintonge and Angoulême areas, and the pyramidal dome over the crossing is very much in the manner of the Church of St-Ours at Loches.

The chancel is graceful in its clarity and simplicity.

In the transept crossing are a number of Plantagenet tombs (**gisants des Plantagenêts**★), good examples of Gothic funerary sculpture. The figures of Henry Plantagenet (died 1189), of Richard the Lionheart (died 1199) and of Eleanor of Aquitaine (died 1204) are in painted tufa, while the figure of Isabel of Angoulême, John Lackland's wife (died 1218), is of polychrome wood.

Cuisine (kitchen)★★

This highly individual structure, 27m – 89ft high, dates from around 1160 and was restored in 1902. It is a rare example of a Romanesque kitchen, with a tiled roof characteristic of the Poitiers area. It is built up in alternately square and octagonal stages. Its main function was as a smoke-house (meat and fish, especially salmon). Its fireplaces, arranged in pairs, could be lit according to the direction of the wind.

◗◗ **Église St-Michel**★

FOUGÈRES★★

MICHELIN MAP309 O 4

GREEN GUIDE BRITTANY

In the 19C Fougères was the most industrialised town in Brittany, having abandoned cloth-making in favour of shoe production. The area formed part of the frontier region taken from the Franks in AD 850 by **Nominoé** ( see VANNES). 1 pl. A.-Briand – 35300 – ☎ 02 99 94 12 20. ↝ Guided tours of the town: Fougères, which is listed at a "Town of Art and history," offersdiscovery tours conducted by guide-lecturers approved by the Ministry of Culture and Communication. Information at the tourist office or on www.vpah.culture.fr.

Château de Fougères

Château★★ – ⏱ *Apr-Sep: daily 9.30am-noon, 2-6pm (mid-Jun to mid-Sep: 9am-7pm); Feb, Mar and Oct-Dec: 10am-noon, 2-5pm.* ⏱ *Closed Jan and 25 Dec.* ✆ *3.51€ (children: 1.83€).* ☎ *02 99 99 79 59.* It is set on a rocky promontory protected by an easily-flooded" meander which formed an effective defence right up to the invention of artillery. The first fortifications date from the 10C, built in response to the entry of the Vikings into Normandy under the terms of the Treaty of St-Clair-sur-Epte of 911.

Baron Raoul II began to rebuild in stone in 1173. In the 13C the castle's mighty towers served to protect Brittany from Capetian France; round or square, with their machicolations and stonework of schist strengthened with granite, they mark the progress of military architecture. After its important role in the War of the Breton Succession (☟ see *JOSSELIN*) in the 14C, the castle was partly demolished by Richelieu in pursuit of his centralising policy designed to limit the power of the great feudal lords.

◗◗ **Église St-Sulpice**★; **Jardin public**★ (Gardens).

Cap FRÉHEL★★★

MICHELIN MAP 309 I 2

GREEN GUIDE BRITTANY

Located near the lighthouse *(30min there and back on foot)*, this is one of the most magnificent sights **(site –** ⓟ *Access to the cape: Jun-Sep: 8am-8pm,* ✆ *2€ per vehicle.)* the Breton coast has to offer. The action of the waves has worn away the softer rocks around, and the great cliff of red sandstone rises 70m – 230ft above the reefs at its foot.

Despite the abundant rainfall, the porosity of the rock and the exposure to wind mean that only plants which are well adapted to dry conditions can flourish here (heather and rushes).

Th**e panorama**★★★ from the clifftop is superb, taking in the Channel Islands and the Cotentin Peninsula.

◗◗ Phare (lighthouse – ➥ *Jul to mid-Sep: guided tours 10am-noon, 2.30-6pm.* ☎ *02 96 41 40 03.*); boat trips.

Le FUTUROSCOPE★★

MICHELIN MAP 322 I 4

GREEN GUIDE ATLANTIC COAST

This vast 70ha – 173 acre development on the northern outskirts of Poitiers was created to introduce the public to the realities of modern technology and to give an insight into future developments in a world dominated by screen images.

The complex, the European Park of the Moving Image **(Parc européen de l'image)** or more simply **Le Futuroscope,** (⏱ *Apr to early Nov: 9am-1-pm (mdinight with show); early Nov to early Jan: 9am-6pm, school and public holidays and certain weekends: 9am-7pm.* ✆ *32.01€ (children: 22.11€, low season 22.11€ (children: 15.24€).* ☎ *05 49 49 30 80.)* presents a modernistic architectural universe of steel and glass which was conceived by the French architect Denis Laming; it is dominated by a symbolic sphere above the Communication Pavilion **(Pavillon de la Communication)**. Numerous attractions, both educational and purely entertaining, are on offer.

Advances in the field of communications are on display in several buildings and halls. Among the most astonishing shows are the **Lac enchanté** and its **Théâtre Alphanumérique** which present performances and productions incorporating the technology of the future. **Kinémax, Omnimax, Solido, Showscan** and **Imax 3D** will enable the visitor to view films from a different angle (3D films, hemispherical cinema, etc). **Images-Studio**★★★, a vast glass structure, shows what goes on behind the scenes.

Cirque de **GAVARNIE**★★★

MICHELIN MAP 342 L-M 6

GREEN GUIDE LANGUEDOC ROUSSILLON TARN GORGES

The village of Gavarnie lies near the upper end of a blind valley high in the Central Pyrenees; its fame is due to its cirque, a natural amphitheatre forming one of Europe's most magnificent mountain landscapes.

Visit

2hr round trip on foot from the village; horses or donkeys can be hired.

The Cirque de Gavarnie rises in a series of huge steps (formed by more resistant strata and marked by permanent deposits of snow and ice) to the crest-line from which a number of peaks stand out at more than 3 000m – 10 000ft. The base of the cirque is 3 1/2km – 2mi across while the crest-line extends over 14km – 9mi.

Innumerable falls cascade down the rock walls, the greatest of them (the Grande Cascade) 422m – 1 385ft high, fed by meltwater from the Marboré snowfields and from the frozen lake of Mont-Perdu.

Downstream from the cirque, below the restaurant, the waters of the torrent have carved a gorge through the rock bar, and a pine forest has colonised the stony wastes of the moraine. Further downstream other typically glacial features like hanging valleys and secondary moraines make their appearance; together with the extensive grasslands, they compose a landscape of great serenity and charm. Some distance further northwards, as the torrent approaches the little town of Luz-St-Sauveur it has carved a deep and narrow gorge through the marble outcrop.

The splendours of Gavarnie excited people's imagination well before **Victor Hugo** sang its praises; the great cleft in the rock wall visible from as far away as Gèdre has long been known as Roland's Breach (La Brèche de Roland). The dying Christian knight is supposed to have tried in vain to smash his sword Durandal against the rock here in order to stop it falling into the hands of the pursuing infidels. In fact, the rearguard of Charlemagne's army was ambushed by the Basques 115km – some 70 miles to the west at the Pass of Roncesvalles in 778.

The Song of Roland **(Chanson de Roland)** was the first French verse-chronicle *(chanson de geste)*. Probably 11C in date, it is outstanding in epic literature in that it depicts the psychological state of its hero as defeat and death loom, rather than simply concentrating on his glorious feats of arms or celebrating the courage of Charlemagne's 12 peers as they tried vainly to fight off their attackers.

GORDES★

POPULATION 2 031

MICHELIN MAP 332 E 10

GREEN GUIDE PROVENCE

The **site**★ of Gordes is a spectacular one; the village's buildings rise in sun-soaked tiers up the rocky slopes on the edge of the Vaucluse plateau. The Vaucluse forms one of the distinct landscapes of the southernmost Alps; its succession of limestone outcrops carry an impoverished *garrigue* vegetation, though some of its lower-lying areas support vines and fruit-trees in spite of the difficulties of irrigation.

Château

Daily 10am-noon, 2-6pm. Closed Jan 1 and 25 Dec. 4€. 04 90 72 02 75. www. gordes-village.com.

The Renaissance château which stands on the village's highest point, was built by Bertrand de Simiane on the site of a 12C fortress. The austere north face is flanked by round machicolated towers; the monumental south façade is relieved by mullioned windows and small turrets. There is a fine Renaissance doorway in the courtyard the great hall *(first floor)* the splendid chimneypiece **(cheminée★)** of 1541 is adorned with ornate pediments and pilasters as well as shells and flowers.

Excursions

Abbaye de Sénanque ★★
4km – 2.5mi north. Founded in 1148, this is a characteristically Cistercian abbey, in a remote **site**★ conducive to the contemplative life and the renunciation of self. The buildings grouped together to form the monastic community are almost complete; the abbey church is notable for its purity of line and lack of distracting ornamentation, and for the table tracing the links between the daughter houses of the Cistercian Order in the 12C.

Village des Bories★
3.5km – 2mi southwest. Corbelled drystone structures of this kind are to be found from Iceland to the Middle East as well as in many other parts of France. In Provence they have existed for almost 4 000 years and seem to have been built in great numbers on the Vaucluse between the 14C and the 19C. Their purposes appear to have been manifold, some serving as field shelters, others as dwellings. They are marvels of craftsmanlike handling of the simplest of materials.
The village consists of a number of dwellings as well as structures for threshing, baking, oil pressing, and housing animals.

GRAND COLOMBIER★★★

MICHELIN MAP 328 H 5

GREEN GUIDE BURGUNDY JURA

At 1 571m – 5 154ft the Grand Colombier forms the highest point in the Bugey area. The viewpoint at the summit is one of the finest in the whole of the Jura and the only one accessible by car. In geological terms, the structure here consists of limestone beds forming a dome which has been subsequently eroded, exposing the older rocks making up its core.

Visit

From Virieu-le-Petit to Culoz
29km – 18mi. The road rises steeply (maximum gradient 19%) passing first through splendid fir-woods. At the summit with its cross and triangulation-point there is the widest of panoramas, taking in the Jura, the Dombes plateau, the valley of the Rhône, the Massif Central and the Alps. The features of the landscape read almost like a geological section, with the domes of anticlines and troughs of synclines clearly distinguishable.
In the distance the Grand Fenestrez crowned by an observatory (**Observatoire**★★) rears up from the Culoz plain which can be reached by car via a boldly-designed hairpin road.

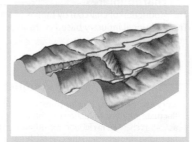

Diagram showing the typical structure of the folded Jura
The synclines form valleys (vals) running parallel to each other, separated by anticlinal ridges (monts).
Transversal valleys (cluses) cut across anticlines to link two main valleys.
A high-level depression (combe) occupies a hollowed-out ridge: it has steep inward-facing scarps (crêts).

Écomusée de la **GRANDE LANDE**★

MICHELIN MAP 335 G-H 9-10

GREEN GUIDE ATLANTIC COAST

The Grande Lande Open-air Museum comprises three separate sites in the heart of the Parc naturel régional des Landes de Gascogne. Between them they evoke the daily life and traditional activities of the region in the 18C and 19C.

The clearing was once inhabited by three families; its 30 or so buildings have been restored or replaced on their original site. As well as the master's dwelling (marquèze), there is an array of other structures serving a variety of purposes, none of them with foundations and relying for their stability on the soundness of their timber construction. A flock of sheep, hives of tiny black bees and an orchard complete the picture of life as led in this locality.

The **Landes** were once a marine depression, subsequently filled with fine sands deposited by the Pyrenean glaciers of Quaternary times. These sands are quite distinct from those on the coast. The vast tract is poorly drained, and below the surface is a hard impermeable pan, further reducing its fertility.

Visit

♿ ⏰ *Tourist steam train from Sabres every 40min Jun to mid-Sep: daily 10am-noon, 2-5.20pm; Apr-May and mid-Sep to end Oct: Mon-Sat 2-4.40pm, Sun and public holidays 10am-noon, 2- 4.40pm.* ✆ *8.40€.* ☎ *05 58 08 31 31.*

Marquèze
Built in 1824 of stout beams and cob walls and with a three-pitched roof.

Les Brassiers
The more modest servants' quarters.

Moulin de Bas
The corn-mill.

Les charbonnières
The production of charcoal by means of slow combustion.
The traditional industry based on resin products is featured at Luxey *(22km – 14mi northeast)*.

Man's Conquest over Nature

Since Roman times, the pine forest growing on the better-drained soils has tended to fluctuate in extent, reflecting the changing demands made on it by the local population as well as changes in climatic and other conditions. In the late 18C, Brémontier followed his success in stabilising the coastal dunes when he fixed some 4 000ha – 10 000 acres of inland sands by planting pines, broom and gorse in a matrix of faggots.

The problem of drainage remained to be tackled. It was solved in 1857 by Chambrelent who enabled the area to be put into productive use by means of a system of ditches and filtering wells. Napoleon III set a good example by purchasing the 8 000ha – 20 000 acre Solferino estate. By 1890, the area under maritime pines was 840km2 – 325sq mi; today the area under woodland continues to grow at the expense of arable and pasture land. The pines of the Landes would be capable of supplying the whole of France's needs for resin products, though because of competition from Asia the present proportion is a mere 6%. But the wood serves any number of useful purposes: sawn timber, veneers, paper pulp, wood charcoal, wood alcohol...

GRENOBLE★★

POPULATION 400 141

MICHELIN MAP 336 H 6 -7

GREEN GUIDE FRENCH ALPS

Undisputed capital of the French Alps, modern Grenoble is a flourishing city of broad boulevards. It was held back in the past by the precarious nature of its communication links; though well-sited on the roads leading from the Rhône valley to Turin and Cannes, frequent floods and challenging gradients made travelling an uncertain business.

▶ **Orient Yourself:** Grenoble, which is listed as a "Town of Art and History," offers 2hr guided tours in Jul and Aug on Sat at 10am for 7€. Information at the tourist office or on www.vpah.culture.fr.

Sights

Fort de la Bastille

Access by cablecar. Allow 1 hr. 🕐 *Jul-Aug: Tue-Sun 9.15am-12.15pm, Mon 11am-12.15pm; Jun and Sep: Tue-Sat 9.15am-11.45pm, Mon 11am-11.45pm, Sun 9.15am-7.25pm; Mar-May and Oct: Tue-Sat 9.30am-11.45pm, Mon 11am-7.25pm, Sun 9.15am-7.25pm. Nov-Feb: Tue-Sun 10.45am-6.30pm, Mon 11am-6.30pm.* 🕐 *Closed 2nd and 3rd week in Jan.* ∞ *5.70€ round trip, 3.90€ single.* ☎ *04 76 44 33 65.*

The fort was built in the 16C and strengthened in the 19C. Its function was to protect the approaches to the city.

It has the best **view**★★★ over the town set magnificently between the Vercors plateau to the southwest, the long narrow Taillefer ridge to the southeast and the Chartreuse Massif (Massif de la Chartreuse) to the north. Far below is the Isère, flowing in stately fashion from the Grésivaudan; it is joined here by the vigorous waters of the Drac which has forced the bigger stream to the north. Between them, the two rivers bring down some 20 000 tons of material a day. Their mingled waters have carved out the valley separating the Chartreuse and Vercors massifs, which forms an important communications axis.

Vieille ville (Old Town)★

The vast quantities of material brought down by the restless River Drac ("that most brutal, most violent of Alpine tributaries" R Blanchard) formed an alluvial fan on which by the late 3C a fortified Roman town was sited, close to the present-day Place Granette (celebrated by Stendhal) and on either side of the Grande-Rue, itself a Roman road. By the 13C the town had spread northeastwards as far as the Isère, where today a number of courtyards and porches dating from the 16C can be found (no 8 Rue Brocherie, nos 8 and 10 Rue Chenoise).

In the reign of Henri IV the city was captured by Lesdiguières, commander of the armies of Piedmont and Savoy, who fortified it further, thereby accommodating the urban growth due to the beginnings of industrial activity. His son-in-law, Marshal Créqui, extended this work to the west. Later fortifications, the Enceinte Haxo, doubled the area of the city to the south and catered for the expansion which took place at the end of the 19C.

The inventor Vaucanson (1709-82) was born in the old town. He designed a water-pump, a slide-lathe and various devices to regulate silk-throwing. But he was led astray by his success, and is best known for his wonderful automata.

Cathédrale

On the right of the chancel is an unusual Flamboyant **ciborium**★ of the 14C in polychrome stone.

Palais de Justice (Law Courts)★

To the left is a wing in Flamboyant style; the right wing is of Renaissance date, still with a certain irregularity in the arrangement of the windows from one floor to the other. Between the wings are an emblazoned porch and the apse of the chapel, also in Flamboyant style.

Musée de Grenoble★★★

🕐 *Wed-Mon 10am-6pm.* 🕐 *Closed Tue, 1 Jan, 1 May, 25 Dec.* ∞ *5€, no charge 1st Sun in the month.* ☎ *04 76 63 44 44. www.museedegrenoble.fr.*

Built on the bank of the river Isère in the heart of the old town, this museum, inaugurated in 1994, is an example of architectural sobriety. In the main hall, the collection is concentrated on the first floor. On each side of a white gallery, alcoves house 16C-19C works. Further on, the rounded end of the building

Interior with Aubergines by Matisse

Musée de Grenoble/© Succession H. Matisse

is the setting for a collection of modern and contemporary art where the natural lighting is modulated according to each work of art.

Huge windows enable the visitor to observe the numerous and massive sculptures which enhance the parvis and the Parc Michallon, outside the north building.

This is one of France's most important provincial museums. The collections include fine modern works like Matisse's *Interior with Aubergines* and Picasso's *Woman Reading* as well as Old Masters like de Champaigne's *John the Baptist*, Rubens' *Pope Gregory surrounded by Saints* or de La Tour's *St Jerome*. Most art movements after 1945 are represented: Abstraction lyrique, New Realism, "Supports-surfaces", Pop Art and Minimalism.

Église-musée St-Laurent

North bank, on the outskirts. The 11C-12C Romanesque church is built over its predecessor which dates back to Merovingian times. The latter constitutes the crypt **(crypte St-Oynand★)**. It has four apses, a colonnade whose shafts are of Roman date, and capitals carved with primitive Christian motifs.

⬤⬤ **Musée Dauphinois★** ♿ ⓧ *Oct-May: Wed-Mon 10am-6pm; Jun-Sep: Wed-Mon 10am-7pm.* ⓧ *Closed Tue, 1 Jan, 1 May, 25 Dec. No charge.* ☎ *04 76 85 19 01. www. musee.dauphinois.fr–* popular art and traditions.

Musée de la Résistance et de la Déportation★ ♿ ⓧ *Jul-Aug: Wed-Mon 10am-7pm; Sep-Jun: Mon, Wed-Fri 9am-6pm, Sat-Sun and public holidays 10am-6pm.* ⓧ *Closed Tue, 1 Jan, 1 May, 25 Dec.* ☎ *04 76 42 38 53.*

Château de **GRIGNAN**★★

MICHELIN MAP 332 C 7

GREEN GUIDE PROVENCE

The old town of Grignan is dominated by its château which was the home of Count François de Grignan, Louis XIV's Lieutenant-General of Provence. In 1669, at the age of 40, with two marriages already behind him, he married Françoise-Marguerite, the daughter of Mme de Sévigné, who became a frequent visitor. The letters written by mother to daughter over a period of 27 years were to create a new literary genre; full of keen observation, wit and spontaneity, they are an inexhaustible source of information to historians of the age of Louis XIV.

Visit

ⓧ *Guided tours* ⬤⬤ *(1hr) Jul-Aug: daily 9.30am-11.30am, 2-6pm; Sep-Jun: daily 9.30-11.30am, 2-5.30pm.* ⓧ *Closed 1 Jan, 25 Dec and Tue from Nov-Mar.* ⬤ *5.20€.* ☎ *04 75 91 83 55.*

Built in 1556, the Renaissance south front of the château was restored early in the 20C following a fire. With its superimposed columns, moulded pilasters, mullioned windows and shell-decorated niches, it marks the arrival of Renaissance architecture in Provence.

The original courtyard is flanked by a Gothic pavilion and opens out onto the terrace constructed over the Church of St-Sauveur. From here there is a **view**★ over the Tricastin area, Mount Ventoux and the plain of the old Comtat Venaissin.

Inside the château are evocative furnishings (**mobilier**★) of many periods, Louis XIII, Régence and Louis XV.

GUÉRANDE★

POPULATION 11 665

MICHELIN MAP 316 B 4

GREEN GUIDE BRITTANY

Secure behind its well-preserved ramparts, Guérande has kept the look of a proud little medieval town which once sent its delegates to the States of Brittany. It is set between the marshlands of the Grande Brière (now a Regional Nature Park) and the extensive salt-marshes of the former gulf. Until the 15C it was a port of some importance which shipped quantities of salt to the Baltic, but then lost out to the more dynamic port towns of Nantes on the Loire and Le Croisic at the entrance to the gulf.

Visit

Remparts★

Begun in 1343, the ramparts were completed only in 1476 in the reign of Duke Francis II (Governor's Residence – Logis du Gouverneur). They are a reminder of difficult and insecure times when towns were forced to protect themselves with such elaborate defences.

Collégiale St-Aubin★

Built between the 12C and the 16C, the church has a striking west front in granite. Embedded in a buttress on the right is an outdoor pulpit. On the south side, a 16C portal in the form of a porch is distinguished by Renaissance motifs.

The nave with its high Gothic arches was reroofed in brick in the 19C. The capitals are decorated with grotesque figures and foliage. The chancel is lit by a magnificent stained-glass window showing the Assumption of the Virgin Mary (much restored in the 19C); to the north is another window depicting the Life of St Peter. There is a Louis XIV pulpit, and, to the south, a "crypt" with a 6C sarcophagus.

Presqu'île de Guérande★

In the Roman era, a great sea gulf stretched between the rocky island, Ile de Batz, and the Guérande ridge. This was probably where Julius Caesar defeated the Veneti fleet in the 6C BC. The sandy Pen Bron Point has not quite reached the island; a channel remains open opposite Le Croisic through which the sea flows at high tide. The exposed mud-flats are suitable for oyster and mussel farming. The sea water in the marsh supplies the salt pans.

Abbaye **d'HAMBYE**★★

MICHELIN MAP 303 E 6

GREEN GUIDE NORMANDY

The 12C abbey of Hambye is charmingly sited in the green valley of the Sienne. Its ruins evoke the serenity of Benedictine life and seem to gain from having the heavens as their vault.

Visit

Église abbatiale★★
🕐 *Apr-Oct: daily 10am-noon, 2-6pm.* 💶 *4€.* ☎ *02 33 61 76 92.*

The group of buildings is dominated by the abbey church with slender columns and sharply pointed arches around the choir (1180-1200). The high bell-tower whose upper stage is pierced by round-headed arches was once crowned by a lantern.
The monastic buildings frame the former cloisters. The chapter-house is noteworthy; it is a masterpiece of Norman Gothic, divided into two by six central pillars, the final one of which gathers together the arches of the apse in a masterly way.

Château de **HAUTEFORT**★★

MICHELIN MAP 329 H 4

GREEN GUIDE DORDOGNE BERRY LIMOUSIN

More like a Loire château than a Périgord fortress, the Château de Hautefort rises up proudly on its hilltop site, overlooking its extensive and well-kept grounds. Although substantial traces of the former medieval castle are still to be seen, the building is essentially the work of the architect Nicolas Rambourg. A native from Alsace, he rebuilt it between 1625 and 1670 in accordance with the rules of Classical architecture then very much in vogue, albeit keeping domes based on the 16C circular plan such as those at Valençay château on the Loire river.

In the 11C, the castle passed into the hands of the de Born family whose most famous offspring was Bertrand de Born, the troubadour, born here in about 1140. The virtuous and beautiful Marie de Hautefort (1616-91) added to the place's fame. Lady-in-waiting to Anne of Austria, she inspired Louis XIII's platonic love. Thereafter, she presided over the salons of the so-called *Précieuses*, ladies dedicated, not without a certain pretension, to refinement in spoken and written expression.

Château de Hautefort

Visit

🕐 *Guided tours* 👣 *(1hr) Jun-Sep: daily 9.30am-7pm; Apr-May: daily 10am-12.30pm, 2pm-6.30pm; Feb-Mar and Oct-Nov: daily 2-6pm. Last admission 1hr before closing.* 💶 *8€. Garden: self-guided visits.* ☎ *05 53 50 51 23.*

The **château** was badly damaged by a fire in 1968 but has since undergone a meticulous programme of restoration.

The interior has fine Flemish tapestries saved from the flames, a 17C Felletin landscape, some good pieces of furniture and above all some unusual paved floors. The tower has magnificent chestnut timberwork (**charpente**★★).

Château du **HAUT-KŒNIGSBOURG**★★

MICHELIN MAP 315 I 7

GREEN GUIDE ALSACE LORRAINE CHAMPAGNE

This vast mock-medieval edifice in pink sandstone overlooks the Alsace plain from its lofty rock rising through the treetops of the Vosges forest (**panorama**★★ from the tall bastion).

Little remains either of the 12C castle or of the rebuilding carried out by the Counts of Thierstein at the end of the 15C, since the place was besieged, plundered and then dismantled in 1633 by Swedish troops in the course of the Thirty Years War.

Visit

🕐 *Jun-Aug: 9.30am-6.30pm; Mar and Oct: 9.45am-5pm; Nov-Feb: 9.45am-noon, 1-5pm. Last admission 30min before closing.* 🕐 *Closed 1 Jan, 1 May, 25 Dec.* 💶 *7€ (18-25 years: 4.50€), no charge 1st Sun in the month (Oct-Mar).* ☎ *03 88 82 50 60.*

The present building is the outcome of an almost complete reconstruction which was carried out on the orders of Emperor William II between 1900 and 1908 during the period when Alsace and Lorraine had been reincorporated into Germany. In the neo-feudal style popular at the time, it provoked bitter controversy, offending archeologists and architectural purists.

Le **HAVRE**★

POPULATION 250 000

MICHELIN MAP 304 A 5

GREEN GUIDE NORMANDY

The **port**★★ of Le Havre is where the great urbanised axis stretching from Paris down the Seine finally meets the sea. It is France's second, and Europe's third, most important harbour and has car-ferry links to both Britain and Ireland.

▶ **Orient Yourself:** The town consists of a large port and industrial area as well as the residential village of Ste-Adresse and the old port of Harfleur. The newer part of town centers around the Espace Niemeyer, which provides an ultra-modern architectual facelift to the urban landscape on place Gambetta.

🔄 **Don't Miss:** Avenue Foch is a fine promenade bordered by lawns and shaded by trees which opens onto the seafront by the Porte Océane.

🕐 **Organizing Your Time:** Give yourself about an hour and a half and take a walk around the modern town starting from the place du Général-de-Gaulle.

🅿 **Parking:** Between the Bassin du Commerce and the Espace Niemeyer (Place du Gén.-de-Gaulle) you will find two parking lots.

A Bit of History

A Judicious Choice – By 1517 the harbour at Harfleur had silted up. To remedy the situation, François I ordered the building of a new port which was to be called "Havre-de-Grâce" (Harbour of Grace). The marshy site selected by Admiral Bonnivet seemed unpromising, but his choice was a happy one since the tide remained at the flood two hours longer here than elsewhere. The port area has subsequently spread some 20km – 12 miles upstream with a parallel development, mostly on the north bank, of chemical, engineering and motor industries, shipyards and refineries.

Le Havre's Great Men – These include Bernardin de Saint-Pierre (1737-1814), author of the novel *Paul et Virginie (*1787); its mingling of exotic and pastoral elements won him a prominent place in French literature. Claude Monet made the name of Ste-Adresse famous through his *Terrace at Ste-Adresse* (in the Metropolitan Museum in New York), painted in 1867. This is a key work of Impressionism, with fleeting effects of light and a wonderful clarity of subject. The old town and resort of **Ste-Adresse**★★ is still a pleasant place; from the clifftop at La Hève there are fine views out over the estuary and the English Channel.

André Siegfried (1875-1959) is noted for his sociological and economic studies of Britain and America and for his work on French politics, while Arthur Honegger (1892-1955) was responsible for breathing fresh life into the composition and staging of choral works (*King David*, 1924).

Sights

Quartier moderne (Modern Town)★

The bombing which preceded Le Havre's liberation on 13 September 1944 was a total disaster for the town. The old centre was obliterated and more than 4 000 people were killed; the besieged Germans completed the destruction by a thorough dynamiting of the port facilities.

The architect **Auguste Perret** (1874-1954), a pioneer of modern architecture already famous for his innovating work with reinforced concrete and promotion of standardised components, was given the task of rebuilding the devastated town from scratch. His initial concept involved a vast deck covering all the new city's services (energy, pipelines, gas, traffic). The very boldness of his scheme led to its rejection. Perret consequently abandoned his advanced ideas and laid out the town using the principal elements of the old street pattern. But the design of his buildings remained in an uncompromisingly modern idiom.

Place de l'Hôtel de Ville★

One of the largest squares in Europe, it is notable for the contrast of verticals (the town hall with its tower, 10-storey blocks) and horizontals (the three-storey buildings lining the square's irregular sides).

Avenue Foch★

The vista leading down to the Ocean Gate (Porte Océane) and the sea is emphasised by the balconies of the buildings lining the avenue and by the regular rows of trees.

Église St-Joseph★

The tall bell-tower soars to a height of 109m – 325ft. Inside, the church's walls are a lattice of stained glass through which the light pours.

Rue de Paris

Gives lateral views of the Commercial Dock (Bassin de Commerce) and leads to the South Promenade (Front de Mer Sud).

Musée des Beaux-Arts André Malraux★

&. ◷ *Mon, Wed-Fri 11am-6pm; Sat-Sun 11am-7pm.* ◷ *Closed Tue, 1 Jan, 1 and 8 May, 14 Jul, 11 Nov, 25 Dec.* ⊜ *3.80€, 5€ during the lighthouse exhibit.* ☏ *02 35 19 62 62. www.ville-lehavre.fr.*

Built entirely of glass and metal it houses the **Collections Eugène Boudin**★. This painter was a citizen of Le Havre by adoption; he was responsible for freshening up the palette of the painters of the Barbizon School and was much admired by Baudelaire who called him "King of the Skies" *(Yellow Boats at Étretat, Breton Church Interior)*. There is also a good selection of pictures by Raoul Dufy, a native of Le Havre *(Amphitrite, Sea Goddess)*.

Excursion

Pont de Normandie★★

This cable-stayed bridge was inaugurated in January 1995. It crosses the Seine estuary from the out-skirts of Le Havre to Honfleur. The bridge has a record-breaking main span of 856m (2 808ft) between its 214m (705ft) high towers and a clearance of 50m (164ft) at high tide.

Pont de Normandie

Cascade du HÉRISSON★★★

MICHELIN MAP 321 F 7

GREEN GUIDE BURGUNDY JURA

High up at the foot of the cirque of Chaux-de-Dombief is little Lake Bonlieu, drained by the River Hérisson (hedgehog). The river crosses the narrow Frasnois plateau, then, in the space of 3km – 2mi drops via a series of rapids and falls through its famous wooded gorge to the Champagnole plain 200m – 650ft below.

Visit

▶ *Follow the footpath which starts 8km – 5mi east of Doucier as far as the Ilay crossroads – 3 hr there and back.*

The path climbs over a series of limestone outcrops rising above areas of alluvial deposits where lakes have formed and where a rich vegetation flourishes. The limestones were laid down over a period of 35 million years during Jurassic times; it is they that form the succession of splendid falls, the **Éventail**★★★ (Fan Falls), the **Grand Saut**★★ (Great Leap), Château Garnier, the **Saut de la Forge**★ and Saut Girard.

HONFLEUR★★

POPULATION 8 272

MICHELIN MAP 303 N 3

GREEN GUIDE NORMANDY

Honfleur lies at the foot of the hill, **Côte de Grâce**★★, overlooking the wide waters of the Seine estuary. Bathed in the soft light of the northern sea, it is the most picturesque of ports, appealing greatly to 19C painters like the English water-colourist Bonington as well as many French artists such as the Normandy-born Eugène Boudin and later the Impressionists. Erik Satie composed some of his music in Honfleur, and writers lived and worked here too, like the historian Albert Sorel, the humorist Alphonse Allais and the poets Henri de Régnier and Lucie Delarue-Mardrus.

Many maritime ventures began on the quayside at Honfleur. Paulmier de Gouneville sailed from here to Brazil in 1503, and in 1506 Jean Denis explored the mouth of the St Lawrence River. In 1608 Samuel de Champlain set out to found Quebec City and in 1681 La Salle started the voyage which was to make him the first European to descend the Mississippi all the way to the sea, thereby opening up those vast territories to which he gave the name Louisiana in honour of his king, Louis XIV.

▶ **Orient Yourself:** Honfleur, which is listed as a "Town of Art and History," offers discovery tours: 5€ for 1hr30min visits, 7€ for a guided all-day visit and 11€ for a guided evening visit (2 people). Information at the tourist office or on www.vpah.culture.fr.

Visit

Le vieux Honfleur (Old Honfleur) ★★

The streets and quaysides of the ancient port are full of character. The old harbour **(Vieux bassin★★)** shelters a fishing fleet as well as yachts and pleasure-craft. A richly varied townscape, the delight of painters and photographers, is formed by the fine stone residences along the Quai St-Etienne, the narrow, slate-faced houses on the Quai Ste-Catherine, the church (Église St-Etienne), the Governor's House (Lieutenance), all seen against the foreground of masts and rigging.

Nearby is the **Église Ste-Catherine**★ with its detached bell-tower (**clocher**★) (🕐 mid-Mar to mid-Nov daily 10am-noon, 2-6pm; 🕐 closed Tue, 1 May, 14 Jul; ⊛ 2.10€; ☏ 02 31 89 54 00). The church was rebuilt after the Hundred Years War by the carpenters from the adjacent shipyards. All around are houses built in like fashion, making up a fine group of timber buildings, an unusual phenomenon in Western Europe.

The **Rue Haute**, a former pathway outside the fortifications, has kept many fine houses of brick, stone and timber once lived in by shipbuilders.

◖◗ Musée Eugène Boudin 🕐 *Mid-Mar to end Sep: Wed-Mon 10am-noon, 2-7pm: Oct to mid-Mar: Wed-Mon 11am-5pm.* 🕐 *Closed Tue, Jan to mid-Feb, 1 May, 14 Jul, 25 Dec.* ⊛ *5.20€.* ☏ *02 31 89 54 00*– paintings in the Honfleur tradition. **Pont de Normandie**★★ (🕯 *see LE HAVRE*).

Old harbour

Honfleur - Address Book

For coin ranges, see the Legend at the back of the guide.

EATING OUT

Le Bistrot des Artistes – *14 pl. Berthelot -* ☎ *02 31 89 95 90 -* 🕐 *closed Jan and Mar, and Wed except July to Sept.* Antiques, paintings of the sea, photos of Honfleur and leatherette wall seats make up the decor of this restaurant with a Parisian bistro flair. Tables near the window have a lovely view of the Vieux Bassin. On the menu: salads and slices of bread with various toppings.

Au Gai Luron – *20 pl. Ste-Catherine -* ☎ *02 31 89 99 90 -* 🕐 *closed 3 weeks in Jan, 1 week late June, Oct, Wed evening and Thu.* This little place next to Ste-Catherine Church has a pleasant rustic setting (the house dates from the 14C), a pretty, flowery terrace, and a relaxed and happy ambience going for it. Market cuisine and attractive seafood platters.

La Tortue – *36 r. de l'Homme-de-Bois -* ☎ *02 31 89 04 93 -* 🕐 *closed Jan.* This venerable half-timbered house features two elegant dining rooms in pastel shades adorned with paintings by a local artist. Well-prepared traditional cuisine, tasty house pastries and a vegetarian fixed-price menu.

Au P'tit Mareyeur – *4 r. Haute -* ☎ *02 31 98 84 23 - jule.rastacoop@freesbee. fr -* 🕐 *closed 5 Jan to 5 Feb, Mon andTue.* This minuscule restaurant right near the harbour has a decided maritime slant, in the kitchen as well as the dining area. The bill of fare changes often, but between the fixed-price menu and the suggestions du jour, fish and seafood fans can look forward to a delightful meal.

Au Vieux Honfleur – *13 quai St-Étienne -* ☎ *02 31 89 15 31.* This restaurant by the old harbour extends its terrace along the quay when the weather is fine. Al fresco or inside, nice and warm among bibelots, posters and paintings, you'll be able to savour Norman dishes and seafood while gazing upon the splendid basin.

WHERE TO STAY

Manoir du Plessis – *1175 rte de Caudebec - 76940 Vatteville-sur-Mer -* ☎ *02 35 95 79 79 - aplvatteville@free.fr - 5 rooms.* This brick manor of the Napoleonic epoch is worth a halt, if only to savour the sovereign calm. Rooms with a bath have decided character; those without are functional, if uninspired. Fox hunting and painting courses offered.

Le Vieux Pressoir – *Hameau le Clos-Potier - 27210 Conteville - 13.5km/8.2mi from Honfleur via D 580, rte de Pont-Audemer then left on D 312 -* ☎ *02 32 57 60 79 - 5 rooms.* Located in the heart of the countryside, this 18C wood-sided farm is

meant for lovers of quietude and authenticity. Each room overflows with 19C and 20C furniture and objects discovered in second-hand shops. Children will be delighted with the duck pond.

Le Belvédère – *36 r. Émile-Renouf -* ☎ *02 31 89 08 13 -* 🕐 *closed Jan - 9 rooms -* 🍽. This venerable old house owes its name to the belvedere crowning the roof. The renovated bedrooms benefit from the ambient tranquillity. Mealtime, the glass-covered restaurant and small terrace offer an unbeatable view of the Pont de Normandie.

Hôtel Otelinn – *62 cours A.-Manuel -* ☎ *02 31 89 41 77 -* 🅿 *- 50 rooms -* 🍽. At a distance from the city centre, this hotel has the considerable advantage of proposing rooms at reasonable prices. Small and functional, they make for an agreeable halt. A garden and a terrace give you the opportunity of basking in the gentle Norman sun.

Le Clos Deauville Saint-Gatien – *4 chemin des Brioleurs - 14130 St-Gatien-des-Bois - 9km/5.4mi S of Honfleur via D 579 -* ☎ *02 31 65 16 08 - hotel@clos-st-gatien.fr -* 🅿 *- 60 rooms -* 🍽. The charm of the Norman countryside a few short miles from the shore characterises this half-timbered house nestled in a verdant setting. Comfortable, cosy rooms. Three pools, one covered, a sauna and a fitness room: careful not to strain your muscles!

SHOPPING

La Cave Normande – *13 r. de la Ville and 12 quai Ste-Catherine -* ☎ *02 31 89 38 27 and 02-31-89-49-28 -* 🕐 *9am-12pm, 11pm in summer.* This is where you'll find top-quality Calvados and can fill your car with cider, perry and pommeau in anticipation of the long cold winters.

SPORT

Centre équestre du Ramier – *Chemin du Ramier - 14600 Équemauville - S of Honfleur, towards Équemauville, follow signs -* ☎ *02 31 89 49 97 or 06 60 15 42 28 -* 🕐 *reception: Wed, Sat-Sun and public holidays 9am-5pm; other days by appointment.* Located in the heart of the (authentic!) Norman countryside, this lovely riding centre has 15 training horses available. Rides last for 1hr-1hr 30min.

LEISURE

Jolie France – *Quai de la Quarantaine -* ☎ *02 31 89 58 01 -* 🕐 *early Apr to end Sept: daily; schedule follows tides - closed rest of year.* The longest cruises available from Honfleur follow in the wake of Proust and Baudelaire. In the space of 1hr 30min, you'll discover the Pont de Normandie, a view of Le Havre, Vasouy and La Côte de Grâce. If the sun chooses to shine, this outing is a pure delight.

🚲 **Station Total** – *Cours Jean-de-Vienne - ☎ 02 31 89 91 73 -* 🕐 *daily 6am-10pm, cycle hire 9am-6.30pm - 1hr: 3.81€, 5hr: 11.43€, all day: 13.72€, weekend: 22.87€.* Original! Rent a bicycle from the only cycle hire business in town, right here in a gas station.

TAKE A BREAK

Le Perroquet Vert – *52 quai Ste-Catherine - ☎ 02 31 89 14 19 -* 🕐 *Fri-Wed 8.30am-2am; Easter-Sep: daily 8.30am-2am -* 🕐 *closed mid-Nov to mid-Dec.* Housed in a 17C building, this former sail workshop has been converted into a convivial café-tearoom with a fine terrace overlooking the harbour. Occasional concerts.

Pom'cannelle – *60 quai Ste-Catherine - ☎ 02 31 89 55 25 -* 🕐 *9am-7.30pm.* These home-made ice creams and sherbets are an absolute must. In addition to liquorice and apricot, you must try this blissfully anti-dietetic concoction: ice cream flavoured with "confiture de lait," a gooey milk caramel.

ON THE TOWN

L'Albatros – *32 quai Ste-Catherine - ☎ 02 31 89 25 30 - Martigny@wanadoo.fr -* 🕐 *Apr-Sept: daily 8am-2am; Oct-Mar: daily 8am-1am.* Baudelaire loved Honfleur, and this café is named after one of his most famous poems. The terrace, where the quality of light changes with the passing hours, offers an exceptional view of the harbour.

La Petite Chine – *14 r. du Dauphin - ☎ 02 31 89 36 52 -* 🕐 *Tue-Fri 11am-7pm, Sat-Sun 10am-7pm.* Decorated in blue and yellow, Monet's favourite colours, this pretty little pastry shop and tearoom looks out on the wharf. Try the regional specialities: gingerbread, *tarte paysanne* (farmers' pie) and apples in calvados. Music and a library are at the customers' disposal.

HUNSPACH★★

POPULATION 615

MICHELIN MAP 315 L 3

GREEN GUIDE ALSACE LORRAINE CHAMPAGNE

Carefully preserved and free from incongruous modern additions, Hunspach is one of Alsace's most charming villages. Flowers fill the streets of timber-framed houses with their projecting roofs and bull's-eye windows (a Baroque feature). Many of the buildings are in fact old farmhouses, with yards opening off the street; orchards, vines and long-handled pumps complete the picturesque scene.

Excursion

Seebach★

5km – 3mi northeast by D 249. This is a typical flower-decked Alsatian village with its half-timbered houses adorned with awnings and gardens; the harmony is, however, broken by a few buildings lacking in style.

ISSOIRE★★

POPULATION 13 559

MICHELIN MAP 326 G 9

GREEN GUIDE AUVERGNE THE RHÔNE VALLEY

This old Auvergne town is situated at the point where the Pavin valley meets the flatter fertile country of the southern Limagne. In 1540 the town became a notable centre of Protestantism.

More recently it has acquired an industrial character, with important engineering works (heavy pressing machinery and aluminium alloys).

Visit

Ancienne abbatiale St-Austremoine ★★

Built around 1135, this is the largest Romanesque church in the Auvergne. It was extensively restored in the 19C (west front, roof, bell-tower, many of the capitals, the polychrome interior decoration).

The east end (**chevet**★★) is a fine example of Auvergne Romanesque, generously and harmoniously proportioned and rich in detail (cornices, ornamental brackets, mosaic stonework and sculpture).

Inside, an impression of strength and solidity, characteristic of these Auvergne churches, is given by the four great arches at the crossing and by the ambulatory with its ribbed vault. The influence of the Mozac School of sculpture is clearly seen in the capitals (**chapiteaux**★ – c 1140) carved from the local volcanic rock; particularly fine are those showing the Last Supper and Christ washing the feet of the disciples.

In the narthex is a 15C mural of the **Last Judgement**★, a favourite subject of the time, here treated with great verve and a degree of satire.

Château de **JOSSELIN**★★

MICHELIN MAP 308 P 7

GREEN GUIDE BRITTANY

This stronghold has stood guard over the crossing of the Oust for 900 years.

A Bit of History

The **War of the Breton Succession**, which started in 1341, set rival heirs to the Duchy against each other, Jeanne de Penthièvre, granddaughter of Jean II of Brittany, and Jean de Montfort, Jean III's half-brother. The struggle, long and confused, overlapped with the early stages of the Hundred Years War. Jeanne was married to Charles de Blois and her claim, supported by the Valois rulers of France, was based on established Breton custom. The ousted De Montfort allied himself to the Plantagenets who had won the great naval battle of Sluys the previous year. He was able to persuade them to set a terrible example by laying waste the area around Tréguier; this action took place during the period which also saw the triumph of English arms at Crécy and Calais.

The garrison at Josselin faced the defenders of Ploërmel Castle, 12km – 8mi to the east; between them they ravaged the countryside without any decisive outcome. A solution to the impasse was sought by arranging a contest between 30 knights from each camp. The **Battle of the Thirty** took place in 1351, half-way between the two towns. Ploërmel's champions consisted of four Bretons, six Germans and 20 Englishmen. Josselin emerged victorious, but even this dramatic settling of accounts did not prove decisive.

The war was finally brought to an end in 1364 by the death of Charles de Blois at the Battle of Auray. In 1365 de Montfort was acknowledged as ruler of the Duchy, albeit subject to the Capetian kings of France.

Visit

🕐 *Guided tours* ⚓ *(45min) mid-Jul to end Aug: daily 10am-6pm; Jun to mid-Jul and Sep: daily 2-6pm; Apr-May and Oct: Sat-Sun, public and school holidays 2-6pm.* 🎫 *6.80€ (children: 4.70€).* ☎ *02 97 22 36 45.*

After the war the **château** was rebuilt by Olivier de Clisson. His work can still be seen in the massive walls overlooking the river; their medieval robustness contrasts with the refinement of the upper parts belonging to the reconstruction of the 15C-16C. The marriage of Anne of Brittany to Charles VIII of France in 1491 had led to a lessening of tension between the Duchy and the French kingdom, and John of Laval was able to rebuild the old castle in accordance with the new ideas of Renaissance architecture. What had been a fortress now became a palace. The transformation is particularly evident in the courtyard, where the **façade**★★ featuring an ornate roof **balustrade** has a splendid variety of motifs: pinnacles, tracery and mouldings.

Inside there is an innovative staircase with straight ramps.

In the 17C the keep and five of the towers were demolished on the orders of Richelieu. A park was laid out in 1760, and in 1882 the castle was restored.

▶▶ **Basilique Notre-Dame-du-Roncier**★ – **Mausoleum**★ of Olivier de Clisson.

Forêt de la JOUX★★

MICHELIN MAP 321 F-G 5-6

GREEN GUIDE BURGUNDY JURA

This is one of France's finest coniferous forests; adjoining it are other forests, the Forêt de Levier, the Forêt de Chapois and the Forêt de la Fresse, making up a vast wooded tract of some 670km² – 174sq mi.

Visit

Route des Sapins★★

45km – 28mi from Levier to Champagnole. The drive is marked by a number of remarkable individual trees including the splendid Président de la Joux.

Life in the Jura has always been intimately bound up with the forest and its manifold uses; these ranged from timber, to firewood and furniture. The modern forest feeds industry and is managed in such a way that the removal of timber in any one year does not exceed the annual increment of new growth.

Sapin Président de la Joux

This is the most famous fir tree in the area. It is more than 200 years old and 45m – 148ft tall.

Abbaye de JUMIÈGES★★★

MICHELIN MAP 304 E 5

GREEN GUIDE NORMANDY

The great abbey in its splendid setting on the Lower Seine forms one of the most evocative groups of ruins in France.

A Bit of History

It was founded in the 7C by Saint Philibert and within 50 years housed a community of 700 monks and 1 500 lay-brothers. Its great wealth was based on the generosity of the Merovingian rulers and on the tithes drawn from a vast area.

Destroyed by the Vikings, the abbey was raised again in the early 11C by a new generation of builder abbots. It suffered in the Wars of Religion and was subject to the abuses of commendam rule. The few remaining monks were scattered at the outbreak of the French Revolution. In 1793 it was put up for auction and one of its later owners saw fit to use it as a source of building stone, blowing up the chancel and lantern-tower in the process. In 1852 a new owner saved it from complete destruction but by then the great edifice was already a ruin.

Visit

Allow 30min. ⏰ *Jul-Aug: daily 9.30am-6.30pm; mid-Apr to end Jun and early Sep to mid-Sep: Mon-Fri 9.30am-1pm, 2.30-6.30pm, Sat-Sun and public holidays: 9.30am-6.30pm; mid-Sep to mid-Apr: daily 9.30am-1pm, 2.30-5.30pm.* ⏰ *Closed 1 Jan, 1 May, 1 and 11 Nov, 25 Dec.* ⚐ *4.60 €, no charge 1st Sun in the month (Oct-Mar).* ☎ *02 35 37 24 02. www.monum.fr.*

The most striking feature of the abbey is the west front of the **Église Notre-Dame** with its two magnificent towers, 43m – 141ft high, the oldest and grandest of any Norman abbey.

The power of the building to move the beholder is enhanced by the absence of vaults which permits the eye to soar freely skywards. The ruins seem to express deeply spiritual qualities too, from the stately double bays of the nave (1052-67) and the single remaining wall of the lantern-tower with its great high arch, to the bases of the walls of the chancel, the ambulatory and the axial chapel.

To the south of the abbey is the **Église St-Pierre**; the porch and first few bays of the nave with their intersecting arcades are typical of the architecture of Carolingian times in Normandy.

KAYSERSBERG★★

POPULATION 2 755

MICHELIN MAP 315 H 8

GREEN GUIDE ALSACE LORRAINE CHAMPAGNE

Located where the Weiss valley meets the Alsace lowlands, Kaysersberg commands what was in Roman times an important route between Gaul and the Rhineland. In the Middle Ages it was one of the confederation of 10 free cities known as the Decapolis, set up to resist feudal demands on their burgeoning urban culture.

A Bit of History

Its flower-bedecked streets have many old houses, some of them dating from the 16C, and behind the pretty little town rise the serried ranks of vines.

It was here that **Albert Schweitzer** (1875-1965) was born, at **no 12** Rue du Général de Gaulle (next to the **Musée** Albert-Schweitzer) (&️ 🕐 *Easter to 11 Nov: daily 9am-noon, 2-6pm; weekends of the Christmas market: 9am-noon, 2-6pm;* 🕐 *closed Dec-Apr;* ☞ *2€, children 1€;* ☎ *03 89 47 36 55).* In his early years he was a gifted organist, specialising in the works of Bach; he became a philosopher, with a doctoral thesis on Kant, and a theologian. At the age of 30 he began to study medicine, with the aim of succouring the sick of Gabon, where he built his first hospital near Lambaréné "on the edge of the primeval forest" in 1913.

During the First World War he was interned for a time as a German national. In 1924 he returned to Africa. He was able to found two further hospitals, thanks to the proceeds of the recitals he gave in Europe and in Colorado in 1949 and to the resources which he was able to command after winning the Nobel Peace Prize.

Albert Schweitzer was in the forefront of the struggle to relieve the sufferings of the Third World and was also a powerful advocate of Franco-German reconciliation. His writings are considered as classics, particularly in Japan and the United States.

▶▶ **Église**★ (church) – **altarpiece**★★. **Hôtel de ville**★. **Vieilles maisons**★ (Old houses). **Pont fortifié**★ (bridge). **Maison Brief**★.

KERNASCLÉDEN★★

POPULATION 434

MICHELIN MAP 308 L 6

GREEN GUIDE BRITTANY

The group formed by pilgrimage church and hospital grew up in the 15C under the protection of the powerful Rohan family.

Visit

Église★★

Built in granite between 1430 and 1455, the church typifies the Breton version of Flamboyant Gothic. It has a characteristic belfry with a balcony, a spire with foliated decoration, buttresses with pinnacles, a roof balustrade and two **porches** on the south side (one of them with statues of the **Apostles**★). Inside there is a fine window at the east end and an untypically low and heavy granite vault.

The frescoes (**fresques**★★ – 1470-85) which have made the church famous are probably the work of a local workshop whose painters were familar with the work of the miniaturists of the Loire Valley.

The choir vault depicts 24 scenes from the Life of the Virgin, notably the Resurrection (over the triumphal arch), the Burial of the Virgin (south side) and above all the Annunciation and the Marriage of the Virgin (north side). The artists have used much ingenuity to overcome the difficulties presented by the ribs and concave surfaces of the vaulting.

In the north transept the elegance of the celestial choir (note particularly the folds of their clothes) recalls the refinement of the court surrounding the Rohans.

On the wall of the south transept is the Passion, and a Dance of Death with the dead dragging the living to their doom against a background of sulphurous yellow symbolic of the Beyond. Below, the damned are depicted undergoing an extraordinary variety of torments.

Château de **LANGEAIS**★★

MICHELIN MAP 317 L 5

GREEN GUIDE CHÂTEAUX OF THE LOIRE

As early as the 10C the great Angevin ruler Foulques Nerra built a sturdy keep to command the Loire Valley. Completed in 994, now in ruins in the park of the château, it is considered to be the oldest such building in the whole of France.

A Bit of History

Anne of Brittany's Marriages – In 1488 Duke François II of Brittany, an implacable adversary of the French Crown, died leaving a daughter, Anne, aged 11. As sole heir to the Duchy, Anne was an attractive match. To begin with, she followed her father's preference for Maximilian of Habsburg; the couple were married by proxy, but the "penniless emperor" could never afford to come to Nantes.

The 21-year-old Charles VIII favoured the union of Brittany with the French Crown; he broke with his wife Margaret of Austria and pressed Anne to do the same with Maximilian. Advised by her tutors, Anne was well aware of what the English occupation of the previous century and the ravages of the War of the Breton Succession had done to her duchy; faced with the subordination of Brittany to the interests of Tudors or Habsburgs, she chose to integrate her inheritance with a France still suffused with the prestige of Saint Louis. The wedding took place at Langeais on Tuesday 16 December 1491. Anne was still only 14.

Charles VIII was killed accidentally in 1498. While he was away campaigning in Italy, Anne showed herself to be a wise ruler of both duchy and kingdom. At the age of 22, still the sole heir to Brittany since she had no living descendant, and possessed of a certain attractiveness despite somewhat mean features and the handicap of a limp, she married Louis XII, Charles' cousin, whose marriage to Joan of France had been annulled by the Church. She presented him with two children, one of them Claude, subsequently the wife of François I to whom she brought Brittany as her dowry (1514).

Fearful of the Breton threat to the Loire Valley, Louis XI began the present **château** in 1465. It was completed in the unusually short time of four years, but events a mere 22 years later made it redundant.

Visit

🕐 *Apr to mid-Jul and Sep to mid-Oct: daily 9.30am-6.30pm; mid-Jul to end Aug: daily 9.30am-7pm; mid-Oct to end Mar: daily 10am-5.30pm.* 🕐 *Closed 25 Dec.* ⟐ *6.50€ (children: 4€).* ☎ *02 47 96 72 60.*

Seen from outside, the château still looks like Louis' medieval fortress, with its drawbridge, towers, battlemented sentry-walk and almost windowless walls. But the façade facing the courtyard has the features of a Renaissance country house, including pointed dormers, turrets, sculptures and mullioned windows.

The apartments (**appartements**★★★) have kept their medieval layout, one room commanding the next through narrow doors and laid out along diagonal lines. The last owner, Jacques Siegfried (a mill- and ship-owner and banker from Le Havre), refurnished the interior in a much more thoroughgoing way than is the case with most such châteaux, with the result that Langeais now gives a good impression of aristocratic life as lived in the reign of Louis XI and in the early Renaissance period.

The rooms contain fine Flanders tapestries together with some *mille-fleurs* tapestries, examples of the girdle of the Franciscan Tertiaries and the interlaced monograms K and A (Charles VIII and Anne of Brittany).

On the first floor are an early four-poster bed, a credence table and a Gothic chest. In the Charles VIII Room is a 17C clock with a single hand.

LAON★★

POPULATION 26 490

MICHELIN MAP 306 D 5

GREEN GUIDE NORTHERN FRANCE AND THE PARIS REGION

This ancient town dominates the surrounding countryside from its magnificent hilltop site★★, a 100m – 330ft high limestone outlier rising abruptly from the plain. Its defensive potential was noted by the Carolingian kings who made it their capital for 150 years, from the reign of Charles le Chauve (the Bald) (840) to Louis V (987). It was only in the reign of Hugh Capet that the capital was moved to the Île-de-France. At the time of the communal movement directed against episcopal rule the city was the scene of bloody and destructive riots (1111 and 1114).

The city was the birthplace of the three **Le Nain** brothers, adept painters of rural life. The works of Louis Le Nain (1599-1648) were particularly successful. They show a prosperous peasantry already enjoying the high standard of living which Colbert was to promote some 30 years later.

▸ **Orient Yourself:** Laon, which is listed as a "Town of Art and History," offers 1hr30min guided tours in Jul and Aug on Sat-Sun, public holidays and Fri afternoon. From Apr-Jun and Sep to All Saints' Day tours are offered on Sat-Sun and public holidays. 5€ (3€ for a panoramic tour from a tower of the cathedral). Information at the tourist office or on www.vpah.culture.fr

Visit

Cathédrale Notre-Dame★★

The present cathedral was begun in 1160 and completed towards 1230. It is in the early-Gothic style, still caught up in the Romanesque idiom (as in its Norman-style lantern-tower). The west front is a masterpiece, with its deep porches and stepped towers flanked by openwork turrets.

The immensely long **nave**★★★ shows the persistence of Carolingian traditions, but "nowhere else did the development of 12C Gothic achieve such breadth and unity" (Henri Focillon). The elevation is four-storeyed, with great arches carried on circular columns, a gallery with bold double arches, a blind triforium and a clerestory. In the nave, transept and chancel the bays are marked – still in a less emphatic way than at either Sens (1140) or Senlis (1153) – by a pattern of major and minor clustered columns, the former with five, the latter with three engaged columns.

▸▸ **Quartier de la Cathédrale**★★ (cathedral area); **Rempart du Midi**★ (southern ramparts) – **views**★; **Musée**★ ◷ *Jun-Sep: Tue-Sun 11am-6pm; Oct-May: Tue-Sun 2-6pm.* ◷ *Closed Mon, 1 Jan, 1 May, 14 Jul, 25 Dec.* ⊜ *3.20€, no charge Sun (Oct-Mar).* ☎ *03 23 20 19 87* – painting and archeology.

Chapelle des Templiers★ ◷ *Jun-Sep: Tue-Fri 9am-6pm, Sat-Sun and public holidays 11am-6pm; Oct-May: Tue-Fri 9am-6pm, Sat-Sun and public holidays 2-6pm.* ◷ *Closed Mon, 1 Jan, 1 May, 14 Jul, 25 Dec.* ☎ *03 23 20 19 87.*

Église St-Martin★*Call tourist office or the church in advance for guided tour.* ☎ *03 23 20 26 54.* **Porte de Soissons**★.

Château de LAPALISSE★★

MICHELIN MAP 326 I 5

GREEN GUIDE AUVERGNE THE RHÔNE VALLEY

The little crossroads town has grown up at the foot of the château which has commanded the crossing of the Besbre since the 11C. Its most famous owner was Jacques II de Chabannes (1470-1525), a Marshal of France who distinguished himself in the conquest of Milan but who was killed by a blast from a harquebus fired during the Battle of Pavia.

Visit

🕐 *Guided tours* 🔁 *(1hr) Apr-Oct: daily 9am-noon, 2pm-6pm. Last admission 1hr before closing.* 🎫 *5€ (children: 2.50€).* ☎ *04 70 99 37 58.*

Little remains of the medieval castle. The present building, started at the beginning of the 16C, is very much in the style of the early Renaissance, the work of Florentine craftsmen brought from Italy by Jacques. The courtyard façade is enlivened by heraldic motifs and polychrome brickwork, by sandstone courses on the towers and around the windows, by bracketed lintels and mullioned windows, by medallions in the portal of the central tower, by foliated scrolls, pilasters and Corinthian capitals.

Inside, there is interesting Louis XIII furniture in the main reception room. The **Salon doré**★★ has a coffered ceiling and 15C Flemish tapestries. The chapel, built in granite, is in Flamboyant style, and there is a fine timber ceiling in the service range **(communs)**.

Grotte de **LASCAUX**

MICHELIN MAP 329 I 5

GREEN GUIDE DORDOGNE BERRY LIMOUSIN

The world-famous cave paintings of Lascaux were discovered by accident on 12 September 1940 by a young man looking for his dog which had disappeared down a hole. Most of the paintings appear to date from the end of the Aurignacian period, others from the Magdalenian. They cover the walls and roofs of the cave with a bestiary of bulls, cows, horses, deer and bison, depicted with such skill as to justify Abbot Breuil's epithet "the Sistine Chapel of prehistoric times".

Visit

Lascaux II★★

🕐 *Guided tours* 🔁 *(45min) Apr-Jun and Sep: daily 9.30am-6.30pm; Jul and Aug: daily 9am-8pm; early Oct to mid-Nov: daily 10am-12.30pm, 2-6pm; mid-Nov to end Apr: daily except Mon 10am-noon, 2-5.30pm.* 🕐 *Closed 25 Dec.* 🐾 *Be careful! During the summer the ticket office is located at Montignac, next to the Tourist Office under the arcades. The sale of tickets starts at 9am and closes when 2 000 tickets have been sold (which happens quite quickly in the high season).* 🎫 *8€ (children: 4.50€).* ☎ *05 53 05 65 65.*

The cave itself is not open to the public, but one may visit a full-size replica, which has reproductions of many of the paintings.

Les Îles de **LÉRINS** ★★

MICHELIN MAP 341 D 6

GREEN GUIDE FRENCH RIVIERA

The **islands** *(boat service from Cannes)* are clad in a rich vegetation of pines, cypresses and eucalyptus and have a fascinating historic and archeological heritage. The fine view back to the coast of the mainland stretches from Cap Roux to Cap d'Antibes.

Visit

Île Ste-Marguerite★★

Regular boat service from Cannes: Cie Esterel Chanteclair – Quai St-Pierre – Quai des îles. 🎫 *10€ (5-10 years: 5€).* ☎ *04 93 39 11 82.*

A Celto-Ligurian population once lived here and the place formed a safe anchorage off the marshy coast of La Napoule Bay. There are fine **forest walks** to the headland (Pointe du Bataigner, du Dragon, de la Convention), as well as through the botanic collection and along the avenue, Allée des Eucalyptus géants. Pines of many species soar above an undergrowth of arbutus, tree heathers, cistus, thyme and rosema

Fort Royal was built for coastal defence by Richelieu. During the Thirty Years War it was occupied by the Spanish for two years (1635-37); reconstructed by Vauban in 1712, it was restored under the Convention. It served as a prison for Huguenot pastors, for the Man in the Iron Mask (1687-98) and for Marshal Bazaine, condemned in 1873 as a traitor for his role in the Franco-Prussian War. From the terrace there is an extensive **view**★ of the coast.

Île St-Honorat★★

Regular boat service from Cannes (Quai Laubœuf): Société Planaria – Abbaye de Lérins – Île St-Honorat. ⌖ 9€ round trip (children: 5€). ☎ 04 92 98 71 38.

St Honoratus founded one of the first monasteries of Roman Gaul here in the early years of the 5C. It became one of the most famous and powerful of the period, not least because Provence was not yet affected by the barbarian invasions.

In 1073, the monks built a crenellated keep (**donjon**★) on a headland on the south side of the island. It was here that they took refuge from the raids of pirates from the Barbary Coast. It has two-storeyed cloisters, fine stonework and a remarkable **view**★★ from its battlements.

The monastery itself was rebuilt in the 19C in a neo-Romanesque style.

LESSAY★

POPULATION 1 719

MICHELIN MAP 303 C 4

GREEN GUIDE NORMANDY

Lessay lies on the edge of moorland country whose harsh beauty was sung by Barbey d'Aurevilly (1808-89), who helped establish a distinct Norman literature. The town comes to life every September at the time of the Holy Cross Fair.

Visit

Église abbatiale★★

Founded in 1056, this is not only one of the most perfect examples of Romanesque architecture in Normandy, but also a tribute to the extraordinary skill and devotion of the chief architect of the Historic Monuments Institute, Yves Froidevaux, who rebuilt the church after it had been blown up by the Wehrmacht in 1944.

From the east there is a fine view of the rounded apse backed by a flat gable and dominated by the massive tower.

Inside, there are the typically Norman features of great nave arches, triforium and inspection gallery running underneath the clerestory windows. But Lessay also marks the architectural transition from groined vaults (as used in the 11C aisles) to quadripartite vaults, used somewhat crudely in the choir (end of the 11C), then with greater confidence in the nave (beginning of the 12C). This revolutionary development led directly to the great achievements of Gothic architecture, with its high-flung vaults and walls of glass.

Centre historique minier de LEWARDE★★

MICHELIN MAP 302 H 5

GREEN GUIDE NORTHERN FRANCE AND THE PARIS REGION

The Lewarde Mining Heritage Centre (Centre Historique Minier de Lewarde) is housed in the converted building of the Delloye Colliery which closed in 1971. The museum's design has adapted the original structure to provide exhibition rooms, a restaurant, a lecture room, etc.

Visit

🕐 *Guided tours* ⚬⚬ *(1hr30min) Mar-Oct: daily 9am-7.30pm; Nov-Feb: Mon-Sat 1-7pm, Sun, school and public holidays 10am-7pm. Last admission 2h before closing.* 🕐 *Closed Jan, 1 May, 25 Dec.* ⚬ *10.60€ high season, 9.40€ low season. (children: 5.30€/4.70€).* ☎ *03 27 95 82 82.*

A tour **(visite)**, partly guided by ex-miners, follows the miners' different activities up to the descent in the cage; from cloakroom, shower room – or "hanging room" (salle de pendus) because of the hooks on which the clothes, boots and helmets were hung – lamp room, infirmary. A small train leads to Pit no 2 where the descent to the seams is by lift. A 450m – over 3/4 mile long circuit traces the evolution of mining work since the 1930s. A tour of the processing building (extraction machines, coal-screening room) and the pit stables completes the visit. A vast collection of fossils is also on display, shown in the context of the formation of the mining basin 300 million years ago.

LILLE★★

POPULATION 950 265

MICHELIN MAP 302 G 4

GREEN GUIDE NORTHERN FRANCE AND THE PARIS REGION

Lille is the centre of a sprawling megalopolis which includes the industrial cities of Roubaix and Tourcoing and which has a total population of nearly a million. The early development of the city was slowed down by the disadvantages of its poorly drained site; nevertheless, its position at the head of the navigable river Deule made it the point of exchange between industrial Flanders to the north and agricultural Artois to the south. This medieval commercial role later changed to an industrial one, with cloth predominating in the 14C and wool in the 16C; by the middle of the 19C, Lille had become the epitome of the overcrowded, polluted, northern industrial city.

A plan to restore the old district has successfully preserved its artistic heritage, while modernisation has proceeded apace with new buildings in some areas and the creation of the new town of Villeneuve-d'Ascq and the building of the Euralille centre.

▶ **Orient Yourself:** Lille is laid out on an axis stretching east to west, with the new town leading into the old town leading into the citadel. **Centre Euralille** (east Lille) has spacious walkways and two floors containing more than 130 shops, a hypermarket, private apartments, and a business school. Lille, which is listed as a "Town of Art and History," offers 2hr discovery tours conducted by guide-lecturers approved by the Ministry of Culture and Communication. Tours of Old Lille are on Sat at 3pm and 5pm for 7€. Evening tours and beer tasting in Jul and Aug on two Wed per month at 8pm for 9€. Other theme tours offered in the summer. Contact the tourist office or www.vpah.culture.fr.

🕐 **Organizing Your Time:** Old Lille will take 2hr30min to see everything. The citadel, about 2hr. The tourist office publishes a weekly journal, *Sortir*, listing all of the city's current events, concerts and art exhibitions.

A Bit of History

The Battle of Bouvines – The fall of Gaillard Castle (🕐 *see Les ANDELYS)* in 1204 marked the beginning of King Philippe Auguste's campaign to win back his kingdom from the Plantagenets. As a counter-measure, John Lackland allied himself with the German Emperor Otto IV who had his own reasons for wishing to weaken the French king. Their strategy was to defeat Philippe by means of a pincer movement. John landed at La Rochelle, but was defeated at Roche-aux-Moines near Angers on 2 July 1214 by Philippe's son. Setting out from Aachen, Otto and his mercenaries took the invasion route through Flanders, only to be soundly beaten by the king here on the plain of Bouvines *(12km – 8mi southeast)*. This first great victory of the House of

Vauban, a Military Genius

Sébastien Le Prestre (1633-1707) was born at St-Léger *(25km – 16mi southeast of Avallon in the Morvan)*. Better known as the Marquis de **Vauban**, he was one of the truly great figures of the age of Louis XIV, a soldier who personally conducted 53 sieges, an engineer who created the French army's corps of engineers and who studied the science of gunnery, and not least an architect and town planner who redesigned ports, dug canals, spanned the Eure at Maintenon with a fine aqueduct, and built from scratch 33 new fortresses as well as improving no fewer than 300 others (many have of course disappeared). Appointed Commissioner of Fortifications in 1678, he took his inspiration first of all from his predecessors, bringing their work to a new peak of perfection; in the case of Belfort he added a second external line of defences as well as strengthening the existing bastions by means of demilunes and a deep moat, while at Neuf-Brisach his innovations included supplementing the internal walls with bastions and placing demilunes in front of the redoubts. But above all he was able to assimilate new inventions and changes in tactics, and to adapt his designs to the particular characteristics of the site.

His main concern was to defend France's new, expanded frontiers. His work thus took him to Flanders, the Ardennes and Alsace, to the Franche-Comté, to the Pyrenees, the Alps and to many places along the country's coastline. Some of his fortresses proved their worth to the retreating French and British forces in 1940.

Capet strengthened the monarchy and won popular support. It also marked the end of 60 years of conflict between the House of Anjou and the kings of France. The outbreak of the Hundred Years War lay far in the future.

From Burgundian to Spanish and French rule – In the 15C Lille belonged to Burgundy; in 1454 Philippe le Bon (the Good) was responsible for the fine brick-built Palais Rihour. But the marriage of Marie de Bourgogne to Charles V brought first Austrian, then Spanish rule.

On 27 August 1667, after only nine days of siege, Lille fell to the armies of Louis XIV, subsequently becoming the capital of France's northern provinces. This stimulated activity of all kinds and the city's growth was rapid.

20C – In October 1914 Lille, which was poorly defended, surrendered after three days of spirited resistance to six Bavarian regiments. Some 900 buildings were destroyed. During the Second World War, in May 1940 Rommel's tanks and six infantry divisions laid siege to the town. The French troops finally capitulated on 1 June 1940.

Sights

La Citadelle★

🕐 *May to end Aug:* 🚶 *guided tours (2hr) Sun and public holidays 3-5pm.* 🎫 *7€.* ☎ *03 20 21 94 21.*

Within four months of Louis XIV's troops entering the town, Vauban began to reconstruct the citadel. The great complex is set in a marshy site of some 1 700ha – 4 200 acres which could be flooded when necessary. With its masterly handling of brick and sandstone, its economical design, its logical plan and its response to the geometry of artillery, it was the great engineer's masterpiece, the "queen of citadels".

Within the Royal Gate (Porte Royale), the citadel consisted of 12 barrack blocks, the arsenal and several magazines, all laid out around the vast Parade Ground (Place d'Armes). Its defensive strength was such that it took Marlborough and his Dutch allies 62 days to break into the city and a further 48 to reduce the citadel itself. The high quality of construction is evident in the allegorical pediments of the Royal Gate, in the lively treatment of the tympanum of the arsenal and in the vaulting of the Ste-Barbe postern-gate. The Jesuit-style chapel has unfortunately lost its Classical decoration. Many patriotic French people met their end in the Turenne Bastion during both World Wars.

Le Vieux Lille★★

The renewal of Lille's old district began in 1965 when architecture enthusiasts became aware of the beautiful façades of the 17C – 18C buildings hidden under unsightly plasterwork. The distinctive Lille stye combines brick and carved stonework. The town also retains remarkable monuments from the period of Spanish rule.

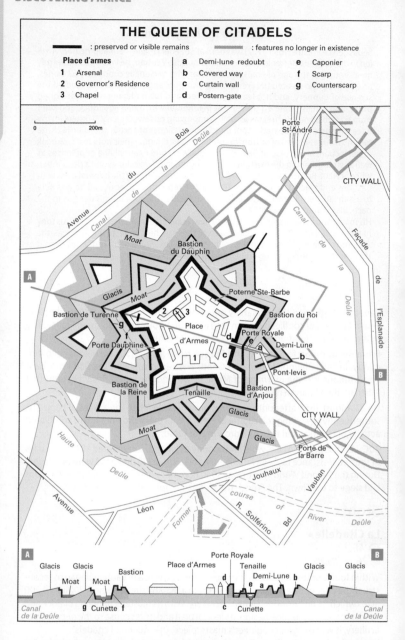

THE QUEEN OF CITADELS

━━━ : preserved or visible remains   ▬▬▬ : features no longer in existence

Place d'armes
1 Arsenal
2 Governor's Residence
3 Chapel

a Demi-lune redoubt
b Covered way
c Curtain wall
d Postern-gate

e Caponier
f Scarp
g Counterscarp

Vieille Bourse

The Old Exchange built in 1650 is an example of the persistence of the Louis XIII style adapted to Flemish tastes (doors with broken pediments, caryatids supporting the entablatures, columns, pilasters and window-surrounds in sandstone, fruit and floral decoration and a little bell-tower). The whole building proclaims the importance of textile manufacturing in the life of the city as well as paying tribute to great men and their contributions to progress with the statues lining the arcades.

Hospice Comtesse★

🕐 Mon 2-6pm, Wed-Sun 10am-12.30pm, 2-6pm. 🕐 Closed Tue,1 Jan, Easter Sun and Mon, 1 May, 14 Jul, 1st Sat-Sun-Mon in Sep, 25 Dec. 👝 2.30€, no charge 1st Sun in the month. ☏ 03 28 36 84 00.

The hospital was rebuilt in 1650 after a fire. It is a fine example of local building, with its monumental gateway, its walls of brick and sandstone, and the superb **timber roof**★★ of its Great Hall (Salle des malades).

Lille - Address Book

TOURISM INFORMATION

🏛 *Palais Rihour, pl. Rihour, 59000 Lille,* ☎ *0 891 562 004 (0,225E/mn). www. lilletourism.com.*

For coin ranges, see the Legend at the back of the guide.

EATING OUT

🍺 **La Taverne de l'Écu** – *9 r. Esquermoise.* ☎ *03 20 57 55 66.* Successively a cabaret, a brothel, then a movie theatre, La Taverne has finally found its true calling as a very lively microbrewery. Combine bustling waiters, a gay, noisy atmosphere and mugs overflowing with tasty home-brewed ale and you have one of Lille's favourite watering holes. Traditional fare plus a few regional specialities.

🍺 **Flam's** – *8 r. de Pas* – ☎ *03 20 54 18 38.* 🕐 *Closed 25 Dec and 1 Jan.* Satisfy your flammküche yen by ordering one in this restaurant – one of thirteen such in France – specialised in the confection of the inimitable Alsatian tarte. The most popular tables are in the upper dining room, facing the oven.

A LEISURELY MEAL

🍴 **Domaine de Lintillac** – *43 r. de Gand.* ☎ *03 20 06 53 51.* 🕐 *Closed 2 wks in Aug, Sun-Mon.* The red facade of the building will lead you directly to this rustic restaurant in old Lille. Wicker baskets hang from the beams and the walls are lined with pots of preserves from southwest France. The plentiful cuisine of the Périgord region is honoured here.

🍴 **Le Bistrot des Brasseurs** – *20 pl. de la Gare.* ☎ *03 20 06 37 27.* The reputation of "The Brewers' Bistro," founded in 1928, is almost as widespread as that of its neighbour, Les 3 Brasseurs, and for good reason! The beer is drawn directly from the brewers' vats of this northern institution. Lively fun of the traditional tavern style; regional fare.

🍴 **Restaurant Le Lapin à Z'os** – *19 pl. de la République, 59830 Cysoing – 15km/9mi SE of Lille via D 955.* ☎ *03 20 79 48 49.* 🕐 *Closed Sat lunch, Sun evening, Tue lunch and Mon – reserv. recommended.* This enjoyable restaurant located on the city's main square features an amusing bric-a-brac decor starring none other than Mr. Rabbit himself. The long-eared creature also has the leading role in the kitchen, where he is prepared in a variety of manners. Diners who aren't keen on lapin may prefer the mussels, served in a pot.

🍴 **Le Passe-Porc** – *155 r. de Solférino* – ☎ *03 20 42 83 93.* 🕐 *Closed 29 Jul to 19 Aug and Sun – reserv. required.* A bistro after our own hearts. The tiled floor, wall seats and enamelled plaques on the walls act as the backdrop for a remarkable collection of pigs. The hearty ambience and plentiful fare are in perfect harmony with the amusing surroundings.

🍴 **Aux Moules** – *34 r. de Béthune* – ☎ *03 20 57 12 46.* 🕐 *Closed Christmas and New Year's.* A multitude of mussels (*moules*) and a few other Flemish specialities await customers in this 1930s style brasserie located in a lively pedestrian street. A must for bona fide shellfish fans and friends.

🍴 **T Rijsel (Estaminet)** – *25 r. de Gand,* ☎ *03 20 15 01 59.* 🕐 *Closed first 3 wks of Aug, Sun-Mon.* A sure bet, this *estaminet* is located in a street crowded with restaurants. The appealing Flemish décor features photos, posters and advertisements, while the appetizing regional menu is presented in the form of an old school notebook.

🍴 **Alcide** – *5 r. des Débris-St-Etienne, 59800 Lille.* ☎ *03 20 12 06 95 – bigaradeasynet.fr.* 🕐 *Closed mid-Jul to mid-Aug and Sun evenings.* In a picturesque narrow street near the Grand'Place, this bistro, founded in 1830, although renovated, still retains its original charm. Regional specialities and incomparable mussels (*moules*) and chips.

🍴🍴 **La Robe des Champs** – *10 r. Faidherbe.* ☎ *03 20 55 13 74.* This pretty yellow and blue restaurant in the town centre gives pride of place to the noble potato and its many disguises. Whether your dish was originally concocted in Lille, Paris or rural France, your taste buds will surely be gratified.

🍴🍴 **La Tête de l'Art** – *10 r. de l'Arc.* ☎ *03 20 54 68 89.* 🕐 *Closed first 3 wks of Aug, Sun and evenings except Fri-Sat – reserv. essential Sat-Sun.* A charming, lively restaurant is hidden behind the pink facade of this manor built in 1890. Follow the hallway to discover the inviting dining room where denizens of Lille gather for traditional meals. A good selection of wines at reasonable prices.

🍴🍴 **Le Bistrot de Pierrot** – *6 pl. de Béthune.* ☎ *03 20 57 14 09 – pierrot@ bistrot-de-pierrot.com.* 🕐 *Closed Sun and public holidays.* Pierrot, the colourful owner of this friendly bistro, is also a local television personality who reveals his culinary secrets on a regional station. A few Flemish specialities figure among the wide variety of dishes offered, with a nice assortment of wines to boot.

🍴🍴 **Restaurant La Cave aux Fioles** – *39 r. de Gand.* ☎ *03 20 55 18 43.* 🕐 *Closed Sat lunch, Sun and public holidays – reserv. required evenings.* Don't be put off by the gloomy passageway that leads to this restaurant housed in two 17C and 18C residences – the interior is unexpectedly warm and pleasant: brick, wood, beams and paintings by area artists. Check out the collection of commodes upstairs. Convivial ambience; bistro cuisine.

WHERE TO STAY

B & B (Bed and Breakfast) – 78 r. Caumartin – ☎ 03 20 13 76 57. ◐ Closed 15 Jul-15 Aug – ⊟ – 3 rms. "B & B" as in Bed and Breakfast, as well as in Béatrice and Bernard, the current owners of this house built during the reign of Napoléon III. The comfortable rooms – non-smoking only – have been nicely refurbished; two of them have sloping ceilings. Cosy sitting room, breakfast room looking out onto the garden.

Station Bac St-Maur – 77 r. de la Gare, Bac St-Maur, 62840 Sailly-sur-la-Lys – 7km/4.2mi SW of Armentières. ☎ 03 21 02 68 20. ◐ Closed Nov-Mar – ⊡ – 6 rms: – ⊿ 6.50€ . Continue your travels while staying put by taking a room in this old train station converted into a hotel-restaurant. Fans of railway's golden years will enjoy lodging in one of the six compartments of this wagon dating from the 1930s. All aboard!

Chez Julie – 8 r. de Radinghem, 59134 Beaucamps-Ligny – 12km/7.2mi W of Lille. Take A 25, exit no 7, then D 62, Rte du Radinghem. ☎ 03 20 50 33 82 – ⊟ – 3 rms. One quickly feels at home in this nice red-brick smallholding on the edge of a village near Lille. The pastel-toned bedrooms are well-maintained; a piano, a wood-burning stove and traditional Flemish games round out the breakfast room.

La Ferme Blanche – R. Pasteur, 59840 Lompret – 7km/4.2mi NW of Lille – ☎ 03 20 92 99 12 – dadeleval@nordnet.fr. ◐ Closed 15 days in Aug – ⊟ – 3 rms. A bumpy lane leads to this pretty white farmhouse behind an electric gate (video surveillance). The simple rooms are comfortably installed in the old barn. Small swimming pool in the courtyard.

Hôtel Flandre Angleterre – 13 pl. de la Gare. ☎ 03 20 06 04 12, hotel-flandre-angleterre@wanadoo.fr – 44 rms – ⊿ 7€. Situated opposite the train station and near the pedestrian streets, this family-run hotel presents modern rooms that are comfortable and cosy. Recommended for its location and affordability.

As Hôtel – 98 r. Louis-Braille, 59790 Ronchin – 3km/1.8mi SE of Lille via the motorway dir. Paris, exit no. 1: Ronchin. ☎ 03 20 53 05 05 – ⊡ – 65 rms: – ⊿ 8€ – restaurant 17/68€. This cubic hotel offers recently refitted rooms, all with new bedding, and a pleasant dining room in shades of yellow and black. A convenient stopover just off the A1 motorway.

Hôtel Brueghel – 5 parvis St-Maurice ☎ 03 20 06 06 69, hotel.brueghel@wanadoo.fr – 60 rms – ⊿ 7.50€. This Flemish-style house is conveniently located in the pedestrian part of town quite near the train station. The rooms have old-fashioned charm and modern bathrooms. The lift, the woodwork and the knick-knacks give the place a nostalgic appeal.

La Viennale – 31 r. Jean-Jacques-Rousseau, Centre-Vieux-Lille. ☎ 03 20 51 08 02, http://laviennale.free.fr – 12 rms: – ⊿ 5€. Sculpted woodwork, ceilings with gilded mouldings, period furnishings and Chinese vases. This 18C house has a deliciously kitsch appeal. The spacious rooms, each unique, are named after flowers. Lovely walled garden.

ON THE TOWN

L'Échiquier (Bar of the Alliance Hotel), 17 quai de Wault – ☎ 03 20 30 62 62. ◐ Mon-Sat 10am-1am, Sun and public holidays 10.30am-11pm. ◐ No musical events Jul-Aug. This bar, installed in the majestic 17C setting of a former Minim convent, is attached to the Alliance Hotel. A harpist performs Mon-Thu 7.30pm-9.30pm, followed by a pianist Mon-Thu 10pm-11.30pm, Fri and Sat 7.30pm-11.30pm, Sun 4pm-7pm. Rich selection of champagne and cocktails.

Les 3 Brasseurs – 22 pl. de la Gare (Opposite the Lille-Flandres train station), ☎ 03 20 06 46 29 – ◐ daily 11am-12.30am. ◐ Closed Aug. The pungent scent of hops greets visitors to this brasserie, a veritable Lille institution. Sample one or all of the four kinds on beer on draught drawn directly from the tuns behind the counter. Flammekueches, sauerkraut and regional fare are on hand for the pleasure of nibblers and the ravenous alike.

Planet Bowling – ZA du Grand-But, 59000 Armentières. ☎ 03 20 08 10 50, www.planetebowling.com – ◐ Sun-Thu 11am-2am, Fri-Sat 11am-4am. An American-style complex featuring 32 bowling alleys, 20 American billiards tables, a children's play area, Internet hook-ups, plus karaoke Sundays, and cabaret and comedy shows Fridays and Saturdays. One huge restaurant.

The Tudor Inn After Burn Café – 12 r. de la Vieille-Comédie (Pl. Rihour), ☎ 03 20 54 53 35 – ◐ Mon-Sat 11am-3am, Sun 3pm-3am. ◐ Closed Christmas and New Year's. An enormous sword dominates the bar of this pub specialised in cocktails, with or without alcohol. Other café highlights include afternoon teas, merry "happy dips" from 6.30pm to 9pm (before-dinner drinks served with appetizers) and "lounge cocktails" later on.

SHOWTIME

Useful tip: The Office de Tourisme publishes a weekly journal, Sortir, listing all of the city's current events, concerts and art exhibitions.

Théâtre Le Grand Bleu – 36 av. Max-Dormoy. ☎ 03 20 09 88 44, www.legrandbleu.com – ◐ ticket office 9am-noon, 2pm-6pm; performances 8pm, Wed and Sat 3pm, Sun 5pm. ◐ Closed Aug – adults: 10€ (children: 8.50€). This performance hall caters to a young audience. Some of its events appeal to children as young as five years old, others are designed for teens. Dance, circus, theatre, storytelling, hip-hop and other nice surprises.

Les Folies de Paris – *52 av. du Peuple-Belge, 59000 Armentières. ☎ 03 20 06 62 64, www.foliesdeparis.com – ⏰ Tue-Sat dinner: 8pm; show: 10.30pm. Sun 1pm and 3pm. ⏰ Closed Aug – tickets 39€, 49€, 59€.* This cabaret and dinner show is the area's biggest. It is frequented by a crowd of Lillois and their Belgian neighbours, especially when the work week is over.

Orchestre National de Lille – *30 pl. Mendès-France, 59000 Armentières. ☎ 03 20 12 82 40, www.onlille.com – ⏰ Mon-Fri 9am-12.45pm, 2pm-6pm. ⏰ Closed Aug - tickets start at 10€.* Since 1976, The Orchestre National de Lille gives an average of 120 concerts per season. Performances are held in the Lille area, the Nord-Pas-de-Calais region and abroad (30 countries altogether). The varied repertoire, featuring performances for young audiences, original pieces, established musicians and fresh talent, exemplifies this orchestra's motto: 'taking music to all who would hear it.'

Théâtre de Marionnettes du Jardin Vauban – *R. Léon-Jouhaux, Chalet des Chèvres in the Jardin Vauban, 59000 Armentières. ☎ 03 20 42 09 95. ⏰ Open Easter-Oct – tickets 4€.* An outdoors puppet show of the Guignol tradition starring characters of local repute, such as Jacques de Lille and Jean-Jean La Plume.

Théâtre Mariska – *2 pl. de la Gare, 59830 Cysoing – 15km/9mi SE of Lille via D 955. ☎ 03 20 79 47 03, www.mariska.fr. ⏰ 8.30am-noon and 1.30-5.30pm. ⏰ Closed Aug – tickets 5€.* Created in 1970, this marionette puppet theatre is housed in a typical Flemish residence. The company gives nearly a thousand shows a year, on site and throughout the region, plus workshops for would-be puppeteers. Impressive collection of 120 puppets.

SPORT & LEISURE

Prés du Hem – 🧒 *7 av. Marc-Sangnier - 59000 Armentières - ☎ 03 20 44 04 60 - voile-armentieres@nordnet.fr - ⏰ closed Jan-Feb - admission 2.50€.* This outdoors activities centre offers a wide range of activities, including a mini-train, a pleasure steamer, miniature golf, a farm animal zoo and a bird preserve. Water sports, swimming, fishing and pedalos on a 44ha/110 acre lake.

Ch'ti vélo – *10 av. Willy-Brandt. ☎ 03 28 53 07 49. ⏰ Daily 7.30am-7.30pm (Sat, Sun and public holidays, 9am-7.30pm – 1€/hr, 5€/day, 12€/week. Reservations required.* Cycling.

SHOPPING

Furet du Nord – *15 pl. du Gén.-De-lle. ☎ 03 20 78 43 43, contact@furet. ⏰ Mon-Sat 9.30am-7.30pm. ⏰ Closed .* This bookshop, founded in 1936, over 7,000m² and 9 different

levels: a bibliophile's paradise. Stairs, footbridges and a number of passageways take you to your chosen destination: books, games, music, videos, comic books, stationery or the ticket agency.

Leroux SAS – *86 r. François-Herbo (south-eastern suburb), 59310 Orchies. ☎ 03 20 64 48 00, lamaisondelachicorée@free.fr – write to make a reservation. ⏰ Tue-Thu 1pm-5pm. ⏰ Closed Jul-Aug.* A visit to this factory teaches all about chicory – cultivated locally – and demonstrates how it is transformed into powder, liquid or special, flavoured products.

Marché de Wazemmes – *59000 Armentières. ☎ 08 90 39 20 04.* Tues, Thur and especially Sun mornings, the Wazemmes market takes over the Place de la Nouvelle-Aventure and its great covered market built of red brick. Food stands alternate with second-hand bric-a-brac in a merry market for shoppers of all categories.

Rue Basse – *59000 Armentières.* This is Lille's main street for antique dealers; you will also find other unusual shops here, such as the Bleu Natier selling furniture, decorative objects, artistic gifts and handcrafted jewellery.

Rue de Gand – Paved, animated and highly colourful, La Rue de Gand is well worth a visit. Butcher shops, taverns, bars and especially restaurants serving various types of cuisine line the pavements.

VISITS AND TOURS

Lille by bicycle – *www.lilletourism.com - May-Aug: departure from Palais Rihour the 1st and 3rd Wed of the month, 3-5pm; 7€ (under 16: 6€).* Cycle hire available. Enquire at the *Office de Tourisme.* A guided ride through Lille's boulevards, streets and alleys.

Tourist packages – The Office de Tourisme, *☎ 0 890 392 004* , offers a variety of package deals (discovery, Christmas market, culture, Lille flea market, cabaret) that may include one or several nights in a hotel, a City Tour, museum admission or a show, etc.

Tour of Lille – A tour of Lille by mini-bus (1hr) – *⏰ May-Oct: dep. hourly from 10am to 6pm (except Mon, Sun and public holidays: 1pm and 6pm); Nov-Apr: dep. hourly from 10am to 5pm (except Mon, Sun and public holidays: 1pm). 8€ (children under 12: 6€).* Rendez-vous at Palais Rihour. The visit is commented in several languages. Bus accessible to persons of reduced mobility. Schedule sometimes varies: enquire at the Office de Tourisme, *☎ 03 20 21 94 21.*

TRANSPORTATION

Lille Métropole City Pass – This inclusive ticket gives you access to metropolitan Lille's public transportation network (Transpole) plus 25 interesting sites and tourist attractions in Lille, Roubaix,

Muséé tbc

ourcoing, Villeneuve-d'Ascq and Wattrelos. The passes are valid 1 day (15€), 2 days (25€) or 3 days (30€). Information and sales in the Offices de Tourisme of the cities cited, through the Comité Départemental du Tourisme du Nord and via ☎ 0 820 42 40 40, www.transpole.f.r

Musée des Beaux-Arts★★★

 ♿ ⏰ *Wed, Thu, Sat-Sun 10am-6pm, Mon 2-6pm, Fri 10am-7pm.* ⏰ *Closed Tue, 1 Jan, 1 May, 14 Jul, 1st Sat-Sun in Sep, 1 Nov, 25 Dec.* ⊚ *4.60€, no charge 1st Sun in the month.* ☎ *03 20 06 78 00.*

The imposing building (1885-92) has recently been renovated and extended. The collection includes many masterpieces of French painting, among them the *Mystical Fountain* by Jean Bellegambe (early 16C) with its symbolic treatment of renewal and redemption, a serenely Classical Nativity by Philippe de Champaigne (1674), a beautifully modelled portrait of Madame Pélerin by Quentin de la Tour, and another portrait, J Forest (1746), by Nicolas de Largillière.

▶▶ **Demeure de Gilles de la Boé**★. **Rue de la Monnaie**★, **Église St-Maurice**★. **Porte de Paris**★.

LIMOGES ★

POPULATION 170 065

MICHELIN MAP 325 E 5-6

GREEN GUIDE DORDOGNE BERRY LIMOUSIN

Limoges originated as a ford over the River Vienne at the meeting-point of the great Roman highways from Lyon to Saintes and from Bourges to Bordeaux. Nevertheless, it was only in the early 19C that it became a commercial centre of considerable importance, requiring a fleet of 5 000 wagons and 20 000 horses to handle its road traffic. Then came the manufacture of porcelain, which moved here from St-Yrieix (40km – 25mi south) where there were kaolin deposits but no workforce. Later, shoe-making became established, based on the already-existing tanneries.

A Bit of History

Famous citizens

The town has been the birthplace of a large number of great men, including:

Léonard Limosin (1505-76), an enameller and painter who worked with Primaticcio at Fontainebleau and who was the leading figure in the 16C Limoges School of enamel-workers;

Pierre Vergniaud (1753-93), a prominent Girondin in the Legislative Assembly and later in the Convention;

Jean-Baptiste Jourdan (1762-1833), the victor of the Battle of Fleurus in 1794 which opened up Belgium to the French armies;

Thomas Bugeaud (1784-1849), promoted corporal at the Battle of Austerlitz, who later pacified Algeria and oversaw its colonisation;

Sadi Carnot (1837-94), who became President of France in 1887;

Auguste Renoir (1841-1919), one of the initiators of Impressionism.

Sights

ENAMEL AND PORCELAIN

Musée de l'Évêché★

The museum is housed in the former Bishops' Palace and features a stunning col... of some 300 *champlevé or cloisonné* enamels *(ground floor)* by Limoges ma...

Limoges Enamel

Enamel has been known since the days of Antiquity. In the 12C L.
important centre of production, partly thanks to the variety of mine...
the surrounding area; its exquisite wares were exported all over Europe.
consists of crushing leadglass, coloured with metal oxides, applying it to...
face, gold, silver or copper, then heating it to a temperature of up to 800 °C,
in a crystalline effect. In the 12C Limoges specialised in champlevé enamels, in...
the enamel is poured into grooves let into a copper surface, then polished level...
the metal. In the 14C painted enamels made their appearance.
In the reign of François I, Léonard Limosin was made Director of the Manufactory,
which produced enamels of great brilliance and colour.

Musée Adrien-Dubouché★★

🕐 *Daily except Tue 10am-12.25pm, 2-5.40pm (Jul and Aug: Open continuously).* 🕐
Closed 1 Jan, 1 May, 25 Dec. 🎫 *4€ (children: no charge), no charge 1st Sun in the month.*
☎ *05 55 33 08 50. www.musee-adriendubouche.fr*

The masterpieces of this most decorative of the arts assembled here illustrate the evolution in time and space of all branches of ceramics. Limoges ware is dealt with in showcases 61 and 62 (when its beginnings were closely linked with production at Sèvres), in the saloon (salon d'honneur – 19C work), and in the left wing of the ground floor (contemporary work).

Porcelain – All vessels made from baked clay come under the generic term **pottery**, but porcelain has certain important characteristics of its own, notably its whiteness, its hardness and its translucence; when baked, it becomes vitrified.

Soft-paste porcelain was first made in Europe in the 17C and 18C in an attempt to recapture the perfection of Chinese porcelain. A white clay was used, given a first firing and then ground and mixed to yield the paste. The paste, which was not particularly easy to work, was then formed into the shape of the vessel or object required, to which glazes and enamels were applied before firing at a temperature of some 1 400 °C. From the 18C new enamels unable to withstand such high temperatures were used, and consequently a third and even a fourth firing took place with progressively lower temperatures, allowing a great variety of colour as well as the use of gold.

It was soft-paste porcelain that made Sèvres' reputation from the 1760s on.

Hard-paste or true porcelain was first produced in Europe in Meissen early in the 18C and came to France around 1770. It is based on kaolin (a very pure kind of clay) and feldspar. It is particularly translucent, resists scratching with steel and gives off a pure tone when rung. The vessel is formed directly from the paste and fired at a temperature of around 500 °C. A first coat of enamel is then applied and a second firing at a high temperature takes place, followed sometimes by other firings at lower temperatures to take account of more vulnerable enamels.

Biscuit-bake is the term used to describe firing at a high temperature when no coloured enamel has been applied.

Faience or **tin-glazed ware** is an imitation of porcelain, made from a soft and porous paste, to which an opaque white glaze of tin oxide is applied which can then be decorated. The oldest and most difficult decorative process is one in which the decoration is applied and given a single firing at a high temperature, thereby limiting the choice of colours and excluding any subsequent retouching.

Most porcelain factories use broadly the same operational processes, the differences in the product depending on the skill of the workforce, the size and form of the objects produced, the way in which they are decorated and in the relative proportion of certain ingredients.

Limoges porcelain from the Comte of Artois manufactory, Musée Adrien-Dubouché

. the Legend at the back

...UT

...François – *Pl. de La Motte, Halles ...ales* - ☎ *05 55 32 32 79* - 🕐 *closed 5-25 ...g, Sun and public hols*. Housed in the ...alles de Limoges, a listed historical monument, this friendly bistro bases its menu on produce from the market. From the dining room, decorated with a fresco of sculpted wood, you can see the chef at work. Good value for money. Opens at 5.30am.

🍽 **Chez Alphonse** – *5 pl. de la Motte* - ☎ *05 55 34 34 14* - 🕐 *closed Mon eve, Sun and public hols*. Tucked away behind the *halles*, this bistro is a popular local haunt. Tables decorated with chequered tablecloths and a menu which is written up on the blackboard.

🍽🍽 **Le Pont St-Étienne** – *8 pl. de Compostelle* - ☎ *05 55 30 52 54* - 🕐 *closed Christmas-1 Jan - reserv. required at weekends*. Attractive bay windows with views of the old stone bridge and the river. The à la carte menu features a number of imaginatively named dishes. Summer terrace.

🍽🍽 **Les Petits Ventres** – *20 r. de la Boucherie* - ☎ *05 55 34 22 90* - 🕐 *closed 8-15 Jan, 2-17 May, 5-22 Sep, Sun and Mon*. Classic French cuisine is to the fore in these two typical 15C houses, run by two young and enthusiastic owners. The cuisine is high on quality with traditional dishes based on liver, tongue, pig's trotters, tripe etc.

🍽🍽 **Le Bœuf à la Mode** – *60 r. François-Chenieux* - ☎ *05 55 77 73 95* - 🕐 *closed 1 to late-Aug, Sat lunchtime and Sun*. If you love eating meat, then this is definitely the place for you! Excellent cuisine served in a friendly and traditional ambience.

🍽🍽 **L'Escapade du Gourmet** – *5 r. des 71ème-Mobiles* - ☎ *05 55 32 40 26* - 🕐 *closed 10-26 August, Sat lunchtime, Sun eve and Mon*. A Belle-Époque decor of wood, frescoes, moulded ceilings and coloured glass is the backdrop to this popular traditional restaurant located between the château and the Cité Episcopale. Classical French cuisine. Good-value-for-money.

WHERE TO STAY

🛏 **Hôtel de la Paix** – *25 pl. Jourdan* - ☎ *05 55 34 36 00* - *31 rooms*. This Napoléon III-style hotel in the heart of the city features an entertaining phonographic collection. Bright and airy bedrooms, some with wicker furnishings. Friendly atmosphere.

🛏🛏 **Hôtel Jeanne-d'Arc** – *17 av. du Gén.-de-Gaulle* - ☎ *05 55 77 67 77* - *hoteljeanned'arc.limoges@wanadoo.fr* - 🕐 *closed 20 Dec-7 Jan* - 🅿 - *50 rooms*. This pleasant, well-located hotel is close to the city's famous train station. The well-mantained bedrooms and pleasant breakfast room have managed to retain their old French charm.

🛏🛏 **Chambre d'hôte M. et Mme Brulat** – *Imp. du Vieux Crezin - 87220 Feytiat - 5km/3mi E of Limoges. Take the A 20, exit 35, and head towards Feytiat; in Crézin follows signs to Le Vieux Crézin* - ☎ *05 55 06 34 41* - ✉ - *3 rooms*. Peace and quiet reign supreme in this large stone house in the middle of the country, yet just 10min from the centre of Limoges. Comfortable bedrooms, relaxing lounge, and a games room with billiards and darts. Friendly family atmosphere.

BARS AND CAFÉS

La Parenthèse – *Cours du Temple - 22 r. du Consulat* - ☎ *05 55 33 18 25* - 🕐 *closed Sun and evenings*. This tea room sells home-made pastries and serves family-style meals at lunchtime. Either sit outdoors in the 16C courtyard or in the dining room painted with a mural of Montmartre. A restful and relaxing retreat.

Brasserie Artisanale St Martial – *8 pl. Denis-Dussoubs* - ☎ *05 55 79 37 98* - 🕐 *open Mon-Thu, 3.30pm-1am; Fri-Sat, 3.30pm-2am* - 🕐 *closed Sun and 15 Aug*. This brewery (in the true sense of the term), established over 10 years ago, perpetuates an old local tradition. Beer has been brewed in the region since the 18C; in the 19C there were no fewer than 50 brewers in the Limoges area.

Café des Anciennes Majorettes de la Baule – *27 r. Haute-Vienne* - ☎ *05 55 34 34 16* - 🕐 *open Tue-Wed, 10.30am-1am; Thu-Sat, 10.30am-2am* - 🕐 *closed mid-Jul to mid-Aug*. This renowned local bar is the venue for regular concerts and plays.

L'Irlandais – *2 r. Haute-Cité* - ☎ *05 55 32 46 47* - 🕐 *open Apr-Oct, daily, 10am-2am; Nov-Mar, Mon-Sat, 4pm-2am, Sun, 2pm-midnight; concerts Wed-Sun; Thu, Irish evening with live music*. This Irish pub is run by a fisherman from Brittany who has travelled the world and has already established a bakery and a pub in Ireland, and a concert violinist who has played in royal circles. Over the past three years they've hosted jazz, Celtic music and other concerts here. Juggling shows on the terrace during the summer months.

ENTERTAINMENT

Cinemas - The main cinemas are around place Jourdan (Colisée et Lido) and Denis-Dussoubs (Grands Écrans). The Théâtre Municipal (rue Jean-Jaurès) hosts performances of ballet, opera, musicals and pop concerts. For theatre, head for La Limousine (rue des Coopérateurs) and Expression 7 (rue de la Réforme).

SHOPPING

Most of the city's shops are located in the area around the castle. The main boutiques selling porcelain are along boulevard Louis-Blanc and along the streets heading west from the city centre. Discount shops selling seconds and end-of-line products include Michel Morel (boulevard Louis-Blanc) and Cygne Bleu (place des Jacobins). Art et Feu (rue de la Boucherie) sells original enamel works.

Le Pavillon de la Porcelaine – *Av. du Prés.-John-Kennedy* - ☎ *05 55 30 21 86 - pavillon-porcelaine@haviland-limoges.com - ⊙ open daily, 9am-7pm - ⊙ closed Sun in Jan, 1 Jan, 1 May and 25 Dec.* This factory outlet belongs to Haviland, the American family which settled in Limoges in 1842 and began crafting prestigious porcelain sets for kings, queens and other famous names. The visit includes the museum and a demonstration of porcelain production, which includes a film on a large screen. A wide choice of table and decorative ware is on sale in the boutique.

Paul Buforn – *4 pl. de la Cité* - ☎ *06 70 54 30 40 - ⊙ open Tue-Sat, 10am-12.30pm and 2-7pm - ⊙ closed Oct and public hols.* The impassioned enameller will delight in telling you all about his profession, its tradition and its techniques. He can also provide information about enamel-making workshops, as well as offer advice and appraisals on individual antique pieces. In the past, Limoges was home to a hundred or so enamel artisans, a number that has dwindled to just thirty today.

Buissières – *27, r. Jean-Jaurès* - ☎ *05 55 34 10 44 - ⊙ open Mon-Sat, 9am-7pm.* This chic confectioner, established in 1848, is one of Limoges' must-see places where the Art-Deco decor is almost worth a visit on its own. Evocatively named chocolates, pastries and desserts, including the house speciality black chocolate with chestnut cream.

GUIDED TOURS

The tourist office is able to provide information on guided, theme-based visits (2hr) of the old town, which take place during school holidays. *5€.* ☎ *05 55 34 46 87.*

Virtually all the porcelain produced at Limoges is of the hard-paste type. Production began in 1771, some 30 years later than at Strasbourg or Niderviller in Lorraine, stimulated by the discovery of a particularly pure deposit of kaolin at St-Yrieix by a local surgeon, one Darnet.

Ville (Town)

Early on in its evolution, Limoges developed two rival centres, known as City (Cité) and Castle (Château).

Cité

Overlooking the Vienne, this is the historic core of Limoges. It spreads out around the **Cathédrale St-Étienne★** which has a fine portal **(portail St-Jean★)** and which has kept its **rood screen★** of 1533, now located at the west end of the nave. In the chancel are a number of **tombs★**.

Château

The castle quarter is the modern centre of Limoges, with busy shopping streets. **St-Michel-des-Lions★** is an old hall-church which has retained its original rectangular plan.

It was in this part of the town that the great abbey, Abbaye St-Martial, was sited. Originally founded on the grave of a third-century missionary, by the 11C it had become one of the important Romanesque churches on the pilgrimage route to Santiago de Compostela, just as important as St-Rémi at Reims or St-Sernin at Toulouse. It stretched southwestwards from today's Place de la République but was demolished at the time of the French Revolution *(its plan is traced out on the paving)*.

◖◗ Cour du Temple★.

LISIEUX★★

POPULATION 23 703

MICHELIN MAP 303 N 5

GREEN GUIDE NORMANDY

Lisieux is the market centre of the Auge region. With its closely-packed hedge-rows, thatched cottages and old manors, this is a pastoral countryside of great charm, the quintessence of the Normandy sung by the poetess Lucie Delarue-Madrus.

A Bit of History

St Teresa of Lisieux – Thérèse Martin (1873-97) was born at Alençon into a deeply religious family. Her father was a watchmaker, her mother a lace-maker. On the death of her mother the family moved to Lisieux, to the house known as Les Buissonnets. At the age of 15, Thérèse left the family home for good, having been given the Pope's permission to enter the Carmelite Order.

In the convent, "Little Teresa", as she wished to be known, scaled the steep stairway towards perfection. "A soul such as she needs no dispensations" said her Prioress. Teresa's short life ended in the Carmelite hospital only a few days after she had finished the manuscript of her *History of a Soul*. She was canonised on 17 May 1925.

The Pilgrimage – Teresa's house, **Les Buissonnets** (◷ *Palm Sun to end Sep: 30min audio tours daily 9am-noon, 2-6pm; mid-Jan to end Mar and Oct: daily 10am-noon, 2-5pm; Nov to mid-Dec: daily 10am-noon, 2-4pm;* ⊜ *no charge;* ☎ *02 31 48 55 08; http://therese-de-lisieux.com)*, can be visited. Her effigy can be seen in the Carmelite Chapel **(Chapelle du Carmel)** and there is a reliquary chamber (Salle des Souvenirs) where relics are displayed.

Mass pilgrimages take place to the vast basilica on its site to the southeast of the town.

Excursions

Manor Houses of the Pays d'Auge

The farmhouses and manors of this tranquil landscape are set within an enclosure planted with apple trees and defined by a hedge. All the buildings are timber-framed, from the house itself, to the cider-press, apple-store, stables and dairy grouped around it. Among the finest are the moated site at **Coupesarte** *(16km – 10mi southwest)* and **Château Crèvecœur★** *(18km – 11mi west)* with its museum devoted to the story of petroleum research (musée de la recherche pétrolière).

◖◗ Cathédrale St-Pierre★.

LOCHES★★

POPULATION 7 133

MICHELIN MAP 317 O 6

GREEN GUIDE CHÂTEAUX OF THE LOIRE

Modern Loches lies mostly on the left bank of the Indre, at the foot of the fortified bluff which dominates the valley and which set natural limits to the growth of the medieval town.

▶ **Orient Yourself:** Loches, which is listed as a "Town of Art and History," of 2hr discovery tours conducted by guide-lecturers approved by the Min Culture and Communication. Information at the tourist office or on ww culture.fr.

Visit

Cité médiévale★★

The medieval town is contained within a continuous wall some 1 000m yd long in which there are only two gates.

To the south, the great square keep **(donjon★★)** (🕐 Apr-Sep: daily 9am-7pm, daily 9.30am-5pm; 🕐 closed 1 Jan and 25 Dec; 🎫 5€, 12-18 years: 3.50€; 📞 0. 07 86) was built by the Counts of Anjou in the 11C on even earlier foundation the 13C, it was strengthened by wide ditches hewn into the solid rock, by buttre towers and the Martelet Tower with its impressive dungeons, then given additiona. accommodation including service buildings.

In the centre of the old town is a church, **Église St-Ours★**, with its Angevin porch built around a Romanesque portal, and pyramid vaults in its nave.

To the north is the **Château★★**(🕐 Apr-Sep: daily 9am-7pm; Oct-Mar: daily 9.30am-5pm; 🕐 closed 1 Jan, 25 Dec; 🎫 5€, 12-18 years: 3.50€; 📞 02 47 59 01 32), begun at the end of the 14C as an extension of the 13C watchtower known as Agnes Sorèl's Tower **(Tour Agnès Sorel)**. Part of the royal apartments are medieval (Vieux logis), part Renaissance (Nouveau logis). It was in the great hall of the Vieux Logis on 3 and 5 June 1429 that Joan of Arc persuaded the Dauphin to undertake his coronation journey to Reims.

There is a tiny Flamboyant oratory dedicated to Anne of Brittany decorated with the ermine of Brittany and the girdle of St Francis, and, in the Charles VIII Room, a recumbent figure **(gisant d'Agnès Sorel★)** of Charles VII's "Lady of Beauty".

◖◖ Porte Royale★ – Ramparts★ and walk round the outside of the ramparts.

LOCRONAN★★

POPULATION 796

MICHELIN MAP 308 F 6

GREEN GUIDE BRITTANY

Locronan is sited at the foot of its granite hill at the meeting point of the roads from Quimper to Châteaulin and from Crozon to Douarnenez.

The little town once flourished on the proceeds of flax-growing and on the manufacture of sailcloth which was exported from the port of Douarnenez.

The traditional crafts of the area are evoked in the museum and in a number of workshops; they include the making of baskets, glass and clogs, stone-masonry, and above all the weaving of flax, wool, cotton and silk.

Sights

Place de l'Église★★

This little square with its well is like many others in Brittany, having grown up over the centuries in a haphazard way without any overall plan, but with a unity due to the consistent use of granite. Because of the strength of the westerly winds, the walls on that side of the weavers' houses are windowless. In the 17C many of the houses were given an additional storey in stone. The lofts are lit by means of dormer windows let into the roof.

Église St-Ronan et Chapelle du Penity★★

This is a 15C pilgrimage church with stone vaults. Its architect endowed it with the plain east end current in Brittany at the time, thereby letting more light into what would otherwise be a somewhat dark interior. Behind the altar, the main window has fine 15C stained glass depicting scenes from the Passion. The pulpit **(chaire★)** of 1707 has panels illustrating the life of St Ronan.

The chapel (Chapelle du Penity) in the south aisle has a 16C altarpiece with a low relief **bas-relief★)** of the Last Supper, a St Michael in armour (on the pillar) weighing souls, an early-15C effigy of St Ronan, carved from the dark kersanton stone.

Conservatoire de l'Affiche en Bretagne – collection of posters.

POPULATION 19 144

MICHELIN MAP 321 D 6

GREEN GUIDE BURGUNDY JURA

‗owes the second part of its name (saunier = salt-merchant) to the salt-works ‗ch, like those at Salins (52km – 32mi northeast), are based on deposits laid ‗own in Secondary times and subsequently uncovered by erosion. The town is also a spa, applying its salty waters to the treatment of rheumatism and problems associated with growth.

The town's most famous son was **Claude Rouget de l'Isle** (1760-1836) who wrote the music, and possibly the words too, of "the Marseillaise". His statue stands at the western end of the Promenade de la Chevalerie and the theatre clock picks out a couple of bars of the national anthem before striking the hour. He was a Captain of Engineers, but more of an artist than a soldier. His "Marching Song of the Army of the Rhine", one among many of his compositions, owes its definitive title to the men of Marseilles who sang it in Paris during the insurrection of August 1792; it became an official national song in July 1795, was forbidden at the time of the Restoration, but was proclaimed the national anthem on 14 February 1879.

Visit

Rue du Commerce★

The town was ravaged by fire between 25 June and 4 July 1636 when it was attacked by Condé on Richelieu's orders. Seven years later, the population was amnestied by Mazarin and allowed to return. The Rue du Commerce was rebuilt in accordance with a detailed plan in the second half of the 17C; it is elegantly laid out on a slight curve and is famous for its great variety of shops with their attractive displays.

What might have been a monotonous piece of planning reflects instead a local love of independence and appreciation of good design. Note particularly the high roofs with their mansards and tall chimneys, the 146 stone arcades (some of them of Romanesque date) of many different shapes and sizes, the trapdoors leading to the cellars, sculpted heads, and balconies and window decoration in wrought iron.

No 24 is the birthplace of Rouget de l'Isle.

Excursion

Cirque de Baume★★★

19km – 12mi east. This is one of the most spectacular of the blind valleys characteristic of the western rim of the Jura. The action of water has been particularly significant here in undermining the upper beds of limestone, which have caved in, thus forming the impressive gorge we see today. The viewpoint at Roches de Baume *(near the D 471)* gives splendid prospects over this great natural amphitheatre with its 200m – 650ft walls marking the boundary between the high plateau of the western Jura and the Bresse plain.

Source de la **LOUE**★★★

MICHELIN MAP 321 H 4

GREEN GUIDE BURGUNDY JURA

The River Loue rises in one of the blind valleys which penetrate deeply into the high plateau of the Jura. In its setting of high cliffs and luxuriant vegetation, it is one of the region's finest natural sites.

Visit

The fully-formed river appears from a cave at the foot of a 100m – 300ft high cliff. The cave should be entered for the power of the waters surging up from the underground world to be fully appreciated. The source is fed by rain falling on the plateau and by water loss from the Doubs and Drugeon rivers into the porous and highly fissured limestone near Pontarlier.

The Loue rejoins the Doubs downstream from Dole.

LOURDES★★★

POPULATION 16 300

MICHELIN MAP 324 L 4

GREEN GUIDE LANGUEDOC ROUSSILLON TARN GORGES

This little market town, sited at the meeting point of mountain and plain, became a pilgrimage place of world renown in the 19C.

Geological Notes

The town's setting – The summit of the **Béout** mountain ( *reached by cable-car then 45min round trip on foot)* is littered with great erratic blocks which give some idea of the power of the Quaternary glaciers. The **view**★ is an object lesson in physical geography; it extends northwards from the exits of the Lavedan valleys over the morainic terraces through which the Pau torrent winds its sinuous course, to the glacial rock-bar on which the castle is sited, and finally to the great terminal moraine which forces the stream to make an abrupt turn to the west.

Rosaire

Carcanague/IMAGES TOULOUSE

Lourdes - Address Book

...n categories, see the Legend at the ...k of the guide.

EATING OUT

Pizza Da Marco – *R. de la Grotte -* ☎ *05 62 94 03 59 -* ⏱ *closed Sun and Mon.* This is a pleasant place, decorated with photos and engravings. The pizzaïolo is set up in the front room, but it is nicer to sit in the other one. Crispy pizza and efficient service.

Brasserie de l'hôtel de la Grotte – *66 r. de la Grotte -* ☎ *05 62 42 39 34 - booking@hoteldelagrotte.com - 1 Apr-31 Oct.* Agreeable contemporary surroundings comprising ochre coloured dining room, veranda and terrace, and a menu to suit all budgets. Extravagant diners can decamp to the more formal adjacent restaurant.

Le Magret – *10 r. 4 Frères-Soulas -* ☎ *05 62 94 20 55 - pene.philippe@ wanadoo.fr -* ⏱ *closed 5-26 Jan and Mon.* This little restaurant occupies a rustic style dining room with exposed beams and straw-bottomed chairs. Pilgrims and locals alike can enjoy traditional southwest cuisine without pretention.

WHERE TO STAY

Cazaux – *2 chemin Rochers -* ☎*05 62 94 22 65 - hotelcazaux@yahoo.fr -* ⏱*closed end Oct-Easter - 20 rooms.* This small hotel just outside the town centre offers scrupulously kept, fresh-looking rooms, a friendly welcome and reasonable prices among other things. It is near the market.

Chambre d'hôte M. and Mme Vives – *28 rte de Bartrès – 65100 Loubajac - 6km/4mi NW of Lourdes on D 940 towards Pau -* ☎*05 62 94 44 17 - nadine.vives@ wanadoo.fr -* ⏱*closed 11 Nov until Feb holidays -* 🛏 *- 6 rms.* If you like the countryside, peace and quiet and a farm atmosphere, then this is the place for you. Sheep, chickens and ducks are raised and consumed here against a stunning backdrop of the Pyrenees. Four rooms with beams and sloping ceilings, and two others with a terrace. Fine garden and children's play area.

Chambre d'hôte Le Grand Cèdre – *6 r. du Barry - 65270 St-Pé-de-Bigorre -* ☎ *05 62 41 82 04 - chp@grandcedre.com -* 🛏 *- 4 rms.* This lovely 17C manor is sure to charm you. Each room is in a different style: Art déco, Louis XV, Henri II, Louis-Philippe. Dining room, music room and superb park with a glasshouese and a vegetable garden.

Chambre d'hôte Les Rocailles – *65100 Omex - 4.5km/3mi SW of Lourdes on D 13 then D 213 -* ☎*05 62 94 46 19 - muriellefanlou@aol.com -* ⏱*closed 1 Nov-Easter -* 🛏 *- 3 rms.* We fell in love with this sweet little place! The owner used to be a costume designer at the Paris Opera and

has decorated this small stone house with taste and refinement. Warm woods blend harmoniously with shimmering fabrics.

Hôtel Solitude – *3 passage St-Louis -* ☎*05 62 42 71 71 - contact@ hotelsolitude.com -* ⏱*closed 6 Nov-31 Mar - 281 rms.* This large imposing modern hotel on the banks of the Pau, a Pyrenean stream, has a small rooftop swimming pool. The dining room is a rotunda and has a terrace overlooking the river. The rooms with their little red armchairs are comfortable. We recommend those on the side of the river.

Hôtel Impérial – *3 av. du Paradis –* ☎*05 62 94 06 30 - hotelimperial.lourdes. fr@gofornet.com -* ⏱*closed 16 Dec-31 Jan - 93 rms.* This 1935 hotel, which has been completely renovated in its original Art Deco style, is near the cave. The rooms are pleasant and furnished in soothing mahogany tones. Large classic style dining room and drawing room opening onto a small garden.

SIT BACK AND RELAX

La Louisiane – *13 r. Lafitte B.P. 20 -* ☎ *05 62 94 60 15 - Jul-Oct: Mon-Sat 8.30am-7.15pm; Nov-Jun: Mon-Sat 9am-7.15pm - closed holidays.* This coffee shop opposite the market square offers a peaceful interlude with top quality beverages. Try the coffee (12 varieties of different roast), or one of the 80 varieties of tea or 6 of hot chocolate on the menu.

LEISURE ACTIVITIES

Golf – *Chemin du Lac -* ☎ *05 62 42 02 06 - www.golfdelourdes.com - 9am-5pm (winter), 9am-6pm (summer).* Pleasant 18 hole course.

La Truite des Pyrénées – *65400 Lau-Balagnas -* ☎ *05 62 97 02 05 - Mon-Sat 9am-noon and 3-5pm; Jul-Aug: 9am-noon and 3-7pm.* Everything you need to know about trout fishing (equipment and instruction available). There is also an exhibition about fish-farming and a shop.

Sports Nature – *65270 St-Pé-de-Bigorre -* ☎ *05 62 41 81 48 - www.sport-nature.org – early Apr-15 Sep: open 24hrs a day; winter: every day 8.30am-5.30pm.* Outdoor activity center with camping and *gite* accommodation.

Lourdes Forest – *Leave town on D 937; just before St-Pé, cross the river to the left then turn right onto the forest road.* The woods, planted with maples, oaks and beeches, offer picnic facilities and are ideal for jogging.

Lac de Lourdes – *Leave town W along D 940 and turn left onto the path leading to the edge of the lake via l'Embarcadère restaurant.* Lying at an altitude of 421m/1 381ft, the 11m/36ft-deep gl... lake offers water sports facilities (...

supervised bathing), fishing and golf (Lourdes 18-hole golf course to the south). From the shores of the lake there are fine views of the Pyrenean foothills. A footpath runs round the lake.

Voie Verte des Gaves – This is a 17km/10.6mi-long cycle track between Lourdes and Soulom to the west.
Information from Association française de développement des Véloroutes et Voies Vertes - Délégation Grand Sud-Ouest - 9 rue Bourdon - 31200 Toulouse - ☎ 05 61 11 87 09.

The pilgrims' town – On 11 February 1858, **Bernadette Soubirous** (1844-79) had the first of the 18 visions which led to Lourdes' becoming a world-famous centre of the cult of Mary, with the grotto and its surroundings attracting pilgrims from all five continents, with a special place reserved for the lame and the sick (70 000 pilgrims out of over 55 million visitors).

Principal dates

1858: the first visions.

1862: Bernadette becomes a novice at the Sisters of Charity convent of St-Gildard at Nevers.

1866: the building of the first sanctuary is begun.

1871: construction of the upper basilica.

1886: opening of the crypt.

1889: Basilica of the Rosary built in Romano-Byzantine style.

1925: beatification of Bernadette (followed by canonisation in 1933).

1959: St Pius X Underground Basilica built.

Visit

Grotto area

Appropriate dress essential.
In the summer months the great local, national and international pilgrimages are held here. The degree of spirituality is evident in the scale of the ceremonial and the devotion of the participants.

Esplanade

500m – 550 yards long, the site of daily processions.

Basilica of the Rosary

In neo-Byzantine style. The two curving approach ramps have fixed the image of the great building in the popular mind.

Crypt

A realm of devotion, contemplation and silence.

Upper Basilica

Dedicated to the Immaculate Conception and with a vast nave of five bays.
St Pius X Underground Basilica: ellipse-shaped, one of the world's largest sanctuaries.

Grotto of the Miracles

The site of the visions, where the most moving manifestations of faith take place.

A typical day during a pilgrimage

Until 5am the only access, Entrée des Lacets, is to the Way to the Cross (Chemin du Calvaire). At 9am pilgrims gather at Esplanade du Rosaire for a celebration of the Virgin in Majesty (Easter to 31 October). Then a ceremony for the sick is held in the grotto; a forest of candles twinkle along the alleyway and on the candelabrum in front of the grotto. Twenty outlets near the cave supply holy water to the faithful from the source which surged in front of Bernadette. The sick are immersed in marble pools. At 4.30pm a procession (Procession du Saint Sacrement) leaves from the grotto to the Esplanade du Rosaire, where the Blessing of the sick is celebrated. Finally at 8.45pm a candle-lit procession takes place from the grotto to the Esplanade and Parvis du Rosaire.

Fountains
Lourdes water collected by pilgrims.

Pools
Immersion of the sick.

Stations of the Cross
Overlooking the basilicas and the Pau torrent.

◐◐ Château★ (Musée du Folklore Pyrénéen★). Musée Grévin de Lourdes (Wax museum).

Excursions

Grottes de Bétharram★★
14km – 9mi west. This is one of the most popular natural attractions in the Pyrenees area. The caves comprise five separate galleries, one above the other. The vast roofs of porous rock of the upper level, a striking column which is still growing and is a typical example of the evolution of stalagmites and stalactites, a collapsed pot-hole 80m – 262ft deep, a narrow fissure through which the river flows are fascinating examples of concretions and underground erosion.

Pic de Pibeste★★★
2hr20min climb from Ouzous on D 202. This peak – alt 1 349m – 4 426ft – provides one of the best viewpoints in the central Pyrénées.

LUNÉVILLE

POPULATION 20 711

MICHELIN MAP 307 J 7

GREEN GUIDE ALSACE LORRAINE CHAMPAGNE

The development of Lunéville parallels that of Lorraine itself, owing much to the enterprise of the ruling Dukes and beginning with an upsurge of intellectual and artistic activity in the 17C. In 1620, **Georges de la Tour** (1593-1652), born at Vic-sur-Seille *(26km – 16mi north)* became the town's official painter. He seems to have been a ruthless opportunist, but his work, with its mastery of nocturnal effects, has a serene, almost mystical quality. In the 18C, under Duke Leopold, Lunéville was for several years the seat of the ducal court, a concession by Leopold to his Duchess, Charlotte, who enjoyed life here, whereas the Duke himself much preferred Nancy.

A Bit of History
The wide streets of the town, the great park and the **château**★ *(musée: ◷ daily 10am-noon; 2-6pm; ☎ 03 83 74 06 55)* of 1719 were all designed by Boffand, who took Versailles as his model. The prestige of the House of Lorraine is expressed in the château's great colonnaded portico and in the wealth of statuary and trophies, while the roofs are concealed behind a high balustrade.

Later in the 18C, Duke Stanislas, "The Magnificent," held court here several times, and continued Leopold's work on the splendid edifice.

On 9 February 1801, the Treaty of Lunéville was signed, thereby giving Habsburg recognition to France's eastern frontier which the conquests of the Revolution had pushed to the Rhine. One of its unforeseen consequences was to promote German unity by consenting to a reduction in number of the multitude of German states and principalities.

◐◐ Parc des Bosquets★. Boiseries★ de l'Église St-Jacques (panelling).

LYON★★★

POPULATION 1 262 223

MICHELIN MAP 327 H-I 5

GREEN GUIDE AUVERGNE THE RHÔNE VALLEY

Two millennia of history, a site at the meeting point of the Rhône and Saône corridors and an exceptionally enterprising population have combined to make Lyon France's second city. Its past periods of greatness, in Roman and Renaissance times, are matched by its present industrial, commercial and cultural dynamism.

▶ **Orient Yourself:** Truly the heart of the city, la Presqu'île offers great views of the quays of the Saône River and Vieux Lyon. Department stores, boutiques, movie theatres and bars line rue de la République, well-known for its 19C architecture. Stretching from north to south, rue du Président-Herriot and rue Paul-Chenavard are also good for shopping. Guided tours of Lyon are available from the tourist office.

🕓 **Organizing Your Time:** Check the tourist office for the **Lyon City Card,** which suggests possible itineraries for one, two and three day visits. A one day visit proposes spending the morning on foot in Vieux Lyon, then visiting the terrace on Fouvière and the Roman theatres by using the funicular railway (with the exception of the museums found there); in the afternoon, tour the musée des Beaux-Arts or take a walk in the Croix-Rousse neighborhood.

🅿 **Parking:** Lyon has many underground parking garages strategically placed throughout the city. Many have been designed by famous architects who truly made them into works of art worth visiting in their own right.

Sights

La Colline de Fourvière
(Fourvière Hill)

A Celtic, then Gallic settlement, Lyon was chosen as a base camp by Julius Caesar for his conquest of Gaul. Under Augustus it became the capital of the Roman Empire's "Three Gauls" (Aquitaine, Belgium and the province around Lyon) complementing the older province centred on Narbonne. Agrippa was responsible for choosing Lyon as the hub of the road system, constructed originally in pursuit of political ends. It was here that the great route coming north from Arles met the other highways from Saintes, Orléans and Rouen, from Geneva and Aosta, and from Chalon with its links to Amiens, Trier and Basle.

The manufacture of pottery became established here as early as the first century AD, only to move later to La Graufesenque on the Tarn (🕭 *see MILLAU).* The Amphitheatre of the Three Gauls on the hill, Colline de la Croix-Rousse, was joined by the Temple of Rome and of Augustus and by the Federal Sanctuary where the noisy annual assembly of the 60 tribes of Gaul was held under Roman supervision.

Christianity reached Lyon via Vienne by the middle of the 2C, brought by soldiers, traders and Greek missionaries. In 177, there were riots on the occasion of the annual assembly, and Saints Pothinus and Blandina, along with 48 others, became the city's first Christian martyrs. Twenty years later, Saint Irenaeus, head of the Church in Lyon, was to meet the same fate. According to St Gregory of Tours, the Gospel was reintroduced to Lyon around 250 by Roman missionaries, and, under Constantine, Christianity is supposed to have flourished here as in the other cities of the Empire.

Fourvière

The name of the hill is derived from the old forum *(Forum vetus)* which was still here in the reign of King Louis I in the 9C. Its site is now occupied by the pilgrimage chapel (with its Black Virgin) next to the basilica of 1870. Roman Lyon had numerous public buildings, including the imperial palace (the Capitol) giving onto the forum, a theatre and an odeon (both rebuilt) on the slope of the hill, baths, a circus building and several temples, as well as the amphitheatre on the east bank of the river.

The terrace to the north of the basilica forms a splendid **viewpoint** overlooking the confluence of the Rhône and Saône and encompassing the hills and Dauphiné plain over which the great city has spread.

Illumination, Colline de Fourvière

Musée de la Civilisation Gallo-Romaine★★

♿ 🕐 *Mar-Oct: Tue-Sun 10am-6pm; Nov-Feb: Tue-Sun 10am-5pm.* 🔈 *Guided tours Sun at 3pm.* 🕐 *Closed Mon, 1 Jan, 1 May, 1 Nov and 25 Dec. On other public holidays call in advance.* 🎫 *3.80€ (under 25 years: 2.30€).* ☎ *04 72 38 81 90.*

The most striking exhibit is perhaps formed by the Claudian Tables (**Table Claudienne★★★**) of bronze, discovered in 1528. They record the speech made by Claudius in AD 48 which gave the citizens of Gaul the right to become senators. It is possible to compare this ponderous "official" version with the more witty and revealing transcription made by Tacitus.

Le Vieux Lyon (Old Lyon)★★★

The medieval and Renaissance quarter of Lyon, the precursor of today's city, extends along the west bank of the Saône at the foot of the Fourvière hill.

Primatiale St-Jean★

🕐 *Daily 8am-12.05pm and 1.55-7.30pm (Sun: 7pm). No Sun morning visit.* 🔈 *Guided tours with Frère Alain Gautier Sat and Sun afternoons, also 3rd Wed in the month from 3-6pm.* ☎ *04 78 54 76 21.*

Begun in 1192, today's church was preceded by a number of sanctu-

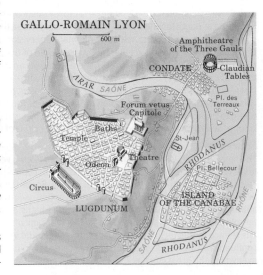

aries, including an early-Christian baptistery, remains of which are on the north side of the building. The cathedral was enlarged in the reigns of Philippe Auguste and St Louis, beginning with the Romanesque east end. The 280 medallions adorning the west front were begun in 1310; in their wealth of detail and great variety they are comparable with those of Rouen cathedral or the chapel of the Papal Palace at Avignon, though the juxtaposition of the sacred, profane and grotesque is sometimes disconcerting.

Inside, the chancel (**chœur**★★), together with the apse, is the oldest part of the church. The apse, with its fluted pilasters below a blind arcade and a frieze of palm-leaves, is typical of Romanesque architecture of the Rhône valley. It is lit by a 13C stained-glass axial window with a fine medallion depicting the Redemption. There is a 14C astronomical clock (**horloge astronomique**★) with original ironwork.

Quartier St-Jean★★

Lyon was incorporated into the French kingdom at the beginning of the 14C. In the Middle Ages it was a border town facing the Dauphiné, Savoy, and the Holy Roman Empire. Charles VII made it a trading centre of European importance when he founded the twice-yearly fair in 1419. Louis XI introduced the weaving of raw silk imported from the Levant and from Italy, but local opposition led the only silk-mill to transfer its operations to Tours. Forty-four years later, Louis doubled the number of fairs; long-distance trade was encouraged and patterns of commercial activity developed which were far in advance of the time; accommodation at inns and hostels was improved, and clearing houses were set up, forerunners of the great bank founded in the 16C. Trade flourished, and with it came a period of great prosperity for the city, its merchants, bankers and high officials. Lyon seethed with activity and ideas; its streets were lined with elegant Flamboyant Gothic façades with asymmetrical window patterns; behind them, down narrow alleys, lay courtyards like the ones at nos 11 and 58 in Rue St-Jean. More numerous are houses of Renaissance date, decorated with Italianate motifs (polygonal turrets, superimposed galleries, basket-handle arches and corner signs like the figure of the ox at the junction of Rue du Bœuf – Hôtel Paterin, 4 Rue de la Juiverie), sculpted in the 16C by John of Bologna.

The **Hôtel de Gadagne**★ houses the **Musée historique de Lyon**★ (Kids 🕐 Wed-Mon 10.45am-6pm; 🕐 closed Tue, 1 Nov, 11 Nov, 25 Dec, 1 Jan, 1 May, 8 May, Thu of the Ascension, 14 Jul, 15 Aug; ∞ 3.80€, no charge under 18 years; ticket includes entry into Musée international de la Marionnette; ☎ 04 78 42 03 61)and the **Musée internatio-nal de la Marionnette**★(as for the Musée historique de Lyon), the latter created by Laurent Mourget (1769-1844), whose **Guignol** is the very embodiment of the spirit of the Lyon populace.

With the development of the characteristic forms of the French Renaissance come superimposed orders, as in the Hôtel Bullioud (8 Rue de la Juiverie) with its gallery and corner pavilions by the local architect **Philibert Delorme**.

Printing had been invented in Korea in 1403, then again at Mainz in 1447. It made its first appearance on the banks of the Saône in 1485. The world of the transcriber or of the illuminator would never be the same again. The spread of books transformed Europe with its diffusion of learning, in literature, science and technology and accounts of voyages. The Reformation, born from widespread reading of the Bible, came about some 50 years after the invention of the printing press.

This was also the age of **Louise Labé**, known as la "Belle Cordière" (Rope-maker's wife), whose salon became a centre for literature and the arts; among those writing was the Lyon poet Maurice Scève.

By 1548 there were almost 400 printers working in the city, including Sébastien Gryphe, Guillaume Rouille and Étienne Dolet, the publisher of Marot and of Rabelais (�”️ see CHINON); the latter served as a doctor at the Pont-du-Rhône hospital for three years, carrying on a correspondence with Erasmus and Du Bellay. It was Du Bellay who published **Rabelais'** Pantagruel in 1532 and Gargantua in 1534 to coincide with the Lyon fairs.

It was here that the Florentine Angelo Benedetto produced white porcelain. Other manufacturers were active too, including Julio Gambiu, who moved away to Nevers around 1565.

Musée de l'Imprimerie et de la Banque★★

♿ 🕐 Wed-Sun 9.30am-noon, 2-6pm. ∞ 3.80€ (under 18 years: no charge). ☎ 04 78 37 65 98.

The museum traces the evolution of printing from its very beginnings in Lyon, from the first wood engravings to the discovery of typography and to photocomposition, as well as evoking the great age of banking (Guérin, Crédit Lyonnais) post-1863 with its support for silk-making, trade generally, and the great Paris-Lyon-Mediterranean Railway.

One of the main features of the old town is the numerous passages or alleyways known as "traboules" – from the Latin trans ambulare meaning "walking through." The passageways run perpendicular to the streets and link the buildings by means of corridors with vaulted or coffered ceilings leading to inner courtyards.

La Presqu'île (Lyon's Peninsula)

The modern centre of the city is sited on a long tongue of alluvial material brought down by the Rhône. The formation of the "Peninsula" has shifted the junction of the two rivers 4km – 2.5mi southwards since Roman times.

The area was first of all a military encampment, then its proximity to the two rivers made it a favourable place for trading and warehousing. Finally it became the very core of the city; its development along Classical lines begun under Henri IV and Louis XIII was continued in the 18C and 19C, until the urban area spread outwards to the modern suburbs and beyond. The great city's character comes across not only in the busy Rue de la République with its fine 19C façades and elegant shops, but also in the pleasantly shaded Place de la République (FT) with its trees and fountains.

The era of invention – Lyon played a leading role in science and technology at this time. Among its eminent men should be noted the following:

The brothers Jussieu (Antoine, Bernard and Joseph), 18C botanists;

Claude Bourgelat, a passionate devotee of horse-racing, who founded Europe's first veterinary school;

Jouffroy d'Albans who sailed up the Rhône in his "pyroscaphe," the first steam paddleboat;

Marie-Joseph Jaquard who built a power-loom in 1804;

André Ampère, a deep thinker as well as a mathematician, the inventor of the galvanometer, electromagnetism, and electrodynamics;

Barthélemy Thimonnier, who invented the sewing machine in 1829;

Jean-Baptiste Guimet, who, in 1834, succeeded in making the dye ultramarine;

Émile Guimet who founded an oriental museum here in 1879;

Claude Bernard, a physiologist, who established the glycogenic function of the liver in 1853;

The **Lumière brothers** (Auguste and Louis), the creators of cinematography;

Marius Berliet (1866-1949), motor manufacturer (♨ *see below*);

Louis Lépine, a civil servant, who introduced traffic regulations as well as setting up a competition for the promotion of French inventions and other products;

Hector Guimard, one of the founders of Art Nouveau in architecture, the designer of the entrances to the metro stations of Paris;

The **brothers Voisin**, both aviators and car designers with a sharp eye for aerodynamic forms.

Place Bellecour

Planned by Henri IV in 1609, the project could not be started until 50 years later, when the city had finally succeeded in purchasing the land.

The designer was Robert de Cotte, who arranged the avenues of trees on the south side of the square in such a way as to disguise its irregular shape. The buildings lining the square were razed during the Terror in retribution for the city's resistance to the Convention. "Lyon is no more," it was triumphantly proclaimed at the time, but the square was rebuilt in the 19C.

Hôtel-Dieu

The plans for this, one of the kingdom's most important buildings, were drawn up by Soufflot in 1740. It marks a significant stage in the evolution of French architecture with its long façade facing the Rhône, its projecting central section with Ionic columns and its dome rising from a square base and crowned with a square lantern. The way in which the transoms of the windows are decorated with linen motifs evokes its function as a hospital. A balustrade relieves the great length of the main façade and disguises the low roofs.

Silk

Silk, the fibre from cocoons produced by caterpillars of the Bombyx moth, otherwise known as silkworms, was discovered in China and was brought to France by Louis XI in 1466. The French silk industry did not really begin to evolve until the 16C; at this time Lyon was chosen as the central silk depot, and large-scale cultivation of mulberry bushes on which silkworms feed was undertaken. The industry's expansion continued under Louis XIV, with notable innovators such as Philippe de Lassalle playing a major role, but this was brought to an abrupt end by the outbreak of the French Revolution. It received a new lease of life under Napoleon's Empire, finally reaching its peak in c 1850; shortly after this a devastating silkworm plague broke out, decimating the French silkworm breeding centres. Subsequently the industry has had to adapt to contend with strong foreign competition, the discovery of artificial fibres and mass industrialisation. Nevertheless, Lyon silk has remained a standard of quality for the fashion world and among French luxury fabrics.

Sericulture, or the production of silk, involves the raising of silkworms in special silkworm farms *(magnaneries)* from the egg to cocoon stage. After the spinning stage, the raw silk obtained is not strong enough to be woven and so undergoes a preparatory process, reeling, in which silk fibres are wound together to form a single strand. Bobbins of this thread are arranged on a special frame, then unreeled in batches onto a warp frame. Next the warp is stretched onto a drawloom to form parallel threads, across which the weft threads are drawn by a shuttle. To allow the shuttle to pass along with the weft, various mechanical systems for raising the warp threads were developed; the most famous was Jacquard's (using punched cards). Various types of plain weave using silk thread are possible: taffeta, silk serge and satin. The manufacture of fancier, figured fabrics (with decorative motifs in coloured threads) requires a more complex system, using cords known as semples operated by means of strings *(lacs)*. For woven pile fabrics such as velvet, it is necessary to have a second set of warp threads which form the pile. Silk can also be processed after it has been woven, for example by silkscreen printing or the manufacture of figured or watered silk.

Place des Terreaux

This is sited where the Saône flowed into the Rhône in Roman times. The older inhabitants of the city are particularly fond of the square with its fountain **(fontaine★)** by Bartholdi, which has four eager horses representing rivers bounding oceanwards. The town hall dates from the reign of Louis XIII, although its façade was rebuilt by Robert de Cotte after a fire and is typically 18C, with a dome and a rounded tympanum supported by atlantes.

Musée des Beaux-Arts★★

♿ ⊙ *Mon, Wed, Thu and Sat-Sun 10am-6pm, Fri 10.30am-6pm. Temporary exhibits: same hours as museum except Fri 10.30am-8pm.* ⊙ *Closed 1 Jan, 1 May, 8 May, Easter Mon, Ascension Day, 14 Jul, 15 Aug, 1 Nov, 11 Nov, 25 Dec.* ⊛ *3.80€.* ☎ *04 72 10 17 40.* Reorganisation in progress until end of 1998. The museum is housed in the Palais St-Pierre (ES), formerly a 17C Benedictine abbey. It presents a remarkable survey of art through the centuries throughout the world. Its collections are organised into five separate departments: painting, sculpture, art objects, antiquities and graphic art. The high-

Ciselé velvet; Lyon, Second Empire

Basset, Courtesy Musée des Tissus, Lyon

lights of the selection of European painting include **The Ascension**★ by Perugino, an imposing *St Francis* by Zurbaràn, and *The Adoration of the Magi* by Rubens. Also illustrated is the evolution of French painting from the 17C (Philippe de Champaigne) to the 19C (*Femme au perroquet* by Delacroix) and 20C (*Corbeille de Fruit by Chagall*).

There is a very fine collection of ancient art: temple doors from Mehamoud (Egyptian section), a remarkable kore (statue of a young girl) from the Acropolis (Ancient Greece).

Musée des Tissus★★★

♿ ⏰ *Tue-Sun 10am-5.30pm.* ⏰ *Closed public holidays, Easter and Pentecost.* 🎟 *5€ (under 18 years: no charge). Ticket also valid for the musée des Arts décoratifs.* ☎ *04 78 38 42 00.*

Apart from its exhibits devoted to very early examples of the weaver's art, the collection consists mostly of Lyon silk from the 17C onward, by masters such as Philippe de Lasalle. There are Louis XV lampas and embroidered satins, embroidery, and cut velvets of the Empire and Restoration periods. The museum also houses the **Centre International d'études des textiles anciens.**

On the slopes of the hill, Colline de la Croix-Rousse, is a network of covered passageways called Traboules (FS), once used to protect the precious sheets of silk from the weather. They proved their worth during the French Revolution too and were much used by the Resistance in the Second World War.

▶▶ Musée lyonnais des arts décoratifs★★ *(same ticket as the Musée des Tissus).* Musée des Hospices civils – pharmacy★ ♿ ⏰ *Mon 1.30-5.30pm, Tue-Fri 10am-noon, 1-5pm.* ⏰*Closed public holidays.* 🎟 *3.40€.* ☎ *04 72 41 30 42.* Basilique St-Martin d'Ainay – capitals★. Église St-Nizier – Virgin with the Infant Jésus★ ⏰ *Daily except Mon mornings 7am-7pm.* Église St-Paul – Lantern-tower★. Montée de Garillan★ (hill). Parc de la Tête d'Or★. Place Rouville – view★.

Excursions

Museum★★

♿ ⏰ *Tue-Sun 10am-6pm.* ⏰ *Closed Mon, 1 Jan, 1 May, 1 Nov and 25 Dec.* 🎟 *Since Jan 2003, the ticket price has been reduced to 2.30€ because of the closing of the grande salle. No charge Thu.* ☎ *04 72 69 05 00.*

Entrance Boulevard des Belges. The museum was founded by the industrialist, Emile Guimet, who was also the founder of another museum of the same name in Paris; it houses fine collections of Far Eastern and Egyptian art as well as remarkable specimens in the Paleontology section.

Musée Henri-Malartre★★

At Rochetaillée, 10km – 6mi north of the bridge, Pont Clemenceau.

The château and its ancillary buildings house a collection the greater part of which was brought together by Henri Malartre. He found his true vocation in 1931 when he discovered, among a lot of old iron, a Rochet-Schneider car of 1898 complete with engine still in working order.

The earliest automobiles in France were Cugnot's trolley of 1769, Beau de Rochas' four-stroke Otto of 1862, Bollée's *"Obéissante"* of 1873 and the steam-driven Jacquot of 1878.

At the beginning of this century there were some 150 manufacturers of motor vehicles in the area. One of them was **Marius Berliet** (1866-1949). He built his first streamliner in 1896, but then based his reputation on the robustness of his chassis, on his monobloc motors (1913) and on the reliability of his CBA lorries (for their role on the Voie Sacrée, 👆 see *VERDUN*). He brought out diesels in 1931, then heavy trucks of 20 and 30 tons in 1932.

Some of the exhibits are unique such as the Rochet-Schneider (1895), the Gobron-Brillié(1898), the Luc Court (1901) and the Thieulin (1908). Others marked an era in technological developments such as the Model "T" Ford (1910), the Peugeot BB (1913) and the Boisin four-door saloon (1932). The Scotte steam-powered omnibus (1892), the Mildé electric-powered car (1900), and the prototype of the Citroën 2 CV (1936), transformed into a van during the Occupation, were both unique and technologically in advance of their time.

Also of note are a De Dion Bouton coupé-docteur (1900), a Marne taxi (1914), a set of three Sizaire cars (1908, 1924, 1927), a Bugatti convertible (1930), Hitler's armoured Mercedes (1942) seized in 1945 at Berchtesgaden, and a Hispano-Suiza (1936) used by General de Gaulle after the Liberation of Paris.

Le MANS★★

POPULATION 189 107

MICHELIN MAP 310 K 6

GREEN GUIDE CHÂTEAUX OF THE LOIRE

Le Mans, a large modern town, stands on the banks of the Sarthe at its confluence with the Huisne; it is a thriving provincial capital which hosts several fairs every year, including a Spring Fair (late March to early April), a great Four-Day Fair (mid-September), an Onion Fair (first Friday in September). Its industrial activity is closely associated with the manufacture of racing cars and Grand Prix events (24-hour Le Mans circuit, Bugatti circuit). It is also an important insurance centre.

The citizens of Le Mans are fond of good food; local specialities include potted pork *(rillettes)*, plump pullets *(poulardes)*, capons *(chapons)* accompanied by sparkling cider, as well as the delicious *reinette* apple.

▶ **Orient Yourself:** Le Mans, which is listed as a "Town of Art and History," offers discovery tours conducted by guide-lecturers approved by the Ministry of Culture and Communication. Information at the tourist office or on www.vpah.culture. fr.

A Bit of History

The historic centre of Le Mans **(Vieux Mans★★)** stands on the site of a Celtic settlement, overlooking the lowlands on either side of the Sarthe. This part of the city is still enclosed within its 4C Gallo-Roman ramparts, some of the few still extant in western France (Queen Berengaria's House – **Maison de la Reine Bérengère★** and Red Pillar House – Maison du Pilier Rouge).

Sights

Cathédrale St-Julien★★

The transition from nave to choir is one of the clearest demonstrations anywhere – even for the architecturally uninitiated – of the great technical and stylistic changes which took place over a period of some 160 years.

Nef romane

1060-1120. The west front is in a very archaic style; behind it extends the Romanesque nave, strengthened and stone-vaulted in 1158, its simplicity relieved by a series of arcades. The Ascension Window *(the second in the south aisle)* dates from 1140 and has remarkable stained glass.

The River Sarthe at Le Mans

Studio 3 Bis/MICHELIN

Outside, the arches of the south porch are pleasingly decorated with dog-tooth moulding, and the doorway (**portail**★★) has splendid statue-columns. The flying buttresses were added in 1419.

Chœur et transept gothiques

1217-1448. The Gothic choir which lacks a triforium was completed in 1254; with its two-stage elevation, it is of a graceful simplicity. Below the clerestory windows runs that characteristically Norman feature, an inspection gallery. There is a double ambulatory whose inside gallery rises to a height of 22m – 72ft at triforium level. The whole is lit by 13C stained-glass windows (**verrières**★★) on three levels; in the chapels opening out onto the outer ambulatory, in the inner ambulatory and in the clerestory.

Note how in the south transept (1385-92) the junction has been effected between the Gothic choir and the older, Romanesque transept.

The north transept was built between 1425 and 1448 in identical style. In the baptismal chapel are two remarkable Renaissance tombs (tombeauxaa); the one on the left in Italianate style was made for Charles V of Anjou, brother of King Réné, and exhibits a taste for Antiquity; the other tomb is that of Guillaume du Bellay (a cousin of the poet Joachim du Bellay), who is shown recumbent on a sarcophagus ravishingly decorated with nautical divinities.

Outside, the **chevet**★★★ is a spectacular demonstration of the boldness and ambition of its architect, and of his consummate understanding of the interplay of forces in such a complex undertaking. It should be viewed from the foot of the steps leading to Place des Jacobins. The famous Y-shaped flying buttresses "seem not so much to prop the structure as to hoist it skywards with their vertical impetus" (Henri Focillon – *The Art of the West*).

Musée de l'Automobile de la Sarthe★★

&. ⏱ *Jun-Sep: daily 10am-7pm; Oct-May: daily 10am-6pm; Jan: Sat-Sun 10am-6pm. Last admission 1hr before closing.* ⏱ *Closed 1 Jan, 25 Dec.* ⊛ *6€ (children under 11 years: 2€).* ☎ *02 43 72 72 24. www.sarthe.com/auto/museeint.htm.*

5km – 3mi south, in the Le Mans circuit. By the middle of the 19C, Le Mans had become an industrial city. In 1873, **Amédée Bollée** (1844-1917), a bell-founder, built his first automobile, 104 years after Cugnot's trolley. He named it *L'Obéissante* (Obedient), a 12-seater break with a maximum speed of over 40km – 25mi per hour (it is now in the Musée des Techniques in Paris), and followed it with *La Mancelle* (Lady of Le Mans), helped by his sons, Amédée and Léon.

On 26 June 1906, the first Grand Prix took place, on the 103.180km – 64.11mi long Sarthe Circuit. The victor was Szisz, driving a Renault fitted with Michelin detachable rims. In 1923 the 24-hour Le Mans race was initiated.

The museum (rebuilt in 1991) has something of the air of a sanctuary, laid out as it is in the heart of the 24-Hour Circuit. It enables the visitor to appreciate some of France's contributions to the evolution of the automobile; 115 vehicles are displayed in a modern setting and using the most advanced techniques.

Pride of place is given to the Bollée models manufactured at Le Mans as well as to the electrically-powered Krieger car of 1908. The inter-war period is represented by prestige cars: a Hispano-Suiza chauffeur-driven drop-head coupé (1929), a Voisin "aerodyne" (1935), a 1939 Bugatti, a caterpillar-tractor *Scarabée d'Or Citroën* that took part in the renowned *Croisière Jaune* (1931). Also of note is the only existing prototype of the 1952 gas turbine Socema Grégoire.

The section on racing cars, in particular those that won the 24-hour Le Mans Grand Prix, presents a superb collection of outstanding automobiles, including a 1924 Bentley, a 1929 Ferrari, a 1974 Matra, a 1983 Rondeau, a 1988 Jaguar, a 1991 Mazda and a 1922 Peugeot.

◖◗ Maison de la Reine Bérengère★ – ethnographical collection. Musée de Tessé★ &. ⏱ *Jul-Aug: Tue-Sun 10am-12.30pm, 2-6.30pm; Sep-Jun: Tue-Sat 9am-noon, 2-6pm, Sun 10am-12.30pm, 2-6pm. Last admission 45min before closing.* ⏱ *Closed Mon and certain public holidays, call in advance. Last admission 45min before closing.* ⊛ *4€ (under 18 years: no charge).* ☎ *02 43 47 38 51. www.ville-lemans.fr–* paintings. Église de la Couture★. Église Ste-Jeanne d'Arc★. Notre-Dame de L'Épau★ *4km – 2mi east.*

MARAIS POITEVIN★

MICHELIN MAP 316 H-L 8-9 AND 324 D-G 2

GREEN GUIDE ATLANTIC COAST

The vast Poitou marshlands occupy what was once a wide bay, the Golfe du Poitou. Up until the beginnings of historical times, the tides washed the foot of the old cliffline, and the barely perceptible rises which form the sites of today's villages were once islands. The marsh rests on a bed of hardened marine silts; it is drained by an extensive network of channels and protected from floods and high water by dikes and sluices.

The lack of a stable foundation forced the builders of the railway between Luçon and La Rochelle to make a long detour and to align the track on the firmer ground of the old shoreline and the "islands."

Visit

The marsh has a total area of some 80 000ha – 197 680 acres. The larger part, nearer the sea, consists of "dry" **marshland**, with dark soils requiring the application of fertiliser. Here can be seen the punt-like craft of the mussel breeders. Inland lies the **"wet" marshland**, known as "green Venice" because of the abundant duckweed in its watery labyrinth. Well-treed with poplars, alders and willows, it is grazed by cattle as well as producing good market-garden crops.

The work of reclamation, involving the digging of drainage channels, the building of sluices and the parcelling out of the new-won lands, was begun by the monks from the abbeys as early as the 11C, and continued, once the Wars of Religion were over, by Henri IV.

The marsh is linked to the ocean by a bay **(anse d'Aiguillon)**. It is protected from the waves by a headland **(Pointe d'Arçay)** and its sandbanks, and by the Aiguillon dike built by a team of Dutch engineers.

The bay is in the process of silting up and evolving into a marsh. It has already shifted southwards and westwards. The effect of currents is added to by that of the tides which transport material eroded by the waves or brought down by the river Sèvre. The deposition of this material is tending to even out the irregularities in the line of the coast and to provide good conditions for oyster and mussel breeding. The bay makes a grand sight at high water, but it is only when the tide is out that its full interest is revealed.

◖◗ Boat trips★★.

MARSEILLE★★★

POPULATION 1 087 370

MICHELIN MAP 340 H 6

GREEN GUIDE PROVENCE

The 19C Romano-Byzantine Basilica of **Notre-Dame-de-la-Garde** stands in a commanding position overlooking this great Mediterranean seaport. The **view**★★★ from the church is immense, taking in the islands standing guard in the bay, the harbour, and the background of limestone hills as well as the sprawling city itself.

▸ **Orient Yourself:** Marseille is centered around the old port, which features nice glimpses of large ships along the quai des Belges, as well as a daily fish market. The relatively recent improvements to the quaiside of the Rive-Neuve has given way to several cafés and restaurants (Quartier des Arsenaux). Marseille, which is listed as a "Town of Art and History," offers guided tours for 6.50€. Information at the tourist office or on www.marseille-tourisme.com.

⊛ **Don't Miss:** The **Corniche Président -J.-F.-Kennedy** is a promenade that runs nearly 5km - 3mi. For a pleasant and timeless evening, choose an outdoor restaurant in the tiny fishing port called **Vallon des Auffes.** Marseille is famous for its *bouillabaisse* (full-flavoured seafood soup), the *aïoli* (garlic sauce) and *pieds-et-paquets* (stuffed tripe and sheep trotters).

Marseille - Address Book

GUIDED TOURS:

Lecture tours – Contact the tourist office.

Histobus – 🚌 A guided tour of the city by bus (3hr). Sun 2.30pm (daily Jul-Oct). 11.43€ (children: 4.57€). ☎ 04 91 91 92 10.

Taxis Tourisme – 🚕 Guided tour with an audio guide (from 1hr to 1 day). From 30.49€ to 86.90€. To book, contact the Tourist Information Centre.

Tourist train – There are two itineraries: to N.-D.-de-la-Garde going past the Basilica of St-Victor and in the old town (the Panier and Vieille Charité quarters). Departures: quai des Belges. Not available mid-Oct to Easter. 4.57€ for 1 circuit (children: 2.29€), 7.62€ for both.

Cathédrale de la Major – Mid-June to end of Aug: Daily except Mon and Sun. 9am-6.30pm. Low season Mon to Thur 9am-noon, 2-5.30pm, Fri and Sat-Sun 9am-noon, 2.30-6pm.

Basilique de N.-D.-de-la-Garde – 🚶 Guided tours possible by appointment. ☎ 04 91 13 40 80.

GETTING AROUND TOWN

Metro – This is the most convenient mode of transport; the two lines operate from 5am to 9pm. From 9pm to 1am the metro is substituted by the "fluobus". Tickets are sold in the form of magnetic cards and are valid for a single trip (carte solo), 1 day (carte journée) or for several journeys (carte liberté: 7.62€ or 15.24€). *Free network maps are given out at ticket offices. Information:* ☎ *04 91 91 92 10.*

Ferry Boat – Trips from place aux Huiles to the town hall. *8am to 6.30pm, weekends in the summer from 8am to 8.30pm. 0.76€ for a trip across and back, 0.46€ one-way.*

Guided tours are available for all ages and tastes: lecture tours on the history and architecture of Marseille, coach tours, taxi tours and a tourist train.

ENTERTAINMENT

Programmes are listed in local newspapers (*La Provence, La Marseillaise*), in a free weekly paper, Taktik, distributed by the Tourist Information Centre, cultural centres and at the paper's head office, 55 cours Julien. The Tourist Information Centre also distributes a small magazine, In Situ, which is published every three months.

Pastorals – In December and January pastorals are performed at the Mazenod theatre (88 rue d'Aubagne) and the Nau theatre (9 rue Nau).

Theatres – Marseilles boasts over 20 active theatres: classical and contemporary plays at the Théâtre National de Marseille-la-Criée, directed by Gildas Bourdet (30 quai de Rive-Neuve), at the Gymnase (4 rue du Théâtre-Français), at the Toursky (poetry and Mediterranean theatre, 16 passage Léo-Ferré) and at the Lenche (4 place de Lenche). "Art et Essai" at the Merlan-Scène nationale (avenue Raimu), at the Bernardines (17 bd Garibaldi) and at the Chocolat-Théâtre (59 cours Julien).

Classical music and dance – Classical music and opera at the Opéra municipal (2 rue Molière). Dance at the Ballet National now directed by Marie-Claude Pietragalla (20 bd de Gabès). A varied musical programme at the Cité de la Musique (4 rue Bernard-du-Bois) and at the Pharo auditorium.

Modern music – Rock concerts, jazz, reggae, etc. at the Espace Julien (39 cours Julien). Large concerts at the Marseille Dôme, with its huge cement arch: a vast room holding 8 000 where world-famous singers perform.

Cinema – Art house cinema: Le César (place Castellane), Breteuil (rue Breteuil), Paris (rue Pavillon) and Les Nouvelles Variétés (on the Canebière). Several multiplex cinemas on the Canebière and along avenue du Prado, near the Rond-Point.

Art galleries – All art events take place in the old warehouses of the Friche de la Belle-de-Mai, rue Jobin. There are also several galleries in rue Sainte, rue Neuve-Ste-Catherine, in the Arcenaulx quarter and on cours Julien.

SHOPPING

Markets – Fish market every morning on quai des Belges, food markets are open every morning (except Sunday) in cours Pierre Puget, place Jean-Jaurès (la Plaine), place du Marché-des-Capucins and avenue du Prado. La Canebière has a flower market every Tuesday and Saturday morning; this market is also set up on avenue Prado every Friday morning.

Every second Saturday of the month cours Julien has a book market and second-hand books and records can be bought daily outside the Palais des Arts. Finally, there is a fleamarket on Sunday mornings in avenue du Cap- Pinède.

Books – Librairie-galerie-restaurant des Arcenaulx, place d'Estienne-d'Orves, head office of the Jeanne Laffitte "regional" publications. Librarie maritime – 26 quai de Rive-Neuve – ☎ 04 91 54 79 26. Mon-Sat, 9am-noon and 2-7pm.

Le Cabanon des Accoules – 24 montée des Accoules – ☎ 04 91 90 49 66). Specialised in the manufacture of santons, in the picturesque Quartier du Panier.

Santons Marcel Carbonel – 47 rue Neuve-Ste-Catherine – ☎ *04 9154 26 58 – www. santonsmarcelcarbonel.com – 🛍 shop: Tue-Sat 10am-noon, 2-7pm; workshop:* 🚶 *guided visits Mon-Fri 8am-1pm, 2-5.30pm.* Visit the workshop where the famous santons are made, as well as the shop.

Marseille soap – *Au Père Blaize, 4-6 rue Méolan* – ☎ *04 9154 04 01.* Herbalist. This shop has remained unchanged since 1780 and sells a wide range of herbs: star anise, thyme, marjoram, pesto, rosemary as well as medicinal plants.

La Compagnie de Provence – *1 rue Caisserie* – ☎ *04 91 56 20 94 – lcdp@free.fr* – ⏰ *Mon-Sat 10am-1pm, 2-7pm,* ⏰ *closed public holidays.* Marseille soap and natural products: bath products, body care, decorations for the home.

Four des Navettes – *136 rue Sainte* – ☎ *04 91 33 32 12 – navettes@aol.com* – ⏰ *Daily from 7am.* It is impossible to celebrate Candlemas without *"navette"* which protect houses from sickness and catastrophe! In the oldest bakery of the city people buy these biscuits **flavoured** with orange blossom; their recipe has been jealousy guarded for two centuries. There is also lavender flavoured chocolate, replete with the scent of Provence.

Provençal fabrics – Souleïado, 101 rue Paradis and in the shops on rue Vacon.

Pétanque – *La Boule bleue, Z.I. La Valentine, montée de St-Menet, 13396 Marseille cedex 11,* ☎ *04 91 43 27 20.* The place to buy the balls used for the traditional game of pétanque, which is always followed by the traditional aperitif of pastis.

LEISURE ACTIVITIES

Thalassa-Form Le Grand Large – *42 avenue du Grand-Large* – ☎ *04 96 14 05 40.* This sea-water spa has a range of health and beauty treatments for all the family.

EVENTS

Fiesta des Suds – In October and over some weekends throughout the year, this "southern fiesta" brings together the melting pot of races present in Marseille and vibrates with the music, traditions and atmosphere of the Mediterranean. It takes place in the J4 dock, near the entrance of the Joliette basin.

Festivals – Theatre and dance in various spots of the city (June-July). Island festival in July.

Pétanque competition – La Marseillaise *pétanque* world championship (in July): selection of games in the Borély park, finals on the Vieux Port. A very popular event frequented by show business celebrities who, after a few throws, let the champions take over.

Folklore – International folklore festival at Château-Gombert which takes place at the beginning of July.

⏰ *For coin ranges, see Legend at the back of the guide.*

EATING OUT

Specialities – As well as the celebrated *bouillabaisse*, the so-called fisherman's dish made with rockfish and found in most restaurants, and the famous *aioli* (garlic sauce), another speciality of

Marseilles is a dish made with tripe called *pied-et-paquets*.

◠ **Dégustation Toinou** – *3 cours St-Louis* - ☎ *04 91 33 14 94* – ⏰ *closed Aug.* This is a real institution and inhabitants of Marseille aren't wrong about these things. They flock here to eat oysters and seafood. Platters are paraded on every floor of this contemporary style building with its wood and burnished metal decor. Reasonable prices a stone's throw away from the Vieux Port.

◠ **Salon de thé Couleur des Thés** – *24 rue Paradis* - ☎ *04 91 55 65 57* – ⏰ *closed 15 Aug-1Sept and Sun.* Located on the first floor of a building in the city centre, this tearoom has all the intimacy of a plush, pleasantly decorated apartment. On offer are a salad buffet, charcuterie, savoury tarts and homemade pastries. Fifty varieties of tea which can also be purchased in bulk.

◠ **La Cloche à Fromage** – *27 cours d'Estienne-d'Orves* – ☎ *04 91 54 85 38.* Here you can help yourself to a wide selection of cheeses: from the mildest to the most pungent varieties, there is something for everyone! There is a wonderful terrace in the summer. A few dishes without cheese also available.

◠◠ **Chez Vincent** – *25 rue de Glandeves* – ☎ *04 91 33 96 78* – ⏰ *closed Aug and Mon* – 🍴. Behind a modest façade lies a simple, bistro-style restaurant, whose owner, Rose, has been cooking here since the 1940s and is much appreciated by the locals. Generous helpings of regional cooking.

◠◠ **Les Arcenaulx** – *25 cours d'Estienne-d'Orves* – ☎ *04 91 59 80 30* – ⏰ *closed 8- 23 Aug and Sun.* Dine surrounded by the books which cover the walls of this restaurant which is combined with a bookshop and publishers, located in the orignal setting of the warehouses of the 17C Arsenal des Galères. Large terrace on cours d'Estienne-d'Orves. Sun-kissed cooking.

◠◠ **Shabu Shabu** – *30 rue de la Paix-Marcel-Paul* – ☎ *04 91 54 15 00* – ⏰ *closed 28 Jul-1Sept, Mon lunchtime and Sun – booking recommended at weekends.* Every kind of Mediterranean fish prepared as sushi right before your very eyes! The decor here is Japanese but the chef is French, and passionate about Japanese cooking. A most unusual place, not least because it is one of the very few Japanese restaurants in the city.

◠◠ **Chez Fonfon** – *140 Vallon-des-Auffes* – ☎ *04 91 52 14 38* – ⏰ *closed 2-24 Jan, Sun evening and Mon lunchtime.* The dining room of this renowned restaurant dominates the Vallon des Auffes harbour. Every morning fresh fish and seafood is brought in by "pointus", the local fishing boats.

◠◠ **L'Épuisette** – *156 Vallon-des-Auffes* – ☎ *04 91 52 17 82* – ⏰ *closed 20 Aug-*

2 Sept, Sat lunchtime, Sun evening and Mon.
Get a front seat for stormy days! Located
above the rocks and facing the Frioul
islands, this restaurant almost feels like a
ship advancing through the sea. Well-
presented food with daily specials.

WHERE TO STAY

Chambre d'hôte Villa Marie-Jeanne
– *4 rue Chicot* – ☎ *04 91 85 51 31* – ⌖ –
3 rooms. A very special address in
Marseille, this 19C building has been
tastefully done up. Situated in a
residential neighbourhood, it blends the
traditional colours of Provence with
antique furniture, wrought iron and
contemporary paintings. Garden shaded
by plane trees and a nettle tree.

Hôtel Edmond Rostand – *31 rue du
Dragon* – ☎ *04 91 37 74 95* – ⌖ *closed
21 Dec-6 Jan* – *16 rooms* – ⌖ *5.49€* –
restaurant 12.20/12.20€. In a smart
residential area of Marseille, this hotel,
whose name bears tribute to the creator
of Cyrano de Bergerac, has been entirely
renovated. Behind the stone façade and
blue shutters are simple, well-kept rooms.
Snacks available for residents only.

Hôtel St-Ferréol's – *19 rue Pisançon*
– ☎ *04 91 33 12 21* – *19 rooms* – ⌖ *6.86€.*
This old house is situated at the heart of
the pedestrian quarter, undoubtedly the
liveliest in Marseille. Each of the little
rooms, decorated with English-style
fabrics and with its own marble bathroom,
bears the name of an impressionist
painter.

New Hôtel Vieux Port – *3 bis rue de
la Reine-Élisabeth* – ☎ *04 91 90 51 42* –
47 rooms – ⌖ *9.15€.* The building is an old
one but has been internally renovated,
and its setting, right beside the Vieux Port,
is ideal. Some rooms have views of the
harbour and the old city. Functional and
well soundproofed.

ON THE TOWN

Café Parisien – *1 place Sadi-Carnot* –
☎ *04 91 90 05 77* – ⌖ *Mon-Wed 4am-9pm,
Thurs-Fri until 1am,* ⌖ *closed public
holidays.* At weekends this baroque style

café hosts musical events based on the
themes presented in the exhibitions that
are organised here every month. The
Torcida Brésil has made this place their
HQ. "Tango aperitif" evenings are also
held, with free entry for guests on the last
Fri of the month.

Le Pelle-Mêle – *8 place aux Huiles* – ☎ *04
91 54 85 26* – *www.pele-mele.com* – ⌖
Tues-Sat from 6pm, ⌖ *closed Aug.* This is a
magnificent venue with a vaulted hall at
the back, where world-famous jazz groups
play.

O'Brady's Irish Pub – *378 avenue de
Mazargues* – ☎ *04 91 71 53 71* – *www.
obradys.com* – ⌖ *daily 11am-1.30am* – ⌖
closed 25 Dec and 1 Jan. Situated near the
seat of the OM and the Stadium-
Velodrome, this award-winning pub is one
of the favourite meeting places of OM
fans. On match nights the game is
broadcast on a giant screen and a lively
atmosphere is guaranteed.

O'Malley's – *9 quai Rive-Neuve* – ☎ *04 91
33 65 50* – ⌖ *daily 4pm-2am.* Irish pub with
a marine decor. There is an authentic and
warm atmosphere and an Irish accent is a
must-have for staff. Traditional Irish music
on Wednesday evenings from 9.30pm.

BOOKS AND FILMS

Books – Nowadays the city is the
backdrop to the mystery thrillers
(nicknamed bouillabaisse mysteries) by
Jean-Claude Izzo (Casino totale and
Chourmo) and Philippe Carrese (Trois
jours d'engatse). Fans of French comic
books – *bandes dessinées* – will enjoy Les
Aventures de Léon Loden, whose hero is a
Marseille-based private eye.

Films – As well as Marcel Pagnol's
celebrated trilogy, which appeals
especially to the nostalgic, the films of
Robert Guédiguian, whose work includes
the well-known Marius and Jeanette, are
redolent with the atmosphere of
Marseille. Lesser-known films like Transit
by René Allio and Bye-Bye by Karem Dridi
also portray the city's unique ambience.

⌖ **Organizing Your Time:** The **Canebière** is the most famous avenue of the city.
Starting down the left-hand pavement of the Vieux Port, take about 2hr to walk
along this street. Afterwards, we recommend going back down the Canebière,
unless it is the season of the santon fair just before Christmas, to the shopping
area which extends south of it. Turn right into boulevard Garibaldi and then
immediately left.

P **Parking:** Getting around Marseille by car is not for the faint-hearted; you need
patience, a philosophical outlook and nerves of steel to cope with the endless
traffic jams, fellow motorists with short tempers (especially towards those who
do not know their way around) and a fondness for sounding their horn at the
slightest delay. If you choose to drive however, there are several underground car
parks around town, most notably the one at place d'Estienne-d'Orves (reached
via place aux Huiles, quai de Rive-Neuve or rue Breteuil). From here Old Marseille
is easily accessed following quai de Rive-Neuve to quai des Belges.

A Bit of History

Marseille owes everything to the sea. It began life as a trading post set up by Greeks from Asia Minor around 600 BC. Its inhabitants soon established other commercial bases both in the interior and on the coast, at Nice, Antibes, the Lérins Islands, Agde, Glanum (St-Rémy), and Arles. By the 3C-2C BC the city they called Massilia covered an area of some 50ha – 125 acres to the north of the Old Port, and the knolls rising above the busy streets were crowned with temples.

A cultural as well as a commercial centre, the city aroused the interest and envy of the Celto-Ligurians of Entremont, and in 123 BC Massilia found it prudent to conclude an alliance with Rome. The Senate took the opportunity thus offered to put its communications with its possessions in Spain on a sounder footing, and began its programme of expansion into Provence and subsequently Gaul.

Seventy years later, when Caesar and Pompey were engaged in civil war, Marseille was obliged to take sides and had the ill fortune to choose the loser. The victorious Caesar besieged the city and sacked it in 49 BC. Narbonne, Arles and Fréjus grew prosperous on the spoils, and Marseille went into decline.

In the 19C, the city's fortunes revived with the expansion of French (and European) colonial activity in the Orient as well as in Africa.

Sights

Basilique St-Victor★

A Christian quarter grew up opposite the old Greco-Roman city. It was here that St Victor is supposed to have met a martyr's death at the very beginning of the 4C, and here too that a fortified abbey is said to have been built in his memory around AD 420.

The basilica was rebuilt in 1040 and its crypt and nave altered at the beginning of the Gothic period. In the crypt (**crypte**★★) are a number of 4C sarcophagi, examples of the individualism which distinguishes Christian art from that of the Classical world. The sarcophagi showing the Council of the Apostles and the Companions of St Maurice are justly famous.

Vieux-Port (Old Port and surrounding area)★★

On the south side of the Old Port is the bust of Vincent Scotto (1876-1952), the composer of much-loved popular melodies, surveying what is almost always a highly animated scene. To the east is the **Canebière**, the city's busy main artery, whose fame has been spread around the world by the mariners of Marseille.

Even after its sack by Caesar, Marseille remained a free city, and its life as a port carried on, with many ups and downs, based on the "Horn" (corne), the original basin sited to the northeast of today's Old Port, which itself came more and more into use as an outer harbour. Nevertheless, the decline of the city as a whole made it difficult to maintain the installations – **Musée des Docks romains**★ *(© Jun-Sep: Tue-Sun 11am-6pm; Oct-May: Tue-Sun 10am-5pm; © closed Mon and public holidays; ∞ 2€,*

View of port, Marseille

La Marseillaise

On 20 April 1792, Revolutionary France declared war against Austria. In Strasbourg, General Kellerman asked Claude Joseph Rouget de l'Isle, a captain in the engineering corps and a composer-songwriter in his spare time, to write a "new piece of music to mark the departure of the volunteers"; the *Chant de guerre pour l'Armée du Rhin (War Song for the Rhine army)* was written during the night of 25 to 26 April. Soon adopted by a battalion from Rhône-et-Loire and carried south by commercial travellers, the Chant reached Montpellier on 17 June. On 20 June, a young patriot from Montpellier on assignment in Marseille, François Mineur, sang it at a banquet offered by the Marseille Jacobin club, located at rue Thubaneau. Enthusiasm was such that the words of the song were passed on to 500 national guards from Marseille, who had been called to arms for the defence of Paris. Renamed *Chant de guerre aux armées des Frontières (War song for the Border Armies)*, the anthem was sung at each of the 28 stages of the journey towards the capital, with growing success and virtuosity. On 30 July, the impassioned verses sung by the warm southern voices, ringing out across the St-Antoine district, was referred to by the electrified crowd as the Chant des Marseillais (Song of the people of Marseille). A few days later, on the storming of the Tuileries, the new anthem was given its definitive name. La Marseillaise became the national anthem on 26 Messidor an III (14 July 1795) of the Republican calendar, and again, after a long period of obscurity, on 14 July 1879.

no charge Sun morning; ☎ *04 91 91 24 62)*– and the original harbour gradually silted up, finally becoming completely blocked in the 11C.

The Crusades, together with the growth of the rivalry between Pisa and Genoa, led to a revival of the city's fortunes in the 12C. Further expansion followed, with the incorporation of Provence into the French kingdom in 1481 and even more with the construction of new quays under Louis XIII (a blow to its old rival Arles).

The archeological site, part of the **Musée d'Histoire de Marseille**★, known as the Garden of Ruins (Jardin des Vestiges – K) gives some fascinating insights into the city's long history. The "horn" formed by the first harbour is dramatically visible, and inside there is a 3C boat recently excavated from the mud.

Centre de la Vieille Charité★★

🕐 *Jun-Sep: Tue-Sun 11am-6pm; Oct-May: Tue-Sun 10am-5pm.* 🕐 *Closed Mon and public holidays.* ⊚ *Musée d'Archéologie méditerranéenne: 2€; Musée des Arts Africains, Océaniens et Amérindiens: 2€; temporary exhibits: 3€; major event exhibits 5€.* ☎ *04 91 14 58 80.*

The old workhouse and hospice (1671 – 1749) has been carefully restored. The **chapel**★ is a masterpiece by Pierre Puget, a Marseille man; it has a little ambulatory and recessed steps allowing the different categories of inmates to make their separate ways to the chapels and galleries, and a central, oval-shaped cupola resting on a drum and supported by Ionic columns and pilasters. The second-floor gallery affords unusual views of the oblong chapel dome.

The rich and varied collections of the **Musée d'Archéologie de Marseille,** comprising some 900 artefacts from the Near East, Greece, Etruria and Rome, make this one of the few provincial museums able to offer a comprehensive survey of ancient Mediterranean civilisations.

▸▷ Musée du Vieux-Marseille★ 🕐 *Jun-Sep: Tue-Sun 11am-6pm; Oct-May: Tue-Sun 10am-5pm.* 🗨 *Call in advance for a guided tour (1hr).* 🕐 *Closed Mon and public holidays.* ⊚ *3€ (children: 1.50€).* ☎ *04 91 55 28 68.* Ancienne cathédrale de la Major★.

Musée Cantini★ 🕐 *Jun-Sep: Tue-Sun 11am-6pm; Oct-May: Tue-Sun 10am-5pm.* 🕐 *Closed Mon and public holidays.* ⊚ *2€ (3€ during temporary exhibits).* ☎ *04 91 54 77 75*– Modern art. Corniche President J.-F.-Kennedy★★.

Musée de la Faïence★ ⅙ 🕐 *Jun-Sep: daily except Mon 11am-6pm; Oct-May: daily 10am-5pm.* 🕐 *Closed public holidays.* ⊚ *2€.* ☎ *04 91 72 43 47.*

Musée Grobet Labadié★★ 🕐 *Jun-Sep: Tue-Sun 11am-6pm; Oct-May: Tue-Sun 10am-5pm.* 🕐 *Closed Mon and public holidays.* ⊚ *2€.* ☎ *04 91 62 21 82*– decorative arts, painting.

Palais Longchamp★ (musée des Beaux Arts★) 🕐 *Jun-Sep: Tue-Sun 11am-6pm; Oct-May: Tue-Sun 10am-5pm.* 🕐 *Closed Mon and public holidays.* ☎ *04 91 14 59 30* ⚯ *Temporarily closed for renovation* – fine arts.

Port★★. Château d'If★★ *About 1hr30min including boat trip and tour of the castle.*
🕐 *Apr-Sep: 9am-5:40pm; Oct-Mar: 9.15am-6.45pm.* ⊚ *4€. Boat service every hour in the summer, every hour and a half in winter. 10€ for the île d'If, 15€ for the îles du Frioul.*

Grotte du **MAS-D'AZIL**★★

MICHELIN MAP 343 G 6

GREEN GUIDE LANGUEDOC ROUSSILLON TARN GORGES

This cave is one of the outstanding natural phenomena of southwestern France as well as a prehistoric site of the first importance.

The River Arize has hollowed out a 420m – 1 380ft tunnel through the Plantaurel heights which once barred its way; a meandering dry valley to the east testifies to its former course. The entrance to the tunnel is formed by a magnificent 65m – 213ft arch, the exit by a much lower opening made in a sheer rock rising to a height of 140m – 460ft.

The site was first excavated by Edouard Piette (1827-1906), who communicated his passion for prehistory to the young seminary student who later became Abbot Breuil. In 1887, Piette discovered a human habitat intermediate between the Magdalenian and the Neolithic, the Azilian.

Visit

🕐 *Guided tours*  *(45min) Jul-Aug: daily 10am-6pm; Jun and Sep: Tue-Sun 10am-noon, 2-6pm; Apr-May: Tue-Sat 2-6pm; Sun, public holidays and spring school holidays (zone A) 10am-noon, 2-6pm; Mar and Oct-Nov: Sun and public holidays 2-6pm.* 🕐 *Closed Mon (except Jul-Aug, school holidays and public holidays)* ⊚ *6.10€ (children: 3.10€), ticket includes museum visit.* ☎ *05 61 69 97 71.*

It was in this cave **(grotte)** that Azilian industry was studied and defined. Practised between 11000 and 9500 BC, it is characterised by miniaturised tools, by flat harpoons made from stags' antlers (the reindeer having moved northwards following the change to warmer conditions after the Wurm glaciation), and by the making of flattened pebbles. The latter carry enigmatic markings done in a red paint made from calcinated ferric oxide; they have been interpreted to be lunar or menstrual calendars, or possibly the beginnings of abstract numbering. The four floors of excavated galleries run for 2km – 1mi through limestone which is sufficiently homogeneous to prevent infiltration and propagation of moisture. Display cases contain artefacts from the Magdalenian (scrapers, chisels, needles, a moulding of a famous neighing horse) and Azilian periods (harpoons made from antlers – the reindeer had moved northwards as the climate became warmer – tips, coloured pebbles, miniature tools).
In the chamber, Salle Mandement, are the remains of animals (mammoths, bears) coated in rubble; these were probably reduced to a heap of bones by subterranean flooding.

MEAUX★

POPULATION 63 006

MICHELIN MAP 312 G 2

GREEN GUIDE NORTHERN FRANCE AND THE PARIS REGION

▶ **Orient Yourself:** Meaux, which is listed as a "Town of Art and History," offers 1hr30min discovery tours conducted by guide-lecturers approved by the Ministry of Culture and Communication. 5€. Information available from the Heritage Dept. ☎ 01 64 34 68 05, or on www.vpah.culture.fr.

A Bit of History

In the early years of the 16C, the bishop of Meaux, Guillaume de Briçonnet, was an advocate of ecclesiastical reform, and the town sheltered numerous adherents of Calvinism. In 1682, the bishopric passed into the hands of **Jacques-Bénigne Bossuet**

(1627-1704), a meagre recompense for the frustrating years spent as tutor to the Dauphin. But Bossuet gave himself wholeheartedly to the task of running his diocese and to the fight against quietism and against Gallicanism, that specifically French movement favouring a reduction of Papal power. In an age when the influence of the pulpit orator equalled that of today's media commentator, the "Eagle of Meaux" was one of the greatest orators of his time, noted particularly for the eloquence of the funeral speeches made on the deaths of the Prince of Condé, known as "Grand Condé" (see ROCROI), and Maria-Theresa, Louis XIV's wife. With his sound Burgundian temperament, he was also one of France's great classical writers, his careful phrasing vibrating with an astonishing lyricism.

Visit

Cathédrale St-Étienne ★

12C-16C. All the major phases of French Gothic architecture are represented here. There are interesting, albeit headless, sculptures on the outside of the south transept, while the central portal of the Flamboyant west front is adorned with a vast composition depicting the Last Judgement, carried out in the 15C but in the style of the 13C. The clarity of the interior is striking, its apparent height enhanced by the removal of the tribunes in the 13C (though their arches have been preserved in the first three bays on the south side of the choir).

◐◐ Episcopal Palace★. Musée Bossuet ◷ Apr-Sep: Wed-Mon 10am-noon, 2-6pm; Oct-Mar: Wed-Sat 10am-noon, 2-5pm, Sun 2-5pm. ◷ Closed Tue, 1 Jan, 1 May, 14 Jul, 25 Dec. ◠ 3€ (under 18: no charge), no charge Wed. ☎ 01 64 34 84 45 – mementoes of Bossuet, archeology, fine arts.

Château de **MEILLANT**★★

MICHELIN MAP 323 L 6

GREEN GUIDE DORDOGNE BERRY LIMOUSIN

This château is a fine example of how stylistic change was allied to the growing desire for domestic comfort towards the end of the 15C, to transform what had been a typical medieval castle into an agreeable country residence. Like the Jacques-Cœur Palace in Bourges and the châteaux at Chaumont and Chenonceaux, it demonstrates the spread of early, Italianate Renaissance motifs in the southern part of the Loire valley.

Among the great families to which the château belonged and who left their mark on it were the Amboises, the Béthune-Charost and the Mortemarts.

Visit

◷ Guided tours ⌁ (45min) Jul-Aug: 9.30am-6pm; May-Jun and Sep: 9.30am-noon, 2-6pm; rest of the year: 9.30am-noon; 2-5.30pm. ◠ 7€ (children: 5€). ☎ 02 48 63 32 05. The medieval south front lapped by the waters of a moat is the only remnant of the old fortress built in the early 14C by Étienne de Sancerre; the towers retain their narrow loopholes although the wall-walk has been demolished. The ornate east façade, which is in a different style recalling that of the châteaux of the Loire, includes two projecting stair turrets in the late-Gothic style featuring a pierced balustrade at the base of the roof, dormer windows adorned with carvings, chimneys with elaborate Gothic balustrades, and in particular the splendidly decorated tower (Tour du Lion) by Giocondo, one of Michelangelo's assistants.
The interior, notably the formal dining room (Grande Salle à Manger) and the Bishop of Amboise's chamber (Chambre du Cardinal d'Amboise), is furnished with period pieces, fireplaces, tapestries and carpets.

Excursion

Bruère-Allichamps

6km – 4mi west. A Roman milestone was found here in 1757. It stands at the centre of the village and is popularly thought to mark the geographical centre of France.

MENTON★★

POPULATION 29 141

MICHELIN MAP 341 F 5

GREEN GUIDE FRENCH RIVIERA

Between mountain and Mediterranean, Menton stretches out agreeably on its sunny **site★★** on the lower slopes of the natural amphitheatre dominated by the heights of Mont Agel, Gorbio and Ste-Agnès. The picturesque qualities of the landscape belie the poverty of its soils and the severe erosion to which it is prone and which is the cause of frequent landslides. On the cliffs around are the remains of fortifications, castellars, evidence of human settlement going back to Neolithic times.

The town was bought by the **Grimaldi** family of Monaco in the 14C, then incorporated into the French kingdom when the county of Nice was annexed.

Menton's gardens are many; together with the abundant olive, orange and lemon trees, they give the town a most pleasant park-like character. The Tropical Garden (**jardin botanique exotique★★**) is outstanding.

▶ **Orient Yourself:** Menton, which is listed as a "Town of Art and History," offers discovery tours on Tue at 2.30pm for 5€. Information available at the Maison du Patrimoine (Heritage Dept.), 24 r. St-Michel, ☎ 04 92 10 97 10 or on www.vpah.culture.fr.

Sights

Hôtel de ville
◔ *Tour of Jean Cocteau wedding hall daily except Sat-Sun 8.30am-12.30pm, 1-5pm.* ◔ *Closed public holidays.* ◈ *1.50€.* ☎ *04 92 10 50 00. www.villedementon.com.*
The town hall is a pretty building in Italianate style, with pilasters and Corinthian capitals and a cream-coloured cornice contrasting with the rosy rendering of the walls. The Registry Office (**Salle des mariages★**) was decorated by Cocteau in 1958.

Vieille ville★★
Allow about 2hr.
The old town nestles underneath the hill just above Rue Longue and Rue St-Michel fragrant with orange trees, whose alignment marks the course of the Roman Via Giulia Augusta.

Parvis St-Michel★★
This is a charming square in the Italian style, laid out on two levels by the Grimaldis, whose monogram can be seen in the pebble mosaic forming the paving. It is bordered by a number of houses in the local style, by a pink-walled chapel (Chapelle de la Conception), and by the **Église St-Michel★** (◔ *Daily except Sat-Sun: 10am-noon, 3-5pm;* ☎*04 93 35 81 63)*, a fine Baroque building dating from the middle of the 17C, extensively restored after the earthquake of 1887.

Rampe St-Michel
Monumental stairway with pebble paving and twin ramps.
◖◗ Promenade du Soleil★★. Musée des Beaux Arts★ (Palais Carnolès) ◔ *Daily except Tue 10am-noon, 2-6pm.* ◔ *Closed public holidays. No charge.* ☎ *04 93 35 49 71*– fine arts. Garavan – gardens★.

Excursion

Roquebrune-Cap Martin★★
2km – 1mi southwest. Roquebrune is a most picturesque hill-top village (**village perché★★**), where the tourist can stroll through the small streets towards the keep (**donjon★**) From the top, wonderful **panorama★★** of the sea, Cap Martin, the Principality of Monaco and the Mont Agel.

METZ★★★

POPULATION 193 117

MICHELIN MAP 307 I 4

GREEN GUIDE ALSACE LORRAINE CHAMPAGNE

From the limestone escarpment of the Côtes de Moselle high above Metz, the Lorraine plateau can be seen stretching away eastwards towards the German frontier. The city itself lies at the meeting point of the Moselle with the Seille, a strategic site whose importance was appreciated by the Romans; it was here that their great highways leading from the Channel coast to the Rhine and from Trier to Italy were linked, their course marked today by Metz' busy shopping street, Rue Serpenoise.

In the 4C, as a response to the threat posed by the Germanic tribes to the east, fortifications were built, together with a basilica which later became the church of a monastery, the original Church of St Peter of the Noviciates (St-Pierre-aux-Nonnains). In the early part of the Middle Ages, the city was the residence of the Merovingian rulers of Eastern Gaul (Austrasia); it then became the capital of the kingdom of Lotharingia (Lorraine), before being attached to the Holy Roman Empire. In the 12C Metz declared itself the capital of a republican city-state, with an elected High Magistrate as ruler. But in 1552, together with Verdun and Toul, it was annexed by a French kingdom seeking to push its frontier eastwards, and its role henceforth was that of a fortress-town standing guard over the border.

▶ **Orient Yourself:** Metz, which is listed as a "Town of Art and History," offers discovery tours daily except Sun and public holidays at 3pm and 4pm. One hour tours are 4€ and two hour tours are 7€. Information at the tourist office or on www.vpah.culture.fr.

A Bit of History

1871-1918-1944 – On the 6 August 1870, the Prussian armies invaded Lorraine, defeating the incompetent Marshal Bazaine in a series of battles and locking up his forces in Metz. On 27 October Bazaine surrendered the city, which seven months later became part of the newly-declared German Empire.

The city lost a quarter of its population, people who chose to resettle in France; artists left and so did many businessmen, at the very moment when industry was expanding rapidly. Metz' loss was Nancy's gain.

The townscape began to take on a Germanic character. In 1898 the cathedral was given a neo-Gothic portal, complete with a statue of the Prophet Daniel looking uncommonly like Kaiser Wilhelm II (though his moustache was subsequently clipped). With its surrounding forts, Metz became the centre of the greatest fortified camp in

Metz Cathedral

Metz - Address Book

PRACTICAL INFORMATION

Tourist Office – *Pl. d'Armes* – ☎ *03 87 55 53 76 - http://tourisme.mairie-metz.fr*

Public transport: Espace-bus – *Pl. de la République* – ☎ *03 87 76 31 11.* The Metz bus service operates all over Metz and the vicinity. **Visi'Pass**: one-day ticket (€3).

Guided tours – 🚶 *Daily except Sun and public holidays 3 and 4pm, €4 (1hr), €7 (2hr), enquire at the tourist office or www. vpah.culture.fr* Metz organises guided tours-conferences by approved government guides to discover the town and its culture.

Tours for disabled visitors – The tourist office has designed a number of visits for disabled visitors so that they can discover the town, its monuments and museum. Wheelchairs loaned.

Illuminations – Metz was awarded the "Illuminated City" prize for its night-time street, square and monument illuminations (*brochure from the tourist office*).

Tourist train – 🕐 *Early Apr to early Oct: leaves at 10.30am, 11.30am, 1, 2, 3, 4 and 5pm and sometimes at 6pm in summer, €5.50 (children: €3.50, lasts 45min,* ☎ *03 87 73 03 08.*

WHERE TO EAT

See the Legend for coin categories.

🍽 **La Migaine** – *1-3 pl. St-Louis* – ☎ *03 87 75 56 67* – 🕐 *closed 1-15 Aug.* You can eat at any time here, from morning to late afternoon. The tearoom in a pretty square surrounded by arcades serves copious breakfasts, meat pies, quiche Lorraine, cakes and tea – the choice is yours. Terrace in summer.

🍽🍽 **La Robe des Champs** – *14 en Nouvelle rue* – ☎ *03 87 36 32 19 - metz@ larobedeschamps.com* . You can't miss the yellow façade and Provençal-style terrace of this pleasant bistro in a pedestrian town centre street. Potatoes, as the name infers ("In its jacket"), take pride of place in this friendly unpretentious establishment.

🍽🍽 **Restaurant du Pont-St-Marcel** – *1 r. du Pont-St-Marcel* – ☎ *03 87 30 12 29 – info@port-saint-marcel.com.* A 17C restaurant not far from St Étienne's cathedral, standing on piles beside a branch of the Moselle. Inside, an amusing contemporary fresco depicts a 17C fairground scene, complete with acrobats and theatre. The staff wear costumes to serve the local cuisine.

🍽🍽 **La Gargouille** – *29 pl. de Chambre* - ☎ *03 87 36 65 77* – 🕐 *closed Mon lunchtime, Tue evening and Wed.* Don't be fooled by the ordinary façade of this restaurant located down from the cathedral: behind it lies a sumptuous interior with velvet-covered seats, cosy little booths and 1900-style decor typical of the Nancy School, all making for a warm ambiance. The food is exceedingly refined: carpaccio de fois gras au sel de Guérande, or joue de bœuf sauce vigneronne. Highly professional service.

🍽🍽 **Restaurant du Fort** – *Allée du Fort – 57070 St-Julien-lès-Metz – 8km/5mi NE of Metz, Bouzonville direction on D 3, then a minor road* – ☎ *03 87 75 71 16* – 🕐 *closed 1-10 Jan, 24 Jul-9 Aug, Sun evening and Wed – booking advisable at weekends.* At the end of a forest track you will be amazed to discover this 1870 fort, evidence of the Moselle's turbulent history. Part of it has been restored to create a restaurant offering Lorraine cuisine.

🍽🍽🍽 **L'Écluse** – *45 pl. de la Chambre* – ☎ *03 87 75 42 38* – 🕐 *closed 5-20 Aug, Sun and Mon.* A taste of Brittany, near the cathedral. The chef's enthusiasm for the region is evident in the decor, inspired by the Breton coast, with blue chairs and a menu that includes seafood served in an attractive, bright dining room.

🍽🍽🍽 **Maire** – *1 r. du Pont-des-Morts* – ☎ *03 87 32 43 12 – restaurant.maire@ wanadoo.fr* – 🕐 *closed Wed lunchtimes and Tue.* There is a superb view of the Moselle from this town-centre restaurant. You will enjoy the young chef's carefully prepared dishes, whether in the salmon-pink dining room with its pale wood furniture or on the attractive terrace.

WHERE TO STAY

🛏 **Chambre d'hôte Bigare** – *23 r. Principale – 57530 Ars-Laquenexy – 9km/5.6mi E of Metz, Château-Salins direction then D 999* – ☎ *03 87 38 13 88* – 🛏 *– 2 rooms.* If the bustle of city life doesn't suit you, a short journey will bring you to this friendly local village house. Simple rooms and reasonable prices.

🛏🛏🛏 **Hôtel de la Cathédrale** – *25 pl. de la Chambre* – ☎ *03 87 75 00 02 – hotelcathedrale-metz@wanadoo.fr* – 🕐 *closed 1-15 Aug - 20 rooms -* 🍽 *€11.* A charming hotel situated in a lovely 17C house that was completely restored in 1997. The attractive rooms have cast iron or cane beds, old parquet flooring and furniture, some of which is oriental. Most rooms face the cathedral, just opposite.

🛏🛏🛏 **Hôtel Bleu Marine** – *23 av. Foch* – ☎ *03 87 66 81 11 – bleumarine-metz@ bplorraine.fr – 62 rooms -* 🍽 *€9.50 - restaurant* 🍽🍽. In an old building (1906) in the station area, this hotel has been completely renovated. Its rooms are modern, spacious and well soundproofed. Buffet meals served. Gym and sauna.

ON THE TOWN

Café Jehanne-d'Arc – *Pl. Jeanne-d'Arc* – ☎ *03 87 37 39 94* – 🕐 *Mon-Thu 11-2am, Fri 11-3am, Sat 3pm-3am* – 🕐 *closed Sun.* One of the most famous cafés in Metz, for its decor, which still includes Gallo-Roman stones, 13C frescoes and 17C stencils. Terrace in the attractive square, where jazz concerts are organised in summer. Relaxed clientele, including students and intellectuals.

SHOWTIME

L'Arsenal – *Av. Ney* – ☎ *03 87 39 92 00 or 03 87 74 16 16* – *www.mairie-metz.fr/ arsenal* – 🕐 *Ticket sales: box office Tue-Sat 1-6pm, by phone Tue-Fri 9am-noon, 1-6pm, Sat 1-6pm* – 🕐 *closed 31 Jul to 6 Aug, 29 Dec-1 Jan, 3-4 Jan, Mon and public holidays.* Built to a 1989 design by Ricardo Bofill within the walls of a former 19C arsenal, this concert hall is said to be the finest in Europe, with "fantastic acoustics", according to Rostropovitch. Apart from the main hall, which can seat 1 354, there is another hall seating 352, an exhibition gallery, and a museum/shop. With nearly 200 events each year, the programme is far-ranging, from contemporary dance to classical music, and from jazz to world music.

SPORTS & RECREATION

Golf – *R. de la Grange-aux-Ormes – Exit Metz-Centre, towards Montigny and Marly - 57155 Marly* – ☎ *03 87 63 10 62* – *www. grange-aux-ormes.com* - 🕐 *summer 8am-11pm, winter 8am-7pm.*
Golf du Château de Chérisey – *38 r. Principale – 57420 Chérisey* – ☎ *03 87 52 70 18* – *www.golfcherisey.com* – 🕐 *9am-6.30pm.* A lovely 18-hole golf course in a hilly, partially wooded site, dotted with ponds. Restaurant inside the château, putting-green and practice.

SHOPPING

Boucherie-charcuterie-traiteur Éric Humbert – *8 r. du Grand-Cerf – Quartier St-Louis* – ☎ *03 87 75 09 38* – *humbert.eric@ wanadoo.fr* – 🕐 *Mon-Thu 8.15am-12.40pm, 2.45-7pm, Fri-Sat 7.30am-12.40pm, 2.30-7pm* – 🕐 *closed 2 weeks in Feb, July, Sun and public holidays.* Eric Humbert has been honoured by an award from a major design magazine, which is explained by the fact that this butcher/delicatessen/caterer is just as talented a designer as he is a cook. He himself designed the avant-garde counters in his otherwise traditional shop, adding a visual treat to that in store for the taste buds. Try the chicken and pistachio sausage, or the foie gras in aspic with Riesling.

CALENDAR

Fontaines Dansantes – *Jul-Sep: Fri, Sat, Sun and public holidays until dusk. Lac aux cynes, beneath the Esplanade (Bd Poincaré).* Dancing fountains...
Grandes Fêtes de la mirabelle – *Late August.* Election of festival ambassadress, folklore and fireworks.
Christmas Market – *December: parade of St Nicholas and the "bogey man". Christmas market: daily from late Nov to Christmas eve, on Place St-Louis, l'Esplanade, Place du Gén.-de-Gaulle and Place du Forum.*

the world. From 1902-08 the area around the station was rebuilt; the station itself was constructed in a style which mixed Rhenish neo-Romanesque and Second Reich symbolism (the Emperor himself designed the bell-tower); an imposing central post office rose nearby, together with hotels providing accomodation for the officers of the garrison and their guests. Metz was in fact the linchpin of the Schlieffen Plan, the strategy to be followed in the event of a future war with France; this envisaged the adoption of a defensive posture to the south of the city coupled with a vast turning movement to the northwest, which would sweep through Belgium and then descend on Paris. In 1914 the plan all but succeeded; the German armies marched steadily forward for six weeks, coming within 50km – 30mi of Paris, only to be thrown back by Marshal Joffre at the Miracle of the Marne.

In the inter-war period, the ring of forts around Metz was incorporated into the Maginot Line. Their defensive strength was such that the Allied armies took two and a half months to eject their German occupants in the autumn of 1944.

Sights

Cathédrale St-Étienne★★★

The cathedral grew out of the joining together around 1240 of two churches which up to then had been separated by an alley-way and had faced in different directions. The 13C and 14C interior recalls the Gothic style of Champagne; its relative narrowness combines with the modest height of the aisles to exaggerate the loftiness of the nave, which does in fact reach 41.77m – 137ft. The late-Gothic chancel, crossing and transepts were completed at the beginning of the 16C.

The stained-glass windows (**verrières**★★★) have led to the cathedral being known as "God's Lantern" (Lanterne du Bon Dieu). They have a total area of 6 500m^2 – about 60 000sq ft. The rose window of the west front is 14C work, the lower part of the north transept window 15C, and the upper part of this window together with the glass of the south transept and the chancel, 16C. Contemporary glass can be seen beneath the towers (abstract designs by Bissière), and above all in the north ambulatory and on the southwest side of the north transept (the *Earthly Paradise* by Chagall).

Musées de la Cour d'Or ★★

Allow about 2hr. ◷ *Daily except Tue 9am-5pm, Sat-Sun 10am-5pm.* ◷ *Closed certain public holidays.* ◉ *4.60€ (under 18 years: no charge), no charge first Sun in the month.* ☏ *03 87 68 25 00.*

The museums are housed in the buildings of a former Carmelite convent (17C), a 15C tithe barn (Grenier de Chèvrement), and several link rooms and extensions. In the basements are the remains of ancient baths.

The complex, which was extended in 1980, brings into play the latest display techniques to present a fascinating survey of times past.

Section archéologique★★★

On display in the archeological section are artefacts found in Metz and the surrounding area. The finds attest to the importance of the town, which was in turn Gaulish, a major crossroads in Gallo-Roman times, and a cultural centre under the Carolingian kings. The **Grenier de Chèvrement**★ is a fine building (1457) used to store cereals given over as tithes.

◖◗ Porte des Allemands★. Place St-Louis★. Église St-Maximin★. Église St-Pierre-aux-Nonnains★ ◷ *Daily except Mon 2-6pm.* ☏ *03 87 39 92 00.*

Massif du **MÉZENC**★★★

MICHELIN MAP 331 H 4

GREEN GUIDE AUVERGNE THE RHÔNE VALLEY

These volcanic uplands in the southern part of the Velay region form the watershed between Atlantic and Mediterranean. They lie at the centre of a belt of igneous rocks cutting across the axis of the Cévennes. The first burst of volcanic activity occurred in Tertiary times, when molten rock was released by the faulting and uplift of the ancient central plateau during the formation of the Alps. A second phase of activity resulted in a series of basalt table-lands, the planèzes, such as the Devès uplands, and a third volcanic period, towards the end of Tertiary times, was responsible for today's rock pinnacles, the sucs. A final set of eruptions released massive flows of lava into the valleys.

Walking Tour

Mont Mézenc

🚶 *2hr round trip on foot from the Croix de Boutières pass.*

Two great lava flows extend downwards from the twin summits of the mountain, from which a vast **panorama**★★★ extends over the Velay. The southern of the two peaks overlooks the luxuriant landscape marked by the sucs and the central part of the huge eroded crater of the volcano, while the north peak with its cross dominates a landscape of huge fields running down to the deep ravines of Les Boutières in the east. Quite close at hand can be seen the village of Les Estables.

Gerbier de Jonc★★

🚶 *1hr30min round trip on foot.*

This lava pinnacle, a typical suc, was of too thick a consistency to flow. Its screes of bright phonolite clatter under the feet of the many who clamber to its summit, from which there is a fine **view**★★. At the foot of the pinnacle, in a stable, is a fountain which is held to be the source of the Loire, though some geographers consider the streams threading the damp pasturelands near Estables to be the river's true origin.

Cascade du Ray-Pic★★

11km – 7mi south of the Gerbier de Jonc – 1hr 30min round trip on foot.

In a harsh setting formed by a succession of lava flows, the Bourges torrent drops in a series of falls, the main one strikingly framed by prisms of basalt. In the bed of the stream, the boulders and pebbles of the dark basalt contrast with those of the much lighter granite.

Lac d'Issarlès★

20km – 12mi east of the Gerbier de Jonc.

This pretty, rounded lake with its blue waters occupies the crater of an extinct volcano, 138m – 450ft deep. It forms part of the Montpezat hydro-electric scheme straddling the Atlantic-Mediterranean watershed and incorporating a 13km – 8 mile tunnel with a drop of 650m – 2 100ft.

Pic du **MIDI DE BIGORRE**★★★

MICHELIN MAP 342 M 5

GREEN GUIDE LANGUEDOC ROUSSILLON TARN GORGES

A vertiginous mountain road winds over the Tourmalet Pass (Col du Tourmalet), whose name "the bad way round" reflects the difficulties heaped upon intrepid travellers by the severity of the elements. From the top of the pass (2 114m – 6 936ft) a toll road (**route à péage**), one of the highest in Europe, leads to the place known as Les Laquets; from here a cable-car or a rough path *(2hr round trip)* gives access to the summit of the Pic du Midi de Bigorre, now reduced in level to the 2 865m – 9 400ft contour in order to accommodate the television transmitter.

Visit

🕐 *High season: departures from La Mongie 9am-4.30pm, last descent from the summit at 7pm; low season: departures from La Mongie 10am-3.30pm, last descent from the summit at 5.30pm.* 🎫 *High season: 23€; low season: 20€ (under 18 years: 12€)* 🕐 *Closed end Apr to early May and early Nov to early Dec.* ☎ *05 62 56 71 14. www.picdumidi.com.*

Panorama★★★

The primary rocks of which the Pic du Midi is made form an isolated mass projecting northwards into the Bigorre lowlands, making a spectacular viewpoint which takes in the Pyrenees from La Rhune to Andorra. To the south rise the summits of the Néouvielle Massif, that extraordinary museum of glacial relief.

Observatoire et Institut de physique du globe du Pic du Midi

The factors favouring the siting here of an observatory include the great height, the purity of the atmosphere and the all-round viewing possibilities. The observatory, founded by General Nansouty, was originally intended for botanical and meteorological studies, but the astronomical function was soon added. It was here in 1706 that the first observations were made of the solar corona during a total eclipse of the sun. In the 19C, Vaussenat set up a 20cm equatorial telescope here, and at the

Dumas/IMAGES TOULOUSE

Pic du Midi de Bigorre

beginning of the 20C, Jules Baillaud and his son built the great observatory dome and installed reflecting telescopes.

Today, the observatory and the Institute of World Physics attached to it form one of the most important scientific stations of its kind in the world, carrying out research into the solar corona, lunar mapping, cosmic radiation and nocturnal luminescence.

MILLAU

POPULATION 21 788

MICHELIN MAP 338 K 6

GREEN GUIDE LANGUEDOC ROUSSILLON TARN GORGES

Millau huddles between two high limestone plateaux, the Causse du Larzac and the Causse Noir, at the meeting-point of the Tarn and the Dourbie. The site of a ford in ancient times, it acquired a bridge in the Middle Ages and became a trading centre of some importance.

A Bit of History

As early as the 2C AD, ewes' milk was used to make Roquefort cheese, a process involving the sacrifice of their lambs. This was turned to advantage by finding uses for lambskin and eventually developing the manufacture of fine gloves.

In its sheltered valley Millau enjoys a much milder climate than that of the harsh plateau high above; with its streets lined with plane trees, its fountains and its bustling air, it has a very southern character. The varied orientation of the edge of the plateau, the depth of the valleys and the rising air currents have made it an important centre for hang-gliding.

Visit

La Graufesenque

🕐 May-Sep: daily 9am-noon, 2-6.30pm; Oct-Apr: daily 9.30am-noon, 2-6pm. 🕐 Closed 1 Jan, 1 May, 1 and 11 Nov, 25 Dec. ⊛ 4€, no charge 1st Sun in the month (1 Oct-1 May). ☎ 05 65 60 11 37.

This 10ha – 24 acre archeological site on the south bank of the Dourbie was an important centre for the manufacture of pottery in ancient times. It flourished for over two centuries, between the reigns of Augustus and Hadrian, activity peaking during Nero's rule.

During the first hundred years of its existence, some 400 potters toiled to produce more than 800 000 numbered pieces in 100 kilns heated to 950°C for a period of two weeks. In spite of transport problems, their wares found customers in Britain, central Europe and around the Mediterranean Sea. Vases, cups, bowls and plates were moulded or turned with great care to patterns which probably originated in Arezzo in Tuscany; they were of high quality, decorated with seals and featuring a vitrified reddish surface.

Around AD 170, the seam of clay began to run out, leading to the decline and then abandonment of the site. Manufacture, on an even bigger scale, then began at Lezoux, near Clermont-Ferrand.

There is an archeological museum **(musée archéologique)** with a fine pottery collection⋆.

Excursions

Chaos de Montpellier-le-Vieux⋆⋆⋆

18km – 11mi northeast – 2hr round trip on foot.

This extraordinary ruined city of rocks extending over some 120ha – 300 acres was formed by the erosive effects of water on the limestones of the Causse Noir. For long inaccessible, it was held by the people of the locality to be the abode of the Devil, but the surrounding dense woodland was eventually cleared, and in 1883 the site was explored by J and L de Malafosse.

The bewildering variety of rock formations (the Sphinx, the Elephant, the Gates of Mycaenae...) is due to the different ways in which the constituents of dolomite react to weathering; the magnesium carbonate has a much greater resistance than calcium carbonate, which decomposes rapidly into sand. The contrasting properties of the rock are further expressed in the pattern of vegetation, with species favouring lime soils and dry conditions (lavender and box) growing in close proximity to plants (thyme, juniper) which prefer siliceous sands.

Caves de Roquefort★

25km – 15mi southwest

The name of the market town of Roquefort located between Millau and St-Affrique is synonymous with one of the most famous of French cheeses, the delicious blue-veined Roquefort. However, not a sign of the town's main economic activity is to be seen in the town itself as production of the cheese takes place underground. Above the town, which lies at the foot of a cliff, is a limestone plateau known as "Combalou," the northeast side of which has collapsed. This has led to the formation of natural caves between the displaced rocks, in which the temperature and humidity are constant. The locals found the conditions ideal for curing cheese.

Roquefort is produced exclusively from full-fat, untreated ewes' milk, neither homogenised nor pasteurised. The dairies turn the milk into a curd to which is added a natural mould, Penicillium roqueforti, which comes from the caves at Combalou. The rounds of cheese are then transported to Roquefort for maturation in the natural caves. A minimum maturing period of three months is necessary for a good Roquefort.

MOISSAC★★

POPULATION 11 971

MICHELIN MAP 337 C 7

GREEN GUIDE LANGUEDOC ROUSSILLON TARN GORGES

Moissac is sited on a low rise overlooking the fertile flood plain near the meeting point of the Tarn with the Garonne. The place is famous for the white Chasselas dessert grape which grows here in abundance.

Visit

Église St-Pierre★

 *Illustration Art: Architecture.* The Benedictines founded an abbey here in the 7C. Its church was consecrated in 1063 and the cloisters **(cloître★★)** completed 35 years later; its capitals depict a great variety of themes and served as a model for similar work all over 12C Europe.

The church originally had dome vaults like those of Périgord, but was transformed in the 15C into a typical southern French building with a single nave. The work of this period is easily recognisable, having been carried out in brick.

The church's south doorway **(portail méridional★★★)** is one of the great triumphs of Romanesque sculpture; in its perfect synthesis of the sculptor's art with the 11C Abbot Roger's profound understanding of the meaning of the Scriptures, it passes beyond beauty into the realm of mysticism.

The subject of the tympanum is the Apocalypse such as it is described by St John. To read Chapter 4 of the Book of Revelation while standing in front of this masterpiece is indeed a moving experience; everything is there, from the "throne set in Heaven," to the "four and twenty Elders with crowns of gold" and the "four beasts (the Evangelists) full of eyes."

Principauté de **MONACO**★★★

POPULATION 27 876

MICHELIN MAP 341 F 5

GREEN GUIDE FRENCH RIVIERA

The Principality of Monaco is a sovereign state covering an area of 192ha – less than a square mile. Inhabited since prehistoric times and later a Greek settlement (5C BC) and a Roman port (1C AD), its history really began when the Grimaldi family bought it from the Republic of Genoa in 1308.

Prince Rainier III ruled the principality from 1949-2005 with the assistance of a National Council. His only son Prince Albert has taken power, but because he has no children, it seems certain that the line of succession will pass to the children of Rainier's daughter Caroline.

▶ **Orient Yourself:** The territory includes the old town on the Rock (Rocher de Monaco); the new town of Monte-Carlo; the port area at La Condamine linking the two; and the Fontvieille quarter. Either walk around Monaco or take the bus, as the city is in a compact area (less than a square mile) and to drive a car around the winding roads can be a precarious venture.

🕐 **Organizing Your Time:** If you do drive, you can park in the underground garage (parking des Pêcheurs creusé) of Le Rocher, and take the elevator. With lots to do in the old town of Monaco, take about 3hr before visiting Monte-Carlo, where you can try your luck in the casino.

Kids **Especially For Kids:** Check out the aquatic life inside the Musée Océanographique, vintage vehicles at the Collection des voitures anciennes, or the displays of dolls from the 18C and automated figures from the 19C at the Musée des Poupées et Automates.

Monaco★★★
Le Rocher (The Rock)★★
This is the historic core of the principality, and its prestigious capital, the miniature city of Monaco. It is built on a rocky peninsula 60m – 200ft above the sea.

Musée Océanographique★★
Kids ♿ 🕐 Jul-Aug: daily 9.30am-7.30pm; Apr-Jun and Sep: daily 9.30am-7pm; Oct-Mar: daily 10am-6pm. 🎫 11€ (6-18 years: 6€). ☎ 00 377 93 15 36 00. www.oceano.mc.
The museum was founded by Prince Albert I who was a leading light in the early days of oceanography. The imposing rooms house the skeletons of large marine mammals (whale, sea-cow...) as well as stuffed specimens. A splendid **aquarium**★★ teems with rare tropical and Mediterranean species of marine life (sea dragon). A live coral reef from the Red Sea is a unique exhibit.

Musée océanographique, Monaco

Monaco - Address Book

TOURISM OFFICE

2a, Boulevard des Moulins – 98030 – ☎ 00 377 92 16 61 66. www.visitmonaco.com

TOURS

🚂 Guided tours of Monaco and day-trips to the surrounding region can be booked at the Monaco Tourism Office.

TELEPHONE

To telephone Monaco from France, dial 00 followed by 377 (code for Monaco) and then the 8-digit telephone number.

CURRENCY AND POSTAGE

Monaco uses Euros just like France, but it has an independent postal system. All letters mailed from within the Principality must have Monégasque stamps.

For coin categories see the Legend at the back of this guide.

EATING OUT

😋😋 **Polpetta** – *2 Rue Paradis* – ☎ 00 377 93 50 67 84 – 🕐 *Closed 10-30 Jun, Sat for lunch and Tue* –🍴. A small Italian restaurant offering three different settings in which to enjoy a tasty tagliatelle alla carbonara or vitello ai funghi: the verandah giving onto the street, the rustic-style dining hall or the cosy, intimate room at the back.

😋😋 **Richart** – *19 Boulevard des Moulins* – ☎ 00 377 93 30 15 06 – www.richart-monaco.com – 🕐 *Closed Sun except in Dec .* The tiny squares of chocolate with their subtle aromas and intricate designs are a delight to behold... and savour! After buying a few boxes of chocolates to take back to friends, sit down in the elegant tea room decorated in white and grey and order one of the light snacks (salads, pastries, savoury tarts) while sipping a cup of delicately scented tea.

😋😋😋 **La Maison du Caviar** – *1 Avenue St-Charles* – ☎ 00 377 93 30 80 06 – 🕐 *Closed 20 Jul-20 Aug, Sat for lunch and Sun.* This prestigious house has been serving choice caviar to Monaco residents for the past 50 years. In an unusual setting made up of bottle racks and wooden panelling, you can also purchase salmon, foie gras or bœuf strogonoff. Definitely worth a visit.

😋😋😋 **Zebra Square** – *Grimaldi Forum, 10 Avenue Princesse Grace* – ☎ 00 377 99 99 25 50 – 🕐 *Closed 6 Feb - 2 Mar* – 🍴. This stylish restaurant has the same sleek decor as its Parisian namesake, featuring modern fusion cuisine and panoramic views over the sea from the terrace. At night the bar is packed with a young and trendy crowd.

😋😋😋😋 **Vistamar** – *Hôtel Hermitage, Place Beauarchais* – ☎ 00 377 92 16 40 00– 🕐 *Closed 24-26, 31 Dec, and lunch Jul-Aug* –🍴. An elegant restaurant specialising in fresh seafood, with one of the best panoramic views of the Principality from its top-floor terrace.

WHERE TO STAY

🛏 **Villa Bœri** – *29 Boulevard Général-Leclerc – 06240 Beausoleil* – ☎ 04 93 78 38 10 – 30 rooms – 🍴. A 1960s building on the French side of the border, fronted by a small garden planted with Mediterranean shrubs and flowers, offers a few rooms, some of which are lacking in modern comforts. Just cross the street and bingo... you are in Monte-Carlo!

🛏🛏 **Hôtel de France** – *6 Rue de la Turbie – Near the train station* – ☎ 00 377 93 30 24 64 – www.monte-carlo.mc/france – 26 rooms – 🍴. Recent renovation work on this hotel has graced it with charming, soundproofed rooms decorated in Provençal hues and a modern breakfast lounge enhanced with metal and wood furniture.

🛏🛏🛏 **Columbus Hôtel** – *23 Avenue Papalins – Fontvieille* – ☎ 00 377 92 05 90 00 – www.columbushotels.com – ✕ 🅿 – 153 rooms – 🍴 Restaurant (😋😋😋😋). Clean, contemporary lines and a soothing palette are combined with cozy fabrics and warm wood furnishings. A lounge bar and Italian-style brasserie with terrace seating attract fashionable locals. Access to a private pool; the heliport is just a block away.

🛏🛏🛏🛏 **Metropôle** – *4 Avenue Madone – Above the Metropôle Shopping Centre* – ☎ 00 377 93 15 15 15 – www.metropole.com – ✕ 🅿 🕐 – 131 rooms – 🍴 – restaurant (😋😋😋😋). This 1886 hotel got a complete facelift from the hot Parisian designer Jacques Garcia, with luxurious fabrics and timeless style. The outdoor pool and solarium have views overlooking the rooftops of the Place du Casino. The restaurant is managed by chef Joël Robuchon.

ON THE TOWN

Café de Paris – *Place du Casino* – ☎ 00 377 92 16 20 20 – www.sbm.mc – 🕐 *Daily 7.30am-2am.* The terraces of this turn-of-the-century brasserie look out onto Place du Casino (for some excellent people-watching) and the Salon Bellevue upstairs commands a superb panorama of the Franco-Italian Riviera.

Casino de Monte-Carlo – *Place du Casino* – ☎ 00 377 92 16 20 00 – www.casino-monte-carlo.com – 🕐 *Daily from noon until the last client leaves.* This is Europe's leading casino, with over a million euros in profits, attributed to gambling and not to slot machines as is the case in other casinos. The gambling salons and lavish dining hall Le Train Bleu, decorated in the style of the Orient-Express, are truly impressive. The terrace overlooking sea is a haven of tranquillity, whether or not you have broken the bank!

La Terrasse (Bar du Vistamar) – *Square Beaumarchais* – ☏ *00 377 92 16 40 00* – *www.montecarloresort.com* – ⏱ *Daily noon - 2.30pm and 7pm-1am.* ⏱ *Closed Jul-Aug at lunch.* This famous bar has been patronised by many celebrities, such as Onassis and Maria Callas. Its superb terrace affords beautiful views of Monaco harbour. The specialities of the house are American cocktails, particularly those made with champagne!

Sass Café – *11 Avenue Princesse-Grace* – ☏ *00 377 93 25 52 00* – *www.sasscafe.com* – ⏱ *Daily 8pm-2am (restaurant; until midnight in winter), 11pm to dawn (piano-bar).* Exclusive bar-restaurant with a cosy atmosphere where members of the local jet set drop in for a fancy vodka or champagne cocktail before meeting up at Jimmy'z.

Le Jimmy'z – *Quai Princesse-Grace* – ☏ *00 377 92 16 22 77* – ⏱ *Daily 11pm to dawn. Reservations recommended.* It would be unthinkable to leave Monte-Carlo without having paid a visit to the legendary Jimmy'z. Formal evening wear is expected in this small but select club where the rich and wealthy love to congregate, whether they come from banking, advertising, fashion, film or the entertainment world... A unique, magic experience.

Stars'N'Bars – *6 Quai Antoine-1* – ☏ *00 377 93 50 95 95* – *www.starsnbars.com* – ⏱ *Daily 11am-midnight; 4am for the dance hall.* This is the great American bar of the moment, where the ambience is slightly more relaxed than in the Principality's other establishments. Stars'N'Bars caters for a younger clientele eager to drink beer, eat a hamburger or two, play billiards, surf on the Internet and dance away the night. The decoration features the paraphernalia of stars. Rock concerts are organised on a regular basis. Terrace with a view of Monaco harbour.

The Living Room Club – *7 Avenue des Spélugues* – ☏ *00 377 93 50 80 31 ou 93 50 88 10* – *monte-carlo.mc/livingroom* – ⏱ *Mon-Sat 11pm to dawn. Exceptionally open on Sun during the Formula 1 Grand Prix.* Select, high-class club where night owls meet up after leaving Jimmy'z. Try their special "Living Room cocktail" or one of their Champagnes. Piano bar music alternates with DJ evenings. Eclectic clientele.

Karé(ment) – *10 Avenue Princesse Grace, in the Grimaldi Forum* – ☏ *00 377 99 99 20 20* – *www.karement.mc* – ⏱ *Thu-Sat 11pm to dawn.* The hottest night spot of the moment is this contemporary tapas bar and dance club located in the Grimaldi Forum. The trendy clientele tend to be younger than in the average Monégasque venues.

SHOWS

lle des Etoiles, Le Sporting – *Avenue ...cesse Grace* – ☏ *00 377 96 06 36 36* – *...w.montecarloresort.com .* International stars perform regularly throughout the summer season at this Sporting Club venue with the retractible roof-top. *Jacket and tie required.*

Le Cabaret – *Place du Casino* – ☏ *00 377 92 16 36 36* – *www.montecarloresort.com* – ⏱ *Shows Wed-Sat from 10.30pm; bar/restaurant open from 8.30pm.* This cabaret run by the Monte-Carlo Casino presents a Bellydance Superstars revue. Exceptionally, it also stages concerts of jazz and contemporary pop.

TOURS AND PUBLIC TRANSPORTATION

BUS

C.A.M. – ☏ *00 377 97 70 22 22* – *www.cam.mc* – ⏱ *Service every 10 minutes from 7.30am-8.30pm* – *Tickets 1.45€ each or 3.50€ for an unlimited day pass.* Five regular bus lines that loop around the Principality. Maps available at the tourism office.

TAXI

Two main **taxi** stands are located near the casino and at the train station. ☏ *00 377 93 50 56 28 or 00 377 93 15 01 01.*

TOURIST TRAIN

Azur Express – *Avenue St-Martin, in front of the Musée Océanographique* – ☏ *00 377 92 05 64 38* – *www.visitmonaco.com* – ⏱ *Operates 10.30-6pm (5pm in winter).* ⏱ *Closed Jan and 15 Nov-26 Dec.* 🎫 *6€.* This small tourist train in Monégasque colours makes 30-minute round-trip journeys around the Principality. Commentary in four languages.

BOAT TRIPS

Aquavision – *Compagnie de Navigation et de Tourisme de Monaco – Quai des Etats-Unis* – ☏ *00 377 92 16 15 15* – *www.aquavision-monaco.com* ⏱ *Jul-Aug departures at 11am, 2.30pm, 4pm and 5.30pm; Jun and Sep daily except Mon departures at 11am, 2.30pm, 4pm; Apr, May, Oct daily except Mon departures at 2.30pm.* 🎫 *11€ (child 8€).* Boat trips affording views of the sea depths, and marine fauna and flora, with commentary in four languages.

HELICOPTER

Héli Air Monaco – *Héliport de Monaco-Fontvieille* – ☏ *00 377 92 05 00 50.* Regular daily service (6min) every 15min between Monaco and the Aéroport de Nice-Côte d'Azur. Also 10-minute sightseeing tours of Monaco (🎫 *50€ per person*) and daily flights between Monaco and Fréjus or St-Raphaël. For details call ☏ *04 94 51 83 83* (Fréjus tourist office).

SHOPPING

All the famous fashion brands have boutiques in Monte-Carlo.

Shops specialising in traditional goods are to be found in the narrow streets of the Rock (*Le Rocher*) opposite the palace.

The Boutique du Rocher in Avenue de la Madone is the official boutique for local arts and crafts.

CALENDAR OF EVENTS

Monte-Carlo Rally – *held every year since 1911 at the end of January.*

Feast of Ste-Dévote – *Monaco's Patron Saint feast, January 27.*

International Circus Festival – *January/February in Fontvieille.*

Sciaratù Carnival – *Monégasque festival during the week of Mardi Gras.*

Rose Ball – *Held every March since 1954 to benefit the Princess Grace Foundation.*

Spring Arts Festival – *Art, music, theatre and dance festival throughout April .*

International Tennis Masters Series – *Held every April.*

Monaco Grand Prix – *every May in the streets of the Principality on a winding circuit (3.145km/2mi).*

Monte-Carlo Golf Open – *on the hills of Mont Agel every June.*

Fireworks Festival – *July and August.*

National Day of Monaco – *Picturesque procession on the Rocher and other cultural spectacles November 19th.*

The museum is also a scientific research centre, and there are exhibits of marine laboratories, the technology of underwater exploration and applied oceanography.

Cathédrale

The neo-Romanesque building contains a number of early paintings of the **Nice School**★★, including a St Nicholas altarpiece by Louis Bréa.

Palais du Prince★

🕐 *Audio guided tours (30min) Jun-Sep: daily 9.30am-6.30pm; Oct: daily 10am-5.30pm.* 🕐 *Closed Nov-May.* ☞ *6€ (children: 3€)* ☎ *00 377 93 25 1831.*

The palace overlooks the **Place du Palais**★, a square ornamented with cannon presented by Louis XIV. With its medieval battlements and walls strengthened by Vauban, the palace makes a most picturesque composition.

An imposing gateway leads into the Court of Honour with its arcades; inside the Palace is the Throne Room and state apartments decorated with fine furniture and hung with signed portraits by Old Masters.

Monte-Carlo★★★

Europe's gambling capital was launched by François Blanc, director of the casino in Bad Homburg in Germany. The place's success has led to building at a very high density indeed, but Monte-Carlo retains its attractiveness with its luxurious casino, its sumptuous villas, its de luxe shops and its pretty gardens.

From the fine terrace **(terrasse**★★**)** of the Casino, the view extends from Monaco to the Bordighera headland in Italy.

Additional Sights

Jardin Exotique★★

🕐 *Mid-May to mid-Sep: daily 9am-7pm; mid-Sep to mid-May: 9am-6pm or until dusk, depending on the month.* 🕐 *Closed 19 Nov and 25 Dec.* ☞ *6.70€ (ticket includes visits to the grotte de l'Observatoire and the musée d'Anthropologie préhistorique).* ☎ *00 377 93 15 29 80. www.monte-carlo.mc/jardinexotique.*

The gardens cascade down a steep rock-face which has its own microclimate supporting a luxuriant variety of vegetation; there are many semi-desert species together with plants from the southern hemisphere.

Collection des voitures anciennes★

🄺 ⌖ 🕐 *Daily 10am-6pm.* 🕐 *Closed 25 Dec.* ☞ *6€ (children: 3€).* ☎ *00 377 92 05 28 56. www.palais.mc.*

Fine old carriages and vehicles from the royal collection are on display. There are also famous cars from the early 20C: Buick, Packard, etc...

▶▶ Grotte de l'Observatoire★ *As for visit to the Jardin exotique.* Musée d'Anthropologie préhistorique★ *As for visit to the Jardin exotique.* Jardins St-Martin★.

Musée Napoléonien★ 🕐 *Jun-Sep: daily 9.30am-6.30pm; Oct to mid-Nov: daily 10am-5.30pm; mid-Nov to end May: daily except Mon 10.30am-12.30pm, 2-5pm.* 🕐 *Closed 1 Jan, 25 Dec.* ☞ *4€.* ☎ *00 377 93 25 18 31. www.palais.mc.*

Musée des Poupées et Automates★.

Musée des Timbres et des Monnaies. ⌖ 🕐 *Jul-Sep: 10am-6pm; Oct-Jun: 10am* ☞ *3€.* ☎ *00 377 93 15 41 50.*

MONTAUBAN★

POPULATION 51 224

MICHELIN MAP 337 E 7

GREEN GUIDE LANGUEDOC ROUSSILLON TARN GORGES

On the boundary between the hillsides of Bas Quercy and the rich alluvial plains of the Garonne and the Tarn, the old bastide of Montauban, built with a geometric street layout, is an important crossroads and a good point of departure for excursions into the Aveyron gorges. It is an active market-town, selling fruit and vegetables from market gardens from all over the region.

The almost exclusive use of pink brick lends the buildings here a distinctive character, which is also found in most of the towns and villages in Bas Quercy and the Toulouse area.

Visit

Place Nationale★

The square, formerly the Place Royale, dates from the foundation of the town in the 12C.

After fire destroyed the wooden roofs or *couverts* above the galleries in 1614 and again in 1649, the arcades were rebuilt in brick in the 17C. The square features a double set of arcades with pointed- or round-arched vaulting. The inner gallery was a covered passageway while the outer gallery was occupied by market stalls.

The ornate elements and warm tones of the brick soften the overall effect, which would otherwise be rather austere, without destroying the stylistic homogeneity.

Musée Ingres ★

🕐 *Jul-Sep: daily 10am-6pm; Oct-Jun: daily except Mon 10am-noon, 2-6pm (mid-Oct to Palm Sunday: closed Sun morning).* 🕐 *Closed 1 Jan, 1 May, 14 Jul, 1 Nov, 25 Dec.* 🎫 *4€ (6€ during special exhibits).* ☎ *05 63 22 12 91.*

The museum is housed in what used to be the bishop's palace. The first floor features some of the artist's best examples of paintings: *Ruggiero freeing Angelica, Ossian's Dream, Jesus among the Doctors*, completed with a selection of his 4 000 **drawings**, displayed in rotation.

◗◗ Vieille ville★ (old town).

MONTHERMÉ★

POPULATION 2 866

MICHELIN MAP 306 K 3

GREEN GUIDE ALSACE LORRAINE CHAMPAGNE

Monthermé has a spectacular site★ just downstream from the meeting-point of the Semoy with the Meuse, which here has hollowed out a meander in the schists of the Rocroi Massif.

Sights

The setting of the little town can be enjoyed from three viewpoints in particular:

Longue Roche★★

1hr round trip on foot. A high spur on the outer side of the meander.

Roche aux 7 Villages★★

5min round trip on foot. Gives wide views★★ over the vast forested expanses of the high plateau of the Ardennes and of the industrial town of Château-Regnault on its r bend dominated by the Quatre Fils Aymon rock.

de la Tour★★

in round trip on foot. Formed from quartzite intruded into the schists.

Excursion

La Meuse Ardennaise★★ (The Meuse Gorge Through The Ardennes)

72km – 45mi. One of Europe's great rivers, 950km – 590 miles in length, the Meuse rises on the Langres uplands. It flows between the escarpment of the Côte des Bars and the dip-slope of the Côte de la Meuse, before penetrating the schists of the high plateau of the Ardennes in a deep gorge. Its meanders here mark the course it traced out in Tertiary times; since then the plateau has been uplifted, but the river has succeeded in entrenching itself in the schists, a process known as superimposition.

From Charleville-Mézières to Givet there is a succession of single meanders (Monthermé, Fumay, Chooz), double (Revin) and even triple ones (Charleville). The valley has long formed a corridor of human activity, with its water, rail and road communications, and with a skilled workforce producing engineering products and domestic appliances. At the beginning of the century, Monthermé was a centre of trade union activity, with considerable conflict between workers and employers.

Downstream from Monthermé the most interesting sites are: the **Roches de Laifour**★ and the **Dames de Meuse**★ opposite one another; Revin, where the old town and the industrial area each occupy their own peninsula; Fumay, with its old quarter, once famous for its quarries producing violet slate; Chooz, with its nuclear power stations; Givet, sited at the exit from a side valley originally fortified by Charles V and strengthened by Vauban. The composer Mehul (1763-1817) was born here, best known for his *Chant du Départ*, a patriotic song of the French Revolution.

MONT-LOUIS★

POPULATION 200

MICHELIN MAP 344 D 7

GREEN GUIDE LANGUEDOC ROUSSILLON TARN GORGES

Mont-Louis occupies a strategic site at the meeting point of three valleys. To the north is the valley of the Aude; its broad upper course is known as the **Capcir**. To the southwest is the Sègre, a tributary of the Ebro, which here flows through the **Cerdagne**, an upland basin; its elevated position (1 200m – 4 000ft) diminishes the apparent height of the surrounding peaks, and its high sunshine level led to the construction here in 1949 of the first "solar oven" (**four solaire**) using parabolic mirrors. Finally, to the west, is the valley of the Têt, which flows out of the Lac des Bouillouses to form the **Conflent**, the major routeway linking the Cerdagne with Perpignan.

Visit

♿ ⏱ *Guided tours* ⟶ *(1hr 30min) Jul-Aug: daily at 10.15am, 2pm, 3.30pm and 4pm.* ⟳ *4€ (children: 2€).* ☎ *04 68 04 21 97.*

The site's importance was confirmed following the **Treaty of the Pyrenees** in 1659, which, by restoring Roussillon to the French crown, made the Pyrenees the legal as well as the natural boundary of France. Louis XIV set about giving his newly acquired lands some more solid protection than that afforded by a signature; the great Vauban carried out his survey of Roussillon and the Cerdagne in 1679, and, from 1681 onwards, directed the construction of Mont-Louis.

Thus came into being this austere little fortified town, completely contained by its massive ramparts (**remparts**★) and protected by its citadel.

▶▶ Four solaire ⏱ *Guided tours* ⟶ *(40min) Jul-Aug: daily 10-11.30am, 2-5.30pm (last admission 6pm); Feb-Jun and Sep-Oct: daily 10-11am, 2-4pm (last admission 5pm); Nov-Jan: daily 10-11am, 2-3pm (last admission 4pm).* ⏱ *Closed 1 Jan, 25 Dec.* ⟳ *5.50€ (children: 4€).* ☎ *04 68 04 14 89. www.four-solaire.fr.*

MONTPELLIER★★

POPULATION 207 936

MICHELIN MAP 339 I 7

GREEN GUIDE LANGUEDOC ROUSSILLON TARN GORGES

By the 11C, Montpellier was already an inland port served by the Maguelone lagoon and by the Camargue canal. At the time of the first Crusades, trade with the eastern Mediterranean encouraged spice merchants to find out more about the medicinal and other plants they were dealing in; one way of doing this was to read the works of Hippocrates, and directly and indirectly this led to the founding here in 1137 of Europe's first medical school. In the space of a hundred years it equalled Salerno in reputation and achieved the status of a university in 1289.

The town had passed by marriage into the hands of the king of Aragon, but was bought back by Philippe VI de Valois in 1349. Louis XIV made it the capital of Lower Languedoc, opening a period of high architectural achievement.

Sights

Promenade du Peyrou★★

This was laid out in 1688 in the upper part of the town by Charles d'Aviler (1653-1700). In the 18C, the construction of the St-Clément aqueduct to supply the town's fountains led to the redevelopment of the site by Jean-Antoine Giral, who cut into the hill, built terraces and camouflaged the reservoir with a charming little octagonal temple. From here there is a fine view★ over the Garrigue and the Cévennes.

Le Vieux Montpellier★★

In the course of the 17C and 18C the townscape of old Languedoc houses was embellished by the addition of fine town residences (hôtels).

The **Hôtel des Trésoriers de la Bourse**★ has kept its fine staircase carried on four central pillars, a Louis XIII feature.

The **Hôtel de Varennes**★ integrates Romanesque and Gothic elements in a harmonious way.

The **Hôtel des Trésoriers de France** has a dignified courtyard with twin columns, superimposed orders and a staircase with a fine wrought-iron grille and straight flights with angle pendentives.

There are many other *hôtels*, with names like Manse, Beaulac, Baudon de Maury, Richer de Belleval, Cambacérès-Murles, Montcalm, St-Côme, each with its own character but all conforming to common rules of taste.

Musée Fabre★★ *Closed for renovation. Call for information* ☎ *04 67 14 83 00 or 04 67 66 13 46*– paintings.

Musée Atger★ *Wed and Fri: 1.30-5.45pm.* *Closed Aug, public holidays and school Christmas holidays. No charge.* ☎ *04 67 66 27 77*– drawings. Quartier Antigone★.

Excursion

La Grande Motte★★★

The resort built in 1967 on poor agricultural land, mostly dunes, between the Or and Ponant marshes, is an original venture. The complex was designed and built by a team of architects and engineers led by Jean Balladur. The design of the main buildings is resolutely modern; the honeycomb pyramids are south-facing. The villas are built in the Provençal style or around an inner courtyard.

It is a holiday-maker's paradise: beaches, fishing, water-sports, seafront promenades, pedestrian precincts and shopping-mall.

Montpellier - Address Book

TRANSPORTATION

Tramway – *Transports de l'Agglomération de Montpellier*, ☎ 04 67 22 87 87. www.tam-way.com

A brand new Montpellier tram has joined local bus lines, allowing passengers to travel just about anywhere within the city and beyond in just a few minutes.

For coin categories, see the Legend at the back of the guide.

EATING OUT

A QUICK BITE

☞ **Simple Simon** – *1 r. des Trésoriers-de-France* - ☎ *04 67 66 03 43* - ⏱ *closed Sun May-Oct and in the evening – reservation recommended.* Simply British, Simple Simon serves a medley of British pastries, an Indian or sweet and savoury dish for lunch, salads in summer and soup in winter. Perfectly cosy setting, with tablemats and a thick carpet. Languedoc wines by the glass, lest we forget our French!

A LEISURELY MEAL

☞☞ **The Salmon Shop** – *5 r. de la Petite-Loge* - ☎ *04 67 66 40 70* - ⏱ *closed Sun and Mon lunchtime - reservation recommended at weekends – 11.28€ lunch - 22.41/36.44€.* Steak-lovers, beware! Salmon rules supreme here, and it is served in every sauce imaginable with one accompanying vegetable: homemade French-fried potatoes. The singular decor represents the interior of a trapper's cabin: wood-panelled walls, old skis, a wooden kayak overhead, old rifles and a totem pole. Relaxed atmosphere.

☞☞ **C'an Jose** – *8 bis r. du Petit-Saint-Jean* - ☎ *04 67 60 70 71* - ⏱ *closed 14 Jul-15 Aug, Sun and Mon.* This establishment in Old Montpellier houses all of Catalonia and the Baleares under its roof. Decorated in yellow and red, naturally, the dining room is covered in photographs of the island of Minorca. Tapas and Catalan, Spanish and Balearic cuisine are served here. Buen provecho!

☞☞ **Le Petit Jardin** – *20 r. Jean-Jacques-Rousseau* - ☎ *04 67 60 78 78* - contact@petit-jardin.com - ⏱ *closed Jan and Mon.* Located on a narrow street in the renovated Écusson quarter, this charming little house welcomes diners to its appealing terrace-garden whenever the weather obliges. Enjoy tasty regional fare as you admire the cathedral from your vantage point under the trees.

☞☞ **Les Bains de Montpellier** – *6 r. Richelieu* - ☎ *04 67 60 70 87* – ⏱ *closed in Feb, Toussaint and Christmas holidays, Mon lunchtime and Sun – reservation recommended.* Whether seated in the shade of the courtyard palm trees, beneath the large glass roof or in one of the little drawing rooms, there's an ambience to suit every guest in the wonderfully well-restored old 'Parisian baths'. Cuisine made from fresh market produce.

WHERE TO STAY

☞ **Hôtel de la Comédie** – *1 bis r. Baudin* - ☎ *04 67 58 43 64* – hoteldelacomedie@wanadoo.fr - *20 rms.* Located just off of La Place de la Comédie, this recently overhauled hotel with a 19C facade offers pleasingly modern bedrooms. Located in a lively Montpellier neighbourhood, it is an excellent starting point for discovering the city. Relaxed ambience.

☞ **Hôtel du Palais** – *3 r. du Palais* – ☎ *04 67 60 47 38 - 26 rms.* This family hotel near the Peyrou gardens and the Place de la Canourgue has small rooms that are stylish and well kept.

☞☞ **Hôtel Maison Blanche** – *1796 av. Pompignane* - ☎ *04 99 58 20 70* – hotelmaisonblanche@wanadoo.fr - 🅿 - *35 rms.* Tempted by a brief stay in Scarlett O'Hara country? This colonial-style wood house comes as something of a surprise in this part of the world. Jean-Edern Hallier sang a song about it; with its gangways and sculpted friezes it will no doubt captivate you as well. Spacious rooms.

☞☞ **Chambre d'hôte Domaine de Saint-Clément** – *34980 St-Clément-de-Rivière – 10km/6mi N of Montpellier on D 17 then D112* - ☎ *04 67 66 70 89* - calista.bernabe@wanadoo.fr - ⏱ *closed Dec-Feb* - 🍽 - *5 rms.* Peace and quiet are guaranteed in this fine 18C farmhouse 10 minutes from the centre of Montpellier. The comfortable bedrooms, decorated with antique furniture and modern paintings, overlook the garden or the swimming pool. Do not miss the fine Portuguese azulejo tiles on the patio.

SIT BACK AND RELAX

Dorian's Kawa – *12 r. Four-des-Flammes* - ☎ *04 67 66 18 71* - *Mon-Sat 8am-7pm* – ⏱ *closed Aug and public holidays.* A tearoom to make a note of – the coffee is excellent and the owner very friendly. The shop sells coffeepots, tea services and English china. Ideal for a break or a tête-à-tête.

L'Heure Bleue – *1 r. de la Carbonnerie* - ☎ *04 67 66 41 05* - ⏱ *Tues-Sat noon-7pm.* This literary tearoom in an 18C mansion is also an art gallery and second-hand shop; as such its decor includes a lavish collection of sculptures and curios. Home-baked pastries and nearly 30 varieties of tea.

STOPPING FOR A DRINK

Café de la Mer – *5 pl. du Marché-aux-Fleurs* - ☎ *04 67 60 79 65* - ⏱ *end Jun-end Aug: Mon-Sat 8am-2am, Sun and holidays*

3pm-2am; rest of the year: 8am-1am, Sun and holidays: 3pm-1am. A large, popular café in the centre of town. Its decor of beautiful coloured mosaics and the large sunny terrace make this a fashionable meeting point for Montpellier residents of all ages.

Grand Café Riche – *Pl. de la Comédie -* ☎ *04 67 54 71 44 -* ◷ *daily 8am-1am; summer: 6am-2am.* This century-old café is an institution in Montpellier. Its large terrace provides a front row seat for observing street entertainment on the Place de la Comédie. Art exhibitions are frequently held here.

La Pleine Lune – *28 r. du Fg-Figuerolles -* ☎ *04 67 58 03 40 -* ◷ *daily 10.30am-1am.* This bar in the Plan Cabannes district is frequented by an inimitable clientele of artists, neighbours and original characters. Happenings, exhibitions by local artists and concerts are organized here regularly. An officially picturesque establishment!

ON THE TOWN

In Montpellier, a student's city, many bars and music cafés are partial to new trends in music and it is quite common to discover a rap concert being performed round the corner from a bourgeois manor. The city's cultural landscape is very diverse, with its jazz enthusiasts, accordion fans and lovers of salsa or classical music.

Rockstore – *20 r. de Verdun -* ☎ *04 67 06 80 00 - www.rockstore.fr –* ◷ *bars: Mon-Sat 6pm-4am; disco: 11pm-4am.* This hotspot of Montpellier nightlife hosts numerous rock groups and organizes techno, rap and sound system evenings. With the huge red American car stuck above the entrance, the techno and rock bars and the disco, the decor mirrors the musical programming.

Centre dramatique national – *Domaine de Grammont, Avenue Albert-Einstein –* ☎ *04 67 99 25 25 : reserv. by phone: 04 67 60 05 45.*

Opéra Comédie – *11 bd Victor-Hugo -* ☎ *04 67 60 19 99 -* ◷ *tickets: Mon 2pm-6pm, Tue-Sat noon-6pm, Sundays of performances – closed Aug.*

Zénith – *Av. Albert-Einstein -* ☎ *04 67 64 50 00 - www.zenith-montpellier.com – performance schedule variable -* ◷ *closed Aug.* Variety and rock shows.

SHOPPING

Aux Croquants de Montpellier – *7 r. du Faubourg-du-Courreau -* ☎ *04 67 58 67 38 –* ◷ *Tue-Sun 7am-7pm, Mon 7am-1pm and 4-7pm ;* ◷ *closed Aug.* This tiny shop has been a mecca for biscuit lovers for over a century with an extensive array of confections available.

Aux Gourmets – *2 r. Clos-René -* ☎ *04 67 58 57 04.* Run by the Fournier family for over 45 years, this shop close to Place de la Comedie offers a wide variety of sweets and cakes.

Librairie Sauramps – *Allée Jules-Milhau (Le Triangle) – Tramway Comédie -* ☎ *04 67 06 78 78 - www.sauramps.com -* ◷ *Mon-Sat 10am-7pm -* ◷*closed public holidays.* This vast, comprehensive bookstore carries a good choice of publications about the area.

Markets – Food markets are open every morning in centre city in the halles (covered markets) Castellane and Arceaux, on the Esplanade Charles-de-Gaulle, the halles Laissac, the new halles Jacques-Cœur in the Antigone district and on the Plan Cabannes. Organic produce is sold Tuesdays and Saturdays Place des Arceaux. On the 3rd Saturday of each month, used-book sellers gather on Rue des Étuves. Avenue Samuel-Champlain in the Antigone district holds a farmers' market Sunday mornings.

A flower market Tuesdays and a flea market Sundays are held in the west at La Paillade, Esplanade de la Mosson.

Maison régionale des vins et produits du terroir – *34 R. St-Guilhem -* ☎ *04 67 60 40 41 -* ◷ *daily (except Sun in Dec) 9.30am-8pm.* All the finest produce of the region is represented here.

CALENDAR OF EVENTS

Montpellier and the surrounding area are rich in all manner of festivals

Festival international Montpellier danse – ☎ *04 67 60 83 60 – www.montpellierdanse.com -* ◷ *late Jun-early Jul.* Traditional music and dance.

Festival de Radio France et Montpellier Languedoc-Roussillon – ☎ *04 67 02 02 01 – www.festivalradiofrancemontpellier.com - first 3wks of Jul.* Concerts, chamber music, jazz, world music...

Festival international cinéma méditerranéen – ☎ *04 99 13 73 73 – www.cinemed.tm.fr -* ◷ *late Oct-early Nov.* Film festival.

Le **MONT-ST-MICHEL**★★★

POPULATION 72

MICHELIN MAP 303 C 8

GREEN GUIDE NORMANDY

Mont-St-Michel has been called "the Wonder of the Western World"; its extraordinary site, its rich and influential history and its glorious architecture combine to make it the most splendid of all the abbeys of France.

▶ **Orient Yourself:** Mont-St-Michel is a granite island about 900m – 984yd round and 80m – 262ft high. As the bay is already partially silted up, the mount is usually to be seen surrounded by huge sand banks which shift with the tides and often reshape the mouths of the neighbouring rivers. It is linked to the mainland by a causeway which was built in 1877.

🅿 **Parking:** Parking is available outside the Tour du Roi near the Porte de l'Avancée.

A Bit of History

The rock of the archangel – At the beginning of the 8C St Michael appeared to Aubert, the bishop of Avranches. Aubert founded an oratory on an island then known as Mont Tombe. This was soon replaced by an abbey, which adopted the Benedictine Rule in the 10C, thereby assuring its importance. Two centuries later the Romanesque abbey reached its peak of development. In the 13C, following a fire, a great rebuilding in Gothic style took place, known as *la Merveille* – the Marvel.

It was then, however, that the Hundred Years War intervened, one of the most critical periods in French history. The greater part of the kingdom, the West, the North and the East passed into other hands. The population suffered decades of misery. The framework of the state weakened to the point at which Henry V of England managed to get himself crowned, in Paris, as King of France. Charles VII himself, son of a madman, was merely a pale incarnation of the idea of royalty.

This sombre century was nevertheless the period when Mont-St-Michel enjoyed its greatest influence. Even though the English blockaded it and besieged it twice (for a time they occupied the adjacent Rocher de Tombelaine), the Mount was the only place in the whole of northern and western France to avoid falling into the hands of the invader, and at no point did it cease being a destination for pilgrimages. The archangel who "watches over God's chosen people" (Book of Daniel) evidently did his work well. Joan of Arc was well aware of all this; her rallying cry was *"St-Michel-Montjoie!"*. St Michael fitted into the plans of Louis XI for strengthening the prestige of his aristocracy when, in 1469, the King founded the Order of St Michael to rival the Order of the Garter created in 1348 by Edward III, and the Order of the Golden Fleece instituted in 1429 by Philip the Good of Burgundy.

It is thus hardly surprising that many sanctuaries have been dedicated to the archangel, nor that there are no less than 76 localities named after him in France.

Visit

L'Abbaye (Abbey)★★★

The original architectural style of the Abbey was determined by the constraints imposed by the rock on which it was erected. The various elements of the complex (barbican, fort, crypt, chapel, cellars, great hall) all had to be built above one another rather in the manner of a skyscraper. Crowned as it is by the Abbey church and the buildings of the Merveille (c 1225), the result bears little resemblance to the conventionally-planned Benedictine monastery.

Mt-St-Michel

Le Mont-St-Michel - Address Book

For coin categories, see the Legend at the back of the guide.

EATING OUT

Auberge de la Baie – *La Rive - 50170 Ardevon - 3km/1.8mi SE of Mont-St-Michel dir. Pontaubault -* 02 33 68 26 70 - *closed Nov and Tue-Wed except during July-Aug.* This restaurant on a departmental road is a welcome break for those who wish to escape from the bustling tourism of Mont-St-Michel, at least for an hour or two. On the menu: traditional and regional dishes, plus a short list of galettes.

Croix Blanche – 02 33 60 14 04 - *closed 1 Jan to 2 Feb.* A tall building housing a main dining room (exposed stones and beams) on the second floor, and a pleasant little terrace opening onto the road circling Mont-St-Michel. A choice of fixed-price menus. Small, well-furnished rooms; some look out onto the ocean.

La Gourmandise – *21 rte du Mont-St-Michel - 50170 Beauvoir - 4km/2.4mi S of Mont-St-Michel -* 02 33 58 42 83 - *closed Nov to Jan and Tue except Jul-Aug .* This tiny village is enlivened by this Breton house transformed into a crêperie. Simple decor, lit up by large bay windows. The extensive menu is concentrated around a choice of crepes and galettes.

La Sirène – 02 33 60 08 60 - *closed 10 Jan to 2 Feb, 15 Nov to 20 Dec and Fri.* Take the spiral staircase to enter the crêperie in this 14C house that was an inn for many years. The frosted-glass windows, their panes separated by metal mullions, confirm the genuine flavour of the place.

Pré Salé – *Rest. belonging to the Hôtel Mercure - 2km/1.2mi S of Mont-St-Michel via D 976 -* 02 33 60 14 18 - *contact@hotelmercure-montsaintmichel. com -* *closed 12 Nov to 6 Feb.* Located along the River Couesnon at the start of the dike, the Hôtel Mercure welcomes you into its bright dining room, recently renovated with tables set comfortably apart from each other. Try the delicious salt-meadow (pré salé) meat from Mont-St-Michel Bay.

La Promenade – *Pl. du Casino - 50610 Jullouville -* 02 33 90 80 20 - *closed Mon and Tue - reserv. advisable.* It would be difficult to find a better view of Mont-St-Michel Bay than that offered by this elegant restaurant-tearoom located on the ground floor of the former casino hotel (1881). Handsome antique furniture and tableware. Menu with an accent on seafood.

WHERE TO STAY

Mme Louet-Gillet Bed and Breakfast – *Le Val-St-Revert - 35610 Roz-sur-Couesnon - 15km/9.3mi SW of Mont-St-Michel via D 797, the coast road to St-Malo -* 02 99 80 27 85 - *- 5 room.* This family house overlooks the bay and offers a beautiful view of Mont-St-Michel and the surrounding countryside. Five rooms where an old world charm lingers on: three on the sea side and a more recent and brighter one with a terrace facing the garden.

Amaryllis Bed and Breakfast – *Le Bas-Pays - 50170 Beauvoir - 2.5km/1.5mi S of Mont-St-Michel dir. Pontorson -* 02 33 60 09 42 - *- 5 rooms -* . This recently built stone house was designed as a B&B. The impeccably clean rooms feature well-equipped bathrooms and a furnished terrace. An extra treat: you can visit the farm next door.

La Tour Brette – *8 r. Couesnon - 50170 Pontorson - 9km/5.4mi S of Mont-St-Michel -* 02 33 60 10 69 - *closed 14-22 Mar, 1-20 Dec and Wed except Jul-Aug -* 10 rooms- *- restaurant* . This small, centrally located hotel is named after the tower that used to protect Normandy from the Duchy of Brittany's assaults. The rooms are not very large but they've just been renovated. Restaurant in a simple setting with a long, traditional menu.

La Bergerie Bed and Breakfast – *La Poultière - 35610 Roz-sur-Couesnon - 16km/9.9mi SW of Mont-St-Michel via D 797, the coast road to St-Malo -* 02 99 80 29 68 - *- 5 rooms.* Located in the former sheepfold, these rooms are not particularly charming, but they are comfortable and benefit from the peaceful atmosphere of the small hamlet. The kitchen set aside for guests is very much appreciated as is the garden where sheep still graze. A self-catering cottage is also available.

Bretagne – *R. Couesnon - 50170 Pontorson - 4km/2.4mi S of Mont-St-Michel via D 976 -* 02 33 60 10 55 - *closed 20 Jan to 5 Feb - 16 rooms -* *- restaurant* . Regional-style house. Admire the lovely 18C wood panels, the grey-marble fireplace and the plate-warming radiator (very unusual!) in the first room. Cosy, typically British bar and spacious, pleasantly furnished rooms.

Les Vieilles Digues – *Rte du Mont-St-Michel - 50170 Beauvoir - 3km/1.8mi S of Mont-St-Michel dir. Pontorson -* 02 33 58 55 30 - *closed Jan - 7 rooms.* This pretty stone house boasts spacious rooms thoughtfully furnished with handsome pieces. The room with a view of Mont-St-Michel is, naturally, a favourite. Agreeable half-timbered breakfast room. Landscaped garden.

e-forme de l'Ouest

m this terrace, there are extensive views over the bay, including the Rocher de
mbelaine, and on 8 November, the autumn Feast of St Michael, the sun sets directly
ehind Mont Dol, where the Saint once wrestled with the Devil.

Église★★

There is a striking contrast between the stern character of the Romanesque nave and
the well-lit Flamboyant choir. The axis of the sanctuary is aligned on the rising sun on
8 May, the spring Feast of St Michael according to the eastern calendar.

La Merveille★★★

This is the name given to the group of buildings on the north side of the mount.
The Guests' Hall (**salle des Hôtes**★) is a masterpiece of High Gothic.
Suspended between sea and sky, the cloisters (**cloître**★★★), with their slim columns
in pink granite arranged in a quincunx pattern, make a magic garden conducive to
serenity and inner joy.
The Refectory (**Réfectoire**★) is filled with light from its recessed windows. It hangs
45m – 148ft high, a bold achievement on the part of its architect who was unable to
use buttresses on the sheer rock-face.
The vast Knights' Hall (**Salle des Chevaliers**★) is divided into four parts. It may be
so named after the chivalric Order established here.

Jardins de l'Abbaye★

From the gardens there is a view of the north face of the mount, the "most beautiful
wall in all the world," according to Victor Hugo.

◑◑   La ville★★ (town) – Grande-Rue★, Remparts★★.

Château de MONTSÉGUR★

MICHELIN MAP 343 I 7

GREEN GUIDE LANGUEDOC ROUSSILLON TARN GORGES

**It was on this fearsome peak that the last episode of the Albigensian Crusade
took place, when its Cathar defenders were massacred and Languedoc eclipsed
by the central power of the French kingdom.**

A Bit of History

At the beginning of the 13C the **Cathars** built a castle here to replace an old, since-
demolished fortress. Forty years later, the stronghold was occupied by some 400 soldiers and adherents to the faith, from whose ranks was drawn the fierce band which
marched on Avignonet (70km – 44mi north) to put to the sword the members of the
Inquisition meeting there. This action sealed the fate of Montségur; in the absence of
Louis IX who was dealing with disturbances in Saintonge, Blanche of Castille ordered
the Crusaders to put the castle to siege. On 2 March 1244 the resistance of the defenders was overcome, but 200 of the faithful refused to retract their beliefs, even after
being granted a fortnight in which to consider the matter. On 16 March, they were
brought down from the mountain to be burnt on a huge pyre at a place known from
then on as the "Field of the Burnt Ones" (Camp des Crémats).

Catharism – the name is derived from a Greek word meaning "pure" – was based on
the principle of the total separation of Good and Evil, of the spiritual from the material.
Its adherents comprised ordinary believers and the *"Perfecti,"* the latter living lives
of exemplary purity in the light of God. Their austerity contrasted awkwardly with
the laxity of the clergy. Their bitter enemy was St Dominic, who died 23 years before
the events of Montségur.

The rebuilding of the **château** was begun in the year following the siege, on the
same **site**★★. It was the third stronghold to be built here, and its ruins crown the
summit (pog) today. Not long after its reconstruction, it became part of the line of
French defences facing the kingdom of Aragon. Its great keep and its fine staircas
concealed from the outside, bear witness to the skill of its builders.

◑◑   Musée archéologique.

MOULINS★

POPULATION 22 799

MICHELIN MAP 326 H 3

GREEN GUIDE AUVERGNE THE RHÔNE VALLEY

Moulins is the capital of the Bourbonnais region. The city was founded by the Bourbon lords at the end of the 11C in the course of their efforts to extend their territory in the direction of Autun, and to control the crossing of the Allier. Over time, the Bourbons' clever manipulation of military, political and marital alliances (Beatrice de Bourbon married Robert, the son of Louis IX) helped them rise first to the rank of counts, then, in 1327, to dukes. In the 15C, their court boasted musicians like Jean Ockeghem, sculptors like Jacques Morel, Michel Colombe and his followers, and above all the painter known as the **Master of Moulins**.

Once Burgundy and Brittany had been incorporated into the French kingdom, the continued independent existence of the Bourbonnais, albeit as a vassal dukedom, became an irritant to the king. François I took advantage of the supposed treason of Charles III, the Ninth Duke, to confiscate his estates. Charles sought the aid of both the Emperor Charles V and England's Henry VIII, and confronted the armies of his sovereign in a series of battles at Pavia, Milan, and finally at Rome, where he was killed (1527). The Bourbonnais was attached to the French Crown in 1531.

Visit

Triptyque du Maître de Moulins★★★

🕐 *Guided tours* 🔊 *(20min) mid-Mar to mid-Oct: daily 9.30am-noon, 2-6pm, Sun 2-6pm; mid-Oct to mid-Mar: daily except Tue 10-noon, 2-5.30pm, Sun 2-5.30pm. Last admission 30min before closing.* 🕐 *Closed 1 Jan, 1 May, 14 Jul, 25 Dec.* 📧 *2€ offering suggested.* ☎ *04 70 20 89 65.*

The **Triptych by the Master of Moulins** is the cathedral's most important work of art, a triumph of late-Gothic painting. It dates from about 1498. The Master has never been conclusively identified; Jean Bourdichon, Jean Perréal and Jean Prévost have all been suggested, while contemporary expert opinion favours Jean Hey. The poses of the figures depicted suggest the Flemish School, while their faces recall the work of Florentine masters. The figures of the donors are painted in a very realistic manner, in contrast to the idealised treatment of the central panel. The painting appears to be rich in symbolism, the use of the numbers 7 and 12, in particular, representing the Gothic idea of perfection.

🔊🔊 Cathédrale★ – stained glass★★. Jaquemart★ (Belltower). Mausolée du Duc de Montmorency★ 🕐 *Guided tours* 🔊 *Jul-Aug: Tue, Thu, and Sat: 4.15pm; Apr-Jun and Sep: Sat 4.15pm.* 📧 *2.40€. Call the Service du Patrimoine in advance.* ☎ *04 70 48 01 32.* Musée d'Art et d'Archéologie 🕐 *Jul-Aug: Wed-Mon 10am-1pm, 2-6pm; Sep-Jun: Wed-Mon 10am-noon, 2-6pm* 🕐 *Closed Tue,1 Jan, 1 May, 25 Dec.* 📧 *3€.* ☎ *04 70 20 48 47. www.musee-moulins.fr.*

MULHOUSE★★

POPULATION 223 856

MICHELIN MAP 315 I 10

GREEN GUIDE ALSACE LORRAINE CHAMPAGNE

Mulhouse (= Mill-house) became a free Imperial city as early as the end of the 13C, and in the 16C formed part of the *Decapolis,* the league of 10 towns of Alsace.

A Bit of History

n the 16C – 17C the Habsburg distrusted this industrial and commercial town, and s resources remained untapped; in addition the Reformed church condemned entation and preached austerity. Between 1466 and 1586, the city's indepen-t spirit led it into an association with the cantons of Switzerland. It joined France ntarily in 1798.

Mulhouse was already established as a textile centre, when, in 1746, three of its citizens, J-J Schmaltzer, the painter J-H Dollfus and the merchant S Koechlin together founded the first mill producing calico cotton fabrics. Their capital investment, use of machinery, division of labour and sales organisation all foreshadowed the techniques of modern large-scale industry. Production advanced by leaps and bounds. In 1812 the Dollfus and Mieg mill was the first to install steam power.

Visit

Hôtel de Ville ★★

Since 1558, the City Hall has symbolised Mulhouse's civic and political liberties. It is a unique example in France of a building (1552) of the Rhineland Renaissance by a Basle architect; the exterior is decorated solely by artists from Konstanz. It was aptly described as a "splendid, golden palace" by the writer Montaigne. The Town Hall was remodelled in 1698 by the local architect, Jeaxn Gabriel, who added the allegorical figures. It is this later decoration which has been restored to its former glory and can be admired today. The coats of arms of the Swiss cantons painted on the main façade on either side of the covered double flight of steps recall the historical link with Switzerland.

Musée de l'Automobile – Collection Schlumpf ★★★

Kids ♿ ⏲ *Apr-Oct: 10am-6pm; Feb-Mar and Nov-Dec: 10am-5pm; Jan: Mon-Fri 1-5pm, Sat-Sun 10am-5pm.* ⏲ *Closed 25 Dec.* 👓 *10€ (children 7-12 years: 5€).* ☎ *03 89 33 23 21. www.collection-schlumpf.com.*

The splendid collection of 500 old vehicles (including those in storage) was lovingly built up over the years by the mill-owning Schlumpf brothers. Industrial troubles and over-enthusiastic buying of expensive items for the collection led to bankruptcy, the acquisition of the museum by an association and its opening to the public in 1982. The collection evokes the history of the motor car over more than a century, from the steam-powered Jacquot (1878) to the Citroën Xénia "2000", and presents 98 European marques including unique or very rare examples. Most of the vehicles are in working order; and several have had famous owners such as French President Poincaré (Panhard X26), King Leopold of Belgium (Bugatti 43 sports car) and Charlie Chaplin (Rolls-Royce Phantom III).

The motor vehicles are aligned along alleyways lined with lamp-posts dating from the 1900s, replicas of those lining the Pont Alexandre-III in Paris. Some of them are real works of art, with elegant bodywork (Peugeot Coach 174, 1927), flowing lines (Bugatti Type 46, with streamlined bodywork, 1933), distinctive wheels, hub-caps, joints (Gardner-Serpollet), beautifully designed radiator grilles (coach Alfa Romeo & C, 1936), radiator caps (Hispano-Suiza stork), famous manufacturers' nameplates (Isotta-Fraschini), fine materials and trims (Renault NM Landaulet, 1924), or controls (Delage F two-seater racer, 1908).

The Bugattis form a collection within the collection. There are some 120 versions of the marque, racing cars, sports cars, luxury cars. Ettore Bugatti (1881-1947) founded his works in Molsheim in 1909. 340 patents attest to the quality and finish of his vehicles which dominated the circuits and won 3 000 first prizes. The highlights of the collection are a Royale limousine, and the Napoleon Coupé owned by Ettore Bugatti himself which ranks among the most prestigious cars.

Other rival marques include Panhard et Levasseur (the 1893 model was the first to be marketed with a catalogue setting out the available models and their variants together with their price), Mercedes (the 300SL model with "butterfly" doors, an exceptional touring car), Alfa Romeo (Disco volante, 1953; only three vehicles were made), Rolls-Royce (the legendary Silver Ghost; some models had silver-plated accessories), Porsche, Ferrari, Gordini, etc... The evolution of the French motor industry is also traced: Peugeot, Renault, Citroën before the Second World War; also the range of other marques which have disappeared owing to consolidation: Ravel from Besançon, Zedel from Pontarlier, Vermorel from Villefrance-sur-Saône, Clément-Bayard from Mézières, and Pilain from Lyon.

Musée français du Chemin de fer★★★

♿ ⚷ *Closed temporarily. Call in advance for times and charges.* ☎ *03 89 42 83 33.*

This well-presented collection relates the evolution of the railways from their origin to the present day. In addition to the different engines, the collection also shows wide variety of equipment: signals, tracks, switches, coupler heads, swing brid etc. In the main hall, visitors will discover the fascinating world of railways: v

films, animated presentations, possibility of going beneath trains, ɪ.
cab or coaches... Highlights include the 1844 Saint-Pierre engine, mac
which ran between Paris and Rouen; the 1852 **Crampton** high-speed tr
– 75 mph); the 232 UI (1949), the last steam engine built. Electric trains are als
with the 1900 first electric version also known as the "boîte à sel" (salt box,
was built to tow trains between the Parisian stations of Orsay and Austerlitz. V
should not miss the BB 9004, the fastest train in 1955, the Bugatti "Présidentie
the **Michelin** tyre-equipped XM 5005 railcars.

◖◗ Musée de l'Impression sur Étoffes★⅙ ◷ *Tue-Sun 10am-noon, 2-6pm.* ◷ *Closeᴅ
Mon, 1 Jan, 1 May, 25 Dec.* ⌆ *6€ (12-15 years: 2€).* ☎ *03 89 46 83 00.*

Musée Historique★★ ◷ *Jul and Aug: Wed-Mon 10am-noon, 2-6.30pm; Sep-Jun:
Wed-Mon 10am-noon, 2-6pm.* ◷ *Closed Tue, 1 Jan, Good Friday, Easter Mon, 1 May,
Mon after Pentecost, 14 Jul, 1 and 11 Nov, 25 and 26 Dec. No charge.* ☎ *03 89 33
78 17.*

Électropolis★ ▦⅙ ◷ *Tue-Sun 10am-6pm.* ◷ *Closed Mon, 1 Jan, Good Friday,
1 May, 1 and 11 Nov, 25 and 26 Dec.* ⌆ *7.50€ (children: 3.50€).* ☎ *03 89 32 48 50.
www.electropolis.tm.fr – musée de l'énergie électrique.*

Parc zoologique et botanique★★ (Zoological and Botanical Gardens) ⅙ ◷ *May-
Aug: 9am-7pm; Apr and Sep: 9am-6pm; Oct-Mar: 9am-5pm; Dec-Feb: 10am-4pm.*
⌆ *8€ (low season and children: 4€)* ☎ *03 89 31 85 10.* Musée du Papier-peint★
(at Rixheim, 6km – 4mi east of Mulhouse) – wallpaper.

Excursions

Collégiale St-Thibaut de Thann★★

Illustration ⌖ *See Introduction: Art – Architecture. 22km – 14mi west.* Its Gothic architecture (14C – early 16C) marks the continuous evolution towards the Flamboyant
style. The west façade is pierced by a splendid doorway (**portail★★**), 15m – 50ft high;
the soaring tympanum surmounting two doors, each topped by a small tympanum,
is noteworthy.

Interior – The height of the nave and chancel is remarkable. The deep chancel is
adorned with 15C statues of the 12 Apostles in multi-coloured stone. It boasts a superb
set of 51 oak stalls (**stalles★★**) dating from the 15C. The carved decoration reveals
the exuberant fantasy of the medieval craftsmen: foliage, gnomes, comic figures
(this unusual feature is described in the chapter on Architecture in the Introduction). The
church is well lit by eight fine 15C stained-glass windows (**verrières★★**).

Église de Murbach★★

21km – 12mi northwest. Built around 1145, this is one of the finest Romanesque
churches in Alsace. It lost its nave in the course of rebuilding in 1738, but its east end
and transepts still stand in the attractive setting of the wooded Guebwiller valley.
Dominated by the transept towers, the flat apse is a masterpiece of harmonious
design. Supported by a number of shallowly-projecting buttresses, it is covered with
lively patterns of arcading. The influence of the great basilicas of the Rhineland is
apparent, as is a decorative sense derived from the master builders of Pisa and Lucca
some 80 years previously, and exemplified here in the contrasting play of light and
dark arches.

Ottmarsheim

7.5km – 5mi east. Although much-restored, the church (**église★**) here goes back to
around 1040. Its layout recalls Charlemagne's chapel at Aachen, a type of plan rarely
found elsewhere, and known as Carolingian or Ottonian. On two levels around a
central eight-sided cupola, it consists of two concentric octagons, the second serving as a kind of ambulatory to the central part of the building. In the east chapels of
both levels are 15C frescoes.

The hydro-electric power station (**centrale hydro-électrique★**) with its impressive
feeder-channel and 185m – 600ft locks is one of the key features of the Grand Canal of
Alsace, itself part of a wider scheme for the management of the Rhine for navigation
and power generation.

NANCY★★★

POPULATION 310 628

MICHELIN MAP 307 I 6

GREEN GUIDE ALSACE LORRAINE CHAMPAGNE

...pital of the industrial area of Lorraine, Nancy is sited on the low-lying land ...etween the River Meurthe and the Moselle Heights (Côtes de Moselle).

▶ **Orient Yourself:** The Old Town is the historic heart of the city, centred on place St-Epvre. When extended outside its original gates, the New Town was born. Nancy is listed as a "Town of Art and History" with brochures and guided tours available from the tourist office to help you make the most of your tour of the town.

🕓 **Organizing Your Time:** Discover Nancy by taxi on one of five routes that features commentary recorded by the tourist office.

A Bit of History

The city was founded in the 11C but its history really begins with the death of Charles le Téméraire (the Bold), Duke of Burgundy, on 5 January 1477. Charles had spent a fortune on undertakings to enhance his prestige and, in an attempt to counter the financial pressures exerted by the Florentine bankers who supported Louis XI, he planned to consolidate his Flemish and Burgundian possessions. In 1476, Charles had ruthlessly incorporated Lorraine into his dukedom, but the standard of revolt was raised in Nancy following his defeat by the Swiss at Murten. Furious, he hastened back to put down the rebellion, but was killed in the course of operations. His body, half devoured by wolves, was found in the freezing mud of an icy pond.

Forty-five years later, the Dukes of Lorraine added Renaissance ornament to their Flamboyant Gothic palace and provided it with a new gallery. To the north of the Triumphal Arch – Arc de Triomphe – the district now known as the old quarter of Nancy (Vieux Nancy) began to take shape.

17C Nancy – Charles III encouraged the laying-out of a new district to the south of Rue Ste-Catherine and Rue Stanislas. The new town (ville neuve) was planned on a regular pattern; it was depicted by the artist Claude Gellée, known as **Claude Lorrain** (1600-82), whose luminous landscapes were sought out assiduously by English milords as souvenirs of the Grand Tour. His Paysage pastoral is in Nancy's Fine Arts Museum.

In 1699, Duke Leopold presented himself to Louis XIV at Versailles, following completion of a mission to Vienna. He was accompanied by his wife, Charlotte, Louis' niece. Their tour of the palace, guided by the the King's architect Mansart, brought home to them the decrepitude of their own palace at Nancy. It seems that it was Louis' gratitude for the services rendered by Leopold at Vienna, rather than affection for his niece, that moved him to lend the couple his architect, who subsequently designed the town hall (**Palais du Governement★**). Though not finally completed until 1753, its balustrade, **Ionic colonnade★** and horizontal entablature are typical of Mansart's work.

18C Nancy – Ever since the Treaty of Munster in 1648, the Duchy of Lorraine had been in a precarious situation; an enclave in French territory, it still formed part of the Holy Roman Empire. Though French in language and culture, its people were proud of their independence and much attached to their princes.

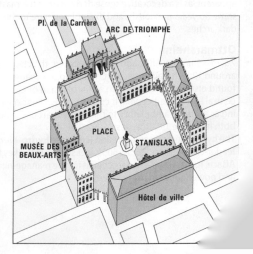

PRACTICAL INFORMATION

Tourist Office – 14 pl. Stanislas, 54000 Nancy - ☎ 03 83 35 22 41, www.ot-nancy.com

Guided tours – Nancy, City of Art, organises 1hr30min guided tours by approved guides. Audioguides with a recorded commentary also available on the Art nouveau theme. *Enquire at tourist office.*

Tourist train – *May-Sep: 45min tour of the historic town by miniature train. Departs from Porte d'Héré (near Place Stanislas) from 10am-noon and 2-6pm, reservations possible.* ⏰ *Closed 14 Jul.* €5.50 (6-14 year olds: €4). ☎ 03 89 73 74 24, www.petit-train.com

City pass – This pass from the Office de tourisme offers 3 services with 13 different possibilities. €13.

WHERE TO EAT

See the Legend at the back of the guide for coin categories.

Les Nouveaux Abattoirs – 4 bd Austrasie – ☎ 03 83 35 46 25 – ⏰ *closed end Jul-mid Aug, Sat, Sun and public holidays.* This rather sombre-looking restaurant in a dull area away from the city centre has dark, old-fashioned dining rooms – but don't let all this put you off! The meat is of excellent quality, which is what gives this authentic restaurant its good name.

Les Pissenlits – 25 bis r. des Ponts – ☎ 03 83 37 43 97 – pissenlits@wanadoo.fr – ⏰ *closed 1-16 Aug, Sun and Mon.* There's always a crowd in this bistro near the market, and with good reason: the atmosphere is relaxed, the cuisine innovative and diverse, and the decor is very pleasant, with its closely packed tables, Majorelle furniture and blackboard. Why not join the crowd!

Le Foy – 1 pl. Stanislas – ☎ 03 83 32 21 44 – ⏰ *closed 29 Jul-21 Aug, Sun evening, Tue evening and Wed.* Climb the lovely stone staircase to reach this first-floor restaurant above the café-brasserie of the same name in place Stanislas. The food is good and served in generous portions. Rustic decor with exposed beams.

Le V Four – 10 r. St-Michel – ☎ 03 83 32 49 48 – ⏰ *closed 1-7 Feb, 30 Aug-9 Sep, Sat lunchtime, Sun evening and Mon.* It may be small, but this restaurant in the heart of the old city is popular among the locals, who enjoy its simple modern decor and its trendy cuisine. Terrace.

Le Gastrolâtre – 1 pl. Vaudémont – ☎ 03 83 35 51 94 – ⏰ *closed 1-6 May, 15-30 Aug, Christmas holidays, Mon lunchtimes, Thu evenings and Sun.* This popular bistro ust behind place Stanislas is run with a ...aster's hand by a media boss. Its mouth-...ering menu and characterful cuisine ...bine local flavours with those from the ... of France.

Grenier à Sel – 28 r. Gustave-Simon - ☎ 03 83 32 31 98 - patrick.frechin@free.fr – ⏰ *closed 23 Jul-15 Aug, Sun and Mon.* This restaurant is in a little-frequented street on the first floor of one of the oldest houses in town. In the large country-style dining room you can enjoy food with a modern flair.

WHERE TO STAY

Weekends in Nancy – Hotel stays of two nights and more are rewarded by a welcome gift and reductions on visits to the town. Ask at the tourist office for the list of hotels and reservation conditions.

Chambre d'hôte Ferme de Montheu – 54770 Dommartin-sous-Amance – 10 km/6.25mi NE of Nancy, Sarreguemines and Agincourt direction – ☎ 03 83 31 17 37 – mgranddidier@wanadoo.fr – 5 rooms – evening meal. This working farm in the middle of the country has lovely uninterrupted views, apart from a nearby high-tension power line. But that's soon forgotten in the peace of the simple rooms with their old furniture. Evening meal by arrangement.

Portes d'Or – 21 r. Stanislas - ☎ 03 83 35 42 34 - contact@hotel-lesportesdor.com - 20 rooms - €6. The main advantage of this hotel is its proximity to the Place Stanislas. The pastel-coloured rooms are not very large, but have modern furniture and are reasonably well equipped.

Hôtel Crystal – 5 r. Chanzy – ☎ 03 83 17 54 00 – hotelcrystal.nancy@wanadoo.fr – ⏰ *closed 24 Dec-2 Jan* – 58 rooms - €8.50. This entirely renovated hotel near the station is a good place to stay in Nancy. Its modern, spacious rooms have been nicely arranged and decorated and feel welcoming. Cosy bar-lounge.

ON THE TOWN

L'Arquebuse – 13 r. Héré – ☎ 03 83 32 11 99 – ⏰ *Tue-Sun 6.30pm-4am, until 5am Fri and Sat.* This high-class bar with a refined decor has a good view of the place Stanislas. A wide choice of cocktails with atmospheric music and disco, attracting a mixed clientele of smart students and businessmen. The place to go after 2am.

L'Échanson – 9 r. de la Primatiale – ☎ 03 83 35 51 58 – ⏰ *Tue-Sat noon-2.30pm, 5.30-9.30pm* – ⏰ *closed public holidays.* A pleasant little wine bar that also serves as the local bistro. A dozen or so wines are available by the glass, which can be accompanied by a savoury snack, and the cellar comprises 500 different wines for sale.

Nouveau Vertigo – 29 r. de la Visitation – ☎ 03 83 32 71 97 – www.nouveau-vertigo.com – ⏰ *Tue-Thu 11am-2am, Fri 11am-4am, Sat 4pm-5am* – ⏰ *closed Mon-Sun.*

he centre-piece of Nancy cultural life, his bar doubles up as a restaurant and venue for café-theatre evenings and concerts (jazz, Afro-jazz, rock and French music). It is often packed, and the drink flows freely, mainly beer and cocktails.

SHOWTIME

Get hold of a programme! – The magazine *Spectacles à Nancy* will keep you informed. *Information from: www. spectacles-nancy.presse.fr*

Shows – The Opéra de Nancy et de Lorraine, Ballet de Nancy, Théâtre de la Manufacture, Centre dramatique national Nancy-Lorraine, Association de musique ancienne de Nancy, Ensemble Poirel, Orchestre symphonique et lyrique de Nancy, Association lorraine de musique de chambre, Gradus Ad Musicam, La Psalette de Lorraine put on numerous concerts and shows each year in various venues around the city.

Opéra de Nancy et de Lorraine – *Pl. Stanislas -* ☏ *03 83 85 33 11 –* 🕐 *daily except Mon and Sun 1-7pm.*

CNN Ballet de Lorraine – *3 r. Henri-Bazin -* ☏ *03 83 36 78 07 - www.ballet-de-lorraine. com –* 🕐 *10am-1pm and 2-6pm.*

Zénith – *R. Zénith - 54320 Maxéville -* ☏ *03 83 93 27 27 - info@zenith-de-nancy.com*

Ensemble Poirel – *R. Victor-Poirel -* ☏ *03 83 32 31 25 - www.nancy.fr* Stages an eclectic selection of theatre, opera, ballet, concerts and readings throughout the year, with shows by well-known and as well as lesser known names.

Théâtre de la Manufacture – *10 R. Baron-Louis –* ☏ *03 83 37 42 42 - manu@theatre-manufacutre.fr –* 🕐 *9.30am-12.30pm, 1.30-7.30pm –* 🕐 *closed Jul-Aug.* Centre dramatique national Nancy-Lorraine

MJC Lillebonne – *14 r. du Cheval-Blanc –* ☏ *03 83 36 82 82 - mjclillebonne@ wanadoo.fr –* 🕐 *Mon-Fri 9am-11pm, Sat 9am-7pm –* 🕐 *closed 2-22 Aug, Sun and public holidays.* Wide choice of socio-educational and cultural concerts, theatre and dance.

Gastronomie en musique – 🕐 *Jul-Aug: evening musical performances on Thu, Fri and weekends near terraces in different areas of the city.*

Patrimoine en musique – Classical concerts in city-centre churches in the afternoons.

RECREATION AND SPORT

Golf – *10 r. du Golf - 54425 Pulnoy -* ☏ *03 83 18 10 18 – www.golfnancypulnoy.com –* *8.30am-7pm -* 🕐 *closed 25 Dec-1 Jan.* 18-hole golf course in woodlands.

L'Est républicain – *R. Théophraste-Renaudot - 54180 Houdemont -* ☏ *03 83 59 80 26 –* 🕐 *9.40pm-12.30am by reservation, no charge.* Guided tour of one of Lorraine's best-known daily newspapers.

SHOPPING

Adam – *3 pl. St-Epvre -* ☏ *03 83 32 04 69 –* 🕐 *Tue-Sat 7.30am-7.30pm, Sun 7.30am-6pm, public holidays and Sun (summer 7.30am-1pm) –* 🕐 *closed Mon.* This confectioner sells St-Epure, a registered trade name, which is made of almond meringue, vanilla cream and crushed nougatine, together with a host of other delights for those with a sweet tooth.

Confiserie Chocolaterie Alain Batt – *30 r. du Tapis-Vert -* ☏ *03 83 35 70 00 –* 🕐 *Mon-Sat 9am-5.30pm, tour by appointment –* 🕐 *closed public holidays.* Before your very eyes, this confectioner will create macaroons and bergamotes de Nancy, plums in marzipan, Chardons de Lorraine, bergamot truffles and chocolates. Products to taste and buy.

Au Duché de Lorraine – *47 r. Henri-Poincaré -* ☏ *03 83 30 13 83 –* 🕐 *Mon-Sat 8.30am-7.30pm, Sun 9.30am-12.30pm.* Fans of the famous bergamotes de Nancy (hard sweets flavoured with citrus rind) and macarons des Dominicains will not be disappointed by those of this confectioner, established since 1840. Also on sale are delightful Lorraine gift boxes, parcels and baskets, all generously filled.

Maison des Sœurs Macarons – *21 r. Gambetta -* ☏ *03 83 32 24 25 – www. macaron-de-nancy.com –* 🕐 *Mon 2-7pm; Tue-Sat 10am-12.30pm, 2-7pm –* 🕐 *closed Sun.* The secret recipe for macaroons has been handed down within the family since the 18C. Other Lorraine specialities are available here: bergamots (a sweet made with essence of bergamot), Berg'amours (crystallized fruits), perles de Lorraine (crystallized fruits with plum liqueur centres), Florentines des sœurs, (fondant-encased praline chocolates) Babas du Roi, gingerbread, etc.

In 1738, following the War of the Polish Succession, Duke François I, son of Leopold and husband of Maria-Theresa of Austria, found himself having to cede Lorraine in exchange for Tuscany. In his place, Louis XV appointed, as ruler for life, his own father-in-law Stanislas Leszczynski, and by 1766 the Duchy had been painlessly incorporated into the French kingdom, a notable success for Cardinal Fleury's foreign policy. Four years later an event took place which can be considered either as an irony of history or as evidence of the cunning match-making of the Viennese court. Marie-Antoinette, daughter of François I and Maria-Theresa, had lost her putative claim to Lorraine years before her birth. In 1770, she married Louis XVI and began her reign at Versa Known as "the Austrian" because of her mother, Marie-Antoinette was, throug father, just as much a Lorrainer and a Frenchwoman. Stanislas was a man of peace, ~~~ of his daughter the Queen of France, a lover of good living and the opposite sex, an~~ passionate builder. He set out to join together the old quarter of Nancy with the "Ne~~ Town" by means of a set-piece of civic design in honour of his son-in-law. The great project was completed in the short space of three years, between 1752 and 1755.

Visit

Place Stanislas★★★

In charge of the work were the architect Emmanuel Héré (1705-63) and Jean **Lamour**, a metal-worker of genius. Héré designed the City Hall (Hôtel de ville) and the flanking buildings with their fine façades. At ground level, the City Hall has a central projecting section with arcades and colossal pilasters separating the windows; on the upper level are balconies and wrought, iron window-ledges. The four flanking buildings are of similar design, though without the centre section; to the north the square is defined by

Place Stanislas

two further buildings, again similar in general treatment, though with only one storey and with an attic and balustrade separated by a later mansard roof. The whole forms a space of exceptional elegance and clarity of structure, ornamented with urns and trophies and with balustrades to conceal the roofs.

Further enclosure is achieved by Jean Lamour's brilliant ironwork. Perfectly integrated into the architectural concept, his gilded railings with their crests and floral decoration are of inimitable gracefulness. He was also responsible for the window-ledges, the balcony and the double curve of the internal staircase of the City Hall.

Palais Ducal★★ and Musée Historique Lorrain★★★ ⑤ *Wed-Mon 10am-12.30pm, 2-6pm.* ⑤ *Closed Tue, 1 Jan, 1 May, 14 Jul, 1 Nov, 25 Dec.* ⌨ *3.10€ (children under 12 years: no charge).* ☎ *03 83 32 18 74.*

Musée des Beaux-Arts★★ ᕫ ⑤ *Wed-Mon 10am-6pm.* ⑤ *Closed Tue, 1 Jan, 1 May, 14 Jul, 1 and 11 Nov, 25 Dec.* ⌨ *4.60€ (under 18 years: no charge), temporary exhibit: 5.40€, no charge 1st Sun in the month 10am-1.30pm.* ☎ *03 83 85 30 72.*

Arc de Triomphe★. Place de la Carrière★. Église★ and Couvent des Cordeliers *Same as the Palais ducal* – Chapel★. Porte de la Craffe★. Musée de l'École de Nancy★★ ⑤ *Daily except Mon and Tue 10.30am-6pm.* ⌨ *2.30€ (children under 12 years: no charge), no charge 1st Sun in the month 10.30am-1.30pm.* ☎ *03 83 40 14 86.* Église de Notre-Dame-de-Bon-Secours★.

NANTES★★★

POPULATION 492 255

MICHELIN MAP 316 G 4

GREEN GUIDE BRITTANY

~~antes is Brittany's largest city, sited at the point at which the mighty Loire ~~comes tidal. The presence of islets (inhabited from the 17C on) in the river had ~~g facilitated the building of bridges, making Nantes the focus of trade and ~~ement between Lower Brittany and Poitou.

~~ent Yourself:** Find a bar or restaurant in the Ste-Croix neighborhood for an ~~entic Nantes evening. Rue Crébillon, which opens onto Place Graslin, is a ~~street for shopping. Three tramway lines and over 60 bus routes make for asy movement throughout the city. Nantes, which is listed as a "Town of Art and History", offers discovery tours by appointment for 6€. Contact the tourist office to make a reservation.

🕐 **Organizing Your Time:** You'll need at least 3hr to visit the château and the surrounding sights (Place Maréchal-Foch, Port-St-Pierre, Cathédrale St-Pierre-et-St-Paul).

🅿 **Parking:** It is not easy to move around Nantes by car. Find parking in one of several lots surrounding the downtown area and move around the city by tramway, bus or foot.

Un bon vin blanc

This expression, well known for being part of a phonetics exercise for Anglo-Saxon learners of French – literally "a fine white wine" – adequately describes the local Muscadet, dry but not too sharp, perfect with seafood. The vineyards are located to the south and east of Nantes, alongside or near the Sèvre and towards Ancenis on the banks of the Loire.

A Bit of History

In the 9C, the city was disputed between Nominoé, the first Duke of Brittany, and the Franks to the east. In 939, it was chosen as his capital by King Alain Barbe-Torte (Crookbeard). By the 14C, Nantes had become a trading port, with a fleet of 1 300 ships, but it was only in the 15C, under Duke François II, that the city reached its full importance.

In the early 18C Nantes grew rich on sugar; cane was imported from the West Indies to be distributed in France or re-exported to England and Scandinavia. This formed part of the profitable "ebony trade", the discreet name given to the triangle of commerce involving the export of fancy goods to Africa, the shipping of slaves to the Indies, and the import of cane. Nantes became France's premier port. But the loss of French territories abroad under Louis XV, the abolition of slavery, the substitution of sugar-beet for cane sugar (a result of the British blockade in the Napoleonic wars) and the increasing size of ships led to the port's decline. In the 19C and 20C the construction of downstream harbour facilities has contributed towards Nantes' continuing prosperity.

Visit

Château des Ducs de Bretagne★★

Restoration in progress. Call in advance for visit information. ☎ 02 51 17 49 00.
"God's teeth! No small beer, these dukes of Brittany!" exclaimed Henri IV on seeing this massive stronghold for the first time. The castle was much rebuilt and strengthened from 1466 on by Duke François II who saw in it the guarantee of his independence from Louis XI. His daughter Anne of Brittany continued the work.

The great edifice is defended by deep ditches of considerable width, which could be flooded when necessary, and by six stout towers with characteristically Breton pyramidal machicolations. The interior reflects the castle's role as a palace of government and residence, known for its high life of feasts and jousting.

Many of its features are of great interest, like the Golden Crown Tower **(Tour de la Couronne d'or★★)**, the main building (Grand Logis) with its massive dormer windows, the Governor's Major Palace (Grand Gouvernement) rebuilt at the end of the 17C, and the well **(puits★★)** with its wrought-iron well-head incorporating ducal crown motifs.

There are two museums in the castle: the **Musée d'Art populaire**★ featuring Breton coiffes, dress and furniture, the Musée des Salorges, a maritime museum *(reorganisation in progress)*. Temporary exhibitions of the latter's collections are held in the Horse-shoe Tower (Tour du Fer-à-Cheval).

Cathédrale St-Pierre et St-Paul

Although the building of the cathedral extended over a period of 450 years, it great unity of style. The use of a white calcareous tufa in the **interior**★★ enh the impression of boldness and purity of line resulting from the moulding pillars which soar without a break in their flight up into the keystones of th

Duke Jean V wished to make it the greatest of all the churches in Brittany to provide a worthy setting for the tomb of his father.

It was here, on 13 April 1598, that Henri IV signed the **Edict of Nantes**, thereby establishing equality between Catholics and Protestants, and explicitly granting privileges to the latter regarding political organisation and the right to maintain fortified strongholds. The Edict had 92 articles, some of them secret; it succeeded others of a similar nature issued by Catherine de' Medici, the first in Europe concerning religious tolerance. This time, however, their efficacy was backed by a ruler in a position to neutralise any lingering opposition to them. In the reign of Louis XIV, some Protestants were persuaded to convert to Catholicism, but the king, misled about the number of conversions, revoked the Edict in 1685 "since it no longer served any useful purpose", thereby provoking the Huguenot exodus of around 200 000 people to England, Holland and Germany and depriving France of some of its most valuable human resources.

In the south transept of the cathedral is the tomb of François II (**tombeau de François II**★★ – 1502), commissioned by Duchess Anne for her father and her mother Marguerite de Foix. It is the work of Michel Colombe and probably also of Jean Perréal; while its recumbent figures and their cortège are still medieval in feeling, the Renaissance is announced by the use of black and white Italian marble, by the arabesques and by the figures of the Virtues.

⊙⊙　Musée des Beaux-Arts★★ ⊙ *Wed-Mon 10am-6pm, Thurs evening 6-8pm.* ⊙ *Closed Tue and public holidays except Easter Monday, 14 Jul and 15 Aug.* ☞ *3.10€ (under 18 years: no charge), no charge Thu evening and 1st Sun in the month.* ☏ *02 51 17 45 00.*

Muséum d'Histoire Naturelle★★ ⛱ ⊙ *Wed-Mon 10am-6pm.* ⊙ *Closed Tue, Easter Monday, 1 and 8 May, 1 and 11 Nov, 25 Dec.* ☞ *3.10€, no charge 3rd Sun in the month.* ☏ *02 40 99 26 20.*

The 19C Town★ Palais Dobrée★ ⊙ *Tue-Fri 1.30-5.30pm, Sat-Sun 2.30-5.30pm.* ⊙ *Closed Mon and public holidays.* ☞ *3€ (ticket combined with the musée archéologique), no charge Sun.* ☏ *02 40 71 03 50* – decorative art.

Musée Jules-Verne★ ⊙ *Mon, Wed-Sat 10am-noon, 2-6pm, Sun 2-6pm. Guided tour* ⚓ *(1hr 30min) Sun 3.30pm.* ⊙ *Closed Tue and public holidays.* ☞ *1.50€. No charge 4th Sun in the month* ☏ *02 40 69 72 52.* Musée archéologique★ *Same as Palais Dobrée.* Jardin des Plantes★. Ancienne Île Feydeau.

Excursions

Safari africain de Port-St-Père★★

20km – 12mi southwest, on D 758. This safari park at the heart of the Pays de Retz has over 1 500 animals roaming free in its 140ha – 350-acre enclosure. The visit includes two circuits: one to be toured on foot, the other by car.

Piste Safari

A 10km – 6mi circuit by car through a series of 13 enclosures takes in a bush and savannah environment where hippopotamuses and elephants disport themselves in ponds, impalas and springboks show off their jumping skills, and tigers prowl menacingly, among other wild species.

Village du Safari

A tour on foot of a bush village inludes a reptile house (**Arche des reptiles**), a dimly-lit vivarium with both snakes and crocodiles; a farm with 20 miniature species; a lake (**Lac des otaries**) where sea-lions can be observed from a viewing platform in the middle; an island (**Ile des siamangs**) where gibbons and howler monkeys taunt colonies of pink flamingoes, marabous and pelicans on the shore. A tropical garden (**jardin exotique**) leads to a wooded area (**Forêt des singes**) inhabited by rhesus monkeys.

St-Nazaire

60km – 38mi west by N165 and N171. A great shipbuilding centre and port, St-Nazaire became an important German submarine base during the Second World War. On 27 March 1942 it was the scene of the heroic deeds of a Canadian-British commando whose aim was to neutralise the installations. The destroyer *Campbeltown* broke through the entrance lock and subsequently blew itself up. The operation was a success, albeit with heavy losses.

NARBONNE★★

POPULATION 45 849

MICHELIN MAP 344 I-J 3

GREEN GUIDE LANGUEDOC ROUSSILLON TARN GORGES

▶ **Orient Yourself:** Narbonne, which is listed as a "Town of Art and History," offers discovery tours conducted by guide-lecturers approved by the Ministry of Culture and Communication. The tours are thematic and centre around the town's monuments. 6.20€. Information available from the Connaître Narbonne association (cultural dept. of the town hall) ☎ 04 68 90 30 66 or on www.vpah.culture.fr.

A Bit of History

The history of this ancient Mediterranean city is a long one; it may well have served as the harbour for a 7C BC Gallic settlement on the Montaurès hill to the north.

After the defeat of Hannibal, and the conquest of Catalonia, La Mancha and Andalusia, the Roman Empire felt the need to secure its land communications with Spain. Narbonne was chosen to be a Senatorial (rather than governmental) colony; the city became the commercial centre of the Celtic province, with an artificial port created by diverting an arm of the river Aude. Finally it was made the capital of Gallia Narbonensis – Provence – and flourished right up to the end of the Empire and the arrival of the Visigoths, who made it the capital of their kingdom.

Some trading activity continued, and Muslim raiders from Spain found the city still worth looting in 793. Medieval shipping made use of the extensive lagoons lining the coast behind the rampart of sand bars. But in the 14C a storm brought the Aude back into its old bed, and Narbonne declined as its bay silted up. The construction of the Canal du Midi at the end of the 17C and the building of the railway in the 19C helped to reverse the process of decline.

Cathédrale St-Just★★

Treasury: 🕐 *Jul-Sep: Mon-Sat 11am-6pm, Sun 2-6pm; Oct-Jun: daily 2-6pm.* 🕐 *Closed 1 Jan and 25 Dec.* ⊚ *2.20€.* ☎ *04 68 90 30 65.*

The present building was begun in 1272, but construction was halted 82 years later in order to preserve the ramparts which would otherwise have been breached to accommodate the nave. The choir remains, its vaulting reaching the dizzy height of 41m – 135ft. It is in the High Gothic style, with a fine triforium – its columns extend upwards into the lancets of the clerestory windows. The great arches of the apse are crowned with battlements and loopholes. The lofty cloisters (1349-1417) are built in crumbling limestone on the site of a Carolingian church.

The cathedral **treasury** has a wonderful late-15C **Flemish Tapestry**★★ featuring the Creation woven in silk and gold thread, a 10C ivory missal plaque and a rare marriage casket in rock crystal with intaglio decoration.

Palais des Archevêques

Many building styles are represented here, from the 12C Old Palace (Palais Vieux), the 13C Madeleine Tower (donjon de la Madeleine) and Gilles Aycelin Tower **(donjon Gilles Aycelin**★*)* (🕐 *Jul-Sep: daily 10am-6pm; Oct-Jun: daily 9am-noon, 2-6pm;* 🕐 *closed 1 Jan, 25 Dec;* ⊚ *2.20€, children under 10 years: no charge;* ☎ *04 68 90 30 66),* the 14C St Martial Tower (tour St-Martial) and New Palace (Palais Neuf), the 17C Archbishops' Residence (Résidence des archevêques) with its Louis XIII staircase to the City Hall (Hôtel de ville), with its 19C façade.

◗◗ Musée Archéologique★★ 🕐 *Apr-Sep: daily 9.30am-12.15pm, 2-6pm; Oct-Jun: daily except Mon 10am-noon, 2-5pm.* 🕐 *Closed 1 Jan, 1 May, 1 and 11 Nov, 25 Dec.* ⊚ *5.20€, ticket provides admission to all the museums (3.70€ for one museum only).* ☎ *04 68 90 30 54.*

Musée d'Art et d'Histoire★. Basilique St-Paul – chancel★ 🕐 *Daily except Sun afternoon.*

Musée Lapidaire★ *Same as Musée Archéologique.*

Excursion

Abbaye de Fontfroide★★

15 km – 9mi southwest. This former Cistercian abbey nestles in a quiet, restful corner of the countryside, planted with cypress trees and reminiscent of the gentle landscape of Tuscany. The fine flame-coloured shades of yellow ochre and pink in the Corbières sandstone used to build the abbey enhance the serenity of the sight, particularly at sunset. Most of the buildings date from the 12C and 13C.

Cirque de NAVACELLES★★★

MICHELIN MAP 339 G 5

GREEN GUIDE LANGUEDOC ROUSSILLON TARN GORGES

This 300m – 1 000ft deep basin, separating the Causses – high plateaux – de Larzac and Blandas, marks the former course of the River Vis before it cut through the base of the meander.

Visit

On the outer sweep of the meander great screes have been formed; the upper parts of the cliffs are made up of exceptionally thick beds, thinning out at the lower levels where traces remain of old buildings and terraces on the marl and clay deposits. On the valley floor a pretty single-arched bridge leads to the village of Navacelles (which once had a priory). The little settlement clings to a rocky outcrop in order to conserve as much as possible of the belt of cultivable land in the former bed of the river.

In contrast to the harsh conditions prevailing on the arid, windswept causses, the valley floor has a mild microclimate which allows figs to be grown.

Massif de NÉOUVIELLE★★★

MICHELIN MAP 342 M 5

GREEN GUIDE LANGUEDOC ROUSSILLON TARN GORGES

In 1976 the Bielsa road tunnel was opened linking France with Lerida in Spain, and making the little mountain resort of St-Lary-Soulan★ an important trans-Pyrenean staging-post.

Driving Tour

St-Lary is the starting-point for the spectacular scenic route *(46km – 29mi round trip)* rising up to 1 362m – 4 435ft and leading, via dark fir-woods and many hairpin bends, to a dam (Barrage de **Cap de Long**★), and lakes **(Lac d'Oredon**★ and **Lac d'Aumar**★).

The Massif de Néouvielle, forming part of the high central spine of the Pyrenees, is made up of granite; it is a veritable museum of glacial topography, with virtually all the features characterising such landscapes, from high, ice-smoothed cliffs and cirques separated by narrow ridges, to hanging valleys, rock-steps and a multitude of lakes and erratic boulders.

The Cap de Long dam forms a key part of the Pragnères hydro-electric scheme with its many miles of tunnels channelling the waters from a number of different valleys to feed the turbines.

NEVERS★

POPULATION 58 915

MICHELIN MAP 319 B 10

GREEN GUIDE BURGUNDY JURA

From the red sandstone bridge spanning the Loire there is a fine view of the old town of Nevers set in terraces on its limestone hill, its tall town houses with their roofs of slate and tile dominated by the high square tower of the great cathedral and the graceful silhouette of the ducal palace.

A Bit of History

As was usual all along the Loire, it was height above the river which was the most important determinant of the town's location. At the meeting-point of the Loire with the Nièvre, Nevers flourished as a port until the 19C when the Loire ceased to be navigable. The abundant and reliable flow of the Nièvre encouraged the development of potteries and iron working along its banks as early as the 16C.

The area around Nevers was known for its everyday pottery in the Middle Ages. Artistic pottery seems to have been brought here in the 1560s by Italian craftsmen from Lyon like Giulio Gambini; at the time the secrets of enamelling were jealously guarded, and the techniques discovered 45 years previously at Rouen by Abaquesne had not spread. Progress at Nevers was encouraged by the humanist Ludovico di Gonzaga, who became Duke of Nevers in 1565, and whose wide interests included the advancement of the arts and technology. In the time of Louis XIII and Louis XIV the town was one of the great centres of faience production, with 12 manufactories employing 1 800 workers and producing some of the finest Blue Persian work ever made. There is a good **collection**★ of Nevers pottery in the museum (**musée municipal**).

Following her visionary experiences at Lourdes, Bernadette Soubirous came to Nevers in 1866 to enter a convent (Couvent de **St-Gildard**★) here. Her body, exhumed three times, was reputedly unaffected by decay; the object of pilgrimages and of the veneration of the faithful, it is displayed in a reliquary in the convent chapel.

Visit

Palais ducal★

The former residence of the Dukes of Nevers is a fine example of the secular architecture of the French Renaissance. The centrepiece of the main façade is formed by an elegant five-sided projecting staircase topped by a small belfry.

Église St-Étienne★

This splendid Romanesque church has a magnificently tiered east end and a beautiful overall pattern of windows in the style of the great abbey church of Cluny. It has a false triforium modelled on Burgundian precedents but above all it is the height of the interior which is impressive, particularly for a building of its date (1063-97); this feat of construction was necessitated by the introduction of a row of windows immediately below the barrel vaulting.

 Cathédrale St-Cyr-et-Ste-Julitte★★. Porte du Croux★.

NICE★★★

POPULATION 475 507

MICHELIN MAP 341 E 5

GREEN GUIDE FRENCH RIVIERA

▶ **Orient Yourself:** The promenade du Paillon divides Nice in two: to the west, the modern city; to the east, the old City, the castle hill, and behind it, the port. To the north on the hill is Cimiez, the ancient Roman settlement. There are 1hr30min guided tours of baroque Old Nice Thu and Sun at 3pm for 3€. Contact the palais Lascaris, 15 r. Droite, ☎ 04 93 62 72 40.

Don't Miss: The panorama from the castle hill.

Organizing Your Time: A full day is necessary for discovering Nice. Spend the morning on the oceanfront and in Vieux Nice; reserve the afternoon for Cimiez, and, if you have time, see the musée des Beaux-Arts, the musée d'Art moderne et d'Art contemporain and the musée des Arts asiatiques.

Parking: It is not easy to move yourself around by car in Nice especially with recent construction work on the tramway (first line to be operational in 2006). As soon as possible, park in one of the many pay lots in the city.

A Bit of History

Some 400 000 years ago, bands of elephant hunters made their encampments on the fossil beach at Terra Amata, 26m – 85ft above the present level of the sea. In the 6C BC, Celto-Ligurians settled on the castle hill; a little later it was the turn of merchants and sailors from Marseille; they established themselves around the harbour, followed by the Romans, who favoured the Cimiez district. In 1388, aided and abetted by the **Grimaldi** family, Count Amadeus VII of Savoy incorporated Provence into his domain and made a triumphal entry into Nice.

As a result of the alliance of 1859 between France and Sardinia, Napoleon III undertook to help drive out the Austrians from Lombardy and the Veneto; in return, France was to receive from the House of Savoy the lands to the west of the Alps and around Nice which had once been hers. A plebiscite produced an overwhelming vote in favour of a return to France (25 743 for, 260 against) and the ceremony of annexation took place on 14 June 1860.

Visit

Le Vieux Nice★

The core of the city, huddling at the foot of the castle hill, has a lively, utterly Mediterranean character.

Château

The landscaped slopes of the castle hill with their umbrella pines shading pleasant walks reach a height of 92m – 300ft. The summit provided a place of refuge for the

Nice Carnival in Place Masséna

A. Philipon/EXPLORER

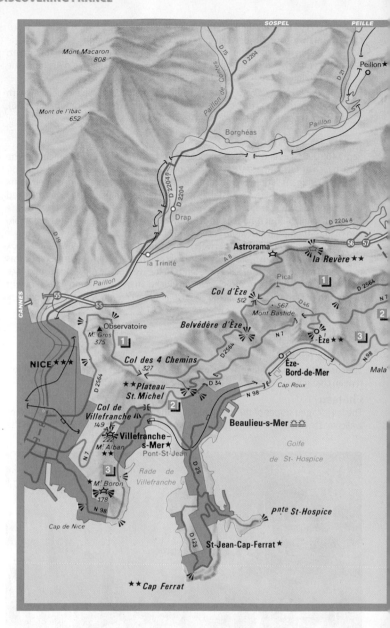

denizens of Cimiez at the time of the fall of the Roman Empire. In the 12C, the Counts of Provence built a castle here which was subsequently strengthened by the Angevin princes and the Dukes of Savoy but was demolished by Louis XIV in 1706. From the top there is a fine **view**★★ over the city, the Pre-Alps and the bay (Baie des Anges).

Place Garibaldi

The square is named after the great fighter for Italian unity who was born in Nice. The ochre walls and arcading of the buildings along its sides recall the urbane elegance characteristic of Piedmontese town planning in the 18C.

Cathédrale Ste-Reparate

This is a fine example of the Baroque style as it developed in Nice. The west front, a pleasant mixture of greens and yellows, is decorated with niches and medallions, topped by an imposing entablature and supported by buttress-pillars with composite capitals. The **interior**★ is enlivened by an elaborate cornice, and in the choir is a frieze outlined in white and gold and decorated with little figures of angels.

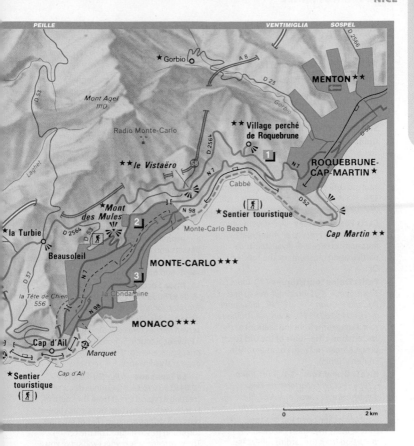

Église St-Jacques★

The west front recalls the Gesù church in Rome. Behind it lies a nave whose severity is relieved by an abundance of sculpture. The barrel vault opens into side chapels containing loggias where the local nobility once worshipped.

Place Masséna

The linear park laid out on what was once the bed of the river Paillon is interrupted by this square begun in 1815. Its buildings with their façades rendered in reddish ochre and their arcades recall the planned urban spaces of Turin.

Cimiez★★

This part of the city originated in the Roman settlement whose growth soon eclipsed that of the older town laid out around the harbour.

Site archéologique gallo-romain★

&. ○ *Daily except Tue 10am-6pm. Last entry 30min before closing.* ○ *Closed 1 Jan, Easter, 1 May, 25 Dec.* ∞ *4€ (includes access to the museum), no charge 1st and 3rd Sun in the month.* ☎ *04 93 81 59 57.*

The archeological site consists mostly of medium-size amphitheatres and the area around the baths.

There is a monastery (**monastère**★) whose church possesses a Pietà of 1475 *(to the right of the entrance)*; though an early work of Louis Bréa, and executed in Gothic style, it is one of his finest achievements, notably in its portrayal of the grieving Mary. To the left of the choir is a later work by the same artist, a Crucifixion (1512) which heralds the Renaissance.

Musée Matisse★★

&. ○ *Daily 10am-6pm.* ○ *Closed Tue, 1 Jan, Easter, 1 May, 25 Dec.* ∞ *4€, no charge 1st and 3rd Sun in the month.* ☎ *04 93 81 08 08. www.musee-matisse-nice.org.*

The museum is housed in the Villa des Arènes; it traces the artist's evolution, from a still-life *(Nature morte aux livres, 1890)* to the *Rococo Armchair (Fauteuil de Rocaille, 1947)* and the *Blue Nude (Nu bleu, 1952)*.

Nice - Address Book

PRACTICAL INFORMATION

Tourism Offices – *5 Promenade des Anglais* – ☎ *0 892 707 707 (0.34€/minute)* – *and at Train Station , Av. Thiers* – *www.nicetourisme.com.*

SIGHTSEEING AND TOURS

Guided tours – 🚶 Tours of the Old Town *(1.5hr)* Tue and Sun at 3pm. 3€. 🚶 *Palais Lascaris, 15 Rue Droite,* ☎ *04 93 62 72 40.* Tours of the Old Town *(2.5hrs)* from the Tourism Office every Saturday at 9.30am, 12€. 🚶 *5 Promenade des Anglais,* ☎ *0 892 707 707 (0.34€/minute).*

Carte Passe -Musées – A 7-day museum pass with free entry to all municipal museums of Nice, 6€. Available at all participating museums or the Tourism Office.

Petits Trains Touristiques – 🕐 *Tours 10am-6pm* – 🕐 *Closed mid-Nov to mid-Dec and 1-15 Jan* – 🚃 *6€ (3€ kids under 9)* – ☎ *04 50 60 05 55 – www.petittrainnice.com.* Departures from the seafront at the Jardins Albert 1re. Tours of the Old Town, port, Château Hill with commentary in English (30min).

Nice le Grand Tour – 🕐 *Tours 10am-5.30pm, hourly departures Jul-Oct, departures every two hours Nov-Jun.* – 🚌 *17€ (children 9€)* – ☎ *04 92 29 17 00.* Double-decker, open top bus tours with commentary in English (90 min), departing from the Jardins Albert 1re. Hop on-hop off the 11 different stops from Promenade des Anglais, Cimiez, Mont Boron, and the Port.

Trans Côte d'Azur – *Quai Lunel* – ☎ *04 92 00 42 30 – www.trans-cote-azur.com* – 🕐 *Operates Feb-Nov Tue, Wed, Fri and Sun at 3pm; Sun-Fri from 15 Jun-15 Sep.* Guided tours *(1hr)* of the coast of Nice, panorama of the Bay of Villefranche and Baie des Anges.

PUBLIC TRANSPORT

Aéroport Nice-Côte d'Azur – ☎ *08 20 42 33 33 (0.12€/min) – www.nice.aeroport.fr* Set up on the left bank of the Var estuary, this is France's second busiest airport.

Buses – The Sunbus network *(10 Avenue Félix-Faure;* ☎ *04 93 16 52 10; www.sunbus.com)* covers the city of Nice and its suburbs. Tickets 1.30€ each, or 4€ for an unlimited one-day pass *(includes airport buses 23, 98, and 99).* The TAM network *(Gare routière, Promenade du Paillon;* ☎ *04 93 85 61 81; www.rca.tm.fr)* has service to other cities such as Antibes, Cannes and Grasse.

TER Train – *SNCF Gare, Avenue Thiers* – ☎ *0 892 35 35 35 – www.ter-sncf.com/paca.* Local train service to Draguignan, Fréjus, St-Raphaël, Cannes, Antibes, Menton Vintimille, Monaco. The Nice-Cuneo line crosses the Bévéra and Roya valleys.

EATING OUT

Salade niçoise, socca, pan-bagnat, poutine, tourte aux blettes, beignets de fleurs de courgettes…to experience the best in local cuisine, look for the restaurants displaying the label "Cuisine Nissarde". A guide to these restaurants is available for free at the Tourism Office. *For coin ranges, see Legend at back of the guide.*

🍴 **Le Pain Quotidien** – *3 Rue St-François-de-Paul (Cours Saleya)* – ☎ *04 93 62 94 32.* This country-style restaurant specializing in brunch has long wooden tables where guests sit side-by-side, an original formula conducive to a friendly, convivial atmosphere. In addition to the bread baskets and tatsy spreads of jam, honey and hazelnut, there is a wide selection of salads and open sandwiches.

🍴 **Nissa Socca** – *7 Rue Ste-Réparate* – ☎ *04 93 80 18 35* – 🕐 *Closed Jan, 10 days in Jun, Mon for lunch and Sun* – 🍴. Pasta, pizza and Mediterranean dishes are served here in two cosy dining areas with a Provençal touch. Simplicity and low prices guaranteed. Old-fashioned bread oven at the entrance.

🍴 **La Tapenade** – *6 Rue Ste-Réparate* – ☎ *04 93 80 65 63* – 🍴. Curious decor re-creating a typical street from the south of France, with its shutters, terra-cotta flower pots and strings of garlic. Do not miss the surprising fresco painted on the ceiling. The warm, friendly owners will serve you a pizza, a tapenade or any other local speciality.

🍴🍴 **Grand Café de Turin** – *5 Place Garibaldi* – ☎ *04 93 62 29 52.* This brasserie, which is over 200 years old, has become an institution in Nice. It serves seafood dishes à la carte at reasonable prices throughout the day. Pleasant, welcoming setting, although a bit noisy on the terrace.

🍴🍴 **L'Escalinada** – *22 Rue Pairolière* – ☎ *04 93 62 11 71 – restaurant-lescalinada@wanadoo.fr* – 🍴 – 🕐 *Closed 15 Nov-15 Dec.* Nestling in the old quarter, this charming restaurant offers attractively presented regional cuisine in a spruce dining room with rustic overtones. Friendly service.

🍴🍴 **Lou Balico** – *22 Avenue St-Jean-Baptiste* – ☎ *04 93 85 93 71* – 🕐 *Closed lunch in Jul-Aug.* Three generations of the same family have been serving classic Niçois dishes in this cosy dining room adorned with a piano and guest book with signatures from around the world.

🍴🍴 **La Table d'Alziari** – *4 Rue François-Zannin* – ☎ *04 93 80 34 03* – 🕐 *Closed 11-22 Jan, 9-20 Aug, 6-17 Dec, Sun and Mon.* Unpretentious family restaurant set up in a small alley of the old district. Typical dishes from Nice and the Provence area, chalked up on a slate, are served in a homey decor, together with wine recommended by the owner.

Capeline – Gilette – 9km/5.5mi from Gilette by D 17 Route de Roquesteron – ☎ 04 93 08 58 06 – ⏰ Open Mar-Oct, weekends only Nov-Feb – ⏰ Closed Wed – Reservation required. Roadside inn whose charm owes much to the lady of the house, clad in a white apron, who officiates in the kitchen and lovingly prepares tasty delicacies exuding Provençal fragrances.

WHERE TO STAY

Star Hôtel – 14 Rue Biscarra – ☎ 04 93 85 19 03 – star-hotel@wanadoo.fr – ⏰ Closed Nov – 24 rooms – ⬜ – 🍽. Small hotel away from the bustling town center offering simple accommodations, some with a balcony. Close to the Etoile Shopping Center.

Villa St-Hubert – 26 Rue Michel-Ange – ☎ 04 93 84 66 51 – hotel-villa-st-hubert@wanadoo.fr– ⏰ Closed 15 Nov-15 Dec – 13 rooms – ⬜. Turn-of-the-century villa near the university campus overlooking a quiet, secluded street. Smallish but well equipped rooms. Flowery patio where breakfast is served in summer.

Claire Hotel – 23 Boulevard Carnot, Impasse Terra Amata – ☎ 04 93 89 69 89 – 10 rooms – ⬜. This converted schoolhouse near the archeological museum has rooms all on one floor (in the old classrooms) and a Mediterranean garden terrace where breakfast is served in the summer. Quiet neighborhood, friendly, family-run atmosphere.

Mercure Marché aux Fleurs – 91 Quai des Etats-Unis – ☎ 04 93 85 74 19 – www.accor-hotels.com – 49 rooms – 🍽 🐾. Centrally located in the Old Town a block from the seafront and the Cour Saleya market. Rooms are simple and colorful, six with balconies facing the sea (and the traffic).

Château des Ollières – 39 Avenue des Baumettes – ☎ 04 92 15 77 99 – 🅿 – 8 rooms – ⬜ 🍽 – Restaurant (🍽🍽🍽) . This princely manor surrounded by a small park behind the Museum of Fine Arts bears witness to the presence of Russian residents in Nice during the last century. Its devastating charm derives from the luxuriously appointed salons, the precious works of art and the large, comfortable suites exuding a hushed, cosy ambience.

La Pérouse – 11 Quai Rauba-Capéu – ☎ 04 93 62 34 63 – 🅿 – 58 rooms – ⬜ 🍽 – restaurant (🍽🍽🍽) . A prime seaside location overlooking the Baie des Anges from the foot of the Château Hill, this cosy Provençal-style hotel features a heated swimming pool and grill restaurant set within a garden against the rocky hill. The top floor terrace has panoramic views over the sea, a hot tub and fitness room.

ON THE TOWN

Casino Ruhl – 1 Promenade des Anglais – ☎ 04 97 03 12 22 – ⏰ Daily 10am to dawn. The casino boasts 300 slot machines and has facilities for French and English roulette, blackjack, stud poker, etc. American bar. Dinner is coupled with live performances on Fridays. Themed evenings on Thursdays.

Le Mélisande – Hôtel Palais Maeterlinck, 30 Boulevard Maurice-Maeterlinck, Cap de Nice – ☎ 04 92 00 72 00 – www.palais-maeterlinck.com – ⏰ Daily 11am-midnight. This bar attached to the luxury hotel whose terrace dominates the sea and offers splendid views of the Baie des Anges. Champagne cocktails, cigars. The Belgian writer Maurice Maeterlinck, 1911 Nobel Prize for Literature, once lived on the premises.

Le Relais – Hôtel Negresco, 37 Promenade des Anglais – ☎ 04 93 16 64 00 – ⏰ Daily 11.30am-1am, until midnight in winter. The sumptuous decoration of this bar belonging to the legendary Negresco Hotel has remained the same since 1913: Brussels tapestry (1683), 18C paintings, replicas of the wall lamps adorning the Ballroom in Fontainebleau Château and a rug similar to that chosen by Napoleon I for the King's Bedchamber in Rome. Piano bar every evening.

Ghost House – 3 Rue Barillerie – ☎ 04 93 92 93 37 – ⏰ Wed-Sat 7.30pm-2am. A sleek and trendy nightclub (dinner and dancing) in the Old Town, with live DJs playing mostly dance and lounge electronic music. Expensive cocktails.

La Trappa – Rue de la Préfecture and Rue Gilly – ☎ 04 93 80 33 69 – ⏰ Daily 5pm-2am. A lively tapas bar with deep, comfortable settees and red walls awaits you at La Trappa, open since 1886. Sip a Cuban cocktail while you listen to Latin American music (DJ weekends). Friendly atmosphere and local wine list.

Les Trois Diables – 2 Cours Saleya – ☎ 04 93 62 47 00 – ⏰ Daily 4pm-2.30am. Cours Saleya is at the heart of Nice and its bustling activity. This broad square is taken over by the terraces of cafés, pubs and restaurants, and notably that of Les Trois Diables. This is undoubtedly most popular among the student nightlife crowd. Regular rock concerts, karaoke evenings, and other themed nights.

Wayne's Pub – 15 Rue de la Préfecture – ☎ 04 93 13 46 99 – www.waynes.fr – ⏰ Daily noon-1am. Genuine Anglo-Saxon pub, with live sports on the big screen and nightly rock concerts. Tea time is from 4pm to 6pm, and cocktail time from 6pm to 7pm.

SHOPPING

Most shops in Old Nice are closed on Mondays.

Shopping streets – The streets surrounding the Cathédrale Ste-Réparate have many shops selling typical Provençal articles: fabrics *(Rue Paradis and Rue du Marché)*, arts and crafts *(Rue du Pont-Vieux and Rue de la Boucherie)*, olive oil and santons *(Rue St-François-de-Paul)*.

Alziari – *14 Rue St-François-de-Paule –* ☎ *04 93 85 76 92 – www.alziari.com.fr –* ⊙ *Tue-Sat. 8.30am-12.30pm, 2.15-7pm.* One of the best addresses in town for olive oil and regional specialities.

La Maison de l'Olive – *18 Rue Pairolière –* ☎ *04 93 80 01 61.* Marseille soaps made from pure olive oil, lotions and scents for the body and home, and regional products such as dried tomatos, lemon jam, marinated capers and olives, and Provençal herbs and spices.

À l'Olivier – *7 Rue St-François-de-Paule -* ☎ *04 93 13 44 97 - nice@olivier-on-line. com.* Every brand of French olive oil with the AOC label is sold in this boutique, originally opened in 1822, in Nice since 2004. Also a fine selection of elegant glassware, dishes, tablecloths.

Confiserie Auer – *7 Rue St-François-de-Paule –* ☎ *04 93 85 77 98 – www.maison-auer.com –* ⊙ *Tue-Sat. 9am-1.30pm, 2.30-6pm.* A gorgeous vintage boutique selling candied fruit and crystallised flowers from the Nice region, as well as chocolates, and calissons from Aix.

Confiserie Florian – *14 Quai Papacino, on the Port –* ☎ *04 93 55 43 50 – www.confiseriefloran.com –* ⊙ *Guided tours of the factory 9am-noon, 2-6.30pm.* Candied fruit, lemon, orange and grapefruit preserve, chocolates and sweets, crystallised petals and delicious jams made with rose, violet and jasmine blossom.

Maison Poilpot - Aux Parfums de Grasse – *10 Rue St-Gaétan –* ☎ *04 93 85 60 77 –* ⊙ *Daily except Mon 9.30am-noon, 2.30-6pm.* This traditional perfumery produces more than 80 different fragrances, including popular Mediterranean scents such as mimosa, rose, violet and lemon.

L'Art Gourmand – *21 Rue du Marché – Old Town –* ☎ *04 93 62 51 79 – www.nice-ville. com-* ⊙ *Open 10am-7pm (Jul-Aug 10am-11pm).* This Old Nice boutique has many treats available to go or eat in: nougats, calisson, candied fruit, cookies, pastries, ice cream and northern France specialities. There's a tea room on the mezzanine decorated with murals.

Fenocchio – *2 Place Rossetti - Old Town –* ☎ *04 93 80 72 52 – www.nice-ville.com–* ⊙ *Open Feb-Oct 10am-1am.* This famous ice cream and sorbet maker has some of the most amazing flavors, from avocado and sun-dried tomato to honey and pine nut. With almost 100 flavors to choose from, you'll have to go back more than once!

Domaine de la Source – *303 Chemin de Saquier – 10km/6mi from Nice on N 202 – St-Roman-de-Bellet –* ☎ *04 93 29 81 60.* A family of horticulturists converted to wine growers run this tiny domain which produces the rare Bellet wines of Nice. There are reds and whites, aged in oak barrels before being bottled. Visitors get a tour of the winemaking process from the friendly owner.

MARKETS

Marché aux Poissons – The fish market is at the Place St-François daily except Monday, 6am to 1pm.

Marché aux Fleurs – The flower market is on the Cours Saleya Tuesday through Sunday morning, 6am to 5.30pm.

Marché aux Fruits et Légumes – The colorful food market on the Cour Saleya takes place Tuesday to Sunday, 6am-1.30pm.

Marché de la Liberation– locals' food market from the Avenue Malausséna to Place Charles-de-Gaulle.

Marché aux Puces – Flea market Tuesday to Saturday 10am-6pm, on Place Robilante.

Marché de la Brocante – Antique market Mondays on Cours Saleya, 7.30am-6pm.

LEISURE ACTIVITIES

Beaches – The Baie des Anges covers a 5km/3.1mi stretch of coastline with smooth pebbles *(galets)*. There are many public beaches placed under close surveillance, and 15 private beaches providing a host of sporting activities.

Hiking – *14 Avenue Mirabeau –* ☎ *04 93 62 59 99 – www.cafnice.org –* ⊙ *Office open Mon-Fri 4-8pm.* CAF (Club Alpin Français) organises one-day hiking tours across the Nice hinterland and Mercantour Park leaving from Nice.

Skiing – *www.guideriviera.com* – The nearby skiing resorts of Auron (☎ *04 93 23 02 66)* and Valberg (☎ *04 93 02 52 27)*, which are only a two-hour drive away, are undoubtedly among the main attractions of the Nice area.

CALENDAR OF EVENTS

There are many traditional festivals throughout the year. Ask at the Tourism Office for a complete schedule.

Nice Carnival – This colorful, extravagant event invariably attracts large crowds every year. Festivities take place around Shrove Tuesday (Mardi Gras) and last for a fortnight. They include processions, floats, firework displays, costume balls and battles where showers of flowers and confetti are thrown!

Cougourdons Festival – Cougourdons are gourds that have been dried and painted. The city of Nice pays homage to these curious vegetables in early April.

Fête de la Mer et de la St-Pierre – A festival celebrating the sea and St-Peter on the port and Quai des Etats-Unis the last weekend in June.

Nice Jazz Festival – The former Roman amphitheatre is the prestigious backdrop

for the jazz festival that is held in Nice the last two weeks of July, attended by leading performers from all over the world. ☎ *0 892 707 407.*
Fête de la San Bertoumiéu – A festival of traditional arts and crafts, regional foods

and entertainment in the Old Town the first weekend in September.
Crèche Vivante Lou Presèpi – A living nativity scene with people and animals, at Place Rossetti the week of Christmas.

Musée Marc-Chagall★★

  Jul-Sep: daily 10am-6pm; Oct-Jun: daily 10am-5pm. Last admission 30min before closing. Closed Tue, 1 Jan, 1 May, 25 Dec. 5.50€, no charge 1st Sun in the month. ☎ 04 93 53 87 21. www.musee-chagall.fr.
The museum was designed to display the 17 great paintings making up the artist's Biblical Message (painted between 1954 and 1967).

Front de mer★★ (seafront). Musée Jules-Chéret des Beaux-Arts★★ *Tue-Sun 10am-6pm. Closed Mon,1 Jan, Easter Sun, 1 May, 25 Dec. 4€, no charge 1st and 3rd Sun in the month. ☎ 04 92 15 28 28.*

Musée d'Art moderne et d'Art contemporain★★ *Tue-Sun 10am-6pm. Closed Mon, 1 Jan, Easter Sun, 1 May, 25 Dec. 4€, no charge 1st and 3rd Sun in the month. ☎ 04 93 62 61 62. www.mamac-nice.org.*

Musée Masséna★ *Closed for restoration*– painting, decorative arts, local history.
Musée d'Art Naïf Jarousry★ *Wed-Mon 10am-6pm. Closed Tue,1 Jan, Easter, 1 May, 25 Dec. 4€, no charge 1st and 3rd Sun in the month. ☎ 04 93 71 78 33.*

Palais des Arts, du Tourisme et des Congrès★ (Acropolis). Chapelle de la Miséricorde★. Église St-Martin – St-Augustin – interior★. *Daily except Mon and Sun afternoon 8.30am-noon, 2-6pm. ☎ 04 93 92 60 45.*

Excursion

Corniches de la Riviera★★★

Circular tour of 41km – 26mi – allow 3 hours. The Lower Corniche road skirts the foot of Mont Boron, giving fine views over Villefranche-sur-Mer and its bay. The highly indented coastline is the result of the recent folding and subsequent drowning of the limestone Pre-Alps.

Both **Cap Ferrat**★★ and nearby headland, Pointe St-Hospice, offer splendid views of the Riviera with its corniche roads; the village of Èze-Bord-de-Mer, the fashionable resort of Beaulieu, Cap d'Ail can all be identified, and rising out of the sea in the distance is Cap Martin.

Clinging like an eagle's nest to its inaccessible rock spike, **Èze**★★ seems the very archetype of a hill village. It was inhabited by the Ligurians and by the Phoenicians, then fortified against raiders from the sea. In 1706 both the village and its castle were demolished on the orders of Louis XIV, but it was rebuilt after 1760.

NÎMES★★★

POPULATION 138 527

MICHELIN MAP 339 L 5

GREEN GUIDE PROVENCE

Nîmes lies between the limestone hills of the Garrigue to the north and the alluvial plain of the Costière du Gard to the south. Its elegant and bustling boulevards are shaded by lotus-trees. The quality of its Roman remains is outstanding.

Emperor Augustus heaped privileges on Nîmes and allowed the building of fortifications. The town, situated on the Domitian Way, then proceeded to erect splendid buildings: the Maison Carrée along the south side of the forum, an amphitheatre able to hold 24 000 people, a circus, baths fed by an imposing aqueduct, the Pont du Gard. In the 2C the town won favour with Emperors Hadrian and Antoninus Pius (whose wife's family came from Nîmes); it continued to flourish and build and reached the peak of its glory.

▶ **Orient Yourself:** Heading northwest along boulevard Victor-Hugo, the Maison Carrée appears in the centre of an elegant paved square separated from the Carré d'art by the boulevard itself. From here you can take the narrow rue de l'Horloge then turn right into place de l'Horloge and then left into rue de la Madeleine to find the main shopping street. Nîmes is a "Town of Art and History" and offers 2hr guided tours. They include a visit to the hôtel Fontfroide (& *see the description under "Sights"*), which is not open to visits otherwise. Tours all year round on Sat at 2.30pm (Jul-Sep: Tue, Thu, and Sat 10am; during school term: Tue, Thu, Sat: 2.30pm). The tour costs 5.50€. Information at the tourist office or on www.vpah. culture.fr.

☺ **Don't Miss:** The amphitheatre **Arènes** and the ancient Roman temple **Maison Carrée.**

◕ **Organizing Your Time:** Those who can't stand the heat should avoid the city in August when it becomes an absolute furnace, even at night. Visitors who object to bull-fighting or crowds are advised not to come during the long weekend of Whitsun (7th Sun-Mon after Easter) when entry just about anywhere is almost impossible, as is finding accomodation.

Ⓟ **Parking:** Entering the city along the canal de la Fontaine and boulevard Victor-Hugo, go around the amphitheatre to get to the underground car park beneath the Esplanade.

Sights

Arènes★★★

◕ *Mid-Mar to mid-Oct: 9am-7pm; mid-Oct to mid-Mar: 10am-5pm.* ◕ *Closed 1 Jan, 1 May, 25 Dec and days when performances are held.* ⊜ *4.80€ (children: 3.50€).* ☎ *04 66 76 72 77.*

This superb structure was built in the reign of Augustus, possibly some 80 years before the amphitheatre at Arles. Its barrel-vaulted galleries are characteristically Roman. To gain a full appreciation of the huge task the Roman architects set themselves and the boldness with which they carried it out, it is necessary to climb to the covered gallery of the top level (from which there are good views over the town), as well as inspecting the first-floor gallery (note particularly the size of the lintels supporting the vaulting) and part of the barrel-vaulted double gallery on the ground floor. The scale of the great structure is extraordinarily impressive, as is the builders' achievement in cutting, transporting and placing stonework of such dimensions with such precision.

Maison Carrée

Although a visit to the amphitheatre is a must at any time, it is during the important corridas when it is packed full of lively crowds that it presents a spectacle closely reminiscent of the past. The taste of the local people for Spanish-style bullfights has never faltered in over 150 years, with the very popular Whitsun and September gatherings now attracting some of the biggest names in bullfighting.

Maison Carrée★★★

◕ *Mid-Mar to mid-Oct: 9am-7pm; mid-Oct to mid-Mar: 10am-5pm.* ◕ *Closed 1 Jan, 1 May, 25 Dec. No charge.* ☎ *04 66 58 38 00.*

Known as the Square House, this is the purest, as well as the bestpreserved, of all Roman temples. It was built

Nîmes - Address Book

Guided tours of the town – 🔊 Nîmes has been listed as a "Town of Art and History" and the guided tours (2hrs), organised by the tourist office, are conducted by guides approved by the Centre des Monuments Nationaux (National Monuments Centre). They include a visit to the hôtel Fontfroide, which is not open to visitors otherwise. All year round: Sat 2.30pm (July to Sept: 10am); during school term: Tue, Thur, Sat: 2.30pm. 5.34€.

An all-purpose ticket (pass) allows entry to all city monuments and museums and can be purchased at the first sight you visit: 9.15€ (children: 4.57€), valid 3 days.

Hôtel Fontfroide – 🔊 Guided tours only.

WHEN (NOT) TO VISIT NÎMES

Those who can't tolerate the heat should avoid the city in August when it becomes a veritable furnace, even at night. Visitors who object to corridas and crowds are advised not to come during the long weekend of Pentecôte (7th Sun-Mon after Easter) when entry to just about anywhere is almost impossible, as is finding accommodation!

ENTERTAINMENT

Programmes – See the daily newspaper *Midi-Libre*, the weekly publication *La Semaine de Nîmes* or its rival the *Gazette de Nîmes*, or *Le César (free)*, provided by the Tourist Information Centre.

Cinema – Art house cinema Le Sémaphore, 25 rue Porte-de-France, ☎ 04 66 67 83 11.

Theatres – L'Armature, 12 rue de l'Ancien-Vélodrome, ☎ 04 66 82 20 52, housed in a hangar which used to be an industrial warehouse, now hosts concerts, plays and exhibitions.

SHOPPING

Maison Villaret – *13 rue de la Madeleine* – ☎ 04 66 67 41 79. Crunchy almond biscuits known as *croquants*.

Brandade Raymond – *34 rue Nationale* – ☎ 04 66 67 20 47. A century dedicating to the producing of this classic Provençal dish!

Wine – *La Vinothèque* – *18 rue Jean-Rebou* – ☎ 04 66 67 20 44. Local wines.

Provençal fabrics – *Olivades* – *4 place de la Maison-Carré* – ☎ 04 66 21 01 31. The textile industry was born during the reign of Louis XI, when the first workshop was founded. In the 18C the textile factories (silk and serge) embraced more than 300 professions and gave work to 10 000 people. The tradition has continued through the centuries with highs and lows and nowadays is represented by prestigious brands such as Cacharel who have made their mark with this shop.

Books – *Librairie Goyard* – *34 bd Victor-Hugo* – ☎ 04 66 67 20 51. For books on the region and on bullfighting.

Markets – Large market on Mon on bd Gambetta. Organic market Fri mornings on av Jean-Jaurès. Flea market Sun mornings in the Costières stadium car park. Evening market, Jul-Aug, Thur 6-10pm ('Les jeudis de Nîmes').

EVENTS

Ferias and bullfighting – There are three ferias in Nîmes: during the so-called "spring" feria which takes place in February, *novilladas* take place throughout the weekend; the Whitsun feria, the most well-known, lasts from the 7th Thursday after Easter to the following Monday and includes a pégoulade along the boulevards, *abrivados*, *novilladas* and corridas throughout the day and evening as well as other entertainments all over the city; the harvest feria, the most typical of all, takes place in mid-September.

Tickets – As well as single tickets you can also buy a pass which gives access to the shows and the best seats. Don't expect to gain access at the last moment at the Whitsun and Harvest ferias, unless you buy tickets on the black market for astronomical prices.

At the ticket office prices vary from 15.24€ to 76.22€ for a *corrida* and from 4.57€ to 7.62€ for a novillada.

Ticket office: 1 rue Alexandre-Ducros, ☎ 04 66 67 28 02.

Amphitheatre – Since 1988, from October to April, the amphitheatre is covered by a detachable dome consisting of an inflatable, transparent cloth held up by an elliptical beam which in turn leans on pilasters which are fixed to the modern parts of the monument. This structure, which forms a spectacular setting for shows held in the winter, can hold up to 7 000 people. As well as ferias, the amphitheatre also hosts rock and pop concerts, fairs and conventions and Davis Cup tournaments.

Le Printemps du jazz – (3rd week in March) Jazz concerts in a variety of venues around town.

For coin ranges see Legend at the back of the guide.

EATING OUT

🍽 **Bistrot des Arènes** – *11 rue Bigot* – ☎ 04 66 21 40 18 – 🕐 *closed Aug, Sat lunchtime and Sun.* Sample the specialities of Lyons restaurants known as bouchon in a delightfully ornate setting crammed with objects including the French puppet Guignol.

🍽 **Le Bistrot au Chapon Fin** – *3 place du Château-Fadaise* – ☎ 04 66 67 34 73 – 🕐 *closed Aug. Sat lunchtime and Sun.* Located behind the church of St Paul, the old façade of this building is more than a little inviting... Inside, the bistro-style decor, with its feria and movie posters and Nîmes paintings, won't disappoint you. Note the collection of cocks! Daily dishes are listed on a blackboard.

🍽🍽 **Le Bouchon et L'Assiette** – *5 bis rue Sauve –* ☎ *04 66 62 02 93 –* ⏰ *closed 2-17 Jan, 29 Apr-2 May, 29 Jul-23 Aug, Tue lunchtime and Wed.* A carefully chosen decor, embellished with paintings and antiques, a warm welcome, and tasty seasonal cooking.

🍽🍽 **Aux Plaisirs des Halles** – *4 rue Littré –* ☎ *04 66 36 01 02 –* ⏰ *closed 12-20 Aug, Sun evenings and Mon except evenings in Jul-Aug.* Everyone in town talks about this place. Once you've got past the discreet façade you will find an elegant yellow room with armchairs draped in fabric, a patio which has been turned into a pretty terrace, excellent, well-presented food and a good wine list.

WHERE TO STAY

🛏 **Hôtel Amphithéâtre** – *4 rue des Arènes –* ☎ *04 66 67 28 51 –* ⏰ *closed 2-15 Jan –* 16 rooms - 🍽 *5.64€.* Near the amphitheatre in a pedestrian street, this small, family-run hotel with its slightly austere façade, is an excellent address for those travelling on a low budget. It offers quite spacious rooms decorated with rustic furniture.

🛏 **Chambre d'hôte La Mazade** – *In the village –* 30730 St-Mamert-du-Gard – 17km/10.5mi west of Nîmes via D 999 and D 1 – ☎ *04 66 81 17 56 –* www.bbfrance. com/couston.html – 🍽 *– 3 rooms: evening meal 14€.* This is a very original family house: each room has designer decor and is bursting with plants and Mexican objets d'art... This picturesque mix of styles makes for an amusing setting! In the evening, dinner is served under an arbour on the terrace which faces the garden.

🛏🛏 **New Hôtel la Baume** – *21 rue Nationale –* ☎ *04 66 76 28 42 – 34 rooms –* 🍽 *8.38€ – restaurant 12.20/20.58€.* This 17C mansion successfully blends contemporary and antique styles. An interior stone staircase leads to the simple bedrooms, a few of which have pretty, French-style painted ceilings.

ON THE TOWN

Behind the numerous ancient buildings in Nîmes lies the hidden shadow of Bacchus and the tendency to view life as a perpetual party. The whole year is marked out by the ferias and the city in general is characterised by a huge number and variety of cafés including Café-concerts, bodegas, Irish pubs or the great fin-de-siècle cafés: each has its own following.

Haddock Café – *13 rue de l'Agau –* ☎ *04 66 67 86 57 – haddock.cafe@libertysurf.fr –* ⏰ *Mon-Fri 11.30am-3pm, 7pm-2am, Sat 7pm-3am.* This wine bar-restaurant cultivates food (wine by the glass, reasonably priced menu) as much the arts. There is a never-ending series of entertainments including concerts, literary and philosophy evenings and art exhibitions. Behind the wide, metal bar Philippe, the owner, presides over what is definitely one of the most dynamic venues of Nîmes' cultural life.

La Grand Bourse – *2 bd des Arènes –* ☎ *04 66 67 21 91 –* ⏰ *daily 7am-1am.* With its Napoleon III style coffered ceiling, a terrace facing the amphitheatre and deep comfortable rattan armchairs, this is the most prestigious café in Nîmes. Excellent, professional service attracts customers of all ages and backgrounds.

Bar Hemingway – *15 rue Gaston-Boissier –* ☎ *02 66 21 90 30 – hotel.imperator@ wanadoo.fr –* ⏰ *daily 8am-11pm.* Opening onto a garden with redwood and cedar trees, a fountain and sculptures, the Hemingway bar of the Hotel Imperator Concorde is an oasis of calm and magic. Photographs evoke the presence in this bar of two lovers of tauromachy: Ava Gardner and Ernest Hemingway, who wrote Death in the Afternnon (1962), a magnificent book about bullfighting.

Le Diagonal – *41bis rue Émile-Jamais –* ☎ *04 66 21 70 01 –* ⏰ *Tue-Thu 5pm-2am, Fri-Sun and the eve of public holidays 5pm-3am.* ⏰ *Closed 3 weeks in Aug.* This 1950s style bar is run by a couple. Rather like the sphinx at the entry of Thebes, the husband poses riddles to customers, if in a rather more convivial atmosphere, judging by the din of the clientele, the board games and the art exhibitions (art previews on the first Thursday of the month). Tapas and house punch, Latino and African music as well as jazz and salsa.

in the reign of Augustus (1C BC) probably by an architect from the Narbonensis (the Roman province in France) and was dedicated to the cult of the emperors. It was inspired by the Temple of Apollo in Rome and is framed by an elegant portico. The carved decoration of the capitals supporting the cornice is outstanding. The architect achieved the harmonious design by varying the number of brackets and the spacing of the columns.

Jardin de la Fontaine★★

In Roman times this site was occupied by a spring, a theatre, a temple and baths. Today's shady gardens exemplify the subtle use of water in the landscapes of Languedoc. They were laid out in the characteristic manner of the 18C, with pools leading into a canal, balustraded walks, porticoes...

◐◑▷ Musée Archéologique★ ◷Tue-Sun 10am-6pm. ◷ Closed Mon, 1 Jan, 1 May, 1 Nov and 25 Dec. ⊜ 4.45€ (children under 10 years: no charge), ticket combined with the Natural History Museum. ☎ 04 66 76 74 80. www.nimes.fr.

Musée des Beaux-Arts★. Musée du Vieux-Nîmes★. Carré d'art★ ⅃ ◷ Tue-Sun 10am-6pm. Last admission 30min before closing. ⌁ Possibility of a guided tour (1hr) Sat-Sun at 3pm and 4.30pm. ◷ Closed Mon, 1 Jan, 1 May, 1 Nov, 25 Dec. ⊜ 4.80€ (children 3.50€), no charge 1st Sun in the month. ☎ 04 66 76 35 70.

NOHANT★

MICHELIN MAP 323 H 7

GREEN GUIDE DORDOGNE BERRY LIMOUSIN

The hamlet of Nohant with its little square shaded by great elms owes its fame to the novelist George Sand (1804-76). This controversial figure, an early fighter for women's right to emotional freedom, was a descendant of Frederick of Saxony, King of Poland, and Aurore, the illegitimate daughter of the Marshal de Saxe who had acquired the Nohant estate in 1793 when it was much more extensive than it is today.

Visit

Château

◷ Guided tours ⌁ (1hr, last departure 1 hour before closing time) Jul and Aug: daily 9.30am-6.30pm; May-Jun: daily 9.30am-noon, 2-6.30pm; Apr and Sep: daily 10-12.30pm, 2-6pm. Oct-Mar: daily 10am-12.30pm, 1.30-5pm. ◷ Closed 1 Jan, 1 May, 1 and 11 Nov, 25 Dec. ⊜ 6.10€ (under 17 years: no charge). ☎ 02 54 31 06 04.

The house, built in the 18C, was extended in the 19C. The literary output generated here – 80 novels and some 12 000 letters – together with the authoress's notoriety, made the place famous throughout Europe. In her pastoral novels George Sand depicted the countryside of the Black Vale – Vallée noire – and the Boischaut, a landscape of small hedged fields with farmsteads half-hidden in the luxuriant greenery. It was here that she received many of the celebrities of the age, Chopin, Liszt, Delacroix...

George Sand's life is touchingly evoked in the theatre designed by Chopin, by the lime-wood marionettes made by her son Maurice for which she sewed the costumes, and in the Blue Room where she died.

Excursion

Église de Vic

2km – 1.5mi northwest. St Martin's Church (Église St-Martin) houses an unusual series of frescoes (fresques★) dating from the early 12C and depicting the Redemption. They are pleasing both as a group and also in the conventional way in which the individual figures are disposed and related to one another. They are related to the art of Aquitaine and even of Catalonia both in technique and in the way in which movement is evoked. Together with Prosper Mérimée, George Sand helped bring them to the attention of the public.

Abbaye de **NOIRLAC**★★

MICHELIN MAP 323 K 6

GREEN GUIDE DORDOGNE BERRY LIMOUSIN

Noirlac is a Cistercian foundation of 1136 whose plan exemplifies the kind of layout envisaged by St Bernard for an abbey of this type. It is the most complete of the 12 surviving Benedictine abbeys in France (out of an original 345), though by no means without its share of upheavals; the Hundred Years War, the Wars of Religion, the commendatory regime, 18C additions, conversion into a porcelain factory in 1822, use as a centre for refugees in the First World War and the Spanish Civil War, and a final role as an old people's home before its restoration in 1975.

Visit

🕐 *Jul and Aug: daily 9.45am-6.30pm; Apr-Jun and Sep: daily 9.45am-12.30pm, 2-6.30pm. Oct-Nov and Feb-Mar: daily 9.45am-12.30pm, 2-5pm.* 🕐 *Closed Dec-Jan (call for specific dates). Call for admission prices.* ☎ *02 48 62 01 01.*

The abbey church (**église abbatiale**) dates from 1150-60. With its plain east end, its great transepts and its vast aisles it follows (like Fontenay Abbey in Burgundy) the plan of the great abbey at Clairvaux. Dating from the end of the Romanesque (in the design of the pillars) and the beginning of the Gothic (vaults still without ribs), it shows clearly how advanced this region was in the development of architectural style. The building of the final two bays of the nave at the beginning of the 13C marked the completion of the great edifice. The modern grisaille glass is the work of Jean-Pierre Raynaud, aided by craftsmen from Chartres and Bourges; it adds a certain subtlety of lighting to the perfect simplicity of the architecture.

Among the conventual buildings, the chapter-house was built in the 12C, and the refectory and the Gothic cloisters in the 13C.

OBERNAI★★

POPULATION 9 610

MICHELIN MAP 315 I 6

GREEN GUIDE ALSACE LORRAINE CHAMPAGNE

Sited where the lower, vine-covered slopes of Mont Ste-Odile meet the plain, its ruined walls eloquent of its ancient independence and its narrow, winding streets lined with high-gabled houses, the little town of Obernai seems to represent the very essence of Alsace. In the 14C it was one of the cities of the urban league known as the Decapolis. A period of great prosperity followed in the 16C, then, in 1679, it was annexed by Louis XIV.

Visit

Place du Marché★★

With its cheerfully-coloured timber-framed buildings, the picturesque market-place is the centrepiece of Obernai, graced by a fountain of 1904 with a statue of St Odile. It has a Town Hall (**Hôtel de ville**★) of the 15C-16C with a fine oriel window and sculpted balcony, a 16C Corn Hall (**Ancienne halle aux blés**★) much restored but with a stork's nest above its doorway, and the Chapel Tower (**Tour de la Chapelle**★), a 13C bell-tower topped by a spire 60m – nearly 200ft above the ground.

 Maisons anciennes★ (old houses).

Excursion

Mont Ste-Odile★★

12km – 7mi southwest. Its associations with St Odile, the province's patron saint, help make this the most popular summit in the whole of Alsace. The high sandstone crag rises 764m – 2 500ft above the plain, offering a spectacular **panorama**★★.

Such a site was bound to attract attention; the Celts were the first to fortify it; their so-called Pagan Wall (**Mur païen**), running for more than 10km – 6 miles is the best-known and the most important of their defensive works, with stonework on a truly Cyclopean scale. The wall was remodelled by the Romans.

At the centre of a magnificent firwood is the convent (**couvent**) built in honour of St Odile. Often added to and restored over time, it is an important place of pilgrimage.

L'OISANS★★★

MICHELIN MAP 333 J 7

GREEN GUIDE FRENCH ALPS

In this region drained by the Romanche flowing down from the Lautaret pass (Col du Lautaret), the population is grouped in villages sited on terraces and reached by narrow roads with spectacular hairpin bends; this contrasts with the Savoie, where the inhabitants live in scattered farmsteads. Like most glacial valleys, that of the Romanche has a self-contained agricultural economy, pasture and arable land complementing each other. Further downstream, as it enters the sub-alpine depression south of Grenoble, the valley becomes one of the industrial corridors typical of the French Alps.

Driving tour

Les Écrins

In character not unlike the other highlands making up the central part of the southern Alps, these bare mountains between the valleys of the Romanche, Drac and Durance look down on more than 100km² – some 40sq miles of glaciers. The Route des Grandes Alpes (see ROUTE DES GRANDES ALPES) gives fine views of the north and east faces of the massif (from the Col du Galibier, the Oratoire du Chazelet, and from La Grave), cut by isolated valleys with their typical way of life and served by long cul-de-sac roads; the best-known is the valley of the Vénéon leading to La Bérarde.

Bassin du Bourg d'Oisans★

Until the 13C the fertile basin was a glacial lake, now filled in by material brought down by the Romanche and its tributary, the Vénéon. This is the economic centre of the region.

Excursion

Vallée du Vénéon★★★

31km – 19mi from Bourg-d'Oisans to La Bérarde. The road up to La Bérarde offers a spectacular lesson in glacial geomorphology made even more dramatic by the scale of the great U-shaped valley and the ruggedness of its high granite walls. It takes in the great rock bar at Bourg-d'Arud with its wilderness of tumbled boulders, the basin of Plan-du-Lac, the terraces of Le Clapier-de-St-Christophe (hairpin bends), Pré-Clot and Champhorent, the moraines planted with conifers and with birches (the pioneer tree of early post-glacial times), waterfalls cascading down from hanging valleys, and a number of compact little villages, before reaching La Bérarde, formerly a shepherds' hamlet and now a climbing centre.

◖◗ Cascade de la Sarennes★. Gorges de la Lignarre★.

ORADOUR-SUR-GLANE★★

POPULATION 1 998

MICHELIN MAP 325 D 5

GREEN GUIDE DORDOGNE BERRY LIMOUSIN

Visit

Access to the ruins of the martyred village via the Centre de la Memoire. The centre offers a permanent exhibit dedicated to the rise of Nazism and the massacre which took place on 10 June 1944. ◷ *Jul-Aug: 9am-7pm; Mar-Jun and Sep-Oct: 9am-6pm; Feb, Nov and early to mid-Dec: 9am-5pm. Last admission 1hr before closing.* ∞ *6€.* ☎ *05 55 43 04 30.*

The stark walls of the burnt-out village of Oradour-sur-Glane have been kept as an eloquent reminder of the horrors of war. On 10 June 1944, a few days after the Normandy landings, an SS Division was being moved from southwestern France to reinforce the front. Harassed by the Resistance, the troops made a characteristically brutal example of this entirely innocent place, massacring its inhabitants (men, women and children), and laying waste the village itself. The 642 victims are buried in the village cemetery; a memorial commemorates the terrible deed.

ORANGE★★

POPULATION 26 964

MICHELIN MAP 332 B 9

GREEN GUIDE PROVENCE

Orange flourished in the days of the Pax Romana as an important staging-post on the great highway between Arles and Lyon. In the 16C, it came into the possession of William the Silent, ruler of the German principality of Nassau, then Stadtholder of the United Provinces. He took the title of Prince of Orange and founded the Orange-Nassau line. Orange is still proud of its association with the royal house of the Netherlands, whose preferred title is Prince (or Princess) of Orange.

It was François de Grignan, Lieutenant-General to Louis XIV in Provence, who captured the town during the war against Holland. In 1678 under the Treaty of Nijmegen, the town became French territory.

A performance during the Chorégies at Orange

▶ **Orient Yourself:** Orange, which is listed as a "Town of Art and History," offers discovery tours conducted by guide-lecturers approved by the Ministry of Culture and Communication. Information at the tourist office or on www.vpah.culture.fr.

Sights

Théâtre antique★★★

🕐 *Jan-Feb and Nov-Dec: 9am-4.30pm; Mar and Oct: 9am-5.30pm. Apr, May, Sep: 9am-6pm. Jun, Jul, and Aug: 9am-7pm.* ⊜ *7.50€ (children under 7 years: no charge).* ☎ *04 90 51 17 60.*

Dating from the reign of Augustus, this theatre is the best-preserved structure of its type in the whole of the Roman world.

The stage wall measures 103x36m – 340x120ft; Louis XIV called it "the finest wall in all the kingdom". Built of granite and African breccia, its outer face is of striking simplicity, interrupted only by the mounts for the poles supporting the awnings shading the audience from the sun.

On the auditorium side, the wall has lost its marble facing and mosaic decoration, its columns and its statues. The great statue of Augustus has been replaced in its central niche; together with some remaining hammer-finished granite blocks, it gives some idea of how the theatre must have appeared originally.

Arc de Triomphe★★

This was built between the years AD 21 and 26. On its north and east sides are reliefs depicting the exploits of the Second Legion in Gaul (weapons both of Gauls and of Amazons), the triumph of Rome (captured Gauls in chains) and Roman domination of the seas following the naval battle of Actium (anchors, oars, warships).

ORCIVAL★★

POPULATION 381

MICHELIN MAP 326 E 8

GREEN GUIDE AUVERGNE THE RHÔNE VALLEY

Many houses in this tiny Auvergne hill-town still have their original roof coverings of tiles cut from the phonolitic lavas of the nearby Roche Tuilière, the core of an ancient volcano.

Basilique Notre-Dame★★

Call in advance, ☎ *04 73 65 81 49.*

Illustration  *see Introduction: Art – Architecture.* Set hard against the hillside and completed around 1130, this basilica is a typical structure of the Auvergne Romanesque, with a many-tiered apse and side-walls strengthened by powerful buttresses and massive arches. The south doorway, dedicated to St John, topped by rows of arches, has elaborate original strapwork and hinges in wrought iron.

Inside, the majestic crossing is lit by 14 windows and supported by sturdy transverse arches, while both chancel and crypt, the latter with a spacious ambulatory, are masterpieces of their kind.

Among the capitals is a 12C one of the Miser or the Money-Lender, illustrating vice, no longer by means of an individual personification, but by its consequences. In the chancel is a **Virgin Enthroned**★ still with its original gilt ornamentation; one side of the face (left) is that of an Auvergne peasant woman, the other (right) of a society lady, an affirmation of the universality of the "throne of wisdom".

Aven d'ORGNAC★★★

MICHELIN MAP 331 I 8

GREEN GUIDE PROVENCE

This extraordinary chasm, Aven d'Orgnac, lies among the woods covering the Ardèche plateau. It was first explored by Robert de Joly (1887-1968) on 19 August 1935. Joly was an electrical engineer, fascinated by cars and planes but above all by speleology; it was due to his efforts that the mysteries of France's underground world were revealed, he himself being responsible for numerous "firsts".

Visit

Kids ⏱ *Guided tours* 🔄 *(1hr) Jul and Aug: daily 9.30am-6pm; Apr-Jun and Sep: daily 9.30am-5.30pm; Oct to mid-Nov: daily 9.30am-noon, 2-5.15pm; Feb-Mar and Christmas vacation: daily 10.30am-noon, 2-4.45pm.* ⏱ *Closed mid-Nov to end Jan.* ✆ *9.20€ (children: 5.70€), ticket combined with museum.* ☎ *04 75 38 65 10.*

Of the four caverns at Orgnac, only **Orgnac I** has so far been opened up to the public. The caverns owe their origin to an underground stream which infiltrated a fault-line in Tertiary times and linked up the Cèze and Ardèche rivers. Over the millennia the slow and silent processes of erosion and corrosion have resulted in the build-up of the extraordinary concretions visible here. Towards the end of the Tertiary era, earthquakes associated with the uplifting of the Alps shattered stalactites and threw down stalagmites, while the Quaternary age, with its alternation of hot and cold periods, brought other changes. A mass of rubble separates the two upper chambers from the lower one, whose stalagmites have developed a variety of forms: bayonet-like spikes marking a resurgence of activity following the removal of an obstruction to the supply of water, "stacks of plates" where the height of the vault has inhibited the formation of pillars, and "pine-cones" where the build-up of material was irregular.

Orgnac III was inhabited 300 000 years ago; the museum **(musée)** has displays on the cultures which flourished between the Rhône and the Cévennes from Paleolithic times to the Bronze Age.

ORLÉANS★

POPULATION 243 153

MICHELIN MAP 318 I 4

GREEN GUIDE CHÂTEAUX OF THE LOIRE

Orléans grew up on the great bend in the Loire between the rich cornfields of the Beauce to the north and the heaths and forests of the Sologne to the south. For a time the city was the capital of France, its cathedral the setting for the coronation in 996 of Hugh Capet's son, Robert II le Pieux (the Pious). Place du Martroi, with its statue of Joan of Arc, is the centre of the historic town. Orléans is now the capital of the Centre region of France (an economic division) and an important administrative and university town.

A Bit of History

The Siege of 1428-29 – This memorable siege was one of the great episodes in the history of France, marking the country's rebirth after a period of despair. It began on 12 October 1428, as the Earl of Salisbury attempted to take the bridge over the Loire and thus link up with the other English forces in central and southern France. Lasting almost seven months, the siege was the scene of one of the first-ever (albeit inconclusive) artillery duels. On 29 April 1429, **Joan of Arc** arrived from Chinon (👁 *see CHINON*); she skirted Orléans to the south and entered the city by the Burgundy Gate (Porte de Bourgogne), several days in advance of the army advancing along the north bank of the river. By 7 May, victory seemed assured, and on the 8th the English capitulated. In Orléans, Joan enjoyed the hospitality of Jacques Boucher, whose fine half-timbered dwelling with its museum is now known as Joan of Arc House **(Maison de Jeanne d'Arc★)**.

Sights

Musée des Beaux-Arts★★

 ♿ *Tue-Sat 10am-12.15pm, 1.30-5.45pm, Sun and public holidays 1.30-6pm.* ♿ *Closed Mon, 1 Jan, 1 and 8 May, 14 Jul, 1 and 11 Nov, 25 Dec.* ⍊ *3€ (under 16 years: no charge), no charge 1st Sun in the month.* ☎ *02 38 79 21 55. www.orleans.fr.*

This museum houses some of the richest collections in France. The painting section constitutes most of the collection, especially the French school from the 16C to the 20C. Among the most famous: Le Nain, P de Champaigne, Courbet, Boudin, Gauguin, Vigée-Lebrun, Rouault, Gromaire, Soutine, Zao Wou-ki and even Max Jacob (better known as a writer).

Cathédrale Ste-Croix★

Construction of the cathedral lasted from the 13C to the 16C. The nave was torn down by the Huguenots in 1568, but rebuilt in composite Gothic style by **Henri IV**, mindful of the city's loyalty to him.

The woodwork **(boiseries★★)** of the choir stalls (1706) includes splendidly carved medallions and panels adorning the high backs.

In the crypt **(crypte)** are traces of the three buildings which preceded the present cathedral, and two sarcophagi, one of which belonged to bishop Robert de Courtenay (13C) who collected the most precious items in the treasury **(trésor)**.

▶▶ Musée historique★. Musée des Sciences naturelles★ ♿ *Daily 2-6pm.* ♿ *Closed 1 Jan, 1 and 8 May, 1 Nov, 25 Dec.* ⍊ *3€, no charge 3rd Sun in the month.* ☎ *02 38 54 61 05.*

Parc Floral de la Source★★ (at Olivet) ♿ *Apr to mid-Nov: daily 9am-6pm (closing time: 7pm); mid-Nov to end Mar: daily 2-5pm.* ♿ *Closed 1 Jan and 25 Dec.* ⍊ *3.80€ (6-18 years: 2.10€). Butterfly glasshouse:* ⍊ *2.50€ (6-18 years: 2.10€).* ☎ *02 38 49 30 00. www.parfloral-lasource.fr.*

Île d'**OUESSANT**★★

POPULATION 1 062

MICHELIN MAP 308 A 4

GREEN GUIDE BRITTANY

The **Île d'Ouessant** is a detached fragment of the Léon plateau on the mainland, 25 km – 16mi away. Two outcrops of granite running northeast-southwest enclose a sunken area of mica-schist much eroded by the sea to form bays to the southwest (Baie de Lampaul) and to the northeast (Baie du Stiff).

Many of the male inhabitants are French Navy men or work for the merchant navy; the few fishermen trap lobsters. The population lives in scattered hamlets or in the little capital of Lampaul, with its tiny harbour and the mausoleum where the Proella crosses representing those lost at sea are assembled.

Where there is shelter from the wind, camellias, aloes and agaves can grow, but the characteristic vegetation of the island is heather and dwarf gorse. The meagre grasses nourish a small flock of sheep. The cliffs of Ushant and its neighbouring islands house numbers of migrating and nesting birds.

Visit

♿ *Leaving from Brest (regular service) aboard the Enez Eussa: departure at 8.30am for Ouessant or Molène via Le Conquet. Leaving from Conquet (regular service) departure at 9.45am, departure from Ouessant 4.30pm: additional departure from Brest or Camaret (summer service): Early Jul to end Aug: aboard the André Colin, departure from Brest at 8am, departure from Camaret at 8.40am, departure from Ouessant at 6pm (except Sun); Apr, May and Jun: additional departure (call for times). Bicycle rental from Stiff during school holidays; in Lampaul, all year round. Information: Compagnie maritime Penn Ar Bed.* ☎ *02 98 80 80 80. Access by plane from Brest-Guipavas airport.* ☎ *02 98 84 64 87.*

Côte Sauvage★★★

■ *4hr round trip on foot starting at Lampaul.* The headlands and inlets of Ushant's rocky northwestern coastline have a rugged and dramatic beauty. In winter the wind

Île d'Ouessant

is master, hurling the breakers against reefs and cliffs with utmost fury. The most spectacular locations include Keller Island (Île de Keller), Penn-ar-Ru-Meur and the Cadoran islet (Îlot de Cadoran).

The 300 or so vessels which pass each day are guided by five great light-houses. The one at **Creac'h**, which houses the **Centre d'Interpretation des Phares et Balises** (& ⏱ *Apr-Sep: daily 10.30am-6.30pm; winter half-term, Christmas and Feb school holidays: 10.30am-5.30pm; rest of the year: daily except Mon 1.30-5pm;* ⏱ *closed 1 Jan and 25 Dec;* ⊚ *4€;* ☎ *02 98 48 80 70)*, a historical museum on lighthouses and beacons, is the most powerful in the world; together wth its counterpart at Land's End in Cornwall it marks the western limit of the English Channel. The light at **Stiff** with its towers built by Vauban in 1695 gives a splendid **view**★★ over the rolling sea. The lighthouses play a vital role; Ushant is notorious for its fogs, treacherous reefs and currents. Over the last hundred years 54 wrecks have been recorded.

Gouffre de PADIRAC★★

MICHELIN MAP 337 G 2

GREEN GUIDE DORDOGNE BERRY LIMOUSIN

Padirac Chasm (Gouffre de Padirac), hollowed out of the limestone mass of the Gramat plateau (Causse de Gramat), is one of the most extraordinary natural phenomena of the Massif Central.

Visit

The chasm *(1hr 30min)* itself is a gigantic well (aven) of striking width (99m – 325ft around its rim) and depth (75m – 246ft to the rubble cone formed by the collapse of the original roof). With its walls covered in vegetation and the overflow from stalagmites, it is one of the most atmospheric of France's underground domains.

Guy de Lavaur (1903-86), a follower of Robert de Joly (👆 *see Aven d'ORGNAC)*, originally devoted himself to the exploration of dry caves, but later turned to the development of techniques for investigating underground watercourses. In 1938 he came to Padirac and succeeded in finding a way through the siphons which had proved inaccessible to his predecessor Édouard-Alfred Martel. As a result of his efforts, the total length of the subterranean network at Padirac rose from 2km – 1.5mi to 15km – 9mi.

The underground river flows 103m – 340ft beneath the surface of the plateau, to reappear on the surface near the natural amphitheatre at Montvalent 11km – 7mi away on the Dordogne. Some 5km – 3mi of its main channel and tributaries have been explored.

The Grand Pilier, Grande Pendeloque of the Lac de la Pluie and the Salle du Grand Dôme are among the most striking of all natural monuments of the underground world.

The rugged relief of southern France conceals caves and chasms which are natural wonders. The following, which are open to visitors, are described in this guide (👆 *see Index)*:

Aven Armand
Aven d'Orgnac
Grotte des Demoiselles
Grotte de Niaux
Gouffre de Padirac

Aven Marzal
Grotte de Clamouse
Grotte du Mas d'Azil
Grotte de Pech-Merle

PARIS★★★

POPULATION 2 152 333

MICHELIN MAP 312 D 2

GREEN GUIDE NORTHERN FRANCE AND PARIS REGION

The dominance of Paris in France's intellectual, artistic, scientific and political life can be traced back to the 12C when the Capetian kings made it their capital.

▶ **Orient Yourself:** The Seine River flows from east to west across the city. Places north of the river are on the *rive droite*, while those to the south are on the *rive gauche*. Paris is divided into 20 arrondissements (districts or neighborhoods), each one with its own local government and characteristics. And each arrondissement is futher divided into a number of neighborhoods determined by history and the people who live there. The metro is the easiest and most economical way of moving around the city. Line 1, which crosses Paris from east to west, services many of the most famous attractions: the Louvre, the Champs-Élysées and the Arc de Triomphe. Line 4 is useful for travelling across the city from north to south. The metro also services the immediate suburbs of Paris, but for those a bit farther out, use the RER or the SNCF suburb trains.

☺ **Don't Miss:** Hôtel des Invalides, Arc de Triomphe, Place de la Concorde, Eiffel Tower, Notre-Dame Cathedral, Sainte-Chappelle, the Marais, the Champs-Élysées, the Latin Quarter, Montmartre, the Louvre, Centre Georges-Pompidou, Musée d'Orsay and the Cité des Sciences et de l'Industrie.

Kids **Especially For Kids:** La Villette which encompasses the Cité des Sciences et l'Industrie, the spherical cinema La Géode and the Cité des Enfants has many interactive exhibits and presentations for children.

A Stroll Through History

Middle Ages (476-1492)
At the time of the fall of the Roman Empire towards the end of the 5C, Paris was a modest township founded seven centuries previously by Gallic fishermen. Following its occupation by the Roman legions of Labienus, the settlement had been extended south of the river to where the remains of the Cluny Baths and a 2C amphitheatre now stand. In the 3C St Denis, Paris' first bishop, had met his martyrdom and the Barbarians had razed the place to the ground. This destruction, together with the threat posed by Attila's hordes (but averted by the intervention of St Genevieve), had caused the inhabitants to withdraw to the security of the Île de la Cité.
Clovis, King of the Franks, settled in Paris in 508. Two years later, he founded an abbey south of the Seine in honour of St Genevieve, just as 35 years previously a basilica had been erected over the tomb of St Denis. In 885, for the fifth time in 40 years, the Norsemen sailed up the river and put Paris to siege; Eudes, son of Robert the Strong, bravely led the local resistance, and was elected king of "France" in 888; from then on, the town became the royal seat, albeit with some interruptions.

The Capetian dynasty (987-1328)
The original abbey of St-Germain-des-Prés was wrecked by the Norsemen; around the turn of the millennium, it was rebuilt in Romanesque style and has been much altered subsequently.
Peter Abelard, master of logic and theology and lover of Heloise, taught in Paris at the beginning of the 11C; in 1136, Abbot Suger rebuilt the abbey church of St-Denis in the revolutionary Gothic style, an example soon followed by Maurice de Sully at

Eiffel Tower

A. Eli/MICHELIN

Notre-Dame. Between 1180 and 1210, Philippe Auguste surrounded the growing city with a continuous ring of fortifications anchored on the Louvre fortress. In 1215 France's first university was founded on the Ste-Geneviève hill.

In 1246, the Sainte-Chapelle was built by St Louis (Louis IX), that sturdy defender of the rights of kings and commoners. A marvel of the Gothic style, it was intended to house the relics of the Passion. The king also founded the Quinze-Vingts (15 × 20 = 300) Hospital to house 300 blind persons, and (together with Robert of Sorbon) the college which was to develop into the mighty Sorbonne.

Seal of the Watermen's Guild (1210)

In the early years of the 14C, Philippe le Bel (the Fair) built the Conciergerie; on 30 October 1307, he ordered the arrest of all the Templars in France, then, after persuading the Pope to dissolve their Order (1314), he had their Grand Master Jacques de Molay and 54 of his associates burnt alive.

The House of Valois (1328-1589)

Philippe Auguste had built a manor house at Vincennes, Louis IX a chapel. Philippe VI added a castle, its keep designed according to the most advanced principles of military architecture. The work was carried on by his son John until his imprisonment in England.

On 22 February 1358, Étienne Marcel, the merchants' provost, succeeded in rousing the townsfolk to break into the Law Courts (Palais de Justice); entering the Dauphin's apartments, he slew two of the future Charles V's counsellors before his very eyes. On becoming king, Charles quit this place of ill memory to set up court, first in the huge Hôtel St-Paul (now destroyed), then at Vincennes. He was also responsible for making the Louvre habitable and providing it with a library; then, in 1370, he built himself a stronghold in the eastern part of the city, the Bastille, which became the centrepiece of a new ring of fortifications.

From the reign of Charles VII onward the monarchs spent much of their time in the châteaux of the Loire Valley, transporting kitchenware and furniture with them. In 1407, the king's brother, Louis of Orléans, was assassinated by followers of John the Fearless, thereby unleashing civil war between the Armagnacs and Burgundians. Paris was delivered up to the English in 1418 and Joan of Arc was wounded in front of the gate, Porte St-Honoré, trying to retake the city in 1429. Paris was only won back for France eight years later by Charles VII.

The Flamboyant variant of the Gothic style was used in the ambulatory of St-Séverin's Church, in the transept of St-Étienne-du-Mont and in the porch of St-Germain-l'Auxerrois which became the royal parish church when the rulers from the House of Valois took up residence in the Louvre. It was at this time that François Villon, thief and reprobate, made his reputation as the poet of the down-and-outs, with a talent far in advance of his time but expressed in a language which was already out of date. Louis XI provided printers from Mainz in the Rhineland with facilities at the Sorbonne. In 1475 the Hôtel de Sens was built; together with the Hôtel de Cluny, it is one of Paris' few surviving late-medieval residences; the influence of the court's Italian artists is apparent in the mouldings of the windows, the brackets and the dormers.

The modern era (1492-1789)

In 1492, the discovery of America marked the start of the modern age. The Neapolitan artists brought back by Charles VIII from his campaigns in Italy were introducing new trends in taste and thought; the influence of the Renaissance became apparent in many ways, in the semicircular arches of St Eustache's Church, in the decoration of the choir screen of St-Étienne-du-Mont and even in the entreaties of Guillaume Budé which persuaded François I to found the prestigious Collège de France.

In the middle of the 16C the Hôtel Carnavalet was built, followed by the Pierre Lescot wing of the Louvre which now forms one side of the impressive courtyard of the old palace, the Cour Carrée; Lescot commissioned Jean Goujon to carry out the sculptural decoration. In 1549, Joachim du Bellay published his *"Defence and Illustration of the French Language"* which became the manifesto of the literary movement known as the *Pléiade*.

In 1559, the court went into mourning for Henri II, fatally wounded in the Rue St-Antoine in the course of a tournament celebrating the wedding of his daughter. His widow, Catherine de' Medici, put Philibert Delorme in charge of the construction of the Tuileries Palace. A few years later Germain Pilon was to sculpt the *Three Graces* in the idealised style of the previous century for the tomb of Henri II. The brothers Androuet Du Cerceau drew up the plans for the Flore Pavilion abutting the Louvre to the west, then set about the construction of the Pont Neuf (New Bridge), which today is the city's oldest surviving bridge. At the same time, Ambroise Paré, a surgeon at the hospital, Hôtel-Dieu, was making great advances in the field of orthopaedics.

On 24 August 1572, the bells rang out from the tower of St-Germain-l'Auxerrois to signal the start of the St Bartholomew's Day Massacre; Henry of Navarre, the future Henri IV, just married to Marguerite of Valois, barely escaped with his life. In 1588, in reaction to the monarchy's centralising policy which had left the country at the mercy of growing Spanish hegemony, the Catholic League turned against Henri III; after the so-called Day of the Barricades (12 May 1588), the king was obliged to flee the city. But with the help of Henry of Navarre, he returned to the attack, only to be assassinated at St-Cloud in 1589 by the monk Jacques Clément. This violent act marked the end of the Valois line.

The Bourbons (1589-1789)

In 1594 Paris opened its gates to Henri IV, the new king who had renounced his Protestant faith and succeeded in pacifying the country. The Arsenal was built to the plans of Philibert Delorme while Louis Métezeau laid out the elegantly symmetrical Place Royale, since renamed Place des Vosges. But on 14 May 1610 in the Rue de la Ferronnerie, this monarch too fell victim to an assassin.

The reign of Louis XIII – 1610-43. Under Louis XIII, Métezeau designed an imposing Classical west front for St-Gervais Church, the first of its kind in Paris; Salomon de Brosse built the Luxembourg Palace for Marie de' Medici; Jean Androuet Du Cerceau laid out the courtyards and gardens of the Hôtel de Béthune-Sully; as well as erecting a church for the Sorbonne with Classical columns on its courtyard side, Lemercier built the Palais-Royal for Richelieu. In 1636, Pierre Corneille, a Rouen lawyer, put on his play *Le Cid* at the theatre in the Hôtel de Bourgogne in the Marais district. Six years later, Lemercier constructed the Clock Pavilion (Pavillon de l'Horloge) forming the centrepiece of the west side of the Louvre's Cour Carrée. In the following year, Cardinal de la Rochefoucauld founded the Hospital for Incurable Diseases; the Laënnec building retains two sides of the original courtyard. On the king's death in 1643, Anne of Austria became Regent, acting in concert with Mazarin and continuing the policies of Richelieu. It was during this period that Guillaume Coustou sculpted the famous *Horses of Marly*. While François Mansart was building the Hôtel Guénégaud and Le Vau was busy with the construction of the Pavilions of the King and Queen at Vincennes, Paris fell prey to the series of disturbances caused by unrest among the nobility and known as the Fronde; the young king came to the conclusion that it might be advantageous to separate Court from city.

The century of Louis XIV – The 23-year-old king began his long and highly personal reign in 1661. The Classical style which had been maturing during the Regency now came into its own. Even more than the splendour of court life, it was the extraordinary advancement of the arts and literature at this time that gave France such prestige in Europe. Under the protection of a king keen to encourage artistic endeavour and promote creative confidence, writers, painters, sculptors and landscapers flourished as never before. In the space of 20 years, the great Le Nôtre redesigned the parterres of the Tuileries; Claude Perrault provided the Louvre with its fine colonnade and built the Observatory; Le Vau completed the greater part of both the Louvre and the Institut de France, the "College of Four Nations" endowed by Mazarin. After building the chapel of the Salpêtrière Hospital, Libéral Bruant drew up his grandiose plans for the Invalides, the barracks founded by the king for his old soldiers.

With the aim of improving the quality of goods and thereby contributing to the country's prosperity, Colbert founded the Gobelins manufactory. Jean-Baptiste Lully created the classical form of opera and collaborated with Molière on his ballet-plays; his recitatives accompanied on the clavichord are masterpieces of measured expressiveness. Lully also founded the Royal Academy of Music.

Bossuet delivered his funeral orations in honour of great figures of the period, while La Fontaine wrote the scabrous anecdotes known as the *Contes et Nouvelles*, followed by his Fables, a wonderful combination of literary enchantment and psychological analysis. At the age of 28 Jean Racine produced his *Andromaque*, the first of the great line of tragedies which include *Britannicus*, *Bérénice*, *Phèdre* and *Athalie*. His verses of "incantatory power but magical simplicity" (G Bréreton) expressed such unbridled passions that he eventually returned in penitence to the Jansenist fold he had once deserted. Molière came back to Paris after a long apprenticeship, notably in the South; out of this came the *École des Femmes (School for Wives* – 1662), followed by *Don Juan, Le Misanthrope, Amphytrion, L'Avare (the Miser), Le Tartuffe (the Hypocrite), Les Femmes Savantes (the Wise Women)*, comedies shot through with *"that masculine gaiety of such sadness and depth to make us mingle tears with our mirth"* (Alfred de Musset). The great playwright died on 17 February 1673 in 40 Rue de Richelieu after being taken ill on stage while playing the role of the *Malade Imaginaire (the Hypochondriac)*.

During this decade, a scandal about the use of poison to secure inheritance and involving the aristocracy touched the throne itself, casting a shadow on a court still avidly in pursuit of youthful pleasures and leading to the disgrace of the king's mistress, Mme de Montespan.

This was the time during which André Boulle gave his name to furniture with elaborate marquetry of tortoiseshell and brass, and when François Couperin became known for his mastery of the harpsichord and his exquisitely elegant suites. La Bruyère's masterly prose and trenchant comment aroused conflicting passions with his *Characters*, while Charles Perrault, brother of the architect Claude Perrault, fascinated his public with his marvellous tales of *Cinderella* and *Sleeping Beauty*. Coysevox sculpted his group of winged horses to grace the Tuileries, and 10 years later Colbert's tomb in the St-Eustache Church. Hardouin-Mansart planned the Place Vendôme and Delamair designed the Palais Soubise and the Hôtel de Rohan in the Marais district. France's "Century of Greatness" came to an end with Louis XIV's death in 1715.

The Age of Enlightenment – On Louis XIV's death, the country found itself, for the second time in its history, under the rule of a five-year-old. The running of the country was therefore put into the hands of a regent, Philippe d'Orléans; the first action of the court was to pack its bags and quit the boredom of Versailles for the gaiety of the capital. A long period of peace accompanied the years of corruption; for 77 years France experienced no foreign incursions. Chancellor Auguesseau continued the work begun by Colbert with his administrative reforms, but the period was also marked by the dramatic bankruptcy of the Scots financier John Law, when the speculation he had fuelled with promissory notes issued from his bank in the Rue Quincampoix finally crashed in 1720.

Literary salons flourished, notably those of the Marquise de Lambert, Mme Du Deffand and Mme Geoffrin, all helping the spread of new ideas. The Palais Bourbon (1722-28), which now houses the National Assembly, was erected at this time.

The Esplanade des Invalides was laid out by Robert de Cotte. The work of the furniture-maker Charles Cressent was characterised by opulent forms and elaborate bronze mounts; in many ways it heralds an age when the fashionable world was enthused by fine furniture, and the craftsmen and shopkeepers of the Rue St-Eustache and the Faubourg St-Antoine were kept busy. Jean-Philippe Rameau expressed his theories in his *Treatise on Harmony* and introduced innovative compositional ideas into his operas and opera-ballets *(Les Indes Galantes)*; in 1723 he composed a number of suites for harpsichord which broke new ground in melodic invention. In 1730 Marivaux wrote the best-known of his delicately amorous comedies, *Le Jeu de l'amour et du hasard (The Game of Love and Chance)*. In 1739, the naturalist Georges Buffon laid out the Jardin des Plantes (Botanical Gardens) and in the following year, the sculptor Bouchardon completed his beautiful *Fountain of the Four Seasons (Fontaine des Quatre Saisons)* in the St-Germain district.

The reign of Louis XV – The personal rule exercised by Louis XV was discredited by his favourites, but was nevertheless marked by a number of personalities such as Charles de la Condamine, a surveyor and naturalist responsible for the discovery of rubber (1751); Jussieu, incumbent of the Chair in Botany at the Botanical Gardens, responsible for a systematic classification of plants (1759) and for many advances in pharmacology; Diderot, author, together with d'Alambert, of the great *Encyclopaedia*, a splendid summary of the technology of the age; Chardin, who had lodgings in the Louvre, devoted himself to working in pastel; Robert Pothier, who wrote the *Treatise of Obligations*; Ange-Jacques Gabriel, the last and most famous of a line of architects linked to Mansart and Robert de Cotte, who between them gave France a hundred years of architectural unity; it was he who designed the magnificent façades fronting the Place de la Concorde, the west front of St-Roch Church and the École Militaire (Military Academy). Finally there was Soufflot, creator of the dome which crowns the Panthéon.

Distinguished furniture-makers were at work too: Lardin with his cabinets and commodes with rosewood inlay, and Boudin with his virtuoso marquetry and secret compartments; they anticipate the masters who were to emerge in the following reign.

The reign of Louis XVI (1774-92) – After making tables and writing-desks, Lacroix showed his skill in the perfect curves of his commodes and cabinets. From his workshops near the Porte St-Martin, Georges Jacob presided over the whole field of furniture-making, making the definitive chairs of the age as well as his famous armchairs *"à la reine"*. But it was above all Jean Riesener with his workshop in the Rue St-Honoré who helped create the Louis XVI style; his commodes and his mahogany desks with bronze decoration are triumphs of sobriety and distinction.

Chalgrin designed the organ-case for the imposing St-Sulpice Church; Gluck wrote Orpheus and exerted his influence over Mehul; Antoine built the Hôtel des Monnaies; Baudelocque pioneered the study of obstetrics; Pilâtre du Rosier rose above the rooftops of the St-Antoine quarter in his "Montgolfière" balloon and sailed across the city; after his *Barber of Seville*, Beaumarchais presented the *Marriage of Figaro* at the Théâtre Français on 27 April 1784, thereby gaining the reputation of a "defender of the oppressed"; nine years after his visionary plans for Arc-et-Senans, Ledoux built 57 toll-houses for the wall enclosing the city; the court painter Élisabeth Vigée-Lebrun portrayed Queen Marie-Antoinette and her children with a seductive grace and tenderness.

Revolution and Empire (1789-1814)

In 1788, the King decided to convene the States-General. The delegates assembled at Versailles on 5 May 1789.

The Constituent Assembly – On 17 June, the States-General transformed itself into a National Assembly which styled itself the Constituent Assembly on 9 July; the monarchy would eventually become a constitutional one.

On 14 July, in the space of less than an hour, the people of Paris took over the Bastille in the hope of finding arms there; the outline of the demolished fortress can still be traced in the paving on the west side of the Place de la Bastille (14 July became a day of national celebration in 1879). On 17 July, in the City Hall (Hôtel de Ville), Louis XVI kissed the recently adopted tricolour cockade. The feudal system was abolished on 4 August, and the Declaration of the Rights of Man adopted on 26 August; on 5 October, the Assembly moved into the riding-school of the Tuileries, and the royal family was brought from Versailles and installed in the Tuileries Palace.

On 22 December, the Assembly divided up the country into 83 départements, thereby carrying out a proposal first suggested by d'Argenson in 1764.

On 12 July 1790 the Church became subject to the Civil Constitution for the Clergy. Two days later, a great crowd gathered on the Champ-de-Mars to celebrate the anniversary of the fall of the Bastille; Talleyrand, Bishop of Autun as well as statesman and diplomat, celebrated mass on the altar of the nation and the king reaffirmed his oath of loyalty to the country.

After his attempt to join Bouillé's army at Metz had been foiled, Louis was brought back to Paris on 25 June 1791; on 30 September, he was forced to accept the constitution adopted by the Assembly which then dissolved itself.

The Legislative Assembly – The new deputies met the following day in the Tuileries Riding School. On 20 June 1792, encouraged by the moderate revolutionary faction known as the Girondins, rioters invaded the Tuileries and made Louis put on the red bonnet of liberty. On 11 July, the Assembly declared France to be in danger, and during the night of 9 August the mob (sans-culottes) instituted a "revolutionary commune" with the status of an organ of government; the next day the Tuileries were sacked and 600 of the Swiss Guards massacred. The Assembly responded by depriving the king of his few remaining responsibilities and confining him with his family in the tower of the Templar Prison (Tour du Temple). Soon after, the "September Massacres" began; 1 200 prisoners, some "politicals", but most of them common offenders, were hauled from the city's jails and arbitrarily executed on the Buci crossroads in a frenzy of fear and panic precipitated by fear of invasion. This grisly event marked the beginning of the Terror. On 21 September, the day after the French defeat at the Battle of Valmy, the Legislative Assembly gave way to the Convention.

The Convention – At its very first meeting, the new assembly, now in the hands of the Girondins, formally abolished the monarchy and proclaimed the Republic. This day, 21 September 1792, became Day 1 of Year One in the new revolutionary calendar, which remained in force until 31 December 1805. On 11 December, the trial of Louis Capet opened at the Riding School. The monarch was guillotined on 21 January 1793 in the Place de la Concorde. At the end of May, beset by difficulties at home and abroad and bereft of popular support, the Girondins fell, to be replaced by the "Mountain" (the extreme Jacobin faction, so-called because they occupied the upper tiers of seating in the Assembly).

One of the acts of the Mountain-dominated Convention was to open the Louvre as a Museum of the Republic, on 10 August 1793. On 17 September,

Louis XVI wearing a "liberty bonnet"

Collection Soalhat/SIPA-PRESS

the Law of Suspects was passed, legalising the Terror. The first to be executed by the revolutionary tribunals were the Girondins, in October 1793. On 8 June 1794, Robespierre the "Incorruptible" presided over the Festival of the Supreme Being. The event was orchestrated by the painter David, beginning in the Tuileries Gardens and proceeding to the Champ-de-Mars.

On 10 June (9 Prairial), the Great Terror began. Over a period of two months, the "national razor", as the guillotine was known, was to slice off 2 561 heads. Among those executed was Lavoisier, former Farmer-General and eminent chemist, responsible for the formulation of the theory of the conservation of mass on which much of modern chemistry rests, and André Chénier, the lyric poet who had condemned the excesses of the regime in his verse. The end of the Terror came with the fall and execution of Robespierre himself, on 27 July (9 Thermidor).

The Thermidorian Convention now attempted to put the sickening spectacle of the scaffold behind it with a policy calculated to promote stability in the nation. Among its most important achievements were measures designed to advance science and learning, including the founding of the École Polytechnique (School of Engineering) by Monge (1794), known for his work on descriptive geometry and electromagnetism; the creation of the Conservatoire des Arts et Métiers (National Technical Institution) on the initiative of Abbot Grégoire, and the setting up of the École Normale (the prestigious pedagogical college). In 1795, the metric system was adopted and the Office of Longitudes founded. Just before the Assembly's dissolution on 25 October, public education was instituted and the Institut de France founded, embracing the nation's learned academies (including the Académie Française).

The Directory and the Consulate – The period of the Directory was marked, in 1798, by the very first Universal Exhibition, but was brought to an end with the *coup d'état* of 9 November (18 Brumaire) 1799, when the Council of Elders persuaded the legislature to move to St-Cloud as a precautionary measure against Jacobin plots. On the following day, Napoleon Bonaparte entered the chamber to address the delegates, but was booed; he was saved by the presence of mind of his brother Lucien, who used the guard to disperse the members. By the same evening, power was in the hands of three consuls; it was the end of the Revolution. In less than five years, the Consulate allowed Napoleon to centralise power, opening the way to the realisation of his Imperial ambitions. A period of consolidation began; the Legion of Honour was created, and Catholic opinion propitiated by a Concordat with the Vatican.

Long before the onset of the Industrial Revolution, Babeuf put forward his "system of socialism" and the mathematician Lagrange was studying the functions and equations of dynamics; Lebon's "thermolamp" inaugurated the era of lighting by gas, and the great anatomist and physiologist Bichat defined the nature of body tissue. In 1803 the Pont des Arts was built, the first iron bridge in France, reserved for the exclusive use of pedestrians. In order to deter the plots being organised against him by royalist *émigrés* and the English, Napoleon ordered the Duke d'Enghien to be executed; the sentence was carried out in the small hours of 21 March 1804 in the moat at Vincennes, sending shock waves throughout the whole of Europe.

The Empire – Proclaimed Emperor of the French by the Senate on 18 May 1804, Napoleon I was anointed on 2 December by Pope Pius VII at Notre-Dame, though it was he himself who actually put the crown on his head in a ceremony immortalised by David. His reign was marked by the promulgation in 1804 of the Civil Code, which he had helped draft himself when he was still First Consul, and which, as the *Code Napoléon*, has since formed the legal basis of many other countries. In order to make Paris into a truly imperial capital, Napoleon ordered the erection of a great column in the Place Vendôme; cast from the melted-down metal of guns taken at the Battle of Austerlitz (Slavkov), it commemorated the victories of his *Grande Armée*. Vignon was commissioned to design a temple which nearly became a railway station before ending up as the Madeleine Church; Chalgrin was put to work drawing up plans for a great triumphal arch (Arc de Triomphe); Brongniart built the Stock Exchange (Bourse); Percier and Fontaine, the promoters of the Empire style, constructed the north wing of the Louvre and the Carrousel Arch (Arc du Carrousel); Gros painted the battles and Géricault the cavalry of the *Grande Armée*.

On 31 March 1814, despite the strong resistance offered by Daumesnil at Vincennes, the Allies occupied Paris. On 11 April, the Emperor, "the sole obstacle to peace in Europe", put his signature to the document of abdication at Fontainebleau.

The Restoration (May 1814-February 1848)

The reign of Louis XVIII – 1814-24. The period of rule of Louis XVI's brother was interrupted by the Hundred Days of Napoleon's attempt to re-establish himself between his sojourn on Elba and his final exile to St Helena. During the years of Louis XVIII's reign, Laënnec invented the stethoscope, wrote his *Treatise on Mediate Auscultation* and founded the anatomo-clinical school together with Bayle and Dupuytren; Pinel studied mental illness at the Salpêtrière Hospital; Cuvier put biology on a sounder footing, formulated the principles of subordination of organs to their function and established a zoological classification; Bertholet studied the composition of acids, Sadi Carnot thermodynamics and temperature equilibrium, and Arago electromagnetism and the polarisation of light; Daguerre laid the foundations of his fame with his dioramas, and Lamartine conquered literary society with his *Méditations Poétiques* – its elegaic rhythms soothed Talleyrand's sleepless nights.

The reign of Charles X – 1824-30. Painting flourished with the brilliant sweep of Delacroix' great canvases and Corot's landscapes. At the same time, Laplace was establishing the fundamental laws of mathematical analysis and providing a firm basis for astronomical mechanics, and Berlioz was composing his *Fantastic Symphony*, the key work of the Romantic Movement in music.

On 21 February 1830, Victor Hugo's drama *Hernani* provoked a literary battle between "moderns" and "classicals" in which the latter were temporarily routed. In the summer, Charles' press ordinances provoked a crisis which led to his abdication; he was succeeded by Louis Philippe, a member of the cadet branch of the Bourbons.

P. WIII/EXPLORER

Coronation of Napoleon by David

The reign of Louis-Philippe – 1830-48. During the 1830s, the mathematician Evariste Galois put forward the theory of sets; his concepts were developed by Cauchy; Victor Hugo wrote *Notre-Dame de Paris* and Alfred de Musset *Caprices*. Chopin, the darling of Parisian society, composed scherzos, waltzes and his celebrated Polonaises. In 1838, while on holiday in Paris, Stendhal wrote *The Charterhouse of Parma*, a masterpiece of psychological observation which can be read on a number of levels. The first news agency was founded by Charles Havas. In 1839, a railway line was opened between Paris and St-Germain. The 1840s saw the publication of the *Mysteries of Paris* by Eugène Sue, the *Count of Monte Cristo and the Three Musketeers* by Dumas and many of the works of Balzac's prodigious Human Comedy as well as the *Treatise on Parasitology* by Raspail; the abuses of the July monarchy were brilliantly satirised in the drawings of Daumier.

At the age of 79, Chateaubriand brought his finely chiselled *Memories from beyond the Tomb* to a triumphant conclusion. On 23 February in 1848, the barricades went up on the Boulevard des Capucines and the monarchy fell; the next day, at the City Hall, amid scenes of wild enthusiasm, Lamartine saluted the tricolour "the flag which has spread the name of France, freedom and glory around the wide world".

Second Republic and Second Empire (1848-70)

Second Republic – The abolition of the National Workshops in June 1848 brought about rioting in the St-Antoine district, in which the archbishop of Paris was killed. In 1849, Léon Foucault proved the rotation and spherical nature of the earth by means of a pendulum (the experiment was repeated in 1855 from the dome of the Panthéon). On 2 December 1851 the short life of the Second Republic was ended by a *coup d'état*.

Second Empire – 1852-70. Two great exhibitions (in 1855 and 1867) proclaimed the prosperity France enjoyed under the rule of Bonaparte's nephew, Napoleon III. **Baron Haussmann**, Prefect of the *Département* of the Seine, was responsible for an ambitious programme of public works which transformed the capital, giving it many of the features which now seem quintessentially Parisian. Among them were the laying out of the Bois de Boulogne and the Bois de Vincennes, and the building of railway stations and the North Wing of the Louvre. But the Baron is remembered above all for the ruthless surgery he performed on the capital's ancient urban tissue, opening up new focal points (Place de l'Opéra) and linking them with great axial roadways (Grands Boulevards), splendid exercises in traffic engineering and crowd control.

ROGER-VIOLLET

Baron Haussmann

In 1852, Alexandre Dumas wrote *The Lady of the Camellias* at the same time as Rudé was working on the memorial to Marshal Ney, which was to be placed on the very spot near the Observatory where the great soldier had been executed in 1815; in Rodin's opinion, it was Paris' finest statue. The following year, Claude Bernard, Professor of Physiology at the Collège de France, analysed the glyco-genic function of the liver and wrote his *Introduction to the Study of Experimental Medicine. In 1857 Baudelaire, the first poet of the teeming modern metropolis, published Les Fleurs du Mal (The Flowers of Evil).* In 1858, the resident organist at the Madeleine Church, Saint-Saëns, composed oratorios and cantatas, and the following year Gounod presented Faust at the Opéra Lyrique. In 1860, Étienne Lenoir registered his first patent for the internal combustion engine, which was to be perfected 28 years later by Fernand Forest.

The year 1863 was marked by the scandals caused by Manet's *Déjeuner sur l'herbe* and *Olympia*; Baltard masked the masterly iron structure of the St-Augustin Church with the stone cladding still obligatory in a religious building; iron was used again by Labrouste, in his case to lend lightness to the supports in the reading room of the National Library (Bibliothèque Nationale); the buildings surrounding the Étoile were given their neo-Classical façades by Hittorf. In 1896, Pierre de Coubertin created the International Olympic Committee.

Republican Continuity (1870 to the present day)

On 4 September 1870, the mob which had invaded the National Assembly was led by Gambetta to the City Hall where the Republic was proclaimed. The new government busied itself in preparing to defend Paris against the advancing Prussians; the St-Cloud château was set on fire and a fierce battle took place at Le Bourget.

The ensuing siege subjected the population of Paris to terrible hardships; food ran out and the winter was exceptionally severe. The city surrendered on 28 January 1871. The revolutionary **Commune** was ruthlessly suppressed by military force, not before the Communards had burnt down the City Hall, the Tuileries and the Audit Office (Cours des Comptes – on the site of what is now the Orsay Museum), pulled down the column in the Place Vendôme and shot their prisoners at the Hostages' Wall in the Rue Haxo. They made their last stand in the Père-Lachaise Cemetery, where those of their number who had survived the bitter fighting were summarily executed at the Federalists' Wall (Mur des Fédérés).

But political institutions were re-established and the nation revived; the Republic was consolidated as France's political regime, notwithstanding Marshal Pétain's so-called French State (État Français), Nazi occupation and the provisional government following the end of the Second World War.

Third Republic – Carpeaux sculpted the Four Corners of the World for the Observatory Fountain, and Émile Littré completed the publication of his renowned *Dictionary of the French Language*. Bizet wrote *L'Arlésienne (the Woman of Arles)* for the Odéon theatre and followed it with *Carmen*, based on a short story by Mérimée.

In 1874, Degas painted *The Dancing Class* and Monet *Impression: Rising Sun*, which, when exhibited by his dealer Nadar, led to the coining of the initially derisive term Impressionism. Later, Renoir worked at the Moulin de la Galette, and Puvis de Chavannes decorated the walls of the Panthéon. The public applauded Delibes' innovatory *Coppélia* and *Lakmé*. Rodin created the *Thinker,* followed by figures of Balzac and Victor Hugo.

In 1879, Seulecq put forward the principle of sequential transmission on which television is based and Pasteur completed his vast body of work. Seurat's Grande Jatte heralded the establishment of the Pointillist school of painting. In the following year, 1887, Antoine founded the Free Theatre (Théâtre libre) based on spontaneous expression. The engineer Gustave Eiffel completed his great tower, centrepiece of the Universal Exhibition of 1889. In the century's final decade, Toulouse-Lautrec painted cabaret scenes and Pissarro Parisian townscapes, and Forain gained fame as a marvellous caricaturist. In the Catholic Institute, Édouard Branly discovered radio-conductors. In 1891, René Panhard built the first petrol-engined motor car, which drove right across Paris, then, two years later, all the way to Nice.

In the year 1894 the Dreyfus affair shook the country, re-awakening old religious enmities; Vincent d'Indy founded the Schola cantorum in 1896 and Debussy composed *Prélude à l'après-midi d'un faune*. The physicist Henri Becquerel discovered radioactivity in the course of his studies on fluorescence, themselves based on the work of his father who had analysed the solar spectrum, and of his grandfather who had worked on batteries and electro-chemistry.

In 1898, the 21-year-old Louis Renault built his first car, then founded his Billancourt factory; in 1902 he patented a turbocharger. The factory turned out cars, lorries, planes and, in 1917, light tanks which contributed to the German defeat in 1918. Nationalised at the end of the Second World War, the firm continued to produce vehicles in large numbers.

In October 1898 Pierre and Marie Curie succeeded in isolating radium and established the atomic character of radioactivity; their laboratory was a shed which has since disappeared, but its outline is shown in the paving pattern in the courtyard of the school at No 10 Rue Vauquelin. At the same time, Henri Bergson was teaching philosophy at the Collège de France and Langevin was conducting his investigations into ionised gases (in 1915, he was to use ultrasonic waves in the detection of submarines); a combination of steel, stone and glass was employed by Girault in the construction of the exhibition halls (the Grand Palais and the Petit Palais) for the 1900 Exhibition; this occasion also saw the bridging of the Seine by the great flattened arch of the Pont Alexandre III.

Archive Laboratoire Curie, Paris

Marie Curie

In 1900, Gustave Charpentier put on a musical romance *Louise*; with its lyrical realism and popular appeal it was a great "hit" of the time. In 1902, Debussy's *Pelléas et Mélisande* was produced at the Salle Favart of the Comic Opera. In 1906, Santos-Dumont succeeded in taking off in a heavier-than-air machine, staying aloft for 21 seconds, and covering a distance of 220m – 720ft. Dalou's bronze group entitled *The Triumph of the Republic* graced the Place de la Nation, while at Montparnasse the re-erected Wine Pavilion from the 1900 Exhibition provided lodgings and studios for Soutine, Zadkine, Chagall, Modigliani and Léger; other innovative artists included the sculptor Maillol and the painter Utrillo, while Brancusi's work was evolving away from cubism towards abstraction *(The Sleeping Muse)*; the Perret brothers built the Théâtre des Champs-Élysées in reinforced concrete; its façade was adorned with eight relief panels by Bourdelle. The theatre was opened in 1913 with a performance of Stravinsky's *Rite of Spring*; its music and choreography outraged an unprepared public.

In 1914 the construction of the Sacré-Cœur Church (begun in 1878 by the architect Abadie) on the Montmartre heights was completed. On the evening of 31 July, the eve of general mobilisation, Jean Jaurès was assassinated.

The Great War of 1914-18 put civilians as well as soldiers to the severest of tests; after three years of conflict, Clemenceau was made head of government, and, by restoring the country's confidence, earned the title of "Father of Victory".

In 1920, the interment of an unknown soldier at the Arc de Triomphe marked France's recognition of the sacrifices made by her ordinary soldiers, the unshaven "poilus" of the trenches.

In the course of the 1920s, Le Corbusier built the La Roche Villa, and Bourdelle sculpted *"France"* at the Palais de Tokyo; Georges Rouault, with his predilection for religious themes, completed his *Miserere*, and Landowsky carved the figure of St Genevieve for the Tournelle Bridge; in the course of a fortnight, Maurice Ravel composed *Boléro* for the dancer Ida Rubinstein; with its subtle instrumentation and rhythmic precision it popularised the name of this aristocratic composer; Poulbot created the archetypal Montmartre urchin; Cocteau wrote *Les Enfants Terribles*; the dynamism of the theatrical scene was marked by many fine actors and producers, notably the Cartel of Four (Cartel des Quatre) consisting of Charles Dullin (at the Sarah Bernhardt Theatre), Gaston Baty (at the Montparnasse), Louis Jouvet (at the Champs-Élysées then the Athénée) and Georges Pitoëff (at the Mathurins).

At the end of the 19C, Émile Roux had studied the causes of and cure for diphtheria; he was now in charge of the Pasteur Institute, and brought to Paris the scientists Calmette and Guérin who had worked on vaccination against tuberculosis.

In 1934, André Citroën brought out the Traction Avant (Front-Wheel Drive) car; 15 years previously, his Type A had been Europe's first mass-produced car; 21 years later, he was to unveil the innovative DS 19.

In 1940, Paris was bombed, then occupied by the German army. Between 16 and 17 July 1942, many victims of the Nazi racial myth were rounded up at the Vélodrome d'Hiver prior to their deportation eastwards; 4 500 members of the Resistance met their deaths in the clearing on Mount Valérien where the National Memorial of Fighting France now stands. Finally, on 19 August 1944, Paris was liberated.

Fourth and Fifth Republics – In 1950, Alfred Kastler, working in the laboratories of the École Normale Supérieure, succeeded in verifying the principle of "optical pumping", which has subsequently become the basis of one of the methods of producing a laser beam. The *Symphony for a Single Man* by Maurice Béjart, presented at the Étoile Theatre on 3 August 1955, was danced to *musique concrète* composed by Pierre Henry and Pierre Schaeffer, and led to many innovations in ballet throughout Europe.

Since 1945 the influence of Le Corbusier (there are few examples of his genius in Paris: Villa La Roche, Cité Universitaire pavilions...), has given a new impetus to architecture: new forms (Maison de Radio-France), structures on piles (UNESCO), sweeping rooflines (CNIT building). The present trend is for glass buildings (GAN and Manhattan towers, Centre Georges-Pompidou, Institut du Monde Arabe). The use of pre-stressed concrete led to technical advances (Palais des Congrès, Tour Montparnasse). But in the main architecture becomes an integral part of town planning: buildings are designed to fit into an overall plan: remodelling of an area (Maine-Montparnasse, les Halles, la Villette, Bercy) or new project (la Défense).

Grand new town-planning initiatives have also been implemented: the Opera house at la Bastille, the Ministry of Finance buildings at Bercy, the Grande Arche at la Défense and the Bibliothèque nationale de France François-Mitterand at Tolbiac are distinctive modern landmarks.

THE CITY'S MONUMENTS
Civil architecture

Palais du Louvre★★★

Neither the Merovingians nor the Carolingians, nor even the Capet kings lived in the Louvre which then lay beyond the city limits; instead, they preferred the Law Courts (Palais de Justice), their *hôtels* in the Marais, the manor at Vincennes, their own châteaux or those of their liegemen in the Loire Valley.

The monarchs and their contribution

Philippe Auguste – Lived in the Law Courts. He built the Louvre fortress on the right bank of the river in order to house his archives.
The original defensive ditches can still be seen *(access via the museum)*. The medieval fortress was sited in the southwestern quadrant of the present Cour Carrée.

Saint Louis (Louis IX) – Lived in the Law Courts, but added a great hall and a chapel to the fortress his grandfather had built.

Philippe le Bel (the Fair) – Lived in the Law Courts, using the Louvre as arsenal and treasury.

Charles V – Lived in the *hôtels* in the Marais. For this king, the Louvre was a place for relaxation; it was here that he kept his library of 973 books (where the Clock Pavilion – Pavillon de l'Horloge – now stands), and protected it with a defensive wall. His "lovely Louvre" is shown in one of the paintings in the Book of Hours known as the *Très Riches Heures du Duc de Berry.*
Charles VI resided in the Hôtel St-Paul. Charles VII, Louis XI, Charles VIII and Louis XII lived in the Loire châteaux, or, when in Paris, in the Hôtel des Tournelles.

François I – Lived mostly on the Loire and in the Marais. He had the old Louvre pulled down, and, in 1546, commissioned Pierre Lescot to build the palace which was to become the residence of the kings of France. Lescot's work 1 is regarded as the most prestigious part of the Louvre; it was he who brought the Italian Renaissance style, already flowering on the Loire, to the banks of the Seine; the façade he built is a delight of proportion, balance and decoration, to which the sculptor Jean Goujon (designer of the nymphs of the Fountain of the Innocents) added his brilliant contribution.

Henri II – Lived in the Louvre. Lescot showed his appreciation of his patron's support by marking the façade with emblazoned monograms interlacing C, H and D (Catherine de' Medici, Henri, Diane de Poitiers).

Charles IX – On the death of his brother François II, the new monarch was only 10 years old; the Florentine **Catherine de' Medici** was made Regent. With Auvergnat blood on her mother's side, this niece of two Popes had been married in France at the age of 14; her qualities of political tolerance were much in evidence in the negotiations

EVOLUTION OF THE LOUVRE PALACE

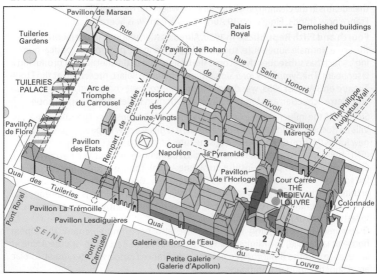

J.-P. Clapham/MICHELIN

The Louvre colonnade

with the Huguenots which led up to the Treaty of St-Germain. She lived in the Louvre on the floor since known as the Queens' Lodging (Logis des Reines) 2, but the idea of residing in the middle of Lescot's building site did not appeal, and she ordered Philibert Delorme (succeeded by Jean Bullant) to build the Tuileries. The site of this new palace was some 500m – 550yd away, just beyond the fortifications built by Charles V, and, to link it with the Louvre, Catherine planned a covered way following the line of the Seine, with a smaller gallery at right angles.

Charles IX completed the southwestern part of the Cour Carrée, the courtyard which is the most impressive part of the Old Louvre to remain, embellishing it with his monogram (K = Carolus).

Henri III – Lived in the Louvre. He was responsible for the southeastern part of the Cour Carrée (which bears the monogram H).

Henri IV – Lived in the Louvre. From 1595, he had the work on the Great Gallery (Grande Galerie) continued by Louis Métezeau (the letters H and G standing for Henri and Gabrielle d'Estrées were all removed, save for a single pair, by Marie de' Medici). He also had the Flora Pavilion (Pavillon de Flore) built by Jacques II Androuet Du Cerceau, completed the Small Gallery (Petite Galerie) (its first floor was occupied by Marie de' Medici and Anne of Austria, hence the monogram AA), and erected the upper part of the Henri III wing in the Cour Carrée, marked by his monogram.

Louis XIII – Lived in the Louvre. Encouraged by Richelieu, he continued with the construction of the Cour Carrée. At the same time as he was building the Sorbonne and the Palais-Royal, the architect Lemercier erected the Clock Pavilion (Pavillon de l'Horloge) together with the northwest corner of the courtyard, a Classical response to Lescot's work (the monogram LA = Louis and Anne). Anne of Austria lived in the Queens' Lodging; the bathroom designed for her by Lemercier now houses the Venus de Milo. In 1638, Charles V's rampart was razed and the moat filled in.

Louis XIV – On the death of Louis XIII, Anne became Regent and moved to the Palais-Royal with the young Louis. Nine years later, however, having been made aware of the palace's vulnerability by the uprising of the nobility (the Fronde), she took up residence in the Louvre again. In 1662, the young king, who had married Maria-Theresa the year before, organised a grand celebration to mark the birth of the Dauphin; the centrepiece was an equestrian fête (a carrousel) which led to the place being named the Place du Carrousel. The king moved into the Tuileries in 1664 for a period of three years. The architect Le Vau was now working at the Tuileries and on the Louvre, his personal style evident in the Small Gallery, started again after a fire in 1661, and in the Apollo Gallery; he continued the enclosure of the Cour Carrée by adding a storey onto the western part of the north wing (monogram LMT = Louis, Maria-Theresa) and by building the Marengo Pavilion (Pavillon Marengo) (with the monogram LB = Louis XIV de Bourbon). All this while he was already busy on the Great Apartment and the Queen's Suite at Versailles.

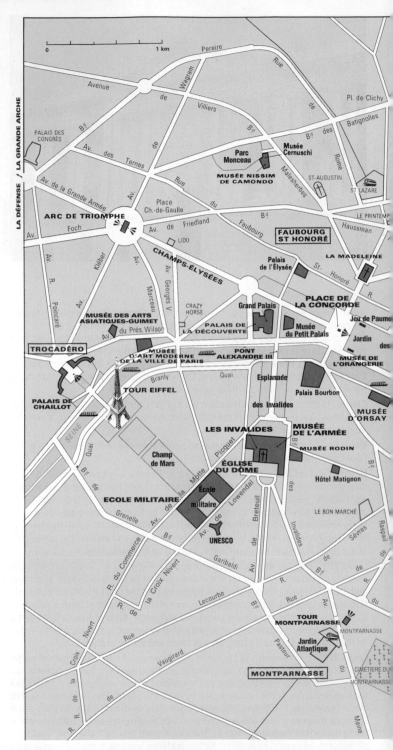

But the palace still needed a monumental façade facing the city; Colbert had just refused permission for a number of projects designed with this in mind. An appeal was made to the master-architect of the Italian Baroque, Bernini, already 67 years old. But his proposals were turned down too, since they would have either destroyed or clashed with Lescot's façade. In the end it fell to Claude Perrault, aided by Le Brun and Le Vau, to design an imposing colonnaded façade. Begun in 1667, but completed only in 1811, it masks Le

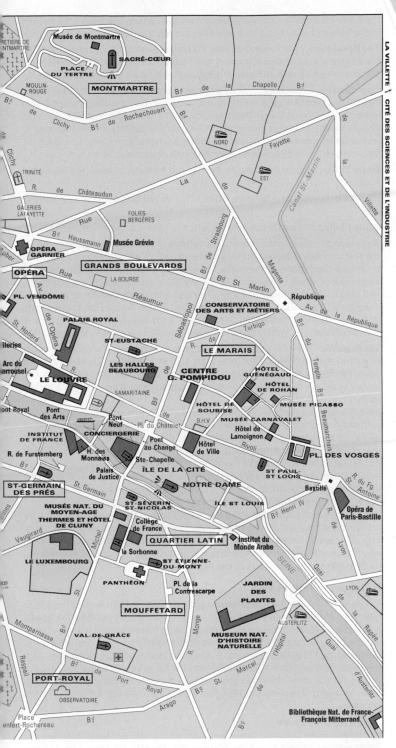

Vau's work on the east side of the courtyard as well as necessitating a solemn extension on the outside of the south wing which made Le Vau's wall into a partition wall.

In 1682, the king left Paris for Versailles. The Louvre now housed the Academy as well as a less desirable population. In 1715, the Court returned to Paris for a period of seven years; the young King Louis XV lived in the Tuileries and the Regent in the Palais-Royal. Coustou continued the work on the colonnade.

Louis XVI resided at Versailles until brought back to Paris on 6 October 1789; he lived in the Tuileries before being incarcerated in the Templar Prison (Prison du Temple).

The Revolution – The Convention used the Louvre theatre for its deliberations. The Committee of Public Safety (Comité du Salut public) convened in the state rooms of the Tuileries which were subsequently appropriated for his own use by Napoleon.

Napoleon I – Lived in the Tuileries. Percier and Fontaine completed the Cour Carrée by adding a second floor to the north and south wings. They also provided a wing linking the Rohan and Marsan Pavilions and gave it a façade identical to Du Cerceau's Grande Galerie, as well as enlarging the Place du Carrousel to enable Napoleon to review his legions and embellishing it with a triumphal arch commemorating the Emperor's victories, its design based on the Arch of Septimus Severus.

Louis XVIII – Lived in the Tuileries. Percier and Fontaine constructed the Rohan Pavilion.

Charles X – Lived in the Tuileries, which was pillaged following the 1830 Revolution.

Louis-Philippe – Lived in the Tuileries, which in 1848 was sacked once more.

Napoleon III – Lived in the Tuileries. He decided to enclose the large courtyard on the north, confiding the task to Visconti, then to Lefuel, whose design was intended to conceal the disparity between the two wings; the architects razed the Hôtel de Rambouillet 3 which had housed the literary *Salon des Précieuses* under Louis XIII, replacing it with the present pavilions. They also restored the Pavillon de Rohan (the monogram LN = Louis Napoléon). Lefuel restored the Pavillon de Flore together with the wing extending it eastwards; his design is a not altogether successful copy of Métezeau's work; the gallery bears the monogram NE (= Napoleon, Eugénie).

The Republic – Since 1873, the official residence of the presidents of the Republic has been the Palais de l'Élysée. During the night of 23 May 1871, the Communards burnt down the Tuileries and half of Napoleon I's North Wing (Aile Nord de Napoléon I), as well as the Pavillons Richelieu and Turgot and the East Wing (Aile Est) attached to the Pavillon de Flore.

In 1875, under the presidency of MacMahon, Lefuel continued the work of Visconti with some modifications; he restored and extended the North Wing (Aile Nord) as well as refurbishing the Pavillon de Marsan and providing it with the monogram RF (République Française); in addition, he rebuilt the Riverside Gallery (Galerie du Bord de l'Eau) and the Pavillons de La Trémoille and de Flore.

In 1883, under the presidency of Jules Grévy, the Palais des Tuileries was demolished; the place where Rameau had once composed his masterpieces was no more, and the city was deprived of one of the key buildings of its architectural history.

In 1984, President Mitterrand voted the "Grand Louvre and Pyramide" project. He commissioned the architect Ieoh Ming Pei to expand the services and reception area of the world-famous museum. Beneath the Cour Napoléon, a vast hall offering information and documentation services is lit up by the glass pyramid **(Pyramide★★)** which marks the main entrance to the museum.

Hôtel des Invalides★★★

The plans for the vast edifice were drawn up by Libéral Bruant between 1671 and 1676; their implementation was placed under the direction of Louvois. The main façade, nearly 200m – 650ft long, is majestic without being monotonous; it is dominated by an attic storey decorated with masks and dormer windows in the form of trophies. Napoleon used to parade his troops in the main courtyard (Cour d'honneur); here the South Pavilion (Pavillon du Midi) forms the façade of the Église St-Louis, the resting-place of some of France's great soldiers; the interior is hung with flags taken from the enemy. It was here, in 1837, that Berlioz' Requiem was performed for the first time.

Église du Dôme★★★

🕐 *Mid-Jun to mid Sep: daily 10am-7pm; Apr and Sep: Mon-Sat 10am-6pm, Sun and public holidays 10am-6.30pm; Jan-Mar and Oct-Dec: Mon-Sat 10am-5pm, Sun and public holidays 10am-5.30pm.* 🕐 *Closed 1st Mon in the month, 1 Jan, 1 May, 1 Nov, 25 Dec.* 👁 *7€.* ☎ *01 44 42 38 77. www. invalides.org.*

The church designed by the master of proportion, **Jules-Hardouin Mansart,** was begun in 1677. It is one of the great works of the Louis XIV style, bringing to a peak of perfection the Classicism already introduced in the churches of the Sorbonne and the Val-de-Grâce, an ecclesiastical equivalent of the secular architecture of Versailles.

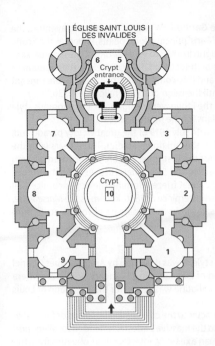

ÉGLISE SAINT LOUIS
DES INVALIDES

1) Tomb of Joseph Bonaparte, elder brother of Napoleon, King of Spain.

2) Monument to Vauban by Etex. The Emperor himself commanded that the military architect's heart be brought to the Invalides.

3) Marshal Foch's tomb by Landowsky.

4) Ornate high altar surrounded by twisted columns and covered by a baldaquin by Visconti. Vaulting decoration by Coypel.

5) General Duroc's tomb.

6) General Bertrand's tomb.

7) At the back – the heart of La Tour d'Auvergne, first grenadier of the Republic; in the centre, the tomb of Marshal Lyautey.

8) Marshal Turenne's tomb by Tuby.

9) St Jerome's Chapel (carvings by Nicolas Coustou). The tomb at the foot of the wall is Jerome Bonaparte's, Napoleon's younger brother and King of Westphalia.

10) The Emperor's tomb.

The façade facing Place Vauban is Doric at ground level and Corinthian above, finished off by a pediment carved by Coysevox. The soaring dome itself is carried on a great drum; the columns support the balconies and the consoles; it terminates in an elegant lantern 107m – 352ft above ground level. In 1735, Robert de Cotte completed the building by replacing the planned south colonnade and portico with the splendid vista offered by the Avenue de Breteuil. On the far side he laid out the Esplanade, and set up the guns captured at Vienna in 1805 by Napoleon to defend the gardens and fire ceremonial salvoes on great national occasions.

The church took on its role as military necropolis when Napoleon had Marshal Turenne (d 1675) buried here.

Église du Dôme

Note also the memorial to Vauban, the great military architect, and the tomb of Marshal Foch. In Visconti's crypt of green granite from the Vosges stands the "cloak of glory", the unmarked red porphyry mausoleum **(Tombeau de Napoléon)** completed in 1861 to receive the Emperor's mortal remains. In 1940, the body of Napoleon's son, King of Rome and Duke of Reichstadt, was brought here too.

Arc de Triomphe★★★

🕙 *Apr-Sep: daily 10am-11pm (last admission 30min before closing); Oct-Mar: daily 10am-10.30pm.* 🕙 *Closed 1 Jan, 1 and 8 May (morning), 14 Jul (morning), 11 Nov (morning), 25 Dec.* ⊚ *7€.* ☎ *01 55 37 73 77.*

Together with the **Place Charles de Gaulle**★★★ and its 12 radiating avenues, the great triumphal arch makes up one of Paris' principal focal points, known as the **Étoile** (Star). The arch was designed by Chalgrin in 1806 to serve as one of the landmarks of Napoleon's imperial capital. But the architect died (in 1811) before the monument had risen very far above the ground, and this, combined with military failures, meant that the work was not completed until the reign of Louis Philippe, in 1836.

The façades of the buildings around the Étoile were designed in a harmonious style by Hittorff as part of Haussmann's plans for the metropolis.

The Arc de Triomphe was the scene on 14 July 1919 of the great victory parade and, on 11 November 1920, of the burial of the Unknown Soldier. Three years later the flame of remembrance was kindled for the first time. The arch is ornamented with much sculpture; the names of 128 battles and 558 generals cover the flat surfaces; caryatids, sculptures in high relief, the great frieze adorning the upper cornice... all pale into insignificance before Rude's masterpiece of 1836; known as the *Marseillaise*, and touched by the breath of genius, it shows the departure of volunteers to fight the invading Prussians (1792).

Place de la Concorde★★★

A perfect expression of the Louis XV style, it was designed by Ange-Jacques Gabriel in 1755 and completed over a period of 20 years. On 21 January 1793, near where the statue of Brest now stands, the guillotine was set up for the execution of Louis XVI and other victims of the Terror.

The square owes its monumental character to the colonnaded buildings defining it to the north, to its octagonal plan, and to the massive pedestals intended for allegorical statues of French cities. Two great urban **axes**★★★ intersect here: one runs from the Église de la Madeleine to the Palais-Bourbon, the other from *Coysevox's Winged Horses (Chevaux ailés)*, which mark the entrance to the Tuileries, to the magnificent marble sculptures (copies) by Nicolas and Guillaume Coustou which flank the Champs-Élysées. The pink granite Luxor obelisk (Obélisque de Louksor), 3 300 years old, covered with hieroglyphics, was brought here from Egypt in 1836. The square's fountains adorned with statues are particularly fine.

Tour Eiffel★★★

Kids ⊙ *Lift: mid-Jun to end Aug: daily 9am-midnight; Jan to mid-Jun: daily 9.30am-11pm. Sep-Dec: daily 9.30am-6pm. ⊜ 4€ (1st floor), 7.30€ (2nd floor), 10.40€ (3rd floor). Stairs: 1st and 2nd floors only, 3.50€. ☎ 01 44 11 23 23. www.tour-eiffel.fr.*

11 fold 28 – J7. The Eiffel Tower is Paris' most famous symbol. The first proposal for a tower was made in 1884; construction was completed in 26 months and the tower opened in March 1889 for the Universal Exhibition (Exposition universelle) of that year.

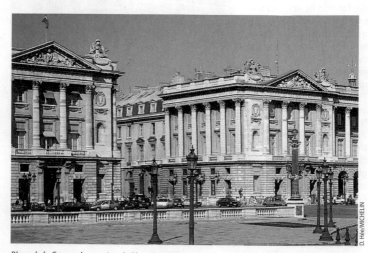

Place de la Concorde, previously Place Louis XV

The structure is evidence of Eiffel's imagination and daring; in spite of its weight of 7 000 tonnes and a height of 320.75m – 1 051ft and the use of 2.5 million rivets, it is a masterpiece of lightness. It is difficult to believe that the tower actually weighs less than the volume of air surrounding it and that the pressure it exerts on the ground is that of a man sitting on a chair.

Palais de Justice and Conciergerie★★

Palais: 🕐 *daily except Sun 8.30am-6pm.* 🕐 *Closed public holidays. Visitors are normally allowed to attend a civil or criminal hearing. Sculpture gallery and children's tribunal:* 🔑 *Closed to the public.* ☎ *01 44 32 50 00.*

Conciergerie: 🕐 *Mar-Oct: daily 9.30am-6pm; Nov-Feb: daily 9.30am-5pm. Last entry 30 min before closing.* 🕐 *Closed 1 Jan, 1 May and 25 Dec.* 💰 *6.10€ (under 17 years: no charge).* ☎ *01 53 40 60 80.*

Known as the Palace (Palais), this is the principal seat of civil and judicial authority. Before becoming the royal palace of the rulers of medieval France, it had been the residence of Roman governors, Merovingian kings and the children of Clovis, the mint of Dagobert and Duke Eudes' fortress.

The Capetian kings built a chapel and fortified the palace with a keep. Saint Louis lived in what is now the Civil Chamber (Chambre Civile).

Philippe le Bel (the Fair) entrusted Enguerrand de Marigny with the building of the Conciergerie as well as with the extension and embellishment of the palace; its Gothic halls of 1313 were widely admired. Later, Charles V built the Clock Tower (Tour de l'Horloge), the city's first public clock; he also installed Parliament here, the country's supreme court. Charles VII abandoned the place to its new occupants, preferring to live elsewhere. Survivals from this period include the Great Hall (Salle des gens d'Armes) with its fine capitals, the Guard Room (Salle des Gardes) with its magnificent pillars, and the kitchens with their monumental corner fireplaces.

The great hall on the first floor was restored by Salomon de Brosse after the fire of 1618; it was refurbished again in 1840 and once more after the fire of 1871.

The First Civil Court is in the former Parliamentary Grand Chamber (Grand'chambre du parlement), the place where the kings dispensed justice, where the 16-year-old Louis XIV dictated his orders to Parliament, where that body in its turn demanded the convocation of the States-General in 1788, and where the Revolutionary Tribunal was set up under the public prosecutor, Fouquier-Tinville.

The entrance to the royal palace was once guarded by the twin towers gracing the north front of the great complex; this is the oldest part of the building, albeit now hiding behind a 19C neo-Gothic façade.

The **Conciergerie** served as antechamber to the guillotine during the Terror, housing up to 1200 detainees at any one time. The Prisoners' Gallery (Galerie des Prisonniers), Marie-Antoinette's cell (cachot) and the Girondins' Chapel (chapelle des Girondins) are particularly moving.

Palais-Royal★★

In 1632, Richelieu ordered Lemercier to build the huge edifice which came to be known as the Cardinal's Palace (Palais Cardinal) when it was extended in 1639. It is remarkable for its impressive central façade, surmounted by allegorical statues and a curved pediment. On his deathbed, Richelieu bequeathed it to Louis XIII, whereupon its name was changed to the Palais-Royal. The king did not outlive his minister for long, and after his death Anne of Austria moved here with the young Louis XIV in preference to the now somewhat old-fashioned Louvre with its never-ending rebuilding and extension.

The first meetings of the Académie Française (founded by Richelieu) were held here in 1635. In 1783, Victor Louis laid out the charming formal gardens and the arcades which enclose them and which house a number of specialist shops and boutiques. In 1787, the same architect built the adjoining Théâtre-Français and in so doing altered the appearance of Lemercier's building which heralded the Classical style.

In 1986, Daniel Buren designed the quincunx of columns, 260 in number and all of different height, which occupy the outer courtyard.

École Militaire★★

Though the original design could not be fully implemented because of lack of financial resources, the Military Academy by Jacques-Ange Gabriel is one of the outstanding examples of French 18C architecture. It was begun in 1752, financed in part by Mme de Pompadour, and completed in 1773. Under the Second Empire, cavalry and artillery buildings of nondescript design were added, together with the low-lying wings which frame the main building. True to its original function, it now houses the French Army's Staff College.

The main façade consists of a projecting central section with great Corinthian columns rising a full two storeys, crowned with a quadrangular dome and ornamented with allegorical figures and military trophies.

The superb main courtyard (**cour d'honneur**★), lined on either side by beautiful porticoes with paired columns, is approached via an exercise yard; the imposing central section and the projecting wings form a harmonious composition.

Panthéon★★

🕓 *Apr-Sep: daily 9.30am-11pm; Oct-Mar: daily 10am-10.30pm.* 🕓 *Closed 1 Jan, 1 and 8 May (morning), 14 Jul, 11 Nov (morning) and 25 Dec.* 🎟 *7€.* ☎ *01 55 37 73 77.*

In 1744, Louis XV had made a vow at Metz to replace the half-ruined church of St Genevieve's Abbey. Fourteen years later Soufflot began the construction of the new building on the highest point of the Left Bank. The scale of the building was such that its collapse was confidently predicted and the pretensions of its architect ridiculed. The present building has been much changed since Soufflot's day; its towers have gone, its pediments have been remodelled, its windows blocked up. In 1791, the Constituent Assembly closed the church to worshippers in order to convert it into the last resting place of the "great men of the epoch of French liberty". Successively a church, a necropolis, headquarters of the Commune, a lay temple, the Panthéon is representative of the time in which churches lost their dominant position in the urban landscape. Still crowned by Soufflot's dome, the great edifice is built in the shape of a Greek Cross. It has a fine portico with Corinthian columns and a pediment carved by David d'Angers in 1831. In the crypt are the tombs of the famous.

Opéra Garnier★★

🕓 *Daily 10am-5pm (unless matinée or special event taking place). Guided tours* 🔊 *(1hr15min) of the public entrance halls and museum, daily at noon (meet at 11.45pm in the entrance hall, next to Rameau's statue).* 🎟 *6€ (children under 10 years: no charge).* 🕓 *Closed 1 Jan and 1 May.* ☎ *01 40 01 25 40. www.operadeparis.fr.*

This is the National Academy of Music, and was until 1990 France's premier home of opera. It opened in 1875 and it is the work of Charles Garnier, who had dreamed of creating an authentic Second Empire style. But the huge edifice, "more operatic than any opera" (Ian Nairn), magnificent though it was, lacked sufficient originality to inspire a new school of architecture. The interior, with its Great Staircase, foyer and auditorium, is of the utmost sumptuousness. Garnier used marble from all the quarries of France, and there is a ceiling by Chagall.

Palais de Chaillot★★

This remarkable example of inter-war architecture was built for the 1937 Exhibition. Its twin pavilions are linked by a portico and extended by wings which curve to frame the wide terrace with its statues in gilded bronze. From here there is a wonderful **view**★★★ of Paris; in the foreground are the Trocadero Gardens with their spectacular fountains, and beyond the curving river the Eiffel Tower, the Champ-de-Mars, and the École Militaire.

The Palais houses the Théâtre de Chaillot, the Musée de l'Homme★★, Musée de la Marine★★, Musée des Monuments Français★★ and Musée du Cinéma Henri-Langlois★.

Ecclesiastical architecture

Cathédrale Notre-Dame★★★

The metropolitan church of Paris is one of the triumphs of French architecture. People have worshipped here for 2 000 years and the present building has witnessed the great events of French history; in many ways Notre-Dame is the cathedral of the nation. Work on the cathedral was begun by Maurice de Sully in 1163. He was already familiar both with the early Gothic of Suger's Cathédrale St-Denis and with the Transitional style, in evidence at Sens, Noyon, Senlis, Laon and in the recently-consecrated choir at St-Germain-des-Prés a short distance away. Notre-Dame is the last great galleried church building and one of the first with flying buttresses. Its successive architects have for the most part kept to the original plan, while at the same time not being afraid to innovate, sometimes in ways which set subsequent standards.

The chancel was built under Louis VII and consecrated in 1182 in the reign of Philippe Auguste. It is still enclosed with sturdy cylindrical columns as near to the Romanesque as to Early Gothic, but the double ambulatory and the tracery reinforcing the wide windows set new trends. Furthermore, there is still a gallery, but, for extra support,

Notre-Dame, east view

there are flying buttresses as used a few years previously at St-Germer-de-Fly. Here, for the first time, they are extended by a spout in order to throw rainwater clear of the foundations, thereby forming the first gargoyles.

By 1210, the first bays of the nave had been built, together with the seatings for the west front; within 10 years the nave was completed, the 28 statues of the Kings' Gallery (Galerie des Rois) were in place, and by 1225 the west front rose as high as the great rose window. In 1245 the bulk of the work was complete and St Louis held a ceremony for the knighting of his son and also placed the Crown of Thorns in the cathedral until the Sainte-Chapelle was ready to receive it. In 1250 the twin towers were finished and the nave provided with side chapels to consolidate the whole structure.

In 1430, the cathedral was the setting for the coronation of the young Henry VI of England as King of France; in 1455, a ceremony was conducted to rehabilitate Joan of Arc; in 1558, Mary Stuart was crowned here on becoming Queen of France by her marriage to François II and, in 1572, the Huguenot Henri IV waited at the door as his bride, Marguerite of Valois, stood alone in the chancel; in 1594 the king converted to the Catholic faith.

The great building was not spared mutilations of various kinds; in 1699 the choir screen was demolished, and later some of the original stained glass was removed to let in more light, and the central portal demolished (18C) to allow processions to move more freely. During the Revolution statues were destroyed and the cathedral declared a Temple of Reason. It was in a much-dilapidated building that Napoleon Bonaparte crowned himself Emperor and the King of Rome was baptised. In 1831, public opinion was alerted by Hugo's novel Notre-Dame de Paris to the state of the building, and in 1841 Louis-Philippe charged Viollet-le-Duc with its restoration. In the space of 24 years, the great architect-archeologist had completed his work in accordance with his own, idealised vision of the Gothic style; though open to criticism, it needs to be seen in the context of the wholesale demolition of the medieval Île-de-la-Cité and its replacement with administrative buildings.

Extérieur (Exterior) – The cathedral square is the point from which the distances along the great highways – routes *nationales* – radiating from Paris are measured. It was the scene, in 1452, of a performance of one of the long mystery plays of the time, *The True Mystery of the Passion (Le Vray Mistère de la Passion)*, by Arnoul Greban; its 35 000 lines took four days to recite.

In the belfry of the south tower hangs Emmanuel, the famous bell weighing 13 tonnes. Its pure tone is said to be due to the gold and silver jewellery thrown by the ladies of Paris into the molten bronze on the occasion of the bell's recasting in the 17C. Above the Kings' Gallery is the great rose window, still with its medieval glass. An enterprise of considerable daring – it was the largest such window of its time – its design is so accomplished that it shows no sign of distortion after 700 years and has often been imitated.

The South Portal, dedicated to St-Anne (Portail de Ste-Anne), has the cathedral's oldest statues and, at the apex of the tympanum, a somewhat stiff Virgin in Majesty, still very much in the Romanesque tradition. The strapwork of the doors is particularly fine.

The Portal of the Last Judgement (Portail du Jugement Dernier), in the centre, depicts Christ in Majesty and, in the archivolts, the Heavenly Kingdom.

To the north is the Portal to the Virgin (Portail de la Vierge), based on the one at Senlis and divided into horizontal registers; it was a model for sculptors throughout the Middle Ages.

The magnificent Cloister Portal (Portail du Cloître – north transept) is 30 years later than the west front portals; with its richly carved gables and smiling figure of the Virgin – the only original large sculpture to have survived – it demonstrates clearly how far the art of sculpture had advanced over the period.

Further east is the Red Door (Porte Rouge), showing the Coronation of the Virgin.

At the beginning of the 14C, the bold array of flying buttresses was sent soaring over ambulatory and galleries to hold in place the high vaults of the east end.

The South Portal (Portail de St-Étienne) was begun in 1258 by Jean de Chelles; it depicts the Martyrdom of St Stephen; few sculpted scenes had ever been so full of feeling.

Intérieur (Interior) – The boldness of its layout and the noble uplift of its lines testify to the pre-eminence of the French school of architecture in the early 13C. The addition of side chapels in the 13C and 14C by guilds and corporations widened the building and made it necessary to extend the transepts. Jean de Chelles took advantage of the opportunity and of the experience gained at the Sainte-Chapelle to construct rose windows of daring dimensions but with exceptionally delicate tracery above a pierced triforium. The rose window in the north transept has particularly fine stained glass of a deep bluish-mauve. Finally, at the entrance to the chancel, on the right, is a Virgin and Child of the 14C, depicted with even greater nobility and idealism than the equivalent in the Cloister Portal, exemplifying the degree to which sculpture had evolved over the course of a hundred years.

Sainte-Chapelle★★★

Daily 9.30am–6pm. Last admission 30min before closing. Closed 1 Jan, 1 May, 1 and 11 Nov, 25 Dec. 6.10€. 01 53 40 60 80.

Only 80 years separate this definitive masterpiece of the High Gothic from the Transitional Gothic of Notre-Dame, but the difference is striking; in the lightness and clarity of its structure, the Sainte-Chapelle exceeds in ambition even the achievements of the Lanceolate style of Chartres and Amiens, pushing Gothic logic to its limits. The relatively modest dimensions of the building allowed its architect, Pierre de Montreuil, to support it by means of conventional buttresses capped by pinnacles.

The chapel was built on the orders of St Louis to house the recently acquired relics of the Passion within the precincts of the royal palace; it was completed in the record time of 33 months. Like other palatine chapels (Laon, Meaux), it is built on two storeys, the upper for the monarch, the lower for the staff of the palace.

Vitraux (Stained glass) – The upper chapel resembles a shrine with walls made almost entirely of stained glass covering a total area of 618m² – 6 672sq ft; 1 134 different scenes are depicted, of which 720 are made of original glass. The windows rise to a height of 15m – nearly 50ft. By 1240, the stained glass at Chartres had been completed, and the king was thus able to call on the master-craftsmen who had worked on them to come to Paris; this explains the similarity between the glass of cathedral and of chapel, in terms of the scenes shown and the luminous colour which eclipses the simplicity of the design.

The theme is Christ's Passion, including its foretelling by the Prophets and by John the Baptist, together with the episodes which lead up to it. The original rose window is shown in a scene from the *Très Riches Heures du Duc de Berry*; the present rose window is a product of the Flamboyant Gothic, ordered by Charles VII, and showing the Apocalypse of St John. It is characteristic of its age in the design of its tracery and in the subtle variations of colour which had replaced the earlier method of juxtaposing a great number of small coloured panes. The glass of the Sainte-Chapelle has been much imitated, even in architecturally inappropriate situations.

Abbaye de St-Germain-des-Prés★★

This most venerable of the city's churches reveals more than visual delights to those who know something of the history of its ancient stones. With the exception of Clovis, the Merovingian kings were buried here. The church was subsequently destroyed by the Normans, but restored in the course of the 10C and 11C. Understandably, the tower rising above the west front has a fortress-like character. Around 1160, the nave was enlarged and the chancel rebuilt in the new Gothic style. "Improvements" followed in the 17C (triforium and chancel windows) and in 1822 a somewhat over-zealous restoration took place.

But the church's years of glory were between 1631 and 1789, when the austere Congregation of St Maur made it a centre of learning and spirituality: the monks studied ancient inscriptions (epigraphy) and writing (paleography); the Church Fathers (Patristics), archeology, cartography... Their library was confiscated at the time of the French Revolution.

Église St-Séverin-St-Nicolas★★

This much-loved Latin Quarter Church has features from a number of architectural styles. The lower part of the portal and the first three bays of the nave are High Gothic; while much of the rest of the building was remodelled in Flamboyant style (upper part of the tower, the remainder of the nave, the secondary aisle, the highly-compartmentalised vaulting of the chancel and the famous spiral pillar in the ambulatory). In the 18C, the pillars in the chancel were clad in wood and marble.

Église St-Eustache★★

This was once the richest church in Paris, centre of the parish which included the areas around the Palais-Royal and the Halles market; its layout was modelled on that of Notre-Dame when building began in 1532. But St-Eustache took over a hundred years to complete; tastes changed, and the Gothic skeleton of the great building was fleshed out with Renaissance finishes and detail.

The Flamboyant style is evident in the three-storeyed interior elevation, in the vaulting of the choir, crossing and nave, in the lofty side aisles and in the flying buttresses. The Renaissance is exemplified in the Corinthian columns and in the return to the use of semicircular arches, and Classicism in P de Champaigne's choir windows and in Colbert's tomb, designed by Le Brun in collaboration with Coysevox and Tuby. In the Chapelle St-Joseph is the English sculptor Raymond Mason's colourful commemoration of the fruit and vegetable market's move out of Paris in 1969.

Église Notre-Dame-du-Val-de-Grâce★★

After many childless years, Anne of Austria commissioned François Mansart to design a magnificent church in thanksgiving for the birth of Louis XIV in 1638. The work was completed by Lemercier and Le Muet. The church recalls the Renaissance architecture of Rome; the dome, rising above the two-tier west front with its double triangular pediment, is particularly ornate and obviously inspired by St Peter's. Inside, the spirit of the Baroque prevails; there is polychrome paving, highly-sculptured vaulting over the nave, massive crossing pillars and a monumental baldaquin with six wreathed columns. The **cupola**★★ was decorated by Mignard with a fresco featuring 200 figures.

Urban Design

Since the sweeping away of much of medieval Paris in the 19C, three central districts have come to typify particular stages in the city's evolution.

Le Marais★★★

Renaissance, Louis XIII and Louis XIV. Charles V's move to the Hôtel St-Paul in the Marais district in the 14C signalled the incorporation of a suburban area into Paris. The area soon became fashionable, and Rue St-Antoine the city's finest street. It was here that that characteristic French town house, the hôtel, took on its definitive form with the collaboration of the finest architects and artists; it became the setting for that other distinctive feature of Parisian life, the literary or philosophical salon.

The **Hôtel Lamoignon**★ of 1584 is a typical example of a mansion in the Henri III style. For the first time in Paris, its architect, Jean-Baptiste Androuet Du Cerceau, used the Giant Order with its flattened pilasters, Corinthian capitals and sculpted string-course.

The Henri IV style makes its appearance in the **Place des Vosges**★★★ designed by Louis Métezeau and completed in 1612. The 36 houses retain their original symmetrical appearance with arcades, two storeys with alternate brick and stone facings and steeply-pitched slate roofs pierced with dormer windows. The King's Pavilion (Pavillon du Roi) is sited at the southern end of the square, balanced by the Queen's Pavilion (Pavillon de la Reine) at the sunnier northern end.

Place des Vosges

Louis XIII's reign heralds the Classical style. In 1624, Jean Androuet Du Cerceau built the **Hôtel de Sully**★ with a gateway framed between massive pavilions and a main courtyard **(cour d'honneur★★★)** with triangular and curved pediments complemented by the scrolled dormer windows; beyond is an exquisite inner courtyard. The early-Louis XIV style is seen in Mansart's **Hôtel Guénégaud**★★ of 1648, with its plain harmonious lines, majestic staircase, and small formal garden one of the finest houses of the Marais; in Le Pautre's **Hôtel de Beauvais**★ with its curved balcony on brackets and its ingenious internal layout; in the **Hôtel Carnavalet**★, a Renaissance house rebuilt by Mansart in 1655; and in Cottard's **Hôtel Amelot-de-Bisseuil**★ of somewhat theatrical design with its cornice and curved pediment decorated with allegorical figures.

The later-Louis XIV style features in two adjoining *hôtels* built by Delamair: the **Hôtel de Rohan**★★ with its wonderful sculpture of the *Horses of Apollo (Chevaux frémissants d'Apollon à l'abreuvoir)* by Robert Le Lorrain; and the **Hôtel de Soubise**★★ with its horseshoe-shaped courtyard and double colonnade. They are characterised by their raised ground floors, massive windows, roof balustrades and by the sculpture of their projecting central sections.

La Voie Triomphale (From the Tuileries to the Arc de Triomphe)★★★

A great axis leading from the courtyard of the Louvre to St Germain had been planned by Colbert, but today's "Triumphal Way" was laid out under Louis XVI, Napoleon III and during the years of the Third Republic.

Arc de Triomphe du Carrousel★

This delightful pastiche of a Roman arch is decorated with statues of Napoleonic military men in full uniform. An observer standing in the Place du Carrousel commands an extraordinary perspective which runs from the Louvre, through the arch, to the obelisk in the Place de la Concorde, then onward and upward to the Grande Arche at the Défense.

Jardin des Tuileries★

The gardens were first laid out in the 1560s by Catherine de' Medici in the Italian style. A century later, they were remodelled by Le Nôtre, who here created the archetypal French garden, a formal setting for the elegant pleasures of outdoor life. The Riverside Terrace (Terrasse du Bord de l'Eau) became the playground of royal princes and of the sons of the two Napoleons, then of all the children of Paris.

Place de la Concorde★★★ – *Page 396.*

Champs-Élysées★★★

In 1667, Le Nôtre extended the axis from the Tuileries to a new focal point, the Rond-Point, which he laid out himself. The avenue was then a service road for the houses facing the Rue du Faubourg-St-Honoré, but very soon refreshment stalls were set up and crowds flocked to the area. In 1724, the Duc d'Antin planted rows of elms to extend the "Elysian Fields" up to the Étoile. In 1729, street lanterns lit the evening scene. Forty-eight years on, and the avenue had descended the gentle slope beyond the Étoile to reach the Seine at the Pont de Neuilly. The buildings lining it included taverns and wine-shops, the later haunt of Robespierre and his friends. Finally, in 1836, the **Arc de Triomphe**★★★ was completed by Louis-Philippe.

The Champs-Élysées became fashionable during the reign of Louis-Napoléon, when high society flocked to the restaurants (like Ledoyen's), to the theatres (like the Folies Marigny and the Bouffes d'Été where Offenbach's operettas were performed), or to receptions in the grand houses (like no 25, today occupied by the Travellers' Club, with its doors of bronze and its onyx staircase).

The avenue has undergone much change since 1914. Its character nowadays is determined by its luxury shops, expensive cafés, and motor showrooms; but it nevertheless remains the capital's rallying point at times of high national emotion (the Liberation, 30 May 1968, the funeral of De Gaulle in 1970, and annually on July 14).

La Défense★★

An outstanding architectural achievement, La Défense has nothing in common with the traditional business districts found in most city centres. A 1 200m – 4 000ft terraced podium, pleasantly punctuated with gardens, fountains, sculptures and shaded spots, runs from the Seine up to La Grande Arche. It is lined with an impressive ensemble of huge towers (Tour Fiat: 178m – 583ft) that compose a dazzling tableau of radiant light.

La Grande Arche★★

🕐 *Apr-Sep: 10am-8pm. Oct-Mar: 10am-7pm (last admission 30min before closing).* 💷 *7€ (children: 5.50€).* ☎ *01 49 07 27 27. www.grandearche.com.*

The Danish architect Johan Otto von Spreckelsen designed this vast hollow cube which stands at the end of the esplanade and houses private firms as well as several ministries. The Cathédrale Notre-Dame with its spire could fit into the space between the walls of the arch. Each side of the cube is 110m – 360ft long. Towering 100m – 328ft above the esplanade, the 1 ha (2.4 acres) terrace-roof is partly taken up by temporary exhibition rooms. From the belvedere visitors will also be able to admire Paris and its suburbs. At the foot of the arch lies the Palais de la Défence **(CNIT)**: it was the first to be built (1958) and has been "rejuvenated". Now it is an important business centre focusing on three main areas of activity: technology, world trade and corporate communication. Nearby stand a car museum **(Musée de l'Automobile de la Colline de la Défense★★)** and the glass sphere of a cinema **(Dôme Imax)** with a giant panoramic screen.

Exterior decoration – La Défense is also noted for its many public sculptures, which turn the district into an informal, open-air museum: *Two Figures (Deux personnages)* by Miro, Calder's *Red Stabile (Stabile rouge),* his very last work, Julio Silva's *Lady Moon (Dame Lune),* Agam's Fountain *(Fontaine),* Moretti's Monster (Monstre), Attila's Cloud Sculptor (Sculpteur de nuages), Leygues' Corollas of the Day (Corolles du Jour), Philoloas' Mechanical Bird (Oiseau mécanique), Derbré's Earth (Terra), etc. The statue representing the Defence of Paris (Défense de Paris), belonging to a different tradition altogether, has been reinstated on its original site.

Bercy – The Bercy area has been redeveloped as part of an ambitious town-planning project for the eastern section of the capital and now boasts: a sports complex, **Palais Omnisports** built by the architects Andrault, Parat and Gavan; the imposing buildings of the Finance Ministry **(Ministère des Finances)** designed by Chemetow and Huidobro – part of the structure rises above the Seine; a Remembrance Garden **(Jardins de la Mémoire)** comprising three planted areas; and over the river, a brand new library **(Bibliothèque nationale de France-François-Mitterrand★)** by Dominique Perrault – four tower blocks in the evocative shape of open books. It is the last of the great town-planning undertakings carried out during the former President's 14 years in power.

POLITICAL CAPITAL

Palais de l'Élysée

The palace has been the Paris residence of the President of France since 1873. It was built in 1718 by Henri de La Tour d'Auvergne and was once the property of the Marquise de Pompadour. During the Revolution it housed a public dance-hall, a gaming saloon, and a picture gallery. In Napoleon's time, Marie-Louise had a boudoir here in a pavilion overlooking the Rue de l'Élysée, and the young King of Rome a set of rooms. It was here, on 22 June 1815, that the Emperor signed his second act of abdication. The architectural treatment of the palace is a reminder of the taste for comfort which accompanied the revival of court and society life during the period of the Régence.

Hôtel Matignon

Like the Élysée, this attractive town house of 1721 exemplifies the early 18C's quest for architectural refinement; it has been the residence of the French Prime Minister since 1958. Between 1808 and 1811 it belonged to the statesman Talleyrand, whose lavish receptions here enjoyed great renown. Its carriage-door (porte-cochère) is flanked by Ionic columns, and the balconies of its projecting central section are adorned with trophies.

Palais Bourbon★

The palace has been the seat of the Lower House of France's parliament, the Assemblée Nationale, for more than 150 years. The role of the Assembly, which consists of directly-elected deputies, is to examine, and where necessary amend, all draft legislation. The vote must be carried on a text after its wording has been approved by both Assembly and Senate.

The palace was built in 1722; during the Revolution, it was the seat of the Council of Five Hundred. The decorative treatment of the façade (1804) which faces the Place de la Concorde was decided upon by Napoleon. The Antique-style south façade giving onto the courtyard has balconies, a roof balustrade and a portico decorated with an allegorical pediment by Cortot.

Palais du Luxembourg★★

This is the seat of the Senate, the French Upper House, which is composed of 283 members chosen by an electoral college consisting of deputies, departmental and municipal councillors. They are elected for a period of nine years, but a staggered system ensures that a third of them are changed every three years. The president of the Senate exercises the functions of Head of State if the Presidency falls vacant.

In 1615, the Tuileries Palace, begun by Catherine de' Medici, had been a-building for half a century. The Regent, Marie de' Medici, had come to dislike the Louvre since the death of her husband the king; she now wished to emulate her cousin Catherine and have a palace of her own which would remind her of the Pitti Palace in Florence.

Palais du Luxembourg

J.-P. Clapham/MICHELIN

The work was given to Salomon de Brosse. The exterior has ringed columns and rusticated stonework of very Florentine character. The splendid courtyard displays the architect's command of the Classical repertory with a Doric ground floor with semicircular window-openings, columns and curved pediments in the central section, portals with columns, an upper storey emphasised with balconies and roof balustrades on the wings. The south façade has a fine central section with a quadrangular dome, a massive pediment, and garden terraces.

In 1625, Marie de' Medici decorated her gallery with huge paintings (now in the Louvre) ordered three years previously from Rubens. They were intended to glorify her person and her reign; the sense of fleeting colour and movement was a new experience in France.

Hôtel de Ville★

It is from here that central Paris is governed. Municipal government was introduced in the 13C, under the direction of leading members of the powerful watermen's guild appointed by Louis IX. The council was headed by a merchant provost, one of whom was Étienne Marcel, "champion of French unity", who openly challenged royal power.

The place has long been the epicentre of uprising and revolt. Throughout the French Revolution it was in the hands of the Commune, and in 1848 it was the seat of the Provisional Government. The Republic was proclaimed from here in 1870, and, on 24 March 1871, the Communards burnt it down. It was rebuilt from 1874; the central section of the main façade is a reproduction of Il Boccadoro's design for François I; the grand staircase is based on a project of Philibert Delorme's, and the decoration gives a good idea of official taste under the Third Republic.

Intellectual Capital

Quartier Latin★★★

The city as a whole functions as the capital of the country's intellectual life; there is nevertheless a particular concentration on the Left Bank, in the Fifth and Sixth arrondissements. On the slopes of the mount, **"Montagne" Ste-Geneviève,** and the surrounding area are concentrated many of the capital's most venerable institutions, around them the ebb and flow of a perpetually youthful tide, the students and other young people who make up the population of the "Latin" Quarter (so-called because Latin was the language of instruction right up to the French Revolution). Here, in the University and other great institutions of learning, the dogmas of Church and State have been continuously challenged for seven centuries, in lecture-hall and library, and sometimes on the street.

The area abounds in publishing houses, many of them highly specialised (fine art, science, languages, philosophy...), in bookshops, purveyors of scientific equipment, and of course in terrace cafés, places in which to refashion the world as well as to have a drink; they include the Flore, the Deux-Magots and Procope, and, in Montparnasse, the Dôme, La Coupole, La Closerie des Lilas...

Institut de France★★

The Institute originated as the College of Four Nations founded by Mazarin for scholars from the provinces incorporated into France during his ministry (Piedmont, Alsace, Artois and Roussillon). Dating from 1662, its building was designed by Le Vau and stands on the far side of the river from the Louvre, on the site of the Nesle Tower which had formed part of Philippe Auguste's ring of fortifications. It is famous for its cupola, its semicircular flanking buildings and the tomb of Mazarin in the vestibule.

The Institute is made up of five academies:

The **Académie Française,** the most prestigious of all. Founded in 1635 by Richelieu, its membership is limited to 40. Its meetings are held beneath the oval cupola of the former chapel. Its members, the "Immortals", devote themselves to upholding the quality of the French language and enshrining it in the great *Dictionnaire de la langue française*, the country's standard dictionary.

The **Académie des Beaux-Arts** dates from 1816. It has 50 members, divided into sections representing painting, sculpture, architecture, engraving and music.

The **Académie des Inscriptions et Belles Lettres** was founded by Colbert in 1663. It deals with literary history and maintains an archive for original documents.

The **Académie des Sciences**, also founded by Colbert, in 1666, has 66 members involved in astronomy, mathematics, medicine, natural sciences and research.

The **Académie des Sciences morales et politiques** was founded by the Convention in 1795. It has 40 members and is concerned with philosophy, ethics, law, geography and history.

Collège de France

Its origins can be traced to six "King's Readers", and it was founded in 1529 by François I at Guillaume Budé's request under the name of the College of Three Languages – Latin, Greek, Hebrew – (Collège des Trois Langues), in order to combat the narrow scholasticism of the Sorbonne. The present buildings date from the time of Louis XIII when the subjects taught were increasing in number; the king renamed it the Royal College of France (Collège Royal de France). Chalgrin supervised a major reconstruction in 1778. Among the great figures of the era of individual research who were active here were Gassendi, Picard and Roberval, and Claude Bernard, who worked in the laboratories for 30 years. It was here, in 1948, that Frédéric Joliot-Curie formulated the laws controlling the process of nuclear fission and built a cyclotron to test his theories.

The college is not subject to administrative constraints dictated by set courses of study and does not award any qualifications. No charge is made for its courses, which are given by leading authorities and often attended by other experts in the particular field.

Sorbonne

This is the most illustrious of all the country's universities. It is the successor to the theological college founded in 1253 by Robert de Sorbon for 16 poor scholars. The first printing press in France was installed here by Louis XI in 1469. For many years, the university's tribunal constituted the highest ecclesiastical authority after that of the Pope. During his period as Rector, Cardinal Richelieu, faced with crumbling university buildings, was responsible for much reconstruction, including that of the church. Rebuilt and extended at the end of the 19C, the Sorbonne is the seat of the Paris-III and Paris-IV Universities.

The church, **Église de la Sorbonne**★, built by Lemercier from 1635 on, is a fine example of Jesuit architecture; the façade overlooking the courtyard is remarkable for its Corinthian columns and its dome. Inside is Richelieu's tomb **(tombeau de Richelieu**★, 1694) by Girardon.

Higher education and research

The prestige of French universities (17 Nobel Prizes between 1901 and 1939) is largely due to the state's encouragement of innovation. Paris alone has 13 universities (five of them, plus the five Technical Universities, in the suburbs) as well as a number of teaching hospitals of equivalent status.

Other institutes of higher education include the Grandes Écoles; these either prepare a student for an advanced course or deliver it themselves. They include the École Normale Supérieure (teacher training), the École Polytechnique (engineering), École des Ponts et Chaussées (civil engineering), École des Mines (mining engineering)... Places are limited, and subject to fierce competition. Many of these institutions have recently been resited in the outskirts of Paris or in the provinces.

The National Centre for Scientific Research (Centre National de Recherche Scientifique), set up in 1941, promotes scientific progress by supporting research of all kinds.

Libraries

Paris has several hundred institutional libraries and 62 municipal ones. Apart from the National Library, the Mazarin Library and the Ste-Geneviève Library, the most popular are those in the Arsenal, the Pompidou Centre (BPI), the Museum of Decorative Arts (Musée des Arts Décoratifs) and the National Technical Museum (Conservatoire National des Arts et Métiers). The latest, the Bibliothèque nationale de France-François-Mitterrand, introduces the latest communication techniques.

Capital of Entertainment

This section gives an outline of the city's wide range of entertainment and cultural attractions. Full information about what is on at any one time is contained in a number of specialised publications like *L'Officiel des Spectacles, Une Semaine à Paris and Pariscope*, or in the daily press.

The monthly booklet *"Paris Selection"*, edited by the Paris Tourist Office, lists the different exhibitions, shows and other events in the capital.

Entertainment

Paris may be said to be one huge "living stage", as it boasts a total of 100 **theatres** and other venues devoted to the performing arts, representing altogether a seating capacity of 56 000. Most of these are located near the Opéra and the Madeleine but from Montmartre to Montparnasse, from the Bastille to the Latin Quarter and from Boulevard Haussmann to the Porte Maillot, state-funded theatres (Opéra-Garnier, Opéra-Bastille, Comédie Fran-

Morris Column

çaise, Odéon, Chaillot, La Colline) are to be found side by side with local and private theatres, singing cabarets and *cafés-théâtres*.

Not to mention television studios and the large auditoriums where radio and TV programmes are regularly recorded in public.

Cinemas, more than 400 in number, are to be found in every part of the city, with particular concentrations in the same areas as the theatres and on the Champs-Élysées.

Music-hall, variety shows and **reviews** can be enjoyed at such places as the Alcazar de Paris, the Crazy Horse, the Lido, the Paradis Latin, the Casino de Paris, the Folies Bergère and the Moulin Rouge.

As well as the Opéra-Garnier, the Opéra-Bastille and the Comic Opera (Opéra-Comique), there are a number of **concert halls** with resident orchestras like the Orchestre de Paris at the Salle Pleyel, the Ensemble Orchestral de Paris at the Salle Gaveau, and the orchestras of the French Radio at the Maison de Radio-France. In

Famous artists

On 19 December 1915, Giovanna Gassion was born to abject poverty on the steps of no 72, rue de Belleville. She later sang in the streets, before becoming a radio, gramophone and music-hall success in 1935 under the name of **Édith Piaf**. Beloved for the instinctive but deeply moving tones of her voice, she came to embody the spirit of France *(La vie en rose, Les cloches)*.

Another famous figure to come from this neighbourhood was Maurice Chevalier (1888 – 1974), film star, entertainer and cabaret singer *(chansonnier)*; he paired with Jeanne Mistinguett at the Folies Bergères (1909) and sang at the Casino de Paris between the wars. Before attaining fame on Broadway in blacktie and boater, he was known at home for songs that are rooted in Belleville: *Ma pomme, Prosper and Marche de Ménilmontant*.

addition there are many other halls in which full-scale performances are put on (Théâtre des Champs-Élysées, Châtelet, Salle Cortot, Espace Wagram, Maison de la Chimie, Palais des Sports, Palais Omnisports de Bercy, Palais des Congrès, Théâtre de la Ville, Zénith…).

Besides this there are nightclubs, cabarets, dens where *chansonniers* can be heard, *café-théâtres*, television shows open to the public, concerts and recitals in churches, circuses…

Exhibitions

The city has a total of 87 museums and over 100 art galleries. In addition, there are around 30 places where temporary exhibitions are held and a whole array of studios (particularly around the Rue St-Honoré, Avenue Matignon and the Rue de la Seine), as well as libraries and other institutions. Between them, they offer the visitor a continuously changing view of past and present artistic achievement and aspiration. The most famous include the Grand Palais, the Palais de Tokyo, the Pavillon des Arts, the Petit Palais, the Pompidou Centre and the Grande Halle de la Villette.

Tourist Paris

Certain parts of the city have come to be identified in the visitor's mind with the very idea of Paris itself.

Butte Montmartre★★★

The "Martyrs' Mound" was a real village before becoming the haunt of artists and Bohemians in the late 19C, and it still has something of the picturesque quality of a village in its steep and narrow lanes and precipitous stairways. The "Butte", or mound, rises abruptly from the city's sea of roofs; at its centre is the **Place du Tertre**★★ with the former town hall at no 3, still enjoying some semblance of local life, at least in the morning; by the afternoon, tourism has taken over, and the "art market" is in full swing.

Not far away from all this activity rises the exotic outline of the **Basilique du Sacré-Cœur** ★★, a place of perpetual pilgrimage. From here, particularly from the gallery of the dome, there is an incomparable **panorama**★★★ over the whole metropolitan area.

Avenue des Champs-Élysées★★★– *Page 403.*

Tour Eiffel★★★– *Page 396.*

Musée du Louvre★★★– *One of the world's great museums.*

Cathédrale Notre-Dame★★★– *Page 398.*

Le Marais★★★– *Page 401.*

Les Deux Magots

J.-P. Clapham/MICHELIN

Quartier de St-Germain-des-Prés★★

Antique dealers, literary cafés, the night life of side streets... all combine to create the reputation of this former centre of international Bohemian life.

Centre Georges-Pompidou★★

♿ ⏰ *Wed-Mon 11am-9pm (last admission 1hr before closing); Museum and exhibitions Mon, Wed, Fri, Sat-Sun 11am-9pm, Thu 11am-11pm.* ⏰ *Closed Tue and 1 May.* ✈ *7€ or 10€, depending on the spaces visited (under 13 years: no charge for the exhibitions, under 18 years: no charge for the museum), no charge 1st Sunday in the month.* ☎ *01 44 78 12 33. www.cnac-gp.fr.*

The Centre seeks to demonstrate that there is a close correlation between art and daily activities. For both the specialists and the general public, this multi-purpose cultural centre offers an astonishing variety of activities and modern communication techniques encouraging curiosity and participation. The Centre includes four departments: the **Bibliothèque Publique d'Information** (BPI), offering a wide variety of French and foreign books, slides, films, periodicals, reference catalogues...; the **Musée National d'Art Moderne – Centre de Création Industrielle** (MNAM – CCI), the former presenting collections of paintings, sculptures and drawings from 1905 to the present time, and the latter demonstrating the relationship between individuals and spaces, objects and signs through architecture, urbanism, industrial design and visual communication; the **Institut de Recherche et Coordination Acoustique/Musique** (IRCAM), bringing together musicians, composers and scientists for the purpose of sound experimentation.

Quartier Latin★★★

With its core on Mont Ste-Geneviève, this home of students and the young of all nationalities extends north to the St-Séverin and Maubert areas, south to the Rue Mouffetard and eastwards to the Jardin des Plantes. Nearby, the **Institut du Monde Arabe**★ celebrates Arab civilisation.

La Défense★★– *Page 403.*

Palais de Chaillot★★ – *Page 398.*

La Villette★★

The **Parc**★ de la Villette is the largest architectural ensemble to be found within the city boundaries. The 55ha – 135 acre site houses an impressive urban complex featuring the City of Science and Industry (Cité des Sciences et de l'Industrie) and its cinema La Géode, the Zenith concert hall, the Paris-Villette Theatre, La Grande Halle and the Cité de la Musique.

Cité des Sciences et de l'Industrie★★★

🌟 ♿ ⏰ *Daily except Mon 10am-6pm (Sun. 7pm).* ⏰ *Closed 1 May and 25 Dec.* ✈ *7.50€ (children under 7 years: no charge).* ☎ *01 40 05 70 00. www.cite-sciences.fr.*
Built in response to the growing need of both children and adults to understand the scientific and industrial world, this living museum encourages visitors to investigate, learn and have fun through a wide range of edifying scenarios.

La Géode★★★

🌟 ♿ ⏰ *10.30am-9.30pm (special times Mon, call in advance), 1 program every hour.* ✈ *8.75€ per program. Reservations recommended.* ☎ *01 40 05 12 12.* ⚠ *Children under 3 and women over 6 months pregnant prohibited. www.lageode.fr.*
This spherical cinema and its circular screen (diameter: 36m – 118ft), which rests on a sheet of water, is a remarkable technical achievement, whose bold conception and perfect execution is the work of the engineer Chamayou.

Museums of Paris

MUSÉE DU LOUVRE★★★

🌟 ♿ ⏰ *Daily except Tue and some public holidays 9am-6pm (Wed and Fri 9am-9.45pm). Temporary exhibitions under the pyramid: 9am-6pm (Wed and Fri 9am-9.45pm).* ✈ *Permanent collection and temporary exhibits (same ticket, except for temporary exhibits in the hall Napoléon) 8.50€ before 4pm, 6€ after 4pm (under 18 years: no charge, under 26 years: no charge every Fri after 4pm), no charge 1st Sun in the month and 14 Jul. Ticket also gives access to the musée Delacroix. Last ticket sold at 5.15pm (9.15pm Wed and Fri). Tickets can be bought in advance at FNAC (* ☎ *08 92 68 46 94) or at Ticketnet (* ☎ *08 92 69 70 73) with 1.10€ surcharge. Tickets do not expire. www.louvre.fr.*

When the Grand Louvre was opened to the public in 1994, the different collections were divided into three large departments, **Sully, Denon** and **Richelieu**, which are located in the two wings and around the Cour Carrée.

▶ **Orient Yourself:** The main entrance to the museum is by the Pyramid. There is also entrance to the museum through the shopping mall of the Carrousel du Louvre, accessed by metro stop Palais-Royal-Musée-du-Louvre (lines 1 and 7), on either side of the arc du Carrousel, or at 99 rue de Rivoli. You will find yourself in the well-lit Napoleon Hall which orients you towards the three wings of the museum: Denon, Richelieu and Sully. There is a bookstore, the restaurant "Le Grand Louvre," and an auditorium.

🕐 **Organizing Your Time:** The information desks here offer a variety of aids and amenities to further enhance your visit. For 5€ you can rent an Audio guide, or you may just want to choose one of the thematic trails (provided on leaflets), which are designed for all ages, and allows you to discover both masterpieces and less well-known works while exploring a particular theme. Whatever you do, formulate a game plan. The Louvre cannot be enjoyed in its entirety in several visits, let alone one day. Decide what it is you'd really like to see, and get to it!

🅿 **Parking: Parking Carrousel-Louvre** is an underground parking garage located on avenue du Général Lemonnier. It is open daily from 7 a.m. to 11 p.m. There are 80 spaces for buses/coaches and 620 spaces for cars. After parking, enter the museum via the shopping mall of the Carrousel by the fortifications of Charles V.

Kids **Especially for Kids:** Children ages 4 and up can take part in one of the many workshops for young people. Call or check the website in advance for details. ☎ *01 40 20 53 17, www.louvre.fr.*

Sully

History of the Louvre *Entresol*
Medieval Louvre *Entresol*
Egyptian Antiquities *Ground and 1st floor*
Greek Antiquities (Salle des Caryatides, Hellenistic Period) *Ground floor*
Oriental Antiquities (Levantine Art) *Ground floor*
Greek Antiquities (Bronzes) *1st floor*
Objets d'art (Restoration and 18C) *1st floor*
French Painting (17C and 19C) *2nd floor*
Beistegui Collection *2nd floor*

Denon

Greek antiquities *Ground and 1st floors*
Etruscan Antiquities *Ground floor*
Roman and Paleo-Christian Antiquities *Ground floor*
Italian Sculpture *Entresol and ground floor*
Northern Schools: Sculpture *Entresol and ground floor*
Objets d'art (Galerie d'Apollon, Crown Jewels) *1st floor*
Italian Painting *1st floor*
Large Format 19C French Painting *1st floor*
Spanish Painting *1st floor*

Richelieu

Special Exhibitions *Entresol*
Islamic Art Entresol
French Sculpture *Ground floor, Cour Marly and Cour Puget*
Oriental Antiquities *Ground floor*
Objets d'art *1st floor*
French Painting (14C-17C) *2nd floor*
Northern Schools Painting *2nd floor*

Oriental Antiquities

Statues of *Gudea* and *Ur-Ningirsu* – Mesopotamia: c 2150 BC

Code of Hammurabi – Babylon: c 1750BC
Frieze of the Archers from Darius' palace – Susa: 6C BC
Low-reliefs from Nineveh and Khorsabad – Assyria: 7C BC
Vase from Amathus – Cyprus: early 5C BC

Egyptian Antiquities

Gebel-el-Arak knife – Egypt: end of prehistoric times
Sphinx of the Crypt – Egypt: end of the Old Kingdom
Jewellery of Rameses II – middle of second millennium
Seated Scribe from Sakkara – Egypt: Fifth Dynasty
Funerary chapel of Akhout-Hetep – Fifth Dynasty

Rameses II's breastplate (19th dynasty)

Fragments from the Coptic monastery of Bawit – 5C

Classical Antiquities

Kore from the Temple of Hera at Samos – Greece: archaic period
La Dame d'Auxerre (Lady of Auxerre) – Greece: archaic period
Apollo of Piombino – Greece: archaic period
Venus de Milo – Greece: Hellenistic period
Parthenon fragments (metopes) – Greece: Classical period
Etruscan terracotta sarcophagus from Cerveteri, Italy: 6C BC
Victoire de Samothrace (Winged Victory) – Greece: Hellenistic period

Sculpture

Limewood *Madonna* from the Church of the Antonites, Isenheim – late 15C
Diana the Huntress (fountain) from Château d'Anet – French Renaissance
The Three Graces (funerary monument for Henri II) by Germain Pilon
The Four Evangelists by Jean Goujon
Madonna and Child (terracotta) by Donatello – Florence c1450
Marble bust of *Voltaire* by Houdon: 1778
The Slaves by Michelangelo – Florence: early 16C

Painting

Malouel's circular *Pietà* – Dijon: early 15C
St Denis Altarpiece by Henri Bellechose – Dijon: 15C
Avignon *Pietà* by Enguerrand Quarton – c 1440
Portrait of *François* I by Jean Clouet – Loire Valley School
St Thomas by Georges de La Tour – 17C
Gilles by Watteau – 18C
Portrait of *Mme Récamier* and *Sacre de Napoléon I (The Coronation of Napoleon)* by David
La Baigneuse de Valpinçon (The Turkish Bath) and *Grande Odalisque* by Ingres
Les Massacres de Chios (Scenes of the Massacres of Chios) by Delacroix – 1824
Le Radeau de la Méduse (Raft of the Medusa) by Géricault – 1819

The Fortune-Teller by Caravaggio (c1590)

Vierge aux anges (Virgin with Angels) by Cimabue – Florence: 13C
Couronnement de la Vierge (Coronation of the Virgin) by Fra Angelico – Florence: 15C
La Joconde (The Gioconda – Mona Lisa) by Leonardo da Vinci – Florence: early 16C
Les Noces de Cana (The Wedding at Cana) by Veronese – Venice: 16C
La Mort de la Vierge (Death of the Virgin) by Caravaggio – Naples: early 17C
Jeune mendiant (Young Beggar) by Murillo – Seville: mid-17C
Vierge d'Autun (Madonna) by Jan van Eyck – Dijon: 15C
Charles I of England by Van Dyck – England: 17C
Vie et règne de Marie de Médicis – allegorical paintings of the *Life of Marie de' Medici* by Rubens
Les Pèlerins d'Emmaüs (Pilgrims at Emmaus) by Rembrandt

Objets d'art

The Regent Diamond and Crown Jewels of France
Ivory figure of the Virgin Mary from the Sainte-Chapelle, Paris: middle of the 13C
The *Hunts of Maximilian* tapestries – Brussels: 1537
The study of the Elector of Bavaria by Boulle – early 18C
Clock in ebony case inlaid with tortoiseshell by Boulle – early 18C
Monkey commode (gilded bronze) by Charles Cressent – 1740
The *Loves of the Gods* tapestries – Gobelins: middle 18C
Writing-desk, table and commode in the Oeben room – middle 18C
Medici vase (Sèvres porcelain, bronzes by Thomire)

MUSÉE D'ORSAY★★★

♿ ◷ *23 Jun to 28 Sep: Tue, Wed, Fri-Sun 9am-6pm, Thu 10am-9.45pm; rest of the year: Tue, Wed, Fri-Sat 10am-6pm, Thu 10am-9.45pm, Sun 9am-6pm. Last admission 1 hr before closing.* ◷ *Closed Mon, 1 Jan, 1 May, 25 Dec.* 🎫 *7€ (children: 5€), no charge 1st Sun in the month.* ☎ *01 40 49 48 14. www.musee-orsay.fr.*

Highlights include: *La Source (The Spring)* by Ingres
Un enterrement à Ornans (Burial at Ornans) by Courbet – 1849
Les Glaneuses (Gleaners) and *L'Angélus du Soir (Angelus)* by Jean-François Millet
Le Déjeuner sur l'herbe and *Olympia* by Manet
La Danse (The Dance), sculpture by Jean-Baptiste Carpeaux – 1869
L'Estaque vue du port et du golfe de Marseille (L'Estaque from Marseille Bay) by Cézanne – 1878
Les Danseuses bleues (Blue Dancers) by Degas
L'Église d'Auvers-sur-Oise (The church at Auvers-sur-Oise) and *Autoportrait (Self-Portrait)* by Van Gogh
Le Cirque (The Circus) by Seurat
Aréarea joyeusetés (Women of Tahiti) by Gauguin – 1892
Jane Avril dansant (Jane Avril Dancing) by Toulouse-Lautrec
Balzac by Rodin – 1897
The Mediterranean by Maillol – 1902
Pendant and chain by René Lalique
Héraclès Archer (Hercules the Archer) in bronze by Antoine Bourdelle – 1909
Les Baigneuses (Women Bathing) by Renoir – 1918

MUSÉE NATIONAL D'ART MODERNE (CENTRE GEORGE POMPIDOU)★★★

Highlights include: *La Rue pavoisée (Street Bedecked with Bunting)* by Dufy – Fauvism: early 20C
Le Guéridon (Table) by Braque – Cubism: 1911
Nus de dos (Nudes) by Matisse – beginnings of Abstraction: 1916
Arlequin (Harlequin) by Picasso – mature Cubism: 1923
La Vache spectrale (Spectral Cow) by Dali – beginnings of Hyper-realism: 1928
Le Phoque (Seal), sculpture by Brancusi – Surrealism in sculpture: 1935
Outside the museum, re-creation of the workshop of the sculptor Constantin Brancusi

HÔTEL DE CLUNY (MUSÉE DU MOYEN ÂGE)★★

◷ *Daily except Tue 9.15am-5.45pm. Last admission 30min before closing.* ◷ *Closed 1 Jan, 1 May and 25 Dec.* 🎫 *5.50€, no charge 1st Sunday in the month.* ☎ *01 53 73 78 16. www.musee-moyenage.fr.*

Highlights include: Ivory casket – Constantinople: early 11C
Gilt altar-front made for Henri II – Basle cathedral: 11C

29 medallions from the stained glass of the Sainte-Chapelle – Paris: 13C

Limoges reliquaries in *champlevé* enamel – 13C

Golden rose given by Pope Clement V to the Prince-Bishop of Basle: early 14C

Eagle of St John (brass lectern) – Tournai cathedral: 1383

Life of St Stephen tapestry – Arras: middle 15C

Altarpiece from Limburg in painted and gilded wood – late 15C

Lady with the Unicorn tapestries – Brussels: late 15C

Mary Magdalene (probable likeness of Mary of Burgundy) – Flanders

The Lady and the Unicorn

MUSÉE DE L'ORANGERIE★★

⚬╍ *Closed for renovation work. Reopening planned for 2006.*

Highlights include: *Portrait of Mme Cézanne* by Cézanne

Baigneuse aux cheveux longs (Woman Bathing) and *Femme à la lettre (The Letter-Writer)* by Renoir

Nude on red background by Picasso – 1906

La Carriole du père Junier (Père Junier's Cart) by Douanier Rousseau – 1908

Maîson de Berlioz (Berlioz' House) and *Église de Clignancourt* by Utrillo

Antonia by Modigliani

Nymphéas (Water-lilies) from Giverny by Claude Monet

Les Trois Soeurs (The Three Sisters) by Matisse

Le Petit Pâtissier (The Little Pastry-cook) and *Garçon d'étage (The Attendant)* by Soutine – 1922

Arlequin à la guitare (Harlequin with Guitar) and *Le Modèle blond (Blond Model)* by Derain

MUSÉE DE L'ARMÉE (HÔTEL DES INVALIDES)★★★

♿ ⏱ *Apr-Sep: Mon-Sat 10am-6pm, Sun 10am-6.30pm; Oct-Mar: Daily 10am-5pm. Last admission 30min before closing.* ⏱ *Closed 1st Mon in the month, 1 Jan, 1 May, 1 Nov and 25 Dec.* ⊚ *7€.* ☎ *01 44 42 37 72. www.invalides.org.*

Highlights include: Seussenhofer's suit of armour for François I – 1539

Model of the city of Perpignan (one of a series ordered by Vauban in 1696)

Napoleon's flag of farewell flown at Fontainebleau on 20 April 1814

The room where Napoleon died on St Helena (reconstruction)

The Armistice Bugle (which sounded the cease-fire at 9pm on 7 November 1918)

CITÉ DES SCIENCES ET DE L'INDUSTRIE (LA VILLETTE)★★★

Highlights include: L'Argonaute (a submarine formerly in use with the French Navy)

Le Nautile (full-size model of research submarine)

Voyager 2 space probe

Model of Ariane 5 rocket (scale 1:5)

Le Robot-mouche (a glimpse into the future development of bionics)

PALAIS DE LA DÉCOUVERTE★★

Kids ♿ ⏱ *Tue-Sat: 9.30am-6pm; Sun and public holidays: 10am-7pm.* ⊚ *6.50€ (under 18 years: 4€), 3.50€ supplementary cost for the planetarium.* ⏱ *Closed 1 Jan, 1 May, 14 Jul, 25 Dec.* . ☎ *01 56 43 20 21.*

Highlights include: Lunakhod (Soviet moon buggy) – 12 November 1970

Fragment of moon-rock – Apollo Mission XVII: 1972

The number Pi and the 703 prime numbers of the 16 000 000 decimals calculated

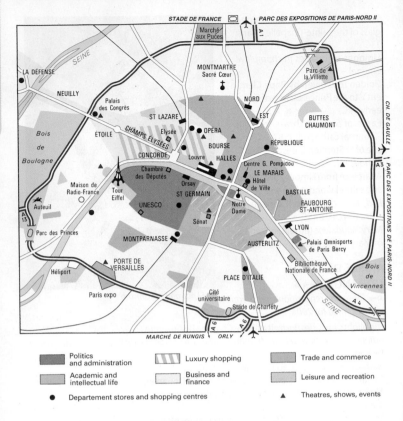

Politics and administration

Academic and intellectual life

● Departement stores and shopping centres

Luxury shopping

Business and finance

Trade and commerce

Leisure and recreation

▲ Theatres, shows, events

CONSERVATOIRE DES ARTS ET MÉTIERS (MUSÉE NATIONAL DES TECHNIQUES)★★

Kids ⊙ *Tue-Sun 10am-6pm (closes at 9.30pm Thu).* ⊙ *Closed Mon and public holidays.* ⊚ *6.50€ (under 18 years: no charge).* ☎ *01 53 01 82 00.*

Highlights include: Microscope belonging to the Duke of Chaulnes – middle 18C
Cugnot's steam-carriage of 1771
Marie-Antoinette's automaton "Dulcimer-Player" – 1784
Jacquard loom
Thimonnier's sewing-machine – 1825
Foucault's pendulum (proving the rotation of the Earth)
L'Obéissante automobile by Amédée Bollée Snr – 1873
The Lumière brothers' cinematographic apparatus – 1895
Transmitting station from the Eiffel Tower
Blériot's No 9 aeroplane (in which he made the first cross-Channel flight)

"Coco" Chanel's headquarters

At the end of 1910, Gabrielle Chanel (1883-1971), the descendant of a family of stall-holders from the Cévennes, and well versed in financial dealings and horse racing, set up shop as a milliner in a basement at 21 rue Cambon. Ten years later she moved to no 31. With her keen business sense, she launched in 1920 the famous "Number 5" perfume, a stable, subtle scent blending floral and animal extracts and artificial stabilisers. Her essential talent, however, was in fabric-cutting and dress-making, applied with skill in the use of "humble" fabrics such as jersey, tweed and plaid. She had an expert eye for colour and designed clothes that relied on line rather than ornament for effect. The reputation of this independent career woman, who was a popular figure in the world of poetry, painting and dance, is based in the main on the success of her tailored suits.

Commercial Capital

Greater Paris is the industrial and commercial capital of France, the country's undisputed centre of economic activity. The distribution and consumption of energy, food, and of products of all kinds take place on a vast scale, and are accompanied by geographical specialisation. Shopping particularly is marked by a high degree of concentration in certain areas, particularly where luxury goods (jewellery, perfume, silk and leather goods) are concerned. The range of goods offered by the great department stores is unparalleled, while the city plays host to numerous trade fairs of national and international significance.

Shopping districts

Most boutiques are concentrated in a few districts whose name alone is suggestive of Parisian opulence.

Champs-Elysées

All along this celebrated avenue and in the surrounding streets (avenue Montaigne, avenue Marceau), visitors can admire dazzling window-displays and covered shopping malls (Galerie Elysée Rond-Point, Galerie Point-Show, Galerie Elysée 26, Galerie du Claridge, Arcades du Lido) devoted to fashion, cosmetics and luxury cars.

Rue du Faubourg-St-Honoré

Here haute couture and ready-to-wear clothing are displayed alongside perfume, fine leather goods and furs.

Place Vendôme

Some of the most prestigious jewellery shops (Cartier, Van Cleef & Arpels, Boucheron, Chaumet) stand facing the Ritz Hotel and the Ministry of Justice.

Place de la Madeleine and rue Tronchet

An impressive showcase for shoes, ready-to-wear clothing, luggage, leather goods and fine tableware.

Department stores

For tourists who are pressed for time, this is probably the ideal solution as most leading names are represented. Department stores are usually open from 9.30am to 7pm Monday to Saturday. **Bazar de l'Hôtel de Ville** (4th arrondissement) – **Galeries Lafayette** (9th) – **Magasins du Printemps** (9th) – **Samaritaine** (1st) – **Au Bon Marché** (7th) – See Michelin plan of Paris No 11.

Antique shops and dealers

Le Louvre des Antiquaires (1st), Le Village Suisse (15th), the Richelieu-Drouot auction room and the rues Bonaparte and La Boétie specialise in antique objects and furniture. Good bargains can also be found by browsing through the flea market at the Porte de Montreuil and Porte de St-Ouen (Saturdays, Sundays and Mondays).

Fairs and Expositions

Paris hosts a great number of world fairs and exhibitions all year round. The following events are among the most important.

Paris – Expo

(Porte de Versailles) International Agricultural Show and World Fair of Tourism and Travel in March; Book Fair in April; Foire Internationale de Paris in April; International Fair of Photography, Video and Sound in late September; International Motor Show in early October (even years); International Boat Show in mid-December.

The bouquinistes

The distinctive dark-green boxes of the second-hand booksellers (bouquinistes) have changed little over the years but their pitches have moved to various locations. They began selling their wares on the riverside when they were little more than pedlars specialising in books on alchemy. Later they congregated on the Pont-Neuf where they set up on collapsible stalls. In the 18C they were chased off the bridge and returned to the quaysides. No stroll along the Seine would be complete without a quick scan of the bouquinistes' stalls as they are an integral part of the Paris scene. Gone are the days, though, when dedicated enthusiasts would pick up manuscripts autographed by famous writers, and other treasures.

Parc International d'Expositions

(Paris-Nord Villepinte) International Fair of Farming Machinery (SIMA) in March; World Exhibition of Computer Science, Office Equipment and Technology (SICOB) in October.

Parc des Expositions

(Le Bourget aerodrome) International Fair of Space and Aeronautics (odd years).

Sports Capital

Among the most popular sporting events held in and around Paris are the International Roland Garros Tennis Championships, the Paris Marathon, the legendary Tour de France with its triumphant arrival along the Champs-Elysées, and several prestigious horse races (Prix du Président de la République in Auteuil, Prix d'Amérique in Vincennes, Prix de l'Arc de Triomphe in Longchamp). The **Parc des Princes** stadium is host to the great football and rugby finals, attended by an enthusiastic crowd, and the **Palais Omnisport de Paris-Bercy (POPB)** organises the most unusual indoor competitions: indoor surfing, North American rodeos, ice figure-skating, tennis championships (Open de Paris), moto-cross races, martial arts, Six-day Paris Cycling Event, and also pop concerts by international stars.

Around Paris

50km – 30mi radius from Notre-Dame Cathedral – Green Guide Northern France and the Paris Region

Barbizon★★

The landscapes of the Forest of Fontainebleau and the Bière plateau inspired a group of landscape painters who worked directly from nature (1830-60) and came to be known as the Barbizon School. Together with their leader, Théodore Rousseau (1812-67), these forerunners of Impressionism favoured dark tones, soft light and stormy skies. The old inn (**Auberge du Père Ganne★**) where they used to stay is now a museum (**Musée de l'École de Barbizon**).

Château de Champs★★

An 18C mansion and landscape. The **park★★** was designed in typically French style, while the internal layout of the **château** broke new ground in its time: the rooms are no longer directly connected with one another and each is provided with a closet and dressing-room; a separate dining room makes its appearance. There is fine Rococo wainscoting (**boiseries★**) and a Chinese Room (**Salon chinois★★**).

Château de Chantilly★★★ – ⚅ *See Château de CHANTILLY.*

Château d'Écouen ★★

The château is a good example of the progress made in architecture between the Early and High Renaissance. It houses a **Musée de la Renaissance★★** which has furniture, tapestries and embroidery, ceramics, enamels...

Enghien★ – ⚅ *See Main Resorts in Introduction*

Château de Gros-Bois★

The early-17C château houses a fascinating **furniture collection★★** of the Classical and Empire periods; it includes a mahogany bed with gilded bronze decoration, porphyry candelabra and bronzes by Thomire, and furniture by Jacob.

Château de Maisons-Laffitte★

Built 1642-51 by Mansart in early-Louis XIV style, the château subordinates considerations of domestic well-being to the creation of grandiose effects (dominance of its site, majestic scale, use of columns and pilasters, lofty pediments).

Meaux★ – ⚅ *See MEAUX.*

Port-Royal-des-Champs★ – ⚅ *See PORT-ROYAL-DES-CHAMPS.*

Rambouillet★

The small town attracts many visitors because of its **château** (Rococo **woodwork★**), its **park★** with formal parterres, water gardens, Royal Dairy (**Laiterie de la Reine★**), Shell Cottage (**Chaumière des Coquillages★**) and the splendid walks offered by its vast forest. The château is the summer residence of the President of France.

Abbaye de Royaumont★★

Founded by Louis IX in 1228. The extent of the original abbey church is indicated by the still-extant bases of its columns, while the splendid Gothic refectory and the 14C Madonna of Royaumont evoke the spirit of the Middle Ages.

Rueil-Malmaison★★

Malmaison is a place of pilgrimage for all those fascinated by the figure of Napoleon. In 1799, three years after her marriage to Bonaparte, Josephine bought the château and its park from the actor Talma. The First Consul spent much of his free time here with her; it was the happiest period of their life together and it was to Malmaison that Josephine returned after their divorce (1809). In June 1815, at the end of the Hundred Days (Josephine had been dead for more than a year), Napoleon fled here, staying with her daughter Hortense until his final departure from France.

Lemercier worked on the château around 1625; the building is interesting for its decoration by Percier and Fontaine and for its **collections★★**, which include busts of the Imperial family, Jacob furniture and many other ornamental objects.

The **Château de Bois-Préau★** has many moving mementoes of Bonaparte's exile and of the eventual return of his remains to France.

Cathédrale St-Denis ★★★– 👜 See Cathédrale ST-DENIS.

St-Germain-en-Laye★★ – 👜 See ST-GERMAIN-EN-LAYE.

Senlis★★– 👜 See SENLIS.

Sèvres★★

Sèvres owes its fame to the porcelain made here. In 1756, on the orders of Louis XV, the original factory at Vincennes was moved to Sèvres, half-way between Paris and Versailles; the government saw the move as an opportunity to assuage the concerns that had arisen as a result of the beginnings of the development of industry. Not unnaturally, Sèvres products are featured in the **Musée National de Céramique★★** which also has examples of the work from the world's other great porcelain makers. On the ground floor is an "Etruscan vase" (19C), while the first floor has plates, cups, dinner services and a range of objects illustrating the differences between hard- and soft-paste porcelain from 1770 onwards.

Château de Vaux-le-Vicomte★★★ – 👜 See Château de VAUX-LE-VICOMTE.

Château de Versailles★★★ – 👜 See Château de VERSAILLES.

Château de Vincennes★★

Green Guide Paris. This "Versailles of the Middle Ages" originated in the manor house built by Philippe Auguste. Louis IX was wont to dispense justice here in the shade of an oak-tree; he also built a chapel. The fortress begun by Philippe VI was completed by Charles V whose place of birth it was.

In the 17C, Mazarin ordered Le Vau to build the King and Queen Pavilions (Pavillons du Roi et de la Reine) together with the portico linking them. The **château** subsequently became a state prison.

Built in 1337, the keep (**donjon★★**) is a masterpiece of 14C military architecture. Henri II completed the chapel (**chapelle★**); the choir has fine stained glass (**vitraux★**) made in 1556 in a Paris workshop.

Ph. Gajic/MICHELIN

Keep, Château de Vincennes

Films about Paris

Hôtel du Nord (1938) directed by Marcel Carné – This film contains the famous line spoken by Arletty. "Atmosphere, atmosphere, do I look like I've got atmosphere?" The Hôtel du Nord still exists, near the Canal St-Martin whose bridges and locks are inseparably linked to the film, although it was, in fact, shot on a studio set.

Les Enfants du Paradis (Children of Paradise, 1943-45) directed by Marcel Carné – Arletty/Garance, Jean-Louis Barrault/Baptiste, Frédéric Lemaître/Pierre Brasseur, Maria Casarès, dialogue by Prévert... – this film is one of cinema's all-time classics.

Gigi (1948) directed by Claude Dolbert – This period movie is full of local colour. The story of a young girl who is brought up by an aunt and is married off to a rake. Not to be confused with the musical version.

Zazie dans le métro (Zazie on the Underground, 1959) directed by Louis Malle – A burlesque comedy which is a screen adaptation of an idea by Raymond Queneau.

A bout de Souffle (Breathless, 1959) – A light touch on the camera and natural settings. Jean-Luc Godard's film laid down the principles of the New Wave.

Les Quatre cents coups (The 400 blows, 1959) directed by François Truffaut – A lively spontaneous Parisian lad, Antoine Doinel, ends up in a Borstal-type institution. The unforgettable shots of the streets of Paris are reminiscent of the photographic art of Doisneau.

Charade (1962) directed by Stanley Donen – Audrey Hepburn is chased through Paris by a gang of ruffians and helped by Cary Grant. Is he or is he not interested in the missing 250 000 dollars?

Last Tango in Paris (1972) – Bernardo Bertolucci directs this fateful story of obsessive love in Paris. Stars include Marlon Brando and Maria Schneider.

Le locataire (The Tenant, 1976) directed by Roman Polanski – A lonely young man falls victim to a conspiracy in an apartment block full of hostile neighbours.

Le dernier Métro (The Last Métro, 1980) directed by François Truffaut – The oppressive atmosphere of Paris during the German Occupation.

La passante de Sans-Souci (1981) directed by Jacques Rouffio – A moving performance by Romy Schneider in her last film. Having fled to Paris (Hôtel George V then Pigalle) to escape Nazi killers, she is finally caught.

Diva (1981) directed by Beineix – Paris serves as a refined context for two very different themes. A beautiful black opera singer gets indirectly entangled with the harsh and violent underworld.

Subway (1985) directed by Luc Besson – This was filmed like a video clip, with musical backing by Eric Serra. The leading actors (Isabelle Adjani and Christophe Lambert) express their love in the labyrinthine world of the Paris métro.

Les amants du Pont-Neuf (1991) directed by Léo Carax – The décors are artificial and heighten the unreal atmosphere of the life led by two young homeless lovers in the middle of the Pont-Neuf while work is being carried out on the bridge.

PAU ★★

POP 85 766

MICHELIN MAP 342 J 3

GREEN GUIDE ATLANTIC COAST

Overlooking the busy waters of the torrent (Gave de Pau), the town has guarded the route to Spain via the Somport pass (Col de Somport) since Roman times. Since 1450 it has been the capital of the Béarn country, in touch with both the lowlands and the high mountains of this ancient southwestern province of France.

A Bit of History

The Béarn and its people – The province has a diversified and attractive agricultural landscape with some arable cultivation, vines (yielding Jurançon, Madiran and rosé wine), and orchards on the spurs separating the river valleys; grazing the mountain pastures are sheep, some of whose milk goes into the making of Roquefort cheese. The inhabitants live in large houses with steep-pitched slate roofs. Since the 11C they have practised a virtually autonomous form of pastoral democracy (fors). They identify strongly with a number of historical figures. **Gaston IV Fébus** (1331-91) was not only a notable huntsman but also an authoritarian ruler who surrounded himself with men of letters; he was the first to fortify Pau. **Jean II d'Albret** acquired the Foix country through his marriage to Catherine de Foix in 1484, but was obliged to abandon southern Navarre to the King of Spain. In 1527, his son Henri II married Marguerite d'Angoulême, the sister of François I: it was she who brought the art of the Renaissance to the castle, and, fired with Reformation zeal, made the place one of the foremost intellectual centres of Europe. Their daughter, **Jeanne d'Albret,** married Antoine de Bourbon, a descendant of Louis IX; this enabled her own son Henry of Navarre (the future Henri IV) to garner the inheritance of the House of Valois on the extinction of the line, thereby "incorporating France into Gascony by way of the Béarn" (Henri IV).

Driving Tour

Boulevard des Pyrénées ★★

From this splendid panoramic road there is a view★★★ over the valley to the Pyrenean foothills, and, in clear weather, far beyond, to the Pic du Midi de Bigorre and the Pic d'Anie.

▶▶ Château★★ ⏰ *Guided tours* 🚶 *(1hr15min) mid-Jun to mid-Sep: daily 9.30am-12.15pm, 1.30-5.15pm; Apr to mid-Jun and mid-Sep to end Oct: daily 9.30am-11.45pm, 2-5pm; Nov-Mar: daily 9.30am-11.45am, 2-4.15pm.* ⏰ *Closed 1 Jan, 1 May, 25 Dec.* 🎟 *4.50€, no charge 1st Sunday in the month.* ☎ *05 59 82 38 07– tapestry collection★★★.*

Musée des Beaux-Arts★ ⏰ *Daily Wed-Sun 10am-noon, 2-6pm.* ⏰ *Closed Tue, 1 Jan and 1 May, 14 Jul, 1 Nov and 25 Dec.* 🎟 *3€.* ☎ *05 59 27 33 02.*

Grotte du PECH-MERLE ★★★

MICHELIN MAP 337 F 4

GREEN GUIDE DORDOGNE BERRY LIMOUSIN

Sited high above the River Célé just before it flows into the Lot, the Pech-Merle cave is of the greatest interest in terms of both prehistory and speleology.

Visit

Kids ⏰ *Guided tours* 🚶 *(1hr) mid-Apr to end Oct: 9.30am-noon, 1.30-5pm. Tour limited to 700 visitors per day (reservations recommended 3 days in advance in Jul and Aug).* 🎟 *7€ (children: 4.50€), ticket combined with the Prehistoric museum.* ☎ *05 65 31 27 05.* *www.pechmerle.com.*

On the lower level of the cave (**grotte**) are paintings of a fish, two horses covered in coloured dots, and of "negative hands" (made by stencilling around hands placed flat against the rock). Something like a three-dimensional effect is produced by the way in which the Late Perigordian artists integrated their work with the irregularities of the rock surface. There are also representations of bisons and mammoths, as well as petrified human footprints from the Early Magdalenian. The upper level has strange, disc-like concretions, "cave pearls", and eccentrics with protuberances defying the laws of gravity.

Pointe de PENHIR★★★

MICHELIN MAP 308 D 5

GREEN GUIDE BRITTANY

The high cliffs and deep inlets of the Crozon Peninsula (Presqu'île de Crozon), which lies between the Brest roadstead to the north and Douarnenez Bay to the south, are the result of the faulting and fracturing of this part of the Armorican plateau. Penhir Point is the most impressive of the four headlands of the Crozon Peninsula. The processes of coastal erosion have worn away the sandstone matrix from which the cliffs were formed, exposing the seams of quartzite. In rough weather, the violence of the waves crashing against the variously-coloured rocks makes a magnificent spectacle. Offshore, the line of isolated rocks known as the Tas de Pois marks where the ancient coastline used to be; there is an unusual view of them from the grassy strip called the Chambre Verte.

Other sites on the Crozon Peninsula★★★

The peninsula has some of the finest coastal landscapes in the whole of Brittany.

Pointe des Espagnols★★

From here there is a panorama of the port of Brest and its approaches.

Pointe de Dinan★★

Fine coastal views. "Le Château de Dinan" (Dinan Castle) is a great rocky mass linked to the mainland by a natural bridge; one day the action of the waves will make it an island. To the north stretch the vast sandy beaches of the Dinan inlet.

Grottes de Morgat★

The caves tunnel into the cliffs at either end of Morgat's sandy bay. Their walls and roofs are attractively coloured, and a covering of seaweed helps protect them from erosion. The **Grotte de l'Autel** (80m – 260ft deep 15m – 49ft high) is probably the most beautiful of all.

Cap de la Chèvre★

The panorama takes in the headlands of Finistère, Raz and Penhir with the Tas de Pois, while Sein Island can be glimpsed in the far distance.

PÉRIGUEUX★★

POPULATION 51 450

MICHELIN MAP 329 F 4

GREEN GUIDE DORDOGNE BERRY LIMOUSIN

Five distinct historical periods have contributed to the formation of this ancient town. First of all there was the Gaulish settlement which prospered in Roman times under the name of Vesunna; its site, the "Cité", is marked by the amphitheatre gardens and St Stephen's Church (St-Étienne). In the Middle Ages, the quarter known as "Puy St-Front" became established on a rise to the north; the cathedral was built here and the area became the heart of Périgueux, eventually in 1251 absorbing the older Cité. In the 18C, the provincial governors, the Intendants, were responsible for a planned northward extension of the city, which linked the two districts by means of broad streets lined with public buildings. At the end of the 19C, the station area was developed, and more recently vast modern suburbs have grown up on the outskirts.

Périgueux - Address Book

EATING OUT

Au Temps de Vivre – *10 r. St-Silain -* ☎ *05 53 09 87 18 -* ⏰ *closed evenings, Sun and Mon - reserv. recommended.* Tucked away in a pleasant street in the old town, this restaurant serves daily specials, plus a selection of savoury and sweet pies. In the afternoon, tea and pastries are served here. The decor is enlivened by the attractive wooden tables and painted chairs.

Au Bien Bon – *15 r. des Places -* ☎ *05 53 09 69 91 -* ⏰ *closed during Feb school hols and in early Nov, Sat lunchtime, Sun, Mon and public hols -* ⌇ The menu here is firmly influenced by seasonal local products. Dine in the rustic interior or outdoors on the summer terrace.

Le 8 – *8 r. Clarté -* ☎ *05 53 35 15 15 - yannick.guichaoua@wanadoo.fr - closed 13-20 Apr, 2-10 Aug, 26 Oct-3 Nov, 25 Dec - 3 Jan, Sun and Mon - reserv. required.* This small, cosy restaurant near the cathedral has established an excellent local reputation for its authentic regional cuisine and an excellent pâté de Périgueux.

Le Clos Saint-Front – *5 r. de la Vertu -* ☎ *05 53 46 78 58 -* ⏰ *closed for several days in early Nov.* This old house, with its exposed beams, fireplace and Louis XVI furniture, is now home to an elegant restaurant which is resolutely devoted to Périgourdine cuisine with an inventive twist. Attractive summer terrace with shade provided by linden, banana and liquidambars trees.

Hercule Poireau – *2 r. de la Nation -* ☎ *05 53 08 90 76 -* ⏰ *closed 24-27 Dec, 31 Dec-3 Jan and Sat-Sun.* The name of this restaurant expresses the good humour of its owners: Hercule Poirot was, of course the Agatha Christie detective of Murder on the Orient Express, among other mysteries. The restaurant, in a vaulted 16C cellar, is popular with locals, who come here for the varied menu which includes several healthy options.

🪙 *For coin categories, see p000.*

WHERE TO STAY

Comfort Hôtel Régina – *14 r. Denis-Papin (opposite the train station) -* ☎ *05 53 08 40 44 - comfort.periguex@wanadoo.fr -* 🅿 *- 45 rooms.* It is easy to spot this hotel as you exit the station, thanks to its newly repainted yellow façade. The rooms are small, functional and colourful. Buffet breakfast. Friendly service and a good location.

Chambre d'hôte La Calade – *Le Bourg - 24420 St-Vincent-sur-l'Isle - 15km/9mi N of Périgueux on the N 21 towards Limoges, then turn right onto the D 705 -* ☎ *05 53 07 87 83 - j.hottiaux@libertysurf.fr -* ⏰ *closed 1 week at the end of Dec -* ⌇ *- 5 rooms.* This farm was built around 1750. The guestrooms, either in the main building or a restored barn are furnished with a mixture of family items, old and new. A large chestnut tree provides welcome shade in the garden.

Hôtel L'Écluse – *24420 Antonne-et-Trigonant - 10km/6mi NE of Périgueux on the N 21 -* ☎ *05 53 06 00 04 - contact@ ecluse-perigord.com -* 🅿 *- 43 rooms - restaurant* 🍽. The River Isle flows gently past the small beach on the hotel property. The rooms on the main façade have balconies which overlook the river. Dine on the terrace in summer.

SHOPPING

Le Relais des Caves – *44 r. du Prés.-Wilson -* ☎ *05 53 09 75 00 - relais.aupert@ wanadoo.fr -* ⏰ *open Tue-Sat, 9am-12.30pm and 2-7.30pm; holidays: mornings only.* The friendly proprietor sells a wide selection of wines from across France, including a few very special vintages. Other local specialities such as fruit preserved in Bergerac wine, wine jam and foie gras are also sold here.

Stéphane Malard – *8 r. de la Sagesse -* ☎ *05 53 08 75 10 -* ⏰ *open mid-Jun to mid-Sep, Tue-Sun, 6.30am-12.45pm and 3.30-7.30pm; mid-Jul to the end of Aug, 6.30am-7.30pm; rest of the year, open Tue-Sat.* Behind the window arcades of his shop, Stéphane Malard sells some of the region's finest delicacies, including confits, foies gras, duck magret and wines. What he doesn't prepare himself, he sources with the greatest care.

La Ferme Périgourdine – *9 r. Limogeanne -* ☎ *05 53 08 41 22 - laferme.perigourdine@ wanadoo.fr -* ⏰ *open in summer, daily 7am-12.30pm and 2.30-7.30pm; rest of the year, daily except Sun, Mon and public hols.* The Thieullent family claims that local cheeses are too fatty, and prefer to ripen and sell cheeses from other parts of France. You will find their careful selection of quality products at the daily morning market (except Monday) on place du Coderc.

Markets – Pl. de Clautre: Wed and Sat morning; pl. de la Clautre (food), pl. Bugeaud and pl. Franche-Ville (clothing): every morning; pl. du Coderc (food); duck and goose product market *(marché au gras)* from Dec-Feb.

BARS AND CAFÉS

Tea for Tous – *Pl. St-Louis -* ☎ *05 53 53 92 86 -* ⏰ *open Tue-Sat, 10am-7pm -* ⏰ *closed Sun and Mon.*

In a building dating from the 16C, this charming tearoom draped in red and yellow fabric offers a selection of teas from the prestigious company Mariage, perhaps accompanied by a delicious home-made pastry. In fine weather, you can sit outside on place Saint-Louis.

Bar St-Silain – *7 pl. St-Silain -* ☎ *05 53 05 02 23 -* 🕐 *open in summer, daily, 10am-2am; rest of the year, Tue-Sat, 9.30am-7pm.* More than a café, this is an outdoor experience! The setting is idyllic, with cane chairs set out on cobblestones under the trees.

Café de la Place – *7 pl. du Marché-au-Bois -* ☎ *05 53 08 21 11 -* 🕐 *open daily, 9am-2am -* 🕐 *closed Christmas and 1 Jan.* Once known as the café for intellectuals, this café is perhaps the most popular in the town? Choose between the lovely outdoor terrace or the early-19C interior.

The Star Inn – *17 r. des Drapeaux -* ☎ *05 53 08 56 83 www.thestarinnfrance.com -* 🕐 *open in summer, 8pm-2am; rest of the year, Mon-Sat, 8pm-1am.* The Anglo-Irish owners have created a home-from-home for their compatriots, with regular events found in a typical British or Irish pub. Three rooms, with lots of old stone, dark wood, tall bookcases and photographs of sailors adorning the walls. Pleasant terrace for the summer months. The inscription next to the bar, "Chevaliers de la Royale Champagne", was carved in the stone in 1778.

LEISURE ACTIVITIES

Gabarre Vésunna – *Quai de l'Isle -* ☎ *05 53 24 58 80 -* 🕐 *departures every hour in summer from 11am-6pm - services do not operate from mid-Sep to mid-June - 6.50€ (child: 4€).* This 50min cruise on the river provides an excellent introduction to the town and its 2 000 years of history. On-board commentary.

▶ **Orient Yourself:** Périgueux, which is listed as a "Town of Art and history," offers 2hr discovery tours conducted by guide-lecturers approved by the Ministry of Culture and Communication. In particular, they cover the Gallo-Roman town (including a visit to the temple of Vesone, which is not open to the public otherwise) or the medieval and Renaissance town (including a visit to the hôtel la Joubertie and the Tour Mataguerre, which are not open to the public otherwise). (🕐 *Jun-Sep: daily except Sun.* ☜ *4.60€ for the Gallo-Roman town tour (10.30am), 5€ for the medieval and Renaissance town (2.30pm and 4pm, 3pm on Sun).* 🚹 *Information at the tourist office or on www.vpah.culture.com.)*

Visit

Domed Churches

The city has two important examples of the domed churches characteristic of Périgord.

St-Étienne-de-la-Cité★

🕐 *Daily except Sun and public holidays 8am-7pm.*

Two of the domes of the original sanctuary have survived. The earlier is thought to have been built in 1117 and may well have been the inspiration for the domed churches of Aquitaine; it is built directly on two massive transverse arches and on two lateral arches; it is dimly lit by a number of small windows opening onto the top of the dome.

The second dome, erected half a century later, is altogether lighter; it rests on pointed arches supported by square pillars made less heavy in appearance by twinned columns, and has a lofty open passage resting on an elegant blind arcade.

Cathédrale St-Front★

Of the original early-Romanesque church there remain only two small domes at the eastern end of the nave. They are octagonal in shape and rest on high drums.

The church was an important stopping-place for pilgrims on their way to Santiago de Compostela since it was here that the remains of St Front, the apostle of Périgord, could be seen. His tomb dates from 1077.

The cathedral was virtually rebuilt from 1852 onwards by Abadie, the architect who designed the Sacré-Cœur in Paris, very much in the spirit of the Second Empire; it nevertheless remains impressive on account of its sheer size and the remarkable simplicity of its lines.

🔁 Quartier du Puy-St-Front★. Rue Limogeanne★. Musée du Périgord★ 🕐 *Apr-Sep: Mon, Wed-Fri 10.30am-5.30pm, Sat-Sun 1-6pm; Oct-Mar: Mon, Wed-Fri 10am-5pm, Sat-Sun 1-6pm.* 🕐 *Closed Tue and public holidays.* ☜ *4€, no charge Oct-May: Mon, Wed, Thu, or Fri noon-2pm.* ☎ *05 53 06 40 70* – prehistory, archeology, ethnography and painting.

PÉROUGES★★

POPULATION 851

MICHELIN MAP 328 E 5

GREEN GUIDE AUVERGNE THE RHÔNE VALLEY

On its hilltop site dominating the Ain valley, this fortified town was originally founded by settlers who came from Perugia in central Italy long before Caesar's invasion of Gaul. One of its lords was **Claude Vaugelas** (1585-1650), who was born at Meximieux a short distance to the east. This influential grammarian of the French language founded his precepts on logic, good taste, clarity of expression and on the language as actually used.

Visit

Cité ancienne★★

Tightly contained within the ramparts, the tortuous streets and ancient houses of the old town of Pérouges have formed the perfect setting for many a period film.

The place was virtually rebuilt in its entirety after the war of 1468 with Savoy. The older buildings are timber-framed with projecting upper storeys. The modest artisans' houses contrast with those of the richer townsfolk and gentry, which have mullioned windows and basket-handle arches, characteristic of the local response to Renaissance influences.

The Upper Gate **(Porte d'en Haut★)** is the principal entrance to the town; the main square, the **Place de la Halle★★★**, has a splendid hostelry and the **Musée du Vieux-Pérouges** (🕐 Apr-Oct: daily 10am-noon, 2-6pm; 🕐 closed Nov -Mar; ⊚ 4€; ☎ 04 74 61 00 88), as well as a Liberty Lime planted in 1792.

 Promenade des Terreaux★ (Outer rampart walk) – Rue des Rondes★.

PERPIGNAN★★

POPULATION 138 735

MICHELIN MAP 344 I 6

GREEN GUIDE LANGUEDOC ROUSSILLON TARN GORGES

Thoroughly French, Perpignan is nevertheless second only to Barcelona in the league of Catalan cities. It is a lively and attractive place, full of memories of great people who have left their mark on the city and its surroundings.

▶ **Orient Yourself:** Enter the centre of the city from the west by boulevard Michelet, from the north by the pont Arago or from the south by the avenue des Baléares. Clothing boutiques are found near rue Mailly. The avenue du Gén.-de-Gaulle located in a very popular part of town is also good for shopping, while the "rue des Olives" (rue de l'Adjudant-Pilot-Paratilla) is well-known for a rôtisseur and two épiceries dating from the early 20C. Perpignan is a "Town of Art and History" with guided tours conducted by guide-lecturers approved by the Ministry of Culture and Communication. Tours run from Jun-Sep daily except Sun at 3pm (Easter and Christmas school holidays at 2.30pm). 4€. Information at the tourist office or by calling 04 68 66 30 30, or on www.vpah.culture.fr.

A Bit of History

In the square which bears his name is a statue to **Hyacinthe Rigaud** (1653-1743). This local man, deeply attached to his home town and to his family, became a celebrated master of portraiture, painting Louis XIV and his courtiers with a rare degree of cool insight into the characters of his sitters. A number of his canvases, including his *Autoportrait au turban (Self-portrait in a Turban)* and his portrait of *Cardinal de Fleury*, are in the Perpignan museum.

Another square, the Place François-Arago, shady with palm-trees and magnolias, is named after the scientist **François Arago** (1786-1853), born at nearby Estagel, who worked on the sun's chromosphere, the polarisation of light, and magnetisation.

In the **Place de la Loge** is the Loge de Mer, the fine 14C and 16C building which long served as stock exchange and maritime tribunal. The square has been the scene of Holy Week processions, political upsets, Louis XIV's celebrations to mark his reconquest of Roussillon, as well as of the *sardanes* which are still danced here in summer.

The sculptor **Aristide Maillol** (1861-1944) was born at Banyuls, the last town on the coast road before the frontier with Spain; the square is graced by his *Venus*, while the nearby Town Hall has his *Méditerranée*; both statues embody that lively southern sensuality characteristic of the artist's female nudes.

Perpignan station found an artistic admirer in the person of the Surrealist painter and master exhibitionist, **Salvador Dali** (1904-89), another Catalan, albeit from just over the border.

Visit

La Ville Catalane (Catalan Perpignan)

Palais des rois de Majorque★

🧒 �🕐 *Jun-Sep: daily 10am-6pm; Oct-May: daily 9am-5pm. Call in advance for guided tour. Last admission 30min before closing.* 🕐 *Closed 1 Jan, 1 May, 1 Nov and 25 Dec.* 🗝 *4€ (children: 2€).* ☎ *04 68 34 96 26.*

The origin of the palace lay in the desire of James I of Aragon to make his younger son ruler of the "Kingdom of Majorca" with its mainland seat in Perpignan. The ephemeral dynasty lasted long enough (68 years) for this characteristically Majorcan stronghold to be built on an eminence overlooking the modest township on the banks of the Rivers Basse and Têt. The plain central courtyard has a Romanesque ground floor and high Gothic arches above; flints and pebbles are used to make decorative patterns in the brickwork.

Among the other characteristic features of this school of architecture are the great hall known as the Salle de Majorque, the lower Queen's Chapel (Chapelle de la Reine) with traces of medieval frescoes on the squinches, the upper chapel with its fine Catalan figure of Christ, and the royal apartments.

Ensemble monumental civique★

The civic buildings make a fine architectural group along Rue de la Loge.

The **Loge de Mer**★ once housed the tribunal regulating Perpignan's sea-trade. Its walls are of the finest stonework with tall Gothic arches at ground level. The windows let into the upper floor are of much later date (1540), as is the roof balustrade.

The Town Hall **(Hôtel de Ville**★) has been rebuilt a number of times. The upper floor is made of bands of pebbles held in place by brick coursing. The three projecting bronze arms are supposed to symbolise the three States representing the city's inhabitants, but in fact were designed to hold flares. The Renaissance courtyard has arcades and 18C wrought-iron grilles.

The **Députation**★ was once the seat of the Catalan "Corts"; it has a high arched doorway and window-openings with delicate columns made of marble from the Montjuich quarry far away to the south in Catalonia proper.

Castillet★

This pink brick citadel is all that survived from the 1904 demolition of Vauban's ramparts. It dates from the reign of Peter IV of Aragon, while the adjacent Notre-Dame Gate was built during the occupation of the city by Louis XI. The **Casa Pairal** (🧒 🕐 *May-Sep: Wed-Mon 10am-6pm; Oct-Apr: Wed-Mon 11am-5.30pm;* 🕐 *closed Tue, 1 Jan, 1 May, 1 Nov and 25 Dec;* 🗝 *4€, under 15 years: no charge.* ☎ *04 68 35 42 05)* is a Catalan folk museum.

Cathédrale St-Jean★

Work on the cathedral was begun by Sancho of Aragon in 1324 but the building was completed only in 1509. The bell-tower is topped by an 18C wrought-iron cage housing a great 15C bell. Inside, the stately single nave is characteristic of the architecture of Languedoc; the altarpieces of the high altar and the north chapels are fine work of the 15C and 16C, and in the Romanesque Chapel of Notre-Dame-del-Correchs is a collection of reliquaries. In an outside chapel, on the south side of the cathedral, is a touching carved wood **Crucifixion**★, known as the Devout Christ. Such realistic depictions of Christ's suffering became widespread in Europe following Louis IX's acquisition of the relics of the Passion which included the Crown of Thorns.

Excursions

Musée de Tautavel (Centre européen de préhistoire) ★★
25km – 15mi northwest of Perpignan, 9km – 5.5mi from Estagel. Tautavel, a little village in the Corbières has become a major centre in the field of prehistory owing to the discovery in 1971 and in 1979 of fragments of human skull, from which it has been possible to reconstruct the appearance of **"Tautavel man"**; this prehistoric hunter roamed the Plaine du Roussillon about 450 000 years ago.

The vast museum makes use of the latest technology and state-of-the-art displays to take visitors on a fascinating journey far back in time. Besides the realistic dioramas, the main attractions are the facsimile of the cave of Caune de L'Arago and a reconstruction of the skeleton of Tautavel man.

La Côte Vermeille★★
South of Perpignan, between Argelès Beach and the Spanish border, small towns and ports huddle in the bays along the indented coastline created as the last foothills of the Montagnes d'Albères drop sheer into the sea.

Collioure★★
Hemmed in between the royal castle and the Church of Our Lady of the Angels (Notre-Dame-des-Anges) with its domed belltower, this picturesque town attracted artists of the Fauve School in the early 20C and is still very popular with painters.

Banyuls-sur-Mer
This resort is also famous for its vineyard which produces a wine served as aperitif and as dessert wine.

The D 86 which runs through the hinterland leads to the Madeloc Tower (Tour Madeloc – alt 652m – 2139ft): wide **panorama**★★ of the Albères, the Côte Vermeille and the Roussillon.

Château de **PEYREPERTUSE**★★★

MICHELIN MAP 344 G 5

GREEN GUIDE LANGUEDOC ROUSSILLON TARN GORGES

The dramatic barrier of the Corbières was defended by a number of strongholds of which the ruins of the Château de Peyrepertuse, separated into two distinct castles on their rocky promontory, are the most imposing.

Visit
🕐 *Apr-May and Oct: daily 9am-7pm; Jun-Sep: daily 9am-8pm; Nov-Mar: daily 10am-5pm.* 🕐 *Closed Jan. No visits during stormy weather.* 🎫 *4€.* 📞 *04 68 45 40 55. www.chateau-peyrepertuse.com.*

Peyrepertuse

D. Pazery/MICHELIN

425

The Lower Castle (Château Bas) to the east came under Aragonese rule in 1162, enabling it to remain aloof to some extent from the troubles of the Cathar period, at least in their early stages. In 1240, it surrendered almost without resistance to the Seneschal of Carcassonne acting in the name of the king. Louis IX subsequently ordered a stairway to be built giving improved access to the castle. Under the terms of the Treaty of Corbeil in 1258, it became part of the fortified French border facing Spanish Roussillon.

The spectacular northern curtain wall running to a dramatic point, together with the ruins of the main building, the keep and chapel, give an idea of the successive stages of improvement and modernisation of the defences which took place over the centuries.

On the far side of the open area separating the two castles, a monumental stairway has been hewn into the living rock. *Use the chains which serve as a handrail.*

The royal castle raised on this western height is known as St George's Castle. It was built in the course of a single campaign, probably by Philip the Bold. There are remains of a cistern and a chapel. From its western extremity the view extends over the fortifications capping the neighbouring crests.

In 1659, the incorporation of Roussillon into France by the Treaty of the Pyrenees stripped Peyrepertuse of its strategic importance, but improvements in artillery had already made it obsolete.

Haras du PIN ★

MICHELIN MAP 310 J 2

GREEN GUIDE NORMANDY

The opening of Deauville's racecourse in 1864 helped spread the English fashion of owning a stable as a status symbol. 800 years previously it had been different; the Saxons had been so taken by the fine figure cut by the Norman horsemen that they had come here to study the breeding of their mounts. Thoroughbreds have been raised here since the beginning of the 18C, flourishing on the rich pastures of the Pays d'Argentan.

Visit

In its setting of elegantly laid-out parkland, the stud-farm (**Haras du Pin**), is one of France's premier centres of horse-breeding. The estate was bought by Louis XIV in 1660 and shortly afterwards Colbert instituted a public stud-farm and Mansart built a château. Dignified buildings, trim hedges and the fresh white paint of estate fences make Le Pin the most attractive of such establishments.

POITIERS ★★

POPULATION 105 268

MICHELIN MAP 322 H -I 5

GREEN GUIDE ATLANTIC COAST

Poitiers was first established in Gallo-Roman times on a promontory overlooking a bend in the River Clain. Fertile land lay around in plenty, but the town's founders chose instead this site which had the advantage of commanding the "Gate of Poitou", the almost imperceptible rise in the land some 30km – 20mi south which divides the Paris Basin from Aquitaine. Key events in France's history have occurred in and around Poitiers, and have left their mark in an array of buildings of exceptional interest.

▶ **Orient Yourself:** Poitiers, which is listed as a "Town of Art and History," offers discovery tours conducted by guide-lecturers approved by the Ministry of Culture and Communication. 5.40€. Information at the tourist office or on www.vpah. culture.fr.

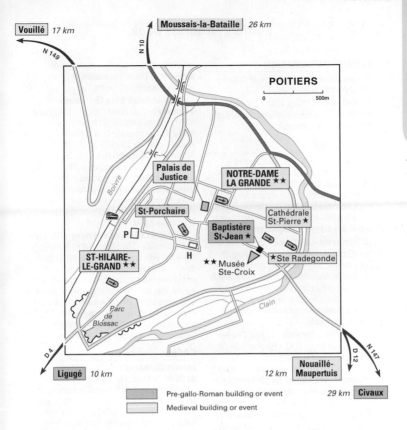

POITIERS

0   500m

| Vouillé | 17 km

N 149

| Moussais-la-Bataille | 26 km

N 10

Palais de Justice

NOTRE-DAME LA GRANDE ★★

Boivre

St-Porchaire

Cathédrale St-Pierre ★

P

Baptistère St-Jean ★

ST-HILAIRE-LE-GRAND ★★

H

★★ **Musée Ste-Croix**

★ **Ste Radegonde**

Parc de Blossac

Clain

D 4

D 12

N 147

| Ligugé | 10 km

12 km | Nouaillé-Maupertuis |

29 km | Civaux |

Pre-gallo-Roman building or event

Medieval building or event

A Bit of History

Antiquity

Poitiers has one of France's most venerable Christian buildings, **Baptistère St-Jean**★ (🕐 Jul and Aug: daily 10.30am-12.30pm, 3-6pm; Apr-Jun and Sep: daily except Tue 10.30am-12.30pm, 3-6pm; Oct-Mar: daily except Tue 2.30-4.30pm; 🕐 closed 1 Jan and 25 Dec; ⊕ 0.80€; ☎ 05 49 41 21 24). The narthex and baptistery proper have the characteristic architecture of 4C Gaul. The narthex was restored in the 10C and is polygonal in form; there are panels of Roman brickwork under its windows, and beneath the gables are strange pilasters with capitals carved in low relief.

The baptistery interior has marble columns and arcades with richly-decorated capitals. Right up until the 17C, the octagonal pool was the city's sole place of baptism, originally by total immersion.

The building, which now houses an interesting lapidary museum, goes back to the time when St Hilary was elected Bishop of Poitiers, 27 years after the Edict of Constantine. Hilary played a leading role in the conversion of Gaul and was an ardent defender of the consubstantial indivisibility of the Trinity at the Council of Milan in the year 355. In 361, he received St Martin at nearby **Ligugé**, becoming his spiritual leader and encouraging him in his promotion of monastic life throughout Gaul.

The Dark Ages

A memorial in the old village of **Vouillé** recalls King Clovis' victory in 507 over Alaric II in a battle marked not only the end of the rule of the Visigoths in Aquitaine, but also the decline of a culture which had straddled the Pyrenees, stretching from Toledo to the foothills of the Massif Central.

Fifty-two years later, in 559, St Radégunde, Queen of France and wife of the Merovingian King Clotaire I, founded a monastery (Monastère Ste-Croix) – where the museum of the same name now stands – near St John's Baptistery (Baptistère St-Jean) and retired thence.

It was on an October Saturday in 732 that Charles Martel (688-741) won his famous victory at **Moussais-la-Bataille** on the banks of the Clain over the invading Arab forces. After a week spent in careful observation, Martel succeeded in drawing the

Poitiers - Address Book

TOURIST INFORMATION

Tourist office – 45 pl. Charles-de-Gaulle - 86009 POITIERS - ☎ 05 49 41 21 24.

Guided tours – ☞ 5.40€. Contact the tourist office for further information or log onto www.vpah.culture.fr

EATING OUT

⊜ **L'Orée des Bois** – 86280 St-Benoît – ☎ 05 49 57 11 44 – ⏰ Closed Sat noon, Sun eve and Mon. This building covered in Virginia creeper is a restful place for a meal away from the bustle of the city centre. There are two country-style dining rooms, one with a fireplace. Traditional local fare.

⊜⊜ **Poitevin** – 76 r. Carnot - ☎ 05 49 88 35 04 – ⏰ closed 19 Apr-2 May, 11 Jul-3 Aug, 23 Dec-3 Jan and Sun. The accent is on traditional regional cuisine in this busy restaurant which is popular with locals. Sample specialities such as mouclade charentaise or farci poitevin in one of four comfortable contemporary-style dining rooms.

⊜⊜ **Les Bons Enfants** – 11 bis r. Cloche-Perse - ☎ 05 49 41 49 82 – ⏰ closed 20-29 Feb, Sun eve and Mon. Amid the many schools of this neighbourhood, this little restaurant with a green façade boasts a large painting of a group of late-19C schoolchildren. The restaurant specialises in regional cuisine. Friendly ambience.

⊜⊜ **La Chênaie** – 6km/3.6mi S of Poitiers. Take the N 10, Hauts-de-Croutelle exit – ☎ 05 49 57 11 52 - ⏰ closed Feb school hols, 26 Jul-8 Aug, Sun eve and Mon except hols. Protected from the road by a garden, this old farm has an attractive dining room with exposed wooden beams, yellow walls and elegant tables. Fine cuisine, served on the terrace in the summer. Friendly service.

⊜⊜ **Maxime** – 4 r. St-Nicholas - ☎ 05 49 41 09 55 - ⏰ closed 13 Jul-18 Aug, Sat (except eve from Nov-Feb) and Sun. Situated near the Musée de Chièvres in a quiet street in the city centre, this restaurant serves traditional French cuisine. Attractive mix of red and yellow hues in the contemporary-style dining room .

⊜⊜⊜ **Le Chalet de Venise** – in the village - 86280 St-Benoît - 4km/2.4mi S of Poitiers via the D 88 – ☎ 05 49 88 45 07 – ⏰ closed 1-10 Mar, 23 Aug-2 Sep, Sun eve and Mon. This charming restaurant is situated just outside Poitiers in the village of St-Benoît. The outdoor terrace overlooking a peaceful garden with a stream is the perfect spot for a meal in summer, while the comfortable dining room has a cosy ambience in winter. Pleasant rooms.

⏱ For coin categories, see p000.

WHERE TO STAY

⊜⊜ **Hôtel Gibautel** – rte de Nouaillé - ☎ 05 49 46 16 16 - hotel.gibautel@ wanadoo.fr - 🅿 - 36 rms. This modern hotel situated opposite a clinic on the outskirts of Poitiers has small, modern and well-equipped rooms.

⊜⊜ **Chambre d'hôte Château de Vaumoret** – r. du Breuil Mingot - 10km/6mi NE of Poitiers. Take the D3 towards La Roche-Posay, then the D 18 to Sèvres-Anxaumont – ☎ 05 49 61 32 11 – ☞ - 3 rms. Although only a few kilometres from Poitiers, this B&B is surrounded by peaceful countryside. Housed in a delightful 17C château in grounds of 15ha/37 acres, the guestrooms here are attractively furnished in traditional style. The perfect place to unwind.

⊜⊜ **Hôtel Château de Périgny** – Périgny - 86190 Vouillé - 17km/12mi NW of Poitiers via the N 149 and a secondary road - ☎ 05 49 51 80 43 - info@château-perigny.cim - 🅿 - 39 rms - restaurant ⊜⊜. Right in the middle of a park, this 15C château is a haven of peace and tranquillity. The rooms are furnished in period or modern style; those in the annexe are a little more basic. Attractive patio-terrace. Contemporary cuisine.

CAFES

Jasmin Citronnelle – 32 r. Gambetta - ☎ 05 49 41 37 26. This delightful tea-room situated opposite a flower-filled courtyard serves a wide variety of teas, pastries and ice cream, as well as quiches and salads at lunchtime. Attractive terrace in summer. Exhibitions of paintings.

Chez Cul de Paille – 3 r. Théophraste-Renaudot - city centre - ☎ 05 49 41 07 35 – Mon-Sat 9am-11pm - ⏰ closed 2nd week of school hols in Feb, in May, for a week in Aug, and Sun. A charming auberge with flagstones on the floor, straw stools and old varnished tables. The graffiti on the ochre walls includes some famous signatures, including those of Arletty, Brel and Coluche.

ENTERTAINMENT

Le Confort Moderne – 185 r. du Fg-du Pont-Neuf - ☎ 05 49 46 08 08 - www. confort-moderne.fr - ⏰ depending on show schedules, 6pm-2am. Ticket office: daily - ⏰ closed Jul-Sep. This cultural association is dedicated to promoting modern music and contemporary arts through concerts, art shows and various original events. Unique in Europe, the fanzinothèque (library for the specialist press) has collected over 20 000 titles which can be consulted on site or borrowed. Bar open during concerts.

Maison de L'Île Jouteau – 5 chemin du Tison - ☎ 05 49 60 06 33 – ⏰ open Tue-Sun noon-10.30pm (midnight during events); open-air café Sun 2-7pm. This charming house is run by an association which organises a variety of cultural events and leisure activities. The programme of festivities includes boat rides, mini-golf, an open-air café and concerts.

SHOPPING

Market – ⏱ *Mon-Sat.* The main food market takes place in the market hall near Église Notre-Dame-la-Grande. There is an excellent choice of fruit and vegetables, fish, meat, cheese and bread.

Bajard – *8 r. Carnot -* ☎ *05 49 41 22 49.* This elegant pâtisserie specialises in home-made cakes and pastries. Specialities include Le Ventou, a macaron biscuit topped with nougat and raspberry coulis, and the Ambré, a mixture of caramel cream and pear mousse. A spiral staircase leads up to the salon de thé.

Rannou-Métivier – *30 r. des Cordeliers -* ⏱ *open Mon afternoon to Sat, 9am-7pm -* ☎ *05 49 30 30 10.* For five generations, the Rannou-Métivier family has perfected its skills in the art of almond confectionery. The award-winning house speciality is the delicious Montmorillon macaroon.

Saracen cavalry onto the lances of his soldiers, cutting them to pieces and thereby saving Christian Europe from Islamic domination.

Romanesque era

This is the period to which Poitiers owes its most important monuments.

Église St-Porchaire

It has a fine 11C belfry-cum-porch.

Église St-Hilaire-le-Grand★★

This great Romanesque edifice was built in 1049; it was an important staging-post on the pilgrimage route to Santiago de Compostela and in architectural terms is Poitiers' most interesting church. In 1100, it was given stone vaults to replace the original wooden roof which had been destroyed by fire. The distance it was possible to span in stone was naturally shorter than in timber, and the designer thus had to reduce the width of the nave and increase the number of aisles; he set up a double row of columns linked ingeniously with the original walls and carrying a series of domes. The final arrangement is the unusual one of a nave flanked by three aisles on either side.

The choir, built over the tomb of St Hilary, is at a higher level than the nave where the crowds of pilgrims would assemble; it has a hemicycle of eight columns with iron grilles dating from the 12C.

D. Mar/EXPLORER

Notre-Dame-la-Grande

Église Notre-Dame-la-Grande★★

The church is a good example of the local version of the Romanesque style as it had developed around 1140. Its harmonious appearance is due to the great height of its rib-vaulted aisles. It has a splendid 12C west **front**★★★, richly decorated with sculpture based on the theme of the Incarnation, including figures of Adam and Eve, the Prophets, the Annunciation, St Joseph and the Infant Jesus being bathed.

Six round columns hold up the choir vault, which was painted in the 12C with a fresco depicting the Virgin in Majesty and Christ in Glory.

Gothic period

For a long time, Poitiers was English, part of Eleanor of Aquitaine's dowry. From the 13C to the 16C, the city was an occasional residence of the French kings, and, during the Hundred Years War, found itself allied with Aquitaine in confronting the forces of the Black Prince.

On 19 September 1356, a famous episode in this interminable Anglo-French conflict took place at **Nouaillé-Maupertuis** on the steep banks of the River Miosson. Jean II le Bon (the Good) was encumbered by the eye-pieces of his helmet, but fought bravely on, harking to his son's cries of "Watch out to your right, father! Watch out to your left!" In the event the French were defeated, largely because of the redoubtable English archers, able to reload their longbows three times as fast as their crossbow-equipped opponents. The Black Prince accepted the exhausted John's surrender, and the King of France passed into comfortable exile in London.

The disaster created a revolutionary situation in France; a wave of popular indignation swept the country at this further manifestation of the aristocracy's neglect of its responsibilities. The eventual result was the signing four years later of the Treaty of Brétigny which gave Poitiers to the English.

In 1372, Du Guesclin retook the town, presenting it to the king's representative, Duke Jean de Berry, brother of Charles V. In 1418, the fleeing Charles VII set up his court and parliament here; four years later he was proclaimed king. In March 1429, in the Gothic Great Hall **(Grande Salle★)** of Poitiers' recently rebuilt Law Courts, **(Palais de Justice)** (◷ *Mon-Fri 8.45am-noon, 1.45-5.30pm;* ◷ *closed Sat-Sun and public holidays; no charge;* ☎ *05 49 50 22 00)*, Joan of Arc was subjected to a humiliating investigation by an ecclesiastical commission, only to emerge three weeks later with an enhanced sense of her sacred mission. The vast hall, scene of solemn audiences, great trials and the sessions of the Provincial Estates, was built under the Plantagenets and restored by Jean de Berry. It has a great gable wall with monumental chimneys, a balcony and Flamboyant windows.

The Renaissance

In the 16C the frontiers of France had been greatly extended, and border problems no longer affected Poitiers. Now the country's third-largest city, it played host to Rabelais, then Calvin and the writers of the Pléiade. In 1569, the place was besieged for seven weeks by a Protestant army under Coligny. In the 18C, under the rule of the centrally-appointed governors known as Intendants, Poitiers became a tranquil provincial capital.

◗◗ Cathédrale St-Pierre★. Musée Ste-Croix★★ ◷ *Jun-Sep: Mon 1.15-6pm, Tue 10am-noon, 1.15-8pm, Wed-Fri 10am-noon, 1.15-6pm, Sat-Sun and public holidays 10am-noon, 2-6pm; Oct-May: Daily except Mon mornings 10am-noon, 1.15-5pm, Sat-Sun and public holidays 2-6pm.* ◷ *Closed 1 Jan, Easter, Whitsun, All Saints' Day and 25 Dec.* ◉ *3.60€, no charge Tue and 1st Sunday in the month (ticket combined with the Musée des Chièvres).* ☎ *05 49 41 07 53. www.musees-poitiers.org* – archeology, ethnology, fine arts. Église Ste-Radegonde★.

PONTARLIER

POPULATION 18 104

MICHELIN MAP 321 I 5

GREEN GUIDE BURGUNDY JURA

Between the 13C and 17C this proud upland town, which still commands the internationally important Besançon-Lausanne highway, was the capital of the area known as the Baroichage. This statelet, consisting of Pontarlier and the 18 surrounding villages, enjoyed an independent regime of republican character which was only extinguished by Louis XIV's conquest of the Franche-Comté. Today, Pontarlier is a busy resort and commercial centre, advantageously sited on the approaches to the Jura mountains.

Excursions

Cluse de Pontarlier★★

5km – 3mi south. The Jura has many such cluses, lateral clefts through the high ridges separating two valleys which enable them to communicate with each other more easily. This example, with the road and railway tightly squeezed together in the narrow defile, is strategically located on the route to Switzerland and overlooked by the Larmont and Joux forts high above.

Lac de St-Point★

8km – 5mi south. Nearly 7km – 4mi long and covering an area of 398ha – 983 acres, it is the largest lake in the Jura, fed by the waters of the River Doubs and attractively sited among mountain pastures and firwoods.

Le PONT DU GARD★★★

MICHELIN MAP 339 M 5

GREEN GUIDE PROVENCE

One of the wonders of Antiquity, this superb aqueduct was built between AD 40 and 60. It formed part of a water-supply system with a total length of 49km – 30mi, stretching from its source near Uzès via a whole series of cuttings, trenches, bridges and tunnels to supply the growing Roman city of Nîmes with up to 20 000 cubic metres – nearly 3/4 million cubic feet of fresh water every day.

▶ **Orient Yourself:** The road bridge is now closed to motor traffic, so you must choose the bank from which you want to view the Pont du Gard.

⊙ **Don't Miss:** James Turrell's **Illuminations,** every evening for 40min after nightfall in Jul and Aug (Jun and Sep: Fri and Sat evenings only), is another way of looking at the Pont du Gard. Lights are used to emphasize the splendour of the site using a variety of colours and intensities.

🅿 **Parking:** The left bank (rive gauche), via the Vers road (D 981 from Uzès to Remoulins), has a large car park (800 spaces); the right bank (rive droite), reached by crossing the River Garden at Remoulins, also has a large car park (600 spaces). Car parks on each bank open from 7am-1am (5€ per day, fixed charged).

Visit

Free access to the bridge at the beginning of the Mémoires de garrigue footpath and at the médiathèque. ☎ *0825 01 30 30.*

The three great rows of arches of the aqueduct rise 49m – 160ft above the valley of the Gardon. One can imagine the effect such a structure must have had on the imagination of the local Gauls, impressing with the power and prestige of Roman achievement, as indeed it still does today. A slight curve in the upstream direction increases its ability to withstand seasonal high waters, while the independent construction of the arches lends a certain flexibility to the whole. Careful calculation of the dimensions of the

Pont du Gard

huge blocks of stone (some of them weighing more than six tonnes) meant that they could be put in place without the use of mortar. The channel on the topmost level was faced with stone in order to maintain water quality and alongside it ran the car-riageway of a Roman road. The Pont du Gard fulfilled its function until the 9C, when lack of maintenance and blocking by deposits of lime finally put it out of use.

Golfe de **PORTO**★

MICHELIN MAP 345 A-B 6

GREEN GUIDE CORSE (IN FRENCH)

The Bay of Porto is one of the most splendid tourist destinations in Corsica owing to its sheer size, range of colours and varied natural sights. Imposing cliffs of red granite contrast with the deep-blue waters. The area is part of a national park, Parc naturel régional de Corse, which is responsible for the protection of its flora and fauna. The park is listed as a World Heritage Site by UNESCO.

Visit

Calanche de Piana★★★
Boat trips (1hr30min) leaving from Porto. ◯ *Apr Sep: departure 2pm, 4pm, 6pm.*
The deep creeks *(calanche)* dominating the Bay of Porto are remarkable; the chaotic landscape is shaped by erosion of the granite, jagged rocks and spherical cavities known as "taffoni".
A road (D 81), which runs through the calanche for 2km – 1mi, affords splendid view-points over the rock piles and the sea. To enjoy this mineral world to the full, it is best to travel the route in both directions. Starting from the terrace of the **Chalet des Roches bleues**, several walks lasting about one hour allow visitors to admire at close range the distinctive form of some of the rocks: the Turtle, the Bishop, a human head (Tête de Poincaré) and a castle.

Réserve Naturelle de Scandola★★★
The Scandola Peninsula (Presqu'île de Scandola) rises to a height of 560m – 1 837ft between two headlands, the Punta Rossa to the south and the Punta Nera to the north. It is the first nature reserve in France combining both sea and land features and is part of the national park. The majestic massif which is of volcanic origin presents great geological diversity. It is the habitat of the last surviving pairs of ospreys; it is the only region of France where these splendid fish-eating eagles are to be found.

The "taffoni"
The large cavities known locally as taffoni are an integral feature of the picturesque landscape of Corsica. The deep cavities piercing the bare rocks along the coast are fascinating, owing to the precarious balance of the vaults, the subtle play of light

and shade and their amazing forms shaped by erosion. In the prehistoric era, they were used as burial places and nowadays they are still used for shelter and remain an intrinsic feature of Corsican culture.

The grainy texture of the rock breaks down as a single crystal particle becomes unstable and starts a process of decay on a gigantic scale under the influence of variations in temperature and humidity; near the sea this is accelerated by corrosion caused by spray. Some kinds of granite consisting of large crystals are more susceptible to this phenomenon: pale-coloured granite from Sant'Ambroggio, grey granite from Calvi, and red granite from Porto and the Piana creeks. Some ancient cavities no longer show any sign of disintegration while others are still crumbling: large flakes drop off the vaults and sand particles can be rubbed off the walls by hand.

Abbaye de **PORT-ROYAL-DES-CHAMPS**★

MICHELIN MAP 311 I 3

GREEN GUIDE NORTHERN FRANCE AND THE PARIS REGION

Much of the 17C in France was marked by religious conflict, not only between Catholics and Protestants, but between Jesuits and Jansenists. One focus of the latter struggle was the abbey of Port-Royal in its valley setting. The abbey dates from 1204. In 1602, its nuns, who had departed somewhat from the strict rules of their calling, were given a new Mother Superior, Angélique Arnauld, only 11 years old at the time. In the space of seven years, this young woman succeeded, mostly by her own example, in restoring the self-respect and prestige of the abbey.

A Bit of History

Jansenism and the "Solitaires" – By 1625, the abbey had become cramped for space, and it was decided to move to new quarters in Paris. In 1633 the Abbot of Saint-Cyran was appointed as spiritual director, and Jansenism, closely related to Calvinism, began to make its influence felt. Jansenius, a former bishop of Ypres in Flanders, had written a book, the *Augustinus*, in which he refuted the view put forward by a Spanish Jesuit that Man could improve himself by his own will, reaffirming instead St Augustine's doctrines on the need for grace and the power of predestination.

By 1648, the Paris buildings had become overcrowded in their turn, and part of the community returned to the original abbey in the Vallée de Chevreuse where Mother Angélique was still in residence. It was now that the convent entered its period of greatest fame and influence. Some of the best minds of the time (Arnauld, the Master of Sacy, Jean Hamon...) settled here, eventually to be known as the *Solitaires*. In the outbuildings referred to as Les Granges (Barns) they founded the most progressive school of the age, called the "Petites Écoles". Racine was one of their pupils. The institution enjoyed a modest degree of success, but it was enough to call down on their heads the disapproval of Richelieu and of the Jesuits, who found their ideas too close to those of Jansenius. The *Solitaires* had to face polemics and persecution; the *Augustinus* was denounced at the Sorbonne in 1641, the *Five Propositions* summarising the work were condemned by Rome in 1653, and in 1656, on suspicion of subversion, the Petites Écoles were shut down. The importance of the issue and the deeply-held convictions on both sides made compromise impossible. In its turn, Port-Royal studied the *Five Propositions* and denounced them too, but pointed out that they were not to be found in the book.

The whole country was affected by the quarrel. The cause of Port-Royal was taken up by Pascal, who carried the offensive into the enemy camp with the publication in 1656-57 of the 18 letters he entitled *Provinciales*, satirising the pettifogging ecclesiastical habit of microscopic textual analysis in order to make an argument out of nothing. His grasp of the truth of the situation was altogether convincing. In 1668, Pope Clement IX, moved by the evident integrity of the *Solitaires*, accepted a formulation to which all parties could subscribe.

With passions calmed, Port-Royal now experienced an Indian summer, albeit still regarded somewhat askance by the Crown as a potential centre of resistance to absolutism. Arnauld was obliged to go into exile in Flanders, and from 1679 the nuns were no longer allowed to take in novices. Thirty years later, the convent was closed and its buildings razed.

Jansenism may have lost the argument about dogma, but the moral stature of its adherents influenced most of the contemporary intellectual élite, La Fontaine, Boileau, Perrault, Saint-Simon, Mme de Sévigné... and the 17C is beholden to it for much of its cultural achievement. It survived until the French Revolution in the policy of Gallicanism and in the collective hysteria of the convulsionaries of St-Médard.

Visit

Musée national des Granges de Port-Royal

🕐 *Mid-Mar to end Oct: daily except Tue 10.30am-6.30pm; Nov to mid-Dec and Jan to mid-Mar: Mon, Wed-Fri 10am-noon, 2-5pm Sat-Sun 10.30am-6.30pm.* 🕐 *Closed between Christmas and New Year.* ⊚ *3€ (under 18 years: no charge), no charge 1st Sun in the month.* ☎ *01 39 30 72 72.*

The spirit of Jansenism is captured in a magnificent painting by Philippe de Champaigne, Ecce Homo, whose power lies in its restraint and profound acceptance of suffering to come. The museum also has a copy of the *Augustinius*. Below the museum there are remains of the famous abbey in the valley.

PROVINS★★

POP 11 608

MICHELIN MAP 312 I 4

GREEN GUIDE ALSACE LORRAINE CHAMPAGNE

The ancient fortified city of Provins sits atop a ridge overlooking the Seine valley and the Champagne chalklands, roughly equidistant from both Paris and Troyes. The town has a famous outline (once painted by Turner), dominated by a tower (Tour de César) and the dome of Église St-Quiriace. Provins' role as an important centre of commerce was confirmed in the 12C when it became one of the two capitals of the County of Champagne. Its annual fairs were renowned, part of a round of such events which also took place at Lagny, Bar-sur-Aube and Troyes. For a number of years in the 13C, Edmund of Lancaster was lord of Provins, at a time when the place was known for its roses, in those days a rare flower. He incorporated a red rose into his emblem; a century-and-a-half later it was this flower which triumphed over the white rose of York in the Wars of the Roses.

▶ **Orient Yourself:** Provins, which is listed as a "Town of Art and History," offers 2hr discovery tours conducted by guide-lecturers approved by the Ministry of Culture and Communication. Tours cost 6.10€ and run from Apr-Sep on Sat-Sun and public holidays at 3pm. No tours 11 and 12 Jun or 28 Aug. Information at the tourist office (☎ 01 64 60 26 26) or on www.provins.net.

Visit

Ville Haute★★

Still protected to north and west by its 12C and 13C wallsaa, its most splendid feature is the Tour de Césaraa, a massive 12C keep with an additional rampart built by the English in the Hundred Years War as an artillery emplacement. There is also a roughly-built 13C tithe barn (Grange aux Dîmes), which belonged to the canons of St-Quiriace.

◖◖ Église St-Ayoul – group of statues★★.

Excursion

Église de St-Loup-de-Naud★

11km – 6mi southwest. The church belonged to a Benedictine priory of the Archbishopric of Sens, and was one of the first in the area to be vaulted in stone.

Erected in the 11C and 12C, it demonstrates the gradual evolution of the Romanesque into Early Gothic (in 1874, the vaulting was subjected to major restoration). The choir dates from the 11C, as does the early-Romanesque cradle-vault next to it. The dome over the crossing, the barely-projecting transepts and the first two bays of the nave were built at the beginning of the 12C. Finally, around 1160, the last two bays of the nave were completed; they are square in plan and have alternating pillars and twin columns on the model of Sens cathedral. The well-preserved doorway (**portail**★★), under the main porch, shows similarities with the Royal Doorway (Portail royal) of Chartres Cathedral; Christ in Majesty surrounded by symbols of the Evangelists on the tympanum, apostles in arched niches on the lintel, statue-columns in the splays, figures in between the arch mouldings. The sculptures of St-Loup mark the beginning of a transition which gave birth to Gothic Realism.

PUY DE DÔME★★★

MICHELIN MAP 326 E 8

GREEN GUIDE AUVERGNE THE RHÔNE VALLEY

With its summit rising to 1 465m – 4 806ft, this is the highest as well as the oldest of all the peaks making up the extraordinary volcanic landscape known as the Puys. Long before the Romans built a temple to Mercury here, the Gauls had erected a sanctuary to their god Lug. In 1648, Pascal was responsible for the experiment which proved Torricelli's theory about atmospheric weight; he arranged for his brother-in-law Florin Périer to take simultaneous readings of the height of a column of mercury on the top of the Puy de Dôme and down in Clermont-Ferrand; the difference was a decisive 8.4cm. On 7 March 1911, only three years after Henri Farman had successfully flown the first kilometre in a closed circuit, the aviator Eugène Renaux and his passenger landed on the summit of the Puy de Dôme five hours and 11 minutes after leaving Paris, thereby winning the Michelin Grand Prix of 100 000 francs.

J. Damase/MICHELIN

Puy de Pariou and Puy de Dôme

Panorama★★★

From the summit there is a vast panorama over the city of Clermont-Ferrand, the Grande Limagne basin, the complex volcanic structure of the Monts Dore and the Puys themselves. The Puys, or the Monts Dômes as they are sometimes known, extend over an area 30km – 19mi long and 5km – 3mi wide; in it, there is a total of 112 extinct volcanoes, all more than 50 000 years old, all distinct from one another and aligned along the fault line which borders the Limagne to the west. Between them they exhibit virtually all the forms of volcanic relief; some, to the north, are of "Peleean-dome" type, with craterless extrusive domes; they include the Puy de Dôme itself, built up by slowly extruded domite, the Clerziou, Puy Chopine and the Grand Sarcoui, all formed from trachytic lava.

Others are of Strombolian type, with craters and cones of ejected material around their vents; some have a single crater (Gravenoire, La Nugère, Les Goules); some have had the sides of their craters ripped out by explosions and have given birth to great lava-flows (La Vache, Lassolas, Louchadière), while the Puy de Côme has a double crater with a cone on the outer rim.

Other kinds of volcanic material have been injected into sedimentary rocks which have subsequently been eroded, leaving pinnacles, as at Puy de Monton and Montrognon, or sills, as at Montadoux.

Elsewhere (Gergovie, Montagne de Serre and Plateau de Chanturgue), lava flows have created the phenomenon known as relief inversion.

PUY DE SANCY★★★

MICHELIN MAP 326 D 9

GREEN GUIDE AUVERGNE THE RHÔNE VALLEY

The Puy de Sancy rises from the Mont Dore massif to 1 885m – 6 184ft, the highest point in Central France.

Visit

Panorama★★★

1hr 30min to the summit and back on foot by a rough path from the top station of the cable railway. With the heights of the Mont Dore massif in the foreground, the immense views extend northeastwards over the Puys and to the Cantal massif in the south.

The Puy de Sancy, the Banne d'Ordanche and the Puy de l'Aiguiller form the centre of the Mont Dore volcanic massif, an area three times greater than that of Vesuvius. Towards the end of the Tertiary era, more than 100 openings spewed forth lava from the great volcano, the successive flows building up to thicknesses of more than 1 000m – 3 300ft. In Quaternary times, radiating valleys were gouged out of the sides of the volcano by glacial action. The Puy de Sancy itself is a trachyte plug whose outer covering has been worn away by erosion. The hedged fields of the valley bottoms give way, between 1 100 and 1 400m (3 600 – 4 600ft), to forest of beech, spruce and fir, while the landscape as a whole is enhanced by the presence of volcanic lakes.

Besse-en-Chandesse★

On the eastern slopes of the massif. This is a mountain village, made of lava, with picturesque **streets** and houses, a barbican and a severe little church (**église**★) with sturdy columns, rough capitals, and a choir screen and stalls decorated with Italian-style grotesques of the 16C.

Around the village are a number of volcanic lakes, each with its own character. The **Lac Pavin**★★ occupies a crater which was formed by the explosion of a pocket of gas on the slopes of the **Puy de Montchal**★★; Lake Chauvet has filled the void left by the effects of an implosion, while Lake Montcineyre and the **Lac Chambon**★★ were formed when the volcano Tartaret erupted into the Vallée de la Couze's floor and blocked the outflow of water.

Le **PUY DU FOU**★★★

MICHELIN MAP 316 K 6

GREEN GUIDE ATLANTIC COAST

On summer evenings the château sparkles under the lights of its famous Son et Lumière show in which a cast of hundreds stages an open-air historical pageant; by day the museum, Écomusée de la Vendée★★, evokes the past of the Vendée region, while various attractions along a trail (Grand Parcours★★) lure visitors into the 12ha – 30 acres of grounds. The name Puy du Fou is derived from the Latin: Puy (from podium) means an eminence, a knoll; Fou (from fagus) designates a beech tree. Thus "A hill where a beech tree grows" or, less lyrically, "Beechmount".

Visit

Château

It is likely that the original castle, built in the 15C and 16C, was never completed; it was in any case partly destroyed by fire during the Wars of the Vendée. There remains nevertheless a fine late-Renaissance pavilion at the far end of the courtyard, preceded by a peristyle with engaged Ionic columns. This now serves as the entrance to the open-air museum. The left wing of the château is built over a long gallery.

Cinéscénie★★★

Early Jun to end Jul: show (1hr45min) Fri and Sat at 10.30pm (last admission 10pm); Aug: Fri and Sat at 10pm; first two Saturdays in Sep. 20€ (children: 8€). Visitors must reserve. 02 51 64 11 11.

The terrace below the rear façade of the château, together with the ornamental lake below it, makes an agreeable background for the spectacular *"Cinéscénie"* in which "Jacques Maupillier, peasant of the Vendée" directs a company of 700 actors and 50 horsemen in a dazzling show. The history of the Vendée is re-lived with the help of an impressive array of special effects, fountains, fireworks, laser and other lighting displays...

Excursion

Le logis de La Chabotterie★

53km – 33mi west of Les Herbiers by D 23, then N 137 to St-Sulpice-le-Verdon. From 1560 a new type of compound appeared in the Vendée area: the fortified enclosure (logis clos). Its unusual feature was that the lord's residence and the outbuildings were grouped around the fortified inner courtyard. This typical architectural complex remained popular until the 18C. After careful restoration, the house, where the royalist leader Charette was taken after his capture (1796) and which is thus directly linked with the war of the Vendée, recreates the refined décor of the 18C combining rustic simplicity and elegance typical of contemporary country society of the Bas-Poitou. The period rooms **(salles historiques★★)** contain authentic furnishings and articles.

Les Lucs-les-Bourgs

Take D 18 left to St-Sulpice-le-Verdon, then left again to the entrance of the village of Les Lucs-sur-Boulogne. Parking available.

On 28 February 1794 numerous villagers, who had taken refuge in the church, were massacred by Republican troops. A monument (1993) commemorates all the victims of the Vendée war.

Le Chemin de la Mémoire des Lucs★

The historic and spiritual trail is a place of remembrance and meditation dedicated to the martyrs and victims of the Terror during the Revolution. This modern project combines vegetation and architectural features, and leads from the banks of the Boulogne to a chapel on the hilltop.

An alleyway **(allée de l'Histoire)** is lined with historical monuments highlighting the principal events of the war, which lasted from March to December 1793.

Le PUY-EN-VELAY★★★

POPULATION 21 743

MICHELIN MAP 331 F 3

GREEN GUIDE AUVERGNE THE RHÔNE VALLEY

The town occupies the centre of a basin created by the collapse of the Vellave plateau. Sediments stripped from the surrounding hills then partly filled the basin in which a gorge was cut by the river Loire. At the end of the Tertiary era, a series of volcanic eruptions convulsed the region leaving huge and resistant cones of basalt flows. Le Puy, capital of the Velay district, is famous for its spectacular site★★★ and splendid monuments, its pilgrimages and its fine lace.

▶ **Orient Yourself:** Le Puy-en-Velay, which is listed as a "Town of Art and History", offers discovery tours for 5€ in Jul and from mid to end Aug daily at 3.30pm (early to mid-Aug: daily at 10am and 3.30pm). Information at the tourist office or on www.vpah. culture.fr. In the summer there is a tourist train that introduces you to the many curiosities of Puy-en-Velay. Saturday is the market day when the place du Breuil and the surrounding streets come alive with activity.

St-Michel-d'Aiguilhe and Rocher Corneille

● **Don't Miss:** The fantastic views from the upper rim of the basin, especially during sunset.

Visit

Musée Crozatier

🕐 *May-Sep: daily except Tue (mid-Jun to mid-Sep: daily) 10am-noon, 2-6pm; Oct-Apr: daily except Tue 10am-noon, 2-4pm, Sun 2-4pm.* 🕐 *Closed from Dec to Jan, 1 May and 11 Nov.* ✎ *3€, no charge Sun (Oct-Apr).* ☎ *04 71 06 62 40.*

On the first floor of the **Musée Crozatier** is a **lace collection**★ of great richness. It includes a magnificent square of 500 bobbins with the pins in place and adorned with glass beads, a complex piece of work begun with gold thread and still awaiting completion; a large shawl of fine silky black wool; an umbrella covered with bobbin lace and decorated with needlepoint – its handle is fashioned from a horse's hoof. Also on display are the first samplebooks (18C), giving hints on salesmanship and identification of the different types of stitch.

Rocher Corneille

🕐 *Jul-Aug: daily 9am-7.30pm; May-Jun and Sep: daily 9am-7pm; mid-Mar to end Apr: daily 9am-6pm; Oct to mid-Mar: daily 10am-5pm.* 🕐 *Closed Dec and Jan (outside Christmas school holidays 10am-5pm and excepting Sundays 2-5pm).* ✎ *3€.* ☎ *04 71 04 11 33.*

Lace

Lace-making was widespread in the area around Le Puy as early as the 17C, though its high point was reached in the 19C, in part due to the efforts of Théodore Falcon (1804-56), who encouraged high standards in both design and quality. Before the First World War, bobbin lace and needlepoint lace were equally popular, but after 1919, the former (also known as pillow lace) became dominant, with threads of linen, silk and wool used to form patterns of great variety and delicacy.

This is an outlier of the volcano of which the Rocher St-Michel was the vent. It is topped by a 16m – 52ft statue of Notre-Dame of France made in 1860 from melted-down cannons captured at the Siege of Sebastopol. The terrace at the foot of the statue offers the best viewpoint over the extraordinary **site**★★★ of Le Puy.

La cité épiscopale (Cathedral Quarter)★★★

The city's growth dates from the 11C, when it took over the urban functions of nearby St-Paulien and when it formed an important destination on the pilgrimage road to Santiago de Compostela in Spain.

The cathedral's fortifications are evidence of the bishops' quarrels with the local lords (the Polignacs, Montlaurs, Mercœurs...) over sovereignty and over the taxes raised from the pilgrims...

In the centre of the old town, the area around the cathedral has a sombre air, with its buildings of granite and lava, narrow arcaded entranceways, mullioned windows, heavy iron grilles and paving stones.

Cathédrale Notre-Dame★★★

Guided tours available, contact the Tourist Office. ☎ *04 71 09 38 41.*

The first building to occupy the site was a Roman temple. This was followed around 430 by a sanctuary dedicated to the Virgin Mary, built at the same time as Santa Maria Maggiore at Rome. Rebuilding and extension took place from the 10C on, and in the 19C major restoration was carried out.

The lofty west front rises from its monumental steps to dominate the Rue des Taules. The windows in the third storey mark the extension to the nave which took place at the end of the 12C and which is supported on massive arcading. The overall impression is a highly ornamental one, due to the pierced or blind Romanesque arches, the use of polychrome granite and basalt stonework, the mosaics in the gables and the columns with carved lava capitals.

The steps continue to rise, giving a good view of the carved doors (which were once painted) of the Golden Doorway (Porte Dorée) with, on the left, a depiction of the Nativity, and on the right, Christ's Passion. In the 10C and 11C, the apse was rebuilt and the transepts and first two bays of the nave erected. At the beginning of the 12C the two adjacent bays were built and vaulted with splendid domes; here there is a carved 14C figure of Christ and a 17C pulpit. The two last bays were added at the end of the 12C.

Cloître★★

🕐 *Jul-Aug: 9am-6.30pm; mid-May to end Jun and Sep: 9am-noon, 2-6.30pm; Oct to mid-May: 9am-noon, 2-5pm.* 🕐 *Closed 1 Jan, 1 May, 1 and 11 Nov and 25 Dec.* ⊛ *4.60€ (children: no charge), no charge 1st Sun in the month (Oct-May).* ☎ *04 71 05 45 52. www.monum.fr.*

Dating from the 11C and 12C, the cathedral cloisters have polychrome mosaics, an allegorical Romanesque frieze at the base of the roof, a fine 12C wrought-iron grillea and, in the Reliquary Chapel (Chapelle des Reliques), a celebrated Renaissance fresco depicting the Liberal Arts.

Chapelle St-Michel-d'Aiguilhe★★

🕐 *May to mid-Jul and Sep: 9am-6.30pm; mid-Jul to end Aug: 9am-6.45pm; mid-Mar to end Apr and Oct to mid-Nov: 9.30am-noon, 2-5.30pm; Feb to mid-Mar and Christmas school holidays: 2-5pm.* 🕐 *Closed 1 Jan and 25 Dec.* ⊛ *2.50€.* ☎ *04 71 09 50 03.*

268 steps lead to the chapel perched on its 82m – 270ft lava pinnacle. Arabesques and polychrome mosaics of Byzantine inspiration decorate the chapel doorway. Inside, the complex vaulting gives some indication of the difficulties the 11C architect had to overcome in transforming the original Carolingian sanctuary; one of his contributions was the addition of a gallery to the narthex. Note two capitals re-used in the smaller gallery, the 10C murals in the apse depicting the heavenly kingdom, and a Romanesque Christ-reliquary carved in wood.

👁👁 Trésor de la cathédrale★★ (treasury). Trésor d'art religieux★★ (Religious Art Collection in the cloisters).

Excursions

Château de Polignac

5km – 3mi northwest. There is a striking view of this medieval fortress from the N 102 main road. Its defences were so strong that its lords were known as the "Kings of the Mountain". From the 17C to the 19C, their descendants held prominent positions in political and diplomatic life.

The ruined walls and keep rise from a basalt platform, a fragment of one of the lava flows from the Mont-Denise volcano which poured along the floor of an ancient valley and then solidified. The strata beneath it were thus protected from erosion, while the material all around was being carried away by the waters of the Loire, the Borne and their tributaries. The resulting tableland stands nearly 100m – some 300ft above the surrounding land, a good example of relief inversion.

Lac du Bouchet★

21km – 13mi southwest. The clear waters of the lake, surrounded by coniferous woodland, occupy the almost perfectly circular crater of an ancient volcano. Around it stretch the extensive Devès uplands, formed by a series of fissure-eruptions and overlying the even older granite foundation of the landscape.

PUY MARY★★★

MICHELIN MAP 330 E 4

GREEN GUIDE AUVERGNE RHÔNE VALLEY

At 1 787m – 5 863ft, Puy Mary is one of the main peaks of the immense Cantal volcano, which when active was a true rival to Etna, with a circumference of 60km – 37 miles and a cone rising to 3 000m – nearly 10 000ft.

Panorama★★★

The summit is reached by a steep path from Pas-de-Peyrol – 1hr30min round trip on foot. Glacial action has decapitated the volcano and worn it down. The view from the top takes in a landscape punctuated by the remains of volcanic vents (Griou, Violent, Élancère, Chavaroche) and lava flows which seem to have only just cooled. The **Pas-de-Peyrol★★** too affords fine views.

The way in which this spectacular geological heritage has been fashioned by man for his various purposes is unusually fascinating. Sharp ridges divide the country up into a series of amphitheatres, in each of which the same set of activities is carefully staged. Meadows and cropland fill the valley bottoms, where the villages are also sited, though in areas less exposed to the sun there are birchwoods, grown for fuel. On the middle slopes are beeches, used for a whole range of purposes, and recently planted conifers. Higher still come the upland pastures, dotted with stone-built huts used until lately as summer-dwellings by shepherds or for cheese-making. Known as burons, they are planted round with ash-trees, a useful source of fodder in times of drought.

The basaltic lava (unlike the trachytes of Mont Dore) yields rich herbage which is grazed by the reddish Salers cattle, who in their turn yield the milk for which Cantal cheese is famous.

QUIMPER★★

POPULATION 59 437

MICHELIN MAP 308 G 6-7

GREEN GUIDE BRITTANY

Quimper was first of all a Gaulish foundation, sited on the north bank of the Odet estuary 16km – 10 miles inland at the tidal limit. Towards the end of the 5C BC, Celts sailed over from Britain (hence the area's name of Cornouaille = Cornwall) and put the original inhabitants to flight. This was the era of the legendary King Gradlon and of the fabulous city of Ys which is supposed to have sunk beneath the waves of Douarnenez Bay. Tales such as these are considered by some authorities to represent the folk-memory of the most recent episodes of marine transgression (the post-glacial rise in sea-level), which would have been witnessed by prehistoric people.

▶ **Orient Yourself:** Quimper, which is listed as a "Town of Art and history," offers 1hr30min discovery tours daily except Sun at 11.30am and 5pm in Jul and Aug. There are also Wed evening tours with entertainment at 9pm. Information at the tourist office or on www.vpah.culture.fr.

Visit

Cathédrale St-Corentin★★

🕐 *Summer: daily 8.30-6.30pm, Winter: daily 8.30am-noon, 1.30-6.30pm.*

The extent to which the choir is out of alignment with the nave is particularly striking. This is a consequence of the re-use of the foundations of earlier buildings which stood on the site. The choir itself (currently undergoing extensive restoration) is remarkable for its deeply-moulded pillars, its imposing triforium and the design of the vault spanning both the ambulatory and radiating chapels.

Dish decorated with Breton figures, HB faïence works (late 19C)

Jean-Yves Uguet

Le vieux Quimper★

The medieval town lies between the cathedral and the Odet and its tributary, the Steyr. There are fine old houses with granite ground floors and timber-framed projecting upper storeys, notably in the Rue Kereona.

◖◖ Musée des Beaux-Arts★★ 🕐 *Jul and Aug: Wed-Mon 10am-7pm; Apr-Jun and Sep-Jun: Wed-Mon 10am-noon, 2-6pm. Nov-Mar: Mon, Wed-Sat 10am-noon, 2-6pm, Sun. 2-6pm.* 🕐 *Closed Tue, 1 Jan, 1 May, 1 and 11 Nov and 25 Dec.* ⊕ *4€.* ☎ *02 98 95 45 20.*

Musée Départemental breton★ 🕐 *Jun-Sep: daily 9am-6pm; Oct-May: daily except Sun morning and public holidays 9am-noon, 2-5pm.* 🕐 *Closed Easter Mon, 1 and 8 May, 25 Dec.* ⊕ *3.80€, no charge Sun after (Oct-May).* ☎ *02 98 95 21 60*– local history.

Musée de la faïence★ 🕐 *Mid-Apr to end Oct: daily except Sun 10am-6pm.* 🕐 *Closed public holidays. Call in advance for guided tour.* ⊕ *4€.* ☎ *02 98 90 12 72. www.quimper-faiences.com.*

Excursion

La Cornouaille★★

Although the area today is limited to the coast and immediate hinterland west of its capital Quimper, Cornouaille was once the Duchy of medieval Brittany, stretching as far north as Morlaix. Brittany's "Cornwall" juts out into the Atlantic just like its counterpart across the Channel. The spectacular coastline with its two peninsulas, **Presqu'île de Penmarch**★ and **Cap Sizun**★★, culminates in the breathtaking **Pointe du Raz**★★★.

Pointe du **RAZ**★★★

MICHELIN MAP 308 C 6

GREEN GUIDE BRITTANY

Formed from a particularly hard-wearing granulite, Raz Point is one of France's most spectacular coastal landscapes. Its jagged cliffs, battered by the waves and seamed with caves, rise to over 70m – 220ft.

Visit

The **view**★★ extends over the fearsome Raz de Sein or tide-race with its multitude of reefs and rocky islands (on the outermost of which is sited the lighthouse, Phare de la Vieille); this was once dry land, but was drowned by the rise in sea-level following the melting of the Quaternary glaciers. The outline of the Île de Sein can be seen on the horizon. To the north lies the headland, Pointe du Van, perhaps less impressive, but having the distinct advantage of being off the tourists' beaten track.

A coastal path *(difficult in places, 1hr 30min round trip on foot –  to be avoided in bad weather or high winds)* leads round the Point; the sheer walls of the Plogoff Inferno (Enfer de Plogoff) dropping down to the boiling ocean are particularly impressive *(safety rope)*. To the north of the Point, **baie des Trépassés** cuts into the schists; it was from here that the bodies of Druids are supposed to have been taken over to Île de Sein for burial.

REIMS★★★

POPULATION 206 362

MICHELIN MAP 306 G 7

GREEN GUIDE ALSACE LORRAINE CHAMPAGNE

Along with Troyes, Reims is one of the capitals of the province of Champagne. The city has always looked towards the Ardennes to the northeast and was the metropolis of Roman Belgica, the forerunner of modern Belgium.

▶ **Orient Yourself:** Reims, which is listed as a "Town of Art and History," offers discovery tours conducted by guide-lecturers approved by the Ministry of Culture and Communication. Information at the tourist office or on www.reims-tourisme. com.

A Bit of History

It was at Reims, in 496, that Clovis was baptised by St Remigius (St Rémi). This was a political event of some significance, since it made the ambitious 35-year-old warrior the only Christian ruler in the chaotic times consequent upon the collapse of the Roman Empire.

Strengthened by the support of the Church, Clovis became a symbol of order in a confused world. Within the space of a few years he had drawn his scattered subjects together; it was he who halted the advance of the Visigoths at Poitiers, subsequently pushing them back, first to Toulouse, then all the way into Spain. With him, the source of political authority in Gaul passed from Provence to the Seine Valley.

At the time of the Carolingians, a feeling for beauty became evident at Reims; ancient texts were carefully copied, manuscripts illuminated, ivory carved and masterpieces of the goldsmith's art created. The period produced Charlemagne's Talisman (now in the Bishops' Palace) as well as the Épernay Gospel. In 816, Louis I the Pious had himself crowned here, as Charlemagne had done at Rome 16 years before. It was from this point that the dynasty acquired a sort of religious character, though it was not until the crowning of Louis VIII, four 400 years later, that the city became the recognised place for coronations, with a ceremonial ever more elaborate and charged with symbolism. By the time of Charles X, 25 kings had been crowned here. The most moving coronation was that of Charles VII on 17 July 1429, which took place in the middle of the Hundred Years War in the presence of Joan of Arc; the Maid of Orléans

Champagne

Though covering only 2% of the total area planted with vines in France, this northernmost of the country's wine-growing regions is perhaps its most prestigious. The product was known in Roman times, when it was a still wine. It was Dom Pérignon (1638-1715), cellar-master of Hautvillers Abbey (Abbaye de Hautevilliers), who had the idea of making it sparkle by means of double fermentation, a process carried out today by the use of cane sugar and yeasts.

The vines are spread over an area totalling 30 000ha – nearly 74 000 acres, on the lower slopes of the chalk escarpment of the Côte de l'Île-de-France for preference. The most renowned vineyards are the Montagne de Reims (robust, full-bodied wines), the valley of the Marne (fruity wines with plenty of bouquet) and the Côte des Blancs (fresh and elegant wines). Champagne is a blended, branded wine, the prestige of the great labels dependent on the expertise of the master-blenders.

Some 215 million bottles are produced in an average year, with over 75 million of them for export.

Reims - Address Book

PRACTICAL INFORMATION

Tourist office - 2 r. Guillaume-de-Machault, 51000 Reims, ☎ 03 26 77 45 25, www.reims-tourisme.fr

Guided tours - Reims, City of Art, organises tours by approved guides. Enquire at tourist office.

WHERE TO EAT

See Legend at the back for coin categories.

Le Vergeur – 32-34 pl. du Forum - ☎ 03 26 47 56 87 – ◑ closed 25 Dec-1 Jan, lunchtime, Fri evenings and Sun. This nice little bistro is not far from the Place Royale. The room used for painting exhibitions is attractively decorated with zinc and old-fashioned wood finish. Lovely sunny terrace.

Univers – 41 bd. Foch - ☎ 03 26 88 68 08 - contact@hotel-univers-reims.com The dining room of this hotel provides an elegant setting to the classical dishes. Excellent value-for-money. Cosy sitting room-bar.

Brasserie Le Boulingrin – 48 r. Mars – ☎03 26 40 96 22 – boulingrin@wanadoo. fr – ◑ closed Sun. This Art Deco-style restaurant dating from 1925 has become an institution in Reims life. The owner is much in evidence, overseeing the operations and creating a congenial atmosphere. The menu is inventive and the prices reasonable.

La Table Anna – 6 r. Gambetta – ☎ 03 26 89 12 12 – latableanna@wanadoo. fr Champagne takes pride of place in the window of this establishment next door to the music conservatory. Some of the paintings adorning the walls are the work of the owner, an artist by heart. Traditional dishes renewed with the seasons.

Continental – 95 pl. Drouet-d'Erlon – ☎ 03 26 47 01 47 – lecontinental-restaurant@wanadoo.fr Right in the centre of the champagne capital, this restaurant proposes classic cooking served in several old dining rooms, the biggest of which is decorated with panelling and a lovely coffered ceiling.

La Vigneraie – 14 r. de Thillois – ☎ 03 26 88 67 27 – lavigneraie@wanadoo. fr Place Drouet-d'Erlon is the centre of the city's nightlife with nightclubs, theatres and cinemas. La Vigneraie, which is just next-door, boasts a fantastic collection of carafes. Tasty classical menu and fine wine list. Excellent value-for-money.

Café du Palais – 14 pl. Myron-Herrick – ☎ 03 26 47 52 54 – ◑ closed Sun and public holidays. This lively café near the cathedral was founded in 1930. With its original glass roof and a warm red decor, it serves generous portions of salad and other daily dishes, which are much appreciated, as are the home-made pastries. You can also enjoy a reasonably priced glass of champagne.

Au Petit Comptoir – 17 r. de Mars - ☎ 03 26 40 58 58 - au.petit.comptoir@wanadoo.fr – ◑ closed 1-5 Jan, 1-7 Mar, 1-15 Aug, 24-31 Dec. This imposing restaurant with its wooden terrace is right behind the town hall. Inside, the black and white decor and studied lighting lend a cosy atmosphere. Traditional cooking and spit-roast dishes.

Da Nello – 39 r. Cérès - ☎ 03 26 47 33 25 – ◑ closed Aug. A Mediterranean welcome awaits you at this Italian restaurant where the tables look onto the kitchen and the pizzas are baked in the oven in the centre of the room. Fresh pasta, grilled dishes and daily specials according to what the market has to offer… and all served with an authentic Italian accent.

WHERE TO STAY

Ardenn Hôtel – 6 r. Caqué - ☎ 03 26 47 42 38 – ◑ closed Dec-early Jan – 14 rooms €31/54 – ☐ €5.50. This hotel, which lies behind an attractive brick façade, has many points in its favour. You will certainly be won over by its location in a quiet little town-centre street, the unfailing cleanliness of the tastefully decorated rooms and the smiling service.

Chambre d'hôte Lapie – 1 r. Jeanne-d'Arc - 51360 Val-de-Vesle - 21km/12.5mi SE of Reims on N 44 and D 326 to the left - ☎ 03 26 03 92 88 – ◑ closed 15 Dec-15 Jan - ⌿ - 5 rooms. Five lovely pastel-toned rooms are available on this farm in the heart of the village. Attractive decor bringing together old and modern styles. The large ground-floor hall, with immaculate walls, is a pleasant setting in which to enjoy breakfast.

Grand Hôtel du Nord – 75 pl. Drouet-d'Erlon – ☎ 03 26 47 39 03 – grandhoteldunord-reims@wanadoo.fr – ◑ closed Christmas holidays – 50 rooms - €6. Mostly refurbished rooms in a 1920s building set in a pedestrians-only square. The rooms facing the back are quieter. Many restaurants and lots going on nearby.

Hôtel La Cathédrale – 20 r. Libergier – ☎ 03 26 47 28 46 – 17 rooms - ☐ €6.50. This smart but welcoming hotel stands in one of the streets that lead to the cathedral. The small rooms have comfortable beds and are bright and cheerful, while the breakfast room is decorated with old engravings.

Crystal – 86 pl. Drouet-d'Erlon – ☎ 03 26 88 44 44 – hotelcrystal@wanadoo.fr - 31 rooms - ☐ €7.50. An astonishing haven of greenery right in the centre of town is the main sales argument of this 1920s house. The renovated bedrooms all have excellent bedding. Breakfast is served in a delightful flowered courtyard-cum-garden in summer.

Hôtel Continental – *93 pl. Drouet-d'Erlon* – ☎ *03 26 40 39 35* – *grand-hotel-continental-restaurant@wanadoo.fr* - 🕐 *closed 21 Dec-7 Jan - 50 rooms* - 🖫 – €10.50. The attractive façade of this central hotel adorns one of the city's liveliest squares. The rooms, renovated in varying styles, are reached by a splendid staircase (avoid the rooms overlooking Bd du Gén-Leclerc). Elegant Belle Epoque sitting rooms.

Hôtel Porte Mars – *2 pl. de la République* – ☎ *03 26 40 28 35* – *hotel.porte-mars@wanadoo.fr* - *24 rooms* - 🖫 €9. It's a pleasure to drink tea near the fire in the cosy sitting room, or enjoy a drink in the sophisticated bar. A delicious breakfast is also served in the attractive glass-roofed dining room decorated with photographs and old mirrors. The comfortable, well sound-proofed rooms all have a personal touch.

ON THE TOWN

Place Drouet-d'Erlon – This square is the prime starting point for anyone wanting to go out on the town. There is something for everyone, whether you are looking for a bar, pub, restaurant, tearoom or brasserie.

La Chaise au Plafond – *190 av. d'Épernay* – ☎ *03 26 06 09 61* – 🕐 *Mon-Sat 7am-8pm; public holidays: open mornings* – 🕐 *closed last week of Feb, 1st week of Mar and 3 weeks in Aug.* Founded in 1910, this bar and tobacconists is famous for the chair that has remained stuck to the ceiling ever since a shell hit the establishment on 12 September 1914. Terrace in summer. Selection of 150 cigars (Cuban, Honduran or from Santo Domingo).

Le César's Club – *17 r. Lesage* – ☎ *03 26 88 24 80* – 🕐 *Mon-Fri noon-3am, Sat-Sun 2pm-3am.* Two former national billiards champions run this attractive club, which offers 21 tables in all (snooker, pool, French billiards). Tournaments on Monday evenings, 8pm. Occasional regional competitions and exhibitions.

SPORTS AND RECREATION

Parc de Champagne – ☎ *03 26 77 45 00.* 🕐 *Mon-Fri 9.30am-6.30pm, Sat 2-7.30pm, Sun 9.30am-6.30pm.* Over 22 hectares of children's play areas and sports facilities.

SHOPPING

Deleans – *20 r. Cérés* - ☎ *03 26 47 56 35* – 🕐 *Tue-Sat 9am-noon, 2-7pm (Fri-Sat 7.30pm); mid-Oct-Apr: Mon-Sat 9am-noon, 2-7pm; Sun 10am-noon* – 🕐 *closed Aug.* Cocoa-based specialities have been made here in the old-fashioned way since 1874. Those to try include Néluskos (chocolate-coated cherries in cognac) and petits bouchons de champagne enclosed in a giant champagne cork made of chocolate.

Fossier – *25 cours Jean-Baptiste Langlet* – ☎ *03 26 47 59 84* – *Mon 2-7pm, Tue-Sat 9am-7pm.* Founded in 1756, the biscuit and chocolate maker Fossier creates the ultimate in Reims confectionary (biscuits roses and croquignoles). Pay a visit to the shop and factory and learn how to "piouler" (stir) your glass of champagne correctly!

La Petite Friande – *15 cours J.-B. Langlet* - ☎ *03 26 47 50 44* - *hjw@sirtem.fr* – 🕐 *summer: Tue-Sat: 10am-noon, 2-7pm; winter: Mon-Sat 10am-noon, 2-7pm.* For more than 170 years, the establishment has prided itself on being the specialists in authentic bouchons de champagne, made with marc de champagne. Another of their delicious creations are bulles à la vieille fine de la Marne.

CALENDAR

Fêtes johanniques – 🕐 *2nd weekend in June.* 2,000 walk-ons in period costume accompany Joan of Arc and Charles VII during a massive street festival.

Flâneries musicales d'été – 🕐 *Jul and Aug.* Over 150 street concerts throughout the town, including shows by major international stars In some of the town's most prestigious and unlikely venues.

had given Frenchmen the first inklings of national identity, and had persuaded the king to make his way to Reims, even though this involved him in crossing the hostile Burgundian territory of Philippe le Bon (the Good).

On 7 May 1945, in a modern technical college near the station, the document was signed which marked the surrender of Germany. Confirmed the day after in Berlin, this brought to an end the Second World War in Europe.

Sights

Cathédrale Notre-Dame★★★

Illustration 👁 see Introduction: Art – Architecture. The present building was begun in 1211. It is one of the great cathedrals of France, built in the Lanceolate Gothic style pioneered at Chartres, but with more sophisticated ornamentation, its window tracery above all. Four architects were involved in its construction; Jean d'Orbay (choir and transepts) up to 1228, Jean Le Loup (who designed a west front to rival Amiens) up to 1244, Gaucher de Reims (nave side of the west front) up to 1252, and Bernard de

Soissons up to 1287. The west front has wonderfully soaring lines and superb 13C sculpture, the output of four workshops, whose masterpiece is the world-famous Smiling Angel (in a splay of the north portal).

Inside is one of the greatest achievements of the Gothic, the west end of the nave, best seen towards the end of the afternoon when the sun lights up the two rose windows.

The martyrdom of the cathedral – Reims was occupied by the German army between 3 and 12 September 1914, and for four years remained in the battle zone. By the end of the war, out of a total of 14 130 houses, only 60 remained habitable. The cathedral, one of the country's most precious buildings in terms of both artistic and historic value, was in ruins. The artillery bombardments of 19 September 1914 and April 1917 had been particularly destructive. The skilful restoration has largely been financed by the Rockefeller Foundation.

Palais du Tau★★

🕒 *May-Aug: daily except Tue 9.30am-6.30pm; Sep-Apr: daily except Mon 9.30am-12.30pm, 2-5.30pm. Last admission 30min before closing.* 🕒 *Closed 1 Jan, 1 May, 1 and 11 Nov, 25 Dec.* ✎ *6.10€ (under 17 years: no charge)* ☎ *03 26 47 81 79.*

Dating from 1690, the former palace of the bishops of Reims was built by Mansart and Robert de Cotte. In it is housed some of the cathedral's original statuary, including the Coronation of the Virgin from the gable of the central doorway, and monumental figures of St Paul and of Goliath. There are also tapestries, among them two huge 15C examples from the Arras manufactory depicting scenes from the life of Clovis.

The treasury has many objects of outstanding interest, such as the 9C Talisman of Charlemagne, the 11C cut-glass Holy Thorn reliquary, the 12C coronation chalice, the St Ursula reliquary with its cornelian casket, the Holy Ampulla reliquary, and a collar of the Order of the Holy Ghost.

Basilique St-Rémi★★

Dating from 1007, this is the city's most venerable church, though successive restorations have left little that is Romanesque and even less that is Carolingian.

The west front was rebuilt in the course of the major restoration of 1170; it is remarkable for its Romanesque south tower. The façade of the south transept with its statue of St Michael was reconstructed in the 14C and 15C.

The sombre interior **(intérieur ★★★)** is remarkable for its extraordinary length (122m – 400ft) in proportion to its width (26m – 85ft). The oldest part of the church consists of the 11C transepts. In the 12C, the choir was rebuilt in the Early Gothic manner, with a blind triforium which is really no more than a roof to the galleries. All around the choir a series of double columns separates the chapel vaults from those of the ambulatory, an elegant solution which found favour throughout the province.

At the same time, the two westernmost bays of the nave were rebuilt and the whole nave given Gothic vaulting, while an imposing gallery was provided above the original aisles which were themselves given ribvaults.

In the choir is the tomb of St Remigius (rebuilt in 1847) with statues of the peers of France, clergy to the right, lay peers to the left, none of whom ever missed a coronation.

◖◖ Musée-abbaye St-Rémi★★ 🕒 *Mon-Fri 2-6.30pm (Sat-Sun 7pm).* 🕒 *Closed 1 Jan, 1 May, 14 Jul, 1 and 11 Nov, 25 Dec.* ✎ *3€, no charge 1st Sun in the month.* ☎ *03 26 85 23 36. www.reims.fr* – local art and architecture, arms and armour. Caves de Champagne★ (Champagne cellars). Musée des Beaux-Arts★ 🕒 *Wed-Mon 10am-noon, 2-6pm.* 🕒 *Closed Tue, 1 Jan, 1 May, 14 Jul, 1 and 11 Nov, 25 Dec.* ✎ *3€, no charge 1st Sun in the month.* ☎ *03 26 47 28 44. www.reims.fr* – paintings; Place Royale★. Porte Mars★.

Musée-Hôtel le Vergeur★ 🕒 *Guided tours ⌕ (1hr) daily Jun-Aug: Tue-Sat 10am-noon, 2-6pm, Sat-Sun 2-6pm. Sep-May: daily except Mon 2-6pm.* 🕒 *Closed between Christmas and New Year's Day, 1 May, 14 Jul, 1 Nov.* ✎ *3.90€.* ☎ *03 26 47 20 75. www.museelevergeur.com* – paintings and sculpture, Dürer engravings. Hôtel de la Salle★.

Chapelle Foujita★ 🕒 *May-Oct: Thu-Tue 2-6pm.* 🕒 *Closed Wed, 1 Jan, 1 May, 14 Jul, 1 and 11 Nov, 25 Dec.* ✎ *3€.* ☎ *03 26 40 06 96. www.reims.fr.* Centre historique de l'automobile française★.

RENNES★★

POPULATION 245 065

MICHELIN MAP 309 L-M 6

GREEN GUIDE BRITTANY

Originally founded by the Gauls, Rennes grew up around the meeting point of the great highways linking St-Malo to Nantes and Le Mans to Brest. When Brittany won its independence in the 12C, Rennes became the capital of the Duchy's eastern march. Its role as the capital of the whole of Brittany dates from the province's incorporation into France in the 16C.

▸ **Orient Yourself:** Rennes, which is listed as a "Town of Art and History," offers 1hr30min discovery tours daily at 10.30am in Jul and Aug, with an additional tour at 9pm on Tue and Thu. 6.10€. Information at the tourist office, "Rennes Ville d'Art et d'Histoire" dept. or on www.vpah.culture.fr.

Sights

Palais de Justice★★
🕐 *Guided tours* ⌛ *daily except Sat-Sun.* 🕐 *Closed 1 Jan, 1 May and 25 Dec.* ✎ *6.10€ (7-15 years: 3.05€). Call the Tourist Office in advance.*
This is the former seat of the Breton Parliament. The splendid south front of the building with its two corner pavilions was designed in 1618 by Salomon de Brosse; it is an early and characteristically severe example of the Classical style of architecture, with a rusticated ground floor in granite supporting an upper storey rhythmically divided up by flattened pilasters. The façade is completed by an elaborately sculpted cornice and a balustrade, above which rises an unusually steeply pitched roof. The building was originally graced by a terrace with a double stairway, but this disappeared in 1726, when the square was replanned on monumental lines by Jacques-Jules Gabriel.

Le vieux Rennes★
The old town was devastated in 1720 by a great fire which raged for eight days and engulfed almost 1 000 houses. Enough buildings were spared however to make a walk through the old part of Rennes an architecturally rewarding experience. The medieval houses crowd picturesquely together in the narrow streets, identifiable, like the Early Renaissance (pre-1580) houses among them, by their timber construction, their projecting upper floors and their sculptured decoration. No 3 Rue St-Guillaume is called the **Du Guesclin** House, although it actually dates from a later period than that of the Breton hero. It has a deeply-carved door flanked by figures of St Sebastian and one of his tormentors with his bow.
Even in the 17C, after the completion of the Law Courts (Palais de Justice), the people of Rennes continued to build in timber; though oversailing upper floors were abandoned and ground-floor walls sometimes built in granite, exuberant timber patterning still found favour. The city's notables had houses built at this time in which the granite ground floor supports one or two upper floors with walls of tufa or Charentes limestone. One such house, the **Hôtel de Brie**★ (8 Rue du Chapitre), with a fine doorway and upper storeys nicely defined by an entablature, is of such refinement that it has been attributed to Mansart.
In the meantime, some of the more distinguished houses were given a central staircase with no newel, a feature particularly characteristic of Rennes. These might have straight or curved flights, be hung from brackets or squinches, or built with a timber frame (good examples are shown below by means of a letter E against the house number).
In the 18C, after the great fire, Rennes was rebuilt according to a plan drawn up by Jacques-Jules Gabriel. The streets were realigned and widened and lined with fine new buildings with granite ground floors, frequently in the form of arcades, and upper floors of stone. In the 19C, urban planning emphasised the unity of the French state; the banks of the River Vilaine were laid out as a grand axis and the city provided with imposing public buildings (high school, city hall, churches...).
The following are Rennes' finest houses:
Rue St-Georges: nos 2 (E), 3, 6, 7, 8, 10, 12, 18, 22 (E), 30, 32;
Rue du Chapitre: nos 3, 6 (**Hôtel du Blossac**), 8 (**Hôtel de Brie**), 11, 18, 22 (E);

Rue de la Psalette: nos 4, 6, 12;

Rue du Champ-Jaquet: nos 5, 11, 13, 15 (E), 19;

Rue St-Guillaume: no 3 **(Maison de Du Guesclin★)**;

Rue St-Sauveur: 18C houses, nos 6, 7, 9.

Musée des Beaux-Arts★

♿ *Wed-Mon 10am-noon, 2-6pm. Guided tours* ••• *(1hr) available.* 🕐 *Closed Tue and public holidays.* ⊚ *4€.* ☎ *02 99 28 55 85. www.mbar.org.*

This important gallery has a fine picture collection. It includes *Le Nouveau-Né* (The Newborn – c 1630) by Georges de la Tour, a masterpiece of glowing colour, subtle lighting and deep tranquillity.

▷▷ Musée de Bretagne★ 🕐 *Wed-Mon 10am-noon, 2-6pm.* 🕐 *Closed Tue and public holidays. No charge.* ☎ *02 99 28 55 84.* Cathédrale St-Pierre – interior★; altarpiece★★.

Écomusée du pays de Rennes★ *(8km – 5mi south)* 🕐 *Apr-Sep: Tue-Fri 9am-6pm, Sat 2-6pm, Sun 2-7pm. Oct-Mar: Tue-Fri 9am-noon, 2-6pm, Sat 2-6pm, Sun 2-7pm.* 🕐 *Closed Mon, public holidays and 2nd week in Jan.* ⊚ *4.60€ (children: 2.30€).* ☎ *02 99 51 38 15.* Jardin du Thabor★.

RIOM★★

POPULATION 18 793

MICHELIN MAP 326 F 7

GREEN GUIDE AUVERGNE RHÔNE VALLEY

Riom lies at the foot of the scarp slope marking the eastern edge of the range of ancient volcanoes known as the Puys. It is the market centre of the Limagne district, a down-faulted Tertiary basin whose rich soils support a prosperous farming industry. Beginning in the 14C, the town was rebuilt in the black granite quarried either at Volvic, the "lava city", from the lava flow which once poured from the Puy-de-la-Nugère, or from the volcano itself. This hard stone is highly resistant to the sculptor's chisel, but is much appreciated by the architect for its strength and durability.

▶ **Orient Yourself:** Riom, which is listed as a "Town of Art and history," offers discovery tours conducted by guide-lecturers approved by the Ministry of Culture and Communication. Information at the service Animation du patrimoine (heritage dept.) or on www.vpah.culture.fr.

Sights

Quartier Ancien (Old Town)

The medieval town is entirely contained within the ring of boulevards laid out on the line of its now-demolished walls. In the Middle Ages it was the capital of the Duchy of Auvergne, then the seat of important courts of law in the 16C and an administrative centre in the 17C, and it is to its former population of lawyers and magistrates that it owes its heritage of fine 16C-18C town houses.

Église Notre-Dame-du-Marthuret★

Dating from 1583, it houses the splendid late 14C – **Virgin with a bird★★★**. This famous sculpture, with its finely modelled face, is a masterpiece of harmonious proportion; it is a product of the school of sculpture patronised by Duke Jean de Berry, the reputation of which rivalled that of the sculptors of Dijon.

Rue du Commerce

The modern sculptures made of lava contrast with the traditional decoration of the houses using the same material (no 36 has 17C caryatids).

Rue de l'Hôtel-de-ville

The 16C **Maison des Consuls★**, no 5 has a corner-turret set on corbels, and Italian-style busts on either side of its doorway. The Hôtel de ville has retained its 16C Renaissance arcades, and statuettes of Hercules and Cupid mounted on small engaged columns.

Rue de l'Horloge

The Renaissance **Clock Tower** (Tour de l'Horloge) replaced a medieval bell-tower; it is crowned by a delightful little 18C domed temple. The 16C **Hôtel Guimoneau**★ has a famous corner-tower staircase, Italian medallions enlivening its façade and balustrade, and statues of the Annunciation and of Venus which recall the work of the Loire School and which have been attributed to Michel Colombe.

▶▶ Ste-Chapelle★ ⊙ *Guided tours* ⏱ *(1hr30min) Jul and Aug: daily except Sat-Sun 11.30am and 4.30pm; Jun and Sep: Tue 4.30pm. Apr and May: Tue 3-5pm. Last admission 30min before closing. Tours specially adapted for the blind and partially sighted.* ⊙ *Closed 1 Jan, 1 and 8 May, 14 Jul, 15 Aug and 25 Dec.* ⊚ *0.50€.* ☎ *04 73 38 99 94.*

Musée régional d'Auvergne★ ⊙ *Jun-Sep: Tue-Sun 10am-noon, 2.30-6pm; Oct-May: Tue-Sun 10am-noon, 2-5.30pm).* ⊙ *Closed Mon, 1 Jan, 14 Jul, 15 Aug, 1 and 11 Nov, 25 Dec.* ⊚ *5.60€, no charge Wed.* ☎ *04 73 38 17 31* – folk art and local customs.

Musée Mandet★ ⊙ *Jun-Sep daily 10am-noon, 2.30-6pm; Oct-May: daily 10am-noon, 2-5.30pm.* ⊙ *Closed 1 Jan, 14 Jul, 15 Aug, 1 and 11 Nov, 25 Dec.* ⊚ *5.60€, no charge Wed.* ☎ *04 73 38 18 53* – painting and decorative arts.

Excursions

Église de Mozac★

2km – 1mi west. This ancient abbey was founded towards the end of the 7C by St Calminus, becoming subordinated to Cluny in 1095. Until its collapse in 1460, the abbey church was one of the finest in Auvergne. Of the building of 1095, all that remains are arches and pillars and the north aisle, together with the 47 capitals **(chapiteaux**★★**)** which are the oldest and perhaps the most beautiful in the whole of the province. They are products of a workshop which was active from the end of the 11C until the middle of the 12C and which enjoyed considerable influence. Those depicting Jonah (1st bay of the nave), the Apocalypse (on the ground in the choir), and the Centaur (3rd pillar on the left), are justly famous, but it is the capital showing the Resurrection which is truly outstanding (on the ground at the end of the nave); it is a faithful account of St Mark's text, but in its sober depiction of pose, gesture and expression, goes beyond the telling of a story to convey inner truths.

The Shrine of St Calminus **(châsse de Saint Calmin**★★**)** in champlevé enamel is an exquisite example of Limoges work with chased and gilded inlay figures.

Église de Marsat

3km – 2mi southwest. The church here has one of Auvergne's great works of medieval art, a 12C **Black Virgin**★★ (in the choir of the north chapel). Few will be untouched by this depiction of Mary as a simple countrywoman, holding out the Child in a maternal gesture of great dignity.

Château de Tournoël★★

8km – 5mi west. This is one of the province's most celebrated castles. It dominates the town of Volvic, famous not only for its lava quarry, but also for its spring water, whose exceptional purity is due to the filtering effect of one of the lava flows from the Puy-de-la-Nugère.

Picturesquely perched on a crag, the castle has two keeps, one round, one square, joined together by ancillary buildings now in ruins. Mullioned windows of Renaissance date look down onto the courtyard, some of them blocked up to avoid the payment of window tax.

Gour de Tazenat★

22km – 14mi northeast. This lovely upland lake (32ha – 79 acres, 60m – 200ft deep) in its wooded setting marks the northern limit of the Auvergne volcanoes, one of whose craters it now fills.

RIQUEWIHR★★★

POPULATION 1 075

MICHELIN MAP 315 H 8

GREEN GUIDE ALSACE LORRAINE CHAMPAGNE

Unlike other French wines, those of Alsace are named according to the grape from which they are made rather than the locality. Protected by the Vosges from cold and wet westerly winds, the region's vineyards benefit from their southeasterly orientation, while the subtle bouquet of their wines is enhanced by the late ripening of the grapes in the soft September sun.

▶ **Orient Yourself:** The rue du Général-de-Gaulle is the main road running east to west from which the museum and the old houses are easily accessed.

🕓 **Organizing Your Time:** An inclusive walking tour of the town may take around 2hr, probably longer if you visit the museums or stop at one of the typical Alsatian restaurants for a meal and to try a glass of the region's famous Riesling.

🅿 **Parking:** Use the parking facilities on the outside of the town: place des Charpentiers, rue de la Piscine, rocade Nord and près de la Poste.

Visit

Village

The tiny village of Riquewihr prides itself on its fine Riesling; the vintners' houses in its picturesque streets were designed with the production of wine more in mind than the comfort of the residents. A variety of building materials enlivens the scene, brick, red sandstone, timber, rendered and painted façades... while every balcony is adorned with flowers. Some of the dwellings (like the De Hugel house of 1494) go back to the end of the 15C, others to Renaissance times (like the Cour de Strasbourg house of 1597); most of them, however, are of 17C date, but they are all ornamented in the Rhineland Renaissance style which persisted longer in Alsace than elsewhere.

Riquewihr - Address Book

PRACTICAL INFORMATION

Tourist office - BP 28, 68340 Riquewihr - ☎ 03 20 36 09 22/0 820 360 922 - www.ribeauville-riquewihr.com

WHERE TO EAT

See p 28 for coin categories.

⊖ **Auberge St-Alexis** – 68240 St-Alexis 6km W of Riquewihr on minor road and path – ☎ 03 89 73 90 38 – 🕓 closed Fri. It's definitely worth venturing into the forest along a dirt track to this former 17C hermitage. You will be rewarded with simple dishes, as authentic as the site, made from local farm produce.

⊖⊖ **Le Sarment d'Or** – 4 r. du Cerf – ☎ 03 89 86 02 86 – info@riquewihr-sarment-dor.com – 🕓 closed 5 Jan-11 Feb, 28 Jun-6 Jul, Sun evening, Tue lunchtimes and Mon. Pale wood panelling, copper light-fittings, fireplace and huge beams create a lovely warm atmosphere in this restaurant. The cooking is traditional and uses seasonal ingredients. Plush, comfortable rooms.

WHERE TO STAY

⊖ **Chambre d'hôte Schmitt** – 3 chemin des Vignes – ☎ 03 89 47 89 72 – 🕓 closed Jan-Mar – ⌿ – 2 rooms. A house with a garden in the higher part of the village, on the edge of a vineyard. The wood-panelled rooms have sloping ceilings. High standard of cleanliness and reasonable prices.

⊖⊖⊜ **Hôtel L'Oriel** – 3 r. des Écuries-Seigneuriales – ☎ 03 89 49 03 13 – hotel.oriel@wanadoo.fr - 19 rooms - 🖙 €9.50. This 16C hotel is easily recognised by its wrought-iron sign. The lack of straight lines in the building, combined with simple decor and old Alsatian furniture and exposed beams, creates a romantic atmosphere. The three new rooms nestled in the annexe are smarter and more modern.

SHOPPING

Féerie de Noël – 1 r. du Cerf – ☎ 03 89 47 94 02 – feerie.de.noel@wanadoo.fr – 🕓 open daily 15 Feb-Jun 10am-12.30pm, 1.45-6pm, Jul-Aug 9.30am-7pm, Sep-Dec 10am-12.30pm, 1.45-6.30pm - 🕓 closed early Jan-mid-Feb, 25-26 Dec. It's never too early or too late to think about Christmas decorations - over 2,000 decorations and ideas for the home and christmas tree.

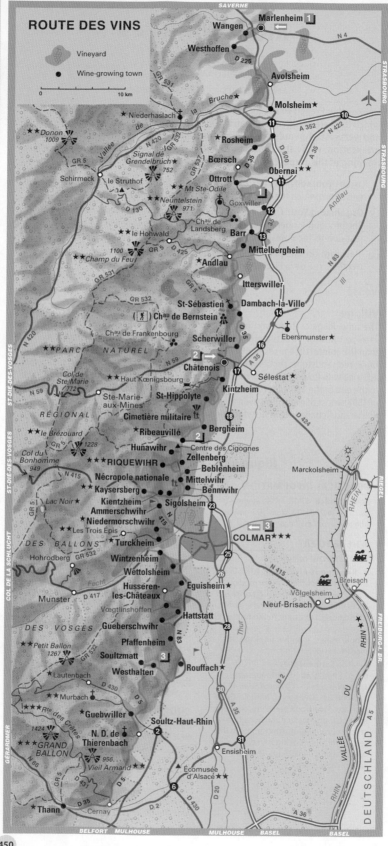

ROUTE DES VINS

Vineyard

Wine-growing town

0   10 km

Riquewihr

◐◐ Porte Dolder★ (1291) ◷ *Jul and Aug: daily 10am-12.30pm, 2-6.30pm; Apr-Jun and Sep-Oct: Sat-Sun and public holidays 10am-12.30pm, 2-6.30.* ◷ *Closed from All Saints' Day to Easter.* ◷ *2€, 3€ (ticket combined with the musée de la Tour des Voleurs) (under 10 years: no charge).* ☎ *08 20 36 09 22 or 03 89 49 08 40* – local history museum. Maisons Liebrich (1535), Kiener (1574), Dissler (1610) and Preiss-Zimmer (1686)★ (old houses).

ROCAMADOUR★★★

POPULATION 627

MICHELIN MAP 337 F 3

GREEN GUIDE DORDOGNE BERRY LIMOUSIN

Clinging dramatically to the cliffs of the gorge cut by the little River Alzou, the tiny medieval town of Rocamadour is one of the most visited places in the Dordogne. All around stretches the Causse de Gramat★, a vast limestone plateau, known as good sheep country and for its pâté de foie gras.

▶ **Orient Yourself:** You can only walk on foot around Rocamadour so park on the plateau and walk into town (or pay and take the elevator) or take the little train that runs into town (fee). To reach the Place St-Amadour (and the seven sanctuaries), take the stairway at Via Sancta or the elevator.

☺ **Don't Miss:** Rocamadour should be viewed from the Hospitalet belvedere *(2km – 1.5mi northeast)*, as well as from the Couzou road. The castle, rising 125m – 420ft above the valley floor, dominates the scene; below it is a picturesque confusion of old houses, stepped streets, towers, gateways, churches and chapels.

A Bit of History

A place of pilgrimage

Long ago, Rocamadour was chosen by a hermit, Saint Amadour, as his place of retreat. Legend identifies him with the figure of Zaccheus, husband of St Veronica, both of whom fled here from the Holy Land. From the 12C onwards, and above all during the 13C, Rocamadour was one of the most popular places of pilgrimage in the whole of Christendom. Just as they do today, souvenir stalls tempted the throngs of tourists, among them Henry III of England, who experienced a miraculous cure here.

A stairway with 216 steps leads to the Place St-Amadour (**or Parvis des églises**) around which are grouped seven sanctuaries, including the Chapel of Notre-Dame or Miraculous Chapel.

Rocamadour - Address Book

TRANSPORT

Getting around by car – The streets of Rocamadour are pedestrianised. Access for vehicles is only permitted for hotel and restaurant customers.

Lift – ⏰ Open Jul-Aug, 8am-8pm, May-Jun, 8am-7pm; Feb-Apr and Sep to mid-Nov, 10am-5pm. 3€ return, 2€single (chidren under 8: no charge). ☎ 05 65 33 62 44.

TOURS

Petit train de nuit – Apr-Sep, departures from porte du Figuier at 9.30pm and 10pm. 5€ (child: 3€). ☎ 05 65 33 67 84 or 05 65 33 65 99. 🌂 Guided tours by little train in seven languages (30min).

EATING OUT

😊🍽 **Le Château** – Rte du Château - ☎ 05 65 33 62 22 - hotelchateau@wanadoo.fr - 🕐 closed 8 Nov-21 Mar. The traditional house is near the château, in a quiet setting. Oaks shade the large terrace and the dining area inside is embellished by a wooden sculpture of a shepherd. The rooms in the hotel are very comfortable whereas the annex offers simpler accommodation. The pool is nice and you can use it summer and winter alike.

😊🍽 **Jehan de Valon** – ☎ 05 65 33 63 08 - hotel@bw-beausite.com - 🕐 closed 16 Nov-7 Feb. Dining room with a view of the valley and a pleasant terrace shaded by lime trees. The menu features traditional regional dishes.

😊🍽 **Le Bistrot Beau Site** – Cité Médiévale - ☎ 05 65 33 63 08 - www.bw-beausite.com - 🕐 daily 7am-9pm - 🕐 closed Nov-Feb. With a shaded terrace above the valley, this chic bistrot lives up to its name. Tables are reserved for diners during meal times, but they also serve breakfast – what better way to start the day?

😊🍽 **Le Mas de Douze** – Les Gîtes de Rocamadour - 4km/2.5mi E of Rocamadour on the D 673 - ☎ 05 65 33 72 80 - 🕐 closed 15 Nov-15 Mar. This restaurant provides some quiet relief from the tourist crowds, yet it is not too far away. The setting is country-style and the dishes hearty regional specialities. You can take a break on the terrace and a dip in the pool. There are eight cottage-bungalows in the park.
🕯For coin categories, see p000.

WHERE TO STAY

😊🍽 **Hôtel du Centre** – Pl. de la République - 46500 Gramat - ☎ 05 65 38 73 37 - le.centre@wanadoo.fr - 14 rooms - restaurant 😊🍽. The warm welcome in this family-style hotel in the town centre will charm you. The rooms with roughcast walls are serviceable. Traditional fare; children's menu.

😊🍽 **Hôtel Les Vieilles Tours** – Rte de Payrac - 4km/2.5mi W of Rocamadour on the D 673 - ☎ 05 65 33 68 01 - les.vieillestours@wanadoo.fr - 🕐 closed 16 Nov-26 Mar - 🅿 - 16 rooms - restaurant 😊🍽. The country house dates from the 16C and the hawk house from the 13C. The tower room is the nicest, if it's available, but the others are attractive too. Nice view of the valley from the garden. Pool. Meals served in the evening only.

😊🍽 **Le Troubadour** – Belveyre - 2.5km/1.5mi NE of Rocamadour on the D 673 towards Brive - ☎ 05 65 33 70 27 - troubadour@rocamadour.com - 🕐 closed 16 Nov-14 Feb - 🅿 - 10 rooms. Seeking peace and quiet? Do not hesitate to book in this restored farmhouse. The garden, pool and surrounding countryside are part of the charm. Simple meals prepared for hotel residents only.

😊🍽 **Chambre d'hôte Moulin de Fresquet** – 46500 Gramat - ☎05 65 38 70 60 - moulindefresquet@ifrance.com - 🕐 closed Nov-Mar - 🅿 - 5 rooms - meals 😊🍽. This very agreeable guesthouse, a renovated mill in a pretty park, is just a short walk from the centre of town. The rooms are stylish and comfortable (non-smoking) and look out over the garden. The welcome is warm and the food delicious.

😊🍽 **Domaine de la Rhue** – 6km/3.7mi NE of Rocamadour on the D 673 and then the N 140 - ☎05 65 33 71 50 - domainedelarhue@wanadoo.fr - 🕐 closed 18 Oct-1 Apr - 🅿 - 14 rooms. Quiet nights guaranteed! The rooms are in the renovated stables of a prosperous 19C farm. The rustic furniture, original wooden beams and posts are in harmony with the view of the countryside. The swimming pool is a modern touch.

BARS AND CAFÉS

L'Esplanade – L'Hospitaland - ☎ 05 65 33 18 45 - bouz06@infonie.fr - 🕐 summer: daily 10am-12.30am; Feb-Mar, Oct-Nov except school holidays: 🕐 closed evenings - closed from mid-Nov to mid-Feb. This new café has an exceptionally good view of the old city and surrounding mountains. The shaded terrace is an ideal spot to relax and admire the site.

Les Jardins de la Louve – Pl. Hugon - ☎ 05 65 33 62 93 - 🕐 in season: 10am-11pm- 🕐 closed mid-Nov to Jan except school holidays. This elegant establishment is a 13C residence that was remodelled in the 15C. The interior is charming, with exposed beams and stone walls. A pleasant terrace under the trees is welcoming in fine weather. Choose from a selection of regional dishes, pizzas, ice cream and teas in the afternoon.

Pâtisserie Quercynoise – Pl. St-Louis - ☎ 05 65 33 63 09 - 🕐 Apr-Nov: daily 8am-midnight. Take a break on the shaded terrace of the pastry-shop and brassiere, and pity the pilgrims of yore who doubtless did not enjoy such delights as they came to the end of their long and weary trail.

SHOPPING

Boutique du Terroir – R. de la Couronnerie - ☎ 05 65 33 71 25 - ◷ hours vary in different seasons – ◷ closed 11 Nov-1 Apr and Sat except Jul-Aug. This culinary artist has won many awards including the Gold Medal at the 1999 Salon Agricole. Foie gras, prepared dishes, black Périgord truffles…this attractive shop has a thousand and one delights, including prize-winning plum brandy.

Ferme Lacoste – Les Alix - ☎ 05 65 33 62 66 - ◷ Mon-Fri 10am-noon, 2.30-6pm, Sat 10am-noon, 2.30-5pm, occasionally open Sun. This handsome farm is home to 100 goats who live to maintain the reputation of the delicious cheese Cabécou de Rocamadour, also known simply as Rocamadour.

La Maison de la Noix – R. de la Couronnerie - ☎ 05 65 33 67 90. This shop sells aperitifs, liqueurs, jams, oils, biscuits, sweets, mustards and vinegars made with walnuts.

Farmers' market - In Miers (10km/6mi from Rocamadour). Fridays in July and August, 5-8pm.

LEISURE ACTIVITIES

Association Rocamadour Aérostat – Domaine de la Rhue - ☎ 05 65 33 71 50 - domainedelarhue@rocamadour.com - ◷ daily by reservation only. Rocamadour is the perfect place to try the most poetic of all forms of transportation – the hot-air balloon. Once the balloon is ready, you will rise up from the valley floor for a flight of about 45min around the site. Naturally, the company may cancel flights when the weather is inclement.

The stream of pilgrims eventually dried up, unsurprisingly, in view of the destruction which was caused by the great rock-fall of 1476 and completed by the Huguenots a century later. In the 19C, the place was restored by the Bishops of Cahors in an attempt to revive the pilgrimages.

◗◗ Hôtel de ville – tapestries★. Musée trésor Francis-Poulenc★ ⦿ ◷ Jul and Aug: daily 9am-6pm; Sep to mid-Nov and Mar-Jun: daily 10am-noon, 2-5pm. ⊜ 4.80€. ☎ 05 65 33 23 30 – sacred art.

ROCHEFORT★★

POPULATION 25 561

MICHELIN MAP 324 E 4

GREEN GUIDE ATLANTIC COAST

▶ **Orient Yourself:** Rochefort, which is listed as a "Town of Art and History," offers discovery tours conducted by guide-lecturers approved by the Ministry of Culture and Communication. Information available from the Service animation du Patrimoine (Heritage Dept.), by calling ☎ 05 46 99 57 17 or on www.vpah.culture.fr.

A Bit of History

In 1664, the French Secretary for the Navy, Colbert, became aware of the vulnerability of France's Atlantic coast to attack by the English. Between Lorient in Brittany and the Spanish frontier there were hardly any defences worthy of the name; the bay at La Rochelle was very exposed and the ancient port of Brouage was silting up. In 1665, he chose a site 22km – 14mi up the River Charente and charged Vauban with extending the defences of the fort already built there. Though the place had few natural advantages as a port, the presence of easily fortifiable islands and promontories facilitated the great engineer's task.

Seven years later, the work, which included a harbour for the navy, was complete, and by 1690 Rochefort rivalled the naval bases of Toulon and Brest. The increasing draught of modern vessels led to the harbour's obsolescence, however, and on 31 December 1926, the base was closed down.

Visit

chefort's fascinating history has left many traces: houses richly ornamented with blatures, window brackets, balustrades and balconies, the stately church, Église uis, of Classical design, the former rope-walk (**corderie★★**), 374m – 1 200ft ong, the great timber hall built by naval carpenters (now a covered market and conference centre), and the Sun Gateway (Porte du Soleil) which formed the entrance to Colbert's arsenal.

Pierre Loti (1850-1923) – Born Julian Viaud, this native of Rochefort and lover of the exotic was intimately familiar as a young man with the life of the port and its links with the wider world. As a naval officer, he sailed the seven seas, evoking the sights and sounds of distant places in a series of novels under the nom de plume Pierre Loti. His house, **Maison de Pierre Loti**★ *(45min guided tours* ⌐◖ *Jul to mid-Sep: 10am-5.30pm, departure every 30min; mid-Sep to end Jun: daily except Tue at 10.30am, 11.30am, 2pm, 3pm and 4pm;* ○ *closed in Jan, 1 and 11 Nov, 25 Dec;* ⊜ *7.65€ (children 3.90€);* ☏ *05 46 99 16 88, reservations necessary)*, now a museum, is equally evocative of his travels.

◖◗ Musée Naval★. Musée d'Art et d'histoire de la ville★. ⌐ *Closed for maintenance.*

Excursion

Moëze

11km – 6mi southwest. In the cemetery is a Hosanna Cross **(croix hosannière**★**)**, also known as the "Temple du Moëze", one of the finest in southwestern France. It crowns a small early – 16C Corinthian temple, whose square plan and porticoes are evidence of growing Renaissance interest in the architecture of the ancient world.

The region's Hosanna crosses are so named because they formed the setting for Palm Sunday celebrations, the "palm" branches strewn on the ground being referred to as "hosannas".

Château de La **ROCHEFOUCAULD**★★

MICHELIN MAP 324 M 5

GREEN GUIDE ATLANTIC COAST

A Bit of History

The property is the seat of a noble family which gave the name François to all its first-born sons and which produced many a soldier, statesman, artist and churchman. In 1494, François I de la Rochefoucauld became godfather to King François I.

François XII (1747-1827) was a characteristic figure of the late 18C, an "Improver" in the English mould, a founder of technical colleges and savings banks, who also set up a model farm to apply the progressive agricultural techniques he had studied in England. In the previous century, **François VI** (1613-1680) had established his reputation as the greatest of France's maxim-writers. In his younger days, this Duke de la Rochefoucauld had been a brave soldier but a somewhat inept plotter; he had been imprisoned by Richelieu, ignored by Mazarin and had fought on the wrong side in the Fronde; almost blinded by a blast from a harquebus, he retired to his country seat. Here, in the West Tower of the castle, a perception of the world sharpened by an understandable pessimism and filtered through a somewhat Jansenist temperament led him to produce the *Maxims* for which he is famous. Expressed in short, incisive phrases, they convey his assumption that it is self-esteem *(amour-propre)* which underlies all human activity. Many of his Maxims have passed into languages other than French:

"Hypocrisy is the tribute vice pays to virtue."

"We are all brave enough to bear other people's misfortunes."

Visit

François I de la Rochefoucauld, encouraged by his wife Anne de Polignac, transformed the severe stronghold (château fort) he had inherited into a sophisticated Renaissance residence, albeit retaining the medieval towers, with its chapel, terrace, 16C façades and dormer windows adorned with candelabra motif.

La ROCHELLE★★★

POPULATION 100 264

MICHELIN MAP 324 D 3

GREEN GUIDE ATLANTIC COAST

The port of La Rochelle is also the capital of the ancient province of Aunis. It is a lively place, much frequented by artists, but still retains that slightly secretive air characteristic of those French towns laid out on Classical lines. It owes its origin to the fort built in the 11C to guard the entrance to the Aiguillon inlet; during the centuries of almost continuous English rule it was an important trading centre, exporting salt and wine, while Genoese ships landed Mediterranean produce on its quaysides.

A Bit of History

A Protestant stronghold – La Rochelle was one of the first places in France where the Reformation took hold, becoming known as the "French Geneva". In 1570, at the end of the Third War of Religion, the town was one of the four fortified places permitted to the Protestants as a guarantee of their liberty of conscience and worship. After the St Bartholomew's Day Massacre, La Rochelle became one of the main centres of Protestant resistance. Besieged by the Duke of Anjou, the town was granted an honourable surrender in 1573 after an English fleet commanded by Gabriel de Montgomery had failed to relieve it but had occupied Belle-Île.

The religious freedoms secured by the Edict of Nantes in 1598 brought several years of peace to La Rochelle. By 1627, however, the town's continued adherence to Protestantism had become intolerable to Richelieu, not least because of its English connection; the Duke of Buckingham had set up camp on the Île de Ré, and English forces had even landed on the mainland.

Richelieu directed the siege of La Rochelle in person. A fortified perimeter, 12km – 7 miles long was created and extended seawards by means of a dike (designed by the architect Métezeau) which blocked the entrance to the harbour. It took 15 months to starve the town into submission. Richelieu made his entrance into La Rochelle on 30 October 1628, followed two days later by Louis XIII. 23 000 citizens had perished in the course of the siege; the 5 000 who had survived were spared, though a number of their leaders, including the mayor, Jean Guiton, who had embodied the spirit of resistance, were forced to leave the place for a period of several months.

Visit

Vieux Port★★

The old port was originally laid out by Eleanor of Aquitaine; its entrance is guarded by two towers, probably built by the English in the 14C and once forming part of the town's ring of fortifications.

Tour St Nicolas★

🕐 *Mid-May to Jul and early Sep to mid-Sep: 10am-12.30pm, 2-6.30pm; Jul and Aug: 10am-7pm; mid-Sep to mid-May: daily except Tue 10am-12.30pm, 2-5.30pm.* 🕐 *Closed 1 Jan, 1 May, and 25 Dec.* ⊛ *4.60€ (under 17 years: no charge), 10€ ticket combined with the Tour de la Chaine and Tour de la Lanterne.* ☎ *05 46 34 11 81.*

La Tour St Nicolas to the east has rested on its foundation of oak piles for six centuries; 42m – 138ft high and with immensely thick walls, it is a fortress in its own right.

La Rochelle has contributed more than its share to the opening up of the world beyond Europe; in the 15C, it was from here that the first colonists embarked for Canada and Jean de Béthencourt sailed off to discover the Canary Islands; in the 16C, the La Rochelle fishing fleet operated in the rich fishing grounds off Newfoundland. Other explorers to set out from here were de la Salle, who sailed down the Mississippi to the Gulf of Mexico in 1681-12, and René Caillié, the first European to get back from Timbuktu alive. La Rochelle's shipowners profited mightily from trade with Canada, Louisiana and above all with the West Indies, where they owned vast estates producing spices, sugar, cocoa, coffee and vanilla; they drew their wealth too from the triangular trade involving the sale of cloth and purchase of slaves in West Africa, transport and disposal of the slaves in America, and a lucrative trip home with a full load of colonial produce.

La Rochelle - Address Book

EATING OUT

🍴 **Le Café de la Mer** – *Port du Plomb - Lauzières - 17137 Nieul-sur-Mer* – *Take the D 106E1 4km/2.5mi W of Nieul-sur-Mer* - ☎ *05 46 37 39 37* – 🕐 *closed Nov-Mar.* Mouclades (mussels in a spicy cream sauce), oysters and crepes in the summer, hearty simmering dishes in the winter. This little restaurant opens its bay windows onto a view of the Île de Ré bridge. Enthusiastic appetites will be more than satisfied with the generous portions.

🍴 **Le Mistral** – *10 pl. Coureauleurs, in the Le Gabut district* - ☎ *05 46 41 24 42* - *restaurant.lemistral@wanadoo.fr* - 🕐 *closed 23 Feb-8 Mar, 23 Oct-4 Nov and Sun to Thu eve except Jul-Aug.* This wood-clad house is located at the heart of the Le Gabut district, a stone's throw from the tourist office. The maritime-style dining room is on the first floor; the terrace, on the same level, overlooks the old fishing port.

🍴 **André** – *pl. de la Chaîne* - ☎ *05 46 41 28 24* – *barandre@wanadoo.fr*. A visit to La Rochelle is not complete without a meal at André! On the old docks, facing the Tour de la Chaîne, this enormous restaurant is comprised of a dozen bistro-style dining rooms where customers sit elbow to elbow to feast on seafood. Nautical ambience, marine paintings and objects de rigeur.

🍴 **À Côté de chez Fred** – *32-34 r. St-Nicolas* - ☎ *05 46 41 65 76* – *barregilles@wanadoo.fr* - 🕐 *closed Sun from Oct-Mar* – *reser. recommended.* Here the fish couldn't be fresher! And no wonder – this little restaurant gets its provisions from its neighbour and sister…the fishmonger. Result: a slate menu that changes as the fishing boats come to moor and an authentic atmosphere just behind the docks.

🍴 **Le Boute-en-Train** – *7 r. des Bonnes-Femmes* - ☎ *05 46 41 73 74* - 🕐 *closed 26 Aug-9 Sep, Sun and Mon.* Near the markets, this charming restaurant serves a variety of quiches and food fresh from the marketplace. Children's drawings adorn the walls of the bistro dining room…grab a crayon and add to their collection. More mature customers may prefer to visit the vaulted cellar to choose their bottle of wine.

🍴 **Le Petit Rochelais** – *25 r. St-Jean-du-Pérot* - ☎ *05 46 41 28 43* – 🕐 *closed Sun except public hols.* A friendly and competent team has taken over this ex-pizzeria cum bistro. The menu chalked on slate and the inviting atmosphere complement food prepared with brio, cooked fresh each day and served with enjoyable wines.

🕯️ *For coin categories, see Legend at back of the guide.*

WHERE TO STAY

🛏️ **Chambre d'hôte Margorie** – *17139 Dompierre-sur-Mer - 8km/5mi NE of La Rochelle on the N 11, then take the road to Mouillepied* - ☎ *05 46 35 33 41* - 🚭 - *4 rooms.* A relaxing stop in the local countryside, this isolated old farm is surrounded by stone walls and its inviting garden is full of flowers and trees. In the outbuildings, the rooms are arranged around a second courtyard; some come with a mezzanine.

🛏️ **Hôtel de la Plage** – *bd de la Mer - 17340 Châtelaillon-Plage* - ☎ *05 46 56 26 02* - *hotelaplage-chatel@wanadoo.fr* - 🅿️ - *10 rooms - restaurant* 🛏️. This tiny hotel facing the beach is nothing fancy, but it is impeccably managed and nicely situated. The small rooms are appealing and soundproofed, and their very reasonable prices should win over the wariest wayfarer. A sure bet.

🛏️ **Hôtel France-Angleterre et Champlain** – *20 r. Rambaud* - ☎ *05 46 41 23 99* – *hotel@france-champlain.com* - *36 rooms.* A spot of the country in the city. On a busy street near the historic district, this old 16C convent features a discrete, pleasant garden - a marvellous place to unwind after a busy day in town. In this genteel setting, the rooms, some quite spacious, are decorated with period pieces.

🛏️ **Hôtel Les Brises** – *Chemin digue Richelieu, (av. P.-Vincent)* - ☎ *05 46 43 89 37* - 🅿️ - *46 rooms.* How delightful to open one's windows in the morning, contemplate the ocean and breathe the sea air…This 1960s hotel is well situated between earth and water. Lovely view from the panoramic terrace and most of the rooms.

🛏️ **Hôtel de la Monnaie** – *3 r. de la Monnaie* - ☎ *05 46 50 65 65* – *info@hotel-monnaie.com* - *31 rooms.* Right behind the Tour de la Lanterne, this splendid 17C mansion where coins used to be made is an agreeable address. You'll appreciate the serenity of the rooms between courtyard and garden, as well as their modern furnishings and spaciousness.

BARS AND CAFÉS

Cave de la Guignette – *8 r. St-Nicolas* - ☎ *05 46 41 05 75* – 🕐 *open Thu-Sat, 3pm-8pm* – 🕐 *closed hols except Ascension Thursday and 8 May.* This charming and colourful wine bar used to be the watering hole of the local fishermen (who have since changed towns). Try the house speciality, la Guinguette, an aperitif made of wine and fruit.

Café de la Paix – *54 r. Chaudrier* - ☎ *05 46 41 39 79* – *open 7am-10pm* - 🕐 *closed Sun, 25 Dec and 1 Jan.* Behind its carved wood facade, this big café covered with mirrors and mouldings has a long history. A hospital in 1709, a theatre during the Revolution, since about 1900 it has been a café popular with visiting artists such as Colette, Jean Gabin, Lino Ventura…

Le Morgane Pub – 99 bd de la Mer - 17340 Châtelaillon-Plage - ☎ 05 46 56 39 19 - lemorganepub@9telecom.fr - ☼ open daily Apr-Sep, 9am-2am; rest of the year, daily except Mon and Tue - ☼ closed Jan. No evil spells cast by the fairy queen of this spot! Instead, the enchantment of enjoying a glass of potion while gazing at the sea from the pub's terrace.

LEISURE ACTIVITIES

Casino de la Rochelle – Allée du Mail - ☎ 05 46 34 12 75 - www.lucienbarriere.com - ☼ casino: open daily, 10am-5am; le Cosy: Wed-Sat, 10:30pm-5am; traditional games:

9pm-5am; restaurant: daily for lunch and dinner. Le Casino Barrière de la Rochelle awaits you with its 120 slot machines. From 9pm on you can also try your hand at traditional gambling games: blackjack, roulette or boule. After 10pm you can catch your breath at the Cosy with a cocktail while planning your next bet. This chic bar merits its name – note the tartan carpet, marble counter, leather armchairs and terrace overlooking the ocean.

Cours des Dames – Cours des Dames. This is the place to go if you want to discover the Charantais archipelago by boat. In this part of the port, several ventures offer cruises to Fort Boyard, l'île de Ré, l'île d'Oléron or l'île d'Aix. You can also charter a boat for an excursion along the River Charente.

In 1890 a new deep-water port was created at La Pallice, capable of taking shipping at all states of the tide.

The 17C and 18C town★★

The 18C **Porte de la Grosse-Horloge**★ leads to the Old Town. Here, as well as timber-framed medieval houses with hung slates to keep out the damp and fine residences of Renaissance date, there are substantial 18C stone town houses adorned with some astonishing gargoyles. Arcades of pleasingly varied design enliven the urban scene, which reaches a climax in the splendid **Hôtel de ville**★. Built in Tuscan style in the reign of Henri IV, this has a courtyard **façade**★ of 1606, with an arcaded gallery. Probably built by the great architect Du Cerceau (himself a Huguenot), it is evidence not only of the growing taste for things Italian but also of the economic recovery following the Wars of Religion.

▶▶ Old Town streets★. Museum d'Histoire Naturelle★★. Musée du Nouveau-Monde★ ☼ Apr-Sep: Mon, Wed-Sat 10am-12.30pm, 2-6pm, Sun 2.30-6pm. Oct-Mar: Mon, Wed-Fri 9.30am-12.30pm, 1.30-5pm, Sat-Sun 2.30-6pm. ☼ Closed Tue, 1 Jan, 1 May, 14 Jul, 1 and 11 Nov, 25 Dec. ☞ 3.50€ (under 18 years: no charge). ☎ 05 46 41 46 50. www.perso.wanadoo.fr/musees-la-rochelle.

Musée des Beaux-Arts ☼ Apr-Sep: Mon, Wed-Sat 2-6pm, Sun 2.30-6pm; Oct-Mar: Mon, Wed-Fri 1.30-5pm, Sat-Sun 2.30-6pm. ☼ Closed Tue, 1 Jan, 1 May, 14 Jul, 1 and 11 Nov, 25 Dec. ☞ 3.50€ (under 18 years: no charge). ☎ 05 46 41 64 65. www.perso.wanadoo.fr/musees-la-rochelle.

Musée d'Orbigny-Bernon★ Apr-Sep: Mon, Wed-Sat 10am-12.30pm, 2-6pm, Sun 2-6pm. Oct-Mar: Mon, Wed-Fri 9.30am-12.30pm, 1.30-5pm, Sat-Sun 2-6pm. Closed Tue, 1 Jan, 1 May, 14 Jul, 1 and 11 Nov, 25 Dec. ☞ 3.50€ (under 18 years: no charge). ☎ 05 46 41 18 83. www.perso.wanadoo.fr/musees.la.rochelle. – local history, ceramics.

Tour de la Lanterne★ Same as Tour St Nicolas. ☎ 05 46 41 56 04. Musée des Automates★ Kids ♿ ☼ Jul and Aug: 9.30am-7pm; Sep-Jun: 10am-noon, 2-6pm. ☞ 7.50€ (children: 5€). ☎ 05 46 41 68 08. www.museeslarochelle.com. Parc Charruyer★.

Excursion

Île de Ré★

The island, which is also known as White Island and has been linked to the mainland by a viaduct since 1988, is a popular resort. Part of the salt-marshes to the north has been set aside as a bird sanctuary.

ROCROI★

POPULATION 2 555

MICHELIN MAP 306 J 3

GREEN GUIDE ALSACE LORRAINE CHAMPAGNE

First laid out in the 16C in a clearing in the Ardennes forest, Rocroi is a typical Renaissance fortified town.

A Bit of History

After the principality of Sedan had been incorporated into France in 1642, the death of Richelieu and the ill health of Louis XIII made a long period of uncertain rule by a regent seem likely. The prospect whetted the expansionist appetites of Philip IV of Spain, for whom the capture of Rocroi would open the way to Paris via the valleys of the Aisne and the Marne.

On 19 May 1643, three days after the death of Louis XIII, a bold manœuvre by the Duke d'Enghien – the future **Grand Condé** – routed the redoubtable Spanish infantry which never succeeded in regrouping. This, the first French victory over the Spaniards for more than a century, reverberated around Europe (it is commemorated by a monument in the leafy countryside 3km – 2 miles to the south). Fortune now began to smile on France, and Mazarin was able to implement Richelieu's foreign policy, using the generation of officers trained by the far-sighted Cardinal.

Later, after his involvement in the disturbances known as the Fronde, Condé went over to the Spaniards, and, in 1658, was responsible for capturing Rocroi for them. But in the following year, the Treaty of the Pyrenees gave the fortress town back to France and Condé to his king.

Visit

Ramparts

The ramparts **(remparts)** of Rocroi were improved by **Vauban**. With their glacis, bastions, demi-lunes and deep defensive ditches they are a fine example of the great engineer's mastery of his art.

RODEZ★

POPULATION 24 701

MICHELIN MAP 338 H 4

GREEN GUIDE LANGUEDOC ROUSSILLON TARN GORGES

The origins of Rodez go back to a stronghold built by the Gauls on the rocky spur high above one of the meanders of the river Aveyron. The layout of the town reflects the ancient rivalry of secular and ecclesiastical power; the areas around both cathedral and castle (near Place du Bourg) were each provided with fortifications.

Visit

Cathédrale Notre-Dame★★

The red sandstone edifice was probably begun in 1277 by Jean Deschamps, who propagated the new Gothic style of the Île de France throughout Central and Southern France. The impressive fortress-like west front was originally a bastion protruding from the city wall. Its Flamboyant Gothic portals were completed in 1475; 35 years later, the construction of the magnificent bell-tower **(clocher★★★)** was begun, incorporating an existing tower of 14C date. The top three storeys are richly decorated, the third with large arches with very pronounced mouldings, the fourth with statues of the Apostles in niches, and the fifth with Flamboyant turrets and pinnacles. The delicate Renaissance belfry is noteworthy.

The interior was completed in the 16C but still in the style of the 13C. Four works in particular are worthy of attention; a rare example of a Romanesque altar-table with scalloped decoration (in the axial chapel); the former rood screen (**jubé**★) of 15C date (in the south transept); and the superb 17C carved wooden organ case (**buffet d'orgue**★) in the north transept. The elegance of the Gothic style is apparent in the soaring elevation of the chancel with its delicate lancet windows, in the slender pillars finely moulded only at the level of the capitals, in the height of the great arches surmounted by a triforium which echoes the pattern of the clerestory. The choir stalls (**stalles**★) are by André Sulpice (15C).

◗◗ Musée Fenaille★★ � ◷ *Tue, Thu and Fri 10am-noon, 2-6pm, Wed and Sat: 1-7pm, Sun 2-6pm.* ◷ *Closed Mon, 1 Jan, 1 May, 1 Nov, 25 Dec.* ☞ *3€, no charge 1st Sun in the month.* ☎ *05 65 73 84 30 – prehistoric and medieval collections, archeology.*

Chapelle de **RONCHAMP**★★

MICHELIN MAP 314 H 6

GREEN GUIDE BURGUNDY JURA

Built by **Le Corbusier** (Charles-Édouard Jeanneret 1887-1965), the Chapelle Notre-Dame-du-Haut high up on its hilltop site is one of the few great works of religious architecture produced by the Modern Movement of the early to mid-20C. The characteristically Corbusian use of fluid, interpenetrating space, first deployed in his La Roche Villa at Paris appears here again to great effect.

Visit

The apparent simplicity of the building's curving lines and asymmetrical surfaces can be deceptive, as can the architect's subtle use of light falling from the "periscopes" in the side chapels, filtering in from the base of the convex vault or streaming through the irregular wall-openings which constitute the building's main decoration. Only slowly does one come to appreciate the fusion of feeling and technology which is the measure of the greatness of this unique work of art.

Château de **ROQUETAILLADE**★★

MICHELIN MAP 335 J 8

GREEN GUIDE ATLANTIC COAST

This imposing medieval castle was built in 1306 for Cardinal Gaillard de la Mothe, a nephew of Pope Clement V, and is part of a compound made up of two forts dating from the 12C and the 14C within a walled enclosure. Six enormous round towers, crenellated and pierced with arrow slits, frame a rectangular main structure; two of them flank the entrance. In the courtyard stands a powerful square keep and its turret. The twinned and trefoiled bays recall other castles belonging to Pope Clement; there are also vast vaulted rooms and monumental chimneys.

Visit

◷ *Guided tours* ⬝⬝⬝ *(1hr) 10.30am-7pm; mid-Apr to end Jun and Sep-Oct: 2.30-6pm; Nov to mid Apr: Sun, public holidays and Zone C school holidays 2.30-5pm. Last admission 1hr before closing.* ◷ *Closed 25 Dec.* ☞ *6.50€ (children 4.80€).* ☎ *05 56 76 14 16. www.chateauderoquetaillade.com.*
The bartizans aligned along the curtain wall and, inside, the decorative paintings (including those in the chapel) and the furnishings represent an excellent example of the restoration of medieval buildings as conceived by Viollet-le-Duc during the Second Empire. He was assisted here by the architect E Duthoit.

ROUEN★★★

POPULATION 380 161

MICHELIN MAP 304 G 5

GREEN GUIDE NORMANDY

With its skyline of towers and spires, Rouen is the capital of Lower Normandy, its importance from Roman times onwards being due to its role as the lowest bridging-point on the Seine; the alignment of its two main streets (Rue du Gros-Horloge and Rue des Carmes) still reflects the layout of the early city. Normandy is as much renowned for its architecture as for its orchards and rich pastures, and Rouen, with its heritage of fine buildings and its many museums, offers its visitors a wealth of artistic delights.

▶ **Orient Yourself:** The quays of the Seine River and the progression of streets surrounding it to the north form a sort of semi-circle which defines the city-centre. It is in this vicinity that you will find the three famous examples of Gothic architecture: Notre-Dame cathedral and the churches St-Maclou and St-Ouen. The other bank of the river contains the city's administrative buildings, as well as some more modern residential neighborhoods and shopping centres. Rouen, which is listed as a "Town of Art and history", offers discovery tours for 6.50€ during Jul-Aug and weekends in Spring and Sep. You can find information at the tourist office, on www.vpah.culture.fr or on www.rouentourisme.com.

⊛ **Don't Miss:** Notre-Dame cathedral.

⏱ **Organizing Your Time:** Take 1hr 30min for the cathedral and 30min for a walk through Old Rouen with its beautiful 15C-18C half-timbered houses.

A Bit of History

Literature and art – Although the birthplace of a number of scientists, it is men of letters and artists who have contributed most to Rouen's fame.

Pierre Corneille was born here in 1606. Trained as a lawyer, he subsequently became the first of France's great tragedians. A quartet of plays *(Le Cid, Horace, Cinna and Polyeucte)* celebrate love, courage, clemency and faith; written between 1636 and 1641, their heroes come from a classical mould, noble beings, able to subordinate both emotion and action to the exercise of will.

Gustave Flaubert (1821-80) was the son of Rouen's chief surgeon. Living for reasons of health at the village of Croisset *(west of the city)*, he seems divided between the wish to portray the human soul in all its detail and a taste for vivid expression. His major works include the celebrated *Madame Bovary* (1857), in which the village of Ry (20km – 12mi east) is described under the name of Yonville, *Salammbô*, and *L'Éducation Sentimentale*.

Théodore Géricault (1791-1824) was the Romantic painter par excellence; his feeling for movement and love of the theatrical are displayed to great effect in works such as the *Raft of the Medusa* (in the Louvre, Paris).

Sights

Cathédrale Notre-Dame★★★

⌖ *Illustration see Introduction: Art – Architecture*. This is one of the finest achievements of the French Gothic. Like the great buildings which preceded it towards the end of the 12C, it is in the Lanceolate style, in spite of having been rebuilt after a terrible fire in 1200. Thanks to the generosity of John Lackland, Duke of Normandy as well as King of England, reconstruction was swift and bold in scope; the transepts were extended and the choir enlarged in accordance with the latest techniques. It had originally been intended to place galleries above the arcades, but by the 13C, the development of flying buttresses at Chartres had made them superfluous.

The spaciousness of the interior is striking. The nave has 11 bays and a sexpartite vault, while the lantern-tower, rising 51m – 167ft from the floor of the crossing, achieves a kind of sublime perfection. The choir, with its 14 soaring pillars and delicate triforium, is a masterpiece of harmonious proportion.

The great edifice seems to have been under repair for most of its existence for varied reasons: a consequence of the fire of 1200, the Hundred Years War, another fire in 1514, the misdeeds of the Calvinists, the hurricane of 1683, the French Revolution, the burning-down of the spire in 1822 and the aerial bombardment of the night of 19 April 1944. This most recent disaster threatened the whole structure, and restoration work still goes on today.

Vieux Rouen★★★

The old town's narrow streets, many of them pedestrianised, are lined with more than 800 timber-framed houses, large and small, elegant or picturesquely askew, all characteristic examples of medieval building techniques. They consist of a skeleton of vertical posts and horizontal beams, reinforced by studwork and diagonals. Infilling is with plaster or rubble. Up until 1520, the upper floors were jettied out for reasons of economy and greater floor-space.

Rouen

S. Sauvignier/MICHELIN

Rue St-Romain★★

One of the old town's most fascinating streets, with many timber-framed houses dating from the 15C to the 18C. No 74 is a Gothic building still with its 15C windows.

Église St-Maclou★★

When compared to the cathedral, the church provides striking evidence of the evolution of the Gothic style. It was begun in 1437 and is a fine example of the Flamboyant style at its purest. Nevertheless its decoration is of the Renaissance (doors, stairs, gallery and organ-case). At the north corner of the west front is a fountain with two manikins performing the same act as their counterpart at Brussels, albeit with somewhat less finesse.

Aître St-Maclou★★

This is a rare example of a medieval plague cemetery. It is enclosed by half-timbered buildings decorated with macabre carvings showing the Dance of Death, skulls and crossbones, grave-diggers' tools...

Église St-Ouen★★

🕑 *Mid-Mar to end Oct: Tue-Sat 10am-12.15pm, 2-6pm, Sun 9am-12.15pm, 2-6pm; mid-Jan to mid-Mar and early Nov to mid-Dec: Tue and Sat-Sun 10am-noon, 2-5pm.*
Built in the 14C, this former abbey church marks the peak of achievement of the High Gothic style. Its architect was complete master of the forces acting on his building, leading them at will via ogee arches on to flying buttresses weighted by pinnacles, thence to foundations beyond the walls. The structural problem solved, he was then able to concentrate on designing the shell of the building. With no structural role, walls could become windows, flooding the interior with light and thereby encouraging an increasingly literate congregation to follow the service with the missals now coming into use.

A few years on, and the Gothic had fulfilled its architectural potential; its final phase, the Flamboyant, is a virtuoso style, delighting in ornamental excess rather than structural innovation.

Rue du Gros-Horloge★★

This bustling street, lined with old houses and given over to pedestrians, is one of the city centre's main attractions for visitors. The Gros-Horloge clock **(BZ N)** on its arch has only one hand; next to it is the belfry from the top of which there is a fine view over the city and its surroundings.

Place du Vieux-Marché★

This modern complex occupies the site where Joan of Arc, aged only 19, was burned at the stake following her trial as a heretic; 25 years later she was rehabilitated. In the centre of the square is the great Cross of Rehabilitation, marking the place where Joan of Arc was burnt. There is also a covered market and a church incorporating stained-glass windows **(verrière★★)** of 16C date.

Rouen - Address Book

For coin categories, see the Legend at the back of the guide.

EATING OUT

☺ **Pascaline** – *5 r. de la Poterne* - ☎ *02 35 89 67 44* - *pascaline.rouen@wanadoo.fr* - *reserv. advisable.* Located next to the courthouse, this restaurant with a bistro façade is very nice. Brasserie decor with handsome wood counters, long seats and yellow walls. Choice of attractive fixed-price menus. Book ahead – it's often full.

☺☺ **Les Maraîchers** – *37 pl. du Vieux-Marché* - ☎ *02 35 71 57 73.* A restaurant with Parisian bistro airs in a half-timbered house. Wall seats, a bar, tables set close to one another, old advertising plaques, hat and jug collections – nothing's missing! Improvised cuisine. Norman-style second dining room on the ground floor.

☺☺☺ **La Couronne** – *31 pl. du Vieux-Marché* - ☎ *02 35 71 40 90.* The decor of this 14C house on the market place is simply superb: beams, carved woodwork, hearths and frescos. It is said to be France's oldest inn. True or false? No one knows, but one thing is certain, their *canard rouennais* (Rouen-style duck) is superlative!

☺☺☺ **Le Beffroy** – *15 r. Beffroy* - ☎ *02 35 71 55 27* - ⏰ *closed Sun evening and Tue* - *reserv. required.* This 16C Norman half-timbered house offers the choice between three pretty dining rooms, all equally inviting. A fine address for savouring plentiful fare prepared with quality ingredients.

☺☺☺ **La Marine** – *At the foot of the bridge (D 982) - 76430 Tancarville* - ☎ *02 35 39 77 15* - *la-marine@wanadoo.fr* - ⏰ *closed 20 Jul to 24 Aug, Sat lunch, Sun evening and Mon.* From the gardens along the Seine to the boats ascending the river to the Tancarville suspension bridge, the landscape is to be thoroughly relished! Fish and shellfish are the stars of the table. Garden and terrace in summer.

☺☺☺☺ **La Butte** – *69 rte de Paris - 76240 Bonsecours - 3.5km/2.2mi SE of Rouen along N 14* - ☎ *02 35 80 43 11* - ⏰ *closed 1-27 Aug, Sun-Mon.* This 17C coaching inn, named after the Butte Montmartre in Paris, is predictably Norman: half-timbered façade, paved courtyard, and inviting, plush dining and drawing rooms. A fine place to appreciate very traditional cuisine.

WHERE TO STAY

☺ **Hôtel des Carmes** – *33 pl. des Carmes* - ☎ *02 35 71 92 31* - *h.des.carmes@mcom.fr* - *12 rooms* - 🍴. Situated in the town centre, not far from the cathedral, this hotel is an appealing halt. The delightfully decorated reception area hints of Bohemia, and the clutter-free bedrooms are charming and well fitted out. A very good address for budget-conscious travellers.

☺ **Le Panorama Bed and Breakfast** – *282 chemin du Panorama, 76480 Duclair* - ☎ *02 35 37 68 84* - ⏰ *closed Nov through Feb school holidays - 4 rooms.* This 1930s villa deserves its name: the view on the winding Seine is remarkable. The brightly coloured rooms are pleasant; lovely view from the breakfast room, charming little garden.

☺☺ **Hôtel Versan** – *3 r. Jean-Lecanuet* - ☎ *02 35 07 77 07* - *hotel-versanrouen@aol.com - 34 rooms* - 🍴. A practical address on a busy boulevard not far from the town hall. The rooms are all similar, functional and well equipped.

☺☺☺ **Hôtel Dandy** – *93 bis r. Cauchoise* - ☎ *02 35 07 32 00* - *contact@hotels-rouen.net* - ⏰ *closed 26 Dec to 2 Jan - 18 rooms* - 🍴. Situated in a pedestrian street downtown, close to place du Vieux-Marché, this little hotel decorated with care has a certain charm. The rooms, rather too cluttered for some tastes, are quite cosy. Breakfast served in a pretty little room.

ON THE TOWN

La Luna – *26 r. St-Étienne-des-Tonneliers* - ☎ *02 35 88 77 18* - *cristolaluna@hotmail.com* - ⏰ *Thu-Sat 7pm-5am.* A tropical Cuban night club right in the centre of town. Currently very much in vogue, this colourful discotheque decorated with frescoes and plants vibrates to a salsa rhythm every night. Electric atmosphere.

Le Bateau Ivre – *17 r. des Sapins* - ☎ *02 35 70 09 05* - ⏰ *Wed-Sat 10pm-4am - closed Aug.* Ever on the lookout for new talents, this bar has been livening up Rouen night life for the past 20 years. Concerts Fridays and Saturdays, ballads and poetry Thursdays, café-theatre or French songs Tuesday evenings. A few programmes are available at the tourist office.

Bar de la Crosse – *53 r. de l'Hôpital* - ☎ *02 35 70 16 68* - ⏰ *Tue-Sat 9am-9pm* - ⏰ *closed early to mid-Aug and public holidays.* When spending time in Rouen, one must pay a visit to this small, unpretentious bar. It owes its fine reputation to its singular atmosphere; between concerts and exhibits, laughter abounds, and it isn't unusual to see tourists and regulars chatting here like old friends.

Big Ben Pub – *95 bis r. du Gros-Horloge* - ☎ *02 35 88 44 50* - ⏰ *Tue-Sat noon-2am, Mon 6pm-2am.* A visit to this pub located beneath the Gros-Horloge is a must. Whether you're having a beer at the ground-floor bar, listening to rock on the second floor or singing on the third, the ambience is guaranteed! Snacks and light meals.

La Boîte à Bières – *35 r. Cauchoise* - ☎ *02 35 07 76 47* - ⏰ *Tue-Sat 3pm-2am* - ⏰ *closed 2 weeks in Aug.* This handsome half-timbered house is a tavern specialized in beer and ale, with a wide range of Belgian brews and 10 different brands on draught. Student clientele, friendly atmosphere. Theme evenings from October to June.

Taverne St-Amant – *11 r. St-Amant -* ☎ *02 35 88 51 34 -* 🕐 *Tue-Fri 11am-4pm, 7pm-2am, Mon and Sat 7pm-2am -* 🕐 *closed 3 weeks in Aug*. Transformed into a bar nearly 30 years ago, this 17C house attracts painters, writers, actors and other regular patrons. Convivial atmosphere. Popular songs evening the last Thursday of the month.

SHOWTIME

Théâtre Duchamp-Villon – *Centre St-Sever, BP 1033 -* ☎ *02 35 18 28 10 - www.theatreduchampvillon.com -* 🕐 *ticket office Mon-Fri 1-5.30pm - consult programme -* 🕐 *closed Jul-Aug and public holidays*. The programme of this newly renovated municipal theatre is deliberately eclectic and international: dramatic creations, contemporary music, jazz, French songs, world music, modern and urban dance, children's shows, movie festivals, conferences, new circus, humour.

Théâtre de l'Écharde – *16 r. Flahaut -* ☎ *02 35 15 33 05 - tickets: at the theatre before performance -* 🎫 *4.50/9€*. Theatre with 100 seats where the troupe's creations and shows for young theatre-goers are performed.

Théâtre des Deux Rives – *48 r. Louis Ricard -* ☎ *02 35 70 22 82 - jean.marc.devaux@theatredes2rives.com - consult programme -* 🕐 *ticket office: Tue-Sat 2-7pm -* 🕐 *closed Sun-Mon and Jul-Aug -* 🎫 *19€*. Classical and modern theatre.

SHOPPING

Faïencerie Augy-Carpentier – *26 r. St-Romain -* ☎ *02 35 88 77 47 -* 🕐 *Mon 9am-8pm, Tue-Sat 9am-7pm - tour of the workshop by appointment*. The last handmade and hand-decorated earthenware workshop in Rouen! They offer copies of many traditional motifs on white and pink backgrounds, from blue monochrome to multicoloured, and from lambrequin to cornucopia. Personalized pieces available.

Hardy –*22 pl. du Vieux-Marché -* ☎ *02 35 71 81 55 -* 🕐 *daily except Sun-Mon 9am-1pm, 2.30-7.30pm*. In this alluring delicatessen, the Hardis offer Rouen specialities such as terrine de canard, duck being a highly prized fowl in this city (also known for its mutton). Mr Hardi's andouilles de Vire and his Caen tripe cooked in calvados and cider, specialities from Normandy, have clinched his reputation.

Chocolatier Auzou – *163 r. du Gros-Horloge -* ☎ *02 35 70 59 31 -* 🕐 *Mon 2-7.15pm, Tue-Sat 9.30am-7.15pm, Sun 9.30am-1pm; Jul-Aug: closed Sun.* 🕐 *Closed 1 Jan and 1 May*. Located in a half-timbered house, this renowned chocolatier will tempt you with his specialities, such as Les Larmes de Jeanne d'Arc (Joan of Arc's Tears: lightly roasted almonds covered with nougatine and chocolate) or L'Agneau Rouennais (a sort of sponge cake) and candied apples.

MARKETS

Place Saint-Marc – Tue, Fri and Sat 8am-6.30pm.

Place des Emmurés – Tue and Sat 8am-6.30pm.

Place du Vieux-Marché – Daily except Mon 6am-1.30pm.

LEISURE

Cavelier de la Salle – ☎ 02 35 52 54 43. Tour of the harbour (under certain conditions) by boat. Info: Office de Tourisme or Port Autonome de Rouen (public relations and communications branch).

Musée des Beaux-Arts★★★

♿ 🕐 *Daily 10am-6pm (South wing closed 1-2pm).* 🕐 *Closed Tue and certain public holidays.* 🎫 *3€, no charge 1st Sun in the month.* ☎ *02 35 71 28 40.*

The museum was renovated in 1992 but until all the work is completed, collections are limited to the 16C and 17C. Among the pictures on display, visitors should see Gérard David's Virgin and Saints, an oil painting on wood, one of the masterpieces of Flemish Primitive art, as well as several choice pieces from the French School: *Diana Bathing* by François Clouet, The *Concert of Angels* by Philippe de Champaigne, and *Venus Arming Aeneas* by Nicolas Poussin. Other outstanding works from European countries are *The Adoration of the Shepherds* by Rubens, *St Barnabé Healing the Sick* by Veronese, and especially Democritus by Velasquez.

Musée de la Céramique★★

🕐 *Wed-Mon 10am-1pm, 2-6pm.* 🕐 *Closed Tue and certain public holidays.* 🎫 *2.30€, no charge 1st Sun in the month.* ☎ *02 35 50 31 74.*

In 1530, a citizen of Rouen, **Masséot Abaquesne**, succeeded in making faience, hitherto a secret process which had originated in Faenza in Italy in the 14C. Rouen's moment of glory in the production of this most aristocratic of ceramics came in the more settled times which followed the troubled start to the 17C. It was at this time that the Poterat workshop flourished.

The liking for chinoiserie and lambrequin ornament, together with royalty's desire to replace outmoded metal plates and dishes with ceramics (🕯 *see Index*), helped assure Rouen's success with ewers, fountains, spice pots... The fine bust of Apollo of c 1740 from the Fouquay workshop exemplifies both taste and technique.

◖◗ Palais de Justice★★ *Contact the tourist office.* Musée Le Secq des Tournelles★★ 🕓 *Wed-Mon 10am-1pm, 2-6pm.* 🕓 *Closed Tue and certain public holidays.* ⊜ *2.30€, no charge 1st Sun in the month.* ☎ *02 35 88 42 92* – wrought-ironwork. Musée des Antiquités de la Seine Maritime. Église St-Godard. Panorama★★★ from Côte-Ste-Catherine *Unaccompanied tours Sat 2-7pm.*

Jardin des Plantes★ 🕓 *Daily 8am to dusk. Greenhouse: daily 9-11.30pm, 1.30-4.30pm. Call 2 weeks in advance for guided tour.* 🕓 *Closed public holidays. No charge.* ☎ *02 32 18 21 30.*

ROUTE DES CRÊTES★★★

MICHELIN MAP 315 G 8, F 8, F 9 AND G 9

GREEN GUIDE ALSACE LORRAINE CHAMPAGNE

In the First World War, the French and German armies confronted each other along the old frontier between the two countries formed by the crest-line of the Vosges. Hugging the ridge is the strategic north-south road planned by French military engineers to serve the front; today it forms a fine scenic route, the Vosges Scenic Road, running for 63km – 39 miles from the Bonhomme Pass (Col du Bonhomme) in the north to Thann in the south. It offers the visitor a splendid introduction to the varied landscapes of these uplands, which include the sweeping pasturelands of the summits, an array of lakes, and the broad valleys of the Fisch and the Thur.

Driving Tour

Col du Bonhomme
949m – 3 114ft high, this is the pass linking the provinces of Alsace and Lorraine.

Col de la Schlucht
1 139m – 3 737ft. This is the steepest, but also one of the busiest of the routes through the Vosges. The eastern slopes are subject to intense erosion because of the gradient of the torrential rivers; at a distance of only 9km – 5mi from the pass, the town of **Munster**★ lies 877m – 2 877ft below, while Colmar, 26km – 16mi away is 1 065m – 3 494ft lower.

Hohneck★★★
1 362m – 4 469ft. Rising near the central point of the range, this is one of the most visited of the Vosges summits. From the top there are superb **views**★★★; to the east, the **Munster Valley**★★ plunges steeply down towards the broad expanses of the Alsace plain, while to the west is the Lorraine plateau, cut into by the valley of the Vologne.

Grand Ballon★★★
1 424m – 4 672ft. The Grand Ballon forms the highest point of the Vosges. From the top *(30min round trip on foot)* the magnificent **panorama**★★★ extends over the southern part of the range, whose physiognomy can be fully appreciated. The eastern and western slopes are quite unlike each other; the drop to the Alsace plain is abrupt, while to the west the land falls away gently to the Lorraine plateau. Glacial action in the Quaternary era is responsible for many features like the massive rounded humps of the summits *(ballons)*, and the morainic lakes in the blocked valleys. Above the tree-line, the forest clothing the hillsides gives way to the short grass of the wide upland grazing grounds known as the Hautes-Chaumes.

Vieil-Armand★★
The war memorial (monument national) marks one of the most bitterly-contested battlefields of the First World War.

ROUTE DES GRANDES ALPES★★★

MICHELIN MAPS 332, 334, 340 AND 341

GREEN GUIDE FRENCH ALPS

Among the many routes which invite the visitor to explore the French Alps, this high-altitude road is the most famous. Rarely far from the frontier, the Great Alpine Road links Lake Geneva with the Riviera, crossing 25 passes in all as it leaps from valley to valley. It is open from end to end during the summer months only.

Two-day programme

By driving hard it is indeed possible to get from Thonon to Menton in two days, but to do so would be to deprive oneself of a number of sights which in themselves would make the trip worthwhile; they include Chamonix with the Aiguille du Midi and the Vallée Blanche, La Grave and the splendid viewpoint at Le Chazelet, St-Véran...

Five-day programme

–Thonon-Beaufort: *144km – 90mi – allow 5hr 30min including sightseeing.*

–Beaufort-Val d'Isère: *71km – 44mi – allow 3hr including sightseeing.*

–Val d'Isère-Briançon: *180km – 112mi – allow 7hr 30min including sightseeing.*

–Briançon-Barcelonnette: *133km – 83mi – allow 6hr 30min including sightseeing.*

–Barcelonnette-Menton: *206mi – 128mi – allow 6hr including sightseeing.*

A Bit of History

The great arc of the Alps running from Vienna to Nice was formed in Tertiary times by earth-movements which brought the plateau-continent of Africa and the Hercynian foreland of Europe closer together, subjecting the deep sedimentary beds laid down in the geosyncline between them to intense pressure, uplifting, folding and transporting them. The High Alps (Grandes Alpes) in France comprise two main divisions. In a central position rise ancient crystalline massifs, remains of the Hercynian system which were eroded, then covered by sedimentary rocks in Secondary times. The shocks of the Tertiary age uplifted them violently; subsequent denudation has left a varied pattern of rounded summits and dramatic pinnacled peaks.

The sparsely populated landscapes of this part of the Alps with their forests of larch are lit by intense sunshine from the clearest of skies. To the east of the crystalline massifs lies the Sedimentary Zone, whose uplifted rocks, often metamorphosed under extreme pressure and heat, have formed broad sunlit valleys which enjoy a mild climate.

During Quaternary times, the landscape was refashioned by the erosive powers of great rivers and by four successive glaciations.

At the foot of the northern High Alps is the Sub-Alpine Furrow (Sillon alpin); running roughly north-south, this broad valley some 177km – 110 miles long is fed by the mountain streams draining into the Isère and the Drac; it forms one of the most important communication routes in the French Alps. The Durance valley plays a similar role in the southern Alps.

The High Alps are approached via a more or less continuous zone of rugged calcareous mountains, the Pre-Alps, which reach their widest extent in the south.

Driving Tour: Thonon to Menton *734km – 458mi*

Thonon★★

From the Place du Château the view extends over the great sweep of Lake Geneva **(Lac Léman★★★)**. On the Swiss shore to the north rise the terraces of the great Lavaux vineyard, and beyond are the mountains of the Vaudois Alps (to the east) and the Jura. Saint Francis of Sales once preached in St Hippolytus' Church (Église St-Hippolyte); its vault **(voûte★)** has retained its original stucco and 18 painted medallions, together with the stucco decoration of its false pillars (visible from the adjoining basilica), all done by the Italian craftsmen who restored the interior in Rococo style in the 18C.

The road rises in a series of steps through the damp beech woodland of the gorges cut by the River Dranse de Morzine. This marks the transition between the gently rolling hill country fringing the great lake and the **Chablais★★** massif, a complex of high ridges and peaks, with rich pastures grazed by Abondance cattle. The most spectacular part of the route is known as the Devil's Bridge Gorge **(Gorges du Pont du Diable★★)**, marked by a number of rock-falls, one of which has formed the bridge attributed to the Evil One.

Morzine★★

The valleys around the resort are dotted with hamlets; the chalets have patterned balconies. All around grow sombre forests of spruce.

After the pass at Les Gets, the small industrial town of Tanninges marks the beginning of the **Faucigny**★★ country. Drained by the Giffre, this is a landscape of pastures and sprucewoods, fashioned by the action of glacial moraines on calcareous rocks deposited here far from their point of origin.

Cluses

The town commands the most important lateral valley *(cluse)* in the French Alps. The River Arve has cut down directly through the folded rocks of the **Aravis** range to make its gorge. Clocks and watches and precision metal products are made here.

Above Cluses, the broad glacial valley of the Arve separates the Chablais and the Giffre (to the northeast) from the Aravis range (to the southwest), also known as the **Genevois**. The upland Sallanches basin is bounded to the north by the dramatic peaks of a number of ranges, but dominating all is the great mass of Mont Blanc itself, the "Giant of the Alps".

La Clusaz★★

The most important ski resort in the **Massif des Aravis** owes its name to the deep gorge or cluse, downstream of it, through which the Nom torrent gushes. The village, situated in the middle of pine forests and mountain pasture, is tightly huddled around the big church characterised by its onion-dome tower. The jagged outlines of the Aravis mountains can be seen stretching away into the distance.

In the summer, La Clusaz offers an excellent setting for walking, and in winter this well-equipped resort provides plenty of thrills for ski enthusiasts.

At the top of the climb out of the valley, Val d'Arly, the Notre-Dame de Bellecombe road gives good views, first of the whole Aravis massif, then of the wooded gorges cut by the Arly.

Col des Saisies

It is at this point that the route leaves the Sub-Alpine Furrow (Sillon alpin); from here as far as St-Martin-d'Entraunes to the south of the Cayolle Pass (Col de Cayolle), its course lies entirely within the High Alps (Grandes Alpes).

The broad depression of the Saisies Pass, 1 633m – 5 358ft high, is one of the most characteristic alpine grazing grounds to be seen along the route; it is browsed by sturdy little reddish-brown cattle as well as by the dark-brown Tarines breed and the white-spotted Abondances. The landscape is studded with innumerable chalets.

Beaufort

This little crossroads town (its church has fine woodcarvings and interesting sculptures) has given its name to the **Beaufortain**★★ country, an area of folded limestone beds on a base of ancient crystalline rocks. Virtually continuous forest cover forms a background to sweeping alpine pastures. Above the 1 450m – 4 750ft contour, the pastoral economy is marked by the seasonal movement of the herds up and down the slopes. The village of **Boudin**★ *(7km – 4mi south)* is particularly picturesque.

Cormet de Roselend★

This long valley, 1 900m – 6 200ft high, links the Roselend and Chapieux valleys. It is a vast, treeless, lonely place, dotted with rocks and a few shepherds' huts.

A rushing mountain stream descends the steep valley, **Vallée des Chapieux**★, in a series of abrupt steps towards **Bourg-St-Maurice**. This strategically-sited town commands the routes coming down from the Beaufortain country and the Little St Bernard (Petit-St-Bernard) and Iseran Passes. Around it is the **Tarentaise**★★ country of the upper Isère valley where transhumance is still practised. By the time the route reaches Ste-Foy in the upper Tarentaise, the landscape has become decidedly more mountainous in character. The Tignes valley (Val de Tignes) is characterised by a striking series of gorges and glacial bars; the avalanche protection works are impressive, as is the Tignes Dam **(Barrage de Tignes**★★**)**, a major engineering feat of the 1950s.

Val d'Isère★★★

In its high valley 1 000m – 3 300ft above Bourg-St-Maurice, this is the most important place in the upper Tarentaise. With an excellent sunshine record, the resort is surrounded by splendid mountain landscapes; to the south and west are the glaciers and peaks (several of them rising to more than 3 500m – 11 500ft) of the Vanoise National Park, an important habitat for alpine flora and fauna, much favoured by walkers.

As the road climbs amid the crystalline massifs, it affords views of the imposing peaks of the Gran Paradiso in Italy to the left and of the Vanoise massif (Grande Motte peak) to the right.

Col d'Iseran★

2 770m – 9 088ft. The road across this high pass was built as recently as 1936; it is the only link between the Tarentaise and the **Maurienne** country to the south. The latter region centres on the long valley of the River Arc; industry is more important here than agriculture, with metal-working and electro-chemical plants at places like Bonneval, Lansevillard, Modane, St-Michel-de-Maurienne and St-Jean-de-Maurienne. The location of settlements has been determined by the sharp breaks in slope marked by glacial bars.

Modane

This is a border town, sited at the French end of rail and road tunnels leading to Italy. The 13 657m – 8.5 mile rail link (completed in 1872) was begun on the initiative of the Sardinian monarchy, which wished to unite those parts of its domain lying to either side of the Alpine barrier. The road tunnel which came into service in 1980 is shorter – 12 870m – 8 miles.

At Valloire, the route once more enters the ancient Hercynian mountains and begins to climb towards the Galibier Pass.

Col du Galibier★★★

2 642m – 8 668ft. From the viewing table there is a superb panorama which takes in the Maurienne country (to the north), and the Pelvoux region (to the south), which is separated from the Briançonnais country by the high ridge of the Massif des Écrins. The pass marks the dividing line between the northern and southern part of the French Alps.

At the pass, **Col du Lautaret**★★, with its fine views of the Meije mountains, turn right in the direction of La Grave in the Romanche valley, then turn left at the entrance to the second tunnel.

Oratoire du Chazelet★★★

From the viewing table, the view extends over the high peaks of the Écrins National Park from the Col des Ruillans on the right to the broken ridges of the Meije (including le Doigt de Dieu – The Finger of God – at 3 974m – 13 025ft). The upper course of the glacier, fed by frequent snowfall, is of a staggering whiteness.

La Grave★

The village has a particularly fine **site**★★ in the Romanche valley at the foot of the Meije. A two-stage cable-car ride takes the visitor to a height of 3 200m – 10 500ft at the col on the western flank of Mont du Râteau, from where there are unforgettable views over the Meije and the Écrins glaciers.

Back at the Col du Lauteret, the route now enters the southern part of the French Alps. At Monêtier in the Guisanne valley, it re-enters the sedimentary zone of the High Alps; oak, beech and ash reappear, the valleys open out and the whole landscape takes on a lighter air.

Briançon★★ – 🍂 See BRIANÇON.

Col d'Izoard★★

2 361m – 7 746ft. The pass is in a desolate setting fringed by dramatic peaks. From the viewing tables magnificent views extend over the Briançonnais to the north and the Queyras country to the south.

The road descends in a series of hairpin bends through a strange landscape of screes and jagged rocks known as the **Casse Déserte**★★. At this high altitude, the processes of erosion are greatly accelerated by the extremes of temperature to which the rocks are exposed.

The high **Queyras**★★ country is centred on the valley of the River Guil. Closed off downstream from the outside world by a series of narrow gorges, and cut off from main communication routes, it has fine examples of alpine houses. Above Château-Queyras, the valley sides are sharply differentiated; the gentler south-facing slopes are covered with well-watered meadows, while the north-facing slopes grow only larches and Arolla pines.

St-Véran★★

Lying between the 1 990m – 6 530ft contour and the 2 040m – 6 690ft contour, this is the highest community in Europe. Its chalets, timber-built on a basement of schist, are a unique example of adaptation to the rigours of a high-altitude mountain life which combines arable cultivation and grazing, forestry, and the exercise of craft skills during the long winters. The south-facing dwellings are sited in groups, most of them with hay-barns and the balconies on which cereals are ripened. The village has a strange sculpture showing Christ's Agony.

The little town of **Guillestre**, with its church characterised by a beautiful porcha is situated at the end of the **Combe du Queyras** ★★, a canyon carved out by the clear and abundant waters of the River Guil.

Embrun★

24km – 15mi southwest of Guillestre. High up on its terrace overlooking the River Durance as it emerges from the mountains, the little town was once a cathedral city, the seat of an archbishop. From the Place de l'Archevêché there are fine views over the valley slopes with their well-cultivated terraced fields. The torrents entering the main valley have spread their debris over its floor in alluvial fans, forcing some of the local roads to follow a tortuous alignment. The upper slopes have been gouged by deep ravines, while dominating the scene are the bare and sombre crests of the high mountains.

The former **Notre-Dame Cathedral**, the finest church in the whole of the Dauphiné Alps, dates from the close of the 12C; it has fine black and white marble stonework and the **north porch** ★ « Le Réal », in North Italian style, is supported on pretty pink columns.

Col de Vars

2 111m – 6 893ft. This pass forms the gateway to the Ubaye valley. The landscape is made up of highly laminated schists; the valley floor, littered with boulders and studded with gloomy ponds, is grazed by flocks of sheep.

Beyond the pass, the south-facing slopes with their scattered hamlets are given over entirely to stock-farming. In its upper reaches, the River Ubaye has cut deeply into the dark schists; its course is frequently impeded by the alluvial fans of the side-torrents which feed it. Near La Condamine, the 19C Fort Tournoux seems part of the high rock on which it is built. After Jausiers, the route enters the Barcelonnette basin; the valley pastures are interspersed with woodland and the scene becomes altogether more cheerful.

Barcelonnette★

The little capital of the Ubaye district was laid out as a bastide on a regular plan in 1231 by Raimond Béranger, Count of Barcelona. It belonged to the House of Savoy until passing to France under the provisions of the Treaty of Utrecht in 1713. On the edge of town are the houses of the "Barcelonnettes" or "Mexicans", locals who made their fortunes in the textile trade in Mexico before returning home. A museum, **Musée de la Vallée**, traces the history of the migrations.

At this point, those visitors who are already familiar with the Cayolle Pass (Col de la Cayolle) can get to the central Var valley

View of La Meije from the Oratoire du Chazelet

via the Restefond Pass (Col de Restefond), the Bonnette Peak (Cime de la Bonnette) (involving an extra climb of 535m – 1 755ft), and the Tinée valley, or alternatively via the Allos Pass (Col d'Allos) and the upper Verdon (36km – 22mi further). See details below.

The road climbs around the flank of Mont Pelat, the highest (3 035m – 10 164ft) peak in the Provence Alps.

Col de la Cayolle★★

2 327m – 7 635ft. This pass links the Ubaye country and the Upper Verdon to the upper reaches of the Var. From the top there are views over the deep valley of the Var towards the Grasse Pre-Alps in the far distance.

The Upper valley of the River Var★★

The source of the Var is on the left as the road drops away from the pass to follow the river as it threads its way through the sombre mountains. At St-Martin-d'Entraunes, the route passes from the High Alps into the sedimentary zone again, this time into the Pre-Alps of Provence. Downstream from Villeneuve, the clear water coursing through the drainage channels draws the visitor's attention to the changes that take place in the landscape of the countryside around Guillaume.

Gorges de Daluis★★

These deep gorges have been cut by the river into thick beds of red porphyry and Urgonian limestone, giving striking colour effects. The road from **Guillaume** to **Beuil** leads to the **Gorges du Cians** situated in the upper stretch of the river Var.

The road climbs steadily to the Col de Valberg offering varied views of the different sides of the valley: woody to the north, compared to the southern one covered with vineyards and fruit trees. The descent towards **Roubion** from the **Col de Couilloie** (1 678m – 5 503ft) reveals the valleys of **La Vionèse** and **La Tinée**.

After the impressive **site**★★ of Roubion (the village is perched 1 300m – 4 264ft up on a ridge), the road travels through a red schistose landscape, enlivened by several waterfalls.

Roure★

This village is characterised by its architectural unity: houses with red schist walls and limestone tile roofs *(lauze)*.

The route then follows the river Vionèse until it flows into the river Tinée at **St-Sauveur-sur-Tinée**. Outside the village, on the left, a small road leads to the striking **site**★ of **Ramplas**, a village built on a ridge.

La Bolline

This pleasant summer resort is situated in the middle of a chestnut grove.

La Colmiane

The chalets and hotels of this winter sports resort are set amidst a wonderful larch forest. From the **Col de St-Martin**, there is a possibility of taking a chairlift up to the **Pic de Colmiane**★★ (beautiful **panorama**★★ from the top).

St-Martin-Vésubie★

From this famous mountaineering centre, visitors can go rambling in the **Vallon du Boréon**★★ or the **Vallon de la Madone de Fenestre**★.

Roquebillière

This large village has been rebuilt six times since the 6C.

La Bollène-Vésubie

The concentric streets of this peaceful village, in the middle of a beautiful chestnut grove, converge on the church, which crowns the hill. The forest, Fôret de Turiniaa, which spreads across the valleys of the Vésubie and of the Bévéra, demarcates the southern border of the Parc national du Mercantour.

Le Massif de l'Authion★★

North of the **Col de Turini**, this massif constitutes a wonderful natural fortress which seems to stand guard over the roads between the Vésubie and Roya valleys. This strategic value has caused it to be, throughout the centuries, the stage for several conflicts. In April 1945, it was the last sector of France to be liberated. A stele commemorates the fierceness of the combat.

After crossing the forest of Turini, the river Bévéra winds its way towards the **Gorges du Piaon**★★ where the corniche road overlooks the river. Before reaching the gorges, the road goes through **Moulinet**, a charming village set in a verdant valley before passing the **Chapelle de Notre-Dame-La-Menour** with its Renaissance façade on the left.

Sospel★

This Alpine resort was once a bishopric, during the Great Schism. On the Nice road, 1 km – 0.6 miles from the centre of the village, stands the **Fort St-Roch** one of the last elements of the "Alpine Maginot line" built in the 1930s.

The road follows the old railway line which used to link Sospel to Menton, along the course of the Merlanson, a tributary of the Bévéra. On the opposite side of the valley, the road to Nice via the **Col de Braus** winds its way, amidst olive groves, towards the capital of the French Riviera.

Menton★★ – 🕭 See MENTON.

ROUTE NAPOLÉON★★

MICHELIN MAP 341 B 5-D 6

GREEN GUIDE FRENCH RIVIERA

This scenic highway (Napoleon's Highway – N 85) runs from the Mediterranean shore at Golfe-Juan to Grenoble, following the route taken by Napoleon on his return from Elba in 1815. Inaugurated in 1932, it leads from the Riviera north-westwards through the southern Pre-Alps and is marked throughout its length by the flying eagle symbol inspired by Napoleon's remark: "The eagle will fly from steeple to steeple until he reaches the towers of Notre-Dame".

The Flight of the Eagle

The Emperor escaped from Elba on 26 February 1815, landing on the beach at Golfe-Juan on 1 March.

2 March: After a brief overnight stop at Cannes, Napoleon and his little troop halted just outside Grasse and then took to the mule tracks of the countryside. The next night was spent at Seranon.

3 March: Midday halt at Castellane and overnight in Barrème.

4 March: The party found its way back onto the main highway at Digne, then passed the night at the Château de Malijai.

5 March: The Emperor lunched at Sisteron, then left the town in an atmosphere of growing enthusiasm. Overnight at Gap.

6 March: At Les Barraques, Napoleon declined the offer of the local peasants to join his force. Overnight at Corps.

7 March: Near Laffrey, the way forward was barred by troops. Ordered to fire, they first hesitated, then broke ranks to shouts of "Vive l'Empereur!" Escorted by the men of the 7th Regiment, Napoleon made his triumphal entry into Grenoble at 7 o'clock in the evening.

Driving Tour: Golfe-Juan to Grenoble

336km – 209mi – allow a whole day. Leading across the southern Pre-Alps to the long valley known as the Sub-Alpine Furrow, the route can be followed throughout the year.

Golfe-Juan

Leave Golfe-Juan by the N7.

Antibes★★

The first settlement here was a trading-post founded by Greek merchants from Marseille in the 4C BC. Reconstructed in the 16C, the castle **(Château Grimaldi)** dates from the 12C, when it was built on the site of a Roman encampment to protect the coast from the incursions of Barbary pirates. Inside, the Picasso Museum **(Musée Picasso** ★**)** has a good selection of the master's works, including drawings, prints and tapestries *(The Lobster, Two Nudes and a Mirror),* as well as paintings *(Still Life with Watermelon)*... The town was purchased from the Grimaldi family by Henri IV because of its strategic position in relation to the Kingdom of Savoy. It was fortified first by François I, then by Vauban. To the west of the **Cap d'Antibes** ★★ stretches the fine sandy beach of Golfe-Juan.

Grasse★★

Prettily located on the slopes of the Grasse Pre-Alps, the old town **(vieille ville** ★**)** has picturesque streets lined with tall Provençal houses. Grasse's most famous son was **Jean-Honoré Fragonard** (1732-1806), the painter best known for his witty depictions of the frivolities of 18C court life. The Salle Fragonarda in the Villa-Musée Fragonard has two of the artist's self-portraits as well as his *Landscape with washerwomen* and *Three Graces.*

C.I. Muzzin/Musée internatinal de la parfumerie, Grasse

For the past three centuries, Grasse has been an important centre of the perfume industry. The products which emerge from the secrecy of the town's laboratories owe much to the sensitivity of certain highly developed "noses". It takes one tonne of jasmine blossom to manufacture just three grammes of the mixture of perfume and wax known as "concrète". Two museums, the **Musée international de la Parfumerie** and the **Musée d'Art et d'Histoire de Provence**, are of interest.

Perfume bottle

To the north of the **Pas de la Faye** with its **view** ★★ over mountains and Mediterranean, the road enters Upper Provence (Haute Provence) through the Seranon valley.

Castellane★

The sheep-grazed valley in which the town is situated is overlooked by the "Roc", a limestone cliff 184m – 604ft high.

The Castellane Pre-Alps extend over a wide area; they consist of a series of bare ridges through which the River Asse has cut its deep valley. To the north of the former cathedral city of Senez lie the Digne Pre-Alps, the most desolate of all the Southern Alps, a harsh landscape with a meagre mantle of garrigue vegetation, deeply scored by the beds of torrents. A complex geological history has produced a series of folded ridges through which the rivers have cut their gorges, as well as long crests of pale rock to the east and broad fertile valleys to the north.

Digne-les-Bains★

Digne spreads out along its valley **site** ★ at the foot of the rise on which its old town is situated. There are dramatic **views** ★ of the whole area from the hill-top village of **Courbons** ★, 6km – 4mi to the north. In the Place General-de-Gaulle is a memorial to **Pierre Gassendi** (1592-1655), born at nearby Champtercier. This natural philosopher was provost of the cathedral here; much of his scientific work was devoted to studying the properties of sound.

At **Malijai**, the route enters the **Durance basin**, an alluvial plain 6km – 4mi wide in places, lying between the Valensole plateau to the east and the Vaucluse to the west. The Durance is the great river of the southern Alps, tracing its meanders through the gravel terraces on which a prosperous agricultural pattern has developed, favoured by the mildness of the climate. The best crops are grown on those sites which have been effectively drained; the wetter areas are occupied by woodland.

Sisteron★★ – ☾ *See SISTERON.*

Gap★

Gap is pleasantly sited in the valley carved out by the glacier which was the ancestor of the Durance. The town's prosperity was built on the rich soils of its agricultural hinterland, one of the most fertile areas of the southern Alps. Founded by the Gauls, Gap became a staging-post along the Roman road from Turin to Valence, then a fortified cathedral town.

The **Col Bayard** (1 246m – 4 088ft) links the southern and northern Alps. From the viewing table at Chauvet on the south side of the pass the view extends over the valley around Gap. To the north is the beginning of the Sub-Alpine Furrow which the road enters by way of the Drac valley, hollowed out in the beds of schist by the action of the Quaternary glaciers. This is an ancient highway, once travelled by merchants on their way to the fairs at St-Bonnet. Terraced villages line the route, their roofs tiled in brown stone. To the left are the precipitous slopes and savage peaks of the Dévoluy Massif, to the right the Valgaudemar valley threading its way deep into the Écrins National Park.

Corps

A small bustling town in the Sub-Alpine Furrow. The road passes through areas of well-cultivated farmland interrupted by glacial bars, one of which has been used in the siting of the Sautet Dam (**Barrage de Sautet**★★ – *5km – 3 miles west*), with its deep lake hemmed in by high canyon-like walls; far below its surface is the hidden confluence of the Drac with the Souloise.

Around La Mure, the Trièves country is overlooked by the broad summit of Mont Aiguille (2 086m – 6 880ft), also known as the "unclimbable mountain" though it was actually conquered as long ago as 1492.

Laffrey★

Just south of the village is the spot known as the **"Prairie de la Rencontre**★**"** where the vain attempt was made to bar Napoleon's progress northwards. The road now descends towards **Vizille**★ and Grenoble.

Abbaye de **ST-BENOÎT-SUR-LOIRE**★★

MICHELIN MAP 318 K 5

GREEN GUIDE CHÂTEAUX OF THE LOIRE

In AD 675, the original abbey founded here on a river terrace well above flood level was presented with the remains of St Benedict and of his sister, St Scholastica, brought all the way from Monte Cassino in Italy. Hitherto known simply as Fleury Abbey, the monastery now rededicated itself to the founder of Western monasticism (St Benedict = St-Benoît in French). The abbey's influence waxed at the beginning of the 9C with the appointment of Theodulf by the Emperor Charlemagne; this great abbot served his master by introducing the study of the Scriptures and of Roman law, and by promoting the conservation of ancient texts.

Visit

Basilique★★

🕐 *Mid-Mar to mid-Nov: Mon-Sat 9-11.30am, 3.15-5.30pm, Sun 3.15-5.30pm.* 🕐 *Closed 1st Fri in the month.* ☎ *02 38 35 72 43. www. abbaye-fleury.com.*

Built between 1067 and 1108, the Romanesque basilica has a fine crypt (**crypte**★) with a double ambulatory and a massive central pillar containing the relics of St Benedict.

The choir (**chœur**★★) is remarkable for its paving (a Roman mosaic brought here from Italy) and for the elegant arcading setting off the plain walls of its elevation, while the crossing carries the cupola of the central bell-tower on superimposed squinches.

Outside, the belfry porch (**clocher-porche**★★) is one of the finest examples of Romanesque art in France. Originally free-standing, it was joined to the basilica when the nave was extended in the middle of the 12C. It evokes in stone the vision of Paradise as described in the Apocalypse of St John,

Porch of the basilica, St-Benoît-sur-Loire

Studio 3Bis/MICHELIN

with three gateways facing each point of the compass (north, south, east and west), ever-open to receive the souls of the elect. A total of 16 sturdy pillars with engaged columns have beautifully carved capitals (c1120) depicting the same theme.

Excursions

Germigny-des-Prés★

5.5km – 3mi northwest. The much-restored church is the oratory (**oratoire**) which Abbot Theodulf built for himself. It is a typical example of Carolingian architecture of the 9C, with an unusual plan, alabaster window-panes filtering the light and above all a remarkable **mosaic**★★ in the dome of the east apse; this conforms to the iconography of the time, which rejected all forms of personal representation of the divinity. Its design centres on the Ark of the Covenant which symbolises the figure of Christ and which is surmounted by two cherubim flanked by two archangels.

ST-BERTRAND-DE-COMMINGES★★

POPULATION 217

MICHELIN MAP 343 B 6

GREEN GUIDE LANGUEDOC ROUSSILLON TARN GORGES

King Herod is supposed to have spent his years of exile in the substantial town which had been founded here in 72 BC by Pompey. In AD 585 the Burgundians descended on the place and laid it waste. For centuries the site lay abandoned, until in 1073 St Bernard saw its potential for the building of a cathedral and monastery. Here the rules of the religious reforms of Pope Gregory VII were applied, making the little city the spiritual centre of Comminges, endowing the awkwardly-shaped county (sandwiched as it was between the territories belonging to the House of Foix-Béarn and dotted with enclaves) with a religious significance far outweighing its political importance.

The sanctuaries of this area, with their wealth of highly-prized relics, were often adorned with sculpture, which here reaches a high point in its development. The Romanesque portal of the cathedral is made up of several independently sculpted panels showing the Adoration of the Magi and a figure of St Bertrand without a halo (i.e. before his canonisation in 1218), recalling the work of the School of Toulouse at St Sernin. The cloisters (**cloître**★★) are built over the 12C-15C ramparts; the south side is open, giving fine views over the Upper Garonne countryside, and there is a famous pillar in primitive style with statues of the four Evangelists.

Visit

Cathédrale Ste-Marie-de-Comminges★

Paid access to the cloisters and on the right of the church (treasury, choir stalls) Free access to the rest of the cathedral. ⏱ *May-Sep: 9am-7pm; Feb-Apr and Oct: 10am-noon, 2-6pm; Jan and Nov-Dec: 10am-noon, 2-5pm. No visit Sun morning and religious holidays. Call ahead for guided tour (cathedral, terraces, and treasury).* ☎ *05 61 89 04 91.*
There are splendid **choir stalls**★★ of 1535 in Italian Renaissance style; features to note particularly include the bishop's throne, a Jesse Tree and a Madonna and Child.

Basilique St-Just★

At Valcabrère, 2km – 1mi northwest. Standing in isolation among the cypresses of a country cemetery, the church was built in the 11C-12C with materials from an older building. Four fine statue-columns grace its north portal, but its most unusual feature is its apse, where a number of triangular niches frame a central opening with a window giving onto a funerary recess.

ST-CLAUDE★

POPULATION 12 704

MICHELIN MAP 321 F 8

GREEN GUIDE BURGUNDY JURA

The historic core of St-Claude sits high up on a site★★ overlooking the meeting-point of the Tacon with the Bienne. Lying as it does in the heart of the Jura forests, the town has long produced wooden articles of all kinds, notably the brier pipes which have been made here for over 200 years (exhibition).

Excursion

Chapeau de Gendarme

8km – 5mi southeast. This geological oddity owes its name to the shape made by the folded beds of limestone. These were originally laid down in Secondary times, but during the Tertiary era were compressed and uplifted at the same time as the

Alps were being formed; they were folded without however being split, and forced upward into dome-like shapes with symmetrical sides, a text-book example of the formation of an anticline.

◐◐ Cathédrale St-Pierre★ – choir stalls★★ – altarpiece★. Place Louis-XI – view★.

Basilique **ST-DENIS**★★

MICHELIN MAP 305 F 7

GREEN GUIDE NORTHERN FRANCE AND THE PARIS REGION

St-Denis is an important manufacturing centre immediately to the north of Paris. It owes its name to the great missionary who became the first bishop of Paris when it was still Roman Lutetia. St Denis was beheaded at Montmartre around AD 250; legend has it that he walked all the way here with his head in his hands before finally expiring.

Visit

🕐 *Apr-Sep: Mon-Sat 10am-6.15pm, Sun and public holidays noon-6.15pm; Oct-Mar: Mon-Sat 10am-5.15pm, Sun and public holidays noon-5.15pm. Guided tours ⌐ daily at 11.15am and 3pm. Last admission 30min before closing.* 🕐 *Closed 1 Jan, 1 May and 25 Dec. ⊗ 6.10€, no charge 1st Sun in the month (Oct-Mar). ☎ 01 48 09 83 54.*

The basilica is of central importance in the evolution of the Early Gothic style in architecture. Although work had begun on the cathedral at Sens eight years earlier, St-Denis precedes Noyon, Senlis and Laon by several years and Notre-Dame at Paris by a good quarter-century. The building is the achievement of two great masters, Abbot Suger in the 12C and Pierre de Montreuil in the 13C.

Suger was responsible for the first two bays of the nave, begun in 1136 and completed four years later, where the Romanesque tribunes and semicircular arches sit together with the pointed arches heralding the Gothic. Similar juxtapositions are evident in the chancel and ambulatory (only the lower part of which survives) completed in 1143, giving "an effect of lightness, of air circulating freely, of supple curves and energetic concentration" (Nikolaus Pevsner). A century later, Pierre de Montreuil rebuilt the upper parts of the chancel and transept, which he treated as a pre-chancel, giving it sufficient width to accommodate the royal tombs. He also built the nave, a masterpiece of High Gothic.

The many royal tombs (**tombeaux**★★★) in chancel and pre-chancel make the cathedral a veritable museum of funerary art from the Middle Ages to the Renaissance; there is a total of 79 recumbent figures. Note the splendid **crypt**★★.

Since the French Revolution the tombs have been empty, but it is nevertheless possible to trace the evolution of this particular form of sculpture as it developed in France. To begin with, the recumbent figure, like the one depicting Clovis, was simply placed on a slab. In 1260, Louis IX ordered symbolic effigies to be carved of all the rulers who had gone before him since the 7C. The first attempt at producing a likeness appears in 1285 with the statue of Philippe le Hardi (the Bold). By the middle of the 14C, authentic portraits (eg that of Charles V – 1350) were the result of the work being commissioned while the subject was still alive.

In Renaissance times, fashion replaced effigies with mausoleums, often of the most elaborate character, with representations of the deceased in highly studied poses. The tomb of Henri II and Catherine de' Medici was designed by Primaticcio in the form of a little temple, with bronze sculptures by Germain Pilon depicting the Virtues and other praying figures.

ST-ÉMILION★★

POPULATION 2 799

MICHELIN MAP 335 K 5

GREEN GUIDE ATLANTIC COAST

St-Émilion, like many towns in wine-producing regions, offers both simple and sophisticated attractions to art lovers and gourmets alike. The town, which is named after the Breton hermit who retired here around 750, is divided into two hill sites with the Royal Castle and Deanery (Doyenné) symbolising the age-old rivalry between the civil and religious authorities. Its sun-baked, pantile-roofed stone houses nestle in an **amphitheatre**★★ on the slope of a limestone plateau.

Visit

🕐 *Jul-Aug: daily 9.30am-8pm; mid-Jun to end-Jun and early Sep to mid-Sep: daily 9.30am-7pm; mid-Sep to end Oct and early Apr to mid-Jun: daily 9.30am-12.30pm, 1.45-6.30pm; Nov-Mar: daily 9.30am-12.30pm, 1.45-6pm.* ⊕ *1€.* ☎ *05 57 55 28 28*

St-Émilion has an unusual underground church (**église monolithe**★) hollowed out of a single rock in the limestone strata between the 8C and the 12C. The nave and two aisles are 38m – 125ft long, 20m – 65ft wide and 11m – 33ft high.

ST-FLOUR★★

POPULATION 7 417

MICHELIN MAP 330 G 4

GREEN GUIDE AUVERGNE RHÔNE VALLEY

This ancient town was once the capital of Upper Auvergne (Haute Auvergne); it occupies a spectacular **site**★★ high above the valley, Vallée du Lander, at the eastern tip of one of the lava flows from the vast Cantal volcano. During the Hundred Years War, its virtually impregnable fortifications helped guard French Auvergne from English Guyenne.

Viaduc de Garabit

J. Damase/MICHELIN

Visit

At the eastern end of the upper town with its old lava-built houses stands the **cathedral**★, erected in the 15C in Southern French style. From the Terrasse des Roches nearby there are extensive views over the rich grasslands of the Planèze de St-Flour; this is an inclined plateau, the result of the piling up on one another of successive lava flows whose mineralogical composition is very diverse.

Excursions

Viaduc du Garabit★★

12km – 7mi south. This daring steel structure carries the Clermont-Ferrand-Millau railway across the **Truyère** valley with its many hydro-electric works built in the **gorges**★★ gouged in the granite plateaux. Its central arch is 116m – 381ft across. The viaduct was built between 1882 and 1884 by Gustave Eiffel using plans drawn up by Boyer.

The river changes its course abruptly just here; long ago, it flowed northward towards the Allier, but the effects of the fold-movements of Tertiary times, together with the blocking of its valley by a lava-flow, meant that its waters were diverted southwestward to feed the Lot. Boat trips are possible on the Grandval.

Site du Château d'Alleuze★★

26km – 16mi west from Garabit via the Mallet viewpoint and the Grandval Dam. The square keep and round towers of this most romantic of ruins loom menacingly over the lake held back by the Grandval Dam. During the course of the Hundred Years War, an adventurer in the pay of the English, one Bernard de Garlan, got hold of the place by trickery. For seven years he terrorised the neighbourhood, until a band of soldiers from St-Flour sent him packing. They also dismantled the castle in order to prevent any recurrence of the trouble in 1405.

ST-GERMAIN-EN-LAYE★★

POPULATION 39 926

MICHELIN MAP 311 I 2

GREEN GUIDE NORTHERN FRANCE AND THE PARIS REGION

▶ **Orient Yourself:** St-Germain-en-Laye, which is listed as a "Town of Art and History," offers discovery tours conducted by guide-lecturers approved by the Ministry of Culture and Communication. 6.50€. ☎ 01 34 51 05 12. Information at the tourist office or on www.vpah.culture.fr.

A Bit of History

Now a pleasant residential town just to the west of Paris, St-Germain's significance in the course of French history goes back hundreds, if not thousands, of years. Proximity to the capital and a strategic site 60m – 200ft above a bend in the Seine persuaded Louis VI le Gros (the Fat) to build a stronghold here. Later, when the Hundred Years War was at its height, the castle was restored by Charles V.

Some of the French kings were born at St-Germain (Charles IX, Henri II, Louis XIV), as were any number of princes, writers, historians, composers... Louis XIII died here. It was here that the negotiations took place between the Huguenot leader Gaspar de Coligny and the representatives of Catherine de' Medici which put an end to the Third War of Religion by means of the Treaty of St-Germain, signed on 8 August 1570; and it was here that in 1641 Richelieu promulgated the edict limiting the rights of the French parliament.

On 28 February 1837, the first passenger-carrying railway line in France was inaugurated; following the alignment of today's RER (Paris Express Network), it linked a ferry landing-stage in Paris with the one at Le Pecq, on the far side of the river from St-Germain.

On 10 September 1919, the Treaty of St-Germain laid down the new frontiers of a defeated Austria and limited the size of her armed forces.

Visit

Château★

Its appearance is still much as it was when François I had it rebuilt by Pierre de Chambiges; over the foundations of the medieval castle the architect raised an edifice more to the taste of the 16C, though his upper brick courses and roof terrace with its ornamental balustrade caused a sensation at the time. The Court spent much of its time here between the reigns of Henri IV and Louis XIV; the latter brought in Mansart, who replaced the corner turrets by pavilions, and Le Nôtre, who designed the park, laid out the enormously long terrace (**terrasse★★**), and replanted the forest.

The château houses the **Musée des Antiquités nationales**★★*(& ⊙ May-Sep: Mon, Wed-Fri 9am-5.15pm, Sat-Sun 10am-6.15pm; Oct-Apr: Wed-Mon 9am-5.15pm ⊙ closed Tue, 1 Jan and 25 Dec; ⊛ 4€, children: no charge; ☎ 01 39 10 13 00; www.musee-anti-quitesnationales.fr);* its priceless collection of archeological exhibits traces French history through space and time from the Paleolithic to the Middle Ages.

Most of the objects displayed are original; they illustrate the slow progress of humanity from the days of the Pebble Culture (some 4 000 000 years ago) to the industries and arts of Paleolithic times (the tiny head of the Lady of Brassempouy, the first known representation of a human face), via the Mesolithic and Neolithic cultures (the Bronze Age, followed by the Iron Age with the Halstatt and La Tène periods), to Gallo-Roman and Merovingian times, when skills decisive for the course of human evolution were developed (weapons, tools, utensils...).

◐◐ Ste-Chapelle★ (in the château). Musée départemental Maurice-Denis★ ⊙ *Daily Tue-Fri 10am-5.30pm, Sat-Sun 10am-6.30pm. ⊙ Closed 1 Jan, 1 May and 25 Dec. ⊛ 3.80€ (under 13 years: no charge). ☎ 01 39 73 77 87. www.musee-mauricedenis.fr* – paintings of the Pont-Aven School and of the Nabis' movement.

ST-GUILHEM-LE-DÉSERT★★

POPULATION 190

MICHELIN MAP 339 G 6

GREEN GUIDE LANGUEDOC ROUSSILLON TARN GORGES

In its remote site★ where the Val de l'Infernet runs into the valley of the Hérault, this 9C village★ grew up around an abbey founded by William of Aquitaine, one of Charlemagne's most valiant lieutenants.

Visit

Église abbatiale★

This is a Romanesque structure of striking simplicity, famed for its possession of a fragment of the True Cross *(in the south transept)*. It has a doorway with dogtooth moulding, and an apse with massive buttresses and an elegant little arcade.

Inside, the width of apse and transept is the result of a rebuilding undertaken in the 11C.

Of the 11C-12C cloisters, nothing remains apart from the ground floor of the north walk and part of the west walk. The vigorously-sculpted 13C capitals which once graced the galleries are now among the treasures of the Cloisters Museum, high above the Hudson in New York.

R. Delon/Castelet, Boulogne-Billancourt

Aragonite bush, Grotte de Clamouse

Grotte de Clamouse★★

3km – 2mi south. The caves run beneath the Larzac plateau. They are a product of the violent earth movements of the Tertiary era, when deep fissures were opened up which subsequently became part of an extensive network of underground streams.
There are remarkable stalactites and stalagmites, but above all it is the splendid crystallisations in varied shapes which impress the visitor (calcite flowers, aragonite bushes, frosted bunches of grapes...).

ST-JEAN-DE-LUZ★★

POPULATION 13 031

MICHELIN MAP 342 C 2

GREEN GUIDE ATLANTIC COAST

A harbour town at the mouth of the river Nivelle, St-Jean-de-Luz is one of the principal centres of the French Basque country.

A Bit of History

The port and the Barre Quarter – As early as the 11C, sailors from St-Jean were hunting whales off Labrador. By the 15C, their quarry had changed to the abundant cod of the great fishing grounds off Newfoundland. When the Treaty of Utrecht forbade this activity, they turned to piracy, creating a fearsome reputation for their home port. Eventually they returned to more law-abiding ways, fishing for sardines off the coasts of Portugal and Morocco and for tuna off Senegal and Mauritania.
The part of the town known as La Barre was where the ship-owners lived; its growth was intimately linked to the fortunes of its fleet. The 16C and 17C brought good times, though the place was burned down by the Spaniards in 1558, then ravaged by high tides in 1749 and 1785. Among the fine old houses, the most venerable is the one which survived the 1558 fire, once the property of Carquiou Kailu.

The marriage of Louis XIV – The marriage of Louis XIV to the infanta Maria-Theresa was held up, first by one of the clauses in the Treaty of the Pyrenees, then by the king's passion for Marie Mancini, but in the end was solemnised here, on 9 June 1660. The king had been staying since 8 May in an imposing dwelling belonging to the ship-owner Lohobiague, which ever since has been known as the **Maison Louis-XIV**★(⏰ *30min guided tours* ☞ *Jul-Aug: Mon-Sat 10.30am-12.30pm, 3-6.30pm, Sun and public holidays 3-6.30pm; Jun and Sep: Mon-Sat 10.30am-noon, 3-5.30pm, Sun and public holidays 3-5.30pm; call for price information;* ☎ *05 59 26 01 56);* the interior is particularly interesting, with a sturdy staircase built by ships' carpenters, 18C furniture in the drawing room and fine panelling in the dining room. Maria-Theresa was lodged in an elegant brick and stone **house** (Maison de l'infante) nearby.
For a while, St-Jean-de-Luz became the capital of France. Court and government moved here, and days and nights were spent in feasting and revelry.

Visit

Église St-Jean Baptiste★★

Work on enlarging the church had began in 1649 and had still not been completed when the royal wedding took place within its walls. It is the finest church in the French Basque country, with a resplendent 17C gilded altarpiece (**retable**★) attributed to Martin de Bidache, a painted wooden ceiling and oak-built galleries on several levels. The main altar is raised above the sacristy, a feature of churches in the ancient Basque provinces of Labourd (in France) and Guipuzcoa (in Spain).

Excursions

Corniche basque★★

14km – 9mi south, then extending southward to Hendaye. The Socoa cliff (**Falaise de Socoa**★), an unusual example of coastal relief, is best seen at low tide. Following the drowning of the former coastline by the waters released by the melting of the Quaternary glaciers, the beds of highly laminated schists were attacked by wave action; the strata dip sharply seaward, projecting sharp saw-tooth ridges of the more resistant rock from the wave-cut platform at the foot of the cliffs.

La Rhune ★★

14km – 9mi southeast, then as far as Sare. Towards the end of the 6C, the Basques were probably pushed northwards by the Visigoths. Those of their number who settled in the plains of Aquitaine intermarried with the other local people, eventually to become the Gascons. But those that remained in the mountains kept their independence and their enigmatic language, thus guaranteeing their very distinct identity.

The mountain called La Rhune ("good grazing" in Basque) is one of the symbols of the Basque country; its **summit** *(accessible by rack-and-pinion railway)* rises to a height of 900m – c 3 000ft, offering a wonderful **panorama**★★★ of the Bay of Biscay, the Landes and the ancient provinces of Labourd, Navarre and Guipuzcoa.

At the foot of the mountain lie the villages of **Ascain**★ and **Sare**★, both with many characteristically Basque features. The houses are timber-framed; the white rendering of the walls makes a pleasant contrast to the reddish-brown colour usually applied to the timber, while the cemeteries adjoining the churches have the typical discoidal tombstones arranged in a circle.

If visitors are lucky, they may see the local people dancing the chaste but passionate fandango or taking part in pigeon-hunts.

ST-JEAN-PIED-DE-PORT★

POPULATION 1 432

MICHELIN MAP 342 E 4

GREEN GUIDE ATLANTIC COAST

The little town owes its name to its position at the foot of the important Roncesvalles pass (port) through the Pyrenees and at the outlet of the Valcarlos defile. In the days when numberless pilgrims trod the dusty road to Santiago de Compostela, St-Jean was the last staging-post in France before the steep ascent towards the Spanish frontier. The pilgrims would normally have taken the Ports de Cize road, now no longer a highway but an official long-distance footpath (GR 65); today's tourist traffic on the Rue d'Espagne still evokes something of the bustle of medieval times.

Visit

The northern side of the town was fortified in the 15C by the Navarrese. In 1512, the place became capital of Lower Navarre, the rump left to the Albret family by Ferdinand the Catholic after he had dispossessed them of their lands in Spain. In the Rue de la Citadelle are a number of red sandstone houses built at this time or in the 16C and 17C, distinguished by their rounded doorways and sculpted lintels.

The fortifications on the far bank of the river protecting the road to Spain, together with the citadel itself, are part of a system of defences designed by Vauban.

ST-MALO★★★

POPULATION 48 057

MICHELIN MAP 309 J 3

GREEN GUIDE BRITTANY

The **site**★★★ of the walled town of St Malo on the east bank of the Rance is unique in France, making the ancient port one of the country's great tourist attractions.

▶ **Orient Yourself:** Starting at the Esplanade St-Vincent, it is possible to walk right around the town on top of the ramparts *(allow 2hr)*. St-Malo, which is listed as a "Town of Art and History," offers discovery tours conducted by guide-lecturers approved by the Ministry of Culture and Communication. Contact the town history museum (musée d'Histoire) in the castle keep (☎ 02 99 40 71 57) or on www.vpah.culture.fr.

🕓 **Organizing Your Time:** Spend half the day seeing the ramparts, château and cathedral, then take the excursion down the Emerald Coast scenic road. There are also several companies that offer a variety of boat tours in the bay of St-Malo (varying prices and times; contact the tourist office for more info, ☎ *02 99 56 64 48*).

Especially For Kids: Le Grand Aquarium.

P **Parking:** Park near the port by the Esplanade St-Vincent.

A Bit of History

The town's real prosperity began in the 16C. In 1534, **Jacques Cartier** had set out from here on the voyage which led to the discovery and naming of Canada; very soon a thriving commerce had begun, based on the abundant furs brought back from the deep interior of the new country by trappers and traders. Cod fishing developed too, as the Breton sailors exploited the teeming grounds off Newfoundland (though this did lead to a reduction in the dried fish export trade). St-Malo waxed rich.

From the end of the 16C, the local ship-owners began to build themselves fine manor houses in the surrounding countryside, as well as tall timber-built residences in the town itself. By the 60s of the following century, their boats were trading around the coasts of the Pacific, and their ever-increasing wealth enabled them to build in granite. But from this time onwards, Parisian architectural fashions and the centralising tendencies of the monarchy began to prevail over local traditions. Anticipating the coming naval rivalry between England and France, Colbert became aware of the vulnerability of his country's western coasts; in 1689, Vauban was commissioned to strengthen the defences of St-Malo, particularly on the landward side of the town to the north and the east. The two countries contested command of the seas and of the lands beyond throughout the 18C; a prominent part in the struggle was played by men from St-Malo such as the privateers Dugay-Trouin and Surcouf, while the

St-Malo

Y. Arthus-Bertrand/ALTITUDE

Falkland Islands were given their French name (Isles Malouines) by colonists who came from here.

In the 19C, the invention of floating docks ended the advantage which the great tidal range of the port had long given its ship-builders and -repairers.

Sights

Remparts★★★

Walking along the ramparts, there are fine views up the valley of the Rance and towards Dinard on the far side of the estuary. Nearer at hand is Grand Bé Island, which low tide leaves stranded; the simple tomb of **Chateaubriand** (born in St-Malo in 1768) is here, facing seaward. Within the walls is the old town, almost entirely rebuilt after near-total destruction in 1944, but in such a way as to recapture the spirit of the place; solid walls of granite, relieved only by horizontal bands between each storey, steep mansard roofs and formidable chimney stacks (essential on this windy western coast), all combine to give an effect of harsh dignity and strong identity. The houses along the Rue de Dinan and those facing the walls are particularly fine.

RP2570

Château★★

This still has the façades of the 17C and 18C barracks.

Cathédrale St-Vincent

The nave vault of 1160 is one of the oldest in Brittany, albeit rebuilt after the last war. It is of Angevin type; at the time Brittany was a Plantagenet fiefdom. However, the effect of lightness achieved elsewhere is absent here, owing to the use of granite and its solidity of appearance (an original vault survives in the north aisle). Note the **stained-glass windows**★ by Jean Le Moal.

Le Grand Aquarium★★

The aquarium offers a fascinating experience as well as presenting collections of great scientific interest, as visitors trace the history of great sailors from St-Malo. Two attractions are of special interest among the many pools and basins: the ring (**Anneau**), a remarkable technical achievement, which is a round aquarium containing 600 000 litres in which shoals of pelagic species of fish swim endlessly; and a life-size reconstruction of a sunken wreck (**Vaisseau englouti**) with preying sharks.

Musée d'histoire de la ville et d'Ethnographie du Pays Malouin (**M²**)★ Apr-Sep: daily 10am-12.30pm, 2-6pm; Oct-Mar: daily except Mon 10am-noon, 2-6pm. Closed 1 Jan, 1 May, 1 and 11 Nov, 25 Dec. 4.80€. 02 99 40 71 57 – history of the town and its famous men. Quic-en-Groigne Tower (E)★ – wax museum.

Fort National★ Guided tours (45min) Jun-Sep: at low tide (times vary according to tides). Contact the St-Malo tourist office. 4€ (children: 2€). 02 99 85 34 33.

Excursion

Côte d'Émeraude★★★

The name has been given to the picturesque northern coast of Brittany stretching from Cancale (**headland – Pointe du Grouin**★★) to **Le Val André**★★ in the west. The Emerald Coast scenic road runs through the major resorts (Dinard, St-Malo) and offers detours to the tips of the numerous headlands, including Fort de Latte★★, **Cap Fréhel**★★★ and **Cap d'Erquy**★ from which the views of the jagged coastline are in places quite spectacular.

ST-MARTIN-DU-CANIGOU★★

MICHELIN MAP 344 F 7

2.5KM – 1.5MI SOUTH OF VERNET-LES-BAINS

GREEN GUIDE LANGUEDOC ROUSSILLON TARN GORGES

This eagle's eyrie (1 055m – 3 460ft above sea-level) is one of the classic sights to be visited in the area around Vernet-les-Bains.

P **Parking:** Park the car in Casteil, then follow a steep road uphill *(over 1hr round trip)*. The abbey can also be reached by jeep. Contact the tourist office at Vernet-les-Bains (☎ *04 68 05 55 35)* or contact Transports Circuits Touristiques (M. Cullell) for departures from Corneilla-de-Conflent, Vernet-les-Bains or Casteil (☎ *6.50€ round trip, ☎ 04 68 05 64 61)*.

Visit

Abbaye

Kids ☉ *Guided tours* ☜ *(1hr) Jun-Sep: Mon, Wed-Sat 10am, 11am, noon, 2pm, 3pm, 4pm, 5pm, Sun and public holidays 10am, 12.30pm, 2pm, 3pm, 4pm, 5pm; Oct-May: Mon, Wed-Sat 10am, 11am, 2pm, 3pm, 4pm, Sun and public holidays 10am, 12.30pm, 2pm, 3pm, 4pm. Possibility of a tour with a story of the site for children (ask for information).* ☉ *Closed Jan.* ☜ *4€ (ages 12-18 years: 3€).* ☎ *04 68 05 50 03.*

The abbey, built on a rocky pinnacle at an altitude of 1 094m – 3 589ft, grew up around a monastic community that was originally founded here in the 11C. After falling into disuse at the Revolution, it was restored from 1902 to 1932 and extended from 1952 to 1972.

Cloître

At the beginning of the 20C, all that remained of the cloisters was three galleries with crude semicircular arches. As part of the restoration a south gallery has been rebuilt overlooking a ravine.

Églises

The lower church (10C) dedicated to Notre-Dame-sous-Terre in accordance with an early-Christian tradition, forms the crypt of the upper church (11C). The latter, consisting of three successive aisles with parallel barrel vaults, conveys an impression of great age with its rugged, simply carved capitals.

On the north side of the chancel stands a bell-tower crowned by a crenellated platform. Near the church, two tombs have been hollowed out of the rock: the tomb of the founder, Count Gulfred de Cerdagne, which he dug out with his own hands, and that of one of his wives.

Site★★★

To appreciate St-Martin's unusual site, after reaching the abbey (30min on foot round trip) take a stairway to the left (itinerary no 9) which climbs through the woods. Turn left past the water outlet. There is an impressive view of the abbey, which lies in the shadow of the Canigou until the late morning. It stands in an imposing site dominating the Casteil and Vernet valleys.

Église de ST-NECTAIRE★★

POPULATION 664

MICHELIN MAP 326 E 9

GREEN GUIDE AUVERGNE THE RHÔNE VALLEY

This little Romanesque church enjoys a spectacular location on the eastern slopes of the Dore mountains (Monts Dore). Built around 1160 as a dependency of the great Chaise-Dieu monastery, it suffered much damage during the French Revolution, and underwent major restoration (towers, west front) in 1875.

Visit

🕐 *Apr-Oct: 9am-7pm; Nov-Mars: 10am-12.30pm, 2pm-6pm. Jul-Aug: guided tours daily except Sun and public holidays 3pm and 5pm* ☎ *04 73 88 50 67.*

The interior has a number of notable features in addition to the dome on squinches; they include the unusual arrangement of nave vaults supported on columns rather than on pillars, a massive narthex and the characteristically Auvergnat mitred arches of the transepts.

The church's 103 **capitals**★★ (most are 12C) are justly famous. Carved from igneous rock (trachyte and andesite), they depict animals, foliage and Bible scenes. The finest of them, in the chancel, seem to owe much to the work of the sculptors of Mozac (🕐 *see RIOM)*; 87 figures illustrate scenes from the Life of Christ (the kiss of Judas, the road to Calvary) and the Resurrection (Holy Women at the tomb, Doubting Thomas).

The treasury **(trésor**★★ – north transept) houses a statue of Notre-Dame-du-Mont-Cornadore (a Virgin in Majesty of the 12C), **a reliquary bust of St Baudime**★★, a 12C Limoges masterpiece with a penetrating gaze and beautifully-rendered hands, as well as a reliquary arm of St Nectaire in repoussé silver and a pair of Limoges book-plates of about 1170.

Excursion

Château de Murol★★

6km – 4mi east. The ruined castle rises from a basalt platform formed by a lava flow from the Tartaret volcano. The site with its polygonal keep was fortified as early as the 12C because of its strategic position between Auvergne and Cantal. At the end of the 14C, it became one of the main seigneurial residences of the province; Guillaume de Murol was responsible for those features which still distinguish the stronghold today (internal courtyard, main tower, and north and east walls) and which serve to remind us both of the medieval obsession with security and of the fiercely guarded independence of the Auvergnat nobility.

A century later, the castle underwent alterations to bring it more into line with Renaissance tastes, including a tilting-ground with grandstand, a tympanum decorated with heraldic devices, and ornamental mantelpieces. But the troubled times associated with the **Catholic League** and the Wars of Religion led to the place being modernised in a military sense, with the building of bastions, watch-towers, as well as an outer wall rising directly from the cliff, all reinforcing the site's natural defensive ability to withstand bombardment or sapping. Now impregnable, the fortress was spared by Richelieu's demolition programme, but fell into ruin in the 19C.

ST-NICOLAS-DE-PORT★★

POPULATION 7 702

MICHELIN MAP 307 J 7

GREEN GUIDE ALSACE LORRAINE CHAMPAGNE

Located on the River Meurthe and the Marne-Rhine canal, St-Nicolas is an industrial town. It is the home of the Solvay Company's soda works, France's oldest, based on a 70m – 230ft thick deposit of rock salt which has been extracted since 1872 by solution and brine pumping. The splendid 15C-16C Church of St Nicolas rises somewhat incongruously from these workaday surroundings.

Visit

Basilique★★

🕐 *Jul to mid-Sep: guided tours (1hr) Sun 3pm.* 💶 *5€. Organ concerts every Sunday in August 5.30pm. No charge. Audio-guided visit daily except Sun and Mon. 10am-noon, 2- 5pm, Sat 2-5pm. Audio devices at the Tourist Office, pl. Croué-Friedman.* ☎ *03 83 48 58 75.*

The building is perhaps the finest example of the Flamboyant Gothic style in Lorraine. It was built between 1481 and 1560, at a time when the style had passed its peak and was indulging in all kinds of extravagant embellishment. A number of the church's features are of this kind, not only the west front with its heavy decoration and sculpture and the delicate arcading which in places relieves otherwise bare walls, but also the false transept; here a pair of bold 28m – 92ft columns (the tallest in France) help hold up the vaulting with its elaborate play of liernes and tiercerons. The transept is lit by windows with unusually complex tracery.

The influence of the neighbouring province of Champagne can be seen in the inspection gallery running below the transept windows. The side chapels were built in Renaissance style after the completion of the main part of the building.

ST-OMER★★

POPULATION 14 434

MICHELIN MAP 301 G 3

GREEN GUIDE NORTHERN FRANCE AND THE PARIS REGION

A market centre of some importance, St-Omer has kept many fine town houses dating from the Classical period. The town lies at the junction of Inland Flanders, with its watery landscapes of poplars, elms and willows, and Coastal Flanders, won from the sea in medieval times and now dominated by industry and arable farming.

A Bit of History

38km – 24 miles to the south lies the site of the Battle of **Agincourt** (Azincourt), where, on 25 October 1415, France suffered its gravest defeat of the Hundred Years War at the hands of Henry V of England. The French cavalry, lacking any sort of unified command, moved in extended order against a less numerous but highly mobile foe; their horses, weighed down by their riders' armour and stumbling in the heavy ground, made good targets for English bowmanship. Once unhorsed, the knights in their armour were no match for the agile English infantrymen. The captured Duke of Orleans became the prisoner-poet of the Tower of London.

The disaster bled the French nobility white; ten thousand of their number had been cut down, while English casualties were negligible.

"O God, thine arm was here", cried Shakespeare's Henry V,

"When, without stratagem,

But in plain shock and even play of battle,

Was ever known so great and little loss

On one part or the other?"

Now Normandy lay open to invasion, Paris was defenceless against John the Fearless of Burgundy and nothing stood between Henry V and the crown of France he coveted. The battle is commemorated by a cross and an inscription on a standing stone. A border town, St-Omer was in turn part of the Holy Roman Empire, Flanders, Burgundy and then Spain, finally passing into French hands in 1677. The town's industry, predominantly metal-working, chemicals and glass-making, is concentrated in the Arques district.

Visit

Cathédrale Notre-Dame★★

Completed at the end of the Hundred Years War, the building shows signs of the influence of the English Perpendicular style; the tower is treated with an overall pattern of lancet arches and, inside, the triforium of transept and chancel has very tall, slender colonnettes.

Works of art★★ are numerous and of high quality; there is 18C woodwork (pulpit base with scenes from the life of St Dominic, choir-stalls panelling, organ-case), and very rare 13C floor tiles in the ambulatory and chancel. Others survive in the two radiating chapels and in the first bay of the south transept, with subjects such as the Shrouding of the Virgin, the liberal arts, signs of the Zodiac... They are probably the work of 13C sculptors who originally came from Italy.

◗◗ Hôtel Sandelin★ ♿ ◷ *Wed-Sun 10am-noon, 2-6pm.* ◷ *Closed public holidays.* ✉ 4.50€. ☎ 03 21 38 00 94. www.m3. dnalias.com/sandelin. ☎ 03 21 38 00 94 – decorative arts. Ancienne Chapelle des Jésuites★. Jardin Public★ (gardens).

ST-POL-DE-LÉON ★

POPULATION 7 261

MICHELIN MAP 308 H 2

GREEN GUIDE BRITTANY

St-Pol is one of the main market-gardening centres of the rich band of fertile soils running all round the Breton coast from St-Malo to St-Nazaire. Where the wind can be kept out, the otherwise mild climate allows excellent crops of vegetables to be grown, artichokes, onions, early potatoes, cauliflowers, salad vegetables... eagerly bought in the markets of Paris and on the far side of the English Channel. Mechanisation means that much of the characteristic pattern of tiny fields bounded by stone walls is doomed to disappear.

Visit

Chapelle du Kreisker★

The chapel was rebuilt around 1375; in the 15C, when the coastal towns were prospering from their sea-borne trade, it housed the meetings of the town council. In about 1430, Duke John V of Brittany, who had spent his boyhood at the Burgundian court, then married Joan of France, felt it opportune to introduce the Gothic style into Brittany in order to boost his prestige. But the response of the Breton architects was to adapt Flamboyant Gothic to local ways; they shunned highly designed and decorated façades which were difficult to reconcile with the dour qualities of the granites of the region, and favoured a flattened apse (a reflection of the influence of both English architecture and that of the mendicant orders). They thereby eliminated the problems caused by vaults with a circular or polygonal plan, as well as enabling the interior to be lit by a single large window. In addition, the use of a coffered ceiling and a lightweight slate roof allowed them to dispense with flying buttresses.

The chapel was subsequently enlarged, and, between 1436 and 1439, given its belfry (clocher★★), the finest in the province. Interest in it has increased owing to the loss of the tower of Notre-Dame-du-Mur at Morlaix on which it is supposed to have been modelled. In its vertical emphasis, it is reminiscent of the churches of Normandy; it has a pointed steeple and pinnacles so delicate they had to be tied into the main structure by braces to enable them to resist the force of the wind. The tall openings below reinforce this impression. The English Perpendicular style is recalled by the mullions of the windows, by the overhanging balustrade and by the entablatures expressing the different levels.

Ancienne cathédrale★

The old cathedral was erected on 12C foundations in the 13C and 14C. This fine building with its characteristically Breton balustraded belfry was restored by the Dukes of Brittany from 1431 onwards. Seven bays of the nave still have their original vaults; the nave itself, unlike most of the rest of the cathedral where local granite was used, was built in Caen stone, a clear indication of Norman influence. Norman too is the inspection gallery which runs below the triforium.

In the north side of the chancel, below the funerary niches, are a number of wooden reliquaries with skulls dug up in a nearby cemetery, while in the sanctuary a palm tree carved in wood contains a ciborium for the Host (1770).

Excursion

Roscoff★

5km – 3mi north. The harbour town with its fishing fleet and important export trade (vegetables) to Britain also has ferry services linking Brittany to Plymouth and Cork. It is a flourishing resort and a medical centre using sea-water treatment.

Not far from the harbour in the town centre is the church of **Notre-Dame-de-Kroaz-Batz**★ with its remarkable lantern-turret belfry (clocher★) of Renaissance date. Inside, four alabaster **statues**★ grace the altarpiece of one of the altars in the south aisle.

ST-QUENTIN★

POPULATION 69 188

MICHELIN MAP 306 B 3

GREEN GUIDE NORTHERN FRANCE AND THE PARIS REGION

On its hill overlooking the Somme, the industrial town of St-Quentin was granted the charter guaranteeing its civic privileges as early as 1080.

▶ **Orient Yourself:** St-Quentin, which is listed as a "Town of Art and History," offers discovery tours conducted by guide-lecturers approved by the Ministry of Culture and Communication. Information at the tourist office or on www.vpah.culture.fr.

A Bit of History

The Battle of St Quentin and its aftermath – In August 1557, the Constable of France, Montmorency, had been taken prisoner by the Spaniards besieging St-Quentin and his forces scattered. His king, Henri II, was plagued by worries, not only about the consequences of this grave defeat, but also about the course the Reformation was taking; to the grumblings of the peasants was added the malignant effect of German-influenced Protestant preachers on the morale of the army. The successes of the Duke of Guise at Calais (recovered by France after 211 years of English occupation) and Thionville were not enough to reassure him. The **Treaty of Le Cateau-Cambrésis** was signed on 2 April 1559 with England and with Spain the following day, but the final negotiations leading up to it had unsettled the king even more, making him acutely aware of his country's vulnerability.

Historians still argue about the significance of this treaty. It certainly restored Calais to France, gave implicit recognition of her rights over Metz, Toul and Verdun, and put an end to the conflicts in Italy. Some see in it a failure on France's part to make its provisions work in her favour, and consider Henri II to have been duped by Philip II of Spain into relinquishing no fewer than 189 strongholds, together with Nice, Bresse, Savoy, Corsica, the Italian territories dependent on Florence and Siena... According to others, more subtle considerations were at work. Faced with heresy at home and abroad, it suited the king to effect a reconciliation with the Catholic powers at whatever cost, even if this meant putting off the acquisition of secure frontiers to some uncertain point in the future. It is conceivable that the continued pursuit of such a policy could have spared France the disasters of the Wars of Religion. But it was not to be; three months after the signing of the treaty, Henri II succumbed to the effects of a wound received in the course of a joust. He was succeeded by François II, a sickly 15-year-old; in the period which followed, the lack of any strong authority meant that the political crisis grew worse.

Sights

Musée Antoine-Lécuyer

🕐 Jul-Aug: Mon, Wed-Sat 10am-noon, 2-6pm, Sun 2-6pm. Sep-Jun: Mon, Wed-Fri 10am-noon, 2-5pm, Sat 10-noon, 2-6pm, Sun 2-6pm. 🕐 Closed Tue,1 Jan, 1 May, Whitsun, 14 Jul, 1 Nov, 25 Dec. ✍ 2.50€, no charge Wed. ☎ 03 23 06 93 98.

The artist Maurice Quentin de La Tour (1704-88), known above all for his works in pastel, was born and died in St-Quentin. The museum houses a total of 78 of his **portraits**★★, masterpieces all in their anatomy of personality, whether it be impulsive, malicious, ironic, mocking, kindly, cynical... His introspective self-portrait also has this penetrating quality.

Basilique★

This is a building in Lanceolate style, with the elevation characteristic of this version of the Gothic. In addition, it has a double transept and an ambulatory of the type prevalent in the neighbouring province of Champagne; on its south side is an arrangement of twin columns supporting the chapels in the manner of the church of St-Remi at Reims. Traced out on the floor of the nave is a rare example of a labyrinth.

Visit

L'Abbatiale★★

🕐 *Open all day. Use discretion in visiting during religious services. Guided tour (1hr15min plus 30min for the film) of the church and the abbey buildings. Tour and film have fixed hours according to the season, call in advance.* 🕐 *Closed Jan, 11 Nov, 25 and 31 Dec.* 6€ *(12-18 years: 4.50€).* ☎ *05 49 84 30 00.*

The abbey church was mostly built in the space of 50 years, between 1040 and 1090. The base of the tower dates from the 11C; above it rise two storeys added in the 12C and a slender 14C steeple (rebuilt in the middle of the 19C). Inside, tall columns divide the nave from the transepts, and in the six chapels which open off the choir and transepts are Romanesque altar-tables still with their original carved inscriptions.

The fame of St-Savin rests on its stunning series of Romanesque **murals**★★★, the finest in the whole of France. They seem to have been painted around 1100 by a single team of artists over a period of only three to four years. The colours consist only of black and white, green, and reddish or yellowish ochre; they were applied flat, without gradations. Some of the paintings have withstood the ravages of time (and men) better than others; they include a monumental treatment of the Apocalypse (in the narthex), the Creation (nave), the Book of Abraham (in the vaulting of the first three bays of the nave), then the stories of Moses, Abel, Noah and Joseph (in the remaining six bays), Christ in Majesty, the Evangelists and the Saints (in the crypts).

Enclos paroissial de **ST-THÉGONNEC**★★

MICHELIN MAP 308 H 3

GREEN GUIDE BRITTANY

The parish close (enclos paroissial) is one of the most characteristic features of the Breton landscape, particularly in the Elorn valley, on the slopes of the Arrée Hills and in the Léon district. The one at St-Thégonnec is among the most famous of these monumental groupings of church, cemetery, calvary and charnel-house.

A Bit of History

Parish closes began to develop in this form during the second half of the 16C at the time of the Counter-Reformation. They formed a powerful instrument in the hands of the Roman Catholic Church, helping it to consolidate its dogmas and to promote the veneration of apostles and saints in opposition to spontaneous local cults. Their effectiveness was increased by the presentation of their subject matter somewhat in the manner of a strip cartoon, with exaggerated features and dramatic gestures.

Much of the religious life of the community (masses, sermons, processions) took place in the close, emphasising the indivisibilty of the living and the dead.

This parish close is approached through a Renaissance triumphal arch **(porte triom-phale**★) (1587), lavishly decorated with cannon balls, shells, pilasters and little lanterns. The calvary **(calvaire**★★) dates from 1610. It is the work of Rolland Doré, and the last of its type to be carved from the mica-rich igneous rock known as **kersanton**. On the lower arm of the cross are figures of angels collecting Christ's blood, while the base shows scenes of the Passion and Resurrection. Note particularly the depiction of Christ's tormentors and also the symbolic use of clothing, with Our Lord and His followers dressed according to Christian tradition, while the representatives of worldly power wear the fashions of the time of Henri IV. The funerary chapel **(chapelle funé-raire**★) of 1676 illustrates the survival of traditional decorative motifs in the province (altarpiece with spiral columns and a Holy Sepulchre in painted oak).

The 15C church **(église**★) was rebuilt and refurnished several times in the 17C and early 18C in an entirely harmonious way. The pulpit **(chaire**★★) has a remarkable polygonal base (1683) carved by master carpenters from the naval yards at Brest, as well as a fine medallion at the back and a Louis XV sounding-board.

By the end of the 17C, Anglo-French naval rivalry had brought to an end the Léon district's maritime prosperity; local patrons of the arts now had little money to spare and the artists themselves suffered a diminution of their imaginative powers. St-Thégonnec was to be the last of the great parish closes of Brittany.

Excursion

Enclos paroissial de Guimiliau★★

8km – 5mi southwest. This example of a parish close pre-dates the one at St-Thégonnec by some 30 years. The calvary (**calvaire**★★, 1581) has an attractively naïve quality; its 200 figures are full of a sense of vigorous movement and are carved in a robust way which recalls the sculpture of the Romanesque period, notably in the episodes from the life of Christ and the scenes from the Passion depicted in the frieze. Also of interest is the terrifying sculpture showing the Gates of Hell, with the struggling figure of Catel Gollet (Lost Kate in Breton), the flirtatious serving-girl who failed to reveal all at Confession. The funerary chapel of 1642 has an outdoor pulpit of earlier (15C) date. The church (**église**★) has a Renaissance **porch**★★ dating from 1606 with an unusual wealth and variety of ornament; the arching depicts scenes from both the Old and the New Testaments. Panelled vaulting is a feature of the interior, which has a fine Baroque baptistery (**baptistère**★★) with a canopy and spiral columns decorated with pampres and foliage. The pulpit (**chaire**★), with its sculpted panels of about 1675, is also in the Baroque style.

ST-TROPEZ★★

POPULATION 5 754

MICHELIN MAP 340 O 6

GREEN GUIDE FRENCH RIVIERA

The foothills of the Maures Massif rise behind the narrow streets of the village of St-Tropez.

Visit

The harbour where luxury yachts are moored teems with life. The old fishing village which was discovered by the painter **Paul Signac** and attracted the major figures of the Post-Impressionist School – paintings in the **Musée de L'Annonciade**★★ (🕐 *Jul-Oct: Wed-Mon 10am-1pm, 3-10pm; Dec-Jun: daily 10am-noon, 2-6pm;* 🕐 *closed Tue, Nov, 1 Jan, 1 May, Ascension Day, 25 Dec;* 4.50€, 5.50€ *during temporary exhibits, Jul-Oct;* ☎ *04 94 97 04 01*) – has become a fashionable resort frequented by writers and

---

St-Tropez - Address Book

For coin ranges, see the Legend at the back of the guide.

EATING OUT

Régis Restaurant – *19 Rue de la Citadelle* – ☎ *04 94 97 15 53* – *info@regisrestaurant.com* – 🕐 *Closed 30 Oct-15 Mar.* Pasta in all shapes and sizes, cooked in various ways, as well as sushi and wok stir-frys, attract a regular clientele to this restaurant located on a steep, narrow street in St-Tropez. The food is served on the terrace or inside one of the small dining areas decked out in white.

La Cantina el Mexicano – *16 Rue des Remparts* – ☎ *04 94 97 40 96* – *elmexicano@wanadoo.fr* – 🕐 *Closed Nov to Mar and for lunch.* After sipping your tequila, savour generous helpings of Mexican cuisine in this typical setting characterised by religious statues, painted wood furnishings and vases. Even the bathroom warrants a visit! Youngish clientele. Friendly, relaxed ambience.

Leï Salins – *Plage des Salins* – ☎ *04 94 97 04 40* – 🕐 *Closed 15 Oct-31 Mar.* Open-air beach restaurant offering a tasty bill of fare consisting of salads and grilled, freshly caught fish. Charming seaside location coupled with attractive surroundings.

La Table du Marché – *38 Rue Georges-Clemenceau* – ☎ *04 94 97 85 20.* Gourmets will love this temple of gastronomy located near Place des Lices, open at all hours of the day. In addition to the restaurant offering traditional French cuisine, La Table du Marché is also known for its homemade pastries that can be purchased on the premises: croissants, cakes and the legendary "gendarme de St-Tropez" – mouthwatering chocolate mousse in the shape of a policeman's cap filled with vanilla crème brûlée. Who can resist?

Au Vieux Gassin – *Place deï Barri - Gassin* – ☎ *04 94 56 14 26* – 🕐 *Closed Jan, and dinner in winter.* A ravishing little hilltop village serves as the backdrop for this popular restaurant. A terrace with panoramic views is partially enclosed and heated in cooler weather, taking over a large section of the charming Place deï Barri. The regional menu had a few "exotic" specialities. Extraordinarily friendly service.

Leï Mouscardins – *Port (Tour du Portalet)* – ☎ *04 94 97 29 00* – *- info@lei-mouscardins.com* – ⏱ *Closed 9 Jan-4 Feb, 14 Nov-17 Dec, and Tue off-season.* Tucked away behind the harbor, near Tour du Portalet, this restaurant pays homage to Mediterranean tradition. It has a faithful following of food lovers, lured by its creative and lovingly prepared cuisine, presented to you in two dining rooms opening out onto St-Tropez Bay.

WHERE TO STAY

Hôtel Lou Cagnard – *Avenue Paul-Roussel* – ☎ *04 94 97 04 24* – ⏱ *Closed 3 Nov-27 Dec* – 🅿 *– 19 rooms* – 🚭. Enjoy breakfast seated in the shade of a mulberry tree in the tiny garden of this pretty Provençal house, just off Place des Lices. At night you'll be lulled to sleep by the chirping of cicadas... Highly reasonable prices for St-Tropez.

Bello Visto – *Place deï -Barri – Gassin* – ☎ *04 94 56 17 30 or 04 94 56 47 33* – ⏱ *Closed Jan and Nov* – *9 rooms* – 🚭 – *Restaurant (*🍴*).* There's truth in the name of this small family-run hotel and restaurant posted on the place of the ramparts (*barri*), at the top of Gassin. The majority of the rooms, like the terrace, profit from a "beautiful sight" over the Massif des Maures and the gulf of St-Tropez. Dining room with fireplace and Provençal cuisine.

Bastide des Salins – *4km/2.4mi southeast of St-Tropez* – ☎ *04 94 97 24 57* – *info@labastidedessalins.com* – ⏱ *Closed 6 Oct-31 Mar* – 🅿 *– 14 rooms* 🚭. You will be greeted like friends of the family at this old Provençal house surrounded by extensive leafy grounds. Barely 5 minutes from Place des Lices and yet totally isolated, this hotel offers large rooms decorated in the Provençal spirit, appointed with great simplicity.

Hôtel Ponche – *Place Révelin* – ☎ *04 94 97 02 53* – *hotel@laponche.com* – ⏱ *Closed 1 Nov-13 Feb* – *18 rooms* – 🚭 – *Restaurant (*🍴*).* The rooms of this cosy hotel occupy four village houses formerly belonging to fishermen; the blue one was a favourite of Romy Schneider's. You will be under the charm of the rooftop terraces nestling between the citadel and the bell-tower. The warm, bright hues and considerate service make the Hôtel Ponche an absolute must.

ON THE TOWN

St-Tropez has two facets. In summer, it is a town for the rich and wealthy and is given over to sailing, bathing, entertainment and nightlife. However, in winter, it looks more like a ghost town. Indeed, most businesses close down between November and April and the swinging bars, restaurants and hotels that have made the reputation of St-Tropez are completely deserted.

Bar du Château de la Messardière – *Route de Tahiti* – ☎ *04 94 56 76 00* – *www.messardiere.com* – ⏱ *Mid-Mar to mid-Oct from 6pm.* This bar belongs to one of the Riviera's most prestigious hotels. Hushed, cosy ambience in the piano bar of this former 18C private residence. The terrace commands nice views of St-Tropez Bay.

Chez Nano – *2 Rue Sibille* – ☎ *04 94 97 72 59* – ⏱ *Daily 7pm-3am* – ⏱ *Closed Feb-Mar.* A must for any visitor to St-Tropez. Frequented by wealthy yacht owners and foreign patrons, Chez Nano exudes a cosy atmosphere and is often used as a venue for painting exhibitions.

Bar Sube – *15 quai de Suffren* – ☎ *04 94 97 30 04* – ⏱ *Open 6-11pm, until 3am Jul-Aug* – ⏱ *Closed 5-31 Jan.* This is one of the most beautiful bars of the city. Model boats decorate the interior, where the leather armchairs and fireplace make for a cordial and comfortable place. Small tables are installed on the balcony, with prime views of the old port.

WORKING OUT

Artemis – *Route des Plages* – ☎ *04 94 97 86 69* – *artemis-stkwanadoo.fr* – ⏱ *Jul-Aug Mon-Sat 9am-9pm; Sep-Jun Mon-Fri 9am-8pm, Sat 9am-2pm.* This gym club features an unusual method unique in France, aimed at establishing a personalised programme for members: all the relevant information about their state of health is fed into a computer that decides on the number and nature of the fitness sessions. Artemis also has beauty treatments available.

FOR YOUR SWEET TOOTH

La Tarte Tropézienne – *Place des Lices* – ☎ *04 94 97 71 42* – *www.tarte-tropezienne.com* – ⏱ *Daily 6.30am-10pm.* It was in this pâtisserie that the famous tarte tropézienne saw the light of day, invented in 1955 by Polish baker Alexandre Micka: a round delightfully moist, brioche cake flavored with orange blossom, filled with custard and sprinkled with crystallised suger.

Sénéquier – *Quai Jean-Jaurès* – ☎ *04 94 97 00 90* – ⏱ *Daily 8am-7pm; Jul-Aug 7am-3am* – ⏱ *Closed mid-Nov to mid-Dec.* The sidewalk terrace and crimson chairs of this tea room are famous throughout the world or so say the locals! Renowned personalities such as Jean Marais, Errol Flynn and Colette would come here for a cup of delicately fragrant tea, an iced coffee, a delicious ice cream or a few squares of homemade nougat.

SHOPPING

Markets – Tuesdays and Saturdays on Place des Lices.

Foire de la Ste-Anne – Fair on Place des Lices, every July 26.

Shopping streets – The most lively shopping streets are Rue Clemenceau, Rue Gambetta and Rue Allard, offering an impressive selection of local arts and crafts: pottery, glassware etc.

Les Sandales Tropéziennes – *16 Rue Georges Clemenceau* – ☎ *04 94 97 19 55* – *www.nova.fr* – 🕐 *Oct-Mar Tue-Sat 9.30am-noon and 2.30-6.30pm; Apr-Sep daily until 8pm.* The Rondini house has been crafting St-Tropez sandals since 1927. The distinctive, namesake model in natural leather is the most popular, but the snakeskin version sells well, too!

Le Petit Village – *La Foux* – *near the commercial center just outside Gassin* – *Gassin* – ☎ *04 94 56 32 04* – *infos@ petitvillage.com* – 🕐 *Open Jun-15 Sep 8.30am-1pm, 2.30-7.30pm; rest of the year 8.30am-12.30pm, 2.30-6.30pm* – 🕐 *Closed Sun.* This showroom brings together the wines from eight prestigious vineyards on the St-Tropez peninsula in a location just off the busy La Foux intersection. Includes the famous Château de Pampelonne vineyard. Free tastings and many regional products for sale.

TRANSPORT

MMG boat trips – ☎ *04 94 96 51 00.* Regular services to Ste-Maxime leaving from St-Tropez operate Apr to end of Oct, 10.40€ round-trip; to Les Issambres Jun-Sep, 11.20€ round-trip; to Port-Grimaud Apr-Oct, 9€ round-trip; to Les Cannebiers Bay at 3.30pm leaving from St-Tropez, 8€ round-trip and at 3pm leaving from Ste-Maxime, 11.80€ round-trip.

LEISURE ACTIVITIES

Maison du Tourisme du Golfe de St-Tropez – *Gassin* – ☎ *04 94 55 22 00.* This tourist office issues a list of all the companies based in St-Tropez Bay that specialise in deep-sea diving.

---

artists and more recently by celebrities from the entertainment world. Two Bravades, or "acts of defiance", take place each year. The first is a religious procession in honour of St Tropez, the second commemorates an event of local history which took place in 1637.

Massif des Maures★★★

The long, low parallel ranges of the massif unfold from Fréjus to Hyères. Its fine forests of pine, cork oak and chestnut trees have been devastated by fire. Chapels, monasteries and small villages are dotted in the hinterland, while the coast is fringed by coves and bays.

SAINTES★★

POPULATION 25 874

MICHELIN MAP 324 G 5

GREEN GUIDE ATLANTIC COAST

Saintes was already a regional capital in Roman times, with a bridge over the Charente aligned on today's Rue Victor-Hugo. In the Middle Ages, the town was an important staging-post on the pilgrims' route to Santiago de Compostela. Two great religious establishments developed on its outskirts, St-Eutrope on the west bank of the river, the Abbey for Women (Abbaye aux Dames) on the east bank.

Bernard Palissy (1510-90) came from Périgord. He was known for his works on technology and philosophy; his greatest fame nevertheless came from the glassware and pottery made here in a studio close to one of the towers of Saintes' ramparts. His total commitment to this work (he is even supposed to have chopped up his furniture to fire his kiln) enabled him to discover for himself the technique of making enamel, a secret jealously guarded by Masséot Abaquesne at Rouen for more than 20 years.

The historic core of the town, built on the site of the Gallo-Roman city, has been restored and pedestrianised.

▶ **Orient Yourself:** Saintes, which is listed as a "Town of Art and history," offers discovery tours from end Jun to mid-Sep. 6€. Information is available at the Heritage workshop, by calling ☎ 05 46 74 23 82 or on www.vpah.culture.fr.

Visit

Roman Saintes – The Arch of Germanicus (**arc de Germanicus**★) was built in AD 19 at a point on the east bank of the Charente where the roads from Poitiers and Limoges converged on the Roman bridge. An archeological museum houses objects saved when the ruins of the Roman city were demolished. To the west, on the slopes of the west bank of the river, is an amphitheatre (**arènes**★), one of the oldest (1C AD) in the Roman world.

Romanesque Saintes – On the west bank, the crypt (**crypte**) of the Église St-Eutrope once served as a parish church (**église inférieure**★) to the pilgrimage church above. This upper part of the building was monastic in origin; it has retained two very fine capitals from the pillars of the former transept *(visible from the gallery)*.

On the east bank is the church (**église**★) of the Abbaye aux Dames (🕐 *Apr-Sep: daily 10am-7pm; Oct-Mar: daily except Mon in early Nov 1-6pm;* 🕐 *closed between Christmas and New Year's Day;* ☜ *3€, no charge under 16 years;* ☎ *05 46 97 48 48; 1hr30min guided tour* ☜ *available end Jun to 3rd Fri of Sep, contact the Tourism Office* ☎ *05 46 74 23 82)*. It is a notable achievement of Romanesque local style, with fine carving in the excellent local stone showing the influence of the sculpture gracing St Peter's Church at Aulnay. The design of the west front (**façade**) is typical; it has rich carving in the arching, particularly around the central portal, featuring angels, symbols of the Evangelists, martyrs and the Elders of the Apocalypse. The harmoniously proportioned tower, with its rotunda divided up into twin bays and its mosaic arcading, is topped by a conical roof covered in fish-scale tiles.

◖◗ Musée des Beaux-Arts★ 🕐 *May-Sep: daily 1.30-6pm; Oct-Apr: daily 1.30-5pm.* 🕐 *Closed Mon, 1 May.* ☜ *1.50€ (under 18 years: no charge), no charge Sun and Wed.* ☎ *05 46 93 03 94.www.saintes.fr.*

Excursion

Église de Rioux

15km – 9mi south. Among the many fine Romanesque churches of the Saintonge countryside, this one is well known for its west front and particularly for its apse (**chevet**★). This is divided into sections by columnar buttresses and has an extraordinary wealth of geometric motifs emphasising windows, arcades and even the bonding of the stonework. With this display of decorative perfection, the Saintonge Romanesque can be said to have reached the end of its evolution, any further development being attributable to the virtuosity of individual sculptors.

SALERS★★

POPULATION 439

MICHELIN MAP 330 C 4

GREEN GUIDE AUVERGNE THE RHÔNE VALLEY

High up among the vast grazing-grounds of the volcanic Cantal uplands, Salers has long been a market centre and staging-post for travellers. The tiny town seems to have been laid out to confuse possible attackers, with a maze of tortuous streets leading to the main square.

Visit

This square (**Grande-Place**★★) is something of a stage-set, overlooked by the corner-towers and turrets of the grand lava-built houses of the local notables; the effect is completed by a fountain.

External staircases, arched doorways and dormer windows peering out from the schist-tiled roofs are among the features characterising the 15C and 16C houses. The Renaissance building known as the Ancien Bailliage has typically Auvergnat window-mouldings and angle-towers, while the canted Flojeac House (Maison de Flojeac) protects its windows behind massive iron grilles; the Hôtel de la Ronade is distinguished by a Gothic turret rising five storeys high.

The church (**église**★) has a 12C porch with a very simple doorway, as well as a tower (restored in the 19C) with mitred arches very much in the local Auvergne style. Inside there is a fine polychrome sculpture of the **Entombment**★ dating from 1495.

Fort de **SALSES**★★

MICHELIN MAP 344 I 5

GREEN GUIDE LANGUEDOC ROUSSILLON TARN GORGES

Ever since Roman times Salses has guarded the main road linking France and Spain at the pinch point where the Corbières range approaches the Mediterranean shore. The site's strategic importance was not lost on Ferdinand of Aragon, who erected a fort here in 1497 to protect the northern frontier of a Spain which, since 1493, had once more included Catalan-speaking Roussillon (the place still marks the language frontier between Languedoc and Catalan today).

Visit

Allow 1hr. Kids ⏱ *Jun-Sep: daily 9.30am-7pm; Oct-May: daily 10am-12.15pm, 2-5pm. Possibility of a guided tour (upper sections of the fort) upon request. Last admission 1hr before closing.* ⏱ *Closed 1 Jan, 1 May, 1 and 11 Nov, 25 Dec.* ☞ *6.10€ (under 18 years: no charge), no charge 1st Sun in the month (Oct-Mar).* ☏ *04 68 38 60 13.*

Designed for Ferdinand by Francisco Ramirez, the fort is an unusual example in France of such a structure of Spanish type, albeit subsequently much modified by Vauban in the 17C. Salses changed hands more than once during the long years of Franco-Spanish conflict, but finally, in September 1642 – Perpignan had just been retaken by Louis XIII – its Spanish garrison marched forth from its gates and headed southwards for the last time. Seventeen years later, the Treaty of the Pyrenees ended the border problem by incorporating Roussillon into France. Nevertheless, Vauban's considered opinion was that the fort was obsolete; in 1691 he reduced the height of the keep and protected the walls and bastions with convex additions designed to make shells ricochet off them.

Église **SAN MICHELE DE MURATO**★★

MICHELIN MAP 345 E 4

GREEN GUIDE CORSE (IN FRENCH)

On its lonely hilltop site just to the north of the village of Murato, this little church is a good example of the archeological and tourist attractions in Corsica.

Visit

⏱ *Daily except Sun 9am-noon, 2-5pm, Wed and Sat 9am-noon. Call the town hall in advance.* ☏ *04 95 37 60 10.*

Built around 1280, it belongs to the end of the second period of the Pisan Romanesque; as it developed in the island, this style was often characterised by polychrome stonework and a degree of sculptural decoration. The green serpentine and white limestone have been expertly cut into blocks of different sizes to avoid any impression of monotony.

The sculpture has a strangely naïve quality; crudely fashioned figures of animals and people decorate the west front, while the side windows are surrounded with foliated scrolls and strapwork, and the apse has ornamental brackets and modillions.

SAORGE★★

POPULATION 362

MICHELIN MAP 341 G 4

GREEN GUIDE FRENCH RIVIERA

The Upper Roya valley★★ has been carved out between the schists of the Mercantour massif and the limestone rocks of the southern Pre-Alps. Its gorges★★ form a spectacular setting★★ for the village of Saorge clinging to the steep south-facing slopes which rise abruptly from the river far below.

Visit

The place is dominated by the belfries of its churches and monasteries, which overlook terraces and balconies, tall old houses with open-fronted drying lofts and roofs tiled with heavy stone slabs. A maze of stepped and tunnelled streets completes this highly picturesque townscape.

Excursion

Notre-Dame-des-Fontaines★★

17km – 11mi northeast via St-Dalmas-de-Tende. The key to the chapel is kept at La Brigue.
A temple dedicated to water gods once stood in this lonely valley at the foot of Mont Noir (Black Mountain). The chancel of the present building dates from the 12C; the nave added in the 15C was raised in height in the 18C and given a new ceiling.
Most of the chapel's well-preserved **frescoes**★★★ were painted by the Piedmontese artist Giovanni Canavesio between 1472 and 1492; in late-Gothic style, they form a veritable catechism in pictures. The 500 figures illustrate the artist's great mastery of movement and expression. The walls of the nave are covered with scenes from Christ's Passion (including an extraordinary depiction of the Death of Judas), while the west wall is occupied by a vast fresco of the Last Judgement.
The triumphal arch at the entrance to the choir is the work of another artist from Piedmont, Giovanni Baleisoni; his treatment of scenes from the Life of the Virgin and the childhood of Jesus is altogether more delicate.

SARLAT-LA-CANÉDA★★★

POPULATION 9 909

MICHELIN MAP 329 I 6

GREEN GUIDE DORDOGNE BERRY LIMOUSIN

Sarlat is the capital of the Périgord Noir (Black Périgord) country, the well-treed agricultural region bounded by the Dordogne and Vézère rivers. The town grew up around the Benedictine abbey founded in the middle of the 9C, from whose rule the townspeople managed to free themselves in 1299. The wealth of the surrounding countryside poured into the town, enabling it to support a prosperous population of merchants, clerics and lawyers, among them Étienne de la Boétie (1530-63), friend of Montaigne, philosopher, and one of the first translators of Classical Greek literature into French. Sarlat reached its peak during the 13C and 14C. During the Hundred Years War, many of its houses were neglected and required major restoration once peace returned; cumulative extensions over the course of the centuries have left a number of them with Renaissance upper storeys built over a medieval ground floor, the whole topped by roofs laden with Classical details. The town has long played host to busy fairs and markets, and such traditional activity still takes place every Saturday, when the produce of the season is bought and sold, poultry, cereals, horses, nuts, geese, foie gras, truffles...

▸ **Orient Yourself:** The town developed on a north-south axis. The old town is accessible by the avenue Thiers and Gambetta. In the summer, you have to visit the old town by foot. Sarlat, which is listed as a "Town of Art and History," offers discovery tours from Apr-Oct for 5€. Evening tours are available from Jun to end Sep for 6€. Information at the tourist office, on www.vpah.culture.com or on www.ot-sarlat-perigord.fr.

🅿 **Parking:** There are 12 parking lots in town, 8 of which can be used at no charge. We suggest you find spot on one of the short streets surrounding the old town.

Sights

Vieux Sarlat (Old Town)★★★

A conservation programme begun in 1964 has safeguarded Sarlat's exceptional townscape. In the 19C, the ruler-straight Rue de la République was driven ruthlessly through the irregular network of medieval streets, dividing the popular west from the more refined east. But there are houses of great charm all over the town, many with attractive courtyards. Most are ashlar-built from the fine golden limestone of the area, and this stone is used for the roofs too. Unlike the slates or schists of other regions, it is cut in thick slabs, and the roof-beams consequently have a heavy load to carry. The tiler often had to distort the profile of the roof, which however has the advantage of leaving lots of small openings to improve the ventilation of the timber structure below.

The finest houses include: **Maison de la Boétie**★, a Renaissance building of 1525; the **Hôtel de Malleville**★ consisting of three medieval dwellings knocked into one another in the 16C; the **Hôtel de Plamon**★, every storey of which was built in a different century, and the Présidial, which was once the seat of the royal court of justice. The 12C Lantern of the Dead (Lanterne des Morts) was probably used as a funerary chapel.

◐◐ ▸ Place des Oies★ – Rue des Consuls★.

Town house, Rue Montaigne

S. Sauvignier/MICHELIN

SARTÈNE ★

POPULATION 3 525

MICHELIN MAP 345 C 10

GREEN GUIDE CORSE (IN FRENCH)

The writer Prosper Mérimée thought Sartène, 305m – 1 000ft above the Bay of Valinco, the "most Corsican of Corsican towns". The area around has been occupied by man for more than 5 000 years and there are abundant traces (dolmens and menhirs) from the time of the megalith builders, notably at Cauria and Palaggiu. The warlike Torreans too left their mark in a number of places like Alo Bisucce, Cucuruzzu and in particular Filitosa (⌖ *see FILITOSA*). Corsica's medieval history is based to a great extent on the chronicles of Giovanni della Grossa (1388-1464), who was born and died at Grossa *(12km – 7mi west of Sartène)*. In his early days he was a determined opponent of the Genoese, but later he allied himself to their cause, taking part in many of the decisive events in the island's history. Finally he became a lawyer and recorded his stirring times in writing. Between the 16C and the 18C, Sartène suffered at the hands of pirates from the Barbary coast, so much so that it was deserted by part of its population.

Sights

Place de la Libération

The shady square is the focus of local life. It is overlooked by the **Église Ste-Marie**, built in granite. To the left of the main entrance are the chains and the heavy cross of oak borne by Catenacciu, the anonymous red-robed penitential figure at the centre of the nocturnal procession on Good Friday. This procession (**procession du Catenacciu★★**) is probably the island's most ancient ceremony.

Vieille ville (Old Town)★★

Go through the arch of the Town Hall (Hôtel de ville) and take the street opposite (Rue des Frères-Bartoli). The narrow stone-flagged alleyways, occasionally stepped or vaulted, are lined by tall granite-built houses with a fortress-like air. The **Quartier de Santa Ann★★★** has a particularly characteristic townscape of this kind.

 Musée de préhistoire corse★.

SAUMUR ★★

POPULATION 30 301

MICHELIN MAP 317 I 5

GREEN GUIDE CHÂTEAUX OF THE LOIRE

Dominated by its château on a chalky spur overlooking the meeting-point of the Thouet with the Loire, Saumur is famous for its wines and the French army's prestigious cavalry school.

A Bit of History

The town owed its early prosperity to the wooden bridge which crossed the Loire via two islands (the Île d'Offrand and the Île Millocheau, now joined together). It formed the only crossing point over the river between Tours and Ponts-de-Cé downstream from Angers, at the time of pilgrimages to Santiago de Compostela. In the 13C, the monks from the Abbaye de St Florent undertook to replace the original structure by one of stone, constructed at the rate of one arch a year. Though often carried away by floods, this bridge was always rebuilt.

Like all the towns along the great river (Decize, Nevers, La Charité, Cosne, Gien, Orléans, Blois...), Saumur's site was chosen, regardless of orientation, on whichever bank offered the better protection from high waters. The attractive old houses facing the Loire have walls of pale tufa and steeply-pitched slate roofs.

Saumur's long association with the horse began in 1763, when the crack corps known as the Carabiniers Regiment was sent here, under the command of Louis XV's brother ("Monsieur"). It was a time when the refinement of riding technique which had begun under de Pluvinel (Louis XIII's Master of the Horse) had become fashionable among the aristocracy. The National Equitation Centre (École Nationale d'Équitation) was founded in 1972, incorporating the famous **Cadre Noir** (Black Squad) which had originally consisted solely of army instructors. This aspect of the town's identity is evoked in the museum in the Château, and in the **Musée de l'École de Cavalerie**★ (*presently closed; the museum will reopen in a new location; call the Tourism office for information;* ☎ *02 41 40 20 60*) which has displays on post-18C military history and on the development of horsemanship. In addition, there is a **Musée des Blindés**★★ (* May-Sep: daily 9.30am-6.30pm; Oct-Apr: daily 10am-5pm; last admission 1hr before closing; closed 1 Jan and 25 Dec. 5.50€; ☎ 02 41 53 06 99; www.musee-des-blindes.asso.fr*), with displays of armoured vehicles both French and foreign from 1918 onwards.

Visit

Château★★

 Château's interior closed for maintenance. Visit of the exterior only. Apr-Oct: Wed-Mon 10am-1pm, 2-6pm; Nov-Mar: Wed-Mon 10am-12.30pm, 2-5.30pm. Possiblity of a guided tour (call in advance Apr-Oct). Last admission 30min before closing. Closed Tue. 2€ (under 11 years: no charge). ☎ 02 41 40 24 40.

In the 14C, the château was rebuilt on the foundations of the medieval fortress originally erected by Philippe Auguste and Louis IX. As a consequence, it has a somewhat irregular layout. In the 15C, with the return of more peaceful times following the end of the Hundred Years War, Good King René (* see Index*) endowed his "castle of love" with sumptuous decorative detail in late-Gothic style. The château is shown in this state, albeit in a somewhat idealised landscape, in one of the miniatures from the *Très Riches Heures du Duc de Berry* (* see Index*). In the late 16C, at the time of the Wars of Religion, the place was refortified, as Saumur was one of the strongholds of French Protestantism.

There are two museums in the château, the **Musée du Cheval**★ with fascinating collections of riding equipment and a number of pictures (including work by Stubbs), and the **Musée des Arts décoratifs**★★, which has a fine display of works of art from the Middle Ages and Renaissance, including a collection of faience and French porcelain from the 17C and 18C.

During the Military Tattoo (Carrousel) held in July, the Musée des Blindés presents a number of armoured vehicles restored at the school and driven by cadets.

Excursion

Zoo de Doué★★

The zoo is situated on the western edge of Doué-la-Fontaine on the road to Cholet (D 960). Some 500 animals roam more or less freely in this remarkable cave setting enhanced by acacia trees and bamboo groves, cascades and rocky overhangs. Visitors can walk among the birds of prey in the vulture pen (fosse aux charognards) while in the large quarry reserved for leopards (canyon aux léopards), there are observation posts to view three sets of cats: snow leopards, Persian leopards and jaguars. A school of penguins disport themselves in a creek (crique aux manchots). A gallery (Galerie des Faluns) gives a glimpse of the fauna which existed on the site some 10 million years ago.

SAVERNE★

POPULATION 10 278

MICHELIN MAP 315 I 4

GREEN GUIDE ALSACE LORRAINE CHAMPAGNE

The town has given its name to one of the main routes through the Vosges uplands, the Saverne Gap (Col de Saverne). To the west is the plateau of Lorraine; to the east, steep wooded slopes dropping down to the lowlands of the Rhine valley and the other towns of Alsace.

Visit

Château★

This splendid red sandstone palace replaced the old residence of the prince-bishops of Strasbourg which was burnt down in 1779. It was rebuilt by the high-living Cardinal de Rohan who endowed it with a monumental Louis XVI **façade**★★ giving onto the park. It has a central peristyle with eight massive Corinthian columns; to either side extend long wings with fluted pilasters supporting an attic floor and a roof balustrade, while at each end stands a projecting corner pavilion.

Maisons anciennes★ (old houses).

Excursion

Église de Marmoutier★★

6km – 4mi south. This former abbey church was built around 1150-1160. Its fine west front **(façade ouest★★)** in the red sandstone of the region is in Romanesque style incorporating Carolingian and Rhineland influences.

The façade is articulated by horizontal bands carried on low arches and by flattened buttresses, giving a highly compartmentalised effect. The central bell-tower is set back somewhat and flanked by two octagonal corner towers. The overall impression is one of unalterable solidity, barely relieved by minor decorative touches such as the foliage scrolls on the austere capitals in the porch.

SEDAN★

POPULATION 21 667

MICHELIN MAP 306 L 4

GREEN GUIDE ALSACE LORRAINE CHAMPAGNE

The ruler of Sedan, Count de la Marck, built a fortress on a rocky outcrop here in 1424. His descendants served a variety of overlords, the Holy Roman Emperor, the King of France... without however neglecting the proper interests of their town.

A Bit of History

In the 16C, Sedan turned Protestant; a military academy was founded in the town which was attended in his youth by Turenne (Henri de la Tour d'Auvergne). This great soldier was born in the castle here in 1611; of serious and scrupulous character, he became progressively more adventurous as his experience broadened. In an age still preoccupied with the techniques of the siege, he advocated more mobile ways of making war. In the course of the Thirty Years War, he showed almost incredible bravery, beating the impetuous Condé at Bléneau and opening the gates of Paris to Louis XIV in 1652. The victories won by him at Arras and in the sanddunes near Dunkirk brought Spain to the negotiating table and led to the Treaty of the Pyrenees. In 1675, he was slain by a cannon-ball. His funeral elegy, composed on the same lines as that of the Grand Condé, was given by Bossuet.

The end of the Second Empire – On 1 September 1870, the French army executed a bold manœuvre designed to relieve General Bazaine besieged in Metz. But the attack failed, and the troops fell back on Sedan and its fortifications. On 2 September, the ailing Napoleon III met Bismarck, who had him escorted to the château at Bellevue. It was here that the Emperor's plenipotentiary was forced to sign the humiliating surrender of the French forces to the future Kaiser William I. Napoleon himself was taken to Kassel, then eventually to exile in England.

Visit

Château fort★★

🕐 *Guided tours* 👟 *(1hr30min) daily mid-Mar to end Jun and early Sep to mid-Sep: 10am-noon, 1.30-5.30pm; Jul and Aug: 10am-6pm; mid-Sep to mid-Mar: daily 1.30-4.30pm, Sat-Sun, public and school holidays 10am-noon, 1.30-6pm.* 🕐 *Closed Mon (non-season and excluding holidays) 1 Jan and 25 Dec.* 👓 *6.90€ (children: 4.60€).* ☎ *03 24 27 73 73. www.sedan-bouillon.org.*

With a total area of 35ha – 86 acres, this was the most extensive stronghold in 15C Europe. Built on a rocky spur, its 30m – 100ft high walls had bastions added to them in the 16C. At the beginning of the 17C, it was extended and given extra height by Turenne's father. The timber construction inside the Great Tower (Grosse Tour) is a remarkable piece of 15C master carpentry. The castle's apartments are laid out on seven floors. In the south wing is a museum.

SENLIS★★

POPULATION 14 439

MICHELIN MAP 305 G5

GREEN GUIDE NORTHERN FRANCE AND THE PARIS REGION

At the centre of a rich agricultural region, Senlis was already a prosperous place in Gallo-Roman times. Later, the Merovingian rulers made it their place of residence, followed by the Carolingian kings; eventually Senlis became a royal domain, the kernel of the Île-de-France, itself the core of the future kingdom of France. The old part of the town, to the south of the cathedral, is sited on the Gallo-Roman settlement which preceded it; it has a number of old dwellings in the characteristic style of the Valois area, built of brick and soft limestone. Many of the streets are still paved with big flagstones.

▶ **Orient Yourself:** Senlis, which is listed as a "Town of Art and History", offers 2hr discovery tours on Sun and public holidays at 3pm from end Mar to end Jun (Jul and Aug: Sun at 5pm; Sep: Sun at 3pm). 5€. Information at the tourist office or on www.vpah.culture.fr.

Visit

Cathédrale Notre-Dame★★

👓 *Illustration Art: Architecture.*
Begun in 1153 with the support of Louis VII, it is one of the first churches in the Île-de-France to be built in Transitional style. The choir was completed in 1180 and the west front 10 years later. Of this first building a few features survive. They include the choir and the insensitively restored west front, as well as three bays of square plan on either side of the transept; these have sexpartite vaults held up by columns alternating with piers of massive proportions; the elevation here includes a gallery on the Norman model.

Old town, Senlis

S. Sauvignier/MICHELIN

Around 1240, the building of a false transept involved the loss of four columns and the shifting of two piers to the centre of the nave, thereby breaking the continuity of the pattern previously established. At the same time, the south tower was given its spire.

The Flamboyant Gothic appearance of the cathedral is the result of the restoration undertaken between 1513 and 1560, following a great fire in 1504. The transept and its arms were rebuilt, as were the upper parts of the elevation; the roof was given extra height, the new vaults being supported on flying buttresses. The base of the building was extended by adding a second run of aisles with complex lierne and tierceron vaulting. Pierre Chambiges, the son of Martin Chambiges who had worked at Sens, Beauvais and Troyes, was in charge of building the south doorway; whether because of tradition or out of respect for his father, he continued to work in the Flamboyant style (with luxuriant sculpted ornamentation, mouldings, balustrades and galleries). He also added features of Early Renaissance type, like basket-handle arches and cable-moulding.

The tall spire (**flèche**★★) of the south tower soars 78m – 256ft heavenwards, its verticality emphasised by the gables which have the additional function of converting the square plan to the octagonal and of keeping the whole composition in a state of equilibrium. The rigorous geometry of the design is relieved by the crockets and by the dormers and gables which set a trend all over the Valois area until the 16C.

◗◗ Musée d'Art et d'Archéologie★ ◷ *Feb-Oct: daily except Tue 10am-noon, 2-6pm, Wed 2-6pm, Sat-Sun and public holidays 11am-1pm, 2-6pm; Nov-Jan: daily 10am-noon, 2-5pm, Sat-Sun and public holidays 11am-1pm, 2-5pm.* ◷ *Closed 1 Jan, 1 May and 25 Dec.* ⊚ *4€ (under 16 years: no charge).* ☎ *03 44 32 00 83.* Vieilles rues★ (old streets).

Chapelle royale St-Frambourg★ ◷ *May-Oct: Sat-Sun and public holidays 3pm-6pm; Nov-Apr: Sun. 3-5pm.* ⊚ *4.50€.* ☎ *03 44 53 39 99. www.fondation-cziffra.org* – Fondation Cziffr★.

SENS★★

POPULATION 27 082

MICHELIN MAP 319 C 2

GREEN GUIDE BURGUNDY JURA

In Gallo-Roman times, Sens was the capital of the province of Senonia. Later, at a time when Paris was little more than an overgrown village, the city was extended outwards to new limits still marked by the line of today's boulevards. Its central position in relation to Burgundy, Champagne and the Île-de-France gave it an administrative and ecclesiastical importance lasting for centuries; for a long time it was the Bishop of Sens who crowned French kings, and the bishopric of Paris was subordinate to the archbishopric of Sens until 1627.

Visit

Cathédrale St-Étienne★★

In its general conception this is the very first of France's great Gothic cathedrals, its foundations laid in the years 1128-30, though most building took place between 1140 and 1168.

The influence of the Romanesque can still be discerned in a number of features, like the slightly pointed "Burgundian" arches of the nave, a series of twin openings at tribune level with a false gallery, as yet no triforium, and, in the side chapels, a combination of rounded and pointed arches. But it is the Gothic which is decisive. There is use throughout of quadripartite vaulting; the choir has sexpartite vaults of square plan resting on massive pillars alternating with slender columns, and the ambulatory has pointed arches, still awkwardly asymmetrical.

Following the collapse of the south tower of the west front in 1268, the building was restored and altered, with the probable addition of flying buttresses. In the 13C and 14C, the clerestory windows were given extra height; then, in the 15C and 16C, the transepts were built in Flamboyant style.

Outside, the decorative features include the pier of the central portal, the famous statue of St Stephen (in style intermediate between the Schools of Chartres and Amiens), and the Flamboyant gable of the north portal, the work of Martin Chambiges.

Inside, the eye is drawn to the **stained glass**★★; this is of 12C date in the ambulatory and north side of the choir, while the Jesse Tree and St Nicholas in the south transept and the rose window of the north transept are all Renaissance works by master glaziers from Troyes. The ambulatory, the chapels opening off it, and the choir all have very fine grilles of wrought and gilded ironwork (18C).

◐◑ Musée, Trésor (treasury) and Palais Synodal (Bishops' Palace)★ ⓘ *Jul-Aug: Wed-Mon 10am-6pm; Jun and Sep: Wed-Mon 10am-noon, 2-6pm. Oct-May: Mon, Thu-Fri 2-6pm, Wed, Sat-Sun and public holidays 10am-noon, 2-6pm.* ⓘ *Closed Tue, 1 Jan and 25 Dec.* ◈ *3.40€, no charge 1st Sun in the month.* ☎ *03 86 64 46 22.*

Prieuré de **SERRABONE**★★

MICHELIN MAP 334 G 7

GREEN GUIDE LANGUEDOC ROUSSILLON TARN GORGES

In its remote and stony setting among the austere Aspres mountains, the former priory contains some of the finest Romanesque sculpture in Roussillon. The schist-built structure sits well in this wild landscape, its severity relieved somewhat by the use of delicate pink marble.

Visit

Allow 30min. 🄺🄸🄳🅂 ⓘ *10am-6pm. Last admission 30min before closing.* ⓘ *Closed 1 Jan, 1 May, 1 Nov, 25 Dec.* ◈ *3€ (children: 2€).* ☎ *04 68 84 09 30. www.cg66.fr.*

The chapel gallery (**tribune**★★) of about 1080, originally intended to serve as the choir, was moved to the centre of the nave at the beginning of the 19C. It is an unusual feature to have survived and has wonderful decoration in low relief as well as exceptionally richly carved capitals. The latter show traces of oriental or Lombard influence, for example in the symbolic treatment of the lions and in the integration of the figures of animals in the total composition. A delightful south-facing **gallery**★ (Promenoir des Chanoines) overlooks the ravine far below.

SISTERON★★

POPULATION 6 594

MICHELIN MAP 334 D 7

GREEN GUIDE FRENCH ALPS

Sisteron lies between the Laragne valley to the north and the valley of the middle Durance to the south. As well as marking the historic boundary between Dauphiné and Provence, this is also the northern limit of the cultivation of the olive.

Visit

Citadelle★

ⓘ *Jul-Aug: daily 9am-7.30pm; Jun and Sep: daily 9am-7pm; Apr: daily 9am-6pm; May: daily 9am-6.30pm; Oct: daily 9am-5.30pm; Nov: daily 10am-5pm.* ◈ *4.80€ (children: 2.40€).* ☎ *04 92 61 27 57. www.sisteron.com.*

Major restoration had to be carried out following the heavy bombing carried out by the Americans on 15 August 1944. Of the 12C fortress little remains other than the keep and the sentry walk-since the defences were virtually rebuilt in the 16C by Jean Évrard, Henri IV's military engineer and predecessor of Vauban. The important N85 highway tunnels its way through the rock on which the citadel is built. From

the Guérite du Diable there is an impresssive view over the **site**★★
limestone beds were dramatically folded to form the Baume Rock (Roch.
which the ice of Quaternary times then refashioned into a glacial bar.

 Église Notre-Dame★ ⏰ *Open Easter to All Saints' Day. Contact the tou*
☎ *04 92 61 12 03 or 04.92.61.12.03.*

Excursion

Signal de Lure★★

Alt 1 826m – 5 990ft. 27km – 17mi southwest. The Lure mountains are a bleak limestone
range, an extension eastwards of Mont Ventoux, with the same friable rock which
quickly breaks down into a mass of debris, and the same pattern of vegetation; on
the south-facing slopes, garrigue and lavender and evergreen oaks; on the northern
flank of the mountains, beeches, firs and larches and patches of grazing. From the
summit there is a vast panoramic **view** stretching as far as the Mediterranean, the
Vercors Massif and Mont Ventoux.

SOLIGNAC★★

POPULATION 1 345

MICHELIN MAP 325 E 6

GREEN GUIDE DORDOGNE BERRY LIMOUSIN

Before becoming trusted adviser to the Frankish king Dagobert, the legendary
figure of St Eligius (St Eloi) had been a goldsmith, learning the intricacies of the
art at Limoges. In the year 632, he founded an abbey here in the valley of the
Briance by the side of the old Roman road linking Limoges with Périgueux.

Visit

Église abbatiale★★

Rebuilt around 1175, the abbey church shows Limoges influence in its use of granite
and in certain characteristic mouldings, but its domes are based on the ones at
Souillac in Quercy erected 35 years previously.

The abbey's outside appearance is strikingly robust; the elevations of north wall and
apse are particularly harmonious. From the steps of the porch there is a fine general
view of the beautifully proportioned **interior**; the overall impression is one of great
purity and simplicity, a result of the architect's careful control of the layout and his
use of materials of high quality. The multiple domes are supported by great pointed
arches and pendentives; as well as being among the last of their kind to be built in
Aquitaine, they are some of the finest examples to be seen in the region.

There are many other features of interest in the abbey; the first bay of the lateral
inspection gallery has capitals of archaic design, while there is an extraordinarily
deformed dome over the choir and one of ovoid shape covering the north transept.
One of the crossing pillars is painted with an impressive portrait of St Christopher.

SOUILLAC★

POPULATION 3 459

MICHELIN MAP 337 E 2

GREEN GUIDE DORDOGNE BERRY LIMOUSIN

Souillac evolved originally as a river port at the upper limit of navigation on the
Dordogne and its present role as a market town goes back to this time too. The
wn spread out on the alluvial plain of an old meander around a Benedictine
y whose golden age was in the 12C after which decline set in, hastened by
ubled times of the Hundred Years War and the Wars of Religion.

...église abbatiale

... for the former abbey church was Cahors Cathedral, but at Souillac the ... improved on the original by making his pillars much less massive and giving ... weight to the main arches. The latter are cleverly integrated with the transverse ... to form the square base on which four pendentives and a cornice of corbels ... support the slender arch-stones of the three domes.

...he discreet elegance of the exterior of the Romanesque east end of the church finds its counterpart inside in the harmonious arrangement of the chapels opening off the hemicycle of the choir.

The west front was mutilated by the Huguenots in 1573; the fragments of the former portal (**ancien portail** ⋆) have been rearranged on the inside of the doorway. The right engaged pillar which was once the central pillar of the doorway is richly decorated; on the right are the forms of concupiscence associated with the different stages of life, in the middle, their effects (monsters devouring each other), and, on the left, the remission of sin by the sacrifice of Isaac, with Abraham's hand held back by the messenger of God.

To the left of this pillar is the fine-low relief figure of **Isaiah** ⋆⋆ – its affinities with the depiction of Jeremiah at Moissac are obvious; there is the same expressiveness and virtuosity, but the sculptor has moved beyond the conventional approach of his model.

◯◯ Musée National de l'automate et de la robotique⋆ 🧒 ⏱ *Jun and Sep: daily 10am-noon, 3-6pm; Jul-Aug: daily 10am-7pm; Apr-May and Oct: daily except Mon 10am-noon, 3-6pm; Nov.-Mar: daily except Mon and Tue 2.30-5.30pm.* ⊚ *5€ (children: 2.50€).* ☏ *05 65 37 07 07* – automata, robots.

La Haute **SOULE** ⋆⋆

MICHELIN MAP F-G-H 4-5

GREEN GUIDE ATLANTIC COAST

The Saison or Mauléon torrent is the principal axis of the Soule region, one of the original seven provinces in the Basque country. The province shares many cultural influences with the Béarn including the style of houses, and has retained the dances and folk traditions most characteristic of the Basque region.

The Upper Soule is separated from the St-Jean-Pied-de-Port basin by the Iraty and Arbailles massifs forming a difficult barrier owing to the rough terrain and dense woodland cover. This region is suitable for fishing and forest rambles, and in winter, cross-country skiing.

The passes of the Haute Soule region are on the migration route of wood pigeons as the birds fly from the Poitou, the Massif Central and the North Pyrenees to their wintering ground. Hunting and shooting are popular sports in the area.

Visit

Ahusquy

A mountain inn (restored) stands in a panoramic **site** ⋆⋆ which was a place where Basque shepherds gathered.

Col d'Aphanize

Wild horses graze on the slopes around the pass. The pastureland here is the summer home of many flocks of sheep. Just east of the pass the **view** ⋆⋆ opens out wide: from Pic des Escaliers immediately south to Pic de Ger to the southeast on the horizon.

Forêt des Arbailles ⋆⋆

This forest of beech trees covers the higher reaches of a sandstone bastion silhoue... against the sky.

Crevasses d'Holçarté★

Access by a track signposted GR 10 past the bridge, Pont de Laugibar. After a steep cʳ
the entrance to the gorges ("crevasses") cut through the limestone to a depth of 20ᵗ
– 656ft. The path rises to the top of the Olhadubi tributary gorge which is crossed bʸ
a dizzily impressive footbridge slung high up above the torrent.

Fôret d'Iraty★

This forest of beech groves straddling the frontier supplied wood for masts to the
French and Spanish navies from the 18C onwards. It is one of the largest wooded
areas in Europe.

Gorges de Kakouetta★★

*It is recommended that this excursion, which can be tiring and sometimes daunting,
should be undertaken when the flow of water is reduced (from early June to late October).
Access by D 113, the road to Ste-Engrâce. Cross the river Uhaïtxa by a footbridge, climb
the slope on the far side and then proceed down the gorges.*

The beginning of the narrows (Grand Étroit) is the most grandiose section of the
Kakouetta gorges.

This splendid canyon, more than 200m – 656ft deep, is no more than 3m to 10m
(11ft – 33ft) wide. The path, frequently difficult, crosses the torrent by footbridges
and ends within sight of a waterfall formed by a resurgence. A cave boasting huge
concretions marks the end of the walk.

STRASBOURG★★★

POPULATION 388 483

MICHELIN MAP 315 K 5

GREEN GUIDE ALSACE LORRAINE CHAMPAGNE

**Strasbourg's name comes from the German meaning "city of the roads", and the
place is indeed a meeting point for the highways, railways and waterways linking the Mediterranean with the Rhineland, Central Europe, the North Sea and
the Baltic via the Belfort Gap and the Swabian Basin. Since 1949, Strasbourg has
been the seat of the Council of Europe.**

▶ **Orient Yourself:** On the banks of the river Ill, Strasbourg was built around its
famous cathedral whose exterior can be enjoyed best from rue Mercière. If you
follow the rue des Grandes Arcades you will come across Place Kléber, the most
famous square in the city. A 1hr 30min audio-guided tour enables visitors to
discover the cathedral, the old town and the Petite France at their own speed.
Audio devices available in the tourist office for 6€ (30€ deposit). There are also
"Town of Art and History" tours offered through the tourist office for 6.80€. Call
☎ 03 88 52 28 28 or visit www.ot-strasbourg.fr.

Strasbourg - Address Book

PRACTICAL INFORMATION

Tourist Offices – *17 pl. de la Cathédrale,
67000 Strasbourg,* ☎ *03 88 52 28 28, www.
ot-strasbourg.fr - Pl. de la Gare, 67000
Strasbourg,* ☎ *03 88 32 51 49 www.
strasbourg.com - Pont de l'Europe, 67000
Strasbourg,* ☎ *03 88 61 39 23.*

Parking – Eight car parks situated on the
outskirts of town are at the disposal of
ᵥisitors (from €2.40 to €2.70; tram ticket
ᵒffered) who are invited to take a tramway
ᵗᵒ town. The location of these car parks
ᵢⁿdicated by a square panel with the
ˢ P+R on a blue background.

Tramways – *CTS – b 03 88 77 70 70.* 4 lines
link many tourist places and sights in and
around Strasbourg. *Lines A, B and C
operate Mon-Sun 4.30am-0.30am; line D
operates Mon-Sat 7am-7pm except during
the summer school holidays.*

Buses – *CTS – b 03 88 77 70 70.* 26 lines
crisscross the Strasbourg conurbation; in
addition, 11 intercity buses link the city
with the most beautiful Alsatian villages.

Tickets – A **Unipass** *(€1.20)*is a single-
journey ticket valid for an hour on the bus
and tram network; A **Tourpass** *(€3.10)* is
valid for 24 hours for an unlimited number

...urneys. A **Familipass** *(€4.20)* is valid ...24 hours for an unlimited number of ...urneys, for a family of 2 to 5 persons ...travelling together *(minimum: 1 adult and 1 child)*.

Strasbourg Pass – Issued by the Tourist office, this pass allows free or half-price admission to 10 sights and monuments. *Valid for 3 days, it is on sale in the Tourist office information centres (place de la Cathédrale, place de la Gare and Pont de l'Europe) and in some hotels. €10.60.*

Guided tours – The town organises guied tours (1hr 30min) by approved guides. *€6.80. Enquire to the tourist office.*

Audio-guided tours – The itinerary, meant to last 1hr 30min, enables visitors to discover the cathedral, the old town and the Petite France at their own speed. A leaflet is given with the Walkman *(deposit: €30). 24-hour hiring cost: €6. Apply to the Tourist office.*

Mini-train – *Apr to Oct.* Departure place du Château, next to the cathedral, every half-hour or every hour depending on time of year. *€4.80. ☎ 03 88 77 70 03. Guided tour of the old town (50min) with a stop at Barrage Vauban.*

Vélocation – *4 rue Maire-Kuss – ☎ 03 88 43 64 30.* Bike hire service. Strasbourg has an extensive network of cycle tracks (300km/186.4mi).

Taxi 13 – ☎ *03 88 36 13 13.* This association suggests tours of the main tourist sights.

Boat trips on the Ill – ♿ Guided trips (1hr 10min)along the River Ill *(departure from the Palais Rohan pier)* taking in the Petite France, past Barrage Vauban, then the Faux Rempart moat as far as Palais de l'Europe. *Apr to Oct: 1hr 10min, departure every half-hour 9.30am-9pm; Nov-Dec and Jan-Mar: 4 departures a day 10.30am, 1pm, 2.30pm and 4.30pm. €6.80 (children €3.40).*

Boat trips on the Rhine and tour of the **harbour** – ♿ Departure from the Promenade Dauphine pier. *Jul-Aug: guided trip (2hr 15min) at 2.30pm. €8 (children €4). ☎ 03 88 84 13 13, www. strasbourgport.fr*

Flights – *Aéro-Club d'Alsace – aérodrome du Polygone (BX) – Strasbourg-Neudorf – ☎ 03 88 34 00 98.* Prices vary *(between €34 and €82)* according to the length of the flight, between 15min and 45min. Around Strasbourg: Château du Haut-Kœnigsbourg, Rhine Valley…

WHERE TO EAT

See the legend at the back for coin categories.

🍽 **Pommes de Terre et Cie** – *4 r. de l'Écurie - ☎ 03 88 22 36 82 – booking advisable*. If you want a change from choucroute, this friendly restaurant mainly serves dishes with jacket potatoes and meat, fish or cheese. Blue and yellow decor. Local produce.

🍽 **Aux Fines Gourmandises** – *5 pl. Corbeau- ☎ 03 88 36 09 92 - brm1@noos. fr – booking advisable in summer*. Internet enthusiasts will love this spacious restaurant-tea room with its internet café. Wde choice of dishes including tartes flambées and choucroute and a delicious selection of pastries.

🍽 **Flam's** – *29 r. des Frères, (quartier historique) - ☎ 03 88 36 36 90 - freres@ flams.fr – booking advisable at weekends*. This half-timbered house very close to the cathedral houses a restaurant specialising in flammekueches. The three dining rooms and two cellars have been redecorated in lovely bright colours. Note the superb 15C painted ceiling.

🍽 **Au Hanneton** – *5 r. Ste-Madeleine - ☎ 03 88 36 93 76 – closed Tue lunchtime and Mon – booking advisable*. This tiny winstub faithfully follows Alsace tradition with its warm, intimate country decor, its friendly atmosphere and regional specialities such as fish choucroute and Munster cordon bleu. Lovely terrace for sunny days.

🍽 **La Stub** – *4 r. du Saumon - ☎ 03 88 21 05 00 – closed 24-31 Dec*. This recent winstub successfully combines modern and traditional Alsace rustic styles. The restaurant is arranged around the famous kacheloffe (earthenware stove where food was cooked in former times). The menu offers a selection of regional specialities including baeckeoffe.

🍽 **Zum Strissel** – *5 pl. de la Grande-Boucherie – ☎ 03 88 32 14 73 – closed 27 Jan-7 Feb, 3 Jul- 2 Aug, Sun and Mon*. An authentic wine bar, run by the same family since 1920. The much-loved decor consists of wood panelling, decorative wrought iron, stained-glass windows depicting Bacchus and a 14C wine press. Regional cooking accompanied by Alsace wines, including the famous kaefferkopf d'Ammerschwihr.

🍽🍽 **Le Pigeon** – *23 r. des Tonneliers - ☎ 03 88 32 31 30 – closed 3 weeks in Jan and 18 Jul-12 Aug*. This typical winstub, which takes its name from the two pigeons sculpted on the façade, is situated in one of the oldest residences in Strasbourg (take a minute to look at the listed wooden staircase). Decor and cuisine in keeping with Alsace tradition.

🍽🍽 **Art Café** (at the Musée d'Art Moderne et Contemporain) – *1 pl. Hans-Jean-Arp - ☎ 03 88 22 18 88 - artcafe@ mames.com – closed Mon, public holidays and according to the museum opening times* You will be hard pushed to find a lovelier view of Strasbourg than that afforded by the terrace of this restaurant on the first floor of the Musée d'art moderne et contemporain. Very fashionably designed interior to match the location and the trendy cooking. Brunch on Sunday and public holidays.

La Choucrouterie – *20 r. St-Louis –* ☎ *03 88 36 52 87 – closed Aug, Sat and Sun lunchtimes.* This 18C coaching inn was the last place in Strasbourg to make pickled cabbage. Feast and have fun in a slightly chaotic setting, with music, cabaret or theatre dinners, as you like. Alsace cuisine served with local white wine.

Caveau Gurtlerhoft – *13 pl. de la Cathédrale –* ☎ *03 88 75 00 75.* Sample regional and traditional cooking in the lovely cellars of this 14C canonical building near the cathedral, with their splendid vaulting and massive pillars. Mouth-watering menus and fixed-price lunch. Unhurried service.

La Coccinelle – *22 r. Ste-Madeleine - ☎ 03 88 36 19 27 – closed 15 Jul-15 Aug, Sat lunchtime and Sun – booking advisable.* Wood panelling, beams, copperware, stained-glass windows and photos from the beginning of the 20C lend this winstub (in the family since 1976) its typical Alsace feel. Regional cooking with a few home-made specialities: the classic choucroute, but also quenelles de foie (liver quenelles), jambonneau rôti (roast knuckle of ham) and bœuf gros sel (beef). Good choice of wines served by the jug.

Pont St-Martin – *13-15 r. des Moulins - ☎ 03 88 32 45 13 – booking advisable.* This ever-popular restaurant in a venerable half-timbered building is in the heart of the picturesque Petite France district, just above the water. Typical Alsace interior of panelling, wainscoting and checked tablecloths. Regional cooking.

La Taverne du Sommelier – *Ruelle de la Bruche (Krutenau distict) –* ☎ *03 88 24 24 10 – closed fortnight in Aug, Christmas and New Year's Day - booking essential.* The type of little restaurant it's always a pleasure to discover. The decor of yellow walls and lithographs is perfect to set off the intimate atmosphere. The cooking follows the seasons, while the wine list features wines from the Languedoc region and the Rhône Valley.

Petit Ours – *3 r. de l'Écurie (quartier des Tonneliers) –* ☎ *03 88 32 13 21 – booking advisable.* Great little restaurant decorated with Tuscany-inspired colours. Light floods through the bay windows of one room, and the non-smoking cellar is also very pleasant. Each dish (mostly fish) is characterised by a particular herb or spice.

Au Renard Prêchant – *34 r. de Zürich –* ☎ *03 88 35 62 87 – closed lunchtime on Sat, Sun and public holidays.* A 16C chapel in a pedestrian-only street, which takes its name from the murals decorating its walls telling the story of the preaching fox. Rustic dining room, pretty terrace in summer, and reasonable fixed-price lunches.

L'Arsenal – *11 r. de l'Abreuvoir –* ☎ *03 88 35 03 69 – baderyvonne@noos.fr – closed Aug, Sat lunchtime (except Oct-Dec), Sun and public holidays.* This 18C half-timbered house is in the Krutenau district near the university, and serves tasty food at very reasonable prices. The decor is rustic, with wooden benches and rendered walls. Strong regional influence in the cuisine.

Brasserie Kirn – *6-8 r. l'Outre -* ☎ *03 88 52 03 03 – closed Sun evening.* This restaurant set in what used to be a butcher's, is reminiscent of the 1900s with its lovely central cupola and attractive stained-glass windows. For more intimacy, try the tables in the booths. Brasserie-style food.

Le Clou – *3 r. du Chaudron –* ☎ *03 88 32 11 67 – closed Wed lunchtime, Sun and public holidays.* This small wine bar in a little street near the cathedral is always popular, with its typical decor, friendly atmosphere and good Alsace cooking. Well-known locally.

La Maison des Tanneurs, known as "Gerwerstub" – *42 r. du Bain-aux-Plantes –* ☎ *03 88 32 79 70 – maison. des.tanneurs@wanadoo.fr – closed 29 Dec-21 Jan, Sun and Mon.* A picture-postcard restaurant on the banks of the Ill, in a cobbled street in the Petite France district. Inside, the rooms are panelled with dark wood and have Alsatian furniture. Typical regional cuisine.

WHERE TO STAY

Patricia – *R. du Puits -* ☎ *03 88 32 14 60 – booking advisable - 20 rooms -* ⌑ €5. Two small wooden printers are a reminder that this venerable residence (listed façade) was the home of the regional printers' in the 19C. It is now a hotel with quiet, bright rooms where TV is banished and smoking not permitted.

Chambre d'hôte La Maison du Charron – *15 r. Principale – 67370 Pfettisheim – 13km/8mi NW of Strasbourg on D 31 –* ☎ *03 88 69 60 35 - maisonducharron@proveis.com –* ✉ *– 5 rooms.* The owner of this 1858 property has done up the rooms himself, making each one individual by using different woods, while his wife's hobby is patchwork. Small garden, stabling for horses and two holiday cottages.

Hôtel de L'Ill – *8 r. des Bâteliers -* ☎ *03 88 36 20 01 - info@hotel-ill.com – closed 29 Dec-6 Jan - 27 rooms -* ⌑ €6.50. Renovated hotel with family atmosphere. The rooms are of differing sizes and impeccably clean, while the traditional-style breakfast room has a cuckoo clock. You can take a boat trip on the River Ill just a stone's throw away.

Couvent du Franciscain – *18 r. du Fg-de-Pierre –* ☎ *03 88 32 93 93 - info@hotel-franciscain.com – closed 24 Dec-9 Jan -* 🅿 *- 43 rooms -* ⌑ €8. At the end of a cul-de-sac you will find these two buildings, which are joined by a pleasant hall. We recommend the rooms in the new wing. The breakfast room is in the cellar. A good option within walking distance of the old city.

Hôtel Cardinal de Rohan – *17 r. Maroquin* – ☎ *03 88 32 85 11* – *info@hotel-rohan.com* – *36 rooms* – ⚟ *€10.* Named after the nearby palais de Rohan, this little hotel is also near the cathedral. Its quiet, pleasant rooms are furnished in Louis XV style, and those on the south side have air conditioning.

Hôtel Pax – *24 r. du Fg-National* – ☎ *03 88 32 14 54* – *info@paxhotel.com* – *closed 23 Dec-4 Jan* – *106 rooms* – ⚟ *€7* – *restaurant* ⚟⚟. A family hotel in a busy street on the edge of the city's old district. Its plain rooms are well kept, and its restaurant serves regional dishes. You can eat in the vine-shaded courtyard in summer.

Hôtel Beaucour – *5 r. des Bouchers* – ☎ *03 88 76 72 00* – *beaucour@hotel-beaucour.com* – *49 rooms* – ⚟ *€11.* Those who like staying in lovely places will enjoy this city-centre hotel spread out in several old houses. Attractions include the flower-decked courtyard, cosy rooms and regional furniture in an inviting decor.

ON THE TOWN

Bar des Glacières – *5 r. des Moulins* – ☎ *03 88 76 43 43* – *www.regent-hotels.com* – *5pm-2am.* This is the hotel bar of the luxurious Regent Petite France, which was a mill for 800 years before becoming an ice manufacturer's until the late 1980s. No effort has been spared to ensure that you spend a relaxing evening here: the fine contemporary decor, the riverside terrace, a good choice of cocktails and the best whiskies. The discreet jazzy background music adds the final touch.

L'Opéra-café (in the public opera house) – *Pl. Broglie* – ☎ *03 88 75 48 26* – *daily 11-1.30am except Sun 2-8pm* – *closed 25 Jul- 16 Aug, 24-26 Dec and 31 Dec.* The purple and gold decor in this theatre bar evokes the world of the stage. A classy setting for an intimate date over a glass of whisky or wine – or a hot chocolate with the family. Painting and photography exhibitions.

SHOWTIME

Demandez le programme! – To find out the programme of theatres, concerts, seminars, exhibitions and sporting events, get a copy of the monthy Strasbourg actualités or Hebdoscope, with weekly listings fro arts and shows.

SHOPPING

Markets – The markets are generally open from7am-1pm. Traditional market Tue and Fri place Kléber, Wed rue Krutenau and rue de St-Gothard. Direct from the grower market on Sat, pl. du Marché-aux-Poissons. Flea market (9am-6pm) Wed and Sat, r. du Vieil-Hôpital and pl. de la Grande-Boucherie. Book market (9am-6pm) Wed and Sat, pl. and r. Gutenberg and r. des Hallebardes. Christmas market in Dec.

Un Noël en Alsace - *10 r. des Dentelles, Petite France* - ☎ *03 88 32 32 32* - *www.noelenalsace.fr* - *daily except Sun morning 10am-12.30pm, 1.30-7pm (from Jul, Sun 2-6pm)* - *closed Jan-Feb.* It's Christmas every day in this 16C building in the heart of the Petite France district. Tinsel, little wood figurines, twinkling stars and coloured baubles: you name it, they have it!

Au Paradis des Pains d'Epices - *14 r. des Dentelles, Petite France* - ☎ *03 88 32 33 34 32* - *www.paindesoleil.com* - *daily 9am-7pm except Mon mornings.* Scents of orange, honey, cinnamon and cardamom greet you as you enter this tiny shop located in a timber-framed house dating from 1643. Heaven on earth for gingerbread fans: soft or crunchy, sweet or savoury, even iced varieties to tempt you.

CALENDAR

Folklore shows – *Mid-Jul to early Aug, Square Louise-Weiss. Local, national and international dancing.* ☎ *03 88 60 97 14.*

European Fair – *Early Sep, Parc des Expositions du Wacken.* Over 1000 exhibitors representing a wide range of activities. *Enquiries:* ☎ *03 88 37 21 21.*

Strasbourg, Christmas Capital - Countless events and shows all over town: Christmas market (Christkindelsmärik), illuminations, giant Christmas tree, exhibitions, nativity scene and concerts. *Programme available from tourist office.*

🕭 **Don't Miss:** Notre-Dame Cathedral and the Musée de l'Œuvre Notre-Dame.

🕐 **Organizing Your Time:** Allow a whole day to see the old town.

🅿 **Parking:** Eight parking areas along the outskirts of Strasbourg allow you to leave your car and travel into the town centre by tram (2.40€ or 2.70€).

A Bit of History

On 14 February in the year 842 the **Strasbourg Oaths** were sworn by two of the sons of Louis the Pious (himself the son of Charlemagne). One year before the Treaty of Verdun, the brothers Charles and Louis undertook to be loyal to one another in their attempt to frustrate the ambitions of their elder brother Lothair. Protocol demanded that each declare the oath in a language comprehensible to his brother's entourage; thus it was that the text read out by Louis the German is considered to be the oldest such document in a Romance language, the first written example of the language which has evolved into modern French. The same can be said for the German text.

Some Strasbourg figures – Strasbourg remained a free city within the Holy Roman Empire even after the virtual incorporation of the rest of Alsace into France by the Peace of Westphalia in 1648, but eventually submitted to annexation by Louis XIV in 1681.

Among the many great people born here were:

François Kellermann (1735-1820), the hero of Valmy, acting under the orders of Dumouriez, then the commander responsible for putting down the Lyon rising of 1793, finally a supporter of the Bourbon Restoration and a member of parliament;

Frédéric de Dietrich (1748-93), ⓒ *see below: the Marseillaise;*

Sébastien Érard (1752-1831), famous maker of grand pianos and harps;

Jean-Baptiste Kléber,   *see below: Place Kléber;*

Jean-Pierre Clause (1757-1800), celebrated chef, cook to the Marshal de Contades and the populariser of *pâté de foie gras;*

Gustave Doré (1832-83), the caricaturist and illustrator;

Charles de Foucauld (1858-1916), who began his career as an army officer, but subsequently became a missionary in Algeria and wrote a pioneering work on Morocco, a then unknown country. He later became a Benedictine monk, living as a hermit in the remote Hoggar mountains of southern Algeria; here he collected Tuareg poetry and wrote the first French-Tamahag dictionary before dying at the hands of assassins;

Jean Arp (1887-1966), one of the great post-war generation of artists, who moved from Surrealism to Abstraction, then to even more revolutionary forms of expression.

The Marseillaise – On 24 April 1792, Frédéric de Dietrich, Strasbourg's first constitutional mayor, threw a farewell celebration for the volunteers of the Army of the Rhine. The conversation turned to the need for a marching song to match the troops' enthusiasm. Dietrich asked Rouget de Lisle (ⓒ *see LONS-LE-SAULNIER)* to compose "something worth singing"; de Lisle set to, working through the night with pen and violin. By the morning he had finished; with Dietrich's niece accompanying him on the piano, he sang his "marching song for the Army of the Rhine". Not long after, it was adopted by the Federates of Marseille, and ever since has been known as the Marseillaise.

Sights

Cathédrale Notre-Dame★★★
🕐 *Apr-Oct: Mon-Fri 9am-5.30pm, Sat-Sun 10am-5.30pm; Nov-Mar: Mon-Fri 9am-4.30pm, Sat-Sun 10am-4.30pm.* ✎ *3€ (under 18 years: 1.50€).* ☎ *03 88 43 60 32.*
In 1176, the cathedral was rebuilt in red Vosges sandstone on a site above flood-level but nevertheless using bundles of oak piles as a foundation (these were recently reinforced with concrete).

Externally, this is still a Romanesque building as far as choir, transept and lantern-tower are concerned. The famous Gothic spire **(flèche★★★)** is an architectural masterpiece, its verticality emphasised by its forward position immediately over the west front. An unmistakable landmark, visible over much of the Alsace plain, it rises to a height of 142m – 466ft. The openwork octagon supporting it was erected between 1399 and 1419 by a Swabian architect and given an extra 7m – 23ft in height during the course of construction for reasons of prestige. Its final stage was designed and built between 1420 and 1439 by a Cologne architect, using techniques from the previous century; it is particularly notable for the projecting structures carrying the external staircases. The High Gothic west front **(façade★★★)** was the work of Erwin von Steinbach. It is decorated with a wealth of sculpture (statues and low-reliefs of many different periods), especially in the central portal **(portail central)** with its double gable and delicate lancets masking part of the rose window. The three lower levels of the tympanum have particularly fine 13C work, including depictions of the Entry into Jerusalem, scenes of the Passion and Resurrection, and the Death of Judas; in the arching can be seen the Creation, the story of Abraham, the Apostles, the Evangelists and the Martyrs.

In the south doorway **(portail Sud)** is a famous portrayal of the Seducer about to succeed in tempting the most daring of the Foolish Virgins (she is undoing her dress). The statues of the Church and Synagogue (copies) on the south side of the cathedral are equally celebrated.

Inside, the nave elevation is a straightforward example of the High Gothic style of the 14C, with an openwork triforium and wide aisles lit by elegant window-openings.

In the south transept is the 13C Angel pillar (**pilier des Anges**★★) or Last Judgement (**du Jugement dernier**); its delicate statuary, on three levels, raises Gothic art to a peak of perfection. Stained-glass windows (**vitraux**★★★) from the 12C, 13C, and 14C are remarkable.

The astronomical clock (**horloge astronomique**★) (🕐 *Clock chimes at 12.30pm;* 👁 *1€;* 🔑 *may be closed for exceptionally long services or concert rehearsals*) nearby, dating from 1838, continues to draw crowds with its automata ringing out the quarter-hours (the figure of Death has the privilege of sounding the hours) and the crowd of figures brought out to mark midday (12.30pm).

Musée de l'Œuvre Notre-Dame★★★

🕐 *Daily 10am-6pm.* 🕐 *Closed Mon, 1 Jan, Good Friday, 1 May, 1 and 11 Nov, 25 Dec.* 👁 *4€ (under 18 years: no charge), no charge 1st Sun in the month.* ☎ *03 88 52 50 00. www.musees-strasbourg.org/F/oeuvre_nd.html.*

Housed in a number of old dwellings just to the south, this museum greatly enhances the visitor's appreciation of the cathedral. Its great treasure is the famous Head of Christ (**Tête de Christ**★★) from Wissembourg in northern Alsace. In addition, there is the oldest stained glass in existence and above all, many of the cathedral's original statues, including the Church and the Synagogue, the Wise and Foolish Virgins. The architect's drawings of the west front and the spire are here too.

Palais Rohan★

This was the residence of the Prince-Bishops of Strasbourg, among their number Armand, who built the place, and high-living Louis, who was involved in the affair of Marie-Antoinette's necklace.

The palace was built between 1732 and 1742 to the plans drawn up by Robert de Cotte, a quarter-century after the de Rohans' Parisian mansion had been completed; its architecture reflects the more relaxed style ushered in by the reign of Louis XV. It is a fine building in the Classical manner, with a curving entrance colonnade ornamented with statues and trophies, a main courtyard defined by balustraded galleries, a façade with dressings of pale limestone, a fine entablature, and mansard roofs lit by bull's-eye windows. The Prince-Bishops' state rooms are considered to be among the finest French interiors of the 18C. The building's most elegant façade is the one overlooking the River Ill; it has tall Corinthian columns, a dome and a balustraded terrace.

Musées★★

The palace houses museums with rich collections.

Musée des Arts décoratifs★★

♿ 🕐 *Wed-Mon 10am-6pm.* 🕐 *Closed Tue, 1 Jan, Good Friday, 1 May, 1 and 11 Nov, 25 Dec.* 👁 *4€ (under 18 years: no charge), no charge 1st Sun in the month.* ☎ *03 88 52 50 00.*

The museum includes the State Apartments (**Grands Appartements**) and tells the story of the city's crafts and craftsmen. It has one of the finest **ceramic collections**★★ in France, particularly rich in Strasbourg and Niderwiller faience and porcelain.

Musée des Beaux-Arts★

As for the Musée des Arts décoratifs.

The Musée des Beaux-Arts is known for its Italian paintings (Primitives and Renaissance), its Spanish works (Zurbaran, Murillo and Goya) and 15C-17C Netherlandish Old Masters. On no account should the visitor miss Nicolas de Largillière's 1703 portrait of *La Belle Strasbourgeoise*, the elegant, black-robed beauty.

Musée archéologique★★

As for the Musée des Arts décoratifs.

The Musée archéologique covers the period between the Quaternary era and the end of the first millennium AD. There are displays on prehistory, extinct animals, ceramics, and on Roman and Merovingian times.

La cité ancienne★★★

Two parts of the old city evoke the delightful spectacle of a bygone Alsace of timber-framed houses with the whole array of traditional features, wooden galleries, loggias on brackets, windows with tiny panes of coloured glass, as well as the overhanging upper storeys which continued to be built here in the post-1681 years even though they had been banned in France proper. Each house can be enjoyed for its own sake; together, they compose the most ravishing of townscapes.

Quartier de la cathédrale★★★

In the cathedral quarter, two especially attractive buildings give onto the **Place de la Cathédrale**★; at the corner with the Rue Mercière there is the Pharmarcie du Cerf **(F)** of 1268, supposedly the oldest pharmacy in France, and on the north corner is the Kammerzell House **(Maison Kammerzell★)** of the same date with frescoes and wooden sculptures. Other streets and squares, like the Place du Marché-aux-cochons-de-lait (Sucking-Pig Market Square), Rue Mercière and Rue des Cordiers, complete the pleasures of a stroll.

Petite France★★

This is the city's well-preserved historic core. It owes its name to a former French hospital and was once the abode of fishermen, tanners and millers. The arms of the Ill were provided with locks giving shipping from the Rhine access to the back door of virtually every shop. With its gabled Renaissance houses reflected in the green waters of the river, it forms a charming urban scene, notably in the **Rue du Bain-aux-Plantes★★**.

Place Kléber

This is the city's most famous square, named after Jean Kléber (1753-1800), the hero of the battles of Mainz (1793), Fleurus and Maastricht, who was assassinated in the course of Napoleon's campaign in Egypt.

Place Kléber

▶▶ Cour du Corbeau★. Covered Bridges★. View from the Barrage Vauban★★ ◷ *Wed-Mon 9am-7.30pm. No charge.* ☎ *03 88 60 90 90.* Musée alsacien *Jan-Apr and Jul-Aug: Wed-Mon 10am-6pm; May, Jun, and Sep-Dec: Wed-Mon noon-6pm.* ◷ *Closed Tue, 1 Jan, Good Friday, 1 May, 1 and 11 Nov, 25 Dec.* ⊜ *4€ (under 18 years: no charge), no charge 1st Sun in the month.* ☎ *03 88 52 50 01.*

Musée d'Art Moderne et contemporain ★★ &. ◷ *Tue, Wed, Fri, Sat 11am-7pm, Thu noon-10pm, Sun 10am-6pm.* ◷ *Closed 1 Jan, Good Friday, 1 May, 1 and 11 Nov, 25 Dec.* ⊜ *5€ (under 18: no charge), no charge 1st Sun in the month.* ☎ *03 88 23 31 31.* Musée historique. Église St-Thomas – mausoleum of Marshal de Saxe★★. Orangerie★. Palais de l'Europe★. Boat trips.

Gorges du **TARN**★★★

MICHELIN MAPS 330 H-J 8-9 AND 338 L-N 5

GREEN GUIDE LANGUEDOC ROUSSILLON TARN GORGES

The deep gorges cut by the Tarn through the harsh limestone plateaux (causses) to the south of the Massif Central make up one of France's most spectacular natural landscapes. The source of the Tarn lies high (1 575m – 5 167ft) in the granitic uplands of Mount Lozère; tumbling torrent-like down the slopes of the Cévennes, the river then enters the most spectacular section of its course at Florac.

Driving Tour: From Florac to Millau

83km – 52 miles – allow about 4hr.

The river flows through a deep canyon, joined by side valleys like those of the Jonte and the Dourbie. Escape from the valley bottom is by means of roads which twist and turn up the precipitous slopes to join the roughly-planed surface of the Méjean causse; its porous limestone is deeply fissured and hollowed out to form the caves for which the region is famous.

View of Gorges du Tarn from Roc des Hourtous

Most visitors come here when the summer sun is beating down, but the scene should also be appreciated in the kindlier conditions of spring and autumn, when the mantle of vegetation is better able to assert itself and local life is flourishing. Nor should the spectacle of winter be missed, when every feature has its frosty outline. Above the river's pebbly bed are piled up the successive beds of limestone, some of them 50m – 165ft thick, evidence of the huge scale of the sedimentation which took place over almost inconceivably long stretches of time during the Secondary era. Rocky debris from the mountains fringing the warm and shallow seas of these remote times was washed down to mingle with the remains of corals and crustaceans, spongy tissues and the skeletons of fish; subjected to the heat generated by their own increasing weight, these accumulations slowly built up to form this massive addition to the Earth's crust which extends all around the southern fringe of the Massif Central, here reaching an astonishing thickness of some 600m – 2 000ft. Some idea of the great force of the Alpine uplift can be gained when it is realised that the earth movements of the time raised this great plinth of stone 1 000m – 3 300ft above its original level. At the same time faulting and fracturing occurred in a number of places (as is proved by the non-conformity of the strata on opposite sides of the river), thus opening the way (south of Ste-Énimie and between the Cirque des Baumes and Le Rozier) to the formation of today's gorges.

No trace of the underground realm of chasms **(Aven Armand**★★★**)** and caverns is visible at the surface; those who venture into this unsuspected world are rewarded by the extraordinary spectacle presented by the dissolution of the limestone, and by the strange forms of the stalactites and stalagmites.

In contrast to the gorges of the Verdon and the Ardèche, one never inhabited, the other depopulated, the hostile landscape here has been humanised by centuries of determined human effort. Thus there are villages on the flatter patches of cultivable land which occur on the valley bottom and sides (Ste-Énimie, La Malène, Les Vignes...) and the castles of lords and robber-barons on the more easily-defended sites overlooking the river. On the plateau above are isolated farms based on the better soils of the little depressions known as dolinas; the drystone walls once made by piling up the boulders collected laboriously from the fields are now supplemented by electric fences, and the thoughtless forest clearance of the 19C is being made good by the planting of Austrian pines.

Les Détroits (The Straits)★★
This is the narrowest part of the valley, hemmed in by plunging cliffs of coloured limestone.

Cirque des Baumes★★★
Below Les Détroits, the gorge widens, forming this magnificent natural amphitheatre.

Rocher de Cinglegros

This huge detached rock rears up over the Lafont Farm (Mas de Lafont) on the left bank of the river.

Le Point Sublime – Adds 26km★★★

16mi to the journey between La Malène and Les Vignes. This splendid viewpoint above the Cirque des Baumes overlooks both canyon and causse.

Roc des Hourtous – Adds 25km★★

16mi to the journey between La Malène and Les Vignes. Dramatic vista downstream towards Les Détroits and the Cirque des Baumes as well as wide views over the causse.

Abbaye du **THORONET**★★

MICHELIN MAP 340 M 5

GREEN GUIDE FRENCH RIVIERA

Of the "three Cistercian sisters of Provence" (the others being Silvacane and Sénanque), Le Thoronet is the earliest; it was founded in 1136, when St Bernard was still alive. It is one of the most characteristic of Cistercian abbeys, as well as one of the most austere.

Visit

The plain architecture of the abbey **(abbaye)** is unrelieved by decoration, save in the chapter-house, where two roughly-sculpted capitals relieve the prevailing rigour. The abbey church **(église★)** has a simple beauty. Built from 1160 onwards, it has remarkable stonework which was cut and assembled without the use of mortar (notably in the oven-vaulted apse).
The cloisters **(cloître★)** of about 1175 have kept their four barrel-vaulted walks; the change of level is more obvious here than in the church and is still causing problems of subsidence.

TOUL★

POPULATION 17 752

MICHELIN MAP 307 G 6

GREEN GUIDE ALSACE LORRAINE CHAMPAGNE

For many years from the 11C onwards, Toul was ruled by its bishops, whose interests frequently failed to coincide with those of their subjects. Together with Metz and Verdun, the city was one of the three Imperial Bishoprics which were annexed by Henri II in 1552 and were finally recognised as belonging to the French crown by the Peace of Westphalia in 1648.

Vauban came here at the end of the 17C to redesign the fortifications, the Metz Gate in particular. After the loss of France's eastern provinces in 1871, Toul became part of the defensive system created in the early days of the Third Republic by General Séré de Rivières; this was based on huge half-buried polygonal forts like the one at Villey-le-Sec (7km – 4mi east) which was intended to secure the strategically vital Toul Gap.

Visit

Cathédrale St-Étienne★★

1221-1496. The influence of the very Early Gothic architecture of the neighbouring province of Champagne (Notre-Dame-en-Vaux Church and Châlons-en-Champagne Cathedral) makes itself felt in the cathedral's very simple elevation (consisting only of main arches and clerestory), in its east end (a straightforward apse with tall 13C windows), and in the inspection gallery running round the aisles at the base of the windows. The highly pointed arches of the first five bays of the nave are in the High Gothic style of the 14C.

The west front (façade★★), almost overloaded with architectural ornament, lost its statuary at the time of the French Revolution. A number of features like the tympanums with window openings are characteristic of the architecture of the late 15C, while the triangular gable is of earlier date. The other gables are later and herald the awakening Renaissance, as do the upper parts of the façade and the little central lantern. The cloisters (cloîtrea) adorned with fine gargoyles are among the most extensive in France.

◐◐ Église St-Gengoult★ ◷ Jul to mid-Sep: daily except Mon 10am-noon, 2-5.30pm. ☎ 06 20 42 51 74 – Cloisters★★.

Musée d'Art et d'Histoire★ ◷ Apr-Oct: daily 9.30am-noon, 2-6pm; Nov-Mar daily 9.30am-noon, 2-6pm, Sun 2-6pm. ◷ Closed Tue, 1 Jan, Easter, Easter Mon, 1 May, 1 Nov, 25 Dec. ◌ 3€ (under 18 years: no charge). ☎ 03 83 64 13 38.

TOULON★★

POPULATION 437 553

MICHELIN MAP 340 K 7

GREEN GUIDE FRENCH RIVIERA

Backed by high hills whose summits are crowned by forts, Toulon is France's second most important naval base.

A Bit of History

The siege of 1793 – In 1793, an anti-revolutionary uprising had gained control of the whole of Corsica, pitting the monarchist Paoli (◖ see CORTE) against the loyalist Napoleon Bonaparte. Paoli enjoyed British support, and the warships of the Royal Navy controlled the waters between the island and the Toulon anchorage. The city had remained faithful to the monarchy, in whose cause it had welcomed an Anglo-Spanish fleet into its fine harbour.

The Revolutionary government in Paris, threatened as it was by both internal and external enemies, had to take action. On 15 December, its troops attacked. The British were in possession of strongpoints on the St-Mandrier peninsula and between La Seyne and Fort Balaguier (known as Little Gibraltar). The French infantry blockaded the city on the east while the artillery threatened it from the northwest. Captain Bonaparte (who had left Corsica in June) took bold advantage of the situation, redeploying his guns in order to subject the British positions to direct fire. Little Gibraltar fell, and on the night of 18 December, the British evacuated their troops, taking part of the population with them.

Repression was harsh; however, Napoleon intervened and the Revolutionary government's threat to raze the city to the ground was not carried out.

Sights

La rade★★

Construction of Toulon's Old Port (Vieille darse) began under Henri IV. Richelieu appreciated the strategic advantages of the roadstead and ordered the building of the first naval installations. In the reign of Louis XIV, the base was extended and the New Port (Darse Neuve) laid out by Vauban. In the 19C, the Mourillon extension and the Castigneau basin were built, completing the naval base which had become the home port of the French Mediterranean Fleet.

Beyond the harbour lies the magnificent Outer Roadstead (Grande Rade), approached via the Inner Roads (Petite Rade), guarded to the north by the Royal Tower (Tour Royale) and the main jetty, to the south by Vieille Point; it is here that the naval base with all its installations and repair yards is located. The still-considerable remains of the French fleet had anchored here after the disaster of Mers-el-Kébir in 1940, when the Royal Navy had turned its guns on the ships of its defeated ally in order to

Toulon - Address Book

PRACTICAL INFORMATION

Tourism Office –Place Raimu – ☎ 04 94 18 53 00 – www.toulontourisme.com.

Guided tours of the city – Guided tours *(1.5hr)* starting out from the Tourism Office are a great opportunity to discover the old town of Toulon: Jul-Aug Tue-Thu at 10am; Sep-Jun Wed and Fri at 2pm.

Train Touristique – ☎ 04 94 36 01 32. 5€ *(chiid 2.50€)*.

Departs from the Carré du Port for a tour with commentary *(50min)* of the Old Town to the beaches at Mourillon and the Tour Royale.

EATING OUT

For coin ranges, see the Legend at the back of the guide.

Al Dente – *30 Rue Gimelli* – ☎ 04 94 93 02 50 – *spaa.aldente@wanadoo.fr* – Closed Sun for lunch. The main reason for coming here is the remarkable choice of pasta dishes and Italian specialities, with additional menus at highly affordable prices. Regular customers also appreciate the modern decor bursting with color.

La Chamade – *25 Rue de la Comédie* – ☎ 04 94 92 25 58 – Closed Aug and Sun. This simple restaurant with the discreet façade is a local favorite for its bright and cheerful interior, carefully laid out tables with plenty of space between them for intimacy. The cuisine is fresh and modern, based on what the chef finds in season at the market that week.

L'Eau à la Bouche – *54 Rue Muiron* – ☎ 04 94 46 33 09 Closed Easter vacation, 1-6 Jun, Dec holidays, Mon (except Jul-Sep) Sat lunch and Sun. Situated next to the Mourillon arsenal on the route to the Tour Royale, this restaurant is decorated with a naval theme. The menu is drawn up on a chalk board, with plenty of seafood specialities.

Chez Daniel "Restaurant du Rivage" – *La Seyne-sur-Mer – 4km/2.4mi south of La Seyne by Route de St-Mandrier and country lane* – ☎ 04 94 94 85 13 – Closed Nov, Sun evening and Mon Sep-Jun. A small rocky inlet is the choice setting for this seafood restaurant that knows the true meaning of Provençal life. The freshly caught fish offered to diners may come from the sea or from the big fish tank set up on the premises. One of the dining rooms proudly displays a collection of old barouches and farming tools.

WHERE TO STAY

Les 3 Dauphins – *9 Place des 3 Dauphins* – ☎ 04 94 92 65 79 – *14 rooms* – . The windows of this recently renovated hotel give onto a tiny square dominated by a bust of Raimu. The smallish rooms have been tastefully appointed and decorated in cheerful shades. Charming welcome and service.

Grand Hôtel Dauphiné – *10 Rue Berthelot* – ☎ 04 94 92 20 28 – *contact@ grandhoteldauphine.com* – *55 rooms* – . This centrally located hotel is the perfect starting-point for a tour of the old city and its intricate maze of streets. The lively rooms hung with printed fabric are above all functional.

Val'Hôtel – *Avenue René-Cassin, ZA Paul Madon – La Valette – Take exit 5 off the A 57, behind the Leroy-Merlin store, follow signs to ZI de Toulon-la-Valette* – ☎ 04 94 08 38 08 – www.val-hotel.com – – *42 rooms* – – *Restaurant ()*. This hotel offers several advantages: a lush garden setting; tlarge, colorful rooms with balcony or terrace; and inexpensive weekend rates. Hopefully, these features will soon make you forget the motorway exit nearby.

La Corniche Best Western – *17 littoral Frédéric-Mistral across from the Port St-Louis and near the Mourillon beaches* – ☎ 04 94 41 35 12 - *info@cornichehotel.com* - – *80 rooms* – . This hotel just two steps from the beaches at Mourillon has views over the sea, perfect for those looking for a seaside holiday atmosphere.

New Hôtel de l'Amirauté – *4 Rue Adolphe-Guiol* – ☎ 04 22 19 67 – *58 rooms* – . In the center of town, this hotel is a good opportunity to combine a business trip with the delights of tourism. The decor is reminiscent of the large luxury liners of bygone times. Functional, efficiently soundproofed rooms.

ON THE TOWN

Like many big cities, Toulon swarms with people. The city is lively at night as well as by day, thanks to the many bars, cafés and restaurants. Request a list of bars and restaurants that feature nightly concerts, karaoke, dancing, piano bars, etc., from the Tourism Office.

Café-Théâtre de la Porte d'Italie – *Place Armand-Vallée* – ☎ 04 94 92 99 75 – Check the programme of events. This café-théâtre presents clarinet and jazz concerts, stand-up comedy and pantomime shows year round.

Opéra de Toulon – *Boulevard de Strasbourg* – ☎ 04 94 92 70 78 */ 04 94 93 03 76* – operadetoulon@wanadoo.fr. Built in 1862, the Opéra de Toulon is ranked 2nd in France on account of its seating capacity and remarkable acoustics. The 2005-2006 season included *The Magic Flute, Pétrouchka, Aïda, Boléro,* and a Wagner festival.

Zénith-Oméga – *Place des Lices* – ☎ 08 36 68 06 86 – www.zenith-omega-toulon.com. This concert hall organises various events such as stage productions, classical concerts, pop music, alongside international fairs and exhibitions.

TRANSPORT

Pedestrian area – The district in the old part of town bordered by Rue Anatole-France, Avenue de la République, Avenue de Besagne and Boulevard de Strasbourg is closed to traffic.

Buses – The RMTT (☎ *04 94 03 87 03, www.rmtt.com*) provides an efficient bus service covering Toulon and its outskirts. Plans, timetables and tickets can be obtained from the newsstand on Place de la Liberté.

Boat shuttle service – *SITCAT/RMTT on Quai Cronstadt or 720 Avenue du Colonel-Picot* – ☎ *04 94 03 87 03*. There are several daily services to and from La Seyne-sur-Mer, Les Sablettes, Tamaris and St-Mandrier-sur-Mer.

These lines are part of the local transport system and they charge the same rates as the buses.

Pass Téléphérique – This day pass is good for the entire RMTT network (bus and boat) and allows RT access to the téléphérique on Mont Faron. 5€.

CULINARY SPECIALITIES

The café terraces on Quai Cronstadt provide a good view of the life of the old port – Bar du Soleil, La Gourmandise and Le France. The natives of Toulon *(moccots)* particularly enjoy *l'escabèche de sardine, la cade* (a flat cake made from chickpeas, similar to socca in Nice), *la pompe à l'huile* (a hard cake, oiled and flavoured with orange water) and the famous sweet doughnut *(chichifregi)* which can be bought from the stalls in the Lafayette market. Several restaurants specialise in fish dishes (Place du Théâtre and Rue Jean-Jaurès).

In Mourillon many restaurants have terraces which are ideal places to sit and try the seafood dishes (Corniche Henri-Fabre, Port St-Louis).

SHOPPING

The best place to go shopping is the area around Rue Jean-Jaurès, Rue Hoche, Place Victor-Hugo and Rue d'Alger. Rue Lamalgue (near the Port St-Louis) is a good market street for gourmet treats.

Provençal Market – Tuesday through Sunday mornings on the Cour Lafayette.

Côté Tissus – *8 Rue de la Fraternité* – ☎ *04 94 46 37 92* – ⏰ *Tue-Sat 9am-noon, 2.30-7pm*. Delightful boutique with stone walls that sells Provençal fabric. The arch on the right reminds visitors that a river flowed through the premises over 100 years ago.

Les Navires de la Royale – *30 Rue des Riaux* – ☎ *06 14 45 19 38* – ⏰ *Mon-Sat 9am-noon, 2-6pm*. Amateur sailors should make a point of visiting this shop, owned by Jean-Michel Delcourte, an enthusiastic lover of all things maritime! His days are spent making and restoring all sorts of boats, ranging from yachts to schooners to catamarans.

Palmer – *62 Cours Lafayette* – ☎ *04 94 92 22 65* – ⏰ *Tue-Sat 8am-12.30pm, 3-7pm*. Over 150 herbs and spices from all corners of the world are sold in this colorful little boutique. Also dried fruits, beans, nuts... the friendly owner is more than happy to give advice.

Puyricard – *10 Boulevard Berthelot* – ☎ *04 94 91 64 10* – ⏰ *Mon afternoon to Sat 9am-7pm*. This prestigious chocolate boutique sells delightful pralines, ganaches, pâtes d'amande, caramels, calissons, candied fruits, sugared chestnuts, and nougat de Sault, all direct from its kitchens in Aix-en-Provence.

Grosso – *9 Rue Lamalgue* – ☎ *04 94 46 37 22*. Monsieur Grosso has been making cheeses for over 25 years, and 70% of the cheeses in his boutique come from his own farms nearby. Known for his brebis and goats' cheeses, he also sells Iberian ham and Corsican dried sausages.

HAVING A DIP

Mourillon beach ☆ – *To the east, along Littoral Frédéric-Mistral, between Fort St-Louis and the water sports center*. First-aid posts, restaurants, bathroom facilities. To avoid paying the fee charged by the Mourillon car park, go there by bus ! Lines 3, 13 and 23 (Mourillon) or 7 and 23 (Magaud and Méjean coves) will drop you at the beach. The long Toulon beach, separated from the road by a large park, consists of four curved stretches of coastline covered with fine sand or gravel, or a combination of both, depending on their location. The lands descends into the sea on a gradual slope and bathers are sheltered by the piers.

Méjean and Magaud beaches – *From Le Mourillon, follow directions to La Garde-Le Pradet*. At the entrance to La Garde, Chemin de la Mer leads to two natural sandy beaches, the twin coves of Magaud *(on the left)* and Méjean *(on the right)*.

SIT BACK AND RELAX

Le Tigre – *Sommet du Mont Faron* – ☎ *04 94 88 08 00* – ⏰ *Jun-Sep: daily 9.30am-10pm; Oct-May: daily 10am-6pm*. This café-restaurant perched atop Mont Faron commands outstanding views of Toulon anchorage. The Souza family, who own the nearby zoo, settled here in April 2000 and will be delighted to explain the local sights to you (binoculars available). Warm welcome.

Bar à Thym – *32 Boulevard de Cunéo* – ☎ *04 94 41 90 11 / 04 94 41 90 10* – *www.barathym.com* – ⏰ *Mon-Tue 6pm-1am; Wed-Sat 6pm-3am; May-Sep 6pm-5am*. Popular watering hole for the younger generation. The impressive choice of beers (over 100, including 12 draught beers) is a definite asset. Choose between the live concerts *(Tue-Wed-Thu)* or the evenings run by a disc jockey. Special evenings on a particular theme are also organised *(Fri-Sat)*.

prevent them falling into German hands. The same danger threatened in July 1942; in response to the Allied landings in North Africa, the Germans had swiftly overrun the hitherto-unoccupied part of France. Caught by surprise and unable to escape, 60 warships scuttled themselves, only a few submarines managing to make their way to the open sea.

Port★

To the west of the Quai Cronstedt (landing-stage for boat-trips) is the Navy Museum (Musée de la Marine). Once the entrance to the old Arsenal, its doorway is a Louis XV masterpiece; it is flanked by sculptures of Mars and Bellona and has marble columns with Doric capitals framing tableaux of maritime motifs. The balcony of the former Town Hall (Hôtel de ville) is supported by two splendidly muscular **Atlantes**★, the work of Pierre Puget.

Mont Faron★★★

This is the easternmost of the limestone ranges which were raised up in Provence on the fringe of the great earth movements associated with the formation of the Alps in Tertiary times.

Musée-mémorial du Débarquement en Provence★

    Jul-Sep: daily 9.45am-12.45pm, 1.45-6.30pm; May-Jun: daily except Mon 9.45am-12.45pm, 1.45-6pm; Oct-Apr: daily except Mon 9.45am-12.45pm, 1.45-5.30pm. Last admission 1hr before closing. 3.80€. *04 94 88 08 09.*

From the tower, Tour Beaumont (507m – 1 663ft), there are fine views inland as well as a magnificent seaward **panorama**★★★ over the Hyères Islands, the Toulon roadstead and the whole of the coast between Sanary and Bandol. The diorama explains the course of the landings which took place on the night of 14-15 August 1944, and of the subsequent liberation of the coast between Antheor and Marseille. This second front supplemented the one already opened up by the Normandy landings, and forced the Wehrmacht to beat a rapid retreat to avoid being cut off.

    Corniche du Mont Faron★★ (corniche road). Musée de la Marine★ *Apr to mid-Sep: daily 10am-6.30pm; mid-Sep to end Mar: daily except Tue 10am-noon, 2-6pm.* *Closed mid-Dec to end Jan, 1 May.* 4.60€ *(under 18 years: no charge).* *04 94 02 02 01. www.musee-marine.fr.* Vieille ville★ (old town). Navire de débarquement "La Dives" (landing craft) – museum.

TOULOUSE★★★

POPULATION 608 430

MICHELIN MAP 343 G 3

GREEN GUIDE LANGUEDOC ROUSSILLON TARN GORGES

Toulouse has long been the focus of very diverse influences; it is linked with the Mediterranean via the low Lauraguais Pass and with the Atlantic via the Garonne, while the valleys running down from the Pyrenees keep it in touch with Spain. Many of the great movements of population which have taken place since Roman times have consequently left their mark in this area.

The city was the capital of the Visigothic kingdom, and enjoyed considerable prosperity between the 9C and 13C under the Raymond dynasty, whose court was considered to be one of the most cultured in Europe. Alas! the Albigensian crisis of the 13C put an end to the power of these rulers, giving the Capetian kings the chance to push their frontier southwards into Languedoc.

In 1323, Europe's oldest literary society was founded here to further the cause of the language of southern France (Langue d'Oc). Later, in the 16C, the city flourished again because of a boom in what at the time was the most widely-cultivated of all dye plants, woad, which yielded a blue-black colour.

▶ **Orient Yourself:** The east side of the Place du Capitole is the main meeting point for local residents. Rue St-Rome is a pedestrian shopping street stretching south away from the Capitole. Other shopping streets are Rue d'Alsace-Lorraine, Rue Croix-Baragnon, Rue St-Antoine-du-T., Rue Boulbonne, Rue des Arts and the pedestrian sections of Rue des Filatiers, rue Baronie and Rue de la Pomme. There is also a shopping mall, St-Georges, in the centre of the city. Take the "Town of Art and History" tour offered through the tourist office to become better acquainted with the city.

◉ **Don't Miss:** From the **St-Michel bridge,** you can get a great view of the the city, especially towards the end of the day when sun picks up the warm red tones of the brickwork.

◷ **Organizing Your Time:** If you plan on visiting most of the museums check the tourist office for special passes that guarantee reduced rates. Take the 2hr guided tour of Toulouse to get a better idea of where you want to spend the rest of your time in France's sixth-largest urban centre.

ℙ **Parking:** Cars can be parked free of charge in the "transit car parks" and you can then take the bus or metro into the city.

Toulouse - Address Book

EATING OUT

A QUICK BITE

◔ **La Faim des Haricots** – *3 r. du Puits Vert - ☎ 05 61 22 49 25 - schongfrance@yahoo. com - ◷closed Sun - ⊟*. A mere stone's throw from the Capitole, this vegetarian restaurant gives diners a choice of varied, plentiful fixed-price menus at painless prices. The warm decor blends brick and yellow shades; the mezzanine is also very appealing.

◔ **Jean Chiche** – *3 r. St-Pantaléon - ☎ 05 61 21 80 80 - ◷ closed evenings.* This pleasant patisserie and tearoom is close to the Capitole. The menu offers a choice of around a dozen light meals, plus cakes and ice creams.

◔⊜ **L'Autre Salon de Thé** – *45 r. des Tourneurs - ☎ 05 61 22 11 63 -lautres*

alondethe@yahoo.fr - ◷ closed lunch, Mon, Tue. Delicious pastries and nouvelle cuisine are on offer in this restaurant-tearoom right in the city centre. Tea is taken in a small sitting room in the comfort of armchairs set beneath an impressive chandelier. Popular with the locals.

⊜⊜ **Le Petit Bacchus** – *16 r. Pharaon - ☎ 05 62 26 54 87 - ◷ closed Aug, Sat and Sun – reservation recommended.* The walls of this charming wine bistro are covered with a great array of miscellany. Interesting selection of regional vintages, enormous salads and 'Croustons', a worthy house speciality using toast made of famous Poilâne bread.

A LEISURELY MEAL

⊜⊜ **La Madeleine de Proust** – *11 r. Riquet - ☎ 05 61 63 80 88 - ⊟*. Childhood memories inspire the original, carefully designed decor of this restaurant featuring yellow walls, waxed tables, antique toys, an old school desk, a time-worn cupboard. The cuisine gives the starring role to vegetables that have fallen out of common use.

🍷🍴 **La Cave des Blanchers** – *29 r. des Blanchers -* ☎ *05 61 22 47 47 –* 🕐 *closed Tues.* An attractive spot, situated among other restaurants on a street which is very popular in the evenings. Vaulted ceiling and pink brick inside, while in summer diners can eat on the pavement terrace. Regional cuisine blending characteristic sweet and sour flavours.

🍷🍴 **La Régalade** – *16 r. Gambetta -* ☎ *05 61 23 20 11 –* 🕐 *closed Sat lunch, Sun and 2 weeks in Aug.* Located between the Capitole and the Garonne, this small restaurant's pink brick facade leads to a pleasant interior of exposed beams, modern art, wood furniture and bistro chairs. Bountiful traditional fare.

🍷🍴 **Bon Vivre** – *15 bis pl. Wilson -* ☎ *05 61 23 07 17 -* 🖥. With its terrace giving onto Place Wilson and an attractive interior decorated with photos of Gers (where the proprietor was born), this is an appealing spot with a solid traditional menu.

🍷🍴🍴 **Le Mangevins** – *46 r. Pharaon -* ☎ *05 61 52 79 16 –* 🕐 *closed Aug and Sun.* In this local tavern where salted foie gras and beef are sold by weight, the bawdy, fun atmosphere is enhanced by ribald songs. There is no menu, but a set meal for hearty appetites. Anyone in search of peace and quiet should look elsewhere!

🍷🍴🍴 **Colombier** – *14 r. Bayard -* ☎ *05 61 62 40 05 - colombier@wanadoo.fr -* 🕐*closed Aug, 1 Sep. 25 Dec, Sat lunch, Sun - reservation recommended.* Opened in 1874, this is an essential stopping point for culinary pilgrims in search of authentic cassoulet. Delightful dining room with pink bricks and wall paintings. Friendly and efficient service.

🍷🍴🍴 **Le Châteaubriand** – *42 r. Pargaminières -* ☎ *05 61 21 50 58 –* 🕐 *closed end Jul-21 Aug .* The atmosphere in this little restaurant in old Toulouse is particularly pleasant. Cosy interior with a parquet floor, red brick walls, a huge mirror and houseplants. Southwestern cooking on the menu.

🍷🍴🍴 **L'Envers du Décor** – *22 r. des Blanchers -* ☎ *05 61 23 85 33 –* 🕐 *closed Sun and Mon -* 🖥. Cuisine of the southwest with some exotic touches is served in this restaurant in a small, busy street not far from the Garonne. Dice, cards, and theatre contribute to the playful ambience; perhaps you will win yourself a second meal. Good luck!

🍷🍴🍴 **7 Place St-Sernin** – *7 pl. St-Sernin - b 05 62 30 05 30 –* 🕐 *closed Sat lunch, Sun.* This pretty 19C house typical of Toulouse stands opposite the basilica. Bright red and yellow Catalan colours, contemporary furniture and a display of paintings from a local art gallery garnish the dining room. Contemporary cuisine.

🍷🍴🍴 **Brasserie de l'Opéra** – *1 pl. du Capitole -* ☎ *05 61 21 37 03 -* 🕐 *closed Sun.* The brasserie of the Grand Hôtel de l'Opéra is the essential place to go and see and be seen. The inviting decor, leather wall seats and autographed photos of the many artists who have spent time here create a special atmosphere. Cuisine of southwest France.

🍷🍴🍴 **Le Bellevue** – *1 av. des Pyrénées - 31120 Lacroix-Falgarde - 13 km au S de Toulouse par D 4 -* ☎ *05 61 76 94 97 -* 🕐 *closed 20 Oct-20 Nov, Tue and Wed.* A cosy traditional ambience with windows overlooking the Ariège; in summer the large riverside terrace gets busy so reservation is advised.

🍷🍴🍴 **Au Gré du Vin** – *10 r. Pléau -* ☎ *05 61 25 03 51 –* 🕐 *closed Aug, Christmas-New Year, Sat, Sun and public holidays – reservations required.* A casual restaurant opposite the Musée Paul-Dupuy. The rustic setting, pink brick walls, convivial ambience, good selection of wines by the glass and simple, toothsome fare make this a popular address.

🍷🍴🍴 **Brasserie "Beaux Arts"** – *1 quai Daurade -* ☎ *05 61 21 12 12.* The atmosphere of a 1930s brasserie is recreated here with bistro-style chairs, wall seats, retro lighting, wood panelling and mirrors. The cuisine, in keeping with the decor, features seafood, sauerkraut and a few regional specialities.

🍷🍴🍴🍴 **Toulousy-Les Jardins de l'Opéra** – *1 pl. du Capitole –* ☎ *05 61 23 07 76 - toulousy@wanadoo.fr -* 🕐*closed 1-7 Jan., 29 Jul-28 Aug, Mon lunch and Sun.* The excellent restaurant of the Grand Hôtel de l'Opéra. Sophisticated cuisine in luxurious surroundings.

WHERE TO STAY

🍷🍴 **Hôtel de France** – *5 r. d'Austerlitz -* ☎ *05 61 21 88 24 - contact@hotel-france-toulouse.com - 64 rms.* In business since 1910, this attractive hotel is situated a few steps from the Place Wilson. The rooms are of various sizes; though not luxurious, they are shipshape and affordable. Some of the largest come with a balcony.

🍷🍴 **Hôtel le Capitole** – *10 r. Rivals -* ☎ *05 61 23 21 28 - hotelcapitolewanadoo.fr - 33 rms: 42/75€ -* 🍽 *8€.* Situated very near to the Place du Capitole, this old mansion has a brick facade that has just been redone. Some of the spacious bedrooms are sparkling new, and half are air-conditioned. A bonus: breakfasts are served 'til noon.

🍷🍴 **Hôtel St-Sernin** – *Pl. St-Senin -* ☎ *05 61 21 73 08 -* 🅿 *- book in advance – 18 rms.* Some rooms at this family hotel have fine views of the famous basilique St-Sernin; all are simply decorated with yellow or pale pink walls and well presented. Open fireplace in the breakfast room.

🍷🍴 **Ours Blanc** – *25 pl. Victor-Hugo -* ☎ *05 61 23 14 55 - victorhugo@hotel-*

oursblanc.com – 38 rms. Situated opposite the marché Victor-Hugo, this hotel has simple yet comfortable rooms (recently renovated) which are air conditioned and sound proofed; bright breakfast room with some attractive pictures embellishing its walls.

🍽☕ **Hôtel Castellane** – 17 r. Castellane - ☎ 05 61 62 18 82- castellanehotel@wanadoo.fr 49 rms. This small hotel close to the Capitole is slightly set back from the main thoroughfare. The simple, practical rooms are housed in three different buildings; some rooms are particularly well suited to families. Breakfast is served on the veranda.

🍽☕ **Park Hôtel** – 2 r. Porte-Sardane - ☎ 05 61 21 25 97 - contact@au-park-hotel. com - 44 rms:. An excellent location within a stone's throw of the city's most prominent sights. Renovated, functional rooms (most of which are air-conditioned), effective double glazing, mini-gym… What more could one need?

🍽☕ **Hôtel des Beaux Arts** – 1 pl. du Pont-Neuf - ☎ 05 34 45 42 42 - contact@hoteldesbeauxarts.com – 19 rms. A handsome 18C building on the raised banks of the Garonne. The rooms are rather compact but pleasant: a select decor, silky fabrics, nice furniture and a cosy atmosphere prevail. Some rooms overlook the river.

🍽☕☕ **Hôtel Mermoz** – 50 r. Matabiau - ☎ 05 61 63 04 04 - reservation@hotel. mermoz.com - 🅿 – 52 rms. The inner flower garden of this hotel near the city centre provides a haven of calm. Many decorative touches, notably portraits of pilots, bring aviation's early years to mind. Spacious rooms furnished in 1930s style.

🍽☕☕ **Chambre d'hôte Château des Varennes** – 31450 Varennes - 18km/11.2mi E of Toulouse on D 2, Revel road - ☎ 05 61 81 69 24 - j.mericqwanadoo.fr - 🍴 - 5 rms. This 16C pink brick château and its main courtyard are very impressive. The guest rooms, reached via a stately double stairwell, are elegant indeed; the 'Bedouin' room is particularly colourful. Marvellous vaulted cellars and a park with splendid old trees.

SIT BACK AND RELAX

Maison Octave – 11 allée Franklin-Roosevelt - ☎ 05 62 27 05 21 - octave.fm@wanadoo.fr - 🕙 daily noon-midnight. Come to this famous ice cream parlour for a overwhelming choice of sherbets, ice cream, vacherins. Over thirty different flavours to enjoy in the parlour or take home.

ON THE TOWN

Bar La Loupiote – 39 r. Réclusane - ☎ 05 61 42 76 76 - 🕙 Mon-Fri 5.30pm-1.30am, Sat 7pm-2.30am - 🕙 closed Aug, 5 Jan, 1 May, 20 Dec. Café-theatre, concerts, board games, art and photography exhibitions: the local music and theatre crowd flocks to this bar where conviviality and good humour prevail.

Le Bibent – 5 pl. du Capitole - ☎ 05 61 23 89 03 - 🕙 daily 7am-1am. Classified as an historic monument because of its Belle Époque decor, this roomy café has a superb terrace giving onto the Place du Capitole.

Le Père Louis – 45 r. des Tourneurs - ☎ 05 61 21 33 45 – 🕙 Mon-Sat 8.30am-2.30pm, 5-10.30pm – 🕙 closed 1 week in Spring, 3 weeks in Aug, Christmas-1 Jan and public holidays. First opened in 1889 and now a registered historical building, this wine bar is a local institution. The portrait of Père Louis, the founding father, conspicuously observes goings-on from above; his debonair visage also adorns wine bottle labels. Wine is sipped around fat-bellied barrels; an appetizing choice of open-faced sandwiches is available evenings.

Place du Capitole – The famous central square of the city is a pedestrians-only meeting place where numerous markets are held. It is surrounded by alluring terraces, notably those belonging to the Brasserie Le Bibent (magnificent panelling), Le Café des Arcades and the Brasserie de l'Opéra, all facing the Capitole. To the right, Mon Caf is a typical establishment.

SHOWTIME

The magazine Toulouse Cultures (monthly and its Agenda Cultures (every 2 months) list all current and upcoming events. Don't forget the tourist office website: www.ot-toulouse.fr and the mairie's website: www.mairie-toulouse.fr

Cinémathèque de Toulouse – 69 r. du Taur, BP 824 - ☎ 05 62 30 30 10 / 11 - contact@lacinemathequedetoulouse.com - 🕙 Tue-Sat 2pm-10pm, Sun 2pm-7pm. This cinematic citadel, founded in 1950 by Raymond Borde, was overseen by Daniel Toscan du Plantier between 1996 and 2003. Numerous theme cycles and film festivals. Exhibition hall, library and bar.

SHOPPING

Markets – The Sunday morning country market held round the Eglise St-Aubin is where farmers come sell their fruit, vegetables and poultry, live or butchered. Wednesday and Friday from November to March, geese, ducks and foie gras are sold Place du Salin. Saturday mornings an organic farmers' market is held Place du Capitole. Sunday mornings L'Inquet, a renowned flea market, takes place around the Basilique St-Sernin. Used-book sellers gather around Place St-Étienne Saturdays and Place Arnaud-Bernard Thursdays (many are present at L'Inquet as well). Another flea market is held in Allée Jules Guesde the first weekend of each month.

Shopping streets – The main shopping streets are Rue d'Alsace-Lorraine, Rue Croix-Baragnon, Rue St-Antoine-du-T., Rue

Boulbonne, Rue des Arts and the pedestrian sections of Rue St-Rome, Rue des Filatiers, Rue Baronie and Rue de la Pomme. There is also a shopping mall, St-Georges, in the centre of the city.

Busquets – *10 r. Rémusat -* ☎ *05 61 21 22 16 - www.extrawine.com -* ◷ *Mon afternoon-Sat, 9.45am-12.45pm, 2.15-7.15pm -* ◷ *closed Sun and public holidays.* Connoisseurs of wines from the southwest, *foie gras, cassoulet, confit,* and other regional specialities will be in seventh heaven in this shop founded in 1919.

La Maison de la Violette – *Bd de Bonrepas - Canal du Midi -* ☎ *05 61 99 01 30 -* ◷ *Tue-Sat 10am-12.30pm, 2pm-6.30pm.* The celebrated Toulouse violet is the star of this shop housed on a pastel-coloured barge. The very hospitable owner's enthusiasm for this noble flower is contagious – let her guide you through an array of violet-scented perfumes, liqueurs, sweets and cosmetics.

Librairie des Arcades – *16 pl. du Capitole -* ☎ *05 61 23 19 49.* This shop specialises in comic books.

Ombres Blanches – *50 r. Gambetta -* ☎ *05 34 45 53 33 - info@ombres-blanches.fr -* ◷ *Mon-Sat 10am-7pm.* Toulouse's biggest bookshop.

Privat – *14 r. des Arts -* ☎ *05 61 12 64 20.* This publisher and bookshop is a local institution.

Atelier du Chocolat de Bayonne – *1 r. du Rempart-Villeneuve -* ☎ *05 61 22 97 67 -* ◷ *Mon-Sat 9.30am-7.30pm -* ◷ *closed early-mid Aug, Christmas, New Year.* All the chocolates in this shop are guaranteed 100 % pure cocoa with no added fat. Faced with such abundance, it is difficult to make a choice: chocolate flavoured with cinnamon, orange or ginger, or rather chocolate from Madagascar, Java or Ecuador??

Olivier Confiseur-Chocolatier – *20 r. Lafayette -* ☎ *05 61 23 21 87 -* ◷ *Mon-Sat 9.30am-12.30pm, 1.45pm-7.15pm.* Olivier, a master chocolate maker, produces irresistible chocolate specialities, including the famous candied violets, capitouls (almonds covered in dark chocolate), *Clémence Isaure* (Armagnac-soaked grapes covered in dark chocolate), *brindilles* (nougatine covered in chocolate praline) and *Péché du Diable*, The Devil's Sin, (dark chocolate ganache with orange peel and ginger). Heaven help us!

RECREATION

Le Capitole – *Quai de la Daurade -* ☎ *05 61 25 72 57 -* ◷ *Apr and Oct daily at 10.30am, 3pm and 4.30pm; May-Sep daily at 10.30am, 3pm, 4.30pm and 6pm -* 8€ *(children: 5€); Jul-Aug: night cruises, 9pm, 10pm -* 5€ *(children: 3.50€).* Embark upon the pleasure steamer Le Capitole for a cruise along the Garonne. You'll discover

the Pont Neuf, the Saint-Michel lock, the untamed banks of the Île du Grand Ramier… A sightseeing tour full of sights worth seeing!

Parc toulousain – Set on an island in the river Garonne, the Parc toulousain offers four swimming pools, three outdoors and one covered; the Stadium, where the Stade Toulousain rugby team plays; the Parc des Expositions and the Palais des Congrès.

Péniche Baladine – ☎ *05 61 80 22 26 or 06 74 64 52 36 - www.bateaux-toulousains. com - departs quai de la Daurade.* ◷Oct-May: open Wed, Sat, Sun and public holidays; Jun-Sep and school holidays: open every day, Canal du Midi cruises (1hr 15mins) depart at 10.50am and 4pm, Garonne cruises (1hr 15mins) depart at 2.30pm, 5.30pm and 7pm. 7€. Details of night cruises on request.

Golf club de Toulouse – *31320 Vieille-Toulouse -* ☎ *05 61 73 45 48.* 18 holes.

Golf club de Toulouse Palmola – *Rte d'Albi - A 68 sortie N° 4 - 31660 Buzet-sur-Tarn -* ☎ *05 61 84 20 50 - www. golfdepalmola.com -* ◷*9am-6.30pm -* ◷*closed Mar.* 18-hole golf course. Clubhouse with restaurant, tennis court and swimming pool.

Golf Seilh – *R. de Grenade - 31840 Seilh -* ☎ *05 62 13 14 14 - www.macva-latitudes-toulouse.co -* ◷*Mon-Fri 8am-6.30pm, Sat and Sun 8am-7pm -* ◷*closed 1 Dec, 25 Dec.* Golf Latitudes Toulouse Seilh; two 18-hole golf courses.

CALENDAR OF EVENTS

Fête de la violette – *First or second weekend in Feb -* ☎ *05 62 16 31 31.* Growing, selling, exhibiting… the ideal opportunity to learn all about the flower that is the city's emblem.

Printemps du rire – *Late Mar -* ☎ *05 62 21 23 24, www.printemps-du-rire.com.* Spring comedy festival.

Garonne le Festival – *Late Jun -* ☎ *05 61 32 77 28, www.garonne-rioloco.org.* Visitors from all over the world congregate for concerts and other events.

Piano aux Jacobins – *Sep -* ☎ *05 61 22 40 05, www.pianojacobins.com*

Le Printemps de Septembre – *Late Sep -* ☎ *01 43 38 00 11, www. printempsdeseptembre.com.* Festival of photography and visual arts.

Festival Occitania – *Oct -* ☎ *05 61 11 24 87, www.ieotolosa.free.fr.* Regional culture celebrated through various media (cinema, poetry, song etc…).

Jazz sur son 31 – *Oct -* ☎ *05 34 45 05 92, www.jazz31.com.* Large jazz festival established 18 years ago.

Cinespaña – *Octobre -* ☎ *05 61 12 12 20, www.cinespagnol.com.* Spanish cinema.

An Aeronautical Capital

As early as 1917, strategic industries like aircraft manufacturing were being set up in southwestern France, as far away as possible from the country's vulnerable eastern border. In the inter-war period, Toulouse became the starting-point of France's first scheduled air service.

Clément Ader (1841-1925) – Born at nearby Muret. This pioneer experimented with a balloon at Toulouse in 1870 and also designed a dirigible. On 9 October 1890, he succeeded in flying a short distance in a heavier-than-air machine.

Pierre Latécoère (1883-1943) – Built aircraft for the French army during the First World War. On Christmas Day 1918, assisted by Cornemont, he carried out a test flight to investigate the possibilities of a link with Barcelona.

Didier Daurat (1891-1969) – With a great talent for leadership, he became director of the airline set up by Latécoère, then ran Aéropostale, and finally headed Air France. On 10 March 1919, he inaugurated the first airmail service to link Toulouse and Casablanca (though the official opening was not until 1 September).

Émile Dewoitine (1892-1979) – Founder of Toulouse's aviation industry and builder of the Dewoitine 520 fighter plane.

Antoine de Saint-Exupéry (1900-44) – A pilot on the Toulouse-Casablanca route, he was responsible for investigating the Dakar link which was eventually inaugurated on 1 June 1925. He also flew extensively in South America and was the author of internationally acclaimed works like *Night Flight* and *The Little Prince*.

Jean Mermoz (1901-35) – Pioneered the trans-Andean route between Rio and Santiago. In 1930, he set up the first airmail route between France and South America. He died aboard his seaplane *Croix-du-Sud*.

Henri Guillaumet (1902-40) – Helped Latécoère set up the trans-Andean route and completed a total of 393 flights over this formidable mountain barrier.

21 April 1949 – Jean Gonord piloted the Leduc 010 on its maiden flight. The plane's ram jet, designed by René Leduc, was the precursor of the engines powering the high-speed aircraft of later decades.

27 May 1955 – Maiden flight of the Caravelle, piloted by P Nadot. This was one of the world's first jet airliners, second only to the ill-starred British Comet.

2 March 1969 – André Turcat took off in the supersonic Anglo-French Concorde with its distinctive tapering fuselage designed by Servanty. It is the first supersonic plane used for commercial transport.

1992 – The Airbus A330 with a capacity of 395 makes its maiden flight.

A Brick-Built City

In the Early Middle Ages, Toulouse was one of France's most important centres of cultural and artistic activity. Today, little remains of this distant period other than the great St-Sernin Church and the Romanesque sculptures in the Augustinians' Museum.

Pont Neuf and the city of Toulouse

Dumas/IMAGES TOULOUSE

The city's medieval growth could not be catered for by building in stone, the nearest quarries being 80km – 50 miles distant. The problem was solved by using the Garonne clays to manufacture the bricks which are such a characteristic feature of the Toulouse townscape. Robust, cheap, easy to use, but perhaps less decorative than stone, brick added a further layer of austerity to that wished for by the mendicant orders who were so influential here.

Basilique St-Sernin★★★

The great church was built to honour the memory of the Gaulish martyr St Sernin (or Saturninus). A first phase of construction lasting from around 1080 to 1118 was in a mixture of brick and stone, a second phase in brick alone.

St-Sernin was one of a number of major Romanesque pilgrimage churches on the route to Compostela like Cluny, St-Martin at Tours, St-Martial at Limoges, St-Hilaire-le-Grand at Poitiers, St-Remi at Reims and Santiago de Compostela itself, which, often provided with five aisles to accommodate the throngs of pilgrims, form a distinct grouping; it was on these great institutions that the medieval Papacy relied for the consolidation of its temporal power, the Reconquest of Spain from the Moors and the extirpation of the Cathar heresy. These churches also played a role in the realisation of Capetian designs on Languedoc.

St-Sernin's octagonal bell-tower is particularly characteristic of the area, with five levels of twin arches built in brick, the upper two of which are provided with little pediments.

Église des Jacobins★★

Daily 9am-7pm. Possibility of a guided tour (1hr). 2.40€, no charge 1st Sun in the month. 05 61 22 21 92. www.jacobins.mairie-toulouse.fr.

This was the first church of the Preaching Friars, an order founded at **Fanjeaux** *(20km – 12mi south of Castelnaudary)* in 1215 by St Dominic, and intended by him to help in the fight against the Cathar heresy. To the poverty demanded by St Francis of his followers, Dominic added a solidly-based knowledge of theology and a training in eloquence which enabled his disciples to overcome their opponents in argument and spread true doctrine.

The church is the key building in the evolution from 1230 onwards of Southern French Gothic as influenced by the mendicant orders.

The first rectangular-shaped church, built between 1230 and 1235, was enlarged in the middle of the century, then again between 1275 and 1292 in order to accommodate the growing fraternity. This was the point at which major changes were made in the apse and elevation of the nave. The size of the edifice, combined with the impossibility of providing it with external support (because of ownership and circulation problems), ruled out the construction of a single nave, and the building's original division into two parts had to be retained. A decisive factor in the choice of roofing method was the recent destruction in a fire of the Order's timber-roofed church at Bayonne; thus it was that the architect here resorted to the expedient of a marvellous ribbed vault and the "palm-tree" of the chancel with its splendid array of 22 radiating arches. All this in 1292, 170 years before the great pointed vaults of the Late Gothic.

The tower dates from 1298, several years later than the upper stages of the tower of St-Sernin; with its great height, octagonal plan, pedimented arches and rhomboid openings, it became the model for the towers of the major churches of Southern France (just as the gable-wall of the adjoining Church of Notre-Dame-du-Taur formed the prototype for many village churches).

Violets

According to tradition violets, which originate in Parma, were brought back to Toulouse in the 19C by French soldiers returning from the Napoleonic wars in Italy. They proved very popular with the locals and in particular with florists, perfumers, and confectioners who specialised in the famous crystallised violets. At the beginning of the 20C some 600 000 bunches were despatched each year to Paris, Northern Europe and even as far as Canada. Unfortunately the delicate flower succumbed to disease. From 1985 scientists made a determined attempt to save the little mauve flower. Ten years later in vitro cultivation was a success. Nowadays the glasshouses of Lalande, north of Toulouse, are once more filled with the characteristic perfume of violets and Toulouse has regained its emblem.

Capitole★

This is Toulouse's City Hall, its name being derived from the "capitouls" or consuls who administered the city when it was ruled by the Raymonds. With its Ionic pilasters and alternating use of brick and stone, it is a fine example of the urban architecture of the 18C.

Cathédrale St-Étienne★

There is a fascinating contrast here between the nave completed in 1212, a vast hall in the Mediterranean tradition designed to accommodate large numbers of people, and the chancel, begun 60 years later on the pattern of the Gothic churches of Northern France. The architect of this later addition was Jean Deschamps, who took it upon himself to propagate this style throughout Languedoc once it had become part of the Capetian realm.

The nave and chancel are not aligned on the same axis and hardly seem to form part of a whole. The original plan had envisaged a more or less total reconstruction, but in the event the old nave was retained, and the link between it and the chancel cleverly improvised by some architectural virtuosity in what should have been the north transept.

Musée des Augustins★★

  ♿ 🕐 *Wed 10am-9pm, Thu-Mon 10am-6pm. Possibility of a guided tour (1hr15min).* 🕐 *Closed Tue, 1 Jan, 1 May, 25 Dec.* 👓 *2.40€, no charge 1st Sun in the month.* ☎ *05 61 22 21 82. www.augustins.org.*

The museum is housed in the former convent; in the chapter-house there is a famous Pietà. The superb collection of Romanesque sculpture (**sculptures romanes★★★**) (mostly 12C), much of it in grey Pyrenean marble, comes for the greater part from the cloisters of St-Sernin and St Stephen's, and from Notre-Dame-de-la-Daurade. The influence of Moissac (♿ *see MOISSAC*) is evident (La Daurade was a priory attached to the abbey there), as is that of Chartres and St-Denis, where Gilbertus, the sculptor responsible for the cloisters of St Stephen's, may well have worked.

  ◖◖   Hôtel d'Assezat★. Musée St-Raymond★★ ♿ 🕐 *Jun-Aug: daily 10am-7pm. Sep-May: daily 10am-6pm. Possibility of a guided tour (1hr15min).* 🕐 *Closed 1 Jan, 1 May and 25 Dec.* 👓 *2.40€, no charge 1st Sun in the month –* archeology.

   Muséum d'Histoire naturelle★★ ⚊ *Closed for renovation work at present, reopening 2006.*

   Musée Paul-Dupuy★ 🕐 *Jun-Sep: Wed-Mon 10am-6pm; Oct-May: Wed-Mon 10am-5pm.* 🕐 *Closed Tue and public holidays. Call in advance for a guided tour (1hr15min).* 👓 *2.40€, no charge 1st Sun in the month.* ☎ *05 61 14 65 50 –* applied arts from medieval times to the present.

Le **TOUQUET**★★★

POPULATION 5 596

MICHELIN MAP 301 C 4

GREEN GUIDE NORTHERN FRANCE AND THE PARIS REGION

Le Touquet was simply the name given to a stretch of uninhabited sand dunes at the mouth of the River Canche, when, in 1837, the area was purchased by a speculator who planted it up with maritime pines and later, in 1876, divided it into residential plots. At the beginning of the 20C, a British company, the "Le Touquet Syndicate" moved in and built the first of many exclusive holiday dwellings. By 1912 the place had developed to such an extent and become so fashionable among the leisured classes, not only of England but also of Paris, that it took on the name of Le Touquet Paris Plage.

Today, not only is the "Pearl of the Opal Coast" a favoured resort among the well-to-do families of France's industrial North, but it also enjoys an international reputation, with its range of facilities, which include casinos and a hydrotherapy centre as well as golf, tennis, riding, land-yachting...

The town is divided into two: there is the well-treed residential area with its luxury villas, some of them modern, but many in that hybrid style known as "Anglo-Norman"; then there is the resort itself, stretching out along the magnificent beach of fine sand. The town centre is laid out on a grid pattern and the main shopping streets are Rue St-Jean and Rue de Paris.

TOURNUS★

POPULATION 6 568

MICHELIN MAP 320 J 10

GREEN GUIDE BURGUNDY JURA

Originally founded by the Aidui tribe, Tournus became a Gallo-Roman settlement on a river-terrace on the right bank of the Saône, then later an important stopping-place for river traffic.

The sanctuaries erected over the tomb of St Valerian from Merovingian times onwards made it one of the earliest centres of monasticism in France. In the 9C, monks from Noirmoutier fled here from the Vikings, bringing with them the relics of St Philibert. The place's wealth excited the envy of the Hungarian hordes, who sacked it in 937.

Visit

Église St-Philibert★★

The reconstruction of the church was begun 25 years after the Hungarian raid. A number of features date from this period, including the crypt (**crypte★**), where the persistence of Carolingian tradition can be seen in the layout of the chapels and the barrel vault of the ambulatory, as well as the narthex, whose enormous circular abacus pillars are one of the great achievements of this early phase of the Romanesque. The west front dates from the 10C-11C; it was built like a castle keep, down to having loophole slits (the machicolations are a 19C addition).

At the beginning of the 11C, after a fire in 1006, work was started on the nave. The splendid cylindrical pillars are almost unique in the history of medieval architecture, and the early-12C vault is highly original too; its five transversal barrel vaults offered a number of structural advantages by eliminating lateral thrusts, allowing longitudinal pressures to cancel each other out, and making use of narthex and transept for support as well. In view of this, it is surprising that it remained an isolated example, with no imitators.

The rapid development of the Romanesque style can be traced in both transept and choir, the latter with a barrel vault on divergent transverse arches.

TOURS★★

POPULATION 271 927

MICHELIN MAP 317 N 4

GREEN GUIDE CHÂTEAUX OF THE LOIRE

Built in white tufa and roofed in slate, the old dwellings of Tours fill the isthmus between the Loire and its tributary the Cher. The place originated in Gaulish times, becoming an important centre of trade and administration under the Romans. The peaceful atmosphere of the Loire valley with its exceptionally clear light may be responsible in part for the many great figures associated with the city in one way or another.

▶ **Orient Yourself:** Tours, which is listed as a "Town of Art and history," offers discovery tours conducted by guide-lecturers approved by the Ministry of Culture and Communication. Information at the tourist office or on www.vpah.culture.fr.

Tours Address Book

EATING OUT

📠 **Bistrot de la Tranchée** – 103 av. Tranchée – ☎ 02 47 41 09 08 – charles. barrier@cegetel.net – 🕐 closed 5-26 Aug, Sun and Mon. Dark wood panelling, bottles of wine, comfortable wall sofas and old-fashioned pizza ovens (remnants of the previous restaurant) make up the decor of this pleasant bistro. Enjoy a good selection of small dishes typical to this type of restaurant. Definitely worth a visit.

📠📠 **Léonard de Vinci** – 19 r. de la Monnaie – ☎ 02 47 61 07 88 – 🕐 closed Sun evening and Mon – reservation required in evenings – A taste of Tuscany in the heart of the Touraine. This Italian restaurant's claim to fame is that it doesn't serve pizzas! A chance to discover different Italian dishes, in a decor that highlights models of Leonardo da Vinci's inventions.

📠📠📠 **La Furgeotière** – 19 pl. Foire-le-Roi – ☎ 02 47 66 94 75 – 🕐 closed 1-15 Jan, Feb school holidays, 1-7 Jul, Tue and Wed – This restaurant has a charming decor, with half-timbering and limestone. The owners love life, good food and their work. Original, inventive cuisine should satisfy all appetites.

📠📠📠📠 **La Roche Le Roy** – 55 rte de St-Avertin – ☎ 02 47 27 22 00 – 🕐 closed Feb school holidays, 1-25 Aug, Sun and Mon. The restaurant in this Touraine manor house was created under a lucky star and will be much appreciated by gourmets. Sample the cooking, which varies with the seasons, in the intimate dining room or the pretty enclosed courtyard in summer, and enjoy fine wines from the cellar hewn into the cliff face.

WHERE TO STAY

📠 **Italia** – 19 r. De Vildé – ☎ 02 47 54 43 01 – 🅿 🕐 closed 3-10 Jan – 🛏 7€. This hotel is in a quiet part of town that has a little bit of everything. The service here is excellent and the rooms are recently renovated, comfortable and well kept. There is a charming covered veranda and small garden area for those eating breakfast.

📠📠 **Chambre d'hôte Le Moulin Hodoux** – 37230 Luynes – 14km/8.75mi W of Tours on N 152 and minor road – ☎ 02 47 55 76 27 – 🛏 – 4 rooms. In a peaceful country setting not far from Tours, near the castle at Luynes, this 18C-19C watermill provides comfortable, well-equipped rooms. In the lovely garden there are tables, chairs and a barbecue for visitors' use, as well as a swimming pool.

📠📠📠 **Central Hôtel** – 21 r. Berthelot – ☎ 02 47 05 46 44 – 🅿 – 40 rooms – 🛏 8.39€. A quiet, comfortable hotel in the old part of Tours, near the busy pedestrian-only districts. The staff are reserved but pleasant. There is a small, peaceful garden to enjoy behind the hotel in summer, and you can eat breakfast on the terrace.

ON THE TOWN

Aux Trois Pucelles – 19 r. Briçonnet – ☎ 02 47 20 67 29 – 🕐 Mon-Fri 7.45am-midnight, Sat 9am-3.30pm. The oldest bar in Tours is in a 15C building. Away from the bustle of place Plumereau, this café is popular among university students. The owner may tell you how it got its name (Three Young Virgins").

Le Corsaire – 187 av. de Grammont – ☎ 02 47 05 20 00 – 🕐 daily except Sun 6pm-4am. A smart bar offering a choice of over 400 cocktails. The decor is designed to look like a boat's hold, with real portholes and ship's lanterns. Discreet clientele and atmospheric music, mainly jazz.

Le Hamac – 21 r. de la Rôtisserie – ☎ 02 47 05 25 71 – 🕐 daily 7pm-2am. A peaceful cocktail bar which is a popular place to go in the evening in Tours. An ideal place for an ice cream (from a choice of 40) or a cocktail (180). Romantic couples will appreciate the sofas on the first floor.

SIT BACK AND RELAX

Le Gambrinus – 69 bis r. Blaise-Pascal – ☎ 02 47 05 17 00 – 🕐 daily except Tue 10am-2am – 🕐 closed in Aug. This bar specialises in Belgian beers, offering around 100, some of which are not normally available in France. Regular clientele.

Le Vieux Mûrier – 11 pl. Plumereau – ☎ 02 47 61 04 77 – 🕐 Tue 2pm-2am, Wed-Sat 11am-2am, Sun 2pm-1am. This is one of the oldest cafés in place Plumereau, and it has that extra hint of character that is so often missing from modern establishments, with a decor reminiscent of a museum. Lovely terrace in the square.

Pub St James – 7 r. des Orfèvres – ☎ 06 60 77 44 97 – 🕐 daily 6pm-2am. A truly English place with the friendly atmosphere of a pub with its regulars (not many students among them). Specialities: beers and 25-year-old whiskies.

Famous Men of Tours

St Gatien, the first bishop of Tours (3C), who helped convert Gaul to Christianity;

St Martin (316-97), whose veneration by the common people made the "city of St Martin" into a place of pilgrimage as well as an important crossroads;

Gregory of Tours (6C), the chronicler of Merovingian times;

Tours – Place Plumereau

Alcuin of York (late 8C), who helped implement Charlemagne's revival of intellectual life and who founded an illustrious school of calligraphy;

Jean Fouquet (1420-81), Charles VII's portrait-painter;

Louis XI (1423-83), responsible for introducing silk and velvet manufacture to the city;

Jean Bourdichon (1457-1521), miniaturist and portrait-painter in the reign of Charles VIII, who decorated the field of the Cloth of Gold for François I;

Jean Clouet (1485-1541), François I's court painter;

Pierre Ronsard (1524-85), the highly individualistic poet who passed his last 20 years as Prior of nearby St Cosmas';

Anatole France (1844-1924), the somewhat sceptical but nevertheless optimistic humanist who stayed at La Béchellerie and St-Cyr-sur-Loire;

Henri Bergson (1859-1941), the philosopher of the pre-war years whose work was devoted to bridging the gap between metaphysics and science and who stayed at La Gaudinière.

Sights

Le Vieux Tours (OLD TOWN)★★

The city long prided itself on its craftsmen, and even at the end of the 19C there were still three guilds jealously guarding their traditions. The **Musée du Compagnonnage** contains many fine examples of the work of master craftsmen like roofers and slaters, blacksmiths and locksmiths, saddlers and carpenters...

Château★

This is a heterogeneous collection of buildings ranging in date from the 4C to the 19C. The lower parts of the wall on the west side go back to Roman times and here too is the 11C residence of the Counts of Anjou; the Guise Tower (Tour de Guise) with its machicolations and pepper-pot roof is of the 13C-15C, while the dormer-windowed Governor's Lodging (Logis du Gouverneur) is 15C and other additions were made as recently as the 17C-19C.

Cathédrale St-Gatien★★

Following a fire, the cathedral was rebuilt from 1235 onwards. The work lasted all of 250 years; the choir dates from the reign of Louis IX and the nave from the age of Charles VII and Duke John of Brittany. The latter was probably responsible for commissioning a master glazier from Rennes to make one of the cathedral's stained-glass windows. The west front was completed under Louis XI and Charles VIII; in Flamboyant style, it has an openwork tympanum and triangular gable, while the design of the lantern crowning the twin towers is characteristic of the Early Renaissance.

The stained glass ranges in date from the 13C (high windows in the chancel) via the 14C (transept rose windows) to the 15C (rose window of the west front).

In the south transept chapel is the tomb of the children of Charles VIII; mounted on a base carved by Geronimo di Fiesole, it is the work of the sculpture workshop founded by Michel Colombe. The choir is lit by a rare 18C chandelier.

La Psalette★

🕐 *Guided tours* ⬅ *(1/2hr) Jun-Sep: Mon-Sat 9.45am-12.30pm, 1.30-6pm, Sun 1.30-6pm;*
Apr-May: Mon-Sat 10am-12.30pm, 2-5.30pm, Sun. 2-5.30pm; Mar: Wed-Sat 9.30am-
12.30pm, 2-5.30pm, Sun 2-5.30pm; Oct-Feb: Wed-Sat 9.30am-12.30pm, 2-5pm, Sun
2-5.30pm. Call in advance for a visit Sun morning. 🕐 *Closed 1 Jan, 1 May and 25 Dec.*
2.50€. ☎ *02 47 47 05 19.*

This is the name given to the cathedral cloisters where canons and choir-master used to meet. The tiny Archive Room (Salle des Archives) of 1520 and the vaulted Library (Librairie) are reached by means of a spiral staircase, Gothic in structure but Renaissance in the way in which it is detailed.

Place Plumereau★

This busy and picturesque square is located at the old "meeting of the ways" (carroi); it is bordered by fine 15C residences built of stone and timber. On the corner with the Rue du Change and the Rue de la Monnaie is a carved corner post with a somewhat mutilated depiction of the Circumcision.

Musée des Beaux-Arts★★

🕐 *Wed-Mon 9am-12.45pm, 2-6pm. A guided tour in sign language is given the 4th Sat in the month.* 🕐 *Closed Tue, 1 Jan, 1 May, 14 Jul, 1 and 11 Nov, 25 Dec.* 4€. ☎ *02 47 05 68 73.*

In the former Bishops' Palace (17C-18C), its rooms are beautifully decorated with Louis XVI panelling and silk hangings made locally.

It houses works of art from the châteaux at Richelieu and Chanteloup (now demolished) as well as from the great abbeys of Touraine. The collection of paintings consists mostly of French works of the 19C-20C, but there are also two outstanding Mantegnas, a Resurrection and Christ in the Garden of Olives (late 15C).

Excursions

Prieuré de St-Cosme★

♿ 🕐 *Apr-Sep: daily 9am-7pm; Oct-Mar: daily 9.30am-12.30pm, 2-5pm.* 🕐 *Closed 1 Jan and 25 Dec. 4.50€ (12-18 years: 3€).* ☎ *02 47 37 32 70.*

3km – 2mi southwest on the south bank of the river. Leave Tours by the Pont Wilson. Now in ruins, this is the priory to which the poet Ronsard retired. He lived and died in the Prior's Lodging (Logis du Prieur), a charming little 15C dwelling, and is buried in the church.

Château de Plessis-lès-Tours

3km – 2mi southwest after crossing the Pont Wilson. This modest brick building is all that remains of the substantial château built here by Louis XI and where he spent much of his time. The room in which he died still has the linenfold panelling much favoured in the 15C. This Louis was a restless monarch, more of a politician than a military man; he succeeded in imposing his authority on the country and in bringing the Hundred Years War to an end, after which he turned his attention to restoring France's devastated economy. He incorporated into his kingdom not only the Duchy of Burgundy, but also the Somme towns, Artois and the Franche-Comté (all in 1477), followed by Maine and Anjou in 1481 and Provence in 1486. Conscious of the importance of monarchical prestige, he feigned good health in his declining years in spite of serious illness.

👁👁 Rue Briçonnet★. Place Grégoire-de-Tours★. Hôtel Gouin★ 🕐 *Apr-Sep: daily 9.30am-12.30pm, 1.15-6.30pm; Oct-Mar: daily 9.30am-12.30pm, 2-5.30pm.* 🕐 *Closed 1 Jan and 25 Dec. 4.50€ (12-18 years: 3€).* ☎ *02 47 66 22 32* – Musée de la Société archéologique de Touraine★. Historial de Touraine★ (in the castle).

Jardin de Beaune-Semblançay★. Musée des Équipages militaires et du Train★ 🕐 *Daily except Sat 1.30-5.30pm. Last admission 1hr before closing. No charge.* ☎ *02 47 77 33 07.*

TRÉGUIER★★

POPULATION 2 799

MICHELIN MAP 309 C 2

GREEN GUIDE BRITTANY

Tréguier is a little medieval city, overlooking the wide estuary of the Jaudy and Guindy rivers, one of the drowned valleys known as abers which are so characteristic of the Breton coast.

A Bit of History

The place was converted to Christianity in the 6C by St Tugdual, a monk of Welsh origin, and soon became the seat of a bishop. The most popular Breton saint, the ecclesiastical judge Monsieur **Saint-Ives** (1253-1303), lived here; he was often depicted in the act of even-handedly dispensing justice between rich and poor alike and hence became the patron saint of well-versed lawyers.

The town and its surroundings were no strangers to misfortune. In 1345-47 the area was devastated by the English allies of Jean de Montfort in retribution for having supported Jeanne de Penthièvre in the War of the Breton Succession. In 1592 it was pillaged by the Catholic Leaguers for having taken the part of Henri IV, then punished again in 1789 for its oppostion to the taxes and clerical reforms introduced at the time of the French Revolution.

Sights

Cathédrale St-Tugdual★★

🕐 *Jun-Sep: daily 9am-6.30pm; Oct-May : daily 9am-noon, 2-6pm. Guided tours* 👣 *(30min) in Jul and Aug 10am-noon, 2-6pm. No charge.* ☎ *02 96 92 30 51.*

Begun in 1339, this is one of the finest buildings of its kind in Brittany, Anglo-Norman in style in spite of the use of the local granite. The exterior is notable for its Romanesque Hastings Tower (Tour d'Hastings) and the balustrades adorning the slate roofs, as well as for the two porches on the south side; the larger one with its statues of the Apostles is known as the People's Porch (Porche du Peuple), the other with its much-eroded statuary is the Bell Porch (Porche des Cloches).

Within, the Lanceolate version of the Gothic survives in the three-storeyed elevation. A frieze sculpted in white tufa runs underneath the blind triforium, while in the south transept there is a graceful window (**Grande Verrière**★) with Flamboyant Gothic lancets (**fenêtre**★) adorned with a depiction of the Mystic Vine symbolising the Church in Brittany. In the ambulatory is a 13C wooden figure of Christ, and the nave has a copy of the tomb of St Ives built by Duke John V.

Cloître★

🕐 *Jul-Aug: daily 9am-7pm; Oct-Jun: daily 9am-noon, 2-6pm.* ⊛ *3€ in high season (low season: no charge).* ☎ *02 96 92 22 33 or 02 96 92 30 51.*

The cloisters 1458) are among the few to survive in Brittany. Timber-roofed and with a carved frieze, it has 48 elegant arches giving onto a hydrangea-planted courtyard.

Maison de Renan

🕐 *Jul and Aug: daily 10am-noon, 2-6pm. Apr-Jun and Sep: Wed-Fri 10am-noon, 2-6pm; Sat-Sun and public holidays 2-6pm.* 🕐 *Closed 1 Jan, 1 May, 1 and 11 Nov, 25 Dec.* ⊛ *4.60€ (under 18: no charge), no charge 1st Sun in the month (Apr-May).* ☎ *02 96 92 45 63. www.monuments.fr.*

The timber-framed house (**maison natale**) where the writer **Ernest Renan** (1823-92) was born is devoted to his memory (musée), and his statue stands in the Place du Martray.

Forêt de **TRONÇAIS**★★★

MICHELIN MAP 326 D 3

GREEN GUIDE AUVERGNE RHÔNE VALLEY

This splendid forest, "one of the finest in France, indeed in Europe" (JL Reed), lies at the southeastern end of the great plains of central France, bounded by the rivers Allier and Cher.

Today's forest covers a total area of 10 954ha – 27 067 acres. It passed into the hands of the French Crown when François I put an end to the independence of the Bourbonnais in 1527. A steady process of deterioration set in, which was reversed by the great Colbert in 1670; anxious to maintain the supply of ship timber for the expanding French navy, he instituted measures for the conservation and renewal of the woodland. However, in 1788 an iron foundry was opened, and to satisfy its demands for charcoal, two-thirds of the area was converted from high forest to a coppice regime, thereby destroying much of the resource slowly built up over the preceding century.

In 1832 a new policy of conservation was adopted, and since 1928 six blocks of high forest totalling 650ha – 1 606 acres have been managed on a long rotation of 225 years.

▶ **Orient Yourself:** For one or two months in the summer, there is a departure from the rond de Trançais. Contact the forestry commission office. ☏ 04 70 46 82 00 or the CPIE, ☏ 04 70 06 14 69. For information on tourist activities, contact the Association du Pays de Tronçais in Cérilly. ☏ 04 70 67 55 89.

Visit

The forest consists largely of sessile oak. The finest stands are called the **Hauts-Massifs**★★★; here there are a number of exceptional individuals with their own names, some of them more than 300 years old. To the east of the Gardien clearing are the Carré, Émile-Guillaumin and Charles-Louis-Philippe oaks, and to the west of the Buffévent clearing in the Richebout block other venerable trees bearing the names Jacques-Chevalier, de la Sentinelle and des Jumeaux. The Tronçais region straddles the boundary between the north and south of France. To the north is the country of langue d'oïl, four-wheeled carts, and slate or flat-tiled roofs; to the south, langue d'oc, carts with only two wheels, and roofs covered with pantiles in the Roman fashion.

 Séries de l'Ouest★ – Western forest stands – Futaie Colbert★ – Colbert Stand – Étangs de St-Bonnet★, Pirota et Saloup★ – ponds.

TROYES★★★

POPULATION 122 763

MICHELIN MAP 313 E 4

GREEN GUIDE ALSACE LORRAINE CHAMPAGNE

Troyes shares with Reims the distinction of being one of the capitals of the province of Champagne, though the city looks southeast towards Burgundy and the Langres plateau rather than northwards to the Ardennes. The town developed in the Seine valley on the great trade route between Italy and the cities of Flanders; in the Middle Ages it was host to two huge annual fairs, each lasting for three whole months, and attracting merchants and craftsmen from all over Europe. But by the end of the 14C the pattern of commercial exchanges had changed, and these great gatherings fell into decline.

▶ **Orient Yourself:** The outline of the old part of the city bears a curious resemblance to a champagne cork, with the area around the cathedral forming the head. Place Alexandre Israël is the town centre, where numerous activities are organized throughout the year, and also where a variety of shops are found. More shopping can be done in the area around the factory outlets on the way out of Troyes (St-Julien-les-Villas and Pont-Ste-Marie sites). From early Jul to mid-Sep take the "Town of Art and History" tour at 2.30pm for 5.50€. Also, audio tours can be booked all year round. Visit the tourist office or www.tourisme-troyes.com for more information.

🕐 **Organizing Your Time:** Allow 4hr to visit Vieux Troyes.

🅿 **Parking:** If you are visiting the old town, park the car behind the town hall (place Alexandre-Israël or along boulevard Gambetta).

A Bit of History

A number of important figures either were born in Troyes or worked here. They include:

Saint Loup (383-478) who was born at Toul. An associate of Saint Germanus of Auxerre, he founded an abbey and became Bishop of Troyes, saving the city from Attila's assault;

Maison du Boulanger and Tourelle de l'Orfèvre

Christian of Troyes (1135-83), author of verse-chronicles and of romances celebrating courtly love;

Jean Juvénal des Ursins (1350-1431), the magistrate who conducted on behalf of Charles VI the negotiations with John the Fearless which led to the signing of the Treaty of Arras (1414), which it was hoped would put an end to the war between Armagnacs and Burgundians;

Pierre Mignard (1612-95), the painter, a master of colour, who portrayed Mazarin, Mme de Sévigné, Turenne, Colbert. He also designed the dome of the Church of Notre-Dame-du-Val-de-Grâce in Paris;

François Girardon (1628-1715), the sculptor, famous for the tomb he designed for Richelieu and for his contribution to the statuary in the gardens at Versailles.

The Treaty of Troyes giving Henry V of England sovereignty over France was signed on 21 May 1420 by Charles VI (the Mad), the possibility of the "so-called" Dauphin Charles VII succeeding to the throne being excluded because of the notorious misconduct of Isabel of Bavaria.

Troyes has long been France's most important centre of hosiery manufacture. The industry was introduced here at the very beginning of the 16C, followed by cloth-making, dyeing, paper-making... and prosperity. The city's wealth enabled it to overcome the great fire of 1524; houses and churches were quickly rebuilt in a style showing both the Italianate influence of the artists who came here from Fontainebleau around 1540 as well as the persistence of local, medieval traditions.

In an area lacking suitable stone there is nevertheless fine sculpture, especially the work of Jean Gailde and Jacques Julyot. Early sculpture reflects troubled times, as in the *St Martha* by the Master of Chaource in the city's St Mary Magdalene Church (Église Ste-Madeleine). Later work, like the *Virgin with the Grapes* in St Urban's Church (Église St-Urbain) is more refined, while finally the Italian Il Fiorentino introduces a note of southern gracefulness. Stained glass was made here too, eventually becoming a kind of painting on glass, with the artist using and re-using for economy's sake the same cartoons for different projects. Advances were made in graphic skills, with elaborate designs like Jesse Trees divided into several parts, or involving a variety of closely juxtaposed scenes explained by means of a written commentary (the ancestor perhaps of the strip cartoon). Grisaille work can be seen in St Pantaleon's Church (Église St-Pantaléon), and the green glass made in the province is famous.

The hosiery industry – From 1505 onward the hosiers of Troyes were making hats and bonnets, and knitting socks and stockings. They acquired guild status in 1554. In 1746, looms were installed in the city's Trinity Hospital in order to give employment to destitute children. Troyes is still France's hosiery capital, with some 300 different enterprises at work.

Troyes - Address Book

PRACTICAL INFORMATION

Tourist office – *16 bd. Carnot, 10014 Troyes – ☎ 03 25 82 62 70 - www.ot-troyes.fr*

Guided tours – 🔎 Troyes, City of Art and History, organises 1hr 30min tours by approved guides of the town. *Early Jul-mid-Sep at 2.30pm, €5.50.* The rest of the year audioguides can be reserved and theme tours are organised from Oct to Jun. *Enquire at the tourist office or on www. tourisme-troyes.com*

Tourist circuit – The city has created two well signposted tours of the city's most noteworthy sites. Brochure from the tourist office.

Le Vitrail – *4 r. Brulard* – ☎ *03 25 73 38 87.* Technical tours by appointment with Mr Vinum, who restored the cathedral stained-glass windows, of St-Urbain and St-Pantaléon Churches.

WHERE TO EAT

See the Legend for coin categories.

🍽 **L'Ancolie** – *130A bd de Dijon - 10800 St-Julien-les-Villas - 4km/2.5mi N of Troyes on N 71, Dijon direction - ☎ 03 25 78 12 95 – closed Sun evenings and Wed evenings.* This restaurant, nestled among the boutiques of Marques Avenue, is an ideal spot to refuel during a shopping spree. We recommend sampling the regional cooking in the dining room or on the flower-decked terrace in summer. Good wine list and catering service.

🍽🍽 **Aux Crieurs de Vin** – *4-6 pl. Jean-Jaurès* – ☎ *03 25 40 01 01* – 🕐 *closed Sun and Mon.* Wine connoisseurs will appreciate this establishment, which is part wine and spirits shop, part atmospheric pre-1940s style bistro. The cuisine will also please enthusiasts, with produce fresh from the market and a good choice of fish.

🍽🍽 **Bistrot DuPont** – *5 pl. Charles-de-Gaulle – 10150 Pont-Ste-Marie – 3km/1.8mi NE of Troyes on N 77 – ☎ 03 25 80 90 99* – 🕐 *closed Sun evening and Mon.* Flowers and smiles from the staff provide a fine welcome. In a simple but carefully planned setting, the cheap and cheerful dishes suit the style of the bistro. Terrace in summer.

🍽🍽 **Auberge de la Cray'Othe** – *31 Grande-Rue - 10190 Messon - 12km/7.5mi W of Troyes on N 60, Sens direction and D 83 to the left - ☎ 03 25 70 31 12* – 🕐 *closed 2 weeks in Jan, 2 weeks in Sep; open from Thu-Sun lunchtime – booking necessary.* This beautiful farm houses a pleasant restaurant decorated with paintings of the village and surrounding area. Connoisseurs will love the authentic local dishes such as coq au cidre du pays d'Othe and the tasty farmhouse terrines.

🍽🍽🍽 **Le Bistroquet** – *Pl. Langevin* – ☎ *03 25 73 65 65* – 🕐 *closed Sun except lunchtimes from Sep-June.* This restaurant is situated in the centre of the pedestrianised part of Troyes, and is reminiscent of a Parisian brasserie. The large dining room is attractively lit by a decorated glass ceiling, and has leather seats, indoor plants and a lively atmosphere. All dishes are based on fresh ingredients. Terrace with shrubs and garden lights.

WHERE TO STAY

🛏 **Les Comtes de Champagne** – *56 r. de la Monnaie -* ☎ *03 25 73 11 70 -* 🅿 *- 36 rooms -* ☕ *€5.* It is said that the four 12C houses which make up this hotel used to belong to the counts of Champagne who minted their coins here. Renovated rooms; those with kitchen facilities could be ideal for families. The impressive fireplace in the breakfast room testifies to the age of the premises.

🛏🛏 **De La Bonne Fermière** – *Pl. de l'Église - 10450 Bréviandes - 5 km/3mi S of Troyes -* ☎ *03 25 82 45 65 -* 🅿 *- 13 rooms -* ☕ *€6.50.* This peaceful little hotel has just been given a new look with gay springtime colours and new beds. Friendly service and excellent value.

SHOPPING

Specialities – First and foremost, andouillettes (chitterling sausages)… grilled, unaccompanied or drizzled with olive oil flavoured with browned fines herbes and garlic. Try them with mustard au vin de champagne or Meaux mustard and accompanied by mashed potatoes, kidney beans or fried onion rings, dipped in milk or beer, then in flour.

Other specialities include Chaource cheese, cider or champagne choucroute, rosé des Riceys, and cacibel (aperitif made with cider, blackcurrant and honey).

La Boucherie Moderne – *Halle de l'Hôtel-de-ville* ☎ *03 25 73 32 61/03 25 73 32 64 -* 🕐 *Tue-Thu 7.30am-12.45pm, 3.30-7pm, Fri-Sat 9.30am-7pm, Sun 9am-12.30pm.* Stock up on andouillettes made by Gilbert Lemelle, the largest French manufacturer of these sausages.

Charcuterie Audry-Chantal – *Halles de l'Hôtel-de-Ville-Case 37 –* ☎ *03 25 73 27 74 –* 🕐 *Mon-Thu 8am-12.45pm, Fri-Sat 7.30am-7pm, Sun 9am-12.30pm - closed 3 weeks in Jul and 2 weeks in Feb.* A good place to buy real home-made Troyes andouillettes (chitterling sausages).

Jean-Pierre-Ozérée – *Halles de l'Hôtel-de-Ville -* ☎ *03 25 73 72 25 –* 🕐 *Tue, Wed, Thu 7.30am-12.45pm, 3.30-7pm, Fri-Sat 7.30am-7pm, Sun 9am-12.30pm.* Maturing of cheeses, including Chaource, Mussy and Langres. A useful alternative if you don't have time to go to the production site yourself.

Patrick Maury – *28 r. du Gén.-de-Gaulle -* ☎ *03 25 73 06 84 –* 🕐 *Tue-Fri 8.30am-*

12.45pm, 2.45-7pm; Sat 7.30am-8pm.
Opposite the market you will find this tiny boutique prized for its specialities. Andouillette de Troyes is of course the star buy, but black pudding and other home-made charcuterie come a close second.

Le Palais du Chocolat – *2 r. de la Monnaie - ☎ 03 25 73 35 73 - www.pascal-coffet.com – ○ Tue-Fri 9am-12.15pm, 2-7.15pm; Sat 9am-7.15pm; Sun and public holidays 9am-1pm.* An emporium of chocolate, as well as ice cream, sorbets and pastries. Among the specialities are tuiles chocolatées et aux amandes (chocolate almond thins), cristallines de Troyes and liquorice ganache which taste all the better in this magnificent setting.

Market – Daily market in the Place St-Remy halls. The main market is held on Saturdays. There is another in the Chartreux area on Wed and on Sun morning. A country market is held every third Wed of the month on Boulevard Jules-Guesde.

Shopping districts – Numerous activities are organised throughout the year in the town centre. Shopping may be done in the area around the factory outlets on the way out of Troyes (St-Julien-les-Villas and Pont-Ste-Marie sites).

Domaine du Moulin d'Eguebaude – *10190 Estissac ☎ 03 25 40 42 18.* Guided visits of this fish farm. Rooms and table d'hôte.

Marques Avenue – *114 bd de Dijon – ☎ 03 25 82 00 72 – ○ Mon 2-7pm, Tue-Fri from 10am, Sat from 9.30am.* With 80 boutiques, Marques Avenue is the biggest centre for fins de séries (end-of-line) discount fashion stores in Europe. Here you will find all the big brand names, both French and foreign.

Mc Arthur Glen – *Voie des Bois - 10150 Pont-Ste-Marie - ☎ 03 25 70 47 10 – ○ Mon 2-7pm, Tue-Fri 10am-7pm, Sat 9.30am-7pm - ○ closed 1 May.* Opened in 1995, the village includes 80 end-of-line shops along an outside covered gallery.

ON THE TOWN

La Chope – *64 av. du Gén.-de-Gaulle - ☎ 03 25 73 11 99.* Wide selection of beers, whiskies and cocktails.

La Cocktaileraie – *56 r. Jaillant-Deschainets - BP 4102 – ☎ 03 25 73 77 04– ○ Tue-Sat 5pm-3am.* The clientele of this smart bar ranges from businessmen discussing stock options and the Dow Jones to young lovers whispering sweet nothings. A hundred or so cocktails are on offer, around 45 whiskies and many prestigious champagnes, as well as ice cream. A small reception room can be hired for private parties and meetings.

Le Bougnat des Pouilles – *29 r. Paillot-de-Montabert – ☎ 03 25 73 59 85 – ○ daily 6pm-3am.* The high-quality vintages in this wine bar are sought out by the young proprietor himself, among the smaller producers in the region. The walls are often hung with exhibitions of painting and photography. The atmosphere is very peaceful and the music an easygoing blend of jazz, blues and world music. Concerts twice a month.

Le Chihuahua – *8 r. Charbonnet – ☎ 03 25 73 33 53 – ○ Mon-Sat 6pm-3am.* This fashionable cellar bar also has dancing. Each Thursday a theme night takes place (e.g. tequila, techno) and a rock concert is organised once a month. The barman's Tex-Mex cocktails are brilliant.

Le Tricasse – *16 r. Paillot-de-Montabert – ☎ 03 25 73 14 80 – ○ Mon-Sat 3pm-3am – ○ closed Sun.* This most famous of Troyes' nightspots is in a smart area and offers a glorious mix of music, from jazz to salsa to house (DJ every Saturday night). It is frequented by students from the business school and engineers, among others. Rum, champagne, cocktails and wines are the house specialities.

SHOWTIME

Théâtre de Champagne – *R. Louis-Mary – ☎ 03 25 76 27 60 / 61 - ○ location: Mon-Fri 10am-12.30pm, 2-6pm, Sat 10am-12.30pm, 2-5pm – ○ closed Jul-Aug.* Opera, comedy, arthouse theatre, variety shows.

Théâtre de la Madeleine – *R. Jules-Lebocey - ☎ 03 25 43 32 10 – ○ Mon-Sat 10am-12.30pm, 2-6pm.* Arthouse theatre, comedy, variety shows.

Sights

Musée de Vauluisant★

○ *Jun-Sep: daily except Tue 10am-1pm, 2-6pm; Oct-May: daily except Mon and Tue 10am-noon, 2-6pm.* ○ *Closed public holidays.* ⊚ *3€ (under 25 years: no charge). No charge 1st Sun in the month (except during special exhibits).* ☎ *03 25 73 05 85.*
The 16C **Hôtel de Vauluisant★** contains the **Musée de la bonneterie** with exhibits depicting the industry's evolution, including historic looms and other machinery and a variety of products, some of which go back to the 18C.

Le Vieux Troyes★★

The outline of the old part of the city bears a curious resemblance to a champagne cork, with the area around the cathedral forming the head. The majority of the old

houses are timber-framed, with vertical members held together by horizontal beams rather than by timbers set obliquely or in the form of a St Andrew's cross as elsewhere in France. The most elegant infill is the characteristic local chequer-board pattern made from brick, slate or chalk rather than the cob or daub commonly employed.
The streets with the best examples of such houses are Rue Champeaux, Ruelle des Chats, Rue de Vauluisant, as well as the Cour du Mortier d'Or.

Maison de l'Outil et de la Pensée ouvrière★★

🕙 *10am-6pm.* 🎫 *6.50€ (children under 12 years: no charge).* 🕐 *Closed 1 Jan and 25 Dec.* ☎ *03 25 73 28 26. www.maison-de-l-outil.com.*

Housed in the Hôtel du Mauroy, it is a fine architectural setting for the fascinating range of objects displayed. The dignity of labour is celebrated here in the subtle but never gratuitous diversity of forms as much as in the individual character and highly specialised function of each object. Though some are conventionally beautiful or pleasingly ornamented, one is more touched in the end by the way in which tools like hammers have been shaped over time by the hand that has used them as well as by the material they have been in contact with.

Église Ste-Madeleine

This church is Troyes' oldest place of worship. Much rebuilt in the 16C, it is famous for the rood screen (**jubé★★**) made by Jean Gailde; this has scalloped ogee arches with no intermediate supports, fine glass (**verrières★**) – the Passion, the Creation, a Jesse Tree – as well as a statue of St Martha (**statue de Sainte Marthe★**) of striking gravity.

Cathédrale St-Pierre et St-Paul★★

The cathedral was begun in 1208. Work on the vast edifice continued into the 16C, enabling the regional Gothic style to be traced over the whole period of its evolution. The chancel is remarkable for its three-storeyed elevation, carried out entirely in openwork, a pioneering achievement on this scale.
It was completed in 1228, followed by the transepts in 1300 and the vaulting of the nave in 1497.
In 1506 the architect Martin Chambiges came to Troyes, having already worked at Sens. He was responsible for the design of the elaborate west front in the Flamboyant style, worked on until 1556 by his son Pierre, his son-in-law and his grandson Jean Bailly. The stained-glass windows (**vitraux★★**) of the cathedral cover a total area of 1 500m2 – about 16 000sq ft. One of the supreme achievements of this art form, they transform the building into a cage of glass.
Most periods are represented: the 13C by the large-scale figures in the choir and the scenes of the Passion in the east window; the 14C by the transept clerestory windows; the end of the 15C by the Jesse Tree with its fine figures and foliage (upper part of the glass in the sixth bay on the south side of the nave); the 16C by the great western rose window with the celestial court painted by Jean Soudain in 1546; and the 17C by Linard Gontier's Mystic Wine-Press (Pressoir mystique) of 1626 in which the Church reasserts itself at the time of the Counter-Reformation.

Musée d'Art moderne★★

♿ 🕙 *Daily 11am-6pm.* 🕐 *Closed Mon and public holidays.* 🎫 *5€.* ☎ *03 25 76 26 80.*
This is the collection built up since 1939 by Pierre and Denise Lévy, noted hosiery manufacturers. It comprises thousands of items dating from 1850 to 1950, many of them donated to the State and now on display in the former Bishops' Palace.
Lévy was on good terms with many artists, visiting their studios and becoming firm friends with some of the great figures of our age. Particularly well represented here are the **Fauves**, who, together with Braque, Dufy, Matisse and Van Dongen "made colour roar". Derain too, one of the first to appreciate the art of Africa, is very much present, as is Maurice Marinot, a local artist and glass-maker.

◖◗ Basilique St-Urbain★. Église St-Pantaléon★. Musée St-Loup – Fine art and archeology★. Pharmacie★ de l'Hôtel-Dieu (**M⁵**). ♿ 🕙 *Jun-Sep: daily except Tue 10am-1pm, 2-6pm; Oct-May: Mon, Wed and Sat-Sun 10am-noon, 2-6pm.* 🕐 *Closed public holidays.* 🎫 *2€ (under 25 years: no charge), no charge first Sun in the month.* ☎ *03 25 80 98 97.*

VAISON-LA-ROMAINE★★

POPULATION 5 663

MICHELIN MAP 332 D 8

GREEN GUIDE PROVENCE

Founded 60 years before Caesar's conquest of Gaul, Vaison-La-Romaine still evokes the life of a Gallo-Roman city.

Before the legions came, the place had been the capital of a Celtic tribe, the Vocontii. Under Roman rule it became the seat of great landed proprietors, a flourishing city possibly as large as Arles or Fréjus, one of the centres of Transalpine Gaul and subsequently of Narbonensis. It fell into ruin at the time of the barbarian invasions.

A Bit of History

Ruines romaines★★

The layout of modern Vaison has allowed two parts of the Roman city to be excavated. The La Villasse quarter **(quartier de la Villasse)** lies to the southwest of the Avenue Général-de-Gaulle on either side of a paved central street; there are shops, houses and a basilica. The Dolphin House (Maison du Dauphin) dating from 30 BC is particularly interesting, as is the House of the Silver Bust (Maison du Buste-d'argent). The Puymin quarter **(quartier de Puymin)** lies to the east of the avenue. Here there is the House of the Messii (Maison des Messii) with its atrium, peristyle and baths, as well as the Roman Theatre.

The latter structure *(approached via a tunnel)* dates from the time of the Emperor Augustus; the pits containing the machinery and curtain have been well preserved and the tiers of seating were reconstructed in 1932 by the then Inspector-General of Historical Monuments, Jules Formigé, though it is left to the visitor's imagination to visualise what the stage wall (like the one at Orange) must have looked like.

◖◗ Musée archéologique Théo-Desplans★. Ancienne cathédrale Notre-Dame – High Altar★, cloisters★ – Chapelle de St-Quenin.

Château de VALENÇAY★★

MICHELIN MAP 318 G 9

GREEN GUIDE CHÂTEAUX OF THE LOIRE

A Bit of History

The medieval castle which once stood here was rebuilt by Jacques d'Étampes from 1540 onwards. Even more than at Azay-le-Rideau 22 years previously, the defensive features of the traditional castle are used here in a purely decorative way; there are harmless turrets, an entrance pavilion disguised as a keep, sham machicolations, and a sentry-walk held up on brackets rather than on corbels as hitherto.

The Italian influence of the Early Renaissance is well represented too, in a number of distinctive features like the steeply-pitched roofs with their dormer windows and chimneys treated as miniature Classical temples, the balustraded entablature, the windows separated by pilasters and tableaux in stone, and the superimposed Orders arranged according to the Vitruvian canon (published a few years previously, in 1521).

The west wing was added in the 17C and altered in the 18C.

In 1803, the estate was acquired by **Charles-Maurice de Talleyrand-Périgord** (1754-1838), paid for almost entirely by Napoleon, at the time still First Consul.

For almost a quarter of a century, the château served as a glittering background to the masterly manœuvres in international diplomacy conducted by its illustrious owner, who held high offices of state from the time of Louis XVI to the Restoration.

Visit

🕐 *Apr-Jun and Sep to early Nov: 9.30am-6pm. Jul and Aug: 9.30am-7.30pm.* ⟲ *8.50€ château and show (children: 4.50€).* ☎ *02 54 00 10 66. www.chateau-valencay.com.*

Inside the château are fine furnishings of the Régence and Empire periods, including 18C Savonnerie carpets, the round table from the Congress of Vienna (in fact it came from the Kaunitz Palace, the French Embassy at the time of the Congress), and a portrait by Élisabeth Vigée-Lebrun of Talleyrand's wife, the Princess of Benevento.

VANNES★★

POPULATION 45 644

MICHELIN MAP 308 O 9

GREEN GUIDE BRITTANY

Vannes lies at the highest point to which tides flow at the head of the Morbihan Gulf.

▶ **Orient Yourself:** Vannes, which is listed as a "Town of Art and History," offers discovery tours daily except public holidays from 10.30am-3pm in Jul-Aug (Apr-Jun and Sep: Wed and Sat 3pm). You might also enjoy discovering Vannes with an evening walking tour on Fri at 10pm. Contact the Service Animation du Patrimoine (Heritage Dept), Hôtel de Roscanvec, 19 r. des Halles. ☎ 02 97 01 64 00. 4.50€.

A Bit of History

In pre-Roman times, it was the capital of the **Veneti**, a tribe of Central European origin, some of whose number had settled in the Veneto in northeastern Italy. One of Gaul's most powerful peoples, they were intrepid sailors, crossing the seas to trade with the inhabitants of the British Isles. They nevertheless suffered a terrible defeat at sea in 56 BC at the hands of the Romans, losing 200 ships in a single day. Immobilised by a dead calm and lacking any form of long-range weaponry, their navy was an easy prey for the Roman galleys with their battering rams, grappling irons and tough mariners ready to storm aboard. This was a triumph for Caesar, earning him the loyalty of the legions and ensuring his popularity in both Senate and Forum. Brittany's fate was to become a backwater for a very long time indeed.

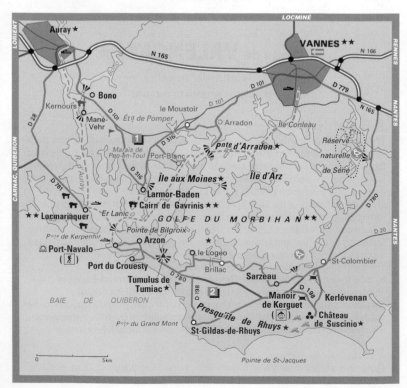

In the 9C, Vannes was the place where Breton unity was sealed. Nominoé had already been made a count by Charlemagne; in 826, he was raised to the rank of duke by Louis the Pious, mindful of the advantage to himself of giving the province to a Breton rather than to a Frank.

Ten years later, Nominoé made Vannes his capital; in 850, he put an end to his tutelage under Charles the Bald by seizing the eastern and southern marches of Brittany from the Franks, going on to push back the Normans, then taking measures to reduce the influence of the high clergy

Sights

Vieille Ville (OLD TOWN)★★

Surrounded by ramparts (**remparts**★), the area around the cathedral, the successor to a much more ancient place of worship, still has the air of a medieval town. Among the old half-timbered houses built over a granite ground floor with pillars, arcades and lintels is a 14C market hall known as **La Cohue**★. Its upper floor served as the ducal law-court right up until 1796, the ground floor as a market until 1840.

There are fine houses bordering **Place Henri IV**★ and in the adjoining streets. Note the timber cross-braces, corbelling, granite pilasters and 16C slate-hung gables.

Cathédrale St-Pierre★

Of robust granite construction, it has a north aisle with a balustraded terrace and sharply-pointed granite gables in Breton Flamboyant style separating the chapels.

Inside, the 15C nave is covered by a heavy ribbed vault of the 18C, concealing the original timber roof.

▶▶ Ramparts★. Musée d'Histoire et d'Archéologie★ ⊙ Mid-Jun to mid-Sep: daily 10am-6pm. ⊗ 3€. ☎ 02 97 01 63 00.

Aquarium du Golfe★. 🅺 ♿ ⊙ Jun-Aug: daily 9am-7.30pm; Apr-Jun: daily 10am-12.30pm, 2-7pm; Feb-Mar and Sep-Oct: daily 10am-12.30pm; 2-6.30pm; Nov-Jan: daily 2pm-6pm. Last admission 30min before closing. ⊙ Closed 1 Jan, 25 Dec. ⊗ 8.50€ (children 4-11 years: 5.50€). ☎ 02 97 40 67 40. www.incontournables56.com.

Excursions

Golfe du Morbihan★★

This little inland sea was formed when the land sank and the sea-level rose as a result of the melting of the great Quaternary glaciers, drowning the valleys occupied by the Vannes and Auray rivers. The indented coastline and the play of the tides around the countless islands make this one of Brittany's most fascinating maritime landscapes.

Château de Suscinio★

This was once the summer residence of the Dukes of Brittany. There is a rare 13C decorated tiled floor (accessible via a spiral staircase with 94 steps). The massive buildings lining the courtyard are now partly ruined.

A gun-emplacement at the foot of the northwest tower may well date from the time of the War of the Breton Succession.

Port-Navalo★

The little port and seaside resort guards the entrance to the Gulf. There are fine views.

Ensemble mégalithique de Locmariaquer★★

This group of megaliths is an important part of a programme of conservation and restoration of megalithic sites. Three megaliths can be found on this site: the **Grand Menhir brisé** (probably broken on purpose into five pieces, after it had served as a landmark for sailors); the **Table des Marchands** (a recently restored dolmen as well as the tumulus underneath) and the **Tumulus d'Er-Grah** (where excavations are presently under way).

Presqu'île de Quiberon★

Quiberon used to be an island, but over the years sand has accumulated north of Penthièvre Fort to form an isthmus linking it to the mainland. The peninsula's rocky and windswept western shore is known as the **Côte Sauvage** (Wild Coast), but to the east there are sheltered sandy beaches. The ferries for **Belle-Île**★★ leave from Quiberon harbour.

▶▶ Cairn de Gavrinis★★. Golfe de Morbihan en bateau★★★ (boat trips).

Massif de la **VANOISE**★★★

MICHELIN MAP 333 M-N-O 4-5-6

GREEN GUIDE FRENCH ALPS

This famous massif lies between the valleys of the Arc and the Isère. It was proclaimed a national park in 1963 and consists of two concentric areas. The outer zone (1 450km2 – 560sq miles) includes some of the largest skiing resorts in the world, including the Three Valleys (les **3 Vallées** – Courchevel, Méribel, Les Menuires-Val Thorens), and l'**Espace Killy** (Tignes and Val d'Isère). The central zone (530km2 – 205sq miles), accessible to ramblers, is a remarkable natural site subject to strict regulations. La Vanoise Massif, which is dotted with charming villages and lovely forests, remains nonetheless a high mountain area: 107 summits exceed 3 000m – 9 900ft and the glaciers cover a total surface of 88km2 – 34sq miles. The massif is noted for the extreme diversity of its fauna (marmots, ibexes, chamois) and flora (around 2 000 species). Some of the more attractive sites are listed below. Visitors are advised to wear sturdy walking shoes.

Visit

Val-d'Isère★★★

A prestigious meeting-place for winter sports enthusiasts, this resort commands an impressive view broken by a series of high peaks (Grande Sassière, Grande Motte).

Rocher de Bellevarde★★★

Access by cable railway. Splendid views of the Tarentaise and Mont-Blanc.

Refuge de Prariond★★

2hr round trip on foot. A pleasant walk with varied landscapes (gorges, rock faces).

Réserve naturelle de la Grande Sassière★★

A superb backdrop of lakes and glaciers frame Tignes Dam. The park boasts a wealth of animal and plant species which may be easily observed. From the Saut car park, one may reach **Lac de la Sassière**★★ (1hr on foot) and the **Glacier de Rhême-Golette**★★ (2hr30min), at an altitude of 3 000m – 9 900ft.

Tignes★★★

Alt. 2 100m – 6 890ft. The resort was built around Tignes Lake in a **site**★★ dominated by the breath-taking view of the Grande Motte Glacier (3 656m – 12 052ft). We strongly advise the following route to seasoned ramblers who do not balk at five to six hours' walking: **Col du Palet**★★, **Pointe du Chardonnet**★★★ (very steep slope) or the **Col de la Croix des Frêtes**★★, the **Lac du Grattaleu**★, **Col de Tourne**★.

Lac Blanc and the Col de Soufre

Peisey-Nancroix★

This village, nestling in the lush **Vallée de Ponturin★**, traditionally opens onto the park and is linked to the skiing area of Les Arcs.

Lac de la Plagne★★

4hr round trip on foot. A beautiful route in a delightful, flowery setting, at the foot of the summit (Sommet de Bellecôte, 3 417m – 11 269ft) and Mont Pourri (3 779m – 12 398ft).

Pralognon★

Alt. 1 400m – 4 600ft. One of the main stopping-places for ramblers in La Vanoise Massif.

Col de la Vanoise★★

Alt. 2 517m – 8 260ft. 4hr round trip. Views of the Grande Casse (3 855m – 12 705ft).

Col d'Aussois★★★

Alt. 3 015m – 9 950ft. Ascent 5hr. Sweeping panorama. These two passes may also be reached from Termignon and Aussois en Maurienne.

La Saulire★★

Alt. 2 738m – 7 986ft. Access by cable-car. View of La Vanoise Massif and the Oisans.

Réserve naturelle de Tuéda★

A beautiful forest planted with cembra pines at the edge of Tuéda Lake.

Cime de Caron★★★

Alt. 3 198m – 10 550ft. 2hr 30min round trip by cable-car and cable railway. Breath-taking panorama of the Écrins, the Tarentaise and Mont-Blanc.

Château de **VAUX-LE-VICOMTE**★★★

MICHELIN MAP 312 F 4

GREEN GUIDE NORTHERN FRANCE AND THE PARIS REGION

The splendid château built by **Nicolas Fouquet** lies at the heart of French Brie, a countryside of vast arable fields relieved by the occasional copse or spinney.

A Bit of History

Fouquet had been Superintendent of Finances since the days of Mazarin; his vast fortune was founded on the dangerous habit of confusing the credit of the state with his own. In 1656, he decided upon the construction of Vaux, the palace which was to symbolise his success. As architect, he chose Louis Le Vau, already familiar with Maisons-Lafitte, as interior decorator, Charles Le Brun, assisted by Girardon and de Legendre; as landscaper, André Le Nôtre; as major-domo, the famous chef Vatel; as poet-in-residence, La Fontaine.

By 1661, Vaux looked as it does today. A connoisseur, a man of lavish tastes, but sadly lacking in political judgement, Fouquet had counted on being appointed in Mazarin's place right up to the moment when Louis XIV decided to take power into his own hands. Furthermore, he had alienated Colbert, and, even worse, had made advances to one of the King's favourites, Mlle de La Vallière.

By May, the decision to place him under arrest had been taken. On 17 August, the unwitting Fouquet threw the most sumptuous of festivities among the Baroque splendours of Vaux. Hoping to impress the young Louis, he succeeded only in offending his monarch more deeply by the unparalleled extravagance of the proceedings. Dinner was presented on a solid gold service, at a time when the royal silverware had been melted down to repay some of the expenses of the Thirty Years War! On 10 September, Fouquet was arrested at Nantes, put under lock and key, his property confiscated, and his brilliant team of designers put to work on Versailles.

Visit

🕐 Mid-Mar to early Nov: daily 10am-6pm. 🎫 12€ (children: 9.50€). 🕯️ Visit by candlelight May to mid-Oct: Sat 8pm-midnight (Jul-Aug: Fri and Sat). 🎫 15€ (children: 13€). ☎ 01 64 14 41 90. www.vaux-le-vicomte.com.

Le Vau's château is the definitive masterpiece of the early Louis XIV style. It is majestic in its impact, with lateral pavilions fully integrated into the composition as a whole, high roofs graced by numerous chimneys, and a raised ground floor commanding the extensive gardens. It is to be understood as the central feature of a grandiose designed landscape, an archetype of immense influence over the whole of Europe in the course of the following century and a half.

Le Brun's talent is here made manifest in all its richness and diversity. He began work in 1659,

Chateau de Vaux-Le-Vicomte

A. Cassaigne/MICHELIN

but the central rotunda in the Grand Salon with its 16 caryatids remained unfinished; his King's Bedroom (Chambre du Roi) anticipates the splendour of the Royal Apartments at Versailles.

In the gardens (**jardins**★★★) (🕐 As for the château), Le Nôtre showed himself to be the master of perspective, with terraces, urns, clipped-box hedging, water features and orange trees (later removed to Versailles) all contributing to the overall scheme.

At Vaux, the essentially decorative preoccupations of early Classicism (as at Villandry) are left behind, and Baroque virtuosity is tempered by a sense of majesty. The three main bodies of water, the moats, the twin canals in the centre of the composition and the Grand Canal, all reveal themselves unexpectedly in a most dramatic fashion.

From the final circular basin known appropriately as la Gerbe, (the spray) there is a fine view back over this wonderfully harmonious composition of building and landscape.

◖◗ Musée des Équipages★ 🕐 As for the gardens.

VENDÔME★★

POPULATION 17 525

MICHELIN MAP 318 D 5

GREEN GUIDE CHÂTEAUX OF THE LOIRE

At the foot of a steep bluff, which is crowned by a castle, the River Loir divides into several channels. Vendôme stands on a group of islands crowded with bell-towers, gables and steep slate roofs.

Visit

Ancienne Abbaye de la Trinité★

🕓 *Apr-Oct: daily except Tue 10am-noon, 2-6pm; Nov-Mar: daily except Sun: 10am-noon, 2-6pm.* 🕓 *Closed 1 Jan, 1 May, 25 Dec.* 🎟 *2.80€ (under 16 years: no charge).* ☎ *02 54 77 26 13.*

Founded in 1040 by Geoffroy Martel, Count of Anjou, the Benedictine abbey expanded considerably and became one of the most powerful in France, so that the abbot was automatically raised to the rank of cardinal. The abbey became a pilgrimage centre where pilgrims flocked to venerate the Holy Tear which Christ had shed at Lazarus' tomb and which Geoffroy Martel had brought back from the Crusade.
RP2800

Église abbatiale★★

The abbey church is a remarkable example of Flamboyant Gothic architecture. The harmonious 12C bell-tower standing alone to the west served as a model for the old bell-tower of Notre-Dame de Chartres. The remarkable west front highlighted by a great incised gable contrasts with the plain Romanesque tower.

ntérieur – The transept, all that is left of the 11C building, leads to the chancel and ambulatory with its five radiating chapels. The nave is remarkable for the width of the triforium and the height of the clerestory. In the 14C chancel are fine late-15C stalls **(stalles★)** decorated with naïve scenes. The axial chapel contains a window dating from 1140 depicting the Virgin and Child (Majesté Notre-Dame).

◖◗ Musée★ 🕓 *Apr-Oct: daily except Tue 10am-noon, 2-6pm. Nov-Mar: daily except Sun 10am-noon, 2-6pm.* 🕓 *Closed 1 Jan, 1 May, 25 Dec.* 🎟 *2.80€ (under 16 years: no charge).* ☎ *02 54 77 26 13.*

Mont VENTOUX★★★

MICHELIN MAP 332 E 8

GREEN GUIDE PROVENCE

Though hardly the equal of the soaring peaks of the High Alps, Mount Ventoux enjoys an isolated position far from any rival summit, making it a commanding presence in this part of Provence, visible over vast distances especially when topped in winter with a sparkling coat of snow. It is the most spectacular of the limestone uplands constituting the Southern Alps, one of the series of great synclinal folds running from Apt in the south to Nyons in the north which recall in the simplicity of their structure the ridge and valley morphology of the Jura.

The massif is served by a scenic route 67km – 42mi long between Vaison and Carpentras; its upper section is blocked by snow from 15 November to 15 March. The road was used for motor racing until 1973, and the ascent is a major challenge in those years when it features as part of the Tour de France.

Driving Tour

Vaison-la-Romaine★★ – 👣 *See VAISON-LA-ROMAINE.*

Shortly after leaving the little town of Malaucène, the road passes close to the Le Groseau Vauclusian Spring (Source vauclusienne du Groseau) which emerges from several fissures at the foot of an escarpment. Forests of fir trees follow, interspersed with grazing land, and the view then opens out over the Toulourenc valley where the folds of friable limestone have been buried beneath deep accumulations of scree. Mount Serein (1 428m – 4 685ft) appears, followed by the Dentelles de Montmirail and the Baronies Massif.

Sommet★★★

1 909m – 6 263ft. The top of the mountain consists of a vast field of white shingle from which protrudes an array of masts and instruments, air force radar equipment, a TV transmitter, a weather station... Mount Ventoux, the Windy One, is so named because of the mistral which blasts it with a force unequalled elsewhere. On average, the temperature here is 11 oC – 52 oF lower than in the valley. The flora includes specimens of polar vegetation such as the Spitzbergen saxifrage and the Icelandic poppy.

In the early morning and late afternoon, as well as in autumn, the vast **panorama**★★★ extends from the Écrins Massif to the northeast to the Cévennes and the shore of the Mediterranean.

Below the resort of Chalet-Reynard on the descent southward are fine stands of Aleppo and Austrian black pine and Atlantic cedar, as well as beeches and oaks. Finally, beyond St-Estève, vines and fruit-trees make their appearance.

Massif du **VERCORS**★★★

MICHELIN MAP 332 F-G 2-3

GREEN GUIDE FRENCH ALPS

The Vercors is the most extensive of the Pre-Alpine massifs. Protected by sheer cliffs of Urgonian limestone, it is a natural citadel, inside which grow fine forests of beech and conifers interspersed with lush pasturelands. In places, the immensely thick limestone has been cut into by the rivers to form deep and spectacular gorges.

In 1944, the Vercors saw one of the French Resistance's most tragic episodes. Since the previous year, a number of clandestine military formations had been taking to the forests of the area in order to organise its defences. They were joined in the spring of 1944 by several thousand more, as well as by young people evading the German labour draft. In June of that year, the Wehrmacht stepped up its assault on the Resistance's positions, determined to secure its communications in the face of Allied progress up the Italian peninsula and the impending break-out from Normandy. The maquisards fought off a number of attacks, but the enemy returned with reinforcements on 19 July and brought in parachute troops on 21 July. With many of their number lost, the surviving members of the Resistance were given the order to disperse on 23 July. 700 of the inhabitants and defenders of the Vercors had died; several of its villages lay in ruins.

Just to the north of the rebuilt village of Vassieux-en-Vercors is a cemetery (Nécropole national) with the graves of some of those who died in the course of that terrible summer, and at the Col de Lachan stands a monument to the fallen (Mémorial du Vercors).

Driving Tour

Gorges de la Bourne★★★

The lack of a road through the gorge meant that for many years the Lans area led its own life, orientated towards Grenoble rather than to the rest of the massif. The unusually regular walls of the gorge open out progressively downstream; its entrance is marked by the old cloth town of Pont-en-Royans with its houses clinging picturesquely to the rock face.

Combe Laval★★★

One of the finest sights in the Vercors. The road clings dizzily to a vast limestone wall rising 600m – some 2 000ft above the upper valley of the Cholet.

Grands Goulets★★★

An epic piece of construction dating from 1851, the narrow road was hewn directly into the rock. From its upper section it is possible to see the river beginning the process of eroding an as yet intact geological formation. The village of Les Barraques-en-Vercors was destroyed by enemy action in January 1944.

Col de Rousset★★

Go as far as the southern entrance to the disused tunnel. The pass marks the climatic as well as the morphological boundary between the northern and southern Alps. There are spectacular views, not only of the road twisting its way downwards, but also of the great limestone walls protecting the Vercors, of the Die valley 960m – 3 150ft below, and of a succession of bare ridges extending into the far distance.

Grand Canyon du **VERDON**★★★

MICHELIN MAP 334 E-F 10

GREEN GUIDE FRENCH ALPS

A tributary of the Durance with its source high up at the Allos Pass, the Verdon has cut Europe's most spectacular canyon through the Castellane Pre-Alps; here is one of the continent's wildest landscapes, a place which has resisted all human attempts to tame it.

Visit

Grand Canyon

The canyon extends 26km – 16 miles from the meeting-point of the Verdon with the Jabron in the east to where it flows into Ste-Croix Lake in the west at the Galetas bridge. In places the river has followed fault-lines in the domed structures formed in the Jurassic limestone; elsewhere the phenomenon of antecedence is evident, where it has cut down through the rock along the line of its original course, a result of the uplifting of the area during the Alpine-building period.

The boundaries of the successive beds of limestone are picked out by the growth of box and evergreen oak.

The opposite rims of the canyon are between 200-1 500m (about 650-5 000ft) apart. Its depth varies from 250-600m (about 800-2 000ft), while the width of its floor ranges from 8-90m (about 25-300ft). The dizzy height of the canyon's walls impresses on one the sheer scale of the Jurassic sedimentation, in terms of both time and the quantity of material deposited.

La Corniche Sublime★★★

South bank scenic route. The steep and twisting (20km – 12mi) road was engineered so as to open up the most spectacular views. They include: the **Balcons de la Mescla**★★★ overlooking the swirling waters where the Verdon is joined by the Artuby; the bridge, Pont de l'Artubya, linking sheer walls of rock; the Fayet tunnels above the Étroit des Cavaliers (Knights' Narrows), and the **Falaise des Cavaliers**★ (Knights' Cliff) 300m – 1 000ft high.

La route des Crêtes★★★

North bank scenic route. The road (23km – 14mi long) links a series of viewpoints overlooking the most spectacular section of the canyon. Further to the east, the viewpoint known as the **Point Sublime**★★★ dominates the downstream section of the canyon and the impressive narrows called the **Couloir de Samson**★★★.

Castellane★ – ⚘ *See ROUTE NAPOLÉON.*

Moustiers-Ste-Marie★★

The small town is the centre for the Valensole plateau, a depression filled with material brought down by the Verdon. It has an extraordinary **site**★★ at the foot of a cleft in the limestone cliff, across which a knight returning from the Crusades stretched the chain which can still be seen today. The church has a **tower**★ with arcading in Lombard style. Faience was introduced here in 1679; the most sought-after pieces are those for which the decoration was fired at high temperatures (⚘ *see LIMOGES*) and which have charming hunting scenes executed in blue monochrome.

Falaise des Cavaliers, Gorges du Verdon

D. Faure/SCOPE

VERDUN★★

POPULATION 20 733

MICHELIN MAP 307 D 4

GREEN GUIDE ALSACE LORRAINE CHAMPAGNE

The Gauls were the first to build a fortress here on the left bank of the Meuse. They were followed by the Romans, but Verdun entered the mainstream of history with the signing of the **Treaty of Verdun** in 843. By its terms, Charlemagne's realm was divided up among his grandsons, contrary to their father's wish for its preservation as a single unit. The Emperor, Lothair, received the central zone (Northern Italy, Provence, the Rhineland and the Low Countries); Louis, the Germanic countries, and Charles the Bald, Gaul. At the time, this signified little more than a convenient distribution of the different parts of an estate, but the repercussions have been felt throughout the centuries to the extent that the treaty has been referred to as "the most significant in all the continent's history". Louis the German, however, was dissatisfied with his portion; of an expansionist bent and dreaming of more clement skies, he launched what might be considered the first of all Franco-German wars in 858, following the death of Lothair. Charles was only able to resist the attack thanks to the support of the clergy led by the Bishop of Reims. *Place de la Nation, 55016 Verdun, ☎ 03 29 86 14 18. www.verdun-tourisme.com.*

Visit

Ville haute★

The seat of a bishop, the fortified upper town rises in stages from the banks of the Meuse. It was besieged by the Duke of Brunswick on 31 August 1792, underwent an occupation of several weeks, but was then relieved following the victory at Valmy. It was besieged again in 1870 at the start of the Franco-Prussian War, then occupied for three years. In the First World War, Verdun was the scene of some of the bloodiest fighting of the Western Front, in a battle that lasted 18 months. The city's historic buildings include **Cathédrale Notre-Dame★**, laid out like the great Romanesque basilicas of the Rhineland, and the Bishop's Palace (**Palais épiscopal★**) constructed by Robert de Cotte in the 18C.

◖◗ Citadelle souterraine (Underground Citadel).

Champ de bataille de **VERDUN**★★★

The name of Verdun is indissolubly linked to the decisive struggle on which the outcome of the Great War turned. The gaze of the world was fixed for a year and a half on the paroxysm of violence endured by both sides, in a battle which brought forth the uttermost in steadfastness and courage.

At the outbreak of war in August 1914, Verdun lay a mere 40km – 25 miles from the Franco-German frontier, though the **Schlieffen Plan** did not anticipate any significant military activity in this area. However, following the battle of the Marne and the ensuing stalemate of trench warfare, the German High Command decided on an attack on Verdun in order to take the French right wing from the rear and sow panic and confusion.

The 21 February 1916 dawned bright but numbingly cold; a devastating bombardment preceded the Germans' frontal assault on the French lines; the attack was contained for a while by the bravery of Colonel Driant and his Chasseurs, but within four days Douaumont Fort had fallen. This was the moment at which General Pétain took effective charge of the battle; by the time of his replacement in April 1917, it was clear that the German attempt to break the staying-power of the French army had failed. Verdun, the hinge of the whole Western Front, could not be taken.

The Germans now attempted to close the jaws of the trap in a series of battles which raged throughout March and April in the Argonne, around Les Éparges; and, closer to Verdun, on Hill 304

Casemate

L'illustration – L. Bertrand/EXPLORER

and the other eminence known chillingly as the Mort-Homme (Dead Man's Hill). This phase is known as the "Battle of the Wings". There then followed a battle of attrition, intended to "bleed the French white". But on 11 July, the final German offensive ground to a halt in front of the Souville fort, a mere 5km – 3 miles from the city, and the Crown Prince's troops were given orders to assume a defensive posture.

The French counter-offensive began in October 1916. By 20 August 1917, the Hell of Verdun, which had cost the lives of over 700 000 men, was over.

Battlefields *10km – 6mi northeast of Verdun*

La Cote 304 – The hill was first attacked by the Germans on 20 March 1916 but held out for three months. It was retaken by the French on 24 August.

Douaumont – The 15 000 war graves overlooked by the memorial tower, the cloisters and the underground ossuary (nécropole) make this the most moving of all the battlefield sites.

Fort de Douaumont – The fort, with its subterranean passages, casemates, and its defences bearing for all time the scars inflicted by both French and German shells, had been occupied as from 5 August 1915 only by a skeleton force of French Territorial gunners; it fell, almost by accident, to a small party of Germans on 25 February 1916, and was not retaken until, at great cost, 24 October.

Les Éparges – This long spur extends outwards from the Meuse Heights to dominate the Woëvre plain. It fell to the German attackers on 21 September 1914 and became the scene of some particularly bloody mine warfare. It was retaken on 10 April 1915. There is still evidence of the conflict in the shape of gaping craters opened up by the sappers' mines. The visitor should also see the monument and viewing table at "Point X" at the far extremity of the spur, as well as "Point C", and the Trottoir Cemet-ery (Cimetière du Trottoir).

Fleury-devant-Douaumont – Fleury was taken by the Germans on 23 June and retaken by the French on 18 August 1916. Where the village once stood are now only pinetrees and a number of mounds. There is a modern chapel, dedicated to Notre-Dame of Europe.

Butte de Montfaucon – This rounded hillock was occupied by the Germans in 1914 and only retaken on 28 September 1918 by American troops who stormed its slopes in the face of determined opposition.

Le Mort-Homme – A key location in the Battle of the Wings. The German assault on it was launched from the Montfaucon heights; the fight went on throughout March and April, but the top of the hill did not fall until 23 May. It was an empty victory, for further advance proved impossible, and the hill fell to the French again on 30 August 1917. Though the Germans may have reached the summit, "they did not pass".

Tranchée des Baïonnettes – A battalion of men from Brittany and the Vendée was buried alive here as they waited with fixed bayonets for a ferocious bombardment to end.

Fort de Vaux – Taken by the Germans on 7 June 1916 and recaptured on 2 November.

Château de **VERSAILLES**★★★

MICHELIN MAP 311 I 3

GREEN GUIDE NORTHERN FRANCE AND THE PARIS REGION

Versailles is the creation of the French monarchy at the moment of its greatest splendour. Consisting of the **château**, the gardens (jardins), and the Trianon, it is a wonderfully harmonious composition of building and landscape, the definitive monument of French Classicism. In the words of Pierre Gaxotte, "Versailles taught Europe the art of living, good manners and well-bred behaviour, wit, love of truth, tolerance, human values, a love of beauty and of work well-done, the secret of being rather than merely seeming, and a concern that all should shine".

▶ **Orient Yourself:** Versailles is only 18km-11mi from Paris, easily reached by taking line C of the RER to Versailles-Rive gauche, or by SNCF rail link from the stations St-Lazare (to Versailles-Rive droite) or Montparnasse (to Versailles-Chantiers). The town was originally conceived in the symbol of the sun, with the château at the centre and the three main avenues radiating away like rays of light. Today the place du Marché is the town's focal point, offering a variety of delightful restaurants, shops, cafés, brasseries and weekly markets. Take one of the "Town of Art and History" tours offered by the tourist office to get better acquainted with not only the château and its gardens, but also the town itself.

Louis XIV by LeBrun

RMN

 Don't Miss: The Grand Canal is shaped like a large cross. Rent a rowing boat and enjoy an impressive view of the palace and its gardens.

 Organizing Your Time: A variety of guided tours for the interior of the palace are offered, ranging from 1-2hr. Allow 3hr for the gardens, and even more time if you wish to visit the Grand and Petit Trianons. The park is best seen when the Grands Eaux (fountains) are in operation *(weekends and holidays in summer)*.

 Especially for Kids: Beyond the Petit Trianon is the Queen's Hamlet **(Le Hameau de la Reine)** where farm animals (ducks, black pigs, goats...) roam about, serving as a great attraction for children.

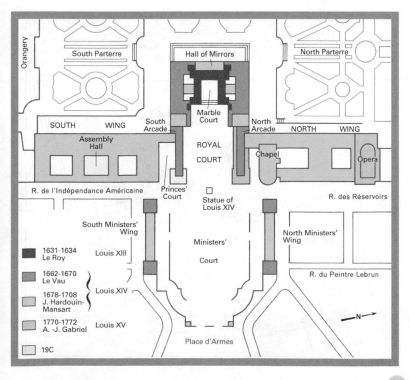

Monarchs – Court – Government

Louis XIII – Born 1601 – Marries Anne of Austria in 1615

Louis XIV – Born 1638 – Marries Maria-Theresa in 1660

1648   The Peace of Westphalia puts an end to the Thirty Years War, giving France most of Alsace and establishing French as the language of diplomacy.

1659   The Treaty of the Pyrenees puts an end to hostilities with Spain, giving France Roussillon, the Cerdagne and Artois.

1661   On the death of Mazarin, Louis decides to take the government into his own hands – Arrest of Fouquet – Colbert appointed Superintendent of Finance – Persecution of the Protestants.

1664   The Port-Royal controversy.

1667   The War of Devolution, fought in support of Louis' claim to the Spanish Netherlands, is ended in 1668 by the Treaty of Aix-la-Chapelle (Aachen); the southern part of today's Belgium (Wallonie) becomes part of France.

1672   War with Holland ended by the Peace of Nijmegen

1674   Conquest of the Franche-Comté

1682   On 6 May, the Royal Court and the Government move into Versailles.

1683   Maria-Theresa dies on 30 July. "The only time she ever upset me" was Louis' comment. She had used her splendid bedroom for only just over a year. The King now moves out of the North Wing of the palace and into the Marble Court.
Revocation of the Edict of Nantes – Audience with the Doge of Genoa.

1685 1686 Reception of the Siamese Ambassadors – War of the League of Augsburg terminated by the Treaty of Ryswick (Rijswijk).

Full appreciation of Versailles demands a knowledge of Classical mythology and its symbols, the château and its gardens being in effect a temple dedicated to worship of the Sun God.

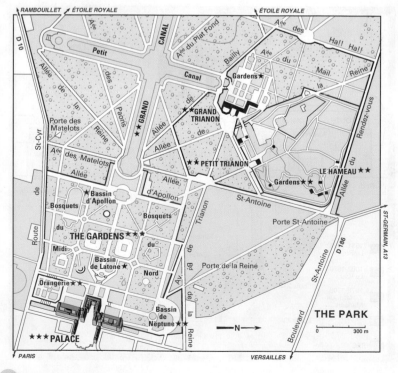

Versailles - Address Book

TOURISM INFORMATION

2bis av. de Paris, 78000 Versailles, ☎ 01 39 24 88 88. www.versailles-tourisme.com. For coin ranges, see the Legend at the back of the guide.

EATING OUT

⊜ **La Brasserie du Théâtre** – *15 r. des Réservoirs – ☎ 01 39 50 03 21 – reserv. advisable evenings.* The walls of this 1895 brasserie situated next to the theatre, as its name would suggest, are covered with photos of artists who have frequented it over the years. 1930s style décor, covered terrace and traditional cuisine.

⊜ **Le Bœuf à la Mode** – *4 r. au Pain, (Pl. du Marché Notre-Dame) – ☎ 01 39 50 31 99.* ① *Closed Christmas weekend.* A typical 1930s bistro with a convivial, relaxed atmosphere. The decor – red wall-seats, knick-knacks, posters, mirrors – is a hit and the regional specialities are delicious. Very busy on market days.

⊜⊜ **La Bodega** – *4 bis r. de la Paroisse – ☎ 01 30 21 01 73.* ① *Closed 25 Dec to 1 Jan, Mon lunch and Sun – reserv. requested weekends.* Come have a royal time at the gates of the château! Tapas, caracoles and other dishes with an Hispanic flavour will satisfy epicureans in quest of the exotic. And to round out the bodega experience, weekend evenings continue late into the night at the Bagheera piano bar.

⊜⊜ **Le Baladin** – *2 r. de l'Occident (quartier St-Louis) – ☎ 01 39 50 06 57 – sebat@wanadoo.fr.* ① *Closed Sun evening and Mon lunch in summer – reserv. advisable.* This genial establishment is nestled in the old St. Louis neighbourhood. The dining room, decorated in tones of grey and yellow, is pleasant and the terrace under the horse chestnuts is very popular in fine weather. Delightful, savoury fare.

⊜⊜ **Au Chapeau Gris** – *7 r. Hoche – ☎ 01 39 50 10 81 – auchapeaugris@club-internet. fr.* ① *Closed 22 Jul to 22 Aug, Tue evening and Wed – reserv. required.* This restaurant, said to date back to the 18C, is a veritable institution hereabouts. Quintessential Versailles ambience and décor are the setting for appetizing, traditional cuisine. Nothing too wild, just a reliable, very much sought-after establishment.

⊜⊜ **Valmont** – *20 r. au Pain – ☎ 01 39 51 39 00 – levalmont@wanadoo.fr.* ① *Closed Sun evening and Mon.* This nicely restored old house on the Place des Halles is bound to catch your eye. Venture inside and appreciate the first-rate reception, charming decoration, modern colours, elegant tables and succulent cookery. A meal to look forward to!

WHERE TO STAY

⊜⊜ **Hôtel Versailles** – *7 r. Ste-Anne, Petite Place – ☎ 01 39 50 64 65 – info@ hotel-le-versailles.fr – P – 46 rms – ⊠ 10€.* This renovated hotel is situated in a quiet side street not far from the château. The Art Deco style rooms are spacious, bright and elegant. Cosy bar-lounge and terrace where breakfast is served in summer.

⊜⊜ **Résidence du Berry** – *14 r. d'Anjou – ☎ 01 39 49 07 07 – resa@hotel-berry.com – 39 rms – ⊠ 10€.* Located in the Saint-Louis quarter, this 18C edifice has been entirely restored by Les Bâtiments de France. Comfort and top-quality materials await you in rooms with time-worn beams overhead. In summer breakfast is taken on a veranda that opens onto the patio.

ON THE TOWN

Cinéma Le Cyrano – *7 r. Rameau – ☎ 08 36 68 70 25 – cinemacyrano@wanadoo.fr –* ① *1-10:30pm. 8.50€ and 7€.* 8 screens, for up to 1 650 viewers.

Cinéma Le Roxane – *6 r. St-Simon – ☎ 01 30 21 31 50.* ① *Daily 1pm-midnight.* Cinema, cine-club, lectures, chamber music concerts.

Théâtre Montansier – *13 r. des Réservoirs – ☎ 01 39 24 05 06 –* ① *tickets: Tue-Sat noon-7pm.* ① *Closed mid-Jul to end Aug.* Classical, modern and comic theatre productions, plus dance and children's shows. An eclectic, wide-ranging programme.

Fenêtres sur cour – *Passage de la Geôle, Quartier des Antiquaires – ☎ 01 39 51 97 77 –* ① *Mon-Wed 9:30am-4pm, Thu-Sun 9:30am-11pm.* ① *Closed 3 wks Aug.* A restaurant-salon de thé under a glass roof. The bric-a-brac décor - tile floor, carpets, lamps, chandeliers, plaster statues and paintings - is in perfect harmony with the neighbourhood antique shops. Appetizing wine menu. In summer, tables are set outdoors on the Place de la Geôle.

SHOPPING

Shops – The principal shopping streets are the Rue de la Paroisse and the Place du Marché, the Rue Royale and the Rue du Général-Leclerc. One may also stroll through Les Manèges, opposite the Rive-Gauche station. You'll find many antique dealers in the Passage de la Geôle, near La Place du Marché.

Major stores – From the FNAC (books, CDs, cameras, etc.) to Printemps or BHV (department stores), the shopping complex Le Centre Commercial de Parly II, on your way out of Versailles toward St-Germain, has it all.

The table on the previous pages draws attention to key events and major artistic achievements in the creation of the palace and its setting, a process extending over more than 150 years.

External events are indicated in red.

👁 Visitors whose time is limited should concentrate on the items in bold type which are starred.

The enjoyment of even the shortest of visits will be greatly enhanced if the Michelin Green Guide Northern France and the Paris Region (in English) is used.

Artists and Their Masterpieces

1610-43

1624   Louis XIII has a modest hunting lodge built in this game-rich area.

1631   Philibert Le Roy designs the first château, built of brick, stone and slate.

1643-1715

1661   Le Brun is made responsible for the interior, supervising a gifted team of painters, sculptors, carvers and interior decorators.

1664   A great May festival is organised, called "Pleasures of the Enchanted Island" (Plaisirs de l'Ile enchantée), featuring three acts of Molière's Tartuffe.

1666   The gardens' splendid fountains are inaugurated.

1667   The Grand Canal is dug.

1668   Le Vau extends the palace by encasing it in an "envelope" of stone; he builds the six rooms making up the Grand Apartment and lays out a spacious terrace overlooking the gardens. The **Grands Appartements**★★★ (🕐 Apr-Oct: daily except Mon 9am-6.30pm; Nov-Mar: daily 9am-5.30pm. Last admission 30min before closing. 👁 7.50€ (under 18 years: no charge). ☎ 01 30 83 76 20) comprise the King's Suite on the north and the Queen's Suite to the south, facing the sun. Le Vau restores the **cour de Marbre**★★, built in brick with stone dressings and reserved for the King's private use; it has fine raised paving in black and white marble, façades graced by 40 busts (some of them by Coysevox), mansard roofs decorated with urns, and a colonnaded portico supporting the wrought-iron balcony of the King's Bedchamber.

Château de Versailles

The gardens (**Jardins**★★★) are laid out by Le Nôtre. They are a masterpiece of the French landscape style, going beyond the evocation of the idea of majesty (as at Vaux-le-Vicomte) to celebrate the supreme authority of the monarch by the systematic use of Classical symbolism. Among the 200 statues of this open-air sculpture museum are Keller's bronzes in the Water Gardens (Parterres d'eau), the Latona Basin (Bassin de Latone), Louis XIV's recommended starting point for a tour of his domain, Tuby's splendid Apollo in his chariot, low-reliefs by Girardon... On 18 July, a Grand Royal Entertainment is held in the gardens.

1671   Le Brun undertakes the decoration of the State Apartments; his use of the choicest materials is characteristic of the early Louis XIV style.

Portraits are painted by Rigaud and Van Loo.

1672   Boulle delivers the first items of his furniture featuring showy marquetry of tortoiseshell and brass.

1674   Lavish summer festivals are held. Le Brun designs 24 statues for the gardens. On 18 August, Racine presents the première of his Iphigenia in an open-air theatre close to the Orangerie.

1678   Lulli presents his Alceste in the Marble Court. Desjardins, Le Hongre and the Marsy brothers work on the Diana Fountain (Fontaine de Diane). Jules Hardouin-Mansart, a nephew by marriage of François Mansart, adds to the palace in the late Louis XIV style, giving it a grand first floor over the raised ground floor, columns to break up the monotony of horizontal lines, fine windows and roof sculptures. He completes the **Galerie des Glaces**★★★ begun by Le Brun, and built over Le Vau's terrace; this splendid reception room lies between the War Salon and the Peace Salon; its mirrors catch the rays of the setting sun. Its decoration was completed in 1687.

1680   The King's Kitchen Garden (Potager du Roi) is laid out by La Quintinie.

1683   The King's favourite musician, La Lande, composes divertimenti and ballets. The sculptor Puget carves his Milo of Crotona followed by his Perseus and Andromeda.

1684   Jules Hardouin-Mansart designs the Orangerie.

1688   Jules Hardouin-Mansart builds the Grand Trianon (or Marble Trianon) with its peristyle by Robert de Cotte, and Empire and Restoration furniture.

1701   War of the Spanish Succession; the French victory over the Dutch and Austrians led to the Peace of Utrecht in 1713 and the final definition of France's northern frontier.

1702   Suppression of the camisard revolt.

1715   Reception of the Persian Ambassadors – On 1 September, Louis XIV dies.

Louis XV – Born 1710 – Marries Maria Leszczinska in 1725

1715-22   Philippe d'Orléans rules as Regent from 1715-23. Court and Government move from Versailles to Paris between.

1729   Birth of the Dauphin, father of Louis XVI.

1733   War of the Polish Succession (fought in Italy), ended by the Treaty of Vienna in 1738.

1740   War of the Austrian Succession (Peace of Aix-la-Chapelle in 1748).

1745   The Dauphin is married to Marie-Josèphe de Saxe, the Spanish Infanta.
1756   The Seven Years War (ended by the Peace of Paris in 1763).

1757   Attempted assassination of Louis XV by Damiens.

1774   Louis XV dies of smallpox.

1776   The Genevan banker, Necker, is appointed Controller-General.

Louis XVI – Born 1754 – Marries Marie-Antoinette in 1770

1783   The independence of the United States is confirmed by the Treaty of Versailles on 3 September.

1785   The Affair of the Queen's Necklace: Cardinal de Rohan arrested.

1699   The Royal Chapel is built by Hardouin-Mansa rt (completed in 1710 by Robert de Cotte and decorated by Van Cleve and Claude Lorrain, with frescoes by Coustou and Coypel).

1701   The King's Suite is designed by Hardouin-Mansart; the room is laid out around the axis formed by the course of the sun (shown today with its summer furnishings of 1723).

1712   Hercules' Salon (Salon d'Hercule), on the site of the former chapel, is begun. Completed in 1736, it has a ceiling by Lemoyne.

1715-74

1729   The Queen's Bedchamber is redecorated, and finally completed by Boucher.

1738   The private suites are redecorated.

1739   The cabinet-maker Gaudreau produces a splendid medal cabinet.

1742   Nattier is appointed court portrait-painter.

1754   Passement makes his astronomical clock with its bronze figures by Caffieri.

1755   Ange-Jacques Gabriel designs the cabinet room of the Council of Ministers.

1762   Ange-Jacques Gabriel starts work on the "Petit Trianon" (woodwork by Guibert).

1768   Ange-Jacques Gabriel builds the Royal Opera with its splendid auditorium; Pajou's decorative scheme anticipates the Louis XVI style.

1769   The celebrated roll-top desk for the King's Corner Room (Cabinet de travail du roi) is completed; it is a masterpiece of French cabinet-making by Oeben and Riesener.

1774-93

1774   Ange-Jacques Gabriel completes the Petit Trianon and, together with the sculptor Rousseau, creates the King's Library (Bibliothèque du roi).

1775   Coustou's statues are placed in the Queen's Grove (Bosquet de la Reine).

1783   The Hamlet (Hameau) is laid out in the gardens of the Petit Trianon – the Queen's Private Suite (Cabinet intérieur de la reine) is decorated by Mique.

1787	Portrait of Marie-Antoinette with her children by Mme Vigée-Lebrun. The formal session of the States-General opens in the town on 5 May. The Real Tennis-Court Oath is sworn on 20 June. 14 July: the Fall of the Bastille. 27 August: Declaration of the Rights of Man.
1789	6 October: the mob force the royal family to return to Paris.

Revolution – Empire – Restoration – Republic

1792	10 August: fall of the monarchy.
1793	21 January: Louis XVI guillotined on Place de la Concorde.
1871	18 January: the German Empire is proclaimed in the Hall of Mirrors.
1875	The National Assembly meets in the Opera. The Wallon Amendment forms the basis for the establishment of the Third Republic.
1919	28 June: the Treaty of Versailles terminates the First World War.

From 1790 to today

1791	The Fête de la Fédération is celebrated with gusto in Paris, Louis XVI swearing loyalty to the Revolutionary Constitution.
1810	The painter David finishes his sketch depicting the Real Tennis-Court Oath.
1833	The Apartments are demolished (with the exception of the central section of the first floor) in order to house a museum.
1837	The palace becomes a museum of the history of France.

VÉZELAY

POPULATION 571

MICHELIN MAP 319 F 7

GREEN GUIDE BURGUNDY JURA

The picturesque village of Vézelay is built along the ridge of a rocky spur among the northern foothills of the Morvan countryside. Its fame is due to its wonderful basilica.

A Bit of History

The Celts were the first to settle this hilltop site. In 878 an abbey was founded here, and in 1050 it was dedicated to Mary Magdalene. The place soon became one of France's great pilgrimage destinations and a sanctuary was built. It suffered destruction by fire more than once. It was here that St Bernard preached the Second Crusade in 1146. In 1279, however, the monks of St-Maximin in Provence discovered the bones of Mary Magdalene in a cave; the certification of the relics as authentic led to the decline of Vézelay as a place of pilgrimage; it was pillaged by the Huguenots, razed at the time of the French Revolution and given its coup de grâce by lightning.

In 1840, Prosper Mérimée, who was in charge of the national survey of the country's heritage, came to Vézelay; recognising the value and significance of the ruin, he appointed the young Viollet-le-Duc as architect in charge of its restoration.

Visit

Basilique Ste-Madeleine★★★

First built between 1096 and 1104 and restored following the fire of 1120. The principal external features are the fine Romanesque body of the church (to which flying buttresses were added in the 13C), St Antony's Tower (Tour St-Antoine), and a particularly harmonious chevet with radiating chapels. From the terrace, there is a fine **view**★ over the valley of the River Cure.

In the dimly-lit narthex (1140-60) is the marvellous tympanum **(tympan**★★★**)** of the central doorway. Dating from around 1125 (and thus preceding the one at Autun), it shows Christ blessing the 12 Apostles before sending them out into the world. Proportion is used to reinforce the meaning of the composition; of superhuman size, the figure of Christ is shown with hands extended outwards, passing on to the disciples something of His divine power, while the extraordinary length of His legs seems to elevate Him beyond all earthly contingencies. In contrast, the figures of the Apostles and the heathen are of much more modest dimensions. The sculptor's great talent is made manifest in his treatment of the Apostles and of the fantastic figures in the lintel, and in his depiction of the signs of the Zodiac and labours of the month, as well as in his masterly handling of the folds of clothes (notably Christ's robes).

The Romanesque nave of 10 bays, rebuilt between 1120 and 1135, is unusually large and exceptionally well lit. Here in Burgundy it stands out by virtue of a number of features, including semicircular arches, the lack of tribunes or false triforium, the boldly-patterned stonework, the pillars with engaged columns (rather than pilasters), and especially the use, even in the nave, of ribbed vaults. The greatest contribution to the basilica's decoration is made by the many capitals **(chapiteaux**★★★**)** adorning the pillars; these were sculpted from 1106 onwards, and depict Biblical scenes, the lives of the saints, moralising subjects and weird beasts, all with a verve and dynamism which anticipates subsequent work at Autun. The magnificent Gothic choir (1185-1215) seems to have been influenced by the great new churches of the North of France.

VICHY★★★

POPULATION 27 714

MICHELIN MAP 326 H 6

GREEN GUIDE AUVERGNE RHÔNE VALLEY

Pleasantly sited in the Allier valley, and well-endowed with lush parks and luxurious thermal establishments, Vichy is a famous spa town. The virtues of the waters drew visitors here in Roman times and in the 17C, while it is primarily to Napoleon III that the place owes its reputation as a luxury health resort.

In medieval times, the river crossing was commanded by a castle. Later, the town grew during the reign of Henri IV. More recently, Vichy gave its name to the government of the French State, the regime led by Marshal Pétain which ruled the country under close German supervision from 12 July 1940 until 20 August 1944.

Visit

Le Quartier Thermal (Spa)★
The florid spa architecture of the second half of the 19C is well represented by a number of constructions such as the Grand Casino of 1865, the Napoleon Gallery (Galerie Napoléon) of 1857, the covered galleries bordering the park (Parc des Sources) which formed part of the 1889 Paris Universal Exhibition before being re-erected here, and the Great Baths (Grand établissement thermal) of 1900.

VIENNE★★

POPULATION 29 449

MICHELIN MAP 333 C 4

GREEN GUIDE AUVERGNE RHÔNE VALLEY

Vienne is favoured with a sunny site★ on the east bank of the Rhône. The town overlooks the bend formed by the river as it makes its way through the crystalline rocks marking the last outcrops of the Massif Central.

Originally the capital of the Allobroges tribe, Vienne came under Roman rule 60 years before Caesar's conquest of Gaul. In the 3C and 4C, the city was the centre of the vast province known as the Viennoise stretching from Lake Geneva to the mouth of the Rhône. Great public buildings were erected at the foot of Mount Pipet, opposite **St-Romain-en-Gal**, the Gallo-Roman city (**cité gallo-romaine**★) with its houses and shops. In the 5C, Vienne became the capital of the Burgundians, who ruled over the east bank of the Rhône before being chased away by the Franks in 532. Ruled subsequently by its archbishops, the city became the object of the rivalry between the Kingdom of France and the Holy Roman Empire, until its final incorporation into France at the same time as the Dauphiné, in 1349.

▶ **Orient Yourself:** Vienne, which is listed as a "Town of Art and History," offers 2hr discovery tours conducted by guide-lecturers approved by the Ministry of Culture and Communication. 6€. Information at the tourist office or on www.vpah.culture.fr.

Sights

Temple d'Auguste et de Livie★★
This Classical temple was first built in the reign of Emperor Augustus shortly before the beginning of the Christian era; it seems likely that it was then reconstructed, somewhat carelessly, under Claudius, about 50 years later. At the time it would have dominated the Forum to the east. Its good state of preservation is due to its successive re-use as a public building of various kinds (Church, Jacobin club, tribunal, museum, library), and subsequently to its restoration by Prosper Mérimée in 1850.

It is identifiable as Roman work by the way in which its 16 Corinthian columns rise from a podium rather than directly from the ground in the Greek manner. In the pediment are traces of a bronze inscription to the glory of Augustus and Livia.

Cathédrale St-Maurice ★★

The present building was begun around 1230 by the architect Guillaume de l'Œuvre who redesigned the 11C chevet, giving it additional height and providing it with a ribbed vault. There followed major modifications to the seven Romanesque bays of the nave (identifiable by their fluted pilasters) with the provision of columns, a triforium and clerestory windows, making possible the construction of the choir vault at the same height. Finally, in the 14C, the final four bays of the nave were built, together with the west front and its portals.

Only 35 years after its completion, the cathedral suffered much mutilation during the Wars of Religion. It underwent extensive restoration in the 19C (vaults, arching of the portals, rose window). But much remains to be admired inside, including the fine Renaissance window in the south aisle *(to the right of the choir)*, the 13C low-relief between the sixth and seventh chapels in the north aisle depicting Herod and the Magi, and the rare 11C Bishop's Throne *(in the apse behind the high altar)*.

The inner niches contain episodes from the life of Christ; in the equivalent central niche is a depiction of the corresponding Old Testament event, while the outer niche portrays the Prophet who foretold the episode; thus in the third level on the right can be seen (reading from inside to outside), firstly Christ's descent into Hell, then Lot leaving Sodom in flames, and finally the Prophet Hosea.

Théâtre romain★. Église St-André-le-Bas★ *For guided tours, same times as for the cloister.* ☎ 04 74 85 50 42. .

Cloître de St-André-le-Bas★ *Apr-Oct: Tue-Sun 9.30am-1pm, 2-6pm; Nov-Mar: Tue-Fri 9.30am-12.30pm, 2-5pm, Sat-Sun 2-6pm; Theatre open Apr-Aug: Mon 9.30am-1pm, 2-6pm, Nov-Mar: Sat-Sun 2-5pm.* Closed 1 Jan, 1 May, 1 and 11 Nov, 25 Dec. *2€.* ☎ 04 74 85 50 42 Ancienne église St-Pierre★ – Musée Lapidaire★ *Same times as for the cloister.*

Jardins et Château de **VILLANDRY**★★★

MICHELIN MAP 317 M 4

GREEN GUIDE CHÂTEAUX OF THE LOIRE

In 1536, Jean Le Breton, who had been France's ambassador in Italy, rebuilt the château here on the foundations of an earlier one. The new building had a number of features which made it unusual in Touraine: ditches and canals, an esplanade and a terrace, rectangular pavilions in place of round towers, and, above all, its gardens.

Studio 3 Bis/MICHELIN

Gardens, Château de Villandry

Visit

Château★★

🕐 *Feb and early Nov to mid-Nov: 9am-5pm; Mar: 9am-5.30pm; Apr-Jun and Sep-Oct: 9am-6pm; Jul and Aug: 9am-6.30pm; Christmas vacation: 9.30am-4.30pm. Guided tours (2hr, call for times) except in Feb, Dec and Sundays May-Sep (during which time you can take a self-guided tour with a leaflet).* 🕐 *Closed the rest of the year.* ∞ *7.50€ (château and gardens).* ☎ *02 47 50 02 09. www.chateauvillandry.com.*

The interior is distinguished by Louis XV panelling in the Great Salon and Dining Room, by the fine ramped staircase in wrought iron, and by a surprising 13C Mudejar ceiling from Spain, brought here by Joachim de Carvallo.

Jardins★★★

🕐 *Mid-Jun to mid-Sep: daily 9am-7.30pm; Apr to mid-Jun and mid-Sep to end Sep: daily 9am-7pm; Oct: daily 9am-6.30pm; Mar: daily 9am-6pm; Feb and early Nov to mid-Nov: daily 9am-5.30pm; mid-Nov to end Jan: daily 9am-5pm.* ∞ *5€ (7.50€ château and gardens (children: 3.50€, 5€).* ☎ *02 47 50 02 09. www.chateauvillandry.com.*

In 1906, Dr Carvallo, founder of the French Historic Houses Association (Demeure Historique), bought the Villandry estate and began to restore the gardens. The plan of the gardens shows both the influence of the agricultural writer **Olivier de Serres**, and the synthesis of the monastery garden with the Italian garden proposed by Jacques II Androuet Du Cerceau.

Covering a total area of 7ha – 17 acres, the gardens have many fascinating features. There are three terraces one above the other, separated by shady avenues of limes and vines; the highest is the water garden with its mirrorlike stretch of water, then comes an ornamental garden with box clipped into patterns symbolising the varieties of love: tragic (sword and dagger blades), fickle (butterflies and fans), tender (masks and hearts), and passionate (broken hearts). Finally there is a kitchen garden with 85 000 plants contained in clipped-box beds. The use of the humblest of vegetables (cabbage, celery...), chosen for their culinary value, symbolism, therapeutic value or colour, is here raised to an art form of great delicacy and seasonal interest.

VILLEFRANCHE-DE-ROUERGUE★

POPULATION 12 291

MICHELIN MAP 338 E 4

GREEN GUIDE LANGUEDOC ROUSSILLON TARN GORGES

Villefranche was once a staging-post on the Roman road from Rodez to Cahors. In 1252, Alphonse de Poitiers, brother of Louis IX, founded a bastide here. The little fortified settlement became a market town, linking the wheatlands on the Quercy causse to the west with the rye-growing areas to the east; the yield of the infertile plateaux was increased by the application of lime, made possible after the building of the railway at the beginning of the 20C.

Visit

Bastide★

The old town on the north bank of the River Aveyron has kept many of the typical features of a planned urban foundation of the 13C. Its cobbled streets, connected by narrow alleyways, are laid out on a grid pattern, and there is a central square (**Place Notre-Dame★**) with covered walks, dominated by a large metal figure of Christ. The tall, severe houses are characteristic of the Rouergue area; a number of them have high open balconies with provision for drying grain. The President Raynal House (Maison du Président Raynal) with its 15C façade is particularly striking, and the Dardennes House (Maison Dardennes) has a fine galleried courtyard.

There is a fortified church (**Église Notre-Dame★**) with splendid ironwork around the font.

Chartreuse St-Sauveur★

🕐 *Jul to end Sep: daily 10am-noon, 2-6pm. Possibility of a guided tour* 🔍 *(1hr).* 🔖 *3.50€.* ☎ *05 65 45 13 18.*

Built in 1461 in an unusually-pure Gothic style. The little cloisters are a monastic masterpiece of Flamboyant architecture.

VILLEQUIER★

POPULATION 822

MICHELIN MAP 304 E 4

GREEN GUIDE NORMANDY

On the banks of the Lower Seine, Villequier is the point at which ships change the pilot who has brought them through the channels of the estuary for the one who will take them up the river to Rouen. It is also a key site in the literary history of France.

A Bit of History

The Vacquerie House is now the **Musée Victor-Hugo**★. As well as commemorating this Grand Old Man of literature (and in particular, his ties with Normandy), the museum evokes his relationship with his companion Juliette Drouet and the short life of his beloved daughter Léopoldine.

"À Villequier" – In September 1843, Victor Hugo (1802-85) is at the height of his literary fame; at his fine home in Place des Vosges in Paris (also a **museum**), he learns of the death in an accident of his 19-year-old daughter, Léopoldine, married only seven months previously to Charles Vacquerie.

Under the impact of this terrible blow, Hugo stopped writing for a whole year; then, on 4 September 1844, at a single sitting, he composed the poem *"À Villequier" (At Villequier)*, later included in his volume of poems entitled *Les Contemplations*, dedicated to the memory of his daughter. Critics have seen in these elegiac lines some of the finest verse in the French language.

YVOIRE★★

MICHELIN MAP 328 K 2

GREEN GUIDE FRENCH ALPS

This picturesque village bedecked with flowers has retained its medieval character. It enjoys a magnificent site on the shores of Lake Geneva (Lac Léman), at the tip of a headland separating the Petit Lac and the Grand Lac. Its marina is very popular with Swiss residents.

Visit

Village Médieval (Old Town)★

Pedestrian access only. Rebuilt in the 14C on the site of a former fortress, Yvoire has kept part of its original ramparts including two gates protected by towers and its castle *(not open)* with a massive square keep framed by turrets. The bustling streets lined with old houses and craft shops lead to delightful squares decked with flowers which afford fine views of the lake.

From the end of the pier there are views of the Swiss coast, the town of Noyon and the Jura mountains.

◉◉ Jardin des Cinq-Sens★ ♿ 🕐 *Mid-May to mid-Sep: daily 10am-7pm; mid-Apr to mid-May: daily 11am-6pm; mid-Sep to mid-Oct: daily 1-5pm. Summer:* 🔖 *8€ (4-16 years: 4.50€); Spring and Autumn:* 🔖 *6.50€ (3.50€).* ☎ *04 50 72 88 80. www.jardin5sens.net* – Boat trips on the lake.

Little Red Riding Hood

But Little Red Riding Hood had her local map with her, and so she did not fall into the trap. She did not take the path through the wood and she did not meet the big bad wolf. Instead, she chose the picturesque touring route straight to Grandmother's house, and arrived safely with her cake and her little pot of butter.

The End

A

INDEX

MAPS AND PLANS

COMPANION PUBLICATIONS

LOCAL MAPS

For each site in this guide, you will find map references which correspond to local maps (nos 301 to 345) of France.

MAPS OF FRANCE

For all of France, there are 5 formats at a 1:1 000 000 scale to choose from: France no 721, the whole country on a single sheet with an index of place names; no 722, reversible, divided north/south; no 724, north of France; no 725 south of France; and the collection of atlases. Atlases to France are published in several formats for your convenience: spiral, paperback and hardback all include the Paris region, town plans and an index of place names. Now available in a mini format as well. You may also wish to consult no 728 France Administrative, showing regions, departments, main roads, distance tables, universities.

MOTORWAYS

Other useful maps include no 726 Route Planning, with motorways, alternative routes, journey times and 24-hour service stations.

ROUTE PLANNING VIA INTERNET

Michelin is pleased to offer a route-planning service on the Internet: www. Via Michelin. com. Choose the shortest route, a route without tolls, or the Michelin recommended route to your destination; you can also access information about hotels and restaurants from The Michelin Guide, and tourist sites from The Green Guide.

Bon voyage!

St-Lô
303
Quimper
308
St-Brieuc 309
Rennes
Vannes
Nantes
La Roche-
sur-Yon 316
La Rochelle
324
Bordeaux
335
Mont-
de-Marsan
336
Pau
342
Tarbes
Auch
343
Caen
Rouen
Évreux
304
Versailles
311
Chartres
310
Angers 317
Tours
323
Poitiers
322
Niort
325
Guéret
329
Périgueux
330
Cahors
Agen
337
Montauban
338
Albi
Toulouse
Amiens
Beauvais
305
Lille
Arras
301
302
Laon
306
Chalons-en-
Champagne
Charleville-
Mézières
307
Strasbourg
315
Colmar
312
Orléans
Blois 318
Auxerre
319
Nevers
320
Chaumont
Troyes
Épinal
313
314
Vesoul
Besançon
321
Lons-le-
Saunier
328
Annecy
333
Chambéry
Bourg-en-
Bresse
326
Moulins
Clermont-Fd
327
Lyon
Limoges
Tulle
331
Le Puy
St-Étienne
Valence
332
Privas
Rodez
Nîmes
339
Digne
Gap
334
Avignon
340
Nice
341
Mende
Montpellier
Carcassonne
344
Perpignan
Bastia
345
Ajaccio

Legend

★★★ **Highly recommended**

★★ **Recommended**

★ **Interesting**

Tourism

	Sightseeing route with departure point indicated	**AZ B**	Map co-ordinates locating sights
	Ecclesiastical building		Tourist information
	Synagogue – Mosque		Historic house, castle – Ruins
	Building (with main entrance)		Dam – Factory or power station
	Statue, small building		Fort – Cave
	Wayside cross		Prehistoric site
	Fountain		Viewing table – View
	Fortified walls – Tower – Gate		Miscellaneous sight

Recreation

	Racecourse		Waymarked footpath
	Skating rink		Outdoor leisure park/centre
	Outdoor, indoor swimming pool		Theme/Amusement park
	Marina, moorings		Wildlife/Safari park, zoo
	Mountain refuge hut		Gardens, park, arboretum
	Overhead cable-car		Aviary, bird sanctuary
	Tourist or steam railway		

Additional symbols

	Motorway (unclassified)		Post office – Telephone centre
	Junction: complete, limited		Covered market
	Pedestrian street		Barracks
	Unsuitable for traffic, street subject to restrictions		Swing bridge
	Steps – Footpath		Quarry – Mine
	Railway – Coach station		Ferry (river and lake crossings)
	Funicular – Rack-railway		Ferry services: Passengers and cars
	Tram – Metro, underground		Foot passengers only
Bert (R.)...	Main shopping street		Access route number common to MICHELIN maps and town plans

Abbreviations and special symbols

A	Agricultural office (Chambre d'agriculture)	**P**	Local authority offices (Préfecture, sous-préfecture)
C	Chamber of commerce (Chambre de commerce)	**POL.**	Police station (Police)
H	Town hall (Hôtel de ville)		Police station (Gendarmerie)
J	Law courts (Palais de justice)	**T**	Theatre (Théâtre)
M	Museum (Musée)	**U**	University (Université)
			Hotel
			Park and Ride

Some town plans are extracts from plans used in the Green Guides to the regions of France.

NOTES

NOTES